International Directory of
COMPANY
HISTORIES

International Directory of
COMPANY
HISTORIES

VOLUME 71

Editor

Jay P. Pederson

ST. JAMES PRESS

An imprint of Thomson Gale, a part of The Thomson Corporation

THOMSON
™
GALE

Detroit • New York • San Francisco • San Diego • New Haven, Conn. • Waterville, Maine • London • Munich

THOMSON

™

GALE

International Directory of Company Histories, Volume 71

Jay P. Pederson, Editor

Project Editor
Miranda H. Ferrara

Editorial
Virgil Burton, Donna Craft, Louise Gagné,
Peggy Geeseman, Julie Gough, Linda Hall,
Sonya Hill, Keith Jones, Lynn Pearce,
Maureen Puhl, Holly Selden,
Justine Ventimiglia

Imaging and Multimedia
Randy Bassett, Lezlie Light

Manufacturing
Rhonda Dover

Product Manager
Gerald L. Sawchuk

For permission to use material from this product, submit your request via Web at http://www.gale-edit.com/permissions, or you may download our Permissions Request form and submit your request by fax or mail to:

Permissions Department
Thomson Gale
27500 Drake Rd.
Farmington Hills, MI 48331-3535
Permissions Hotline:
248-699-8006 or 800-877-4253, ext. 8006
Fax: 248-699-8074 or 800-762-4058

Cover photograph (Nestlé headquarters building, Vevey, Switzerland) reproduced by permission of Nestlé S.A.

While every effort has been made to ensure the reliability of the information presented in this publication, Thomson Gale does not guarantee the accuracy of the data contained herein. Thomson Gale accepts no payment for listing; and inclusion of any organization, agency, institution, publication, service, or individual does not imply endorsement of the editors or publisher. Errors brought to the attention of the publisher and verified to the satisfaction of the publisher will be corrected in future editions.

LIBRARY OF CONGRESS CATALOG NUMBER 89-190943
ISBN: 1-55862-546-1

BRITISH LIBRARY CATALOGUING IN PUBLICATION DATA
International directory of company histories. Vol. 71
I. Jay P. Pederson
33.87409

Printed in the United States of America
10 9 8 7 6 5 4 3 2 1

CONTENTS

Company Histories

PREFACE

The St. James Press series *The International Directory of Company Histories (IDCH)* is intended for reference use by students, business people, librarians, historians, economists, investors, job candidates, and others who seek to learn more about the historical development of the world's most important companies. To date, *IDCH* has covered over 7,100 companies in 71 volumes.

Inclusion Criteria

Most companies chosen for inclusion in *IDCH* have achieved a minimum of US$25 million in annual sales and are leading influences in their industries or geographical locations. Companies may be publicly held, private, or nonprofit. State-owned companies that are important in their industries and that may operate much like public or private companies also are included. Wholly owned subsidiaries and divisions are profiled if they meet the requirements for inclusion. Entries on companies that have had major changes since they were last profiled may be selected for updating.

The *IDCH* series highlights 10% private and nonprofit companies, and features updated entries on approximately 50 companies per volume.

Entry Format

Each entry begins with the company's legal name, the address of its headquarters, its telephone, toll-free, and fax numbers, and its web site. A statement of public, private, state, or parent ownership follows. A company with a legal name in both English and the language of its headquarters country is listed by the English name, with the native-language name in parentheses.

The company's founding or earliest incorporation date, the number of employees, and the most recent available sales figures follow. Sales figures are given in local currencies with equivalents in U.S. dollars. For some private companies, sales figures are estimates and indicated by the abbreviation *est.* The entry lists the exchanges on which a company's stock is traded and its ticker symbol, as well as the company's NAIC codes.

Entries generally contain a *Company Perspectives* box which provides a short summary of the company's mission, goals, and ideals, a *Key Dates* box highlighting milestones in the company's history, lists of *Principal Subsidiaries, Principal Divisions, Principal Operating Units, Principal Competitors,* and articles for *Further Reading.*

American spelling is used throughout *IDCH*, and the word "billion" is used in its U.S. sense of one thousand million.

Sources

Entries have been compiled from publicly accessible sources both in print and on the Internet such as general and academic periodicals, books, annual reports, and material supplied by the companies themselves.

Cumulative Indexes

IDCH contains three indexes: the **Index to Companies**, which provides an alphabetical index to companies discussed in the text as well as to companies profiled, the **Index to Industries**, which allows researchers to locate companies by their principal industry, and the **Geographic Index**, which lists companies alphabetically by the country of their headquarters. The indexes are cumulative and specific instructions for using them are found immediately preceding each index.

Suggestions Welcome

Comments and suggestions from users of *IDCH* on any aspect of the product as well as suggestions for companies to be included or updated are cordially invited. Please write:

The Editor
International Directory of Company Histories
St. James Press
27500 Drake Rd.
Farmington Hills, Michigan 48331-3535

AB	Aktiebolag (Finland, Sweden)
AB Oy	Aktiebolag Osakeyhtiot (Finland)
A.E.	Anonimos Eteria (Greece)
AG	Aktiengesellschaft (Austria, Germany, Switzerland, Liechtenstein)
A.O.	Anonim Ortaklari/Ortakligi (Turkey)
ApS	Amparteselskab (Denmark)
A.Š.	Anonim Širketi (Turkey)
A/S	Aksjeselskap (Norway); Aktieselskab (Denmark, Sweden)
Ay	Avoinyhtio (Finland)
B.A.	Buttengewone Aansprakeiijkheid (The Netherlands)
Bhd.	Berhad (Malaysia, Brunei)
B.V.	Besloten Vennootschap (Belgium, The Netherlands)
C.A.	Compania Anonima (Ecuador, Venezuela)
C. de R.L.	Compania de Responsabilidad Limitada (Spain)
Co.	Company
Corp.	Corporation
CRL	Companhia a Responsabilidao Limitida (Portugal, Spain)
C.V.	Commanditaire Vennootschap (The Netherlands, Belgium)
G.I.E.	Groupement d'Interet Economique (France)
GmbH	Gesellschaft mit beschraenkter Haftung (Austria, Germany, Switzerland)
Inc.	Incorporated (United States, Canada)
I/S	Interessentselskab (Denmark); Interesentselskap (Norway)
KG/KGaA	Kommanditgesellschaft/Kommanditgesellschaft auf Aktien (Austria, Germany, Switzerland)
KK	Kabushiki Kaisha (Japan)
K/S	Kommanditselskab (Denmark); Kommandittselskap (Norway)
Lda.	Limitada (Spain)
L.L.C.	Limited Liability Company (United States)
Ltd.	Limited (Various)
Ltda.	Limitada (Brazil, Portugal)
Ltee.	Limitee (Canada, France)
mbH	mit beschraenkter Haftung (Austria, Germany)
N.V.	Naamloze Vennootschap (Belgium, The Netherlands)
OAO	Otkrytoe Aktsionernoe Obshchestve (Russia)
OOO	Obschestvo s Ogranichennoi Otvetstvennostiu (Russia)
Oy	Osakeyhtiö (Finland)
PLC	Public Limited Co. (United Kingdom, Ireland)
Pty.	Proprietary (Australia, South Africa, United Kingdom)
S.A.	Société Anonyme (Belgium, France, Greece, Luxembourg, Switzerland, Arab speaking countries); Sociedad Anónima (Latin America [except Brazil], Spain, Mexico); Sociedades Anônimas (Brazil, Portugal)
SAA	Societe Anonyme Arabienne
S.A.R.L.	Sociedade Anonima de Responsabilidade Limitada (Brazil, Portugal); Société à Responsabilité Limitée (France, Belgium, Luxembourg)
S.A.S.	Societá in Accomandita Semplice (Italy); Societe Anonyme Syrienne (Arab speaking countries)
Sdn. Bhd.	Sendirian Berhad (Malaysia)
S.p.A.	Società per Azioni (Italy)
Sp. z.o.o.	Spólka z ograniczona odpowiedzialnoscia (Poland)
S.R.L.	Società a Responsabilità Limitata (Italy); Sociedad de Responsabilidad Limitada (Spain, Mexico, Latin America [except Brazil])
S.R.O.	Spolecnost s Rucenim Omezenym (Czechoslovakia
Ste.	Societe (France, Belgium, Luxembourg, Switzerland)
VAG	Verein der Arbeitgeber (Austria, Germany)
YK	Yugen Kaisha (Japan)
ZAO	Zakrytoe Aktsionernoe Obshchestve (Russia)

$	United States dollar	ISK	Icelandic krona
£	United Kingdom pound	ITL	Italian lira
¥	Japanese yen	JMD	Jamaican dollar
AED	Emirati dirham	KPW	North Korean won
ARS	Argentine peso	KRW	South Korean won
ATS	Austrian shilling	KWD	Kuwaiti dinar
AUD	Australian dollar	LUF	Luxembourg franc
BEF	Belgian franc	MUR	Mauritian rupee
BHD	Bahraini dinar	MXN	Mexican peso
BRL	Brazilian real	MYR	Malaysian ringgit
CAD	Canadian dollar	NGN	Nigerian naira
CHF	Swiss franc	NLG	Netherlands guilder
CLP	Chilean peso	NOK	Norwegian krone
CNY	Chinese yuan	NZD	New Zealand dollar
COP	Colombian peso	OMR	Omani rial
CZK	Czech koruna	PHP	Philippine peso
DEM	German deutsche mark	PKR	Pakistani rupee
DKK	Danish krone	PLN	Polish zloty
DZD	Algerian dinar	PTE	Portuguese escudo
EEK	Estonian Kroon	RMB	Chinese renminbi
EGP	Egyptian pound	RUB	Russian ruble
ESP	Spanish peseta	SAR	Saudi riyal
EUR	euro	SEK	Swedish krona
FIM	Finnish markka	SGD	Singapore dollar
FRF	French franc	THB	Thai baht
GRD	Greek drachma	TND	Tunisian dinar
HKD	Hong Kong dollar	TRL	Turkish lira
HUF	Hungarian forint	TWD	new Taiwan dollar
IDR	Indonesian rupiah	VEB	Venezuelan bolivar
IEP	Irish pound	VND	Vietnamese dong
ILS	new Israeli shekel	ZAR	South African rand
INR	Indian rupee	ZMK	Zambian kwacha

International Directory of

COMPANY
HISTORIES

A-Mark Financial Corporation

100 Wilshire Boulevard
Third Floor
Santa Monica, California 90401
U.S.A.
Telephone: (310) 260-0315
Toll Free: (800) 827-4653
Fax: (310) 319-0310
Web site: http://www.amark.com

Private Company
Incorporated: 1965 as A-Mark Coin Company
Employees: 112
Sales: $2.8 billion (2004)
NAIC: 523130 Commodity Contracts Dealing; 423940
     Jewelry, Watch, Precious Stone, and Precious Metal
     Merchant Wholesalers

A-Mark Financial Corporation operates in the realm of precious metals, offering gold, silver, platinum, and palladium products and a range of supporting services. The four-decade-old operation serves clients, including government mints, across the globe. Privately held, A-Mark traditionally has revealed few in-depth details about its business.

Golden Opportunities: 1965 to the Mid-1980s

Steven C. Markoff laid the groundwork for A-Mark Financial Corporation when he was yet a teenager, according to the *Los Angeles Business Journal.* A coin collector, Markoff established A-Mark Coin Company in 1965 and entered the rare coins and precious metals trading business. In 1972, the U.S. Treasury granted A-Mark a special license for dealing in gold. When gold ownership was extended as a right to all U.S. citizens in 1974, the company seized the opportunity to expand its business.

The company reached an industry high watermark in 1976, purchasing the LaVere Redfield silver dollar collection. The 11-ton, $7.3 million cash purchase consisted of 411,000 coins.

Four years later came another boon: The price of silver skyrocketed. The metal became very precious at $50 an ounce.

Family heirlooms and coin collections were melted down to take advantage of the 1980 price surge, the *Houston Chronicle* recounted. During the year A-Mark traded millions of ounces of silver. In 1981, the company minted its first proprietary one-ounce silver bar.

A-Mark Precious Metals, Inc. sales topped $1 billion for 1983. The following year, the company began encapsulating and certifying gold coins through its Guaranteed U.S. Gold program. Also in 1984, A-Mark received designation as exclusive distributor for the Mexican one-ounce Silver Coin Libertads by Banco de Mexico, the Mexican central bank.

Another precious metal took center stage in the mid-1980s. The majority of the world's platinum supply came from South Africa. Fear of economic sanctions directed toward South Africa in response to their apartheid policies had driven up the price on the metal during the summer of 1986. No large supplies of platinum were in existence nor were there substitutes for its use in products such as the catalytic converter, an air pollution device. Moreover, investors had taken a shine to the metal.

''Growing investor demand for the metal comes at the same time as supplies are threatened, says Bruce Kaplan, senior vice president of A-Mark Precious Metals Inc. of Beverly Hills, Calif. Until about two years ago, platinum was considered strictly an industrial metal, Kaplan says,'' David Flaum reported for the *Houston Chronicle.*

Gold had no such supply shortage problems. But prices were rising, in response to fears related to the mounting federal deficit and the potential for defaults among debtor nations, such as Mexico. A-Mark continued to build its connections in the market, receiving rights as Exclusive Western Hemisphere Distributor of Australian Gold Coin Nugget Proof sets by Australia's Gold Corporation during 1986.

Silver, on the other hand, was in a slump caused by the oversupply created as the decade began. Kaplan told the *Houston Chronicle* the traditional gold-to-silver price ratio of 35:1 had shot up to 70:1. ''That is 'causing speculators to salivate,' '' he said. Compounding oversupply problems was several years of downturn in industrial use, although the metal had begun

3

Company Perspectives:

Honesty, Integrity, and Reliability: Our Corporate Culture reflects our founding principles and philosophy of placing honesty, integrity, and reliability at the forefront of our dealings.

seeing an upswing during 1985. Silver was found in medical, photographic, and electrical component applications.

Mercurial Precious Metals Market: Late 1980s

A policy change early in 1987 opened the door for more firms to become authorized distributors of the American Eagle gold and silver bullion coins. The U.S. Mint altered its net worth requirements to allow companies to use letters of credit to reach the minimum standards—a stipulation that fell away after a six-month period of solid performance. A-Mark, already an authorized distributor of silver bullion coins, had protested the policy that excluded it from the network of distributors, according to the *American Metal Market.* The resulting out-of-court settlement with the firm prompted the new rules. Once authorized as a dealer of the Gold Eagle coins, A-Mark quickly became one of the U.S. Mint's largest customers.

Gold, by June 1987, was trading at about $455 per ounce, up from less than $290 per ounce in early 1985. Mining stocks and gold mutual funds thrived. "Gold has become downright respectable. No longer is the typical gold buyer an oddball preparing for imminent financial catastrophe. 'Mr. and Mrs. Main Street are buying now,' " A-Mark's Kaplan told *U.S. News & World Report.*

Coins were accessible to everyday investors, affording the advantages of variable purchase size, ease of transport, aesthetic qualities, and ready resale when compared with an investment such as gold bars. When the American Eagle was first introduced demand outstripped production, driving up the premium, or markup price, for a time. Other gold coins included the Canadian Maple Leaf, the Chinese Panda, and the South African Krugerrand.

Mass-produced bullion coins were judged for their value based on metal content. Numismatic coins—valued for rarity, condition and beauty, in addition to metal content—presented more of a challenge for investors. "You can't just pick up the paper and see what a coin is worth," A-Mark's Kaplan told the *Journal Record.* "You have to really know your stuff."

Platinum was the precious metal leader around mid-1988, trading above $600 per ounce. Kaplan told the *Wall Street Journal* the metals market had been bullish for about the past two years. By 1988, large brokerage houses, such as Merrill Lynch, Prudential-Bache, and Shearson Lehman Hutton, had entered into coin marketing.

The Gold Corporation, wholly owned and guaranteed by the state of Western Australia, issued a platinum coin in 1988. The only other non-special issue platinum had been offered in 1983 by the Isle of Man—located between England and Ireland.

Kaplan told the *Los Angeles Times* that it "looks like it's going to be blockbuster. It's not just because it's the first platinum bullion from a major, popular country, but because (people) love the koalas [featured on the coins]. It's like the (Chinese) panda. It's a wonderful design concept."

As platinum made inroads in investment metal, word of a technological development drove down its price. Ford Motor Co. announced that it had come up with a catalytic converter made without the use of platinum. The automotive application accounted for the leading use of platinum, followed by jewelry. Kaplan told the *Wall Street Journal* that downturn for the metal was "sheer overreaction," given the Ford program was perhaps years in the making.

During the spring of 1989 another precious metal created a stir with revelations regarding scientific experiments. Palladium prices climbed in response to news that it played a key role in a cold fusion. But in terms of portfolio potential, little palladium was available for trade.

Gold, meanwhile, had been pulled out of the ground in record levels during 1988, increasing supply. Concurrently, rising interest rates drew investors to other markets. Moreover, relative peace in the Middle East created a political climate less than conducive to gold buying. But jewelry and industrial demand continued to be strong.

Although the top-selling Canadian Maple Leaf retained much of its strength and the South African Krugerrand remained popular in the resale market due to its lack of premium over gold price, other gold coin sales suffered. Kaplan told the *Jewelers Circular Keystone* that gold coin sales were a "disaster area."

Solidly Established: 1990s

By 1990, A-Mark was one of the largest wholesalers of precious metals, with banks, brokerage houses, refiners, jewelers, investment advisors, coin dealers, and government mints its main clients. The company had evolved along with the industry, growing as the market grew. "Since I've gotten into it, it's gone from a cottage industry to a fairly established market with very large players," Markoff told the *Los Angeles Business Journal.*

David Tobenkin wrote: "A-Mark was one of the first major dealing houses to supply gold coins and bars to mutual funds holding physical gold. The same services are extended to banks, brokerage and coin dealers." In addition, A-Mark aided in its own success through endeavors such as advertising support for dealers and inventory storage and financial programs for industrial users of precious metal.

A-Mark acquired Deak International Goldline (U.S.A.) in 1991. The company sold retail precious metals and provided bulk storage services through bank depositories, according to the *Wall Street Journal.* A-Mark purchased the business from Thomas Cook Currency Services Inc., whose ultimate parent company was Midland Bank PLC.

In 1995, the privately held A-Mark still was revealing only that its revenues exceeded $1 billion. Sales figures aside,

Key Dates:

1965: A-Mark Coin Company is incorporated by Steven C. Markoff.
1972: A-Mark is granted special license by the U.S. Treasury for dealing in gold.
1981: A-Mark mints a proprietary one-ounce silver bar.
1983: A-Mark Precious Metals, Inc. tops $1 billion in sales for the fiscal year.
1987: The company fights to gain status as an authorized dealer of Gold Eagle coins by the U.S. Mint.
1997: The company arrives on the World Wide Web.
1998: The product line is expanded to include platinum alloys.
1999: A-Mark Financial Corporation, now established as the parent company of A-Mark Precious Metals and other subsidiaries, is ranked 51st on the *Forbes* list of top privately held companies.
2000: A-Mark is recognized by the *Los Angeles Business Journal* as the second largest privately held company in Los Angeles.
2001: The New Issues and Collectibles division is established.

A-Mark's business was one of slim margins. Mark Albarian, a company director, told the *Los Angeles Business Journal,* "Wholesale mark-ups on precious metals can be 1 percent or less, and mark-ups for retail can be as little as 1 to 3 percent." Most of A-Mark's transactions took place in the wholesale market. Although the company made large-volume purchases, the majority of the metal was traded, not held. Any speculative buying was only a "very small" part of the company's business according to Albarian.

Among the company's wholly owned subsidiaries serving its customers were Precious Metals Finance Corp., offering help to finance precious metal purchases; Goldline International Inc., selling to the general public; Superior Stamp & Coin, a Beverly Hills auction company; and A.M. Handling Company, a melt/assay facility. All of the company's operations were based within Los Angeles County. But the company's transactions took place across the United States and around the globe. A-Mark employed just 89 people to run all of its operations.

In 1997 A-Mark arrived on the World Wide Web. The product line was expanded the next year to include platinum alloys, including ruthenium, iridium, and cobalt.

During 1999 *Forbes* listed A-Mark Financial Corporation as the 51st largest privately held company in the United States, and in 2000 it was recognized by the *Los Angeles Business Journal* as the second largest privately held company in Los Angeles.

Risky New Millennium

A-Mark had established a New Issues and Collectibles division in 2001 "to market established and proprietary collectibles products and expand international distribution of all its product." But events across the continent brought nearly all commerce to a halt for a time.

In September, New York's World Trade Center was attacked and destroyed. The *Financial Times* used the event to explain gold's enduring reputation as a safeguard of wealth. "In excess of 379,000 troy oz (almost 12 tonnes) of gold in Scotia Mocatta's underground depository, beneath 4 World Trade Center, lie buried under the mounds of rubble. Experts think that it remains intact."

The stock market took a beating following 9/11, helping precious metal prospects. Even though the stock market had rallied by the time the decade headed into its middle years, the precious metal market benefited from continuing global tension.

The Royal Canadian Mint introduced its 25th anniversary Maple Leaf gold coin in 2004. As an official distributor for the mint, A-Mark was on the bandwagon, promoting its virtues. In addition to coins, A-Mark continued to offer precious metals in bar, wafer, and grain form, as well as services such as leasing, consignment, hedging, and finance.

The company's fortunes would continue to rise and fall with that of precious metals, but A-Mark had the experience of four decades of continuous operation on its side.

Principal Subsidiaries

A-Mark Precious Metals, Inc.; A-M Handling Company; Goldline International Inc.

Principal Competitors

Chicago Mercantile Exchange Holdings Inc.; Anglo American PLC; Degussa AG; Signet Group PLC; Zale Corporation; DGSE Companies.

Further Reading

"A-Mark Precious Metals Deal," *Wall Street Journal,* April 1, 1991.
"Americans in Rush for Canada's Gold and Silver Coins," *Vancouver Sun,* December 19, 1988, p. C5.
Brennan, Judith I., "Strategizing on Metals: Small Investors Should Play Precious Metals Cautiously, Experts Say," *Orange County Register,* April 17, 1989, p. C1.
"Dealers: Gold Looks Good in the Long Term," *Orlando Sentinel,* November 22, 1987, p. D2.
Flaum, David, "Precious Metals/Profits Still May Be Possible in Gold, Platinum," *Houston Chronicle,* September 21, 1986, p. 4.
Jacobson, Aileen, "Smart Money/Investing: Gold As Portfolio Insurance," *Newsday,* September 23, 1987, p. 53.
McGrath, Anne, "Getting Your Gold Fix from Coins," *U.S. News & World Report,* June 15, 1987, pp. 53+.
Porter, Sylvia, "Gold Coin Collecting Capitalizes on Monetary System Comments," *Journal Record* (Oklahoma City), November 5, 1987.
Roberts, Adrienne, "Why Crises Put a Gloss on Gold: People Instinctively See the Yellow Metal As a Safe Haven, But Some Investors Find It More Useful Than Others, Says Adrienne Roberts," *Financial Times,* September 22, 2001, p. 22.
Schmitt, Bill, "Mint Clears Way for More Eagle Coin Distributors," *American Metal Market,* January 19, 1987, p. 2.
Sheeline, William E., "Golden Hopes," *Fortune,* June 6, 1988, pp. 14+.
Shor, Russell, "Gold Demand: Jewelry Booms, Investors Yawn," *Jewelers Circular Keystone,* May 1989, pp. 68+.

Tobenkin, David, "A-Mark: Wholesaler Strikes Gold with Precious Metals," *Los Angeles Business Journal,* February 5, 1990, pp. S10+.

Valentine, John, "Futures Markets: Platinum Rises Further As It Continues to Lead Precious Metals Prices Higher," *Wall Street Journal,* June 2, 1988, p. 1.

——, "Futures Markets: Precious Metals Futures Stand Ground As Dollar Weakens, Inflation Fears Loom," *Wall Street Journal,* May 19, 1988, p. 1.

——, "Platinum Cash Prices, Futures Plummet on News Ford Is Testing a Converter Without the Metal," *Wall Street Journal,* December 16, 1988, p. 1.

Yoshihara, Nancy, "Australia Sees Solid-Gold Opportunity in New Platinum Coin," *Los Angeles Times,* October 17, 1988, p. 3.

Young, Douglas, "Local Coin Collector Builds $1 Billion Firm," *Los Angeles Business Journal,* August 21, 1995, pp. 45+.

—Kathleen Peippo

ADESA, Inc.

13085 Hamilton Crossing Boulevard
Carmel, Indiana 46032
U.S.A.
Telephone: (317) 815-1100
Toll Free: (800) 923-3725
Fax: (317) 249-4603
Web site: http://www.adesa.com

Public Company
Incorporated: 1989 as ADE Management, Inc.
Employees: 12,000
Sales: $931.6 million (2004)
Stock Exchanges: New York
Ticker Symbol: KAR
NAIC: 423110 Automobile and Other Motor Vehicle
   Merchant Wholesalers

ADESA, Inc. is one of the leading providers of wholesale used vehicle auction services and financing in North America. The company operates more than 50 used vehicle auctions and 30 salvage vehicle auctions, as well as loan offices affiliated with each. ADESA also owns a vehicle importation service, a web-based auction service, auto reconditioning facilities, and other related subsidiaries. The company controls about one-fifth of the North American auto-auction market.

Beginnings

ADESA officially traces its roots to 1989, when Mike Hockett formed a company called Auto Dealers Exchange Management, Inc. in Birmingham, Alabama. Hockett had grown up in the car business in Indianapolis, Indiana, where his father had owned a used car lot and a Ford dealership before taking control of an auto auction in 1964. Young Hockett began to manage the latter in 1966, running it for more than a decade. In 1979 he joined with a partner to open a vehicle auction in Indianapolis, and they subsequently bought others in Illinois and in Birmingham, Alabama. In 1989 he split with his partner to manage the Birmingham auction on his own.

Several firms had begun buying up clusters of the nearly 400 U.S. wholesale vehicle auctions in the 1980s, and Hockett now sought to grow his company in a similar manner. Over the next several years he bought other auctions near Cincinnati, Memphis, and Lexington, Kentucky, and in 1992 he and Gary Pedigo, president and co-owner of Indianapolis Auto Auction, formed ADESA (Auto Dealers Exchange Services of America) Corp., basing it in Indianapolis. Hockett, 49, was named president and CEO. The company's auctions had sold 173,000 vehicles, worth close to $1.4 billion, in 1991. The firm employed 925.

Wholesale vehicle auctions fell into two categories: consignment sales, where dealers, banks, fleet operators, and wholesalers sold vehicles, some of them for salvage; and factory sales, at which car manufacturers auctioned cars repurchased from rental companies to their franchised dealers. ADESA's auctions were divided equally between the two types. The company's revenues were derived primarily from fees it collected on each sale.

Each of the firm's sites typically held two auctions per week, at which cars were sold as often as once every five seconds. All buyers at the auctions were licensed dealers, and the general public was not admitted. In addition to auctioning vehicles, the firm also reconditioned cars, transported them, and provided financing to dealers. A total of 43 percent of the company's revenues came from auctions, while 25 percent was derived from reconditioning and 19 percent from transportation.

Initial Public Offering in 1992

Shortly after forming ADESA, Hockett and Pedigo announced plans to sell shares to the public to help fund further acquisitions, as well as to pay for construction of a new auction in Buffalo, New York, of which the firm would own 80 percent. In April 1992 two million shares of stock were sold at $11.50 each. Hockett retained controlling interest, with 56 percent of the total.

After the initial public offering (IPO) was completed, the firm purchased the remaining 20 percent of the Buffalo auction, and the fall of 1992 saw the purchase of Concord Auto Auction in Acton, Massachusetts, for $16 million. Revenues for the year topped $45 million, up from nearly $29 million the year before. Net earnings stood at $3.6 million.

Company Perspectives:

ADESA, Inc. helps its business-to-business customers throughout North America succeed by providing a comprehensive array of superior, customer-focused vehicle remarketing and financing services.

In the spring of 1993 ADESA acquired two auctions in Knoxville, Tennessee, which it would continue to operate until a new, larger facility in the area was completed. In July the firm entered Canada, purchasing Montreal Auto Auction in Quebec province, the second largest auto auction in the country. ADESA would later build a new facility there. The company also secured $20 million in bank loans to fund more growth, and in the fall sold an additional 2.5 million shares of stock.

ADESA's Canadian operations were soon expanded with the acquisitions of auctions in Halifax, Nova Scotia, and Ottawa, Ontario. The latter site offered a salvage auction every other week, which was the company's first foray into the sales of wrecked vehicles for parts.

In January 1994 the firm acquired a company called Automotive Finance Corporation, which would enable it to better provide customers with onsite financing. The following month Gulf Coast Auto Auction, Inc. of Bradenton, Florida, and Northfield Auto Auction Corp. of Cleveland also were acquired. Their names were changed to ADESA Sarasota/Bradenton and ADESA Cleveland, respectively, in keeping with the company's usual practice.

In the spring the firm bought a vacant General Motors (GM) plant in Framingham, Massachusetts, for $8 million, to which it would relocate its Concord auction. The 2.9 million-square-foot facility would comprise the nation's largest indoor auction site. It was primarily purchased to enable ADESA to hold auctions in the winter without interruptions from bad weather.

The summer of 1994 saw an agreement reached with General Motors Canada to sell 42,000 rental repurchase vehicles over a three-year span in that country. In August another auto auction was acquired in Miami, Florida, and in September one was purchased in Austin, Texas. Two months later Gary Pedigo sold most of his stake in ADESA and left the company to buy a Chevrolet dealership in Indianapolis.

Acquisition by Minnesota Power & Light in 1995

In January 1995 Minnesota Power & Light (MP&L), an electric utility company, bought 80 percent of ADESA's stock for $162 million. ADESA management, who held most of the remainder, would remain in charge. The deal brought more money for growth, while also helping to diversify the power company's portfolio. MP&L had earlier purchased wastewater treatment, mining, and paper milling and recycling operations, though it had sold the latter two to fund the acquisition of ADESA.

In mid-1995 ADESA began construction of a new auction facility in Ottawa, Ontario, and began tearing down a former Johns-Manville asbestos plant in New Jersey to build an auction

there. In the fall the company's Canadian division merged its salvage operations with Impact Auto Auctions of Canada, after which it would operate salvage auctions in six locations. The latter half of the year also saw ADESA purchase an auction in Billings, Montana, and reorganize its top management to improve efficiency. During the year 475,000 cars were sold at the firm's auctions, and its finance arm loaned more than $100 million to 2,400 dealers.

In early 1996 MP&L boosted its ownership stake in the firm to 83 percent, and ADESA bought another auction near Milwaukee. In the summer, after founder Mike Hockett and several other top executives had reportedly attempted to purchase the firm and take it public, the utility exercised its option to buy them out. After the $44 million deal was completed, the head of ADESA's Canadian unit, James Hallett, was named president and CEO. In the fall ADESA bought an auction in Pennsylvania and three in Texas. Earnings for the year topped $3.7 million on sales of $183.9 million.

Completion of the company's two most ambitious auction facilities, the former factory sites in Massachusetts and New Jersey, were now putting a strain on its finances. Spending on the latter had ballooned from $18 million to $37 million, and $20 million had been spent at the Framingham site, double the original estimate. In the latter case the indoor auction's advantages were offset by the challenges of efficiently operating such a large facility, and two-thirds of the 2.9 million-square-foot building had been torn down. Because of these and other financial problems, new CEO Hallett began taking a more measured approach to growth by slowing down the rate of acquisitions, adding services at existing sites, and marketing ADESA's business to new customers.

The spring of 1997 saw a stake bought in an auction in Sacramento, California, and the sale of the firm's Bradenton, Florida auction. In the fall the company spent $15 million to double its vehicle-hauling fleet to approximately 180 vehicles, and created a separate business, Great Rigs, Inc., to perform vehicle transport duties for it and other companies. ADESA also bought 28 acres in Halifax, Nova Scotia, to build a new auction facility there.

In 1998 the firm formed an alliance with competitor ADT Automotive, through which ADESA's finance unit would offer loans at all 28 ADT auctions. In the spring of 1999 the company bought auctions in Des Moines, Iowa, and Vancouver, British Columbia. Construction of an additional Canadian auction near Calgary, Alberta, was started in October, and it began operations the following year.

Adding More Than Two Dozen Auctions in 2000

In early 2000 ADESA bought an auction in San Diego and a partially completed one near Los Angeles. The firm also was preparing to reopen its Concord, Massachusetts site after exceeding the capacity of its Framingham location.

In June the company bought Canadian Auction Group (CAG), the owner of 13 auctions and dealer financing sites around Canada. CAG had sold 200,000 vehicles and taken in $68 million in the most recent 12-month period. ADESA also

Key Dates:

1989: Mike Hockett forms Auto Dealers Exchange Management, Inc. in Alabama.
1992: Hockett, with four auctions, and Gary Pedigo, with one, form ADESA, launching its initial public offering (IPO).
1993: The company's first Canadian auctions are purchased.
1994: Automotive Finance Corp. and a Massachusetts GM plant are acquired; Pedigo leaves.
1995: Minnesota Power & Light buys control of ADESA; Impact Auctions is purchased.
1996: Minnesota Power buys the remainder of the firm; James Hallett replaces Hockett as CEO.
1997: Great Rigs, Inc. trucking subsidiary is formed.
2000: The company acquires the 13-site Canadian Auction Group and eight ADT auctions.
2001: Auto Placement Center and ComSearch are purchased; the company's *Global Vehicle Remarketing* report debuts.
2002: Great Rigs is sold.
2003: LiveBlock Internet auctions are introduced.
2004: ADESA is spun off on the New York Stock Exchange; David Gartzke is named CEO.

acquired the remaining interest in Impact Auto Auctions of Canada that it did not own.

Less than a week later, the company reached an agreement to buy eight auctions from ADT Automotive and a ninth from Manheim Auctions. Their combined sales for the previous year was put at $130 million. The nine sites were located in Phoenix, San Francisco, Atlanta, Kansas City, Seattle, Colorado Springs, Tampa, Orlando, and in Clearwater, Florida.

The $251 million deal had come about after Manheim agreed to buy ADT's chain of auctions, full ownership of which would violate federal antitrust laws. Afterward, ADESA moved its finance offices out of the 28 former ADT sites that Manheim would keep. In August, two additional auctions were purchased in Arkansas. When those deals were completed, ADESA would own 57 auctions in the United States and Canada.

In December 2000 the firm bought International Vehicle Importers, Inc., a Flint, Michigan-based vehicle importer. ADESA's holdings now also included a half-dozen auctions that specialized in heavy equipment and trucks, a vehicle remarketing company called PAR, and AutoVIN, a firm that performed inspections of cars coming off-lease.

Acquisition of APC and ComSearch in 2001

January 2001 saw the purchase of two Rhode Island-based firms, Auto Placement Center, Inc. (APC) and ComSearch, Inc., for a total of $62.4 million. The latter was a web-based provider of parts location and insurance adjustment audit services, and APC ran eight salvage auctions in New England. ADESA also published the first edition of *Global Vehicle Remarketing,* a 68-page statistical report on the used vehicle industry. The

publication was intended to inform the industry, media, and lawmakers, as well as help to raise ADESA's profile. A quarterly report, *Pulse,* was added later.

In May 2001 the firm bought an auction in Tulsa, Oklahoma, and in October Brian Warner was appointed president, with Jim Hallett remaining in charge as CEO. Later in the year, ADESA bought a salvage auction in North Carolina.

In the summer of 2002 the company was restructured to combine its marketing and sales departments, and the commercial remarketing staff was moved from offices to auction sites. The firm also sold its trucking unit, Great Rigs, Inc., and replaced its San Francisco-area auction with a new $60 million facility located on 230 acres. The 12-lane auction was California's largest. The site it replaced was later taken over by an ADESA Impact salvage auction.

The year 2002 also saw a new salvage auction opened in Orlando, Florida, and the firm's Industry Relations and Analytical Services department starting to supply monthly reports to the U.S. Bureau of Economic Analysis. ADESA recently had added other services to its portfolio, including AutoScan diagnostic certification programs, EndTrust end-of-term leasing services, Auction Management Computer Systems, and Micro 21 dealer software. The company's revenues reached $844 million during the year, with profits of $93 million.

January 2003 saw Brian Warner reassigned to head the company's Canadian operations, while Jim Hallett took back the title of president. In October the firm's parent, now known as ALLETE, Inc., announced that it would spin off ADESA as a separate entity. One share of ADESA stock would be issued for each share owned in ALLETE. The move was taken to increase shareholder value, as ADESA now accounted for almost two-thirds of ALLETE's revenues.

The fall of 2003 also saw a new auction facility opened near Atlanta, Georgia, to serve Chrysler Group dealers. The eight-lane auction was situated on 260 acres and featured a 90,000-square-foot reconditioning center. The company had by now also introduced LiveBlock, which enabled dealers to participate in auctions at certain sites via the Internet. ADESA had acquired the technology from a Canadian firm. The following spring saw the company move its headquarters to a new building in the Indianapolis suburb of Carmel, after first considering offers from several other cities.

Returning to Public Ownership in 2004

In June 2004 the spinoff from ALLETE got underway with the sale of 6.25 million shares of stock on the New York Stock Exchange. The remaining 93 percent of the firm's shares were distributed to ALLETE shareholders in September. ADESA had by now also issued $125 million in bonds, as well as securing $525 million in loan commitments from a total of 29 banks.

After the spinoff was complete ALLETE CEO David Gartzke left that firm to become CEO, president, and chairman of ADESA, which he had been helping run since the previous summer. The year 2004 also saw the firm open a new salvage auction in Sacramento, California, and an auction in Mexico, its first in that country. ADESA was now planning expansions to several of its existing sites, including Manville, New Jersey, and Montreal. The firm also was working with Toyota Financial Services to offer direct vehicle sales between dealers over the Internet. LiveBlock was now available at an increasing number of ADESA auction sites as well, with 6 percent of sales at such sites made to online bidders. Sales for the year topped $931 million, and income hit $105.3 million.

In early 2005 ADESA completed the repurchase of some 4.4 million shares of stock to boost its value. The firm also upgraded LiveBlock, which was now offered at most of its sites, so that bidders could view multiple auctions at the same time. Expansion continued during the year with the construction of a new salvage auction near Hartford, Connecticut. The firm's 2005 Global Remarketing Report projected continuing growth in the market, with U.S. used vehicle sales expected to rise from 42.7 million in 2004 to 44.4 million in 2005, and 47.7 million in 2009.

In more than 15 years of steady, sometimes rapid growth, ADESA, Inc. had assembled the second largest chain of used-vehicle auctions in North America. The company had added complementary businesses in financing, reconditioning, importation, and other services along the way, and was now expanding its Internet sales capabilities.

Principal Subsidiaries

ADESA Corporation, LLC; Impact Auto Auctions, Inc.; Automotive Finance Corporation; PAR, Inc.; AutoVIN, Inc.; ComSearch, Inc.; Automotive Recovery Services, Inc.; ADESA Importation Services, Inc.

Principal Competitors

Manheim Auto Auctions Inc.; Copart Inc.; Insurance Auto Auctions Inc.

Further Reading

Andrews, Greg, "Auto Auction Firm Goes Public, Ends Hoosier Dry Spell for IPOs," *Indianapolis Business Journal,* April 20, 1992, p. 3.

Barker, Robert, "A Divorce with a Tidy Deal for Investors?," *Business Week,* June 14, 2004, p. 97.

Evanoff, Ted, "Automotive Services Company Ponders Incentives to Leave Indianapolis," *Indianapolis Star,* May 3, 2002.

Feaver, Christopher, "Auctioning Used Cars for the Lord: ADESA's Mike Hockett Builds Small Business into Public Company," *Indianapolis Business Journal,* January 24, 1994, p. 10B.

Kukolla, Steve, "ADESA Sells 80%: Auto Auction Firm to Shoot for No. 1," *Indianapolis Business Journal,* January 9, 1995, p. 1.

Love, Myron, "Auctioning Autos Goes High Tech at ADESA – On-Line Inventory Helps Move Cars," *Winnipeg Free Press,* May 30, 2003, p. F4.

Maurer, Katie, "ADESA Planning New Carmel Headquarters," *Indianapolis Business Journal,* October 28, 2002, p. A3.

Miller, Joe, "Auction Chain Turns Gluttony into Growth," *Automotive News,* January 11, 1999, p. 32.

Morrison, Patrick, "ADESA Writes Book on Used-Car Industry," *Indianapolis Business Journal,* April 30, 2001, p. 21.

O'Malley, Chris, "ADESA Pushes Virtual Business," *Indianapolis Business Journal,* January 3, 2005, p. A3.

Passi, Peter, "Duluth, Minn.-Based ALLETE to Spin Off Profitable Automotive Division," *Duluth News-Tribune,* October 25, 2003.

Postman, Lore, "Rift Leads to $44 Mil. Buyout," *Indianapolis Business Journal,* September 9, 1996, p. A1.

Sawyers, Arlena, "ADESA, Manheim Divvy Up ADT's Auctions," *Automotive News,* July 3, 2000, p. 345.

Smith, Bruce C., "Independence Is Road to Profit for ADESA Auto Auction House of Carmel, Ind.," *Indianapolis Star,* August 18, 2004.

Thomas, Charles M., "Hockett Firm Seeks $57 Million to Grow," *Automotive News,* March 9, 1992.

Wernle, Bradford, "ADESA Adds Haulers," *Automotive News,* September 7, 1997, p. 18.

——, "ADESA Turns onto a More Conservative Route," *Automotive News,* September 30, 1996, p. 6.

——, "ADESA: You'll Be Sold on Auctions," *Automotive News,* May 20, 1996, p. 3.

——, "Indoor ADESA Boston Auction Helps Buyers Beat the New England Winter," *Automotive News,* February 10, 1997, p. 18.

—Frank Uhle

Agnico-Eagle Mines Limited

145 King Street East, Suite 500
Toronto, Ontario M5C 2Y7
Canada
Telephone: (416) 947-1212
Toll Free: (888) 822-6714
Fax: (416) 367-4681
Web site: http://www.agnico-eagle.com

Private Company
Incorporated: 1972
Employees: 549
Sales: $126.8 million (2003)
Stock Exchanges: New York Toronto
Ticker Symbol: AEM
NAIC: 212221 Gold Ore Mining

Agnico-Eagle Mines Limited is a Toronto-based Canadian gold producer, with its shares trading on the Toronto Stock Exchange and the New York Stock Exchange. The company no longer mines its founding properties, the silver-producing Agnico mine and Eagle Gold mine, instead limiting its mining activities to the LaRonde Mine in northwestern Quebec, which possesses proven and probable gold reserves of 5.3 million ounces and produces silver, copper, and zinc as a byproduct of the gold mining process. Agnico-Eagle's other properties, not currently in production, contain gold reserves of another 2.6 million ounces. The company also is conducting exploration on 56 properties located in eastern Canada and the western United States. It is pursuing opportunities in northern Mexico as well and owns a stake in the Surrikuusikko gold field in Finland. For many years Agnico-Eagle has been one of the lowest cost producers in North America, a company that has steadfastly refused to engage in hedging (selling future gold production at a set price as a precautionary measure), instead selling all of its production at the spot price of gold.

Merger of Agnico and Eagle: 1972

Agnico-Eagle was created in 1972 by Canadian businessman Paul Penna when he merged Agnico Mines Limited and Eagle Gold Mines Limited. The origins of the Agnico property can be traced to 1903, at a time when northern Ontario remained wilderness. A pair of timber scouts, James McKinley and Ernest Darragh, were boating along the shore of what was then known as Long Lake when they noticed the sun reflecting off the rocks in a curious manner. They investigated, and took samples of the rocks they found, which were then assayed in Montreal. The report showed that the men had found silver, an astounding 4,000 ounces to the ton. The boom town of Cobalt sprang up, as more than a dozen silver mines opened in the area over the next few years. Silver was so prevalent in Cobalt that in the early years mining was done at the surface, and only later were the first shafts dug. Production peaked in 1911, a year in which Cobalt shipped 31 million ounces of silver, or roughly one-eighth of the world's silver production. In the 1930s the area appeared to be played out, as repeatedly the silver veins refused to yield beyond 300 feet below the surface. Some of the original claims continued to be picked over for a number of years, and during the 1950s the area was revitalized by the mining of cobalt, used in the United States in cutting tools, heat-resistant alloys, and cancer radiation therapy. But this market dried up as well when new sources of cobalt became available in the United States.

A handful of Cobalt-area silver mining companies remained operational into the 1950s, but the cost of production was higher than the price of silver. In 1953 they banded together to form Cobalt Consolidated Mining Co. Four years later the company took a new name, Agnico Mines Ltd., its name combining the symbols of silver (Ag), nickel (Ni), and cobalt (Co). By employing new diamond drills and other modern mining techniques, the company was able to recover high-grade silver and began to buy up other mining properties in the area. In 1960 Agnico discovered a major silver deposit, but poor management squandered the company's opportunities and unwisely opted to lease out two of its best properties. It was at this time that Paul Penna, a new Agnico shareholder, began building a stake in the company and took steps to seek control through a proxy fight.

Penna was born Paul Phineas Osheroff in 1922, one of seven children in a family of Russian Jewish immigrants raised in a tough section of Toronto. Growing up poor, he tried to make money any way he could. When just eight, he attempted to become a caddy at the exclusive St. Georges's Golf & Country

Company Perspectives:

We have set out to build a company that focuses on quality, growth and a strong financial position, while retaining full leverage to gold process.

Club, but was turned away because he was too small. When he grew bigger he returned to the country club to become a caddy, and in the process developed a passion for golf. At the age of 14 he quit school to become a full-time caddy at the Weston Golf & Country Club. He rose early each morning to play the course and hone his game, then for the rest of the day carried the bags of the rich and influential men who were club members. It was during his days as a caddy that Penna assumed a less Jewish-sounding name. Long called Penny because of his middle name Phineas, he modified it to Penna, thus becoming Paul Penna.

Paul Penna Becoming Involved in Mining in the 1930s

Naturally athletic, Penna was a superb golfer, but lacked the necessary killer instinct to become a professional. Penna began running a pro shop, but because it was a seasonal business he was in need of work during the winter months. He found it as a messenger with one of the men whose bag he carried at the Weston golf club, Eddie de Palma. According to Mike Macbeth in his *Silver Threads Among the Gold,* de Palma was a loud-talking, big-spending mining promoter and a Detroit resident who left the United States after the Securities and Exchange Commission tightened its regulations in the 1930s. De Palma set up a bucket shop in Toronto and began promoting penny stocks, selling shares of Canadian mines to the unsuspecting. Penna, always an eager learner—outside of the classroom, at any rate—paid close attention to the salesmen making their telephone pitches, so that when de Palma gave him a chance to try his hand at it, Penna became an instant success. While the older men concentrated on the U.S. calls, Penna handled the Canadian prospects, taking advantage of his natural enthusiasm and charm, and soon becoming de Palma's top salesman. One of the secrets to his success, however, may have been that he naively believed what he was pitching. He invested a large percentage of his commissions in the same dubious properties he was selling on the phone.

Penna was a millionaire by the age of 24, but he also was exhausted and suffering from a stomach ulcer, and just as he was coming to understand that he was a seller (and buyer) of worthless stocks, he found himself swept up in a housecleaning effort launched by the Ontario Securities Commission. De Palma was especially targeted, as were de Palma's salesmen—especially his boy wonder. Penna had his license suspended for six months; he was out of work and, soon, broke. His license was reinstated but Penna lost his enthusiasm for stock promotion, drifting from broker to broker over the next few years, before deciding to become a golf teacher.

Although disenchanted with stock promotion, Penna remained fascinated by the mining industry. After getting married and experiencing the death of his father, he was mature enough

in 1956 that he decided to go into business with his brother Norman to develop properties into producing mines. While Norman scouted for prospects in the field, Penna, contending with the stigma that was still attached to his name from his days with de Palma, struggled to raise the necessary capital for drilling and exploration. A key success was a silver mine in the Cobalt area, Deer Horn Mines Ltd., which Penna and his brother bought in 1963. Penna also began investing in the nearby Agnico properties and became outraged by the company's inept management. He and his brother formed the Share-holder's Protective Committee and began sending out letters to fellow shareholders severely questioning Agnico's leadership. A proxy war for control of the company ensued and Penna's group won out.

Although Agnico's disheartened employees were wary of Penna, having become well aware of his bucket-shop past during the proxy fight, they were quickly won over by his willingness to supply them with much needed equipment and the assurance that from that day forward Agnico would no longer be leasing its properties to outsiders. He also demon-strated his belief in the company's properties by sticking with an effort, rather than quitting once a vein appeared to end. Instead of assuming that the region's silver was to be found no deeper than 300 feet, he backed his geologist, Brian Thorniley, who had a gut feeling that another layer of silver would be found around the 1,500-foot level. It was a costly gamble, but it paid off when silver was discovered at the deeper level, a deposit that the company would exploit for decades to come. Penna also benefited from rising silver prices, so that by the end of the 1960s Agnico was a profitable concern.

Also during the 1960s Penna began his involvement with Eagle Gold Mines, which was launched in 1945 as Jack Lake Mines Ltd., a base metals company with a few claims in Quebec. In 1961 the company, now known as New Jack Lake Uranium Mines Ltd., acquired some property in Joutel that it hoped might contain copper and zinc. A year later it assumed yet another name, Equity Explorations Ltd., and as such began a drilling program in 1964. Penna in the meantime was confident about the state of Agnico and now scouting around for new prospects. He kept tabs on Equity, which looked like it had a promising copper mine in its Joutel property. But when gold began to appear as the drills cut deeper, Penna was quick to buy up Equity stock, which was selling around 20 cents a share. In March 1965 assay reports were so promising that Equity's stock jumped to nearly $2 a share and the company was able to take advantage of sudden interest to sell $800,000 of new shares. But the bubble soon burst when assays conducted by the Quebec Securities Commission offered a less optimistic report, leading to a panic and total collapse in the price of Equity stock. While others were unloading their shares, however, Penna was buying. He kept buying even as Equity was accused of salting its sample with additional gold. More tests were done by the Commission and it was shown that despite the salting of the sample, there was still plenty of true gold in the new samples. Moreover, Equity drilled deeper and found even more promising amounts of gold. But Equity's management was now under a cloud of suspicion and it could no longer effectively operate the company. As a result, Penna was able to wrest away control and was elected president in November 1966.

Penna immediately took steps to turn the Joutel site into a producing mine. One of the first things he did was change its name; in February 1967 Equity became Eagle Gold Mines. Over the next three years nearly $9 million was invested to ready the property for mining, but in early 1970 Penna received grim news: The 1967 estimate on how much it would cost to bring the mine into production had been rendered invalid by rising material and construction costs. The $3 million price tag had ballooned to more than $5.5 million, money that the company could not raise. Penna was forced to shut down the operation, but rather than following the normal procedure of flooding the mine to preserve the timbers and excavation, he opted to spend about $3,000 a month to maintain the property, lest his action threaten future attempts to raise new money. Nevertheless, the news destroyed the value of Eagle stock. Penna, who had bought a lot of shares on margin, soon found his broker selling off his holdings, despite promising not to sell.

The next two years were a difficult period for Penna, who traveled around the world looking for money to shore up Eagle. All the while, Agnico was flourishing. A friend put Penna in contact with Jake Moore, the head of Brascan Ltd., who suggested that Penna should use Agnico's money to bail out Eagle. Since Agnico was an Eagle investor, it made sense to Penna that Agnico had a vested interest in helping out Eagle. With cash to spare, Agnico was in a position to do so. Using Agnico's money, Eagle was able to pay off its debt, and with rising gold prices in the world, the Eagle mine was able to attract investment from the Toronto-Dominion Bank to complete the mine. Then, in 1972 the two mining companies merged, becoming Agnico-Eagle Mines Limited. Two years later, in February 1974, the Eagle mine became operational, just in time to take advantage of record gold prices. In addition, more gold reserves were discovered at a deeper level. Eagle was now earning money, and the symbiotic relationship between Agnico and Eagle became apparent: Within ten years Eagle would come to the rescue of Agnico. With the price of silver down, the company could now afford to stockpile silver until prices rebounded, depending on the revenues of the gold mine.

Always on the lookout for new opportunities, Penna accumulated other mining properties along the way. In 1971 he bought the Telbel property adjoining Eagle, which he had tar-

geted years earlier. He bought it for the rock-bottom price of $76,000. After Telbel went into production in 1985 it would prove to contain 500,000 ounces of gold. Another mining property with which Penna became involved in the 1970s was the LaRonde Mine, which grew out of Dumagami Mines, incorporated in 1961. While the property showed some promise, no one other than Penna became overly excited by the periodic drilling results. Another company he controlled, Mentor Exploration and Development, began buying shares in Dumagami in the mid-1970s. Then starting in 1978 he began stockpiling shares for both Mentor and Agnico-Eagle, so that by 1982 Penna controlled 36.3 percent of the venture. He and the other major shareholder, Noranda Mines, began developing the property, and eventually Penna bought out Noranda's interest. By the mid-1980s the mine was put into production. A man instrumental in the project, and who had brought Eagle into production, was Don la Ronde. Troubled with a bad heart, he died at the age of 55 in 1986. To honor him, Penna renamed the mine at Dumagami the LaRonde Mine. It was folded into the Agnico-Eagle operations in 1989.

Agnico-Eagle prospered during the 1980s until gold and silver prices plunged at the end of the decade. The company closed its silver mines in late 1988 and a few months later sold off its real estate investments (a diversification effort launched in 1986). The company also wrote off some older, played-out mines, leading to significant losses on the balance sheet. A disgruntled shareholder attempted to mount a proxy fight but the effort petered out in 1990. A few weeks later, a major gold discovery was located in the LaRonde property, an event that bolstered Agnico-Eagle's stock price, and led to the company focusing its attention on this property. In the next three years Agnico-Eagle raised $179 million in stock and bond offerings to bring the LaRonde Mine into production.

Penna's Death in 1996

Penna died in August 1996 at the age of 73, setting off rumors that Agnico-Eagle might be the subject of takeover bids. Over the years Penna, who had owned a majority stake in the company, had been able to thwart any attempts by larger mining companies to take over the company. Although Agnico-Eagle remained independent, it began to turn over its aging management team and board of directors. Upon Penna's death, 73-year-old Wencel A. Hubacheck was named the new CEO. But within two years, a younger man, Sean Boyd, the company's chief financial officer, was tabbed to lead the company into the future.

Partially because of weak gold prices, Agnico-Eagle failed to produce a profit from 1996 until 2002. The company continued to focus on the LaRonde Mine and the area surrounding it, where other promising deposits were uncovered. The company also sought opportunities elsewhere in the world. In 2004 it acquired an interest in a Finnish company, Riddarhyttan Resources AB, gaining a stake in the Surrikuusikko gold deposit located some 500 miles north of Helsinki. Later in 2004 Agnico-Eagle acquired Contact Diamond Corporation, picking up 56 properties in Canada and the United States to explore. Contact Diamond's Reno, Nevada-based office also evaluated exploration opportunities in northern Mexico. Early in 2005, Agnico-Eagle entered into an option agreement to acquire a project in northern Mexico's Sierre Madre gold belt.

Principal Subsidiaries

Sudbury Contact Mines Limited; Mentor Exploration and Development Co., Limited.

Principal Competitors

Barrick Gold Corporation; Newmont Mining Corporation; Placer Dome Inc.

Further Reading

Hasselback, Drew, "Agnico-Eagle Foresees Gold Bull Market," *National Post,* June 22, 2002, p. FP6.

Macbeth, Mike, "You Can Take a Flier on This One," *Canadian Business,* April 1983, p. 46.

——, *Silver Threads Among the Gold,* Toronto: Trans-Canada Press, 1987.

Rudnitsky, Howard, "Gold Digger," *Forbes,* September 11, 1995, p. 82.

—Ed Dinger

Air Berlin GmbH & Co. Luftverkehrs KG

Saatwinkler Damm 42-43
Berlin 13627
Germany
Telephone: +49 (0)1805 737 800
Fax: +49 (0)30 41 02 10 03
Web site: http://www.airberlin.com

Private Company
Incorporated: 1991
Employees: 2,300
Sales: DEM 1.28 billion (2005 est.)
NAIC: 481111 Scheduled Passenger Air Transportation;
481211 Nonscheduled Chartered Passenger Air
Transportation; 488190 Other Support Activities for
Air Transportation

Air Berlin GmbH & Co. Luftverkehrs KG is Germany's leading low-fare airline. Begun as a charter operator, Air Berlin has repositioned itself, in large part, as a scheduled carrier. It follows a low-cost business model with emphasis on direct, scheduled flights from a number of regional airports, rather than a hub-and-spoke system. Air Berlin specializes in flying to sunny vacation spots in the Mediterranean, the Canary Islands, and North Africa, as well as major business destinations in Europe. The airline makes more than 200 trips each week to the airline's first destination, the Spanish island of Mallorca, which it uses as a hub for service to mainland Spain. The airline's passenger count approached 14 million in 2005. It is the second largest airline in Germany after Lufthansa AG. Air Berlin's 200-person maintenance division handles all but the heaviest maintenance in-house. It also does third-party work. An engineering department allows the airline to handle minor modifications. Air Berlin has a holding in and a close alliance with NIKI, the airline formed from the remnants of Aero Lloyd Austria. As of 2005, company founder Kim Lundgren owned 26 percent of Air Berlin's shares.

Origins

Air Berlin was shaped by the forces that divided and reunited its namesake city. During the Cold War, only civil aircraft from the Allied occupying nations (the United States, the United Kingdom, and France) were allowed to fly into Berlin. In the late 1970s, an American started a company to provide flights for tour operators from the German capital to holiday destinations. Its two main clients, reported *Frankfurter Allgemeine Zeitung,* would be Hanover's TUI (Touristik Union International) and NUR-Touristic of Frankfurt.

Air Berlin Charter Company was established in Oregon in 1978 by former Pan Am pilot Kim Lundgren. It was originally a subsidiary of Lelco, an agricultural business of Kim's father Leonard Lundgren. It was renamed Air Berlin, Inc. in 1982 and Lundair, Inc. in 1992.

The first charter flight, from Berlin's Tegel Airport to Palma de Mallorca, Spain, occurred on April 28, 1979. Flights to the United States soon followed. A leased Boeing 707 was used briefly, replaced by a pair of Boeing 737s in 1981. According to *Air International,* the company posted its first profit in 1986.

German Registry in 1991

East and West Germany were reunified on October 3, 1990, and the occupation of the country by the Allies ended. On April 16, 1991, Lundgren established a new, German-registered company, Air Berlin GmbH & Co. Luftverkehrs KG, in partnership with Joachim Hunold, former marketing executive at holiday airline LTU (Lufttransport-Unternehmen GmbH), and other investors. On November 1, 1991, the German-registered Air Berlin took over Air Berlin Inc.'s operations. Its capital had been increased to DEM 7.5 million. Hunold became the airline's managing director.

Service from secondary airports was part of Air Berlin's plan to offer "blanket coverage." Originally based at Berlin's Tegel Airport, in 1992 the airline began flying from the sleepy provincial airport of Münster/Osnabrück. Other airports in-

15

cluded Paderborn/Lippstadt, Nuremberg, and Dortmund, as well as Dresden, Erfurt, Leipzig/Halle, and Rostock-Laage in the former East Germany. Air Berlin developed a primary hub at Nuremberg. Air Berlin GmbH had also expanded its client base, reported *Frankfurter Allgemeine Zeitung,* adding several tour operators, including Cologne's ITS.

Passenger count exceeded one million in 1994. In 1995, the company operated a fleet of eight jets and had 90 employees, according to *Flight International*'s "World Airline Directory." Air Berlin thrived in the 1990s, ordering at least 16 new Boeing 737s during the decade to meet demand.

Scheduled Flights in the Late 1990s

A company spokesperson told *Air Transport World* that changes in the package tour market prompted Air Berlin to begin operating as a low-cost, scheduled carrier in 1997. It started running the Mallorca (Majorca) Shuttle to its top destination from several cities in Germany. At the same time, Air Berlin began selling seats through its own call center for the first time. Internet sales were added three years later.

A series of Spanish cities—Alicante, Almeria, Jerez de la Frontera, and Malaga—were added to the roster in the late 1990s due to increased interest in the Iberian mainland. Majorca was used as a secondary hub.

Air Berlin managed to grow its business even in the depressed aviation environment of 2001 and 2002. Passenger count grew by a third to 5.5 million in 2001 as sales climbed from DEM 407 million to DEM 562 million. After the September 11 terrorist attacks on the United States, its customers avoided Egypt, visiting Spanish destinations instead, reported *Die Welt.* According to *Financial Times Deutschland,* routes to Spain accounted for 70 percent of revenues, with half of sales direct to passengers and half to tour operators.

2002 City Shuttle

Air Berlin began offering scheduled flights to several European business centers through its City Shuttle program in October 2002. London, Milan, Vienna, and Barcelona were the first of these destinations. The lowest of these fares was DEM 39 one-way. A number of other airlines were entering the low-fare market at the same time, both to European capitals and to holiday destinations. What set Air Berlin apart, noted *Flight International,* was its emphasis on direct departures from a number of regional airports, rather than a hub-and-spoke system. A spokesperson told the *Observer* that the smaller airports Air Berlin used were often near city centers, making them more appealing to business travelers. Another appealing feature was a new frequent flyer program.

Air Berlin had 16 Boeing 737s at the time of the City Shuttle launch, which precipitated a huge fleet expansion. Another 15 aircraft were added within six months. The company also leased three BAe 146s and three Fokker 100s. As the fleet grew, the airline's 200-person maintenance division was preparing to add hangar space and perform heavier maintenance duties, both for the airline itself and for third parties, according to *Flight International.*

Air Berlin carried a record 9.6 million passengers in 2003 as revenues rose from DEM 696 million to DEM 894 million. It was Germany's second largest airline after Lufthansa AG. Revenues rose to DEM 1.05 billion in 2004, when the airline served 12 million passengers.

In 2004, the airline took a 24 percent holding in the "NIKI" airline being rebuilt from insolvent Aero Lloyd Austria by airline entrepreneur (and Formula One champion) Niki Lauda. Joint marketing agreements were part of the deal, billed as the world's first low-fare airline alliance. Air Berlin had begun flying to NIKI's base of Vienna, which it planned to use as a springboard into Eastern Europe, reported *Air Transport Intelligence.* By this time, Air Berlin had about 50 Boeing 737s in its fleet.

Another cooperation agreement, with German rival Hapag Lloyd Flug AG, was announced in July 2004. Hapag Lloyd was one of two airlines owned by travel group TUI AG and focused on holiday trips to the Mediterranean. TUI's other airline, Hapag Lloyd Express, connected major European cities and was not part of the code-sharing deal with Air Berlin.

According to *Aviation Week & Space Technology,* the European airline industry was expected to undergo some form of consolidation after spawning approximately 50 new airlines since the turn of the millennium. In 2004, *Air Transport World* counted 14 budget airlines in Germany alone. Unlike Air Berlin, however, many of these were unprofitable.

A massive aircraft order positioned Air Berlin to become the third largest low-fare airline in Europe, said *Aviation Week & Space Technology.* Primarily a Boeing operator for most of its history, in late 2004 Air Berlin ordered 70 A320 aircraft valued at $4.2 billion from Airbus. Ten of these were earmarked for NIKI, which already had an all-Airbus fleet of five A320s. Options were placed on another 40 planes. By the time of this

Key Dates:

1978: Air Berlin Inc. is incorporated in Oregon, in the United States, by a former Pan Am pilot.
1979: The first flight connects Berlin with the holiday destination of Palma de Mallorca, Spain.
1986: The company posts its first profit.
1991: Air Berlin GmbH & Co. Luftverkehrs KG is established in Germany by Kim Lundgren and local partners.
1994: The passenger count reaches one million.
1997: Air Berlin restructures operations as a low-cost, scheduled airline.
2002: City Shuttle is launched.
2004: Turnover exceeds DEM 1 billion; Air Berlin takes 24 percent holding in new ''NIKI'' airline.

order, charters accounted for only 10 percent of the airline's capacity.

2005 Euro Shuttle

The City Shuttle and Majorca Shuttle programs were combined into the ''Euro Shuttle'' in January 2005. The new name reflected Air Berlin's range of operations. It was a significant presence in the domestic Spanish market and also was growing its London (Stansted) to Majorca traffic. The airline was expecting to carry 13.8 million passengers in 2005.

Principal Competitors

easyJet PLC; GermanWings GmbH; Hapag Lloyd Express GmbH; Lufthansa AG; Ryanair PLC.

Further Reading

''Air Berlin—Breaking the Mould,'' *Air International,* December 7, 2004.

''Air Berlin Grows Rapidly (Air Berlin Wachst Kraftig),'' *Die Welt,* January 3, 2002.

''Air Berlin Increases Capital Base,'' *Frankfurter Allgemeine Zeitung,* July 19, 1991, p. 22.

Atkins, Ralph, and Jens Flottau, ''Air Berlin and TUI to Expand Links,'' *Financial Times* (London), July 6, 2004, p. 28.

Boles, Tracey, ''German Airlines Eye European Budget Sector,'' *Sunday Business* (London), January 12, 2003.

Flottau, Jens, ''Growth Spurt; Air Berlin's Surprisingly Large Aircraft Order Bodes Well for Industry, Ill for Its Competitors,'' *Aviation Week & Space Technology,* November 29, 2004, p. 46.

——, ''Joining Forces; Alliance by Low-Cost European Airlines Could Launch Industry Trend,'' *Aviation Week & Space Technology,* January 19, 2004, p. 408.

Genger, Jenny, and Jens Flottau, ''Holiday Flight Operator Air Berlin Enters Low-Cost Market (Air Berlin Folgt Dem Trend Zum Billigflieger),'' *Financial Times Deutschland,* September 4, 2002.

Hill, Leonard, ''The New Breed: Cut-Price Flights Reshape the German Market, But the Airlines May Not All Survive,'' *Air Transport World,* February 1, 2004, p. 44.

——, ''An Old Hand at Low Fares: Air Berlin Melds Tour-Operator Sales with Rising Seat-Only Business,'' *Air Transport World,* January 2003, pp. 45 + .

Kaminski, David, ''Air Berlin Takes 24% of New Lauda Carrier Niki,'' *Air Transport Intelligence,* January 9, 2004.

Kingsley-Jones, Max, ''Airbus Sees Off Boeing to Win Air Berlin Mega-Deal; All-737 Operator Signs $4.2 Billion A320 Order, Including a Batch for Austrian Partner Niki,'' *Flight International,* November 9, 2004, p. 12.

Morgan, Oliver, ''Cut-Price Crisis: Does No Frills Mean No Profits?,'' *Observer,* Bus. Sec., May 9, 2004, p. 3.

Phelan, Michael, ''Bringing It Home; As Low-Cost Airlines Reach Critical Mass, They Are Pulling More Ground Services and Technical Support In-House to Achieve Maintenance Efficiencies,'' *Flight International,* May 20, 2003, p. 42.

Pilling, Mark, ''Air Berlin Sets Growth Path,'' *Airline Business,* December 1, 2004, p. 20.

Wastnage, Justin, ''Air Berlin to Double Fleet in Bid for Low-Fare Supremacy; German Carrier Starts Negotiations with Airbus and Boeing About Expansion Ambitions,'' *Flight International,* April 8, 2003, p. 17.

—Frederick C. Ingram

Akamai Technologies, Inc.

8 Cambridge Center
Cambridge, Massachusetts 02141-1401
U.S.A.
Telephone: (617) 444-3000
Toll Free: (877) 425-2624
Fax: (617) 444-3001
Web site: http://www.akamai.com

Public Company
Incorporated: 1998
Employees: 535
Sales: $210.0 million (2004)
Stock Exchanges: NASDAQ
Ticker Symbol: AKAM
NAIC: 541512 Computer Systems Design Services

With its headquarters located in Cambridge, Massachusetts, Akamai Technologies, Inc. maintains a massive distributed computer network, composed of more than 15,000 servers in more than 65 countries. The network provides software and services to help companies, government entities, and other customers ensure reliable delivery of web content and applications. Rather than just supplementing a customer's server capacity, in effect acting as a mirror site or caching service, Akamai uses sophisticated programming to monitor web traffic, makes extra copies of high-demand content, and spreads out requests, routing them to a server in the geographic proximity of the end user. In this way, customers do not have to maintain an excessive number of servers to handle peak traffic and are able to weather usage spikes without overloading their systems. In addition, Akamai offers an array of professional services, including Internet architectural design, implementation, performance optimization, and security. Akamai maintains offices in nine U.S. cities, as well as offices in Europe and the Pacific Rim.

Company Origins in Mid-1990s Challenge

Originally developed by the U.S. military, the Internet was little more than a collection of linked computers before Dr. Tim Berners-Lee, a British computer scientist, invented a software program in 1989 called the World Wide Web, which provided easy access to the quickly accumulating resources of the Internet. The program supplied an address (universal resource locator, or URL) to documents, which were encoded with hypertext markup language (HTML), and linked for easy retrieval by hypertext transfer protocol (HTTP). Coupled with a graphic interface, Mosaic, which became the backbone of web browsers, the Internet enjoyed explosive growth in the 1990s. Berners-Lee joined the faculty of the Massachusetts Institute of Technology (MIT) in 1994, heading the W3 Consortium for the Laboratory for Computer Science, very much devoted to making sure the Web developed into the universal tool he envisioned it to be. But by 1995 he became concerned that traffic problems could have a deleterious effect on the growth of the Web, in particular the "hot spot" or "flash crowd" phenomenon, when large numbers of web users try to access the same site at the same time, leading to a bottleneck that would not only bring down a site but create a domino effect, with the network around the site becoming a casualty. Moreover, the future of the Internet was jeopardized because of a general lack of speed, leading wags to call the Internet the "World Wide Wait." In 1995 Berners-Lee issued a challenge to his MIT colleagues to improve the way in which Internet content was delivered.

Among the people who accepted the challenge was Tom Leighton, a professor of Applied Mathematics, who headed the Algorithms Group at MIT's Laboratory for Computer Science. Although initially regarded as an academic exercise, the task of speeding up the Internet offered MIT math students a chance to work on a problem with a real-world application. Over the next two years, Leighton, his colleagues, and graduate students worked with little sense of urgency, since no one at the time gave any thought to building a company around the results of their research. Among the graduate students who used this work as a basis for their theses was Daniel Lewin, who devised key algorithms that would become part of a system that efficiently routed Internet traffic, achieved in part by spreading copies of high-demand material over a network of distributed servers.

Prototype Ready in 1998

A chance conversation with an MIT business student led Lewin to suggest that he and Leighton use their research to enter

MIT's Sloan School of Management's annual entrepreneur contest. Lewin's motivation was simple enough: He needed his share of the $50,000 prize to pay off some student loans. Although their business proposal failed to win the 1998 competition, it was among the six finalists out of 100 entries, prompting Leighton and Lewin to continue their work. By August 1998 they had developed a prototype of their system that worked to their satisfaction. Some major customers interested in working with them on beta trials were lined up, and the partners began taking steps, including the licensing of some MIT intellectual property, to form a company to exploit their research. For a name they chose Akamai, a word they found after coming across a Hawaiian dictionary on the Web and looking up the word for "intelligent." Akamai was also a colloquial term for "cool."

Akamai found no shortage of interested investors. In a first round of venture capital, the start-up company received $8.3 million from Boston's Polaris Ventures and New York's Baker Communications. A second round was conducted a few months later, garnering $35 million from Polaris and Baker, plus newcomers Battery Ventures of Wellesley, Massachusetts, and TCW Group of Los Angeles. In addition, Akamai was able to sell interests in the company to other high-tech companies. Akamai and Cisco Systems Inc. began discussing a technology-sharing agreement, which led to Cisco buying a 4 percent stake for $50 million, followed a few weeks later with Microsoft Corporation acquiring a 1 percent stake for $15 million. To that point, Akamai's software was being run on a Unix-based operating system, Linus. The Microsoft deal called for Akamai to develop a version of its software that could be run on Microsoft's NT operating system. Later, Apple also paid $12.5 million to get a piece of the action.

Akamai's business model also attracted the attention of seasoned executive George H. Conrades, a 30-year veteran of IBM who rose to the rank of senior vice-president for U.S. Operations and later headed technology research and development firm BBN until it was acquired by GTE Corp. He then became a partner at Polaris and after the venture capital firm began investing in Akamai he became a member of the start-up's board and served in an advisory capacity. He was subsequently tabbed to serve as Akamai's chairman and CEO, taking over in April 1999 when the company became operational. Akamai's chief executive officer, Paul Sagan, was another experienced hand, the former president of Time Inc. New Media and founder of Time Warner Cable's Road Runner high-speed cable service.

Going Public in 1999

From the outset Akamai boasted an impressive roster of clients, including Yahoo, CNN, About.com, and Go Network. The first product was called FreeFlow. The service, as described by *Network World* in a January 1999 profile, "delivers customers' web pages via Akamai's global network of distributed web servers. . . . The Akamai network determines where hits are coming from and shifts copies of the pages sought to Akamai servers nearest the source of the demand. When demand drops, the network cuts back on the number of servers delivering content. Customers don't have to add hardware or change Internet access to use the service. With faster response times, Akamai customers will be able to post more complex pages." FreeFlow was able to achieve this feat because "the network uses server software based on a blend of four families of algorithms: randomized, online, flow and consistent hashing. The software runs on each server, distributing intelligence around the network so adjustments are made without intervention from a central site. . . . If one server goes down, others become aware and pick up the slack." FreeFlow was put to the test in October 1999 when it was used by NetAid to support the webcast of a concert to draw attention to the problem of world hunger. Despite the immense traffic to the NetAid site, there were no crashes or delays, a far cry from the debacle that took place several months earlier when Victoria's Secret attempted to webcast a fashion show without the support of a dynamic system like FreeFlow.

Very quickly Akamai became a Wall Street darling, involved in a sector (essentially any company even remotely connected to the Internet) that was proving irresistible to investors. The company took advantage of the interest by announcing in August 1999 an initial public offering (IPO) of stock, in the hope of raising about $86 million by selling shares in the $16 to $18 range. Morgan Stanley Dean Witter served as lead manager of the offering, joined by co-managers Donaldson, Lufkin & Jenrette, Salomon Smith Barney, and Thomas Weisel Partners LLC. But when the IPO was actually conducted in October, demand for shares was so strong—due in no small measure to the success of the NetAid concert—that Akamai commanded a price of $26 a share, selling 9 million shares to raise $234 million and netting $216.5 million. Moreover, as soon as shares began trading on the NASDAQ they soared in value to more than $145 a share, a 458 percent gain in the first day on heavy trading, the fourth steepest climb ever for a U.S. stock in its first day. As a result, 42-year-old Leighton and 29-year-old Lewin were worth on paper $1.4 billion each. Conrades owned enough stock to be worth nearly $960 million. Even MIT graduate students who performed summer and part-time work for stock options were now millionaires. Akamai itself had a market capitalization of about $13 billion, an incredible number given that it was now worth more than Sears, Roebuck & Co.

With its coffers full and high-priced stock at its disposal, Akamai began to fill out its business through external means. In early 2000 it paid $200 million in cash and stock to acquire Network24 Communications Inc., a Cupertino, California-based streaming media company, the addition of which helped Akamai to move toward offering live Internet broadcasting services to additional web sites. A few weeks later, Akamai engineered a much larger deal, agreeing to trade $2.8 billion in stock to pick up InterVU Inc., another streaming media company. Until this time, Akamai was limited to working in Apple's QuickTime stream format, so that customers working in another format would have to provide Akamai with a streaming media file. The addition of InterVU allowed Akamai to create streaming media files in Real Networks' popular RealVideo and Microsoft's Windows Media formats, thereby broadening the company's customer base. Later in 2000, Akamai completed another strategic acquisition, paying $6 million in cash and stock for Santa Clara, California-based CallTheShots, Inc., a private company developing technology that would allow web sites to deliver customized content to users without incurring the expense of a larger infrastructure.

The price of Akamai stock peaked on December 31, 1999, at $344.88 a share. The outlook for the company continued to look rosy in 2000, but as the tech sector began to sour, along with the economy in general, Akamai got caught up in the downward spiral when the dotcom bubble began to burst. The company had quickly ramped up its hiring and bought a lot of real estate, only to see a large percentage of its customers going out of business, unable to afford its service, or delaying investments. During the first half of 2001 Akamai lost more than 12 percent of its recurring contracts. The price of its stock began to plummet as a result, and the company was forced to make deep cuts in staffing and to terminate leases. Akamai shares closed 2000 trading in the $21 range, a drastic change from the same time the prior year, but an enviable price compared with what was to follow. Akamai eventually bottomed out in 2002, worth little more than 50 cents per share.

In 2001 Akamai recorded sales of $163 million and a net loss of $2.4 billion, albeit the bulk of that loss was the result of restructuring and other charges. With those items excluded the company's loss totaled $429.1 million. The year also was marked by personal tragedy. On September 11, 2001, Lewin was a passenger on one of the airliners that terrorists crashed into New York's World Trade Center. Ironically, the act that cost his life also demonstrated the value of the Internet trafficking system he helped to develop, as the Internet was besieged with requests for information from people keeping track of events and Akamai's customers were able to cope with the spike in demand. Although the company continued to lay off staff in the remaining months of 2001, its performance on September 11 led to an increase in customers and played a significant role in Akamai beginning to rebound in 2002.

Akamai launched a new product in 2002, EdgeSuite, and began targeting large companies interested in establishing a significant web presence. EdgeSuite was essentially a more robust version of FreeFlow: combining the earlier dynamic traffic control features with added security features, increased speed on digital downloads, and the ability to deliver streaming media. A rash of new customers responded, including FedEx Corporation, Staples, MTV, and The Bombay Company. Akamai was also successful in attracting government customers, selling EdgeSuite to the Federal Bureau of Investigation (FBI), whose web site had experienced an increased level of traffic after September 11. As a preferred government vendor, Akamai also began selling its services to other federal government customers,

such as the U.S. House of Representatives, who used Akamai to stream hearings on the Web. Despite this success, there was still more bitter medicine to be swallowed in 2002, as the company continued to shed workers. Employment that crested at 1,300 in 2000 stood at 550 at the end of 2002. The company was also the recipient of unwanted publicity when it was disclosed by the *Boston Globe* that Akamai was using college servers to deliver content from teen-pornography web sites and help offshore gambling sites to speed content delivery. Few people had realized that Akamai's system of spreading Internet content to geographically advantageous servers relied on college servers as well as company-owned servers. Schools benefited from the relationship because they gained faster Internet access and paid less money for more bandwidth. At first Akamai downplayed the controversy, maintaining that pornography and gambling represented less than 1 percent of its revenues and that it was not going to renew contracts with online gaming companies and no longer sought new business from what a spokesperson referred to as "adult content sites." Within a couple days the *Boston Globe* reported that the objectionable material was no longer mirrored on the college servers it checked.

Akamai's comeback continued in 2003, as reflected by the rising price of its stock, which traded below $2 at the beginning of the year and above $10 at the end. By February 2004, the price reached the $16 range, so that over a five-month period Akamai increased its market capitalization by $1.4 billion. The reasons for renewed investor confidence included Akamai's cost-cutting measures, increasing sales, and a restructuring of debt that took place in 2004. The outlook was also brighter because the market was beginning to come to the company, which had been criticized for overbuilding a network, intended for a much larger Internet of the future. But with the rising use of streaming technology to deliver music, movies, sports, and software, Akamai now found itself well positioned to service customers looking to take advantage of this demand. In 2004 Akamai became profitable for the first time, posting net income of $34.4 million on sales of $210 million.

One nettlesome concern for Akamai that continued to trouble the company in 2004 was its involvement in costly litigation to protect intellectual property. Initially Akamai fought with competitor Digital Island, and the matter continued with Cable & Wireless after the latter acquired Digital Island. Akamai won a patent infringement suit in 2002. But in that same year, Akamai became embroiled in a patent dispute with Santa Clara, California-based Speedera Networks, with both parties trading lawsuits and countersuits. Akamai accused Speedera of stealing trade secrets, while Speedera called Akamai a legal bully. In March 2005 both sides were weary of the distraction and the legal costs and, after six months of negotiations, agreed to settle their differences by joining forces. In a $130 million stock deal, Akamai acquired Speedera and quickly began to merge their operations and grow the combined company. In an odd way, the litigation was a benefit. According to Speedera's CEO Ajit Gupta, "We have been joined at the hip through litigation, so we know each other very well."

Principal Subsidiaries

AKAMAI Ltd.; AKAMAI GmbH; AKAMAI SARL; AKAMAI JAPAN; KAHUA HK Limited.

Principal Competitors

Kontiki, Inc.; SAVVIS, Inc.; Communications Corporation; Cable and Wireless PLC.

Further Reading

Greene, Tim, ''Start-Up Seeks to Unclog Web,'' *Network World,* January 18, 1999, p. 6.

Lee, Dan, ''Akamai Buys Rival Speedera,'' *San Jose Mercury News,* March 17, 2005.

McLaughlin, Tim, ''Akamai Founders Net Cool Billions,'' *Boston Herald,* October 30, 1999, p. 20.

Penenberg, Adam L., ''Speed Racer,'' *Forbes,* September 20, 1999, p. 200.

Poe, Robert, ''Helping Web Sites Dish It Out,'' *Upside,* March 2000, p. 80.

Soule, Alexander, ''With Akamai Rebound, CEO Is in Line for Stock Windfall,'' *Boston Business Journal,* February 20, 2004, p. 1.

Walker, Leslie, ''Akamai Strives for a Safer, Speedier Net,'' *Washington Post,* September 30, 2004, p. E1.

—Ed Dinger

Alpine Confections, Inc.

119 East 200 North
Alpine, Utah 84004
U.S.A.
Telephone: (801) 756-6916
Toll Free: (800) 377-4368
Fax: (801) 756-7791
Web site: http://www.fanniemay.com

Private Company
Incorporated: 1999
Employees: 900
Sales: $125 million (2005 est.)
NAIC: 311320 Chocolate and Confectionery Manufacturing from Cacao Beans; 311330 Confectionery Manufacturing from Purchased Chocolate; 311340 Nonchocolate Confectionery Manufacturing

Alpine Confections, Inc. owns a number of candy companies, including Maxfield Candy Company, Kencraft, Inc., and Harry London Candies Inc. The Fanny Farmer and Fannie May brands were acquired from bankrupt Archibald Candy Corporation in 2004. Alpine also produces confections under license for Hallmark and Mrs. Fields'. Canadian brands include Dolce d'Or and Botticelli, produced at the Dynamic Chocolates plant in Delta, British Columbia.

Utah Origins

Robert B. Murray and his son, R. Taz Murray, acquired Salt Lake City's Maxfield Candy Co. in August 1993 for $1.8 million. Bob Murray had become a business professor at Brigham Young University after flying jets in the Korean War.

Maxfield was known for its boxed chocolates and chocolate-enrobed cream sticks. It had been formed in 1947 by A. Vard Maxfield. His son, Neal, was president of the company when it was sold to the Murrays.

Taz Murray then became business partners with a former classmate at Harvard Business School, David Taiclet. (After getting their MBAs, they had worked for a time at Cargill and

Deloitte & Touche, respectively.) The expanded partnership acquired another Utah confectioner, Kencraft, Inc., in 1994.

Kencraft had been founded in 1969 by Ken and Marlene Matheson of Salt Lake City. Their first products were hollow sugar Easter eggs with figures inside. The Mathesons moved to Utah County in 1972.

Kencraft's big break came when a New York buyer noticed the novelty candies at a Chicago trade show. The operation moved into a 900-square-foot building at the Alpine Valley Lumber Co. in the town of Alpine. This became Kencraft's permanent home and the site of a 90,000-square-foot factory.

A pair of "Peppermint Place" retail outlets, one adjacent to the plant, opened in 1991. By 1993, the company was making 800 different products, including lollipops, chocolate truffles, candy canes, and confections designed to celebrate a number of holidays. Many of the items were adorned with hand-formed figures and branded with names such as Candy Climbers, Puppet Pals, and Bubble Gum Buddies. Kencraft employed 215 people, many of them "craftsy" Mormon women who decorated the candies.

Under new management, Taiclet told *Candy Industry,* employment became less seasonal for Kencraft's production workers as the company built up inventory. They also added incentives for productivity. The Utah Department of Workforce Services cited Kencraft as a "Top Family Friendly Company."

Late 1990s Licensing

In the late 1990s, Maxfield Candy updated its logo and packaging for its own brand, All American Chocolates. A new boxed chocolate line aimed at the Hispanic market called "¡Coleccion Festiva!" (Festive Collection) was tested, reported *Professional Candy Buyer.* The assortment included some tropical fruit centers such as mango and lime.

Maxfield had entered a deal to produce confections under license for Mrs. Fields' Original Cookies in 1997, and spent two years developing the concept before its Christmas 1999 launch. Some of the candies, dubbed "Decadent Chocolates," featured centers based on established Mrs. Fields' cookies flavors such

Key Dates:

1919: The Fannie May and Fanny Farmer brands are established.
1922: Ohio's Harry London Candies is founded.
1947: Maxfield Candy Company of Salt Lake City is formed.
1969: Utah's Kencraft, Inc. is launched.
1991: Vancouver's Dynamic Chocolates is formed.
1993: Robert and Taz Murray acquire Maxfield Candy.
1994: Kencraft is acquired by Taz Murray and David Taiclet.
1998: Dynamic Chocolates is acquired.
1999: Alpine Confections, Inc. holding company is formed.
2002: Alpine wins the Hallmark Chocolatier licensing deal.
2003: The Fannie May, Fanny Farmer, and Harry London brands are added.

as Chocolate Chip Cookie Dough and Debra's Special Oatmeal Raisin Caramel, noted *Professional Candy Buyer*. The Kencraft unit gained a license for Disney characters in 1998; licenses eventually followed for the Peanuts gang, Raggedy Ann and Andy, Curious George, and others.

Custom orders accounted for half of Kencraft's business in 2000, according to one executive. The unit was beginning to expand overseas, forming a Polish joint venture with the Dutch company Luijckx BV Chocolade. Exports accounted for 5 percent of sales at the time.

In 1998 Alpine acquired Vancouver's Dynamic Chocolates, Inc., maker of Dolce D'or Seashell Treasures chocolates and Botticelli "Hedgehogs." Dynamic had been established by Richard Foley in 1991. Six years later, it moved its operations to one of North America's largest and most advanced chocolate molding plants, a 55,000-square-foot factory. A majority of its revenues came from outside Canada.

Formation of a Holding Company in 1999

In the five years after the Maxfield purchase, four other candy companies had been acquired by the group: Kencraft Candy, Fernwood Candy, De La Mare Taffy, and Dynamic Chocolates—manufacturer of the Botticelli brand. (Maxfield also produced chocolates under the Mrs. Fields' brand.) A holding company, Alpine Confections Inc., was formed in 1999.

Candy Industry estimated the Kencraft unit's 2001 sales at $15 million. The company was producing ten million candy sticks and candy canes a year and employed 360 people.

Kencraft was the exclusive candy maker for the 2002 Winter Olympics in Salt Lake City. In a much larger licensing deal, Alpine began producing boxed chocolates for the Hallmark Chocolatier brand in 2002. These were distributed in the thousands of stores that carried Hallmark cards.

Sales were $80 million in 2003, when Alpine had 900 employees. The company had two manufacturing facilities in Utah and one in Vancouver, where its Dynamic Chocolates unit supplied the Canadian market with Dolce d'Or and Botticelli branded items.

Adding Big Brands in 2003

In 2003, Alpine acquired Harry London Candies Inc., a Canton, Ohio maker of premium chocolates, for a reported $13 million. Harry London had become insolvent after borrowing heavily to expand. It had been founded in 1922. Before its bankruptcy, Harry London had eight retail stores and 270 employees in addition to a 200,000-square-foot factory. Alpine kept this facility active. Harry London's sales were about $20 million a year.

In 2003, Alpine and North Development Company won a bid to acquire the Fannie May and Fanny Farmer brands from the insolvent Archibald Candy Corporation of Chicago. The price was $39 million, which included 31 Midwest area retail stores. These were reopened in the fall of 2004.

At its peak, Archibald had operated the largest candy chain in the nation, with hundreds of stores and 3,000 workers. It had been founded by H. Teller Archibald, who opened the first Fannie May candy shop in Chicago in 1919. Archibald bought another venerable boxed chocolates brand, Fanny Farmer, in 1995. Fanny Farmer dated back to 1919 and was said to be named after legendary cookbook author Fannie Farmer (though the names were spelled differently).

Fannie May's Mint Meltaways (mint chocolate centers in chocolate or pastel candy), Trinidads (chocolate center inside a coconut/pastel shell), Pixies (nuts and caramel enrobed in chocolate), and other candies inspired legendary devotion from consumers in the Midwest, who stockpiled them as Archibald went through its bankruptcy. Alpine had resumed production of these confections, however, even before it had completed the Fannie May acquisition, reported the *Salt Lake Tribune*.

"The brand stood to take a huge hit if it went away for a year," explained Taz Murray. The *Chicago Tribune* reported that Murray's partner, Dave Taiclet, had first become acquainted with Fannie May Pixies during his Indiana boyhood. "We love the brand," said Taiclet. "We want to do everything we can to protect and grow it."

According to the *Chicago Tribune,* Alpine had to begin running three shifts at its Utah plant to keep up with demand. Fannie May chocolates were popular as fundraising items; 1,500 charitable groups sold $2.6 million worth of the candy a year.

Principal Subsidiaries

Dynamic Chocolates, Inc. (Canada); Fannie May Confections Inc.; Harry London Candies Inc.; Kencraft, Inc.; Maxfield Candy Company.

Principal Competitors

Chocoladefabriken Lindt & Sprüngli AG; Godiva Chocolatier Inc.; Guylian USA Inc.; Nestlé Confections & Snack (Nestlé USA); Rocky Mountain Chocolate Factory, Inc.; Russell Stover; World's Finest Chocolate, Inc.

Further Reading

"Alpine Confections Kicks Off Hallmark Partnership," *Candy Industry,* August 1, 2002, p. 12.
Babbit, Christi, " 'Tis Always the Season for Candy Confections," *Deseret News* (Salt Lake City), November 8, 1999, p. B1.

Crown, Judith, "Fannie and Fanny Fight Dusty Image; Parent Plans Careful Shifts at Candy Store," *Crain's Chicago Business,* February 21, 1994, p. 4.

Dorrell, Kathryn, "Dynamic Approach to Chocolate Processing," *Food in Canada,* June 1998, p. 15.

Eddington, Mark, "Alpine's Kencraft Turns Sweet Profit," *Daily Herald* (Provo, Utah), December 11, 1994, p. 1.

Fannie May Confections Inc., *More Than 84 Years of Fannie May—A Success Story,* Chicago: Fannie May Confections Inc., c. 2004.

Fuhrman, Elizabeth, "Alpine Wins Court's Blessing for Harry London Purchase," *Candy Industry,* August 2003, pp. 14–15.

Kurtz, Rod, "Testing, Testing...," *Inc.,* June 2004, p. 35.

Lloyd, Jennifer, "Leaders & Success: Fannie Merritt Farmer," *Investor's Business Daily,* September 9, 1999, p. A4.

Mitchell, Lesley, "Utah Retail Firm to Market Bankrupt Brands," *Salt Lake Tribune,* February 24, 2004.

Oberbeck, Steven, "Nutrition Labels: A Big Problem for Small Utah Businesses," *Salt Lake Tribune,* July 18, 1993, p. F1.

——, "Sweets Firm Bitter Over Competition; Maxfield's Candy Names Former President in Suit," *Salt Lake Tribune,* May 28, 1997, p. D4.

Pacyniak, Bernard, "Utah's Candy Medalists," *Candy Industry,* February 2002, pp. 24+.

"Purchase of Maxfield's Helps Propel Alpine to Very Sweet Success," *Deseret News,* June 25, 2000, p. M3.

Rave, Jodi, "Candy Makers Settle Lawsuit on Trade Secrets; Neal's and Maxfield's Dispute Illustrates Competitiveness of Utah Sweets Industry," *Salt Lake Tribune,* April 21, 1998, p. B5.

Russell, John, "Bankruptcy Court Approves Sales of Green, Ohio-Based Chocolate Maker," *Knight-Ridder Tribune Business News: Akron Beacon Journal,* July 23, 2003.

Schmeltzer, John, "Chicago Loses Another Icon As Archibald Candy Corp. Shuts Down," *Chicago Tribune,* February 26, 2004.

——, "Fannie May Candies' Sales, Demand Greater Than Anticipated," *Chicago Tribune,* December 14, 2004.

——, "Utah-Based Candymaker to Acquire Fannie May," *Chicago Tribune,* January 15, 2004.

——, "Utah Candy Firm Takes Over Fannie May Brand, Plans to Keep Name," *Chicago Tribune,* February 26, 2004.

Smith, Erika, and Gloria Irwin, "Green, Ohio-Based Chocolate Maker to Become Subsidiary of Utah Company," *Knight-Ridder Tribune Business News: Akron Beacon Journal,* April 29, 2003.

Tarantino, Teresa, "Going for the Gold," *Professional Candy Buyer,* July/August 2000.

Warchol, Glen, "A Card and a Box of Chocolate," *Salt Lake Tribune,* August 7, 2002, p. B4.

——, "Sweet Increase," *Salt Lake Tribune,* September 21, 2003, p. E1.

Wharton, Tom, "Alpine, Utah, Factory Produces Hand-Made Candy for International Chains," *Salt Lake Tribune,* December 19, 1999.

—Frederick C. Ingram

Alticor Inc.

7575 Fulton Street East
Ada, Michigan 49355-0001
U.S.A.
Telephone: (616) 787-6000
Fax: (616) 682-4000
Web site: http://www.alticor.com

Private Company
Incorporated: 1959 as Amway Sales Corporation and
     Amway Services Corporation
Employees: 13,000
Sales: $6.2 billion (2004)
NAIC: 325620 Toilet Preparation Manufacturing; 325611
     Soap and Other Detergent Manufacturing; 551112
     Offices of Other Holding Companies; 454390 Other
     Direct Selling Establishments

Alticor Inc. is the holding company for four businesses, the most well-known of which is Amway Corporation, the pioneer of multilevel marketing (MLM). Amway Corporation sells its own products as well as brand name products from other companies through a network of more than three million independent distributors worldwide. Unlike many other MLM firms, Amway offers a broad selection of items, ranging from cleaning products, cosmetics, and vitamins to travel services, discount car purchases, and catalog merchandise. Amway derives roughly 80 percent of its sales from Asia. Alticor's other businesses are Pyxis Innovations, Quixtar, Inc., and Access Business Group. Pyxis serves as the corporate development arm for the organization. Quixtar, which generates more than $1 billion in annual revenue, sells personal care products, health supplements, laundry care products, and a range of other merchandise on the Internet. Access Business Group develops, manufactures, and distributes products for Amway, Quixtar, and unaffiliated companies.

Origins

Amway's history represents a recent chapter in the long history of direct selling, which began in the American colonial period with unorganized Yankee peddlers selling tools and other items door to door. By the 1800s, direct selling decreased with the advent of mass merchandising, such as department stores and mail-order sales. In the later 19th century and early 20th century, however, some manufacturers found direct sales had advantages over the sales of their products in large stores. They preferred the personal touch, with salesmen making home demonstrations of their products exclusively. By the 1920s door-to-door salesmen were marketing brushes, cooking utensils, and other products. Retail stores fought back with local laws on peddlers. The federal government's regulations of company-employee relations led to the independent contractor solution. As independent contractors, salesmen were no longer employees: they were independent businessmen who bought products for resale. The first network marketing began in 1941 when two men created a mechanism to distribute Nutrilite vitamins. Within this mechanism, in addition to making money in retail sales, distributors earned a bonus on the sales of those individuals whom they personally recruited.

Amway's story began with the friendship between two youths who would become the founders. Jay Van Andel, born in Grand Rapids, Michigan, in 1924, and Richard M. DeVos, born in the small nearby community of Ada in 1926, became friends at Christian High School in Grand Rapids. Their common Dutch heritage of hard work, thrift, and entrepreneurship drew them together.

Both served in the Army Air Corps during World War II. Returning to Michigan after the war, they founded Wolverine Air Service to offer flying lessons. After selling Wolverine and a couple of other small businesses, the two young men bought a schooner and sailed off to see Latin America. The vessel sank in the Caribbean, and the two spent the next six months in South America; when they returned to Michigan, they started the JaRi Corporation to import and sell Caribbean handicraft.

In 1949 DeVos and Van Andel became distributors of vitamins for the Nutrilite Company of California. They enjoyed modest success from their own retail sales and from bonuses earned on the sales force they created in the Midwest. However, increasing government regulations and an internal conflict in Nutrilite led Van Andel, DeVos, and several other leading Nutrilite distributors to start their own venture. In April 1959 they

25

Company Perspectives:

Our products and services help people live better lives by offering them the opportunity to have their own businesses. The business services we offer help companies develop, manufacture and distribute their own products, using our 40 plus years of expertise. The wellness, body & beauty and home products we create and manage are some of the best in the world, helping make life cleaner, easier, healthier and more beautiful for those that use them.

created The American Way Association, later renamed the Amway Distributors Association, to protect the independent distributors. They chose as their first product a biodegradable liquid organic cleanser made by a small Michigan firm, the kind of high-demand merchandise that could be easily sold by MLM. By September 1959 the Amway Sales Corporation and the Amway Services Corporation were begun to assist the distributors. Van Andel and DeVos, with the help of their wives and a handful of employees, began operations from offices in their basements. Van Andel created sales literature and supervised new product development; DeVos motivated and trained new distributors.

The company rapidly expanded. The first full year of operations in 1960 resulted in gross sales of $500,000. That figure doubled in each of the next two years, and in 1964 it reached $10 million. Thousands of distributors signed up each month. The expansion was so rapid that as soon as the company moved into new facilities, they were already crowded. In the company history, *Commitment to Excellence: The Remarkable Amway Story,* DeVos noted, ''We were always scrambling, just trying to catch up on back orders, working to train people adequately.''

In 1964 the business underwent a major reorganization. The three divisions—sales, services, and manufacturing—were merged to create the Amway Corporation, with Van Andel as chairman of the board and DeVos as president. Major business decisions were always made jointly by the two founders.

A laundry detergent, SA8, was introduced in 1960. Amway's reputation for selling soap was based primarily on its experience with this product. Other products included a dishwashing liquid, aerosol shoe spray, cookware, hair products, and cosmetics. In 1962 Amway started international growth, with its expansion into Canada. In 1968 the Personal Shoppers Catalog allowed distributors to sell merchandise made by other companies. Catalog sales increased thereafter.

The 1960s also brought some false starts and problems for the new firm. It began marketing underground fallout shelters, for example, in an era when civil defense against atomic warfare was a priority, but gradually consumers lost interest in the shelters. Other short-lived products included 110-volt automobile generators and water-conditioning units. It was not surprising that some items were not successful, however, for by 1968 the company was selling more than 150 products through its 80,000 distributors.

In July 1969 Amway's aerosol manufacturing plant burned completely to the ground. Losses were estimated at $700,000.

The next day plans were made for a temporary substitute supplier and a new facility. Six months later the new facility was completed and the company moved in.

Growth and Controversy: 1970s–80s

The 1970s began with a change in corporate structure. Van Andel and DeVos remained board chairman and president, respectively, but four vice-presidents were added to handle the daily burden of a rapidly expanding firm. In addition, 30 regional warehouses were replaced by seven new regional distribution centers in Georgia, Michigan, Texas, California, New Jersey, Washington, and Colorado. Overseas expansion in the 1970s began with Australia in 1971, a choice that was partly influenced by the common culture, language, and economic system. Operations in the United Kingdom began in 1973. Other European operations began with West Germany in 1975, France in 1977, and the Netherlands and the Republic of Ireland in 1978. The Asian market was opened with ventures into Hong Kong in 1974, Malaysia in 1976, and Japan in 1979.

Diversification and acquisitions marked Amway's experience during this time. In 1972 the company purchased Nutrilite Products, Inc., the firm that had introduced Van Andel and DeVos to direct selling. Moreover, to reward and train its key distributors, the company acquired a yacht, Enterprise II, to serve as a floating conference center. A luxury resort and hotel complex on Peter Island in the British Virgin Islands was purchased in 1978, another amenity used to motivate Amway distributors. To house distributors coming to corporate headquarters, the firm bought the dilapidated Pantlind Hotel in Grand Rapids. The hotel, renovated and renamed Amway Grand Plaza Hotel, along with the newly constructed adjoining Grand Plaza Tower, marked a significant addition to downtown Grand Rapids.

Amway's growth was predicated on the success of its independent distributors. Lacking formal control over the distributors, Amway relied on bonuses and incentives to motivate them. As the company grew, distributors built larger and larger sales organizations. Their status and income increased and were marked by achievement levels identified as ''pin levels.'' The first major milestone of a successful distributor was reaching the level of Direct Distributor (DD), thus buying products and literature directly from the corporation instead of from a sponsor or other DD. Soon after Amway's origin, it began recognizing further sales milestones by using the names of jewels in achievement awards. The first Ruby DD was awarded in 1962, followed by Pearl, Emerald, and Diamond, in each instance the award including a decorative pin in which the specific stone was mounted. In 1966 the first Double Diamond level was reached, the Triple Diamond in 1969, Crown in 1970, and the highest level, Crown Ambassador DD, in 1977. By Amway's 25th anniversary in 1984, there were 24 Crown DDs and 15 Crown Ambassador DDs. Almost all of these 39 distributors were married couples; 28 were based in the United States.

The corporation kept in touch with its distributors through a monthly magazine, the *Amagram,* and provided a wide variety of sales literature, audiocassettes, and videocassettes. Although much of the product promotion was done by distributors, Amway also sponsored advertising in magazines, newspapers, radio, and TV. Its advertising costs were much less than other

Key Dates:

1959: Jay Van Andel and Richard M. DeVos start The American Way Association.
1964: The business is renamed Amway Corporation.
1971: Amway expands overseas for the first time.
1979: After years of investigation, the Federal Trade Commission declares Amway's business model is legitimate.
1989: Amway fails in an attempt to acquire Avon Products, Inc.
1992: The founder's children, Dick DeVos and Steve Van Andel, assume control over the company.
2000: Amway restructures and creates Alticor Inc. as a holding company.
2002: Doug DeVos is named president of Alticor.
2004: Sales eclipse $6 billion for the first time.

corporations, allowing Amway to introduce new products inexpensively.

Amway's most important legal battle was its successful defense against the allegation that it was engaged in an illegal "pyramid scheme," characterized in part by making money on recruiting new distributors. The Federal Trade Commission (FTC) in 1969 began investigating several companies, including Amway and Nutrilite, filing formal charges against Amway in 1975. Three months of FTC hearings began in May 1977, and a ruling by the full FTC in 1979 declared Amway's MLM plan legitimate. The decision was based on findings that distributors were not being paid to recruit new distributors, that products had to be sold for distributors to receive bonuses, and that the firm was willing to buy back excess distributor inventory. Lawyer Rodney K. Smith in his book *Multilevel Marketing,* after reviewing several cases, concluded, "Amway is not and never has been an illegal pyramid scheme."

In another legal controversy, the Canadian government charged Amway with not paying millions of dollars in customs duties on goods imported from the United States. In 1983, after pleading guilty in the criminal case, Amway paid a CAD 25 million fine in an out-of-court settlement. *Maclean's,* Canada's leading weekly news magazine, reported in a November 1983 issue that the fine was "the largest sum that a Canadian court has ever levied and one of the heaviest criminal penalties ever imposed against any corporation in the world." A separate civil case was continued by the Canadian government to collect the duties it should have been paid in the 1970s. Amway again settled out of court, this time in 1989 for CAD 45 million, 40 percent of the amount the Canadian government tried to collect.

Other serious problems occurred in the first half of the 1980s, when, for the first time, Amway sales declined. Some of the major distributors sold their businesses, and a substantial number of top executives either quit or were demoted or fired. The pyramid allegations surfaced again, not against the corporation, but against certain distributors who advised their sales groups to downplay retail sales, buy Amway merchandise for their own use, and purchase many motivational items, such as tapes and books, from the distributor.

One corporate executive, COO William W. Nicholson, previously a secretary to President Gerald R. Ford and a key player at Amway headquarters since 1984, oversaw the introduction of many new products and services. According to Nicholson, a turning point was reached in 1985 when MCI decided to market its long distance telephone services through Amway. By 1990 Amway was gaining more than 40,000 new clients per month for MCI. Offering its customers discount purchases on new cars was another Amway innovation; by 1988 this service competed with five other discount autobuying services, including the American Automobile Association. Other new items in the Amway inventory included Visa credit cards, prepaid legal services, real estate, and Tandy computers. The increase in high-tech merchandise and services was a dramatic shift for Amway, but the bulk of its sales remained in traditional products such as home care items. According to some analysts, Amway's transition to include more services reflected a general U.S. movement from a goods-and-manufacturing economy toward a service economy.

Not all new ventures worked well for Amway. The Mutual Broadcasting System (MBS), with its hundreds of affiliated radio stations, was purchased in 1977, but inexperience in the field, unfulfilled goals, and lack of profitability, according to DeVos, led to the sale of MBS in 1985. Having retained one satellite division from the original purchase, Amway manufactured and sold satellite dishes for some time, but the last division was eventually sold in 1989.

Probably the most publicized Amway activity in the late 1980s was its failed bid to take over Avon Products, Inc. Amway and corporate raider Irwin L. Jacobs jointly acquired 5.5 million Avon shares, 10.3 percent of the company's stock, in 1989. One week later, without Jacobs's cooperation, Amway offered to buy Avon for $2.1 billion in cash. Although a billion dollars in debt, Avon rejected the bid, citing Amway's evasion of Canadian customs duties and an incompatible corporate culture. In May 1989 Amway withdrew its bid. *Business Week,* in a May 1989 issue, characterized the bid as Amway "flexing its muscles for the first time"; although the bid failed, it was a good indication of Amway's financial strength.

Amway and its founders also became significant sponsors of the arts in the 1980s. In 1982 Jay Van Andel chaired the Netherlands American Bicentennial Commission, while the company sponsored an art exhibit at Amsterdam's Stedelijk Museum. Amway also supported tours of the Hong Kong Children's Choir and the Malaysian Youth Symphony Orchestra. In Grand Rapids, Michigan, the company helped fund an Art Museum, Arts Council, and the Gerald R. Ford Presidential Museum.

Amway also made commendable efforts to be environmentally responsible. Several of Amway's early products were biodegradable, and its SA8 detergent was available in a phosphate-free formula to limit pollution of waterways, and products were concentrated, reducing the amount of packaging that ended up in landfills. After chlorofluorocarbons were reported as hazardous to the ozone layer, Amway modified its aerosol products to delete those compounds. In 1989 Amway was a main sponsor of the two-month-long Icewalk, an expedition to the North Pole, designed to focus attention on environmental issues. In cooperation with the American Forestry

Association, Amway also participated in the Global ReLeaf Program, to plant 100 million trees by 1992. In fact, on June 5, 1989, Amway received the United Nation's Environmental Programme's Achievement Award for Excellence, becoming one of two corporations to gain that honor. That same day the firm announced that it would end all animal testing in its research programs and that it would not cooperate with the Cosmetics, Toiletry and Fragrance Association's campaign against the ban on animal testing. In the area of recycling, Amway was named Michigan Recycling Coalition's 1992 Recycler of the Year, for its onsite recycling center and recycling practices in its operations and product development.

Despite the legal battles and occasionally unfavorable media characterizations of Amway, and direct selling in general, the concept was becoming increasingly popular. According to the Direct Selling Association (DSA), total retail sales were approximately $9.7 billion in 1988, up 10.3 percent from 1987, and Amway accounted for about 16 percent of that total. A 1976 Harris poll of U.S. households found that 16 percent of the respondents had tried direct selling. The boom was influenced by shifts in employment trends. First, more women had moved into the workplace and were selling Amway products; in fact, the DSA reported that in 1988, 81.4 percent of all salespeople were women. Moreover, instability in corporate employment had prompted increasing numbers of workers to consider alternative vocations, particularly those in which much of the administrative activities might be handled in home offices.

Amway's European expansion also continued throughout the 1980s, with operations established in Switzerland and Belgium in 1980, and in Spain and Italy in 1986. In 1985 Panama became the first Latin American base of Amway operations, followed by Guatemala in 1986. Amway de Mexico was established in June 1990 with headquarters in Monterrey and distribution centers in Mexico City, Guadalajara, Tijuana, and Juarez. Amway's success depended in part on its ability to adapt its product line to suit local cultures. In Japan, for example, the company began marketing a small induction range made by Japan's Sharp Company, which proved ideal for the small homes of Japan and sold well when demonstrated in the home by Amway distributors. Perseverance and high quality goods resulted in 1988 sales of $536 million for Amway (Japan) Ltd., Amway's largest overseas subsidiary.

International Expansion During the 1990s

Based on rapid international expansion, strong family leadership, and good financial condition, Amway remained a strong force in the 1990s. When Van Andel and DeVos, whose children had begun in the business in the mid-1970s, retired from the company in the early 1990s, all eight of the Van Andel and DeVos children were in leadership positions. Dick DeVos was named president in 1992, and Steve Van Andel was appointed company chairman. Jay Van Andel planned to remain active with the company as senior chairman and member of the policy board.

With the failure of communist economies in Eastern Europe and other nations, Amway's promotion of free enterprise became increasingly noteworthy in the years ahead. During the first half of the 1990s, Amway's territories expanded into Korea, Hungary, Brazil, Portugal, Indonesia, Poland, Argentina,

the Czech Republic, Turkey, and Slovakia. In addition to tapping into new, emerging economies, foreign expansion was possibly part of Amway's strategy to offset slowing U.S. sales, prompted, according to one article in an October 1994 *U.S. News & World Report,* by regulatory investigations and media criticism of the company. In 1991, for example, Procter & Gamble won a $75,000 judgment from a group of Amway distributors, who were accused of spreading rumors that Procter & Gamble's products were instruments of Satan. Nevertheless, Amway's overall performance did not suffer; in 1994, sales increased by 18 percent over 1993 to total $5.3 billion. Dick DeVos estimated that 70 percent of 1994 sales came from abroad and predicted that figure would increase to 75 percent by fiscal 1996. In 1994 Amway moved its entrepreneurial business into the Eastern European market and also targeted Vietnam and China as its newest markets.

Japan was probably one of Amway's most successful foreign markets in the 1990s. In a culture where many Japanese businesspeople were accustomed to staying with one company for their entire career, Amway offered new economic freedom. In fact, word of mouth recommendations allowed Amway to operate in Japan without spending any money on advertising up until around 1989. In 1990, over 500,000 Japanese belonged to Amway, making the company one of the largest and most profitable foreign companies in Japan. In 1989 Amway (Japan) Ltd. had over $500 million in sales and $164 million in pretax profits, comprising about one-third of Amway's worldwide business. By the mid-1990s, revenues had more than doubled and the Japanese subsidiary had grown to include 816,000 salespeople. Public offerings of stock in Amway Japan and Hong Kong-based Amway Asia Pacific in 1994 proved a huge success, raising $6.7 billion. DeVos and Van Andel reaped the rewards, more than doubling their net worth in one year. Together, the pair were worth an estimated $9 billion by the end of 1994, vaulting the founders into the exclusive ranks of the ten richest people in the United States, according to *Forbes* magazine.

The strong reception to the public offerings in Asia was indicative of Amway's strength in the 1990s. The company was achieving success not only in Asia, but in markets throughout the world as well, deriving nearly all of its growth from international expansion. Between 1990 and 1996, Amway established 20 new foreign affiliates, increasing the number of countries and territories in which it operated to more than 75. Concurrent with the company's aggressive expansion overseas, sales soared, increasing 300 percent between 1990 and 1996 to reach $6.8 billion. The vibrant growth of Amway's international business, which accounted for more than 70 percent of companywide sales, could not have come at a better time because domestically the company's vitality was beginning to wane. Sales in the United States were flattening by the mid-1990s, unaided by persistent accusations of rumormongering that tarnished the company's image. The strident growth of the company outside North America, however, more than offset its anemic domestic performance, underpinning the seamless transition to the second generation of DeVos and Van Andel management.

Much of the company's success during the latter half of the decade depended on continued growth in foreign markets, but continued growth did not arrive. The foray into China, financed by the 1994 public offering of Amway Asia Pacific, ran into a pernicious obstacle in 1998, when the Chinese government banned direct selling because of concerns it would spawn illegal activity. Eventually, Amway was able to sidestep the prohibition by selling products through sales representatives that did not buy products and resell them, as traditional Amway distributors did. A more crippling blow was delivered by the faltering Asian economy in the late 1990s, the effect of which was readily discernible on Amway's balance sheet. Sales peaked at $7 billion in 1997 before falling 18.5 percent the following year to $5.7 billion. For the first time in more than ten years, Amway posted a decline in sales.

While the company waited for economic conditions in Asia to improve, new areas of growth were explored that hinted at an entirely revamped Amway for the future. In 1998 the company strayed far from its core business by teaming with Virginia-based Columbia Energy Group to sell natural gas and electricity in deregulated markets. Initially, Amway began selling natural gas in Georgia, intending to expand into electricity and to broaden its geographic reach as other states became deregulated. The company's other prominent venture during the late 1990s sparked the greatest excitement, leading some industry pundits to hail it as the boldest move in Amway's history. In September 1999, the company established a new company named Quixtar to sell consumer products on the Internet. With Quixtar, Amway used the same marketing concept as it did in its traditional business: distributors purchased products at volume discounts and earned commissions on the sales and bonuses from the sales of new recruits. Apart from Quixtar's business being conducted electronically, the greatest difference between Amway and its new company was the conspicuous absence of the Amway name. Years of negative publicity stemming from the numerous lawsuits filed by Procter & Gamble had stained the Amway name, observers contended, prompting Amway to distance itself from a questionable reputation by adopting a new name. Additionally, by excluding the Amway name from its Internet venture, the company hoped to attract younger customers and younger distributors. The expectations for the new business were high, with the most far-reaching predictions calling for Quixtar to eventually supplant Amway's traditional business. President and co-CEO Dick DeVos did not foresee the ultimate elimination of Amway's traditional business, maintaining both companies could coexist well into the future, but his confidence in Quixtar's potential was unequivocal. "Eventually," he informed *Cosmetics International* in June 1999, "Quixtar ought to be larger than Amway," giving Amway a lofty goal to pursue as it entered the 21st century.

New Identity with the New Century

Quixtar's creation did much to alter the Amway organization at the dawn of the new millennium, representing one of the reasons the company decided to change its corporate identity after four decades of existence. News of the change occurred in May 2000 after Amway reported discouraging financial results for 1999, a 12.3 percent decline in revenues. The company announced it was restructuring its operations to restore its financial vitality, a sweeping effort that involved a reduction in its workforce by 1,300. The most visible aspect of the restructuring program was the unveiling of a new corporate title for the entire organization. In October 2000, the umbrella organization

for Amway and its affiliated companies was introduced as Alticor Inc., a name derived from abbreviating the Latin words for high, heart, mind, and judgment. The name change in no way marked the end of the Amway name or its direct-selling business. Amway continued to operate, recording its greatest growth in Asia, but it operated alongside Alticor's three other businesses: Quixtar; Pyxis Innovations, the corporate development arm of the parent company; and a new company formed in 2000, Access Business Group. Access Business Group developed, manufactured, and distributed products for both Alticor and non-Alticor companies, counting its two sister companies, Amway and Quixtar, and its two largest customers.

One of the primary reasons for the name change was to help foster the growth of Amway's diversification, to free Quixtar and Access Business Group from being associated with the Amway name during their maturation. Direct-selling and multilevel marketing had its many detractors, a negative perception that fell squarely on Amway, the most successful of the breed. Quixtar, Access Business Group, and any other companies that executives in Ada thought to create later would fare better operating under a banner that did not bear the Amway name, company officials reasoned. The success of Amway under the Alticor name presented little opportunity for criticism about the name change. The Amway organization under the Alticor name thrived in the early 2000s, recording encouraging financial gains as it transitioned through one of its few senior management changes.

Dick DeVos announced his retirement in the spring of 2002. His departure, slated for the end of August 2002, was marked by his statement, quoted in the April 17, 2002 issue of *Internet Wire*. "When I arrived," DeVos said, "we were a company that was still questioning whether we could transition past the active involvement of our founders. Now, as I prepare to leave, we have transformed into a more international corporation, sustained by a strategic vision, and with management befitting a leading global company." DeVos left, accepting the position of chairman of the World Federation of Direct Selling Associations, leaving his youngest brother, Doug DeVos, the chief executive officer of Amway and Quixtar for the previous two years, to take his title as Alticor's president. After little more than a month in his new position, Doug DeVos took stock of what he saw and appropriately described his company. "We're basically an Asian company," he said in an October 18, 2002 interview with the *Grand Rapids Press*.

By 2004, Alticor had recorded its fifth consecutive year of revenue growth, posting the largest dollar increase in its history in 2004, when sales jumped 27 percent to $6.2 billion. A good portion of the growth was attributed to new businesses such as Quixtar, which eclipsed $1 billion in sales for the year, but the driving financial force of Alticor continued to be Amway, a direct-selling operation that was achieving its greatest success overseas, in Asia particularly. In China, for example, through its subsidiary Amway China Co. Ltd., sales exceeded $2 billion in 2004, the highlight of other substantial gains in Japan, Thailand, India, and Malaysia. "All eight cylinders are hitting," Alticor's chairman, Steve Van Andel, said in an October 21, 2004 interview with the *Grand Rapids Press*, expressing the mood of the company as it pressed ahead.

Principal Subsidiaries

Access Business Group, LLC; Pyxis Innovations; Nutrilite Products, Inc.; Amway Gesellschaft m.b.H. (Austria); Amway of Australia Pty. Ltd.; Amway Belgium Company; Amway (U.K.); Amway China Co. Ltd.; Limited; Amway France; Amway (HK) Limited (Hong Kong); Amway Italia s.r.l. (Italy); Amway (Japan) Limited; Amway (Malaysia) Sdn. Bhd.; Amway Nederland Ltd. (Netherlands); Amway of New Zealand Ltd.; Amway de Panama, S.A.; Amway (Schweiz) AG (Switzerland); Amway De España S.A. (Spain); Amway Asia Pacific Ltd. (Hong Kong); Amway (Taiwan) Limited; Amway (Thailand) Ltd.; Amway GmbH (Germany); Amway de Mexico; Amway Communications Corporation; Amway Hotel Corporation; Amway Global, Inc.; Amway International, Inc.; Quixtar Inc.

Principal Competitors

Avon Products, Inc.; CCL Industries Inc.; PFSweb, Inc.

Further Reading

"Amway Takes a Bold Step into Cyber-Selling," *Cosmetics International,* June 25, 1999, p. 7.

"Amway Tries Energy," *Crain's Detroit Business,* November 16, 1998, p. 33.

Biggart, Nicole Woolsey, *Charismatic Capitalism: Direct Selling Organizations in America,* Chicago: University of Chicago Press, 1989.

Bott, Jennifer, "Amway Changes Name, Mission," *Detroit Free Press,* October 25, 2000, p. B8.

Butterfield, Stephen, *Amway: The Cult of Free Enterprise,* Boston: South End Press, 1985.

Conn, Charles Paul, *Promises to Keep: The Amway Phenomenon and How It Works,* New York: G.P. Putnam's Sons, 1985.

——, *An Uncommon Freedom: The Amway Experience & Why It Grows,* New York: Berkley Publishing Group, 1983.

Cross, Wilbur, and Gordon Olson, *Commitment to Excellence: The Remarkable Amway Story,* Elmsford, N.Y.: The Benjamin Company, 1986.

"Dick DeVos to Retire As Alticor President," *Internet Wire,* April 17, 2002.

Eisenstodt, Gale, and Hiroko Katayama, "Soap and Hope in Tokyo," *Forbes,* September 3, 1990, p. 62.

"The $4-Billion Man: Rich DeVos Bet on Capitalism and Won," *Success,* May 1993, p. 10.

Gopwani, Jewel, "Ada, Mich.-Based Direct-Sales Firm Finds Fortune in Asia," *Detroit Free Press,* October 22, 2004, p. B12.

Grant, Linda, "How Amway's Two Founders Cleaned Up: Strong Overseas Sales Helped Richard DeVos and Jay Van Andel Add Billions to Their Fortunes," *U.S. News & World Report,* October 31, 1994, p. 77.

Holzinger, Albert G., "Selling America to the Japanese," *Nation's Business,* October 1990, p. 54.

Klebnikov, Paul, "The Power of Positive Inspiration," *Forbes,* December 9, 1991, p. 244.

Kirkbride, Rob, "Alticor Sales Soar 27 Percent," *Grand Rapids Press,* October 21, 2004, p. C1.

——, "Alticor Still Value-Driven Under New Leadership," *Grand Rapids Press,* October 18, 2002, p. A10.

——, "The Style of Doug DeVos," *Grand Rapids Press,* January 25, 2004, p. F1.

Morgello, Clem, "Richard Johnson of Amway Japan: Challenging Japan's Sales Culture," *Institutional Investor,* May 1994, p. 23.

Muller, Joann, "Amway Tailors Marketing Approach to Individual Foreign Cultures," *Journal of Commerce and Commercial,* July 8, 1991, p. 4A.

Ruzicka, Milan, "Amway Wins Converts in Former East Bloc," *Journal of Commerce and Commercial,* June 3, 1994, p. 1A.

Shaw, Anita, "Amway: A Global Approach to the Future," *Soap—Cosmetics—Chemical Specialties,* November 1996, p. 66.

Smith, Rodney K., *Multilevel Marketing: A Lawyer Looks at Amway, Shaklee, and Other Direct Sales Organizations,* Grand Rapids, Mich.: Baker Book House, 1984.

Tate, Nancy Ken, "Amway's Green Roots Go Deep," *American Demographics,* April 1991, p. 18.

Vlasic, Bill, "Amway II: The Kids Take Over—Dick DeVos and Steve Van Andel Try to Shed Old Baggage," *Business Week,* February 16, 1998, p. 60.

Xardel, Dominique, *The Direct Selling Revolution,* Cambridge, Mass.: Blackwell, 1993.

—David M. Walden
—updates: Beth Watson Highman; Jeffrey L. Covell

Andrews Kurth, LLP

600 Travis, Suite 4200
Houston, Texas 77002
U.S.A.
Telephone: (713) 220-4200
Fax: (713) 220-4285
Web site: http://www.andrewskurth.com

Private Company
Incorporated: 1902 as Andrews & Ball
Employees: 900
Sales: $176 million (2003 est.)
NAIC: 541110 Offices of Lawyers

Andrews Kurth, LLP is one of the ten largest law firms in the state of Texas, with more than 400 lawyers. The firm offers services in a number of different areas, with specializations in corporate/securities work, litigation, bankruptcy, taxes, trusts and estates, and public law. The firm's clients have included energy companies El Paso Corp., Conoco, and Enron, as well as Goldman, Sachs & Co., Aetna, Howard Hughes, the government of Argentina, and various U.S. federal agencies. Andrews Kurth has offices in Houston, Dallas, Austin, and The Woodlands, Texas; Washington, D.C.; New York; Los Angeles; and London.

Beginnings

Andrews Kurth traces its roots to 1902, when Frank Andrews and U.S. Congressman Thomas Ball founded a law firm in Houston, Texas. Andrews & Ball's early years saw them perform work for railroad companies including Gulf Coast Lines, which they helped set up. In 1904 former Appellate Judge Sam Streetman joined the firm, after which it became known as Andrews, Ball & Streetman. Other early clients included local banks such as Bankers Trust Company and Union National Bank, both of which the firm helped found. In 1913 a new attorney, Melvin Kurth, joined the group.

In 1914 Andrews, Ball & Streetman assisted Howard Hughes, Sr., in the formation of the Hughes Tool Company, beginning an association that would last for seven decades. In

1915 Frank Andrews was appointed receiver of the bankrupt Gulf Coast Lines, which was reorganized in 1917 as the New Orleans, Texas, & Mexico Railroad with Andrews as chairman. By now the firm had grown to employ 13 lawyers.

During World War I Frank Andrews served as chairman of the Draft Board, and two of the three lawyers who left the firm to serve abroad were killed. The 1920s saw an expansion of the firm's railroad work with new clients Missouri Pacific Lines and International & Great Northern. In 1923 Andrews, Ball & Streetman won a $2 million judgment in a receivership case, one of the largest in Texas to that time. Much work continued to be performed for Hughes Tool Company, which was taken over in 1924 by Howard Hughes, Jr., after his father's death. In 1929 the firm's offices were moved to the 22nd floor of Texas' tallest skyscraper, the Gulf Building.

Leadership Changes During the Depression

The Great Depression saw the firm struggle with a decline in work as well as the deaths of four of its five senior partners in 1932 and 1933. Melvin Kurth and Robert Kelley took on leadership roles, with Kurth taking the firm's top position in 1936 after Frank Andrews's death. Much work came from New Deal agencies the Reconstruction Finance Corporation and the Federal National Mortgage Corporation, as well as General Crude Oil Company and Southland Paper Mills, Inc., which the firm helped organize in 1933 and 1938, respectively.

World War II had a major impact on the firm, which saw ten of its 23 lawyers enter the service while the workload of the rest increased due to the bustling wartime economy. In 1946 the firm lost its railroad business when a key partner left, and it reorganized as Andrews, Kurth, Campbell & Bradley and continued working for other clients including Hughes Tool.

During the 1940s the firm secured a $1.2 million tax refund for Hughes Tool, as well as representing Howard Hughes, Jr., before a Congressional committee that was investigating the construction of his massive wooden airplane, dubbed the "Spruce Goose" by pundits. In 1951 Andrews, Kurth, Campbell & Bradley won a record court settlement in Oklahoma for Hughes Tool in a patent infringement suit.

Company Perspectives:

Straight talk is how we communicate—with clients, colleagues, courts and adversaries. It's our promise to give you advice instead of just options, the bottom line instead of lawyer-speak, and the truth about where you stand and what we think. Though our individual styles may vary, our constant goal is to cut through confusion and help you succeed.

Straight talk is what countless law firm clients across the country have asked for—and what we think you deserve.

These are the straight talk rules we live by: don't hide behind legalese; choose a direction; adopt the client's perspective; tackle problems head-on; find simple solutions; meet deadlines; stay in touch; tell clients what they need to know, not just what they want to hear; know what comes next; respect our client's time; bridge the gap.

Highlights of the 1950s included a growing specialization in the complex legal issues related to the natural gas pipeline industry, with new clients including El Paso Natural Gas Co. and newly formed Pacific Northwest Pipeline Company. The firm also began working with Southwest Forest Industries, Inc. and helped charter Southern National Bank.

In the 1960s the firm, now known as Andrews, Kurth, Campbell & Jones, gained national recognition for its bankruptcy and corporate reorganization practice after it assisted in the reorganization of Westec. In 1963 the firm moved into new quarters in the Humble Building and formed a new management committee to lead it after Melvin Kurth's retirement that year.

Work during the decade included representing El Paso Natural Gas in a drawn-out antitrust case, and advising Howard Hughes on the $546 million sale of his majority stake in Trans World Airlines, as well as his subsequent move into Las Vegas real estate.

In the early 1970s the firm's work for Hughes included advising on the $150 million public offering of shares in the Oil Tool Division of Hughes Tool, and winning the reversal of a $145 million antitrust judgment which reached the U.S. Supreme Court. In 1974 Transcontinental Gas Pipeline Co. (Transco) retained the firm as its financing and regulatory counsel, and it began to take on lawsuits over so-called "take or pay" natural gas sales contracts to industrial customers.

Estate of Howard Hughes Brings Work in 1976

On April 5, 1976, reclusive billionaire Howard Hughes died. Because he had not left a will, the disposition of his business empire fell to the courts. Andrews, Kurth, Campbell & Jones was kept busy looking into claims of kinship, liquidating assets, dealing with tax issues (three states initially claimed Hughes as their legal resident), and resolving litigation. Though numerous purported wills soon appeared, naming heirs that ranged from Western movie actor Hopalong Cassidy to a Utah service-station operator who had supposedly once given Hughes a ride in the desert, none was ultimately deemed valid.

The 1980s saw the firm's bankruptcy work grow, and it handled the filings of such companies as Braniff, Continental Air-

ways, Global Marine, Republic Bank, and Texas financiers the Hunt brothers. The Savings and Loan meltdown was the firm's biggest source of work during the decade, as it represented the Federal Savings and Loan Insurance Corporation (FSLIC) in closing and liquidating the assets of numerous bankrupt thrifts.

In 1984 the firm, now using the name Andrews & Kurth, opened a new office in Dallas through a merger with a five-lawyer litigation firm. It had earlier opened a one-person office in Washington, D.C., that primarily represented Transco.

The mid-1980s saw resolution of tax claims against the Hughes estate by the U.S. Internal Revenue Service and the states of California and Texas. By 1985 Andrews & Kurth employed 128 lawyers. Some 35 percent of its work consisted of litigation, 32 percent was corporate or securities law, 11 percent was tax work, 6 percent was trusts/estates, and 5 percent was labor law. In 1986 P. Dexter Peacock took over as head of the firm's managing committee. He was keen to see it grow in size and diversity, and over the next five years Andrews & Kurth would more than double its ranks of lawyers.

In the early 1980s the firm's tax lawyers had developed a new business entity called the master limited partnership (MLP), which was structured somewhat like a corporation and traded on stock exchanges, but was taxed as a partnership, thus avoiding corporate income tax. By mid-1987 nearly 100 MLPs were trading on major stock exchanges and officials of the Reagan administration were publicly decrying the threat the lost taxes posed to the federal budget. The firm's development of the concept had helped make it the national leader in setting up MLPs.

In 1988 an office was opened in Los Angeles, which was expanded the following year through the acquisition of the nine-lawyer oil and gas specialty firm Bright & Brown. By 1990 Andrews & Kurth employed 270 lawyers and was the seventh largest law firm in Texas. Major clients included Santa Fe Energy Co., Transco, El Paso Natural Gas, Aetna Life & Casualty, Amerada Hess, and Goldman Sachs & Co. Annual revenues were estimated at $67 million.

In 1990 the firm opened an office in New York with three lawyers, which soon grew to 24 through the acquisition of Ross & Korff. The following year saw Andrews & Kurth begin the lengthy process of settling the affairs of the bankrupt Bank of New England, and also begin helping Argentina privatize its state-owned oil and natural gas companies. The latter were sold at public offerings in 1992 and 1993 for a total of $7 billion. The firm's work for Argentina raised its profile in Latin America, and led to a steady stream of work south of the border.

Restructuring in 1992

Andrews & Kurth was run as a democratic organization, with partners voting on everything from critical issues to the type of flooring used in the firm's elevators. Though staff numbers had been rising steadily since the mid-1980s, profits per partner were declining, and the lack of strong central leadership saw the firm reach a state of crisis by late 1991, as it reportedly edged close to dissolution. To improve matters, the new head of the firm's managing committee, Alfred H. Ebert, Jr., chose Washington, D.C. partner Rush Moody to head a restructuring committee. After two months it submitted a report

Key Dates:

1902: Frank Andrews and Thomas Ball form a law firm in Houston, Texas.
1914: Firm helps Howard Hughes, Sr., form Hughes Tool Company.
1936: Melvin Kurth takes over leadership of firm.
1946: Firm becomes known as Andrews, Kurth, Campbell & Bradley.
1950s: Gas pipeline law becomes a specialty.
1976: Death of Howard Hughes brings firm work sorting out his estate.
1980s: Firm's lawyers develop master limited partnership corporate structure; company more than doubles in size to 270 lawyers by end of decade.
1992: Firm restructures; Rush Moody is named managing partner.
1996: Partners vote to seek national practice, name Howard Ayers managing partner.
2001: Merger with Mayor, Day, Caldwell & Keeton brings over 100 new lawyers; firm begins work on Enron bankruptcy.
2003: Name is shortened to Andrews Kurth.

that urged the firm be run more like a corporation, with a CEO and a board of directors making most decisions, and only major issues requiring a vote of all of the firm's partners.

Though Moody was recommended for the role of managing partner/CEO by his own committee, he initially turned down the job, finally signing on in April 1992, while Ebert took the title of board chairman. Moody worked swiftly to right the ship, taking such measures as reducing the firm's support staff from 377 to 311, downsizing the underperforming Dallas office from 33 lawyers to nine, and paring the management committee, which was reduced from 11 members to 7. The firm's timekeeping and billing methods were also examined and found to be highly inconsistent, and Moody streamlined them and set new billing deadlines.

Successes of the year included finalizing the spinoff of El Paso Natural Gas from Burlington Resources, and assisting in the return of medieval artwork stolen from Quedlinburg, Germany, by a Texas soldier during World War II. The year 1992 also saw Andrews & Kurth lose a lucrative contract working for the Federal Deposit Insurance Corporation (FDIC), to which it had billed some $6.7 million since 1988. The firm's 1991 charges were audited, and the FDIC declared $855,000 in fees unacceptable, the highest amount among several firms that were examined. Though Andrews & Kurth admitted to some errors, it also complained that the audit was arbitrary and unfair.

The firm got back on track in the early 1990s, opening a new office in the Houston suburb of The Woodlands and adding staff to its Dallas office. By 1995 Andrews & Kurth's annual revenues stood at $96 million, with per-partner profit payouts of $435,000. The firm was now deriving 30 percent of its revenue from corporate/securities work, 28 percent from litigation, and 14 percent from real estate.

The mid-1990s also saw much mergers and acquisitions work, including assisting with the 1996 purchase of Tenneco by El Paso Energy for $4.2 billion, as well as helping set up a number of public stock offerings. The firm also added a one-person office in London, England, during this period.

In the spring of 1996 Andrews & Kurth began preparing for Rush Moody's retirement as managing partner, as it began to grapple with deciding on whether to pursue becoming a national practice, or remaining a regional one. The partners ultimately voted to strive for a national practice while retaining full-service offices in Houston and Dallas. They also made new changes to the management structure, shortening terms on the managing committee from three years to one, and chose a new managing partner, Howard Ayers, who would take control the following year.

In the first half of 1997 Andrews & Kurth lost more than 25 lawyers, including ten who left to form their own litigation practice in Houston, leaving a total of 230. After Ayers took control the firm's energies were refocused, and partnership share payments began increasing faster than revenues as a whole.

The last details of the Howard Hughes estate were finally worked out in 1999 when his Las Vegas properties were merged to create Rouse Company, for which the estate's beneficiaries were issued ownership shares. A total of more than 100 people ended up sharing the estate, with legal fees estimated to have amounted to more than any single person's share. By now Andrews & Kurth had 243 lawyers, and its annual revenues had reached $114 million.

In February 2000 the firm announced that it would raise associate lawyer base salaries by 20 percent, to $104,000 from $86,000. The move was made to remain competitive with other large law firms, which had also begun raising their associates' pay dramatically.

2001 Merger Bringing Over 100 New Lawyers

Having lost ten partners in 2000, Andrews & Kurth rebounded in October 2001 when it merged with the 107-lawyer Mayor, Day, Caldwell & Keeton, after absorbing that firm's public law group earlier in the year. The year 2001 was a boom year for bankruptcy and energy work for the firm, as the depressed economy took its toll on corporations and gas prices soared. Energy clients now included Enron Corp., El Paso Corp., NRG Energy, and Conoco. The firm also opened a new office in the state capital of Austin during the year.

By the end of 2001 Andrews & Kurth had more than 350 attorneys, including four recently added in a merger with Austin-based Cavazos, Lanagenkamp, Morin & Ferraro, and 22 newly hired associates. The growth put the firm into the top 100 U.S. law firms for the first time, and made it one of the ten largest in Texas. Revenues now stood at $164 million.

In December 2001 Enron filed for bankruptcy protection, the largest such filing in U.S. history. Andrews & Kurth, which had been paid $13 million by the energy company over the preceding 12 months, would act as one of several special counsels in the case, though it did not take a lead role.

The firm celebrated its centennial in 2002, and grew to employ 400 lawyers during the year. More were added in 2003 when groups were absorbed from the Austin office of Brobeck, Phleger & Harrison (specializing in technology), the Dallas office of Arter & Hadden, and from Dorsey & Whitney, a Washington, D.C.-based group of Internet law specialists. The firm also began work on a branding campaign in 2003, which led to a decision to streamline its name to Andrews Kurth.

The Enron bankruptcy examiner's final report, issued in November 2003, concluded that outside counsel from Andrews Kurth and Vinson & Elkins had likely aided and abetted Enron executives' breaches of fiduciary duty, though it noted that they were probably not legally culpable. Several Enron creditors asked the bankruptcy judge for permission to sue the two firms for their roles in helping set up the numerous ''off-the-books'' partnerships that appeared to have been used to artificially boost the corporation's profits. Andrews Kurth declared it had done nothing wrong, and vowed to defend itself.

Despite such controversy, in 2004 the firm reached the top rankings nationally for its work in several areas, including corporate law, equities, and municipal bonds. In January 2005 Andrews Kurth represented El Paso Corporation in a $179 million production company acquisition, and several months later the firm won a $458 million judgment for Paragon Trade Brands against Weyerhaeuser Company.

More than a century after it began, Andrews Kurth LLP had grown into one of the ten largest law firms in Texas, with specialties in corporate and securities law, litigation, estates, taxes, and other matters. It was now nationally ranked in a number of specialty areas, and its growth was continuing through mergers and the hiring of new lawyers.

Principal Competitors

Akin Gump Strauss Hauer & Feld, L.L.P.; Vinson & Elkins L.L.P.; Fulbright & Jaworski L.L.P.; Baker and Botts L.L.P.; Locke Liddell & Sapp LLP; Bracewell & Patterson L.L.P.; McCall, Parkhurst & Horton.

Further Reading

''Andrews & Kurth Retools, Slims Down,'' *Texas Lawyer*, April 27, 1992, p. 38.

Boardman, Amy, ''Battle-Hardened Troops Clean Up in New England—A&K Team Tapped by Boston Bank's Trustee,'' *Texas Lawyer*, May 6, 1991, p. 1.

Greene, Jenna, ''Enron Creditors Taking Aim at Law Firms,'' *Legal Times*, December 2, 2002, p. 3.

Himelstein, Linda, ''FDIC Audits May Recoup $100 Million; Agency Drops Andrews & Kurth After Docking Firm $855,000,'' *Texas Lawyer*, February 3, 1992, p. 2.

Horner, Kim, ''A Gusher,'' *Texas Lawyer*, July 1, 1996, p. 1.

Jeffreys, Brenda Sapino, ''Andrews & Kurth Loses 10 Corporate Partners,'' *Texas Lawyer*, May 22, 2000, p. 7.

——, ''Andrews & Kurth Targets and Snares Public-Law Group from Major, Day,'' *Texas Lawyer*, March 19, 2000, p. 4.

——, ''Big Changes Force A&K to Look Inward,'' *Texas Lawyer*, June 2, 1997, p. 1.

——, ''Impact Players: Howard T. Ayers,'' *Texas Lawyer*, December 8, 2000, p. 64.

——, ''Let the Games Begin; Andrews & Kurth Strikes First with 20 Percent Associate Pay Hike,'' *Texas Lawyer*, February 28, 2000, p. 6.

——, ''Measured Success: Andrews & Kurth Has Figured Out That Size and Revenue Don't Necessarily Determine a Firm's Fortune,'' *Texas Lawyer*, June 28, 1999, p. 1.

——, ''Seven-Year Niche; Boston Bank Liquidation Keeps Andrews & Kurth Raking in East Coast Work,'' *Texas Lawyer*, September 28, 1998, p. 1.

Jeffreys, Brenda Sapino, and Miriam Rozen, ''Final Enron Report Criticizes V&E and Andrews & Kurth,'' *Texas Lawyer*, December 1, 2003, p. 1.

Kessenides, Dimitra, ''Calming the Waters at Andrews & Kurth,'' *American Lawyer*, November 1994, p. 45.

Lancaster, Hal, ''Shrinkage in Estate of Howard Hughes Fails to Deter Claims,'' *Wall Street Journal*, March 3, 1978, p. 1.

Philley, Alicia, and Brenda Sapino, ''Andrews & Kurth Tops State's Life Insurance Counsel,'' *Texas Lawyer*, September 11, 1995, p. 1.

Robbins, Mary Alice, ''Estate and Son of Deceased Partner Sue Andrews & Kurth,'' *Texas Lawyer*, February 23, 2004, p. 5.

Sapino, Brenda, ''Corporate Firm Joins Andrews & Kurth in NY; Month-Old Branch Grows to 23 Lawyers,'' *Texas Lawyer*, October 8, 1990, p. 4.

Turner, Wallace, ''Legal Dispute Over Howard Hughes' Newly Profitable Empire Is Approaching Climax,'' *New York Times*, June 3, 1979, p. 14.

——, ''Legal Fees at Issue in Hughes Probate,'' *New York Times*, February 15, 1977, p. 13.

—Frank Uhle

airBaltic

A/S Air Baltic Corporation

Riga International Airport
Riga LV-1053
Latvia
Telephone: +371 720 7069
Fax: +371 7224282
Web site: http://www.airbaltic.com

Private Company
Incorporated: 1995 as Air Baltic Corporation SIA
Employees: 500
Sales: LVL 33.5 million (2003)
NAIC: 481111 Scheduled Passenger Air Transportation

A/S Air Baltic Corporation (airBaltic) is Latvia's national airline. The two main shareholders are the government of Latvia and the Scandinavian airline group SAS AB. airBaltic operates a fleet of about 14 aircraft (Boeing 737 jets and Fokker 50 turboprops). The carrier flies to about 20 European destinations from hubs in Riga, Latvia, and Vilnius, Lithuania. Its primary focus is the Baltic Sea region.

Origins

Latavio, the local branch of Aeroflot, provided air transportation during the Soviet occupation of Latvia, which lasted from 1940 to 1991. At the fall of the Soviet Empire, Latavio had 22 jet aircraft and 14 turboprops, according to *Flight International.* It employed about 550 people in 1995.

The regional aviation market was attracting interest from outside investors because of its untapped growth potential. In 1991, the American company Baltic International USA (BIUSA) attempted to acquire a share in Latavio. According to *Flight International,* BIUSA wanted to develop Riga, Latvia, into a regional hub.

These ambitions were temporarily scaled back, however, in the face of resistance from neighboring republics Lithuania and Estonia. While the old Latavio stayed in place, BIUSA launched a smaller project with a pair of the Tupolev Tu-134 airliners to fly

to just Germany and Switzerland. Baltic International Airlines, a joint venture between BIUSA (40 percent) and the Latvian state (60 percent), was established in June 1992. Baltic International's fleet grew to include three Western-made jets as the route network expanded to London's Gatwick Airport.

Forming Air Baltic in 1995

Latavio was eventually shut down after a failed privatization attempt. In the meantime, it was relegated to charter flights as another local airline was organized. Air Baltic Corporation SIA (later known as airBaltic) was formed as a limited liability corporation in August 1995. It was a partnership between the Latvian State, which owned 51 percent of shares, the Scandinavian airline group SAS AB, which held 28.5 percent of shares, and three other investors: BIUSA (8 percent), Swedfund International AB (6.2 percent), and IO Danish Investment Fund for Central and Eastern Europe (6.2 percent). AirBaltic was led by a management team from SAS.

The company's first plane was a 30-seat Saab 340 turboprop. The first flight occurred on October 1, 1995. An Avro RJ70 (British Aerospace 146), a small regional jet, was added to the fleet in January 1996. According to *Airclaims,* airBaltic also used a pair of Boeing 727s from the Baltic International fleet.

AirBaltic employed fewer than 200 people at the time. Reuters reported its most lucrative routes were to Helsinki, Copenhagen, and Stockholm; the latter two routes were operated in cooperation with SAS. Passengers included a higher than average percentage of business travelers.

Weathering Change in the Late 1990s

The company replaced its Saab 340 aircraft with Fokker 50 turboprops in the late 1990s. The Fokkers were a bit larger, with 46 seats each. There were also changes to management personnel. SAS veteran Rudi Schwab was named head of airBaltic in 1997. He succeeded Kjell Fredheim, another Scandinavian executive.

In late 1998, airBaltic's capitalization was boosted from LVL 2.4 million ($4.2 million) to LVL 15.5 million. airBaltic became a joint stock company on January 25, 1999. By this

Company Perspectives:

airBaltic aims to be a strong regional carrier. The goal is to assure regular air transport between Riga and Vilnius to Europe's major cities, for the prices that are competitive not only with other airlines, but also with the prices of bus, car, train or ferry.

In parallel with direct flights, airBaltic provides convenient connections through Scandinavian transit hubs— Copenhagen and Stockholm.

airBaltic's service priority is to provide business people and tourists with a wide range of travel options.

Alongside business travel, airBaltic wants to increase tourism travel. This sector has a lot of potential to grow, as Baltic countries represent a place worth visiting, not only for cultural aesthetes, but also for those with special interests in nature and history. To develop this sector airline is introducing one-way fare structure with low prices and opening new direct flights for the travellers.

Key Dates:

1995: A/S Air Baltic Corporation is formed as a joint venture of Latvian State, SAS, and other investors.
1997: The cargo department is launched.
1999: airBaltic becomes a joint stock company.
2001: The company posts its first after-tax profit.
2004: Latvia's entry into European Union brings opportunity, competition.

time, the airline had begun direct service to Moscow, and Russia's Transaero Airlines had acquired a 0.35 percent shareholding. SAS had boosted its holdings to 38 percent. This was increased to 49 percent in late 2001 as SAS bought out the other Danish and Swedish investors for a reported SEK 80 million ($9 million).

Russia underwent a major economic crisis in the late 1990s, prompting airBaltic to suspend unprofitable routes such as Minsk, Warsaw, Prague, and Moscow. A couple of joint marketing agreements in 1999 helped airBaltic extend its reach. Hungary's Malev partnered on a Riga-Budapest route, while Estonian Air and airBaltic teamed up to develop Tallinn and Riga as gateways from Scandinavia.

airBaltic posted a net loss of LVL 1.4 million ($2.4 million) on sales of LVL 25 million in 2000, but it made its first operating profit and was showing other signs of progress. The company had a 39 percent market share, and had boosted its load factor (the ratio of seats sold to available seats) from 37 percent to 52 percent.

In the Black in 2001

airBaltic began the millennium with a new headquarters building at Riga International Airport. A new cargo terminal was opened there in 2001. Jens Helmo Larssen was named company president in June of that year. An SAS veteran, he succeeded Christian Kirchainer, who had led airBaltic since 1999. Bertolt M. Flick, a German, became CEO in early 2002.

The company broke even in 2001, posting its first after-tax profit of LVL 56,000 ($88,000) on revenues of LVL 28 million. About 249,000 passengers were carried during the year, an increase of 14 percent. These gains came in spite of the after-effects of the September 11 terrorist attacks on the United States, including a significant increase in the cost of insurance.

Passenger count rose slightly in 2002, to about 262,000. During the year, the company introduced new Baltic Shuttle

fares. For example, noted Britain's *Financial Times,* one could fly one-way from Riga to Hamburg for EUR 49. Flights to neighboring capitals Vilnius and Tallinn could be had for just EUR 30 one-way. These were popular with passengers but not with some national civil aviation authorities eager to protect their state airlines. Finland and Austria eventually agreed to the fares but Poland refused.

Another European business center, Amsterdam, was added to the network in November 2002. CEO Bertolt Flick told the *Baltic Times* the company was growing its tourist business by adding new flights to Berlin and Vienna. At the same time, the company withdrew its weekly Frankfurt flight when Lufthansa began flying to Riga on Sundays. Minsk and Brussels were two other new destinations for 2003, the latter inspired by Latvia's impending entrance into the European Union in May 2004.

The first leased Boeing 737 entered the fleet in late 2003. It replaced an Avro RJ 70 on the Riga-Copenhagen route. Another half-dozen 737s were added in 2004. The company posted a profit of LVL 1.1 million on operating income of LVL 33.5 million in 2003.

In the EU in 2004

The airline carried 589,288 passengers in 2004, a hefty 75 percent increase over 2003's 336,000 passengers. New, low one-way fares fueled growth. Another factor was the opening of a second hub in Vilnius, Lithuania. According to company President Bertolt Flick, an increase in passenger volume was necessary to offset the steady fall in ticket prices. The route network continued to expand, adding Dublin, Oslo, and Milan, the latter offered as a holiday destination on the Mediterranean. The new 737s also allowed for economical service to London— historically the highest volume route from Riga.

Latvia's membership in the EU had opened airBaltic to low-cost competition from distant lands, such as Ireland's Ryanair. Flick pointed out to the *Baltic Times,* however, that airBaltic had already had considerable success of its own using a low-fare model. It remained the dominant player at booming Riga International Airport, which served more than one million passengers in 2004, up 50 percent from the previous year. airBaltic's own passenger count rose a heart-stopping 75 percent during the year, thanks in part to EU-inspired traffic.

airBaltic entered 2005 with a fleet of seven Boeing 737 jets and a half-dozen Fokker 50 turboprops. The route network continued to spread south in the spring of 2005, with scheduled services added to Istanbul and Barcelona. Flick told the *Baltic*

Times, however, that the airline was focused on increasing flight frequency to meet skyrocketing demand rather than adding destinations.

In the spring of 2005, service from Riga to Liepaja, on Latvia's west coast, was reintroduced for the first time in 45 years. It was not expected to be a profitable route. Ventspils and Daugavpils were other domestic destinations under consideration.

Principal Divisions

Cargo.

Principal Competitors

Estonian Air AS; Finnair Oy; Lietuvos Avialinijos (Lithuanian Airlines); Ryanair PLC.

Further Reading

"Advanced Cargo Terminal Sets into Motion in Riga Airport," *Baltic News Service,* June 12, 2001.

"AirBaltic, Ryanair Set to Go Head-to-Head in 2005," *Baltic Times,* January 19, 2005.

"Air Baltic's Operation Results Always Lagged Behind," *Baltic Business Daily,* January 17, 2000.

"Airlines Step Up the Competition," *Baltic Times,* June 3, 2004.

Arklina, Ilze, "One Airline's Future," *Baltic Times,* April 18, 2002.

——, "SAS Increases Its Stake in Latvian Airline," *Baltic Times,* November 1, 2001.

Bray, Roger, "Boom Time for Baltic Carriers," *Financial Times* (London), March 3, 2005, p. 12.

Ceplis, Kristaps, "AirBaltic Plans on Becoming One of Region's Main Airlines," *Latvian News Agency,* August 20, 2003.

"Estonian Air and airBaltic Sign Cooperation Agreement," *Estonian News Agency,* July 6, 1999.

"Finland, Austria Seek to Curb Airline Competition: Latvian Transport Ministry," *Baltic News Service,* March 22, 2002.

"Flights to Liepaja Return After 60-Year Absence," *Baltic Times,* March 16, 2005.

George, Nicholas, "Flying High with Much Lower Fares," *Financial Times* (London), FT Report—Latvia, November 25, 2003, p. 4.

Gravitis, Martinsh, "Interview—Air Baltic Says SAS Happy, Moscow Disappoints," *Reuters News,* May 26, 1998.

Jeziorski, Andrzej, "Latvian Passenger Tax Hits Air Baltic's Target," *Flight International,* June 18, 1997, p. 21.

——, "Made for Each Other?," *Flight International,* July 2, 1997.

Khamsi, Roxanne, "A One-Way Ticket to Better Business," *Baltic Times,* February 26, 2004.

Lannin, Patrick, "Latvia's Air Baltic Says First Year Below Target," *Reuters News,* October 1, 1996.

——, "New Latvian Airline Optimistic As Set for Take Off," *Reuters News,* September 20, 1995.

"Latvian airBaltic Carrier 1.514 Mln Lats in Red in 2000," *Baltic News Service,* April 24, 2001.

"Latvian Air Company Gets New President," *Baltic News Service,* June 14, 2001.

"Latvian Airlines Plot New Courses," *Flight International,* October 18, 1995, p. 13.

"Latvian National Airline AirBaltic Adds Boeing 737 to Its Fleet," *Baltic News Service,* November 20, 2003.

"Latvian National Airline Sees Passenger Load Soar, 2004 Profits Healthy," *Agence France Presse—English,* January 17, 2005.

"Latvian National Carrier Sees Improved Results As Efficiency Programme Bears Fruit," *Airclaims Airline News,* May 4, 2001.

"Latvia's National Air Co. AirBaltic Plans Domestic Flights," *Baltic Business Daily,* May 11, 2004.

Maslen, Richard, "Strategic Partnerships Key to Profitable AirBaltic Operation," *Airclaims,* October 6, 2000.

"National Carrier AirBaltic Still Leads in Riga Airport," *Baltic Business Daily,* November 9, 2004.

Nimmo, Ben, "EU Regulations Bring Boom to Baltic Skies," *Baltic Times,* March 2, 2005.

Peach, Gary, "AirBaltic, Ministry Rankle Another Competitor," *Baltic Times,* October 24, 2002.

"The Russians Are Coming," *Baltic Times,* January 28, 1999.

"SAS Increases Stake in airBaltic," *Airline Industry Information,* October 26, 2001.

"Six Airlines Still Dominant at Riga Airport," *ETA Economic Bulletin,* April 14, 2002.

—Frederick C. Ingram

←ESTONIAN AIR

AS Estonian Air

Lennujaama tee 13
11101 Tallinn
Estonia
Telephone: (372) 6 401 101
Fax: (372) 6 016 092
Web site: http://www.estonian-air.ee

Private Company
Incorporated: 1991 as Estonian Air
Employees: 309
Sales: EUR 56.6 million ($75.19 million) (2003)
NAIC: 481111 Scheduled Passenger Air Transportation;
481112 Scheduled Freight Air Transportation; 481211
Nonscheduled Chartered Passenger Air Transportation
Handling; 488119 Other Airport Operations

AS Estonian Air is the national airline of Estonia. Based in Tallinn, Estonian Air flies five mid-size Boeing 737 airliners to about a dozen destinations in Europe. It serves about 500,000 passengers a year. Traditionally, almost 90 percent of revenues have come from scheduled passenger operations. Estonian Air also operates charter flights and flies mail and cargo. Scandinavia's SAS Group is a major shareholder, with a 49 percent holding. The Estonian government owns 34 percent of shares; the remaining 17 percent are held by AS Cresco, an Estonian investment group.

Origins

Estonia was part of the Soviet Union for 50 years. During this time, a local division of Aeroflot provided air services, carrying 800,000 passengers a year at its peak, according to *Flight International.*

After the fall of the Soviet Union, Estonia regained its independence and on December 1, 1991, established a national airline, AS Estonian Air. Destinations to Germany, Finland, and Sweden were among the first served, a continuation of service from the Soviet airline Aeroflot. The airport operations were separated from Estonian Air in September 1992.

According to *Airline Business,* Estonian Air carried 160,000 passengers in its first full year (1992). Its loss of $310,000 on revenues of EEK 100 million ($7.8 million) was mostly due to unprofitable domestic routes, where the average fare was just $2.30. However, other airlines were already offering competition on the lucrative international routes.

By January 1993, Estonian was flying to Helsinki, Stockholm, Frankfurt, Copenhagen, and Amsterdam. It was increasing frequency of service to the West from the one to four weekly flights typical of the Soviet era, noted *Airline Business.* Though a tiny country of less than two million people, Estonia was hoping to justify having its own airline by billing itself as a gateway between East and West.

The carrier joined the International Air Transport Association (IATA) soon after its founding and in 1994 formed a joint venture with Amadeus Holding, the global computer reservation service.

Estonian Air faced competition by sea as well as by air on the 45-mile (85 kilometer) route between Tallinn and Helsinki. The airline's monthly passenger count on this route doubled to 6,000 immediately following the tragic sinking of the ferry *Estonia* in September 1994.

Westernization in the Mid-1990s

Estonian Air underwent two major changes in the mid-1990s that made it more of a Western-style airline. The small fleet of Soviet aircraft was replaced with new Western planes, and the airline was partially privatized.

The carrier had inherited from Aeroflot a fleet of about a dozen 72-seat Tupolev Tu-134s (only five of which were being used) and four smaller 26-passenger Yakovlev Yak-40s. These jets were relatively inefficient and noisy by Western standards. Estonian had also inherited a dozen propeller-driven An-2 biplanes.

Estonian began leasing its first U.S.-made Boeing 737, configured for 109 passengers, in 1995. A second one entered the fleet the following year. The mid-size Boeing 737 was the global standard for low-cost carriers. In 1996, a pair of Fokker

Key Dates:

1991: Estonian Air is formed in newly independent Estonia.
1995: First Western-made aircraft enter the fleet.
1996: Maersk Air and Cresco Ltd. invest in Estonian Air's privatization.
2003: SAS Group acquires Maersk's 49 percent shareholding.
2004: European Union membership brings open skies to Estonia.

50 turboprops were leased from Maersk Air for the short-haul commuter routes.

The Russian-made aircraft Yaks and Tupolevs were retired by the end of 1996. At about the same time, according to *Aviation Week,* Aeroflot was compensated $700,000 for the spinoff of its Estonian division. Settling this claim allowed Estonian Air to resume suspended flights to Moscow.

Estonian had about 500 employees in 1995, down from 676 two years earlier. The head count continued to drop, as the Boeings required fewer crewmembers and less maintenance. By 1997, Estonian had 380 employees—100 of whom were with the ground handling operation at Tallinn Airport, according to *Aviation Week.* The airline's pilots and flight attendants were unionized around January 1997.

The airline was partially privatized in September 1996, with Maersk Air A/S of Denmark acquiring 49 percent of shares and Cresco Ltd., an Estonian investment group, taking 17 percent. The government retained a 34 percent stake. The airline was valued at about EEK 60 million ($10 million). Estonian got a new president, former Maersk Travel Managing Director Borge Thornbech. Maersk won the privatization deal over a higher bid from SAS Group, due to its plan to develop Estonian Air as an independent airline, rather than subsume it to its own group.

According to *Aviation Week,* scheduled international operations accounted for 86 percent of total revenues of EEK 365 million ($27.2 million) in 1996. Revenues rose to EEK 558 million by 1998.

Cooperative Marketing in the Late 1990s and Beyond

Estonian's frequent flyer program, Blue Star, was introduced in 1997, followed the next year by the debut of the "Blue Velvet" business class. Estonian began participating in SAS's EuroBonus frequent flyer program in 1999.

There were other cooperative agreements in the late 1990s. In 1997, Estonian joined AVIS in offering a Fly & Drive package. Estonian code-shared with Finnair from 1996 to 1999 on flights between Tallinn and Helsinki. (After this relationship ended, Finnair formed an Estonian subsidiary, Aero Airlines AS, to compete on this route, which Finnair had originally flown from 1924 to 1940.)

Estonian Air began code-share flights with SAS to the Scandinavian capitals in 1999. The SAS deal provided vital access to traffic from the Star global airline alliance (Finnair was joining the rival oneworld alliance). "Scandinavia has no direct service to Minsk (Belarus) or Kiev (Ukraine) and our aim is to become a regional mini-hub for those destinations," company President Borge Thornbech told *Air Transport Intelligence.* Yet another cooperation agreement was signed with Latvia's national airline, airBaltic, in mid-1999.

The airline was maintaining links with Eastern Europe, where its destinations included Moscow, Kiev, Riga, and Vilnius. However, the Minsk, Belarus route was canceled in July 2000 due to low traffic. Aeroflot Russian Airlines became Estonian's codeshare partner on the Tallinn-Moscow route in 2001.

Tallinn Airport opened a new cargo terminal in 1998. Its passenger facilities were subsequently upgraded at a cost of $32 million in time for the new Millennium. Estonian Air was then operating three Boeing 737s and two Fokker 50s to 13 destinations. The airline had been intending to replace the Fokkers with regional jets, but this would be delayed first by an economic crisis in Russia, then by the effects of the September 11, 2001 terrorist attacks on the United States.

Online in 2000

A travel portal, travelUp.net, was launched in 2000. It allowed customers to book hotels and rental cars in addition to flights. The site was revamped and renamed reisi.net in 2002.

There were some leadership changes at the time. In 2000, Maersk Air executive Jorn Ericksen became Estonian's president. He would be succeeded two years later by Erki Urva.

According to the *Baltic Times,* Estonian Air reported a sevenfold increase in the cost of insurance following the 9/11 terrorist attacks on the United States. The airline temporarily switched to leased aircraft as it lined up coverage. However, Estonian was not as affected by the subsequent industry crisis to the same degree as other airlines. In fact, in 2001, it posted its first profit, EEK 15 million ($882,000), on revenues of EEK 800 million. During the year, a joint venture with Air BP, Estonian Aviation Fuelling Services Ltd., was established at Tallinn Airport. Profits more than doubled in 2002 to EEK 39.2 million as revenues reached EEK 838 million.

SAS AB agreed to buy Maersk Air's 49 percent shareholding for SEK 180 million ($22 million) in September 2003. In a press release, SAS (Scandinavian Airlines) pointed out that it had been the first Western European airline to open scheduled flights to the country. SAS was also involved in small airlines from neighboring countries. The region's growth and strategic location were keys to SAS's investment. SAS was intending to acquire majority stakes in both Estonian Air and Latvia's airBaltic, but postponed these plans until their effects on the carriers' traffic rights with Russia could be worked out.

Revenues rose slightly to EUR 56.6 million in 2003. In November of the year, the company's last Fokker 50 turboprop came off lease, leaving an all-Boeing fleet. Estonia's upcoming membership in the European Union (EU) called for the additional capacity.

Open Skies in 2004

Estonia's entry into the European Union (EU) in May 2004 opened the national airline to both competition and opportunity.

More European destinations had been added, including Berlin, Oslo, and Brussels, home of EU headquarters. New competition included low-cost airlines from distant bases, such as the United Kingdom's easyJet.

Earnings slipped from EEK 81 million to EEK 29 million in 2004. While Estonian lost some market share, the local air market was booming. The airline carried more than 500,000 passengers during the year. Erki Urva, CEO for two years, stepped down in January 2005.

Principal Subsidiaries

Amadeus-Eesti AS (60%); Eesti Aviokütuse Teenuste AS (Estonian Aviation Fuelling Services Ltd.) (51%).

Principal Divisions

Airline Services; Handling Division.

Principal Competitors

Aero Airlines AS; Air France; Alitalia - Linee Aeree Italiane S.p.A.; A/S Air Baltic Corporation (airBaltic); easyJet Airline Company Limited; Finnair Oyj; Iberia Líneas Aéreas de España SA; KLM Royal Dutch Airlines; Lietuvos Avialinijos (Lithuanian Airlines); Virgin Atlantic Airways Limited.

Further Reading

Chuter, Andy, "Estonian Revival," *Flight International,* July 7, 1999, p. 32.
"Demand Grows for Tallinn Flights Since Sinking of Estonia Ferry," *Aviation Daily,* November 10, 1994, p. 4.
"Estonian Air Hires New Head, Retires Last of Russian Fleet," *Commuter/Regional Airline News International,* November 11, 1996.
"Estonian Air Prepares for Its First Western Jets," *World Airline News,* March 27, 1995.
Ionedes, Nicholas, "SAS to Buy 49% of Estonian Air," *Air Transport Intelligence,* September 12, 2003.
Jasper, Chris, "Estonian Becomes Star Feeder with SAS Deal," *Air Transport Intelligence,* December 4, 1998.
Kaminski, David, "Estonian Air Sacks Chief Urva," *Air Transport Intelligence,* January 5, 2005.
Kurm, Kairi, "Baltic Airlines Eye Price Hikes," *Baltic Times,* October 10, 2001.
——, "Estonian Air Hit by Global Airline Crisis," *Baltic Times,* October 4, 2001.
——, "Estonian Air Posts Profit Despite Industry Woes," *Baltic Times,* April 11, 2002.
Morrison, Murdo, "Estonian Air Gears Up for Expected Traffic Increase," *Flight International,* July 17, 2001.
Morrocco, John D., "Estonian Air Leaps from East to West," *Aviation Week and Space Technology,* June 16, 1997, p. 112.
"National Carrier Should Not Be Sold to Competitors, General Director Says," *BNS Baltic Business News,* January 29, 1995.
O'Connell, Melanie, "Estonian Air Prepares for Open Skies," *Baltic Times,* July 3, 2003.
"One-on-One with Toomas Leis," *Commuter/Regional Airline News,* September 13, 1999.
"SAS Group Acquires 49 Percent of Estonian Air," *Waymaker,* September 11, 2003.
Thompson, Jackie, "Bilateral Problems Hit SAS Plans," *Airline Business,* August 1, 2004, p. 19.
Wagland, Maria, "Estonian Air Eyes Third 737 for Growth: CEO," *Air Transport Intelligence,* August 12, 2002.
——, "Estonian Air Operating Profits Up a Quarter to EUR 3.7m," *Air Transport Intelligence,* February 18, 2004.
——, "Estonian Air Takes Fourth 737-500, Adds Berlin, Oslo," *Air Transport Intelligence,* June 30, 2003.
——, "Estonian Fleet Back in the Sky," *Air Transport Intelligence,* October 5, 2001.
Warburton, Simon, "Star Links Drive Estonian Air Growth," *Air Transport Intelligence,* December 10, 1999.
Whitaker, Richard, "Baltic Beginnings—Estonian Air Looks Westward," *Airline Business,* May 1, 1993, p. 44.

—Frederick C. Ingram

Aztar Corporation

2390 East Camelback Road, Suite 400
Phoenix, Arizona 85016-3452
U.S.A.
Telephone: (602) 381-4100
Fax: (602) 381-4108
Web site: http://www.aztar.com

Public Company
Incorporated: 1989
Employees: 9,800
Sales: $816.2 million (2004)
Stock Exchanges: New York
Ticker Symbol: AZR
NAIC: 721120 Casino Hotels; 551112 Offices of Other
    Holding Companies

Aztar Corporation, a spinoff from the late 1980s restructuring of Ramada Inc., is a mid-tier U.S. casino operator owning and operating geographically diverse properties. Aztar operates three major casino hotels: the Tropicana Casino and Resort in Atlantic City, the Tropicana Resort and Casino in Las Vegas, and the Ramada Express Hotel and Casino in Laughlin, Nevada—as well as two Casino Aztar riverboat casinos in Evansville, Indiana, and Caruthersville, Missouri. Combined, the five properties encompass more than 300,000 square feet of casino space with in excess of 9,100 slot machines and 300 gaming tables. Aztar manages 5,700 casino hotel guestrooms, 200,000 square feet of meeting space, various entertainment facilities, and more than 60 restaurants and lounges.

The Late 1980s Restructuring of Ramada

The late 1980s were difficult years for Ramada Inc. as increased competition in the hotel industry led to declining profits and, ultimately, losses. The company posted profits of $17.2 million in 1985, $10.3 million in 1986, and $4.9 million in 1987. On the way to posting a $5.1 million loss in 1988, the company decided in October of that year to restructure by selling its restaurant and hotel groups and retaining only its

gaming operations, deemed by company officials as the Ramada assets with the best future. The restructuring was also undertaken to prevent a hostile takeover that the company felt was ''grossly inadequate from a financial standpoint.'' Ramada sold its 152-restaurant Marie Callender chain early in 1989 to the Wilshire Restaurant Group Inc. for $54.5 million. It then reached agreement with New World Hotel (Holdings) Ltd. of Hong Kong to sell all of its hotel operations, including more than 800 hotels and motor inns worldwide, and the Ramada name for $540 million. New World's price included $280 million to be paid to Ramada shareholders and the assumption of approximately $260 million of Ramada's debt.

Before the New World deal could be consummated, a complicated restructuring had to occur, including a new financing plan, and approvals had to be granted by Ramada's shareholders and the gaming regulators of New Jersey and Nevada. The approval process occurred twice because the initial restructuring arrangement was changed because of a downturn in the junk bond market. The original plan had Aztar raising $400 million through the issuance of $230 million in junk bonds and $170 million in first-mortgage notes backed by the company's TropWorld Casino in Atlantic City. The revised plan dropped the junk bonds altogether. It also reduced the amount paid to Ramada shareholders from $7 per share to $1 (but the shareholders would receive one share of Aztar stock for each share of Ramada stock instead of a half-share) and Aztar's initial debt load from $423 million to $189 million. Experts on gaming companies viewed the revised plan as a much healthier one for the new company because they believed $423 million was too great of an initial debt for the company to handle through casino revenues.

The restructured company was to be run by former senior managers of Ramada and its gaming division, including Richard Snell (who was chairman, president, and chief executive of Ramada and became chairman and chief executive of Aztar), Paul E. Rubeli (executive vice-president and head of Ramada's gaming division, who became president and chief operating officer of Aztar), and Robert M. Haddock (who retained the same title with Aztar that he held with Ramada—executive vice-president and chief financial officer). Aztar's board was initially composed of nine former Ramada directors, with Had-

Company Perspectives:

Our product concept is the creation of fun, fantasy, excitement and entertainment in a casino gaming environment. Each of our casinos is designed and operated to serve the unique demographics of its particular market. Our staff is dedicated to the principles of friendliness and service. Our goal is to enhance through operating excellence the value of our shareholders' investment in our company while maintaining a prudent financial position.

dock filling in the tenth slot that had been vacated. In December 1989 the revised plan was approved overwhelmingly by Ramada shareholders. The gaming regulators of Nevada and New Jersey also approved the plan that month, leading to the closing of the hotel sale. The new Aztar Corporation was born, with a name coined to play on the word ''star'' combined with the beginning of the word ''Aztec,'' a reference to the gold- and silver-rich Aztec Empire, whose wealth the new gaming company wished to strive for. Aztar's headquarters remained in Ramada's main office in Phoenix. (The first two initials of the new company name were said to be only coincidentally the same as the two-letter postal abbreviation for Arizona.)

Aztar at Its 1989 Birth

Following the completed restructuring, Aztar's assets consisted of three of the four gaming properties that had been owned by Ramada (in July 1989, in the midst of the restructuring, Ramada closed Eddie's Fabulous 50s Casino, a standalone casino in Reno, Nevada, because of declining revenues). In 1989 the TropWorld Casino and Entertainment Resort was the largest casino in Atlantic City with 1,014 rooms. Located on the famous boardwalk, it also boasted 80,000 square feet of exhibit and meeting space and a casino area of 88,000 square feet. Previously called the Tropicana, it had just been reopened in September 1988 after the completion of a two-year, $200 million expansion. As part of a company strategy to develop ''megafacilities,'' the expansion featured the addition of a two-acre indoor entertainment venue called Tivoli Pier, an attraction that aimed to replicate the peak of the Atlantic City boardwalk. It included various high-tech attractions and games, strolling performers, and a Ferris wheel four stories high. Other TropWorld amenities included the 1,700-seat TropWorld Showroom (at the time the largest in Atlantic City), 18 restaurants and bars, a health club, a miniature golf course, a comedy club, and retail shops. In the face of this major expansion, Aztar would need to absorb the TropWorld's start-up costs and also await major improvements in Atlantic City's infrastructure that were scheduled to be completed over the next several years, including expansion of highway, rail, and airport access and the construction of a new convention center. Company officials believed that the TropWorld was well positioned to take advantage of the increased tourism and convention business that these improvements promised to bring.

In Las Vegas, Aztar had inherited the Tropicana Resort and Casino, which was located on the southeast corner of Las Vegas Boulevard and Tropicana Avenue. Following the completion of a major expansion in 1986, Ramada had introduced a tropical island theme to the casino, calling it ''The Island of Las Vegas.'' The Tropicana featured 1,910 rooms, 100,000 square feet of exhibit and meeting space, and 45,000 square feet of casino space (with 993 slot machines and 72 table games). The facility also featured several other attractions, including the famous ''Folies Bergère'' show, more than a dozen restaurants and bars, and a five-acre water park. With water one of its major themes, the Tropicana was the first casino to offer swim-up slot machines and blackjack. While 1988 had been the casino's best year ever, company officials believed it was ready for further growth, in particular with the expected mid-1990 opening of the Excalibur Hotel & Casino directly across Las Vegas Boulevard. They believed the new 4,000-room facility would bring additional people to the southern end of the ''Strip,'' where the Tropicana stood alone, unable to attract the many gamblers who like to move from casino to casino.

The third casino in the original Aztar threesome was the Ramada Express Hotel and Casino in Laughlin, Nevada, a fast-growing gambling mecca located in extreme southeastern Nevada near both the California and Arizona borders. Construction of the Ramada Express, the newest but smallest of the three casinos, was completed in 1988. A Victorian-era railroad theme was established in 406 rooms and 30,000 square feet of casino space, with ''The Gambling Train of Laughlin'' transporting guests from the parking lot to the front door. Although it featured fewer facilities than the larger Aztar properties, the casino enjoyed a significant share of this much-smaller market and had an ideal location in the middle of Laughlin's gambling district.

Early 1990s Struggles

The initial few years after the restructuring were difficult ones for Aztar. Revenues fell from $522.3 million in 1989 to $508.2 million in 1990 to $481.3 million in 1991. Following an operating profit of $67.4 million in 1990, Aztar managed only a $61.4 million profit in 1991. Many factors contributed to the company's struggles. In 1990 a breach of contract case, which was originally brought against Ramada in the early 1980s and assumed by Aztar following the restructuring, cost the company $34.3 million. Competition was increased with a casino building boom in 1989 and 1990, which saw the completion of the 3,000-room Mirage and 4,000-room Excalibur in Las Vegas, a 2,000-room Hilton in Laughlin, and Atlantic City's 1,250-room Taj Mahal (which made TropWorld the second largest casino in Atlantic City). This increased capacity greatly exceeded demand with the onset of economic recession, and in particular when the Persian Gulf crisis of late 1990 and the war in early 1991 greatly decreased travel and tourism traffic. Adding to the difficulties for the Nevada casinos was California's severe recession, while TropWorld felt the impact of the deep recession in the northeastern United States.

Aztar's management—now led by Rubeli who took over the CEO slot in February 1990 and then the chairman position two years later—adopted several strategies to address the difficult environment. While many casinos battled each other for customers through such bargains as reduced room rates, package deals that included transportation, and cheap buffet-style meals, Aztar decided not to chase after people lured by these bargains because they did not tend to spend much money gambling. Rather

Key Dates:

1989: Ramada Inc. divests its restaurant and hotel operations to concentrate on its three hotel casinos; company is renamed Aztar Corporation.

1992: A $75 million expansion of the Ramada Express casino in Laughlin, Nevada, begins.

1993: Aztar purchases full control of the TropWorld casino in Atlantic City.

1995: Operations begin at Aztar's two riverboat casinos, in Evansville, Indiana, and Caruthersville, Missouri.

1996: Following a $75 million expansion, the TropWorld casino is renamed Tropicana Casino and Resort.

2002: Company takes full ownership of the Tropicana in Las Vegas.

2004: A $285 million expansion of the Atlantic City Tropicana is completed, featuring the addition of The Quarter entertainment and retail complex.

than trying to attract all potential gamblers, the company decided to take a niche approach to its marketing by concentrating on what they called the "high end of the middle market." Such customers spend between $100 and $400 gambling during an average day. In Las Vegas, for example, this placed the Tropicana between such lower-end casinos as Circus Circus, whose guests spend less than $100 per day, and upscale casinos such as Caesars Palace, a facility for high rollers. In essence, the company sought to attract fewer people who would spend more in their casinos than to seek a high volume of gamblers. To this end, Aztar eliminated many of the bargains it once offered. One strategy to reach its desired clientele and to encourage repeat visitors was the initiation of a program modeled after airline frequent-flier programs. Another tactic was to deemphasize baccarat, favored by high rollers, and concentrate on slot machines.

While the company pursued its new marketing strategy in Atlantic City and Las Vegas, it decided in 1991 to expand its Ramada Express casino in Laughlin. Laughlin had also seen a huge increase in hotel rooms in 1990 and 1991 (nearly doubling to more than 8,000 rooms), but Aztar management saw a window of opportunity for expansion during the next two years based on the limited capacity of Laughlin's water and sewer system. Because the Ramada Express had been designed to accommodate 1,200 rooms (at the time it was built, Ramada lacked sufficient capital to build it to its capacity), it could be expanded with its current water and sewer allocations. Aztar calculated that other casinos could add only an additional 1,500 rooms in Laughlin based on their water and sewer capacities. In late 1992, the $75 million expansion began. Upon its completion in September 1993, Aztar had increased the hotel space of the Ramada Express to 1,500 rooms with the addition of an 1,100-room tower, and also added 20,000 square feet of additional casino space (for a total of 50,000 square feet), a new parking garage, and additional meeting space and restaurants.

The company's strategies began to pay off with revenues beginning to turn around in 1992. That year Aztar realized a 6 percent increase in revenues over the previous year, from $481.3 million to $512 million. The slow but steady growth continued the next two years with revenues of $518.8 million in 1993 and $541.4 million in 1994. Evidence that the company's marketing strategy was working came in the form of increased revenue from slot machines, up 19 percent in 1992. Aztar was also able to solidify its financial position during this period. Late in 1992 the company refinanced $171 million in high-yield notes, reducing its debt payments in the process. In 1993 it bought out the limited partners that had owned a majority interest in the TropWorld property for approximately $62 million in cash, gaining complete control over Aztar's largest asset.

Mid- to Late 1990s Expansion of Existing Casinos and into Riverboat Casinos

Having cleaned up its finances and showing improved results, Aztar in the mid-1990s turned its attention to expansion, while continuing to vigilantly protect its solid trio of original casinos. With the Tropicana in the weakest position in the increasingly competitive Las Vegas market, the company undertook a minor renovation project in 1993. Where it once stood alone on the southern end of the Strip, the Tropicana now shared a corner with both the 4,000-room Excalibur and the newly opened 5,000-room MGM Grand, with another new neighbor, the 2,500-room Luxor, nearby. While this boom in what became known as "The New Four Corners of Las Vegas" promised to bring increasing numbers of people to the vicinity of the Tropicana, company officials felt they needed to redesign the casino's front entrance and facade to entice additional walk-in business from the surrounding resorts. With a "Caribbean Island" theme highlighting the design, the renovations were completed in early 1994. These included new stores accessible from the street, a "Wildlife Walk" connecting the casino's two towers and featuring natural displays of live birds and other tropical wildlife, and other improvements. At about the same time, the state of Nevada completed construction of a skywalk system connecting "The New Four Corners of Las Vegas," an improvement that promised to increase traffic among the Tropicana and its neighboring casinos.

Aztar was beginning to feel the effects of competition from outside the cities in which its casinos operated, and decided that its first new developments should occur in these nascent gambling areas. By 1993, 14 states had legalized casino gambling and additional states had approved or were considering legalized gambling on riverboats or Indian reservations. The company's first target would be riverboat gambling operations in the Midwest. The riverboat strategy followed closely Aztar's increasing emphasis on slot machine players, since this type of gambling venue is typically dominated by slot machines. In early 1995 the Indiana Gaming Commission approved Aztar's plan for a riverboat casino in downtown Evansville. The $100 million project included a 310-foot, 2,500-passenger riverboat, a casino onboard with 1,250 slot machines and 70 gaming tables, a hotel with 250 rooms, a pavilion entertainment complex, and parking for 1,600 vehicles. The company estimated that the casino, which commenced operations in late 1995, becoming the first casino property in Indiana, could draw 2.3 million visitors each year, provided competition did not arise within nearby Louisville.

Meanwhile, a smaller $55 million riverboat project opened in the spring of 1995 in Caruthersville, Missouri, a town in southeastern Missouri on the Mississippi River about 90 miles north of Memphis, Tennessee. This facility featured a 600-passenger riverboat with a casino of 500 slot machines and 30 gaming tables, an entertainment and ticketing pavilion, parking for 1,000 vehicles, and a recreational vehicle (RV) park. At the same time, Aztar was also pursuing several other riverboat facilities. In early 1995 Newport News, Virginia, selected the company to develop a riverboat casino, but Aztar had to await legislative consideration of the legalization of gambling in the state before proceeding. For these and future operations, Aztar decided to use a brand-name marketing strategy to connect the riverboat casinos. "Casino Aztar" was tied to the particular site, as in "Casino Aztar Caruthersville."

The company also undertook a major addition to the Trop-World casino in Atlantic City, including a new hotel tower with 604 rooms (including six large penthouse suites), additional restaurants, a large poker room with an expanded baccarat and Asian game room, and other new facilities. The $75 million expansion, completed in the summer of 1996, gave the casino more than 1,600 hotel rooms, making it the largest hotel in New Jersey. Upon completion, the casino reassumed the Tropicana Casino and Resort name.

In order to finance the TropWorld addition and the new riverboat casinos, Aztar secured a financing package from a group of ten banks late in 1994. The package totaled $280 million, the fourth largest such package ever made within the gambling industry, with $73 million to refinance debt on the Tropicana and $207 million in revolving credit secured by the TropWorld and Ramada Express properties. Further financing was provided in 1996 by the issuance of an additional 6.3 million shares of common stock through two secondary offerings, raising net proceeds of $55.8 million.

These funds were also earmarked for enhancements to the Casino Aztar in Evansville. Late in 1996 the riverboat casino gained a 44,000-square-foot passenger pavilion featuring passenger ticketing facilities, three restaurants, a sidewalk cafe, an entertainment lounge, and a gift shop. Also added to the site were a 1,600-space parking garage and a 250-room hotel.

Aztar's biggest long-term capital project involved the Tropicana Resort in Las Vegas. The Tropicana had on the one hand benefited from its New Four Corners location as two more megaresorts opened nearby, the Monte Carlo and New York-New York. On the other hand, the aging casino, which opened in 1957, was at a serious competitive disadvantage compared to its glittering new, "hot" casino resort neighbors. Ultimately, Aztar aimed to completely overhaul the casino or even raze it to make room for an entirely modern, "must-see" destination. Financially, Aztar was in no position to undertake such a project in the late 1990s, and the management also wanted to wait and see how well the market absorbed all the new properties sprouting up on or near the Strip. Another issue was the ownership of the site. Although Aztar managed the casino and its various operations, the land and buildings themselves were owned by a 50-50 partnership between Aztar and the Jaffe family (the latter's interest dating back to when the casino first opened). Before undertaking any large-scale renovation or the building of a new property on the site, Aztar wanted to have full ownership. In February 1998 the company purchased an option

to buy out the Jaffe family for $120 million. A year later, this 18-month option was then extended to 2002.

Early 2000s and Beyond

Throughout the late 1990s and into the early 2000s, while its competitors built $1 billion properties and/or acquired smaller casino operators, Aztar concentrated on paying down and refinancing its debt and repurchasing stock. The former helped drive net interest expense down from $60.5 million in 1997 to $37.6 million in 2001. Not coincidentally, Aztar's net income figures in the early 2000s were much higher than those of the late 1990s—$58 million in 2001, for example, compared to $4.4 million in 1997.

Much stronger financially, Aztar in February 2002 exercised its option to buy out the Jaffe family from the Tropicana Las Vegas property and then began conducting feasibility studies on future developments at the site. By 2003 Aztar had developed tentative plans for the 34-acre site. They called for the property to be divided into two interconnected 17-acre sites. For the northern site, the company envisioned a new development encompassing 2,500 hotel rooms and suites; a 120,000-square-foot casino; 200,000 square feet of dining, entertainment, and retail facilities; a four-acre rooftop pool recreation deck overlooking the Strip; and a 3,800-car parking garage. The project was projected to cost at least $700 million, part of which would need to be raised through the capital markets. The company planned to hold onto the southern site for future solo or joint development or sale to another party. At least twice, Aztar delayed making a final decision on whether to go ahead with the redevelopment in Las Vegas. Part of the reason for these delays was a simultaneous major—and sometimes troubled—expansion of the Atlantic City Tropicana.

Construction began on the $285 million expansion in April 2002. One component of the expansion was a 2,400-space state-of-the-art parking garage. On October 30, 2003, a part of the ten-story garage collapsed while under construction, killing four workers and injuring 20 others. The tragedy forced the temporary closure of the casino's 600-room tower and of major entrances to the property. Gambling and lodging revenue was therefore lost, construction was set back, and Aztar now had to contend with numerous lawsuits arising from the collapse. These difficulties were compounded by a five-week strike by some of the Atlantic City Tropicana workers in the fall of 2004. The expansion was finally completed in November 2004, eight months later than originally planned.

The centerpiece of the addition was a 200,000-square-foot dining, entertainment, and retail center dubbed "The Quarter"—a Las Vegas-style resort destination for Atlantic City that followed the successful opening in July 2003 of the Borgata, a $1.1 billion Las Vegas-style casino resort. The Quarter was designed to capture the ambience of Old Havana in its pre-Castro heyday. (The original Tropicana casino was in fact located in Old Havana. Opened in 1939, it continued to operate under Fidel Castro right into the early 21st century as a nightclub only, famous for its risqué floor shows.) Upon opening, The Quarter included more than two dozen shops ranging from the traditional (Brooks Brothers) to the trendy (Chico's) to the whimsical (Houdini's Magic Shop); nine restaurants, including several imported from New York City (e.g., Carmine's) and Philadelphia (e.g., Cuba Libre Restaurant & Rum Bar); and lounges, clubs, a karaoke bar, and an IMAX theater. The expansion also included a new 502-room hotel tower geared to the convention trade. The entire top floor of the new tower was dedicated to boardrooms and hospitality suites with ocean views, providing the Tropicana with another 20,000 square feet of meeting and convention space.

This expansion ended up being the final large project in Rubeli's career at Aztar. After having led the company since just after the Ramada spinoff, Rubeli retired in March 2005. Taking over as chairman, president, and CEO was Haddock, who had served as president and CFO since May 2002. Haddock assumed the top position at a crucial time, when Aztar was evaluating the rollout of the Atlantic City expansion and also reviewing the market in Las Vegas to weigh the prospects for the proposed redevelopment of the Tropicana property located in that gambling mecca. While the decision on whether to go ahead with the huge Las Vegas project remained pending, rumors continued to circulate about a possible sale of the company, either to another casino operator or perhaps a private equity fund.

Principal Subsidiaries

Adamar Garage Corporation; Adamar of Nevada; Adamar of New Jersey, Inc.; Atlantic-Deauville, Inc.; Aztar Development Corporation; Aztar Indiana Gaming Company, L.L.C.; Aztar Missouri Riverboat Gaming Company, L.L.C.; Hotel Ramada of Nevada; Ramada Express, Inc.; Ramada New Jersey, Inc.; Ramada New Jersey Holdings Corporation; Tropicana Enterprises.

Principal Operating Units

Tropicana Casino and Resort; Casino Aztar Evansville; Casino Aztar Caruthersville; Tropicana Resort and Casino; Ramada Express Hotel and Casino.

Principal Competitors

Harrah's Entertainment, Inc.; MGM Mirage; Caesars Entertainment, Inc.; Mandalay Resort Group; Trump Hotels & Casino Resorts, Inc.; Boyd Gaming Corporation; Argosy Gaming Company.

Further Reading

Benston, Liz, "Aztar Remains Bullish on LV Tropicana Redevelopment Plan," *Las Vegas Sun,* February 12, 2004, p. 3.

——, "CEO Tries to Quell Talk of Tropicana Overhaul," *Las Vegas Sun,* April 24, 2003, p. 3.

——, "Decision on Tropicana Delayed," *Las Vegas Sun,* February 3, 2005, p. 3.

Berns, Dave, "Aztar Buys Option for Tropicana," *Las Vegas Review-Journal,* February 4, 1998, p. 1D.

——, "Aztar Plans to Own Entire Tropicana Site," *Las Vegas Review-Journal,* January 31, 2002, p. 1D.

Bhatt, Rob, "Fresh Face, Old Property," *Las Vegas Business Press,* February 16, 1998, p. 10.

Binkley, Christina, "Garage Collapse Delays Expansion at the Tropicana," *Wall Street Journal,* November 3, 2003, p. B4.

Curran, John, "Casino Reels from Crash's Aftermath," *Bergen County (N.J.) Record,* November 2, 2003, p. A3.

Edwards, John G., "Aztar Plans Major Remake of Tropicana," *Las Vegas Review-Journal,* November 1, 1995, p. 8E.

Giblin, Paul, "Aztar Dives into Three Riverboat Casino Ventures," *Business Journal—Serving Phoenix and the Valley of the Sun,* December 3, 1993, p. 3.

Gilbertson, Dawn, "Improving Its Hand: Phoenix Casino Operator Poised for Rebound," *Phoenix Gazette,* May 14, 1992.

Jarman, Max, "Aztar's Fortunes Coming Up 7s," *Arizona Business Gazette,* July 15, 1993, p. 5.

Novotny, Jean, "Ramada to Be 'Aztar' After Hotel Sale," *Arizona Republic,* July 4, 1989.

Reich, Peter, "Aztar Is Born: Ramada to Give Up Hotel Biz," *Phoenix Gazette,* December 13, 1989.

——, "Ramada's New Name Reflects Changes," *Phoenix Gazette,* July 4, 1989.

Ruber, Ilana, "Aztar to Ante Up 6 Million Shares," *Business Journal—Serving Phoenix and the Valley of the Sun,* June 14, 1996, pp. 1+.

Smith, Rod, "Garage Collapse Hampers Aztar's Results," *Las Vegas Review-Journal,* February 12, 2004, p. 8D.

Strow, David, "Tropicana Looking at LV Options to Expand," *Las Vegas Sun,* January 30, 2002, p. 1.

Stutz, Howard, "Report Says Aztar Better If Broken Up," *Las Vegas Review-Journal,* March 29, 2005.

"$280 Million Package for Gaming Company," *Arizona Republic,* October 7, 1994, p. E1.

Whaley, Sean, "Gamers OK Ramada Restructuring," *Las Vegas Review Journal,* December 13, 1989.

Yoshihashi, Pauline, "Ramada Bets Its Fate on Casino Industry," *Wall Street Journal,* December 29, 1988.

—David E. Salamie

Barry Callebaut AG

Westpark, Pfingstweidstrasse 60
8005 Zurich
Switzerland
Telephone: +41-44-801-61-57
Fax: +41-44-801-61-53
Web site: http://www.barry-callebaut.com

Public Company
Incorporated: 1842 as Cacao Barry; 1850 as Callebaut
Employees: 8,933
Sales: CHF 4.04 billion ($3.18 billion) (2004)
Stock Exchanges: Zürich
Ticker Symbol: BARN
NAIC: 311320 Chocolate and Confectionery
    Manufacturing from Cacao Beans

Franco-Belgo-Swiss Barry Callebaut AG is the world's largest manufacturer of chocolate and cocoa products for industrial and consumer use. Barry Callebaut has its corporate headquarters in Zurich, Switzerland, while maintaining its French and Belgian roots. Barry Callebaut operates 30 cocoa processing and chocolate production facilities in 22 countries in Europe, North America, Latin America, and the Asia/Pacific region. The only vertically integrated chocolate concern in a $60-billion-in-sales industry, Barry Callebaut processes 15 percent of the world's cocoa production, supplying an estimated 35 percent of the world's gourmet chocolatiers. The company's history comprises the heritages of two companies, Belgian chocolate maker Callebaut and its French rival Cacao Barry. The two companies merged in the mid-1990s, a deal orchestrated by Swiss financier Klaus J. Jacobs, whose company, Klaus J. Jacobs Holdings, owns a majority stake in Barry Callebaut.

300 Years of Chocolate History

Both Cacao Barry and Callebaut trace their origins to the 19th century, yet both companies entered their respective core markets—cocoa and chocolate production—in the early decades of the 20th century. Cacao Barry was founded in 1842 by Charles Barry in Meulan, France. The Barry family entered cocoa production in 1920, building a facility in Meulan that would remain one of Cacao Barry's most important production facilities through the end of the century.

Belgium's Callebaut family entered the trade in 1850, operating a brewery, malt, and dairy company, before turning to chocolate production in 1911. The Callebaut family's original chocolate products were chocolate bars; chocolate *couverture,* or covering, products—extending the company's production of industrial use chocolate—were introduced in 1925. By then the Barry family company had been taken over by another family, the LaCarre family. The LaCarres would keep the Cacao Barry name, however.

Barry and Callebaut operated, in large part, complementary product lines throughout the century, with the former processing raw cocoa for use by chocolate producers such as the latter. Nevertheless, Barry would gain a reputation for its own fine quality chocolate products—and especially its industrial use chocolates. Meanwhile, Callebaut's small family-run operation benefited from the increasing worldwide interest in Belgian chocolates, considered by many to be the finest chocolates in the world. Callebaut began exporting its products in 1950, building up the Callebaut name in the European and North American markets.

During this time Barry began imposing itself as one of the world's premier cocoa products producers. Seeking to extend its activity to complete control of the cocoa production process, Barry initiated partnerships with the principal cocoa-producing countries. This course would lead the company to implant itself on the African continent. In 1952 Barry opened production facilities in Cameroon and in the chief cocoa bean producing nation of the Ivory Coast.

Barry's expanding grip on cocoa processing and cocoa products manufacturing would lead the company to withdraw from the consumer products segment in the mid-1960s in favor of continuing to boost its share of the industrial use cocoa market. At the same time, Barry sought to expand its presence in the chief cocoa consuming markets, principally the European and North American markets. This expansion would lead the company to build or acquire factories in England, Canada, and in the United States, where the company acquired US Cocoa, one of the United States' leading cocoa powder producers.

Mergers and Acquisitions: 1970s–90s

Barry's expansion continued in the 1970s, including the acquisition of Italy's Sicao. Callebaut also was extending its presence in Italy, building a plant and opening one of its Chocolate Schools there. Meanwhile, Barry's control of the cocoa market increased with the acquisition of Cacao Processing United in Louviers, France; under Barry's leadership, the Louviers plant specialized in cocoa bean processing, grinding, and pressing, for the production of the principal cocoa products: cocoa powder, cocoa liquor, and cocoa butter. In 1974, Barry would take over one of its chief domestic competitors, with the acquisition of Belgium's Goemaere.

The 1980s, however, would see changes in ownership for both Barry and Callebaut. The Callebaut family business was taken over by Interfood, a subsidiary of Tobler-Suchard, maker of chocolate and cocoa consumer products. The Callebaut family did not withdraw from chocolate-making entirely: in 1982 Bernard Callebaut moved to Canada, where he founded Chocolaterie Bernard Callebaut. In 1983 Interfood was in turn bought up by Klaus J. Jacobs, then in the process of building a consumer chocolate empire. The resulting Jacobs Suchard became one of the world's leading chocolate manufacturers.

Barry, too, had lost its independence. In 1982 the company was taken over by fellow French concern Sacré et Denrées. Nevertheless, Barry, like Callebaut, continued operations under its own name. A crucial step in Barry's expansion was taken in 1985, when the company acquired Bensdorp, of Bussum in The Netherlands. The Bensdorp name was already known worldwide. Founded in 1840 by Gerard Bernadus Bensdorp, this company built its success on two processes that became important for the overall cocoa trade. These processes were the alkalization—or "Dutching"—of cocoa, and the separation of cocoa butter from the cocoa mass. The main Bussum facility was established in 1884, and it remained in operation through the 20th century. Under Barry's ownership, Bensdorp continued to produce its own branded cocoa products.

Jacobs Suchard continued its own expansion drive, acquiring the United Kingdom's S&A Lesne in 1985. In 1987 Jacobs Suchard purchased the Brach candy company, based in Chicago, Illinois, a move intended to enable Jacobs Suchard, by then with annual sales topping $3 billion, to enter the U.S. consumer candy market. This acquisition, however, proved somewhat disastrous and would lead Jacobs into a retreat from the consumer chocolate market. Soon after the Brach acquisition, Klaus J. Jacobs Holdings announced its agreement to sell off its consumer candy holdings to the Philip Morris Group for a purchase price worth nearly $2 billion. These operations were combined with Philip Morris's Kraft foods subsidiary to form the Kraft-Jacobs-Suchard division.

Klaus Jacobs, however, would retain Jacobs Suchard's industrial chocolates divisions. Jacobs would also be left holding the Brach candy subsidiary, which later merged with Tennessee-based rival Brock's in the 1990s. With his chocolate holdings pared down, Jacobs once again consolidated around the Callebaut industrial use chocolates operation. Jacobs would retain 100 percent control of Callebaut, keeping the company private until after its late 1990s merger with Cacao Barry.

In 1987 Barry added a new cocoa processing plant in its Meulan, France base. Not long after, the company found itself under new ownership. In 1992 the Société Centrale d'Investissement (SCI) acquired control of Cacao Barry. Under SCI's ownership, Barry expanded in the United Kingdom, adding a chocolate production unit there. SCI's losses—which reached FRF 8.3 billion in 1994—would, however, lead the investment group to bring in a new partner in that year, selling 49 percent of Cacao Barry to the Compagnie Nationale à Portefeuille (CNP), an investment vehicle held by the Albert Frère group.

Two years later, Klaus Jacobs gained access to Barry by purchasing, through Callebaut, CNP's share of Barry, before acquiring complete control from SCI. The purchase price was reportedly near $400 million. The merger, named Barry Callebaut, with headquarters at Jacobs' Zurich base, created the world's leading producer of industrial use cocoa and chocolate. The merger also brought Jacobs back into the ranks of the world's leading chocolate manufacturers.

The company's existing operations underwent a restructuring, reinforcing the two companies' mostly complementary operations, while combining the two companies' brand recognition. Barry Callebaut's brand lines now included the Bensdorp brand of cocoa powders; the Barry and Callebaut brands of gourmet chocolate and cocoa products; and the new Barry Callebaut brand of industrial use cocoa powder, butter, liquor, and chocolate.

The merger nearly fell through, however. The company's extensive international implantation required it to receive clearance from the antitrust review boards of the countries concerned. The company met the most resistance in Callebaut's Belgian home, where the merger was, in fact, rejected. Barry Callebaut won out, however, on a technicality (the review board handed down their decision too late), and the merger was allowed to be completed. As part of the merger, Barry Callebaut agreed to sell off part of its Goemaere cocoa production unit.

Barry Callebaut's antitrust difficulties forced it to postpone a planned public offering. This was finally achieved in June 1998, when Barry Callebaut placed a listing on the Zurich Stock Exchange. Klaus Jacobs remained in control of the company, with nearly 70 percent of its shares. The public offering gave Barry Callebaut further impetus for a reinvigorated expansion campaign.

Barry Callebaut sought to extend its dominance of the Western European and North American chocolate markets—the primary chocolate markets worldwide—to those of other parts of the globe. On the Barry side, the company already had entered the Eastern European market in 1995, with the construction of Cacao Barry Polska, a chocolate production facility. Callebaut, meanwhile, had been looking to expand in the booming Asian market, where chocolate was beginning to find some popularity, by opening sales offices in Singapore and Hong Kong. In 1997 the company began construction on a state-of-the-art chocolate production facility in Singapore, with plans to extend distribution from there to such markets as Vietnam, China, Hong Kong, the Philippines, and Japan, as well as covering the New Zealand and Australian markets.

Barry Callebaut also moved to consolidate its main markets. In 1998 the company acquired Van Leer Chocolate, based in the United States. This acquisition was followed by the acquisition of Carma-Pfister AG, a Swiss-based chocolate company, in January 1999. These moves were followed soon after by the acquisition of Chadler Industrial de Bahia. The February 1999 purchase of Brazil-based Chadler was aimed at enabling Barry Callebaut to enter the South American market.

De Maeseneire Taking the Helm in 2002

Barry Callebaut held sway as a chocolate giant at the end of the century, but the company's formidable size did not make it immune to the problems suffered by smaller chocolatiers. Barry Callebaut's stock price languished, as it recorded several years of lackluster profits. The financial malaise led to a change in leadership, prompting Schmid to relinquish his post as chief executive officer to focus exclusively on serving as the company's chairman. To replace Schmid, the company recruited Patrick G. De Maeseneire from Adecco, S.A., a Swiss temporary employment agency partly owned by KJ Jacobs AG. De Maeseneire was named chief executive officer in June 2002 and quickly began reorganizing the company's plants, striving to rid the network of inefficiency. For example, a plant in New Jersey that was involved in a gamut of chocolate and cocoa manufacturing activities was given the sole task of making liquid chocolate. De Maeseneire also began serving the private label businesses operated by retail chains such as Wal-Mart and Aldi in Germany. ''We asked ourselves, 'Why will outsourcing happen in the computer and car industries and not in the food industry?,' '' De Maeseneire said in an April 11, 2005 interview with *Forbes*. ''Well, it is happening,'' he added.

De Maeseneire's actions produced encouraging results. Within two years of his arrival, Barry Callebaut's shares doubled in value. Sales and earnings per share recorded double-digit increases, adding to the vibrancy of the company. The first years of De Maeseneire's tenure also included several significant acquisitions that added to investors' confidence. In mid-2002, the company strengthened its consumer business by acquiring a German chocolate company named Stollwerck, paying $225 million to gain control over the company's 17 brands, with the addition of Stollwerck's Sarotti label regarded as the jewel of the bunch. The following year, Barry Callebaut acquired a company familiar to KJ Jacobs AG, purchasing Brach's for a bargain price of $16 million in assumed debt. In 2004, the company acquired a Danish-Swedish chocolate and cappuccino vending products company named AM Foods K/S. As the company plotted its future course, some analysts were convinced the company was looking to complete the acquisition of a premium brand, suggesting that Neuhaus, a Belgian label, was within De Maeseneire's sights. De Maeseneire, in his interview with *Forbes*, brushed off the suggestion. ''We don't want to be a European company only,'' he said. ''We want to be a global company.''

Principal Subsidiaries

Barry Callebaut Sourcing AG; Barry Callebaut Schweiz AG (Switzerland); Chocolat Alprose S.A.; Barry Callebaut Belgium N.V.; Barry Callebaut Services N.V. (Belgium); Barry Callebaut Belgium N.V.; Pierre Iserentant S.A. (Belgium); Barry Callebaut Brasil S/A (Brazil); Societe Industrielle Camerounaise des Cacaos S.A. (Cameroon); Chocolateries Confiseries Camerounaise Chococam, S.A. (Cameroon); Barry Callebaut Canada Inc.; Barry Callebaut Manufacturing France S.A.; Barry Callebaut France S.A.; Stollwerck France S.A.R.L.; Chocogab S.A. (Gabon); Barry Callebaut Deutschland GmbH (Germany); Gubor Schokoladenfabrik GmbH (Germany); Van Houten GmbH & Co. KG (Germany); Stollwerck AG (Germany); Thuringer Schokoladenwerk GmbH (Germany); Wurzener Daurbackwaren GmbH (Germany); Barry Callebaut Ghana Limited; Barry Callebaut Manufacturing Italia SRL (Italy); Barry Callebaut Italia SpA (Italy); Stollwerck Italia SpA

(Italy); Societe Africaine de Cacao SA (Ivory Coast); Societe Africaine de Cacao SA (Ivory Coast); SACO Chocodi Site (Ivory Coast); SN Chocodi SA (Ivory Coast); Barry Callebaut Japan; Vernell Inc. (Mexico); Barry Callebaut Sales Nederland B.V. (Netherlands); Luijckx B.V. (Netherlands); Hoogenboom Benelux B.V. (Belgium); Dings Décor (Netherlands); Barry Callebaut Polska Sp.z.o.o (Poland); Barbara Luijckx Sp.z.o.o (Poland); Barry Callebaut Russia LLC; Chocosen SA (Senegal); Barry Callebaut Asia Pacific (Singapore) Pte. Ltd.; Van Houten (Singapore) Pte. Ltd.; Barry Callebaut Iberica S.L. (Spain); Barry Callebaut Sweden AB; Barry Callebaut (UK) Ltd.; Brach's Confections, Inc. (U.S.A.); Barry Callebaut USA Inc.; Barry Callebaut Cocoa USA Inc.

Principal Divisions

Industrial Business; Food Service/Retail Business.

Principal Competitors

Hershey Foods Corporation; Mars, Incorporated; Nestlé S.A.

Further Reading

"Barry Callebaut AG Completes Acquisition of AM Foods K/S," *Nordic Business Report,* September 2, 2004, p. 12.

"Brach's Purchased by Callebaut," *Candy Business,* September-October 2003, p. 6.

"Callebaut Opens New Markets with Stollwerck Buy," *Candy Business,* May-June 2002, p. 6.

"Candy Maker Callebaut Enriches Its Business," *Daily Deal,* April 29, 2002, p. 32.

Forcino, Hallie, "Joining Strengths: Merger Synergies Benefit Barry Callebaut," *Candy Industry,* June 1, 1997, p. 72.

Hall, William, "Wraps Come Off of Chocolate's Best-Kept Secret," *Financial Times,* June 5, 1998.

"Industry Leader: Terry O'Brien; Brach's CEO Talks About the Challenges, Successes and Changes at the Century-Old Candy Company," *Candy Business,* January-February 2005, p. 14.

"Le groupe chocolatier Barry Callebaut reprend le suisse Carma-Pfister," *Les Echoes,* January 19, 1999.

Morais, Richard C., "The Gnomes of Cocoa," *Forbes,* April 11, 2005, p. 110.

Parry, John, "Chocolate Man Won't Melt Away," *European,* July 11, 1996, p. 21.

Tiffany, Susan, "Cacao Barry Accepts Challenge of an Emerging Market," *Candy Industry,* May 1, 1996, p. 32.

"Swiss Financier in £250m Cocoa Deal," *Financial Times,* July 10, 1996.

—M.L. Cohen
—update: Jeffrey L. Covell

Belleek Pottery Ltd.

Main Street
Belleek, Fermanagh
BT93 3FY
United Kingdom
Telephone: +44-28-6865-8501
Fax: +44-28-6865-8625
Web site: http://www.belleek.co.uk

Private Company
Incorporated: 1859 as D. McBirney & Co.
Employees: 600
Sales: EUR 40 million ($55 million) (2004 est.)
NAIC: 327112 Vitreous China, Fine Earthenware and
  Other Pottery Product Manufacturing

Belleek Pottery Ltd. has operated for more than 150 years as Northern Ireland's leading manufacturer of porcelain giftware. The company has achieved an international reputation for the high quality of its porcelain, known as Parian china, and the intricacy of its designs. Belleek's gift range includes lamps, picture and mirror frames, platters, vases, bowls, candlesticks, clocks, and other items, mostly in a flowery, Victorian-era style. Belleek's target consumer market traditionally has been an older, more conservative age group. In 2003, however, the company launched a new line of contemporary designs, Belleek Living, in an effort to extend its customer base to a younger market. In addition to its production facilities in the town of Belleek, in Fermanagh, Northern Ireland, Belleek manages its own network of retail shops in the United Kingdom and Ireland, with a sixth store opening most recently in Newry at the end of 2004. In the 1990s and early 2000s, Belleek expanded through acquisitions, adding Aynsley China Ltd., based in Staffordshire, England; Galway Irish Crystal Ltd., in Ireland; and Donegal Parian China Ltd., which, like Belleek, specializes in the production of marble-like parian china. Belleek is owned by U.S.-based Chairman George Moore, and run by a local management team under John Macguire. In 2004, Belleek recorded sales of more than EUR 40 million ($55 million).

Victorian Era Origins

The town of Belleek was founded in 1610 by two brothers, Edward and Thomas Blennerhassett, from Norfolk, England, who had been granted farming estates in County Fermanagh along the River Erne. The town took its name from a large flagstone, known as Beal Leice in Gaelic, at the foot of a waterfall. The flagstone had been a prominent river crossing point for some centuries. The location next to the river also provided a powerful source of energy for operating water-powered mills. The Blennerhassett family built a castle in Belleek, originally called Hassett's Fort.

Sir James Caldwell purchased the Blennerhassett estate, which encompassed the town of Belleek and its castle, changing its name to Castle Caldwell. Over time, however, the castle and the estate fell into disrepair. It was only with the arrival of John Caldwell, returning from military service in the Americas to take over the family estate, that Castle Caldwell was restored. Caldwell passed the estate on to his daughter, who married John Bloomfield and produced a son, John Caldwell Bloomfield.

Born in 1823, the younger Caldwell inherited the family estate in 1849, at a time when the surrounding population was still reeling from the devastation of the Potato Famine. As owner of Belleek and its surrounding areas, Caldwell sought ways to provide employment for his tenants and alleviate their poverty.

Caldwell commissioned a geological survey of the region and discovered large clay deposits, as well as kaolin, flint, feldspar, and shale. Caldwell quickly organized a business around the deposits, establishing a mill on a small island in the River Erne from which to grind the clay and raw materials for making slip, a liquid potter's clay. By 1853, the quality of the Belleek slip provided the basis for an award-winning dinner service produced by Worcester Porcelain Company for the Dublin International Exhibition.

With all the ingredients needed to fashion crockery, Caldwell decided to build a pottery workshop at Belleek as well. For this, Caldwell enlisted the aid of architect Robert Williams Armstrong, who had built up a specialty designing potteries in the British Midlands and who had been working for Worcester in the early 1850s. Armstrong agreed to design the pottery and lead development of the works. The pair then found a financial backer in David McBirney, a prominent businessman from Dalkey, near Dublin. In exchange for McBirney's investment, the company became known as D. McBirney & Co.

Construction began on the pottery in 1857, and although the factory was not completed until 1860, the company was able to launch production of its first earthenware pieces before the end of 1857. Built at a cost of £40,000, the factory was designed to accommodate as many as 500 workers. The company's initial production remained limited to earthenware, relatively cheap to produce. With few skilled workers in the region, earthenware provided another advantage in that it could be made with relatively little training. The company's production at first fell into a predominantly utilitarian category, with items such as floor tiles, hospital sanitation goods, and even insulators for telephones.

Yet Bloomfield, Armstrong, and McBirney had their sights set on a higher goal, that of creating decorative porcelain pieces. The company began experimenting with adapting the Belleek clay in order to produce parian porcelain. This type of porcelain had been developed in Stoke-on-Trent, a major pottery center in England, in 1844. Using a mixture of glass and rock, the resulting slip produced a porcelain said to resemble the marble found on the Greek island of Paros.

The Belleek pottery's early attempts to develop its own parian china proved fruitless. In the early 1860s, however, Bloomfield went to England, offering higher wages and better living conditions to skilled pottery craftsmen if they would move to Belleek. Fourteen men agreed, among them William Bromley, who became the company's foreman, and William Gallimore, who became its chief modeler.

Belleek finally succeeded in producing a small amount of parian china in 1863. Production grew strongly after that, and by 1865 the company had begun to ship its porcelain to the rest of the United Kingdom, before turning to a still more international market. Led by Armstrong, the company established high-quality standards for its porcelain—and each piece became subject to Armstrong's approval. Rejected pieces were then destroyed—a policy the company continued over the next 150 years. Indeed, even in the early 21st century, Belleek continued to throw away some 20 percent of its production.

Earthenware, therefore, remained the company's primary revenue source. Over the next decade, the company continued to plow its profits back into the development of its parian china. By 1872, the company at last reached a level of perfection. In that year, Belleek displayed its goods at the Dublin Exposition, featuring both its tableware and its decorative parian pieces, including statues and a double-spouted Chinese tea urn. The company captured gold medals in both of these categories.

The company's success was crowned when Queen Victoria herself ordered a tea set from the company. Belleek china now became highly fashionable and sought after throughout the world. The company began receiving orders from other members of the British nobility, as well as elsewhere in Europe, and from as far away as India and the United States as well. In 1880, the company's fortunes were further aided by a new gold medal at the Melbourne International Exhibition.

The death of McBirney in 1882 caught the company off guard, however, when his son and heir, Robert McBirney, announced his intention to sell off the company—which in the meantime had eaten up much of McBirney's fortune. Armstrong, who also had put his entire life savings into the company, attempted to resist the sale, claiming to have made a gentleman's agreement with McBirney. Armstrong launched a legal battle to retain control of the company, yet died just two years after McBirney.

Bloomfield, McBirney, and Armstrong had one last success, although none of the founding partners lived to see it. For many years, the company had fought to bring the railroad to Belleek in order to make it easier to haul much-needed coal to fire the company's kilns and to provide a more secure means of transporting its finished goods. In 1886, a connection was finally made to Belleek, when the line from Enniskillen was extended to Ballyshannon, passing through Belleek.

After Armstrong's death, the Belleek pottery was sold off to a group of investors for just £4,500, accompanied by a 999-year lease fixed at a rent of £50 per year. The company was renamed as Belleek Pottery Works Company Ltd. The pottery's new directors were more interested in profits than Belleek's less than profitable parian china creations, and the company shifted its focus to its earthenware production. As a result of this shift in focus, the company, which by then boasted one of the United Kingdom's strongest pools of porcelain artisans and craftsmen, lost a number of its most highly trained and talented staff.

Nonetheless, Belleek works at last made its first profit by the end of 1884. The business did not entirely stop production of parian china, and managed to win a new gold medal at the Adelaide Exhibition in 1887, and then again in Paris in 1900. By then, however, parian china had lost its fashionable status, in favor of other porcelain designs. Worse for the company, the Erne Drainage Board had begun an effort to control the water levels on the River Erne—including blasting away the waterfall that had provided a primary source of power for the company.

Parian China Specialist for the 1950s

The outbreak of World War I dealt a new blow to the company, as new orders slowed to a stop and wartime restrictions essentially put a halt to production. By the end of the war, the company's staff had dwindled from nearly 200 to less than 50. In 1919, the company was sold to Bernard O'Rourke, for £10,000, on the condition that the site remain in operation as a pottery.

The company's new owners now refocused the pottery on the production of parian china. Belleek entered a new period of growth, hampered only by a rapid succession of managers. Stability came to the company in the 1930s, with the arrival of the Arnold family, first through Harry Arnold, who joined as manager in 1934. Arnold turned over the manager's position to brother Eric Arnold in 1941, who retained that position into the late 1950s.

World War II brought a new challenge to the company, as wartime restrictions once again forced the company to cut back on its production. Belleek again turned to the production of earthenware for its survival, although the company managed to produce a small number of parian china objects during this period.

An impediment to the group's production of parian china had long been the need for kilns capable of firing at extremely high temperatures for a long period of time: The initial biscuit firing period alone required a 24-hour firing cycle at temperatures above 1,400 degrees Celsius. Belleek at last solved its production problem with the installation of two new high-temperature, coal-fired kilns in 1946. The new kilns enabled the company to focus its entire production on parian china, and the company ceased production of earthenware that year.

Orders once again filled the company's books as new generations of porcelain enthusiasts embraced Belleek's highly intricate, if somewhat kitsch, designs. The coal-fired kilns were soon replaced by the company's first electric-powered kilns. These provided for still more consistent, high-temperature operation, and enabled the company to solidify its worldwide reputation for high-quality porcelain. By the end of the decade, the company employed some 250 people.

Expanding for a New Century

Belleek's highly identifiable designs nonetheless left the company vulnerable to changing fashions. By the early 1980s,

the company had once again run into financial difficulty. In 1883, the Northern Ireland Industrial Development Board launched a rescue effort, installing Roger Troughton in place as the company's managing director. Troughton led a restructuring, which included cutting the company's payroll in half to just 120 workers.

Troughton's efforts paid off, and the company returned to profitability. When the Industrial Development Board decided to put the company up for sale in 1984, Troughton himself led a consortium of investors to buy the company. Under Troughton, Belleek launched its own collector's society, which grew to an international membership of more than 6,000, and helped boost the company's profile among global porcelain collectors.

Troughton sold out to Powerscreen International, a maker of quarry handling machinery then in the midst of a diversification effort. The price of the sale stood at £2.2 million. Under Powerscreen, the Belleek works was refurbished, and a new visitor's center was established. The visitor's center quickly became a major tourist attraction in the region. Belleek also launched a new, higher-end ''designer'' line, boosting its range of production to more than 250 items, with prices ranging from $25 to more than $4,000.

By 1990, Powerscreen had abandoned its diversification strategy. In that year, Belleek was acquired by George Moore, a native of Drogheda, in Ireland, who had moved to California, for £3.7 million. Moore, who remained in the United States, brought in a new management team headed by Managing Director John Macguire.

The new owner and management team now led the Belleek works into a new era of expansion. Over the next decade the company rebuilt its production facilities. By 1998, the company's factory had quadrupled in size, to more than 120,000 square feet. The company's sales also were booming. From just £2 million in sales ($3.5 million) in 1993, the company sales climbed to more than $55 million in 2004.

Part of the company's growth came through an acquisition program instituted in the mid-1990s. The company first purchased Galway, Ireland-based Galway Irish Crystal. This purchase was followed by the 1996 acquisition of Donegal Parian China, a company founded in 1986. Then in 1997, Belleek added operations in England's Stoke-on-Trent, still a major hub of the U.K. pottery industry, with the purchase of Aynsley China, founded in 1775 by John Aynsley. That company had played an important role in developing the method for producing bone china.

Into the 2000s, Belleek remained one of the world's leading names for high-quality decorative porcelain products. In 2003, Belleek launched an effort to appeal to a new generation of porcelain buyers (noting, in particular, the rising popularity of bridal registries) with the launch of a new, more modern design-oriented line, Belleek Living. Belleek appeared to have found the recipe for continued success in the new century.

Principal Subsidiaries

Aynsley China Ltd.; Donegal Parian China Ltd.; Galway Irish Crystal Ltd.

Principal Competitors

American Greetings Corporation; Waterford Wedgwood PLC; Villeroy und Boch AG; Longaberger Co.; Kyocera Fineceramics GmbH; Rosenthal AG; Lladro S.A.; Pamesa Ceramica S.L.; Josiah Wedgwood and Sons Ltd.; The Porcelain and Fine China Companies Ltd.

Further Reading

''Belleek Adds to Portfolio,'' *News Letter,* November 29, 2000, p. 17.

''Belleek Pottery Group Purchases Aynsley China,'' *HFN The Weekly Newspaper for the Home Furnishing Network,* June 16, 1997, p. 33.

''Belleek Signs New US Deal,'' *News Letter,* June 25, 2004.

Chapman, Sandra, ''Something Old, Something New at Belleek Pottery,'' *NewsLetter,* May 2, 2003.

Godson, Lisa, ''Designer Ireland: No. 183: Belleek Living,'' *Sunday Times,* May 18, 2003, p. 15.

Karl, John, ''Belleek China: Pride of the Irish,'' *Sarasota Herald Tribune,* December 2, 2000.

McCaughren, Samantha, ''Belleek's EUR 2.4m Facelift to Target Younger Market,'' *Irish Independent,* April 16, 2003.

McGurk, Helen, ''Pottery Is Living Proof of Vibrant Marketing,'' *News Letter,* October 12, 2004, p. 4.

''Pottery Firm Breaks New Ground with Living Range,'' *News Letter,* April 15, 2003, p. 3.

''Pottery Firm's 'Belleek' Future,'' *Newsletter,* January 10, 2003.

—M.L. Cohen

Bill Barrett Corporation

Bill Barrett Corporation

1099 18th Street, Suite 2300
Denver, Colorado 80202
U.S.A.
Telephone: (303) 293-9100
Fax: (303) 291-0420
Web site: http://www.billbarrettcorp.com

Public Company
Incorporated: 2002
Employees: 110
Sales: $169.9 million (2004)
Stock Exchanges: New York
Ticker Symbol: BBG
NAIC: 211111 Crude Petroleum and Natural Gas
   Extraction

Bill Barrett Corporation is a publicly traded, independent oil and gas exploration and development company, concentrating its efforts on five major Rocky Mountain sites: the Wind River Basin, the Uinta Basin, the Piceance Basin, the Powder River Basin, and the Williston Basin. All told, Barrett's portfolio includes more than 450 producing wells and 820,000 net undeveloped acres in nine oil and gas basins in the Rocky Mountains. The Denver, Colorado-based company is headed by legendary wildcatter William J. Barrett, lured out of retirement by his sons.

Founder's Career Launch in the 1950s

Along with nine brothers and sisters, Bill Barrett grew up on a Kansas farm, and then in the 1950s enrolled at Kansas State University. After two years, however, when his father suffered a stroke, he was forced to return home to take over the family poultry business. Because of the Korean War, Barrett was drafted, although an eye problem kept him stateside. Following his stint in the Army, he returned to the poultry business, but it was obvious that it was too small to allow both him and his brother an adequate living while supporting their parents. Instead, he took advantage of the GI Bill and resumed his studies at Kansas State, ultimately receiving a master's degree in geology in 1957. He then went to work as a stratigrapher, studying

rock strata for El Paso Natural Gas, thereby beginning his long association with Rocky Mountain oil and gas exploration, due to El Paso's discovery of the Desert Springs Field in the Green River Basin area of southwestern Wyoming.

Barrett left El Paso for Pan-American Petroleum Corp. in 1963, and then four years later became chief geologist for Wolf Exploration Co., where he made his reputation as an exceptional "oil finder." As described by a 1993 *Denver Business Journal* article, "Finding oil is like fitting together a jigsaw puzzle. The geologist combines as many pieces of information as possible, such as seismic data or well histories, and then produces a solution after lots of tedious work." According to Barrett, "A lot of hard work probably helps improve the luck factor." Barrett's first major discovery for Wolf in the mid-1960s was the 24-mile-long, 15-mile-wide Highlight field in Wyoming. He then discovered an even larger field, the Madden field in the state's Wind River Basin.

When Wolf elected to relocate from Denver to Houston, Barrett decided to stay in the Rockies while also shifting gears and becoming an entrepreneur. In 1969 he joined forces with Chuck Shear to form BNC Exploration (BNC referring to "Bill 'n Chuck"), for which he served as vice-president of exploration. Two years later BNC merged with Rainbow Resources, a company that enjoyed success in the Rockies and further solidified Barrett's reputation. The Williams Companies bought Rainbow for $40 million in 1978, a deal that required Barrett to sign a three-year noncompete agreement. After sitting on the sidelines during this period, Barrett emerged in 1981, using his share of the Williams money to launch a sole proprietorship operating under the corporate umbrella of Aeon Energy, before becoming an independent entity, Barrett Energy Company. He took the company public in 1983 by way of a reverse merger with AIMEXCO Inc., renaming it Barrett Resources.

Over the next 20 years Barrett Resources grew into one of the largest energy companies in Colorado, despite less than favorable conditions. In the early 1980s major oil companies began to pull out of the region, but Barrett, sensing opportunity, remained and was able to secure several important leases from the majors. At the same time, he was a disciplined businessman who refused to take on debt, unlike many competitors who became overly aggressive in the early 1980s. Instead, Barrett Resources sold interests in the wells it discovered, initially retaining about 12.5 percent. As the company established itself, it increased its ownership position to 25 percent, until finally it was strong enough to own projects in their entirety. This conservative approach to risk management served the company well during the oil and gas crash of the mid-1980s, allowing Barrett Resources to survive while many other energy companies fell by the wayside. The company was also well positioned to prosper in the 1990s after the market rebounded. In 1994 Barrett Resources drilled a discovery well that led to the discovery of the Cave Gulch Field, one of the largest discoveries in the Rockies in many years.

In and Out of Retirement: Late 1990s and Early 2000s

Bill Barrett retired in July 1997, but less than a year later, as an energy recession began to take hold, he returned as chief executive officer to lead the company, which he feared had begun to drift off course during the short time he was absent. He told the *Rocky Mountain News* in a 1999 interview, "After working primarily in the Rocky Mountains, we had gotten involved in exploration in the Gulf of Mexico and in Peru. We wound up overspending our cash flow and taking on more debt than I was comfortable with." Barrett was able to shore up the company, so that it was in a position to enjoy another growth spurt after commodity prices rebounded.

In March 2000 Barrett retired again. The company he built now became a takeover target for a major oil company, Royal Dutch/Shell Group, which in March 2001 made an unsolicited bid of $1.8 billion. Barrett Resources resisted the overture, instead putting itself up for sale in the hope of attracting a better deal from a "white knight" bidder. Another buyer soon emerged in the familiar form of the Williams Companies, which had bought out Bill Barrett's Rainbow venture 25 years earlier. Although Shell upped its offer for Barrett Resources, Williams offered more, nearly $2.8 billion in cash and stock, driving Shell from the field.

Some of Barrett's sons had worked for Barrett Resources, but after it was sold to Williams, they were at loose ends. In October 2001, Fred and Terry Barrett, both trained geologists, approached their 73-year-old father and urged him to join them, along with a number of like-minded Barrett Resources employees, to launch a new Barrett energy company based in Denver. Bill Barrett, who had not lost his love for geology, was won over by his sons' enthusiasm and agreed to serve as CEO and chairman of the new venture, which traded on his sterling reputation as an oil finder by adopting the name Bill Barrett Corporation. His stature was such that the new company was able to lure away the entire management team from his previous venture, all of whom had worked together for 15 to 20 years and were expert at locating oil and gas in the Rocky Mountains.

As a result of assembling such an experienced team, Barrett had no difficulty in raising seed money. An initial investment of $27.5 million came from members of the management team as well as family members. The first round of outside financing lasted just two months, with a number of investors having to be turned away. The company raised $107.5 million from Warburg Pincus, Goldman Sachs Capital Partners, and JP Morgan Partners. In addition, the company supplemented its war chest with another $175 million in credit. Another important factor in the company's ability to raise money was fortuitous timing: In the early months of 2002, gas prices began increasing steadily and there was a perception in the marketplace that gas prices would continue to climb. Barrett also wasted little time in its effort to acquire desirable assets. In March 2002 the company paid $73 million for gas properties in Wyoming's Wind River Basin. A month later it spent another $8 million for gas properties in the Uinta Basin in Utah. The company also signed a deal with the Apsaalooke Crow Native American tribe to drill for coalbed methane on tribal lands in Montana. Barrett closed 2002 with the $62 million purchase of properties in Wyoming's Powder River Basin, the Cooper Reservoir field, and oil properties in the Williston Basin of North Dakota. As a result, at the end of 2002 Barrett owned 119 billion cubic feet equivalent (Bcfe) of natural gas and crude oil and liquid gas. For the year 2002, Barrett posted revenues of $16 million and a net loss of $3.8 million. Most of the sales came from the Wind River properties acquired in March and developed late in the year. They were to provide an even greater payoff in 2003.

Barrett acquired more Powder River Basin properties in March 2003, paying $35 million. By the end of the year the company's proved reserves grew to 204 Bcfe. Due to an increase in the company's production activity, as well as a rise in oil and natural gas prices, Barrett's balance sheet showed a marked improvement over the previous year. In 2003 the company recorded operating revenues of $75.3 million, resulting in a net loss on the year of approximately $500,000, overall an excellent performance for a start-up venture.

Going Public in 2004

From the outset, Barrett hoped to make an initial public offering (IPO) of stock after 18 months to two years. In the spring of 2004, Barrett took the necessary steps to make its IPO and waited for the right market conditions before pulling the trigger. Again, the Bill Barrett name carried great weight with Wall Street investors, who were well familiar with his career and impressed with his experienced team. Although the asking price was high, given the young company's asset value and project cash flow, investors lined up to become involved in the offering, which was reportedly oversubscribed two or three times. With Goldman, Sachs & Co. acting as the lead underwriter and the involvement of JP Morgan, Lehman Brothers Inc., Credit Suisse First Boston LLC, Morgan Stanley & Co. Incorporated, Petrie Parkman & Co., Inc., and First Albany Capital Inc., the IPO was conducted in December 2004. Barrett sold nearly 15 million shares, netting $347 million. After the offering, Barrett's institutional backers—Warburg Pincus, Goldman Sachs, and JP Morgan—continued to own more than a 50 percent interest in the company. Listed on the New York Stock Exchange, the shares quickly rose in value, from the initial price of $25 per share to a high of $35, before settling around $30 early in 2005 because of softening in natural gas prices.

Key Dates:

1958: William J. Barrett launches an energy career as a geologist.
1981: Barrett forms Barrett Energy Company.
1983: Barrett Energy becomes publicly traded Barrett Resources.
2001: Barrett Resources is sold to the Williams Companies.
2002: Bill Barrett and sons start Bill Barrett Corporation.
2004: The company goes public.

While it devoted much of 2004 preparing for its IPO, Barrett continued to grow its portfolio of oil and gas properties. For the year, it invested $347 million, including $138 million to purchase Gibson Gulch properties located in northwest Colorado's Piceance Basin. The company also drilled 285 wells during the year, experiencing an impressive success rate in excess of 95 percent. Barrett finished the year with 292.3 Bcfe, a 43 percent increase over the previous year. Moreover, the company posted total revenues for the year of nearly $170 million. Although it lost $5.3 million in 2004, Barrett had increased its exploration expenses from $6.1 million in 2003 to $36.2 million in 2004, an investment that resulted in a sizable improvement in discretionary cash flow and helped to position the company for long-term growth.

Bill Barrett indicated that despite his age he planned to continue serving as the company's CEO for several more years. Waiting in the wings to succeed him were sons Fred Barrett, president of the company, and Terry Barrett, vice-president.

Principal Divisions

Northern Division; Southern Division.

Principal Competitors

Double Eagle Petroleum Co.; KCS Energy, Inc.

Further Reading

Cummins, Chip, "Williams Cos. to Buy Barrett Resources for About $2.38 Billion in Cash, Stock," *Wall Street Journal,* May 8, 2001, p. A4.

Hubler, Eric, "Legendary Colorado Energy Explorer Prepares to Take Firm Public," *Denver Post,* June 8, 2004.

Locke, Tom, "Bill Barrett Corp. Expected to Go Public," *Denver Business Journal,* April 16, 2004, p. A3.

——, "Bill Barrett: Wildcatter of the Year," *Denver Business Journal,* April 23, 1993, p. 3A.

Toal, Brian A., "Starting Over, Aiming Higher," *Oil & Gas Investor,* June 2002, p. 35.

Tyson, Ray, "Barrett Back in Business with Rockies Firm," *Gas Daily,* April 5, 2002, p. 1.

—Ed Dinger

biogen idec™

Biogen Idec Inc.

14 Cambridge Center
Cambridge, Massachusetts 02142
U.S.A.
Telephone: (617) 679-2000
Fax: (617) 679-2617
Web site: http://www.biogenidec.com

Public Company
Incorporated: 2003
Employees: 4,266
Sales: $2.21 billion (2004)
Stock Exchanges: NASDAQ
Ticker Symbol: BIIB
NAIC: 325414 Biological Product (Except Diagnostic)
Manufacturing; 533110 Owners and Lessors of Other
Non-Financial Assets

Biogen Idec Inc., formed through the 2003 merger of Biogen Inc. and IDEC Pharmaceuticals Corporation (Idec), is a biotechnology company focused on developing treatments for cancer and autoimmune and inflammatory diseases. The company's portfolio of approved drugs includes Rituxan and Zevalin, both of which treat B-cell non-Hodgkin's lymphoma. Biogen Idec also markets Amevive, a drug to treat psoriasis, and the best-selling treatment for relapsing multiple sclerosis, Avonex. Based in Cambridge, Massachusetts, the company maintains facilities and offices in San Diego and abroad. Biogen Idec operates throughout Europe and in Canada, Japan, and Australia.

Origins

Idec began the long and difficult journey of taking a drug from discovery to market in 1985. The company was founded in San Francisco to develop and to commercialize drugs to treat immune system cancers and autoimmune and inflammatory diseases, a costly, time-consuming, and risky undertaking for a start-up biotechnology company. Ahead, Idec faced the daunting task of developing an effective drug and shepherding it through the numerous regulatory stages required to gain approval from the U.S. Food and Drug Administration (FDA).

The process would take years to complete, and it would require vast sums of capital, promising to drain the financial reserves of any but the largest pharmaceutical concerns. Idec's success would hinge on the effective mixture of science and business, two disciplines that often were at odds with one another. The demands of science called for time and money for research and development, while the demands of business called for revenues and profits. As Idec began its journey in 1985, the company would have to find a way to satisfy both its scientific and business needs.

Much of Idec's initial work centered on monoclonal antibodies as a way to treat non-Hodgkin's lymphoma, specifically B-cell lymphoma, a cancer of the immune system afflicting approximately 240,000 people in the United States. Monoclonal antibodies were used to bind to specific cells, such as tumor cells, and either deplete or suppress the targeted cells, leaving the healthy cells unharmed. Although monoclonal antibodies were known for their discriminatory ability to damage targeted cells, Idec's scientists employed a plan-B strategy in treating non-Hodgkin's B-cell lymphomas, working on a product to reduce total B cell levels, thereby eliminating a patient's normal and malignant B cells. The approach was based on clinical studies demonstrating that normal, healthy B cells regenerated within months. The other part of Idec's research and development efforts focused on treating autoimmune and inflammatory diseases, afflictions such as rheumatoid arthritis, psoriasis, and multiple sclerosis. Monoclonal antibodies also worked well in combating autoimmune and inflammatory diseases, succeeding by their ability to target specific cells.

Idec scientists labored for years developing monoclonal antibodies, chewing through millions of dollars as they performed their pioneering work. Not surprisingly, a scarcity of funds plagued the company early on, a problem that would hound Idec for years. In 1991, in a bid to alleviate some of the financial pressure it was experiencing, the company completed an initial public offering of stock, debuting on the NASDAQ. The proceeds from the stock offering provided some help, enabling the company to progress toward its first major hurdle. In 1993, Idec began Phase I clinical trials with a monoclonal antibody product it had given the temporary name IDEC-C2B8. Phase I trials were concluded before the end of the year, paving the way for the start of Phase II trials. Once Phase II trials were concluded, the end of the regulatory approval process was in sight, but Idec's management team, led by Dr. William H. Rastetter, faced a formidable problem. Idec did not have the money to pay for Phase III trials.

Idec's string of annual losses had inflicted a heavy toll on the company. Its financial performance in the years leading up to its most profound crisis offered a glimpse at the precarious financial state of the company. In 1994, the company collected $7.4 million in revenue and posted a loss of $18 million. Idec lost another $17.2 million in 1995 on revenues of $23.6 million, its tenth straight year of recording an annual loss. Since its inception, Idec had racked up more than $80 million in losses, leaving it dangerously short of cash as it reached the critical Phase III patient study portion of the FDA approval process. By 1995, the company had enough money to stay afloat for perhaps two more years, but it did not have enough money to pay for Phase III trials. It was at this juncture of the company's development when a company-saving agreement was forged.

1995 Agreement with Genentech

Idec's chief executive officer, William Rastetter, joined the company in 1986, roughly a decade after earning his doctorate in chemistry from Harvard University. After spending seven years on the faculty at the Massachusetts Institute of Technology, Rastetter joined a company named Genentech, Inc., one of the largest biotechnology companies in the world. Rastetter served in various capacities at Genentech, directing the company's Biocatalysis and Chemical Sciences groups and serving as the director of corporate ventures at the company. It was through Genentech's intervention that Idec was able to continue conducting clinical trials on IDEC-C2B8. The two companies signed a collaboration agreement in March 1995 that provided the funding for the further development of IDEC-C2B8, a drug that would become known as Rituxan. During the next several years, Genentech invested approximately $60 million on Rituxan's development, getting in return a majority of the sales and profits Rituxan would generate if it earned FDA approval.

FDA Approval of Rituxan in 1997

Idec ceded the bulk of the financial spoils of its development efforts, but the partnership with Genentech kept the Rituxan project moving forward. Phase III trials were concluded in February 1997, and with the help of Genentech's regulatory expertise, the company filed for final approval from the FDA. In November 1997, after 12 years of work, the company received welcome news. The FDA greenlighted Rituxan, making it the first monoclonal antibody to be approved as a cancer therapeutic.

Rituxan, which offered an alternative to chemotherapy, quickly became the leading treatment for non-Hodgkin's lymphoma. The drug's success, even with the majority of the financial rewards going to Genentech, dramatically improved Idec's finances and its standing within the biotechnology community. With what quickly became the leading treatment for B-cell non-Hodgkin's lymphoma to its name, the company gained global recognition as a skillful pioneer in the industry. Further, the embrace of Rituxan by the medical community enabled the company to record its first annual profit in 1998, beginning what became a string of profitable years for Idec.

With Rituxan proving to be a market winner, Idec focused on the next drug it intended to commercialize. In 1993, the same year the company began Phase I trials with Rituxan, Idec began clinical studies of a drug that would become known as Zevalin. Zevalin, a therapeutic designed to treat B-cell non-Hodgkin's cancer as well, was a radioimmunotherapy product, one that, as *Business Week* noted in its October 29, 2001 issue, added "a second line of defense" to Rituxan. As Zevalin passed through various regulatory phases, the drug demonstrated an ability to kill malignant cells with radiation, promising to give Idec two products to combat the sixth leading cause of cancer death. In September 2001, the FDA's advisory panel voted 13 to two to recommend Zevalin for treating non-Hodgkin's lymphoma patients. The FDA, which rarely ruled against the recommendation of its advisory committee, approved Zevalin in February 2002, making it the first radioimmunotherapy to enter the market. Unlike with Rituxan, Idec was not forced to strike a partnership with another company to bring Zevalin to market, which meant the company could collect all the sales and profits generated by its new cancer treatment. In a February 25, 2002 interview with the *San Diego Business Journal*, Rastetter offered his reaction to Zevalin's approval by the FDA. "It feels good," he said. "We have our first product that we have [taken] 100 percent ourselves from the discovery to the marketplace."

By the time Zevalin was approved, Rituxan had become a phenomenal force in the pharmaceutical industry. In 2002, the drug generated $1.47 billion in sales, but Idec, because of its agreement with Genentech, collected only $370 million of the total. With Zevalin, the company hoped to register another success, one that would be enjoyed entirely by itself, but Idec was not depending solely on Rituxan and Zevalin to guarantee its financial health. The company was working on other drugs to develop a product pipeline that would provide a steady stream of new pharmaceuticals. In the fall of 2002, Rastetter met with Jim Mullen, the chief executive officer of another biotechnology firm, Cambridge, Massachusetts-based Biogen, Inc. The pair discussed working together to develop treatments for autoimmune disorders, but their conversation led to a relationship far deeper than a collaborative agreement.

Biogen Merger Announcement in 2002

When Rastetter and Mullen began working on a licensing agreement for future drug development, they realized the complementary nature of their technologies. Within a space of months, Rastetter and Mullen began hashing out an agreement to merge their companies, a union that would combine Idec's expertise in developing cancer treatments with Biogen's expertise in developing Avonex, the first multiple sclerosis product to achieve $1

Key Dates:

1985: IDEC Pharmaceuticals Corporation (Idec) is founded.
1991: Idec completes its initial public offering of stock.
1993: Clinical studies begin on Rituxan and Zevalin.
1995: Idec signs a collaboration agreement with Genentech, Inc. for the further development of Rituxan.
1997: Rituxan is approved by the Food and Drug Administration (FDA).
2002: Zevalin is approved by the FDA.
2003: Idec completes a merger with Biogen, Inc., creating Biogen Idec Inc.
2004: The company moves into a new, $400 million complex in Oceanside, California.

billion in sales, and Amevive, a psoriasis treatment. The merger was announced in June 2002, a stock-for-stock transaction valued at approximately $6.5 billion. The announcement sparked widespread interest, ranking as the largest biotechnology merger between two independent companies. The union promised to create the third largest biotechnology company in the world, trailing only Amgen Inc. and Genentech. The greatest advantage gained by merging the companies was the enormous size of the combined organization, which would have far more money to spend on research and development and would realize cost savings from shared manufacturing facilities. "There's been a trend over the last two to three years in biotech where companies are looking for girth, they're looking for mass," an industry analyst commented in a June 24, 2003 interview with *Investor's Business Daily.* "What does girth give you?," the analyst asked. "It can make growth more difficult, but on the upside it creates a more diversified company."

The merger of Idec and Biogen was completed in November 2003, creating a new company named Biogen Idec Inc. Under the terms of the transaction, Idec shareholders owned 50.5 percent of the combined company, while Biogen shareholders were given a 49.5 percent interest in the new company. Biogen was roughly three times larger than Idec in terms of sales and number of employees, but technically Idec acquired Biogen because of a change-of-control provision in Idec's agreement with Genentech. Despite the technical aspect of the merger, a dominant strain of Biogen was seen in the merged company. Biogen Idec adopted Cambridge as its headquarters, the headquarters of Biogen Inc. For leadership, the title of chief executive officer was awarded to Jim Mullen, while Rastetter assumed the role of executive chairman. These two executives took charge of a company with annual sales estimated at $1.5 billion, the same figure the pair had available to spend on promoting the development of the new company. A new, powerful player in the business of biotechnology had emerged, one whose origins sprang from the roots of two small biotechnology start-ups that had hit the jackpot in drug development.

In the wake of the merger, the industry waited and watched to see if the marriage of two of the rising stars in biotechnology created a company superior to its two parts. Undoubtedly though, the company figured as a heavyweight in the biotech-

nology industry. In 2004, Biogen Idec began moving some operations into a sprawling campus near San Diego in Oceanside, a construction project begun by Idec in 2001. The six-building, $400 million complex befitted one of the industry's premier players. That same year the company posted sales of $2.21 billion. In the years ahead, the company intended to use its "girth" to develop a diverse portfolio of therapeutic products to rival the remarkable success of Idec's Rituxan and Biogen's Avonex, two products to inspire future generations of Biogen Idec researchers.

Principal Subsidiaries

Biogen Idec MA Inc.; Biogen Idec U.S. Corporation; Biogen Idec U.S. Limited Partnership; Biogen Idec Holding I Inc.; Biogen Holding II Inc.; The Biogen Idec Foundation Inc.; Biogen Idec (RTP) Realty L.L.C.; Biogen Idec Realty Corporation; Biogen Idec Realty Limited Partnership; Biogen Idec U.S. West Corporation; Biogen Idec U.S. Pacific Corporation; Biogen Idec Nobel Research Center, L.L.C.; Biogen Idec Trade Services Building, L.L.C.; Biogen Idec Manufacturing Operations, L.L.C.; Biogen IDEC Canada Inc.; Biogen Idec Austria GmbH; Biogen Idec Belgium S.A./N.V.; Biogen Idec B.V. (Netherlands); Biogen Idec International B.V. (Netherlands); Biogen Idec (Denmark) A/S; Biogen Idec (Denmark) Manufacturing ApS; Biogen Idec Finland Oy; Biogen Idec (France); Biogen Idec GmbH (Germany); Biogen Iberia SL (Spain); Biogen Idec Limited (U.K.); Biogen Idec Norway AS; Biogen Idec Portugal; Biogen Idec Sweden AB; Biogen Idec (Switzerland) GmbH; Biogen Dompe S.R.L. (Italy); Biogen Dompe AG (Switzerland); Biogen Idec Australia Pty. Ltd.; Biogen Idec Japan Ltd.; Idec Seiyaku (Japan); Biogen Idec (Bermuda) Investments Limited; Biogen Idec (Bermuda) Investments II Limited; Biotech Manufacturing C.V. (Netherlands).

Principal Competitors

Bristol-Myers Squibb Company; Corixa Corporation; GlaxoSmithKline PLC.

Further Reading

Allen, Mike, "Merger Puts Idec Among Top Bio Firms," *San Diego Business Journal,* June 30, 2003, p. 1.
Bell, Rick, "A Much-Needed Shot in the Arm," *San Diego Business Journal,* September 4, 2000, p. 66.
Graebner, Lynn, "Biotech Company Scouts Area for Factory," *Business Journal Serving Greater Sacramento,* November 18, 1996, p. 1.
Herper, Matthew, "Bio Dreck," *Forbes,* July 21, 2003, p. 34.
Howell, Donna, "Idec Pharmaceuticals Scoops Up Biogen in the Largest Biotech Merger Since '01," *Investor's Business Daily,* June 24, 2003, p. A1.
Krasner, Jeffrey, "Biogen, Idec Complete Merger," *Boston Globe,* November 13, 2003, p. B3.
Webb, Marion, "Idec to Reap Huge Benefits with Drug's Approval," *San Diego Business Journal,* February 25, 2002, p. 11.
——, "It's Celebration Time at Two Local Biotech Firms," *San Diego Business Journal,* February 8, 1999, p. 13.
——, "Risky Business," *San Diego Business Journal,* July 15, 2002, p. 12.

—Jeffrey L. Covell

The Bombay Company, Inc.

550 Bailey Avenue
Fort Worth, Texas 76107-2155
U.S.A.
Telephone: (817) 347-8200
Fax: (817) 332-7066
Web site: http://www.bombaycompany.com

Public Company
Incorporated: 1987 as Bombay Company
Employees: 5,500
Sales: $575.3 million (2004)
Stock Exchanges: New York
Ticker Symbol: BBA
NAIC: 442110 Furniture Stores; 454110 Electronic
   Shopping and Mail-Order Houses

The Bombay Company, Inc. is a retailer of large furniture, small, occasional furniture, home accessories, and wall decor. The firm operates more than 500 stores across North America, most of which are flagship Bombay units with a few dozen each of the BombayKIDS and Bombay Outlet formats. Traditionally a mall-based retailer, Bombay in the early 2000s began pursuing an off-mall strategy, and by the end of 2004 more than one-quarter of the units were in off-mall locations. Another key strategy for the company is to offer a unique product line: More than 95 percent of the products it sells have been designed or styled specifically for Bombay. The company made its initial mark selling traditional, dark-stained English-style wooden furniture but has since broadened its lines to include other styles. In addition to running its core stores, Bombay also sells products through catalogs and on the Internet and operates a small wholesaler, Bailey Street Trading Company, which distributes furniture to other retailers.

Mail-Order Beginnings

The Bombay Company got its start in 1975 as a mail-order business based in New Orleans. The company sold mahogany-stained reproductions of small 18th- and 19th-century English furniture pieces, such as plant stands, nightstands, and butler's tables, which were manufactured in the Far East. After running

advertisements in upscale magazines such as the *New Yorker,* Bombay Company shipped its goods to customers in flat boxes, for assembly. Usually, all the customer had to do was screw the legs on. Entrepreneur Brad Harper, who founded the company with a partner, named the enterprise ''Bombay Company'' in an effort to conjure up the glory of the British Empire at its height. Most people, however, missed the reference.

By the end of the 1970s, Bombay Company was racking up annual sales of about $1.5 million, offering 12 different items of accent furniture through ads in magazines. Overall, however, the company was losing money. The quality of the products it sold was uneven, as its distant Asian manufacturers proved unreliable. Also, The Bombay Company's growth was severely limited by its reliance on mail order.

In 1979 Bombay signed an agreement with Canadian entrepreneur Robert E.M. Nourse to begin selling its products in Canada. For rights to the Canadian market, Nourse paid one dollar, plus a 4 percent royalty on sales. Since Canadian mail-order opportunities were extremely limited, Nourse set out to convert The Bombay Company into a successful retail property.

Early 1980s Move into Retail

In April 1980 Nourse's first Bombay Company store opened in Toronto's Eaton Centre mall. Nourse had concluded that The Bombay Company was able to offer customers three things that made location in a mall advantageous: value, fashion, and instant accessibility. Value was provided by the fact that the company's products, manufactured in Taiwan and other East Asian countries, were not high-priced.

Fashion, the hook to lure customers out of the mall and into The Bombay Company store, was provided by an elaborate store design. Under the watchful eye of a designer, the company's 2,000-square-foot space was transformed into a replica of England's Fountain Court, located at Henry VIII's palace, Hampton Court. In order to pay for this renovation, and other start-up expenses, Nourse invested $125,000 of his own money, and borrowed an equal amount from a bank.

To justify this expense, and the high rent of a mall space, Bombay needed to attract impulse buyers. Since Bombay Company products came boxed flat, a large number of them could be kept in stock without taking up an excess amount of space for storage. Because of this, customers could take home their purchases right after deciding to buy them. In this way, The Bombay Company introduced an element of immediate gratification to the furniture market, in contrast to a traditional furniture store, where customers ordered items, and then waited six to 12 weeks for delivery. In The Bombay Company store, 35 styles of furniture were available to be carried out of the store at the time of purchase. With these elements of a successful retail operation in place, The Bombay Company store in the Eaton Centre mall was an immediate success.

Three months after the opening of the Toronto Bombay Company store, in July 1980, Harper sold 80 percent of the U.S. operations of The Bombay Company to a Fort Worth-based holding company called Tandy Brands, Inc., for $26,000 plus assumption of the company's debts. The Bombay Company's new corporate parent was a miniconglomerate, spun off from the Tandy Corporation in 1975. In July 1981 Tandy Brands acquired the remaining 20 percent of The Bombay Company.

After a year of successful operation of the Eaton Centre Bombay Company outlet, Nourse was looking for additional financing to buy further inventory and expand his store. Since the general financial climate for borrowing money at that time was highly forbidding, he felt that he had no choice but to sell out to Tandy. In August 1981, Tandy also bought out Nourse's Canadian operation. "I had mixed feelings about [Tandy] buying me out," Nourse later told *Inc.* magazine. "If capital had been available at a reasonable cost, I never would have sold. But at the time it was the only way to grow the company."

Under the terms of the sale, Nourse retained control of the Canadian operations of The Bombay Company. With the influx of money from Tandy, he was able to build 13 stores by 1983, all of which proved profitable.

South of the Canadian border, however, the situation looked very different. Tandy had built 36 Bombay Company stores since taking over the company, and the business was hemorrhaging money, having racked up $3 million in losses in just three years. By the end of 1983, the situation had become desperate. In an effort to revive its American operation, Tandy's chief executive officer moved to merge the company's successful Canadian operations into its money-losing American operations, and put Nourse in charge of both.

Mid-1980s Turnaround with the Nourse Husband-and-Wife Team at the Helm

Nourse took control of the consolidated Bombay Company operations at the start of 1984. His strategy for renovating the company's ailing American operations was to implement the profitable store model that he had developed in Canada in The Bombay Company's American locations. To do so, however, it was necessary to close a number of unprofitable American stores in weak locations. Within three months of Nourse's arrival, nine of the company's 36 stores had been shut down. "We saw our concept as selling home decor in malls and other high-traffic locations," Nourse later told *HFD—The Weekly Home Furnishings Magazine,* an industry journal. "A number of the stores were in bad locations; that first year we closed more stores than we opened."

In addition to pruning unprofitable stores, The Bombay Company revamped its product line, under the direction of Nourse's wife, Alexandra "Aagje" Nourse, an advertising executive who had taken responsibility for the company's design operations. Under her direction, the company shifted away from masculine, military style furniture, which looked like it might have been used in a British military campaign of the previous century, toward more feminine and traditional Chippendale, Hepplewhite, and Queen Anne styles. In addition, the company began to market more home accessories, such as mirrors and lamps, and also started to offer printed fabrics for decorating. To keep customers interested, a constant flow of new products was moved through the store, and seven different catalogs a year alerted customers to the presence of new items.

In 1984 The Bombay Company began to open additional stores, relying on the other subsidiaries of Tandy Brands for financing. At the end of the fiscal year, the company posted a loss of $3 million, but by the middle of 1985, The Bombay Company was back in the black, turning a profit of $500,000. With these gains, The Bombay Company began to step up its plans for expansion. Its first targets for growth were areas of the United States where traditional furniture was best accepted: the mid-Atlantic states, the Southeast, the Midwest, and the Pacific Northwest. By 1986, the company was operating stores in 75 different locations, and earnings had hit $2 million. In 1987 the number of Bombay Company stores reached 114.

In 1988 and 1989 The Bombay Company moved its expansion into the Sunbelt for the first time, opening stores in Los Angeles and southern Florida, with exterior architecture carefully calibrated to blend with other surrounding structures. "We have to be careful," Robert Nourse told *HFD* in 1989. "We always wondered about the Sunbelt. But our Southern California stores and our store in Palm Beach are going gangbusters."

By April 1989, The Bombay Company had opened 190 mall stores, and the company's revenues had reached $79 million, up from $55 million the year before. The company had introduced a line of products with neoclassical styling, to complement its other Georgian and Victorian offerings. In September 1989 Bombay opened a flagship East Coast store on Madison Avenue in Manhattan, which soon began turning in record sales.

Emerging As a Solo Firm in the Early 1990s

While The Bombay Company was steadily growing, its corporate parent, Tandy Brands, was gradually streamlining its operations, shedding other properties and companies that were smaller and less profitable than The Bombay Company. In 1984 it closed two chains of retail stores, Western World and Ryon's,

Key Dates:

1975: Brad Harper founds The Bombay Company, selling small furniture pieces by mail order.

1979: Robert E.M. Nourse acquires Bombay's Canadian rights.

1980: Nourse opens the first Bombay Company store in Toronto's Eaton Centre mall; Harper sells an 80 percent interest in the U.S. operations to Tandy Brands, Inc.

1981: Tandy Brands acquires the remaining 20 percent stake; Nourse sells the Canadian operation to Tandy Brands but continues to manage it.

1984: Nourse is put in charge of both U.S. and Canadian Bombay Company operations; aided by his wife, Aagje, Nourse revitalizes the company.

1990: After divesting nearly all of its other operations, Tandy Brands changes its name to The Bombay Company, Inc.; Bombay launches the Alex & Ivy chain.

1992: Company tests larger format Bombay Company stores.

1993: Bombay commits itself to converting nearly all of its outlets to the larger "superstore" format.

1995: The Alex & Ivy chain is shut down.

1996: The board of directors fires both Robert and Aagje Nourse.

1998: First Bombay Outlets are opened.

2000: Company shifts focus to off-mall locations.

2002: Company opens its first BombayKIDS outlet.

and two years later, Tandy sold its Tex Tan Western Leather division for about $3 million. In March 1987 the company sold its Grate Home and Fireplace Company for $1.6 million. By the end of the decade, it had effectively centered its operations on The Bombay Company. Accordingly, on November 9, 1990, the company changed its name to The Bombay Company, Inc., and two months later, it completed the final transfer of its other accessories operations to its shareholders.

In the midst of this consolidation and concentration on the home furnishings market, The Bombay Company also moved to expand its franchise in this area. In the fall of 1990, the company opened three new concept test stores in Southern California. Called Alex & Ivy (named after Aagje Nourse's two cats), these outlets offered the same type of merchandise as Bombay Company stores, but with a more relaxed, country theme. Robert Nourse characterized Alex & Ivy merchandise in a 1990 *HFD* article as "more casual, yet traditional stylings. They will include European country, Italian Renaissance, French country and some traditional Swedish country . . . lots of painted finishes . . . a little more whimsical than Bombay."

The stores were opened in areas where The Bombay Company did not already have retail outlets. A second test of another three stores was planned for locations right next door to Bombay Company stores, to measure how much their success would come at the expense of their older retail sibling. Both store chains were planned to take advantage of the same structure for

manufacturing and distribution, and to appeal to the same demographic group of customers: well-educated women, with higher than average incomes.

"We constantly had comments from Bombay customers who said, 'I love your stores, but it isn't exactly our kind of furnishings,' " Aagje Nourse told *HFD* in 1994. "We . . . had hopes we could do something that was the other side of Bombay's lifestyle." Each Alex & Ivy store was slated to look exactly like all the others, arranged according to elaborate plans from the company headquarters, and the merchandise mix was set at half furniture, half accessories, such as quilts, pillows, lamps, and wall art.

Despite the recession of the early 1990s, which flattened The Bombay Company's earnings somewhat, the company continued to post strong growth in sales. By mid-1990, sales had reached $112 million, and earnings were at $12.3 million. By the middle of 1991, 43 more stores had been opened, nudging revenues up by a quarter to $140 million, but earnings had remained flat.

By the start of 1992, The Bombay Company's steady stream of new products had started to produce stores that were cramped with merchandise. In an effort to alleviate this problem, and to shake up the company's entrenched retail formula, the company opened a superstore in lower Manhattan as an experiment. The new store had about 3,500 square feet of space, instead of the usual 1,700. When this concept showed promise, The Bombay Company converted two more stores to the new, larger format.

In February 1993 The Bombay Company decided to convert almost all of its retail outlets to superstores. "I believe a business, and certainly a retail business that changes so quickly, has to keep reinventing itself or it will whither and die," Robert Nourse told *Inc.*, in explaining the chain's decision to leave its original store concept behind.

By the end of 1993, The Bombay Company had opened 100 superstores, and plans were on the board to add 50 more each year. In November of that year, the company marked the opening of its 400th store. In its Alex & Ivy operation, The Bombay Company had opened 26 stores, in California, Texas, Connecticut, Delaware, Georgia, Maryland, New Hampshire, New York, and New Jersey. Revenues from these combined operations reached $232 million, and earnings were at $16 million.

This pattern of strong growth continued in 1994, after The Bombay Company reported a strong holiday sales season at the end of the previous year. With these results, the company decided to expand its program to double the size of its stores in its fledgling Alex & Ivy chain as well. Tests of the "international country" concept had demonstrated that it appealed to a different set of customers within the company's basic demographic target, and that sales lost in The Bombay Company stores to Alex & Ivy outlets equaled only 5 percent of business.

In January 1994 the company began to install a new merchandising computer system, to speed up customer transactions and upgrade inventory controls. In addition, the company laid plans to open a fourth distribution center in Atlanta to provide goods to its newly enlarged stores. This facility joined three other distribution sites located in Texas, Pennsylvania, and Canada.

Mid-1990s Downfall

Sales began stagnating in the spring of 1994, at the same time that profits were being hurt by higher operating costs, partly stemming from higher inventory levels. Wall Street began pummeling the stock because of the disappointing results, and Bombay's shares fell by more than 70 percent by early 1995. One problem was that the company had expanded its larger format stores too quickly—and without enlarging the product line to fill up the larger space. The poor results, coupled with clashes with Robert Nourse, led to the ouster of executive vice-president Michael L. Glazer in January 1995. Glazer had been in charge of day-to-day operations since early 1991. Another problem area was the Alex & Ivy chain. It too had been expanded too rapidly, reaching 62 units by January 1995. By that time, it was losing about $2 million per year. Glazer had had a plan to quickly get Alex & Ivy to break even, but Nourse abruptly shut down the chain in January 1995, incurring a $30 million charge that resulted in a net loss of $14.7 million for 1994.

Bombay's struggles continued. Numerous managers left the company in 1995 following Glazer's departure, including two of four regional managers, both the vice-president and the director of store operations, the chief merchandising officer, and one-third of the 36 district managers. When Nourse had failed to turn Bombay around by September 1996, the board of directors ousted both him and his wife. The board chairman, Carson R. Thompson, who was Bombay's CEO from 1982 to 1991, was named president and CEO on a temporary basis.

Under Thompson, Bombay slashed inventory and changed its merchandise mix. Believing that the product lines had become too upscale, the firm eliminated some of its more expensive items in favor of moderately priced pieces and also returned to a tighter focus on the traditional dark-wood styles that were the chain's trademark. More accessories were also added to the mix, along with a collection of upholstered chairs and sofas. Furthermore, a new store design was introduced, one that, according to the industry journal *HFN*, resembled "a turn-of-the-century mercantile building." The breakneck growth of the past was halted, as only a handful of new stores were opened in 1997.

Thompson left the company in March 1997. Taking over on an interim basis was Robert S. Jackson, a board director. Finally in February 1998 Carmie Mehrlander was brought onboard as president and chief operating officer. She was a veteran retail manager, with stints at Sears, Roebuck and Co.; Home Shopping Network, Inc.; Abraham & Straus; and R.H. Macy & Co., Inc. Over the next two years the leadership gradually transitioned to Mehrlander, who was named CEO as well in February 2000.

An Evolving Company: Late 1990s and Early 2000s

Under the new leadership, Bombay continued to evolve in the late 1990s and into the new century. In 1998 the company moved into the outlet mall market, opening the first Bombay Outlets, which offered both clearance items from the flagship stores and merchandise that had been specifically developed for outlet customers. At the Bombay stores, a key new marketing strategy was to develop and offer to customers entire collections of furniture and accessories, rather than simply selling individual, unrelated items. These collections focused on four rooms of

the home: living room, dining room, bedroom, and home office. After largely following a mall-based strategy for most of its existence, The Bombay Company also began testing off-mall locations. The idea was to lower operating costs while improving profitability based on consumers' increasing preference for non-mall shopping venues. By 2000 Bombay had committed to gradually shift toward off-mall sites: when leases for its mall stores expired, some of them would be closed and replaced by nearby off-mall stores. Furthermore, many of the new stores to be opened would likewise be in off-mall locations. By early 2002 nearly 10 percent of Bombay stores were located outside an enclosed shopping mall.

Other efforts in the early 2000s focused on pursuing further channels for growth. In March 2000 the company formed Bailey Street Trading Company, a wholesale subsidiary charged with selling Bombay products to other retailers and the contract trade. Late in 2001 Bombay introduced a children's furniture and home accessories line that was available via a mail-order catalog and an Internet web site. This was followed by the opening of the first BombayKIDS store, in Dallas in March 2002. Several more BombayKIDS opened in the fall, and the new format proved a huge success as the launch was well-timed, coming in the midst of a booming market for children's home furnishings. The first BombayKIDS store, like many of the subsequent ones, was opened adjacent to a regular Bombay store. The two stores, which occupied 9,000 square feet of space, had separate entrances but also sported a connecting passageway inside. By the end of 2003 there were 35 BombayKIDS stores located across North America.

Unfortunately, the management team's focus on these new—and still very small—initiatives distracted them from the core Bombay outlets. The product lines there were allowed to become stale and dated. Worse, the company missed the entire post-9/11 home-focused craze that became known as nesting or cocooning. The managers canceled merchandise orders and marketing campaigns, believing that American consumers were unlikely to be interested in purchasing such things as candlestick holders and four-poster beds in the new environment. The fall person for these questionable decisions was Mehrlander, who resigned under pressure in August 2002.

While the CEO position remained vacant, James D. Carreker was named nonexecutive chairman in December 2002. He then became CEO as well in June 2003. Carreker was a former CEO and chairman of hotelier Wyndham International, Inc., and he had experience at several retailers, including Federated Department Stores, Inc.; Burdines, Inc.; and Sanger-Harris, Inc. The new executive led Bombay through a turnaround year in 2003. As it sold off accumulated inventory through heavy markdowns, Bombay refreshed its merchandise selection and introduced a new, three-tier pricing scheme. The company enjoyed its best results in a decade: Net income jumped 37.9 percent to nearly $10 million, while revenues increased 20.7 percent, reaching $596.4 million. Same-store sales (that is, sales at stores open at least 12 months) surged 13 percent. Revenues from the company's nonstore business, which encompassed e-commerce, catalog, and wholesale, grew 8 percent. Late in the year, Bombay reached an agreement with e-commerce leader Amazon.com, Inc. to sell Bombay, BombayKIDS, and Bombay Outlet products through Amazon's home and garden store. During the year, an increasingly confident

Bombay Company boosted its store count by 49, the largest amount of store openings in a decade.

Bombay strengthened its alliance with Amazon in May 2004 when it reached an agreement to hand over complete management of its e-commerce operations to Amazon. Although its store count surpassed the 500-unit mark for the first time during 2004, Bombay slowed its store openings midyear because of disappointing sales. The company divested its Bailey Street Trading wholesale operation late in the year in order to reallocate resources to its core retail businesses. Despite such moves, The Bombay Company failed to capitalize on the momentum established in 2003. Overall revenue fell 4 percent during 2004, while same-store sales plummeted 12 percent. In the highly competitive retail environment—particularly in the middle of the market, where Bombay operated—it was difficult to determine whether these results were a momentary blip on a longer-term turnaround or the beginning of a new period of struggle.

Principal Subsidiaries

The Bombay Furniture Company of Canada; BBA Holdings, Inc.; The Bombay Furniture Company, Inc.; BMAJ, Inc.; The Bombay Company de Mexico, S.A. de C.V.; Bombay International Inc.; Bailey Street Trading Company.

Further Reading

Caminiti, Susan, "Selling Instant Gratification," *Fortune,* June 28, 1993, p. 102.

Chakravarty, Subrata N., "Queen Anne at the Mall," *Forbes,* June 24, 1991, pp. 78+.

Duff, Mike, "Bombay Hones Core Operations, Moves Off-Mall," *DSN Retailing Today,* May 3, 2004, pp. 4, 45.

Finegan, Jay, "Survival of the Smartest," *Inc.,* December 1993, p. 78+.

Gilbert, Les, "Bombay Company Sets Alex & Ivy Test," *HFD—The Weekly Home Furnishings Magazine,* February 19, 1990, p. 16.

——, "Three Fundamentals Fuel Bombay Company," *HFD—The Weekly Home Furnishings Magazine,* February 26, 1990, p. 16.

Halkias, Maria, "Balm for Bombay: Retailer Seeks Remedy After Growth Spurt Falters," *Dallas Morning News,* January 13, 1995, p. 1D.

——, "Bombay Closing Alex & Ivy," *Dallas Morning News,* January 14, 1995, p. 1F.

——, "Bombay Fires Pair of Execs: Nourses' Removal Comes As a Surprise," *Dallas Morning News,* September 6, 1996, p. 1D.

Howell, Debbie, "Bombay Reaches Out to Parents with Launch of Kids Concept," *DSN Retailing Today,* April 22, 2002, pp. 6, 29.

Hutchinson, Harry, "Bombay's on a CEO Search," *HFN—The Weekly Newspaper for the Home Furnishing Network,* April 7, 1997, p. 6.

Jones, John A., "Bombay Company's Furniture Sales Still Growing Strongly," *Investor's Business Daily,* February 7, 1994.

Keeton, Laura E., "Bombay to Take Charge to Close Alex & Ivy Unit," *Wall Street Journal,* January 16, 1995, p. B4.

Lee, Louise, "Bombay, amid Falling Sales, Aims to Refinish Strategy," *Wall Street Journal,* May 13, 1997, p. B4.

——, "Bombay Co. Ousts Nourse As CEO and President," *Wall Street Journal,* September 6, 1996, p. B2.

Norton, Leslie P., "One-Trick Elephant?," *Barron's,* March 14, 1994, pp. 17+.

Santorelli, Dina, "Country Road, Take Me Home," *HFD—The Weekly Home Furnishings Magazine,* March 21, 1994, pp. 15+.

Seymour, Liz, "Bombay Company Breaks with Convention," *HFD—The Weekly Home Furnishings Magazine,* April 17, 1989, pp. 20+.

Spence, Rick, "Local Boy Makes Good Down South," *Profit,* Spring 1994.

Welles, Edward O., "The Fall of Bombay," *Inc.,* January 1996, pp. 48–52, 54–55.

Werner, Holly M., "Bombay Sets Stage for a Rebound," *HFN—The Weekly Newspaper for the Home Furnishing Network,* May 18, 1998, p. 8.

—Elizabeth Rourke
—update: David E. Salamie

Boyne USA Resorts

1 Boyne Mountain Road
Boyne Falls, Michigan 49713
U.S.A.
Telephone: (231) 549-6060
Toll Free: (800) 462-6963
Fax: (231) 549-6896
Web site: http://www.boyne.com

Private Company
Incorporated: 1947 as Boyne Ski Lodge, Inc.
Employees: 1,200
Sales: $316 million (2004 est.)
NAIC: 721110 Hotels (Except Casino Hotels) and
    Motels; 713920 Skiing Facilities; 713910 Golf
    Courses and Country Clubs; 451110 Sporting Goods
    Stores

Boyne USA Resorts is one of the leading operators of ski and golf resorts in North America. The firm's properties include Big Sky Resort in Montana, Crystal Mountain in Washington State, Brighton Ski Bowl in Utah, Cypress Mountain in British Columbia, and Boyne Mountain, Boyne Highlands, and the Inn at Bay Harbor in Michigan. Boyne also operates a Michigan-based chain of ski and golf shops, a sightseeing chairlift in Gatlinburg, Tennessee, and a golf course in Naples, Florida. The company is owned and run by the family of founder Everett Kircher.

Beginnings

Boyne USA Resorts traces its roots to the year 1947, and a Michigan skiing fan named Everett Kircher. Born in 1916 to German immigrants in St. Louis, Kircher had moved as an infant with his family to Detroit. He received his first set of skis at nine, and later took ski trips to Lake Placid, New York, and Sun Valley, Idaho, where he became an accomplished downhill skier.

After briefly attending the University of Michigan, Kircher began working at his family's Studebaker car dealership in the Detroit suburb of Rochester. Frustrated by the lack of skiing options in Michigan, which then had just one private and one public ski hill, in the mid-1940s he and two partners put up $5,000 each to create a ski area of their own. After looking at ten possible sites, in 1947 they bought 40 acres of land in the northwest corner of Michigan's lower peninsula, on which an 1,150-foot mountain stood. The seller was so incredulous that Kircher wanted to use the undeveloped, remote site for skiing, that he sold it to him for a dollar.

After buying the land Kircher left the auto dealership and moved his young family north. He soon began clearing trees to create two ski trails, which had been laid out by Victor Gottshalk, a German ski instructor he had worked with at Sun Valley. Gottshalk alerted Kircher to the fact that Sun Valley was willing to sell one of its single-chair ski lifts, and he bought it with $2,000 of his own money, his partners having by now gotten cold feet. The lift, which could transport 400 skiers per hour, had originally been built in 1936, and in fact was the very first chairlift ever constructed. It was a sizable improvement over existing devices such as tow ropes and "J-bars," and its status as the first ski lift in the Midwest immediately put Kircher's operation on the map.

On New Year's Day, 1948, the Boyne Mountain Ski Club opened with two ungroomed slopes, still bumpy from the stumps of trees that had been removed. Lift tickets were priced at $5 per day, and facilities consisted of a small warming lodge and an unpaved parking lot. Although the lift's gearbox froze up on the first day, and Kircher and his small staff had to occasionally shovel snow from the woods onto the ski trails to cover them, his faith in the concept remained strong, and in the off-season he converted the chairlift into a double-seater.

Boyne's first years were not easy ones, but Kircher's tenacity and love for the sport of skiing, as well as the continuing improvements he made to the facility, helped bring in more business each season. To teach the sport to beginners, he hired Stein Eriksen, an Olympic gold medalist from Norway. Eriksen soon recommended Othmar Schneider, a gold medalist from Austria, who would run the Boyne ski school for many years. By the early 1950s Boyne Mountain was selling up to 500 family ski packages per week, and attracting 1,500 skiers on weekends.

Opening of Gatlinburg Sky Lift: 1954

In 1953 Kircher was asked to build a chairlift in Gatlinburg, Tennessee, by the owner of a local hotel, who had read about the installation of the Boyne lift in *AAA* magazine. The canny Kircher responded that he would build it only if he could own it, and after securing a 99-year lease on the property, he installed a used chairlift he had bought for $3,000 from a ski resort in California.

From the time it began operations in 1954, the Gatlinburg Sky Lift, which overlooked the Great Smoky Mountains National Park, proved a highly profitable enterprise. With the steady revenue it provided, Kircher was able to add features to Boyne Mountain, and later buy a second ski hill, Harbor Highlands, a few miles to the north. It was opened in 1964 under the name Boyne Highlands with the first triple-chair ski lift in the world.

In addition to being a sharp businessman, Kircher had by now shown himself to be a talented engineer and inventor. Over the years he developed a variety of new techniques and equipment for grooming slopes, as well as a patented snow-making machine. The Boyne Snowmaker (also known as the Highlands Snow Gun) used just one-fourth the power of earlier snow-making equipment, was quieter, and was the first to operate at temperatures just below freezing. Like a number of Kircher's other innovations, it came to be used widely within the industry.

Opening of Heather Golf Course: 1967

Seeking to attract business during the warm summer months, in part so that he could keep his staff employed year-round, Kircher had early on added a golf course called Hemlock at Boyne Mountain, which he had built himself using his father's Ford tractor. He became even more interested in golf after buying Boyne Highlands, and in 1965 hired renowned designer Robert Trent Jones to plan a new course for the bottom of the hill. Dubbed Heather, it opened in 1967 and was soon named to *Golf Digest*'s list of the top 100 courses in the country.

By 1970 Boyne Country U.S.A., as Kircher's operation had become known, was the largest ski area in the upper Midwest. Though the hills were not huge, they offered well-groomed slopes, guaranteed snow via an extensive network of snow-making machines, and short waits for ski lifts. Boyne now had a total of four ridges within a 27-mile radius that featured 53 different ski slopes, the most recent additions being Thunder Mountain and Walloon Hills. Kircher also had an extensive instructional program, with a staff of nearly four dozen.

Overnight accommodations were available at Boyne Mountain, whose Boyne, Boynehof, and Edelweiss Lodges offered a total of 170 rooms, each with a private bath, while the Boyne Highlands Lodge had space for 250 guests. The four ski areas operated a total of 12 chairlifts, three T-bars, three Pomalifts, and four rope tows. The most expensive lift ticket was $7.50 per day. Adding to his earlier innovations, Kircher had also introduced the world's first quadruple lift in 1969.

The late 1960s saw Boyne's business fall off as Midwesterners began taking advantage of cheaper airfares and travel packages to ski resorts in the Rocky Mountains, and Kircher fought this tide by ramping up his golf offerings (adding the Alpine course to Boyne Mountain in 1970), and by seeking out convention business. In 1972 he opened the Boyne Mountain Civic Center, which featured meeting rooms with a capacity of 850.

Acquisition of Big Sky: 1976

The 1970s also saw Kircher begin looking at adding a ski operation in the West. After passing on chances to buy resorts in Jackson Hole, Wyoming, and Telluride, Colorado, he settled on Big Sky, Montana, which had been steadily losing money since opening in 1974. In 1976 Kircher acquired the resort for $1 million and the assumption of $7.5 million in debt.

Big Sky at this time featured three lifts, a gondola, and the 200-room Huntley Inn, named after cofounder Chet Huntley, the NBC newscaster. Its two peaks measured 11,166 feet and 8,800 feet, making it Montana's tallest ski area. After the acquisition, Kircher's organization began upgrading, adding accommodations and new runs.

Growth at Boyne's Michigan resorts continued during the 1970s and early 1980s, with additions including a tennis center and a cross-country ski center. New golf courses were also opened in 1974 and 1985. In the late 1970s the money-losing Walloon Hills area was donated to a charitable organization that offered skiing opportunities to handicapped children.

The year 1986 saw Kircher expand his Western holdings with the purchase of a resort in Brighton, Utah. Operated since the late 1930s, the Brighton Ski Bowl boasted a 10,200-foot peak. Boyne soon began adding new lifts and accommodations.

In 1989 Boyne Highlands opened its third golf course, as well as the Heather Highlands Inn Convention Center, which featured 72 suites of rooms. The following year a new country club and golf center were also added. The Donald Ross Memorial course at Boyne Highlands duplicated famous holes at Ross-designed courses around the United States. The year 1990 also saw installation of Michigan's first high-speed detachable chairlift at Boyne Highlands.

Developments of the early 1990s included construction of a new conference center at Big Sky and new lodging at Boyne Highlands and Brighton Bowl, as well as the 1992 acquisition of a golf course in Naples, Florida, that became known as Boyne South Resort. A new golf course and new ski runs and chairlifts were also added to Boyne Highlands and Boyne Mountain, including the first high-speed six-seat chairlift in the United States.

In 1994 the company signed an agreement to build and manage the Bay Harbor Golf Club and the Inn at Bay Harbor, part of a new resort located on five miles of Lake Michigan coastline near Petoskey that had once been the site of a cement plant and limestone quarry. Bay Harbor, which was being developed by CMS Land Company and Victor International, would also feature luxury homes, condominiums, and a yacht harbor.

In 1995 the $3 million Lone Peak Tram was opened at Big Sky Resort, which enabled it to claim the most total vertical feet of skiing in the United States, 4,180. The tram utilized two cylindrical cars, each of which could carry 15 passengers to a height of 11,150 feet, just 16 feet below the tip of the mountain. Expert skiers could descend on the peak's most challenging runs, while others could enjoy the view of Yellowstone National Park and three different states. Also during the year the firm abandoned a five-year effort to secure approval to expand Brighton Ski Bowl, after encountering strong opposition from environmentalists and area residents.

Purchase of Crystal Mountain Resort: 1997

In early 1997 Boyne reached an agreement to acquire Crystal Mountain Resort in Washington State, which had been operating in the red for some time. It was situated near Mount Rainier on 4,300 acres of land leased from the U.S. Forest Service. Founded in 1962, it boasted the state's largest vertical drop (3,100 feet), ten lifts, conference facilities, and other accommodations. The company committed to spending $15 million over ten years to make improvements. At about the same time Boyne acquired a 50 percent stake in the 18-hole Crooked Tree Golf Club in Petoskey, Michigan, near Bay Harbor.

In 1998 the *Wall Street Journal* named Bay Harbor one of the top five destination resorts in the U.S., and *Golf* magazine rated Boyne's new Arthur Hills-designed course there eighth on its list of the top 100 public courses in the country. Boyne USA

Resorts, as the firm was now known, continued to be headed by 82-year old-founder Everett Kircher, though many of the day-to-day operations were now managed by his four children. Stephen, a talented golfer who had helped design the course at Bay Harbor, ran the firm's Michigan and Montana operations, while John was in charge of its Western holdings, Amy handled the golf and real estate operations of Boyne South, and Kathryn was in charge of Boyne Design Group, which designed interiors for the company's resorts.

Expansion continued in the fall of 1999 when Boyne USA Resorts bought 51 percent of Bavarian Ski Village and Golf Shops, a 50-year-old, Michigan-based chain of eight shops located in the Detroit suburbs, Ann Arbor, East Lansing, and Grand Rapids. They were subsequently remodeled and re-christened Boyne Country Sports, with the Bavarian Village name used for ski departments within the shops. The stores soon boosted their clothing offerings and began to sell lift tickets and travel packages to Boyne properties.

In December 1999 the 130-room Inn at Bay Harbor officially opened, winning favorable reviews for its plush appointments. The month also saw Boyne founder Everett Kircher named to *Ski* magazine's list of "The 100 Most Influential Skiers of All Time."

In March 2000 a new ten-story, $45 million hotel, the Summit, opened at Big Sky, part of the company's ongoing efforts to bring the resort into the black. It had lost money for all 19 years of Boyne's ownership, due to a myriad of problems including its out-of-the way location and inherited sewage, power, and construction issues. Early the next year Boyne also announced plans for a new $400 million, ten-year expansion, which would add chairlifts, more than 100 shops and restaurants, a spa, and more conference facilities. A new Holiday Inn Express hotel opened at the resort during the year as well.

Acquisition of Cypress Mountain: 2001

In February 2001 the Boyne USA empire expanded yet again with the purchase of Cypress Mountain near Vancouver, British Columbia. It offered both cross-country and downhill skiing, with night skiing on some runs and limited amenities including a cafeteria. The one-time public recreation area had been run by a private company since 1984.

In August 2001 the U.S. Forest Service issued a draft environmental-impact statement which approved most of Boyne's plans for a $100 million expansion to Washington's Crystal Mountain, which included a tram to the peak, more runs and lifts, a new retreat center on a ridge, and other additions. Later in the year, construction was halted on the recently begun Boyne Mountain Grand Lodge and Spa as lenders pulled back lines of credit due to the tightening economy and the post-September 11 travel industry slowdown. On January 16, 2002, Boyne USA Resorts founder Everett Kircher died at the age of 85.

In 2003 it was announced that portions of the 2010 Winter Olympics would be held at Cypress Mountain near Vancouver, which was slated to receive numerous improvements by that time. In the fall the Inn at Bay Harbor became affiliated with the exclusive Renaissance Hotels & Resorts chain, and construction resumed at the Boyne Mountain Resort and Spa.

In early 2004 Boyne USA filed a lawsuit against Moonlight Basin ski area, which was building a resort on the other side of Montana's Lone Peak from Big Sky. The suit charged Moonlight Basin with using an avalanche control device to fire explosives toward Big Sky, as well as other forms of trespassing.

In 2005 the $70 million Boyne Mountain Resort and Spa was opened to the public, along with a new indoor water park, which was touted as the largest in Michigan. The additions were part of a $250 million, multiyear program to evolve Boyne Mountain into a four-season family destination. Other attractions were also in the works, including a live music series.

Nearly 60 years after Everett Kircher paid $1 for an undeveloped mountain on a dirt road in northern Michigan, Boyne USA Resorts had grown into one of the largest ski and golf resort operators in the United States. The firm was in the midst of its most ambitious renovation efforts to date, which would add hundreds of millions of dollars worth of new infrastructure and accommodations to its properties.

Principal Operating Units

Boyne Mountain; Boyne Highlands; The Inn at Bay Harbor; Bay Harbor Golf Club; Gatlinburg Sky Lift; Big Sky Resort; Crystal Mountain; Brighton Resort; Boyne South Resort; Cypress Mountain (Canada); Boyne Country Sports.

Principal Competitors

Vail Resorts Inc.; Intrawest Corp.; American Skiing Co.; Booth Creek Ski Holdings, Inc.

Further Reading

Alva, Marilyn, "Skiing Mogul Everett Kircher," *Investor's Business Daily*, September 17, 2003.

Anderson, Scott, "Boyne Founder Isn't Packing Up His Skis Anytime Soon," *Grand Rapids Press*, August 30, 1998, p. F5.

"Boyne USA Founder Helped Shape Ski, Golf Industries; Everett Kircher Dies at Age 85," *Grand Rapids Press*, January 18, 2002, p. B1.

Bradley, Carol, "Huntley's Dream Is 25 Years Old—Would He Recognize It?," *Associated Press Newswires*, December 25, 1999.

DuFresne, Jim, "Boyne-Bavarian Village Merger May Greatly Impact Industry," *Grand Rapids Press*, October 23, 1999, p. D3.

——, "Boyne New Runs Draw Intermediates, Families," *Grand Rapids Press*, March 8, 1997, p. D4.

——, "First-Ever Chairlift Still in Use at Boyne," *Grand Rapids Press*, January 15, 2000, p. D3.

——, "Kircher: Skiing Remains King at Boyne USA," *Grand Rapids Press*, January 15, 2000, p. D3.

——, "Kircher's Vision Shaped State Ski, Resort Industry," *Grand Rapids Press*, January 15, 2000, p. D1.

French, Brett, "Big Sky Expands with New Resort," *Billings Gazette*, April 30, 2004, p. B1.

Grass, Ray, "Ski Resort of the Week: Brighton," *Deseret Morning News*, March 3, 2005, p. C2.

Hill, Kelly, "Boyne Transforms into Four-Season Resort Destination," *Grand Rapids Press*, April 10, 2005, p. 8.

Holt, John, "Good Times Are Dawning at Big Sky," *Denver Post*, December 9, 1990, p. 1T.

Kamb, Louis, "Ski Area Expansion Closer for Crystal Mountain," *Seattle Post-Intelligencer*, August 23, 2004, p. A1.

Kircher, Everett, Stephen Kanisse, and Robert Vincent, *Everett Kircher, Michigan's Resort Pioneer,* Bloomfield Hills, Mich.: Vincent and Associates, 1998.

"Michigan-Based Boyne USA Sues Moonlight Basin Ski Area in Montana," *Associated Press Newswires*, February 19, 2004.

Mottram, Bob, "New Owner, and New Features, Highlight Season for Crystal Mountain Ski Area," *Associated Press Newswires*, December 12, 1997.

Phipps, John E., "New Jewel Sparkles on Little Traverse Bay," *Grand Rapids Press*, June 27, 1999, p. M1.

Roelofs, Ted, "Sloping Upward; After 2 Years, Work Resumes on Boyne's $70 Million Lodge," *Grand Rapids Press*, December 28, 2003, p. A1.

Saxon, Wolfgang, "Everett Kircher, Ski Resort Owner, Dies at 85," *New York Times*, January 24, 2002, p. 7.

"Shareholders Vote to Sell Home-Owned Ski Area," *Associated Press Newswires*, March 28, 1997.

Strauss, Michael, "Boyne Falls Not the Alps But Is Enticing to Skiers," *New York Times*, Dec. 14, 1972.

——, "Skiing Is on the Upswing in the Upper Midwest," *New York Times*, January 18, 1970.

Sylvain, Rick, "Isolation at Big Sky Resorts Blessing—And Curse," *Salt Lake Tribune*, February 6, 1994, p. H2.

Thompson, Chris, "International Instruction: Ski School at Boyne Highlands Sports Austrian Flavor," *Grand Rapids Press*, January 5, 1991, p. D1.

White, Dana, "Next Stop, Lone Peak; Will a Much-Anticipated Tram Give Big Sky, Montana, Big-Time Visibility?," *Skiing*, February 1, 1996, p. 26.

Woolf, Jim, "Brighton Ski Resort Abandons Expansion," *Salt Lake Tribune*, June 19, 1995, p. D1.

—Frank Uhle

Britannia Soft Drinks Ltd. (Britvic)

Britvic House, Broomfield Road
Chelmsford, Essex CM1 1TU
United Kingdom
Telephone: +44-1245-261871
Fax: +44-1245-267147
Web site: http://www.britvic.co.uk

Private Company
Founded: Mid-1800s as British Vitamin Products Company
Sales: £600 million ($1.1 billion) (2004)
NAIC: 312111 Soft Drink Manufacturing

Britannia Soft Drinks Ltd. is the holding company for its more well-known business, Britvic, the number two-selling soft drinks company in the United Kingdom. Britvic commands a strong stable of brands, including the Britvic fruit juices and mixers lines. The company also holds the franchises for producing and bottling Pepsi Cola and 7Up in the United Kingdom. Other prominent national and regional brands include Robinsons, R Whites lemonades, the youth-oriented Tango brand, and J20, targeting the 18- to 45-year-old segment. Britvic has been making acquisitions in the first half of the 2000s in order to boost its portfolio. In 2000, for example, the company acquired Orchard Drinks and Purdey's, followed by the purchase of Red Devil, an "energy" drink, in 2002. At the end of 2004, the company boosted its profile in the fast-growing bottled water market with the purchase of the Ben Shaws water division of soft drinks maker Birkby. Britvic itself is controlled by the Intercontinental Hotels Group, which owns 50 percent, as well as minority investors Allied Domecq and Whitbread, each holding 23.75 percent. PepsiCo Inc. owns the remainder of the company. Britvic called off its planned 2005 initial public offering, although the company was committed to launching a public offering before 2008. In 2004, Britvic's sales reached approximately £600 million ($1.1 billion).

Pharmacist Origins in the 19th Century

Britvic originated as a pharmacy side business in Chelmsford, in Essex, England, in the mid-19th century. The Victorian era, and a prevailing hostility toward alcoholic beverages, en-couraged the development of a whole new range of so-called "soft drinks." Many of the new beverages used carbon dioxide injected into water, a method developed toward the end of the 18th century and popularized by Schweppes in London.

The rising popularity of "effervescent" drinks in the mid-19th century coincided with the development of new bottle-stopping technologies and early industrialized production techniques. At the same time, the appearance of early advertising methods enabled many beverages to achieve a certain degree of recognition, even on a national scale. A large number of drinks makers, many of them pharmacists with laboratory experience, began developing their own soft drink recipes, mixing fruit juices, sugar, and other ingredients. Pharmacists were especially drawn to the development of healthful beverages, such as tonics and other soft drinks. Although a few beverages managed to achieve a degree of recognition on a national level, many others became solid regional or local favorites.

The British Vitamin Products Company, as the Chelmsford business became known, developed a broad range of soft drinks through the end of the 19th century and into the 20th century. In addition to the highly popular lemonades, the company developed its own tonic recipes, and also produced nonalcoholic ales. The company also began bottling and selling mineral waters.

The company's transition to its modern form began toward the middle of the 20th century. By the 1930s, the British Vitamin Products Company had come under the leadership of Ralph Chapman. Recognizing that the Depression era had begun to take a toll on the health of his soft drink customers, Chapman conceived of a means of bottling fruit juices in order to supply much-needed vitamin C at affordable prices. In 1938, Chapman began packaging fruit juices in small bottles, using a method that enabled him to bottle juices without the need for preservatives.

Consumer response was immediately favorable, and Chapman began plans for a wider rollout of the bottled juice line. Yet the outbreak of World War II halted the company's plans. Restrictions were put into place not only on the sale of fruit juices, but, as part of the sugar rationing effort, on the soft drink industry in general. During the war, the government rationalized the soft drink industry, nationalizing the sector and establishing a narrow field of just six permitted "standard" drinks.

The restrictions on the soft drink industry were lifted after World War II. By 1949, the company was finally able to roll out the full-scale launch of its fruit juice line. The company became the first in England to bottle fruit juices, and the small-format bottles, marketed under the Britvic brand name, became a popular soft drink choice.

Soft Drink Boom in the 1950s

Soft drink consumption in general rose steadily in the United Kingdom through the 1950s. A number of factors contributed to the new success of the category, not the least of which was the appearance of television—keeping people at home and on their couches—and the concurrent appearance of new advertising possibilities. Britvic profited from the rising demand, and in the early 1950s built one of the largest fruit drink processing and bottling facilities in the world.

The growing sales of soft drinks placed pressure on other parts of the U.K. beverage sector, namely the alcoholic beverage producers. This encouraged a number of the country's winemakers, distillers, and brewers to extend their operations to include soft drinks into the mid-1950s. Among them, Vine Products, a group involved in the wine trade and that also produced the sparkling drink Babycham, as well as a number of liquors and other alcoholic beverages, bought control of Britvic in 1954.

The 1960s saw an intensification of the consolidation of the British beverage sector. In 1961, Britvic became part of a larger operation when Vine Products merged with Showerings and Waterways to form Showerings, Vine Products & Waterways. Later in the decade, that company entered talks with brewing giant Allied Breweries. In 1968, Allied agreed to purchase Showerings, Vine Products & Waterways, for more than £100 million. Britvic then became the operating company for Allied's soft drinks division.

The link with a major brewer—and its vast, nationally operating network of "tied" pubs—became the signal for an extension of the Britvic brand into new product categories. In 1973, for example, the company launched a new line covering the "mixer" soft drinks category, producing its own tonic, bitter lemon, and dry ginger ale. Britvic's relationship to Allied gave it ready access to its parent company's pub network, ensuring strong sales.

Britvic also joined in the newly developing diet drink category, launching its first effort, Slimsta, in the early 1970s. By then, the company adopted its brand name as its own, becoming Britvic Limited in 1971. In another move to take advantage of Allied's pub network, Britvic also launched draught versions of its most popular soft drinks, starting in 1972.

Through the end of the 1970s and into the 1980s, Britvic continued to seek new brand formulas to attract the British soft drink consumer. In 1977, for example, the company launched an adult-oriented beverage, Britvic 55, which was available only in pubs.

Acquiring Scale for the New Century

In the meantime, Britain's soft drinks producers had been facing increasing pressure from a new type of competitor. Cola drinks had been introduced from the United States in the 1950s and, backed by strong marketing campaigns, had succeeded in capturing a major share of the U.K. market. The popularity of U.S. soft drinks, especially Coca-Cola and Pepsi (produced and bottled under license in the United Kingdom), led Britvic to seek its own U.S. brands to license. In 1982, the company launched its first licensed soft drink, Dr. Pepper. This launch also marked the U.S. brand's first appearance in the United Kingdom. The company backed up the launch with a marketing drive costing some £600,000.

In 1985, Allied Lyons sold 50 percent of Britvic to Australia's Castlemaine-Tooheys, part of Alan Bond's booming conglomerate in the 1980s, in a share swap deal. By 1986, Bond had turned Britvic around, selling it off to the Bass brewery, pubs, and beverages group. Bass then merged Britvic with its other soft drink holdings, including Britannia Soft Drinks and Canada Dry Rawlings, which also owned HD Rawlings, producer of the R. White soft drinks brand. The resulting company was renamed as Britvic Soft Drinks Limited.

The newly enlarged Britvic began acquiring new brands for its portfolio. In 1986, the company acquired the Tango soft drink brand, originally launched in the early 1950s. Under Britvic, Tango was successfully repositioned as an "edgy" youth brand.

In 1987, Britvic scored a major coup, when it acquired the U.K. production and bottling rights for the Pepsi brand, as well as for PepsiCo's recently acquired 7Up brand. Under Britvic, Pepsi, which had struggled to make headway against Coca-Cola's dominance in the United Kingdom, now rose to become one of the country's major brands.

Into the early 1990s, majority owner Bass, under pressure from the British Mergers and Monopolies Commission, appeared set to sell its 51 percent stake in Britvic to PepsiCo. Yet the deal, which would have included the 20 stakes held by both Allied-Lyons and Whitbread, ran into disagreements, and by 1994, the parties agreed to call off negotiations.

Instead, Britvic began seeking new expansion opportunities. In 1994, the company gained the license for launching Liptonice in the United Kingdom, another brand in the PepsiCo stable. In 1995, the company purchased rival U.K. soft drinks maker Robinsons. That company had been founded in the early 19th century as Robinson & Bellville, becoming famous for its Barley Water, and for its association with the Wimbledon tennis tournament, before becoming part of the Reckitt Coleman foods group. Backed by Britvic's marketing muscle, the Robinsons brand entered a new growth phase, and by 1998 had grown into the country's 11th largest seller in the supermarket and grocery channel.

Britvic's next major expansion effort came in 2000, when the company acquired Orchid Drinks. That company had been part of the Camerons Brewery, operated by the Brent Walker group, before being spun off in a management buyout in 1992. The addition of Orchid brought Britvic a number of new brands, including Amé, Purdey's, and Aqua Libra.

The rising sales of bottled waters led Britvic to enter this area as well in 2001, with the acquisition of the marketing rights

Key Dates:

1938: British Vitamin Product Company (Britvic), originally founded in the mid-19th century to produce soft drinks, develops a method for bottling fruit juices without preservatives; production is suspended at the outbreak of World War II.

1945: Britvic begins construction on a new processing and bottling facility, then the largest in the world.

1949: The Britvic fruit juice brand is relaunched.

1954: Vine Products, maker of Babycham, among other beverages, acquires Britvic; the company later becomes part of the Allied Breweries group in the late 1960s.

1971: The company changes its name to Britvic Limited.

1972: The company launches mixer soft drinks.

1973: A draught version of the company's soft drinks is launched.

1977: Britvic 55, a pub-only adult soft drink, is launched.

1982: The company acquires the U.K. license for the Dr. Pepper brand.

1985: Castlemaine Tooheys acquires 50 percent of Britvic.

1986: Castlemaine Tooheys sells its stake in Britvic to Bass, which merges Britvic with its other soft drink holdings, including Britannia Soft Drinks and Canada Dry Rawlings, as Britvic Soft Drinks Limited; Britvic acquires the Tango soft drink brand.

1987: Britvic acquires the U.K. license for Pepsi and 7Up.

1994: Britvic acquires the U.K. license for Liptonice.

1995: Britvic acquires Robinsons, maker of the Barley Water soft drink.

2000: Britvic acquires Orchid Soft Drinks, maker of adult drinks Amé, Aqua Libra, and Purdey's.

2002: Britvic acquires the Red Devil energy drink.

2004: Britvic announces its plan to list on the London Stock Exchange in 2005.

2005: Britvic announces its decision to suspend the public offering.

for the Abbey Well brand in parts of the United Kingdom. The following year, Britvic bought Red Devil, an ''energy'' drink, in order to capture a share of the relatively young ''stimulant drink'' market.

Into the mid-2000s, Britvic's ownership once again appeared up in the air. In 2000, Bass announced its intention to split off its brewery operations as a separate company and transform itself into a new company, the hotels operator Six Continents, subsequently renamed as Intercontinental Hotels Group. As part of its transformation, the company let it be known that it was interested in selling off its majority stake in Britvic's parent company, Britannia Soft Drinks.

Britvic was put up for sale in 2001. Yet PepsiCo, which held some 10 percent of Britvic—and, more important, owned the Pepsi brand, which by then had become a major source of Britvic's sales and profits—balked at the sale. Among the reasons given for ending the offer was PepsiCo's reluctance to allow Britvic into the hands of private equity investment groups. A future sell-off of Britvic might open the possibility of PepsiCo's arch-rival Coca-Cola gaining control of its British bottler.

Britvic's other shareholders, however, continued to push for a means to reduce or sell off their stakes in the company. By the end of 2004, the companies had negotiated a new 15-year licensing agreement with PepsiCo, a move that served to nullify any threat of a takeover by Coca-Cola. As part of the agreement, PepsiCo agreed to the principle of a public offering by Britvic by 2008 at the latest. Britvic then announced its intention to list on the London Stock Exchange in early 2005.

Yet in January of that year, after poor weather in the summer season had depressed the company's net profits, Britvic's shareholders announced that they were suspending the plan for a public offering, citing fears that the company would not be fully valued. Regardless of its ownership structure, Britvic remained a key player in the British soft drinks industry in the new century.

Principal Subsidiaries

Britvic.

Principal Competitors

Procter & Gamble Company; PepsiCo Inc.; The Coca-Cola Company; Sara Lee Corporation; Groupe Danone; Cadbury Schweppes PLC; Interbrew SA-NV; SABMiller PLC; Mitchell and Butlers PLC; AG Barr PLC.

Further Reading

Almond, Siobhan, and Josh Kosman, ''Buyout Firms Prepare for Third Round in Britvic Auction,'' *Daily Deal,* September 14, 2001.

Benady, David, ''Brands Shift Upscale to Escape Food Curbs,'' *Marketing Week,* February 24, 2005, p. 25.

''Britvic Aims New Tango Variant at Older Market,'' *Marketing Week,* February 17, 2005, p. 8.

''Britvic: No Soft Touch,'' *Super Marketing,* November 18, 1994, p. S8.

Hall, Richard, ''Their Cup Runneth Over,'' *Grocer,* May 5, 2001, p. 58.

''IHG to Sell Hotels Worth Pounds 1 bn and Float Britvic,'' *Financial Times,* March 12, 2004, p. 22.

Kemeny, Lucinda, ''UK-Based Drinks Maker Britvic Postpones Seeking Stock Market Listing,'' *Daily Mail,* January 16, 2005.

——, ''UK Drinks Company Britvic Gets Ready for Floatation,'' *Daily Mail,* December 26, 2004.

Lewis, Ellen, ''Charge Your Glass for Britvic's Marsden,'' *Brand Strategy,* February 2003, p. 14.

''A New Peak for Mountain Range,'' *Grocer,* February 12, 2005, p. 53.

Walsh, Dominic, ''Domecq Insists That Britvic Price Tag Is Too Low,'' *Times,* October 22, 2004, p. 52.

Yelland, Jane, ''Britvic Buys Ben Shaws Division,'' *Huddersfield Daily Examiner,* November 2, 2004, p. 2.

—M.L. Cohen

THE BRITISH MUSEUM

The British Museum

> **Great Russell Street**
> **London WC1B 3DG**
> **United Kingdom**
> **Telephone: +44-20-7323-8000**
> **Fax: +44-20-7323-8616**
> **Web site: http://www.thebritishmuseum.ac.uk**
>
> *State-Owned Company*
> *Incorporated:* 1753
> *Employees:* 1,047
> *Sales:* $103.9 million (2004)
> *NAIC:* 712110 Museums

Founded in 1753, The British Museum is not only one of the world's oldest, but also one of the world's largest museums, with a collection spanning more than seven million objects. The museum's range of art and antiquities reaches back some two million years, and the museum remains one of the most important repositories of artifacts retracing human civilization. Among the objects found at the museum are treasures such as the Rosetta Stone, which provided the means for decoding Egyptian hieroglyphs; the Elgin Marbles, a collection of sculptures from the ancient Greek Parthenon; the Black Obelisk; and African and Asian collections. The museum also boasts a prominent collection of artifacts from the time of the Roman occupation of Britain. The British Museum has provided free and unlimited access to its collections for nearly 200 years, and remains one of the country's top tourist attractions. Each year, the museum records more than 5.5 million visitors. The museum is supported by government grants, through the Department of Culture, Media and Sport, as well as through corporate sponsorships and through ancillary sales of gifts, books, and other merchandise, sold directly by the museum or under license. Yet these funds are rarely enough to cover the museum's entire budget, and the museum often operates under budget deficits that have reached as high as £8 million in the early 2000s. Neil MacGregor, formerly with the London Gallery, is the British Museum's director.

18th-Century Origins

As with the world's other great museums, including the Louvre in Paris and the Hermitage in Saint Petersburg, the British Museum is the result of the surge in interest in ancient cultures and civilizations that took place during the Renaissance era. The period saw the appearance of a great many naturalists, archeologists, anthropologists, botanists, ornithologists, and the like, many of whom, whether working in an amateur or professional capacity, amassed extraordinary collections of artifacts, specimens, and species from all over the world.

Britain's status as a naval and colonial force placed it at the center of this new breed of scientific exploration. The scope of the British empire made it possible for its subjects to scour the Earth in search of new treasures. Among them was physician and naturalist Sir Hans Sloane, born in 1660. Sloane's interest in naturalism led him to accept the position as physician to the governor of Jamaica in 1687. In less than two years, Sloane had collected more than 800 species of plants and other living specimens. Back in London, Sloane became quite wealthy, serving as physician to, among others, King George I, Queen Anne, and King George II.

Sloane's interest in collecting remained unabated, however. Indeed, Sloane went on to buy the collections of others, such as those of William Charlton and James Petiver. Sloane's collection of books, coins, artifacts, and natural history specimens had grown so large that he was forced to buy a neighboring house in order to have enough space. At his death in 1753, Sloane's collection consisted of more than 71,000 items.

Sloane's will sought to preserve the integrity of his collection by stipulating that the entire collection become the property of King George II and the British people, in exchange for a payment of £20,000 to Sloane's two daughters. Failing that, the collection was to be sold off in pieces to various overseas institutions. Although the king at first remained uninterested in the collection, the British parliament quickly passed an act establishing a new British Museum. At the same time, the museum was to incorporate another government holding, the Cotton collection of manuscripts, held by the government since 1700. Parliament also decided to spend £10,000 for the purchase of the Harleian manuscripts. These three collections then formed the basis of what was to become one of the world's largest and most respected museums.

The museum's collection was boosted in 1757 when King George II added another collection of manuscripts, the Old Royal Library. At the same time, the museum received the copyright to these publications. A location was found in the Montagu House, a mansion in the Bloomsbury section of London, which was to remain the museum's site into the 21st century. The museum's gardens were first opened to the public in 1757. In 1759, the museum itself was ready to open its doors to the public.

From the outset, the British Museum was established as belonging to the British people, with free access offered to all. In the early years, however, admission was granted on the basis of tickets, which were obtained in advance. Visits were limited to escorted tours in small groups. These practices were abandoned in 1810, when the museum ended the ticket system and escorted visits were no longer required.

By then, the museum's collection had grown substantially. Among the objects acquired during the 19th century were the famed Rosetta Stone, from which Egyptian hieroglyphs were decoded, acquired in 1802, and the Charles Townley collection of classical sculptures. This collection led to the establishment of a new Townley Gallery, focused on classical and Egyptian artifacts.

Golden Age in the Late 19th Century

The British Museum's important—if controversial—association with Greek civilization took off in 1814 when the museum bought the Phigaleian Marbles, a series of sculptures from the Temple of Apollo in Bassae. Two years later, the museum acquired the Elgin Marbles as well, a series of sculptures from the Parthenon sold to the museum by Lord Elgin.

In 1823, Robert Smirke designed a new building to house the museum's growing collection, which included the King's Library, donated to the museum by King George IV. Work on the new building was to last until 1852. Upon its completion, the museum launched construction of a new structure, the Reading Room, which was completed in 1857.

Into the mid-19th century, the British Museum not only emerged as one of the world's foremost repositories of ancient human civilization, but also had become an active participant in the search for more of the world's treasures. The museum

began sponsoring excavations and other scientific explorations, such as the work conducted by Austen Henry Layard in the 1840s in Assyria.

The last half of the 19th century saw the museum enter its Golden Age with the emerging triumph of science over religion and the development of new scientific disciplines, particularly the development of new conservation techniques. The museum, therefore, not only played a prominent role in the discovery and categorization of new artifacts, it also became an important part of the effort to conserve and restore the world's antiquities. The museum's development in conservation techniques ultimately resulted in the creation of a temporary research laboratory in 1920, which in turn led to the founding of the permanent Research Laboratory in 1931.

Other important additions continued to flow into the museum through the end of the century. In 1863, for example, Charles Turtle Wood, under the museum's auspices, began excavating at the Temple of Artemis in Ephesos, considered one of the Seven Wonders of the Ancient World. In 1869, the museum received the famed Island Statue from Queen Victoria. By then, too, the museum had been given the collection of ethnographical and prehistoric artifacts gathered by Henry Christy, on his death in 1865.

The museum began introducing electricity in the 1870s, lighting the Reading Room first in 1879 before extending lighting throughout the museum in 1890. The Reading Room would host the studies of a number of prominent personalities of the era, including Charles Dickens, Karl Marx, and Vladimir Ilich Lenin.

Financial Crises into the 21st Century

An important moment in the museum's history came in 1880 when the museum's natural history collections were transferred to a new building in South Kensington. The transfer process was completed in 1883, and the site later became known as the British Natural History Museum.

Into the World War I period, the museum continued to expand, adding the White Wing, fronting Montagu Street in 1885, and the King Edward VII Galleries, completed in 1914. Fears of bombing at the end of World War I led the museum to close and move part of its collection to safety in 1918. The museum was to come under still heavier threat during World War II, however. Evacuation began in 1939. In 1941, the building was hit by an incendiary raid. For the duration, however, much of the museum's collection was housed in an underground facility at Bradford on Avon.

Changes were in store for the museum during the postwar period. The first discussions were held in 1943 on splitting off the museum's library. In 1963, the passage of the New British Museum Act formally separated the museum and its natural history component. This act was followed ten years later with the British Library act of 1972 creating a single British Library, which included the museum's libraries. The new library was established in 1973; the collection, however, remained at the museum until the opening of a new library at St. Pancras in 1997.

Funding for the museum, and the willingness to increase the museum's budget, varied considerably with successive British

Key Dates:

1753: The British Museum is established by an act of Parliament, based on the collections of Sloane, Cotton, and Harleian.
1759: The British Museum is first opened to the public.
1810: The ticket admission system ends.
1842: Construction begins on a new, permanent building.
1931: The museum establishes a dedicated Research Laboratory, the first in the world devoted to development of conservation techniques.
1963: The New British Museum Act formally separates the natural history collection, establishing the British Natural History Museum.
1972: The museum library is placed under a new, separate body, the British Library.
1973: The British Museum Company Ltd. and the British Museum Press are launched.
1997: The library moves into a new facility at St. Pancras.
2000: The $145 million Great Court is opened.
2003: The museum celebrates its 250th anniversary.

governments, and the British Museum often found itself confronting fresh financial crises. Forced to find new ways of supplementing its budget—and barred from charging admission—the museum turned to merchandising in the early 1970s. In 1973, the museum established The British Museum Company Ltd., which became responsible for operating the museum's retail wing, as well as overseeing its wholesale sales, production of replicas of objects in the collection, and licensing of the museum brand and logo. The museum also established the British Museum Press that year, which became the world's leading museum-based publishing company.

Yet these funds were not always enough to overcome the museum's increasingly recurrent budget crises. In the mid-1990s, the museum's financial difficulties erupted in a scandal, when, in 1996, a commission discovered that the museum had been operating without an accountant. This discovery came on top of an extended period of relative budget indifference: For more than a decade, the government-provided increases in the museum's annual budget failed to keep up with inflation. As a result, by the time a new financial crisis emerged in the early 2000s, the museum's budget had in fact decreased by some 30 percent in real currency.

Adding to the museum's difficulties was a massive project, worth some $145 million, to cover the Great Court. Yet funding for the project, in large part through the National Lottery, came with a catch: that the Great Court, and hence the museum itself, remain open until late at night. Yet the Great Court proved far less attractive—at least in the evening—than had been expected, and the expenses of keeping the museum open only added to the museum's financial woes.

Worse, the tourist drop-off after the September 11 attacks in 2001 saw a huge slump in admission, which fell to just 4.2 million from the museum's more usual 5.5 million visitors per year. At the same time, the museum had been planning a new expansion, a new study center slated at a cost of $118 million, as a centerpiece for its future strategy. Yet the museum was forced to recognize that it could not afford to operate the new center, and the project was dropped after incurring more than $17 million in expenses.

By 2002, the museum was operating with a deficit of more than £6.5 million. Forced to cut back on services, it closed many of the galleries and opened a number only part-time. The museum also began a painful staff-cutting exercise, sinking employee morale. By June 2002, the threat of further staff cuts led to a strike among the museum's employees—the first time the museum had been shut down by strike since its founding.

In response, the museum brought in a new director, Neil MacGregor, who had formerly headed the London Gallery, to direct the British Museum. MacGregor joined in time to help celebrate the musuem's 250th anniversary in 2003. Yet the new director also joined in time to confront a new and growing controversy, that of the demands by certain countries for the return of their artifacts. A famous example of this trend was the Greek government's demand for the return of the Elgin Marbles, a request steadfastly refused by the British Museum. After more than 250 years, the museum remained a symbol of the Renaissance era's thirst for knowledge, and one of the world's leading repositories for the history of human civilization.

Principal Subsidiaries

The British Museum Company Ltd.; The British Museum Press.

Principal Competitors

Metropolitan Museum; The Louvre; Berlin State Museum; Smithsonian Institution; State Hermitage Museum.

Further Reading

Appleyard, Bryan, ''Roll Away the Stones,'' *Sunday Times,* November 30, 2003, p. 10.
''British Museum Shut by First Strike in History,'' *Evening Standard,* June 17, 2002, p. 4.
Brooks, Richard, ''British Museum Plans £6.5m Cuts to End Crisis,'' *Sunday Times,* June 23, 2002, p. 9.
Djokotoe, Edem, ''British Museum Would Rather Export Cultural Diplomacy Than Return Artefacts—MacGregor,'' *Africa News Service,* February 25, 2005.
Irving, Mark, ''Displaying a Mix of Ancient and Modern,'' *Financial Times,* December 1, 2001, p. 10.
Jury, Louise, ''Renewed Financial Crisis at British Museum Raises Question of Blame,'' *Independent,* May 21, 2002, p. 2.
Lyall, Sarah, ''Financial Troubles, Staff Cuts and Low Morale Plague a Top Tourist Attraction,'' *New York Times,* July 23, 2002, p. E1.
Milner, Catherine, ''Cash-Strapped British Museum to Sell £30m London Properties,'' *Sunday Telegraph,* January 20, 2002, p. 10.
Waterfield, Giles, ''The Collectors' Collection,'' *Sunday Telegraph,* September 15, 2002.
Wilson, David M., *The British Museum: A History,* London: The British Museum Press, 2002.

—M.L. Cohen

Campbell Soup Company

One Campbell Place
Camden, New Jersey 08103-1799
U.S.A.
Telephone: (856) 342-4800
Toll Free: (800) 257-8443
Fax: (856) 342-3878
Web site: http://www.campbellsoupcompany.com

Public Company
Incorporated: 1922
Employees: 24,000
Sales: $7.11 billion (2004)
Stock Exchanges: New York Philadelphia Swiss
Ticker Symbol: CPB
NAIC: 311422 Specialty Canning; 311330 Confectionery
Manufacturing from Purchased Chocolate; 311412
Frozen Specialty Food Manufacturing; 311421 Fruit
and Vegetable Canning; 311423 Dried and
Dehydrated Food Manufacturing; 311812 Commercial
Bakeries; 311813 Frozen Cakes, Pies, and Other
Pastries Manufacturing; 311821 Cookie and Cracker
Manufacturing; 311919 Other Snack Food
Manufacturing; 311941 Mayonnaise, Dressing, and
Other Prepared Sauce Manufacturing

Campbell Soup Company is the number one maker of soups in the world, holds the top position in that category in Europe, and dominates its home market of the United States with a commanding 69 percent share. The company divides its operations into four areas. North American soup and "away from home" products includes the flagship condensed and ready-to-serve soup lines, Swanson broths, and the firm's entire Canadian business, as well as the distribution of soups, specialty entrees, beverages, other prepared foods, and bakery products through various food-service channels. North American sauces and beverages comprises Pace Mexican sauces, Franco-American canned pastas and gravies, V8 vegetable juices and other beverages, Campbell's tomato juice, and all of the company's operations throughout Latin America and the Caribbean region, including Mexico. The

biscuit and confectionery segment is made up of three subsidiaries: Pepperidge Farm, Incorporated, which specializes in cookies, crackers, breads, and frozen bakery products under the Pepperidge Farm, Goldfish, and Milano brands; Australia-based Arnotts Ltd., maker of salty snack foods, biscuits, and crackers; and Godiva Chocolatier, Inc. Campbell's manufacturing facilities include 20 plants in the United States and another 27 overseas located in Australia, Belgium, Canada, France, Germany, Indonesia, Ireland, Malaysia, Mexico, the Netherlands, Papua New Guinea, Sweden, and the United Kingdom. The company generates about 64 percent of its sales in the United States, 15 percent in Europe, 13 percent in Australia and the Asia-Pacific region, and 8 percent in other countries.

Early History

The roots of the Campbell Soup Company can be traced back to 1860, when Abraham Anderson opened a small canning factory in Camden, New Jersey. In 1869 Philadelphia produce merchant Joseph Campbell became Anderson's partner, forming Anderson and Campbell. The company canned tomatoes, vegetables, jellies, condiments, and mincemeat. In 1876 Anderson and Campbell dissolved their partnership and Campbell bought Anderson's share of the business, changing its name to Joseph Campbell & Company. In 1882 a partnership was formed between Campbell's son-in-law, Walter S. Spackman; Campbell's nephew, Joseph S. Campbell; and Arthur Dorrance, Spackman's personal friend who brought a cash infusion to the partnership. At this time the company was renamed Joseph Campbell Preserving Company. The name was changed again in 1891, to Joseph Campbell Preserve Company. The senior Campbell maintained daily involvement in the company until his death in 1900.

In 1896 the company built a large factory in Camden and expanded its product line to include prepared meats, sauces, canned fruits, ketchup, and plum pudding. The next year Arthur Dorrance hired his nephew John Thompson Dorrance, a chemical engineer and organic chemist. By 1899 John Dorrance had successfully developed a method of canning condensed soup. This innovation helped Campbell outstrip its two soup-canning competitors. While others were still shipping heavy, uncondensed soup, Campbell was able to ship and sell its product at

Company Perspectives:

In July 2001, we launched a bold plan—and made a massive commitment—to transform Campbell Soup Company. Despite many challenges, it is now clear that we have renewed, revitalized, and reinvigorated our company and put it back on a growth track. We've rebuilt our organization, recharged our brands, and reinforced our market positions around the world. We are clearly better as a company, and ready for the next phase of our transformation: driving quality growth in everything we do.

one-third the cost. There were five original varieties: Tomato, Consommé, Vegetable, Chicken, and Oxtail. Around this same time, Campbell introduced its famous red-and-white label for its soups. As the company began increasing the variety of soups it offered, it began canning less produce, eventually leading, in 1905, to a change in company name to Joseph Campbell Company. John Dorrance became director of the company in 1900.

Campbell's soup began finding its way into American kitchens at a time when the prepared-food industry was growing rapidly yet was still small. By 1904 the company sold 16 million cans of soup a year. That same year, in order to provide workers with something to do in the middle of the day when the soup stock was in the midst of its long simmering time, the company began making and selling Pork and Beans. Also that year, the Campbell Kids were introduced as advertising characters. Boasting 21 varieties of soup by this time, Campbell began to eye a bigger market; in 1911 Campbell began selling its products in California, thus becoming one of the first companies to serve the entire nation.

In 1910 Dorrance was made general manager of the company, and in 1914 he became president. Dorrance focused on soup and discontinued the marginal line of ketchups, preserves, and jams. In 1915 Dorrance became sole owner of Campbell when he bought out his uncle, Arthur Dorrance. A marketing genius, Dorrance boosted sales of soup by pushing the idea of using condensed soup as an ingredient in easy-to-make recipes. The first of many Campbell cookbooks, *Helps for the Hostess,* was published in 1916.

In 1912 Campbell began growing its own produce in an effort to standardize quality. This program was the first of an ongoing series of efforts Campbell made to grow what it processed. At that time, during the eight summer weeks in which tomatoes were harvested, the Campbell plant devoted its entire effort to the production of tomato soup and tomato juice. During World War I almost half of Campbell's sales were from these two products. Meantime, in 1915, Campbell acquired the Franco-American Food Company. In addition to being the first American soup-maker, Franco-American was also a producer of other foods. Although the use of the Franco-American brand for soups was halted, the brand continued for spaghetti and other pasta products.

Incorporated in 1922

In 1922 the company was incorporated as the Campbell Soup Company, centering the company on its most famous and

profitable product. One year later, Arthur C. Dorrance, John Dorrance's brother, became Campbell's general manager. In 1929 Arthur C. Dorrance was made a director and vice-president of the board of directors. When John Dorrance died in 1930, Arthur C. Dorrance was elected president.

Throughout this period Campbell continued to grow. In 1929 the company opened a second major facility in Chicago. In the early 1930s Campbell opened Campbell Soup Company Ltd., in Canada, as well as Campbell's Soups Ltd., in Great Britain. In 1936 Campbell began making its own cans and in 1939 its agricultural research department was formed. On the product front, both Cream of Mushroom and Chicken Noodle soups were introduced in 1934, Campbell's Tomato Juice debuted in 1938, and Cream of Chicken hit store shelves in 1947. Campbell began backing these introductions with radio advertising in 1931, using the famous "M'm! M'm! Good!" slogan. Meantime, the company published its first full-length cookbook in 1941, titling it *Easy Ways to Good Meals.* In 1942 sales topped $100 million for the first time. Arthur C. Dorrance died in 1946, and James McGowen, Jr., became president. The following year Campbell began growing its own mushrooms in Prince Crossing, Illinois, and it opened its third soup plant, in Sacramento, California. In 1950 the first Campbell television commercials were broadcast.

Acquisition of Swanson: 1955

Despite this growth, Campbell was slow to diversify. In 1948 the company acquired V-8 juice, but its first major purchase was not made until 1955, when it bought the Omaha, Nebraska-based C.A. Swanson & Sons, producers of the first complete-meal frozen entrees called TV dinners.

In the midst of this growth, W.B. Murphy was elected president, following McGowan's retirement in 1953. In 1954 Campbell took its stock public on the New York Stock Exchange and, in 1957, the company formed an international division to oversee its foreign concerns. In 1958 sales exceeded $500 million for the first time and Campbell established Campbell's Soups, S.p.A. in Italy. This venture was followed, in 1959, by the opening of subsidiaries in Mexico and Australia.

Several Acquisitions Marking the 1960s

Throughout the 1960s Campbell was conservatively managed and quite successful. In that decade the company opened two mushroom growing facilities and 11 new plants on three continents. New products continued to be rolled out, with two particularly noteworthy: Franco-American SpaghettiOs, which debuted in 1965, and Goldfish crackers, introduced by Pepperidge Farm in 1962. During the decade Campbell's growth—which underwent a slight shift in emphasis—began to include regular acquisitions in addition to internal expansion. In 1961 Campbell acquired Pepperidge Farm, Incorporated, a maker of quality baked goods, and a similar Belgian company, Biscuits Delacre. In 1965 Campbell created a foodservice division and, in 1966, began marketing EfficienC, its own brand of foodservice products through that division. Also in 1966 Campbell formed Godiva Chocolatier to distribute the Belgian-made chocolates in the United States. In 1974 the company completed a purchase of the European Godiva company and became its sole owner. Campbell created Champion Valley Farms, Inc., a pet food concern, in 1969.

During the 1970s the company's slow but steady growth continued. Campbell, which had built its fortune on Dorrance's invention of condensed soup, introduced the Chunky brand of ready-to-serve soups in 1970. This became a highly successful enterprise. In 1971, for the first time, Campbell's sales topped $1 billion. In 1972 Murphy retired and was replaced as president by Harold A. Shaub. Also that year, Swanson introduced Hungry Man meals, a line of frozen dinners with larger-than-average portions.

Diversifying in the 1970s and 1980s

In 1973 Campbell acquired Pietro's Pizza Parlors, a chain based in the Pacific Northwest. This led, in 1974, to the forma-

tion of a restaurant division, and heralded Campbell's intention to add more restaurants to its growing list of subsidiaries.

In 1978 Campbell purchased Vlasic Foods, Inc., a Michigan-based producer of pickles and similar condiments, for approximately $35 million in capital stock. This acquisition gave Campbell the lead over archrival H.J. Heinz Company in the pickle-packing business. Campbell added seven small European food producing companies and three domestic operations in 1979. That same year sales topped $2 billion for the first time. In 1978 Campbell made a brief and unsuccessful foray into the Brazilian soup market.

The diversification movement started by Shaub in the early 1970s prepared the company for long-term growth. Campbell's debt remained low and the company's new products and acquisitions provided it with popular brand names in a variety of food industry sectors. Campbell realized that the key to growth in this mature market was diversification. Shaub changed a long-standing policy on new product development requiring a profit within the first year. His most notable innovation, however, was his decentralization of marketing for major product lines.

To sustain these growth-oriented policies, Campbell broke its tradition of relying on internally generated funds to finance its efforts. In June 1980 the company entered the debt market with a $100 million ten-year offering. As a cautious food producer, Campbell's earnings had always been healthy, but Shaub hoped to increase both sales and profit margins. A key reason for Shaub's determination to allow Campbell to diversify was the recognition that the market for many of these products had matured and growth had slowed.

In 1980 R. Gorden McGovern succeeded Shaub as president and Campbell made two acquisitions—Swift-Armour S.A. Argentina and a small American poultry processing plant used by Swanson for its frozen chicken dinners. Campbell's efforts in Argentina were not entirely fruitful, with much of the difficulty related to currency-transaction adjustments. Also in 1980 Campbell acquired additional bakery, pasta, and pickle operations.

In 1981 McGovern reorganized Campbell's management structure, dividing the company into two new divisions—Campbell U.S.A. and Campbell International—and about 50 business groups. This new structure was meant to foster entrepreneurship and heighten management's sensitivity to consumer opinion, long a weakness at Campbell. The company acquired Snow King Frozen Foods, a large producer of uncooked frozen specialty meats, and introduced the wildly successful Prego spaghetti sauce nationally in 1981. In 1982 Campbell acquired Mrs. Paul's Kitchens, a processor of frozen prepared seafood and vegetables. Several of the company's subsidiaries also made major purchases. Vlasic Foods acquired Win Schuler Foods, a specialty foods producer, and Pepperidge Farm completed the purchase of an apple juice processor, Costa Apple Products, with markets primarily on the East Coast. Also in 1982, Juice Bowl Products, a fruit juice processor, was acquired.

A variety of other acquisitions in the early 1980s added Annabelle's, a restaurant chain; Triangle Manufacturing, a manufacturer of physical fitness and sports-medicine products; a fresh produce distributor; a Puerto Rican canning company; and an Italian manufacturer of premium biscuits.

Marketing Emphasis Began in the 1980s

McGovern further increased emphasis on marketing and new product development in an effort to shift the company away from its production-oriented focus. McGovern also introduced Total Systems, a worker-oriented system designed to increase quality and efficiency that was similar to the successful worker management strategies employed by many Japanese companies.

One of McGovern's primary concerns was turning Campbell into a ''market-sensitive food company.'' After McGovern publicly referred to some of the company's Swanson TV dinner line as ''junk food'' in 1982, Campbell initiated Project Fix in an effort to upgrade food quality and improve packaging of its older products. As McGovern told *Business Week* in 1983, one of the most important facets of his makeover was helping the company personify ''somebody who is looking after [consumers'] well-being.'' The 1983 Triangle Manufacturing purchase and 1982 formation of a health and fitness unit were both designed to meet that goal. Campbell's involvement in frozen fish, juices, and produce were also part of the new market sensitivity urged by McGovern.

In addition, Campbell attempted to market products regionally and according to age group. The central marketing system was broken into 20 regions to allow tailoring of advertising and marketing to fit each region's peculiar demographics. For instance, the company sold spicier nacho cheese soup in Texas than in the rest of the country. The company also aimed its national brands at regional audiences, with spots featuring local celebrities and locally arranged promotions. Campbell, which reached half the nation's homes just by sponsoring the television show *Lassie* in the 1950s, spent 15 percent of its advertising budget in regional efforts in 1983. That figure was expected eventually to reach 50 percent.

McGovern increased Campbell's sales and earnings significantly in his first few years. His encouragement of new product development and line extensions may have been overzealous. The company introduced frozen entrees to compete with Stouffer's, dried soups to challenge Lipton, and name-brand produce such as Farm Fresh mushrooms and tomatoes, complemented by exotic varieties of mushrooms, refrigerated salads and pasta sauces, and juices. In all, Campbell introduced 334 new products in the first half of the 1980s. This included several costly mistakes, such as the 1984 failure of Pepperidge Farm's Star Wars cookies, which did not fit the brand's high-quality image. Yet spurred on by successes such as Le Menu frozen dinners, McGovern concentrated on marketing and new product development. In 1985, however, the company decided to cut back on new product gambles and McGovern reevaluated his goals and returned the company's focus to product quality and efficiency.

Throughout this period, during which it became increasingly clear that McGovern's plan was destined to fail, acquisitions and group formations continued, but at a pace reminiscent of the old Campbell. The company purchased a Belgian food producer and 20 percent of Arnotts Ltd., an Australian biscuit manufacturer, in 1985. In 1986 the company bought two more American food companies and established Campbell Enterprises to oversee non-grocery products. Meanwhile new products were gradually but steadily introduced.

In 1984 John T. Dorrance, Jr., the son of condensed soup's inventor, retired as chairman of the board and became director of the board's executive committee. He was succeeded as chairman by William S. Cashel, Jr. Dorrance and other members of his family, however, still controlled 58 percent of Campbell's stock and showed no interest in selling, keeping the company safe from takeover.

By 1987 McGovern began selling off some of Campbell's less successful ventures. In 1987 the company sold its disappointing Valley Farms pet food, Triangle physical fitness, and Juice Works beverage businesses. In 1988 the Pietro's pizza and Annabelle's restaurants were also sold, taking Campbell out of the restaurant business entirely.

However, Campbell also bought several smaller companies in 1987 and 1988 that were more compatible with its traditional lines of business. These included a French cookie maker, the Open Pit barbecue sauce line, an American olive producer, and Campbell's largest acquisition to date, Freshbake Foods Group PLC, a British producer of frozen foods. Also in 1988, Robert J. Vlasic, whose Vlasic Foods Campbell had purchased in 1978, became chairman of Campbell.

Campbell's management crisis was exacerbated by the death, in April 1989, of John Dorrance. Dorrance's 31 percent of the company's stock was split between his three children, who demonstrated an interest in preserving family control of the company. The remaining 27 percent of the family-owned stock was split among other members of the clan, some of whom (representing about 17.4 percent of the company's stock) expressed a desire to sell Campbell. Chairman Vlasic, however, had loaded the board with family members loyal to the company (six of the 15 board members were family members, including John Dorrance's three children), so a proxy battle never materialized.

McGovern—who failed in an attempt to merge the company with the Quaker Oats Company in 1989—left Campbell that same year. His final attempt to recoup Campbell's losses, a $343 million restructuring program, earned him little praise. Although sales had doubled during his term, profits had dropped 90 percent as a result of his aggressive capital commitments. From 1988 to 1990 alone, earnings fell from $274.1 million to $4.4 million.

Back to Basics in the 1990s

In January 1990 David W. Johnson was elected president and CEO. Johnson came to Campbell from Gerber Products Company, where he had been successful in streamlining that company's operations. Johnson employed a back-to-basics strategy that called for drastic restructuring. The new CEO oversaw the divestment of whole businesses, including mushroom farms, a salmon processing plant, the refrigerated salads line, and cookie maker Lazzaroni. By June 1991, Johnson had closed or sold 20 plants worldwide, reduced the company's 51,700 person workforce by 15.5 percent, and pulled unprofitable lines from store shelves. While Johnson purported to support marketing, he also cut Campbell's advertising budget.

Johnson was most interested in promoting the company's core product, soup. Even into the early 1990s, Campbell soups had 66 percent, or $1.6 billion, of the $2.6 billion U.S. soup market, which contributed almost half of the conglomerate's $570 million in operating profits.

In anticipation of the North American Free Trade Agreement, Johnson also supervised the merging of Campbell's Canadian operations, some Mexican companies, and the U.S. businesses into one division called Campbell North America. Late in 1991, Campbell also focused on the impending European Community's single market, which promised 344 million consumers (50 percent more than the United States) and had potential for future growth. The cookie subsidiary of Campbell Soup, Campbell Biscuits Europe, got a head start on the market in February 1990, when it reorganized its European corporate structure, consolidated marketing, and standardized packaging.

By the end of 1991, some indicators showed that Johnson's efforts had paid off: Campbell's earnings through the first three quarters of 1991 had risen 33 percent, making the company's profits the second fastest-growing in the food industry. But some analysts warned that the profits came at the expense of core brand promotion, which was cut in 1991. The growth in earnings was not based on sales increases, which only rose 1.9 percent during the same period.

Johnson was given an overall good rating in the quick turnaround at Campbell. In 1992 the company made bolder goals, with a vision expressed as "Campbell Brands Preferred Around the World." The plan made further preparations for the European Community's single market and expanded those efforts around the world. The company was reorganized into three multinational divisions: Campbell North and South America grouped Campbell's Swift-Armour subsidiary in Argentina with the previously organized North American group; Campbell Biscuit and Bakery united Pepperidge Farm in North America with Delacre in Europe and Australia's leading biscuit company, Arnotts Ltd. (of which Campbell by then owned 58 percent); Campbell Europe/Asia was a growth-oriented division that comprised the company's "greatest opportunity and challenge," according to the 1992 annual report.

In 1993 Vlasic retired as chairman, with Johnson taking on this additional title. Also, Bennett Dorrance, a grandson of condensed soup inventor John Dorrance, was named vice-chairman of Campbell Soup. Bennett Dorrance represented the Dorrance family's interests on the board of directors and took an active role, particularly in tying executive pay to performance and putting oversight practices into place. The family's power was soon diminished somewhat, after Bennett's brother, John T. Dorrance III, sold most of his stake in the company by late 1996, leaving the family in control of 44 percent of the stock. No attempts at a takeover—hostile or otherwise—were immediately evident, however.

Johnson continued to restructure Campbell as the decade continued. The company recorded a $300 million restructuring charge in 1993 in relation to the divestment of several underperforming units. That year also saw the launch of a new soup campaign using the slogan "Never Underestimate the Power of Soup." The Mrs. Paul's frozen seafood line was sold to Pillsbury Co.'s Van de Kamp's unit in 1996. Altogether, Johnson dumped $500 million worth of noncore, underperforming assets from 1990 through 1996.

Simultaneously Johnson led Campbell Soup in a more aggressive overseas push and sought out compatible acquisitions. In addition to a big push into the Mexican soup market, the company in 1993 began selling V8 vegetable juice in Europe and established a joint venture with Nakano Vinegar Co. Ltd. to market Campbell's soups in Japan. In January 1995 Campbell completed the largest acquisition in its long history, paying $1.1 billion for Pace Foods Ltd., the leading maker of Mexican sauces (picante and salsa) with 1994 sales of more than $200 million. Later in 1995, the company picked up Greenfield Healthy Foods, the number one maker of fat-free brownies and cookies for the health and convenience store markets, and Fresh Start Bakeries, a supplier of baked goods to fast-food restaurants. The latter, however, was sold in 1999.

Campbell Soup continued its overseas push with the 1996 purchases of Homepride, the leading cooking sauce brand in the United Kingdom, and the Cheong Chan soup and sauce business in Asia; and the 1997 acquisition of Erasco Group, the leading seller of canned soup in Germany, from Grand Metropolitan PLC for $210 million. Also in 1997 Arnotts acquired the Sydney, Australia-based Kettle Chip Company. Campbell then the following year spent about $290 million to purchase the remainder of Arnotts, making it a wholly owned subsidiary. Campbell also extended its soup business in Europe through the $180 million acquisition of the Liebig soup business of France. Even with all of these foreign maneuvers, Campbell was far from a goal Johnson had set in 1993 of increasing overseas operations to 50 percent of sales by 2000. The figure had stood at 28 percent in 1993 and had risen to 31 percent in 1994, but by 1998 was back at 28 percent.

Despite the lack of progress toward this goal, Johnson had succeeded in improving Campbell Soup's profitability thanks to his aggressive restructuring efforts. The company's net profit margin stood at 10.4 percent for 1996, compared to 5 percent for 1988 and 6.5 percent for 1991. But Johnson was not finished with his tinkering. Campbell recorded restructuring charges of $204 million in 1997 and $262 million in 1998 related to plant closures and the divestment of nonstrategic businesses. Jettisoned in 1997 were the Marie's salad dressing and dip unit, the company's Argentinean beef operations, and its German chilled foods business, Beeck-Feinkost GmbH.

After the installation of Dale F. Morrison as president and CEO (with Johnson remaining chairman), Campbell Soup made its most dramatic divestment yet. In March 1998 the company completed the spinoff of its Specialty Foods segment, which included seven noncore businesses. The $1.5 billion spinoff created a new public company, Vlasic Foods International Inc., which included Vlasic pickles, Swanson frozen foods, Swift Armour meats in Argentina, Open Pit barbecue sauce, U.K. canned foodmaker Stratford Upon Avon, Gourmet Specialty Foods of Germany, and a fresh mushroom business in the United States. This move left Campbell Soup with four main core business segments: soups, sauces and beverages, biscuits and confectionery, and foodservice. The 1998 dealmaking was not quite over, however, as Campbell sold Delacre, its European biscuit business, to United Biscuit (Holdings) PLC for $125 million in cash in June—leaving Pepperidge Farm and Arnotts as its mainstays in biscuits and crackers. In June the company sold its can-making assets to Stamford, Connecticut-based

Silgan Holdings Inc. for $123 million. In August Campbell completed the purchase of Fortun Foods, maker of StockPot soup, the market leader in premium refrigerated soups, a rapidly growing segment of the foodservice sector.

According to *Business Week,* Morrison warned employees in the fall of 1997, "We are driving the incredibly shrinking company." Reduced to a much more manageable core of leading brands, Campbell faced a number of challenges. In addition to the slower than expected growth in international sales, Campbell's canned soup sales in the United States were on the decline, leading to the implementation in 1998 of the largest advertising campaign in company history, which centered around a new slogan, "Good for the Body, Good for the Soul." It was clear by this time that increasingly convenience-minded consumers were losing their appetites for condensed soups—both for eating as soups and for using to prepare meals. Campbell therefore also introduced in 1998 and 1999 several new convenience products in an attempt to recharge sales. These included ready-to-serve Tomato soup in a resealable bottle; Campbell's Soup to Go single-serving, microwavable soups; and the Campbell's Select line of ready-to-serve soups. The cans for the ready-to-serve soups were soon redesigned with easy-open pop-top lids, but the most noticeable change for the entire Campbell's soup line was the first major overhaul of the labels since the now-iconic design was first used more than 100 years previous. In the fall of 1999 the new labels debuted. While they remained red and white, the *Campbell's* script logo was smaller and each can showed a steaming bowl of the variety inside. In July 1999, meantime, Johnson retired from his remaining position as chairman. A longtime member of the board, Philip E. Lippincott, succeeded him.

Launch of Revitalization Drive in Early 2000s

Johnson's retirement proved short-lived. The board of directors and the founding Dorrance family, which continued to own more than 50 percent of the company, had grown dissatisfied with the company's performance, particularly its stock price. Under pressure from the board, Morrison tendered his resignation in March 2000. Johnson was brought back on an interim basis while a search for a permanent successor was launched. During this interregnum, Johnson reintroduced the famous "M'm! M'm! Good!" slogan in Campbell's advertising, replacing the poorly received "We Have a Soup for That" campaign.

In January 2001 Douglas R. Conant was brought onboard as the new president and CEO. A 25-year food industry veteran, Conant had experience at three of the largest food companies in the world: General Mills, Inc., the Kraft Foods unit of Philip Morris Companies Inc., and Nabisco Holdings Corp. He had most recently served as president of Nabisco Holdings' Nabisco Foods unit, a maker of snacks such as LifeSavers candies and Planters Nuts and condiments such as Grey Poupon mustard.

Just weeks after Conant began at Campbell, the company announced its biggest acquisition since the 1995 purchase of Pace. In a deal completed in May 2001, Campbell paid Unilever about $900 million for several dry soup and bouillon brands in Europe, including Oxo, Batchelors, Heisse Tasse, Blå Band, and Royco. These additions made Campbell the largest soup seller in most of Europe and increased its share of the overall

European soup market from 20 percent to 30 percent. In August 2001 George M. Sherman, former CEO of Danaher Corporation and a Campbell director since 1995, was named chairman, replacing Lippincott.

In July 2001 Conant launched a three-year "transformation plan" to revitalize the ailing company. Dividends were slashed to free up funds to improve the quality of the soup line and significantly increase marketing outlays not only for soups but also for nonsoup brands such as Prego and Franco-American. On the quality front, Campbell began overhauling the way it made soups, most notably by switching to a "cold-blending" process, which allowed ingredients to be added at different points in the cooking process rather than all at once. This process helped the broth stay clear and the vegetables retain their crunch. Other improvements were in the form of an increase in the amount of a key ingredient. For example, the amount of chicken in Chunky Chicken Corn Chowder was increased by one-third, while Alphabet soup gained 40 percent more letters. In addition, as sales of Campbell's condensed soups continued to fall—increasingly because of the rise of private-label competition—the company pushed to develop new lines of convenience soups. In 2002, for example, Campbell's Soup at Hand debuted. Designed for on-the-go eating, these sippable soups were sold in an easy-open, plastic, microwavable container that could be held in one hand like a soda can. The next year, Campbell began selling its Chunky and Select soups in microwavable bowls. The company also expanded its product portfolio through acquisition during this period. In 2002 Campbell strengthened its position in the Australia snack food market by acquiring Snack Foods Limited, that country's number two maker of salty snacks. Also acquired that year was Erin Foods, the second largest dry soup company in Ireland.

Results for 2003 were somewhat lukewarm but better than that of the previous several years. Although condensed soup sales continued to fall, overall sales increased 9 percent, to $6.68 billion, aided by an 8 percent increase in ready-to-serve soup shipments and continued strong performance for the V-8 and Pace brands and at the Pepperidge Farm and Godiva subsidiaries. More changes were implemented during 2004 to build upon the success of the previous three years. Campbell's North American business was reorganized into four units: U.S. soup, sauces, and beverages; operations in Canada, Mexico, and Latin America, plus the company's foodservice business; Pepperidge Farm; and Godiva. A new plan to "drive quality growth" included the layoff of 400 employees from the worldwide payroll of 25,000, the implementation of a new sales and distribution system in Australia, and $32 million in pretax charges for these initiatives. Campbell set goals of attaining net sales growth of 3 to 4 percent per year and earnings per share growth of 5 to 7 percent per year. Among other developments in 2004, Campbell dropped the Franco-American name from its SpaghettiOs line of canned pasta products in favor of the Campbell's name in an attempt to leverage the strength of the flagship brand. In addition, Sherman retired as chairman. Replacing him was Harvey Golub, former chairman and CEO of American Express Company and a Campbell director since 1996.

Principal Subsidiaries

Arnotts Ltd. (Australia); Campbell Australasia Pty. Ltd. (Australia); Campbell Cheong Chan Malaysia Sdn. Bhd.; Campbell

Company of Canada; Campbell Foods Belgium n.v./s.a.; Campbell Foodservice Company; Campbell France S.A.S.; Campbell Japan Inc.; Campbell Soup Asia Ltd. (Hong Kong); Campbell Soup Ireland Limited; Campbell Soup Sweden AB; Campbell Soup Trading (Shanghai) Co. Ltd. (China); Campbell Soup UK Limited; Campbell Southeast Asia Sdn. Bhd. (Malaysia); Campbell's de Mexico S.A. de C.V.; Campbell's Germany GmbH; Campbell's Netherlands B.V.; Campbell's U.K. Limited; Continental Foods S.A. (France); Erin Foods Limited (Ireland); Eugen Lacroix GmbH (Germany); Godiva Chocolatier, Inc.; Joseph Campbell Company; Pepperidge Farm, Incorporated; Sinalopasta S.A. de C.V. (Mexico); Snack Foods Limited (Australia); Stockpot Inc.

Principal Competitors

General Mills, Inc.; Kraft Foods Inc.; H.J. Heinz Company; Unilever; Sara Lee Bakery Group; Kellogg Company.

Further Reading

Barrett, Amy, "Campbell Soup: Hail to the Chef," *Financial World,* June 11, 1991, pp. 52–54.

——, "Campbell's Wet Noodles," *Business Week,* January 25, 1999, p. 48.

——, "Souping Up Campbell's," *Business Week,* November 3, 1997, pp. 70, 72.

Berman, Phyllis, and Alexandra Alger, "Reclaiming the Patrimony," *Forbes,* March 14, 1994, p. 50.

Branch, Shelly, "Campbell Bets on Famous Old Slogan to Pull It Out of Sales Slump," *Wall Street Journal,* September 6, 2000, p. B1.

——, "Campbell's Soup Shipments Rise As Buyers Stock Pantries," *Wall Street Journal,* November 15, 2001, p. B4.

——, "Campbell to Buy Soup Brands of Unilever," *Wall Street Journal,* January 30, 2001, p. B11.

Briggs, Jean A., and Barbara Rudolph, "Mmm, Mmm, Not So Good," *Forbes,* December 7, 1981, pp. 44+.

"Campbell: Now It's M-M-Global," *Business Week,* March 15, 1993, pp. 52–54.

"Campbell Soup: Widening Its Menu and Looking Beyond Food," *Business Week,* August 11, 1980, pp. 85+.

Collins, Douglas, *America's Favorite Food: The Story of Campbell Soup Company,* New York: Abrams, 1994, 216 p.

Donlon, J.P., "Top Spoon Stirs It Up," *Chief Executive,* November 1996, pp. 44–47.

Dugas, Christine, and Anthony Bianco, "Marketing's New Look: Campbell Leads a Revolution in the Way Consumer Products Are Sold," *Business Week,* January 26, 1987, pp. 64+.

Dwyer, Steve, "Red Alert: The Soup's Back On," *Prepared Foods,* September 1997, pp. 14–16, 18, 21, 23.

Eklund, Christopher S., "Campbell Soup's Recipe for Growth: Offering Something for Every Palate," *Business Week,* December 24, 1984, pp. 66+.

Ellison, Sarah, "Campbell Hopes Portable Soups Will Reheat Its Sluggish Sales," *Wall Street Journal,* February 18, 2003, p. B4.

——, "Inside Campbell's Big Bet: Heating Up Condensed Soup," *Wall Street Journal,* July 31, 2003, p. A1.

Fairclough, Gordon, "Campbell's Recipe for Higher Profit: Reheat Soup Sales," *Wall Street Journal,* May 19, 1999, p. B6.

"From Soup to Nuts and Back to Soup," *Business Week,* November 5, 1990, pp. 114, 116.

Glosserman, Brad, "Campbell Soup Works for Spill Over Effect," *Japan Times Weekly International Edition,* May 11–May 17, 1992, p. 17.

Grant, Linda, "Stirring It Up at Campbell," *Fortune,* May 13, 1996, p. 80.

Hays, Constance L., "Will Goldfish Tactics Help Campbell's Soups?," *New York Times,* October 18, 1998, sec. 3, p. 4.

A History, Camden, N.J.: Campbell Soup Company, 1988.

Mastrull, Diane, "Campbell and Pace Recipe: A Mixing of Disparate Cultures," *Philadelphia Business Journal,* February 17, 1995, pp. 1, 27, 28.

Nulty, Peter, "The National Business Hall of Fame," *Fortune,* March 11, 1991, pp. 98–103.

O'Connell, Vanessa, "Campbell Decides Its IQ Health Meals May Be Ahead of the Curve for Foods," *Wall Street Journal,* April 27, 1998, p. B8.

——, "Campbell Sees Profit Shortfall and Stock Gets Creamed," *Wall Street Journal,* January 12, 1999, p. B4.

——, "Changing Tastes Dent Campbell's Canned-Soup Sales," *Wall Street Journal,* April 28, 1998, pp. B1, B25.

——, "How Campbell Saw a Breakthrough Menu Turn into Leftovers," *Wall Street Journal,* October 6, 1998, pp. A1, A12.

Pehanich, Mike, "Brand Power," *Prepared Foods,* Mid-April 1993, pp. 38–40, 42.

Saporito, Bill, "Campbell Soup Gets Piping Hot," *Fortune,* September 9, 1991, pp. 142–48.

——, "The Fly in Campbell's Soup," *Fortune,* May 9, 1988, pp. 67+.

"Seizing the Dark Day," *Business Week,* January 13, 1992, pp. 26–28.

Sim, Mary B., *History of Commercial Canning in New Jersey,* Trenton, N.J.: New Jersey Agricultural Society, 1951.

Weber, Joseph, "Campbell Is Bubbling, but for How Long?," *Business Week,* June 17, 1991, pp. 56–57.

——, "M'm! M'm! Bad! Trouble at Campbell Soup," *Business Week,* September 25, 1989, pp. 68+.

——, "What's Not Cookin' at Campbell's," *Business Week,* September 23, 1996, p. 40.

Wentz, Laurel, "Europe: How Smart Marketers Cash In," *Advertising Age,* December 2, 1991, pp. S-1, S-9.

Wimp, Marilyn, "Campbell Spins Off Frozen Food, Pickles," *Philadelphia Business Journal,* March 27, 1998, p. 20.

—updates: April Dougal Gasbarre; David E. Salamie

CN

Canadian National Railway Company

935 de La Gauchetière Street West
Montreal, Quebec H3B 2M9
Canada
Telephone: (514) 399-5430
Toll Free: (888) 888-5909
Fax: (204) 987-9310
Web site: http://www.cn.ca

Public Company
Incorporated: 1919 as Canadian National Railway
   Company Limited
Employees: 22,679
Sales: CAD 6.55 billion ($5.46 billion) (2004)
Stock Exchanges: Toronto New York
Ticker Symbols: CNR (Toronto); CNI (New York)
NAIC: 482111 Line-Haul Railroads; 482112 Short Line
   Railroads; 483113 Coastal and Great Lakes Freight
   Transportation; 488210 Support Activities for Rail
   Transportation; 488510 Freight Transportation
   Arrangement

One of the six major North American railways, known as Class 1 railways, Canadian National Railway Company (CN) operates the largest rail network in Canada and the only transcontinental network in North America. In Canada, the CN network encompasses 12,900 route miles in eight Canadian provinces, including the nation's five major ports—Vancouver and Prince Rupert, British Columbia, on the Pacific; the key Great Lakes port of Thunder Bay, Ontario; and Montreal and Halifax, Nova Scotia, on the Atlantic. The U.S. network comprises 6,400 route miles in 16 states, connecting the Canadian network to the U.S. Midwest (including Chicago) down to the Gulf of Mexico and the ports of Mobile, Alabama, and New Orleans. The company is also able to offer its customers access to Mexico and the U.S. Southwest through a marketing alliance with the Kansas City Southern Railway Company, with the two networks interconnecting in Jackson, Mississippi. The diversified freight transported over CN rails are well balanced among petroleum and chemicals, grain and fertilizers, coal, metals and minerals, forest products, automotive products, and intermodal services (the movement of trailers and containers on railroad freight cars). CN also holds interests in two overseas railways: 42.5 percent of English, Welsh & Scottish Railway Holdings Limited of Great Britain and 33 percent of Australian Transport Network Limited.

CN was formed in the post-World War I era through the integration and nationalization of two of the country's largest railroads, Canadian Northern and Grand Trunk. Although they were not the first railroads to come under government control, these two systems formed the basis of Canada's largest transportation conglomerate. After 78 years as a Crown corporation, CN was privatized through an initial public offering (IPO) on November 28, 1995. This was the largest privatization in Canadian history, raising CAD 2.26 billion for the government of Canada. Key post-privatization events included the 1999 acquisition of Illinois Central Corporation, the scuttling by regulators of a proposed merger with Burlington Northern Santa Fe Corporation in 2000, and the acquisitions of Wisconsin Central Transportation Corporation (2001), the rail and marine holdings of Great Lakes Transportation LLC (2004), and BC Rail Ltd. (2004).

The Grand Trunk and Canadian Northern Predecessors

CN was created as a result of the near-collapse of the Canadian Northern and Grand Trunk railways not long after the end of World War I. When a postwar economic depression undermined the railroads' finances, the consolidation provided a way for the companies to avoid defaults on CAD 1.3 billion in loans. It also gave Canada the second largest railway system in the world, with almost 100,000 employees and over 22,000 miles of track, nearly twice as much as its nearest competitor.

Canada's railroads had enjoyed the support of government since the colonial era, when the Grand Trunk (GT) emerged as the dominion's first major railway. Incorporated in 1852, GT soon dominated the railway boom concentrated in central Canada between Montreal and Toronto. Close government cooperation came in the form of land grants, loans, and loan guarantees. The railway's first president, John Ross, also held a high government position.

Company Perspectives:

Success in any business depends on motivated people managing valuable assets to deliver safe and reliable customer-focused service while conscientiously controlling costs. These five elements are key to delivering our service and keeping our promise to "do what we say we will do." Understanding how these interconnected elements work together is crucial for everybody in the company, and is part of a concept we call "How We Work and Why."

Railroad and government officials, however, envisioned disparate goals for GT—profits for its British shareholders on the one hand and settlement of the vast western territories on the other. The public and private interests in the railway clashed before the end of the decade. In 1858 British Columbia became a Crown colony and western settlement became government policy. A transcontinental railway would bind the colonies together and prevent American squatters from seizing the territory before Canadians had a chance, and as the Dominion's largest railway, the GT would naturally have been the vehicle of choice for this western movement. Expensive construction projects, however, had drained finances to the point that the company could not make interest payments on its loans, and shareholders—who had yet to receive the dividends promised at the company's inception—would not agree to what they saw as a losing venture. Under pressure from both the government and the company's investors, Ross and most of his board of directors resigned in 1858. GT's English shareholders sent Edward Watkin, a British railway executive who represented England's preeminence in the industry, as Ross's replacement.

Watkin and his managing director, Charles J. Brydges, continued the traditional mix of public and private support for the GT, but concentrated on financial reorganization and capital improvements. By 1865 they had built up traffic by 50 percent, increased net earnings, and made plans to replace iron rails with steel, upgrade from wood fuel to coal, and standardize rail gauges.

As did his predecessor, Watkin had a vision of a coast-to-coast railway that would promote western settlement and bring about confederation. Two factors stood in the way: shareholders who wanted customers to be settled in the West before they would build a railway to serve them, and the Hudson's Bay Company, owner of the territory between the eastern and western colonies. In 1863 Watkin engineered the takeover of the Hudson's Bay Company by a London-based finance company, bringing the possibility of a coast-to-coast railway even closer. In 1869, however, Watkin was ousted by those shareholders, led by Captain Henry W. Tyler, who opposed investment in the intercolonial railway. The Canadian government bought out the Hudson's Bay Company, and Grand Trunk began an era of eastern consolidation under Tyler.

During the 1880s, Tyler oversaw the absorption of 16 railways and expanded freight service to the United States. His concentration on American markets was rewarded—25 percent of the railway's earnings came from meat and grain traffic

between Chicago and New England. In 1882 GT took over its largest competitor, the Great Western, and in 1888 it assumed control of Ontario's Northern Railway.

In the midst of all this consolidation, Prime Minister John A. MacDonald, gave up his attempts to persuade Tyler and the GT to build to the western coast. Instead he contracted with a new system, the Canadian Pacific Railway, to build a transcontinental railway from the West. This would turn out to be a momentous decision—privately held Canadian Pacific Railway remained CN's largest rail competitor into the early 21st century.

Tyler's 18-year reign at Grand Trunk was brought to an end by economic recession and, as with his predecessors, 20,000 fickle stockholders who blamed him for the loss of government support that, instead, sustained the Canadian Pacific during the "lean years." Tyler's successor, Sir Charles Rivers Wilson, hired Charles Melville Hays—an American with railroad experience—to manage the nearly 5,000 miles of Grand Trunk track. Hays brought American management techniques to the still British-owned GT, made such physical improvements as better brakes and improved grades, and rebuilt the suspension bridge over the Niagara River into the United States. All these changes improved service and, by the end of the century, operating expenses had been reduced by 10 percent. Hays also satisfied English shareholders by enabling the company to finally pay out dividends on its shares. He quickly realized, though, that without service to the west, the Grand Trunk was just a "feeder line" for the western markets served by Canadian Pacific.

Formidable competition also came from the Canadian Northern railroad, owned by William Mackenzie and Donald Mann, partners in Mackenzie Mann & Co. Limited. The men, who met when both were working for Canadian Pacific, acquired their first railway in 1896, after they had decided to branch out on their own. Concentrating on the prairies to the north, Mackenzie and Mann built up the Canadian Northern by consolidating many small "farmer's railroads" into a system that offered transportation to 130 communities, with the motto "Energy, Enterprise, Ability." They built connecting lines with the help of provincial grants and controlled 1,200 miles of track, serving Canada's breadbasket by 1902.

By 1896 all of Canada was booming; Prime Minister Sir Wilfred Laurier heralded the arrival of "Canada's century." That year Grand Trunk's Charles M. Hays was finally able to announce the railroad's plan to open a line to the Pacific at the port of Prince Rupert. Grand Trunk Pacific (GTP), created as a subsidiary, was Hays's strategy for breaking out of the corner into which the railroad had been backed and ensuring Grand Trunk's future. He had tried to buy out the Canadian Northern, but Mackenzie and Mann hoped to build their own transcontinental railroad. In 1902, however, it was Mackenzie's turn to suggest that the two exchange traffic instead of building duplicate track, but by then Grand Trunk was too deep into GTP. The competition between Grand Trunk and Canadian Northern would prove to be the ruin of both systems.

The Grand Trunk Pacific line was completed in 1914, but it was an empty victory. The Panama Canal opened that same year, drawing a steady stream of traffic from Vancouver and making that city into a major port, while Prince Rupert lan-

Key Dates:

1852: Grand Trunk (GT) railway is incorporated.

1896: Canadian Northern begins building its railway system.

1914: GT completes its transcontinental railway, from Moncton, New Brunswick, to Prince Rupert, British Columbia.

1915: Canadian Northern finishes its transcontinental line from Vancouver to Montreal.

1917: Canadian Northern is taken over by the Canadian government.

1919: The Canadian government incorporates Canadian National Railway Company Limited (CN) as a Crown corporation, which includes Canadian Northern and a number of other railroads.

1923: CN completes takeover of GT, creating one of the world's largest railway networks with more than 22,000 miles of track.

1992: Canadian and U.S. rail holdings are consolidated to create CN North America; Paul Tellier is named CEO and begins major cost-cutting effort.

1995: Canadian National Railway is privatized through a CAD 2.26 billion initial public offering (IPO).

1998: CN and Illinois Central Corporation (IC) enter into a marketing alliance with the Kansas City Southern Railway Company.

1999: CN acquires IC for CAD 2.4 billion; company agrees to a $6 billion merger with Burlington Northern Santa Fe Corporation (BNSF).

2000: The U.S. Surface Transportation Board issues moratorium on rail mergers, scuttling the BNSF deal.

2001: Wisconsin Central Transportation Corporation is acquired.

2004: CN completes two acquisitions: the rail and marine holdings of Great Lakes Transportation LLC and BC Rail Ltd.

guished. In addition, British ships no longer enjoyed the strong presence in the North Atlantic that they once did, further reducing traffic for Prince Rupert and GTP. The event that might have helped to keep Grand Trunk in private hands had it been undertaken 20 years earlier was now contributing to its failure. Meanwhile, Canadian Northern completed its transcontinental line from Vancouver to Montreal in 1915.

Post-World War I Formation of Canadian National

By 1916 both Canadian Northern and Grand Trunk were on the brink of receivership. Overextension had stressed finances: Canada had at least twice as many railway miles per capita as the United States, much of it duplicating service. A royal commission recommended nationalization of the two, including Grand Trunk's subsidiary, GTP. It took four years to bring the former competitors together—in addition to the National Transcontinental and the Intercolonial, two government lines—to form one of the country's first Crown corporations, the Canadian National Railway Company Limited, created on June 6, 1919.

The amalgamation brought together over 90 different railways to form a system divided into four geographical regions:

the Atlantic, with headquarters in Moncton; the Central, headquartered in Toronto; the Grand Trunk Western, a U.S. system with headquarters in Detroit, Michigan; and the Western region, headquartered in Winnipeg. Each region had its own general manager and superintendents. CN's officers were all drawn from the various systems, which helped to unify the previously rival railways.

The reorganization was directed by David B. Hanna, former vice-president of the Canadian Northern. Despite the CAD 1.3 billion debt assumed by the newly formed system, Hanna began a program to rehabilitate the railroad's physical property and bring it up to par with that of the Canadian Pacific. His task was made more difficult by a postwar industrial recession, a flu epidemic, and history-making bad weather, but the program was supported by Prime Minister Mackenzie King's Liberal government and the healthy economy of the 1920s. Hanna also began to focus on new markets for CN, especially Asia and Europe. The Canadian Government Merchant Marine, a shipping arm of the CN created in 1919, helped open Asian markets and increased the level of competition with Canadian Pacific, which was already well established in the Pacific basin.

By 1923 Grand Trunk had been officially assimilated into the Canadian National system and Sir Henry Thornton became president. Now fully formed, CN stood as one of the world's largest railroads with more than 22,000 miles of track and more than 100,000 employees. CN also operated express services, a telegraph company, a chain of hotels, and a steamship line. On the railroad side, Thornton continued to improve lines, equipment, and service and also reduce expenses. To entertain train travelers he established the first radio network in both Canada and North America in 1923. Ten years later the network was sold to the federal government, and it would evolve into the Canadian Broadcasting Corporation.

CN began to compete with Canadian Pacific for the Asia-to-New York silk trade in 1925. Competition between the two was fierce—every hour saved between the two coasts meant higher profits, because insurance on raw silk, a perishable commodity, ran as high as 6 percent per hour. The CN's "silkers," trains carrying the precious cargo, traveled at speeds up to 90 miles per hour and took precedence over all other trains, including express passenger lines. They averaged just four days to cross the continent. The largest CN silker ran in October 1927. The 21-car train carried 7,200 bales of silk worth CAD 7 million. The success of CN's Asian freight service was encouraging, but the worldwide depression that began in 1929 brought an end to that optimism.

1930s Through 1950s:
Financial Travails, Wartime, and Labor Strife

Caught in the midst of trying to increase both the quality and quantity of services, the railway was shocked by the severity of the unexpected depression. In 1930 the support of the Liberal government was lost and by 1932 Thornton was forced to resign and business had been curtailed. By that time the system's earnings had fallen 40 percent below those in its peak year of 1928, and CN was carrying only half the traffic it had two years earlier. A smaller-than-normal grain crop and a drop in the Japanese silk trade worsened the effects of the Great Depression.

The year 1932 was the low point of the depression for Canadian National, with operating revenues decreasing a further 20 percent from those of the previous year. The depression was not the only force moving against the CN: new modes of transportation were quickly being developed to compete with the outdated railway system. Passengers preferred the convenience of buses, cars, and airplanes; shippers preferred the lower-cost, specialized services of the trucking industry.

Trade picked up after 1932, when the British Empire employed such protectionist measures as quotas and increased customs duties on non-empire trade. Although business was generally improving by 1936, the depression and decreased Asian trade brought about the demise of the Canadian Government Merchant Marine. A brief trade war with Japan was settled in 1935, and CN enjoyed good trade relations with that country until 1941, when the United States, Britain, and Canada froze all Japanese assets during World War II.

In the meantime, in another quirky aspect of CN's history, the Canadian government in 1937 established Trans-Canada Air Lines (TCA) as a national airline and made it a subsidiary of Canadian National Railway. TCA, renamed Air Canada in 1964, remained a CN subsidiary until 1977 when it became a direct subsidiary of the federal government.

The years of World War II provided a boom in transportation that enabled Canadian National to make interest payments on all of its publicly held debt and to make its first profits. At the close of the 1940s, however, the company's debts began rising, freight volumes were falling, and passenger service appeared doomed. Donald Gordon, a banker and chairman of the World War II War Prices and Trade Board, was selected as president of CN. Gordon invested in the conversion from steam to diesel and modernization of the aging railway's physical properties—three-fourths of the system's locomotives were over 30 years old. In 1952 the Canadian government gave Gordon the debt relief he needed. Recapitalization cut the system's interest charges by more than CAD 22 million per year.

In addition to the financial difficulties facing CN, there were growing problems on the labor front. Technological advances made within the rail industry cut staffing requirements: automation of train control and clerical operations decreased the need for office staff, while diesel locomotives and higher capacity freightcars allowed carriers to operate longer and heavier trains and lengthened the distance between service stops, affecting train and repair personnel. While rail management worked to maximize productivity gains, rail labor unions fought to save their members' jobs.

Tensions between management and labor came to a head several times during the 1950s. A strike by 120,000 Canadian railway workers in August 1950 brought rail transport to a halt, shutting down traffic from coast to coast. A government injunction sent the strikers back to work within two days. Other strikes were threatened during the 1950s, but arbitration kept the trains running.

Gordon accomplished many goals during the 1950s and 1960s. These achievements included decentralized management, replacing old rolling stock with new specialized containers, adding road transport to CN's roster of services, introducing computerized processes, and improving employee training. In spite of these measures, the railroad was still commonly viewed as a tool for national development, rather than a profit-making venture. As technology continued to diminish the role of railways, Canadian government and CN officials allowed the system to become mired in deficits. Changing regulations, irregular funding, and other political machinations were often caused by party changes. These issues limited CN's ability to grow and diversify in an age when the company could not afford to be confined to rail transport.

Deregulation and Increasing Autonomy: 1960s–80s

In the late 1960s deregulation and revision of government support put CN on the road to stability and increased profits. The National Transportation Act of 1967 removed nearly all the constraints on rates that had bound both the CN and Canadian Pacific. The legislation also compensated railways for unprofitable passenger services and branch lines that had been deemed necessary for the public welfare. CN was able to end its unprofitable passenger service in Newfoundland in 1969 as a result of the new law.

During the 1970s, CN's management concentrated on increasing autonomy and profitability. The organization of profit centers improved managerial accountability and highlighted areas of government-enforced losses. CN also concentrated on diversification, spreading the company's interests into telecommunications, hotels, and oil exploration. This measure took pressure off the company's slowing railway business.

In 1976 the Canadian government formed Via Rail Canada Inc. as a nationwide passenger rail service. Via Rail gradually began taking over responsibility for passenger train operation from both CN and archrival Canadian Pacific, a process largely complete by 1979. This relieved both railroad companies of the burden of running unprofitable passenger services.

Much of the railway's success in the 1980s was credited to increased independence from government constraints. The 1983 Western Grain Transportation Act brought an end to the 84-year-old Crow's Nest Pass Act, which had fixed shipping rates at 1925 levels. Only 20 percent of the actual transportation expenses had been covered, costing Canada's railways CAD 300 million per year.

The legislative changes freed capital for investment in such technical improvements as double tracks that prevented bottlenecks, speeded rail traffic, and improved the system's ability to compete with U.S. railroads. The late 1980s also saw CN enter the stack-car market. Having a stack of two freight containers required hefty investments in new lift equipment and higher tunnel clearances, but the added capacity increased efficiency and helped CN compete for lucrative contracts to transport Asian auto parts.

In 1987, 46-year CN veteran Ronald Lawless was appointed president and CEO of the transport company. Over the course of his five-year tenure, the executive oversaw a series of massive cutbacks, slashing employment from 100,000 to 40,000; eliminating over 40 percent of the railway's CAD 3.4 billion debt; and divesting (per a 1988 government order) the corporation's hotel, telecommunications, and trucking operations.

Two major strikes in the late 1980s marred a decade-long record of good labor relations. The Associated Railway Union's

50,000 members walked out over wages, pensions, and job security in August 1987. By the sixth day of the strike, government legislation that levied fines against workers who stayed off the job ended the stoppage. The legislation came in handy less than a week later, when 2,500 members of the Brotherhood of Locomotive Engineers threatened to strike. In an effort to head off labor disputes, CN established a forum for labor and management in 1991.

The early 1990s proved to be less financially stable for Canadian National than the previous decade. A recession reduced traffic that had already been siphoned off by competitors in the trucking and U.S. rail industries. Lingering regulatory constraints and high taxes further hampered the company's fiscal performance. To improve profitability, Canadian National's gas and oil subsidiary, CN Exploration, was privatized in 1991 and the proceeds from the sale were used to reduce the federal deficit. Early in 1992 the railway combined its U.S. subsidiary, the Grand Trunk Corp., with its Canadian rail interests, thereby creating CN North America. The reorganization was part of an effort to exploit continental markets, provide more efficient, cost-effective service to CN's shippers, and increase cross-border business, which stood at about 25 percent of annual sales.

1992–95: Cost Cutting and Privatization Under Tellier

But in spite of Lawless's various cutbacks and reorganizations, an internal study completed in 1990 showed that CN was still one of North America's least competitive railways. Revenues declined 22 percent from 1988 to 1992, when the company suffered a CAD 893.7 million loss. When Lawless was called away to wield his budget axe at Via Rail in 1992, CN hired Paul M. Tellier as president and CEO. It did not take the new executive long to assess the situation. In 1993, he warned that the company's annual losses would continue to surge, reaching CAD 1.5 billion by 1998, unless drastic measures were taken. Although some questioned this career civil servant's knowledge of the rail industry, Tellier was able—by 1994—to effect CN's first profit since 1990. It was not an easy task.

Tellier first cut employment at all levels. To show fiscal leadership and decentralize management, he slashed administrative layers by half in some cases. By 1993, he had reduced overall payroll to 32,700 employees. Although these layoffs cost CN CAD 80 million in 1993 alone (the company was obliged to buy out unionized workers' employment security contracts at an average of CAD 80,000 each) they promised increased productivity in the years to come.

Tellier even initiated merger negotiations with longtime rival CP Rail in 1992. When those talks broke down, the two firms tried to work out a deal to combine their beleaguered eastern operations, which together had lost over CAD 2 billion in recent years. More than one industry analyst had noted that overcapacity, especially east of Winnipeg, was a serious and ongoing threat to both players' profitability. A 1993 review by the National Transportation Act Review Commission asserted that "oversized rail networks" had plagued the industry in general since the 1920s; at CN in particular, 90 percent of its tonnage traversed only one-third of its total trackage. Nonetheless, late in

1994, Transport Minister Douglas Young put the brakes on CP Rail's CAD 1.4 billion offer to purchase CN's eastern assets, noting that the purchase price undervalued the property by at least 50 percent and threatened to reduce competition as well.

After years of denying that CN was being groomed for a launch on the public markets, legislation to that very effect was introduced in May 1995. The bill proposing Canadian National's privatization restricted individual share ownership to 15 percent and called for the creation of an employee stock option plan. In light of Quebec's flirtations with succession, the legislation also required the company to maintain its headquarters in Montreal and remain bilingual. Unlike previous IPOs of nationalized businesses, this one did not restrict share ownership to Canadians. The sheer size of the offering, at least CAD 1.6 billion, was expected to overwhelm the Canadian stock market. The federal government anticipated an estimated CAD 1 billion return on the sale.

Before being ready to go to market, however, CN still required some "primping." As part of an effort to cut debt by 50 percent, and therefore make its massive stock flotation attractive to domestic and international investors, the firm sold to the government its real estate holdings, which included the CN Tower in Toronto and 85,000 acres of property, for about CAD 500 million. Thus, prior to the offering, the company's only significant nonrail holding was wholly owned subsidiary Canac, which was involved in worldwide consulting on transportation and in project management.

These final moves enabled CN to proceed with the offering, which was completed on November 28, 1995. All of the company's shares were sold to investors via the Toronto, Montreal, and New York stock exchanges. Through an employee stock ownership plan, 42 percent of the shares went to CN employees. The offering raised CAD 2.26 billion ($1.65 billion) for government coffers, representing the largest privatization in Canadian history.

Post-Privatization Efficiency Drive and Acquisition of Illinois Central

Although CN suffered a CAD 1.08 billion loss in 1995 stemming from special charges of CAD 1.45 billion—primarily representing a writedown of the value of assets, most notably in the troubled eastern Canadian part of its network—1996, the firm's first full year as an investor-owned company, was its most profitable year in history. CN was able to post an operating profit of CAD 610 million and a net profit of CAD 142 million on revenue of CAD 4.16 billion, despite a special charge of CAD 381 million taken in the fourth quarter. The charge was taken in connection with plans to lay off an additional 2,250 workers in 1996 and 1997. A reduction in labor costs of CAD 95 million helped CN lower its operating ratio to 85.3 percent in 1996, compared to the 89.3 percent figure for the preceding year. Tellier had placed an emphasis on lowering CN's operating ratio, a key yardstick of a railway's efficiency, and profitability, that compared expenses with revenues (the lower the figure the better).

Another aspect of Tellier's efficiency drive was to eliminate unprofitable track and reduce the amount of overcapacity in the railway system. Thousands of miles of track were sold or abandoned in the mid- to late 1990s. He also invested heavily in information technology to allow CN to cut turnaround times, improve service, and operate with thousands fewer railcars. By 1997 Tellier had cut the operating ratio to 78.6 percent, which while much improved was still higher than those of the top U.S. railroads. In October 1998 CN announced plans to cut an additional 3,000 jobs, earning Tellier the enmity of many workers and union leaders.

Tellier also staked the future of Canadian National on the growth in north-south traffic of industrial products, automobiles, and commodities such as forest products engendered by the North American Free Trade Agreement (NAFTA), which took effect in 1994. He told *Barron's* in 1999, ''We want to be the NAFTA railroad.'' To that end, he engineered the $2.4 billion acquisition of Illinois Central Corporation (IC), completed in July 1999. The Illinois Central had been chartered in 1851 as the first land grant railroad in the United States. By 1999 it had grown into a 3,450-mile railroad, and the most efficient one in North America, its operating ratio in 1997 standing at 62.3 percent. Its trackage extended south from Chicago to New Orleans. This made a perfect fit with CN's system, which traversed Canada from Vancouver to Halifax and reached into the United States as far as Chicago. Combined, the two systems totaled 18,700 miles—the fifth largest in North America—and comprised the only railway on the continent connecting the three coasts of the Atlantic, Pacific, and the Gulf of Mexico. The resulting Y-shaped system had little overlap, which eased the concerns of regulators troubled by other recent rail combinations that had disrupted rail service and upset customers. It also meant that no significant layoffs were necessary from the combined workforce of 24,600.

In April 1998, after the merger had been announced but well before its completion, CN and IC entered into a deal that extended the reach of the combined system to the U.S. Southwest and into Mexico. The two companies reached a marketing alliance with the Kansas City Southern Railway Company (KCSR) through which CN could offer its customers coordinated interline train service throughout the three networks. The KCSR system ranged from Springfield, Illinois, where it could interchange with CN/IC, through Kansas City and Tulsa, Oklahoma, and then into the south, where another major interchange was established in Jackson, Mississippi. KCSR track also ranged west into Texas, including both Dallas and Houston, and the alliance also offered shippers access to Mexico's largest rail system, Transportacion Ferroviaria Mexicana, S.A. de C.V. (Grupo TFM), which was in a separate alliance with KCSR.

Following the acquisition of IC, Tellier remained president and CEO of CN, but he ceded control of day-to-day operations of the railroad to the former head of Illinois Central, E. Hunter Harrison, who was named executive vice-president and chief operating officer. Unlike Tellier, Harrison was a veteran railroad man, having entered the industry in 1964 as a carman/oiler. He was given much of the credit for making IC such an efficiently run railroad, particularly by implementing ''scheduled railroading,'' whereby freight trains were operated on a more precise schedule than had been typical. Under Harrison, CN too would become a scheduled railway, enabling it to considerably increase its usage of locomotives, freight cars, and train crews.

Early 2000s: Failed BNSF Merger, Several More Acquisitions

The impact of the IC deal was immediately felt as CN posted record profits of CAD 751 million in 1999, up from CAD 266 million the previous year. The operating ratio was down to 70.7 percent by the end of that year. It was from this position of strength that Canadian National agreed to combine its rail systems with those of Burlington Northern Santa Fe Corporation (BNSF) in a $6 billion deal that would have created a new holding company called North American Railways Inc. and the largest railroad on the continent with a network covering more than 50,000 route miles. In March 2000, however, the U.S. regulatory authority over the rail industry, the Surface Transportation Board (STB), issued a 15-month moratorium on rail mergers. The STB was concerned that the CN-BNSF merger could cause irreparable harm to the industry, setting off a ''final round'' of rail consolidation, the eventual result of which could be just two transcontinental railways. After a U.S. Court of Appeals upheld the moratorium in July, CN and BNSF called off the merger rather than endure a lengthy delay.

Disappointed that the deal was blocked but undeterred from his determination to see CN grow, Tellier completed the acquisition of Wisconsin Central Transportation Corporation (WCTC) in October 2001 for about $800 million in cash plus the assumption of $400 million in debt. CN thereby added about 2,150 miles of track, the key addition being a stretch of track running between Chicago and the twin port cities of Duluth, Minnesota/Superior, Wisconsin, that enabled CN to secure a main link between western Canada and the U.S. Midwest. CN also inherited WCTC's interests in several overseas railroads, including 42.5 percent of English, Welsh & Scottish Railway Holdings Limited of Great Britain and 33 percent of Australian Transport Network Limited.

In the last major moves of his tenure at CN, Tellier announced in November 2002 that the company would slash its workforce by 5 percent, or 1,146 jobs, and take a $173 million charge to settle growing personal injury and asbestos claims in the United States. The reasons for the job cuts were twofold: a drought in western Canada that reduced CN's grain shipping revenue and the efficiency drive that cut the number of locomotives and railcars the company needed, leading in turn to a reduced need for workers. At the end of 2002, Tellier left CN to become president and CEO of Bombardier Inc., the Canadian maker of transportation equipment. Harrison was the choice to succeed Tellier at CN.

The leadership transition was a smooth one as CN posted sharp increases in both profits and revenues in 2003 and 2004, culminating in the latter year in record net income of CAD 1.26 billion ($1.08 billion) on best-ever revenues of CAD 6.55 billion ($5.46 billion). The CAD 17.8 million lost as a result of a monthlong strike in early 2004 by 5,000 CN workers, all members of the Canadian Auto Workers union, was more than offset by the completion of two more significant acquisitions. In May 2004 CN acquired the rail and marine holdings of Great Lakes Transportation LLC (GLT) for CAD 547 million ($395 million). GLT was a group of rail and water carriers that catered particularly to the needs of the steel industry in the Midwest and that provided CN with additional links between western Canada and Chicago. It included the 200-plus-mile Duluth, Missabe and Iron Range Railway Company, an iron ore carrier; the Bessemer & Lake Erie Railroad Company, a transporter of coal, iron ore, and limestone between the port of Conneaut, Ohio, and steel mills in Pittsburgh; and Great Lakes Fleet Inc., a firm that owned and operated eight vessels carrying bulk commodities on the Great Lakes.

In July 2004 CN finalized its purchase of BC Rail Ltd. from the government of British Columbia for CAD 1 billion. The deal gave CN ownership of the BC Rail franchise and the right to operate over its more than 1,400 miles of track under a long-term lease. The province retained ownership of the track itself, but CN assumed responsibility for track maintenance. The BC Rail trackage ran from North Vancouver to Fort Nelson in the far northern reaches of the province. CN immediately announced plans to cut BC Rail's workforce to 950 employees, from 1,380, sparking a great deal of criticism. This acquisition strengthened CN's position in forest products shipping and also enhanced its access to the U.S. West Coast. Industry observers suggested that additional acquisitions were possible given CN's success in integrating the deals, its strong profits and cash flow, and its continued position as the most efficient railroad among the North American majors.

Principal Subsidiaries

Grand Trunk Corporation (U.S.A.); Illinois Central Corporation (U.S.A.); Illinois Central Railroad Company (U.S.A.).

Principal Operating Units

Western Canada Region; Eastern Canada Region; United States Region.

Principal Competitors

Canadian Pacific Railway Limited; Union Pacific Corporation; Burlington Northern Santa Fe Corporation; CSX Corporation; Norfolk Southern Corporation.

Further Reading

Bertin, Oliver, "CN Chops 3,000 More Jobs," *Globe and Mail,* October 21, 1998, p. A1.
——, "CN to Cut Rail Lines Across Canada," *Globe and Mail,* July 3, 1996, p. A1.
——, "CN Unites Continental Rail System," *Globe and Mail,* July 2, 1999, p. B1.
Bertin, Oliver, and Susan Bourette, "CN Corrals Illinois Central," *Globe and Mail,* February 11, 1998, p. B1.
Bonney, Joseph, "CN + Grand Trunk = CN North America," *American Shipper,* February 1992.
Branswell, Brenda, "The Axe Falls Again," *Maclean's,* November 2, 1998, pp. 62+.
Bruce, Harry, *The Pig That Flew: The Battle to Privatize Canadian National,* Vancouver: Douglas and McIntyre, 1997, 168 p.
Chipello, Christopher J., "Bombardier Names New CEO, Canadian National's Teller," *Wall Street Journal,* December 16, 2002, p. B4.
——, "Hopes High for 'New' Canadian National," *Wall Street Journal,* December 7, 1995, p. B9.
Chipello, Christopher J., and Daniel Machalaba, "Canadian National Railway Buys Wisconsin Central for $800 Million," *Wall Street Journal,* January 31, 2001, p. A10.
"CN Wins Bid for BC Rail," *Railway Age,* January 2004, pp. 14, 17.
Dorin, Patrick C., *The Canadian National Railways' Story,* Seattle: Superior Publishing, 1975, 206 p.
Freeman, Alan, "CN Shares May Fetch $1.5 billion," *Globe and Mail,* May 6, 1995, p. A1.
Gallagher, John, "Network Builder: Exports into U.S., Steel Industry Supply 'Partnership' Drive CN's Latest Acquisitions," *Traffic World,* October 27, 2003, pp. 31–32.
Jang, Brent, "CN Buys U.S. Line to Boost Western Exports," *Globe and Mail,* October 21, 2003, p. B1.
——, "CN Joins Double-Stack Parade," *American Shipper,* February 1989.
——, "CN Plans Share Buyback As Profit Rises in Quarter," *Globe and Mail,* October 28, 2004, p. B8.
——, "CN Wins BC Rail in $1-Billion Cash Deal," *Globe and Mail,* November 26, 2003, p. B1.
Johnson, Bruce, "How CN Competes with U.S. Stack Trains," *American Shipper,* June 1988.
——, "Trans-Canada Double Track Nears Completion," *American Shipper,* September 1988.
Kaihla, Paul, "Back on the Rails," *Maclean's,* January 13, 1997, pp. 36+.
Koch, George, "Full Throttle: Canada's Railroads—and Their Profits—Come Steaming Back," *Barron's,* September 13, 1999, p. 24.
Lipin, Steven, and Christopher J. Chipello, "Canadian National Railway to Acquire Illinois Central in $2.4 Billion Accord," *Wall Street Journal,* February 11, 1998, p. A4.
Machalaba, Daniel, "Burlington Northern, Canadian National Scuttle Plan to Combine Railroad Lines," *Wall Street Journal,* July 21, 2000, p. A4.
Machalaba, Daniel, and Steven Lipin, "Burlington Northern Agrees to Merger: Canadian National Rail Deal for $6 Billion Will Form Leader in North America," *Wall Street Journal,* December 20, 1999, p. A3.
MacKay, Donald, *The Asian Dream: The Pacific Rim and Canada's National Railway,* Vancouver: Douglas and McIntyre, 1986, 223 p.
——, *The People's Railway: A History of Canadian National,* Vancouver: Douglas and McIntyre, 1992, 328 p.
McArthur, Keith, "Tellier Still Has a Few Spikes to Drive at CN," *Globe and Mail,* November 16, 2000, p. B1.
McKenna, Barrie, "Ottawa Big Winner in CN Sale," *Globe and Mail,* May 31, 1995, p. B1.
Murray, Tom, *Canadian National Railway,* St. Paul, Minn.: MBI Publishing, 2004, 160 p.
Rowan, Geoffrey, "CN Productivity Right Off the Tracks," *Globe and Mail,* 9 October 1991, B1.
Stevens, G.R., *History of the Canadian National Railways,* New York: Macmillan, 1973, 538 p.
Waldie, Paul, "CN Slashes 5% of Work Force," *Globe and Mail,* November 27, 2002, p. B1.
Watson, Thomas, "On Track," *Canadian Business,* May 12, 2003, pp. 24+.
Weaver, Kent R., *The Politics of Industrial Change: Railway Policy in North America,* Washington, D.C.: Brookings Institution, 1985, 291 p.
Welty, Gus, "CN + IC: A Three-Coast Strategy," *Railway Age,* March 1998, p. 33.
——, "CN Turnaround: A Work in Progress," *Railway Age,* August 1996, p. 39.
Wilson-Smith, Anthony, "Rolling South: CN's Merger Plans Would Make It Part of North America's Largest Railroad," *Maclean's,* February 7, 2000, p. 30.

—updates: April Dougal Gasbarre; David E. Salamie

Canadian Tire Corporation, Limited

2180 Yonge Street
P.O. Box 770, Station K
Toronto, Ontario M4P 2V8
Canada
Telephone: (416) 480-3000
Fax: (416) 544-7715
Web site: http://www.canadiantire.ca

Public Company
Incorporated: 1927
Employees: 8,300
Sales: CAD 8.39 billion ($6.97 billion) (2004)
Stock Exchanges: Toronto
Ticker Symbol: CTR
NAIC: 441310 Automotive Parts and Accessories Stores;
    441320 Tire Dealers; 444110 Home Centers; 447110
    Gasoline Stations with Convenience Stores; 448140
    Family Clothing Stores; 454111 Electronic Shopping;
    811191 Automotive Oil Change and Lubrication
    Shops; 811192 Car Washes

Canadian Tire Corporation, Limited is one of the leading retailers in Canada. The company, aided by associate dealers, franchisees, and agents, operates the flagship Canadian Tire chain, which includes more than 450 stores from coast to coast. These stores offer a wide selection of automotive parts, accessories, and services; sports and leisure products; and household goods. About 85 percent of all Canadians live within a 15-minute drive of a Canadian Tire store; nine out of ten adult Canadians shop at one of these outlets at least twice a year; and 40 percent of Canadians shop at Canadian Tire every week. The company also offers online shopping via the Canadian Tire web site and runs the 40-unit PartSource automotive parts specialty chain. The Canadian Tire Petroleum unit is the nation's leading independent retailer of gasoline with about 250 gasoline filling stations, some of which include a convenience store and/or a car wash. Canadian Tire Financial Services finances and manages the Canadian Tire Options MasterCard program, which has more than 3.1 million cardmembers; markets insurance and warranty products; and

offers emergency roadside assistance through the Canadian Tire Auto Club. The company also owns Mark's Work Wearhouse, operator of around 320 men's and women's clothing stores, including approximately three dozen L'Équipeur stores in Quebec; these outlets specialize in business casual and weekend clothing and workwear. Canadian Tire Corporation is a true national institution, so much so that it issues its own "money," was celebrated on a Canadian postage stamp, and has won the nation's highest honor, the Order of Canada. Martha Billes, a daughter of one of the company cofounders, is the controlling shareholder, owning a stake of more than 60 percent.

Early History

Canada Tire was started in 1922 by brothers John W. and Alfred Jackson (A.J.) Billes. The budding entrepreneurs invested their combined savings of CAD 1,800 in an automobile service garage and auto parts depot in Toronto. The company—Hamilton Tire and Garage Limited—stocked a small inventory of repair and replacement goods, including tires, batteries, and automobile fluids. Although the automobile industry was still in its infancy, the Billeses believed surging automobile sales at the time indicated a bright future for their business. Later that year, in fact, Toronto hosted its first "Closed Car Show," in which windshield wipers, automatic starters, and other new car parts were introduced.

The Billeses experienced what could have turned out to be a major setback shortly after they opened their shop: A bridge that routed traffic past their garage was shut down for repairs. To overcome the problem, the brothers converted the garage into an overnight parking facility and took turns sleeping in the garage at night. Then, early in 1923, they moved the entire operation to a better location. The new shop included retail goods and a gas pump. The success of that outlet encouraged the Billeses to open a second retail store nearby. Early gains were largely attributable to A.J.'s marketing savvy. He began offering free road maps in the company's promotional flyers, for example, because maps were rare at the time and valued by customers.

In 1927, after four years of rising sales, the Billeses changed the name of their enterprise to Canadian Tire Corporation, Limited. That same year, A.J., building off of his successful road

Company Perspectives:

Canadian Tire is a growing network of innovative, interrelated businesses achieving extraordinary results through extraordinary people. We help Canadians make a great start in their lives every day by providing them with essential products and services. Canadian Tire customers shop in our retail stores, fill up their cars with gas and choose convenience items at our gas bars, get their vehicles washed at our car wash outlets, find specialized automotive parts at Part-Source, choose clothing at Mark's Work Wearhouse, enjoy the convenience of our universally accepted Canadian Tire Options MasterCard, and benefit from the added value of Canadian Tire ''Money.''

map idea, decided to test a mail-order offer to car owners in southern Ontario and New York state. Response to that effort, in turn, led him to publish a full catalog in 1928 that featured Canadian Tire's retail offerings and allowed customers to order by mail. Thus, the company became a pioneer in the mail-order and catalog auto-parts retailing industry. Indeed, Canadian Tire's mail-order sales swelled in the late 1920s and early 1930s. Even during the Great Depression the company continued to post gains as a result of its low prices, high-quality merchandise, and an emphasis on customer service. Importantly, shrewd marketing always played a role.

Throughout the 1930s and into the 1960s, in fact, Canadian Tire was a leading innovator in its industry. Among A.J.'s most brilliant marketing schemes was Canadian Tire ''money,'' an innovation he concocted in the 1950s. A.J. knew a lot of money could be made from the sale of gasoline from his store pumps. Because of pressure from the big oil companies, however, retailers such as A.J. were unable to lower their prices to undercut competitors. A.J. got around that hurdle by giving his gas customers coupons that they could use for merchandise in his stores. The scheme was a major success and continued to be used, in some form, for several decades. Another of A.J.'s innovations was clerks on roller skates. When A.J. expanded one of his stores into a vacant supermarket he became concerned that the longer aisles would slow down his clerks. Besides speeding up the clerks, the roller skates served as an entertainment gimmick that drew customers.

Among other firsts, Canadian Tire introduced the unconditional tire guarantee in 1931. Until that time, tires were guaranteed only against manufacturing defects. A.J. decided to begin offering an unconditional ''Super-Lastic'' tire guarantee that would cover the tire for almost any mishap. ''In those days the guarantee on tires was only for defects and workmanship,'' A.J. recalled in company annals, ''but customers would come in with a shard of glass or a stone bruise, saying well, I didn't do that. So I introduced the first one-year unconditional tire guarantee. People came in looking for a fight, and there wasn't one.'' Canadian Tire also helped pioneer the profit-sharing concept, giving workers a stake in the profits of the business and generating employee motivation and loyalty.

Canadian Tire expanded in the 1930s as business grew. In 1934 the company opened an associate store in Hamilton,

Ontario. That store was the first in what would become a huge chain of stores that spanned Canada. Although Canadian Tire automotive lines were already stocked in other stores, the new outlets gave the company higher profit margins and more control over its products. As the chain expanded, Canadian Tire's stores and mail-order catalogs began featuring a wide range of parts and supplies—many under the Canadian Tire brand name—including motor and chassis parts, radio equipment, and hundreds of miscellaneous accessories. In addition, Canadian Tire was beginning to branch out into sporting goods such as camping equipment. Gains at the new store spawned a flurry of expansion during the mid- and late 1930s. By 1939, in fact, Canadian Tire was operating an impressive 71 stores in addition to its thriving mail-order business.

Postwar Expansion

World War II caused shortages of many goods, and Canadian Tire was forced to change many of its operating procedures. Nevertheless, the company managed to adapt and even to sustain its healthy growth rate throughout the war years. By 1946, in fact, Canadian Tire had boosted its total number of outlets to 116. As a result of spiraling demand during the postwar economic boom, moreover, sales soared. Canadian Tire built a giant new warehouse that was averaging 57 tons of new inventory daily by 1952. By 1956 even that facility had become too small to serve the company's 160-plus outlets, so Canadian Tire built a large new distribution center. Before the center was opened, President John W. Billes passed away. His brother, A.J., succeeded him.

Canadian Tire continued to prosper under A.J.'s ten-year stint as president. Warehouse and distribution centers were expanded, and the company's network of retail outlets increased to a total of 225 by the mid-1960s. A.J., always open to new ideas, was among the first retailers to use new electronic equipment and computers to handle accounting, inventory, and invoicing tasks. Canadian Tire flourished under his leadership, becoming one of the most successful retailers in Canada. Later, looking back on his career and life, A.J. would give much of the credit for the company's success to his employees: ''If asked what has been my life's most rewarding experience, it is good health, strength, and a destiny which afforded me the opportunity to assist our corporate people in recognizing and more fully exploiting their God-given talents, both for their own betterment and for that of others around them, and while in the process, building a business wherein the spirit of enlightened self-interest continues.''

A.J. stepped aside in 1966; J. Dean Muncaster succeeded him. Muncaster had started out working in a Canadian Tire store before working his way through the executive ranks. Under Muncaster's direction Canadian Tire continued to expand. The company began its own long-distance hauling operation in 1967, which would balloon in size to include more than 700 transport units by the 1990s. A second major distribution facility was built in 1973 to feed the growing Canadian Tire retail chain. In 1979, moreover, the company completed a giant 65-million-cubic-feet, computer-controlled, high-rise warehouse and distribution center that was among the largest of its kind in the world. That facility helped to support the company's new Auto Parts Depot division. The Auto Parts Depot, on the

---

Key Dates:

1922: Brothers John W. and Alfred Jackson (A. J.) Billes purchase Hamilton Tire and Garage Limited, an automobile service garage and auto parts depot in Toronto.
1927: The Billeses incorporate their enterprise as Canadian Tire Corporation, Limited; first mail-order catalog is published.
1931: Company introduces its unconditional tire guarantee.
1934: First associate store opens in Hamilton, Ontario.
1950s: Canadian Tire "money" is introduced.
1982: Canadian Tire buys the U.S.-based White Stores, Inc. automotive retail chain.
1985: The White Stores venture flops and is divested.
1991: Company reenters U.S. market with the establishment of the Auto Source chain.
1994: Multiyear store improvement program is launched.
1995: Canadian Tire announces that it will shutter Auto Source.
1997: Martha Billes, daughter of A.J. Billes, buys out her brothers' stakes in the company, giving her a controlling 61 percent interest.
1999: The PartSource chain begins its official rollout.
2002: Clothing retailer Mark's Work Wearhouse Ltd. is acquired.

---

cutting edge of just-in-time techniques that would emerge in the 1980s, provided speedy daytime and overnight delivery of auto parts to Canadian Tire outlets.

1980s to Early 1990s: Failed U.S. Ventures, Heightened Competition at Home

During the late 1970s Canadian Tire upgraded its existing stores and expanded into British Columbia with a new store format. Then, in 1982, Canadian Tire reached outside its national borders when it purchased the assets of White Stores, Inc., of Wichita, Texas, for $144 million. White Stores was a chain of more than 400 automotive retail stores in the United States. Most of the stores were owned and operated by dealers, but some of the outlets were company owned, and Canadian Tire also took possession of the company's warehouse operations. Canadian Tire attempted to convert the stores into a format similar to that used by its Canadian stores. Unfortunately, the venture flopped and Canadian Tire elected in 1985 to sell the entire division. Shortly thereafter, Muncaster resigned. He was replaced in 1986 by Dean Groussman, the former chief executive of White Stores.

By the mid-1980s Canadian Tire was generating more than CAD 2 billion in annual sales and operating nearly 400 stores throughout Canada (not including the U.S. White Stores division). In addition, the company was operating about 115 gas stations. Besides increasing the number of stores in its portfolio during the 1970s and early 1980s, Canadian Tire had introduced a variety of new merchandise. The company had started selling a large amount of sporting and leisure items, as well as hard-

ware, lawn and garden items, inexpensive furniture and other home products, and even luggage. In essence, Canadian Tire was becoming a general-merchandise discount store with an emphasis on automotive products.

Under Groussman's leadership, Canadian Tire continued to expand its store network and distribution facilities. Between 1986 and 1990, in fact, Canadian Tire added about 75 gas stations and 17 retail stores to its group, pushing sales past the CAD 3 billion mark for the first time in 1990. Meanwhile, net earnings gradually rose to nearly CAD 150 million annually in both 1989 and 1990—Canadian Tire was ranked as the 42nd most profitable company in Canada in 1990—and the company's workforce swelled to nearly 25,000. Encouraged by healthy gains at home, Canadian Tire management decided once again to take a crack at the massive U.S. market. In 1991 the company announced its intent to enter the Indianapolis, Indiana, market with four new stores under the name Auto Source Inc.

Canadian Tire had started its Auto Source experiment in 1990, when it opened two stores under the banner Car Care USA. Those stores, which mimicked the successful Pep Boys centers, incorporated 14 service bays and about 18,000 square feet of space for inventory. In 1991, it decided to change the names of those stores and began construction on two new stores. The design of the new outlets was influenced by the growing trend toward superstores. Thus, the new Auto Source outlets boasted 30,000 feet of retail space and 24 service bays. Auto Source planned to open between 100 and 150 additional outlets in the United States by the close of the century, aiming for CAD 1 billion in sales by that time.

During the early 1990s Canadian Tire opened six more Auto Source outlets, for a total of ten, that were soon generating more than CAD 60 million in annual revenues. Like the company's first attempt in the U.S. market, however, Auto Source proved unprofitable. The venture lost CAD 15.3 million in 1992 alone. Company officials explained that the loss was not unexpected considering that it was a new enterprise. In 1993, however, the division's losses increased. Part of the problem was that Auto Source was attempting a start-up in the midst of a U.S. economic downturn. But losses, according to critics, also stemmed from the fact that the company's U.S. support infrastructure was too great for the ten-store chain. Furthermore, the auto parts industry was facing increasing competition from discount stores such as Wal-Mart Stores, Inc., as well as new entrants into the burgeoning automotive discount superstore industry.

In fact, Canadian Tire's domestic operations were also suffering from increased competition, particularly from invading mega-discounters such as Wal-Mart and Kmart Corporation. Indeed, by the early 1990s Canadian Tire was generating only about one-third of its revenues from automotive-related sales. The other revenue was generated from general merchandise. Canadian Tire was Canada's largest hardware retailer, for example, and a leading supplier of sporting goods. Profits from those items were increasingly being pinched by competition from discount warehouse rivals. Partly as a result of that dynamic, Canadian Tire's financial performance deteriorated in the early 1990s. Although the company's revenues grew to CAD 3.2 billion in 1992 and then to CAD 3.6 billion by 1994, its net income plunged to less than CAD 100 million annually in 1992 and 1993.

Revitalized Under Bachand in the Mid- to Late 1990s

Groussman left Canadian Tire in 1992 and was replaced by Stephen E. Bachand, previously an executive vice-president at Hechinger Company, a home center chain based in Landover, Maryland. Under Bachand's leadership, the company began implementing a strategy to help it compete in the new retail environment. That meant eliminating certain inventory items such as furniture and luggage from some stores and focusing on the company's traditional core products: automotive accessories, hardware, and sporting goods. The big superstores that were popping up across Canada carried all of those items and often had larger selections. But Canadian Tire benefited from intense market penetration—about 80 percent of all Canadian citizens lived within 15 minutes of one of its outlets—and was also known for its high-quality products. Importantly, Canadian Tire launched an aggressive renewal program that called for the enlargement of 240 of its 423 stores by 1998.

Canadian Tire's net earnings plummeted to just CAD 5.5 million in 1994, partly as a result of weak gasoline markets that were slowing the company's gas station division. Early in 1995, moreover, the company decided to shutter its Auto Source chain in the United States and completely bail out of that market. All of the U.S. stores were sold by 1996. Despite this setback, early results from the company's store expansion program were positive and management expected to realize substantial gains as it enlarged existing stores.

On April 3, 1995, company founder Alfred Jackson Billes passed away at the age of 93. His professional accomplishments included investiture in 1976 as a Member of the Order of Canada, the highest recognition a civilian Canadian could achieve. He was also inducted into the Canadian Hardware/Houseware Hall of Fame in 1986.

Canadian Tire's store improvement program continued throughout the late 1990s and into the new decade, by which time the cost of the program would top CAD 1 billion. While some existing stores were expanded to conform to a handful of new prototype layouts (later reduced to three), in many cases brand-new stores were built as replacements. By 1999, when the number of completed outlets stood at 188, the program had been expanded: The firm now planned to convert 350 of its 430 stores to the new formats.

As the company saw dividends from the more modern store designs and improvements in customer service, it also made changes in its management and ownership structure. In the late 1980s and early 1990s relations between the Toronto headquarters and the Canadian Tire dealers had been strained—so strained that the dealers had tried to buy the company in 1987 from the three children of A.J. Billes who held a controlling interest. The brothers, Alfred and David, and the sister, Martha, had been locked in a battle for control of the company before agreeing to sell to the dealers. But security regulators blocked the plan, contending that it was ''abusive'' to nonvoting shareholders. A truce was reached in 1989 that put an end to various lawsuits, but it was not until Bachand came onboard that rela-

tions with the dealers began to be mended. Bachand spent much of his first year meeting with and listening to the dealers, and he also started involving them in corporate strategy sessions. Most importantly, he got them to buy into the store improvement program, which began to pay off handsomely for all involved by the late 1990s. Meantime, the unsettled ownership situation reached a resolution as well. In 1997 Martha Billes bought out her brothers' stakes for CAD 45.4 million, boosting her holding to 61.2 percent.

The latter move came as Canadian Tire was celebrating its 75th anniversary, a milestone that Canada Post Corporation marked by issuing a commemorative stamp. It featured the company cofounders, an early Canadian Tire storefront, and a scene meant to be indicative of the relationship between the company and Canadians.

Another significant development in the late 1990s was the launch of PartSource, a new retail concept that was officially rolled out in 1999 after the testing of a few outlets. About 10,000 square feet in size, PartSource stores sold only automotive parts and were aimed at professional automotive installers and serious do-it-yourselfers. The move was widely viewed as a preemptive strike against the possible encroachment of major U.S. auto parts retailers, such as AutoZone, Inc. and The Pep Boys, into the Canadian market.

Remaining a Canadian Icon in the 21st Century

By 1999, under Bachand's leadership, revenue at Canadian Tire had reached CAD 4.73 billion, while profits had improved to CAD 145.9 million. Bachand announced in early 2000 that he would retire from the company, having successfully transformed Canadian Tire into a more modern operation. He had managed to do so while fending off the aggressive cross-border advances of U.S. retailing giants Wal-Mart and The Home Depot, Inc. Succeeding Bachand was Wayne Sales, who had been second-in-command as executive vice-president of Canadian Tire Retail. An American like Bachand, Sales had joined Canadian Tire in 1991, having previously worked in the United States for Kmart Corporation.

Sales oversaw the launch in 2000 of Canadian Tire's ''Next Generation'' store format, which was designed to be easier for customers to navigate and featured expanded and more upscale kitchen, hardware, and other product lines. Part of the aim with the new format was to attract more female customers. All stores built in 2001 and 2002 were given the new format, and some existing stores were also retrofitted into ''Next Generation'' stores. By 2002, 290 of Canadian Tire's 451 outlets featured one of the newer store formats. In November 2000, meanwhile, Canadian Tire launched its web site, which already by year's end was one of Canada's top five online retail destinations.

In a move that surprised many, Canadian Tire acquired Mark's Work Wearhouse Ltd. in February 2002 for CAD 110.8 million. Mark's operated about 320 outlets across Canada that sold casual clothing and footwear for work and leisure. Under Canadian Tire, it operated as a separate business unit. In 2004 the company began testing Mark's Work Wearhouse ''stores within a store'' inside of select Canadian Tire outlets. The addition of Mark's helped boost overall Canadian Tire revenues to CAD 7.86

billion by 2003. Profits by that time had ballooned to CAD 241.3 million, a 22 percent increase in just one year. Also aiding these stellar results were improvements to the product selection at Canadian Tire outlets, the addition of more gas stations and car washes, and the conversion of its customers from proprietary credit cards to a cobranded MasterCard called Options.

Not resting on its laurels, Canadian Tire began testing a new retail format in 2003 called Concept 20/20. Designed to achieve sales 20 percent higher than an older format Canadian Tire store, the new concept featured an updated layout, new and expanded product assortments, a customer care center, new store signage, and a redesigned exterior facade. Some of the 20/20 stores featured a Mark's Work Wearhouse store-within-a-store. The test stores were so successful—achieving 30 percent higher sales—that Canadian Tire announced that beginning in 2004 Concept 20/20 would supersede the Next Generation format as the prototype for the ongoing store improvement program.

For 2004 profits improved to CAD 291.5 million on record sales of CAD 8.39 billion. The company said that strong holiday buying played a significant role in the 20.8 percent increase in profits and the 6.7 percent jump in revenues. CEO Sales told analysts in early 2005 that the company was considering future acquisitions, building on its successful purchase of Mark's. An expansion of the Mark's store-within-a-store initiative was also under consideration because results had exceeded expectations. Canadian Tire, one of a dwindling number of Canadian-owned retailers, confidently looked to the future as an icon of the Canadian business community, and indeed for many Canadians it was an integral part of their lives.

Principal Subsidiaries

Canadian Tire Financial Services Limited; Canadian Tire Real Estate Limited; Canadian Tire Bank; CTC Capital Corp. (U.S.A.); CTC Holdings Inc. (U.S.A.).

Principal Operating Units

Canadian Tire Retail; PartSource; Canadian Tire Petroleum; Mark's Work Wearhouse.

Principal Competitors

Wal-Mart Stores, Inc.; Hudson's Bay Company; Sears Canada Inc.; Costco Wholesale Corporation; The Home Depot, Inc.; Ace Hardware Corporation; True Value Company; The Forzani Group Ltd.

Further Reading

"Auto Source Loses Money But Gains Experience," *Automotive Marketing,* May 1994, p. 20.
Bachand, Stephen E., "There's a Lot More to Canadian Tire," *Business Quarterly,* Spring 1995, pp. 30–33, 36–39.
Brown, Ian, *Freewheeling: The Feuds, Broods, and Outrageous Fortunes of the Billes Family and Canada's Favorite Company,* Toronto: Harper & Collins, 1989, 339 p.
——, "Trouble in Tireland," *Canadian Business,* November 1989, pp. 95–109.
"Canadian Tire's Journey South Is Uphill All the Way," *Business Week,* February 6, 1984, p. 88H.
Caulfield, John, "Canadian Tire CEO Announces Retirement," *National Home Center News,* January 24, 2000, pp. 1, 12.
——, "Canadian Tire Looks to 'The Next Generation,'" *National Home Center News,* May 1, 2000, pp. 3, 27.
——, "Decisions Lie Ahead for Canadian Tire's New CEO," *National Home Center News,* September 4, 2000, pp. 4, 49.
Deverell, John, "Canadian Tire Remake 'Encouraging' Sales Up 60 Percent in Revamped Stores, Shareholders Told," *Toronto Star,* May 6, 1995, p. E7.
Duff, Mike, "Canadian Tire Rethinks Strategy," *DSN Retailing Today,* July 23, 2001, pp. 3, 26.
Fox, Jim, "Canadian Tire in the Passing Lane: Chain Rolls Out New Store, Merchandising Strategy," *Discount Store News,* September 18, 1995, pp. 11, 111.
——, "Canadian Tire Names CEO," *DSN Retailing Today,* August 21, 2000, pp. 4, 43.
Heinzl, John, "Canadian Tire Opens Parts Stores," *Globe and Mail,* August 7, 1996, p. B4.
Lorinc, John, "Road Warriors," *Canadian Business,* October 1995, pp. 26+.
McBride, Hugh, *Our Store: 75 Years of Canadians and Canadian Tire,* Toronto: Quantum Book Group, 1997, 127 p.
McCann, Julie, "Cutting the Crap: Wayne Sales, the New Man Behind the Wheel at Canadian Tire," *National Post Business,* March 2001, pp. 46–48, 53+.
McFarland, Janet, "Canadian Tire Now Seen As the Last Northern Fortress," *Globe and Mail,* August 14, 2004, p. B5.
McQueen, Rod, *Can't Buy Me Love: How Martha Billes Made Canadian Tire Hers,* Toronto: Stoddart, 2001, 282 p.
Olijnyk, Zena, "In the Driver's Seat," *Financial Post,* October 18, 1997, p. 18.
Olive, David, "Tire on a Roll," *Globe and Mail Report on Business Magazine,* June 27, 1997, p. 17.
Parent, Tawn, "Not Just an Automotive Chain: Canada's Largest Specialty Wholesaler Opens U.S. Headquarters Near Castleton," *Indianapolis Business Journal,* May 28, 1990, p. 1A.
Pearlstein, Steven, "Turnaround in Toronto: Canadian Tire Meets Challenge from United States," *Washington Post,* January 19, 1999, p. E1.
Powell, Chris, "On a Roll: With the Acquisition of Mark's Work Wearhouse, an Ambitious Expansion Strategy, and a New "Let's Get Started" Positioning, Canadian Tire Isn't Sitting on Its Advertising Laurels," *Marketing Magazine,* July 1, 2002, p. 10.
Shalom, Francois, "Is 'the Tire' Going Flat? Tough Competition Is Forcing Canadian Tire Back to Its Strengths," *Gazette,* September 19, 1994, p. C8.
Sheikh, Fawzia, "How Canadian Tire Refocused and Solved Its Identity Crisis," *Marketing Magazine,* December 20–27, 1999, p. 13.
Southerst, John, "Tire Kicker," *Canadian Business,* July 1993, p. 37.
Strauss, Marina, "Canadian Tire to Test New Concept," *Globe and Mail,* May 15, 2003, p. B1.
——, "Sister to Rule at Canadian Tire," *Globe and Mail,* July 22, 1997, p. B1.
Strauss, Marina, and Elizabeth Church, "Canadian Tire Makes Surprise Mark's Work Wearhouse Bid," *Globe and Mail,* December 20, 2001, p. B1.
Total Customer Value: A Special Edition in Memory of A.J. Billes, 1902–1995, Toronto: Canadian Tire Corporation, Limited, 1995.
Wirebach, John, "Canadian Tire Closes U.S. Subsidiary," *Automotive Marketing,* February 1995, p. 6.

—Dave Mote
—update: David E. Salamie

Cascades Inc.

404 Marie-Victorin, P.O. Box 30
Kingsey Falls, Quebec J0A 1B0
Canada
Telephone: (819) 363-5100
Fax: (819) 636-5155
Web site: http://www.cascades.com

Public Company
Founded: 1964
Employees: 15,000
Sales: CAD 3.3 billion (2004)
Stock Exchanges: Toronto
Ticker Symbol: CAS
NAIC: 322121 Paper (Except Newsprint) Mills; 322130
  Paperboard Mills; 423930 Recyclable Material
  Merchant Wholesalers

Cascades Inc., over its 40-year history, has grown from the operator of a single paper mill in a small Canadian town to a corporation with international presence. Owned approximately 40 percent by management, Cascades' main business segments are packaging products, tissue papers, and fine papers, primarily made from the two million tons of paper and board the company recycles annually. The company had nearly 150 operating units in six countries—Canada, the United States, France, England, Germany, and Sweden—during 2004.

Family Plan Looking Good on Paper: 1960s–80s

A father and son team, Antonio and Bernard Lemaire, had a vision of reviving a paper mill in a small town to the northeast of Montreal. Cascades Paper Inc. was established in Kingsey Falls, Quebec, on March 26, 1964, and the pair went on to transform the single mill into a model for subsequent plants.

The Lemaire's concept was to use recycled pulp, a cheap source of material, to manufacture paper for industrial markets. Having limited resources, Cascades needed the support of the local financial institution to buy the mill. Finding success there, the company acquired other shuttered or declining mills. Diver-

sification coincided with growth: Cascades moved into the manufacture of molded pulp, tissue paper, corrugated carton, and boxboard.

In December 1982, Cascades made its initial public offering. Common stock was listed on the Montreal Stock Exchange in January 1983, and then on the Toronto Stock Exchange in October 1984. The move to the public sector facilitated a new phase of expansion, allowing the operation to enter the ranks of the world-class papermakers.

In 1985, Cascades entered the European carton board market, establishing Cascades S.A. in France and taking over three businesses in that country. Exceeding their expectations in terms of output and market share, the company had by 1989 become France's largest cartonboard producer, according to *Pulp & Paper International.* During the year the company bought two additional firms, one in Belgium and one in Sweden. A sole sales organization represented all the European operations. Meanwhile, back in North America, Cascades had established control over more than 20 companies.

Successful Groupings: 1990s

The 1990s would be a decade marked by both acquisition and divestment of businesses. In 1992, Cascades acquired Paperboard Industries and created a subsidiary to combine those assets with Canadian and European boxboard mills. Cascades Paperboard International Inc. then embarked on an effort to reduce debt load and improve profitability through a range of activities including elimination of the Belgium mill, entering a joint venture for another French mill, and restructuring some of the debt of its North American operations.

By 1995, Cascades Paperboard International Inc.—held 63.4 percent by Cascades—was the leading producer of boxboard in Canada and France. Moreover, 43 percent of Cascades' consolidated sales came from its boxboard operations.

Fine papers was Cascades second largest business segment. The cornerstone of the group was Rolland Inc., a company in which Cascades acquired a 73.5 percent interest during 1992. Cascades ranked second among Canadian producers of fine papers and related products, according to *Pulp & Paper.*

Company Perspectives:

Of all the elements that have contributed to Cascades' history of success, the two that have undoubtedly done the most to differentiate Cascades from the rest of the pulp and paper industry are its approach to doing business and its corporate culture. This culture, based on workforce respect and commitment as well as social responsibility and preservation of resources, has been a constant source of innovation and advancement for the Cascades Group. In fact, in many ways Cascades has become a pioneer and leader, largely because of its innovative vision in terms of human resources management, but also because of its commitment to quality, technological development and environmental protection. The Cascades philosophy has also been an important engine for growth and financial performance. Indeed, Cascades has successfully channeled the energy and talent of its employees to build a world-class company, while maintaining the organizational flexibility required to adapt to changing markets.

The containerboard group made up the company's third largest division. Cascades was looking into North American investments and strategic alliances in central Europe and Asia to expand that market and the one for its packaging products division.

Overall, Cascades was producing more than 400 different products during the mid-1990s. They ranged from security papers for stocks, bonds, ballot paper, passports, and travelers checks, to plastics and building materials.

Activity continued into the last half of the decade. During 1997, Cascades agreed to buy a German boxboard mill and entered into a joint venture with a fellow Canadian paper product producer.

The acquisition of the German operation gave Cascades a strong foothold in that market and provided a gateway to others in the region. The 50:50 agreement with Domtar Inc., merging assets of Cascades' containerboard operations and Domtar's packaging division, created a new $1 billion company. As the tenth largest containerboard producer in the fragmented North America packaging market, the new entity would gain immediate market clout.

In 1999, Cascades was ranked second in Canada's paper industry by the Paper Industry Management Association, behind Abitibi-Consolidated Inc. and ahead of Domtar. In addition to its ownership in specialty products, containerboard, boxboard, and fine paper concerns, Cascades held a 73 percent interest in Perkins Papers Ltd., a tissue business, and a 45 percent interest in Boralex Inc., a hydroelectric operation.

Drive for Growth and Innovation: 2000–02

In 2000, Cascades achieved its goal of $3 billion in sales. The strong sales volume was driven by the performance of the packaging sector. But operating margins were hurt by the rising cost of waste papers and energy. During the year the company spent a combined $31 million to acquire Wyant Corporation,

adding to its tissue paper business, and Amor Box Corporation, a containerboard company. Norampac Inc., the company formed through its alliance with Domtar, pulled in a record $1 billion in net sales.

Cascades Inc., through a stock exchange, gained sole ownership of Paperboard Industries International Inc., Perkins Papers Ltd., and Rolland Inc. as 2001 began. The restructuring reduced the Lemaire family's ownership from 46 percent to about 38 percent, according to *Market News Publishing*.

Cascades purchased two U.S. tissue mills during the second half of 2001. The acquisitions moved Cascades up the ranking among North American tissue producers, from seventh to fifth. The companies' products—bathroom tissue, paper towels, paper napkins, and facial tissue—were made from 100 percent recycled fibre and primarily marketed under private labels.

Norampac embarked on the building of a $30 million environmentally friendly steam reformer in 2001. The system would make Norampac's Trenton, Ontario, paper mill ''the cleanest in North America,'' converting pulping liquor into hydrogen-rich fuel gas, steam, and soda ash, all of which would be reused in the papermaking process beginning in 2003. Norampac was the first commercial enterprise to embark on such an effort, according to *Market News Publishing*.

In April 2002, Cascades announced a name change: Paperboard Industries International Inc. was renamed Cascades Boxboard Group Inc. Other subsidiaries, including Rolland and Perkins, would follow suit, according to a *Market News Publishing* release. ''We are proud of our past, and how far we have come, we are confident that our future is bright, and that the unification of the subsidiaries under one name will enable us to offer a much more complete package of products and services to our customers worldwide,'' said Laurent Lemaire, Cascades Inc.'s president and CEO.

Profits for 2002 climbed 55 percent, over 2001, to $169 million. Sales increased by 11.6 percent to $3.4 billion, according to the *America's Intelligence Wire*. Lemaire said, ''During the year, we generated $196 million of free cash flow, which allowed us to pursue our acquisition-driven growth strategy while reducing our indebtedness ratio and increasing our dividend.''

Meeting New Challenges: 2003–05

Shares of publicly traded Domtar and Cascades fell in April 2003, in response to news of an investigation by the Competition Bureau regarding alleged price fixing. Also under scrutiny were Coast Paper Ltd. and Unisource Canada Inc. Cascades said the allegations involved the carbonless paper and fine paper products segments of their business.

After recording its best year ever in 2002, Cascades saw sales drop by 4 percent and operating income slide 60 percent in 2003. The company attributed the declines to the strengthening Canadian dollar, the sluggish economy, rising energy prices, and intensified competition, all driving down pricing.

In response, the company implemented a campaign to control expenses, increase efficiency, and sharpen competitiveness. Cascades believed its decentralized structure, with mills and plants

Key Dates:

1964: Cascades Paper Inc. is founded in small Canadian town.
1982: Company completes its initial public offering.
1985: Cascades enters European market.
1992: Rolland Inc. is acquired.
1997: Company enters containerboard joint venture with Domtar Inc.
2000: Cascades moves up in the ranks among tissue paper makers.
2002: Company begins integration of all business under the Cascades name.
2004: Company weathers second consecutive year of difficult economic climate for Canada's paper industry.
2005: Cascades plans to open sales office in Russia.

operating independently, helped during tumultuous times, allowing for rapid response to changes in their environment.

The management philosophy was recognized in both 2003 and 2004 when the company was named one of Canada's top employers by Mediacorp Canada Inc. in collaboration with *Maclean's* magazine. "In addition to being in the Top 100, Cascades also received the credit for being No. 1 in the Top 10 for financial benefits, amongst others, because of its important financial contribution to employees who want to settle in Kingsey Falls, where the head office and several of the company's paper plants are located," reported *Canada NewsWire*.

In addition to its employees, the company depended on its "leading edge de-inking technology, sustained research and development, and 40-plus years of experience in recycling" to help it continue to bring innovative product to the marketplace. All these attributes were put to the test as difficult conditions persisted during 2004. Cascades maintained profitability on the year, focusing on core business areas of packaging and tissue, but jobs were lost.

In January 2005, Cascades announced plans to open a sales office in Obninski, southwest of Moscow. "The Russian market hovers around 500,000 tonnes of board, which is not an insignificant market, is very promising and comparable to the size of certain markets in Western Europe," Cascades vice-president,

Stephane Thiollier, said in *Canadian Business*. Cascades had sales offices in the Czech Republic, Poland, and Hungary. The global economic environment would dictate how things played out at home and abroad.

Principal Subsidiaries

Cascades Boxboard Group Inc.

Principal Competitors

Domtar Inc.; Georgia-Pacific Corporation; Weyerhaeuser Company.

Further Reading

"Attains $3 Billion in Sales," *Market News Publishing*, May 21, 2001.
"Cascades Amongst the Top 100 Employers in Canada for a Second Year," *Canada NewsWire*, October 19, 2004.
"Cascades Opens Moscow-Area Office in Bid to Tap into Russian Markets," *Canadian Business*, January 12, 2005.
"Domtar, Cascades in C$1 Billion Merger," *Pulp & Paper*, December 1997, p. 19.
Glowacki, Jeremy J., "Cascades Inc.: Emphasizes Boxboard Production and Converting," *Pulp & Paper*, November 1995, pp. 36+.
Johnson, Jim, "Mill Purchases Vault Cascades to 5th," *Waste Paper*, October 1, 2001, p. 12.
"Norampac Announces World's Most Efficient Hydrogen Generator," *Market News Publishing*, November 26, 2001.
"$1 Billion Merger of the Assets of Domtar Packaging and Cascades Containerboard to Create Leading Canadian Producer," *Business Wire*, October 9, 1997.
"Paperboard Industries International Inc. Changes Its Name to—Cascades Boxboard Group Inc.," *Market News Publishing*, April 25, 2002.
"Paperboard Industries International Acquires a Boxboard Mill in Germany," *Business Wire*, May 30, 1997.
"Papermaker's 1999 Top 50: Canada," *PIMA's North American Papermaker*, June 1999, pp. 68+.
Pariat, Maurice, "Cascades Outlines Boxboard PM Plan," *Pulp & Paper International*," November 1989, pp. 60+.
"Perkins Papers Ltd.—Cascades Completes Its Restructuring," *Market News Publishing*, June 8, 2001.
Raghavan, Sudarsan, "Price Probe Sinks Domtar, Cascades Stock," *America's Intelligence Wire,* April 10, 2003.
Sparshott, Jeffery, "Better Sales Aid Papermaker's Profit: Yearly Earnings Up 55%," *America's Intelligence Wire,* January 31, 2003.

—Kathleen Peippo

CDC Corporation

18 Whitfield Rd.
Causeway Bay
Hong Kong
Telephone: +852 2893 8200
Fax: +852 2893 5245
Web site: http://www.cdccorporation.net

Public Company
Incorporated: 1994 as China Internet Corporation
Employees: 1,179
Sales: $182.7 million (2004)
Stock Exchanges: NASDAQ
Ticker Symbol: CHINA
NAIC: 541512 Computer Systems Design Services

Once one of China's hottest internet-focused stocks, formerly known as chinadotcom, CDC Corporation has repositioned itself as a provider of integrated software systems for Enterprise Resource Planning (ERP), Supply Chain Management (SCM), Customer Relationship Management (CRM), Human Resources Management (HRM), and Business Intelligence applications. As part of its change in direction, CDC has made a number of strategic acquisitions, namely of Ross Systems (ERP), IMI Corp. (SCM), and Pivotal Corporation (CRM). The company expects to leverage the technological expertise of these North American businesses in its quest to capture a major share of the soon-to-boom enterprise software market in China, and particularly among mid-sized businesses. In addition, CDC has launched CDC Outsourcing, which provides outsourcing services for companies seeking to establish manufacturing and other operations in China. The company's Mobile Applications and Portal Operations targets the mobile telephone market with software and services for SMS, WAP, MMS, and other mobile telephone applications. CDC was the first Chinese company to list on the NASDAQ. In 2004, the company's sales topped $180 million.

Chinese Internet Pioneer in the 1990s

In 1994, James Chu, who had worked for some time in the U.S. high-tech industry, returned to his native Hong Kong in order to play a pioneering role in introducing the Internet to both that city and mainland China. Chu set up a business, China Internet Corp. (CIC), becoming one of the very first in the market. That early entry also enabled Chu to register three extremely well-chosen domain names: China.com, Hongkong .com, and Taiwan.com.

Soon after forming the company, Chu brought in Peter Yip, who later became the driving force behind CIC's transition into chinadotcom. Like Chu, Yip was a Hong Kong native who had gained a good deal of experience in the United States. After completing studies in computer engineering at the University of Pennsylvania, and receiving an MBA from the Wharton school, in the 1970s, Yip went on to found a number of businesses in the United States, including Yipkon, founded in 1982 and later sold to SHL Systemshouse (later part of MCI).

Yip helped CIC engineer an important partnership via the sale of a one-third stake in the company to mainland China's official news agency, Xinhua. Chu and Yip shared the remaining two-thirds of the company. The association with Xinhua led CIC to put in place an ambitious business plan: that of constructing the China World Web, a countrywide Internet for the Chinese market operating parallel to the global internet. CIC's infrastructure was to serve as an intranet of sorts that enabled communication among the Chinese population, with access to outside sources carefully screened. In this way, the Chinese government hoped to maintain control of information transmitted into the country.

Yip and Chu managed to raise some private investment capital to get the company off the ground. Yet its two attempts in the mid-1990s to take the company public met with a lack of interest from the investment community, in large part because of its relationship with Xinhua. Through 1996, CIC continued its efforts in the development of its Chinese intranet. However, the ability to put the network into place, and the likelihood of being able to "tame" the internet, appeared less and less likely.

By 1997, CIC had changed strategy. The company was now clearly driven by Yip, and that year Chu was squeezed out of the company in a boardroom struggle. Yip now reregistered the company outside of China, in the Cayman Islands, a move to appease potential investors of the threat of a Chinese government clampdown on domestic internet-oriented companies after the transfer of Hong Kong to mainland control. The company also changed its focus, adopting a strategy of developing web portals based on its domain name and offering web design services to Chinese companies eager to establish a presence on the World Wide Web. As a reflection of the group's change in focus, it adopted a new name, China.com Corporation.

A key factor in the company's change in orientation was the launch of a partnership with another fast-rising Hong Kong-based company, The Web Connection. That company had been founded in 1995 by Peter Hamilton, originally from the United Kingdom with a background in law, and Ian Henry, who had come to Hong Kong with a background in marketing. The Web Connection became one of the first to offer web design services in Hong Kong.

Hamilton and Henry provided China.com with the expertise in building web sites and in the construction of a web portal, or an entry point providing links of interest to sites on the Internet. The company meanwhile maintained its association with Xinhua. By 1998, the partnership between China.com and Web Connection had flourished, and in that year, China.com purchased a 51 percent stake in the Web Connection. In February 1999, the two companies were restructured into a new entity, chinadotcom Corporation.

The company now adopted a new strategy based on the mission: "Build, Sell, Distribute," that is, build web sites, sell advertising space, and distribute content through its own portals. The company—in part because of its possession of the china.com domain—became a focal point for the huge surge in interest in the development of China's internet market. While only an estimated four million Chinese had online access in 1999, the number was forecast to soar to as high as 140 million or more by 2005, making China one of the world's largest internet markets.

Yip, along with Hamilton and Henry, now prepared a third attempt to take the company public, scheduling an initial public offering (IPO) on the NASDAQ for July 1999. The IPO was to represent the first time a Chinese company had listed its shares on the high-technology oriented exchange. The investment community nonetheless remained somewhat skeptical about the company, primarily due to its continued association with Xinhua. Indeed, while a number of competitors had sprung up, including Sina.com, Suho.com, and NetEase.com, chinadot-

com's own portal, hampered by Xinhau censorship restrictions, lagged behind in terms of content and in the number of visitors.

Just three weeks before its IPO, however, Yip pulled off a coup, announcing that AOL had agreed to acquire a 10 percent stake in chinadotcom. The association of the company with the world's leading online content provider piqued investor interest, and at the end of its first day of trading, chinadotcom's share price had surged more than 200 percent.

Chinadotcom quickly began amassing a war chest. On top of the $97 million raised in its IPO, the company added nearly $400 million in a secondary offering in January 2000. (Yip, Hamilton, Henry, and other investors pocketed nearly $100 million of that offering.) In March 2000, the company added nearly $170 million more through the listing of 18 percent of its hongkong.com subsidiary on the new GEM (Growth Enterprise Market) board of the Hong Kong Stock Exchange.

Flush with cash, chinadotcom went on a buying spree, picking up part or all of some 50 companies over the next year. While most of the group's investment involved web site developers and content providers, such as look.com, based on sales of duty free cosmetics, a number of the group's purchases also went toward building its technological expertise. Such was the case with its acquisition of Australia's XT3, an Internet integrator, and Hong Kong's e2e Business Solutions, which provided software and information technology (IT) systems services. By the end of 2000, the company's revenues had soared from just $20 million in 1999 to over $120 million. Meanwhile, the company's payroll swelled to 2,400 employees. The company was by then present in most of the major Asian markets.

Reshaping Strategy for the 2000s

Like its competitors, chinadotcom was hit hard by the crash in the Internet sector in mid-2000. The company's stock, which had soared to a peak of $270 per share, collapsed to a low of just $5 per share. Worse for chinadotcom, a new generation of easy-to-use web development software had made its core business more or less obsolete. At its lowest point, the company's market valuation had dipped below even its available cash assets.

Henry left the company soon after, followed by Hamilton in 2001. Web Connection was subsequently rebranded as Ion Global. Chinadotcom then underwent a drastic restructuring, shedding more than 1,100 jobs and cutting costs by some 60 percent over the next year.

Yip now set about rebuilding the company. In this, the company was aided by a strong treasury. Despite its acquisition spree, the company had maintained control of the majority of the capital raised in its offerings. This cash enabled the company to absorb its continuing losses, while reshaping its future strategy.

By 2002, the company had adopted a new two-pronged business model. The first part of that strategy was based on the booming mobile telephone market in China. To this end, the company began making new acquisitions, such as the March 2003 purchase of New Palm (China) Information Technology Co., through Hongkong.com, a provider of SMS (short messaging service) services for the mobile telephone market. The company followed that purchase with a number of other acqui-

Key Dates:

1994: James Chu founds China Internet Corporation in Hong Kong and is joined by Peter Yip, who helps arrange investment from Xinhau news agency.

1997: Company begins partnership with The Web Connection, set up by Peter Hamilton and Ian Henry, changes name to China.com Corporation.

1998: Company acquires majority control of Web Connection.

1999: Web Connection is integrated; company name changes to chinadotcom; becomes first Chinese company to list on the NASDAQ.

2000: Company launches acquisition drive, buying up 50 firms and boosting sales at least fivefold.

2001: Company restructures, shedding 1,100 jobs amid internet stock crash.

2002: Change in strategy is pursued as web site development business becomes obsolete; company begins targeting mobile telephone services market.

2003: Company adds new business in enterprise software development, acquiring IMI (United States) and Pivotal Corporation (Canada).

2004: Company sells off mobile telephone and internet businesses to focus on enterprise software; Ross Systems is acquired.

2005: Peter Yip resigns as CEO; company announces plans to change name to CDC Corporation.

sitions in order to establish a network across mainland China, as well as in Hong Kong and Taiwan.

The other part of the company's new strategy emerged in late 2003 as the company began targeting the provision of enterprise software solutions, particularly to the mid-sized business market in China. This sector was expected to grow strongly into the new decade, in particular because the vast majority of Chinese companies had not yet adopted information systems technology.

To this end, chinadotcom began amassing the technological expertise in order to position itself as a primary provider in this market. In order to acquire this expertise, the company turned to North America, targeting a number of acquisitions to give it a foothold into the full range of enterprise software sectors. The first of these came in September 2003, when the company announced its purchase of a majority share of Industri-Matematik International Corporation (IMI). This company, with U.S. headquarters in New Jersey, brought chinadotcom expertise in supply chain management applications, as well as clients in the United States and Europe.

By the end of 2003, chinadotcom had reached a new agreement, this time in order to acquire Pivotal Corporation, based in Vancouver, Canada. This acquisition, which brought the company Pivotal's successful customer relationship management

(CRM) technology, encouraged chinadotcom to focus its future strategy more narrowly on its growing enterprise software wing. In February 2004, the company announced plans to spin off its mobile and internet businesses as a separate, publicly listed company.

The next prong in chinadotcom's new growth effort came in early 2004 when the company announced the takeover of Ross Systems, based in Atlanta, Georgia, a provider of back office applications, such as Enterprise Resource Planning, and others.

By the end of 2004, the reasoning behind chinadotcom's choice of North America for its acquisitions became increasingly clear, as the company launched a new subsidiary, CDC Outsourcing. The company now hoped to take advantage of the rising numbers of internationally operating companies that had begun outsourcing their manufacturing and other requirements to factories in China. Chinadotcom then began developing software and services targeting this sector.

By then, Yip had taken a leave of absence from the company, followed by his resignation from the company in March 2005. Nonetheless, chinadotcom appeared to be on the growth track, despite continued struggles for profitability. With Yip's departure, and given its selloff of its internet operations, chinadotcom announced its proposal for a change in name, to CDC Corporation. The company had survived the birth pangs of China's technology sector and was expected to become a major player in one of the world's fastest growing IT markets.

Principal Subsidiaries

CDC Software; Industri-Matematik International Corp.; Pivotal Corporation; Ross Systems, Inc.

Principal Competitors

Oracle Corporation; Microsoft Business Solutions; Huawei Technologies Company Ltd; eSoftBank Inc.; China Greatwall Computer Shenzhen Company Ltd.; Sina.com Ltd.; Sohu.com Inc.; ECS Technology China Ltd.; IT United Beijing.

Further Reading

Bonasia, J., "Chinadotcom Buys US Firms to Cover China," *Investor's Business Daily*, April 5, 2004, p. A05.

"Chinadotcom Comes in Penny Short; CEO Takes Leave," *America's Intelligence Wire*, May 14, 2004.

Hui Yuk-min, "Chinadotcom Turns to NASDAQ for Spin-off," *South China Morning Post*, February 4, 2004.

Jordan, George E., "Chinadotcom Remakes Itself to Survive the Bust," *Star Ledger*, December 23, 2003, p. 30.

Krilic, Samir, "Chinadotcom Q4 Loss Widens from Q3, CEO Resigns," *America's Intelligence Wire*, March 9, 2005.

Lau, Justine, "Internet Survivors Find New Strength," *Financial Times*, December 45, 2003, p. 28.

Marcial, Gene G., "How Chinadotcom Works the Phones," *Business Week*, February 23, 2004, p. 130.

"Piecing Together a Software Giant," *Business Week*, May 10, 2004.

—M.L. Cohen

Cenveo Inc.

8310 South Valley Highway, Suite 400
Englewood, Colorado 80112-5806
U.S.A.
Telephone: (303) 790-8023
Fax: (303) 566-7380
Web site: http://www.cenveo.com

Public Company
Incorporated: 1994 as Mail-Well, Inc.
Employees: 10,000
Sales: $1.74 billion (2004)
Stock Exchanges: New York
Ticker Symbol: CVO
NAIC: 322232 Envelope Manufacturing; 322233
  Stationery, Tablet, and Related Product
  Manufacturing; 323110 Commercial Lithographic
  Printing; 323115 Digital Printing; 323119 Other
  Commercial Printing; 323122 Prepress Services;
  422110 Printing and Writing Paper Wholesalers;
  422120 Stationery and Office Supplies Wholesalers

Cenveo Inc. (formerly Mail-Well, Inc.) is one of the largest players in the North American printing industry, specializing in offset and digital printing, custom and stock envelopes, and business documents and labels, and positioning itself as offering one-stop services ranging from design through fulfillment. About three-quarters of the firm's revenues come from its commercial business, which operates under the Cenveo name and serves national and local commercial clients, printing such documents as annual reports, corporate brochures, marketing materials, financial documents, and custom envelopes. Cenveo's resale business, operating under the Quality Park name, accounts for the remainder and produces business forms and labels, custom and stock envelopes, and specialty packaging and mailers, most of which is sold to dealers, such as print distributors, forms suppliers, and retail office products chains. The company operates 84 production facilities and five fulfillment and distribution centers throughout North America.

From its incorporation as Mail-Well, Inc. in February 1994 through 2000, the company bought 59 businesses, serving as a leading consolidator of what it called the "highly fragmented printing industry." Revenues grew from $260 million to $2.43 billion, but the company was saddled with more than $1 billion in debt just when the economy soured. Mail-Well spent the next few years streamlining its operations and jettisoning underperforming lines of business, before emerging in 2004 as a slimmed-down and more focused firm with a new name, Cenveo.

Rocky Mountain Roots

The roots of Cenveo's main predecessor company can be traced back to the 1919 founding in Denver, Colorado, of Rocky Mountain Envelope Co., which was the first consumer envelope manufacturer in that city. The cofounders were Carl L. Tucker and Willett R. Lake, transplanted Missourians, who led the company into the 1960s. During the 1920s, when Denver experienced rapid growth, the company changed its name to Rockmont Envelope Co. in order to distinguish itself from the growing number of firms that had included "Rocky Mountain" in their names. Early on, Rockmont began branding its envelopes with the trademark "Mail-Well."

Rockmont grew steadily over the years, and by the late 1950s had a 100,000-square-foot manufacturing plant in Denver, as well as additional plants in Houston, Los Angeles, and Portland, Oregon. Rockmont also had scattered around the country seven warehouses that served the company's customers in the entire continental United States. With a workforce exceeding 500, Rockmont made all manner of envelopes, ranging from an inch square to a yard wide by 45 inches long. The company had also made modest moves into the manufacture of low-cost stationery, which was sold in supermarkets and drugstores, and of specially designed paper bags for department stores.

In 1960 Rockmont diversified into the production of school supplies, offering a full line of typing paper, filler paper, notebooks, spiral-bound theme books, memo pads, and tablets. By this time the company was one of the largest manufacturers of envelopes in the United States. The company structure had also changed by the early 1960s, as Rockmont Envelope became a subsidiary of Pak-Well Paper Industries, Inc., a Colorado holding

Company Perspectives:

The company name, Cenveo (pronounced senn-VAY-oh) and the Cenveo logo are derived from the unique combination of the syllables "Cen" or center, and "Veo" which relates to vision and understanding. Cenveo represents a central point for creating understanding visually. Cenveo also represents much more—the combined strength of 85 facilities and 10,000 employees coming together under one name and focused on one thing, our customers. The company's new name and logo also provide a visual representation of the center, or hub with dots that signify people, ideas, and more importantly, an understanding of their customer's visual communication needs, with the ability to connect resources to create customized solutions.

corporation headed by Tucker and Lake. In early 1963 Pak-Well was taken public through the sale of 153,620 shares of common stock at $11.50 per share. Pak-Well had revenues of more than $13 million in 1962, and operated plants in Denver, Portland, Houston, Phoenix, Los Angeles, Salt Lake City, and Honolulu.

By the early 1970s, sons of the cofounders had taken over management of Pak-Well, with Richard B. Tucker serving as president and Willett R. Lake, Jr., in the position of chairman. The company posted net earnings of $1.74 million on sales of $53.8 million in 1973.

The road from the early 1970s to the emergence of Mail-Well in 1994 is a rather sketchy one, but Pak-Well eventually fell into the hands of paper company Great Northern Nekoosa Corporation. Pak-Well then became part of Georgia-Pacific Corporation when that paper giant acquired Great Northern for $4.5 billion in 1990. By the early 1990s what was once the diversified Pak-Well had become strictly an envelope maker operating under the Mail-Well Envelopes and Wisco Envelopes names.

Creation of Mail-Well, Inc.: 1994

The early 1990s saw many paper companies exit from the envelope business because profits in that sector had been eroded by postage increases, new technologies, and changes in the customer base. Around this same time, Gerald F. Mahoney had entered the world of entrepreneurship by purchasing a small, one-plant manufacturer of envelopes called Pavey Envelope and Tag Corp. Mahoney had previously served as CFO and in other positions at a number of companies, including a one-time *Fortune* 500 firm that grew very fast through acquisitions before downsizing itself through the spinning off of a number of operations. Mahoney joined with some partners with leveraged buyout experience to form the Houston-based Sterling Group Inc. After Georgia-Pacific decided to exit from envelope making, it reached a deal with Sterling to sell its envelope business for $155.1 million. Sterling also purchased, for $4.4 million, Pavey, which it merged with the Georgia-Pacific envelope business in February 1994 to create Mail-Well, with Mahoney serving as chairman and CEO.

Mail-Well was launched with 16 manufacturing plants that had produced about 13 billion envelopes during 1993. It also

began with debt of $142 million and equity of only $17 million. Mahoney's plan for Mail-Well was clear from the start: he aimed for it to be a major consolidator within a highly fragmented industry. Envelope makers typically served customers within local or regional areas. By growing through acquisition and gaining additional manufacturing and distribution operations, Mail-Well would still be able to serve regional customers but would benefit from economies of scale. Mahoney also reasoned that larger corporations with operations in different regions of the country might prefer dealing with a single envelope supplier that had plants located in each of those regions, rather than having to contract with several different suppliers.

Mahoney's first major acquisition came in December 1994 when Mail-Well paid $97.4 million to purchase American Envelope Company, which had annual revenues of $180 million, from CC Industries. The purchase increased the number of plants to 29 and the number of employees to 4,200, and made Mail-Well the largest envelope manufacturer in the United States. Next, Mail-Well gobbled up Supremex, Inc. for $65.5 million in July 1995. Supremex was the largest envelope maker in Canada, with revenues of $90 million and 11 manufacturing facilities.

Mail-Well's next move was to create a second leg for the company to stand on. In August 1995 it entered the field of commercial printing through the $82.6 million acquisition of Graphic Arts Center, Inc., a leading West Coast-based printer of "high-impact" documents, such as car brochures and annual reports. By this time the company's debt load had reached $370 million, while equity had increased only to $33 million, so Mahoney in September 1995 took the company public on the NASDAQ, raising $64 million. Mail-Well's debt was thus reduced to $310 million, while its equity grew to $100 million. For 1995 the company posted net income of $8 million on net sales of $596.8 million.

The acquisitions in 1996 were more modest ones, but fit into the company strategy of pursuing small commercial printers and envelope printers in geographic areas not already served by Mail-Well. In April 1996 Mail-Well spent $28 million for Quality Park Products, Inc., a Pennsylvania-based printer of envelopes for the office products market, a fast-growing segment and a new area for Mail-Well. In November of that year the company increased its share of the Canadian envelope market to more than 50 percent with the $20 million acquisition of Ontario-based Pac National Group Products, Inc. One month later, Mail-Well's high-impact commercial printing sector was bolstered through the $20 million purchase of Indianapolis-based Shepard Poorman Communications Corporation, a specialist in calendars and computer instruction books. Net sales increased by more than 30 percent in 1996, reaching $778.5 million, while net income more than doubled to $16.9 million. In December 1996 Mail-Well's stock moved from the NASDAQ to the New York Stock Exchange.

Additions of Third and Fourth Legs in the Late 1990s

During 1997 Mail-Well spent about $87 million to acquire six more companies, including envelope maker Griffin Envelopes Inc., based in Seattle, and several firms in the commercial printing field—Seattle-based Allied Printers, Atlanta-based National Color Graphics, Inc., and Western Graphics Communications, headquartered in Cambridge, Maryland. The most significant acquisition of the year, however, was that of Murray Envelope Corporation of Hattiesburg, Mississippi. The addition of Murray provided Mail-Well with a third leg, that of printing services for the distributor market. Among the items that Murray supplied to distributors were envelopes, secure documents, pressure-sensitive labels, index tabs, and mailers. Revenues stood at $897.6 million in 1997, with net income growing to $22.2 million.

In January 1998 Paul V. Reilly was named president and chief operating officer of Mail-Well, having previously served as CFO. Also in early 1998 Mail-Well improved its equity base through a secondary stock offering that raised $90 million in capital. During 1998 the company stepped up its acquisitions activity, purchasing 23 more companies for an aggregate $369.5 million in cash,

stock, and assumed debt. Three of these acquisitions were particularly significant. The addition in January of Fairhope, Alabama-based Poser Business Forms, Inc., which had annual revenues of $90 million, enhanced Mail-Well's printing for distributors sector. In March Mail-Well gained a fourth leg through the purchase of the label division of Lawson Mardon Packaging Inc. This division, which was based in Toronto, had annual sales of $81 million and was the second largest supplier of glue-on labels in North America, with a special focus on the food and beverage markets. Mail-Well's new label group was bolstered in May with the acquisition of the label division of International Paper Company, which included one of the most advanced label printing facilities in the United States. The company's third major acquisition of 1998 also came in May when it acquired Los Angeles-based Anderson Lithograph, a $135 million in revenue firm with a reputation as one of the top commercial printers in the country. Additionally, Mail-Well merged with seven commercial printing companies through the exchange of common stock worth about $118 million. The largest of these companies was St. Louis-based Color Art, Inc., which had revenues of about $75 million in 1997. In June 1998 Mail-Well's stock split two for one. The host of acquisitions helped push revenues up to $1.5 billion for 1998, a 68 percent increase. Net income, however, fell to $21.7 million, reflecting a $21.8 million charge taken late in the year to restructure the envelope and commercial printing operations, including the closure of three facilities and resulting staff reductions.

Mail-Well was able to smoothly integrate this many companies within a short period mainly because of its hands-off, decentralized management style. Mahoney told the *Denver Business Journal:* ''We let them pretty much run the business as they were before and over a period of time the culture evolves as they get to know how we operate.'' One key imperative eventually absorbed by the acquired companies was Mail-Well's keen attention to cost-containment, particularly through an emphasis on productivity gains.

While the acquisition pace slowed somewhat in 1999, Mail-Well made a significant move in the middle of the year when it gained a European beachhead through the $102 million acquisition of Porter Chadburn plc, a publicly traded London-based label manufacturer. Porter Chadburn had revenues of $126 million, 70 percent of which came from the United States, where ten of its 13 plants were located. But the purchase did give Mail-Well its first European operations and moved its label division into the number two position in North America. The company's workforce grew to more than 13,000, while the number of printing plants increased to 110. For the year, Mail-Well's results were its best ever: $64.5 million in net income on record revenues of $1.85 billion.

Early 2000s: From Mail-Well to a Slimmed-Down Cenveo

In February 2000 Mail-Well made its largest acquisition yet, snaring American Business Products, Inc. (ABP) in a deal valued at approximately $334 million. Based in Atlanta, ABP had four operating units, three of which—Curtis 1000, International Envelope, and Discount Label—produced office supplies and products. The fourth, Jen-Coat, was involved in paper extrusion coating and lamination. Although the purchase further diversified Mail-Well's product lines, it also saddled the company with additional debt. Mail-Well's debt-to-capital ratio jumped to an unhealthy 74 percent, and by mid-2000 total debt exceeded $1 billion.

The ill-timing of the ABP acquisition soon became apparent. By the middle of 2000 Mail-Well was beginning to feel the effects of a softening in its core markets, including cutbacks in both direct mail and commercial printing. To decrease its debt burden, the company announced the sale of the noncore Jen-Coat unit to a management-led buyout group for about $100 million. Later in the year a restructuring was launched involving the closure of 11 unprofitable plants and offices and the replacement of several inefficient printing presses. As a result of $28 million in charges incurred thereby—coupled with heavy debt servicing costs—Mail-Well saw its earnings drop to $27.6 million for 2000, despite a 31 percent increase in revenues, to $2.43 billion.

As these travails began to play themselves out, Mail-Well placed a moratorium on further acquisitions. A change in management leadership also occurred. Mahoney, the person who engineered the consolidation strategy, retired in January 2001. Taking the helm as president and CEO was Paul V. Reilly, who had joined the company as CFO in 1995 and later served as president and chief operating officer, and therefore played an instrumental role in the firm's acquisition spree. Reilly took on the additional post of chairman later in 2001.

When the economic recession fully kicked in during 2001, the printing industry was hit harder than the overall economy because of its reliance on the advertising market, which went into freefall. Compounding Mail-Well's difficulties were the continuing debt burden and its hands-off management style. At least on the commercial printing side, Mail-Well found that a number of the companies it had acquired suffered from poor management. Over the next three years, as the company restructured its operations, a greater degree of control and standardization among its far-flung units became a key goal.

In June 2001 the first phase of this restructuring was announced. Intending to concentrate its resources on general commercial printing and envelopes, Mail-Well said it would sell its label and printed office products units. In addition 11 envelope plants were slated for closure in a consolidation and streamlining initiative that involved the laying off of 1,500 workers. The poor economy and restructuring charges led to a net loss of $136.2 million for 2001, while revenues fell sharply, to $1.65 billion.

The divestiture program did not proceed entirely as planned. During 2002 Mail-Well succeeded in selling its Curtis 1000 printed office products distribution business; Mail-Well Label, its main label business; and its filing products division. But it was unable to get the price it was seeking for PrintXcel, a unit selling business forms and labels, envelopes, and related items to print distributors, forms suppliers, and office supply retailers, and the unit was withdrawn from the auction block. The divestiture program was completed in March 2003 with the sale of part of the company's digital graphics operations. As the advertising market remained in its prolonged slump, financial results for 2002 were little improved over the previous year—a net loss of $202.1 million on $1.73 billion in revenues—although the firm did manage to eke out earnings of $2 million before restructuring and impairment charges.

Through its various restructuring efforts, Mail-Well managed to reduce annual expenses by $130 million a year and both cut and restructure its debt. Equally important were further operational changes. Late in 2003 the company announced plans to combine its commercial printing and envelope businesses into a single group for direct sales to national and local accounts. This group, responsible for about three-quarters of overall revenues, was melded together in a key way: Rather than the myriad names that the branches had been operating under over the years—which had confused customers and impeded the development of national or even regional customers—they would all begin operating under the same name, Cenveo. Likewise, in May 2004 Mail-Well itself changed its name to Cenveo Inc., the new moniker (pronounced senn-VAY-oh) derived from the syllables *Cen*, from "center," and *Veo*, relating to vision and understanding. Furthermore, the company's other unit, its resale division, comprised of PrintXcel and other units, began operating under the Quality Park name.

With the printing industry failing to reattain the heights reached in the late 1990s, paper costs increasing, and pricing pressures continuing, Cenveo suffered another net loss in 2004, albeit a more modest one than that incurred in 2001 and 2002. The company lost $19.7 million on revenues of $1.74 billion. In January 2005 Reilly announced plans to resign from his positions with the company, pending the hiring of his replacement. Further implementation of the company's new strategic direction would therefore fall to the new leader.

Principal Subsidiaries

Cenveo Alberta Finance LP (Canada); Cenveo Canada Leasing Company Inc.; Cenveo Commercial Ohio, LLC; Cenveo Corporation; Cenveo Government Printing, Inc.; Cenveo International Holdings, Inc.; Cenveo McLaren Morris & Todd Company (Canada); Cenveo Resale Ohio, LLC; Cenveo Services, LLC; Cenveo Texas Finance, LP; Cenveo West, Inc.; Colorhouse China, Inc.; Discount Labels, Inc.; Graphic Arts Center de Mexico; Innova Envelope Inc. Enveloppe Innova Inc. (Canada); MM&T Packaging Company (Canada); MMTP Holdings, Inc.; PNG Inc. (Canada); Precision Fine Papers Inc. (Canada); Supremex, Inc. (Canada).

Principal Competitors

National Envelope Corporation; R.R. Donnelley & Sons Company; National Service Industries, Inc.; UPM-Kymmene Corporation; Quebecor World Inc.

Further Reading

Aven, Paula, "Mail-Well Seals Acquisitions," *Denver Business Journal,* February 26, 1999, pp. 20B +.
Berta, Dina, "Printer Corrals Rival ABP," *Denver Rocky Mountain News,* January 15, 2000, p. 1B.
Cantarano, Dana, "Mail-Well Sells Lamination Division," *Denver Post,* July 18, 2000, p. C2.
"Cenveo Finds a Comfortable Fit in Its New Corporate Identity and Strategy," *What They Think?,* June 23, 2004, http://members.what theythink.com/allsearch/article.cfm?id = 16623.
Eaton, John, "Investors Take Shine to Mail-Well," *Denver Post,* April 30, 1998, p. C1.

Ford, Katie, ''Mail-Well Inc. Pushes Acquisition Envelope,'' *Denver Business Journal,* February 18, 2000, p. 23B.

''Growth Story,'' *Wall Street Corporate Reporter,* January 19–25, 1998.

Haselbush, Willard, ''Denver-Made Envelopes Carry America's Mail,'' *Denver Post,* September 15, 1957, pp. 1E, 3E.

——, ''Rockmont Envelope Moving to New Plant,'' *Denver Post,* June 30, 1963, p. 1D.

——, ''Rockmont Only Tip of Pak-Well Iceberg,'' *Denver Post,* March 24, 1974, p. 67.

''Mail-Well Buys Label-Making Unit,'' *Pulp and Paper,* April 1998, pp. 19+.

''Mail-Well Executives Note Gains in Big Restructuring,'' *Graphics Arts Monthly,* April 2004, p. 22.

''Mail-Well Reveals Plans to Simplify and Sharpen,'' *Graphics Arts Monthly,* July 2001, p. 26.

Marsh, Virginia, ''Mail-Well Bids £47m for Porter Chadburn,'' *Financial Times,* March 17, 1999, p. 22.

Mayer, Olivia, ''Pushing the Envelope,'' *Colorado Business Magazine,* March 1998, p. 40.

McGhee, Tom, ''Envelope Giant Trimming 1,200 Jobs,'' *Denver Post,* June 14, 2001, p. C1.

Milstead, David, ''Delivering a Turnaround: Douglas County Mail-Well Got Leaner, Met Its 2001 Goals,'' *Denver Rocky Mountain News,* January 26, 2002, p. 1C.

——, ''Mail-Well Planning Job Cuts, Closures,'' *Denver Rocky Mountain News,* September 11, 2002, p. 5B.

——, ''Mail-Well Will Shed Two Divisions,'' *Denver Rocky Mountain News,* June 14, 2001, p. 1B.

Narvaes, Emily, ''Englewood's Mail-Well, Under New Ownership, Is Buying Other Companies and Expanding Quickly,'' *Denver Post,* September 7, 1996, p. D1.

Nelson, Brett, ''Wrong Address: Recovering from a Roll-up Gone Awry,'' *Forbes,* March 17, 2003, p. 78.

Proctor, Cathy, ''Growth Too Much to Deliver,'' *Denver Business Journal,* July 6, 2001, p. 1A.

Raabe, Steve, ''Mail-Well Inc. Sells Adhesive Label Division,'' *Denver Post,* May 23, 2002, p. C1.

''Rockmont Envelope Opens New Building,'' *Denver Post,* November 6, 1963, p. 35.

Schwartz, Jerry, ''Paper Maker Is Selling Off a Major Unit,'' *New York Times,* December 9, 1993, p. D4.

Sherburne, Cary, ''Mail Is Now Cenveo,'' interview with Paul Reilly, *What They Think?,* April 20, 2004, available from http://www.cenveo.com/media/news.asp.

Smith, Jerd, ''Sealed Deal Creates Local Giant: At American Mail-Well, Low Profile Belies Rank As Top Envelope Maker,'' *Denver Business Journal,* January 13, 1995, p. A1.

Svaldi, Aldo, ''Buying Binges Buoy Mail-Well Stock Price,'' *Denver Business Journal,* May 2, 1997, pp. 3A, 63A.

——, ''Mail-Well Annual Profits Decline; CEO Steps Down,'' *Denver Post,* January 26, 2001, p. C2.

——, ''Mail-Well's Proceeds Will Go to Retire Debt,'' *Denver Business Journal,* October 13, 1995, p. A10.

——, ''Mail-Well Unveils New Name: Cenveo,'' *Denver Post,* April 20, 2004, p. C2.

—David E. Salamie

Colgate-Palmolive Company

300 Park Avenue
New York, New York 10022-7499
U.S.A.
Telephone: (212) 310-2000
Toll Free: (800) 850-2654
Fax: (212) 310-2475
Web site: http://www.colgate.com

Public Company
Incorporated: 1806 as The Colgate Company
Employees: 36,000
Sales: $10.58 billion (2004)
Stock Exchanges: New York Euronext Frankfurt London
    Zurich
Ticker Symbol: CL
NAIC: 311111 Dog and Cat Food Manufacturing; 325611
    Soap and Other Detergent Manufacturing; 325612
    Polish and Other Sanitation Good Manufacturing;
    325620 Toilet Preparation Manufacturing; 325998 All
    Other Miscellaneous Chemical Product and
    Preparation Manufacturing; 335211 Electric
    Housewares and Household Fan Manufacturing;
    339994 Broom, Brush, and Mop Manufacturing

Colgate-Palmolive Company's growth from a small candle and soap manufacturer to one of the most powerful consumer products giants in the world is the result of aggressive acquisition of other companies, persistent attempts to overtake its major U.S. competition, and an early emphasis on building a global presence overseas where little competition existed. The company is organized around four core segments—oral care, personal care, home care, and pet nutrition—that market such well-known brands as Colgate toothpaste, Irish Spring soap, Softsoap liquid soap, Mennen deodorant, Palmolive and Ajax dishwashing liquid, Ajax cleanser, Murphy's oil soap, Fab laundry detergent, Soupline and Suavitel fabric softeners, and Hill's Science Diet and Hill's Prescription Diet pet foods. Colgate-Palmolive has operations in more than 200 countries and generates about 70 percent of its revenue outside the United States.

Beginnings

In 1806, when the company was founded by 23-year-old William Colgate, it concentrated exclusively on selling starch, soap, and candles from its New York City-based factory and shop. Upon entering his second year of business, Colgate became partners with Francis Smith, and the company became Smith and Colgate, a name it kept until 1812 when Colgate purchased Smith's share of the company and offered a partnership to his brother, Bowles Colgate. Now called William Colgate and Company, the firm expanded its manufacturing operations to a Jersey City, New Jersey, factory in 1820; this factory produced Colgate's two major products, Windsor toilet soaps and Pearl starch.

Upon its founder's death in 1857, the firm changed its name to Colgate & Company and was run by President Samuel Colgate until his death 40 years later. During his tenure several new products were developed, including perfumes, essences, and perfumed soap. The manufacture of starch was discontinued in 1866 after a fire destroyed the factory.

In 1873 Colgate began selling toothpaste in a jar, followed 23 years later by the introduction of Colgate Ribbon Dental Cream, in the now familiar collapsible tube. By 1906 the company was also producing several varieties of laundry soap, toilet paper, and perfumes. Colgate & Company shifted its headquarters to Jersey City in 1910.

While the Colgate family managed its manufacturing operations on the East Coast, soap factories were also opened in 1864 by B.J. Johnson in Milwaukee, Wisconsin (under the name B.J. Johnson Soap Company), and in 1872 by the three Peet brothers in Kansas City, Kansas. In 1898 Johnson's company introduced Palmolive soap, which soon became the best-selling soap in the world and led the firm to change its name to the Palmolive Company in 1916. The Peets, who sold laundry soap mainly in the Midwest and western states, merged their company (Peet Brothers) with Palmolive in 1926, forming Palmolive-Peet Company. Two years later that firm joined with Colgate & Company to form Colgate-Palmolive-Peet Company, with

105

headquarters in Jersey City. Palmolive-Peet's management initially assumed control of the combined organization.

On October 25, 1929, management signed an agreement to merge the company with Kraft Phenix Cheese Corporation (forerunner of Kraft Foods) and Hershey Chocolate Company. The three companies would continue to operate independently, but they would become subsidiaries of a holding company slated to be called International Quality Products Corporation. Just four days after the deal was signed, however, the stock market crashed, forcing the huge amalgamation to be scuttled. In the wake of the crash, the Colgate family regained control of Colgate-Palmolive-Peet and installed Bayard Colgate as president in 1933.

International Expansion

Colgate & Company had been a pioneer in establishing international operations, creating a Canadian subsidiary in 1913 and one in France in 1920. In the early 1920s the firm expanded into Australia, the United Kingdom, Germany, and Mexico. Colgate or its successor firm next created subsidiaries in the Philippines, Brazil, Argentina, and South Africa in the late 1920s. In 1937 the company moved into India and by the end of the 1940s had operations in most of South America. By 1939 Colgate-Palmolive-Peet's sales hit $100 million.

In the 1940s and 1950s the company also built upon its strategy of growth by acquisition, buying up a number of smaller consumer product companies. Organic growth remained on the agenda as well, and in 1947 the company introduced two of its best-known products, Fab detergent and Ajax cleanser. These acquisitions and new products, however, did little to close the gap between Colgate and its arch-rival, the Procter & Gamble Company, a firm that had been formed in the 1830s and had by now assumed a commanding lead over Colgate in selling detergent products in the United States. Meanwhile, the firm adopted its present name in 1953 and moved its offices for domestic and international operations to New York City in 1956.

In 1960 George H. Lesch was appointed Colgate's president in the hopes that his international experience would produce similar success in the domestic market. Under his leadership, the company embarked upon an extensive new product development program that created such brands as Cold Power laundry detergent, Palmolive dishwashing liquid, and Ultra Brite toothpaste. In an attempt to expand beyond these traditional, highly competitive businesses into new growth areas, Colgate also successfully introduced a new food wrap called Baggies in 1963. As a result of these product launches, the company's sales grew between 8 and 9 percent every year throughout the 1960s. Sales topped the $1 billion mark in 1967.

Lesch assumed the chairmanship of Colgate, and David Foster became president in 1970 and CEO in 1971. Foster was the son of the founder of Colgate-Palmolive's U.K. operations. He joined the company in 1946 as a management trainee and rose through the sales and marketing ranks both in the United States and overseas.

New Strategies for the 1970s

During the 1970s, as environmental concerns about phosphate and enzyme detergent products grew, the company faced additional pressure to diversify beyond the detergent business. In response to this pressure, Foster instituted a strategy that emphasized internal development via a specialized new venture group; joint ventures for marketing other companies' products; and outright acquisitions of businesses in which Colgate could gain a marketing advantage over Procter & Gamble. In 1971, for example, the company began selling British Wilkinson Sword Company razors and blades in the United States and other countries. In 1972 Colgate-Palmolive acquired Kendall & Company, a manufacturer of hospital and industrial supplies. It was originally hoped that the Kendall acquisition would bolster the pharmaceutical sales of Colgate's Lakeside Laboratories subsidiary, which had been acquired in 1960. The partnership never materialized, however, and Lakeside was sold in 1974. The Kendall business proved to be one of Foster's most successful acquisitions. Within two years, the subsidiary was producing sales and earnings results well above the company's targeted goals. On the product development side, meanwhile, Irish Spring deodorant soap was introduced in 1972.

In 1971 the U.S. Federal Trade Commission enacted restrictions on in-store product promotions, such as couponing. In response to these restrictions, Foster began to employ other tactics designed to enhance Colgate's visibility in the marketplace. Two such programs awarded money to schools and local civic groups whose young people collected the most labels and boxtops from selected Colgate products. Under Foster, Colgate-Palmolive also began to sponsor a number of women's sporting events, including the Colgate-Dinah Shore Winner's Circle, a women's professional golf tournament. Foster chose women's sports in an effort to appeal to Colgate-Palmolive's primarily female customer base. He even went so far as to have Colgate buy the tournament's home course, the Mission Hills Country Club in Palm Springs, California, so that he could supervise the maintenance of the greens.

In 1973 Colgate acquired Helena Rubinstein, a major cosmetics manufacturer with strong foreign sales but a weak U.S. presence. Believing that its marketing expertise could solve Rubinstein's problems, Colgate reduced both the number of products in the company's line and the number of employees in its workforce, increased advertising expenditures, and moved the products out of drugstores and into department stores. The following year the company acquired Ram Golf Corporation and Bancroft Racket Company, and in 1976 it bought Charles A. Eaton Company, a golf and tennis shoe manufacturer.

Although total U.S. sales of consumer products appeared to be slowing by the end of 1974, particularly in soaps and detergents, Colgate's international sales continued to carry the company forward. It maintained its leadership position abroad through new product development geared specifically to local tastes throughout Europe as well as through its involvement in

Key Dates:

1806: Company is founded by William Colgate in New York to make starch, soap, and candles.
1857: After founder's death, company becomes known as Colgate & Company.
1873: Toothpaste is first marketed.
1896: Collapsible tubes for toothpaste are introduced.
1898: B.J. Johnson Soap Company (later renamed Palmolive Company) introduces Palmolive soap.
1910: Colgate moves from original location to Jersey City, New Jersey.
1926: Palmolive merges with Peet Brothers, creating Palmolive-Peet Company.
1928: Colgate and Palmolive-Peet merge, forming Colgate-Palmolive-Peet Company.
1947: Fab detergent and Ajax cleanser are introduced.
1953: Company changes its name to Colgate-Palmolive Company.
1956: Corporate headquarters shifts back to New York.
1966: Palmolive dishwashing liquid is introduced.
1967: Sales top $1 billion.
1968: Colgate toothpaste is reformulated with fluoride; Ultra Brite is introduced.
1976: Hill's Pet Products is purchased.
1987: The Softsoap brand of liquid soap is acquired.
1992: The Mennen Company is acquired; Total toothpaste is introduced overseas.
1995: Latin American firm Kolynos Oral Care is acquired; Colgate-Palmolive undergoes major restructuring.
1997: Total toothpaste is launched in the United States; Colgate takes lead in domestic toothpaste market.
2004: Company acquires European oral care firm GABA Holding AG; major restructuring is launched.

the growing markets of less-developed countries in Latin America, Africa, and Asia.

Setbacks Beginning in the Late 1970s

Foster's diversification strategy initially improved earnings, but Colgate's domestic sales, market share, and profit margins were beginning to soften. This was due, in large part, to an economic recession and an advertising cutback the company had made in an attempt to boost earnings. Colgate was consistently losing the marketing battle in personal care products to Procter & Gamble. It had no leading brands and few successful new product introductions because of reduced spending for research and development. In an effort to remedy this problem and broaden its product mix, Colgate moved into food marketing in 1976 with the acquisition of Riviana Foods, a major producer of Texas long-grain rice with its own subsidiaries in pet food (Hill's Pet Products), kosher hot dogs (Hebrew National Kosher Foods), and candy. The Riviana acquisition, however, did not live up to the company's expectations. Along with purchasing a successful rice-milling business, Colgate found that it had also saddled itself with two unprofitable restaurant chains and a low-quality candy company. In 1977 declines in the price of rice seriously eroded Riviana's cash flow.

Helena Rubinstein created additional headaches. Whereas other cosmetic manufacturers had moved their products from department store distribution to higher-volume drugstores, Colgate's management elected to keep Rubinstein products in department stores even though stores' demands for marketing support eroded the company's margins so severely that it lost money on every cosmetic item sold. Colgate finally sold the business in 1980 to Albi Enterprises.

Foster had become chairman in 1975. In 1979, embattled by a series of marketing failures and the pressures of an acquisition strategy that yielded more losers than winners, Foster suddenly resigned, citing ill health. The company's president and chief operating officer, Keith Crane, was appointed as Foster's successor. A 42-year Colgate employee, Crane quickly instituted a new management structure consisting of several group vice-presidents, reunited all domestic operations under one group, and realigned division managers in an attempt to promote a more cohesive organization. Consumer advertising and product research were given renewed emphasis to support the company's basic detergent and toothpaste lines.

Over the next two years, Crane sold a number of Foster's acquisitions that no longer fit with the company's long-term strategic plan, including Hebrew National Kosher Foods, which had been part of the Riviana purchase; Ram Golf; and the Bancroft Racket Company. Crane also put the Mission Hills Country Club up for sale and withdrew Colgate's sponsorship of the sporting events his predecessor had nurtured.

Also during the late 1970s and the 1980s, Colgate found itself named as a defendant in two lawsuits. In 1981 the company lost a suit brought by United Roasters, who successfully argued that Colgate had violated the terms of a contract between the two firms for Colgate to market Bambeanos, a soybean snack produced by United Roasters, and was awarded $950,000. The following year the company was sued by the federal government for alleged job discrimination. According to a complaint filed with the U.S. Equal Employment Opportunity Commission, Colgate had failed or refused to hire people between the ages of 40 and 70 since 1978 and had also deprived employees in that age group of opportunities for promotion.

By the end of 1982 Crane also experienced problems at Colgate. Several attempts at new product development never made it out of the test-market stage. Increased advertising expenditures for a limited number of major brands produced only temporary gains in market share while slowly killing off other products receiving little or no media support. Even Fresh Start detergent, one of the most successful new products to come out of the Foster era, was having problems retaining market share. Thus while Procter & Gamble's sales and margins were increasing, Colgate's were on the decline. To make matters worse, the strong dollar overseas hurt Colgate's international sales, and changes in Medicare policy weakened Kendall's business.

Turnaround Under Reuben Mark, Mid- to Late 1980s

In 1983 Crane relinquished the title of president to Reuben Mark, one of the company's three executive vice-presidents and a member of Crane's management advisory team. Mark also assumed the position of chief operating officer at that time; one year later he succeeded Crane as CEO. Mark built upon his predecessor's restructuring efforts in an attempt to increase profits and shareholder value. Between 1984 and 1986 several inefficient plants were closed, hundreds of employees laid off, and noncore businesses sold, including the remnants of the Riviana Foods acquisition, except for the Hill's Pet Products subsidiary.

In an attempt to refocus the company's marketing and profitability, Mark developed a set of corporate initiatives intended to address business areas ranging from production-cost reduction to new product development, with a heavy emphasis on motivating employees and involving them in company decision-making. In response to the implementation of these ideas, the company's U.S. toothpaste business enjoyed a boost with first-to-the-market introductions of a gel toothpaste and a pump-type dispenser bearing the Colgate brand name. Similar U.S. market share gains were earned by new and improved versions of its Palmolive and Dynamo detergents and Ajax cleaner. Palmolive automatic dishwashing liquid debuted in 1986.

With the company's turnaround firmly underway, business units managed by key executives were formed to develop plans for the company's major product categories. The purpose of each plan was to identify how products under development could be best introduced in domestic and international markets. Two years into this strategic reorganization, coinciding with Mark's appointment as chairman in 1986, Colgate confronted an embarrassing controversy.

Since the early 1920s Hawley & Hazel Chemical Company had marketed a product called Darkie Black and White Toothpaste in the Far East. Colgate had acquired a 50 percent interest in this company in 1985. The following year, the Interfaith Center on Corporate Responsibility, a coalition of Protestant and Roman Catholic groups, demanded that Colgate change what it deemed to be the product's racially offensive name and packaging, which depicted a likeness of Al Jolson in blackface. The company acknowledged the criticism and agreed to make the necessary changes.

Colgate also continued to seek out growth areas in its personal care product and detergent businesses. In 1987 it acquired a line of liquid soap products (including the Softsoap brand) from Minnetonka Corporation, the first transaction the company had made in the personal care area in several years. Building upon its success in launching an automatic dishwashing detergent in liquid form ahead of its competitors, the company also beat Procter & Gamble to the market with a laundry detergent packaged in a throw-in pouch called Fab 1 Shot, although this product failed to sustain consumer interest or reach sales expectations over the long term.

Buoyed by product development breakthroughs and a renewed commitment to consumer products marketing, Colgate sold its Kendall subsidiary and related healthcare businesses in 1988 to Clayton & Dubilier. The sale enabled Colgate to retire some debt, sharpen its focus on its global consumer products businesses, and invest in new product categories. Moreover, Mark's global approach enabled the company to maintain its overall profitability despite not having a leadership position in the United States. Although Colgate lagged behind Procter & Gamble in the toothpaste category, for example, it held a commanding 40 percent share of the toothpaste market worldwide.

Mark's strategy appeared to pay off handsomely. By the end of the third quarter of 1989 Colgate's international operations performed strongly while the profitability of its U.S. operations rose, due mostly to manufacturing-cost economies and greater control over promotional and sales expenses. Not yet ready to concede the U.S. market for personal care products to Procter & Gamble, though, Colgate acquired Vipont Pharmaceutical, a manufacturer of oral-hygiene products, toward the end of that year. Vipont's products, several of which Colgate had already been marketing overseas, enabled Colgate to strengthen the market position it had recently established with the introduction of a new tartar-control formula toothpaste.

Major Acquisitions in the 1990s

Colgate continued to make significant acquisitions in the early and mid-1990s while it attempted to gear up its product development program, which had been unable to introduce more than a few new products each year. In 1991 Colgate acquired the Murphy-Phoenix Company (whose top brand was Murphy's Oil Soap) to bolster its household care segment. That same year, Mark initiated a restructuring aimed at improving the firm's profitability and gross margins, which lagged behind the industry leaders. A major part of the effort was the elimination or reconfiguration of 25 factories throughout the world and an 8 percent reduction in the workforce. Consequently, Colgate took a $243 million charge in September 1991, which reduced significantly the firm's net income for the full year.

Colgate's most dramatic acquisition to date came in 1992 with the $670 million purchase of the Mennen Company, which added to its personal care line the top U.S. deodorant brand, Mennen Speed Stick, and the number two baby-care brand, Baby Magic. In addition, Colgate gained footholds in skin-care and hair products, and the Mennen brands gained the power of Colgate's worldwide distribution and marketing reach. This major acquisition was followed in 1993 by the purchase of S.C. Johnson & Son, Inc.'s liquid hand and body soap brands in Europe and the South Pacific, which enabled Colgate to become the worldwide leader in liquid soap.

Gross margins steadily improved in the early 1990s, reaching 48.4 percent by 1994 (up from 39.2 percent in 1984). This provided Colgate with additional funds for research and development and advertising. The North American sector also experienced gains in gross margins, which resulted in part from pricing increases on Colgate detergents. In turn, this cut into overall North American sales, which declined 8 percent from 1993 to 1994. Mark's strategy was to turn North American sales around through new product introductions such as a variant of Irish Spring soap and an extension of the Murphy's Oil Soap brand into a Murphy's Kitchen Care line of all-purpose cleaners. Under the leadership of Lois D. Juliber, who formerly headed up new product development, the North American sector was able to introduce several products within a short span for the first time.

A hidden jewel within the Colgate empire in the 1990s was its pet foods sector, Hill's Pet Nutrition. The worldwide leader in therapeutic and specialty wellness pet food, Hill's enjoyed a compound annual growth rate of 14.6 percent from 1989 to 1994. During this period the market for premium pet food increased dramatically in Europe and Japan, with Hill's snatching a substantial portion of this growth. Overall, pet foods were one of Colgate's leading profit generators, boasting gross margins of 55 to 60 percent.

Early in 1995 Colgate made another major acquisition with the $1.04 billion purchase of Kolynos Oral Care from American Home Products, which gained it the Kolynos toothpaste brand, the top brand in Brazil and a leader in several other Latin American countries. This purchase pushed Colgate's share of the Latin American oral-care market from 54 percent to 79 percent.

In September 1995 Colgate announced another major restructuring of its operations to close or reconfigure 24 additional factories and cut 3,000 more employees (more than 8 percent of the workforce). Mark said the action was necessary to finance new growth initiatives; Colgate took a $369 million charge as a result. The 1995 figures were also affected by a deepening recession in Mexico, which had accounted for 11 percent of sales and 20 percent of profits in 1994.

Boosting Sales with the Introduction of Total

Beginning in the late 1980s, Colgate had begun development of a toothpaste that contained a gingivitis-fighting antimicrobial agent, triclosan. Researchers found a way to use polymers to bind triclosan to teeth for up to 14 hours, allowing users to fight bleeding gums and bad breath continuously with only two brushings a day. The company began marketing the product overseas in 1992 under the name Total, eventually distributing it to 100 countries. The toothpaste was a major success, and enabled Colgate to increase its worldwide share of that market segment.

In the United States, however, introduction of Total was held up by the Food and Drug Administration (FDA), which required extensive tests to prove the product's effectiveness before Colgate could make gingivitis-fighting claims on package labels. After some five years the agency granted final approval, and Total reached store shelves in December 1997. The company backed it with a $100 million marketing blitz, its largest product introduction to date.

The response was even stronger than anticipated, and cemented Colgate's place as leader of the U.S. toothpaste market, a position it had actually reached in the months prior to Total's introduction. This was the first time since 1962 that ACNielsen's rankings had shown Colgate on top. Following the successful launch, the company's profits and stock price climbed steadily. In December 1998 the FDA also approved a variant of Total, Total Fresh Stripe, which reached stores several months later. A year after Total's release it was the number one toothpaste brand in the United States. Competitors such as Procter & Gamble, which already marketed a triclosan-based toothpaste in Canada, were prevented from mounting a quick response by the lengthy FDA approval process. Powered by Total and the strong U.S. economy, Colgate continued to do well in 1999, with record earnings approaching the $1 billion mark.

New Challenges in the Early 2000s

Under Mark's continued leadership, Colgate-Palmolive maintained its momentum into the early 2000s. By keeping a tight rein on costs, the company boosted its gross profit margin to 54.6 percent by 2002, when net income reached $1.29 billion on sales of $9.29 billion. On the new product front, the Colgate Actibrush battery-powered toothbrush was brought to market in 2000, soon followed by products in the burgeoning at-home tooth-whitening sector, such as Simply White gel and Total Plus Whitening toothpaste. In pet food, the company in 2002 introduced Hill's Science Diet Nature's Best, a new line of premium dog and cat food made with natural ingredients.

Long unable to compete with Procter & Gamble in that firm's mainstay detergent lines, Colgate pulled back from that sector in certain markets. In 2001 it sold its detergent business in Mexico, headed by the Viva brand, to Henkel KGaA, and then two years later off-loaded its European detergent brands to Procter & Gamble. In 2004 Colgate sold its detergent business in Ecuador and Peru. In June of that year, the company completed its first major acquisition since the 1995 purchase of Kolynos. Colgate spent $866 million for GABA Holding AG, a privately held European oral care company based in Switzerland. GABA, operating in 15 countries, had annual sales of about $300 million. Its strength in the pharmacy channel complemented Colgate's leading presence in the European retail market. The addition of GABA boosted Colgate's share of the European toothpaste market to 33 percent.

Although revenues increased another 7 percent in 2004, topping the $10 billion mark for the first time, profits fell 7 percent, to $1.33 billion. Intense global competition—particularly from a resurgent Procter & Gamble—forced Colgate to allocate additional money for advertising, and the firm also had to contend with increased raw material and packaging costs and the growing power of discount retailers such as Wal-Mart Stores, Inc. who were forcing consumer product makers to hold the line on price increases. To free up funds for marketing initiatives and new product development efforts, Colgate launched a sweeping restructuring in December 2004, its first major overhaul since 1995. The latest reorganization, a four-year program, aimed to generate between $250 million and $300 million in after-tax cost savings by 2008 by closing 26 of the firm's 78 factories around the world and eliminating about 12 percent of the workforce, or more than 4,400 jobs. Cumulative after-tax restructuring charges of between $550 million and $650 million were anticipated. As part of the restructuring, further divestments of noncore lines were very possible. As Colgate continued to deemphasize its detergent business, it seemed likely to seek buyers for its Fab and Ajax brands. Just as the restructuring began, however, Colgate faced the prospect of an even more formidable chief foe. Procter & Gamble reached an agreement to acquire The Gillette Company in January 2005 for $57 billion, which would add Gillette's Oral-B toothbrushes and toothpastes to P&G's Crest line. This deal was likely to compound the competitive pressures that Colgate-Palmolive faced, making the successful implementation of the restructuring that much more important.

Principal Subsidiaries

Colgate Flavors and Fragrances, Inc.; Colgate (Guangzhou) Co. Ltd. (China); Colgate Oral Pharmaceuticals, Inc.; Colgate-Palmolive (America), Inc.; Colgate-Palmolive (Asia) Pte. Ltd. (Singapore); Colgate-Palmolive Argentina S.A.; Colgate-Palmolive A/S (Denmark); Colgate-Palmolive Belgium S.A./N.V.; Colgate-Palmolive Beteiligungsgesellschaft mbH (Germany); Colgate-Palmolive Canada, Inc.; Colgate-Palmolive (Central America), Inc.; Colgate-Palmolive (Centro America) S.A. (Guatemala); Colgate-Palmolive Chile S.A.; Colgate-Palmolive Cia.; Colgate-Palmolive (Hellas) S.A.I.C. (Greece); Colgate-Palmolive Compania Anonima (Venezuela); Colgate-Palmolive Company, Distr. (Puerto Rico); Colgate-Palmolive del Ecuador S.A.I.C.; Colgate-Palmolive de Puerto Rico, Inc.; Colgate-Palmolive Deutschland Holding GmbH (Germany); Colgate-Palmolive (Dominican Republic), Inc.; Colgate-Palmolive (Eastern) Pte. Ltd. (Singapore); Colgate-Palmolive España, S.A./N.V. (Spain); Colgate-Palmolive Europe S.A. (Belgium); Colgate-Palmolive Europe Sarl (Switzerland); Colgate-Palmolive G.m.b.H. (Germany); Colgate-Palmolive (Guangzhou) Co., Ltd. (China); Colgate-Palmolive (H.K.) Ltd. (Hong Kong); Colgate-Palmolive Holding Inc.; Colgate-Palmolive Holdings (UK) Limited; Colgate-Palmolive Holding S. Com. p.a. (Spain); Colgate-Palmolive Inc. S.A. (Uruguay); Colgate-Palmolive (India) Limited; Colgate-Palmolive Industria e Comercio Ltda. (Brazil); Colgate-Palmolive Industrial Unipessoal, Lda. (Portugal); Colgate-Palmolive International LLC; Colgate-Palmolive Investments, Inc.; Colgate-Palmolive Ltd. (New Zealand); Colgate-Palmolive (Malaysia) Sdn Bhd; Colgate-Palmolive (Marketing) Sdn Bhd (Malaysia); Colgate-Palmolive Nederland BV (Netherlands); Colgate-Palmolive Norge A/S (Norway); Colgate-Palmolive Philippines, Inc.; Colgate-Palmolive (Poland) Sp. z 0.0.; Colgate-Palmolive Pty Limited (Australia); Colgate-Palmolive (Pty) Limited (South Africa); Colgate-Palmolive Services, S.A. (France); Colgate-Palmolive, S.A. de C.V. (Mexico); Colgate-Palmolive S.p.A. (Italy); Colgate-Palmolive Temizlik Urunleri Sanayi ve Ticaret, A.S. (Turkey); Colgate-Palmolive (Thailand) Ltd.; Colgate Sanxiao Company Limited (China); Cotelle S.A. (France); CPIF Venture, Inc.; GABA Holdings Delaware, LLC; GABA Holding A.G. (Switzerland); Hawley & Hazel Chemical Company (HK) Limited (Hong Kong); Hawley & Hazel Chemical Company (Zhongshou) Limited (China); Hawley & Hazel Chemical (Taiwan) Corporation Ltd.; Hill's Pet Nutrition, Inc.; Hill's Pet Nutrition Indiana, Inc.; Hill's Pet Nutrition Limited (U.K.); Hill's Pet Nutrition Sales, Inc.; Hill's Pet Nutrition Manufacturing, B.V. (Netherlands); Hill's Pet Nutrition SNC (France); Hill's Pet Products, Inc.; Hill's-Colgate (Japan) Ltd.; Inmobiliara Hills, S.A. de C.V. (Mexico); Kolynos Corporation; Mission Hills, S.A. de C.V. (Mexico); Norwood International Incorporated; Softsoap Enterprises, Inc.

Principal Competitors

The Procter & Gamble Company; Unilever; The Clorox Company; S.C. Johnson & Son, Inc.; The Gillette Company; Johnson & Johnson; Alberto-Culver Company; Reckitt Benckiser plc; Sara Lee Corporation; Church & Dwight Co., Inc.; The Dial Corporation.

Further Reading

Abelson, Alan, "Colgate-Palmolive: Overseas Markets Have Put New Sparkle in a Century-Old Concern," *Barron's,* November 25, 1957, pp. 15+.

Behar, Richard, "Colgate's Challenge," *Forbes,* October 3, 1988, pp. 39+.

Byrne, John A., "Becalmed," *Forbes,* December 20, 1982, pp. 48+.

Campanella, Frank W., "Soap to Nuts: Colgate-Palmolive Is Steadily Broadening Its Product Mix," *Barron's,* February 23, 1976, pp. 9+.

"Colgate's Outlook Glows on Rapid Gains Overseas," *Barron's,* January 4, 1960, pp. 20+.

"Colgate: Time to Brush Up That Bottom Line," *Business Week,* November 11, 1985, pp. 134+.

Dash, Eric, "Colgate to Cut Jobs and Use Savings to Spur Sales," *New York Times,* December 8, 2004, p. C1.

Doherty, Jacqueline, "Colgate Squeezed: But Future Looks Brighter," *Barron's,* September 27, 2004, p. 14.

——, "Colgate's Revenge: After Ceding Market Share to P&G, the Toothpaste Titan Is Brushing Up Its Defenses," *Barron's,* April 19, 2004, pp. 19–20.

——, "Fighting Profit Decay," *Barron's,* April 9, 2001, pp. 17–18.

Ellison, Sarah, "Colgate's Fight for Market Share Will Likely Erode Profit," *Wall Street Journal,* December 13, 2004, p. C1.

——, "Colgate to Cut 12% of Work Force and Close a Third of Its Factories," *Wall Street Journal,* December 8, 2004, p. A3.

——, "New Task for Colgate CEO: Grooming His Replacement," *Wall Street Journal,* July 12, 2004, p. B1.

Foster, David R., *The Story of Colgate-Palmolive: One Hundred and Sixty-Nine Years of Progress,* New York: Newcomen Society in North America, 1975, 40 p.

Grant, Linda, "Outmarketing P&G," *Fortune,* January 12, 1998, p. 150.

Hager, Bruce, "Can Colgate Import Its Success from Overseas?," *Business Week,* May 7, 1990, pp. 114, 116.

——, "Colgate: Oh What a Difference a Year Can Make," *Business Week,* March 23, 1992, pp. 90–91.

Kindel, Stephen, "The Bundle Book: At Reuben Mark's Colgate, Attention to Small Details Creates Large Profits," *Financial World,* January 5, 1993, pp. 34–35.

Menzies, Hugh D., "The Changing of the Guard at Colgate," *Fortune,* September 24, 1979, p. 92.

Morgenson, Gretchen, "Is Efficiency Enough?," *Forbes,* March 18, 1991, pp. 108–09.

Nayyar, Seema, "Colgate Buys Its Way Back into the Game," *Adweek,* February 17, 1992.

O'Connell, Vanessa, and Bill Platt, "Colgate to Acquire GABA in Europe," *Wall Street Journal,* December 19, 2003, p. B4.

Ono, Yumiko, "Colgate Slates Cuts in Jobs and a Charge," *Wall Street Journal,* September 21, 1995, p. A3.

Parker-Pope, Tara, "Colgate Places a Huge Bet on a Germ-Fighter," *Wall Street Journal,* December 29, 1997, p. B1.

——, "Colgate Puts Lois Juliber in Line for Top," *Wall Street Journal,* January 20, 1997, p. B1.

Rudnitsky, Howard, "Making His Mark," *Forbes,* September 26, 1994, pp. 47–48.

Sasseen, Jane A., and Zachary Schiller, "For Colgate-Palmolive, It's Time for Trench Warfare," *Business Week,* September 19, 1994, pp. 56–57.

Schwartz, Nelson D., "Colgate Cleans Up," *Fortune,* April 16, 2001, p. 179.

——, "Colgate's Reuben Misses the Mark," *Fortune,* October 18, 2004, p. 46.

Steinbreder, H. John, "The Man Brushing Up Colgate's Image," *Fortune,* May 11, 1987, pp. 106+.

—Sandy Schusteff
—updates: Frank Uhle; David E. Salamie

Community Health Systems, Inc.

155 Franklin Road, Suite 400
Brentwood, Tennessee 37027
U.S.A.
Telephone: (615) 373-9600
Fax: (615) 371-1068
Web site: http://www.chs.net

Public Company
Incorporated: 1985
Employees: 31,100
Sales: $3.33 billion (2004)
Stock Exchanges: New York
Ticker Symbol: CYH
NAIC: 622110 General Medical and Surgical Hospitals

Community Health Systems, Inc. is the largest non-urban provider of healthcare services in the United States, operating more hospitals than any competitor. Community Health owns or leases more than 70 hospitals in a 22-state territory, operating nearly 8,000 licensed beds. In approximately 85 percent of its markets, the company is the sole provider of general hospital services. Community Health acquires rural hospitals that typically operate on a nonprofit basis and are struggling financially. The company invests in its acquired hospitals, expanding services and improving managerial controls to produce profitable hospitals.

Origins

Community Health grew in fits and starts during its first decade, a decade in which two of its founders, Richard Ragsdales and E. Thomas Chaney, assumed an active role in running the company. The company they helped found in 1985 grew to be the biggest of its kind, but much of the company's growth was achieved after they departed. Their business strategy was sound, however, forming a foundation that could be leveraged into creating the more than $3 billion-in-sales company that Community Health became 20 years after the pair acquired their first hospital.

When Community Health began operating in 1985, Ragsdales served as the company's chairman and Chaney served as

its chief executive officer. The first hospital to come under their control was the Fannin Regional Hospital in Blue Ridge, Georgia. The hospital, acquired in January 1986, contained 34 licensed beds, the fewest number of beds acquired by the company during its first 20 years in business. The acquisition was followed by the purchase of two more hospitals, both acquired in September 1986. Community Health purchased the Highland Medical Center, a 123-bed hospital in Lubbock, Texas, and the Russell County Medical Center, a 78-bed hospital located in Lebanon, Virginia.

Community Health's first trio of hospitals provided a blueprint for expansion. The company set its sights on acute-care hospitals operating in rural communities, focusing on towns with populations ranging between 20,000 and 80,000. Suitable acquisition candidates generally were operated as nonprofit hospitals and typically were suffering from financial problems. Community Health, which operated as a publicly traded, for-profit, enterprise, served as a savior of sorts for troubled, rural hospitals, although the company, to be sure, was driven by the need to make money. For Ragsdales, Chaney, and their successors, Community Health's strategy allowed them to lay claim to pursuing both missions: serving the public good and focusing on generating profits.

According to U.S. Census Bureau figures, one-quarter of the country's population lived in rural communities during Community Health's formative decades. These communities were served by hospitals spread far apart, often making a particular community dependent on a single hospital for providing healthcare. Community Health focused its acquisitive efforts on communities in which it would become the sole provider of general hospital services, targeting hospitals that were located more than 25 miles from a competing hospital. The acquisition strategy left Community Health free from any meaningful competitive pressures and it also aided the community the hospital served. The financial well-being of an isolated hospital, obviously, was integral to the health of the community it served, but the continued existence of the hospital delivered another benefit to the community, serving as one of its primary employers. There was resistance to the idea of a corporation taking over control of nonprofit hospitals in certain areas of the country—in the Northeast, for example—but typically communities welcomed the arrival of Community Health, whose intervention rescued financially fail-ing hospitals and often led to an improved level of healthcare.

Community Health, in essence, was in the corporate turn-around business, no different than a corporation buying an ill-managed local manufacturer, improving its management, and gaining a substantially more valuable manufacturing business through its efforts. Community Health made capital improve-ments in the hospitals it acquired and it expanded the services offered by the hospitals, investing in more sophisticated emer-gency rooms, adding physical rehabilitation centers, and adding capabilities such as laser surgery. The company also recruited doctors, frequently a difficult task in the more remote areas of the country, attracting young physicians by offering subsidized office space and other incentives. These changes, combined with the standardization of tasks such as accounting—all pre-sided over from a central office—produced better, more profit-able hospitals, according to Community Health's strategy. By following its strategy, Community Health had acquired 13 hospitals in small towns across the Sunbelt by its fifth year of business, succeeding, according to the December 2, 1991 issue of *Forbes,* in "turning marginal outfits into big moneymakers." Revenues by the end of 1991 reached $138 million, from which the company gleaned $9.3 million in profits.

The revenue total recorded by Community Health at the be-ginning of the 1990s represented only a fraction of the total the company boasted at the decade's conclusion. Although the finan-cial growth was driven by several factors, the 1990s provided ideal conditions for Community Health's acquisition strategy. During the decade, more than 450 community hospitals, most nonprofits, went out of business, tempering the resistance of for-profit companies coming in to salvage nonprofit hospitals. Chaney, who was in charge of the day-to-day management of the company, made his most aggressive move during this period, completing the acquisition of Atlanta-based Hallmark Healthcare in 1994. The acquisition nearly doubled the size of Community Health, giving the company 18 hospitals.

New Owners in the Mid-1990s

Roughly a year after the Hallmark acquisition was com-pleted, a leadership dilemma led to dramatic changes at the

company's Brentwood, Tennessee, headquarters. At the end of 1995, Chaney announced he no longer wanted to lead the company, giving Community Health's board of directors a deadline for his departure that left the governing body scram-bling for a replacement. The company's board, reportedly, be-lieved they could not find a replacement for Chaney by the date of his intended departure, which prompted the directors to put the company up for sale. In March 1996, the New York-based investment banking firm Merrill Lynch was hired to solicit interest in the company. After talking to 20 interested buyers, Merrill Lynch found a suitable buyer, a New York-based pri-vate investment firm named Forstmann Little & Co.

Forstmann Little was led by Theodore Forstmann, a lever-aged buyout specialist who gained fame during the 1980s by decrying the use of junk-bond financing. Forstmann's firm, which had more than $20 billion invested in 20 companies, made its living by acquiring companies and selling them for a profit. In 1990, for instance, the company paid $850 million for Gulfstream Aerospace Corp. and sold the company six years later for $4 billion. In 1994, Forstmann Little paid $1.4 billion for Ziff-Davis Publishing and sold it the following year for $2.1 billion.

Forstmann Little acquired Community Health in 1996, marking the firm's first purchase of a healthcare company. The firm paid $1 billion for Community Health, which at the time operated 38 hospitals in 18 states. The change in ownership made Community Health a privately held company and it led to the appointment of a new leader for the company. In January 1997, Wayne T. Smith was named president of Community Health and selected as its chief executive officer in April 1997. Smith joined Community Health after spending more than two decades working for Louisville, Kentucky-based Humana Inc., joining the healthcare provider in 1973 after serving a four-year stint as a Captain in the U.S. Army Medical Services Corp. Smith rose through the executive ranks at Humana, becoming its president and chief operating officer in 1993.

Under Smith's leadership, Community Health began expanding its portfolio of properties, becoming the largest operator of rural hospitals in the country. The company's acquisition campaign began in earnest in 1998, when Commu-nity Health acquired five hospitals for $188 million. By mid-1999, the company had acquired two more hospitals, giving it a total of 45 hospitals, and had signed letters of intent to acquire five more hospitals. The company, during this period, was enjoying its status as a privately held company, enabling it to quietly develop into the country's largest player. "We haven't really tried to talk too much about what we're doing or how we're doing it," Smith said in an August 16, 1999 interview with *Modern Healthcare.* "We've just been doing it," he added, "and we're getting good results." Converting to public ownership was inevitable, however, primarily because Forst-mann Little wanted to get a return on its investment and secondly because Smith needed to obtain capital to fuel the company's expansion drive. "Our reason for going public again would be to access the public market in terms of dollars for capital," Smith explained in his interview with *Modern Healthcare.* "Whenever the hospital sector improves, we'll be looking for an opportunity to go public and access the capital markets."

Going Public in 2000

Less than a year after Smith hinted at an initial public offering (IPO) of stock, Community Health returned to the ranks of publicly held companies. When investors were offered the opportunity to acquire a stake in the company, they became financially wed to what rapidly was becoming an industry giant. Revenue in 1998 exceeded $850 million, eclipsing the $1 billion mark the following year. In June 2000, the company completed its IPO, raising $245 million from the offering and gaining another $269 million through a secondary offering of stock completed before the end of the year. By the end of 2000, the company's first profitable year since 1995, sales increased 24 percent, reaching $1.34 billion.

Once Community Health entered the public spotlight, it was exposed to greater scrutiny from industry analysts, a target for criticism and praise alike. The appraisal from the pundits was positive, underscoring the soundness of the company's strategy. Community Health adhered to a disciplined acquisition strategy, selecting hospitals that were ailing for reasons that were not related to the market they served. "You can fix bad hospitals; you can't fix bad markets," an analyst noted in the June 24, 2002 issue of *Investor's Business Daily*. Community Health relied on strong management and a centralized office to keep costs down, recouping the investments it made in recruiting health specialists, adding new services, and implementing new information and supply systems by carefully following its acquisition criteria. Once a hospital was purchased, it often took several years for the hospital to reach Community Health's standard of optimal performance—one of the reasons the company was unprofitable during the late 1990s—but after the property's financial performance improved, Community Health gained a valuable money-maker.

As Community Health neared its 20th anniversary, the company held sway as the leader in the rural hospital field. Forstmann Little, which first sold a portion of its stake in the company after its IPO, reduced its stake in the company three times after the IPO. In September 2004, the investment firm sold its remaining 23 percent interest for $560 million, which, combined with the earlier stock sales, nearly tripled the firm's original investment. Theodore Forstmann's first foray into the healthcare sector met with success; for Community Health, the backing of Forstmann's firm spurred the company's growth, making the intervention of new owners a beneficial relationship. Between 1996 and 2004, the company spent $1.8 billion, acquiring 47 hospitals during the period. In the years ahead, the company seemed likely to retain its leadership position as it continued its expansion. Preparing to guide the company forward, Smith estimated there were 375 rural hospitals in the country that met his buying criteria, giving Community Health ample room for growth as it sought to widen its lead over competitors in the years ahead.

Principal Subsidiaries

CHS/Community Health Systems, Inc. Community Health systems Professional Services Corporation; Community Insurance Group, Ltd. (Cayman Islands); Pennsylvania Hospital Company, LLC; Virginia Hospital Company, LLC; Community Health Investment Corporation; CHS Holdings Corp.; Hallmark Healthcare Corporation; Hallmark Holdings Corp.

Principal Competitors

HCA Inc.; Health Management Associates, Inc.; Triad Hospitals, Inc.; Lifepoint Hospitals Inc.; Province Health Care Co.

Further Reading

"Community Health Continues Acquisitions Spree," *Health Care Strategic Management,* November 2002, p. 4.

Gardner, Jonathan, "CHS Settles Fraud Case to Pave Way for IPO," *Modern Healthcare,* March 13, 2000, p. 20.

Kirchheimer, Barbara, "Building a System, Quietly," *Modern Healthcare,* August 16, 1999, p. 18.

——, "A For-Profit Beachhead," *Modern Healthcare,* October 15, 2001, p. 14.

Lau, Gloria, "Community Health Systems Inc.," *Investor's Business Daily,* April 24, 2001, p. A8.

Neumeier, Shelley, "Community Health Systems," *Fortune,* December 2, 1991, p. 110.

"Rural for-Profits See Green Pastures," *Modern Healthcare,* February 26, 2001, p. 16.

Saito-Chung, David, "Rural Hospital Chain Grows by Acquisitions," *Investor's Business Daily,* June 10, 2002, p. B6.

Watkins, Steve, "Community Health Systems Inc.," *Investor's Business Daily,* June 24, 2002, p. A4.

—Jeffrey L. Covell

Compagnia Italiana dei Jolly Hotels S.p.A.

Via Bellini 6
Valdagno
I-36078 VI
Italy
Telephone: +39 0445 410000
Fax: +39 0445 412360
Web site: http://www.jollyhotels.it

Public Company
Incorporated: 1949 as Compagnia Italiana Alberghi
    Turistici
Employees: 2,250
Sales: EUR 233.85 million ($320 million) (2004)
Stock Exchanges: Borsa Italiana
Ticker Symbol: JH
NAIC: 721110 Hotels (Except Casino Hotels) and Motels

Compagnia Italiana dei Jolly Hotels S.p.A. is Italy's leading hotel group, operating 48 hotels throughout the country. Although small by international standards—the company's total room count of just less than 7,900 rooms pales in comparison to industry leaders Intercontinental (520,000 rooms) and Accor S.A. (450,000 rooms)—Jolly Hotels nonetheless dominates the heavily fragmented Italian hotel market. Whereas most Italian hotels remain small, family-owned affairs, Jolly Hotels has built a network of hotels covering most of the country. Jolly Hotels divides its offering into two formats, Classic and Master. Jolly Hotels Classic features three- and four-star accommodations furnished in a simple yet comfortable style. The Classic hotels operate exclusively in Italy, and to a primarily domestic clientele, which helps shield the company from the effects of variations in currency and international tourism trends. The company operates 39 Classic hotels, and owns 32 of these properties; the remaining seven are operated under franchise agreements. The ten Jolly Hotels Master hotels provide four-star accommodations to a more upmarket segment, with more elaborate furnishings. The Master format is also the company's international flagship, with hotels in Brussels, Amsterdam, Paris, New York, London, Berlin, and Cologne. Jolly Hotels also operates three domestic Master hotels, in Rome, Milan, and Bologna. Altogether, Italy accounts for more than 72 percent of the group's sales, which topped EUR 223 million ($320 million) in 2004. The rest of Europe adds 22 percent to sales, and the United States represents 5 percent in sales. Jolly Hotels, listed on the Borsa Italiana, remains majority-controlled by the founding Marzotta family, who owns a 50 percent stake. Spain's NH Hoteles acquired a 20 percent stake in the company in 1999.

Industrialist's Lodgings in the 1950s

The Marzotta family counted among Italy's most prominent industrialists in the mid-20th century. The family's industrial background stretched back to 1836, when Luigi Marzotta founded a woolen mill in Valdagno. Under Marzotta's son, Gaetano, the company continued to prosper into the next century, with a new mill opening in Maglio. Yet the family's leap into the ranks of leading Italian industrial families came with the arrival of the next generation, under Gaetano Marzotta, Jr., at the helm of the Valdagno mill in 1921.

Marzotta continued to expand the company throughout the 1920s and into the 1930s, despite the onset of the Depression and the fascist takeover of the Italian government. A major factor in Marzotta's success was the company's ability to take advantage of the difficulties of its international rivals during this period. The company began exporting its woolens and textiles in the 1930s. As a result, Marzotta often found himself on the road, traveling around Italy and internationally as well.

Emerging from World War II (and the company's nationalization by the Mussolini government), Marzotta sought to step up the growth of his business. During this period, Marzotta's travels led him to expand his business interests in a new direction, the hotel market, in large part in order to provide suitable lodging for himself during business trips.

Marzotta founded Compagnia Italiana Alberghi Turistici in 1949, opening his first hotel that year. If his initial purpose was to provide high-quality accommodations for his own business travels, Marzotta quickly recognized the potential for developing a network of luxury-class hotels catering to a growing tourism market. Indeed, the rise of the Italian economy in the

Company Perspectives:

MISSION: Jolly Hotels constantly aims for Customer satisfaction and focuses particularly on individual customers in the middle/upper bracket of every sector of the hotel and conference markets in Italy and abroad. It offers a constant, distinct and recognisable service both at chain and individual hotel level, through brand diversification too, giving a perception of excellent quality in its chosen market.

Key Dates:

1949: Gaetano Marzotta founds Compagnia Italiana Alberghi Turistici in order to provide accommodations for his business trips.
1960s: The company develops a portfolio of city center and tourist resort locations in Italy, emphasizing medium- and large-scale hotels.
1972: The company launches a redeployment of its portfolio to focus on large-scale hotel properties.
1980: The company begins an acquisition program, adding properties throughout Italy.
1990: The company extends into the international market, with hotels in Brussels, Amsterdam, New York, and Berlin.
1999: Spain's NH Hoteles acquires a 20 percent stake in the company.
2000: The company launches a new hotel acquisition drive, adding six hotels, including Hotel MediaPark in Cologne.
2001: The company acquires the St. Ermin's Hotel, entering the U.K. market.
2002: A franchise strategy is launched, with Hotel Grande Albergo in Terme.
2003: The company completes the $30 million renovation of Madison Towers in New York City.
2005: The company owns and manages 45 hotels, including six franchises.

postwar era had created an entirely new leisure market; at the same time, Italy became a highly popular international tourist destination.

Marzotta began building up a network of hotels through the 1950s and 1960s, focusing on the country's major cities and tourist centers. The boom in the Italian tourism market in the 1960s encouraged the company to begin reshuffling its hotel portfolio and concentrate its further growth on the medium and large-sized hotel markets.

Following the death of Gaetano Marzotta in 1972, the company continued to refine its strategy upward, selling off its smaller hotels. By the early 1980s, the company had completed its reorientation, with a focus entirely on developing a network of large-scale, upper-market hotels in Italy. At the same time, the company gradually withdrew from the tourism and resort markets to focus its portfolio around the country's main urban markets.

Leading Italian Hotel Group in the New Century

With its new strategy in place, the company, which became known as Compagnia Italiana dei Jolly Hotels S.p.A., began a new series of hotel purchases, starting in the 1980s and continuing into the 1990s. During this period, the group acquired some prominent holdings, such as the Jolly Hotel Milanfiori in Milan, the Jolly Hotel Midas in Rome, the Jolly Hotel Plaza in Genoa, and the Jolly Hotel Cavlieri in Pisa.

In support of its expansion, the company developed two hotel formats. The first, Jolly Hotel Classic, provided three- and four-star accommodations throughout Italy. The second format placed the company into the higher-end four-star luxury market, under the Jolly Hotel Master name. This format targeted especially the major urban markets of Rome, Milan, and Bologna.

The Master format also became Jolly Hotels' flagship as it began an international expansion in the 1990s. The company at first targeted Europe's major cities for expansion, buying up the Hotel Lotti in Paris, then adding Jolly Hotels in Amsterdam and Brussels. The company also entered the United States, buying the Madison Towers in New York City. That purchase was originally meant as the first part of a full-scale entry into the U.S. market. The downturn in the economy at the beginning of the 2000s, however, and the collapse of the tourism market following the September 11, 2001 terrorist attacks, forced the company to reconsider its North American objectives.

By the end of the 1990s, Jolly Hotels had become the clear leader in Italy's heavily fragmented hotel industry. With 31

hotels, including five foreign hotels, Jolly Hotels was also somewhat of an anomaly in Italy, where the majority of hotels remained small, family-owned businesses. The company continued to seek further growth opportunities, aided by the arrival of a new major shareholder, NH Hoteles of Spain, which acquired a 20 percent stake in the company in 1999.

Jolly Hotels stepped up its hotel acquisition program at the beginning of the 2000s. In the year 2000 alone the company acquired Hotel Tiepolo in Vicenza, the Hotel Pontevecchio in Lecco, the Hotel Machiavelli in Milan, the Hotel Marina in Genoa, and the Hotel Villa Carpegna in Rome.

Jolly Hotels also sought out new acquisitions abroad, focusing this effort on the European market. In 2000, the company acquired Hotel MediaPark in Cologne. Then, in 2001, the company entered the United Kingdom for the first time, with the purchase of London's St. Ermin's hotel, in Westminster, for £57 million. The company added another hotel in 2001, the Hotel Igea, in Breschia, Italy. The company also launched a major refurbishing effort throughout its two hotel chains. The Madison Towers, for example, underwent a $30 million renovation that raised its status to that of four-star hotel at the end of 2003.

By 2005, Jolly Hotels operated 45 hotels, including 20 properties directly owned by the company, and another 19 operated under long-term management contracts. Jolly Hotels also had begun developing a limited number of franchised properties in the early 2000s. As part of this effort, the company licensed a new franchise, the Jolly Hotel Grande Albergo, in

Terme, in 2002. By 2005, the company's operation included six franchised hotels, primarily in the south of Italy and in Sicily. As Italy's leading hotel operator, Jolly Hotels looked forward to further development of its portfolio, both at home and abroad.

Principal Subsidiaries

Jolly Hotels Belgio S.A.; Jolly Hotels France S.A.; Jolly Hotels Holland N.V.; Jolly Hotels Italia S.p.A.; Jolly Hotels St. Ermin's B.V.; Jolly Hotels UK Ltd.; Jolly Hotels USA Inc.; Jolly Hotels USA Management Inc.

Principal Competitors

Loews Corporation; Radisson Hotels and Resorts; Hilton Group PLC; MARITIM Hotelgesellschaft GmbH; Marriott International Inc.; ACCOR S.A.; Sol Meliá S.A.; CIGA S.p.A.; Société du Louvre S.A.; NH Hotels B.V.; De Vere Group; Jarvis Hotels PLC.

Further Reading

Hubbard, Mary Beth, "Jolly Hotels," *Business Traveler,* May 2004, p. 16.

"Jolly Property Brings a Little Tuscany to New York," *Travel Weekly,* March 8, 2004, p. 91.

"Jolly Seeks More Business Clients," *Travel Trade Gazette UK & Ireland,* March 5, 2001, p. 33.

Milligan, Michael, "Jolly Hotel Madison Is Revamped: Chain's Only US Property Gets $30m Face-Lift to Raise It to Four-Star Level," *Travel Weekly,* December 29, 2003, p. 18.

"Spain's NH Hoteles Takes 19% Stake in Jolly," *European Report,* June 23, 1999.

—M.L. Cohen

Concentra Inc.

5080 Spectrum Drive, Suite 400W
Addison, Texas 75001
U.S.A.
Telephone: (972) 364-8000
Fax: (972) 387-1938
Web site: http://www.concentra.com

Private Company
Incorporated: 1997
Employees: 10,000
Sales: $1.1 billion (2004)
NAIC: 561110 Office Administrative Services

Addison, Texas-based Concentra Inc. is a leading provider of outsourced, specialized cost management services in four markets: workers' compensation, occupational health, group health, and auto liability. The company's goal is to save on healthcare costs while improving patient recovery. The privately owned company maintains a national network of occupational healthcare centers to serve more than 136,000 employer locations as well as insurance companies, group health plans, and other healthcare payers. Concentra's operations are divided among three business segments. The Health segment provides physical therapy and other treatments for work-related injuries and illnesses from 264 centers located across the country. It also provides pharmacy services and drug and alcohol testing. Concentra's care management services handles extended cases, arranging for independent medical examinations and providing case management in order to review and resolve more difficult cases. The network services segment helps to control customer costs by negotiating lower fees and reviewing medical bills for possible repricing. Concentra is majority owned by New York City investment firm Welsh, Carson, Anderson & Stowe.

Concentra's Roots Dating to the Late 1970s

Although Concentra resulted from a number of mergers, the company's corporate lineage is that of OccuSystems Inc., founded by Dr. Richard Rehm in Amarillo, Texas, in 1979. Rehm grew up relatively poor in rural Minnesota, and as a teenager spent his summers working as a straw boss for his grandparents, old-time carnies. According to a *Dallas Business Journal* profile, "Whatever tasks came up each week—dictated by whatever carnie was in jail in that particular town during that particular week—Rehm got the job." In addition to his training in the school of hard knocks, Rehm did well scholastically, becoming a favorite of his Catholic school teachers, and urged by the nuns to become a priest. But Rehm opted for a path perched somewhere between huckster and clergyman, deciding to become a doctor. Rehm received an undergraduate degree from the University of North Dakota and earned a Doctor of Medicine degree from the University of Texas. He returned to Minnesota to complete his Family Practice Residency training at the University of Minnesota, and then moved to remote Buffalo, Wyoming. For three years he practiced family medicine, as one of just two physicians to cover an area 4,000 square miles in size. Then in 1979, Rehm relocated his family to Amarillo, to open an occupational medicine practice in an area that was underserved and that he felt presented an opportunity. As Rehm explained to *Dallas Business Journal,* "It was a $100 billion segment of medicine that nobody paid attention to. ... I wanted to build a better mousetrap in this segment of health care that not only needed quality medicine, but also a more efficient business system applied to it."

Rehm proved to be equally proficient as an administrator, taking an approach that at first glance was counterintuitive. "While other facilities were trying to maximize the dollar volume per patient, we were trying to minimize the dollar volume per patient," he told *Dallas Business Journal.* Rehm's clinic succeeded in treating patients and getting them back to work quickly, thus saving employers money and allowing Rehm to reap the financial benefits of handling a large caseload. His business also got a boost from a six-year association with a weekly television health program that was syndicated on ABC affiliates in seven states. Although he discussed general health topics rather than occupational rehabilitation, and did not use the series to directly promote his clinic, he greatly benefited from the exposure.

With his clinic well established in Amarillo, Rehm was urged in 1985 by a group of insurers and employers to open a

Dallas-area clinic. After establishing a practice in the suburb of Garland, he expanded his presence in the market by acquiring a practice and hiring a physician to run it. Other acquisitions followed, so that by 1990 Rehm was operating four clinics. He was now at a watershed moment, realizing that with the healthcare field undergoing consolidation it was only a matter of time before he was "overrun by a big player," and if he wanted to maintain his independence and medical standards, he would have to become a big player himself.

Hiring a Veteran Executive in 1990

In 1990 Rehm hired John K. Carlyle, a seasoned executive in the medical field, to serve as chief executive officer and raise money to fuel expansion for Rehm's business, which took the OccuSystems name in 1990. A certified public accountant, Carlyle had spent the previous six years serving as chief financial officer of Medical Care International, the largest operator of outpatient surgery clinics in the United States. Carlyle tapped venture capitalists Welsh, Carson, Anderson & Stowe and the Sprout Group for $35 million in seed money and starting in 1991 OccuSystems began gobbling up clinics across the country. Less than two years later the company was operating about 50 clinics in seven states. In 1992 OccuSystems entered the Corpus Christi, San Antonio, Milwaukee, and Des Moines markets, as well as adding another Amarillo clinic. A year later it added Denver, Detroit, Albuquerque, and Santa Fe. Revenues during this period grew from $7.8 million in 1991 to $15 million in 1992 and $47 million in 1993.

In May 1994 OccuSystems Inc. was incorporated in Delaware in a preliminary step to taking the company public. The offering was put off for several months, during which time OccuSystems continued to expand, adding several more markets: Tucson, Reno-Carson City, Oklahoma City, Houston, Waco, and York, Pennsylvania. To help fund this growth while waiting for an opportune moment to make a public offering of stock, OccuSystems sold an 18 percent stake to Travelers Inc. for $15 million. Travelers also spent another $7.8 million to acquire stock from OccuSystems shareholders. Moreover, OccuSystems and Travelers forged a working alliance, agreeing to work together to develop occupational health centers, acquire existing ones, share information, and help develop workers' compensation insurance products. When the offering was finally completed in 1995, OccuSystems raised another $68.7 million.

OccuSystems continued to expand at a steady clip in 1995 and 1996. Early in 1995 the company expanded its presence in the Arizona market by acquiring Occupational Medical Centers, adding eight facilities in Phoenix, as well as a center in Honolulu. OccuSystems also opened a center in Flagstaff, Arizona, in 1995. Later in the year the company acquired Fort Worth-based Advanced Occupational Health Care and three occupational

health centers in Fort Worth and one in Grand Prairie, Texas. Another important development in 1995 was the establishment of the company's first hospital affiliation, with Detroit-based Henry Ford Health System. According to the arrangement between the two parties, the 13 OccuSystems clinics in the Detroit area referred patients to Henry Ford for inpatient and ancillary care, and both organizations would work together to use outcomes in developing best practices. In the next year, similar arrangements were forged with El Dorado Hospital and Medical Center in Tucson and Integris Health in Oklahoma City. Further additions to OccuSystems' chain of clinics in 1996 included Colorado Springs, New Jersey, Tulsa, and Austin. By early 1997, OccuSystems operated 110 centers in 16 states, employing nearly 200 physicians.

OccuSystems Merging with CRA in 1997

Another major turning point in the company's history was reached in April 1997 when OccuSystems agreed to merge with a company of similar size, CRA Managed Care Inc. Instead of OccuSystems' physician network, CRA took a managed-care approach to providing cost containment and case-management services for employees injured or made ill on the job. Based in Boston, CRA was incorporated in 1978 as Comprehensive Rehabilitation Associates, Inc. and enjoyed exceptional growth in the early 1990s, expanding to more than 100 field case-management offices, leading to an initial public offering in 1995, at which point it assumed the CRA Managed Care name. The year before its merger with OccuSystems, CRA posted revenues of $179.7 million and net income of $10.1 million, while OccuSystems cleared $11 million on $170 million in revenues.

The combined company now did business as Concentra Managed Care Inc., a subsidiary of parent company Concentra Inc., an industry powerhouse able to offer one-stop shopping for workers' compensation services, with operations in 49 states, the District of Columbia, and Canada. At this stage Rehm retired, but soon turned his attention to a healthcare start-up called TotalMed, an online medical transcription company. Carlyle, in the meantime, became Concentra's chairman, while CRA's chief executive, Donald Larson, became Concentra's CEO. The former president and chief operating officer of OccuSystems, Dan Thomas, assumed the same positions at Concentra.

In June Concentra added an important component to its business with the acquisitions of First Notice Systems Inc., a Boston-based provider of outsourced call reporting to handle initial workers' compensation and automobile insurance claims. Speedy notification, reporting injuries within 24 hours, was a key factor in reducing medical costs and getting workers back on the job more quickly. Moreover, Concentra would be able to use the injury data captured at the beginning of a case episode to supplement its database of outcome-related information to improve the company's services across the board. Early in 1998 Concentra completed another important acquisition to flesh out its business, buying Preferred Payment Systems, a Naperville, Illinois company specializing in bill review services.

For 1997 Concentra reported revenues of nearly $459 million, a 31 percent increase over the combined totals of OccuSystems and CRA in 1996, and net income of $31.9 million, a 51 percent improvement over the prior year. Although on the

Key Dates:

1979: Dr. Richard Rehm launches an occupational medicine clinic in Amarillo, Texas.
1985: Rehm opens a second clinic in Dallas.
1990: Rehm forms OccuSystems Inc.
1995: OccuSystems is taken public.
1997: OccuSystems and CRA Managed Care merge to form Concentra Inc.
1999: Concentra is taken private.
2003: Concentra tops $1 billion in revenues.

surface Concentra appeared to be off to a solid start, the company was having difficulty integrating its service offerings and fell short of financial expectations, leading to Larson's resignation in September 1998. He was replaced as CEO on an interim basis by Thomas, who was named his permanent replacement several weeks later. After receiving some unsolicited interest in acquiring a major portion, if not all, of the company's stock, Concentra's board engaged a firm to help sort through strategic alternatives. In March 1999 the company agreed to be taken private by Yankee Acquisition Corp., an entity created by Welsh, Carson, Anderson & Stowe for the purpose. The $1.1 billion deal was completed in August, with Welsh, Carson increasing its stake in Concentra from 14.9 percent to approximately 93 percent. Concentra now had the backing of a deep-pocketed parent to help it align its different business segments. An important step in this direction was the formation of a centralized corporate marketing group. The company ended the year reporting a 12 percent increase in revenues to $681 million, and $105 million in earnings before taxes and other costs.

The year 2000 would see the upward trend continue for Concentra. The Health Services business performed especially well and was boosted by the acquisition of eight Atlanta-area occupational medicine centers from Select Medical Corporation. Improvements to systems and infrastructure helped Network Services also to perform well in 2000, while Care Management Services rebounded from a poor 1999 to post acceptable results. All told, in 2000 Concentra experienced a 10 percent increase in revenues over the prior year to $752 million, and pretax earnings of $119 million, a 13 percent increase.

Although the U.S. economy struggled in 2001, Concentra was able to maintain its steady march toward becoming a $1 billion company, recording revenues of $857 million and pretax income of $131 million. By year-end the number of centers the company operated reached 233. Aside from a number of internal initiatives (reorganizing the sales force and upgrading information technology), Concentra also completed a significant acquisition in November 2001, picking up National Healthcare

Resources, Inc. (NHR), a Woodbury, New York-based medical consulting company to the automobile insurance and workers compensation industries. NHR was another company that Welsh, Carson had funded. The two companies complemented one another, with NHR having done well by serving middle market and regional clients and possessing a solid footprint in auto managed care services. As a result, Concentra was strengthened throughout its business segments.

Concentra all but reached $1 billion in revenues in 2002, recording slightly more than $999 million in sales, but it also posted a net loss of $9.6 million. The company took steps in the fall of 2002 to reduce costs, allowing it to pay dividends the following year. In addition, Concentra looked to maintain its growth by acquiring two more Welsh, Carson companies: Em3 Inc., a provider of web content management products, and OccMed Services, developers of a web-based integrated prevention and injury management product. Concentra finally topped the $1 billion mark in 2003 to $1.05 billion, a modest increase over 2002, but the cost containment measures resulted in the company posting net income of $43.3 million. Concentra lost some ground in 2004, due to a number of factors, such as a shortage of flu vaccine and a change in California's workers' compensation fee schedule. For the year 2004, revenues improved to $1.2 billion and Concentra posted a net loss of nearly $10 million. In spite of these short-term problems, Concentra continued to grow and appeared well positioned to enjoy long-term success.

Principal Operating Units

Health Services; Network Services; Care Management.

Principal Competitors

CorVel Corporation; Intracorp; UnumProvident Corporation.

Further Reading

Auerbach, Jon G., "CRA, OccuSystems Agree to Merge, Form New Firm," *Wall Street Journal,* April 22, 1997, p. C20.
Genusa, Angela, "Richard Rehm's OccuSystems Thrives on Chaos," *Dallas Business Journal,* June 24, 1994, p. C17.
Gonzales, Angela, "Two Occupational Health Centers in Giant Merger," *Business Journal—Serving Phoenix & the Valley of the Sun,* January 6, 1995, p. 13.
Jaklevic, Mary Chris, "Convenience Is Key to Firm's Success," *Modern Healthcare,* July 1, 1996, p. 39.
Mabray, D'Ann, "OccuSystems Builds War Chest," *Dallas Business Journal,* June 17, 1994, p. 1.
Tanner, Lisa, "Rising Costs Fuel OccuSystems' Growth," *Dallas Business Journal,* November 5, 1993, p. 7.

—Ed Dinger

DADE BEHRING

Every minute of every day™

Dade Behring Holdings Inc.

1717 Deerfield Road
Deerfield, Illinois 60015
U.S.A.
Telephone: (847) 267-5300
Fax: (847) 267-1066
Web site: http://www.dadebehring.com

Public Company
Founded: 1904 as Behringwerke
Employees: 6,000
Sales: $1.6 billion (2004 est.)
Stock Exchanges: NASDAQ
Ticker Symbol: DADE
NAIC: 339112 Surgical and Medical Instrument
  Manufacturing; 339111 Laboratory Apparatus and
  Furniture Manufacturing; 334516 Analytical
  Laboratory Instrument Manufacturing

Although little known outside its industry, Dade Behring Holdings Inc. is a powerhouse in the medical field. The company designs and manufactures a number of clinical diagnostics tools and equipment and has sales of approximately $1.6 billion annually. Headquartered in Deerfield, Illinois, Dade Behring is especially regarded for its life-saving testing materials for in-vitro and other blood disorders. Though the company filed for bankruptcy protection in 2002, Dade Behring emerged from restructuring quickly, went public on the NASDAQ, and has posted strong earnings ever since.

In the Beginning: 1850s to 1899

Emil Adolf Behring was born in March 1854 in the city of Hansdorf, in Eylau, Prussia (later Germany). He was the eldest son of his schoolmaster father's second marriage. With 12 siblings, money was tight in the Behring household and Emil was forced to leave his college studies and enroll at the Army Medical College in Berlin in 1874. Emil earned his medical degree in 1878, passed his state exams in 1880, and was sent to Poland to fulfill his military service. While in Poland, Emil began studying infectious diseases such as sepsis and the antiseptic qualities of iodine and related compounds. The young doctor began writing about his research and his earliest findings, "The Practical Goals of Blood Serum Therapy," appeared in print in 1882.

The German military paired Emil with pharmacologist Carl Binz (1832–1913) in Bonn, Germany, in the middle 1880s. By 1888 Behring was sent back to Berlin as an assistant at the Institute of Hygiene where he worked with famed bacteriologist Robert Koch (1843–1910), who had been the first to prove that infectious diseases were caused by microorganisms or pathogens. Japanese researcher Shibasaburo Kitasato (1852–1931) was also in Berlin, studying with Koch, and he and Behring carried out numerous experiments to understand how healthy hosts fought off disease. During the course of this research, Behring and Shibasaburo injected healthy animals (usually guinea pigs, rabbits, or dogs) with the tetanus-infected blood of others. The healthy animals then developed "antibodies" (a term coined by Behring and Shibasaburo) to tetanus, fighting off the infection with what was called "passive immunity." The two published their findings in the *German Medical Weekly (Deutschen Medizinischen Wochenschrift)* and were propelled to the forefront of the immunology and serology research field.

In 1890 Koch moved to the Institute for Infectious Diseases and Behring followed. There Behring worked alongside though not peacefully with Paul Ehrlich (1854–1915). By the end of 1891 Behring had used his knowledge of antitoxins to develop a vaccine for diphtheria, successfully tested on animals, and refined for use with humans. The antitoxin, simply called "T.A.," was first marketed commercially in 1892. The following year Behring published the first edition of his *Collected Papers (Gesammelte Abhandlungen),* and in 1894 was named Professor of Hygiene at the University of Halle-Wittenburg. He left Halle in 1985 when he was appointed chair of the Hygienics Department at the medical school of the University of Marburg, and married in 1896. The professor and his bride, who was 24 years his junior, had seven children.

An Emerging Field: 1900–50s

By the dawn of the 20th century, Behring continued to research a long-term vaccination for diphtheria but had also

Key Dates:

1878: Emil Behring earns a medical degree from Army Medical College in Berlin.
1888: Dr. Behring begins working with Robert Koch and Shibasaburo Kitasato.
1891: The first human is given Behring's diphtheria vaccine.
1892: Behring's diphtheria vaccine is marketed commercially.
1901: The first Nobel Prize for Physiology and Medicine is awarded to Behring and the ''von'' is added to his surname.
1904: Behringwerke is established in Marburg, Germany.
1913: The first long-lasting diphtheria vaccine is marketed by Behringwerke.
1935: Behringwerke introduces diagnostic products to the commercial medical market.
1994: Investors buy Baxter International's diagnostics division and Dade medical supply products to form Dade International.
1995: Hoechst AG spins off Behring Diagnostics as an independent company.
1997: Behring Diagnostics and Dade International merge to become Dade Behring.
2002: Dade Behring reorganizes under Chapter 11 and becomes a public company, Dade Behring Corporation.
2003: The company begins selling shares on the NASDAQ.
2004: Dade Behring celebrates its centennial.
2005: The company's customer base reaches 25,000 worldwide.

turned his attention to tuberculosis. The next year, 1901, Behring was awarded the Nobel Prize for Physiology and Medicine, the first such award devoted to advances in medicine for his serum and immunology work. In addition, he was given a large cash sum and ''von'' was added to his name, signifying his ascension in class and rank. In 1904 von Behring published ''The Etiology and Etiological Therapy of Tetanus,'' and was himself stricken with the disease. He had been working with a company called Höchster Farbwerke (which later became Hoechst AG), and in 1904 the firm split and its Marburg labs were taken over by von Behring and renamed Behringwerke.

The doctor/scientist divided his time between his laboratories and his duties at the University of Marburg. In 1913 von Behring produced a long-lasting diphtheria vaccine and turned his considerable skills to eradicating cholera and gangrene. In 1915 von Behring published another edition of his *Collected Papers,* filled with notes and articles related to his lifelong research into battling infectious disease. Two years later, in March 1917, after numerous awards and honorary titles, Emil von Behring died in Marburg, Germany.

Behringwerke reaped the benefits of its founder's tireless research into diphtheria, tetanus, tuberculosis, and other infectious diseases. Considered the father of modern immunology and serology, Dr. von Behring led the company to numerous medical breakthroughs. After von Behring's death, however, the company continued his work, though in a different manner: instead of the development of actual serums and vaccines, the firm produced equipment and products for hospitals and labs to process blood and tissue samples to determine the presence of infectious diseases. By 1935 Behringwerke introduced its first commercial diagnostics products, all of which were well received by the medical community. Within a decade the company had become a leader in the emerging field of medical diagnostics.

Near the end of the 1940s as Behringwerke widened its range of diagnostics products and began working with plasma, Dr. John Elliott founded the Dade Reagents Company to provide consistent, high quality typing and testing of blood. Dr. Elliott had been director of the Dade County Blood Bank in Florida, where hundreds of thousands of blood samples were grouped, typed, tested for various diseases, and stored for future use. Dade Reagents Company was acquired by the Illinois-based American Hospital Supply Corporation in 1956, which wanted to expand into the burgeoning international diagnostics field.

Mergers and Acquisitions: 1960s–90s

In the 1960s and 1970s Behringwerke introduced a widening array of diagnostics products and instruments, as did competitors such as the E.I. du Pont de Nemours & Company and

MicroScan Inc. American Hospital Supply bought MicroScan in 1980, and in 1985 medical conglomerate Baxter International acquired American Hospital Supply and its Dade and MicroScan product lines. Less than a decade later, a group of investors bought Baxter's diagnostics unit for over $440 million, creating a private, independent company named Dade International in late 1994. The new firm became the world's largest company devoted to diagnostics, with sales of over $500 million.

While the ink was barely dry on the creation of Dade International, a company bearing Dr. von Behring's name was spun off from Hoechst AG (which later became Aventis) and rechristened Behring Diagnostics in 1995. Soon after its formation, the company acquired a drug-testing firm called Syva Company and then the well known diagnostics and clinical chemistry division of du Pont in 1996. The next year, 1997, saw the merger of Behring Diagnostics and Dade International to become Dade Behring. The combined operations of the two companies reached sales of $1.2 billion and employed a workforce of 6,400 worldwide.

For the remainder of the 1990s Dade Behring continued to do what it did best: develop and market new testing products and procedures for the diagnostics community. The company remained a leader for testing blood, tissue, and urine but had become overburdened with debt. As Dade Behring approached the 21st century, the company's products remained in top form but were threatened as its financial health spiraled out of control. During this time of uncertainty, a new president and chief operations officer, James Reid-Anderson, stepped in to run the company. Reid-Anderson had joined the company in 1996 as executive vice-president and chief financial officer.

A New Century and New Company, the 2000s

As the millennium began for Dade Behring, the company sustained a long line of medical firsts, introducing faster and more comprehensive testing procedures for a growing range of infectious diseases and health disorders. Revenues in 2000 had now retreated to $1.1 billion and the firm was drowning in debt, leading to Chapter 11 filing by 2002. Remarkably, all creditors signed on for the reorganization and Dade Behring emerged from Chapter 11 protection as the newly public Dade Behring Corporation in 2003. Dade Behring traded on the NASDAQ under the ticker symbol DADE and soon amazed investors and creditors with strong sales and renewed vigor in the diagnostics industry.

By the end of 2003 Dade Behring's recovery had been nothing less than spectacular with sales topping $1.4 billion. While Dade Behring ranked sixth among the world's largest clinical diagnostics firms, it was an international leader in IVD or in-vitro diagnostics testing of bodily fluids. The worldwide IVD industry, which consisted of supplies and equipment for healthcare facilities such as labs and hospitals, had reached more than $20 billion by the early 2000s and Dade Behring had secured a sizable share of the market, with plans for more.

By 2004 Dade Behring continued to defy its critics, exceeding expectations and becoming the poster child for Chapter 11 reorganization with revenues of $1.6 billion and net income of $80 million. The firm's four core product lines—chemistry and immunology, hemostasis, microbiology, and infectious disease diagnostics—maintained solid sales and earnings but increased

year over year since its bankruptcy filing. The firm employed more than 6,000 workers by 2005 and had operations in 43 countries to serve more than 25,000 medical customers.

Principal Subsidiaries

Dade Behring AB; Dade Behring GmbH; Dade Behring Materials; MicroScan Inc.

Principal Competitors

Abbott Laboratories; Diagnostic Products Corporation; Johnson & Johnson; Roche Holding Ltd.

Further Reading

Brennan, Terry, "Dade Behring Confirmed," *Daily Deal,* September 19, 2002.

"Deerfield, Ill.-Based Medical-Test Maker Fix Cuts Debt, Sets Public Trading," *Knight Ridder/Tribune News Service,* October 4, 2002.

Herman, Armin, and Kolbe Jurgeo, *German Nobel Prize Winners,* Munich, Germany: Heinz Moos Verlagsgellsachaft, 1968.

Holman, Kelly, "Dade Behring Sponsors Largely Unhurt," *Daily Deal,* August 3, 2002.

Japsen, Bruce, "Deerfield, Ill.-Based Medical Test Maker to Reorganize Under Chapter 11 Filing," *Chicago Tribune,* August 2, 2002.

Klein, Sarah, "Dade Behring Looks to Expand Lab-Test Niche," *Crain's Chicago Business,* June 16, 2003, p. 22.

——, "Illinois Companies' Earnings Pop," *Crain's Chicago Business,* August 16, 2004, p. 4.

Nobel Lectures, Physiology or Medicine 1901–1921, Amsterdam: Elsevier Publishing Company, 1967.

Sikora, Michael, "Private Equity Firms Probe for Hidden Corporate Gems," *Mergers & Acquisitions,* June 2000, p. 42.

Somasundaram, Meera, "40 Under 40," *Crain's Chicago Business,* November 1, 1999, p. E22.

—Nelson Rhodes

Distribución y Servicio D&S S.A.

Avenida Presidente Eduardo Frei Montalva 8301
Quilcura 7490562, Santiago
Chile
Telephone: (56) (2) 200-5000
Toll Free: (56) (2) (600) 399-6666
Fax: (56) (2) 200-5100
Web site: http://www.dys.cl

Public Company
Incorporated: 1985
Employees: 19,409
Sales: CLP 1.39 trillion ($2.49 billion) (2004)
Stock Exchanges: Bolsa de Comercio de Santiago Madrid
    New York
Ticker Symbols: D&S; DYS (ADRs)
NAIC: 445110 Supermarkets and Other Grocery (Except
    Convenience) Stores; 522210 Credit Card Issuing;
    531120 Lessors of Nonresidential Buildings

Distribución y Servicio D&S S.A. operates a chain of supermarkets and retail food stores in Chile and is, in terms of revenue, the nation's largest retailer. Among its 75-odd stores are huge supermarkets, called hypermarkets, under the Líder and Líder Vecino names. They carry (aside from food) apparel, housewares and furniture, electronics and appliances, office supplies, sporting goods, auto parts, pet supplies, and toys. D&S also operates smaller Líder Express supermarkets, FarmaLíder pharmacies, LíderCafé and CafeBuffet restaurants, and shopping malls.

A Growing Array of Products: 1893–1996

D&S derives from Gratenau y Cía., an import and wholesale distribution company founded in Valparaiso by German businessmen from Hannover in 1893. Adolfo Ibáñez Boggiano joined this company in 1899, and it eventually became Ibáñez y Cía. The company's commercial retail activities began in the 1930s, with the opening of Depósitos Tres Montes outlets in strategic points of Santiago, the capital and chief metropolis of Chile. These were small warehouses selling coffee, tea, and maté. Under the management of Adolfo's son Manuel Ibáñez Ojeda, the Ibáñez stores became self-service in 1944. In 1957, he opened what D&S has called the first supermarket in Latin America, naming it Almac for Sociedad Comercial de Almacenes Ltda., which was the company name at this time. Located in Santiago's Providencia neighborhood, Almac's self-service format, combined with parking lots and a wide range of products, found favor and led to the replacement of the older, smaller Tres Montes stores by Almac supermarkets. There were five of these units in 1966, all in the Santiago metropolitan area, making Supermercados Almac the largest supermarket operator in Chile. They carried (in addition to complete lines of food) liquors, wines, hardware, toys, toiletries, glass products, and notions.

The first of a new supermarket chain, Ekono, was opened in 1984; it targeted the middle class with a marketing campaign based on low prices. Distribución y Servicio D&S S.A. was established in 1985 to act as distributor and service provider for the supermarkets, although its field of operation came to be widened. The business was conceived as a system of independent enterprises. Many of the stores were the property of an Ibáñez family group. Others were administered by D&S but belonged to outside investors, including stores operated as franchises. By 1997 D&S owned 27 of its 36 stores and 91 percent of its selling space and properties in Chile.

The first Ekono hypermarket opened in 1987; its larger sales space allowed the company to include more nonfood products. D&S entered Argentina with a half-share in an Ekono supermarket in 1993. By the end of 1996 the company owned three such stores, in hypermarket form, with annual sales of $120 million. In 1995 D&S introduced its first Líder store, with about 10,000 square meters (more than 100,000 square feet) of selling space. This store, with about 60 percent of the space devoted to such nonfood articles as clothing, electric home appliances, and housewares, represented a new, and soon growing, format for the company. The following year D&S took over the Fullmarket S.A. chain, consisting of two Santiago-area stores and real estate in Temuco, and the O'Clock bakery company. The number of its stores almost doubled between 1992 and 1996. During this period D&S more than doubled its operating profit margins and almost tripled its selling space.

Company Perspectives:

We will be the most innovative, most productive and most profitable firm in the industry. We will be the best distribution and retailing company in the region.

We believe that our duty is to serve God and our country. We will best accomplish this by providing a service that meets the basic needs of thousands of families at a low cost, with high quality and by providing job opportunities and the possibility for employees to grow with our company.

Applying the Wal-Mart Model: 1997–2002

In 1997 D&S was Chile's largest supermarket operation, with Almac, Ekono, and Líder each holding roughly equal shares of the company's roughly 20 percent of this sector. Presto, the company's credit card, was introduced in 1996. D&S became a public company in December 1996, raising some $50 million by selling shares of stock on the Bolsa de Comercio de Santiago. By late 1997, when the company began issuing American Depositary Receipts (the equivalent of shares) on the New York Stock Exchange, its shares had doubled in value. This new offering, including parallel issues to European and Chilean investors, raised $227.7 million. Two more Ekono hypermarkets opened that year, in Iquique and Talca, and a third Ekono opened in a part of Santiago previously without a supermarket. A Fullmarket was converted to a Líder, as was an Ekono. The year ended with nine Almacs, 13 Super Ekonos, nine Hiper Ekonos, and six Líders in Chile and five Ekonos in Argentina. D&S also owned two shopping centers in Santiago.

Manuel Ibáñez's son Felipe Ibáñez Scott became president of the D&S board of directors in 1986. Manuel's son Nicolás Ibáñez Scott became general manager (the equivalent of chief executive officer) in 1994. Energetic and ambitious, he presided over D&S's expansion of the mid-1990s and was named the outstanding entrepreneur of 1997 by the Chilean business magazine *Capital*. Interviewed for the publication by Carolina García de la Huerta, he declared, "We want to compare ourselves with American and English companies, the most efficient in the world. . . . So great is our ambition." Armed with the infusion of funds from stock sales he opened, at a cost of $400 million, 17 new D&S stores in 1998, including five in Argentina, where the number of Ekono stores now reached ten. But the recession that began in Argentina in 1998 resulted in a debt of $100 million and current-account losses of $2 million a month. Faced with a very low market share and poor prospects, D&S sold the Argentine operation to Disco S.A. in 1999 for $150 million. The company lost money that year, principally because of its failed venture.

The sale of the Argentine operation enabled D&S to reduce its debt, which reached $377 million at the end of 1999. The company maintained its policy of aggressive expansion within Chile itself, acquiring new land to build more stores and, it was hoped, fend off multinational competitors such as Carrefour S.A. by saturating the market.

In 2000 D&S introduced Líder Vecino, a format created by converting existing Ekono supermarkets. Within an average of only 3,800 square meters of space, a Líder Vecino held all the different sections of any existing Líder. In 2001 the company launched its newest hypermarket format, named Líder Mercado, with the opening of a store located along one of Santiago's major throughfares. This store offered the broadest assortment of products (50,000 storekeeping units), as well as a music-and-entertainment mezzanine, a flower shop, and a pharmacy inside the health-and-beauty area. This was the first of 19 FarmaLíders installed within the company's hypermarkets by the end of 2001.

By this time D&S had regained its equilibrium and impetus, but Nicolas Ibáñez had lost none of his drive to excel. He rose at six each morning and, after jogging for an hour, arrived at his gym for a little work on the machines and to "touch base" informally with his staff. He was at his desk at eight and expected everybody else at headquarters to be there also. Writing for *Capital*, Lorena Medel called the 44-year-old "a strange mixture of privileged child, pampered by his mother, and authoritarian and disciplinarian adult . . . hyperkinetic as a monkey. . . . He does things that no other entrepreneur would do in Chile, such as prohibiting women in his company from wearing pants. . . . Many executives tremble and some don't even dare look him in the eye." Men were forbidden beards, long sideburns, or long hair, and women were not allowed to wear too much makeup. Smoking was prohibited inside offices, nor was anyone allowed to slip outside and smoke. Employees were required to attend "personal growth" sessions once a year at a mountain retreat in the nearby Andes. A dancing session was held the first Monday of each month, and attendance at the weekly mass given at a company chapel was "suggested."

One of the strengths of D&S was a high level of service with relatively low levels of inventory. The company built its own 60,000-square-meter distribution center in 1996 and, soon after, furnished it with advanced inventory-management software from Atlanta-based E3 Corp. By 2001 the company was using more than 1,800 vendors to supply its stores. D&S also put great emphasis on service to its suppliers. Nevertheless, it did not hesitate to leverage its leadership in groceries and perishables to extract maximum concessions from its suppliers, based on a model borrowed from Wal-Mart Stores Inc. In 1999 D&S extended its deadline for making payments to its vendors from the normal 30 to 60 or 90 days. Those refusing had their products banned from the supermarkets. In the same year a suppliers' group said the company was violating the intellectual property of its members by copying logos, images, and colors so that D&S private-label goods would resemble those of established competing brands. In 2002 Nestlé Chile S.A. publicly complained that D&S was demanding prices lower than those accorded to the competition.

Uncertain Direction: 2003–04

Following a year of lower profit margins, Nicolas Ibáñez suddenly departed D&S at the beginning of 2003 and was replaced by a cousin, Cristóbal Lira Ibáñez. Rumor had it that he did not leave of his own accord but had been told to depart, for a time, by his father. Medel, who interviewed Lira, described the atmosphere at company headquarters as "perhaps less tense . . . more relaxed." The new general manager said the staff was not wearing neckties during the summer and laughingly denied that "our people are required to climb Aconcagua" (at 23,834 feet,

Key Dates:

1893: The wholesale distribution business that eventually leads to D&S is founded.

1957: Manuel Ibáñez Ojeda opens an Almac supermarket in Santiago.

1966: With five units in Santiago, Almac is the largest supermarket chain in Chile.

1984: The company establishes a second supermarket chain called Ekono.

1987: The first Ekono hypermarket opens for business.

1993: D&S enters Argentina with an Ekono supermarket.

1995: D&S introduces its third chain, called Líder.

1996: The company goes public and also introduces its own credit card.

1998: Flush with cash from the sale of stock, D&S opens 17 stores.

1999: Too-rapid expansion results in red ink and the sale of the Argentine operation.

2001: The largest D&S hypermarket has a pharmacy and a music-and-entertainment mezzanine.

2003: All remaining Almac and Ekono stores are re-labeled under the Líder name.

2004: D&S purchases all seven Carrefour hypermarkets in Chile.

the highest peak in the Western Hemisphere). A veteran D&S executive, Lira indicated that the company—with debts surpassing its net worth—would be passing through a phase of consolidation rather than expansion, with an emphasis on improving the distribution network, improving service to the customer, and repositioning the stores in the marketplace. D&S, in 2003, took a long-contemplated action when it converted its four remaining Almac and 23 Ekono stores into Líder Express supermarkets and Líder Vecino compact hypermarkets, respectively. The lone Líder Mercado became a Líder hypermarket.

Lira's stewardship proved to be only temporary. Despite increased sales in the first half of 2004, the company's profit margin fell precipitously. Ibáñez took up the reins of the company again at the beginning of September 2004. Earlier in the year, he had scored a coup by purchasing the seven Carrefour stores in Chile for EUR 100 million (about $124 million), traveling to Paris to outbid Chile's largest department store chain, Falabella. The French-based hypermarket chain had entered Chile in 1998 but had scarcely passed 3 percent of the market in its field. In August, D&S raised $250 million by selling stock in Chile and overseas. The funds from this sale, which reduced the Ibáñez Scott family's stake in D&S from three-quarters to two-thirds of the shares, were dedicated to paying Carrefour, augmenting the Presto credit card venture, and financing a 2004–05 expansion plan that called for seven new stores.

The strategy of D&S seemed to be based on Wal-Mart: namely, continuing to attract customers through everyday low prices and keeping costs down by economy of scale. Extracting maximum profit from the company credit card, Presto, which had a million holders, was part of the effort. D&S was about to issue Transbank, a credit card not tied to its outlets, and it had made an alliance with public-owned BancoEstado. In addition, the company seemed certain to establish a Banco Líder in 2005. For 2004 D&S recorded a paper-thin profit of CLP 5.31 billion ($9.53 million) on revenue of CLP 1.39 trillion ($2.49 billion). Its long-term debt at the end of 2004 was CLP 237.92 billion ($417.96 million). It held 33.5 percent of the supermarket sector in 2003.

In early 2004, D&S was operating 74 stores, of which about 50 were in the Santiago metropolitan area. Twenty-nine were Líder hypermarkets intended to be "one stop" shopping destinations modeled after European hypermarkets. Typically these stores occupied strategic sites at the intersection of major thoroughfares, thereby servicing various communities with one store. The Líder sites had ample parking spaces and were generally developed in combination with an assortment of complementary stores, including food courts, cinemas, and pharmacies. These stores ranged in size from 6,020 to 13,243 square meters, carried a large variety of nonfood items, and had 42 to 76 checkout counters. Six of them were Carrefour Chile stores acquired in January 2004.

The 20 Líder Vecino stores incorporated the characteristics of a Líder hypermarket in a smaller selling area, ranging between 2,400 and 4,720 square meters but typically offering the same items as the traditional hypermarkets. The 25 Líder Express stores were rebranded Almac and Ekono units, operated as traditional neighborhood supermarkets providing a friendly atmosphere and personalized attention and emphasizing food products. They averaged 1,532 square meters in selling area. The 42 FarmaLíder stores also were located in small retail spaces within the hypermarkets. The 24 LíderCafé restaurants and eight CaféBuffet restaurants were located in the hypermarkets. A few larger-format restaurants had been opened in certain Líder stores under the Revive name.

Groceries accounted for 47 percent of sales from retail operations in 2003, followed by perishables, with 34 percent. Apparel, with 6 percent, ranked third. Sales of the company's private-label products came to 14.6 percent of the total. Líder stores accounted for 60.5 percent of total net revenues, while Líder Vecino accounted for 21.1 percent and Líder Express for 12.7 percent. Credit card operations, logistics services, and real estate operations accounted for the remaining 5.7 percent.

D&S owned six shopping centers: four in the Santiago area, and one each in Antofagasta and Viña del Mar. These facilities were 64 percent rented by other merchants rather than the supermarkets themselves. Some 705 retail locations were being rented within the supermarkets. D&S owned 52 of its 68 stores prior to the Carrefour purchase. Its distribution center was in Quilicura, on the outskirts of Santiago.

Principal Subsidiaries

Administradora de Concesiones Comerciales de Hipermercados S.A.; Administradora de Concesiones Comerciales de Supermercados S.A.; Maquinsa S.A.; S.A. Inmobilaria Terrenos y Establecimientos Comerciales.

Principal Competitors

Cencosud S.A.; Supermercados Unimarc S.A.

Further Reading

"Los Amos del Retail Chileno," *Gestión,* December 2004, pp. 8–11.

Barrese, Robert, "Supply and Demand Becomes a Balancing Act," *Food Logistics,* May 15, 2001, p. 51.

Bennett, Peter D., "Retailing Evolution or Revolution in Chile?," *Journal of Marketing,* July 1966, pp. 38–41.

"D&S Hits International Market," *LatinFinance,* November 1997, p. 78.

"La Encrucijada de D&S," *Estrategia,* October 4, 2004, p. 16.

Fazio, Hugo, *Mapa actual de la extreme riqueza en Chile,* Santiago: LOM Ediciones, 1997, pp. 339–40.

Garcia de la Huerta, Carolina, "Fuera de serie," *Capital,* December 1997 supplement, pp. 17–18, 21–22, 25.

González, Felipe, "De cazador A PRESA," *América economía,* February 10, 2000, pp. 36–37.

Goyenche, M. Cristina, "Las redes del 'retail,'" *Capital,* February 2005, pp. 32–33.

Hermosilla, Macarena, "El ultimo 'gallito,'" *Capital,* December 6–19, 2002, pp. 60–62.

Jones, Forrest, "Big Time," *Latin Trade,* December 2004, p. 12.

"Manos a la obra," *Capital,* April 23–May 6, 2004, p. 86.

Medel, Lorena, "Cristóbal Lira empuja el carro," *Capital,* February 28–March 13, 2003, pp. 38–43.

——, "Líder Antilíder," *Capital,* May 4–17, 2001, pp. 22–25.

——, "Su prueba de fuego," *Capital,* July 16–29, 2004, pp. 70–71.

Sullivan, Tara, "La difícil decisión de vender," *América economía,* April 8, 1999, p. 29.

—Robert Halasz

Duracell International Inc.

Berkshire Corporate Park
Bethel, Connecticut 06801
U.S.A.
Telephone: (203) 796-4000
Toll Free: (800) 551-2355
Fax: (203) 207-7145
Web site: http://www.duracell.com

Wholly Owned Subsidiary of The Gillette Company
Incorporated: 1935 as P.R. Mallory & Company
Sales: $2.02 billion (2003)
NAIC: 335911 Storage Battery Manufacturing

Duracell International Inc., owned by The Gillette Company, is the world's leading manufacturer and marketer of high-performance alkaline batteries. Known as P.R. Mallory for decades after its founding in 1935, the company took on the Duracell name in 1978 when it was acquired by Dart Industries. Subsequently, the battery maker was involved in numerous acquisitions and mergers, including one of the largest leveraged buyouts (LBOs) of the 1980s. Duracell's distinctive copper and black color scheme has been around for more than three decades. In addition to its alkaline batteries, the company sells primary lithium, zinc air, and rechargeable nickel-metal hydride batteries as well as a line of flashlights. Gillette—parent to Duracell since 1996—was in line to be purchased by Procter & Gamble in 2005.

Mallory Charging Up with Duracell: 1935–77

P.R. Mallory and his basic business tenets of "invest in research" and "the customer is King" laid the groundwork for Duracell back in 1935. Independent inventor Samuel Ruben entered the picture in 1944 and with Mallory introduced the world's first mercury battery, forerunner of the alkaline battery. The innovation allowed the U.S. military to replace poorly performing zinc carbon batteries used in their equipment during World War II, according to Gillette.

The battery component of Mallory's business grew steadily throughout the post-World War II period, reflecting the booming economy and the rapidly growing market for consumer durables and electronic consumer goods, some of which would require battery power. The first hearing aid button cell used Ruben's mercury battery technology.

During the early 1960s, the company introduced its AA size and AAA size alkaline batteries. The Duracell brand name was adopted in 1964, and the Copper Top graphic came on the scene early in the 1970s.

Although revenues were growing, the company also closely tracked the business cycle because sales of many of its products were at the mercy of consumer buying power, itself a function of wages and earnings. From the early 1960s into the mid-1970s sales grew strongly (the average annual rate was 5 percent from 1963 to 1972); however, company profits reflected the recession of the mid- and late-1960s, with earnings per share hitting a peak of $2.34 in 1966 before falling sharply with the recession. With the beginning of the deep recession in mid-1973, company earnings began to fall sharply.

Mallory's profit margins were respectable in that price-competitive climate, but were under constant pressure. The boom of 1972 allowed the firm to boost sales of electrical and electronic items to industry, complementing consumer sales. Specifically, makers of appliances bought Mallory components to satisfy the growing retail demand for household items, such as laundry units, electric and gas ranges, and dishwashers, among other consumer durables. The company saw this expansion of consumer durables, in particular, as a basis for long-term growth.

The strong growth in consumer durables generated an expanding volume of sales and, thus, economies of scale in production, meaning lower unit costs, higher profit margins, and some insulation from price wars. Therefore, even as the U.S. economy left the fast-growth path of the 1960s and Mallory's margins fell, it was able to weather the downslide of demand that accompanied the recession of 1973. The company's debt load was small, and, although most of its market was domestic, it was well positioned to take on the foreign firms using their low production costs to make headway into the U.S. market in the late 1970s.

In 1977, *Fortune* magazine ranked Mallory as the 507th largest company, with $323 million in sales and profits of $10 million (which put it in the 170th position). Most of the company's sales were to individual consumers and to makers of consumer durables. Industry accounted for the rest of Duracell's sales, mostly electrical contacts, welding products, and special metals for the automotive, power generating, aerospace, and communications industries. Mallory was also a supplier of batteries of all sizes to the military, and its Duracell batteries were used in everything from hearing aids to military communications equipment. Brand building was essential during this time; the company's ad campaign focused on the use of batteries in toys, and the "copper-top" image it created would be very successful in promoting the "long life" of Duracell batteries.

The battery was essentially an undifferentiated product, and niches in the market were primarily established through advertising. To a certain extent, before the 1980s, the technology included transistor batteries and photo and watch batteries. But with the advent of the 1980s, however, Duracell and competitor Eveready began to primarily sell general purpose batteries where image was the only means to promote differentiation. Furthermore, the decade would see a shift in electronic technology. Duracell would have to adapt to the "cellular age," adjusting its products to meet the demand for smaller and smaller cells.

High Voltage Deals: 1978–90

P.R. Mallory was bought by Dart Industries in 1978, becoming Duracell Inc. and kicking off what would be a tumultuous two decades of mergers and acquisitions. Many deals transpired in the 1980s, including one of the largest leveraged buyouts in history.

The 1978 takeover was launched by Dart CEO and President C. Robert Kidder, who had come to Dart from Ford. Mallory fought the takeover but eventually settled on Dart's offer of $46 per share, making the total acquisition worth $215 million. At the time, Mallory was being hit hard by competition from Energizer and Panasonic. Kidder had joined Dart as vice-president of Planning and Development and made the recommendation that Dart acquire Mallory in order to add more consumer business to Dart. After gaining control over Mallory, Dart divested several of Mallory's subsidiaries but kept and promoted Duracell.

Shortly thereafter, Kidder joined Duracell as a vice-president based in Europe, where company growth was slower. Within one year, Kidder was promoted by Chairman Pete Viele to vice-president of sales and marketing for Duracell U.S.A. Kidder would be credited with the forward-looking strategy of creating the "cordless Duracell home" of cellular phones and pocket computers and, most importantly, recognizing the need to capture this market. This market shift pointed to the unique, and perennial, technological parameters of a profitable battery business—companies could not just invent new battery products without an established application for their use. Thus, Duracell's success would be highly dependent on energy technologies, especially in the 1980s and 1990s, built into cellular telephones, camcorders, pocket computers, and other innovations.

By 1980 the company was again on the market, this time as part of a deal between Kraft Inc. and Dart. Kraft, which was owned by Phillip Morris at the time, merged with Dart, owner of Duracell. This marriage would last until 1986, when Dart and Kraft split, with Kraft keeping Duracell.

The battery business, meanwhile, kept with its long-held tradition of introducing value-added features. Duracell began placing "freshness dating" on alkaline battery packaging in 1987—the first consumer battery producer to do so.

In 1988, Duracell was taken over by the investment banking firm of Kohlberg Kravis Roberts (KKR) in what would be one of the largest leveraged buyouts of the 1980s. The central players, Jerome Kohlberg, Jr., Henry R. Kravis, and George R. Roberts, raised $62 million to buy out 35 companies between 1976 and 1989, including Duracell. The purchase price for Duracell was $1.9 billion in 1988. Kidder and the management team that organized the buyout from Kraft became 30 percent owners, Kidder was named president and CEO of Duracell, and the new Kidder team devised a particular marketing and restructuring strategy for the newly independent firm.

At the time, the KKR buyout was viewed as very successful in that, compared to other LBOs, there were no assets sold and no large layoffs. Increased research and development spending, prudent debt management, and cost-cutting measures led to an increased market position for the KKR-controlled Duracell. The buyout was hailed by some as KKR's most successful LBO. Of course Duracell also benefited from the increase in battery demand in the United States as well. Duracell and its major rival, Eveready, together controlled 75 percent of the $3 billion a year market. Another key factor in the success of the LBO was the fact that most of the growth of the business had shifted to long-lasting alkalines (from zinc batteries) so that alkalines accounted for 80 percent of Duracell's revenues in 1989.

In addition, the new marketing strategy for the streamlined company emphasized marketing the Duracell brand around the world, including such new products as Lithium Manganese Dioxide batteries and the Copper Top Tester, a package that allowed consumers to test the power of batteries. These marketing commitments were part of the buyout agreement. The commitment to the fierce mass marketing campaign paid dividends as Duracell distribution became vast. "We're in mass merchandising, food, drug, jewelry, and hardware stores, catalogue showrooms, 7-Elevens, and the Price Club, to name a few," said Kidder.

The LBO firm KKR had a reputation for piling on debt as part of its takeovers, and the future of Duracell was uncertain in spite of its strong marketing position. To maintain a healthy cash flow, and as part of the takeover agreement, they sold two plants. Further, shortly after the buyout, KKR took Duracell public in

Key Dates:

1935: P.R. Mallory founds Duracell's predecessor company.
1944: Inventor Samuel Ruben joins forces with Mallory, kicks off battery business.
1966: Earnings per share hit $2.34 before falling off with recession related drop in consumer spending.
1972: Sales of electrical and electronic items to industry are boosted.
1978: P.R. Mallory is acquired by Dart Industries.
1980: Dart merges with Kraft Inc.
1986: Kraft retains Duracell portion of business after split with Dart.
1988: Kohlberg Kravis Roberts takes over Duracell during leveraged buyout spree.
1989: Duracell goes public.
1996: The Gillette Company acquires Duracell.
2005: Procter & Gamble is set to buy Gillette.

May 1989, and the share values rose from $15 to $20 in the first hour of trading. KKR made a $1.1 billion paper profit, and Kidder made a handsome paper profit as well. KKR still controlled 61 percent of the company's stock while institutions held some 36 percent. Operating profits in the second quarter of 1990 rose 13 percent over the previous year to $194 million.

Back in the battery market, Duracell was closing the gap on market leader Eveready Battery; Eveready held 60 percent of sales in 1986, but by 1989 Eveready's share had fallen to 42 percent and Duracell made a significant gain, to a 36 percent share. Duracell challenged Germany's Varta internationally and in 1988 captured almost half of Europe's alkaline market, despite aggressive advertising by European battery makers, who spent $25 million on advertising that year.

As part of its advertising strategy, Duracell hired the high-profile advertising agency Ogilvy & Mather to promote its new battery tester product. Whereas previous Duracell ads focused on the toy market, these television spots showed people, for example, at a bridal shower, unable to capture the event on film or operate any appliances because their batteries were dead. Of course, had they purchased the Duracell's Tester, they would have known beforehand that the batteries were dead. Promoted as "another Tester-monial," the spots used nonactors in everyday situations where batteries are essential. The spots were very successful.

Established As Power Player: 1991–95

Each year, as part of its marketing strategy, Duracell's higher spending on advertising continued to pay off. Worldwide sales in 1991 were close to $1.5 billion and netted a 43 percent share of the U.S. alkaline market. As of the early 1990s, Duracell was outsold in the U.S. market only by Ralston Purina and was challenged in Europe only by Varta, which is Europe's one major rival to the North American heavyweights.

As Duracell moved into 1993, the unbridled growth of the modern "cellular society"—telephones, computers, compact disc players, and power tools—brought double-digit growth to the battery industry and to Duracell. The consumer battery market had become one of small batteries with more power than ever, with narrow, smaller penlite-type and mini-penlites taking over two-thirds of the market, squeezing out the traditional C and D battery lines.

Duracell was also a leader in the new alkaline manganese battery, whose longer life—up to six times that of zinc carbon—more than compensated for its higher price. Zinc-chloride batteries seemed to be ready to take over the market in the early 1980s but were overcome by the longer-lasting, lower-cost alkaline cell.

As the market for zinc and alkaline cells began to reach its limits in a global market, new challenges faced Duracell in its battle with the largest players in the battery industry. According to *International Management* in 1993, this intense struggle showed no sign of slowing down. One issue that surfaced was recyclability, notably in Europe, adding another dimension to the competitive struggle. The throwaway image of nonrechargeable batteries provoked concern about the environment, with the European Commission, in 1989, giving battery makers a choice: eliminate dangerous metals (notably cadmium and mercury) or collect batteries for recycling. Although some companies, such as Varta, moved to make batteries mercury-free, some argued that the costs associated with recycling outweighed the environmental benefits. In some cases, companies cooperated to deflect costs; Europile, the consumer battery makers association, included Duracell, and Duracell's Richard Leveton chaired the Europile environment committee.

The rechargeable market was also revived, with companies trying to balance the higher costs of new technology with the potential gains from new markets. Duracell, for example, began supplying nickel-metal hydride cell phone batteries to Fujitsu and launched a consumer version of the same product in the early 1990s. Although Duracell had cooperated with other industry leaders on such issues as recyclability and the environment, intensified competition continued in the core markets. In one effort to reap the benefits of new product development, Duracell entered into a joint research project with competitor Varta (Germany) and Toshiba. The company hoped to expand into new products and new geographical markets, especially in Asia. In any case, the ever present competitive warfare of the industry exerted continuing pressure on Duracell to innovate and cut costs. As *International Management* summed up the situation in its April 1993 issue: "The struggle for power shows no sign of running down."

Duracell International Inc., parent company of Duracell Inc., was firmly established as a power player in the early 1990s. The company controlled 79 percent of the U.S. consumer battery market. Its only real competitor was Eveready, which, with Duracell, combined for about 80 percent of the alkaline battery market worldwide. Although best known for its batteries, Duracell produced a variety of electrical components used by manufacturers of consumer durables and many related products bought by industry, various government agencies, and consumers.

During 1994, Duracell moved to strengthen its international presence: establishing in India a joint venture to make and market alkaline batteries; spending in China $70 million to build factories to manufacture alkaline batteries; and striking an alliance with Toshiba Battery Co. of Japan and Varta Batterie of Germany to manufacture rechargeable batteries in the United States. In 1996, Duracell acquired Eveready South Africa. But on the European front, the company was planning a restructuring, in response to the economic slowdown which had limited growth for several years.

Sharp New Owner: 1996–2005

Successful international marketer Gillette entered into its biggest deal to date when it acquired Duracell in 1996 for more than $7 billion. Batteries immediately became its second leading product line, behind razors and blades. Gillette planned to funnel Duracell's products through its marketing channel which spanned more than 200 countries across the globe. According to *Fortune*, Gillette had been looking for a strong addition to its consumer products business during the first half of the 1990s. Gillette also sold Braun electrical appliances; Right Guard and Soft & Dri personal care products; Parker, Paper Mate, and Waterman pens; and Oral-B toothbrushes. All were strong products and Duracell appeared a good match, garnering fiscal 1996 sales of $2.3 billion, with room to grow globally. Gillette's 1995 revenues were $6.8 billion.

The Duracell Ultra was introduced in early 1998, and the company turned its attention to promoting that enhanced performance, higher priced line. Duracell revenue growth, which had averaged about 10 percent annually from 1995 to 1997, dropped off in 1998 and 1999, falling to 4 percent and 6 percent, respectively. Gillette had envisioned a world in which better, more expensive batteries would be embraced as had their shaving innovations. "Consumers [globally] are not trading up to the alkaline batteries as much as I expected," Gillette stock analyst Tony Vento of Edward Jones, told the *Boston Globe* in April 2000. "I think a lot of that is the result of these economic difficulties around the world in the last few years."

While Duracell's Ultra sales did grow in 1999, it was at the expense of their regular alkaline sales, resulting in a net loss of overall market share. Moreover, Duracell, unlike Gillette, had a major competitor pumping out product to match its innovations. Energizer had introduced its own high-end battery to go up against Ultra for use in "high-drain" electronic products. Duracell's cause was not helped much either when *Consumer Reports* concluded the added cost of Ultra batteries outweighed performance benefits.

In 2000, Duracell brought in nearly 30 percent of overall Gillette sales but the battery maker's operating profits had fallen off by 28 percent. The departure of Gillette's top executive in the fall of 2000 was due in part to Duracell's performance, according to the *Boston Globe*. For 2001, Gillette planned the relaunch of its mid-priced Copper Top line, complete with improved performance, new packaging, and the return of TV ads.

Other factors contributed to Duracell's woes in 2000. During 1999 batteries flew off the shelves, driven by the much publicized possibility of power blackouts related to Y2K computer glitches. In 2000 those batteries by and large were still stockpiled in the homes of consumers. During the year, competitors turned to discounting to drive up sales and gain market share.

Promotional spending continued into 2002. Duracell sponsored the World Cup tournament and launched the "Trusted Everywhere" campaign. The company also implemented price cuts in the light of intensified competition. Despite these tactics, Duracell's market share dropped to 45 percent in 2003. Energizer and value-priced Rayovac were beneficiaries.

The unprecedented hurricane season aided Duracell in 2004, as Floridians and others in the Southeast suffered with wave after wave of damaging storms. Demand for digital electronic products improved the outlook of batteries introduced for that segment of the market. The disposable Duracell CP 1 primary prismatic battery, for example, was integral to some new digital cameras. "With devices getting smaller and smaller it becomes harder for manufacturers to incorporate disposable and rechargeable power into digital cameras," Kara Salzillo, manager of grand communications, told *Chain Drug Review* in early January 2005. "With a flat shape and high-power chemistry our new battery fills a void in the market, so we are very optimistic about its possibilities."

In late January 2005, Procter & Gamble Co. (P&G) announced plans to buy Gillette. The combined businesses would create a company with more than $60 billion in annual revenue. The sale was expected to be completed in the fall of 2005. "For Gillette, P&G's broad reach will help it sell more razors and batteries in huge developing markets like China," Jessica Wohl wrote for *Reuters*.

Principal Competitors

Energizer Holdings, Inc.; Varta Aktiengesellschaft; Beghelli S.p.A.; Exide Technologies.

Further Reading

"Alkaline: Duracell, Eveready Joust with AA Upgrades," *Battery & EV Technology*, February 2000.

Boorstin, Julia, "Razor Wars," *Fortune*, March 3, 2003, p. 156.

Bulkeley, William M., "Duracell Pact Gives Gillette an Added Source of Power," *Wall Street Journal*, September 13, 1996, pp. A3, A4.

"Duracell Bolsters Line, Raises Marketing Support," *Chain Drug Review*, July 30, 2001, p. 41.

"Duracell Uses Packaging to Sell Lights," *Packaging*, December 1983.

Erickson, Julie Liesse, "Perrin Leads Duracell's Charge," *Advertising Age,* June 26, 1989.

Farnham, Alan, "What's Sparking Duracell?," *Fortune,* July 16, 1990.

Grant, Linda, "Gillette Knows Shaving—and How to Turn Out Hot New Products," *Fortune*, October 14, 1996, pp. 207–08, 210.

Huhn, Mary, "Batteries and Boxer KO the Competition," *AdWeek*, November 12, 1990.

"Hurricanes, Rechargeable Batteries Big News in 2004," *Chain Drug Review*, January 3, 2005.

Lazo, Shirley A., "Speaking of Dividends," *Barron's,* March 1, 1993.

Levine, Bernard, "Dart-Mallory Accord Seen Mirroring Cap Firms' Woes," *Electronic News*, December 11, 1978.

"Mallory's Profits Sparkle," *Financial World,* November 7, 1973.

Maremont, Mark, "How Gillette Wowed Wall Street: It Structured the Duracell Buy to Juice Up Earnings Immediately," *Business Week*, September 30, 1996, pp. 36–37.

Mendelson, Seth, "Duracell Recharges Its Batteries," *Grocery Headquarters*, June 2004.

Neff, Jeff, "Duracell Market Share Sags in Spite of Turnaround Effort," *Advertising Age*, January 5, 2004, p. 3.

Oliver, Joyce Anne, "Duracell CEO Charged Up About His Company," *Marketing News,* November 11, 1991.

Reidy, Chris, "Gillette Prepares Massive Marketing Campaign for Battery Division," *Boston Globe*, March 29, 2001.

Shipman, Alan, "Power Struggle: The World's Battery Makers Are Fighting Over an Expanding Market As Consumer Demand and Environmental Concerns Put the Combatants on Their Mettle," *International Management,* April 1993.

Sloan, Allan, "Battle of the Titans," *Newsweek*, December 9, 1996, p. 51.

Symonds, William C., "Duracell's Bunny Buster?" *Business Week*, March 2, 1998.

Syre, Steven, and Charles Stein, "The Boston Globe Capital Column," *Boston Globe*, April 26, 2000.

Tilsner, Julie, "Duracell Looks Abroad for More Juice," *Business Week,* December 21, 1992.

Wohl, Jessica, "P&G to Buy Gillette for $55.8 Billion," *Reuters*, January 28, 2005.

—John A. Sarich
—update: Kathleen Peippo

Dyson Group PLC

381 Fulwood Road
Sheffield
S10 3GB
United Kingdom
Telephone: +44 114 230 3921
Fax: +44 114 230 8583
Web site: http://www.dyson-group.com

Public Company
Incorporated: 1958 as J&J Dyson PLC
Employees: 855
Sales: £59.54 million ($114.7 million) (2004)
Stock Exchanges: London
Ticker Symbol: DYS
NAIC: 327124 Clay Refractory Manufacturing

Dyson Group PLC is engineering a transformation for the mid-2000s. The company has pinned its future growth on an extension from its traditional business manufacturing refractories and other ceramics into the high-performance materials market. For this effort, Dyson has acquired two companies at the dawn of the 21st century. The first, Saffil Ltd., purchased in 1999, develops and produces chemical fibers for use as heat insulation for catalytic converters and other applications. The company's Ecoflex support mats, End Cone Insulation, and Ecoform metal matrix reinforcement fibers permit catalytic converters to run hotter more quickly, thereby operating more efficiently for reducing pollution emissions; the materials also permit automakers to move catalytic converters closer to the engine block, further reducing emissions. The second company acquired by Dyson is Millennium Materials Inc., based in Knoxville, Tennessee, which specializes in producing high-performance ceramics and metals products, such as Carolite, an aluminum composite developed to provide greater stability to high-speed computer hard drives. Other Millennium products include foamed ceramics, coatings for asbestos, and ceramic preforms. Dyson continues to produce refractories and industrial ceramics, through subsidiaries Dyson Ceramic Systems and Hi-Por Ceramics, and supplies and services thermal process plant systems through subsidiary Dyson TPM. The company intends to continue to exit low-margin operations as it transitions itself into a high-performance, high-margin specialty products group. The company is listed on the London Stock Exchange and is led by Chairman Tom Brown. In 2004, the company posted sales of nearly £60 million ($115 million).

19th-Century Refractory Group

The Dyson group has its origins in the early 19th century, with the founding of a ceramics factory in Sheffield in 1810. The need for heat-resistant bricks for the newly developing furnaces driving the Industrial Revolution led the company to become an important producer of refractories and related ceramics products. Dyson's primary market became England's steel industry, and the group remained focused on that market into the 1970s.

By the late 1950s, Dyson had grown to include three clay preparation plants, each equipped with modern, gas-firing tunnel kilns, as well as ten intermittent kilns. The company also boasted complete brick shaping and drying facilities, in order to produce a wide variety of refractory shapes used for the production of steel ingots.

Dyson, which came under the ownership control of the Lomas family, began an expansion effort in the late 1950s and early 1960s. In preparation for this, the company launched a public offering, listing on the London Stock Exchange in 1958, becoming J&J Dyson PLC. Nonetheless, the company adopted a two-tier shareholding structure, with control of the voting rights shares remaining within the Lomas family.

Dyson's first major acquisition came in 1962, when the company picked up rival Ceramic Holdings. By 1965, the company had expanded again, this time buying a majority stake in Pickford, Holland, another refractory producer. By 1966, the company had completed its acquisition of Pickford, Holland. The two companies had enjoyed some degree of cooperation for some time, and the addition of Pickford, Holland enabled Dyson to extend its range of refractories.

Diversifying in the 1970s

During this period, Dyson also extended its operations to other areas, such as the supply of laboratory equipment, the operation of motor vehicle and truck dealerships, a building supplies business, as well as an operation producing trailers for automobiles and other vehicles. Nonetheless, the company's primary operations remained focused around servicing the steel industry.

Dyson targeted further growth in its refractories operations through the end of the 1960s. In 1967, the company made its next major acquisition, when it agreed to merge with Price-Pearson Refractories. This raised the company's market value to more than £5.3 million. Two years later, Dyson added another Sheffield-area company, with the purchase of Thomas Wragg and Sons. That business specialized in fireclay refractories.

The global economic slump brought on by the oil crisis in the 1970s severely affected the steel industry. Dyson found itself highly vulnerable to the steel industry slump, which worsened toward the end of the decade. In the late 1970s, therefore, Dyson made the decision to diversify its industrial materials beyond support for the steel industry to expand into the ceramics industry in general.

This decision helped to shield the company from the worst effects of the steel industry crisis. Nonetheless, the difficulties of its major customers caught up with the company by the early 1980s, as it slipped into losses. Dyson's fortunes picked up again only with the revival of the steel industry—soon to go into high speed, driven by a massive and global building boom. By 1984, the company was once again turning a profit.

Dyson began a new growth phase in the early 1990s. In 1990 the company extended into fiber-based coals and logs, buying those operations from Foseco FS Ltd. These operations were renamed Dyson Domestic Ceramics and placed under the company's Dyson Refractories division, extending the company into the production of radiants and slip cast components, especially ceramic fiber components for ovens and other home appliances. The extension of the company's refractories arm into a wider pool of products prompted the company to change the division's name to Dyson Industries in 1992. The rising adoption of ceramic fibers among the group's industrial customers prompted Dyson to abandon slip cast and radiant production in 1993.

Dyson expanded again in 1996, buying up the artificial logs and coals operation from Thermal Ceramics, a producer of ceramic fiber. The company then renamed its fiber-based business as Dyson Ceramics in 1997. The company also began

developing a new nonfiber, porous ceramic production technology, which it debuted in 1999. The company's research and development efforts had resulted in the formation of Dycats, a business producing catalysts and absorbents. By 1999, Dycats had readied itself for commercial operations, and this division was sold to ICI in 1999, for £8.1 million.

High-Performance Strategy for the New Century

Dyson continued to boost its ceramics operations into the 2000s. In 2000, for example, the company bought Wade Ceramics, a ceramic fibers manufacturer based in Stoke-on-Trent, for £1.5 million. That year, also, the company purchased Hewitt Refractories' kiln furniture business for £1.4 million, which was then added to another Dyson holding, Diamond Gimson, operating in Stoke-on-Trent. That acquisition was quickly followed by the purchase of Acme Marls, also based in Stoke-on-Trent in 2000, at a cost of £1.9 million. Following the acquisition of Acme Marls, Dyson merged it with Diamond Gimson and Hewitt, forming Dyson Ceramic Systems in 2001. In another extension of its refractories operations, Dyson bought Willan Metals' refractory division, which was merged into Dyson's Precision Ceramics division.

By then, however, the company had decided to change its strategy and transform itself from a low-margin industrial materials producer into a specialty producer of high-performance materials. The move toward this strategy began in the late 1980s with the appointment of Mike O'Brien as company chief executive. Investor interest in the company consistently had remained low, in part due to its focus on ''old-fashioned'' industry, and in good part because of its archaic two-tiered shareholder system.

Yet although the company weathered the recession of the early 1990s, it began to face increasing pressure from a new range of lower-priced competitors, chiefly from the fast-developing Asian markets. The company recognized that in order to survive, it needed to extend itself into higher-margin, more specialized categories, and for this the group required a stronger capital base. In 1998, therefore, the Lomas family agreed to abandon the two-tiered shareholder system, and all of the company's shares were ranked on an equal basis.

Dyson now began to seek the proper format for carrying out its transformation strategy. In 1999, the group found its first target, when it purchased Saffil Ltd. from ICI for £3 million. That company had been a pioneer in developing fibers providing heat resistance for the new catalytic converters designed by the automotive industry in the late 1970s and early 1980s. The catalytic conversion process, which required high temperatures to achieve maximum efficiency, also required specially designed materials capable of providing heat resistance and insulation.

By 1980, Saffil had begun commercial sales of its material. The company then developed fiber pre-forms for reinforcing engine blocks and pistons in 1985. By the late 1990s, Saffil had become one of the top suppliers of heat-resistant fibers to the worldwide automotive industry. Soon after its purchase by Dyson, Saffil expanded its operations, buying up Fibre Techniques Ltd. This acquisition boosted the company to the level

Key Dates:

1810: Refractory production begins in Sheffield.
1958: The company goes public as J&J Dyson on the London Stock Exchange.
1962: The company acquires Ceramic Holdings.
1965: The company acquires control of Pickford, Holland.
1967: The company merges with Price-Pearson Refractories.
1969: The company acquires Thomas Wragg and Sons.
1977: A diversification drive is launched to reduce reliance on the steel industry.
1990: The company extends operations into fiber-based coals and logs, acquired from Foseco FS Ltd.
1993: The company focuses on ceramic fiber coal products.
1998: Two-tier shareholding structure is abandoned.
1999: The company launches a strategy to transform itself into a high-performance materials group, buying up Saffil Ltd.
2001: The company acquires Millennium Materials, based in Knoxville, Tennessee, as the second stage of its high-performance transformation.
2005: Millennium expects to launch commercial-scale production of the new hard drive material Carolite.

of a Tier 2 Automotive Supplier. Under Dyson, Saffil also expanded geographically, adding new subsidiaries in Japan and the United States, as well as a production plant in South Africa.

Dyson's shift into high-performance materials continued into 2001. In that year, the company acquired Millennium Materials Inc. Based in Knoxville, Tennessee, Millennium had carved out a strong niche as a producer of advanced materials, especially new lightweight metal and ceramics materials. Among the company's most promising products was its aluminum composite substrate, Carolite. This material targeted the computer hard drive market, promising a more stable surface so that hard drives could achieve higher speeds. Millennium began cooperating with the world's top hard disk manufacturers in order to adapt its technology to their specifications. By the end of 2004, the company announced that it was ready to launch large-scale commercial production of the new material.

In the meantime, Dyson shed much of its now noncore operations, including the low-margin portions of its ceramics business, as well as nonrelated businesses, including its automotive dealerships, sold off in 1999. Instead, Dyson concentrated on reinventing itself as a high-performance materials specialist. As CEO O'Brien described the group's transformation to the *Financial Times:* "It is evolutionary. We were always in materials technologies at high temperature; our expertise is the development of materials to fit specific applications." Dyson appeared in shape to reach its 200th anniversary in 2010.

Principal Subsidiaries

Dyson Ceramic Systems; Dyson Industries PLC; Dyson Refractories; Dyson TPM; Hi-Por Ceramics Ltd.; Millennium Materials Inc.; Saffil Ltd.; Saffil America Inc.; Saffil Japan Ltd.

Principal Competitors

Corhart Refractories Corporation; RHI AG; Minerals Technologies Inc.; Industrie Ceramiche CISA-CERDISA S.p.A.; Amalgamated Metal Corporation PLC; Didier-Werke AG; Imerys TC; Holcim France S.A.; CERIC S.A.; CeramTec AG; Flemings Fireclay Manufacturing Ltd.; Diploma PLC.

Further Reading

Blackwell, David Harold, "Drive for High Performance," *Financial Times,* January 26, 2002, p. 3.
"Dyson Buys in More Boffins," *ERT Weekly,* January 23, 2003, p. 7.
Hopkins, Gordon, "Dyson Edges Ahead on Lower Turnover," *Financial Times,* December 10, 2004, p. 26.
Jenkins, Patrick, "Dyson's Transformation Plan Will Result in Lower Dividends," *Financial Times,* June 27, 2002, p. 26.
Reece, Damian, "Exciting Dyson Looks High Enough for Now," *Independent,* December 10, 2004, p. 51.
"Shares in Dyson Group at All-Time High," *Financial Times,* December 3, 2003, p. 48.

—M.L. Cohen

eHarmony.com Inc.

300 N. Lake Avenue, Suite 111
Pasadena, California 91101
U.S.A.
Telephone: (626) 795-4814
Web site: http://www.eharmony.com

Private Company
Founded: 1998
Employees: 120
Sales: $100 million (2004 est.)
NAIC: 516110 Internet Publishing and Broadcasting

If you are single and looking for long-term love, eHarmony .com Inc. wants to find you the ''perfect mate.'' With traditional values and modern matchmaking possibilities, eHarmony.com has taken the electronic dating scene by storm. Founder Dr. Neil Clark Warren, a clinical psychologist, has specialized in relationships for nearly four decades and has written several best-selling books. Using the patented and trademarked Compatibility Matching System, eHarmony has united more than 10,000 couples in marriage in its short history and, during 2005, had more than six million registered users.

In the Beginning: 1950s to Early 1990s

Warren was born in Des Moines, Iowa, in 1934. His father was a car dealer and his mother, whose maiden name, Clark, he added to his own, was a homemaker. Warren graduated from Pepperdine University with a bachelor's degree, and went on to earn a master's in divinity from Princeton Theological Seminary in 1959, the same year he married Marylyn Mann. The couple soon moved to Chicago where Warren worked as a staff counselor and taught at the University of Chicago.

After receiving his Ph.D. in 1967, Warren accepted a teaching position at Fuller Theological Seminary in Pasadena, California. He began as an assistant professor and within a year was promoted to associate professor, a post he held until 1974 when he was named dean of the graduate school of psychology. During his years at Fuller, Warren had gone into private prac-

tice and founded Associated Psychological Services in 1971. In his years as a practicing psychologist, Warren counseled couples and began to see a pattern in why marriages ended in divorce. He researched marriage and divorce and began conducting what he termed ''divorce autopsies'' to determine why so many marriages failed. He found one simple fact over and over—that many couples simply were not with the right person and never should have been married in the first place. To help couples make the right choices and avoid the agony of divorce, Warren believed compatibility was the key to a strong, long-term relationship.

Warren's first book, *Make Anger Your Ally* (Doubleday, 1983) was the author's attempt to understand the power of anger and turn it into a productive rather than destructive part of life. His next book came almost a decade later, a relationship-themed ''how-to'' book about finding the perfect mate. *Finding the Love of Your Life* (Focus on the Family, 1992) detailed ten ''principles'' guiding how to choose the right mate for life. The popularity of this book led to the formation of Neil Clark Warren and Associates (NCW&A) in 1995 to market Warren's approach to relationships. As he traveled the country for speaking engagements and appeared on talk shows, Greg Forgatch, who was married to Warren's eldest daughter, Lorraine, ran the company.

Warren's straightforward principles about life and love gained him acclaim across the country. His message was sincere and, though he was a devout Christian, nonsectarian. He touted ''mastering the art of intimacy'' in *Finding the Love of Your Life,* as well as the importance of family support, emotional health, and being willing and able to completely commit oneself to a relationship. Warren's next book, *Finding Contentment* (Thomas Nelson, 1997) followed along the same lines of thought, as did *The Triumphant Marriage: 100 Extremely Successful Couples Reveal Their Secrets* (Focus on the Family, 1995) and *Learning to Live with the Love of Your Life, and Loving It* (Tyndale House, 1995).

In his next books, Warren went from finding the perfect mate to sustaining a healthy marriage. He outlined new principles or ''special somethings'' that made marriages work, discussing issues such as trust, intimacy, and communication.

Finding Contentment (Thomas Nelson) came out in 1997 and
secured an ever growing audience for Warren's declarations on
relationships. As he gained recognition for his no-nonsense
approach to love and marriage, Warren continued to counsel
and began an extensive research project, interviewing some
5,000 couples across the United States. This project, undertaken
with Forgatch in 1997, led to the personality and compatibility
profile later developed for eHarmony.

Cupid Online: 1998 and 1999

The eHarmony concept was created in 1998 by Warren and
Forgatch, to take Warren's scientific approach to love and
marriage to the masses. Forgatch was eHarmony's "idea" man
and chief executive, while Warren used his three decades of
clinical psychology to make the concept work. Everyone involved with eHarmony had high hopes about its science-meets-
love matchmaking capabilities; yet to Warren finding a soul
mate was more than a business proposition, it represented the
single most important milestone in a person's life. Finding a
mate was tantamount to lifelong fulfillment and happiness—
and he knew this firsthand, having been married to Marylyn
for 40 years.

The eHarmony concept began with an in-depth 436-item
personality profile covering 29 different "dimensions" of personality, such as character (curiosity, intellect, appearance),
"emotional makeup" (anger, mood, and conflict issues), family
values (background, education, spirituality), and traits (humor,
sociability, ambition). Whereas some singles found the questionnaire tedious and exhausting, others applauded its thorough
nature and found the results revealing and insightful. This, too,
was no accident; Warren and Forgatch figured that only those
truly committed to finding an appropriate mate would complete
the entire process.

Once an interested person completed the questionnaire,
eHarmony would search its database for matches, but only for
individuals who met at least 25 out of the 29 compatibility
areas, on either a local or worldwide basis. The results, according to the company's web site, would be "matches unlike those
on any other online dating service" and "scientifically evalu-

ated to be uniquely compatible" with each prospective eHarmony member. Once a match was found, however, love-seekers
needed to officially become an eHarmony member by paying
$49.95 for a one-month trial membership, $99.95 for three
months, $149.95 for six months, or $249.95 for a year-long
membership. eHarmony guaranteed at least one match per
month (though there were often dozens), with the hope of
falling in love for what Warren considered "the right reasons."

The catch, however, was that only singles over the age of 21
and looking for a serious long-term relationship needed to apply;
eHarmony was not for casual daters and routinely turned away
up to 20 percent of its prospective clients. eHarmony also turned
away anyone who had been married more than three times, as
well as those suffering from serious mental health problems such
as depression (they were asked to take some time to heal before
signing up for membership). Next came a four-step process for
deciding which mate(s) truly met a member's dating and relationship criteria, the possible exchange of photos, and eventually
setting up an actual face-to-face meeting. The process apparently
worked wonders for many lonely singles, as touted in numerous
articles about eHarmony and popular print and broadcast advertising. Warren, however, did not advocate a quick trip to the
altar; he believed couples should continue to explore their relationship and not rush into marriage—taking up to two years
before tying the proverbial knot.

Conquering the Internet: 2000–03

In 2000 Warren published *Catching the Rhythm of Love*
(Thomas Nelson) as he turned his attention more fully to eHarmony. The official web site, eHarmony.com, was launched on
August 22, 2000, with $3 million in venture capital from Fayez
Sarofim & Company. Although the World Wide Web was
littered with the carcasses of numerous dot.com failures, Warren and Forgatch believed in eHarmony not only because it was
vastly different from anything else on the Internet, but because
it could offer single men and women a real chance at finding
their soul mates. Even Warren's wife of 45 years, Marylyn, was
on board, serving as the company's senior vice-president and
media consultant after a decades-long career in public relations.

Within three months of its debut, eHarmony had 20,000
registered users and was quickly gaining the attention of web
singles. Warren continued to write and publish, with *Love the Life
You Live* (with Les Parrott, Ph.D., Tyndale House, 2002) and
*Date or Soul Mate? How to Know If Someone Is Worth Pursuing
in Two Dates or Less* (Thomas Nelson, 2003). While eHarmony
certainly was not the first online dating service, it had made a big
splash and sent ripples through the industry. Its toughest competition came from InterActive Corporation's Match.com, which
offered love matches for as low as $19.95 per month and allowed
singles to post photos and personal information. Other rivals
included True.com at $29.99 per month, which minimized the
"creep factor" by running prospective matches through criminal
databases, and Matchnet.com's successful JDate and Ameri-
canSingles, which offered a wide array of online dating services
for varying prices per month.

By 2003 consumers spent more than $300 million on U.S.
dating sites according to online researcher Jupiter Communications, Inc. In response to eHarmony's popularity, Match.com,

Key Dates:

1959: Neil Clark Warren and Marylyn Mann marry.
1967: Warren begins private practice as a clinical psychologist.
1992: Warren's first relationship book, *Find the Love of Your Life,* is published.
1995: Match.com launches an online dating service.
1998: eHarmony is founded in Pasadena, California, by Warren and Greg Forgatch.
2000: The eHarmony web site (eHarmony.com) is launched.
2002: Warren coauthors *Love the Life You Live* (Tyndale House).
2003: Warren's *Date—or Soul Mate?* is published by Thomas Nelson.
2004: eHarmony scores with radio and television ads by Donat/Wald; hits at the site climb to more than 10,000 daily.
2005: eHarmony.com forms a partnership with marketing firm Third Age Inc.

which had become the Internet's top dating service, began offering its own version of compatibility and personality testing at its sites. Match.com had brought in revenues of $185 million for 2003 (up from $125 million in 2002) and its success prompted its parent company, InterActive, to file initial public offering papers. Although there seemed to be considerable interest, InterActive backed off and withdrew its papers within a week.

While eHarmony had garnered a solid reputation by 2003, the company had tapped only a small portion of the millions of singles looking for love. Marketing efforts in the last half of the year brought notice, with more than 300,000 new members signing up and bringing the firm's total registered users to about 3.5 million. According to *Internet News* (May 13, 2004), eHarmony had become the fastest growing online love connection, averaging more than a million visits to its web site per month (out of an estimated 35 million visits to online dating sites worldwide) with as many as 10,000 new visitors per day taking its in-depth personality profile. Other matchmaking web sites cashing in on the phenomenon included Playboy.com, personals listings at Monster.com and Yahoo!, as well as Dating.com, Dreammates .com, Cupid.com, Friendster.com, and a slew of others.

Diamonds Are a Girl's Best Friend: 2004 and Beyond

In 2004 eHarmony experienced unprecedented growth, through strategic alliances and aggressive marketing. As a result of its advertising success in 2003, eHarmony initiated another major advertising campaign, determined to become a household word. Spending upward of $10 million on radio and $40 million on television ads, eHarmony reached millions of prospective clients through its marketing efforts, led by Donat/Wald of Santa Monica, California. Popular 2004 ads featured real-life couples who had found each other through eHarmony, touting, "Who knew science and love were so compatible?" Another of Dr. Warren's taglines, "Fall in love for all the right reasons,"

was featured in radio and television advertisements. Competitor Match.com also had begun publicizing its success stories, reporting an average of 40 or so wedding announcements per month, and remained the Internet's largest online dating site with 12 million users.

eHarmony also made news in 2004 through its partnerships with Friendster.com and the Gannett Corporation's newspaper empire. Friendster.com, one of the Internet's pioneering social networks, signed on with eHarmony to offer members online matchmaking, while Gannett, owner of the widely read *USA Today,* agreed to have its personal ads linked to eHarmony's site. Near the end of the year eHarmony sought financing and received $110 million in funds from two venture capital firms. Although eHarmony, a private company, did not publicize its year-end revenues, the figure was estimated at around $100 million for 2004.

Early the following year, 2005, eHarmony entered a partnership with Third Age Inc., a marketing and research firm specializing in Baby Boomers. The joint venture was formed to help older single Americans—the 40-plus crowd, which was estimated at around 100 million—find love and lasting relationships like eHarmony's younger clientele. On Valentine's Day in 2005 eHarmony celebrated its success by delivering gifts to all of its married members. Warren commented in a press release, "Valentine's Day so often focuses only on romantic love—but eHarmony members know successful relationships must be founded on the deeper values that can sustain love year-round." eHarmony marked the occasion with an appropriately heart-shaped glass bowl from Tiffany & Company, delivered to thousands of members who had found their "perfect mate" through eHarmony.com.

With a title familiar to any eHarmony member, Warren published *Falling in Love for All the Right Reasons: How to Find Your Soul Mate* (Center Street, New York). The book reiterated Warren's caveat that strong relationships began with compatibility. His message resonated with millions of singles seeking love, as eHarmony averaged from 10,000 to 15,000 new visitors each day and a worldwide membership of more than six million. As the company grew and outdistanced much of its competition, the biggest question concerning eHarmony's future seemed to be whether the company would go public. Warren and Forgatch were mum on the subject, but it was not outside the realm of possibility.

Principal Competitors

Cupid.com; Dating.com; Dreammates.com; Lavalife; Matchmaker.com; Matchnet; Match.com; PerfectMatch.com; Soulmate.com; True.com; Yahoo! Personals.

Further Reading

Cullen, Lisa T., "Cupid Academy," *Time,* February 16, 2004, p. 67.
"eHarmony Selects eGain's Solutions to Provide Exceptional Customer Service," *Internet News,* May 13, 2004.
"Entrepreneur of the Year Finalists," *Los Angeles Business Journal,* June 23, 2003, p. 29.
Haynes, Monica L., "Couples Match Up Thanks to Popular Web Site," *Pittsburgh Post-Gazette,* December 28, 2004.

Hein, Kenneth, "Matchmaker eHarmony Makes Note of Successes," *Brandweek,* November 29, 2004, p. 13.

Hsu, Caroline, "The Testing of America," *U.S. News & World Report,* September 20, 2004, p. 68.

Kharif, Olga, "Charity, But Not Love," *BusinessWeek Online,* December 3, 2004.

Merx, Katie, "Finding a Match at eHarmony," *Crain's Detroit Business,* December 6, 2004, p. 26.

Metz, Cade, "Lucky in Love," *PC Magazine,* October 5, 2004.

Mulrine, Anna, "Love.com," *U.S. News & World Report,* September 29, 2003, p. 52.

Reitman, Valerie, "We Clicked," *Los Angeles Times,* April 26, 2004.

Shabelman, David, "eHarmony Scores $110 Million," *Daily Deal,* December 23, 2004.

—Nelson Rhodes

Embotelladora Andina S.A.

Avenida Andrés Bello 2687
Las Condes, Santiago
Chile
Telephone: (56) (2) 338-0520
Fax: (56) (2) 338-0530
Web site: http://www.koandina.com

Public Company
Incorporated: 1946
Employees: 4,124
Sales: CLP 413.75 billion ($742.29 million) (2004)
Stock Exchanges: Bolsa de Comercio de Santiago New
    York
Ticker Symbols: ANDINA; AKO
NAIC: 312111 Soft Drink Manufacturing; 312112 Bottled
    Water Manufacturing

Embotelladora Andina S.A. is the largest producer of soft drinks in Chile and the chief producer, bottler, and distributor of Coca-Cola soft drinks in Chile. It also produces and distributes these products in parts of Argentina and Brazil, where it is one of the largest soft drink producers. In addition to its Coca-Cola soft drinks business, Andina through its subsidiaries produces and distributes fruit juices, other fruit-flavored beverages, and mineral water in Chile under trademarks owned by The Coca-Cola Company. In Argentina, the company, through a subsidiary, distributes ready-to-drink juices and produces and sells mineral water. In Brazil, subsidiaries distribute beer and mineral water and also sell and distribute ready-to-drink juices and energy drinks.

Always Coca-Cola: 1946–85

Embotelladora Andina was founded by Carlos Vial Espantoso and other Chilean and U.S. investors in 1946 with the exclusive license to produce and distribute Coca-Cola products in Chile. Four years later, the company made a transition from the individual bottle toward the 24-bottle case, and Coca-Cola distribution was extended from the traditional sales point to a wide variety of institutions. In 1960 it opened a new Santiago plant that also

served as its headquarters. During the short-lived socialist government of 1971–73, Andina was nationalized, but in 1975 the state's 51 percent stake was sold for perhaps only one-seventh of its market value to an investment group whose five members included Alejandro Banados and Sergio Vergara. The company added fruit juices in 1975 and mineral water in 1978.

By 1985—at the tag end of a severe recession in Chile—the owners of Embotelladora Andina were in deep financial trouble. Revenue had dropped by almost half since 1980. Inversiones Andes, their group, owed $20 million, a fortune at this time, since interest rates averaged 10 to 15 percent a month for those who could obtain a loan at all. To raise money, it had in recent years sold the right to distribute Coca-Cola products in most areas outside the Santiago metropolitan region. To extricate itself from its debts, Inversiones Andes agreed to turn over its license to a new Chilean investment group, subject to approval by Coca-Cola, which set tough conditions: more capital, debt renegotiation, greater market participation, more investment in marketing, and the surrender of the franchise in Vina del Mar—Chile's chief beach resort. In late 1985 Coca-Cola chose the new licensee itself—Inversiones Freire Ltda.

This new group consisted of four men. Jaime Said Demaría, the oldest, was a member of a family of Arab origin, prominent in business. During the 1960s and 1970s he directed the largest rayon factory in Chile. His cousin José Said Saffie was the most successful member of the clan, active in banking and real estate as well as industry. José Antonio Garcés had been an executive in a Said enterprise before branching out into cosmetics and real estate. Alberto Hurtado Fuenzalida, also a seasoned executive and entrepreneur, named the group for a relative who had been president of Chile in the 1920s. They paid Inversiones Andes $5 million for its 75 percent of Andina. The other shares belonged to Vial Espantoso's heirs and to public stockholders.

Expansion into Argentina and Brazil: 1994–2002

Inversiones Freire had two immediate pieces of luck: First, Chile started to pull out of the recession, and second, rival beverage enterprise Compañía Cervecerias Unidas S.A. (CCU), the nation's Pepsi-Cola licensee, quarreled with PepsiCo Inc.

and retired from this sector of its business for two years. In addition, the group's connections allowed it some breathing space in dealing with Embotelladora Andina's creditors. In 1989 the company had net income of CLP 1.55 billion ($5.21 million) on net sales of CLP 28.48 billion ($95.76 million).

Embotelladora Andina entered Brazil in 1994 by purchasing 61.5 percent of Rio de Janeiro Refrescos S.A., the Coca-Cola bottler in the nation's former capital, for $120 million, plus the assumption of $31 million in debts. The following year Andina raised most of the money to pay for this purchase and future acquisitions by selling more than seven million American Depositary Receipts (the equivalent of shares) on the New York Stock Exchange, thereby collecting $127.4 million. Another $20 million was raised in a Santiago stock offering. During 1995 the company began production of plastic bottles in Chile—primarily for its own use—through a subsidiary, Envases Multipack S.A. Near the end of 1996 Rio de Janeiro Refrescos opened a $36 million plastic bottle production facility.

Also in 1995, the company, with the approval of Coca-Cola, entered Argentina by purchasing majority control of Embotelladoras del Atlántico, S.A. (Edasa), the parent company for the Coca-Cola bottlers in the Mendoza and Rosario territories, for about $45 million. It brought its stake in this enterprise to 95 percent the following year, when it also acquired the Córdoba territory and bottling plant, this time from parent Coca-Cola itself, by purchasing a 79 percent interest in Inti S.A.I.C. for $68 million. Edasa, which established its headquarters in Córdoba, also acquired full control of Complejo Industrial Pet S.A.I.C. (Cipsa), supplier of plastic bottles for the Coca-Cola system in Argentina, Paraguay, and Uruguay, for $76 million. Although Cipsa held a majority interest in a bottling plant in Buenos Aires, Embotelladora Andina was unable to obtain the franchise in Argentina's giant metropolis. Coca-Cola awarded the license instead to Mexican-based Fomento Economico Mexicano S.A. de C.V. (Femsa), its largest franchisee in Latin America.

In spite of this setback, Embotelladora Andina remained the largest of Coca-Cola's four Chilean-based franchisers and one of its anchors for doing business in South America. Coca-Cola, in 1996, purchased 49 percent of Vital S.A., Andina's fruit juice and mineral water subsidiary, and 6 percent of Andina itself. The following year it purchased 5 percent more of Andina, increasing its ownership of the company to 11 percent. Embotelladora Andina also sold its agribusiness subsidiary in 1996 and repurchased Coca-Cola's share of Vital in 1998.

Embotelladora Andina, at the end of 1996, was producing 71 percent of all carbonated soft drinks in Chile and 91 percent of all cola drinks there. In addition to its licensed Coca-Cola

beverages, fruit juices and mineral water accounted for 14 percent of Andina's sales in that country. In Brazil, Rio de Janeiro Refrescos was, in addition to producing and distributing Coca-Cola products, distributing Heineken and Kaiser beer brands and a brand of mineral water. In Argentina, Edasa and Inti were only producing and distributing Coca-Cola beverages. Andina's revenues were heading toward $1 billion a year, and the company was employing 6,500 workers, compared with 350 when it was purchased in 1985.

This expansion looked better on paper than in fact. Chilean operations were highly profitable and efficient. In Brazil, however, Rio de Janeiro Refrescos had to share income with independent distributors who could not easily be eliminated (because, for example, they operated in certain neighborhoods of the city where even the police dared not enter). In addition, many local people preferred a noncola fruit drink called guaraná. Rio Refrescos was making and selling such a drink, but its brand was not as popular as those offered by rivals Companhia Cervejaria Brahma, S.A. and Companhia Antarctica Paulista Industria Brasileira de Bebidas e Conexos. In addition, powerful Brahma cut the prices of its beer and soft drinks to frustrate the newcomer. Andina's subsidiary was forced to close one of its three plants and lay off 800 employees. In Argentina, Edasa inherited short-term debts at high interest rates and operations in Mendoza and Rosario that had been losing money for three years.

Embotelladora Andina invested $1 million in 1999 in Chile to offer retailers carrying its beverages—the small sweet shops, kiosks, and bakeries, for example—training in new sales and marketing techniques. Edasa opened a new Córdoba production facility in 1999 and shut down the Mendoza and Rosario plants in 2002, concentrating all drink production operations in Córdoba. The following year Edasa took over Cipet, thereby placing all business conducted in Argentina in Córdoba. Andina, in 2000, became the Coca-Cola bottler for three Brazilian territories in addition to Rio de Janeiro by purchasing them from the franchise holder for $74.5 million. But Brahma had created new problems for the Brazilian operation by becoming a distributor for rival PepsiCo. Shortly after, this competition grew even stronger when Brahma and Antarctica merged to form Companhia de Bebidas das Americas (AmBev).

Embotelladora Andina in 2003–04

Coca-Cola's soft drinks accounted for 86.6 percent of Embotelladora Andina's net sales in 2003. The company accounted for 66.8 percent of total soft drink sales by volume in its Chilean territory, 54 percent in its Brazilian territory, and 52.1 percent in its Argentine territory. In Chile, its soft drinks, aside from Coca-Cola products, were Quatro, NordicMist Ginger Ale and NordicMist Tónica, and Tai. In Brazil, in addition to Coca-Cola products, its soft drinks were Schweppes Club Soda, Tónica, and Citrus, and three guaraná drinks. In Argentina, aside from Coca-Cola products, the operation's soft drinks were Quatro Pomelo and Quatro Limonada, three Schweppes soft drinks, three Crush soft drinks, and Tai Lima-Limon and Naranja.

Through Vital, Embotelladora Andina was producing and selling juices and mineral water under the labels Andifrut (natural fruit juices), Néctar Andina (fruit nectars), Kapo (artificially flavored fruit drinks), Hi-C (fruit refreshment with vitamins),

Key Dates:

1946: Embotelladora Andina is founded to produce and distribute Coca-Cola products in Chile.

1978: The company is producing fruit juices and mineral water as well as soft drinks.

1985: Financially troubled Embotelladora Andina is sold to a new investment group.

1994: Andina enters Brazil by purchasing a majority share of Rio de Janeiro's Coca-Cola bottler.

1995: The company finances this purchase by going public and selling stock shares.

1996: Andina now also holds three important Coca-Cola franchises in Argentina.

2000: Andina becomes the bottler for three more Coca-Cola franchised territories in Brazil.

and Vital (mineral water), all trademarks owned by Coca-Cola. In Brazil, the company was distributing beer under the Kaiser, Bavaria, Heineken, and Santa Cerva labels and mineral water under the Bonaqua and Caxambu labels. It also was selling and distributing three ready-to-drink juices named Kapo and energy drinks named Burn and Nestea. In Argentina, the company was distributing Hi-C ready-to-drink juices and producing and selling Kin carbonated soda and Kin mineral water (with and without carbonation).

Embotelladora Andina's main production facility in Chile was in Santiago, for soft drinks. The juice plant was in Renca and the mineral water plant in Rengo. There were two production facilities in Brazil, in Jacarepaguá and Vitória, both for soft drinks. In Argentina, soft drinks were being produced in Córdoba and plastic bottles in Buenos Aires.

Embotelladora Andina had sales of CLP 413.75 billion ($742.29 million) in 2004. This was a gain of only 4 percent over the 2003 total, but the company's net profit of CLP 40.16 billion pesos ($72.05 million) was a 148 percent increase over the previous year's figure. Of Andina's revenues, Chile accounted for 48 percent, Brazil for 31 percent, and Argentina for 21 percent. Of its operating profit, Chile provided 67 percent, Brazil, 20 percent, and Argentina, 13 percent.

Soft drinks accounted for 85 percent of revenue in Chile, 92 percent in Brazil, and 99 percent in Argentina. The long-term debt was CLP 280.55 billion ($503.32 million) at the end of 2004. Inversiones Freire and entities controlled by it owned about 52.6 percent of the Series A shares of common stock at the end of 2003. These shares had preferred voting rights and thereby controlled the company.

Principal Competitors

Companhia de Bebidas das Américas; Buenos Aires Embotelladora S.A.; Compania Cervecerias Unidas S.A.

Further Reading

Hinchberger, Bill, "Andina's Andrés Olivos," *Institutional Investor,* June 1995, p. 170.

Pérez Villamil, Ximena, "El cuarteto andino," *Capital,* July 1997, pp. 15–16, 18–20.

Sullivan, Tara, "En buena compania," *América economía,* October 8, 1998, p. 68.

Vera, Héctor, "Servicio al cliente," *América economía,* November 18, 1999, p. 79.

Waxler, Caroline, "Losing Fizz," *Forbes,* January 27, 1997, p. 120.

—Robert Halasz

Empresas Almacenes Paris S.A.

Coyancura 2241
Providencia, Santiago
Chile
Telephone: (56) (2) 233-3302
Toll Free: (600) 400-8000
Fax: (56) (2) 336-7210
Web site: http://www.almacenes-paris.cl

Wholly Owned Subsidiary of Cencosud S.A.
Incorporated: 1973 as Inmobiliaria San Antonio S.A.
Employees: 3,500
Sales: CLP 422.52 billion ($758.02 million) (2004)
NAIC: 321912 Cut Stock, Resawing Lumber, and
  Planing; 452111 Department Stores (Except Discount
  Department Stores); 522110 Commercial Banking;
  522210 Credit Card Issuing; 531120 Lessors of
  Nonresidential Buildings; 551112 Offices of Other
  Holding Companies; 561510 Travel Agencies

Empresas Almacenes Paris S.A. and its subsidiaries sell clothing and accessories and home supplies through a network of department stores in Chile. Through its subsidiaries, the company also offers investments in securities, bonds, and real estate and owns a bank. It is also engaged in personal insurance, tourism and travel, furniture manufacturing, and the development of shopping malls.

A Century of Retailing: 1900–99

Almacenes Paris got its start in 1900, when José María Couso, a Spaniard who had previously lived in Chile, returned and opened a furniture store in Santiago, then a city of 300,000 inhabitants. The small store, which originally had only five employees, was named Paris and carried Italian merchandise copied from French models. This was soon replaced by copies made by local artisans. Later the business expanded into rugs and tapestries, mattresses, and other bed furnishings. Still later, the business began selling more home furnishings, such as glassware, china, porcelain, cutlery, and bathroom supplies.

After that it became a true department store, with clothing the principal area. Couso sold the business to his son-in-law, Antonio Gálmez, in 1910. The Gálmez family remained in charge of the store throughout the 20th century.

Despite a severe economic crisis, Almacenes Paris achieved an important goal in 1983 when it became the first Chilean department store to branch out from the center of Santiago, opening a store on Plaza Lyon. It added to these operations in 1991 by establishing branch stores in two Santiago shopping malls, Parque Arauco and Plaza Vespucio. After that it opened still another store in another Santiago mall, Plaza Oeste, in 1994, and its first store outside Santiago in Plaza del Trébol in Concepcion in 1996. All these establishments varied in size between 8,000 and 15,000 square meters (roughly 88,000 to 165,000 square feet). One of the smallest (if not the smallest) was the original Alameda store. Established before anyone gave a thought to parking, it had found a solution through an arrangement with a neighboring hotel.

In 1996 the Almacenes Paris chain consisted of seven department stores. It ranked second in its field, behind Falabella, and concentrated on middle-income clients. The company went public that year, selling 30 percent of its shares on the Bolsa de Comercio de Santiago to about 1,000 investors. It was now a holding company embracing more than a dozen subsidiaries. Almacenes Paris was, for example, heavily engaged in real estate, having taken percentages in Plaza del Trebol and Plaza Oeste. During the last months of 1996, it purchased a stake in the formation of two new malls where it was planning to open stores, one in the Puente Alto area of Santiago and the other in La Serena. The company also purchased a 50 percent share of Tecnopolis, a chain of computer stores.

Almacenes Paris was the first department store chain to issue its own credit card. By the end of 1998 it also had disseminated 1.3 million credit cards and was planning to open new stores in Temuco, Viña del Mar, and the Tobalaba neighborhood of Santiago. Almacenes Paris also had just signed an agreement with El Corte Inglés, Spain's leading department store, to offer travel and tourism services to Chileans in collaboration with the latter's travel agency. Finally, the company had opened Paris Express, a virtual store enabling prospective customers to shop

Key Dates:

1900: A furniture store, named Paris, opens in Santiago.
1983: Almacenes Paris is Chile's first department store to open a branch outside central Santiago.
1991: The company opens branch stores in two Santiago shopping malls.
1996: Almacenes Paris, Chile's second largest department store chain, goes public.
1998: The company purchases the two Chilean stores of J.C. Penney Co., Inc.
2000: Almacenes Paris celebrates its centennial by commissioning a new headquarters building.
2003: The company forms a credit alliance with Chile's largest bank, Banco Santander-Chile.
2004: The Gálmez family sells a substantial stake in the company to outside investors.
2005: Cencosud S.A. purchases Almacenes Paris.

by computer. In 2002 the chain was making one-third of its sales online.

Since Santiago—the metropolitan area holding half of all Chileans—was saturated with department stores, large chains were looking to services for growth. Almacenes Paris, for example, was offering insurance through an alliance with the giant U.S.-based company Marsh & McLennan Cos., Inc. In this respect it was taking advantage of its experience dealing with the public and the gigantic database that it had established on its customers. The financing that Almacenes Paris and other department stores had extended to their customers had reached 21 percent of all consumer credit in Chile and 2 percent of the gross domestic product by April 1998. More than ten million of the nation's 14 million inhabitants had a credit card from one of the multistore chains, who were carrying on a war not only among themselves but also against bank credit cards. Falabella, for example, was even offering motorists the convenience of paying their annual automobile tax by credit card.

The other important development in 1998 for Almacenes Paris was its purchase of the Chilean assets of J.C. Penney Company, Inc., consisting of a store in Santiago's Parque Arauco mall and another in the city's high-end Alto Las Condes mall. J.C. Penney had entered Chile in 1995 with a U.S. management team and a U.S. model for selling merchandise that did not take into account the more conservative tastes of the locals, or even, in considering the range of clothing sizes, their relatively smaller bodies.

Forming New Credit Alliances: 2000–03

As the 21st century dawned, Almacenes Paris was still Chile's second largest department store chain, with 14 stores and some 10,000 direct or indirect employees. The company celebrated its centennial by commissioning a new $17 million, 22-story corporate headquarters named Torre Paris in Santiago's high-end Providencia commercial district. The structure, which housed offices, commercial space, and five levels of underground parking for 200 cars, featured a curved glass facade shaped in a shiplike form that maximized the usable area of the small triangular site. Three smaller stores, in Calama, Los Angeles, and Talca, opened in 2002, giving Almacenes Paris's 16 outlets more selling space (about 1.5 million square feet) than any of its competitors.

By the end of 2002, however, financial analysts regarded Almacenes Paris as falling behind its rivals, and this judgment was reflected in falling prices for its stock shares. In August of that year management hired the U.S. consulting firm of McKinsey & Co. to draft a five-year strategic plan for the chain, to suggest new areas of business and store formats, to study the possibility of using the company's credit card to establish alliances with other retailers, to implement the new bank that Almacenes Paris—like rivals Falabella and Ripley—was organizing, and to consider expanding into other countries. In addition, the chain reorganized itself, establishing four independent divisions for retail, industry, real estate, and financial services. The goal remained to emphasize payment by credit, which accounted for more than half of consolidated profits.

By this time the number of credit cards issued by Almacenes Paris had reached 2.9 million. The goal had always been to finance the sales of the chain's own merchandise, which represented 75 percent of total sales. The company also had established, however, pay-by-credit-card alliances with Farmacias Cruz Verde, the Dental Free clinic, and Todocuenta, which was responsible for collecting the telephone bills issued by Telefónica CTC Chile and the cellular telephone company Smartcom. In this respect it was also holding conversations with the Santa Isabel supermarket and Shell service station chains.

In 2003 the company's new Banco Paris established an alliance with the 32 branches of Banco Santiago Express that gave it more than 40 offices dedicated to financial services, a portfolio of 70,000 customers, and annual revenue of some $130 million. The agreement called for Banco Santander-Chile, the nation's largest private bank, to transfer its Santiago Express division, including all of the division's assets, to Banco Paris. This was valued at a little less than $50 million. In return, Almacenes Paris turned over to Banco Santander-Chile assets corresponding to those of Paris's credit card customers denominated "prime" and gave its customers access to Santander-Chile's automatic teller machines. Paris also extended to Santander-Chile clients access to its debit card facilities and financial products, plus the same store benefits enjoyed by its own customers. The agreement was for a term of at least five years. In spite of the new alliance, Almacenes Paris, in 2003, fell to third place, behind Ripley, in revenue among department store chains.

Under New Ownership: 2004–05

In August 2004, in what the Chilean business magazine *Capital* called the deal of the year, the Gálmez family sold 52.4 percent of Almacenes Paris to Inmobiliaria e Inversiones Aconcagua S.A. The purchaser represented Quiñenco S.A., the holding company owned by the Luksic group, whose founder, Andrónico Luksic Abaroa, was the richest man in Chile; Consorcio Nacional de Seguros S.A., the nation's largest insurance group, representing Eduardo Fernández León and Juan Hurtado Vicuna; and Jorge Gálmez Puig, the largest individual shareholder, a great-grandson of the founder of Almacenes Paris and a brother of the company's general manager. Jorge Gálmez became president of the company (the equivalent of chairman of the board). The new general manager (equivalent to chief executive officer) was Pablo Turner González, who had been serving in the same capacity for Falabella but defected because he was offered not only a salary but also stock participation. Public stockholders reacted enthusiastically to the changes, lifting company shares 60 percent in value.

By the end of the year Turner had brought in a new but seasoned management team headed by two executives from Ripley's Peru operation. They quickly departed to Asia, with the mission of diversifying Almacenes Paris's sources of merchandise, in large part derived from the United States and Europe. Turner put another Ripley executive in charge of the home-products division and an old friend and fellow University of Chicago alumnus in charge of sales channels. The company vowed to open new stores and upgrade the existing ones, stock a better mix of products, and offer attractive end-of-season discounts.

But Almacenes Paris was soon rocked by another shakeup, apparently unforeseen, when Gálmez, who held 27 percent of the company's shares, decided to accept a buyout offer for the company from Cencosud S.A., the largest retailer in America's Southern Cone (Chile and Argentina). Cencosud's founder, Horst Paulmann Kemna, had been seeking to acquire the company for two years. After unpublicized talks with Gálmez, Paulmann issued a tender offer for all the shares in February 2005. Quiñenco and Consorcio rejected it and, backed by the real estate firm Parque Arauco S.A., made a counteroffer that was 15 percent higher. Paulmann then successfully sweetened his own offer with an addition of about $50 million. The deal closed in mid-March 2005, with Cencosud committed to paying for 72.67 percent of Almacenes Paris by issuing one share of its own stock for every 1.1144 shares of Almacenes Paris. Cencosud was to pay CLP 960 (about $1.63) for each of the other 27.33 percent of the shares. Almacenes Paris would cease

to be a public company and would presumably become another subsidiary in Cencosud's retail empire, which included the Chilean supermarket chains Jumbo S.A. and Santa Isabel S.A.

Principal Subsidiaries

Administradora de Creditos Comerciales ACC S.A.; Almacenes Paris Comercial S.A.; Paris Corredores de Seguro Ltda.; Sociedad Comercial de Tiendas Ltda.

Principal Divisions

Financial Services; Industry; Real Estate; Retail.

Principal Competitors

Comercial Eccsa S.A.; S.A.C.I. Falabella.

Further Reading

Aldunate, Felipe, "De tenderosa banqueros," *América economía,* November 5, 1998, pp. 22–23.

Barista, David, "Paris Tower Sails into Santiago," *Building Design & Construction,* April 2003, pp. 68–69.

Fazio, Hugo, *El mapa de extrema riqueza en Chile,* Santiago: LOM Ediciones, 1997, pp. 302–03.

"Los galacticos," *Capital,* January 2005, pp. 44–45.

Gama, Julio, "Mirando el futuro, siempre," *America economia,* August 2, 2001, p. 18.

Kaffman, Luis, "Penny Wiser in Chile," *Business Latin America,* October 18, 1999, p. 2.

Medel, Lorena, "En qué está Almacenes Paris?," *Capital,* December 30, 2002–January 30, 2003, pp. 42–44.

——, "La gran jugada," *Capital,* December 5–18, 2003, pp. 43–47.

"Paris bien vale otra OPA," *Capital,* March 11–23, 2005, pp. 26–27.

"This Latin Tiger Is Friendly," *Chain Store Age,* April 1996, supplement, pp. 13–14.

Zegers, V., and M. Angelica, "Celfin suma y sigue," *Capital,* March 24–April 7, 2005, pp. 36–40.

—Robert Halasz

Endo Pharmaceuticals Holdings Inc.

100 Painters Drive
Chadds Ford, Pennsylvania 19317
U.S.A.
Telephone: (610) 558-9800
Fax: (610) 558-8979
Web site: http://www.endo.com

Public Company
Incorporated: 1997
Employees: 492
Sales: $615.1 million (2004)
Stock Exchanges: NASDAQ
Ticker Symbol: ENDP
NAIC: 325412 Pharmaceutical Preparation Manufacturing

Endo Pharmaceuticals Holdings Inc. is a publicly traded company based in the Philadelphia, Pennsylvania area, dedicated to the niche of pain management. Endo develops and sells both branded and generic prescription pharmaceuticals, with its manufacturing contracted out to third parties. Endo's branded products include Percocet, using oxycodone and acetaminophen to treat moderate to moderately severe pain; Percodan, using oxycodone and aspirin to treat less severe pain; the Lidoderm patch, used to relieve pain caused by shingles; and Frova, using frovatriptan to treat migraines. The company also offers branded pharmaceuticals to relieve serious coughing and congestion: Hycodan, Hycomine, and Hycotuss. On the generic side, Endo markets Morphine Sulfate ER (extended release) tablets to treat moderate to severe pain, and Endocet, a generic equivalent to Percocet. Endo markets its products to primary care physicians and specialists, as well as to other healthcare professionals and retail pharmacies. The company is 60 percent owned by investment firm Kelso & Company.

Company Heritage Dating to the 1920s

The heritage of the Endo name dates to 1920 when five brothers of the Ushkow family established Endo Laboratories, a small pharmaceutical company, in Manhattan, New York. The family-run business eventually relocated to Long Island, and then in 1969 was acquired by E.I. du Pont de Nemours & Company, better known as DuPont. Just three years earlier DuPont had become involved in the pharmaceutical industry after one of its researchers developed an antiviral drug called Symmetrel, effective in treating flus. The primary reason DuPont acquired Endo was because of its marketing capabilities. Unfortunately Endo's marketing efforts failed to achieve the kind of growth DuPont was looking for in Symmetrel, due in large measure to the bureaucracy of the parent company. By the early 1980s Endo was generating about $100 million in annual sales, hardly enough to prompt DuPont, which had more than $22 billion in annual sales at the time, to take much notice. Endo began developing other drugs, although in 1983 DuPont decided to stop using the Endo name for its pharmaceutical division.

In 1989 DuPont and giant pharmaceutical Merck and Company entered into a research and marketing arrangement. This collaboration led a year later to the two parties creating an independent joint venture, The DuPont Merck Pharmaceuticals Company, to which DuPont contributed its pharmaceutical holdings. The resulting company proved to be a cipher to customers, who were unsure what to make of its mix of injectable drugs, off-patent brands, and the other products it distributed for other companies. In the fall of 1993 Dupont Merck decided to achieve some focus by establishing a subsidiary to serve as its generic division. For a company name executives drew on the old Endo name, which surveys showed that despite a decade-long absence was still remembered positively by 85 percent of pharmacists. The division was formed in early 1994.

The first successful product offered by Endo Laboratories LLC in May 1994 was cimetidine, a generic equivalent of SmithKline Beecham's Tagamet, followed a few months later by a generic version of Glucotrol. In December 1994 Endo began distributing products marketed by West Point Pharma, Merck's generic operation. Endo also secured the marketing rights to some of the multisource products produced by DuPont Merck, as well as developing its own generics through a strong research and development effort.

Heading Endo was President Carol Ammon, supported by Louis Vollmer, vice-president of sales and marketing, both of whom, along with college friend Mariann MacDonald, head of

Company Perspectives:

Endo's vision is to become a premier specialty pharmaceutical company anchored in pain management, with a balanced focus in complementary therapeutic areas.

DuPont Merck's generic-drug manufacturing, had grown up on Long Island, virtually in the shadow of the old Endo plant. MacDonald, in fact, had gone to work for Endo in 1969 before it was acquired by DuPont, and Ammon joined the company four years later, at a time when the old entrepreneurial spirit of the company was still present. The three of them had successfully lobbied DuPont Merck to reinstate the Endo name for the new generic division.

Ammon and MacDonald had worked together for years and were close friends. They now became part of a team put together by DuPont Merck to determine what to do about some old pain medications, such as Percodan launched in the 1950s and Percocet launched in the mid-1970s. The patents had long expired and the products were now losing sales to cheaper generics. Faced with the choice of either investing in these drugs to expand their markets or selling them, the recommendation was to sell. In effect, Endo wanted to cast off its pain management franchise, an area to which Ammon had devoted much of her career. She recognized that pain management was an underserved area, neglected by major pharmaceutical firms in search of high-margin sectors. But she also observed a changing attitude in the public about pain management that presented a niche opportunity for a small company willing to focus on it. Prior generations, hardened by the experience of the Great Depression and World War II, were far more stoic about enduring pain than members of the Baby Boom generation, who were less interested in pleasing a doctor and more than willing to acknowledge when they were experiencing uncomfortable pain. In the early 1990s pain management became a specialty and physicians could now take their residency in it. Moreover, hospitals were now rated on how well they assessed and treated pain.

Management Team Launch of Endo Pharmaceuticals in 1997

According to a *Philadelphia Inquirer* company profile in 2003, ''Ammon recalls how she ran into the office of her colleague and longtime friend, MacDonald. . . . 'Look, we can buy these products. Do you want to?' MacDonald's answer, 'Yes.' 'Maybe you want to go home to talk to your husband? We may not have a job if this doesn't work out.' MacDonald didn't hesitate. 'No, I'm in.' '' They then recruited Vollmer as a third partner and began meeting with Wall Street investment firms, eventually settling on a partner, Kelso & Co., which helped it to raise $277 million in equity investment and loans. In August 1997 the three bought 35 branded and generic medicines from DuPont Merck along with the Endo name, and in November they incorporated Endo Pharmaceuticals Holdings Inc.

Although there were few success stories of companies that succeeded in combining branded drugs with generics, Endo's management team was not concerned, since all three of them

were experienced in both areas. Their focus was on the therapeutic niche, pain management, which they sought to serve with either brands or generics. By offering generics of the very same brands it sold, Endo was not cannibalizing sales, but actually growing it, since brands and generics served different markets. Moreover, the selling of generics allowed for maximum use of manufacturing capacity.

Endo established its headquarters in Chadds Ford, Pennsylvania, and a laboratory on Long Island, where it conducted research on analgesic drug technology, supplemented by the work of specialty research and development firms. The company also formed two divisions: Endo Laboratories, to market multisource brands including Percocet, Percodan, Symmetrel, Hycotuss, Hycomine, and Hycodan; and Endo Generic Products, which started out with 25 generic products, including cimetidine, captopril, and etodolac. To quickly get up to speed, branded sales were assigned to a contract sales force. Generics, on the other hand, were less labor-intensive, so inside people were able to handle that business.

While R&D efforts began to put products in the pipeline, Endo looked to build sales on some of its well-known branded products. The flagship product, Percocet, for example, was so established that the vast majority of prescriptions for generic oxycodone/acetaminophen were written down as Percocet. With further study of prescriptions, it became apparent to Endo that physicians would order Percocet if it were available in doses other than just five milligrams. The company sought and received FDA approval on different doses, adding 2.5-, 7.5-, and 10-milligram versions, and as a result Percocet experienced strong growth, despite the lack of patent protection. Sales increased from $40 million in 1997 to $214 million in 2003.

Another Endo success story of the 1990s was Lidoderm, a drug that was not developed by the company. Instead, it was the work of a retired pharmaceutical chemist who concocted a homemade salve to relieve the suffering of his wife, who was enduring the pain of shingles (a recurrence of the chicken pox in adults) on her back. Diana Hind was part of the 20 percent of patients in whom shingles damaged the nerves in skin, resulting in constant, severe pain—postherpatic neuralgia. To receive just six hours of relief, she had to endure 45 minutes of injections of lidocaine, spaced every half-inch across her back and just under the surface, lest the anesthetic enter the bloodstream and cause harmful side effects. Before his retirement, Mr. Hind headed a company that developed eye and skin drugs, and he now used that expertise to mix a homemade salve using lidocaine, which he then applied to his wife's back one night in a makeshift patch of plastic wrap and tape. When she woke up in the morning, the pain had vanished. Mr. Hind then developed a 5 percent lidocaine solution hand-sized patch, which gained FDA approval and which Endo began marketing as Lidoderm in 1999. Sales of Lidoderm were strong and steady, reaching about $40 million in 2001 and more than doubling a year later to $83.2 million.

Endo also looked to grow by external means. In November 1999 it reached an agreement to acquire Algos Pharmaceutical Corporation, a New Jersey-based biotech company that also specialized in pain management products. After some adjustments in the terms, the $250 million stock swap closed in July 2000. As a result, Endo received new pain management drugs,

1920: Endo Laboratories is founded by the Ushkow family.
1969: DuPont acquires Endo.
1983: DuPont drops the Endo name.
1994: The Endo name is revived as a generic division for the DuPont Merck joint venture.
1997: A management team acquires the DuPont Merck pain management drugs and the Endo name.
2000: Endo becomes a public company by acquiring Algos Pharmaceutical Corporation.
2001: A secondary stock offering is completed.

the most important of which was MorphiDex, which combined morphine and dextromethorphan to provide relief from moderate-to-severe cancer pain. Because Algos was a public company, Endo was able to become a public company as well.

Stock Offering Highlight of 2001

Endo's balance sheet reflected strong growth since the company's formation, due primarily to the launch of new doses of old products. Endo posted a net profit of $201,000 in 1998, then a year later saw sales increase 28 percent to $138 million and net income to $3.26 million. Sales grew another 43 percent in 2000 to $187.4 million. Endo was established enough that it was able to use its public status to make a secondary stock offering in September 2001, raising about $140 million, which was used to pay off bank debt.

Endo's growth did not come without difficulties, however. The company suffered a setback in 2002 when MorphiDex failed to demonstrate in a late-stage clinical trial that it performed better than simple morphine in relieving pain. Endo abandoned the project and investors dealt out punishment, bidding down the price of its stock. Endo also became entangled in litigation, a not uncommon distraction in the pharmaceutical industry. In October 2000, The Purdue Frederick Company sued Endo, alleging that Endo had infringed on patents relating to OxyContin by developing a generic form of the drug. Endo prevailed because it was able to show that Purdue had made misrepresentations on its drug application, claiming to have made a discovery without actually conducting any clinical studies. As a result, a judge ruled the patent invalid, allowing Endo to proceed. Purdue filed further suits, lost, and appealed. The matter was aired at trial conducted at the U.S. Court of Appeals in Washington, D.C., in November 2004, with the result expected sometime in 2005. In early 2001 Endo sued Watson Pharmaceuticals Inc., a California generic-drug maker with whom it had considered forming an alliance. During 1998 talks, Endo shared its plans to develop a new Percocet product, one that

included Tylenol's active ingredient, acetaminophen. Watson, which had signed a confidentiality agreement, then ended the talks and subsequently sought FDA approval for a generic version of Endo's new Percocet variant. Despite Endo's suit, Watson ultimately gained FDA approval and began marketing its generic product. Endo also became involved in litigation with GlaxoSmithKline P.L.C. in 2001, a challenge that proved successful, concerning Endo's attempts to sell a generic form of Paxil, an anti-depression drug.

Endo increased sales to $252 million in 2001, due to the launch of new strengths of Percocet and the strong growth of Lidoderm. Those two drugs again led the way in 2002 and 2003. Endo increased sales by 58 percent to $399 million in 2002, followed by another jump of 49 percent to $595.6 million in 2003. Also of note in 2003 was the move of R&D operations from Garden City to a more modern location, a 24,000-square-foot center in Westbury, located on Long Island. In 2003 Endo added a pair of painkillers, paying $120 million to British biotech SkyePharma for the rights to Depomorphine and Propofol IDD-D, along with options on other products.

In 2004 Endo launched a pair of branded drugs: Frova and DepoDur, and along with continued strong growth in Lidoderm, the company was able to increase sales to $615.1 million. Although this was not a sizable gain over the previous year, the company was able to increase net income to $143.3 million in 2004, more than doubling the $69.8 million recorded in 2003. Endo also strengthened its pipeline, which included some near-term products. Given the growing pain management sector, Endo was well positioned to enjoy sustained growth.

Principal Subsidiaries

Endo Pharmaceuticals Inc.; EPI Company; BML Pharmaceuticals, Inc.; Endo Pharma Canada Inc.

Principal Competitors

Pain Therapeutics, Inc.; Pfizer Inc.; Purdue Pharma L.P.

Further Reading

"Endo Makes Mark in Generics," *Chain Drug Review,* August 28, 1995.

Loyd, Linda, "Gamble of Pain-Killing Medicines Pays Off for Chadds Ford, Pa., Businesswomen," *Philadelphia Inquirer,* March 9, 2003, p. E1.

Salvatore, Peggy, "Endo Pharmaceuticals Revived by 3 Ex-Execs," *Philadelphia Business Journal,* December 12, 1997, p. 6.

Sellers, L.J., "Feeling No Pain," *Pharmaceutical Executive,* November 2004, p. 80.

Zoeller, Janice, "Endo: On Its Own Again," *American Druggist,* October 1992, p. 26.

—Ed Dinger

Equistar Chemicals, LP

1221 McKinney Street, Suite 700
Houston, Texas 77010
U.S.A.
Telephone: (713) 652-7200
Fax: (713) 652-4151
Web site: http://www.equistarchem.com

Wholly Owned Subsidiary of Lyondell Chemical Company
Incorporated: 1997
Employees: 3,165
Sales: $9.31 billion (2004)
NAIC: 325188 All Other Inorganic Chemical
   Manufacturing

A subsidiary of Lyondell Chemical Company, Equistar Chemicals, LP is a Houston-based manufacturer of petrochemicals and polymers. In the chemical segment Equistar is the largest North American producer of butadiene, the second largest North American producer of ethylene and propylene, the largest U.S. producer of diethyl ether and industrial ethyl alcohol, and also a major U.S. producer of ethylene oxide and ethylene glycol. In addition, Equistar manufactures specialty chemicals such as benzene, TDI toluene, DCPD, and piperylenes. Equistar's polymer products include polyolefin resins, polyethylene, wire and cable resins and compounds, and tie-layer resins. In addition, Equistar maintains 1,400 miles of pipelines in Texas and Louisiana to serve both Equistar and Lyondell facilities, transporting a variety of chemicals as well as natural gas, diesel, butane, and propane. Altogether, Equistar maintains 16 manufacturing facilities, located along the Gulf Coast of Texas and Louisiana, the midwestern states of Iowa, Illinois, and Ohio, plus a facility in Newark, New Jersey.

Parent Company's Origins in the Mid-1980s

Lyondell was created in 1985 as a subsidiary of Atlantic Richfield Company (ARCO), which during the 1960s became actively involved in building a petrochemical business. With Halcon International it forged a joint venture in 1966 called Oxirane Chemical Company, which used a Halcon-developed process to produce propylene oxide. By 1980 Oxirane was doing $1 billion in annual worldwide sales, at which point ARCO bought out Halcon and folded the operation into ARCO Chemical. During the early 1980s, however, ARCO Chemical did not perform as well as expected. ARCO Chemical was on the verge of selling off the olefins business when in 1985 the parent company stepped in to combine these assets under a new unit called Lyondell Petrochemical Corporation. The Lyondell name was drawn from the Lyondell Country Club in Channelview, Texas. On that site in 1955 Texas Butadiene and Chemical Corporation built a plant, which was purchased by Richfield Oil Corporation in 1962. It then became part of ARCO following the merger of Richfield and Atlantic Refining Company in 1966. Three years later ARCO merged with Sinclair Oil & Refining Company, which in 1918 built its first refinery on the 720-acre Allen Ranch in Houston. Among the assets Lyondell inherited was the Allen Ranch facility and the petrochemical complex that replaced the Lyondell Country Club.

As early as 1988 Lyondell began discussing the possibility of combining its operations with another chemical company, Quantum Chemical Company, the largest producer of polyethylene in the United States. Quantum's heritage dated to 1906 and the creation of U.S. Industrial Alcohols, which brewed denatured ethanol from Cuban molasses. In 1939 the company moved into synthetic resins, changing its name to U.S. Industrial Chemical, and a dozen years later merged with National Distillers and soon began producing polyethylene in Illinois. This business grew so much that by the early 1980s National Distillers and Chemicals decided to focus on chemicals. It bought a petrochemicals company, divested all of its nonchemical assets, in 1987 assumed the Quantum name, and soon entered into talks with Lyondell about a merger, an effort that failed but laid the groundwork for the creation of Equistar a decade later.

Formation of the Company from a Joint Venture in 1997

In the meantime, Lyondell and Quantum went their separate ways. After a strong 1988, Lyondell was spun off by ARCO, which took advantage of the subsidiary's peak performance to sell half of the business to the public for $1.4 billion. ARCO also took $500 million out of the company as a special distribution, resulting in Lyondell gaining independence, but with a debt burden of $760 million. Lyondell shares began trading on the New York Stock Exchange and quickly tanked. But free of ARCO's control, Lyondell was able to establish its own course and unleash a hidden entrepreneurial spirit. In 1990 the company completed its first acquisition, the low-density polyethylene and polypropylene plants from Rexene Products Company, valuable additions because they consumed Lyondell's ethylene and propylene and helped the company move into the polyolefins market. Among other deals, Lyondell acquired Occidental Chemical Corporation's high-density polyethylene business in 1995. During this same period, Quantum began to struggle and changed ownership in 1993, acquired by British conglomerate Hanson PLC. In 1996 Hanson elected to focus on its building materials and crane manufacturing operations and spin off its tobacco, manufacturing, energy, and chemical businesses. Quantum was packaged with SCM Chemical, a titanium dioxide maker, and Glidco, which produced terpene-based aroma chemicals, to form a new company, Millennium Chemicals. Because its three component businesses shared little in common, an offer to combine the old Quantum assets with those of Lyondell's was gladly accepted.

In 1997 Lyondell and Millennium petrochemical and polymer assets were used to form Equistar Chemicals, LP. Lyondell held a 57 percent stake in the joint venture and Millennium held the balance. Under terms of the agreement, Equistar assumed $745 million of Lyondell's debt and made a $1 billion cash payment to Lyondell, which necessitated the borrowing of another $750 million. Lyondell's chairman and CEO took over as Equistar's CEO, and he served as co-chairman of the partnership's six-member governance committee along with Millennium CEO William M. Landuyt. Handling day-to-day operations was President and COO Eugene Allspach, a Millennium executive. The melding of Lyondell and Millennium assets was a good fit, and even before the parties received approval from the Federal Trade Commission and Equistar was officially operational on December 1, 1997, the two companies were hard at work integrating the operations in order to realize an anticipated $150 million in cost savings. About a third of that amount would be the result of a 10 percent staff reduction. Equistar also seized on a chance to save about $70 million by dedicating plants to specific grades of resin. Essentially, the company hit the ground running, a $5 billion powerhouse that was the largest North American producer of polyethylene and ethylene, with management determined to take advantage of synergies to become the low-cost producers of these commodities.

From the outset, Equistar was in the market for a third joint venture partner. In March it announced that it had found one in Occidental Chemical Corporation, which agreed to add its ethylene, propylene, ethylene oxide, and derivatives business to Equistar. Assets included a pair of olefins plants in Texas and Louisiana; a 50 percent ownership stake in PD Glycol, which operated ethylene oxide/ethylene glycol (EO/EG) plants in Beaumont, Texas; Occidental's ethylene oxide, ethylene glycol, and ethylene oxide derivatives operations; and more than 950 miles of olefins pipelines and two Texas storage wells that would benefit Equistar's other operations. As a result of the merger, Equistar controlled $7 billion in assets and in pro forma sales in 1997 generated $6 billion. It was now North America's largest olefins producer and the second largest in the world. It was also one of the top three producers of ethylene, propylene, butadiene, and polyethylene in North America and the world. Lyondell, which operated the company for the partnership, owned 41 percent of Equistar, while Millennium and Occidental each controlled a 29.5 percent stake. As part of the deal, Equistar assumed $200 million in further debt and borrowed another $500 million in order to make a cash disbursement of $75 million to Millennium and $425 million to Occidental Petroleum, Occidental Chemical's parent company, which was in the process of redeploying $4.7 billion in assets. For Equistar, the addition of the Occidental assets allowed it to seek even greater synergies in its efforts to become the most efficient and cost-effective producer in its arena of chemical commodities.

In 1999 a struggling Millennium signaled that it was interested in selling its stake in Equistar in order to raise cash and buy back a large portion of its stock. In August Lyondell showed some interest but quickly backed off after the price of its own stock began to dip, due to investor concerns about the amount of debt Lyondell had taken on in the 1998 $5.6 billion acquisition of Arco Chemical. The company made certain that Wall Street now heard its pledge to make debt reduction its top priority. Millennium, according to press accounts, held some exploratory talks with potential buyers of its stake in Equistar, but Lyondell's and Occidental's right of first offer proved problematic. In order to clear the way for a sale, Millennium in early 2000 made the necessary offer to Lyondell and Occidental. Neither of the partners were interested, both expressing satisfaction with their current positions. Millennium was now free to seek a buyer, but it was never able to complete a deal.

Industry Slump in the Early 2000s

As the economy began to slow down in 2000, Equistar was adversely impacted, but higher natural gas prices caused more of a problem, forcing the company to cut back on natural gas-based ethylene production and the shuttering of some facilities. Poor conditions for the chemical industry continued in 2001, leading to further erosion in Equistar's sales and margins. Lyondell also struggled to perform, posting a net loss of $150 million in 2001. Nevertheless, Lyondell was in a stronger position than many other chemical companies, and in 2002 it was able to use its stock to buy out Occidental's interest in Equistar, giving it a 70.5 percent share of the joint venture. Millennium had the right to purchase Occidental's shares on a pro rata basis, but was content with its 29.5 percent stake and declined to participate in the sale—while reiterating its willingness to participate in the governance of the partnership, to help optimize cash flows and, of course, increase the value of its piece of Equistar. Lyondell's CEO Dan Smith explained to investors on a conference call that the rationale for the deal from Lyondell's

---

Key Dates:

1997: Lyondell Chemical Company and Millennium Chemicals form Equistar as a joint venture.
1998: Occidental Chemical Corporation becomes the third joint venture partner.
2002: Lyondell acquires Occidental's Equistar interest.
2004: Lyondell acquires Millennium, gaining 100 percent ownership of Equistar.

---

perspective was "cash flow driven," adding, "It gives us greater command of a greater cash flow stream to shape up our balance sheet much quicker. That's our number one, two, and three focus." From Occidental's point of view, exchanging an illiquid stake in Equistar for a stake in Lyondell made sense, because Occidental could now raise money if needed by selling some or all of its 30 million-plus shares of newly issued Lyondell Series B common stock.

Poor industry conditions persisted in 2002, leading to Equistar's revenues dropping to $5.4 billion in 2002, after sales of $5.9 billion the year before, and a loss of $1.3 billion. High crude oil and natural gas liquid prices continued to be a problem in 2003, but the cost of ethylene production was offset by rising prices for ethylene and its derivatives. As a result, revenues rebounded in 2003 to more than $6.5 billion, but maintenance and financing expenses and employee severance costs led to another net loss of $339 million. Lyondell, in the meantime, recorded a net loss of $302 million in 2003.

To improve its standing in the chemical industry, Lyondell took a major step in April 2004 by reaching an agreement to acquire Millennium in a stock swap, thereby assuming 100 percent control of Equistar. The deal closed on November 30 of that year after shareholders of both companies gave their approval. According to Smith, Lyondell had "achieved the global depth and breadth necessary for long-term success." Because Lyondell would now report the consolidated results of three wholly owned businesses—Equistar, Millennium, and Lyondell's intermediate chemicals and derivatives business—"the true size of the Lyondell enterprise will be more apparent," Smith told reporters. In 2003 Lyondell possessed a market capitalization of $6.5 billion, making it North America's third largest independent, publicly traded chemical company. After enduring a protracted slump in petrochemicals, Lyondell was poised to reap the benefits of an upswing in the cycle, a turnaround led by Equistar, whose 100 percent contribution to the Lyondell balance sheet was a key to the company's future.

Principal Operating Units

Chemicals; Polymers; Pipeline.

Principal Competitors

The Dow Chemical Company; ExxonMobil Chemical Company; Huntsman International L.L.C.

Further Reading

Chang, Joseph, "Lyondell to Buy Occidental Stake in Equistar in $400 MM Stock Deal," *Chemical Market Reporter,* February 4, 2002, p. 1.

Denton, Timothy, "Equistar Poised to Slash Costs and Optimize," *Chemical Market Reporter,* December 1, 1997, p. 1.

Hoffman, John, "Equistar Grows into a Global Olefins Power," *Chemical Market Reporter,* March 30, 1998, p. 1.

Westervelt, Robert, "Lyondell Completes Acquisition of Millennium Chemicals," *Chemical Week,* December 1–December 8, 2004, p. 9.

——, "Lyondell: Gaining Leverage in the Upturn," *Chemical Week,* December 22–December 29, 2004, p. 15.

——, "Millennium, Lyondell Wish Upon Equistar," *Chemical Week,* October 8, 1997, p. 14.

Wood, Andrew, "Equistar: A Match Made in Heaven?," *Chemical Week,* March 11, 1998, p. 40.

——, "Equistar Makes Financial Sense," *Chemical Week,* March 25, 1998, p. 38.

—Ed Dinger

ESCADA

ESCADA AG

Margaretha-Ley-Ring 1
Aschheim
D-85609
Germany
Telephone: +49 89 99 44 0
Fax: +49 89 99 44 11 11
Web site: http://www.escada.com

Public Company
Incorporated: 1979
Employees: 2,886
Sales: EUR 625.5 million ($800 million) (2004)
Stock Exchanges: Frankfurt
Ticker Symbol: ESC
NAIC: 315234 Women's and Girls' Cut and Sew Suit,
    Coat, Tailored Jacket, and Skirt Manufacturing;
    315191 Outerwear Knitting Mills; 315232 Women's
    and Girls' Cut and Sew Blouse and Shirt
    Manufacturing; 315233 Women's and Girls' Cut and
    Sew Dress Manufacturing; 315999 Other Apparel
    Accessories and Other Apparel Manufacturing;
    316992 Women's Handbag and Purse Manufacturing;
    316999 All Other Leather Good Manufacturing

ESCADA AG (Escada) is Germany's leading luxury fashion brand and a leading player in the global luxury clothing market. Based in Aschheim, Germany, Escada has scaled down its range of brands into the mid-2000s to focus especially on its core, high-end Escada Collection, including the Escada haute couture line. The Escada brand also includes a line of sportswear under the Escada Sport label, and a range of Escada Accessories, manufactured by the company itself. In addition, Escada licenses its brand for a number of items, including eyewear, perfumes, ties and scarves, as well as a beauty care collection produced by Wella, and a line of jewelry. As part of its repositioning, Escada has sold or spun off most of its former brands, including BiBa, cavita, and its mid-range Laurel brand, which were placed under a new vehicle, Primera Group. In addition to designing and producing clothing, Escada operates a 400-store international retail network, with stores in most of the world's main fashion markets. The Escada line remains the group's strongest, at 66 percent of sales. Most of Escada's fashions, especially its high-end and haute couture designs, are produced in its factories in Germany. The company also sources some 25 percent of its production from Italy, and from a company-owned facility in Portugal. Germany accounts for 27 percent of the company's sales, which topped EUR 625 million in the company's 2003–04 fiscal year. The rest of Europe accounts for more than 28 percent of sales, while the North American markets add about 21 percent to sales. Escada has been targeting growth in the Asian markets, which accounted for just 14.5 percent of sales in 2004. Company founder Wolfgang Ley remains its CEO. Escada has been listed on the Frankfurt Stock Exchange since 1986.

Launching German Fashion Success in the 1970s

Escada was founded in the early 1970s by husband-and-wife team Wolfgang and Margaretha Ley as a knitwear company in Munich, Germany. Sweden's Margaretha Ley had already established a successful career, first as a model for Vienna's Fred Adlimueller, then as a runway model for Parisian designer Jacques Fath in the 1960s. Prior to her modeling career, however, Ley had worked for Sweden's royal tailor Leja, where she gained experience in designing and producing clothing. In the late 1960s and early 1970s, Ley also worked as a designer for German clothing firm Mondi.

Ley, 37 years old, brought this experience to her marriage with 36-year-old entrepreneur Wolfgang Ley. The couple married in 1974 and launched a contract knitwear business in 1976. The couple found it easy to balance their marriage and working relationships, with Wolfgang Ley taking charge of the financial, administrative, and manufacturing end of the business, and Margaretha Ley establishing the company's reputation for design. As Margaretha Ley explained in an interview in the late 1980s, the company was divided into "two businesses. In Munich we have two buildings—one for design and one for administration. I don't see Wolfgang for weeks unless he's at home."

Margaretha Ley quickly established a reputation for her strong sense of bright colors; Ley was said to have explained that her choice of vivid colors came in reaction to her childhood in

151

Company Perspectives:

The core business of the ESCADA Group covers the following business areas: ESCADA Collection (including Couture), ESCADA Sport, ESCADA Accessories, and Licenses (glasses, perfume, ties and scarves and a jewellery collection). The strategic decision to concentrate on the core brand ESCADA and its effective exploitation will ensure profitable growth in the future.

Sweden, where the northern light tended to mute colors. Ley's designs, and the company's commitment to the high-quality, luxury goods segment, helped the company grow quickly.

The late 1970s saw the rise of a new breed of clothing company—the designer label. In 1979, the Leys decided to join the designer trend and establish their own brand name. For this the company chose the name Escada, after a thoroughbred race horse in Ireland.

Escada proved a success from the start. At the end of its first year, the company had posted revenues of DEM 22 million. The success of the high-end Escada line encouraged the company to add a second, "bridge" label, called Laurel, featuring designs targeting the mid-price sector. The Laurel label became as successful as its parent, even, by the end of the decade, outselling the Escada brand by number of pieces.

Yet Escada remained the group's flagship. The high-priced line was, as Margaretha Ley herself once described it, "for the working woman with a certain amount of money." Ley's collection was also extensive, designed to clothe a woman from head to toe. By the early 1990s, the Escada line featured more than 1,200 pieces, and included jewelry, handbags, accessories, gloves, scarves, and footwear.

Wolfgang Ley quickly steered the group on to an international course. In this, the group was aided by the surge in interest in German fashions during the 1980s, which saw the rise of international labels such as Hugo Boss, Jil Sander, and Joop!, as well as Mondi. Escada itself claimed the position as leader of the country's high-end and couture segments.

Escada expanded rapidly during the 1980s, an expansion aided by the launch of its own chain of retail stores. The company began establishing stores in most of Europe's major cities, as well as in New York, Japan, and elsewhere. The company's entry into the United States came as early as 1981; after several years of losses, the U.S. subsidiary succeeded in generating profits by mid-decade. By 1986, the company's sales had topped $100 million. The United States alone accounted for some 21 percent of the group's sales.

By then, the Leys had begun to eye a still more ambitious expansion strategy, based on building a multi-brand, diversified operation. In order to fuel its expansion, the company turned to the public market. In 1986, Escada went public, listing its stock on the Frankfurt Stock Exchange. The Leys nonetheless retained 76 percent of the group's common stock (later reduced to 51 percent).

Tragedy and Crisis in the 1990s

The public offering enabled the company to go on a buying spree in the late 1980s. The company scored first with the 1987 purchase of Munster, Germany's Schneeberger. That company boosted the group's production capacity, and also gave it an entry into the private-label sector, particularly Schneeberger's focus on plus-sized women's dresses. Next up, Escada purchased Kemper, also based in Germany, which specialized in the production of women's clothing. The addition of Kemper also brought the company its first licensed brand, Cerruti 1881, produced under license from Cerruti starting in 1988.

Escada also began developing other labels to be produced in-house to complement its growing Escada and Laurel lines. During the 1980s and into the early 1990s, the company launched or acquired a number of labels, including its own Crisca label, and the Apriori and Natalie Acatrini labels. The company's knitwear segment grew significantly in 1989 when the company reached an agreement to acquire 80 percent of California-based St. John Knits. Like Escada, St. John was a family-controlled company targeting the high-end and luxury segments. The acquisition not only gave Escada a manufacturing presence in the United States, it also boosted its presence in major department stores such as Nieman Marcus, Nordstrom, and Saks Fifth Avenue.

The St. John purchase was also part of a larger company strategy to establish itself as a force on the U.S. fashion scene. The company began adding new stores, doubling its U.S. presence to nine stores in the early 1990s, including a flagship store in Manhattan. The company also acquired New York's Badgley Mischka in 1992.

The extension of the Escada range into the accessories and related categories led the company to boost its production capacity, and to expand its range of production expertise. The company continued to seek new markets in which to extend its brand, and in 1990 launched its own collection of perfumes and fragrances. This in turn led to the creation of Escada Beaute and the development of an in-house line of beauty care products. By the end of 1991, Escada's sales had climbed past DEM 1.4 billion ($897 million).

Tragedy struck the company in 1992, however, when Margaretha Ley died at the age of 56. To make matters worse, the company's sales snapped on the global recession of the early 1990s. Escada's rapid expansion finally caught up with the company, leaving it heavily in debt, even as a number of its operations sank into the red. By the end of 1992 the company's losses, including extraordinary items, neared DEM 120 million (approximately $60 million). Escada's losses continued into 1993, topping DEM 37 million ($17 million). In order to pay down its debt, the company sold off its 80 percent stake in St. John Knits that year. The company also moved its accessories production to France in 1994, forming the new subsidiary Escada Development in Paris.

Refocusing on the Core in the New Century

Escada called in American designer Todd Oldham to help it relaunch its collection, now known as Escada Margaretha Ley. The company also continued restructuring, shutting down its

Key Dates:

1974: Wolfgang and Margaretha Ley marry and begin to design and produce knitwear for the contract market.
1976: A knitwear manufacturing company is established.
1979: A clothing collection is launched under the Escada label.
1980: A secondary, mid-priced line, called Laurel, is launched.
1981: The company enters the U.S. market.
1986: Escada goes public on the Frankfurt Stock Exchange in order to fund an ambitious expansion.
1987: Women's large-size dressmaker Schneeberger is acquired.
1988: Kemper is acquired.
1989: St. John Knits of California is acquired.
1990: The Escada Beaute division is launched.
1992: Margaretha Ley dies; the company begins restructuring to stop losses.
1993: The company sells St. John Knits to pay down debt.
1994: The company launches the accessories subsidiary Escada Development in Paris.
1998: The company acquires Parfum Gres in Paris for Escada Beaute.
2002: As part of a new restructuring, the company sells Escada Beaute to Wella Group.
2003: Escada spins off Laurel as a separate company, which is then placed into Primera Group.
2004: Escada refocuses operations around the core Escada label and launches the Escada Kids line.

unprofitable divisions, including closing most of its money-losing stores, especially under the Laurel brand. Into the mid-1990s, the company also restructured its operations into clearer divisions, including Escada Sports, to encompass its sportswear lines, and Escada Development for its accessories. The company continued to boost its Escada Beaute division, including through the acquisition of Parfum Gres Producions, based in Paris, in 1998.

Yet a new international economic downturn at the dawn of the 21st century forced Escada to rethink its strategy once again. In 2002, for example, Escada decided to exit the beauty care business, selling off Escada Beaute—including the license to its brand name—to Wella Group AG. The company also began plans to restructure its operations again, this time refocusing its operations around its core Escada label.

In 2002, the company spun off its Laurel division as a separate company, Laurel GmbH. The company then announced its interest in selling Laurel, as well as its other noncore holdings, including Kemper and Primera. The latter division housed a number of Escada brands, including BiBa and cavita. Instead of carrying out the sale of Laurel, however, Escada regrouped Laurel under the Primera Group.

Escada's restructuring continued into 2003, with the announcement that it was dropping its lingerie collection, which had been produced in partnership with Huber Holding of Austria. Escada's restructuring efforts appeared to pay off, as the company, which had posted losses in the early years of the 2000s, moved into profits by the end of 2004. In that year, as well, the company boosted the Escada brand family with the launch of a new children's clothing collection, Escada Kids. Escada now turned its attention to boosting its position in the fast-growing luxury goods markets in the Far East, especially in the booming Chinese market. After nearly 30 years, Escada remained a force in the international designer clothing market.

Principal Subsidiaries

apriori Textilvertriebs GmbH; BiBa Mode GmbH; cavita fashion GmbH; ESCADA (Asia) Ltd. (Hong Kong); ESCADA (U.K.) Limited; ESCADA (USA) Inc.; ESCADA CANADA Inc; ESCADA DEVELOPMENT S.A.R.L. (France); ESCADA France S.A.R.L.; ESCADA Holding B.V. (Netherlands); ESCADA Italia S.r.l; ESCADA Japan Co., Ltd.; ESCADA Korea Limited; ESCADA Maglia Italia S.r.l.; ESCADA Sweden Retail AB; Grupo ESCADA España S.A; Laurèl GmbH; PRIMERA (Asia) Ltd.; PRIMERA AG; PRIMERA Holding GmbH.

Principal Competitors

Christian Dior S.A.; LVMH Moët Hennessy Louis Vuitton S.A.; Esprit AG; Hugo Boss AG; Inditex Industria de Diseno Textil S.A.; Marzotto S.p.A.; Cortefiel S.A.; Donna Karan International Inc.

Further Reading

Drier, Melissa, and Karyn Monget, "Escada Leaves Intimate Apparel," *WWD*, June 2, 2003, p. 15.
"Escada Group Spinoff Seeking Laurel Buyer," *WWD*, July 11, 2002, p. 2.
Ko, Kenneth, "Luxury Brand Builds Up Presence in City," *South China Morning Post,* October 3, 2004.
McGuinness, Damien, "Escada Off to Strong Start in '05," *WWD*, March 4, 2005, p. 11.
Murphy, Robert, "Escada in Black As Sales Climb 5.2% in Quarter," *WWD*, June 9, 2004, p. 5.
Weil, Jennifer, "Escada Exits Beauty, Wella Licenses Brand," *WWD*, March 5, 2002, p. 2.
Weisman, Katherine, "Escada's New 'House' Keys Ambitious Growth Plan," *WWD*, March 14, 1996, p. 10.

—M.L. Cohen

F&W Publications, Inc.

4700 E. Galbraith Road
Cincinnati, Ohio 45236
U.S.A.
Telephone: (513) 531-2690
Fax: (513) 531-0798
Web site: http://www.fwpublications.com

Private Company
Founded: 1913
Employees: 800
Sales: $300 million (2004 est.)
NAIC: 511120 Periodical Publishers; 511130 Book
  Publishers

F&W Publications, Inc. is a Cincinnati, Ohio-based publisher of about 60 special interest magazines and books, 3,000 of which are in print, focusing on hobbies and other ''consumer enthusiast'' categories. The private company also runs a dozen niche book clubs, maintains about 30 free and fee-based web sites and produces conferences, trade shows, contests, and education programs. F&W's oldest periodical and flagship publication is *Writer's Digest,* offering instruction and other information to aspiring writers. Other major F&W subject areas include antiques and collectibles, art, automobiles, crafts, gardening, genealogy, outdoors and hunting, sports, toy collecting, and woodworking. The key to the company's success has been the ability to combine magazine and book publishing with clubs in its various niches, with the business of all three supporting one another. For most of its history the company has been run by the Rosenthal family, but since its sale to outsiders in 1999 F&W has enjoyed dramatic growth.

Heritage Dating to the Early 1900s

F&W was founded in Cincinnati in 1913 as a publisher of automotive periodicals by Edward Rosenthal, who three years earlier had launched the magazine *American Chauffeur,* which later took the name *Automotive Service Digest.* The company soon branched out into other subject areas. In 1921 *Writer's Digest* was launched, proving so successful that the Writer's Digest Books imprint was created, initially to publish *Writer's Market,* and became the basis for the company's book division. Over the next 50 years the company moved in and out of a number of categories. One important publication during the early years was *Farm Quarterly.* The company's name actually stood for *Farm Quarterly* and *Writer's Digest.* Although *Farm Quarterly* was sold in 1970, the F&W name was retained.

F&W did not achieve significant growth until the third generation of the Rosenthal family, the founder's grandson Richard H. Rosenthal, took charge in the 1970s, at a time when annual sales were in the $4 million range and the company employed just 29 people. He had first joined the company in 1957 as the marketing manager for *Writer's Market,* and now expanded on the marketplace concept with the launch of a number of titles: *Artist's Market* in 1975, *Photographer's Market* in 1979, *Songwriter's Market* in 1980, *Fiction Writer's Market* in 1983, and *Poet's Market* in 1986. F&W also built upon the Writer's Digest franchise by introducing the Writer's Digest Book Club in 1979.

One of the most important events that shaped F&W's development was the 1982 acquisition of Fletcher Art Services, which took the company into the fine arts category. Fletcher adopted the name of North Light Books and was supplemented by North Light Book Club. In 1983 F&W launched *The Artist's Magazine,* a monthly targeting commercial artists, which became a major success. Later in the decade, F&W acquired another monthly, *Decorative Artist's Workbook,* geared toward decorative painters, followed by the purchase of *HOW,* dedicated to graphic design. This category was then fleshed out with the publishing of the *Decorative Artist's Workbook* and the launch of the Graphic Design Book Club and Decorative Artist's Book Club. Also of note during the 1980s, the company revived *Story* magazine after a 22-year absence. The publication quickly surpassed its former popularity, becoming the largest literary magazine in the country.

F&W continued to enjoy steady growth in the 1990s, adding woodworking as one of its niches by publishing *Popular Woodworking* magazine and launching the WoodWorkers Book Club. The company also added to its slate of fine art publications with the introduction of *Watercolor Magic.* A children's magazine, *Spark!,* also was launched. According to *Cincinnati Business*

Courier, F&W generated about $38 million in annual revenues in 1991, making it one of the 100 largest private companies in the Cincinnati area. Despite difficult economic conditions, the company was growing revenues and income at a healthy 20 percent clip in the early part of the decade. Rosenthal expressed no interest in selling any of his properties, despite occasional offers, nor was he interested in taking the company public, telling *Cincinnati Business Courier,* "Normally when a company goes public, they need cash, which we don't. Or sometimes the owners want to get out, and I have no interest in that." As far as his lack of interest in leaving Cincinnati for a larger media market, he explained, "We get a better handle of who our customers are by being here. . . . Really, the only con about being here is that we have to train virtually everyone we hire. There isn't that reservoir of experienced people in the field in Cincinnati."

In 1998 F&W acquired *I.D.,* an international design magazine with 27,000 subscribers published eight times a year catering to design and technology professionals that fit in well with two other F&W publications, *HOW* and *Print.* F&W also added a pair of book clubs from Rodale Press: the Successful Sewing Book Club and the I Love Quilting Book Club. In addition, the company also took advantage of the opportunities presented by the Internet in the latter half of the 1990s to establish supporting web sites. Sales reached $65 million in 1998.

Founding Family's Sale of the Company in the Late 1990s

Rosenthal told the press in 1999 that he felt F&W was on the verge of another major growth spurt, but because he wanted to retire to devote more time to his philanthropic endeavors, and neither of his two children were interested in running the business, he decided it was time to sell the company. Thus, in May 1999, he contracted New York investment banker and business broker Veronis, Suhler & Associates to find a buyer, although he wanted to retain a minority stake in the business. There was no lack of suitors, with some 70 parties expressing interest. From this list Rosenthal took his time in selecting a buyer. In December 1999 he finally settled on Citicorp Venture Capital, which was willing to meet his conditions that the company remain in Cincinnati and the buyer commit to growing the business. Moreover Citicorp, which paid a reported $111 million for the company, agreed to Rosenthal's handpicked successor, Stephen J. Kent, an acquaintance for several years and a man that Rosenthal believed was well suited to growing a company through acquisitions. The 46-year-old Kent held an MBA from Harvard Business School and moved to Cincinnati to became a Procter & Gamble brand manager. He struck out on his own in the early 1980s, building up several local companies, including the EyeWorld chain of optical stores.

Soon after taking charge, Kent met with his managers and told them he projected taking F&W to the $100 million mark within a

year. "People looked at me with faces that suggested I had just landed from some planet," he later told *Cincinnati Business Courier.* It actually took F&W two years to reach that target, but Kent was quick to begin making acquisitions to position F&W to enjoy dramatic growth. The first deal was the June 2000 purchase of U.K. publisher David & Charles Group, which was a like-minded enthusiast book publisher that also ran several book clubs, focusing on arts, crafts, hobbies, and gardening. In addition to the David & Charles assets that complemented F&W's existing program, the acquisition provided F&W with an opportunity to grow its business in the United Kingdom and Europe. David & Charles also brought with it a children's unit, which did not fit in with F&W; it was sold to Gullane Entertainment in 2001. Also in 2001, the company added to its craft holdings by acquiring Memory Makers, a Denver-based publisher devoted to the increasingly popular scrapbooking hobby. Despite the emphasis on external growth, F&W did not lose sight of internal opportunities. In 2001 it became involved in custom publishing by taking over the in-flight magazine of Comair, *Comair Navigator.* Not only did F&W get a toehold in custom publishing, an area that was worth more than $1 billion and growing, it found a way to repackage material originally used in a specialty magazine for a general audience. As a result of the additional business, F&W grew sales to $106 million in 2001, and net income approached $20 million.

Ownership of F&W changed hands again in 2002, as Kent and other senior executives along with William F. Reilly and the financial backing of Providence Equity Partners paid $130 million to Citicorp Venture Capital for the company. Reilly took over as F&W's chairman working out of New York, while Kent stayed in Cincinnati to run the company as president. Reilly was a seasoned executive in media and publishing, the former president of Macmillan, Inc. After taking that publisher to new heights, in 1989 he founded K-III Communications, later renamed Primedia, funded by investors Kohlberg, Kravis, Roberts & Company. Primedia published more than 200 specialty magazines, including *New York, Seventeen,* and *Motor Trend.* Over the course of a decade Primedia grew into a $1.5 billion publisher. But Reilly was ousted in 1999 after the price of its stock faltered and he fell out with his backers over the direction to take the company, in particular his reluctance to more fully embrace the Internet. He signed a noncompete agreement to receive a $1 million per year severance package, and was attracted to F&W because he believed as a niche publisher it did not violate his agreement. Primedia was not in complete accord, but the two parties eventually worked out an arrangement to release both of them from their obligations.

Acquisition of Krause Communications in 2002

Reilly expressed no interest in turning F&W into a company the size of Primedia, opting for a still challenging goal of growing F&W into a $500 million company within five years. The new regime wasted little time in aggressively building up F&W. In 2002 F&W completed the $120 million acquisition of Krause Communications, a deal that Reilly had been pursuing the past two years. Based in Wisconsin, the employee-owned company had been founded in 1952 by Chet Krause, a hobbyist who launched a publication aimed at coin collectors who wanted to trade through the mail. He ventured into other specialty interests over the years, including arts and crafts, antique cars, comics, firearms, music, sports cards, and toys. By the time F&W acquired the company it was publishing 46 periodicals as well as 750 reference and how-to books. There were few redundancies with F&W, making Krause an excellent fit. Two divisions were formed, with the Krause president, Roger Case, taking over as president of the magazine division for F&W, and F&W's Budge Wallis serving as president of the book division. Both men reported to Kent. Thus, in one stroke, F&W greatly expanded its slate of magazines and reached the $250 million level in annual revenues. Moreover, the additional titles provided F&W with a platform for future growth, as it was able to apply its successful formula of growing categories by developing synergies between magazines, books, and book clubs. In separate transactions in 2002, F&W expanded into the gardening subject by acquiring the 100-year-old *Horticulture* magazine and covered graphic design by adding *Print – America's Graphic Design Magazine.*

F&W continued its momentum in 2003, acquiring *Pastel Journal,* a magazine serving pastel artists. More important, F&W completed another major acquisition, adding Adams Me-dia Corp., a 24-year-old Avon, Massachusetts-based publisher of 140 lifestyle, self-help, and inspirational books each year and a backlist of 750 titles. Adams published three popular series that employed the phrases "The Everything" (*The Everything Get-A-Job Book*), "Cup of Comfort" (*A Cup of Comfort for Friends*), and "Knock 'Em Dead" (*Knock 'Em Dead Business Presentations*).

F&W continued to add magazines in 2004, picking up *Scuba Diving Magazine* as well as *Country's Best Log Homes.* At the end of the year F&W's revenues reached $300 million, on pace to achieve Reilly's ambitious goal of $500 million within five years.

Principal Divisions

Book Division; Magazine Division.

Principal Competitors

Martha Stewart Living Omnimedia Inc.; Meredith Corporation; The Reader's Digest Association, Inc.

Further Reading

Barker, Beth, "Writing the Book on Publishing," *Cincinnati Business Courier,* September 30, 1991, p. 1.
Boyer, Mike, "Citibank Arm Buys F&W," *Cincinnati Enquirer,* December 3, 1999.
Eckberg, John, "F&W Publications Looking for Buyer," *Cincinnati Enquirer,* May 4, 1999.
Manly, Lorne, "A Primedia Founder Is Going to a Smaller Magazine Venture," *New York Times,* March 4, 2002.
Sims, Rebecca, "Fast 50: F&W Publications Inc., F&W Revenues Soar on Acquisitions," *Cincinnati Business Courier,* December 3, 2004, p. B9.

—Ed Dinger

Fallon Worldwide

901 Marquette Avenue
Minneapolis, Minnesota 55402-3281
U.S.A.
Telephone: (612) 321-2345
Fax: (612) 321-2346
Web site: http://www.fallon.com

Wholly Owned Subsidiary of Publicis Groupe S.A.
Founded: 1981 as Fallon McElligott & Rice
Employees: 500
Gross Billings: $900 million (2005 est.)
NAIC: 541810 Advertising Agencies; 541830 Media
  Buying Agencies; 541840 Media Representatives;
  541890 Other Services Related to Advertising

With 25 years in the business, Minneapolis-based Fallon Worldwide has emerged as one of the world's most creative advertising agencies, with international offices in Brazil, Hong Kong, Japan, London, and Singapore. The agency was a national powerhouse in the 1990s as Fallon McElligott, but changed its name and aspirations after being bought by the Paris-based Publicis Groupe S.A. in 2000. The firm has been named Agency of the Year multiple times by several trade organizations and won numerous awards for its quirky fare, such as the "Cat Herders" (for EDS), "The Hire" short films (for BMW of North America), Citibank's humorous identity theft sketches, and the "But I did spend the night at a Holiday Inn Express last night" promos for Holiday Inn Express. Fallon Worldwide's annual billings swelled from less than $150 million in 1990 to more than $1 billion in 2000, with a growing list of blue-chip clients that has included Amazon.com, British Broadcasting Company (BBC), Dave & Buster's, Dyson Ltd., Foster's Lager, Ikea, Lee Jeans, MTV, Sony Corporation, Starbucks, and United Airlines.

The Beginning: 1981–85

Fallon McElligott & Rice was established in 1981 and named for its three cofounders: Patrick Fallon, Tom McElligott, and Nancy Rice. Fallon and McElligott had first met in the late 1970s when both were moonlighting with a freelance agency

called Lunch Hour Ltd. After a year of planning, Fallon, McElligott, Rice, and Irv Fish formed a new, independent agency. Fallon was the agency "suit"—the executive in charge of cultivating and coddling clients. Copywriter McElligott, once crowned the "King of Print," provided the creative genius that would become the agency's hallmark. Rice served as art director, and Fish was brought on board as chief financial officer. The new partners crafted a mission statement that remained essentially unchanged for the next 20-odd years: "To be the premier creative agency in the nation that produces extraordinarily effective work for a short list of blue chip clients."

Fallon McElligott & Rice (FMR) put the art of advertising above practically all else, even a client's comfort level. McElligott once told an *Inc.* magazine interviewer that his intention was to give clients the kind of advertising that "makes the palms sweat a little" or "makes you a bit nervous." He added, "In my opinion, at least, these are the only ads worth running." The print medium was the agency's particular forte throughout the 1980s. FMR developed a recognizable style during this period, with ads featuring bold headlines. A piece for the Episcopal Church asked, "Whose birthday is it anyway?" above pictures of Jesus Christ and Santa Claus. A trade campaign for *Rolling Stone* magazine titled "Perception/Reality" juxtaposed images belonging to the magazine's perceived audience—hippies in Earth shoes with psychedelic-painted Volkswagen buses, against its actual readership—yuppies in Nikes with Ford Mustangs, in order to convince high-end advertisers to place ads in the periodical.

FMR exhibited a talent for promoting not only its clients' brands and products, but itself. The agency won numerous regional and national awards and used these credentials to draw media coverage as well as new clients to its midwestern headquarters. Fallon reflected on the group's early success in a 1989 *ADWEEK* article saying, "Virtually everything we touched worked dramatically in the marketplace." FMR won accounts with Federal Express, Hush Puppies Shoes, Jack Daniels Distillery, the *Wall Street Journal,* Lee Jeans, and Porsche U.S.A. Critical acclaim came early, too. Just two years after its founding, FMR was named ad agency of the year by *Advertising Age* magazine. The agency's style set the trend for cutting-edge advertising, especially print, throughout the 1980s. Annual bill-

---

Company Perspectives:

To be the world's premier company using creativity to drive business growth and success for clients with whom we share the genetic need for excellence.

---

ings mounted from about $24 million in 1984 to more than $110 million by 1987.

In 1985 Nancy Rice left the firm to form her own agency, Rice & Rice, with her husband Nick. That same year, the remaining principals sold a majority interest in their agency to Scali, McCabe & Sloves, itself owned by international advertising powerhouse Ogilvy & Mather, for an estimated $6 million. To reflect the departure of Rice, the company shortened its name to Fallon McElligott (FM).

From its outset, FM cultivated a familial atmosphere with a flat organizational structure, few titles, and a very relaxed corporate culture. Some competitors dubbed it "Camp Fallon," yet the low-key atmosphere fostered a high rate of job satisfaction and low turnover. Although FM, like many other regional and national agencies, had now become part of the global family of Ogilvy & Mather, it strove to maintain this aesthetic paradise.

Controversy and Reversals: 1987–92

Fallon McElligott suffered a self-inflicted black eye in 1987. Dr. Neala Schleuning, director of the Mankato (Minnesota) State University Women's Center, attended a workshop on marketing given by Fallon McElligott employee Charles Anderson in the fall of 1987. Offended by what she perceived as sexist language (such as several references to prostitution and the agency's "Bitch Bitch Bitch" campaign for the *Dynasty* television series), Schleuning wrote a critical letter to Anderson. Anderson responded by sending her a photo of an East African Dinka tribesman pressing his face to a cow's hindquarters. His accompanying letter suggested Schleuning go to Africa and "put a stop to the Dinka's horrible social practices."

The astonishingly unprofessional behavior did not stop there. When Schleuning reported the incident to Fallon and McElligott, they responded by sending her a pith helmet and offering to pay her way to East Africa—but not back. Schleuning took the correspondence to the Minnesota Women's Consortium, which sent copies to FM's clients and the local news media a week before Christmas 1987. Not surprisingly, what came to be known as "the Dinka incident" launched a firestorm of controversy in the press and among FM's clients. Fallon apologized in writing to Schleuning on New Year's Eve, but the damage had already been done. In the year to come, the agency lost a total of $22 million in billings, including the U.S. WEST, Federal Express, and *Wall Street Journal* accounts. Morale at "Camp Fallon" soon hit the skids.

FM's troubles continued in 1988, when Tom McElligott resigned over "disagreements with management about the future creative direction" of the firm. McElligott later admitted he had struggled with alcoholism, though all involved stressed this had nothing to do with his departure. He went into a month

of treatment and did not return to the advertising business until late 1989. Although the agency had dropped "Rice" from its name when Nancy Rice left in 1985, it retained the celebrated McElligott name.

After McElligott's departure, Pat Burnham, who had served as associate creative director, took over as creative director in 1989. The first of many talented creative people hired by McElligott, Burnham inherited a team little diminished by the loss of its star. FM had begun to recover by 1989, winning accounts with Aveda Corporation, Amoco Oil Company, and an estimated $35 million worth of annual billings from Ralston Purina. In order to manage its growth, the agency limited its clientele to less than 25 accounts at any time.

In 1990 Pat Fallon was called to New York City to turn around parent company Scali, McCabe & Sloves (SMS). SMS had lost its flagship client, Volvo, after pitching a television ad featuring a reinforced Volvo withstanding the weight of a "monster truck." Fallon's presence not only helped inspire confidence among SMS employees, but with its remaining clients as well. After spending two years in the hub of the advertising world, Fallon had secured SMS's future and chose not to stay in the Big Apple but to return to Minneapolis to make his namesake firm "the premier creative agency in the *world.*" Fallon thought he found the stepping stone to global eminence when FM was invited to pitch for the Compaq and MasterCard accounts in 1992. But after investing more than $250,000 and months of nights and weekends, the agency lost both clients to competitor Ammirati & Puris. A major shakeup at FM followed these missed opportunities.

Independent Again: 1993–99

In 1993 Fallon and several other top executives borrowed $14 million to buy the agency back from Scali, McCabe & Sloves (by this time owned by WPP Group PLC). The same year, Fallon asked for and received Creative Director Pat Burnham's resignation. New hires shed light on the agency's redirection: In Burnham's place came Bill Westbrook, a "rainmaker" adept at pitching potential clients, something Burnham had been unwilling or unable to do. To its creative core the agency added an integrated marketing department as well as design, editing, interactive, direct marketing, promotion research and planning, public relations, and account planning services. Westbrook further shook up FM's egalitarian culture by adopting the title president/creative director, and promoting or recruiting several group directors to report to him.

The reorganization worked; by the end of 1996 FM had won accounts with BMW, Prudential, Ameritech, United Airlines (domestic only, international was handled by Young & Rubicam because Fallon supposedly lacked a global presence), Mercury Marine, Holiday Inn, the USA Network, and even McDonald's, which awarded it the Arch Deluxe campaign. The firm capped off the year by winning the $150 million Miller Lite account. Total billings for the year reached an estimated $500 million, and the agency again won *Advertising Age*'s Agency of the Year award. Client turnover, however, plagued the agency for the next several years.

Fallon McElligott had resigned the McDonald's Arch Deluxe account and lost the Prudential campaign by 1997. The

Key Dates:

1981: Fallon McElligott & Rice is founded in Minneapolis.

1983: Fallon McElligott & Rice is named *Advertising Age*'s Agency of the Year.

1985: "Rice" is dropped from the agency's name after cofounder Nancy Rice leaves to create her own firm.

1987: The "Dinka Incident" costs the company $22 million in lost accounts.

1988: Tom McElligott leaves, and the firm is sold to Scali, McCabe & Sloves.

1990: Scali, McCabe & Sloves loses its flagship client and brings Pat Fallon in to turn the agency around.

1992: Fallon returns to Minneapolis, but his agency falters.

1993: Fallon and partners raise funds to buy Fallon McElligott back from Scali, McCabe & Sloves.

1996: The agency first wins United Airlines' domestic advertising account.

2000: The company is bought by the Paris-based Publicis Groupe S.A. and changes its name to Fallon Worldwide.

2001: The agency scores big with its mini movies for BMW, run on television and the Web.

2002: New offices open in Sao Paolo (Brazil), Hong Kong, and Singapore.

2003: Fallon Tokyo opens in Japan, one of the world's top advertising markets.

2004: Fallon Worldwide resigns the coveted $350 million Subway account.

2005: The agency agrees to reduced fees for the bankrupt United Airlines.

agency hoped to make up for the lost billings by winning the $75 million Domino's Pizza account then under review. Later that year, Westbrook announced he would cut back on his day-to-day duties, raising speculation the agency would be hiring yet another creative director in the near future. One element—perhaps the most important—appeared constant, however: Pat Fallon. Having guided his agency through a number of difficulties to acclaim, Fallon still strove to maintain his agency's creative excellence.

By the end of the decade mergers and acquisitions continued to sweep the advertising industry, with European conglomerates gobbling up the top U.S.-based agencies. WPP Group and Interpublic, both based in the United Kingdom, were the world's first and second largest advertising powerhouses. WPP Group owned J. Walter Thompson, Ogilvy & Mather Worldwide, and Young & Rubicam, while Interpublic had McCann-Erickson, Campbell-Ewald, and Lowe Lintas. Third-ranked Omnicom had the acronyms: BBDO, DDB, and TBWA/Chiat Day. The newest power player, however, would have a profound impact on the future of Fallon McElligott, which finished the year with gross billings of $670.4 million.

Publicis Riding Herd: 2000

Publicis Groupe S.A., based in Paris, France, made no secret of its intention to rival WPP Group and Interpublic. Although

Maurice Levy, chief executive of Publicis, failed in his takeover bid for Chicago's True North Communications (though he owned 10 percent of the company and was its largest shareholder), he did succeed in buying Chicago's Frankel & Company, the majority of Burrell Communications (49 percent), and New York's DeWitt Company. Levy wooed Pat Fallon, but few believed he would sacrifice his agency's hard-won independence. Levy, however, convinced Fallon that his agency would thrive under the aegis of Publicis, and many industry insiders were shocked when the deal went through. In February 2000, Fallon McElligott became a wholly owned subsidiary of Publicis, just as another stand-alone king, Hal Riney, had capitulated. San Francisco's Hal Riney & Partners, like Nelson, DeWitt, and Frankel, had become a part of Publicis as well. These acquisitions gave Publicis extensive holdings in the United States, covering the East and West Coasts, and especially the Midwest.

The U.K.-based Saatchi & Saatchi was next on Levy's hit list, and was added to the Publicis fold by the fall of 2000. In little more than two short years, Publicis had become a powerhouse owning several of the world's most prominent agencies, placing it in the top five advertising behemoths, behind WPP Group, Interpublic, Omnicom, and Havas Advertising. For FM, little seemed changed about the firm or how it conducted business. In a *Chicago Tribune* (June 25, 2000) article, Fallon was quoted as saying, "We love [Publicis]. . . . They're there when we want them; they coach us, mentor us, guide us and take care of us, but they don't get in our pants."

Fallon McElligott was indeed in good company, as its sibling agencies represented many of the world's blue-chip corporations. Frankel was behind the resurgence of fast-food giant McDonald's; Saatchi served Procter & Gamble and Johnson & Johnson; Publicis itself had Coca-Cola and Nestlé; and Fallon still had United Airlines, along with Citibank and EDS (for whom Fallon created the much-loved "Cat Herders" commercial). In a move befitting its new status, FM shed some of its old image and changed its name to focus on itself as a "brand." Fallon McElligott became Fallon Worldwide (FW), with firm outposts taking on the name of their location, such as Fallon London and Fallon New York (its Publicis siblings followed suit as well—Saatchi & Saatchi Worldwide, Nelson Communications Worldwide, etc.). In addition, FW launched a new entity, Fallon Brand Consulting, to identify and develop new branding strategies.

At the end of 2000 FW and Young & Rubicam were told United Airlines would consolidate its advertising (domestic and international) into one global account, awarded to only one agency. Although FW had handled the bulk of United's advertising, since domestic ads accounted for two-thirds of the airline's nearly $100 million advertising budget, the firm was determined to win the whole enchilada. To help with the endeavor was a new creative director, Bob Moore, renowned in the advertising world. Fallon Worldwide's gross billings for 2000 reached a phenomenal $1.0 billion.

A New Era: 2001–04

In January 2001 FW scored a coup: The agency beat out rival Young & Rubicam for United's domestic *and* international advertising, due in part to the agency's increased global positioning as part of the Publicis empire. Next came Gateway's $250 million account, followed by FW's five critically acclaimed mini movies for BMW of North America, excerpted on television and shown in their entirety on the Web. Each short film, known under the overall title of "The Hire," featured British actor Clive Owen and a star-studded supporting cast, top-notch directors (Ang Lee, Guy Ritchie), fast shiny cars, and plenty of high-octane driving. The campaign was considered "advertainment," an immensely successful merger of entertainment and genius product placement. Even movie critics applauded the short films, with Elvis Mitchell of the *New York Times* quoted in *Advertising Age* (July 23, 2001) as calling the mini thrillers "the marriage of commerce and creativity, straddling the ever-dwindling line between art and merchandising."

In the terrorist attacks in September 2001 FW's New York office was damaged and major client United Airlines was devastated. United was not FW's only client to experience hardship in late 2001 and the company itself was forced to lay off 15 percent of its U.S. workforce, the first time the agency ever let employees go in its 20-year existence. Nevertheless, FW forged ahead, believing international expansion was the key to its growth. Two offices in Asia (Hong Kong, Singapore) and one in Brazil (Sao Paolo) were slated to open in 2002.

As the economy strengthened in 2002, so did FW, with new clients (L'Oréal, SoBe drinks, Dyson vacuums) and new hires for its struggling New York office. Parent company Publicis also had been on the prowl, buying U.S.-based agency Bcom3 Group in the fall. Yet by the end of the year FW had lost its footing again (despite great ads for PBS and more mini film installments for BMW), losing two of its longstanding clients, Timex and Nikon, as well as Creative Director Bob Moore. Fallon rebounded again in 2003 by winning the much desired $350 million Subway account and opening an office in Tokyo, Japan, one of the world's top advertising markets. In addition, FW won several awards at the 2003 International Advertising Festival for its BMW (mini films), Citibank (identity theft voiceovers), and Lee Jeans (the return of Buddy Lee) work. The BMW films, which continued to spur the car manufacturer's sales, also became a popular exhibit at New York's Museum of Modern Art.

The rollercoaster ride continued in 2004 as FW resigned the massive Subway account over creative differences, which forced another round of layoffs. The agency also lost several top executives to rivals, including Executive Creative Director and former President David Lubars. Lubars was replaced with British ad man Paul Silburn, from TBWA London, owned by Omnicom. Despite the negatives, however, FW still created memorable ads for Starbucks, Citibank, and United Airlines. When United was forced to seek bankruptcy protection, FW agreed to reduced fees to keep the account.

Mastering the Game: 2005 and Beyond

By 2005 FW had grown into an international power, long one of founder Pat Fallon's dreams. Fallon continued to believe in his quirky and wholly original agency, which he believed relied mostly on "courage and integrity." Commenting to *SHOOT* magazine back in 2001, Fallon had summed up Fallon Worldwide's *raison d'être,* which had remained true in its

nearly 25 years of existence: "Obviously creativity is centered around courage. Our clients hire us for the right reasons; nobody accidentally hires this agency, because we're very clear from the first meeting what we are, what we expect, and how we work with our clients. We're not for everyone. The clarity of our kind of self-identity has been a strong tool over the years."

Principal Divisions

Fallon Brand Consulting; Fallon Hong Kong; Fallon Interactive; Fallon London; Fallon Los Angeles; Fallon Minneapolis; Fallon New York; Fallon Sao Paolo; Fallon Singapore; Fallon Tokyo.

Principal Competitors

BBDO Worldwide; Ogilvy & Mather Worldwide; TBWA Worldwide; True North Communications; Young & Rubicam Worldwide.

Further Reading

"Adman Tom McElligott," *Inc.*, July 1986, pp. 30+.

Canabou, Christine, "Free to Innovate," *Fast Company*, November 2001, p. 60.

Cohen, Warren, "More Adventures in Advertising," *U.S. News & World Report*, January 20, 1997, p. 53.

Cooper, Ann, "Coming into Fallon Country," *ADWEEK Eastern Edition*, January 17, 1994, p. 34.

DeSalvo, Kathy, "Fallon McElligott," *SHOOT*, December 13, 1996, p. 33.

——, "Future Fallon," *SHOOT*, June 14, 1996, p. 21.

Donaton, Scott, "France Is Again a Superpower, If Only in the Advertising World," *Advertising Age*, July 10, 2000, 28.

Dunlap, Bill, "Creative Is King: Fallon Takes to the Global Stage," *SHOOT*, December 7, 2001, pp. 25+.

Froiland, Paul, "Creativity Unlimited," *TC* [Twin Cities], June 1985, pp. 55–62, 64–65.

Geiger, Bob, "Fallon Loses McElligott," *Advertising Age*, December 12, 1988, p. 1.

——, "Rice Leaves FMR to Form Own Shop," *Advertising Age*, August 5, 1985, p. 1.

"Global Growing Pains," *Advertising Age*, January 14, 2002, p. S15.

Goetzl, David, "How Fallon Bested Rivals for United Account," *Advertising Age*, January 29, 2001, p. 12.

——, "United Shops to Duke It Out for Global Biz," *Advertising Age*, December 11, 2000, p. 1.

Goldman, Debra, "Camp Fallon," *ADWEEK Eastern Edition*, April 27, 1992, pp. 22+.

——, "Pat Fallon Plays Mr. Fix-It—And Helps Scali Around," *ADWEEK*, March 16, 1992, p. 9.

Harragan, Betty L., "The $10 Million Blunder," *Working Woman*, May 1988, p. 94.

Heitzman, Beth, "Fallon Buys Back Freedom from WPP," *ADWEEK*, October 25, 1993, p. 5.

Jaffe, Andrew, "Reach for the Skies," *ADWEEK*, April 10, 1995, p. 25.

Keller, Martin, "Fallon McElligott Grows Up," *Corporate Report-Minnesota*, January 1991, pp. 61+.

Kiley, David, and Beth Heitzman, "Fallon McElligott: Creative Coming Attractions," *ADWEEK*, May 10, 1993, p. 1.

"The Kings of Madison Avenue," *Campaign*, April 23, 2001, p. S16.

MacArthur, Kate, "After 9/11: Fallon's New York Office Recuperates," *Advertising Age*, August 5, 2002, p. 14.

Madison, Cathy, et al., "Most Valuable Player; Pat Burnham," *ADWEEK*, February 4, 1991, p. CR4.

——, ''National Agency Report Cards; The Year in Review,'' *ADWEEK,* April 7, 1997, pp. 28–34.

——, ''Tom McElligott: The Demanding One Is Back,'' *ADWEEK,* November 20, 1989, p. 34.

''Paris-Based Firm Becomes Powerhouse After Failing to Buy Chicago Firm,'' *Chicago Tribune,* June 25, 2000.

Rich, Andrew, ''Adlife in Minneapolis,'' *Madison Avenue,* October 1986, p. 52.

Sellers, Patricia, ''Leo Burnett: Undone by an Upstart,'' *Fortune,* May 26, 1997, pp. 98–102.

Shahoda, Susan, ''Tom McElligott Exits from Fallon McElligott,'' *Back Stage,* December 16, 1988, p. 1.

Sharkey, Betsy, ''Frozen Out: For Ten Years Pat Burnham Was the Creative Center of Arguably the Country's Most Creative Shop,'' *ADWEEK,* March 22, 1993, p. 28.

Spadoni, Marie, ''Fallon McElligott Rolls Stone into the '80s,'' *Advertising Age,* August 18, 1986, p. S1.

Vagnoni, Anthony, ''Behind the Wheel,'' *Advertising Age,* July 23, 2001, p. 12.

Watts, Jenny, ''Fallon Opens Trio of Global Offices,'' *Campaign,* October 12, 2001, p. 5.

''World's Top 25,'' *Advertising Age,* April 23, 2001, p. S31.

—April Dougal Gasbarre
—update: Nelson Rhodes

Freixenet S.A.

Joan Sala 2
Sant Sadurni d'Anoia
E-08770
Spain
Telephone: +34 93 891 70 00
Fax: +34 93 818 30 95
Web site: http://www.freixenet.es

Private Company
Incorporated: 1928
Employees: 1,260
Sales: EUR 514 million ($590 million) (2004 est.)
NAIC: 312130 Wineries

Freixenet S.A. is one of Spain's leading producers of cava (Spain's sparkling wine alternative to champagne) and a leading producer of still wines as well. Founded in 1861, the company has been producing cava since 1914, including its world-renowned Carta Nevada, launched in 1941, and Cordon Negro, launched in 1974. More recently, the company has released premium Cordon Negro Vintage Cava Brut, launched in 2001. Lower wages and lower production costs in general have enabled Freixenet to position its award-winning cavas at prices far lower than France's premium champagne. Freixenet also has established an international presence, with sales to more than 150 countries. International sales account for more than 50 percent of the group's total. The company also has become an international wine producer, with wineries in the United States (Gloria Ferrer), Australia (Wingara Wine Group), and France (Yvon Mau in Bordeaux and Henri Abelé in the Champagne region), as well as vineyards in Mexico, Argentina, and Chile. This expansion is also part of the group's efforts, begun in the 1980s, to gain scale in the still wines category. By 2005, still wines represented 40 percent of the group's annual sales. Freixenet remains a private company controlled by the founding Ferrer family, led by Chairman and CEO Jose Luis Bonet Ferrer and his cousins Enrique Hevia Ferrer and Eudaldo Bonet Ferrer.

Founding a Sparkling Wine Dynasty in the 19th Century

Grape-growing and winemaking were long a part of Spanish culture, with evidence of Spanish wines dating back to pre-Phoenician times. For the most part, the country's wineries remained small, local affairs, and even into the beginning of the 20th century, Spanish wines stimulated little interest from the international wine community. If the country's wines had not yet reached levels meeting international wine standards, Spain's wine industry flourished, and into the 20th century the country boasted the world's largest number of acres of vineyards. At the same time, the country continued to develop and refine its own wine types, including its soon-to-be-famous cava.

A product of the Pinedes region south of Barcelona, cava (the word means "cave" in Spanish) employed French champagne-making techniques, but used only local grape varieties, including Macabeu, Parellada, and Xarello. Like champagne, cava was fermented in the bottle, producing a sparkling wine. While cava had long been a regional and national favorite (one company, Cordorniu, traced its own origins back to 1551), the sparkling wine's greatest success came through the efforts of a relatively young company, Freixenet.

Based in the tiny village of Sant Sadurni d'Anoia, south of Barcelona, Freixenet had its roots in the mid-19th century, when Francesc Sala I Ferrés founded a winery, Casa Sala, in 1861. That winery later became the first in the region to begin exporting its wines by the end of the century.

Sala's son Joan Sala i Tubella became head of the family business toward the end of the 1800s and launched the company into the production of cava as well. Sala's daughter, Dolors Sala i Vivé married Pere Ferrer i Bosch, whose family owned another local wine estate, La Freixeneda, in existence since the 13th century. It was this generation that transformed the small family-owned winery into one of the world's leading producers of sparkling wines.

In 1914, the Ferrers decided to focus their winery exclusively on the production of cava. The company also adopted a new name, Freixenet, and adopted a new label, Freixenet Casa

Sala. Freixenet also built new cellars for aging its sparkling wines. These cellars, constructed in Sant Sadurni d'Anoia, later became renowned for their beauty. They were also among the world's largest, holding more than 150 million bottles at the beginning of the 21st century.

International Sparkling Wine Leader from the 1950s

By the 1920s, Freixenet's cava began to be recognized for its high quality, and sales grew steadily through that decade. The company formally incorporated as Freixenet in 1928, and by 1930 had begun its first exports. In 1935, the company established its first international subsidiary, opening an office in New Jersey, in the United States, as its exports to that country began to climb.

The Spanish Civil War spelled disaster for the company, when Pere Ferrer and a son were kidnapped and killed. Instead of folding, however, the company, now led solely by Dolors Ferrer, went on to still greater triumphs. A new turning point in the company's history came in 1941, with the launch of a new cava label, Carta Nevada. Packaged in a distinctive frosted white glass bottle, Carta Nevada proved a huge success both in Spain and abroad and, despite the difficult export market during World War II, helped establish Freixenet as one of the world's leading sparkling wine names.

A large part of Freixenet's success in the latter half of the century came through the efforts of another of Dolors's sons, Jose Ferrer i Sala, who took over as head of the company in 1957. Into the early 1970s, Freixenet grew to become Spain's leading cava house, backed by the continued success of the Carta Nevada brand. The company's marketing efforts were also particularly successful, and later campaigns were to feature notable personalities such as Liza Minelli, Shirley MacClaine, Raquel Welch, Sharon Stone, Penelope Cruz, Antonio Banderas, and others.

The introduction of a classification system, codifying production methods, grape varieties, and aging methods, among other factors, helped establish higher wine standards for the country's wine industry. Cava became an early beneficiary of the new Denominacion de Origen appellation (DO), introduced in 1970.

Ferrer in particular recognized a new opportunity to promote the Freixenet brand on an international level. With lower production costs, but often boasting equal or superior quality, Spain's cavas were able to position themselves as low-priced alternatives to premium-priced champagne and other sparkling wine types. Freixenet adopted this pricing policy especially with the launch of a new, internationally oriented label, Cordon Negro. Launched in 1974, and packaged in a distinctive specially ground black bottle, Cordon Negro became a huge success for Freixenet and served as its flagship. By the early 2000s, the company's exports reached more than 150 countries.

Ferrer spotted a new opportunity in the early 1980s—the introduction of cava-styled sparkling wines in the newly emerging Sonoma County wine center in California. Ferrer bought land (a former cow pasture) in Carneros and began planting vines there, establishing a new winery, named Gloria Ferrer after his wife, in 1986. By then, Freixenet also had expanded its sparkling wine production elsewhere, launching the Dolores Sala Vivé winery in Querétaro state in Mexico, in 1980.

Adding Premium Still Wines in the New Century

While remaining committed to its sparkling wine production, Freixenet sought to extend its portfolio into the premium still wines category. The company made its first extension into this market in 1985, when it acquired Rene Barbier, a Pinedes region winery founded by Avignon native Léon Barbier in the late 19th century.

Through the 1990s and into the new century, Freixenet continued to add to its portfolio of still and sparkling wines. The company added a new Pinedes area winery, Segura Viudas, a sparkling wine producer that had begun marketing its label in 1969. The company then began seeking to expand beyond the Pinedes DO region, acquiring Valdubón in Ribera de Duero,

Morlanda in Priorat, and Vionta in Rías Baixas. The company then grouped these wineries under an umbrella label, The Heredad Collection.

Freixenet's expansion continued into the 2000s. In 2001, the company turned to Australia, buying up the Wingara Wine Group for $18 million. That company's operations included the Katnook, Riddoch, and Deakin wine estates in Coonawarra and Mildura, with more than 2,400 acres of vineyards, and a strong export business, particularly to the United Kingdom and North America.

In 2001, also, Freixenet entered the French still wine market, buying up the Bordeaux region's Yvon Mau. The company also moved into the French champagne market, buying Reims-based Henri Abelé, one of the oldest of the region's champagne producers. By then, Freixenet had passed to a new generation of the Ferrer family, under Josep Ferrer, after father Jose's retirement in 2000.

Back at home, Freixenet found a new outlet for its cava division, when it acquired Chandon Cava from the French luxury products group LVMH for $12.8 million in 2003. That same year, the company launched a new luxury cava label, Cordon Negro Vintage Cava 2001, designed to meet a price point between premium cava and the higher-priced champagnes.

As it moved toward mid-decade, Freixenet showed no signs of slowing down. The company entered Argentina in the early part of the decade, before launching its own winery there in 2003. That year, also, the company began establishing a wine producing presence in Chile as well. By 2004, Freixenet had launched its first Chilean label, Terra Nova.

At the end of 2004, Freixenet grew again, this time with the EUR 10 million purchase of Santamaria Lopez, a winery located in the well-known Rioja region. The company then announced its interest in expanding into another increasingly popular wine producing market, South Africa. A number of observers suggested that the group's further expansion might require a public offering; nonetheless, the founding Ferrer family retained tight control of their company. By 2005, Freixenet had succeeded in balancing its portfolio, with still wines representing some 40 percent of the group's sales of more than EUR 514 million in 2004, while remaining the world's leading seller of sparkling wines.

Principal Subsidiaries

Freixenet (Dws) Ltd. (U.K.); Freixenet Alpes GmbH (Switzerland); Freixenet Argentina, S.A.; Freixenet Atlantic (U.S.A.); Freixenet Australia; Freixenet Canada; Freixenet Caribe (Cuba); Freixenet France S.A.R.L.; Freixenet GmbH; Freixenet Japan Inc; Freixenet Mexico, S.A. de C.V.; Freixenet Nordic AB (Sweden); Freixenet Portugal Lda.; Freixenet Sp. z.o.o. (Poland); Freixenet S.p.A. (Italy); Freixenet USA; Z.A.O. Freixenet (Russia).

Principal Competitors

LVMH-Moet Hennessy Louis Vuitton S.A.; Dr. August Oetker KG; Allied Domecq PLC; Sapporo Holdings Ltd.; Pernod Ricard S.A.; Larios Pernod Ricard S.A.; Bacardi Espana S.A.; Osborne Compania S.A.; Ricard S.A.; Marie Brizard et Roger International S.A.; Remy Martin et Cie S.A.; J Garcia Carrion S.A.

Further Reading

Bates, Joe, ''Cava's Chance to Make a Splash: Long-Term Changes in the Champagne Market Could Mean Growth Opportunities for Sparkling Wine Producers,'' *Duty Free International,* February 1, 2004, p. 27.

''The Freixenet Group Has Entered into a Long-Term Distribution Agreement with Chateau Lascombes,'' *StateWays,* September-October 2004, p. 9.

''Freixenet Is Still Confident,'' *Grocer,* May 22, 2004, p. 70.

''Freixenet's Glass Runneth Over,'' *Business Week,* May 24, 1999, p. 23.

''Freixenet's Sparkle Has a Vintage Quality,'' *Grocer,* November 15, 2003, p. 65.

Phillips, Richard, ''The Spanish Grapes of Wrath,'' *Independent on Sunday,* November 30, 1997, p. 8.

Walker, Larry, ''Heredad/Freixenet Takes Terror Seriously,'' *Wines & Vines,* January 2001, p. 120.

—M.L. Cohen

Gold's Gym International, Inc.

358 Hampton Drive
Venice, California 90291
U.S.A.
Telephone: (310) 392-3005
Toll Free: (800) 457-5375
Fax: (310) 452-3269
Web site: http://www.goldsgym.com

Private Company
Incorporated: 1965
Employees: 30,000
NAIC: 713940 Fitness and Recreational Sports Centers

Gold's Gym International, Inc. is one of the largest fitness club chains in the world, one of few global players in a highly fragmented market. The company operates primarily through franchising. Gold's Gym claims 2.5 million members worldwide, and some 600 gyms found in 27 countries. The chain began with a single establishment, which became the center of the sport of bodybuilding in the United States. Though Gold's was originally known as a no-frills gym for serious weightlifters, the chain has modified its image to appeal to a broader class of consumers. Gold's Gym offers classes such as group exercise, yoga, Pilates, and spinning, as well as personal training and pure weightlifting. The private company earns income through franchising, operating company-owned gyms, and through selling apparel and accessories licensed with the Gold's logo. The company was founded by Joe Gold in 1965. Gold sold the company in 1970, and it changed hands several times since then. In 2004 the firm was acquired by the Texas-based investment group TRT Holdings.

Joe Gold's Gym

The Gold name still graces the company Joe Gold sold after only five years of running it. Though his ownership was brief, Gold gave the chain its image and its intrinsic tie to the sport of bodybuilding. Gold also designed much of the weightlifting equipment associated with the sport. Joe Gold was born in Los Angeles in 1922, and he built his first gym at his parents' house while he was a teen, using found objects such as junked car parts for weights. Body-building was not much of a recognized sport during Gold's youth, though even then the area around Santa Monica beach near Los Angeles was familiarly known as "Muscle Beach." Gold became a Muscle Beach regular until he left Los Angeles to join the Navy during World War II. During his service, he was injured by a bomb blast and spent months in the hospital. He served in the Navy again during the Korean War, and also joined the Merchant Marines. He brought his homemade weights with him whenever he shipped out.

Gold opened his first gym in New Orleans in 1951, called Ajax Gym. But at that point, he was not much interested in the business end of running the gym, and he soon abandoned the venture. By 1954 he was back in Los Angeles, where he landed work as a manly backdrop for comedienne Mae West. In 1963, Gold began an arrangement with the Muscle Beach Weightlifting Club in Santa Monica, California, to build an indoor facility. The partnership did not work out, so eventually Gold went it alone, and opened Gold's Gym, in Venice, California, in 1965. (The moniker "Muscle Beach" soon migrated to Venice as well.) In an interview with *Flex* magazine (March 2002), Gold claimed that his gym was "the first bodybuilding gym made for bodybuilders. . . . In fact, I'm not bragging," he continued, "but I think for bodybuilders it was the best-built gym in the world at that time." Gold had designed and built all the equipment himself, and nothing else like it existed. The gym attracted serious bodybuilders, not only from California, but from all over the world.

Bodybuilding at the time was a hobby confined to a small group of competitors. The sport first got wide recognition in 1977, as a result of the movie *Pumping Iron,* featuring bodybuilder Arnold Schwarzenegger. Schwarzenegger, later a movie actor and then governor of California, came to Gold's Gym in 1968. He was a regular there in the very early years of his career, and became a lifelong friend of Joe Gold. Many of the greats of the sport worked out at Gold's Gym in the 1960s. However, Joe Gold himself grew discontented with running the place, and in 1970 he sold Gold's Gym for $50,000. The new owners were Bud Danitz and Dave Sachs. Gold went back to being a merchant marine until in 1977 he opened another gym,

World Gym. His connection to Gold's Gym lasted only those first five years.

Growth of the Chain in the 1980s

Joe Gold sold his business a few years too early. The book *Pumping Iron* was published in 1975, and when the movie debuted in 1977, Arnold Schwarzenegger became a household name, and bodybuilding transformed from an obscure backwater sport to the proud hobby of men and women alike. Celebrities from other sports fields, as well as actors and entertainers, were drawn to bodybuilding. Many sought out Gold's, both because it had been featured in *Pumping Iron* and because it differed from many other gyms of the time in its plainness and simplicity. While other gyms featured comfortable changing rooms, racquetball courts, juice bars, and other accoutrements, Gold's was bare, gritty, and unadorned. An article in *IronMan* (May 1975) described the famous Gold's as "definitely not a plush gym" that was only about as big as "a medium-sized store." Nevertheless, it was the "in" gym, soon attracting not only the greats of bodybuilding but non-athletes such as singer Linda Rondstadt, who used the gym to get in shape.

Gold's Gym changed hands again in 1977, bought by bodybuilder Ken Sprague. That year Gold's hosted the Mr. America contest. In subsequent years, Gold's hosted other major bodybuilding competitions, including the first national championship contest for women. In 1979, another group of investors bought Gold's. These were two bodybuilding champions, Pete Mrymkowski and Tim Kimber, along with architect Ed Connors. The price for the gym was $100,000, merely twice what Joe Gold had sold it for in 1970. This latest change in ownership, however, marked a new era for the gym.

The new owners began franchising the Gold's name. Ed Connors opened the first franchise in 1980 in San Francisco. The chain developed quickly, and by 1988, there were 220 Gold's Gyms in the United States, and another 50 in foreign countries. The Gold's image loosened up to attract more mainstream consumers. The rise in Gold's Gym's franchise business followed an increasing interest in fitness in general in the United States. Gold's aimed to attract both women and men, finding new customers in people who wanted to stay fit and healthy, and so going beyond its core audience of serious weightlifters. Gold's also began selling clothing in 1980, and then added a line of nutritional supplements. These were sold exclusively

through the gyms until 1988. By that year, the company was bringing in 80 percent of its revenue from clothing sales.

The company increased its sales of accessories in the late 1980s. In 1988 it began selling its clothing at department stores and sporting goods stores as well as in its own franchises. The company next made an arrangement with a Los Angeles company, American Marketing Works, to extend the Gold's logo to a wider array of consumer goods. The Gold's logo of a straining weightlifter began appearing on shoes, vitamins and nutritional supplements, sunglasses, skincare products, and even children's clothes. With the signing of this licensing agreement in 1990, Gold's also began national advertising. In the early 1990s, Gold's had over 300 gyms around the world, as it expanded across Europe and ventured into Japan, Greece, and Australia. While the original Gold's had been the mecca for bodybuilders worldwide, by the early 1990s, Gold's managers described the chain as catering to families and people interested in fitness. Though the logo showed a grunting muscleman, the chain's image had softened considerably.

Competition in the 1990s

Health club membership rose quickly in the 1990s as more and more people used gyms to exercise and stay fit. In 1987, health club membership nationwide stood at 13.8 million, with most members in the 18- to 34-year-old age group. Over the next decade, health club membership climbed to 22.4 million, and there was an especially sharp increase in memberships among people 35 and older. Membership grew strongly in the South and West in the United States. Gold's was one of just a few big players in the health club market. By 1993, the chain had about 400 gyms worldwide. At that time they were all franchises except the Venice, California location. With the Gold's name recognized coast to coast, the company stepped up its marketing. In 1993 it brought out a line of sports drinks, licensed through a division of Everfresh Beverages. Gold's brand Isotonic Quenchers and Super Teas competed against market leader Gatorade and other similar products from major beverage manufacturers. The sports drinks line was a fast-growing market category, and Gold's hoped to extend its reputation in the fitness field to its new products. *Advertising Age* (April 12, 1993) summed up the new line's appeal as "drinks for people who take fitness seriously." Though Gold's still maintained its roots as the crusty gym for serious weightlifters, its facilities were not as bare as they had once been. A new Gold's franchise in Manhattan, for example, which opened in 1994, boasted 30,000 square feet of space, including a pool and 3,000-square-foot aerobic facility, a far cry from the modest store-sized Venice gym. The Manhattan gym had extensive weightlifting equipment, but it also offered child care, boxing lessons, self-defense classes, and a computerized nutritional analysis program.

Gold's largest competitors were Bally Total Fitness Centers Corp. and Fitness Holdings, Inc., owner of 24 Hour Fitness. These two companies owned their own gyms instead of franchising. Most of the industry was still made up of very small operators, however. Only about a third of all U.S. health clubs in the mid-1990s were owned by companies with two or more clubs, meaning most were single-location businesses. In the mid-1990s Gold's continued to press its licensing arrangements, leveraging its well-known name and logo. The company brought out a line of bath and beauty products in 1997, which included such things as herbal shampoo and floral-scented body spritzer. Gold's had roughly a dozen licensing arrangements with different companies by that time. It had a Gold's Visa card; produced men's, women's and children's clothing; sold vitamins and muscle rubs; and cross-marketed the well-known "Buns of Steel" line of fitness videos, giving out free two-week Gold's memberships to consumers who purchased the Warner-Vision video. Gold's was able to sell its goods both through its own franchises and through nationwide retailers. By 1997, some 40 percent of Gold's revenue came from licensing. About half its licensing revenue was from gym equipment, and most of the rest was from clothing.

With the overall growth in the fitness club industry, Gold's expanded its franchising. Between 1994 and 1997, the chain added 50 franchises in the United States, for a total of 450. Gold's international market also grew strongly. In 1994 the company had 30 overseas franchises, and by 1997 that number had grown to 54. Even with this solid growth, because Gold's Gyms were owned by franchisees, not the company, Gold's admitted it sometimes had trouble keeping up with its large competitors. Some Gold's franchisees even sold their gyms to rival companies such as Fitness Holdings and another major player, Town Sports International. In a June 29, 1998 interview with the *Los Angeles Business Journal*, Gold's co-owner and CFO Ed Connors speculated that the company might merge with some of its bigger franchise operators, and then take the company public. Connors claimed the company was exploring a public offering, though with no time table or sense of urgency.

In 1999, at least part of this plan came to fruition. Two brothers, Kirk and John Galiani, who owned eight Gold's franchises in the Washington, D.C. area, bought the parent company. The deal was estimated to be worth between $50 million and $100 million. The Galianis had bought their first Gold's franchise in 1990 and rapidly built up a presence around Washington. They were alarmed to see fellow franchisees sell out to rival companies because they did not have enough capital to expand. The Galiani brothers bought Gold's Gym with the intent to double the number of franchises over the next five years. The brothers also planned to grow through acquisitions and through building new company-owned gyms. The Galianis, like the previous owners, also hoped to take the company public at some point.

Changes in the 2000s

The new owners made significant changes at the company. The Galianis broke the company into three business units, corporate, franchising, and licensing. The corporate unit owned and managed 19 gyms by 2001. Gold's also added 100 franchises in two years. The company gave franchisees more power, binding them into a national vendor program so they could buy in bulk for better rates than as individual gym owners. Its licensing area also grew, with new arrangements inked with major companies, such as the women's fitness clothing company Marika Group, Inc. and Icon Health and Fitness, manufacturer of home fitness equipment. All seemed to be going well for the company under its new management. Yet the Galiani brothers stepped down from leadership of Gold's in 2001. They were

the company's major shareholders and they retained their seats on the board, but the brothers claimed to want to return to what they knew best, operating individual gyms. The Galianis would focus on their Washington, D.C.-area gyms, with plans to build more over the next few years.

The Gold's chain continued to lead the field in the number of gyms it had around the world. Growth in the United Kingdom was particularly strong in the early 2000s. Gold's had first come to the United Kingdom in 1990 under a licensing arrangement with the American singer Jermaine Jackson. But Jackson's venture did not flourish, and the Gold's brand was not then a success in England. The license later changed hands, and under the leadership of Karl Sandhu of Vistastar Leisure, the brand expanded dramatically. Refurbished Gold's in the United Kingdom were large, around 20,000 square feet, with attached restaurants and bars run by contractors. One newly remodeled English Gold's was built inside an Art Deco theater from the 1930s. The new Gold's featured a five-floor gym, a pool, spa, sauna, and ice-filled "igloo room." It retained the theater's original decorated ceiling and its Wurlitzer organ. This kind of facility was a far cry from the early Gold's, and yet the British licenser Vistastar used the celebrity status of the original Gold's and its many Hollywood connections to market the new model. The company hoped to build 40 to 50 corporate-owned Gold's Gyms in the United Kingdom over the next ten years, and also to franchise perhaps a hundred more.

While marketing in Britain seemed to proceed with confidence and panache, domestic advertising did not go smoothly. Gold's hired a new advertising agency in 2003, hoping specifically to shed what it called the "intimidation factor" of its hardcore bodybuilding past and create a friendlier image. This seemed to be what Gold's had been doing for years. But the company ditched its new agency after only five months, amid concern that the corporation, the agency, and the franchise-holders were at cross-purposes. The company hired a new advertising agency in 2004, and developed a new slogan, "Train anyway," and its first television advertising campaign in five years. In June 2004, the company announced it had been bought by a new group of investors. The sale price was estimated at $160 million. The new owner was an Irving, Texas-based investment group called TRT Holdings. New marketing under TRT's ownership concentrated on unifying an image for the franchisees. Advertising focused on stories of people who had successfully trained at Gold's, and the gyms' décor was to use historical photographs of famous Gold's patrons such as Schwarzenegger and the early Venice Gold's of Muscle Beach.

Principal Competitors

Bally Total Fitness Centers Corp.; Fitness Holdings, Inc.

Further Reading

Antuck, Al, "The Famous Gold's Gym," *IronMan*, May 1975.
Bittar, Christine, "Gold's Gym Will Weigh in with New Ads, Message," *Brandweek*, June 21, 2004, p. 12.
Chamis, Eleni, "Execs Take a Breather," *Washington Business Journal*, September 14, 2001, p. 3.
Flass, Rebecca, and Griswold, Alicia, "Gold's Tries to Shed 'Intimidation Factor'," *Adweek*, June 9, 2003, p. 20.

——, "Henderson and Gold's Gym: 'It Was Doomed'," *Adweek*, November 4, 2003, p. NA.

"Gold's Gym Is Pressing Its Way into the Manhattan Fitness Scene," *New York Times*, August 21, 1994, p. CY4.

Hinsberg, Pat, "Gold's Gym Wants Marketing Muscle," *Adweek*, January 8, 1990, p. 4.

Horak, Terri, "Exercising Options: As the Health-and-Fitness Craze Cools Down, Familiar Brands and Cross Promotions Heat Up," *Billboard*, October 18, 1997, p. 64.

Israel, Betsy, "The Muscle Merchant of Venice," *GQ*, March 1991, pp. 242–247, 314.

Johnson, Branwell, "Fitness Chains Strive to Diversify Offerings," *Marketing Week*, October 21, 2004, p. 23.

Klein, Frederick C., "On Sports: Bodybuilding Czar Joe Gold," *Wall Street Journal*, December 8, 1989, p. 1.

Maglera, Marcy, "Gold's Steps in Beverage Ring," *Advertising Age*, April 12, 1983, p. 12.

Merritt, Greg, "Good As Gold," *Flex*, March 2002, p. 174.

Milton, Tina, "Karl Sandhu: Going for Gold's," *Leisure & Hospitality Business*, May 2, 2002, p. S12.

Pristin, Terry, "Health Clubs Consolidate As Membership Grows," *New York Times*, August 16, 1998, p. 35.

Schwarzenegger, Arnold, "Heart of Gold," *Muscle & Fitness*, November 2004, p. 24.

Sims, Calvin, "Argentine Women Break Social Barriers to Pump Iron," *New York Times*, December 20, 1995, p. C3.

Stoughton, Stephanie, "Brothers Stake Their Claim to Gold's Gym," *Washington Post*, August 27, 1999, p. E01.

Taub, Daniel, "A Golden Name," *Los Angeles Business Journal*, June 29, 1998, p. 3.

—A. Woodward

Haynes Publishing Group P.L.C.

Sparkford, Yeovil, Somerset
BA22 7JJ
United Kingdom
Telephone: +44 1963 440635
Fax: +44 1963 440825
Web site: http://www.haynes.co.uk

Public Company
Incorporated: 1960 as J.H. Haynes & Co. Ltd.
Employees: 295
Sales: £39.01 million ($71.45 million) (2004)
Stock Exchanges: London
Ticker Symbol: HYNS.L
NAIC: 323117 Books Printing; 334612 Prerecorded
    Compact Disc (Except Software), Tape, and Record
    Reproducing; 511130 Book Publishers; 511190 Other
    Publishers

Haynes Publishing Group P.L.C. publishes repair manuals for automobiles and other vehicles. Its traditional production process involves complete disassembly, step-by-step instructions, and copious photographs. Best known for its advice on the upkeep of cars, Haynes also offers titles concerning the care of men, women, and babies. The Sutton Publishing subsidiary offers history-related titles. The company sells more than one million books a year in the United Kingdom alone.

Origins

John Haynes started his publishing empire at age 16. While still a student he wrote and hand-illustrated a 48-page guide describing the work he did making a sports car out of an Austin Seven. The booklet, *Building a 750cc Special,* found a receptive mail-order market via an ad in an automotive magazine (*Motor Sport*). The 250 copies sold out in ten days, noted a detailed history of the company by one of its former editorial directors, Jeff Clew.

Haynes set up a partnership with his younger brother David in 1957, and produced a handful of automotive titles while training as a pilot officer with the Royal Air Force in Germany. After his military service ended (he later rejoined the RAF), Haynes set up

his own publishing company in a small office on London's Regent Street. It was officially founded as J.H. Haynes & Co. Ltd. on May 18, 1960. Unfortunately his nearby warehouse and "Sporting Motorists' Bookshop" caught fire, so in 1962, Haynes transferred this operation to his parents' garage in Yeovil, England.

In 1965 Haynes produced his first proper repair manual, featuring step-by-step instructions and photographs. An Austin Healey "Frogeye" Sprite, dismantled while Haynes was stationed in Aden with the RAF, was the subject vehicle. The first run of 3,000 copies sold out within six months, according to Clew. Haynes was soon obliged to lease new space for the growing business.

His brother's business, David M. Haynes & Co. Ltd., was handling the printing. David sold this to J.H. Haynes when he himself reentered the RAF in 1967. (David Haynes would return to Haynes Publishing in 1979.)

The business expanded rapidly throughout the 1970s and 1980s. In 1972 the company acquired a former Unigate creamery in Sparkford, 120 miles east of London, which became the site of its headquarters.

In 1973, Haynes capitalized upon a unique opportunity to buy what was then Britain's leading automotive publisher, G.T. Foulis & Co. Ltd. The family-owned company also published general interest books. The same year saw the introduction of Haynes's first motorcycle titles, as well as the addition of a warehouse in Leeds to facilitate deliveries to northern England and Scotland. (It would be closed in 1991.)

Haynes Publishing began selling manuals in the United States for European and Japanese imports. The U.K. books were briefly distributed by New York's Drake Publishing in the early 1970s. Haynes then set up a subsidiary, Haynes Publications Inc., in Los Angeles in 1974. In the late 1970s Haynes began producing manuals for American cars, first in Los Angeles and then for a time at the company's Somerset, England base.

Public in 1979

Haynes listed shares on the London Stock Exchange on November 29, 1979. Thirty percent of employees took advan-

---

Company Perspectives:

Haynes Publishing Group P.L.C. is the worldwide market leader in the production and sale of automotive and motorcycle repair manuals.

Every Haynes manual is based on a complete vehicle stripdown and rebuild in our workshops, so that the instructions to our customers are inherently practical and easy to follow.

The Group publishes many other DIY titles as well as an extensive array of books about motor sport, vehicles and general transport. Through its subsidiary Sutton Publishing, the Group also publishes a range of military and general history books and biographies.

---

tage of an offer to buy discounted shares. A holding company had first been created to link the various businesses in the United Kingdom and United States. Group turnover was about £5 million a year.

Haynes ventured further into mainstream publishing with the 1981 acquisition of Oxford Illustrated Press (OIP) from Blackwells. The tiny company produced 35 titles, including the popular *Classic Car* series. Two years later, Haynes acquired another 18 automotive titles from Gentry books. In 1985, 64 Frederick Warne transportation-related titles were acquired from Penguin Books. Not all attempts at expansion were successful. The company made a disastrous foray into magazine publishing in 1983 with *Automobile Sport*.

An advertising and PR agency, Camway Autographics Limited, was formed in January 1984, named after the West Camel farmhouse where early printing operations had been established. Haynes Garages Limited was established in 1985 to handle the group's car buying.

As Haynes grew, it acquired state-of-the-art printing equipment. During the 1970s this was supplied by U.S. manufacturers. The company was able to acquire a five-color Heidelberg press from Germany in 1985 at a cost of £500,000. A second one was added in 1990.

John Haynes's collection of classic vehicles became the nucleus of the Sparkford Motor Museum, later called the Haynes Motor Museum, which officially opened in July 1985 in conjunction with the company's 25th anniversary celebration. Located near the publishing plant, the museum began with 26 autos and three motorcycles. A unique aspect was that all of the vehicles were driveable; the facility even began renting out its 1971 Rolls-Royce Corniche convertible for weddings, noted Clew. The highlight of the collection was a very rare, $1 million Duesenberg Model J once owned by *Los Angeles Times* publisher Otis Chandler.

In 1987, Haynes acquired another press, the Oxford Publishing Company (OPC), from Cassell PLC. OPC brought 200 titles to the line of railroad books Haynes had been starting to develop.

U.S. sales got a big boost when the Auto Shack (later AutoZone) chain began stocking Haynes titles in 1987. A $1

million warehouse was subsequently acquired in Nashville, Tennessee. According to Jeff Clew, the company ended the decade with a 40 percent market share in the United States.

Patrick Stephens Limited, an imprint established in 1967, was acquired from HarperCollins for £750,000 in 1989–90. Haynes also bought Regency Reprographics (Bath) Limited, which extended its color printing capabilities.

The company cut back its general publishing program and laid off some U.K. workers during the recession of the early 1990s. The group managed to break even in 1990–91 on sales of £19.2 million.

U.S. Printing in 1993

Haynes North America Inc. was formed in 1991 to look after the company's U.S. publishing operations. Haynes Publications Inc. continued to distribute the books. Haynes formed Odcombe Press in Nashville in July 1993. Prior to this, titles for the American market had been printed in England.

By the mid-1990s, the group was posting record profits; two-thirds of sales came from outside the United Kingdom. Haynes developed a series of Spanish language manuals and established distribution subsidiaries in France and Sweden. By 1998 Haynes led the market in Scandinavia and was developing business in Russia. Haynes began producing manuals for the Australian car market in 1997. A major motion picture about the *Titanic* buoyed international sales of titles related to the doomed ocean liner.

Another notable success was *The Bike Book: Everything You Need to Know to Help You Enjoy and Maintain Your Bicycle*, which was launched as cycling was peaking in popularity. It eventually sold 500,000 copies worldwide, noted Clew, and spawned a series of titles related to touring. Other new do-it-yourself lines in the late 1990s covered home improvement and camping.

Oxford Publishing Company, the railway specialist, was sold off to Ian Allan Publishing in 1998. Haynes also folded the G.T. Foulis imprint. A diagnostic garage equipment unit was launched in 1999 but sold off after four years.

Navigating Challenges After 2000

Revenues were £28.2 million in 2000, with a pretax profit of £4.1 million. During the year, Haynes acquired U.K.-based history publisher Sutton Publishing Limited from Guiton Group Ltd. for £4 million. Sutton had 2,000 titles in its backlist and annual revenues of about $9 million.

Haynes began printing its U.K. automotive manuals at the U.S. plant, allowing its British presses to concentrate on general publishing. The Sparkford plant had just undergone a £2 million upgrade and had recently begun taking on printing projects for third-party publishers.

The company posted the first loss in its history (£700,000) in the 2001 fiscal year, though revenues were up 18 percent. During the year, Haynes acquired the consumer business of its main U.S. rival, Chilton, from WG Nichols, which continued to produce automotive manuals for the professional market. (A bid

Key Dates:

1960: Haynes Publishing is founded.
1965: The first "Haynes Owners Workshop Manual" is published for the Austin Healey "Frogeye" Sprite.
1973: The first motorcycle titles are launched; G.T. Foulis & Co. Ltd. is acquired.
1974: A U.S. subsidiary is established.
1979: Haynes goes public on the London Stock Exchange.
1981: Oxford Illustrated Press is acquired.
1985: The Haynes Motor Museum officially opens.
2000: History specialist Sutton Publishing Limited is acquired.
2001: Haynes acquires rival Chilton's consumer business.
2002: Australian rival Gregory Automotive Publications is acquired for £2 million.

to acquire Chilton five years earlier had been blocked by antitrust regulators.) Another U.S. publisher, Clymer Publications Inc., had stopped producing car manuals several years earlier but remained a competitor in the motorcycle market. Haynes bought its main Australian rival, Gregory Automotive Publications, for £2.1 million in 2002.

The General Publishing division began producing manuals for the care and maintenance of human beings. The first, *The Man Manual: The Practical Step-By-Step Guide to Men's Health,* was published in 2003 in collaboration with the Men's Health Forum. It was followed the next year by *The Baby Manual* and *The Sex Manual.* This diversification helped Haynes post record pretax profits of £7.1 million for fiscal 2002–03.

Another reason for the turnaround, reported the *Financial Times,* was the very successful Max Power series of manuals, whose name was licensed from an auto customization magazine popular among young men. Each Max Power manual featured more than 1,000 color photographs, the better to show off the highly stylized alterations that designers put into the vehicles.

By 2004 the company was selling more than one million books a year in the United Kingdom alone. Haynes achieved a pre-tax profit of £8.3 million on revenue of £39 million for the fiscal year ended May 2004.

Principal Subsidiaries

Editions Haynes S.A.R.L. (France); Haynes Manuals Inc. (Australia); Haynes Manuals, Inc. (U.S.A.); Haynes North America, Inc; Haynes Publishing Nordiska AB (Sweden); J.H. Haynes & Co. Ltd.; J.H. Haynes (Overseas) Ltd.; Odcombe Press LP (U.S.A.); Sutton Publishing Limited.

Principal Divisions

Automotive; General Publishing; Book Manufacturing.

Principal Operating Units

North American and Australia; United Kingdom and Europe.

Principal Competitors

Bentley Publishers; Clymer Publications Inc.

Further Reading

Blackwell, David Harold, "Sexed Up from Trusty Wagon to Mean Machine: The Haynes Group Has Helped Revive Its Vehicle Repair Manuals by Taking a Cue from Laddish Car Culture," *Financial Times,* September 16, 2003, p. 17.

"Choice of Finishing Focus at Haynes Publishing," *Printing World,* December 11, 2000, p. 10.

Clark, Michael, "Haynes Publishing Offer by Tender," *Times* (London), November 30, 1979, p. 24.

Clew, Jeff, *Haynes; The First 40 Years: 1960 to the New Millennium,* Somerset, England: Haynes Publishing Group P.L.C., 2000.

Garrett, Jade, "Daewoo Pulls Work As Goodwill Gesture After Haynes Dispute," *Campaign,* March 10, 2000, p. 11.

"Haynes Finds Little Mileage in Manuals," *Printing World,* October 23, 2000, p. 17.

"Haynes Manuals Reports First Ever Loss," *Printing World,* August 6, 2001, p. 6.

"Haynes Seeks More Trade Work," *Printing World,* February 10, 2003, p. 15.

"Managing Director Says Haynes Publishing Recent Acquisition, Partnership and Consolidation Poises It for Market Growth," *Wall Street Transcript,* October 27, 2003.

—Frederick C. Ingram

Hospira, Inc.

275 North Field Drive
Lake Forest, Illinois 60045
U.S.A.
Telephone: (224) 212-2000
Toll Free: (877) 946-7747
Fax: (224) 212-3350
Web site: http://www.hospira.com

Public Company
Incorporated: 2004
Employees: 14,000
Sales: $2.64 billion (2004)
Stock Exchanges: New York
Ticker Symbol: HSP
NAIC: 325412 Pharmaceutical Preparation Manufacturing

Hospira, Inc. is a hospital products company that manufactures medication delivery systems, generic pharmaceuticals, and intensive care pharmaceuticals. Hospira's pharmaceutical products include generic injectables used in areas such as anesthesia, cardiovascular, infectious diseases, and pain management. The company's medication delivery systems include electronic infusion pumps, needle-free syringes, and intravenous administration sets that provide patients with fluids and medications. The company operates globally, but derives 85 percent of its revenues from sales to hospital customers in the United States. Hospira operates 15 manufacturing facilities in the United States and abroad.

Origins

When Hospira began trading on the New York Stock Exchange on May 3, 2004, the debut marked the start of a "new" company, a company with roots stretching back nearly 70 years. Hospira was new in name only, constituting one substantially sized arm of one of the largest pharmaceutical companies in the world. When the HSP ticker symbol was unveiled, it was the result of an announcement made nine months earlier, from the offices of senior executives at Abbott Laboratories.

Abbott Laboratories began in the kitchen of its founder, Dr. Wallace C. Abbott. In the late 1880s, Dr. Abbott began producing alkaloid extracts in pill form, a pioneering achievement that greatly increased the effectiveness of drugs such as morphine, quinine, strychnine, and codeine—all classified as alkaloid extracts. Before Dr. Abbott began experimenting in his apartment's kitchen, alkaloid extracts were available only in liquid form, which made them susceptible to spoilage and thus less effective. Dr. Abbott's work formed the basis of his company, incorporated in 1900 as Abbott Alkaloidal Company. The company developed into a diversified pharmaceutical concern over the course of the next several decades, using a laboratory in Rocky Mount, North Carolina, to develop new sedatives, tranquilizers, and vitamins. In 1936, the ever-widening business scope of the company brought Abbott Laboratories into the field of anesthetics, a move that marked the beginning of what later became Hospira.

In 1936, two Abbott Laboratories scientists, Ernest Volwiler and Donalee Tabern, developed sodium pentothal. The introduction of sodium pentothal, a barbiturate used for intravenous anesthesia and in the treatment of some mental diseases, coincided with the company's production of dextrose and saline intravenous solutions in bulk form, creating the original business foundation of Abbott Laboratories' hospital products business—the basis of Hospira. During the next two decades, investment in research and development paid dividends, as Abbott Laboratories' new hospital products business became a prominent facet of its overall business. The company introduced the first fully disposable intravenous administration set and a new protein solution for feeding surgical patients intravenously. By the 1950s, Abbott Laboratories' hospital products business held sway as a market leader, ranking as one of the largest suppliers of bulk intravenous solutions in the United States.

Abbott Laboratories' expansion and diversification reached new heights in the decades after the discovery of sodium pentothal. The company, on its way toward becoming a corporate behemoth, pursued several different paths in search of revenue growth, delving into infant and adult nutritionals and medical diagnostic equipment, and going as far afield as involving itself in the manufacture of golf balls—one small part of Abbott Labora-

Company Perspectives:

Our Vision: Advancing Wellness . . . through the right people and the right products. Our vision guides everything Hospira does. ''Advancing'' focuses on the progressive, positive and purposeful approach we take as we look to the future. ''Wellness'' demonstrates a broad commitment to healthcare, supported by our wide variety of products that help improve the well being of patients around the world. Wellness also refers to the overall well being of our customers, our employees, our shareholders and our company. The ''right people''—our employees—are a talented group of dedicated, customer-focused, entrepreneurial individuals who are committed to working under the highest standards of integrity and ethics. Our broad portfolio of products—the ''right products''— provides quality, reliability and cost-effectiveness.

tories' push into the consumer products market. The company's most significant addition to its portfolio of interests happened by accident, a discovery that quickly became the financial bedrock of all of its operations and, in direct proportion to its importance, caused considerable pain to Abbott Laboratories when the discovery proved regrettable. Not long after World War II, an Abbott Laboratories researcher who was working with various chemicals somehow realized that one of them had a sweet taste, a discovery that led to the introduction of cyclamate as a sugar substitute. By 1969, the revenue collected from the sale of cyclamate accounted for one-third of Abbott Laboratories' annual revenue, having become a staple ingredient in diet foods. The following year, cyclamate was banned when the U.S. Food and Drug Administration charged that it was carcinogenic. Within months, Abbott Laboratories received another devastating blow, one incurred by the operations that later became Hospira. Nearly 3.5 million bottles of intravenous solution were recalled after it was discovered that the bottles were sealed with a varnished paper called Golsonite that harbored bacteria. The U.S. Center for Disease Control eventually linked the contaminated solutions to at least 434 infections and 49 deaths, resulting in heavy fines incurred by Abbott Laboratories and the company's plea of no contest to conspiracy charges.

The Roots of Hospira in the 1970s and 1980s

On a more positive note, important new products were developed that became one of Hospira's primary business platforms during the 21st century. During the mid-1970s, Abbott Laboratories' hospital products division entered the electronic flow control market with the introduction of its first electronic drug delivery pump, the prototype of the electronic infusion pumps Hospira marketed when it made its debut as a separate company. In 1984, the division introduced another innovation, a device for patient-controlled analgesia that enabled patients, for the first time, to control the administration of their pain medication. The hospital products division added a new business interest the following year, acquiring Oxitmetrix, a company that manufactured high-technology monitoring systems for the management of critically ill patients. The acquisition marked the division's entry into the critical care business, another principal market for Hospira in the early 21st century.

Despite the disastrous intravenous solution debacle at the beginning of the 1970s, the legacy inherited by Hospira generally lacked drama. From 1936 forward, Abbott Laboratories' hospital products division, relative to the company's other business interests, was a steady yet unprolific money winner. Drug development required vast cash investments, occasionally resulting in pharmaceutical products that rewarded the company with a revenue stream akin to a financial panacea. Hospira's legacy within Abbott Laboratories exuded a character quite different from that of the pharmaceutical company's primary business. Abbott Laboratories' hospital products business never yielded big profits. The division was a slow and steady money machine, never risking nor gaining much financially. The division was reliable, but eventually the senior management at Abbott Laboratories decided to go for high-risk, high-yield businesses, a decision that meant the end of the company's association with its more staid business pursuits. Hospira became the result, a division set free from the oversight of a company that had nurtured its development for seven decades.

The timeline of events that led to Hospira's separation began in August 2003, when Abbott Laboratories' senior executives announced their intention to focus on higher-risk, higher-reward operations that developed patented drugs and medical devices. To narrow its strategic focus, the company bundled its lower growth businesses into what was to become a separate company.

Although it lacked a name, the company was given a leader in August, a 17-year veteran of Abbott Laboratories, Christopher B. Begley. Begley, who served as president of Abbott Laboratories' U.S. hospital business in 2003, served in various management positions during his career at the company, including functioning as the senior vice-president of Abbott Laboratories' chemical and agricultural products division, as the vice-president of AbbottHealthSystems, which marketed the company's products, and as the vice-president of MediSense, Inc., a global unit of the company's diagnostics division. A Chicago native, Begley earned his undergraduate degree at Western Illinois University and a master's degree in business administration at Northern Illinois University.

As Begley prepared to take the helm of Abbott Laboratories' spun-off assets, the business press scrutinized the company he was set to inherit. The hospital products company was large and well established, boasting $2.4 billion in 2003 revenues, 14,000 employees, more than 5,000 customers, and 15 manufacturing sites scattered throughout the world. In a U.S. market whose annual worth was estimated a $9 billion, the nearly $2.5 billion Begley-led operation figured to play a prominent, if not a dominant, role. The company's intravenous therapy products and its acute-care generic injectables (a product of concerted expansion undertaken by Abbott Laboratories during the 1990s) generated the bulk of the new company's revenues. While acknowledging the market leadership the company promised to enjoy once it was officially set free, critics pointed to the nature of the company's business, arguing that the reason Abbott Laboratories wanted to shed the assets did not augur a vibrant financial future for Begley's company. The sales collected by the company's two primary business areas were the definition of steady, derived from long-term contracts that provided a reliable stream of revenue. The businesses, however, were char-

---

Key Dates:

1936: Abbott Laboratories develops sodium pentothal, marking the beginning of a business that developed into Hospira.

Mid-1970s: Abbott Laboratories enters the electronic flow control market with the introduction of its first electronic drug delivery pump.

1984: Abbott Laboratories introduces a device for patient-controlled analgesia.

1985: Abbott Laboratories acquires Oximetrix, marking its entry into the critical care market.

2003: Abbott Laboratories decides to spin off its hospital products business.

2004: Hospira debuts on the New York Stock Exchange.

---

acterized as low-profit-margin enterprises that, historically, had suffered the ignobleness of being labeled as slow-growth ventures. In the nine-month period spanning the August 2003 announcement and Hospira's official birth, the financial community anticipated the debut of a sizable entrant, waiting to see if Begley could inject vitality in a company that, on paper, fell short of sparking excitement on Wall Street.

The Spinoff of Hospira in 2004

In the first week of May 2004, Abbott Laboratories' hospital products business began a new era as Hospira. The company's ticker symbol, HSP, debuted on May 3rd, an occasion marked by Begley, who was given the honor of ringing the Opening Bell at the New York Stock Exchange. Once the formalities were concluded, Begley addressed the industry pundits who characterized Hospira's business as being slow-growth in nature and yielding low profit margins—margins that were narrowing as the company's hospital customers banded together to buy in bulk, driving prices further down. Begley responded by pointing out that Hospira, as a separate company, would receive more attention and more investment than it had under the control of Abbott Laboratories, noting, in a May 3, 2004 interview with *CEO Wire,* that Hospira "has been an under-funded business as it relates to research and development." He promised a substantial increase in research and development spending, planning to increase spending 25 percent during the company's first fiscal quarter and to increase spending at a double-digit rate during ensuing quarters until research and development spending as a percentage of annual sales increased to 5 percent, as opposed to the 3 percent committed during Abbott Laboratories' era of control. In one example of the increase in research and development spending, Begley set his sights on more than 30 injectable drugs scheduled to lose their patent protection in the first few years of Hospira's existence. Before Hospira was spun off, Abbott Laboratories allocated funds to develop only four drugs whose patent expirations were pending.

Hospira's first year as an independent company produced both encouraging and discouraging results. During the company's first fiscal quarter as a publicly traded concern, investors were treated to an 86 percent jump in profits, but the reason for the gain enveloped Begley and his management team in contro-

versy. The company discontinued medical and dental retirement benefits for nonunion U.S. employees, a cut in benefits that resulted in an approximately $40 million gain and triggered allegations that Hospira had violated the Employment Retirement Income Security Act. The allegations led to a class-action lawsuit filed against Abbott Laboratories and Hospira in the U.S. District Court in Chicago in November 2004.

Hospira concluded its first year as an independent company with many questions about its financial vitality left unanswered. The company, Begley stressed, was only halfway through its projected 24-month transition period in separating from Abbott Laboratories. In 2004, sales increased negligibly, rising 0.8 percent to $2.64 billion, while the company's net income increased to $301.6 million, eclipsing the $260.4 million posted in 2003. Looking ahead, Begley planned to continue to increase research and development spending and to increase the company's involvement in overseas business, where Hospira derived only 15 percent of its total volume. Although Hospira was a company with a 70-year legacy, in some ways the company was starting from scratch, working to create a profitable future for itself as an independent enterprise. Recognizing this, Begley broadly described the company's plans for the immediate future in a company press release dated March 2, 2005. "We finished our first year as a public company on a strong note, delivering sales and earnings growth higher than we anticipated," he said. "While building on the momentum generated in 2004, we are still in a period of transition, and our focus in 2005 is on execution. We'll continue to take the steps necessary to advance our success—creating an independent infrastructure and increasing our research and development investment to drive future growth."

Principal Subsidiaries

Hospira Worldwide, Inc.; Hospira S.p.A. (Italy); Hospira Limited (Bahamas).

Principal Competitors

American Pharmaceutical Partners, Inc.; Baxter International Inc.; Becton, Dickinson and Company.

Further Reading

Aragon, Lawrence, "Abbott Seeks Valley Expansion," *Business Journal,* September 30, 1991, p. 1.
Barker, Robert, "Hospira Just May Put You in the Pink," *Business Week,* May 31, 2004, p. 102.
DeWitte, Dave, "Abbott Laboratories' Spinoff Hires Iowa Firm to Identify Top Health Products," *Gazette,* December 15, 2003, p. B2.
"Hospira—CEO Interview," *CEO Wire,* May 3, 2004, p. 21.
"Hospira Launches As New Independent, Global Hospital Products Co.," *AsiaPulse News,* May 4, 2004, p. 32.
Japsen, Bruce, "Former Workers Sue Abbott Over Spinoff of Hospital Products Unit," *Chicago Tribune,* November 9, 2004, p. B3.
——, "Lake Forest, Ill.-Based Hospital Equipment Maker Sees 86 Percent Profit Gain," *Chicago Tribune,* August 11, 2004, p. B4.
Johnson, Ed, "Hospira Slumps As 2005 Outlook Spooks Investors," *America's Intelligence Wire,* January 31, 2005, p. 43.
Sikora, Martin, "U.S. Pension Law Violations Alleged in Abbott Spin-Off," *America's Intelligence Wire,* January 14, 2005, p. 13.

—Jeffrey L. Covell

Hotel Properties Ltd.

50 Cuscaden Rd., Ste. 08-01 HPL House
Singapore 249724
Singapore
Telephone: +65 6734 5250
Fax: +65 6732 0347
Web site: http://www.hotelprop.com

Public Company
Incorporated: 1981
Employees: 4,200
Sales: SGD 320.01 million (2004)
Stock Exchanges: Singapore
Ticker Symbol: HPL
NAIC: 551112 Offices of Other Holding Companies;
237210 Land Subdivision; 721110 Hotels (Except
Casino Hotels) and Motels; 722110 Full-Service
Restaurants

Singapore's Hotel Properties Ltd. (HPL) is a diversified property development group active in four primary areas: Hotels and Hotel Management; Development Properties; Investment Properties/Completed Properties for Sale; and Lifestyle, covering the group's restaurant, food distribution, retail and leisure interests. HPL's portfolio of hotels comprises some 20 hotels in nine countries, including Four Seasons hotels in Singapore, Indonesia, the Maldives, and the United Kingdom; Concorde Hotels in Australia and Malaysia; the Hilton Hotel in Singapore; Le Meridien hotels in Singapore and Vanuatu; and the Hard Rock hotel in Bali. The company's Properties portfolio focuses on the Singapore market, and includes Forum The Shopping Mall, and store units at the Meridien, Ming Arcade, and Orchard Plaza shopping centers. The company also owns four residential properties in Singapore, including the Cuscaden Residence, Four Seasons Park, Nassim Jade, and Robertson Blue. Lifestyle covers HPL's Asian franchise (excluding Japan) for the Hard Rock Café brand, and the company operates Hard Rock Cafes in China, Hong Kong, Indonesia, Korea, Malaysia, the Philippines, and Singapore. Listed on the Singapore stock exchange, HPL remains controlled by founder and business tycoon Ong Beng Seng. In 2004, the company's sales topped SGD 320 million.

Founding a Property Group in the 1980s

Ong Beng Seng was born into a wealthy family in Malaysia, but the family moved to Singapore in 1950 when Ong was just four years old. Ong quickly displayed a talent for making money. Already by the early 1970s Ong had founded a business selling shipping insurance, earning his first fortune. Later described as a secretive, yet flamboyant tycoon (Ong became known as one of the leaders of the Singapore jet-set), Ong married Christina Ong, giving him a powerful father-in-law, Peter Fu Yun Siak. Fu's company, Kuo International, had started out as a timber and wax trader, before expanding into the oil market as well. Christina Ong, meanwhile, had begun building up a portfolio of designer brands—including the Armani franchise—later becoming known as the "Queen of Bond Street," given her extensive holdings in London's fashion center.

Ong Beng Seng joined Fu in business in 1975, emerging as a shrewd trader with a knack for spotting opportunities. In the early 1980s, Ong recognized the potential for entering the property market, and formed Hotel Properties Pte Ltd. in 1981 in order to lead Kuo International's acquisition of hotels and other properties. The company made its first purchase in 1982, acquiring the Hilton Hotel in Singapore. Later that same year, Hotel Properties was taken public with a listing on the Singapore Stock Exchange. At that time the company changed its name to Hotel Properties Ltd.

Through the 1980s, HPL activities revolved especially around property investments, as Ong led the company into the purchase of stakes in various high-profile properties. Such was the case with HPL's purchase of a 50 percent stake in Singapore's Four Seasons Hotel in 1984, in partnership with longtime business ally Prince Al Waleed Bin Talal bin Abdulaziz Al Saud. Prince Al Waleed also became an important investor in HPL.

At the start of the 1990s, HPL's hotel holdings remained quite modest, with just the Hilton and the Four Seasons in Singapore. Yet, as others were fleeing the depressed properties market at the beginning of the decade, the Ongs recognized a fresh opportunity to acquire and develop prestigious properties cheaply. In the early 1990s, the company lay the groundwork for two prominent London hotels, the Halkin, in London's Belgravia neighborhood, and the Metropolitan, also in the West End. HPL also became a prominent investor in the huge Canary Wharf development. Meanwhile, the Ongs continued to build up their stable of prominent designer franchises, including Donna Karan's DKNY, Miu Miu, Calvin Klein, Guess, and Bulgari, among others.

During the 1990s, HPL also extended its interests into the leisure sector, launching restaurant operations, such as the trendy Nobu, opened in the Metropolitan Hotel. Ong also became an investor in Planet Hollywood, joining with Al Waleed in order to rescue the troubled restaurant chain. From there, Ong went on to win the franchise for the Asian region (excluding Japan) for the Hard Rock Café chain, opening restaurants in Beijing, Hong Kong, Bali, Jakarta, Seoul, Kuala Lumpur, Makati, and Singapore. The company also joined in the launch of the new Hard Rock Hotel chain, backing the opening of the Hard Rock Hotel Pattaya in Thailand and the Hard Rock Hotel in Bali. In 1995, also, HPL and Ong visited Australia, where the company picked up a number of properties on that country's Gold Coast, buying, among other sites, the Chevron Hotel for $30 million.

Asian Focus for the New Century

The Ongs appeared to have run into a wall in the late 1990s, as an economic crisis swept through the Asian region. In 1997, the Ongs began selling off a string of their assets, including the Donna Karan Japan franchise, HPL's 50 percent stake in the Four Seasons Hotel in London (sold to partner Al Waleed), and Ong's private jet.

News of the sellout sparked rumors that Ong's financial empire was collapsing, and HPL's share price dropped dramatically. Ong, who had long avoided personal publicity, was forced to hold a rare press conference in order to dispel rumors that his company and fortune were in trouble.

Indeed, the strategy behind the sell-off of the Ongs' and HPL's assets quickly became apparent. As property prices bottomed out in the Asian market, HPL had converted its assets into cash as the company launched its hotel and property interests into a new direction. In the late 1990s, HPL began buying up properties, franchises, and companies, including Concorde Hotels & Resorts, transforming the company into a prominent hotel ownership and management firm in the Asia-Pacific and Indian Ocean markets. The Concorde Hotels purchase also played a part in HPL's plans to develop its Chevron Hotel site into a massive hotel and tavern complex.

In 2001, Concorde Hotels & Resorts changed its name to HPL Hotels & Resorts. The company's portfolio now included three HPL Hotels in Malaysia, an HPL Hotel development in Australia, the Hard Rock Hotel Franchise in Bali and Thailand, as well as hotels in the Maldives and the Cameron Highlands. The company also acquired Elegant Hotel Holding in 2000, launching the renovation of the Elegant Hotel complex in Australia. In 2001, the company decided not to pursue the renovation.

During this time, HPL had also targeted the fast-growing residential market in Singapore, guiding four major condominium developments, including Nassim Jade, launched in 1995, Four Seasons Park, Robertson Blue, and Cuscaden Residence. Another important area of investment was the shopping center sector in Singapore. Among the company's investments were the development of Forum The Shopping Mall, and purchases of store units in three other shopping centers, Meridien, Ming Arcade, and Orchard Plaza.

In 2002, HPL looked beyond the Asian market again, paying British Airways $31 million to acquire the Fitzpatrick Hotel in New York City. Unlike many of its other hotels, where HPL had been developing its interests in hotel management, the company turned over management and operation of the Fitzpatrick to Jolly Tinker Inc.

In 2004, HPL spotted a new opportunity in Macau, where Las Vegas's Sheldon Adelson had begun the development of the new Cotai Strip casino resort development. HPL joined in, signing an agreement to build two hotels in the resort, a 400-room Four Seasons, and a 1,500-room Hard Rock Hotel. The company began negotiations to acquire land as part of an investment expected to cost as much as $200 million.

HPL continued to fine-tune its portfolio into the mid-decade. Instead of pursuing the Concorde/HPL Australia development, the company sold off a large part of that site. Then, in April 2005, HPL announced that it was putting up for sale the rest of the former Chevron complex as well. By then, HPL's total hotel portfolio numbered some 20 hotels in 10 countries. Ong Beng Seng remained at the company's helm, guiding it into the new century.

Principal Subsidiaries

Cleaton Investments Pte Ltd; HPL Hotels & Resorts Pte Ltd; HPL Investment & Investment Development Pte Ltd; HPL Leisure Holdings Pte Ltd; HPL Orchard Place Pte Ltd; HPL Properties (Australasia) Pte Ltd; HPL Properties (SEA) Pte Ltd; HPL Properties (West Asia) Investment Pte Ltd; HPL Properties (West) Pte Ltd; HPL Properties Pte Ltd; HPL Singapore Pte Ltd; HPL Tourism & Leisure Pte Ltd; Luxury Holdings Pte Ltd; Maxford Investments Pte Ltd; Pinedale Holdings Pte Ltd; Poussain Pte Ltd; Super Vista Sdn Bhd.

Principal Competitors

Cheung Kong (Holdings) Limited; New World Development Company Limited; Sino Land Company Limited.

Further Reading

Ashworth, Jon, "Ong Beng Seng Still on Song," *The Times*, March 29, 1994, p. 29.
——, "Ong Constructs Concrete Evidence of Solvency," *The Times*, July 4, 1998, p. 26.
Clarke, Hilary, "Profile: Beng Seng and Christina Ong: Asian Pair Sell West, Buy East," *Independent on Sunday*, March 29, 1998, p. 5.
——, "Saviours of the Planet," *Independent on Sunday*, August 22, 1999, p. 4.
Coleman, Zach, "Singaporean Plans Hotels," *Standard*, May 21, 2004.
"Sales of Queensland Hotels Are Continuing to Track at Record Levels," *Asia Pacific Hospitality Enews*, April 5, 2005.
Shameen, Assif, "A Reclusive Tycoon Fights for the Underdogs—Including Himself," *Asia Week*, June 9, 2000.
"Singapore: Quek Leng Chan to Take over HPL?" *Business Times* (Singapore), October 2, 2001, p. 1.

—M.L. Cohen

IHC Caland N.V.

Postbus 31
Schiedam
NL-3100 AA
Netherlands
Telephone: +31 10 232 09 00
Fax: +31 10 232 09 99
Web site: http://www.ihccaland.nl

Public Company
Incorporated: 1965
Sales: $1.34 billion (2004)
Stock Exchanges: Euronext Amsterdam
NAIC: 336611 Ship Building and Repairing; 333120
    Construction Machinery Manufacturing; 541330
    Engineering Services

IHC Caland N.V. provides engineering and support services for the offshore oil and gas industry and for other industries, including dredging, mining, shipyards, gravel extraction, and others. The company's services include the design and production of offshore loading/unloading systems and even the design, manufacturing, and operation of complete Floating Production Storage and Offloading Systems (FPSO/FSO). The company, through its SBM Group of subsidiaries, builds and leases these turnkey platforms, a concept pioneered by IHC Caland itself, and the company remains the world's leading producer of FPSO/FSO systems. Through subsidiary NKI B.V., IHC Caland also provides design, engineering, and construction services for the building of airport and railroad terminal infrastructures. IHC Caland is also a world-leading provider of customized dredging equipment, an activity related to the company's former status as the world's leading manufacturer of dredging vessels. In 2005, however, IHC Caland completed the sell-off of its IHC Holland shipbuilding operations, representing the end of some 300 years of history. Listed on the Euronext Amsterdam Stock Exchange, IHC Caland posted sales of $1.34 billion in 2004.

Roots in the 16th Century

IHC Caland inherited a tradition of shipbuilding and engineering stretching back as far as 1500 and even earlier, when records indicated that the Zeeland region had already achieved recognition for its shipbuilding activities. The region was particularly active in the manufacture of dredgers, used in the construction of the country's dike system. The Smit family later emerged as one of the region's most prominent shipbuilders and engineers. The Smits originally designed and built windmills, starting in the early 17th century; some of these, such as the windmills on the Kinderdijk, remained popular tourist attractions into the 21st century. By 1687, the Smits also were building ships, especially dredgers.

The company's expertise in dredging enabled it to become a major force in the international markets for this kind of vessel. By the mid-19th century, the Smit yard was producing dredgers for Japan, starting with the delivery of its first in 1857. By the end of the century, Smit also had entered the Chinese market, delivering its first dredger in 1895. Over the next century, the company was to produce 100 vessels for China alone.

By the late 1930s, the Smit family was involved in two major Kinderdijk shipyards, L. Smit & Zoon and J&K Smit. In the early 1940s, the companies received a major order for six tin dredgers from the Billiton Mining Company, then a subsidiary of Royal Dutch Shell, for use in Billiton's Indonesian mining operations. In order to fill the order, the Smit yards joined forces with a number of other prominent yards in the region, including De Klop, based in Sliedrecht; Gusto, based in Schiedam; Verschure in Amsterdam; and Werf Conrad-Stork in Haarlem. Backed by the Billiton order, the six companies formed a partnership in 1943, called Industrieele Handels Combinatie, or IHC. The partnership delivered its first dredger, the Mendanau, in 1947.

The success of the Billiton order led the partners to begin working more closely together during the 1950s. In particular, IHC turned its long history of engineering innovation and expertise to tackle a new market, that of the burgeoning offshore platform industry. In the early 1950s, IHC began developing a new offshore platform construction technology, called Single Point Mooring, or SPM. The company successfully pioneered what was to become an industry standard.

IHC continued to display a knack for innovation. In 1961, the company released its CALM buoy system. Over the next several decades, IHC succeeded in patenting a number of new technologies related to its dual core focus of shipbuilding and offshore systems. Meanwhile the adoption of its technologies, and particularly its SPM systems, led IHC to create the dedicated subsidiary Single Buoy Moorings, or SBM, in 1969. SBM remained a leader in the SPM market, retaining a 50 percent share into the 2000s.

Another growing area for IHC was its production of equipment for the offshore industry. The Gusto yard, which itself stemmed from 1862, became the site of much of IHC's operations in this sector. In 1960, the company launched its first jack-up drilling rig, designed and built at the Gusto year.

United Company in the 1960s

By the mid-1960s, the continued growth of IHC led its partner companies to begin moving to a full-fledged merger. In 1965, the partner companies formed IHC Holland NV Industrieele Handels Combinatie NV, which was then listed on the Amsterdam Stock Exchange, with each member retaining control of a block of shares. The only member of the original partnership that did not join the new company was Conrad-Stork, because it had come under the ownership of rival shipbuilding group VMF.

IHC initially attempted to consolidate its operations and bring them under a single, central leadership. In 1966, the company merged the two Smit companies into a single concern, Smit Kinderdijk. IHC also attempted to bring its other member companies together. Yet by 1968 it became evident that differences in corporate cultures, as well as the strong historical identity of each company, made further consolidation too difficult. Instead, in 1968, IHC adopted a new organizational structure, grouping its operations into three primary divisions. Offshore included Gusto, and then SBM starting from 1969. Dredging included Smit, as well as Verschure and De Klop. The company also set up a separate division for its Mining & Transport Engineering operations.

The economic slump during the 1970s led the company to a first consolidation of its shipbuilding and other operations in the latter half of the decade. The company shut down the Verschure yard in 1980, then merged De Klop with another Schliedrecht shipbuilder, Van Rees. Meanwhile, the shipbuilding operations at the Gusto shipyards were closed in 1978; in that year, instead, Gusto was reformed as Gusto Engineering B.V., focused on drilling and other equipment for the offshore industry.

IHC entered the 1980s with hopes for a resurgence in the international dredging market, and in 1983 commissioned a new modern wharf facility on the former Van Rees site. The company also had extended the IHC Smit Kinderdijk operation, adding new facilities for special construction operations. Smit Kinderdijk also launched a modernization effort, completed in 1986.

Yet the hoped-for upswing in the dredging market did not materialize. With its sales dropping and profits crashing, IHC was forced to undertake a more thorough restructuring. In 1986, the company began shutting down facilities and slashing jobs. By 1987, as its losses continued, the company further reduced its shipbuilding operations to just two sites, Sliedrecht and Kinderdijk. These companies were then merged together to form the single IHC Holland N.V.

By 1988, the last of IHC's founding members had sold its stock, and IHC at least succeeded in acquiring full control of the operation. The company changed its name, to IHC Caland, which served as the holding company for its diversified companies. Among them, SBM had continued to develop strongly, particularly after it pioneered another groundbreaking market for the offshore oil and gas industry. In 1977, SBM built the first Floating Production, Storage and Offloading system, or FPSO/FSO, a turnkey offshore platform complex that was built for and sold to Shell. Yet SBM also conceived another industry first—that of leasing FPSOs. The first of these was built and leased in 1981.

Exiting Shipbuilding for the New Century

Into the 1990s, IHC confronted a declining market for dredgers. In order to reduce its vulnerability to the softening market, the company acquired Dutch shipbuilding company Merwede in 1993. That company, founded in 1905, enabled IHC to begin extending into other shipbuilding areas, notably ferries, while also expanding its position among the worldwide dredger market.

In 1997, IHC again boosted its shipbuilding operations through the acquisition of the Giessen de Noord shipyard. This company also provided expanded capacity for IHC's dredger business. Yet IHC continued to seek expansion opportunities elsewhere as the European shipbuilding industry faced increasingly stiff competition from lower-cost competitors in Asia. The Giessen de Noord purchase became attractive in this light as it brought a new operation, NKI B.V., into the IHC fold.

NKI was founded in 1970 to provide engineering and construction services for airport and other terminal infrastructure projects. By 1974, the company had received its first contract, for Schiphol Airport, and by 1977 won its first international contract, for the Murtala Moh Airport in Lagos, Nigeria. NKI later expanded its operations to include railway terminals as well.

IHC expanded its offshore services division in 2001 through the acquisition of U.S.-based Atlantia Offshore Limited. Founded in 1979, Atlantia focused on the Gulf of Mexico and North Sea markets, designing and constructing fixed platforms. The company's first platform was commissioned in 1984, and by 2005 the company had built more than 150 platforms worldwide. Two years later, IHC added to its design and engineering capacity with the acquisition of Ocean Design, based in Houston.

By then, however, IHC's shipbuilding business was struggling to survive in a depressed market against its lower cost Asian rivals. At the beginning of 2003, the company continued to

Key Dates:

1687: The Smit family of Kinderdijk begins shipbuilding, later specializing in building dredging vessels.

1943: The IHC partnership is created through the combination of six shipbuilders, including two Smit companies, Gusto (founded 1862), De Klop, Verschure, and Conrad-Stork.

1950s: The company begins developing the Single Point Mooring offshore platform system.

1960: Gusto launches the first jack-up drilling rig.

1965: IHC is incorporated, and the company lists on the Amsterdam Stock Exchange.

1966: The Smit companies merge as part of an effort to centralize IHC operations.

1968: IHC changes its strategy and develops a decentralized model.

1969: SBM is created as a dedicated offshore engineering subsidiary.

1977: SBM builds the industry's first FPSO for Shell.

1978: The Gusto shipyards shut down and Gusto becomes an offshore engineering specialist.

1981: SBM becomes the first to build and lease FPSOs.

1986: IHC launches a reorganization, resulting in the consolidation of shipbuilding to just two sites, creating IHC Holland.

1988: IHC becomes IHC Caland, which operates as a holding company for shipbuilding and offshore businesses.

1993: IHC acquires the Merwede shipyard, founded in 1905, diversifying its shipbuilding into ferries and other vessels.

1997: IHC acquires the Giessen de Noord shipyard.

2001: IHC acquires the Atlantia Offshore Systems, focused on the Gulf of Mexico and North Sea markets.

2003: IHC shuts down the Giessen de Noord shipyard and announces plans to spin off its shipbuilding operations, which are combined and reformed as IHC Holland Merwede.

2004: IHC announces its decision to sell the shipbuilding business instead of spinning it off as a separate company.

2005: IHC completes the sale of IHC Holland Merwede.

affirm its commitment to its shipbuilding, and especially its dredger building business. By the middle of that year, with 100 percent of its profits now generated by its offshore business, IHC was forced to concede defeat. In that year, the company closed the Giessen de Noord shipyard. IHC then announced a plan to spin off its remaining shipbuilding operations as a separate and independent company.

Yet mounting losses in the division forced IHC to drop the spinoff plan by October 2003. Instead, the company announced its intention to move out of shipbuilding altogether, and began looking for a buyer for its shipbuilding operations. That operation was completed in March 2005, with the creation and sale of IHC Holland Merwede. Rabobank acquired a 49 percent stake through a subsidiary, while IHC Holland Merwede's management and employees acquired a 33 percent stake. The remainder was bought by Indofin, an investment group owned by the De Bruin family. IHC Caland looked forward to a new future as a specialized engineering group.

Principal Subsidiaries

Atlantia Offshore Limited (U.S.A.); IHC Gusto Engineering B.V.; IHC Holland; Marine Structure Consultants; N.K.I. B.V.; SBM Group; SBM Imodco (U.S.A.); SBM Offshore Systems; SBM Production Contractors; SBM Services.

Principal Competitors

Halliburton Company; Bechtel Corporation; Dragados, S.A.; Edeco Petroleum Services Limited; BJ Services Company.

Further Reading

Bickerton, Ian, "IHC Caland Abandons Ship to Rivals After 300 Years," *Financial Times,* August 26, 2003, p. 22.

——, "IHC Caland Issues Warning, Drops Spin-Off," *Financial Times,* October 7, 2003, p. 26.

——, "IHC Optimistic Over Oil Activity," *Financial Times,* August 31, 2004, p. 24.

Hill, Helen, "IHC Caland Bows Out of Shipbuilding," *Lloyds List,* March 3, 2005.

——, "IHC Caland Optimistic After Shipyard Disposal," *Lloyds List,* February 1, 2005.

"IHC Caland Backs Shipbuilding in Spite of Trying Times," *Lloyds List,* June 23, 2003.

"IHC Caland Goes Ahead with Double Yard Sale," *Lloyds List,* August 6, 2004.

Krane, Jim, "Dutch Oil Drilling Equipment Maker Reports Flat Profits," *AP Worldstream,* January 31, 2005.

Ramstack, Tom, "IHC Caland Bows Out of Shipbuilding," *Financial Post,* August 26, 2003.

—M.L. Cohen

International
IΩR Rectifier
THE POWER MANAGEMENT LEADER

International Rectifier Corporation

233 Kansas Street
El Segundo, California 90245
U.S.A.
Telephone: (310) 726-8000
Fax: (310) 332-3332
Web site: http://www.irf.com

Public Company
Incorporated: 1947
Employees: 5,800
Sales: $1.06 billion (2004)
Stock Exchanges: New York
Ticker Symbol: IRF
NAIC: 334413 Semiconductor and Related Device
  Manufacturing

International Rectifier Corporation (IR) is the oldest independent power semiconductor manufacturer in the world. IR's products, protected by hundreds of patents, control the direction and flow of electrical current, a necessity for manufacturers of myriad electronics products. IR's technologies also help to conserve power. The company develops, manufactures, and sells control integrated circuits, diodes, rectifiers, and its signature product, HEXFET power MOSFET switches. IR derives more than 60 percent of its annual sales from Europe and Asia. The company operates production facilities in Italy, Germany, Mexico, the United Kingdom, and the United States.

Post-World War II Origins

An offshoot of the fast-growing aerospace industry in the Los Angeles area during the 1940s was the rise of attendant semiconductor manufacturers. IR was there from the start, founded on August 9, 1947, by Leon Lidow and his son Eric. Eric Lidow, who would control the company for the next half-century, was born in Vilnius, Lithuania. He attended the Technical University of Berlin, where he earned a degree in electrical engineering in 1937, the same year he immigrated to the United States. In 1940 he cofounded and served as general manager of Selenium Corporation of America, which was acquired by Sperry Corporation in 1944. Lidow stayed on after the acquisi-

tion, serving as vice-president of engineering until teaming up with his father to form IR. The Lidows created IR to put to use advanced processes they had developed for manufacturing selenium rectifiers, which converted alternating electrical current to direct electrical current. Their technology, formally employed on IR's August 9 founding date, was pioneering, predating the development of the transistor by more than four months.

IR started with six employees in an unincorporated area of Los Angeles, marking the beginning of the company's continuous efforts to produce devices with increasingly higher power ratings and superior reliability characteristics. The company's business revolved around controlling the flow and direction of electricity, an engineering feat of fundamental importance in the vast world of electronics, enabling appliances, automobiles, computers, and thousands of other devices, components, and systems to function. To switch and condition electricity, manufacturers relied on power semiconductors, using diodes, rectifiers, transistors, and other devices to make their products operate. IR, with its foundation resting on commercial semiconductor processes and devices based on selenium (a nonmetallic element), emerged as an early leader in the industry. At its start, the company manufactured rectifiers, diodes, and transistors for sale to domestic customers, but quickly demonstrated its talent for developing superior technology and its ambition to expand its presence outside the U.S. market.

From selenium, IR made the technological leap to germanium-based systems, introducing germanium rectifiers in November 1954. Three years later, the company's tenth anniversary was marked by the formation of International Rectifier Corp., Japan Ltd., representing the company's first foray into international expansion. In September 1958, Eric Lidow took IR public, completing an initial public offering of stock that preceded the establishment of the company's second foreign subsidiary, IR, Great Britain Ltd., in December 1958. One year later, Lidow drew the semiconductor industry's attention by besting his germanium rectifiers with the September 1959 introduction of the first silicon rectifier, which, facilitated by the company's previous international expansion, made IR the first company to introduce silicon technology to Japan.

An acknowledged force in the semiconductor industry, Lidow's company proceeded to accumulate an impressive list

181

Company Perspectives:

International Rectifier is a pioneer and world leader in advanced power management technology, from analog and mixed signal ICs to advanced circuit devices, power systems, and components. Technological breakthroughs from IR are setting the pace for innovation in the electronics we all rely upon each day. Inside our factories and automobiles, at our homes and offices, and orbiting our world, IR's power management technology is enabling today's leading-edge computers, appliances, lighting, automobiles, satellites, and defense systems—and creating a pathway to tomorrow's advancements.

---

of technological achievements as it extended its global reach. In 1960, after introducing solar cells two years earlier, IR produced the world's first solar-powered automobile. One year later, the company commenced operations in Italy, followed by the establishment of subsidiaries in India in 1965, Canada in 1966, and Mexico in 1973.

Against the backdrop of IR's geographic expansion, the company's leading role in the technological development of power semiconductors produced disparate financial results. For IR, being the pioneer of widely used technology did not necessarily guarantee long-term financial success, which, as a publicly traded company, was an all-important objective. For instance, based in large part on the company's achievements as a pioneer in silicon control rectifiers, IR's stock swelled to $31 per share in 1966. By 1969, after the company's competitors had successfully jumped on the silicon bandwagon, IR's shares plummeted below $12. The company's technological achievements were exemplary, but, frustrating for Lidow, IR's financial reputation was not. Despite the dozens of pioneering patents held by the company, it began to falter by the 1970s, perceived by investors and industry observers as an organization suffering from stagnation. As the prospect of an industry pioneer withering on the vine began to emerge, the next generation of Lidows was exhibiting talents that soon would breathe new life into IR.

Lidow Sons Beginning to Exert Influence: 1970s

Eric Lidow's two sons, Alexander and Derek, possessed exceptional minds. Alexander, two years younger than Derek, built a photoelectric cell at the age of eight, but nevertheless was overshadowed by his older brother when the two boys were in their teens. Derek graduated from Beverly Hills High School at age 16, setting an example Alexander was unable to match. Alexander did not conclude his studies at Beverly Hills High School until the usual age of 18, which fueled a rivalry between the two brothers that would endure for the next 30 years. "I couldn't let him do better than me," Alexander told a *Forbes* reporter in September 1995, but, for Alexander, matching the academic pace of his brother would prove to be a difficult endeavor. Derek graduated from Princeton summa cum laude at the age of 20, then earned a Stanford Ph.D. in two years. Alexander earned an undergraduate degree in physics from California Institute of Technology in three years and was awarded his Ph.D. in applied physics from Stanford, like his

brother, at age 22. In terms of the ongoing rivalry between the Lidow brothers, the race against one another in the academic world had produced no clear winner. IR would serve as the next proving ground, setting the stage for a brotherly battle that had a profound effect on their father's company. For Alexander, who had suffered the indignity of spending four years in high school, redemption would be found.

Derek and Alexander concluded their academic careers in 1975 and 1977, respectively, joining IR at roughly the same time the semiconductor industry was undergoing a dynamic change in technology. For years, the job of converting alternating current into direct current had been performed by bipolar transistors, but the electronics industry had struck upon a substitute for bipolars in many applications: power MOSFETs. MOSFETs, the acronym for metal oxide semiconductor field effect transistor, were more efficient, faster, and smaller than bipolars, threatening to replace the world market for bipolars, which was valued at roughly $1 billion. The potential for MOSFETs was vast, representing a critical area of development for a specialized power semiconductor manufacturer like IR. Not coincidentally, Alexander Lidow had experimented with the technology surrounding MOSFETs while pursuing his academic work at Stanford. His discoveries signaled the beginning of a new era for IR.

In 1976, one year before he was awarded his Ph.D., Alexander began working on an advanced MOSFET with promising capabilities. The early development of his chip, which broke electrical current into smaller, more usable units, impressed his father, persuading the IR chairman to give his son $100,000 worth of equipment and the aid of one engineer for further development of the chip, dubbed HEXFET because of its hexagonal shape. HEXFET was under development for production by the time Alexander left Stanford, but the price to make HEXFETs a commercial reality was severe. IR accumulated massive debt: "We bet the company, bet again, and borrowed to bet some more on HEXFET," Alexander recalled in a September 11, 1995 interview with *Forbes*. Alexander lobbied his father to shelve IR's existing businesses and concentrate fully on HEXFET chips. "The company had plateaued and was struggling," Alexander reflected in his interview with *Forbes*. "From my perspective, International Rectifier had nowhere to go." Derek disagreed, convinced that if the company invested everything in HEXFET its future existence could be in peril. The brotherly rivalry transmogrified into a feud, but plans went ahead for the commercial debut of HEXFET as long-term debt soared to 88 percent of IR's capitalization.

The HEXFET power MOSFET was introduced in June 1979, and would become IR's mainstay product. By 1983, when sales amounted to $127 million, the rewards of the commitment to HEXFET chips were evident. IR controlled more than half of the fast-growing market for power MOSFETs, maintaining a 12- to 18-month lead over rivals such as Motorola, Hitachi, RCA, and Siliconix. Wall Street was impressed, evinced by a dramatic rise in the company's stock value from $7 per share at the start of the 1980s to more than $40 per share by 1983. The debt incurred from the headlong push into commercializing HEXFETs, however, had not disappeared. In 1983 IR's debt stood at 57 percent of its capitalization and would soon increase as the company prepared to build the most automated semiconductor manufacturing plant in the nation. The $82 million plant,

<table>
<tr><td colspan="2" align="center">**· Key Dates:**</td></tr>
</table>

Key Dates:

1947: Leon Lidow and his son, Eric, form International Rectifier Corporation.
1958: Company offers shares of stock for public trading.
1959: Company introduces the first silicon controlled rectifier.
1979: HEXFET power MOSFET is introduced.
1987: Production at HEXFET America commences.
1992: After splitting the company three years earlier, control over all operations is unified.
1995: Alexander and Derek Lidow are appointed co-chief executive officers.
1999: Alexander Lidow is named sole chief executive officer.
2004: Sales eclipse $1 billion.

called HEXFET America, engulfed the company further in debt, but as with the initial investment in Alexander's hexagonal chip, the potential rewards were convincing. The new plant would enable IR to manufacture HEXFETs in one continuous process, cutting production costs in half and increasing the yearly output per worker to $350,000, or more than double the industry average. The financial hurdles were cleared and HEXFET America, located in Temecula, California, commenced production in April 1987. Behind the scenes, however, the tug and pull between Eric Lidow's two sons tempered the celebratory unveiling of the new plant. The IR chief executive officer and chairman was determined to resolve the problem.

Fraternal Rift Dividing IR in 1989

By the end of the 1980s, the constant bickering between Alexander and Derek over corporate strategy, which had persisted for roughly a decade-and-a-half, had forced Eric Lidow to take action. In 1989 he divided the company in two, giving Alexander control over IR's newer businesses and giving Derek command of the company's older business lines. "I felt both were right," the senior Lidow explained to *Forbes* in 1995, "and both were willing to accept responsibility for their ideas." What appeared as a natural solution to a nagging problem, however, quickly developed into a more pernicious problem. Separated, Alexander and Derek built contrary business groups that were inherently at odds, symbolized by the adoption of computer systems that could not communicate with each other. Further, the split spawned a host of corporate redundancies, with Alexander and Derek operating distinct administrative staffs and sales and marketing departments, creating a tangle of operations that ultimately enveloped IR's customers, who found themselves suffering as a consequence of the Lidow brothers' inability to work together. Eric Lidow, in his late 70s as IR stumbled into the 1990s, looked for another solution.

In 1992 Eric Lidow went to the heart of the problem and hired J. Mitchell Perry, a Palo Alto psychologist. With therapy as the recourse, the process of mending the differences between the brothers began—a difficult process that aimed to resolve a lifetime of issues. Eventually, the relationship improved, opening the lines of communication between Alexander and Derek.

Before the end of 1992, they agreed to reunite their halves of the company, which, sparked by the new spirit of conciliation, led to a new product, the electric power conversion chipset. For decades, the company had sold components piecemeal, rather than combining components—the newer products governed by Alexander and the older products governed by Derek—to create a more comprehensive product. Alexander explained to *Forbes* in 1995: "The minute we got together and compared the things we were doing, it became clear all these [components] worked together synergistically in the process of converting electricity into refined energy." The combined chipset, far smaller and far more inexpensive than separate components, was expected to generate half of IR's sales by the end of the 1990s. Before its promising future materialized, however, there was already cause to celebrate. The reunited brothers and a unified IR produced encouraging results. By 1995, debt had been whittled down to 12 percent of capitalization, sales were up to $429 million, a 30 percent gain from the previous year's total, and earnings reached $39 million, double the total recorded in 1994.

Late 1990s: A Roller Coaster Ride

After three years of watching his sons work together, Eric Lidow was convinced the familial squabbles of the past were over. In 1995 he named his sons co-chief executive officers, with Alexander in charge of manufacturing and technology development and Derek in charge of marketing, computer systems, and strategic planning. Initially, the company's financial performance continued to impress. Revenues slipped past the half-billion-dollar mark for the first time in 1996, rising to $576.8 million, while earnings continued to increase exponentially, swelling to $66.5 million. The following year, however, the company's financial results were negatively affected by oversupply and the costs incurred from restructuring the organization. The 1997 restructuring, aimed at improving efficiency, involved revaluing assets, consolidating administrative and service departments, reducing payroll, and relocating manufacturing operations, among other actions. Restructuring led to a one-time charge of $75 million, contributing significantly to the net loss of $43.2 million registered for the year. Despite the loss, IR expanded manufacturing capacity, confident that it would ultimately gain a substantial return on its investment. Expansion of the Temecula facility was announced in 1997, followed by the disclosure in 1998 of plans to build a $40 million manufacturing plant in Swansea, Wales. As the decade drew to a close, there remained one final chapter in the fraternal story that dominated IR's history, recasting the company for the 21st century.

In May 1999, IR announced it was eliminating one of its chief executive officer positions to pass the powers of joint control to a single individual. Alexander was named the company's sole chief executive officer; Derek, in June 1999, resigned from his post to pursue other interests, although he continued to serve as a member of IR's board of directors. Derek's statement regarding his departure, as quoted in the May 17, 1999 issue of *Electronic News,* explained the move and touched on IR's orientation for the future: "The co-CEO structure played a key role in executing a successful transition through periods of unprecedented demand, volatile market conditions, intense competition, and rapidly developing technology. IR is well positioned with an excellent strategy and exciting new products in an improving marketplace. The board of directors, Alex, and I all feel a single-CEO structure helps IR to achieve its long-range objectives.''

IR at the Dawn of the New Century

With Alexander Lidow alone at the helm, IR recorded the greatest growth spurt in its history, doubling its revenue in a five-year span to become a billion-dollar company. Most other semiconductor makers suffered through the period rather than posting annual double-digit financial growth, as flattening personal computer sales had a corresponding effect on the sales of chip makers who served the personal computer makers. IR, however, was positioned in the one sector of the semiconductor industry immune to stagnant personal computer sales. As the main processors in personal computers became increasingly bigger, they ran increasingly hotter, creating a greater demand for IR's chips that regulated heat. Further, the late 1990s and early 2000s witnessed the proliferation of sophisticated electronic devices that required power management chips. IR's ability to thrive in a lackluster personal computer market was only one aspect of its success story under Lidow's rule.

Lidow invested in new technology and reaped the rewards of diversification. He also changed the profile of IR's business, which, when coupled with the new markets entered via the company's diversification, created a vibrant enterprise. Between 1999 and 2004, Lidow spent $300 million to acquire eight companies. The acquisitions gave the company new technology that enabled it to expand its presence in the aerospace and defense industries. Among the acquired assets were: a silicon-fabrication plant in Wales; Advanced Analog, a California-based company that produced direct-current converters for military planes and ships; and Zing Technologies, a New York-based firm specializing in making radiation-tolerant packaging for circuits. Lidow also began a dramatic shift away from less profitable businesses in favor of higher-profit-margin businesses. Components, which yielded gross margins of 20 percent, accounted for 80 percent of IR's revenue in 1999. By 2004, components contributed 33 percent of IR's revenue, with the production of advanced circuits, which yielded gross margins as high as 65 percent, replacing components as the company's mainstay business. In 1999, advanced circuits accounted for 20 percent of IR's revenue. By 2004, they represented 67 percent of the company's revenue volume.

IR was a substantially larger and more profitable company as it entered the mid-2000s. The company faced a future that promised to call on its expertise in power management, a future in which the chips made by IR were to be used in not just regulating electricity flow but in conserving energy as well. IR's chips were suited for improving the efficiency of scores of devices and appliances, ranging from personal computers to hybrid automobiles to washing machines. Appliances and hybrid vehicles, in particular, figured as two of the most important business areas in IR's future, as Lidow strove to emphasize the diversity of applications for the company's power chips and their ability to conserve power. The company's engineers teamed with Sanyo to develop a new generation of washing machines, air conditioners, and refrigerators that reduced power

consumption by as much as 60 percent. In a hybrid car, IR's circuits switched power between the engine and the electrical motor, presenting what potentially could be a lucrative market for Lidow's engineers to exploit in the future.

Principal Subsidiaries

HEXFET America; Rectificadores Internacionales S.A. de C.V. (Mexico); International Rectifier HiRel Products LLC; Advanced Analog, Inc.; Unisem, Inc.; IR Epi Services, Inc.; International Rectifier Company Ltd. (U.K.); International Rectifier Electronic Motion Systems, Ltd. (U.K.); International Rectifier Corporation Italiana, S.p.A. (Italy); IR Newport Limited (U.K.).

Principal Competitors

STMicroelectronics N.V.; Fairchild Semiconductor International, Inc.; National Semiconductor Corporation; Samsung Group; Siliconix Incorporated; Vishay Intertechnology, Inc.

Further Reading

Crider, Jeff, ''Chip Maker International Rectifier of California Says Profits to Decline,'' *Knight-Ridder/Tribune Business News,* September 13, 1996.
——, ''El Segundo, Calif-Based International Rectifier Plans Temecula Expansion,'' *Knight-Ridder/Tribune Business News,* December 6, 1997.
——, ''International Rectifier Adding to Temecula, Calif.,'' *Knight-Ridder/Tribune Business News,* November 17, 1995.
Detar, James, ''International Rectifier Sales Are Hot Because Its Chips Can Regulate Heat,'' *Investor's Business Daily,* January 14, 2005, p. A4.
——, ''Power Control: Big Business at IR,'' *Investor's Business Daily,* January 22, 2004, p. A8.
Flores, J.C., ''Semiconductor Industry in L.A. Finds Survival in Niche Markets,'' *Los Angeles Business Journal,* March 26, 1990, p. 10.
Haber, Carol, ''IR Settles Suits,'' *Electronic News,* January 11, 1999, p. 10.
Henry, David, ''That Old Electric Surge,'' *Business Week,* July 12, 2004, p. 99.
''International Rectifier Posts Net Loss,'' *Knight-Ridder/Tribune Business News,* July 18, 1997.
''Int'l Rectifier Adopts New Single CEO Structure: Alex Lidow Named to Top Position; Derek Lidow Steps Down,'' *Electronic News,* May 17, 1999, p. 14.
''IR Sets $40M Plant in Wales,'' *Electronic News,* October 5, 1998, p. 46.
Kellner, Tomas, ''Don't Look Back,'' *Forbes,* November 29, 2004, p. 61.
Mathisen, Tyler, ''International Rectifier Corporation—CEO Interview,'' *America's Intelligence Wire,* January 28, 2005, p. 32.
''My Brother, My Rival,'' *Forbes,* September 11, 1995, p. 134.
Palazzo, Anthony, ''Chipmaker Targets Hybrid Cars As Engine for Revenue Growth,'' *Los Angeles Business Journal,* August 9, 2004, p. 27.
——, ''Semiconductor Maker Quiet After Analyst Downgrading,'' *Los Angeles Business Journal,* July 15, 2002, p. 24.
Paris, Ellen, ''Hot Again,'' *Forbes,* November 21, 1983, p. 332.
''Power Chips Get a Jolt,'' *Business Week,* March 19, 2001, p. 96D.
''Profits Up for California's International Rectifier,'' *Knight-Ridder/Tribune Business News,* April 15, 1996.
Serioty, Chris, ''Broad Product Line Shields Chip Maker from Tech Ills,'' *Los Angeles Business Journal,* May 21, 2001, p. 51.

—Jeffrey L. Covell

Kensey Nash Corporation

Marsh Creek Corporate Center
55 East Uwchlan Avenue
Exton, Pennsylvania 19341
U.S.A.
Telephone: (610) 524-0188
Fax: (610) 524-0265
Web site: http://www.kenseynash.com

Public Company
Incorporated: 1984
Employees: 294
Sales: $58.21 million (2004)
Stock Exchanges: NASDAQ
Ticker Symbol: KNSY
NAIC: 541710 Research and Development in the
    Physical Sciences and Engineering Sciences; 325211
    Plastics Material and Resin Manufacturing; 339112
    Surgical and Medical Instrument Manufacturing

Kensey Nash Corporation is a medical technology company skilled in developing puncture closure devices for cardiovascular catheterizations. Kensey Nash's mainstay product is the Angio-Seal Vascular Closure Device, which seals and closes femoral artery punctures made during angioplasty procedures performed with a catheter. From this foundation, the company developed other technologies and devices designed for other medical markets, such as sports medicine and spine. The Angio-Seal, however, accounts for a majority of the company's annual revenue, ranking as the leading device in its market in the United States and Europe. One promising product for the company, which won regulatory approval for use in Europe in 2002 and in the United States in 2005, is the TriActiv Balloon Protected Flush Extraction System. TriActiv, via a small balloon, blocks debris from floating into the bloodstream and flushes and extracts debris from a blood vessel after a treatment procedure. The Angio-Seal device is manufactured, marketed, and distributed by St. Jude Medical, Inc., from whom Kensey Nash receives a royalty payment for each device sold.

Origins

Kensey Nash was founded by two individuals who knew which market they wanted to serve, but who lacked a precise idea of the product they would use to serve their selected market. Dr. Kenneth R. Kensey and John E. Nash formed their eponymous company in 1984 to develop medical products for diagnosing and treating cardiovascular disease. That much was clear from the beginning, but the pair had yet to develop a product or device to aid in cardiovascular treatment. Kensey Nash was a development company, an enterprise that recorded little financial success for more than its first decade of business. The process of finding its place in the broadly defined medical products industry was gradual, beginning with a focus on rotary technology that led to the identification of a market for puncture closure devices. By the late 1980s, Kensey Nash researchers had intensified their development of puncture closure devices, an effort that led to the filing of the company's first patent for the Angio-Seal Device in 1987. The Angio-Seal became Kensey Nash's signature product, a device that served as the primary financial engine driving the company's growth during its first two decades of business.

The market need for Kensey Nash's Angio-Seal was created when an angioplasty was performed with a catheter. The company, literally, filled a hole. An angioplasty requires a cardiologist to insert a thin tube, a catheter, into the femoral artery near the groin of the patient. Once the catheter is inserted, the cardiologist snakes it up the body until it reaches the damaged blood vessels, such as the coronary arteries. Next, a tiny balloon is inflated, which clears the blocked artery. The procedure remained minimally invasive, generally leaving holes just two to three millimeters wide in the femoral artery, but a hole in one of the body's main arteries, no matter how small, had the potential to cause major damage without a monitored and extended recovery process. After a catheterization, a nurse was required to put physical pressure on the femoral artery for up to 30 minutes to prevent blood loss, a problem that was compounded because patients often took anti-clotting drugs as part of the procedure. Once the nurse had applied pressure on the hole for the requisite time, the patient was forced to lay flat for as long as 24 hours under a 10-pound sandbag to keep the wound closed. Kensey

Nash's Angio-Seal promised to dramatically alter the recovery process, virtually eliminating it.

Signing an Agreement with American Home Products in 1991

When Kensey Nash filed its first patent related to the Angio-Seal in 1987, the company was years away from developing a marketable device, one that would require approval from the U.S. Food and Drug Administration (FDA) before it could be sold domestically. As the developmental work was underway, the company forged an immensely important strategic relationship with another company, American Home Products Corporation (AHP). The partnership with AHP was struck in 1991 after Kensey Nash had spent three years developing the Angio-Seal in-house. The terms of the partnership included five agreements between the two companies that included licensing agreements for the United States and abroad, a research and development agreement, and a credit agreement. The relationship with AHP represented a lifeblood for Kensey Nash, giving the company essential funding for the research and development of the Angio-Seal, vital help in gaining regulatory approval in Europe (where the company's puncture closure device first appeared), and the financial wherewithal to conduct clinical trials that were mandatory for FDA approval. Without the partnership with AHP, Kensey Nash would have lacked the financial backing to bring the Angio-Seal to market.

Even with the licensing and milestone payments coming from AHP, Kensey Nash endured bleak financial times during the first half of the 1990s. In 1992, the company collected $4.7 million in revenue, nearly all from licensing and milestone payments. The company posted a profit for the year, netting $65,000, but it would be the last time it recorded net income for several years. Between 1993 and 1996, Kensey Nash racked up more than $17 million in losses. A vastly more promising financial future presented itself when the company celebrated a seminal achievement in its history. In September 1995, the company was granted regulatory approval to sell its Angio-Seal in Europe, a product introduction that revealed the remarkable engineering behind Kensey Nash's puncture closure device.

An Angio-Seal relied on biomedical material, a strength of Kensey Nash. When the catheter was removed from the femoral artery following angioplasty, a special polymer anchor was inserted into the artery that sealed the hole within minutes, thereby eliminating the need for physical pressure on the wound as well as an overnight stay in the hospital. The Angio-Seal also inserted collagen, a protein that induced clotting along the arterial wall to create a biological seal. Adding further to the device's appeal among doctors, patients, and insurance compa-

nies, the entire implant was absorbed into the body within two or three months.

Kensey Nash's management celebrated the debut of Angio-Seal in Europe, as did management at AHP. The device sold for between $165 and $205 in a global market that counted more than 6.5 million cardiac catheterizations being performed each year. Officials at Kensey Nash, eagerly awaiting FDA approval, took their European debut as an opportunity to let the investing public share in the company's potential success. Kensey Nash completed its initial public offering in December 1995, debuting on the NASDAQ. Only three weeks after this defining moment, with the company's stock offering sandwiched between its European debut and its eagerly anticipated U.S. debut, disaster struck. A record snowfall in Kensey Nash's hometown of Exton, Pennsylvania, caused the roof of the company's manufacturing facility to collapse. Only a few short months after finally having a market demand to fulfill, the company could not oblige. Production of the Angio-Seal was shut down for four months, as company officials scurried to get the company back up and running.

FDA Approval in 1996

After its winter misfortune, Kensey Nash received news that wiped away the memory of the January snowfall. In September 1996, one year after winning regulatory approval from the European Economic Community, the company won approval from the FDA. The FDA's approval gave Kensey Nash full access to the roughly 6.5 million cardiovascular catheterizations performed each year worldwide, greatly increasing the company's chance to dominate the market. The company was not alone in the vascular puncture closure market. Two other publicly traded companies were vying for market share. New Jersey-based Datascope received FDA approval for its Vaso-Seal in September 1995, the same month Kensey Nash began selling its Angio-Seal device in Europe. Another company, California-based Perclose, was hoping to receive approval for its vascular puncture closure device in 1997. Up for grabs was a worldwide market estimated to be as high as $1.3 billion. From an investment perspective, some Wall Street analysts preferred Kensey Nash because the company represented a "pure play" in an emerging market. Datascope was an established company deriving substantial revenue from other businesses, thereby preventing an investor to invest solely in vascular closure devices. Perclose, without FDA approval, remained a question mark, perceived by the investment community as too great a risk because it lacked a marketable device. Kensey Nash's esteem within the investment community increased in mid-1997 when the FDA ruled that Angio-Seal devices could be administered by hospital professionals other than doctors, such as medical residents, fellows, and nurses. News of the FDA's approval for expanded use caused Kensey Nash's stock price to increase 33 percent in one day.

As the late 1990s progressed, Angio-Seal proved to be the market winner. By the end of the 1990s, the company controlled 35 percent of the vascular puncture closure market, holding sway as the leader. In March 1999, St. Jude Medical, Inc. acquired the worldwide license for Angio-Seal, becoming Kensey Nash's new partner in the success of the device. Under the terms of the agreement, St. Jude was responsible for manufacturing, market-

Key Dates:

1984: Dr. Kenneth R. Kensey and John E. Nash establish Kensey Nash Corporation.
1987: The first patent is filed for the Angio-Seal device.
1991: Kensey Nash enters a strategic relationship with American Home Products Corp.
1995: Regulatory approval to sell Angio-Seal devices in Europe is granted.
1996: Regulatory approval is granted to begin selling Angio-Seal in the United States.
1999: St. Jude Medical acquires the worldwide license for Angio-Seal.
2000: THM Biomedical Inc. is acquired.
2002: TriActiv is approved for sale in Europe.
2004: Sales of the Angio-Seal device eclipse four million units.
2005: The FDA approves TriActiv for sale in the United States.

ing, selling, and distributing Angio-Seal on a global basis. Kensey Nash, for its part, received a royalty payment (initially 12 percent) for each Angio-Seal sold, an arrangement that made Angio-Seal a pure-profit business for Kensey Nash.

In the wake of the successful worldwide launch of Angio-Seal, the company began developing new products and entering new businesses. In 2000, the company acquired a privately held company named THM Biomedical Inc., paying $11.1 million for the Duluth, Minnesota-based firm. THM, with an 11-patent portfolio, produced a porous, biodegradable plastic that absorbed liquid, which the FDA approved for use in dental work in 1996. After receiving a $1.2 million grant from the U.S. Department of Commerce's Advanced Technology Program, THM began experimenting with the plastic as a device to replace damaged cartilage. In the tests, the absorbent plastic acted as a small container, which carried two special proteins capable of directing cell development. After being implanted in a patient, one of the proteins in the plastic vessel induced cells to emerge as bones while the other protein promoted the growth of cartilage. Once both proteins began fulfilling their respective tasks, the plastic gradually disintegrated into lactic acid, a natural, physiological substance.

Kensey Nash at the Dawn of the 21st Century

As Kensey Nash entered the 21st century, much effort was being directed to the development of a new medical device. Called the TriActiv Balloon Protected Flush Extraction System, the device was designed to provide protection against blockage of a diseased blood vessel undergoing treatment. Use of the TriActiv device entailed inserting a tiny balloon in a diseased blood vessel and positioning it to block debris from floating into the bloodstream. The debris, through the use of a tube, was flushed out of the patient's body. As developmental work on the

TriActiv device neared conclusion, the company established a subsidiary to sell and to market the device in Europe. In January 2002, the company formed Kensey Nash Europe GmbH in Eschorn, Germany. In May 2002, the company received regulatory approval to begin selling TriActiv in Europe, prompting it to form distribution agreements for sales in the United Kingdom, Ireland, Switzerland, Austria, and Italy.

As Kensey Nash observed its 20th year in business, the company had cause to celebrate. Its Angio-Seal device controlled approximately 60 percent of the global market for vascular closure devices, generating $20.9 million in royalty income for Kensey Nash in 2004 (St. Jude collected $251 million in revenue from Angio-Seal devices in 2004). The launch of the device in Japan in late 2003 helped the company sell its four millionth unit in early 2004, a milestone that, under the terms of the agreement with St. Jude, reduced Kensey Nash's royalty payment to 6 percent. Looking ahead, the company was gearing up for the launch of TriActiv in the United States. The company concluded clinical trials in 2004 and received FDA approval in March 2005. As Kensey Nash plotted its future course, it was hoped the success of TriActiv would match the success of Angio-Seal and confirm the company's reputation as a pioneer in the medical devices industry.

Principal Subsidiaries

Kensey Nash Holding Company; Kensey Nash Europe GmbH (Germany).

Principal Competitors

Datascope Corporation; C.R. Bard, Inc.; Bascular Solutions, Inc.

Further Reading

Alva, Marilyn, "Kensey Nash Corp.," *Investor's Business Daily,* September 18, 2001, p. A11.

"Duluth, Minn., Biomedical Firm Is Sold to a Medical Device Company," *Knight Ridder/Tribune Business News,* September 5, 2000.

Egan, Mary Ellen, "The Plot Thickens," *Forbes,* September 16, 2002, p. 166.

George, John, "Artery-Clearing Device to Get Wider Testing," *Philadelphia Business Journal,* October 20, 2000, p. 3.

Gianturco, Michael, "A Play on Catheterization," *Forbes,* December 30, 1996, p. 146.

"Kensey Nash Gets FDA OK for TriActiv System," *America's Intelligence Wire,* March 24, 2005, p. 34.

Lau, Gloria, "Kensey Nash Corp.," *Investor's Business Daily,* May 2, 2003, p. A7.

Shaw, Craig, "Artery Seal Developer Tops '98 All-Time High," *Investor's Business Daily,* June 12, 2003, p. B8.

Stark, Karl, "FDA Approves Pennsylvania Firm's Artery-Repairing Tool for Wide Use," *Knight Ridder/Tribune Business News,* August 12, 1997.

"Warnings of Lower Profits Trim Kensey Nash," *Atlanta Journal-Constitution,* June 13, 1998, p. E5.

—Jeffrey L. Covell

Kforce Inc.

1001 East Palm Avenue
Tampa, Florida 33605
U.S.A.
Telephone: (813) 552-5000
Toll Free: (888) 663-3626
Fax: (813) 552-2493
Web site: http://www.kforce.com

Public Company
Incorporated: 1998 as Romac International, Inc.
Employees: 7,569
Sales: $661.45 million (2004)
Stock Exchanges: NASDAQ
Ticker Symbol: KFRC
NAIC: 561320 Temporary Help Services; 561310
    Employment Placement Agencies

Kforce Inc. is a professional staffing services firm that provides temporary and permanent workers trained in finance and accounting, technology, healthcare, clinical research, and scientific fields. Kforce operates 62 field offices in 24 states, maintaining a presence in 45 markets. The company derives more than 90 percent of its annual revenue from placing temporary workers.

Origins

When the Kforce name debuted in 1999, it was the corporate banner for a nearly 40-year-old business. Kforce was a new name for an old company, one whose size roughly doubled the year before the name change when two competitors, Romac International and Source Services Corporation, joined together to create a new national force in the staffing services industry. Source Services was the larger of the two companies when they merged, but Romac was dominant partner in the corporate marriage, with its absorption of Source Services representing one of a string of acquisitions completed by the company during the latter half of the 1990s.

Both Romac and Source Services were founded during the 1960s, a decade of exponential growth for the staffing services industry. Both companies operated in a niche within the U.S. staffing services industry. The industry, as a definable, organized entity, did not emerge until after World War II, when the economy began relying on a class of workers willing to satisfy the sometimes fleeting employment needs of corporate and industrial America. Once industry and commerce in the United States reached substantial proportions, the need for staffing services existed as a conduit connecting the needs of employers with the needs of employees. To gain the status of a definable, national body, the staffing services industry drew from the maturation of two if its most important constituents, Manpower, Inc. and Kelly Girl Service, both formed in the immediate postwar years.

Both Romac and Source Services had much more in common with Manpower. Manpower began by supplying industrial temporaries during its first year of operation, but diversified its services in subsequent years to include salespeople. By the early 1960s, the company had established a technical division to provide architects, engineers, and draftsmen to its clients, entering into the specialized industry niche that Romac and Source Services would occupy. The 1960s also saw the staffing services industry being used as a strategic tool, evolving beyond a stopgap resource for replacing sick or vacationing employees to become an effective means of cutting costs and contending with the dictates of business cycles. Personnel managers realized the advantages to be gained in tapping into a pool of temporary workers to negotiate through upturns and downturns in business, benefiting from the added fluidity of labor management and realizing significant financial savings from reducing the payment of unemployment taxes.

Romac and Source Services were born during the staffing industry's first decade of meaningful existence. Source Services was the older of the two, starting out in 1962. Romac, which was founded as Romac & Associates, was founded four years later, beginning a rise through the industry's ranks that would take decades before the company's growth could be discernible on a national level. In its gradual rise to what it later became, Romac emulated its more prominent mentor, Manpower. Manpower, which set the tone for the development of generations of staffing services to follow, began a franchising program early in its history. By the time Manpower established its technical division, 75 percent of its more than 300 offices were operated by franchisees. Romac followed suit, selling its first franchises in 1976. Romac was small at this point, a local and regional staffing services firm that was two decades away from asserting itself as a company with a national profile. The company did not begin to demonstrate the inclination of becoming an industry player until the 1990s, a decade when the outsourcing of nearly every corporate function was in vogue and a decade that would see Romac's path cross with the rise of another staffing services firm, Source Services.

Union of Romac and Source Services in the 1990s

During its first decades in business, Romac provided skilled workers to companies involved in accounting, banking, and data processing. Its focus shifted during the decade of its greatest growth, when a new breed of trained employees was sought after by scores of companies. During the 1990s, information technology (IT) specialists were in demand, offering a lucrative business area for staffing services firms who provided skilled labor. Both Romac and Source Services built their businesses around the IT sector, using the field as their mainstay source of revenue. Although both companies also provided workers for the financial and engineering fields and other disciplines that required skilled labor, the recruitment and supply of IT specialists became the bedrock of both companies' financial well-being.

Romac began demonstrating the desire to become a national force one year before its 30th birthday. The occasion that triggered the company's drive to expand was its debut as a publicly traded concern in 1995, when the company maintained more than 20 offices in 19 markets. During the course of three decades, Romac had evolved from a local staffing services firm into a regional firm, a pace of expansion that would be eclipsed by far during the latter half of the 1990s. Romac accelerated its pace of expansion by acquiring other companies, embarking on an acquisition campaign that would see the company complete 13 acquisitions in the three-year period leading up to its seminal deal with Source Services.

Most of the acquisitions completed before the Source Services merger were small in stature, but each added a new area of the national map to Romac's geographic scope. The purchases made in the years leading up to the Source Services deal showed a company making a concerted attempt to broaden its operating

territory. In March 1997, Romac purchased Houston-based Professional Application Resources, Inc., a firm that specialized in providing contract services for IT personnel in Houston and Dallas. Several months later, in September, Romac bolstered its presence in the Chicago area by acquiring Oakbrook, Illinois-based UQ Solutions, Inc., a firm that provided IT personnel. Before the end of the year, Romac entered the Denver market through an acquisition, purchasing, in December 1997, Englewood, Colorado-based DP Specialists of Colorado, Inc., a leading IT consulting firm that specialized in providing highly skilled consultants to the Denver market.

Romac completed its 13th, post-IPO acquisition two weeks before coming to terms with Source Services. At the end of January 1998, the company purchased Washington, D.C.-based CRE, Inc., a leading provider of staffing services within the human resources discipline. Romac by this point marketed itself under the trademarked phrase "The KnowledgeForce Resource," which would serve as the basis for the name it would adopt after the Source Services merger was completed. Romac's chief executive officer, Dave Dunkel, whose responsibilities were increasing substantially with each acquisition, commented on the addition of CRE to Romac's portfolio of assets, marking the occasion with a statement quoted in the January 29, 1998 issue of *PR Newswire*. "This is a major step forward in Romac's ability to offer the capability of a national network of widely recognized human resource experts who can act as an extension of our clients in the execution of their deliverables," Dunkel said.

Days later, Dunkel announced the biggest deal in Romac's history. In mid-February, Romac and Source Services revealed that they had agreed to a $375 million merger in a stock-for-stock deal. The announcement promised to create one of the largest staffing agencies of professional and skilled workers in the country. Romac, thanks to the acquisitions completed since its IPO, was in the midst of a tremendous growth spurt, having increased its revenues from $94 million in 1996 to $181 million in 1997, the last year the firm released annual financial results before it absorbed Source Services. Romac collected its sales total from 31 offices serving *Fortune* 1000 companies in 18 markets, a corporate profile set to become substantially more distinguished with the addition of Source Services' operations. Source Services possessed 54 offices in the United States and one in Canada, providing professional workers trained in the finance, engineering, healthcare, and legal fields. Source Services derived two-thirds of its $295 million in sales in 1997 from providing temporary and permanent workers to the IT industry. Once combined, the new company was projected to have annual revenues of $476 million, a total drawn from 86 offices in 40 markets, including the 25 largest markets in the country.

Although Source Services was larger than Romac, Romac was the surviving entity following the merger. The combined company was named Romac International, a company led by Dunkel that counted Source Services as a wholly owned subsidiary. In 1999, the name of the company was changed to kforce.com, an abbreviation of the company's KnowledgeForce marketing slogan. The name change coincided with the company's decision to re-create itself as an Internet-based business, making the beginning of the 21st century the beginning of a new era of existence for the Dunkel-led organization. More than $50 million was spent moving the company's business online, including $4.5 million spent to air commercials on Super Bowl Sunday in early 2000. The strategic shift was ill-timed, however, occurring just before a national recession, the sweeping collapse of dot.com companies, and a deleterious dip in hiring IT personnel conspired to wreak havoc on the "new" kforce.com and its mainstay business of supplying IT specialists through a web-based service.

Kforce Entering the New Century

Kforce.com's losses mounted at the turn of century, prompting cost-cutting measures and a decision to distance itself from the implosion of the dot-com industry. Although the company continued to conduct business online, management decided to drop the ".com" from the corporate title, making the subtle yet symbolic switch to "Kforce." The company incurred losses for four straight years between 1999 and 2002, recording its most devastating loss in 2002, when Kforce registered a $47 million loss. In 2003, the company arrested its financial slide by posting a profit of $5.1 million on sales of $495.5 million.

Although Kforce's financial performance was far from impressive during the early 2000s, the company did make several positive moves. In 2001, Kforce acquired Emergency Response Staffing Inc., an Arizona-based company that placed nurses in hospitals. The acquisition of Emergency Response was followed by another purchase, one that bolstered Kforce's involvement in the pharmaceutical sector. Scientific Staffing, a Florida-based company that provided lab technicians to the pharmaceutical industry, was purchased.

Kforce's return to profitability in 2003 occurred as the national economy began to show signs that recessive conditions were coming to an end. The improving economic climate renewed interest in the staffing services industry as a whole, ushering in a period of consolidation in a fragmented industry populated by roughly 7,000 firms in the United States. Dunkel and his management team became part of the trend toward consolidation, setting their sights on a Novato, California firm named Hall, Kinion & Associates (Hall Kinion).

Hall Kinion, boasting 300 employees, 2,000 contract workers, and 18 field offices, began looking for a suitor in 2003. Hall Kinion was intent on becoming a billion-dollar company, and forging a partnership with another staffing services firm became central to reaching its financial goal. Hall Kinion shopped itself to 37 different companies, piquing the interest of 21 firms, Kforce included. A bidding war ensued, as each of the parties attempted to gain control of Hall Kinion. Kforce emerged as the winner in late 2003, announcing that it had agreed to pay $63.8 million for Hall Kinion.

As Kforce and Hall Kinion worked on turning their agreement into a completed deal, industry observers assayed the merger. The addition of Hall Kinion to Kforce was expected to increase annual revenues by one-third. The geographic gains were expected to be less meaningful, with only two new markets—Oregon and Utah—added to Kforce's national footprint as a result of the merger. One aspect of the merger that impressed onlookers was Hall Kinion's OnStaff division, a result of the company's acquisition in 2002 of Burbank, California-based OnStaff, which placed accountants, bookkeepers, and loan processors at mortgage companies, banks, and other financial institutions.

As Kforce prepared for the future, the company hoped to establish a new trend of profitability. The merger with Hall Kinion, after being renegotiated for the lower price of roughly $50 million, was completed in June 2004. The union with Hall Kinion was not expected to be the last in Kforce's push toward national dominance. The staffing services industry continued to consolidate during the mid-2000s, offering new opportunities to achieve rapid growth for Dunkel and his senior managers.

Principal Subsidiaries

Source Services Corp.

Principal Competitors

Adecco S.A.; MPS Group, Inc.; Robert Half International Inc.

Further Reading

Barancik, Scott, "Kforce Agrees to Buy Competitor at a Lower Price," *St. Petersburg Times,* April 7, 2004, p. 1D.
——, "Kforce Ends Up Top Merger Suitor," *St. Petersburg Times,* January 3, 2004, p. 1D.
"Florida-Based Romac to Let Employers Bid for Job-Search Candidates Online," *Knight Ridder/Tribune Business News,* June 9, 1999.
Cronan, Carl, "Ybor, 'E-Bor' with Dot-Com HQ," *Business Journal (Serving Greater Tampa Bay),* February 4, 2000, p. 3.
Dib, Felisha, "Web Emphasis, Name Change Boost Kforce," *South Florida Business Journal,* March 30, 2001, p. 37.
Harrington, Jeff, "Kforce Says It's Ready for a Rebound," *St. Petersburg Times,* October 1, 2003, p. 1E.
——, "Kforce.com Earnings Rise, but Investors Want More," *St. Petersburg Times,* July 27, 2000, p. 1E.
——, Staffing Services Firm Plans Headquarters, Call Center in Tampa, Fla.," *Knight Ridder/Tribune Business News,* February 18, 1999.
Hundley, Kris, "Kforce Losses Mount in Stalled Job Market," *St. Petersburg Times,* February 6, 2003, p. 1E.
Sigo, Shelly, "Romac Debuts Video Interview System," *Business Journal (Serving Greater Tampa Bay),* November 12, 1999, p. 3.
"Tampa, Fla.-Based Staffing Firm Will Drop Dot-Com from Name," *Tampa Tribune,* May 1, 2001, p. 32.

—Jeffrey L. Covell

Lear Corporation

21557 Telegraph Road
Southfield, Michigan 48034-4248
U.S.A.
Telephone: (248) 447-1500
Fax: (248) 447-1722
Web site: http://www.lear.com

Public Company
Incorporated: 1917 as American Metal Products
    Company
Employees: 110,000
Sales: $16.96 billion (2004)
Stock Exchanges: New York
Ticker Symbol: LEA
NAIC: 336360 Motor Vehicle Seating and Interior Trim
    Manufacturing; 336322 Other Motor Vehicle
    Electrical and Electronic Equipment Manufacturing

Lear Corporation is the world's leading supplier of automotive interior systems. The company ranks first worldwide in seat systems, second in flooring and acoustic systems and door panels, third in headliners and electrical and electronic distribution systems, and seventh in instrument panels. Of the company's more than 270 facilities located in 34 countries, 165 are involved in production/manufacturing, 52 in administration/technical support, and 45 in assembly. Lear also maintains six advanced technology centers and three distribution centers. Increasingly global in operation, Lear generates about 44 percent of its sales in North America, a significant change from the mid-1990s when North America accounted for more than two-thirds of revenues. Although Lear relies on two clients, car-making giants General Motors Corporation and Ford Motor Company (and their respective affiliates), for about 56 percent of its sales, the company's interior systems can be found on more than 300 vehicle nameplates worldwide. Following a management-led leveraged buyout in 1988, Lear's sales grew from less than $200 million to more than $12.4 billion by 1999, as the company broadened its geographic reach and expanded its product line to encompass the full gamut of the automobile

interior. Seventeen major acquisitions completed between 1994 and 1999 were instrumental in Lear's rise to its globally dominant position.

Establishment and Postwar Growth

Although Lear and its predecessors have always made auto seat components, the company did not make a finished car seat until the mid-1980s. In the near seven-decade interim, it produced everything from plumbing fixtures to office furniture. The business was founded in 1917 by Frederick Matthai as American Metal Products Company (AMP), a manufacturer of tubular, welded, and stamped steel seat frames. Its close proximity to Detroit helped it forge close ties with major auto manufacturers General Motors and Ford. AMP incorporated in 1928, added Chrysler Corporation and International Harvester Company as customers by the early 1930s, and had broken the $1 million sales mark by 1939. Wartime contracts for production of military airplane assemblies and parts and axle housings for military trucks swelled its annual sales to $11 million by 1944.

AMP's revenues declined sharply in the immediate aftermath of World War II, to $7.7 million in 1945, but postwar demand for automobiles combined with a series of acquisitions to usher in a decade of mounting sales and profits. In 1954 AMP acquired Tube Reducing Corp., a New Jersey manufacturer of specialty hydraulic and aircraft parts. A Canadian producer of metal automotive springs was purchased that same year. In 1955 AMP diversified into plumbing and porcelain bath and kitchen fixtures with the acquisition of AllianceWare, Inc., and a producer of office furniture and storage units was also added to the corporate roster during this period. Revenues nearly quadrupled to $30.7 million by 1950, then doubled to $63.5 million over the next five years. Net income kept the pace fairly well, jumping eightfold from $346,000 in 1945 to $3 million in 1950, then increasing to $4.3 million by mid-decade. AMP went public at the dawn of this period of dramatic growth in 1946 with a $2.25 million stock offering.

This era of prosperity reached its summit in 1957, when sales and profits peaked at $72.5 million and $4.7 million, respectively. Revenues slid by 36 percent the following year to $46.4 million and net income plunged to $1.6 million. Although

AMP's revenues began to recover, rising to $64 million in 1963, its profit level hovered between $1.5 million and $2 million.

Acquisition by Lear Siegler in the Late 1960s

By the time it was acquired by and merged into the Lear Siegler conglomerate in 1966, AMP had amassed an array of businesses with products and competencies that would later be combined in the production of a finished automotive seat. General Spring Products and, later, the No-Sag Spring Company, supplied the springs. The Burroughs Division and Middletown Manufacturing Co., Inc. (acquired in 1965) were already making durable metal office furniture, and AMP itself had long made seat components for cars. While AMP was under Lear Siegler's wing, the parent company acquired Central Foam Corporation, making it a sister division. But nearly two decades would pass before Lear combined these disparate functions to manufacture a complete auto seat.

Lear Siegler was a widely diversified producer of aerospace electronics, climate control devices, and plastics. In fact, AMP (renamed the Automotive Group) was one of more than three dozen acquisitions made by Lear Siegler from 1955 to 1970. With the support of this large parent company, the Automotive Group built its first outsourced passenger car seat in 1984 and set up its first just-in-time plant near a General Motors facility soon thereafter. By 1983, the Automotive Group's annual sales had reached $160 million.

Management Buyout in Late 1980s Sparks Rejuvenation

The late 1980s ushered in challenges and opportunities that would transform the Automotive Group from a bit player in automotive components to one of the industry's top stars. In spite of antitakeover measures, Lear Siegler was acquired in 1986 by the Forstmann Little & Co. investment firm in a $2.1 billion leveraged buyout. Determining that the parts were worth more than the whole, Forstmann Little soon began spinning off Lear Siegler's disparate business segments.

Kenneth L. Way, then corporate vice-president of the Automotive Group, led a leveraged buyout of the division in 1988. Way, who had joined the company in 1966, was able to convince Kidder, Peabody to finance the $500 million deal (more than $400 million of it borrowed) that launched Lear Siegler Seating Corporation, headquartered in Southfield, Michigan. He became the company's chairman and CEO in 1988.

Once it had gained its independence, Lear Seating grew rapidly by embracing several important industry trends: out-

sourcing, just-in-time, and globalization, among others. Outsourcing, or contracting parts of the manufacturing process to independent businesses, took the auto industry by storm in the late 1980s. Carmakers found that they could save money and often obtain a better product by putting discrete components up for competitive bid. In the seat segment, for example, Lear and Johnson Controls, Inc. competed for the top market share. Knowing this, a given carmaker could negotiate for better prices, improved features, and higher levels of efficiency than it could gain by keeping production in-house.

Led by Way, Lear strove for excellence on all of these fronts. The company had begun to adopt just-in-time (JIT) manufacturing, which emphasized inventory reduction through efficient and timely production and delivery, in the early 1980s. By 1988, 12 of Lear's American plants were operating on a JIT basis. By locating its production facilities near its clients, Lear cut both storage and shipping costs. In the early 1990s, it added "sequencing" to the JIT equation by integrating its computers with those of its customers. A 1995 *Forbes* article told how Lear's Romulus, Michigan, plant was linked to Chrysler's "Dodge City" factory. "When a pickup starts down 'Dodge City's' line, an electronic message calling for the particular seats for that truck is flashed to Romulus, which can produce the seats and deliver them to Chrysler in 90 minutes." Lear was so enamored with the just-in-time process that in 1993 it made "JIT" a part of some divisions' names, as in "Opel/Eurostar JIT."

Lear also began to apply its specialized expertise to the design of auto seats. As a result, the company had a number of industry "firsts" to its credit, including the patented Sure-Bond process, which adhered seat covers directly to the foam padding inside. This process cut down on labor and waste and broadened the range of design options. During the early 1990s, Lear's innovations included the development of the first child-restraint seat, integration of the seat belt into the seat (instead of the traditional door mounting), and development of a seat with a side-impact airbag. Lear also employed sophisticated computer-aided design and manufacturing systems, used in-depth consumer comfort surveys, and conducted numerous safety and durability tests. These efforts resulted not only in growing sales but also in awards for excellence from customers, including General Motors, Ford, Chrysler, Saab Automobile AB, and Mazda Motor Corporation.

Within just a few years of its management buyout, Lear Seating's sales had multiplied nearly eight times, from around $150 million to $1.24 billion in 1990. That same year, in order to distance itself from its former conglomerate parent, the company changed its name to Lear Seating Corporation.

Acquisitions Fueling Continued Growth in Early to Mid-1990s

Lear undertook a concerted acquisition strategy in the early 1990s, focusing strongly but not exclusively on the international market. The ongoing outsourcing trend allowed Lear to purchase the seat and interior component divisions of several major original equipment manufacturers, diversifying geographically in the process. In 1991 the company acquired Saab's Swedish and Finnish interior operations. AB Volvo's interior business came next, in 1992. In 1993 Lear bought Ford

Key Dates:

1917: Based in Detroit, American Metal Products Company is founded by Frederick Matthai as a maker of steel seat frames, with its first major customers being General Motors Corporation and Ford Motor Company.

1946: Company goes public.

1966: Conglomerate Lear Siegler, Inc. acquires American Metal, which is later renamed the Automotive Group.

1984: The Automotive Group builds its first outsourced passenger car seat.

1986: Forstmann Little & Co. acquires Lear Siegler in a $2.1 billion leveraged buyout.

1988: The Automotive Group is acquired in a management buyout led by Kenneth L. Way, creating Lear Siegler Seating Corporation, headquartered in Southfield, Michigan.

1990: Company changes its name to Lear Seating Corporation.

1993: Lear acquires Ford's North American seatmaking operations.

1994: Fiat Auto S.p.A.'s seat operations are acquired; Lear Seating goes public.

1995: Automotive Industries Holding, Inc. is acquired.

1996: Company changes its name to Lear Corporation; Masland Corporation is acquired.

1999: Through its $2.3 billion acquisition of United Technologies Automotive, Inc., Lear is now able to offer its customers fully integrated automotive interior systems.

2003: GM awards Lear contract to supply full interior systems for Buick Lucerne and Cadillac DTS models, beginning with 2006 model year.

Motor's North American seatmaking operations (Favesa, S.A. de C.V., headquartered in Mexico) for $173.4 million in cash, thereby becoming Ford's seatmaker of choice. Fiat Auto S.p.A.'s seat operations (SEPI S.p.A.) were added in December 1994, and in 1995 Lear formed a joint venture with Spain's Inespo (a foam manufacturer) to supply seats to Volkswagen AG in Brazil. By the mid-1990s, Lear had plants in North and South America, Europe, Thailand, Indonesia, and Australia. At that time, more than one-fourth of Lear's sales were generated outside North America.

Fueled in large part by these acquisitions, Lear's sales and earnings multiplied dramatically in the early 1990s. Sales increased at a 34.9 percent average annual clip, from $1.4 billion in 1991 to $4.7 billion by 1995. Earnings grew from a $22.2 million deficit to a $91.6 million profit during the same period.

Lear went public in 1994 with an offering of 14 percent of its equity. The $103 million raised was applied to Lear's long-term debt, reducing it by about 25 percent. It apparently freed up just enough credit to allow the company to make the biggest acquisition yet in its history. In August 1995 Lear purchased Automotive Industries Holding, Inc. for $881.3 million and made it the AI Division. According to the company's 1995 annual report, AI added more than $300 million in sales and doubled Lear's

potential market to about $22 billion. The acquisition boosted Lear's product line to what it called "full interior systems," including door panels, headliners, and instrument panels, but not airbags and electronics. Because its capabilities now went well beyond merely "seating," the company dropped that word from its name in 1996, becoming simply Lear Corporation. The firm now ranked as the third largest independent (i.e., not owned by an automaker) auto supplier in North America and the tenth largest in the world.

Late 1990s: Becoming a Complete Automotive Interior Supplier

Between 1996 and 1999 Lear completed 13 major acquisitions that helped the company achieve its goal of becoming a complete automotive interior supplier. These deals also vastly expanded the firm's global capabilities, making it much less dependent on its traditional customers, the major North American automakers. The acquisitions helped fuel the company's explosive growth as revenues surged from $6.25 million in 1996 to $12.43 billion in 1999—a near doubling over just four years.

Lear acquired Carlisle, Pennsylvania-based Masland Corporation for $473.8 million in July 1996. Masland was a leading producer of automotive floor systems, including carpeting and floor mats, acoustical products, and luggage compartment trim. In December 1996, in a $91.1 million deal, Lear filled another void in its capabilities by acquiring Borealis Industrier, A.B., a Swedish maker of instrument panels for the European automobile and truck industry, particularly Volvo, Saab, and Scania. With annual sales of $230 million, Borealis also produced door panels, climate systems, and exterior trim.

During 1997 Lear launched plans to consolidate its companywide technical staff at a new technical center to be located near its Southfield headquarters. As part of its drive to court more European business, Lear moved the office of Robert Rossiter, the company president, to Germany, placing him nearer to decision makers on that continent. Two more acquisitions completed that year aided the European expansion. In June Lear bought Dunlop Cox, based in Nottingham, England, a producer of manual and electrically powered seating mechanisms. One month later, Keiper Car Seating GmbH & Co. KG was acquired for DM 400 million (about $252.5 million). The German firm was a leading supplier of automotive vehicle seat systems on a JIT basis for Daimler-Benz AG, Audi AG, Volkswagen, and Porsche AG, and it had ten seating assembly plants in Germany, Hungary, Italy, Brazil, and South Africa. Lear now controlled 23 percent of the European auto seating market. Back home, Lear also acquired the Seat Sub-Systems Unit of ITT Automotive, a division of ITT Industries, in August. The unit was a North American supplier of power seat adjusters and power recliners.

The acquisitions continued in 1998. In May Lear acquired two Italian firms: Gruppo Pianfei S.r.L., producer of door panels, headliners, and plastic interior components at six facilities located throughout Italy; and Strapazzini Resine S.r.L., maker of instrument panels, door panels, sunshades, consoles, and pillar trim at two Italian facilities. The most significant deal that year, however, came in September, when the company paid General Motors $246.6 million for the seating business of

Delphi Automotive Systems. The purchase strengthened Lear's relationship with GM and included 16 plants located in ten countries. As the acquisition spree continued, the need to consolidate the growing array of facilities grew as well. Late in 1998, Lear launched a major restructuring involving the closure of 18 plants worldwide and the elimination of 2,800 jobs, representing about 4 percent of its workforce. To implement the program, aimed at lower costs and improving profit margins, Lear took pretax charges of $133 million, cutting 1998 net income to $115.5 million, almost half the $207.2 million total for the preceding year.

In its largest deal ever, Lear spent $2.3 billion in May 1999 for United Technologies Automotive, Inc., the automotive parts business of United Technologies Corporation. With this acquisition, Lear was able to fill in the last piece missing from its product portfolio. UT Automotive provided Lear with the capability to provide the electrical and electronics infrastructure of a car's interior, an increasingly important, and costly, part of a vehicle, including the components and wiring hidden behind the instrument panel and inside doors. Lear could now offer its customers fully integrated automotive interior systems. Headquartered in Dearborn, Michigan, UT Automotive had 1998 annual sales of approximately $3 billion, 44,000 employees, and 90 facilities in 18 countries. The company's electric motors business had nothing to do with vehicle interiors, so Lear quickly divested it, selling it to Johnson Electric Holdings Limited for $310 million in June 1999.

Consolidating and Paying Down Debt in the More Uncertain Early 2000s

While digesting its latest acquisition, Lear placed a hold on further deals and began to seek out more partnerships and joint ventures, particularly in the electronics area and especially as it made a major push into Asia. The company enjoyed its best year yet in 2000, posting profits of $274.7 million on revenues of $14.07 billion. In October of that year, Rossiter was named CEO, succeeding Way, who remained chairman.

As its acquisitions began to pay off in the early 2000s, Lear used much of its free cash flow to pay down the heavy debt it had incurred during the spending spree. By the end of 2002 it was able to pare its debt to $2.27 billion, a 40 percent reduction from the peak level in September 1999. In 2001, however, Lear was forced to begin grappling with production cuts by major auto makers, and its sales fell. In an effort to generate savings of as much as $50 million per year, Lear launched another major restructuring that year. This one involved 6,500 jobs cuts, or about 6 percent of the workforce, the closure of 21 plants, and $110.2 million in restructuring charges. Net income for the year totaled just $26.3 million.

At the beginning of 2003 Way gave up his position as Lear chairman, handing the title to Rossiter, who also remained CEO. Early that year, Lear won a contract from GM, valued at $825 million annually, giving it full responsibility for the design, engineering, sourcing, manufacturing, and delivery of the entire interiors for the Buick Lucerne (formerly the LeSabre) and Cadillac DTS (formerly the DeVille) full-size sedans beginning with the 2006 model year. This was the first time that GM had vested an interior supplier with this level of responsibility,

and it represented the culmination of Lear's desire to supply fully integrated interior systems.

By 2004, despite the continuing struggles of automakers, Lear was able to post record results: net income of $422.2 million on net sales of $16.96 billion. Strong cash flows enabled the company to further cut its debt load to $1.87 billion, to pay the first cash dividend in company history, and to repurchase nearly two million shares of its common stock. The key target area for future growth continued to be Asia, where Lear formed several new partnerships, bringing the total number of joint ventures in the region to 19—including 12 in fast-growing China. In July 2004 Lear augmented its electrical components capabilities by acquiring GHW Grote & Hartmann GmbH for $160 million. Based in Wuppertal, Germany, with 2003 revenues of approximately $275 million, Grote & Hartmann specialized in terminals, connectors, and junction boxes, mainly for the automotive industry.

Amid sharp production cutbacks at the major automakers, significant declines in sales of large sport utility vehicles, and high raw material costs, Lear announced in April 2005 that its earnings for the year would be lower than expected and that it planned to cut its U.S. workforce and some U.S. plants in order to shift production overseas to lower-cost countries. The company also said that it planned to make additional acquisitions. Longer term, the company anticipated that new business, mainly in Asia, would boost earnings in 2006 and 2007. Thus, a key going forward for Lear was its more diversified customer base: Whereas in the mid-1990s two-thirds of revenues had been generated in North America, the company through its overseas expansion had reduced this figure to 44 percent by 2004.

Principal Subsidiaries

Alfombras San Luis S.A. (Argentina); Asia Pacific Components Co., Ltd. (Thailand; 90.4%); Consorcio Industrial Mexicanos de Autopartes, S.A. de C.V. (Mexico); El Trim (Pty.) Ltd. (South Africa); GHW Engineering GmbH (Germany); Hanyil Co., Ltd. (Korea; 99.8%); Honduras Electrical Distribution Systems S. de R.L. de C.V. (60%); Industrias Lear de Argentina SrL; John Cotton Plastics Ltd. (U.K.); Lear Automotive Corporation Singapore Pte. Ltd.; Lear Automotive France, SAS; Lear Automotive Interiors (Pty.) Ltd. (South Africa); Lear Automotive Morocco SAS; Lear Canada; Lear Car Seating do Brasil Industria e Comercio de Interiores Automotivos Ltda. (Brazil); Lear Corporation Asientos, S.L. (Spain); Lear Corporation Austria GmbH & Co. KG; Lear Corporation Belgium CVA; Lear Corporation Beteiligungs GmbH (Germany); Lear Corporation Canada, Ltd.; Lear Corporation Changchun Automotive Interior Systems Co., Ltd. (China); Lear Corporation Czech s.r.o. (Czech Republic); Lear Corporation Drahtfedern GmbH (Germany); Lear Corporation Electrical and Electronics; Lear Corporation France SAS; Lear Corporation GmbH & Co. KG (Germany); Lear Corporation Holding GmbH (Germany); Lear Corporation Holdings Spain S.L.; Lear Corporation Honduras, S. de R.L.; Lear Corporation Hungary Automotive Manufacturing Kft.; Lear Corporation Interior Components (Pty.) Ltd. (South Africa); Lear Corporation Italia S.p.A. (Italy); Lear Corporation Japan K.K.; Lear Corporation Mexico, S.A. de C.V.; Lear Corporation North West (Pty.) Ltd. (South Africa); Lear Corporation (Nottingham) Ltd. (U.K.); Lear Corporation

Poland Sp. z o.o.; Lear Corporation Portugal - Componentes Para Automoveis, S.A.; Lear Corporation Romania S.r.L.; Lear Corporation Seating Czech s.r.o. (Czech Republic); Lear Corporation Seating France SAS (France); Lear Corporation Silao S.A. de C.V. (Mexico); Lear Corporation Slovakia s.r.o. (Slovak Republic); Lear Corporation Spain S.L.; Lear Corporation (SSD) Ltd. (U.K.); Lear Corporation Sweden AB; Lear Corporation UK Holdings Ltd.; Lear Corporation UK Interior Systems Ltd.; Lear Corporation UK ISM Ltd.; Lear Corporation (UK) Ltd.; Lear Corporation Verwaltungs GmbH (Germany); Lear de Venezuela C.A.; Lear do Brasil Industria e Comercio de Interiores Automotivos Ltda. (Brazil); Lear Electrical (Poland) Sp. z o.o.; Lear Electrical Systems de Mexico, S. de R.L. de C.V.; Lear European Holding S.L. (Spain); Lear Gebaudemanagement GmbH & Co. KG (Germany); Lear Holdings (Hungary) Kft.; Lear Holdings, S.r.l. de C.V. (Mexico); Lear Korea Yuhan Hoesa; Lear (Luxembourg) S.a.r.l.; Lear Mexican Trim Operations S. de R.L. de C.V. (Mexico); Lear Netherlands (Holdings) B.V.; Lear Offranville SARL (France); Lear Operations Corporation; Lear Otomotiv Sanayi ve Ticaret Ltd. Sirketi (Turkey); Lear Rosslyn (Pty.) Ltd. (South Africa); Lear Seating Private Ltd. (India); Lear Seating (Thailand) Corp. Ltd. (97.9%); Lear Sewing (Pty.) Ltd. (South Africa); Lear Teknik Oto Yan Sanayi Ltd. Sirket (Turkey; 67%); OOO Lear (Russia); Rael Handelsgmbh (Austria); Shenyang Lear Automotive Seating and Interior Systems Co., Ltd. (China; 60%); Societe Offransvillaise de Technologie SAS (France); Wuhan Lear-DPCA Auto Electric Co., Ltd. (China; 75%).

Principal Competitors

Johnson Controls, Inc.; Faurecia SA; Intier Automotive Inc.; Collins & Aikman Corporation; Rieter Holding Ltd.; Visteon Corporation; Delphi Corporation; Yazaki Corporation; Sumitomo Corporation; Alcoa Fujikura Ltd.; Valeo.

Further Reading

Flint, Jerry, "King Lear," *Forbes*, May 22, 1995, pp. 43–44.
Hampton, Bill, "Kenneth L. Way," *Chief Executive*, May 1995, p. 32.
Jewett, Dale, "Lear's Way Ends Reign on High Note," *Automotive News*, December 30, 2002, p. 4.
"King Lear: How Competitors View Lear/Automotive Industries Deal," *Ward's Auto World*, August 1995, p. 17.
Kisiel, Ralph, "Buyout Positions Lear As Complete Interior Provider," *Automotive News*, July 24, 1995, p. 14.
Krebs, Michelle, "Integrated Interiors," *Automotive News*, February 27, 1989, p. E20.
McCracken, Jeffrey, "Deal Puts Lear Under the Hood," *Crain's Detroit Business*, May 10, 1999, p. 1.
Palmer, Jay, "King of the Cabin," *Barron's*, August 4, 2003, p. 27.
Phelan, Mark, "Rocking Around the Clock," *Automotive Industries*, October 1995, p. 129.
Plumb, Stephen E., "Lear Expansion Jumping into High Gear," *Ward's Auto World*, December 1991, p. 63.
——, "Scrambling for Seats: Outside Vendors Offer Complete Seating Systems," *Ward's Auto World*, August 1989, p. 51.
Sawyer, Christopher A., "Can't Sit Still," *Automotive Industries*, February 1994, p. 68.
Sherefkin, Robert, "A Good Feeling Inside: Lear Sits Pretty As Master of Auto Interiors," *Crain's Detroit Business*, October 28, 1996, p. 2.
——, "Lear Leaps into the Super Six: Supplier Wins Bid for UT Automotive," *Automotive News*, March 22, 1999, p. 4.
Simison, Robert L., "Lear's Recent Acquisition of a GM Unit Bolsters Its Drive Toward Consolidation," *Wall Street Journal*, September 16, 1998, p. B18D.
Simmons, Jacqueline, "Lear Seating to Sell Shares in Public Offer," *Wall Street Journal*, March 14, 1994, p. A8.
Smock, Doug, "This *Lear*'s the King of Interiors," *Plastics World*, October 1996, pp. 32–33, 36–37.
Sorge, Marjorie, "Do Seats Flog Your Fanny?," *Ward's Auto World*, November 1993, p. 44.
——, "Lear Gets Behind Outsourced Seating Plan," *Ward's Auto World*, February 1995, p. 50.
"Southern Exposure," *Automotive News*, December 27, 1993, p. 8.
Vlasic, Bill, "Get Big—or Get Out," *Business Week*, September 2, 1996, pp. 60+.
White, Joseph B., "Lear Agrees to Pay United Technologies $2.3 Billion for Its Auto-Parts Operation," *Wall Street Journal*, March 17, 1999, p. A4.
——, "Lear's Profit, Sales Soar, but Wall Street Is Unimpressed," *Wall Street Journal*, July 21, 2000, p. B4.
Winter, Drew, "Growing Modular," *Ward's Auto World*, January 1996, p. 57.
——, "In the Driver's Seat: Lear Corp.," *Ward's Auto World*, July 1996, p. 35.

—April Dougal Gasbarre
—update: David E. Salamie

Leucadia National Corporation

315 Park Avenue South
New York, New York 10010
U.S.A.
Telephone: (212) 460-1900
Fax: (212) 598-4869
Web site: http://www.leucadia.com

Public Company
Incorporated: 1968 as Talcott National Corporation
Employees: 5,324
Sales: $2.26 billion (2004)
Stock Exchanges: New York
Ticker Symbol: LUK
NAIC: 524126 Direct Property and Casualty Insurance
    Carriers; 524113 Direct Life Insurance Carriers;
    524114 Direct Health and Medical Insurance Carriers

A holding company, Leucadia National Corporation owns businesses ranging from insurance to telecommunications. Although the roots of Leucadia National stretch back to 1854, Leucadia began to grow through acquisitions in 1980, and from that year forward purchased companies that increased its financial magnitude. Through the course of the company's growth during the 1980s, it became heavily involved in the insurance business, specifically commercial and personal property and casualty insurance, as well as health and life insurance. In addition to these businesses, Leucadia National also owned significant interests in banking and lending, trading stamps, bathroom vanities manufacturing, and motivational services. By the 1990s, the company's acquisition strategy had elevated revenues over the billion dollar mark. But Leucadia's ability to capitalize on its investments appeared to be slipping with its entry into the telecommunications business in the early 21st century.

A Hundred Twenty Years in the Making: 1850s–1970s

Both the Leucadia name and the corporate strategy that engendered its exponential increase in revenues emerged in 1980, but the foundation from which Leucadia was built was formed more than a century earlier, in 1854, when James Talcott, Inc. was established. James Talcott, Inc., incorporated 60 years after it was created as a factoring concern, generated revenue initially by accepting accounts receivable from companies involved in the textile industry and using those accounts as security to provide short-term loans. James Talcott, Inc.'s importance to Leucadia, however, did not arise until the company evolved into a more diversified concern, when it began acquiring numerous financial institutions during the 1950s and 1960s, becoming, in 1968, Talcott National Corporation, a company engaged in commercial financing, real estate mortgage financing, equipment financing and leasing, factoring, and consumer financing.

Shortly after Talcott National came into being, the seeds for Leucadia's emergence were sown. In the early 1970s the company launched an imprudent diversification into insurance, fire engines, leather processing, and machine parts that led to a $20 million loss in 1972. Although the company attempted to recover, the losses resulting from the early 1970s saddled Talcott National with mounting debt. From 1972 to 1977 these losses amounted to $355 million, and the company began to flounder, reeling from successive, unprofitable years during the decade.

Although the company was on the brink of failure, several Utah businessmen, led by a Salt Lake City investor named Brooke Grant, believed they could extricate Talcott National from its financial malaise. The investors formed Uintah National Corp. in 1976 to purchase a controlling interest in Talcott National. They borrowed $6.9 million to buy 1.6 million Talcott National shares, which gave them a 53 percent stake in the company. Grant set out to rebuild Talcott National. Within a year of assuming control of the company, Grant enlisted the help of a young, respected businessman named Ian M. Cumming, who was president of a Utah-based land development company and who would soon become the chief architect of Leucadia's creation.

While working at New York-based Carl Marks & Co., a specialty Wall Street firm active in leveraged buyouts and venture capital, Cumming convinced his company to invest $1.5 million in a small land development company in Utah named Terracor. The company's investment, however, began to sour in the early 1970s, when a deteriorating market for second homes negatively affected Terracor's business, so the Wall Street investment firm sent Cumming to Utah in 1971 to help Terracor effect a recovery. Cumming became president of Terracor within several months after his arrival, then began cutting the company's expenses and repositioning its role in the housing market.

Although Terracor continued to lose money, incurring more than $100 million in debt during the decade, Cumming's talents gained Grant's attention, and he called Cumming, asking for his help in restoring Talcott National's financial health. Cumming was elected as Talcott National's chairman and president in mid-1978. Cumming's leadership of the company was open to much debate several years later, when two lawsuits were filed against him. Once Cumming assumed stewardship of the company, he decided against the plan he and Grant had originally formulated to sell a large group of Talcott National's assets to pay off its debt. Instead, he decided to sell the portfolios of the company's commercial loan offices piece by piece, enlisting the help of Carl Marks & Co. in New York, and recruiting a former Harvard Business School classmate and vice-president at Carl Marks & Co., Joseph S. Steinberg, to assist him in his endeavors at Talcott National.

Acquisition Acumen: 1980s

Once Cumming and Steinberg were together at Talcott National they began engineering a plan to take over the company. They convinced Talcott National's creditor banks to approve a restructuring plan in 1979, then formed a partnership with Carl Marks & Co. and Stern & Stern Textiles, a textiles company that Steinberg had helped acquire while at Carl Marks & Co. Named TLC Associates, this partnership included Cumming, Steinberg, John W. Jordan II, a former Carl Marks vice-president, and Lawrence D. Glaubinger, Stern & Stern's chairman. After some initial disagreements between Cumming and Grant, TLC purchased Uintah and thereby a controlling interest in Talcott National, paying Grant slightly more than $900,000 and two of his remaining partners $28,000 to assume Uintah's $7.4 million in debt.

Several years later, in 1982, after Talcott National had become Leucadia and the company's stock began to soar, Grant filed a lawsuit against Cumming, accusing him of breach of contract and violations of fiduciary duty and security laws. Grant claimed he had not been paid the fair market value for his shares in Talcott National and that he had never received an

additional payment he and Cumming had agreed upon in a peripheral deal during the TLC-Uintah negotiations, accusations that Cumming denied were true.

As this legal battle intensified, Cumming and TLC became the object of another lawsuit that same year, when Senior Corp., Terracor's main creditor, demanded Leucadia stock as partial payment of the more than $100 million debt Terracor owed. Senior Corp. charged that Cumming, who was still president of Terracor while he was working for Talcott National, had used Terracor funds to loan Grant $200,000 after his arrival at Talcott National, and had used Terracor time to negotiate for and acquire Talcott National, which entitled Senior Corp., according to its argument, to a portion of Leucadia.

Both of these cases were settled within the next two years. In the dispute with Grant, Cumming was ordered to pay $4.5 million, which he obtained from Leucadia, and in the lawsuit involving Senior Corp., Cumming and his associates retained their shares in Leucadia and gave Senior Corp. approximately half of the properties owned by Terracor, properties that were worth roughly $20 million at the time.

Part of the underlying reason both Grant and Senior Corp. had pursued their lawsuits against Cumming was attributable to the rapid success Leucadia had enjoyed during its first several years under Cumming's and Steinberg's guidance. From 1980 to 1984, the year the last of Cumming's legal disputes were concluded, the two partners had boosted annual sales at Leucadia from $39 million to $232 million. Essentially all of this growth had been realized through acquisitions orchestrated by Cumming and Steinberg.

In 1980, after changing Talcott National's name to Leucadia National Corporation, Cumming and Steinberg sold the company's factoring unit, James Talcott Factors Inc., the 126-year-old remnant of James Talcott, Inc., to U.K.-based Lloyds & Scottish Ltd. for approximately $123 million. Once divested of the company's factoring unit, Cumming and Steinberg set out to expand Leucadia's operations through acquisition, a strategy they would employ throughout the decade and one they first put into practice in December 1980.

For Leucadia's first acquisition, Cumming and Steinberg selected American Investment Company, owner of a small-loan company and a life insurance firm, which combined were much larger than Leucadia. To finance the acquisition, Leucadia arranged for American Investment to purchase the net assets of Leucadia's consumer finance company, for which Leucadia received $94 million, and then used the money obtained from this sale to purchase American Investment for $73.6 million. Leucadia then made three significant investments in 1982 by first purchasing a 57 percent interest in TFI Companies, Inc., then becoming a 50 percent partner in a newly formed private investment firm managed by John Jordan II, called The Jordan Company. The third investment was the acquisition of Terracor, the company that had originally brought Cumming to Utah. Leucadia purchased the remainder of Terracor after the settlement with Senior Corp. for $5.9 million.

By 1984, Leucadia's partnership in The Jordan Company had given it an interest in ten companies, which added $4.8 million to the company's earnings total for the year. Its most

Key Dates:

1854: James Talcott, Inc. is established as factoring concern.
1968: Acquisitions of financial institutions lead to creation of Talcott National Corporation.
1976: Utah investors gain controlling interest in strapped company.
1979: Ian M. Cumming and Joseph S. Steinberg ban together to take control.
1980: Name is changed to Leucadia National Corporation.
1991: Colonial Penn Group Insurance Co. is acquired.
1997: Colonial Penn is sold for $1.4 billion.
2002: Leucadia acquires initial 44 percent stake in bankrupt Williams Communications.
2003: Company gains 100 percent stake in Williams, now operating under the name WilTelCommunications.

profitable achievement for the year, however, and a striking example of Cumming's ability to generate cash through aggressive corporate tactics, involved an attempted acquisition of Avco Corp., a defense supplier as well as a financial concern. Over a five-month period, Leucadia spent $77.5 million to acquire a 12 percent stake in Avco, then made a $930 million bid for the company. Not wishing to sell, Avco's management decided to buy back the stock Leucadia had acquired for $100 million. This by itself gave Leucadia a $22.5 million profit, but Cumming had secured an agreement with Avco that stipulated if Avco was acquired by another company within a year, then it would pay Leucadia the per-share difference between the price Avco's acquirer paid and the price Avco paid Leucadia to buy back its stock. Within the agreed upon time frame, a company named Textron acquired Avco for $50-a-share, $14.25 more per share than Avco had paid Leucadia, which gave Cumming's company an additional $39.8 million in profit.

By the mid-1980s, among the host of companies Leucadia either owned or maintained an interest in, the corporation's two principal operations were a small-loan company named City Finance, which James Talcott, Inc. had purchased in 1966, and Charter National Life Insurance Company, an insurance firm that sold single-premium life policies. Leucadia's investments were strengthened considerably in 1988, when Leucadia increased its interest to 64 percent in PHLCorp., a company it became involved in during a failed takeover four years earlier. One of PHLCorp.'s main operating properties was The Sperry & Hutchinson Company, Inc., which was later divided into two divisions after Leucadia increased its ownership of PHLCorp. These two divisions were organized as a trading stamp business and motivation services business, which designed and managed incentive programs. The other main operating property belonging to PHLCorp., and the company that enriched Leucadia's insurance holdings, was Empire Insurance and its then 85 percent owned affiliate Allcity Insurance Co. Based in New York and primarily serving the New York City metropolitan area, Empire wrote property and casualty policies, which broadened the scope of Leucadia's insurance operations and added assets to the company valued at more than $200 million. By this time, at the end of 1988, Leucadia was generating roughly $735

million in annual revenues and well on its way toward recording a $1 billion increase in its sales volume in a decade.

Big Deals: 1990s

An enormous step toward that direction was achieved in 1991, when the company acquired Colonial Penn Group Insurance Co. from FPL Group for $150 million. Leucadia's third insurance company, Colonial Penn was a direct marketing insurance company that became an integral component of the company's life insurance business and a nationwide provider of private passenger automobile insurance and homeowners insurance.

The addition of Colonial Penn helped elevate Leucadia's revenues to $1.57 billion in 1992, up from $1.08 billion recorded the year before, and a tremendous increase from the $39 million generated in 1980. By the conclusion of 1993, after 15 years of Cumming's and Steinberg's leadership, the value of Leucadia had increased considerably. The net worth of the company at year's end was $907.8 million, or $32.54 per share, compared to negative $0.22 in 1978 when Cumming and Steinberg assumed management of Talcott National. Leucadia's stock price also demonstrated commensurate growth, soaring from $0.16 in 1978 to $41 by 1993.

As the company planned for the future, it focused on increasing the profitability of its investments rather than increasing their market share or magnitude, a corporate philosophy that Cumming and Steinberg believed, as they wrote in a letter to the company shareholders in 1993, conformed to "the theory that the world can tolerate many mice, but few elephants." Operating according to this strategy, Leucadia looked for further growth in the 1990s.

By the mid-1990s, Leucadia's strategy and success had lent to comparisons with Berkshire Hathaway by some but not all followers of the company. "Where's the similarity to Warren Buffett's outfit? Both companies have at their core an insurance company that uses its assets to place big investment bets. Leucadia's bets, however, are less blue chip than Berkshire's. Leucadia recently bought 7 percent of Rockefeller Center Properties, the REIT that owns the mortgage to the famed Manhattan property. This stock is so dicey several other vulture investors have looked at it and passed," wrote Riva Atlas for *Forbes*.

Leucadia hit pay dirt with Colonial Penn in 1997, when it sold the business to Conseco and GE Capital for $1.4 billion, an 11-fold gain on the investment, according to *Forbes*. The next year, Steinberg and Cumming, facing a dearth of potentially profitable deals during a period of sharply rising stock valuation, said they were liquidating the company. Efforts to find deals in the financially stressed Asian market had also come up empty. The pair would receive about one-third of the $4.5 billion in assets should they be returned to shareholders.

The company's largest operating unit, Empire Group, saw premiums fall by about half between 1997 and 1999, according to *Barron's*. Leucadia's profits during the same period were driven by the sale of its holdings. But Steinberg and Cumming reconsidered their decision to fold up their tent after all and instead distributed $812 million to shareholders in 1999 and reentered the acquisition game.

A New Game: 2000–05

Leucadia reported a loss of $7.5 million in 2001. The company's debt rating took a hit early in 2002. A Standard & Poor's credit analyst said they were ''concerned about Leucadia's erratic reported earning performance, concentration risk in commercial real estate and negative operating cash flow,'' noted Steven Oberbeck.

Leucadia came to the rescue of another company, the bankrupt Williams Communications, in 2002. Williams Companies, an oil and natural gas giant, entered the telecommunications business in 1985 with the stringing of optic fiber cable in decommissioned gas pipes. Williams sold WilTel to LDDS Communications (MCI World Com) in 1995 but retained one strand of fiber in all the pipelines.

During a three-year non-compete period, Williams developed its fiber optic network. About a year after entering the market, Williams Communications went public: the telecom market was hot and the Internet was growing by leaps and bounds.

By the time Williams Communications was spun off as a public company in April 2001, the telecommunications industry was in trouble. The stock, once trading at $60, had fallen to just over $4. The Tulsa-based company filed for Chapter 11 bankruptcy protection a year later.

Leucadia's part of the deal to bring Williams Communications out of bankruptcy included a $330 million investment for a 44 percent stake in the company. The telecommunication company's bondholders received 54 percent of the stock with the remaining 2 percent of new equity held for those investors pursuing class-action claims. Williams Communications would go forward under its old name WilTel Communications Group. The *Daily Deal* reported the transaction was among Leucadia's largest, a quarter of the holding company's $1.2 billion net worth.

WilTel returned to the stock exchange, moving from the NYSE to the NASDAQ in December 2002. The company had been trading over the counter since issuing its new stock. Through a private transaction, Leucadia had upped its ownership to 47.4 percent of the company.

The memory of the worthless Williams Communications stock put a damper on interest in WilTel as did an industry dealing with overcapacity. Moves toward consolidation among its players made WilTel's future even more uncertain. Leucadia acquired the balance of WilTel's outstanding common stock in November 2003. The total cost for 100 percent of WilTel over 2002 and 2003 amounted to $779.2 million in cash and common shares.

Leucadia had other activities in the works during 2003. In January, the company entirely ceased its loan origination business. The automobile loan operations had been cut two years earlier. In September, Leucadia purchased some of the physical, occupational, speech and respiratory therapy services operated by subsidiaries of Symphony Health Services, LLC.

Among its continuing business interests were: a plastic netting manufacturing and marketing operation, domestic real estate ventures, and wineries in Napa Valley, California, and Williamette Valley in Oregon. Leucadia held a 72.5 percent interest in MK Gold Company, which was involved in copper mine development, and a 16.1 percent interest in Olympus Re Holdings, Ltd., a Bermuda-based reinsurer. A lucrative joint venture, Berkadia LLC, formed with Berkshire Hathaway to buy the assets of bankrupt The FINOVA Group Inc., was among the entities in which it held equity but did not control.

Leucadia's largest generator of 2003 revenues was from subsidiary WilTel's fiber optic network. In turn, sales by WilTel to SBC Communications Inc. accounted for 65 percent of that business during 2003. Network competitors included AT&T, MCI, Sprint, Qwest, Level 3, Global Crossing, 360 Network and Broadwing. The industry was rife with bankruptcy, excess capacity, and intense price competition.

During 2004, Leucadia made moves toward taking control of one of its competitors, MCI. Cumming and Steinberg's track record of a 15-year average annual return of 22 percent aside, they were in a risky situation. Adam Lashinsky wrote for *Fortune*, ''Like a host of investment-world icons before it, Leucadia is making huge bets on telecommunications even as that industry gets sicker. And buying into Leucadia is a gamble on two managers who acknowledge that their retirement isn't all that far off.''

In 2005, Leucadia received a jolt when WilTel's largest customer announced plans to buy AT&T Corp. Although it would take time for SBC to receive approval for the deal and its shift of network business to AT&T, Leucadia felt some immediate impact related to the anticipated loss of revenue. Because of the ''material adverse effect'' to the telecommunications operation, WilTel's credit situation degraded and so did Leucadia stock.

WilTel would receive compensation for early termination of its agreement with SBC, but the company faced finding new customers in a difficult market. Moreover, although WilTel had tax credits to be utilized, it could not do so without generating a profit, and should the company be sold, change of ownership would diminish their value.

''I believe Leucadia is in the position of having to acquire something,'' Robert Willens, a Lehman Brothers' tax and accounting analyst told *Barron's*. During 2004, Leucadia had dropped a bid for MCI and came up short in an effort to buy a pipeline company.

In March 2005, Leucadia reported revenue for the past year of $2.26 billion with net income of $145.5 million, according to *Tulsa World*. The WilTel contribution to revenues had climbed to $1.58 billion, up from $231.9 million in 2003. The telecommunications business accounted for 43 percent of the corporate revenue.

Principal Subsidiaries

WilTel Communications, Inc.; MK Resources Company (73%).

Principal Competitors

Berkshire Hathaway, Inc.; The Blackstone Group L.P.; The Enstar Group, Inc.; Wesco Financial Corporation.

Further Reading

Atlas, Riva, ''Another Warren Buffett?,'' *Forbes*, July 31, 1995, p. 125.

Bary, Andrew, ''Baby Berkshire,'' *Barron's Online*,'' June 12, 2000.

''Cashing in the Chips,'' *Forbes*, July 27, 1998, pp. 91+.

''Colonial Penn Life, PA.,'' *Best's Review - Life-Health Insurance Edition*, June 1991, p. 122.

Davis, Melissa, ''Tulsa, Okla.-Based Communications Firm Splits from Parent Company,'' *Daily Oklahoman*, April 24, 2001.

George, John, ''Leucadia Buys Colonial Penn for $150 Million,'' *Philadelphia Business Journal*, April 15, 1991, p. 3.

Hahn, Avital Louria, ''Williams Communications Follows Golden Strand to the NYSE,'' *IPO Reporter*, September 27, 1999.

Lashinsky, Adam, ''A Bottom Feeder Goes Bigtime: Little-Known Value Investor Leucadia National Is Suddenly Attracting Attention Thanks to Its Bold Bid for MCI,'' *Fortune*, August 23, 2004, p. 130.

Nolter, Chris, ''Leucadia Aids WilTel Rebirth,'' *Daily Deal*, October 17, 2002.

Norton, Leslie P., ''Telecom Shocker,'' *Barron's*, February 14, 2005, p. 27.

''Package Deal,'' *Forbes,* April 1, 1976, p. 71.

Oberbeck, Steven, ''Chairman of New York-Based Leucadia Speaks on Rescuing Distressed Firms,'' *Knight Ridder/Tribune Business News*, April 3, 2002.

Rosenberg, Hilary, ''Elusive Leucadia,'' *Barron's,* November 11, 1985, p. 6.

Schwer, Robert B., ''Hidden Value,'' *Barron's,* November 26, 1990, p. 16.

Stewart, D.R., ''Leucadia Earnings Increase,'' *Tulsa World* (OK), March 18, 2005, p. E1.

——,''WilTel Shaken by SBC-AT&T Deal,'' *Knight Ridder/Tribune Business News*, February 3, 2005.

——, ''WilTel Stock Begins Trading,'' *Tulsa World* (OK), December 6, 2002.

''Williams' Second Go-Round Begins: Telecom Crash Victim Returns to Health,'' *Investment Dealers' Digest*, October 21, 2002.

—Jeffrey L. Covell
—update: Kathleen Peippo

LKQ Corporation

120 N. LaSalle St., Suite 3300
Chicago, Illinois 60602
U.S.A.
Telephone: (312) 621-1950
Toll Free: (877) 557-2677
Fax: (312) 621-1969
Web site: http://www.lkqcorp.com

Public Company
Incorporated: 1998
Employees: 2,800
Sales: $424.76 million (2005)
Stock Exchanges: NASDAQ
Ticker Symbol: LKQX
NAIC: 441310 Automotive Parts and Accessories Stores

LKQ Corporation is the largest supplier of used auto parts in the United States. The firm operates a network of more than 40 salvage yards where wrecked vehicles are dismantled and usable parts sold to repair shops or parts reconditioning companies. The remainder of each vehicle, including scrap metals, batteries, fluids, and tires, is sold to recycling firms. LKQ also owns a growing number of self-service facilities at which customers remove parts themselves, and sells aftermarket parts via subsidiaries Global Trade Alliance and Bodymaster.

Beginnings

LKQ Corporation was founded in February 1998 by former Waste Management executive Donald Flynn, who had left that firm when it was acquired by USA Waste Services, Inc. Seeking a fragmented industry to consolidate in much the same way that his former employer had done with garbage hauling, Flynn looked at several possibilities, including scrap metal, before settling on used auto parts.

This $8 billion industry consisted of an estimated 11,000-plus junkyards across the United States, which served more than 200,000 collision and mechanical repair shops by recycling parts from 11 million junked autos per year. Many were old, family-owned businesses, fewer than a third of which had computer inventory systems. A large number still fit the stereotypical image of a desolate place where ''shade-tree mechanics'' were eyed by a menacing dog while removing a part from a rusting wreck.

With financial backing from Waste Management founder H. Wayne Huizenga's new AutoNation car dealership chain (which would be one of the firm's first customers), and Waste Management cofounder and former CEO Dean L. Buntrock, Flynn began looking at acquisition targets around the United States. He sought out the best-run companies in each region, not simply the largest, as he wanted the firm to gain a reputation for the consistency and quality of used parts it offered. With this in mind, his new company took the name LKQ, which was auto industry shorthand for ''like, kind, and quality,'' a standard designation for used parts that were considered as good as new.

Late 1990s Acquisitions

LKQ's first purchase, in July 1998, was Triplett Automotive Recycling of Akron, Ohio, a 50-year old, family-owned firm. Triplett was run by Stuart P. Willen, who in over three decades in the business had developed sophisticated methods of salvaging and recycling parts, resulting in revenue growth of 20 percent-plus for seven years running. Willen was especially concerned about quality, and bought only late-model cars that had been declared ''totaled'' by insurance companies but still had many reusable interior, exterior, and engine parts.

Triplett's buyers would typically attend 15 wrecked vehicle auctions per week, bringing their purchases to a facility with six service bays where approximately 20 cars per day could be dismantled. All reusable parts were removed down to the bare frame, then inspected for remaining service life, reconditioned if necessary, bar-coded, entered into a computer database, and stored systematically. Other recyclers bought batteries, fluids, and tires, while the stripped hulks were flattened by an outside contractor and sold as scrap.

A team of some 20 sales representatives worked with repair shops and auto insurers in northwestern and central Ohio to sell the parts, which generally cost half as much as new ones.

Popular items included engines, transmissions, fenders, front-end assemblies, doors, trunk lids, bumpers, wheels, tail and headlamp assemblies, mirrors, and axles. Key to Triplett's success was its reputation for quality, established over the years through personal relationships with customers.

Stuart Willen, like others who would sell their businesses to LKQ, received stock in the new company to help give him incentive to work hard for his firm's new owners. He took the title of vice-president of the Midwest region, and began working with Floyd to select other companies to acquire. In November 1998 the firm also hired former Waste Management COO Joseph M. Holsten to serve as CEO. The company was now busy striking deals in markets all over the United States.

In September 1999 LKQ bought its 35th parts recycling firm. Hunts Point Auto parts of the Bronx, New York, became LKQ Hunts Point, and as with most of the firm's acquisitions, existing management remained in charge of its operations. The aggregate earnings of LKQ's network now gave the firm total revenues of more than $200 million. The company's facilities served three-fourths of the top 50 markets in the country, and it was in the process of setting up a number of parts distribution centers around the United States.

Some in the industry doubted that a new national conglomerate could successfully, and cost-effectively, win the hard-earned reputation for quality that the best salvage yards had built up. Though the size and national reach of a junkyard network would offer the advantages of a deeper stock of parts for a wider range of vehicles, it was as yet unclear whether customers in one part of the country would have faith that parts shipped from a supplier they did not personally know would be good.

Despite such concerns, LKQ's rapid growth began inspiring competition from several clusters of regional salvage operators, as well as, beginning in April 1999, from a unit of Ford Motor Company called Greenleaf Acquisitions, which began assembling a similar network. In the fall of 1999 the used-parts industry got a boost when a court fined State Farm Insurance $1.2 billion for using aftermarket parts (ones similar to original equipment but manufactured by outside companies) to repair vehicles it insured, rather than original equipment manufacturer (OEM) sourced ones.

In December 1999 LKQ announced it was offering a six month free-replacement guarantee for most parts, the longest in the industry, as well as free parts and labor for any repairs needed on many engines and transmissions. Other parts were guaranteed against rust for life. With only about 10 percent of parts purchased by repair shops coming from salvage sources, LKQ was seeking to improve this percentage with methods

including the warranty upgrade and by educating the consumer and the repair industry on the value of used parts. The company was now pulling back from acquisitions to focus on integrating its network of businesses into a cohesive whole.

In early 2000 the firm signed an agreement with parts distributor Keystone Automotive Industries, Inc., to serve as its exclusive supplier of damaged alloy wheels for remanufacturing, while Keystone was named LKQ's exclusive source of remanufactured wheels for resale. The firm was also moving to form relationships with insurance companies, who were the most influential players in the auto-repair industry. LKQ was named the preferred supplier of used parts for both Allstate and Nationwide Insurance companies.

In 2001 the company's annual sales reached an estimated $250 million, and though revenues ticked upward to $287 million for 2002, LKQ recorded a loss of nearly $39 million during the year. In the summer of 2003 the company, which now had 38 recycling facilities and 12 distribution centers, announced it would make an initial public offering of stock on the NASDAQ to fund further expansion and pay down debt. At this time Donald Flynn held 15 percent of the firm's stock, while Dean Buntrock had 13.4 percent, and several directors owned more than 10 percent. AutoNation, Inc. held just under 10 percent, having sold half of its original 20 percent stake back to LKQ earlier in the year.

The IPO took place in October, and raised $91 million. A short time afterwards, AutoNation disposed of its remaining stake in the company. For 2003, revenues increased to $328 million, with earnings jumping to $14.6 million.

Move into Aftermarket Parts in 2004

In January 2004 LKQ acquired Metro East Salvage, Inc. of Caseyville, Illinois, which was located near St. Louis, Missouri, and in February the company opened a new salvage yard in Pennsylvania and bought four self-service used parts outlets in Tampa, Florida. The firm also paid $30 million to buy Global Trade Alliance, Inc. (GTA), a supplier of aftermarket replacement parts to 15 states in the Midwest. The GTA purchase marked LKQ's first move into aftermarket parts, which cost less than OEM parts, but were considered by some to be of inferior quality. The advantage to LKQ was that it could generally sell aftermarket parts in place of used ones it did not have in stock, and GTA carried many of the frequently damaged body parts it had a short supply of. The replacement parts market at this time was made up of 75 percent OEM, 13 percent aftermarket, and 12 percent recycled OEM.

Early 2004 saw the firm secure a new $75 million line of credit, and in the spring LKQ bought two self-service used parts facilities in Guatemala and one in Costa Rica, as well as Albert Lea Auto Salvage, Inc. of Minnesota. By now several GTA operations had been merged into LKQ facilities, and the company was preparing to expand sales of aftermarket parts to the East and West Coasts. Newly built ''greenfield'' salvage yard facilities were also in the planning stages for Texas and Louisiana.

Sales of used parts dropped during the summer when hurricanes in Florida and along the Eastern seaboard impacted the car repair business. One bright spot for the firm at this time was

Key Dates:

1998: Donald Flynn founds LKQ Corporation to buy auto salvage yards.
1999: Acquisitions reach 35.
2003: Company completes its initial public offering (IPO) on the NASDAQ.
2004: Sales of aftermarket parts begin with acquisition of Global Trade Alliance.

the increasing number of parts being sold via eBay and other online vendors.

In October the company paid $19 million for Foster Auto Parts, Inc. of Portland, Oregon, which operated seven self-service used auto parts facilities in Oregon and Washington. This segment of the market, in which customers removed their own parts from wrecked vehicles, was a new growth area for the industry. The cars involved were typically older models, which were not generally worth the time it took to fully disassemble. A rival firm called Pick-n-Pull had already built a chain of nearly 30 such operations. For 2004, LKQ's revenues topped out at just under $425 million, while earnings hit $20.6 million.

In early 2005 the company bought East Coast aftermarket auto parts supplier Bodymaster Auto Parts, Inc. for $15.4 million. Bodymaster served customers in New Jersey, Delaware, Philadelphia, Baltimore, and Washington, D.C. The firm also boosted its credit facility to $100 million, with options for further increases. In April LKQ acquired A&R Auto Parts, Inc., operator of a salvage yard near Duncan, South Carolina, and a few weeks later bought a self-service auto parts operation near Memphis, Tennessee.

In seven short years LKQ Corporation had built up the largest network of automotive salvage yards in the United States, one that gave it a presence in the majority of the country's top markets. In addition to selling used parts, the company was expanding the amount of aftermarket parts it offered, as well as boosting the number of "remove-it-yourself" used parts facilities.

Principal Subsidiaries

Bodymaster Auto Parts, Inc.; Global Trade Alliance, Inc.; LKQ Holding Co.; Damron Holding Company LLC.

Principal Competitors

Greenleaf Auto Recyclers; Quality Replacement Parts (QRP); Schnitzer Steel Industries, Inc.

Further Reading

"Auto Parts Recycler Files to Make $75 Mln IPO," *AFX International Focus*, July 29, 2003.
Blumberg, George P., "Junkyards Discard an Image, and the Scary Dogs, Too," *New York Times*, October 23, 2002, p. 9.
Bowen, Bill, and Bill Hornaday, "Texas Auto Salvage Yards Merge to Compete with Large National Chains," *Fort Worth Star-Telegram*, March 3, 1999.
Daniels, Steve, "Waste Alums Aiming to Clean Up," *Crain's Chicago Business*, October 18, 1999, p. 1.
Danner, Patrick, "AutoNation Quietly Unloads Shares in Chicago-Based Salvage Firm," *Miami Herald*, October 31, 2003.
Goodrich, Melissa, "Dismantling a Way of Life?," *Recycling Today*, October, 1999.
Griggs, Ted, "Livingston Facility No Junkyard; LKQ Corp. Tries to Keep Pace As Its Revenue Grows," *Baton Rouge Advocate*, February 10, 2005, p. 1D.
Jordan, Gregory, "Guy Here Needs a Part. Guy Over There Has It," *New York Times*, October 27, 2004, p. 22.
"LKQ Corporation Acquires East Coast Aftermarket Business, Increases Credit Facility," *Reuters Significant Developments*, February 1, 2005.
"LKQ Corporation Acquires Global Trade Alliance, Inc., Enters New Credit Facility," *Reuters Significant Developments*, February 23, 2004.
McMorris, Frances, "Auto Parts Recycler Aims for NASDAQ," *Daily Deal*, July 29, 2003.
Price, Dudley, "Salvage Business Growing Up," *News & Observer, Raleigh NC*, May 8, 1999, p. D1.
Taylor, Brian, "On the Fast Track," *Recycling Today*, September, 1999, p. 28.
——, "Road Worthy," *Recycling Today*, September, 2004.
Whiteman, Lou, "LKQ Makes Strong Debut," *Daily Deal*, October 6, 2003.

—Frank Uhle

Lookers plc

776 Chester Rd., Stretford
Manchester
M32 0QH
United Kingdom
Telephone: +44 161 291 0043
Fax: +44 161 864 2363
Web site: http://www.lookers.co.uk

Public Company
Incorporated: 1908 as Lookers Limited
Employees: 3,306
Sales: £1.01 billion ($1.9 billion) (2004)
Stock Exchanges: London
Ticker Symbol: LOOK
NAIC: 441110 New Car Dealers; 423110 Automobile
and Other Motor Vehicle Merchant Wholesalers;
423120 Motor Vehicle Supplies and New Parts
Merchant Wholesalers; 423820 Farm and Garden
Machinery and Equipment Merchant Wholesalers;
423830 Industrial Machinery and Equipment
Merchant Wholesalers; 441221 Motorcycle Dealers;
441310 Automotive Parts and Accessories Stores;
447110 Gasoline Stations with Convenience Stores

Lookers plc is one of the United Kingdom's top five new and used car dealers. The Manchester-based company operates a national network of car dealerships, featuring a wide range of car makes, including the volume brands Vauxhall and Renault, among others. The company also has dealerships for a number of high-end makes, including Ferrari in Northern Ireland and Jaguar in Northern Ireland and Scotland. Other brands in the company's stable include Aston Martin, Audi, Bentley, Citroën, Chrysler, Honda, Jeep, Land Rover, Lexus, Maserati, Mazda, MG Rover, Nissan, Peugeot, Saab, Seat, Toyota, and Volkswagen, as well as motorcycle dealerships for BMW, Ducati, Honda, and Kawasaki. The company also sells agricultural vehicles, equipment and machinery, and operates the United Kingdom's leading wholesale auto parts distributor, FPS Distribution. Lookers has been engaged in an aggressive acquisition

drive since the mid-1990s, beginning with its acquisition of Northern Ireland's leading automotive dealer, Charles Hurst. That company remains Looker's Northern Ireland division. In Scotland, the company operates under the Taggarts Motor name. Lookers is listed on the London Stock Exchange. In 2004, the company's sales topped £1 billion ($1.9 billion).

Automotive Sales Industry Pioneer in the Early 1900s

The appearance of an automotive industry at the beginning of the 20th century quickly inspired the creation of a new industry: automotive sales dealerships. Among the earliest of this new kind of retailer was the company that became known as Lookers. Founded in 1908, Lookers became a prominent car seller in the Manchester area. The company came to represent a number of automobile makers, including smaller, regional manufacturers. Yet Lookers later became especially associated with the stable of makes owned by British Leyland, which represented the majority of Lookers sales into the late 1970s. The company was also active in related areas, such as car repair, as well as sales and engineering of agricultural equipment and machinery.

Lookers went public in 1973, at a time when its sales were just £23 million. The company almost immediately faced a threat, when in 1974, Graylaw Holdings launched a takeover offer. Lookers rejected that bid as too low. Instead, the company began to plot a new growth course. In 1978, it acquired R. Platt & Sons and Platts Agricultural Machinery Exports, boosting its operations in that area.

The slump in auto sales at the end of the 1970s had prompted Lookers to adopt a more significant change in strategy. The company decided to diversify its product offering beyond its reliance on British Leyland makes, adding Talbot, International Harvester, Vauxhall, Peugeot, Fiat, and Mercedes Trucks. The company also began its first acquisitions, taking over, for example, Tipton and Morley, an agricultural engineering company, and a Toyota dealership, both in 1980. By then, British Leyland sales accounted for less than half of the company's total revenues. Among other areas, the company built up a business selling vacation caravans, operating holiday parks, while also boosting its sales of aftermarket car parts.

Key Dates:

1896: Taggarts Motor Group originates as a cycle shop in Motherwell, Scotland.
1908: Lookers Limited is founded in Manchester, England.
1911: Charles Hurst Group is formed in Belfast, Northern Ireland.
1973: Lookers goes public on the London Stock Exchange.
1978: Lookers acquires R Platt & Sons and Platts Agricultural Machinery Exports and launches diversified car dealership strategy.
1980: Lookers acquires agricultural machinery group Tipton and Morley and a Toyota dealership.
1983: Braid Group in Liverpool is acquired.
1996: The company acquires Charles Hurst Group, launching a new acquisition drive.
2003: The company enters Scotland with the purchase of Taggarts Motor Group.
2005: Lookers acquires used car supermarket Bristol Trade Centre.

Lookers strengthened its Vauxhall dealerships with the acquisition of the Braid group, a major dealership group based in Liverpool, for £3 million. That purchase was completed in 1983. By the end of 1984, the first full year including Braid, the company's sales topped £150 million.

Lookers' drive to diversify its dealerships led it to continue acquiring dealerships over the next decade. An important purchase for the company came in 1989, when it acquired SMAC Continental, based in the Southeast, for £14.7 million. That purchase also added SMAC's Mercedes dealerships to Lookers portfolio of makes.

By the beginning of the 1990s, the company's turnover had topped £370 million. Lookers was hit hard by the economic recession at the beginning of the decade, watching its new car sales slide some 30 percent, while sales of farm vehicles and machinery plunged into an extended slump. Another area of business hit hard by the recession was the group's sales of new caravans. Yet Lookers' strong car parts and service arm, particularly in the north, helped compensate for its slipping car sales.

The company continued its acquisition drive into the 1990s. By the middle of the decade, the company boasted more than 50 dealerships in the United Kingdom. Nonetheless, Lookers remained associated primarily with the northern region. This changed in 1996 when the company acquired the Charles Hurst Group. Founded in 1911, the Charles Hurst Group grew to become Northern Ireland's dominant automobile seller, with a market share of some 22 percent. The addition of the Hurst dealerships also gave Lookers a new prize, the Ferrari concession for Northern Ireland.

Joining the Top Five in the New Century

Lookers maintained the Charles Hurst name because of its prominence in Northern Ireland, and quickly began steering part of its acquisition program through the Hurst Group. By the end of 1996, Hurst had made its first acquisition for Lookers, buying Baird Cars in Belfast for £2.7 million. In 1998, Hurst added Neville Johnston Garages, also in Belfast, and its Toyota and Daihatsu dealerships, for £3.3 million.

Lookers itself remained an aggressive player in the consolidation of the British motor vehicle sales market. The acquisition of Hurst had boosted it into seventh position among the top 200 British automobile sellers. The company's fast-growing auto-

motive component encouraged Lookers to exit other areas of operations, such as caravan sales and the operation of holiday parks, sold in 1997.

Meanwhile, Lookers began an investment program, which included the opening of a £4.5 million dealership in Stretford, for sales of Suzuki, Seat, and Mazda cars, in 1999, and investments totaling £20 million in order to open new showrooms in Chester, Liverpool, and Oldham in 2001. The company added a number of existing dealerships as well, such as 452 (Birmingham) and Spekehall Vauxhall, both bought from Vauxhall Motor, and Rystar Aston and Selly Oak Vauxhall, bought from Ryland Group, in 2002. Lookers further strengthened its Vauxhall network that year with the purchase of Elt Brothers, based in Birmingham, for £900,000. In 2002, also, Lookers teamed up with supermarket group Morrisons in an experiment to sell cars from Internet displays in three Morrisons stores.

By 2003, Lookers' network of dealerships had topped 90. The company had built up an extensive network throughout England and Northern Ireland. In that year, Lookers completed its United Kingdom presence with a move into Scotland when, through Hurst, it acquired JN Holdings, better known as the operator of the Taggarts Motor Group in Glasgow and Motherwell. The addition of Taggarts also gave the company a new Jaguar franchise.

In August 2004, Lookers made another significant acquisition, this time boosting its presence in the U.K. aftermarket car parts circuit, when it bought FPS Distribution. Founded as Ferraris Piston Service by the Ferraris brothers in Cricklewood, in north London, in 1928, FPS grew into a national chain during the 1980s after being acquired by Tomkins Plc. By the beginning of the 2000s and a series of owners, however, FPS had fallen into financial troubles, before being rescued in a management buyout in 2001. The addition of FPS transformed Lookers into the United Kingdom's leading distributor of wholesale aftermarket auto parts.

Other dealerships acquired through the end of 2004 included Savoy Honda in Warrington; Vauxhall dealerships in Lisburn and Portadown; Darlington Volkswagen; another Volkswagen dealership in Northallerton; and a Saab dealership in Chester. In February 2005, Lookers added the four-acre used car "supermarket" Bristol Trade Center, paying £8.5 million. By then, the company's sales had topped £1 billion, placing the group among the country's top five car dealerships. Lookers expected to remain a prominent participant in the ongoing consolidation of the British car sales market.

Principal Subsidiaries

Charles Hurst Group; FPS Distribution; Taggarts Motor Group.

Principal Competitors

Inchcape PLC; Pendragon PLC; Imperial Holdings Ltd.; Renault UK Ltd.; Reg Vardy PLC; Arnold Clark Automobiles Ltd.; RAC PLC; C D Bramall Ltd; Citroën UK Ltd.; Camden Motors Ltd.; McCarthy Ltd.; Dixon Motors PLC.

Further Reading

"British Car Dealer Widens Its Business Base," *Daily Mail*, August 22, 2004.

"Car Company Buys Bristol Trade Centre," *Bristol Evening Post*, February 17, 2005.

Cranage, John, "Lookers Paints Rosy Picture for Year Ahead," *Birmingham Post*, March 22, 2005, p. 15.

"Hurst Acquisition Drive Gears up in Scotland," *News Letter*, February 6, 2003, p. 21.

"Looking Good: Car Dealer Confident over Star City Move," *Birmingham Post*, March 10, 2004, p. 20.

McDonough, Tony, "Car Dealer Buys Rivals for £1.5m," *Daily Post*, October 6, 2004, p. 6.

McGurk, Helen, "Car Dealer Gears for Growth," *News Letter*, October 17, 2003, p. 19.

Urquhart, Lisa, "Lookers Banks on New Models," *Financial Times*, August 17, 2004, p. 24.

Wagstaff, Ian, "Parts Warehouse Distributor FPS Acquired by Lookers," *just-auto.com*, July 22, 2004.

Wallop, Henry, "Car Dealership Looks the Part," *Daily Telegraph*, March 22, 2005.

—M.L. Cohen

Love's Travel Stops & Country Stores, Inc.

10601 North Pennsylvania Avenue
Oklahoma City, Oklahoma 73120
U.S.A.
Telephone: (405) 751-9000
Toll Free: 1-800-388-0983
Fax: (405) 749-9110
Web site: http://www.loves.com

Private Company
Incorporated: 1978 as Love's Country Stores, Inc.
Employees: 3,500
Sales: $1.9 billion (2003)
NAIC: 447110 Gasoline Stations with Convenience Stores

Love's Travel Stops & Country Stores, Inc. operates more than 160 truck stops and convenience stores in about two dozen states. There are more than 100 Travel Stops, which offer interstate travelers branded fast food in addition to fuel, as well as certain amenities such as showers and parking for RVs. The stops have space for up to 150 trucks. Many feature attached fast-food restaurants from well-known national chains such as Taco Bell, Subway, and Pizza Hut. There are another 67 Country Stores, or convenience stores. The company is owned by the family of founder and CEO Tom Love.

Origins

The origins of Love's Travel Stops & Country Stores, Inc. date back to January 1964 when Tom Love and his wife Judy opened a self-service gas station in the town of Watonga in western Oklahoma. Tom Love had done a stint in the Marines and had excelled at college football, according to the *Daily Oklahoman*. He dropped out of school early, however, to pursue an entrepreneurial path. He tried ventures such as restaurants and car washes before discovering opportunity in abandoned gas stations. Perhaps business—and oil—ran in his blood. According to the *Shawnee News-Star*, his father F.C. Love had been president of petrochemical giant Kerr-McGee Corp.

After leasing their first filling station in Watonga, the Loves soon opened others in nearby small towns. Their company, called Musket Corp., grew to 40 stations within a few years. Tom Love told the *Journal Record* that the business won customers' loyalty during the Arab oil embargo by sourcing gasoline however possible—even buying at retail from other dealers—in order to keep their pumps flowing 24/7.

Convenience in the 1970s

In 1972 Love's opened its first combination convenience store and gas station in Guymon, Oklahoma. These eventually became known as Country Stores. According to the *Journal Record,* they each cost about $300,000 to open at the time.

Love's Country Stores Inc. was established in 1978—the earliest the Love's name appeared on the stores. By the end of the decade, the enterprise had more than 100 stations.

Travel Stops in the 1980s

The company began focusing on interstate locations in the 1980s. Its first Travel Stop opened in Amarillo, Texas, in 1981. The Travel Stop concept featured amenities geared toward truckers and RV drivers, such as showers, mail drops, and laundry machines.

By 1984, Love's was operating in five states: Oklahoma, Texas, Arkansas, Kansas, Colorado, and New Mexico. The company was renamed Love's Travel Stops & Country Stores, Inc. in late December 1986.

Branded Food in the 1990s

Love's began the 1990s with 125 convenience stores and truck stops, 70 of them in Oklahoma. It had about 2,000 employees. In 1991, the company was named Corporation of the Year by a local chapter of Sales and Marketing Executives International.

Love's began adding branded food outlets to the Travel Stop concept in the early 1990s. An Oklahoma City location had a Grandy's restaurant by 1990. In 1993, a Taco Bell Express was added to another site. Others followed the next year, as well as Pizza Hut express operations at some stores. The new national

Key Dates:

1964: Tom and Judy Love launch the Musket chain with a gas station in Watonga, Oklahoma.
1972: The first Country Store opens in Guymon, Oklahoma.
1978: Love's Country Stores Inc. is established.
1981: The first Travel Stop opens in Amarillo, Texas.
1986: The company is renamed Love's Travel Stops & Country Stores, Inc.
1990: Love's begins adding major branded fast-food franchises to Travel Stops.
1999: The 50th Travel Stop is opened.
2001: The company is renamed Love's Travel Stops and Country Stores, Inc.

fast-food brands boosted sales not only of food, but fuel as well. Some stores offered food by all three licensees—Grandy's, Taco Bell, and Pizza Hut, and some sold it 24 hours a day. Other franchises added during the 1990s included Winchell's Donuts and A&W Root Beer. (All of Love's stores were company owned; Love's itself was the franchisee, according to the *Journal Record.*) Love's also had its own sandwich brand: Fresh Daily Deli and Grill.

Around this time, the company also was installing debit and credit card readers to its fuel pumps. Love's also tried fitting some of the branded fast-food locations with drive-up windows, though a company executive later told *National Petroleum News* that these did not justify their expense.

By 1995, Love's had 2,000 employees and 130 stores in six states. Tom Love told the *Journal Record* that the chain's managers and employees were the reason for its success. "The greatest thing we have is that we were lucky enough to get some good employees with an entrepreneurial spirit who would work hard to implement some of the things we want to do."

The company was trying a new business concept: the "Cowboy's Restaurant Trading Post." The 7,000-square-foot location on the Oklahoma/Texas border featured a 4,500-square-foot Western-themed gift shop and was situated adjacent to an existing Love's Travel Stop. Love's also operated two stand-alone trading posts.

In 1997, Love's had sales of $500 million, reported the *Journal Record,* with 80 percent of sales from fuel. The company was expanding quickly, though the cost of opening a store had risen to $3 million.

New Technology After 2000

The company was renamed Love's Travel Stops and Country Stores, Inc. in January 2001. That year, it began appearing on *Forbes* magazine's list of the 500 largest private companies in the United States. Its expansion was going strong, in spite of a lackluster economy.

As the company grew, it invested in information technology to link and manage its stores. After a trial run in late 2003, it also began offering high-speed WiFi wireless Internet access to customers—a vital attraction for those spending extended stretches on the road. Love's had previously provided web access via landlines. The new wireless service was supplied by Truckstop.net and Sprint.

Love's began providing drivers access to TransCore's freight-matching network in 2003. The next year, it started offering the TRANSFLO scanning service from Pegasus TransTech, which allowed truckers to electronically transmit their documentation to payroll departments at the time of fuel purchase.

Revenues approached $2 billion in 2003. Love's had 3,500 employees and about 150 Travel Stops and Country Stores—67 in Oklahoma alone. The company's operations were split into two units in the fall of the year: Love's Development Companies and Love's Operating Companies.

In 2004 company founder Tom Love gave Oklahoma City University $1 million to start an Entrepreneurship Center. Love himself did not graduate college. Love was a vocal advocate for Oklahoma business and was involved in several civic groups. He was named chairman of the Oklahoma Business Roundtable in 2001. Around that time, Love's plastered a promotional billboard for Oklahoma tourism on one of its trucks.

Love's was first to sign up for a statewide e-mail list developed by the Oklahoma Department of Public Safety as an enhancement to the Amber Alert. The chain's 67 locations blanketed Oklahoma's interstates, making them strategic lookouts in the event of child abduction. According to *Convenience Store News,* Love's Country Stores each had up to 350 customers a day, and the interstate-based Travel Stops saw ten times as many people.

In 2005, Love's was in preliminary negotiations to retail the biodiesel fuel sponsored by famed country singer Willie Nelson. Biodiesel was made from vegetable oils rather than petroleum.

Principal Divisions

Love's Development Companies; Love's Operating Companies.

Principal Competitors

Flying J Inc.; Petro Stopping Centers, L.P.; Pilot Travel Centers LLC; TravelCenters of America, Inc.

Further Reading

"Autograf Car Care Center Unveils 'Touchless Tunnel,'" *Journal Record* (Oklahoma City), July 19, 1985.

Brus, Brian, "OK-Based Love's Travel Stops Sees Opportunities in Willie Nelson Venture," *Journal Record* (Oklahoma City), January 18, 2005.

"Driveup Window of Opportunity," *National Petroleum News,* May 1, 1994, p. 26.

Francis-Smith, Janice, "Oklahoma City University, Love's Build Entrepreneurial Center," *Journal Record* (Oklahoma City), December 22, 1994.

Hartley, Tim, "Musket Builds Grandy's Next to Love's Facility," *Journal Record* (Oklahoma City), July 20, 1990.

"Honors Given at St. Gregory's Alumni Banquet," *Shawnee News-Star,* Shawnee Online, October 3, 2000, http://www.news-star.com/stories/100300/edu__alumni.shtml.

"James Xenos—CIO Has the 'X' Factor for C-Store Innovation," *Executive Technology,* May 1, 2004, p. 34.

King, W.B., "Giving: Convenience Retailers Work to Make This Small But Essential Category [Heath and Beauty Care] a Profitable One," *Convenience Store News,* October 16, 2004.

Lichtenstein, Sacha E., "Looking for Love—$40 Million—in All the Right Places," *Private Placement Letter,* November 10, 2003.

"Love's Makes Name Change," *Shawnee News-Star,* Shawnee Online, January 21, 2001, http://www.onlineshawnee.com/stories/012101/bus__loves.shtml.

"Love's to Get Biodiesel from Music Star?," *Convenience Store News,* January 18, 2005.

"Love's to Offer Pegasus TransTech's Scanning Service," *NPN—National Petroleum News,* March 2004, p. 42.

"Love's Travel Stops Splits Operations into 2 Units," *Journal Record* (Oklahoma City), October 20, 2003.

Marchel, Melissa, "Oklahoma City University Gets $1 Million Gift for Entrepreneurial Center," *Daily Oklahoman,* December 22, 2004.

Mastroberte, Tammy, "Anything But General: Two Retailers Take General Merchandise Out of the Box," *Convenience Store News,* September 13, 2004, pp. 96+.

May, Bill, "Alliances Strengthen Love's Chain," *Journal Record* (Oklahoma City), July 10, 1995.

——, "Love's Adds Fast Food, Fueling with Credit Card," *Journal Record* (Oklahoma City), December 31, 1993.

——, "Love's Attributes Success to Employees," *Journal Record* (Oklahoma City), July 10, 1995.

——, "Love's to Double Sales to $1 Billion in 5 Years," *Journal Record* (Oklahoma City), November 13, 1997.

Page, David, "Oklahoma Business Roundtable Elects Chairman," *Journal Record* (Oklahoma City), July 18, 2001.

Parrott, Susan, "Restaurant, Trading Post New Concept for Love's," *Journal Record* (Oklahoma City), November 4, 1994.

Price, Marie, "Oklahoma to Enhance 'Amber Plan,' " *Oklahoma Business News* (Oklahoma City), September 13, 2002.

"Sales Executives Honor Love's As State Corporation of Year," *Journal Record* (Oklahoma City), February 20, 1991.

Shook, Phil, "C-Store Drive-Throughs Get Mixed Reviews," *National Petroleum News,* April 1995, p. 46.

"Supply Woes Force Truck Stop Marketer into Creative But Costly Solution," *Oil Express,* September 1, 2003, p. 5.

Tatum, Lisa, "Based in Oklahoma City, Love's Travel Store Chain Stays Focused on Future," *Daily Oklahoman,* April 28, 2002.

"Travel Stops to Install TransCore Monitors," *Refrigerated Transporter,* May 1, 2003, p. 24.

Vigna, Jeanne-Michelle, "Family Business; Family-Owned Convenience Stores Hold on to Their Territory in the South Central," *Convenience Store News,* April 16, 2001, p. 99.

Ward, Kathryn, "Double-Duty: Love's New Wireless System Is a Win-Win for Customers and the Company," *Convenience Store News,* November 22, 2004.

Wiley, Elizabeth Camacho, "Oklahoma City-Based Convenience Store Continues Expansion Plans," *Daily Oklahoman,* May 2, 2003.

——, "Oklahoma City-Based Truck Stop Chain to Expand into Seven Additional States," *Daily Oklahoman,* February 3, 2003.

—Frederick C. Ingram

Madeco S.A.

Ureta Cox 930
San Miguel, Santiago
Chile
Telephone: (56) (2) 520-1000
Fax: (56) (2) 520-1140
Web site: http://www.madeco.cl

Public Company
Incorporated: 1944 as Manufacturas de Cobre S.A.
Employees: 2,751
Sales: CLP 324.03 billion ($581.32 million) (2004)
Stock Exchanges: Bolsa de Comercio de Santiago New
    York
Ticker Symbols: MADECO; MAD
NAIC: 322996 Fabricated Pipe and Pipefitting
    Manufacturing; 326112 Unsupported Film and Sheet
    Manufacturing Plastics Packaging; 331316 Aluminum
    Extruded Product Manufacturing; 335929 Other
    Communication and Energy Wire Manufacturing

Madeco S.A. is a Chile-based manufacturer of finished and semifinished metal products made of copper, aluminum, and related alloys. Its principal products include wires and cables; tubes, sheets, coils, and bars; and aluminum profiles. The company also manufactures flexible packaging products. Its factories are mainly in Chile and Argentina, but are also in Brazil and Peru.

Industrial Conglomerate: 1944–86

Madeco is an acronym for Manufacturas de Cobre S.A., which was founded in 1944 by Sociedad Manufacturera de Metales S.A., a Chilean company whose principal shareholders were Americo and Aurelio Simonetti and Corporación de Fomento de la Producción (Corfo), a government-owned development corporation. The purpose was to convert the nation's bountiful copper deposits into copper- and copper-alloy products made within Chile itself. These products were wires and cables, pipes, bars, and sheets. By 1960 Madeco had become Chile's first significant manufacturer of finished and intermediate copper products.

It soon became clear, however, that aluminum was a formidable industrial rival of copper because of its lower price and lighter weight, although it was not a suitable substitute for copper in the manufacture of wires and cables. Madeco began, in 1954, producing aluminum sheets and foil, and also profiles for the construction of windows, doors, and curtain walls. Alusa S.A. was established in 1961 in conjunction with the Zecchetto family to manufacture flexible packaging for use in food, snacks, and cosmetic products. About the same time Madeco began making considerable investments in order to modernize its output of copper and aluminum tubes, pipes, sheets, and plates, and its aluminum foil. In 1966, with the collaboration of the Washington-based Export-Import Bank and capital and technical assistance from General Cable Corp. and the Italian firm CEAT, work began on a cable-producing plant located in Antofagasta. During this decade CEAT bought 30 percent of Madeco, with most, perhaps all, of the rest becoming the property of a group belonging to Andrónico Luksic Abaroa.

Madeco was nationalized under the aegis of Corfo in 1971, following the election of a Marxist-dominated socialist government the previous year. Two years after this government was overthrown by a military coup in 1973, the enterprise was returned to prior management. By 1980 Corfo's stake had been sold to CEAT and Forestal Quiñenco S.A., Luksic's holding company. Although private ownership had been restored, conditions remained difficult for management because the military's government program of economic liberalization exposed the company's products to strong foreign competition. The severe recession of the early 1980s placed Madeco, as well as many other Chilean companies, near bankruptcy. In 1983 Quiñenco purchased CEAT's Madeco stock, raising its stake in the company to about two-thirds of the shares.

Advances and Reversals: 1986–2003

By 1986 the Chilean economy, and Madeco, were doing better. The company's debt, $75 million in 1980, had been reduced to $5 million. The wire and cable business had a reliable client in Compañia de Telecomunicaciones de Chile, the national telephone company. The pickup in the country's economy meant more construction and, therefore, more sales of

Company Perspectives:

Madeco S.A. was incorporated as an open stock corporation in Chile in 1944 and has expanded over the years into Brazil, Peru and Argentina. Today, the Company is a leading Latin American manufacturer of finished and semi-finished non-ferrous products based on copper, aluminum, related alloys and optical fiber as well as a manufacturer of flexible packaging products for use in the mass consumer market for food, snacks and cosmetics products.

tubes, plates, and profiles. Madeco's aluminum foil and sheets were finding new markets in east Asia. The following years saw a flurry of activity. In 1987 Madeco established Colada Continua Chilena S.A. to ensure the opportune production and delivery of copper rod, its principal raw material. The following year Madeco acquired Armat S.A., a manufacturer of minted coins and coin blanks made of copper and copper-based alloys for central banks around the world. Cotelsa S.A. was created in 1989 to manufacture wooden packaging. In 1990 Electromecánica Industrial S.A. (Emisa) was established for the repair of electric motors and servicing of other electrical equipment, and Eléctricas de Quilmes S.A. (Indelqui), an Argentine producer of power-transmission and telecommunications cable, was purchased. Indelqui was also a pioneer in fiber optics. Madeco also acquired Indalum S.A., the other principal manufacturer of aluminum profiles in Chile and, in collaboration with Codelco, Chile's state-owned copper producer, established a copper-tube factory in Beijing.

The next year was also an active one for Madeco. The company founded Ingewall S.A., to design and install curtain walls and Madecotel S.A. to install telephone lines produced by Madeco. Two more companies, Madeco Solar S.A. and Alusa's subsidiary Embalajes S.A., were formed in 1992. The following year Madeco acquired Triple-C, a Peruvian cable producer, and went public, raising $83 million by selling 11 percent of its common stock on the Bolsa de Comercio de Santiago and the New York Stock Exchange. The company continued its expansion in Argentina by acquiring a power-cable plant in Llavallol and also expanded its flexible packaging business into Argentina by acquiring Aluflex S.A.

Madeco was now engaged in a major capital investment and restructuring program intended to allow the company to bring new plants on line. Some $60 million was earmarked for 1994 and 1995, with the bulk of the investment program to go to the construction and packaging segments, which were seen as providing the greatest potential for growth during the next four or five years. But in 1994 Madeco also acquired 60 percent of Decker S.A.I.C.A.F. e I., the largest Argentine manufacturer of copper pipes and also a producer of copper sheets and brass pipes and sheets. Decker was merged with Indelqui in 1998 under the name Decker-Indelqui S.A. Triple-C merged with another large Peruvian cable manufacturer, Indeco S.A., under the Indeco name in 1994. Madeco, in 1996, acquired a minority interest in two Peruvian flexible packaging firms.

Madeco's next big move came in 1997, when it acquired two-thirds of Ficap S.A., Brazil's second largest cable company, for $121 million. Madeco raised about $76 million from stock sales that year to help provide the necessary funds and purchased the rest of Ficap in 1998. The company established a joint venture called Ficap Optel Ltda. in 1999 with Corning Inc., which purchased 25 percent and raised its participation to 50 percent in 2001. Ficap Optel's role was to produce, sell, and distribute optical-fiber cables. As part of the joint venture arrangement, Ficap Optel changed its name to Optel S.A. and purchased Corning's cable-manufacturing operation in Buenos Aires, which was renamed Optel Argentina S.A., while the Brazilian operation became Optel Ltda.

The Argentine recession that began in 1998 and resulted in the government's default on its debts and the devaluation of the peso at the end of 2001 did considerable damage to Madeco. Decker-Indelqui, its producer of wires and cables and brass mills in Argentina, closed its four plants in 2002. Corning withdrew from the Optel joint ventures, describing them as effectively bankrupt. Parent Madeco was in trouble, too, having lost money since 1998. Its shares of stock fell 95 percent in value. These setbacks resulted in managerial changes and a financial restructuring. The company, in 2003, rescheduled about $120 million in bank debt, paying 40 percent up front and agreeing to pay the rest over seven years, with a three-year grace period. Quiñenco provided at least $50 million of the funds needed, and a stock sale in Santiago raised about $7 million more. Madeco completed its debt-restructuring process by collecting about $95 million through a stock offering.

Tiberio Dall'Olio, a former CEAT executive who had been general manager of Madeco between 1980 and 1986, was brought back in 2002 to direct the firm's operations again. He vowed to save money not by laying off personnel but by selling some units abroad and by renovating the company's technology, which he described to the Chilean business magazine *Gestión* as "a little stagnant." He went on to affirm a commitment to "an ambience much more sympathetic and collaborative, less bureaucratic, and more direct in its relations. For example, I always have my doors open to all." Dall'Olio said that he dismissed his subordinates at 6:30 p.m. and considered weekends as "sacred" family time. "The workday atmosphere and interpersonal relations are very important. . . . My people ought to know that I will defend my company as my own, because in a certain way they are my family also. Besides I have a social responsibility, because people ought to feel a certain stability in their work."

Interviewed for another Chilean business magazine, *Capital,* by Lorena Medel, Dall'Olio said that Madeco had been "a gold mine" in the 1980s but had then grown too much. "It's the same as when one eats too much," he maintained. "The body swells and then becomes ill without knowing why." The completion of the financial restructuring enabled him to draft a three-year investment plan that emphasized modernizing the cable plant in Rio de Janeiro, Madeco's largest facility. The plan also called for an increase in the export of tubes and plates to Europe, the United States, and East Asia.

Ingewall was sold in 2002, but by late 2003 Madeco was able to reopen the Decker-Indelqui copper pipe manufacturing operation and the foundry. In 2004 Madeco earned its first profit—CLP 8.51 billion ($15.27 million)—since 1998, on

Key Dates:

1944: Manufacturas de Cobre S.A. (Madeco) is founded.
1954: Madeco begins making aluminum products as well as copper products.
1961: The company enters the flexible packaging field.
1966: Work begins on a cable-producing plant in Antofagasta.
1971–75: Nationalized Madeco is being run by a government agency.
1983: The Luksic group takes majority control of the company, which is near bankruptcy.
1993: Madeco goes public, raising $83 million through sales of stock.
1997–98: Madeco purchases Brazil's second largest cable manufacturer.
1999: A joint venture with Corning Inc. is producing fiber-optic cable in Brazil and Argentina.
2003: Continuing losses result in a restructuring of the company's debt.
2004: Madeco earns its first profit since 1998.

revenues that increased by one-third to CLP 324.03 billion ($581.32 million). The turnaround was in large part due to improved sales from the wire and cable and brass mills divisions. Madeco's long-term debt was CLP 126.38 billion ($226.73 million) at the end of 2004. Its total debt was CLP 298.57 billion ($535.65 million).

Madeco in 2004

Madeco was, in 2004, divided into four areas. By far the largest, accounting for more than half of all revenue, was the wire and cable division. This unit was producing both standard and customized wire and cable products for the telecommunications, energy, mining, and construction sectors, and also for durable goods manufacturers. The seven factories of this division were located in Argentina, Brazil, Chile, and Peru, but the one in Llavallol, Argentina, was not operating, and the Optel ones were doing little other than selling the cables in stock.

Second largest was the brass mills division, producing copper pipes for the construction sector and semifinished materials made from copper, aluminum, and related alloys for use in the fabrica-

tion of electrical components, mechanical parts, and hardware fixtures. Production was at facilities in both Chile and Argentina, with export to 36 countries. The flexible packaging division was manufacturing and selling aluminum foil and plastic wrap in Santiago and San Luis, Argentina. This division included the minority interest in two Peruvian operations. The aluminum profiles division continued to hold first place in its field in Chile and was also the largest distributor in this field in Chile. Quiñenco owned 56 percent of Madeco. Guillermo Luksic Craig, a son of Andrónico Luksic, was chairman of the board.

Principal Subsidiaries

Aluflex (Argentina; 76%); Alusa S.A. (76%); Armat S.A.; Decker-Indelqui S.A. (Argentina); Ficap S.A. (Brazil); Indeco S.A. (Peru; 93%).

Principal Operating Units

Aluminum Profiles; Brass Mills; Flexible Packaging; Wire and Cable.

Principal Competitors

Cabos e Sistemas do Brasil S.A.; Cembrass S.A.; Cimet S.A.; Cobre Cerrillos S.A.; Elaboradora de Cobre Viña del Mar S.A.; Envases del Pacífico S.A.; Pajarbol S.A.; Pirelli Cables S.A.I.C.; Pirelli Energía, Cabos e Sistemas do Brasil S.A.; Themco-Conformadores de Metales S.A.

Further Reading

"Corning Increases Ownership in Brazilian Optical Fiber Cable Manufacturer," *Fiber Optics Business,* May 31, 2001, p. 9.
"Laminando un marco para las exportaciones," *Gestión,* August 1986, pp. 26–29.
"Madeco," *LatinFinance,* November 1993, pp. 52+.
Medel, Lorena, "El gran desafío," *Capital,* March 28–April 10, 2003, pp. 58–61.
Millman, Joel, "Follow the Philosophy of the Ant," *Forbes,* October 12, 1992, pp. 132, 134.
"A Nadie le Gusta Estar Entre los Peores, Pero Estoy Optimista con el Futuro," *Gestión,* October 2003, pp. 11–12, 14–15.

—Robert Halasz

Maines Paper & Food Service Inc.

101 Broome Corporate Parkway
Conklin, New York 13748
U.S.A.
Telephone: (607) 779-1200
Fax: (607) 723-3245
Web site: http://www.maines.net

Private Company
Founded: 1919 as Maines Candy Company
Employees: 1,700
Sales: $1.6 billion (2004 est.)
NAIC: 424410 General Line Grocery Merchant
 Wholesalers

A private company based in Conklin, New York, Maines Paper & Food Service Inc. is one of the leading foodservice distributors in the United States, with annual sales in excess of $1.6 billion. The company's core business is the distribution of a broad line of products throughout New York State and northern Pennsylvania. These customers include restaurants (whether they be single units or regional chains, white table cloth or casual), convenience stores, delis, bars, pizzerias, educational institutions, healthcare facilities, cruise lines, concessionaires, and camps. The broad line of products includes fresh, frozen, dry grocery, paper goods, and beverages. Maines's QSR (Quick Serve Restaurants) division is primarily dedicated to serving the needs of the Wendy's and Burger King fast-food chains. Maines also operates an equipment and supply operation, selling a wide variety of equipment and smallware products while also providing services such as kitchen layout, design, and installation. Maines offers institutional products to independents and the general public through Maines Food & Party Warehouse, two cash-and-carry operations in Johnson City and Syracuse, New York. The company maintains distribution centers in upstate New York, the New York City metropolitan area, Massachusetts, Maryland, Ohio, Illinois, and Tennessee. Maines's service area stretches from Maine in the northeast to as far south as Georgia, as far southwest as Louisiana, encompasses the entire Midwest, and reaches as far west as Montana and Wyoming.

Company Founding in 1919

Maines was launched under modest circumstances in 1919 when Floyd L. Maines, Sr., moved to the Binghamton, New York area and established a candy distribution business in the small town of Conklin. In the first year of operation he sold $30,000 worth of nickel candy bars—Hershey bars, Milky Ways, Reese's Peanut Butter Cups, and the like. It was not until a second generation joined the company in the form of Floyd L. Maines, Jr., that it expanded beyond the candy distribution business. After a five-year stint in the Navy during World War II, the younger Maines took a permanent position with the company in 1947, although according to family lore his first inclination was to become an FBI agent. Nevertheless, he was an aggressive businessman and able to persuade his father that Maines Candy Company, as it was now called, should offer a far more diverse selection of products, including paper goods such as napkins, cups, and straws, as well as fountain supplies and even toys. Nevertheless, it remained a small operation, served by a single small truck and a family station wagon. But the younger Maines also recruited some friends to act as sales reps for the growing company, resulting in steady growth for the next two decades.

A third generation of the Maines family became involved with the company when Floyd Maines, Jr.'s son David came to work for the company in 1970. It was during the early 1970s that Maines finally reached the $1 million mark in annual sales. In 1972 the company decided to become involved in food distribution, hiring a veteran of the business, Jack Olin from Binghamton-based Willow Run Foods, to head the effort. Sales began to climb, but the young blood in the family, David and his younger brother Bill, were determined to reach far greater heights. A profile of the Maines family published by Binghamton's *Press & Sun-Bulletin* in 2002 shared the reflections of longtime customer Frank Kelly, a small franchiser of area Burger King restaurants. Kelly recalled an incident in 1974, at a time when David Maines was 24 and his brother William was an 18-year-old college freshman at Babson College in Massachusetts. Maines showed Kelly "a copy of *ID* magazine, a trade journal for the food distribution industry. It listed Maines Paper & Food Service as an up-and-comer in the business.

213

Company Perspectives:

We are dedicated to the customer and to the service required to make our customers successful. The people, equipment and systems have all been put in place with two thoughts in mind: Be part of the customer's solution! And be as easy to do business with, as possible!

'Frank, when Billy gets back from college, we're going to make a plan and we're going to town,' Kelly recalls David Maines telling him.''

Addition of Frozen Foods Leading to 1970s Growth

Maines was growing at a steady clip by the time Bill Maines joined his brother in the family business in 1978. Annual sales had ballooned to $11 million, due in large part to the expansion into foodservice, and the company's association with Burger King. According to Kelly, "When Burger King went into frozen products, that gave them the opportunity to open their first frozen plant. Once they got to be experts in that, it didn't take much to jump in sales." As the Maines brothers came together and began assuming greater day-to-day control, the company experienced even more explosive growth. Because the product mix now included frozen foods, canned goods, beverages, and cleaning supplies, the company changed its name from Maines Candy Company to Maines Paper & Food Service. According to Frank Kelly, the two brothers were close friends who worked well as a team. He described David, the dynamic salesman who also concentrated on expanding markets, purchasing, and pricing, as "Mr. Outside," and Bill Maines as "Mr. Inside," the one who upgraded the facilities and computerized distribution. The younger brother also proved to be a tough and skillful negotiator.

Fast-food chain sales helped to fuel growth in the 1980s, as did the addition of casual dining customers. Maines also looked to make sales to independents and the general public. In 1984 the company opened its first cash and carry operation in Johnson City. A year later the company grew through acquisition, adding the Ground Round chain to double revenues. As a result, the formerly up-and-coming company cracked *Institutional Distributor* magazine's top 50 food distributors in the United States, ranking 43rd. The company's momentum continued in the second half of the 1980s. To keep pace with sales, warehouse space steadily increased, from 40,000 square feet in the 1970s to 135,000 square feet by 1986. A year later a second distribution center was established in Cleveland, allowing Maines to handle the business of customers with Midwest operations. Maines closed the decade by acquiring a new freezer facility, primarily used to service the all-important Burger King account. Also in 1989, Maines added milk, soft-serve, and shake mixes, as well as a complete beverage program to both the Conklin and Cleveland centers. The cash-and-carry facility also was expanded by 10,000 square feet, to 24,000 square feet, to allow the addition of a full beverage center. By this stage Maines was able to become a virtual one-stop supplier for many multiunit restaurant operators. More than 80 percent of the company's sales came from multiunit operations, with the Conklin distribution center serving these customers in 12 states, from Maine to Virginia, and the Cleveland facility handling western Pennsylvania, Ohio, Indiana, Kentucky, and Michigan.

Sales in 1989 totaled $166.9 million, but that number would grow exponentially during the 1990s. An important step in the company's continuing momentum was the 1990 purchase of Prescott-Pierson Equipment Services, a Binghamton equipment supplier and contracting company, the addition of which allowed Maines to now offer a full line of smallwares and equipment, as well as heating and air conditioning and refrigeration installation and service. Maines supplemented the business by adding a showroom and design consulting service. The Prescott-Pierson operation was moved to a separate Conklin facility, where it formed the basis of the Maines Equipment & Supplies division. While multiunit customers continued to contribute the lion's share of sales, Maines increasingly emphasized sales to independents, so-called street sales, taking advantage of a shifting marketplace. The sale of Buffalo-based S.M. Flickinger Group to a larger company and the decision of Willow Run Foods to exit the street business left Maines with an opening to exploit in much of its territory. The average order from multiunits totaled $3,725 and $850 for independents. To further attract street customers, Maines added several hundred items geared toward independents. It also procured additional storage space in Conklin: 15,000 square feet for refrigerated and frozen items and 60,000 square feet for dry storage. Increasing sales also resulted in the purchase of 14 45-foot trailers and tractors, increasing the company's fleet to 39.

In the early 1990s Maines topped the $200 million mark in annual sales and continued climbing steadily. To keep pace with demand, the company had bolstered warehouse space by acquiring storage in a pair of offsite warehouses, followed by the addition of public storage at two area companies. Maines now maintained five separate locations in the Conklin area, in an efficient setup that caused some pallets to be handled three times as they shifted between warehouses before being shipped to customers. Maines established a senior management team to consider how to reorganize the distribution operation, and it concluded, not surprisingly, that the company needed to consolidate the warehouses and handle distribution in a single, state-of-the-art center that incorporated the latest in technology and equipment. In addition to the consolidation issue, Maines was growing increasingly concerned about the cost of doing business in New York State, burdened by high state taxes and workers' compensation costs, as well as expensive utilities. To gain leverage, the company looked six miles south to Pennsylvania, which soon offered a package of tax rebates and construction premiums if Maines would relocate across the border. Floyd Maines, Jr., then wrote to New York Governor Mario Cuomo to see if New York had a counteroffer. Instead, he heard nothing from the governor's office. At the time, 1994, Cuomo was running for reelection, and the perceived snub threw the Maines family into the waiting arms of Cuomo's opponent, George Pataki, who seized upon the situation and made it into a major campaign issue, even appearing at the Conklin plant to make a public pledge to keep the company in the state. After Pataki unseated Cuomo and came into office he helped to arrange a $20 million economic development package to keep Maines in New York.

Key Dates:

1919: Floyd L. Maines, Sr., launches a candy distribution business.

1947: Floyd L. Maines, Jr., joins the company, which adds paper and other products.

1970: David Maines, son of Floyd Maines, Jr., joins the company.

1972: The company becomes involved in food distribution.

1978: David Maines's brother, William, joins the company.

1987: A second distribution center opens in Cleveland.

1990: Prescott-Pierson Equipment Services is acquired.

1997: The Conklin operations are consolidated in a new headquarters/distribution center.

2000: Chris Mellon becomes the first nonfamily member to be named CEO; the company becomes the largest food distributor in the country when it receives a $3 billion contract to supply food and paper products to 1,700 Burger King restaurants.

Opening a New Distribution Center in 1997

In 1997 the company consolidated its operations, moving into a new $25 million state-of-the-art 340,000-square-foot headquarters/distribution center in Conklin. It featured five different temperature zones for coolers and freezers and shipping/receiving docks, a test kitchen, and learning center complete with a 350-seat auditorium. The new facility also allowed Maines to now offer fresh produce (as part of the Markon fresh produce purchasing/marketing cooperative), fresh poultry, and fresh seafood. Because the center offered such a vast array of items, some 13,000 in all, it relied on a new high-tech warehouse management system, the PkMs system offered by Atlanta-based Manhattan Associates. Although the previous system was appropriate for the smaller Cleveland facility, which offered only a few hundred items, it was woefully inadequate for the new Conklin site. It offered no level of detail beyond total inventory, and offered no capabilities in product rotation, tracking, and productivity management. Under the new system, however, every pallet entering the center was assigned a unique identifier in the form of a barcoded license plate, allowing PkMs to create a history for each pallet and to track its progress, from being received to being shipped. The system's logic capability not only could locate a product in the huge facility but also direct the best way to pick it. Once the bugs were worked out of the system, its data was married to the delivery drivers' handheld scanners, so that the drivers could track, trace, and verify product from the warehouse to the point of delivery.

Other developments in the 1990s included the 1993 opening of a second cash-and-carry operation, located in the Syracuse area. In 1995 the company opened its own truck driving school, Maines Driver Training Institute, to take care of the training needs of its expanding truck fleet. It would expand to train outside drivers as well, providing the training necessary to earn a commercial driver's license (CDL) for interstate transport. It would grow to become one of the most respected truck driving schools in the Northeast.

Maines opened the new century with a number of changes. Floyd Maines had retained the titles of CEO and chairman well past the time his sons had taken over effective control of the business. Then in 2000 the company brought in its first nonfamily member as its chief executive, naming CFO Chris Mellon to the post. He had joined the company two years earlier. David and Bill Maines now became co-chairmen of the company, focusing on the big picture, while Floyd Maines, Jr., became chairman emeritus. The year 2000 was also noteworthy because of a $3 billion contract the company received to supply food and paper products to 1,700 Burger King restaurants, a deal that made Maines the largest foodservice distributor in the country and elevated it to the top ranks of national food distributors with approximately $1.2 billion in annual sales. To accommodate the increased business, Maines opened four new distribution centers in 2000, located in Oxford, Massachusetts; Oakwood Village, Ohio; Farmingdale, New York; and Conklin.

Maines's expansion continued during the first half of the 2000s, as operations were established in Maryland and the Chicago area in 2003. The Chicago facility was acquired from Marriott Distribution Services to accommodate a new $1.4 billion contract serving the 11 midwestern states for Darden Restaurants, Inc., the corporate parent to restaurant chains Red Lobster, Olive Garden, Smokey Bones, and Bahama Breeze. In 2005 Maines acquired a distribution center in Memphis, ideally suited to serve the southern locations of the Wendy's hamburger chain, which in 2005 signed a $2 billion contract. This came on the heels of another $515 million contract with Burger King and other multiyear contracts totaling $5 billion, all signed within two months of each other. Maines was now generating annual sales in excess of $1.6 billion, and there was no reason to suspect that its growth would tail off in the near future.

Principal Divisions

Broadline Distribution; Systems Distribution; QSR Division; Maines Equipment and Supply; Retail; Maines Driver Training Institute.

Principal Competitors

SYSCO Corporation; U.S. Foodservice, Inc.; Performance Food Group Company.

Further Reading

"Maines Paper & Food Services," *Institutional Distribution,* December 1989, p. 112.

"Maines Paper & Food Services," *Institutional Distribution,* December 1990, p. 96.

"Maines Paper & Food Services," *Institutional Distribution,* December 1991, p. 88.

McAdam, Todd, "Deal-Makers: The Maines Family—Mainstays of the Community," *Press & Sun-Bulletin,* July 11, 2002, p. 1A.

McManus, Bob, "How the Empire State Got Its Groove Back," *New York Post,* October 22, 1998, p. 31.

Perkins, Caroline, "75 Years and Growing: Maines Paper & Food Service's Legacy of Expansion," *ID: The Voice of Foodservice Distribution,* November 1, 1994, p. 56.

—Ed Dinger

MasterBrand Cabinets, Inc.

1 MasterBrand Cabinets Drive
Jasper, Indiana 47547
U.S.A.
Telephone: (812) 482-2527
Fax: (812) 482-9872
Web site: http://www.masterbrandcabinets.com

Wholly Owned Subsidiary of Fortune Brands, Inc.
Incorporated: 1998
Employees: 6,000
Sales: $1.5 billion (2004 est.)
NAIC: 337110 Wood Kitchen Cabinet and Counter Top
    Manufacturing

MasterBrand Cabinets, Inc. is part of the Home and Hardware products division of Fortune Brands, Inc. The Jasper, Indiana-based subsidiary is one of the largest cabinet manufacturers in the world, generating more than $1 billion in sales each year, trailing only Masco Corporation in market share in the United States. Through its various units, MasterBrand makes custom, semi-custom, stock, and ready-to-assemble kitchen cabinets, as well as bathroom vanities. Products are sold through specialty retailers, home centers, and lumber outlets. Brands include Aristokraft, Capital Cabinet, Decora, Diamond, Georgetown, HomeCrest, Kemper, Kitchen Classics, Kitchen Craft, Maple Creek, NHB, Omega, Dynasty, and Schrock. In addition, MasterBrand produces Thomasville cabinets on an exclusive arrangement with Home Depot.

Parent Company Lineage Dating to the 1800s

The creation of MasterBrand Cabinets in 1998 was part of a much larger story, the effort of a legendary tobacco company to divorce itself from the very product that made its founders and investors immensely wealthy. Before it became Fortune Brands, MasterBrand's parent was known as American Brands, the direct descendant of The American Tobacco Company, which spawned many of the nation's well-known tobacco companies.

American Tobacco was founded by James Buchanan (Buck) Duke, born in Durham, North Carolina, in 1856. The family farm was ravaged by the Civil War, leaving only a barn of bright leaf tobacco, which was becoming increasingly popular. His father, Washington Duke, sold the tobacco and decided to devote his entire farm to the production of bright leaf. In 1873 W. Duke & Sons built a factory in Durham and began shifting its focus from production to the manufacture and sale of tobacco, which at the time was divided between chewing and smoking tobacco, the latter for pipes or rolled into cigars, since cigarettes had yet to gain widespread popularity. In his early 20s, Buck Duke was already becoming a driving force in the family business, and in the 1880s he pushed the firm into cigarettes, taking advantage of the new mechanized rolling machines capable of turning out 200 cigarettes each minute. This advance, coupled with a modern approach to packaging and advertising, gave Duke a competitive edge. He moved to New York City, the heart of the cigarette business, and took on the leading companies of the day on their own turf. By the end of the 1880s, Duke conquered the U.S. cigarette market.

It was an era of trusts in the United States, led by the success of John D. Rockefeller's Standard Oil. Duke, still in his early 30s, looked to avoid the cutthroat competition that suppressed profits in the cigarette business by joining forces with his five largest competitors. In 1890 The American Tobacco Company was formed, with Duke serving as the president of the combination, which sold four out of every five cigarettes in the United States. Not content to rule only the comparatively small cigarette business, Duke assailed the other more popular sectors of the industry, engaging in price wars until opponents agreed to be swallowed by the industry behemoth, as American Tobacco, eventually, dominated snuff, smoking tobacco, and cigars. He employed the same techniques to challenge British tobacco companies, leading to an agreement between Duke and a British coalition to stay out of each other's country while teaming up to form the British-American Tobacco Company (later renamed B.A.T. Industries), two-thirds owned by Duke and his confederates, to tackle the world market. On the retail side, Duke was also dominant, operating a chain of more than 500 United Cigar Stores.

In the early years of the 1900s President Theodore Roosevelt sought to dismantle the powerful trusts that dominated American business, including American Tobacco. Legal wrangling between Duke's lawyers and the Justice Department came to an end in 1911 when the United States Supreme Court ordered the breakup of American Tobacco. The result was the creation of some of the century's most powerful tobacco companies: Liggett & Meyers, Lorillard, and R.J. Reynolds, as well as a reconstituted American Tobacco Company.

After the breakup, cigarettes finally began to challenge chewing tobacco in popularity, as the new tobacco companies began introducing national cigarette brands, led by the 1913 introduction of Camel by R.J. Reynolds. American Tobacco's chief brand became Lucky Strike. Fueled by tremendous levels of advertising, cigarette consumption soared, finally surpassing chewing tobacco in 1923. Two years later Duke died, but not before creating a philanthropic trust fund, much of which was used to found Duke University.

American Tobacco grew Lucky Strike to new heights during World War II and also pioneered the "king size" cigarette with the introduction of Pall Mall, which soon challenged Camel and Lucky Strike as America's top cigarette brand. The company's cigarette business peaked in the early 1950s, after which it failed to answer R.J. Reynolds's first filtered cigarette, Winston, and assumed an increasingly diminished role in the cigarette industry.

American Tobacco Becoming American Brands in the 1960s

In the mid-1960s American Tobacco began to dip into its coffers to diversify, acquiring non-tobacco assets such as James B. Beam Distilling Company, Sunshine Biscuits, and Duffy-Mott Co., maker of Mott's apple sauce and apple juice. In keeping with the shift away from tobacco, American Tobacco changed its name to American Brands in 1969. As its share of the domestic tobacco market declined, the company continued to diversify, transforming itself into a true conglomerate. Over the next 20 years, American Brands acquired and divested a wide variety of assets. It became involved in office products, financial services, valves and pumps, golfing products, lighting, security through Pinkerton's, and locks through Master Lock Company. American Brands also added to its distilled spirits holdings with the acquisition of seven Seagram Company brands, making Jim Beam America's third largest spirits company.

In 1988 American Brands acquired 15 companies in one stroke with the $1.1 billion acquisition of E-II Holdings Inc, spun off from Beatrice Co. a year before. Although American Brands subsequently cast off most of the assets, including Samsonite luggage and Culligan water treatment, it kept four companies that made hardware and home products, which the company planned to make one of its core businesses—joining tobacco, distilled spirits, financial services, and office products. One of the former Beatrice companies American Brands elected to keep was Aristokraft Inc., marking the company's entry into the kitchen cabinetry field.

Aristokraft was founded in 1954 as United Cabinet Corporation by Stanley G. Krempp. It started out in a small 50-foot by 100-foot building in Celestine, Indiana, then in 1963 moved to Jasper, Indiana, home to many furniture companies, prompting the town to bill itself as the "Nation's Wood Office Furniture Capital." In 1971 the company's Jasper plant became the first in the nation to open an industrial ultraviolet curing line. Growth was so strong that United Cabinet opened two more plants, catching the attention of Beatrice Foods, which bought the company in 1974. Two years later United Cabinet established the Decora semi-custom division to serve the more upscale home owner. The stock cabinet division operated under the Aristokraft name, which in 1983 replaced United Cabinets as the company name, becoming Aristokraft, Inc.

American Brands folded Aristokraft and Decora into a new subsidiary called MasterBrand Industries, the name drawn from the group's most prestigious brand, Master Lock. For the next ten years American Brands did not add to the cabinetry sector. In the meantime it attempted to revive its domestic tobacco business through the introduction of low-price brands. Then, in 1994 in a surprise move, American Brands sold its American tobacco interests to its once-removed corporate cousin, B.A.T. Industries, essentially leaving just British cigarette maker Gallaher in its portfolio (albeit Gallaher represented more than $6 billion in annual revenues). A few months later, American Brands cast off its only financial service asset, Franklin Life Insurance Co., opting to concentrate on consumer goods. The last vestiges of tobacco were removed in 1997 when the company's international tobacco operations were spun off as Gallaher Group PLC in a demerger and the remaining company assumed the name Fortune Brands. No longer involved in the tobacco business, management wanted to further remove the company from its American Tobacco heritage and the stigma investors attached to it. Two years earlier, for example, the company's stock price tumbled on the news of a different tobacco company losing a jury award.

Although Fortune Brands had not added cabinetry assets after acquiring Aristokraft, it had continued to build up MasterBrand Industries' slate of hardware and home-improvement assets, including the Moen brand of kitchen and bathroom faucets. Management's strategy was to focus only on top brands in a category and then leverage the power of the brand to convince consumers to "trade up." For example, Master Lock used its reputation with padlocks to become involved in door locks in 1992, and almost immediately became the number three player in the field. Jim Beam used its brand recognition to introduce more expensive premium bourbons.

Forming MasterBrand Cabinets in 1998

In 1998 MasterBrand Industries acquired struggling Schrock Cabinet Company, selling under the Schrock, Kemper, and Diamond brand names to U.S. home centers and kitchen and bath specialty dealers. Schrock was folded into a newly created subsidiary, MasterBrand Cabinets, Inc., in effect, to create a new major cabinet brand to exploit. In one stroke, the $107.5 million purchase from Electrolux A.B. subsidiary White Consolidated Industries turned MasterBrand Cabinets into the second largest cabinet maker in the United States, after Masco Corporation. Schrock was founded in Arthur, Illinois, in 1961

Key Dates:

1954: Aristokraft is launched as United Cabinet Company.
1969: American Tobacco Company changes its name to American Brands.
1988: American Brands acquires AristoKraft.
1997: American Brands changes its name to Fortune Brands.
1998: Fortune Brands acquires Schrock Cabinet Company, forming MasterBrand Cabinets, Inc.
1999: NHB Group Ltd. is acquired.
2002: Omega Group is acquired.
2003: Capital Cabinet is acquired.

as Schrock Brothers Manufacturing, specializing in handcrafted cabinetry, while Kemper was founded in Richmond, Indiana, in 1926, and upscale Diamond Cabinets started out as Diamond Industries in Grants Pass, Oregon, in 1970. All three became part of White Industries, which Electrolux acquired in 1986.

In its first year MasterBrand Cabinets posted sales of more than $400 million. To support the growing business, the company added two factories in 1999, opening a new Schrock Cabinet production facility in Auburn, Alabama, and buying a 600,000-square-foot plant in Kingston, North Carolina, to make Aristokraft brand cabinets. Well positioned in the value, better-best, and semi-custom cabinet categories, MasterBrand Cabinets looked to fill out its product lines through the October 1999 acquisition of NHB Group Ltd., a Canadian cabinet manufacturer that was strong in the ready-to-assemble and do-it-yourself, frameless kitchen and bathroom cabinet categories, adding about $60 million a year in sales. Moreover, NHB gave MasterBrand Cabinets a presence in the Canadian market, and also strengthened ties to the major home centers to which it sold. Along with the NHB brand, MasterBrand Cabinets added NHB's Kitchen Classics and the Georgetown Collection to its stable of cabinet brands.

MasterBrand Cabinets reached $500 million in sales in 1999 and grew that number to more than $800 million in 2001. The next major step in growing the company was taken in April 2002 when it acquired Waterloo, Iowa-based The Omega Group for $538 million, including the assumption of $127 million in debt. Omega's brands of kitchen and bathroom cabinets—Omega, Kitchen Craft, and Home Crest—generated $325 million in sales in 2001. The company was launched in a barn in 1977 by Bob Bertch, then opened a plant in 1984 and expanded until it encompassed more than 400,000 square feet. It also operated plants in Goshen, Indiana; Clinton, Tennessee; and Winnipeg, Manitoba. Omega was considered a good fit for MasterBrand Cabinets for several reasons. The lines complemented one another, with the Omega brands more involved in the remodeling business rather than new construction. MasterBrand also hoped to take advantage of Omega's relationship with high-end dealers and upscale design centers, such as EXPO Design Centers and The Great Indoors. Further, the addition of Omega created economies of scale, allowing MasterBrand Cabinets to consolidate its purchases of raw materials. It also expanded the company's presence in Canada. Of importance as well in 2002 was an exclusive agreement reached with Home Depot to manufacture the Thomasville cabinet line.

MasterBrand Cabinets grew further through acquisitions with the August 2003 purchase of Capital Cabinet Corp., a company founded in 1946, doing about $30 million in sales to homebuilders in Las Vegas and Southern California, fast-growing parts of the country that management was targeting. MasterBrand Cabinets also continued to grow internally, opening new plants and expanding others. With about $1.5 billion in sales, MasterBrand Cabinets was making a sizable contribution to Fortune Brands' Home and Hardware division, which in 2004 generated nearly $3.8 billion of the parent company's $7.3 billion total revenues. In light of the United States' aging population, a demographic given to home improvement projects, and increasing new home sales, which generally led to more remodeling projects, MasterBrand Cabinets was likely to continue its pattern of strong growth for the foreseeable future.

Principal Operating Units

Aristokraft; Capital Cabinet; Decora; Diamond; Georgetown; HomeCrest; Kemper; Kitchen Classics; Kitchen Craft; Maple Creek; NHB; Omega; Dynasty; Schrock.

Principal Competitors

American Woodmark Corporation; Armstrong World Industries, Inc.; Masco Corporation.

Further Reading

Adams, Larry, "Aristokraft's Rough Mill of the Future," *Wood & Wood Products,* November 1996, p. 50.
"Fortune Brands Buys RTA Cabinet Company," *Wood & Wood Products,* December 1999, p. 18.
Oliver, Suzanne, " 'I Love These Brands,' " *Forbes,* September 25, 1995, p. 94.
Palmer, Joel, "Fortune 500 Consumer Products Company Buys Waterloo, Iowa-Based Omega Cabinets," *Waterloo Courier,* April 9, 2002.
Spykens, Chad, "MasterBrand Cabinets CEO Discusses Growth Plans," *Wood & Wood Products,* April 2003, p. 41.
Winkler, John K., *Tobacco Tycoon: The Story of James Buchanan Duke,* New York: Random House, 1942.

—Ed Dinger

McCormick & Schmick's Seafood Restaurants, Inc.

720 SW Washington Street, Suite 550
Portland, Oregon 97205
U.S.A.
Telephone: (503) 226-3440
Fax: (503) 228-5074
Web site: http://www.mccormickandschmicks.com

Public Company
Incorporated: 1979
Employees: 4,600
Sales: $238.8 million (2004)
Stock Exchanges: NASDAQ
Ticker Symbol: MSSR
NAIC: 722110 Full-Service Restaurants; 722310 Food
   Service Contractors

McCormick & Schmick's Seafood Restaurants, Inc. has more than 50 affordable upscale casual dining restaurants that specialize in fish and other seafood dishes in 21 states and the District of Columbia. Half of these restaurants are located in buildings included in the National Register of Historic Places. Each restaurant's menu is printed daily and contains between 85 and 100 made-to-order dishes that incorporate local, regional, national, and international species of seafood and 30 to 40 varieties of fresh fish. The company operates primarily under the McCormick & Schmick brand. Its other names include M & S Grill, McCormick's Fish House & Bar, and Spenger's Fresh Fish Grotto.

1972–80s: Expanding upon an Established Tradition

McCormick & Schmick's began in 1972 when Bill McCormick, who had been a partner in the rapidly expanding Refectory Steak House chain, purchased Jake's Famous Crawfish Restaurant of Portland, Oregon, for $55,000. McCormick, who was proud of his Irish heritage, had grown up in Rhode Island and had earlier worked for Connecticut General. He moved to Portland, Oregon, from San Francisco in 1968 and fell in love with Jake's, an old-time Portland establishment.

Jake's had been founded almost a hundred years earlier, in 1892, as Mueller and Meyer's, a bar restaurant. Portland's citizens at that time had numbered 90,000, and the city's downtown had not yet been built. Ten years later, the restaurant moved to a new location where it still remained at the time of McCormick's purchase, SW 12th and Stark. In 1920, John Romeltsch purchased the establishment and turned it into a soft-drink parlor to survive Prohibition. A year later, Jacob (Jake) Freiman came on board. Jake was experienced in preparing seafood, especially freshwater crustaceans indigenous to the Pacific Northwest. To be able to serve his crawfish fresh, Jake dug ponds in the restaurant's basement to hold them.

By its 35th birthday in 1927, Jake's Famous Crawfish Restaurant was attracting diners and show people from up and down the West Coast. After dances at the nearby Multnomah Hotel, the restaurant often served a thousand customers before it closed at dawn. By the early 1970s, when McCormick bought the restaurant, Jake's Famous Crawfish was about to close. McCormick, determined to ensure the restaurant's future, read the *Joy of Cooking*, consulted with his restaurant's chefs, and began hanging out at Jake's Bar. According to company literature, within a month, people were lining up at Jake's front door, and McCormick had made the decision to focus on serving seafood.

In 1974, Doug Schmick joined Bill McCormick. McCormick and Schmick founded Traditional Concepts, a restaurant management organization. Schmick, who was of German stock, had grown up in Colfax, Washington. After graduating from Idaho University, he became experienced in restaurant management. Although Schmick had dreamed of becoming an author, he abandoned that dream when fatherhood beckoned. The two men met when Schmick walked into Jake's, and soon thereafter, they opened the first McCormick & Schmick's restaurant in downtown Portland.

McCormick & Schmick's built on Jake's successful formula. Most of McCormick & Schmick's customers were 30 to 60 years old, college educated, and in the middle to upper middle class income bracket. A significant portion of customers were in the postwar baby boomer generation. Jake's enhanced its dining room business by creating a social venue that would appeal to its customers and built a regular clientele through its bar operation. The new restaurant also had a bar and positioned itself to stand out from both independent local seafood restau-

Company Perspectives:

The McCormick & Schmick's mission: Offer excellent, fresh regional seafood served in a traditional manner and a "customer is always right" attitude. Empower managers to create initiative and autonomy. Have tremendous faith in your employees. Believe in flexibility and evolve in the markets you're in in order to allow adjusting styles and culinary trends to customers' preferences. Keep consistent parameters along with individuality. Give back to the communities that support you.

Key Dates:

1972: Bill McCormick buys Jake's Famous Crawfish Restaurant.
1974: Doug Schmick joins McCormick.
1994: Castle Harlan purchases McCormick & Schmick's.
1997: Castle Harlan sells McCormick & Schmick's to Apple South.
2001: Avado sells McCormick & Schmick's to Castle Harlan and Bruckman, Rosser, Sherrill & Co.
2004: The company goes public.

rants and national and regional chains by including 30 to 40 fresh seafood items from throughout the United States and select international locations. It printed its menu daily.

Building upon McCormick & Schmick's successful bar operations, Doug Schmick hit upon the idea of creating a cheap after-work menu. "In the '70s and '80s, it was fried food heaven," Schmick said, looking back in a *Willamette Week Online* article. Wanting to restore the product quality served at the bar during the dinner hour, Schmick decided not only to offer good food, but also to offer it a discount. At the Harborside Restaurant and Pilsner Room, which became McCormick & Schmick's Harborside at the Marina, "[w]e practically gave [food] away," Schmick told *Willamette Week Online.* Then, realizing that people associated the idea of free food with not-so-good food, McCormick & Schmick's decided to "just charge $1.95" and to see what happened next. The trend caught on, and all of the McCormick & Schmick's restaurants began to offer some kind of low-cost food.

1990s: Expansion Along the West Coast

Other restaurants followed. As the chain grew, each new McCormick & Schmick's showcased its bar while also aiming to be classic, timeless, and traditional in its approach toward food. Each restaurant had a high degree of operating autonomy, which it could use for developing some of its own dishes, and held responsibility for its own profits and losses.

Then, in 1994, Castle Harlan Inc., a private investment company known for partnering with existing management, bought McCormick & Schmick's for $24 million with plans of taking it public. By the late 1990s, the company's establishments numbered 16 and were located in four states—Oregon, Washington, California, and Colorado—and the District of Columbia. Restaurants ranged in size from approximately 6,000 to 14,000 square feet and were located in a variety of settings, including office towers, high-end retail, tourist-frequented areas, and the street-level portions of condominium complexes.

Under Castle Harlan direction, McCormick & Schmick's became a leader in the seafood dinner house niche. Success attracted attention, and in 1997, Apple South Inc. bought McCormick & Schmick's chain of about 20 restaurants for $53 million. Apple South had begun in 1978 as a Burger King franchise and in the 1980s developed Applebee's Neighborhood Bar & Grill. In 1998, Apple South changed its name to Avado Brands and, facing financial difficulties, began selling off its Applebee's franchises. By late

1998, it had sold 191, or 70 percent, of its Applebee's restaurants and had another 50 establishments under contract to sell.

McCormick & Schmick's continued to operate independently and retain its existing management under Avado Brands. It also expanded into East Coast states. With approximately 30 restaurants in 2000, the chain reached revenues of $162 million. Its restaurants operated under the names McCormick & Schmick's, Jake's Grill, McCormick's & Kuleto's, Spenger's Fresh Fish Grotto, and McCormick & Schmick's Harborside Restaurant and Pilsner Room.

Avado agreed to sell the McCormick & Schmick's to two buyout firms, one of which was Castle Harlan Inc., for $123.5 million in 2001. The other firm was Bruckman, Rosser, Sherrill & Co. At the time of the purchase, McCormick & Schmick's had 34 restaurants.

2000–05: Instituting Core Menu Items to Facilitate Ongoing Expansion

McCormick & Schmick's grew steadily throughout the early years of the new century. In 2003, it reached revenues of $206 million. In 2004, it opened its sixth restaurant in the D.C. area and its total number of restaurants topped 50. The company held its first public offering on the NASDAQ in 2004 and sold six million newly issued shares for $72 million.

Throughout this evolution, McCormick & Schmick's faced the challenge of protecting the indigenous, local nature of its individual restaurants while taking advantage of the increased buying power and market identity of its growing chain and creating a core menu. "We needed to define specs for certain menu items and products," explained the company's director of culinary development and training, Bill King, in *Seafood Business* in 2005. "This is especially important in an area like fresh seafood, where you're dealing with price volatilities, and indigenous species as well as seafood from all over the world." Many of these core items came up "through the field," having been developed first as a local specialty and then chosen by the chain's culinary management team of eight regional chefs.

As it looked to the future, McCormick & Schmick's leadership felt reason for optimism. Americans had consumed 4.7 billion points of seafood in 2003, an increase of almost 5 percent from the previous year. The National Restaurant Association's forecasts predicted rising industry sales through the year 2005. McCormick & Schmick's opened ten new restaurants in 2004 and planned to open another 20 to 25 new establishments in affluent suburban areas from 2005 through 2008. One of these would be its first new restaurant in the Portland area since 1994 and would be located in a ''lifestyle center'' called Bridgeport Village that would eventually house about 100 stores, ten of them restaurants, in a former abandoned rock quarry. In setting its course for the future, McCormick & Schmick's expected to continue to appeal to casual diners, families, tourists, and business travelers with its diverse menu offerings and reasonable prices.

Principal Subsidiaries

McCormick & Schmick Acquisition Corp.; McCormick & Schmick Restaurant Corporation.

Further Reading

Carey, Dave, ''PE Firm Gains on McCormick IPO,'' *Daily Deal*, July 21, 2004.

Carlos, Brenda, ''McCormick & Schmick Management Group,'' *Hospitality News*, September 2001, p. 8.

Colton, Kim, ''Happy Hour Hallelujah!—Cheap Gets Even Cheaper,'' *Willamette Week Online,* April 30, 2003, http://www.wwcck.com/print.php?story = 3885.

Holman, Kelly, ''One Fish, Two Fish: Castle Harlan Buys McCormick & Schmick Again,'' *Daily Deal*, June 8, 2001.

''Jake's Famous Crawfish Restaurant Hits 100,'' *Oregonian*, June 12, 1992, advertising supplement.

Lang, Joan M., ''Core-Menu Plan Offers Quality, Consistency, and Economy: McCormick & Schmick's Buying Program Protects the Brand While Allowing for Regional Tastes,'' *Seafood Business*, January 2005, p. 28.

Tims, Dana, ''Enticed by Bridgeport Village's Potential, the Restauranteurs Open Their First New Portland Eatery in More Than a Decade,'' *Oregonian*, March 30, 2005.

—Carrie Rothburd

Measurement Specialties, Inc.

710 Route 46 East, Suite 206
Fairfield, New Jersey 07004
U.S.A.
Telephone: (973-808-3020
Toll Free: (800) 236-6746
Fax: (973) 808-1787
Web site http://www.msiusa.com

Public Company
Incorporated: 1981
Employees: 1,353
Sales: $112.8 million (2004)
Stock Exchanges: American
Ticker Symbol: MSS
NAIC: 334519 Other Measuring and Controlling Device
   Manufacturing

With its headquarters located in Fairfield, New Jersey, Measurement Specialties, Inc. (MSI) designs and manufactures sensors and sensor-based consumer products. MSI's sensor division offers a wide range of sensors and transducers using a number of technologies—piezoresistive, piezopolymers, electro-optic, electro-magnetic, micro-electromechanical systems, application specific integrated circuits, and strain gauges—to measure pressure, motion, force, displacement, tilt, flow, and distance. These products are used in such industries as automotive, medical, commercial building, appliances, banking, traffic control, power and utilities, industrial machinery, and aerospace and defense. MSI's consumer division produces bathroom scales, the Accutape brand of distance estimators, Accutire tire pressure gauges, and Park-Zone parking gauges. The company maintains manufacturing facilities and engineering centers in Virginia, France, and China. It also has engineering centers located in Wayne, Pennsylvania; Plainfield, Illinois; and San Jose and Torrance, California. MSI is a public company trading on the American Stock Exchange under the symbol MSS.

Company Shifts from Consulting to Manufacturing in 1980s

The men behind the founding of MSI were Damon Germanton and Donald Weiss, who lived across the street from each other in Kinnelon, New Jersey, and became friends. Weiss held a degree in Economics from City College of New York and was the cofounder of Alkalite, a maker of disposable flashlights. Germanton, on the other hand, was an engineering graduate of Fairleigh Dickinson University and employed at Kulite Semiconductor Products, Inc., where he worked as an engineer and served as operations manager, involved in micromachined sensor technology used in military and aerospace applications. Semiconductor-based sensors, so prevalent in today's products, were in their infancy around 1980 when Germanton took Weiss for a visit of the Kulite facilities. Weiss was immediately impressed with the potential of micromachines and decided he wanted Alkalite to become involved in the field. He began working on Germanton and eventually wooed him away from Kulite. In March 1981 Germanton incorporated Measurement Specialties, Inc. to serve as an engineering consulting firm in sensor technology. His only client was Alkalite and he worked out of the Alkalite offices. In 1984 Weiss sold his share of Alkalite to his partner and joined Germanton at MSI.

Weiss and Germanton were considering keeping MSI as a consultancy, but soon decided to turn to manufacturing. They spent several months thinking about how to apply micromachined silicon strain gauge technology to consumer products and eventually settled on a bathroom scale. They developed a prototype and on that basis were able to raise some private financing. They also convinced Philips Electronics to commit to buying a significant quantity of the scales for its consumer products division. Manufacturing at this stage was done through a subcontractor. MSI was now able to raise further money through an initial public offering (IPO) of stock, conducted in July 1986, netting about $2.5 million. After initially trading on an over-the-counter basis the stock moved to the NASDAQ.

Dissatisfied with the work of its subcontractor, which was not willing to manufacture to MSI's specifications, Weiss traveled to Hong Kong in September 1986, intent on using the money raised from the IPO to establish the company's own manufacturing facility. He built a plant from scratch and remained in Hong Kong to run the company as chairman and chief executive officer, while Germanton, the chief technology officer, remained in New Jersey. Out of necessity Weiss developed a unique business model in Hong Kong that was a key element in the company's early success. While most American companies employed agents to deal with Chinese suppliers and distributors, Weiss, to save money, became a primary actor. But because the Chinese saw middlemen as little more than parasites, albeit necessary ones, he found himself in an advantageous position. Although an ex-patriot, he was still regarded as part of the local business community and could build personal relationships that were of great benefit. MSI had no support from its banks, but was able to develop a way to become self-financing through the use of letters of credit issued by distributors as soon as products shipped. The company could then order more supplies and build the business at an accelerated rate. Weiss was also able to improve the company's finances by taking advantage of its manufacturing capacity to do subcontracting work. As a result of these factors, MSI was able to competitively price its electronic bathroom scale compared to the mechanical ones consumers were more familiar with. Weiss also drummed up sales by directly contacting Hong Kong-based buyers for major retailers. Early on, MSI had more success selling into Europe because U.S. retailers were more reliant on traditional distributor relationships. As the electronic scale became more accepted by consumers, however, the United States emerged as the company's leading market.

First Product Launch: Late 1980s

It was while Weiss and Germanton were sitting in a diner that they conceived of a way to build an application-specific integrated circuit (ASIC) to measure distances. The concept would result in MSI's second product: a digital distance measuring device, which would be sold under the Accutape label as well as retailers' private brand names. After being developed from 1986 to 1987 the product was introduced and began to build up sales. Business became so strong that the company opened a larger manufacturing facility in Hong Kong. But the company's fortunes then slipped unexpectedly. One of its major customers for the measuring product, Stanley Works, was disconcerted about declining margins, unaccustomed to the nature of electronic products. Faced with numerous competitors in the market, it asked MSI for an exclusive on Accutape but was denied. Stanley then decided to simply drop the product, selling its stock of several-hundred-thousand units to a liquidator for under $5 apiece. At the time, MSI was wholesaling the item from $14 to $17 apiece, and now had to contend with a multitude of product being dumped onto the market retailing around $10. As a result, orders immediately dried up; MSI was stuck with far too much capacity in its new Hong Kong plant and saddled with untenable overhead costs.

Weiss returned to the United States to deal with the unfolding crisis. The company's credit lines were withdrawn and the price of the company stock plummeted, eventually dipping as low as 25 cents and leading to the company being delisted from the NASDAQ. MSI also had to contend with a group of dissident shareholders who sued the company. According to Weiss in a 2005 interview, they were attempting to manipulate the stock price for their own benefit in what amounted to a ''greenmail'' effort. He maintains that the group's attorney even asked at what point, ''What's it worth to make us go away?'' The matter went before a court and the dissidents were sanctioned, and MSI's management was content to let the matter rest rather than countersue. Weiss and Germanton had to decide whether they should simply shut down the company or attempt to regroup and develop new products. They chose the latter option, cutting staff and paring down its manufacturing operation, while also developing a third product: a digital tire air pressure gauge, which the company introduced in the early 1990s. Other companies had tried to market similar handheld tire gauges but only MSI, by taking advantage of its low-cost manufacturing operation in Hong Kong, was able to make money at it. The company also picked up much needed revenue by licensing some of its technologies to Dresser Industries.

MSI rebuilt its business, enjoying success with the tire gauge and increased interest in the bathroom scale, although sales of the Accutape product continued to languish. In 1993 the company's stock was able to regain a listing, this time on the American Stock Exchange's Emerging Company Marketplace. In 1995, which ended on March 31 of that year, the company posted record sales in excess of $17 million. By now there was no doubt that the company had turned the corner, but to Weiss MSI had reached an important juncture: It could either make some significant changes to go to the next level or adopt a more-of-the-same strategy. One of his ideas was to close down the Hong Kong plant and move manufacturing to China. Weiss had been at odds with the board for several years, primarily because of his strong support for MSI's sales manager, which many of the board members were inclined to blame for the company's misfortunes earlier in the decade. Now Weiss and Germanton no longer agreed on their vision for the company. Germanton aligned himself with board member Joseph Mallon, recommending a more conservative approach to growing MSI. In effect, the rest of the board mediated the matter and came down on the side of Germanton and Mallon. Weiss decided it was now prudent to leave the company, and in April 1995 he was replaced as chief executive officer by Mallon.

Mallon was well qualified to take the helm at MSI, the M.B.A. on his resume the least of his achievements. He brought three decades of experience in micromachined sensor technology, including a 20-year stint at Kulite. In 1985, with financing from oil services company Schlumberger, he cofounded NovaSensor to make pressure sensors to monitor blood pressure as well as fuel levels. He sold out in 1990 and joined MSI's board in 1992. All told, he had 40 patents to his credit.

Key Dates:

1981: Company is founded.
1986: Company goes public on NASDAQ.
1993: After delisting, company stock renews trading, this time on the American Stock Exchange.
2000: Three acquisitions are completed.
2002: Restructuring effort is launched.
2004: Four acquisitions are completed.

For the first three years, Mallon followed the more-of-the-same approach in running MSI, and business grew at an incremental pace. In 1997 sales topped $25 million and net income totaled almost $1.2 million. Then in August 1998 he completed the first of several acquisitions in an attempt to accelerate company growth. At a cost of nearly $4 million MSI added the Sensors Division of AMP Incorporated, which produced piezo-electric polymer sensors for industrial, consumer products, instrumentation, military, aerospace, and medical uses. MSI was now reorganized into two divisions, Sensor Products and Consumer Products, as the company embarked on a new strategy to sell high-volume sensor products to original equipment manufacturers (OEMs) in addition to consumer products. The company also looked to move production from AMP's plants in Valley Forge, Pennsylvania, to its low-cost Chinese plants.

Acquisition Binge Continuing in 2000

MSI picked up the acquisition pace in 2000, adding three more companies. In January it paid $800,000 for the ultrasonic parking aid product Park-Zone, from Exeter Technologies, Inc. A month later MSI spent nearly $12.4 million to acquire IC Sensors, Inc. from Perkin Elmer Inc., maker of silicon micromachined pressure sensors, accelerometers, and microstructures for use in the industrial, medical, and aerospace industries. In August 2000, MSI spent another $16.8 million for Schaevitz Sensors, which designed and manufactured industrial sensors using strain gauge, linear variable differential transformer (LVDT), reluctive, and capacitive technologies. Schaevitz sensor products were used to measure displacement, tilt, fluid level, pressure, and other factors. The company brought with it production facilities in Hampton, Virginia, and Slough in the United Kingdom. As a result of these acquisitions, MSI grew at a rapid clip. Sales approached $60 million in 2000 and topped $100 million in 2001. Net income, in the meantime, increased to $5.5 million in 2000 and nearly $9 million in 2001.

MSI added another company to the fold in 2001, paying $17.1 million for Terraillon Holdings, a European maker of bathroom and kitchen scales. To pay for the deal, the company completed a successful secondary stock offering in August 2001. The company was now recognized by *Fortune* and *Business Week* as one of the fastest-growing public companies, but to accomplish this growth, MSI took on $54 million in debt, mostly from banks, and below the surface the company's strategy was not unfolding as expected. The plan in a nutshell was to buy companies and move production to the China plants where extra margin could be squeezed out. But it took longer than expected to transfer production. In addition, the company was

hurt by the bankruptcy of Sunbeam Corporation, a major customer accounting for 10 percent of sales, and the economy was turning sour. The company was forced to borrow even more money to keep its head above water, and then in February 2002 it was struck a staggering blow when it learned that its chief financial officer, Kirk Dischino, had failed to notify the company that it was in default of its bank debt. Dischino was promptly fired and replaced. After some study the new CFO concluded that MSI had also been overvaluing its inventory and when Mallon refused to restate prior results, he quit in protest. To make matters worse, it was also revealed that Dischino had sold 40,000 shares of stock shortly before the company's precarious state was revealed. He would eventually plead guilty to insider trading charges, and MSI would pay $7.5 million to settle a class-action suit and a $1 million fine to settle Securities and Exchange Commission(SEC) charges.

The American Stock Exchange halted trading on MSI's stock, and investors who bought shares in the August 2001 offering were quick to sue, claiming the company had been misleading in its prospectus. The banks were also displeased and forced Mallon to step aside as chief executive, replaced by turnaround artist Franklin Guidone. A mechanical engineer by training, he became a consultant with Andersen Consulting and Dallas-based George Group before cofounding a turnaround company, Corporate Revitalization Partners, in Dallas. The appointment of Guidone bought time with the banks, and in less than a month he had a plan to offer them, one in which he would make interest payments while shedding non-core assets and attempting to rebuild the business. The banks agreed to give MSI six months of forbearance, and Guidone went to work. He continued to live in Dallas but flew periodically to New Jersey and the company's other locations. He cut payroll and other expenses, shut down the U.K. operations, sold a California manufacturing plant as well as Terraillon. In 2004 he also sold off the company's Thinner bathroom and kitchen scale business. Operations were now consolidated in the two plants located in Hampton, Virginia, and Shenzhen, China.

Guidone's strategy panned out and MSI was soon on solid footing with its lenders. Sales rebounded, improving to $107.7 million in 2003 and $112.8 million in 2004. Debt was eliminated by the middle of 2003. The company returned to profitability in 2004, earning $21.6 million. MSI was now strong enough to return to a growth mode, and completed a series of acquisitions in 2005. It bought Elekon Industries USA Inc., adding optical sensors sold to the medical and security markets. It then added Entran Devices, Inc. and Entran SA, expanding MSI's presence in the race car and automotive crash-test markets. MSI also acquired Encoder Devices LLC, which used magnetic encoding technology to make fuel pump sensors and had the potential to be applied to medical syringe pumps, flow meters, military, motor, and other uses. In December 2004, MSI made two acquisitions in Europe. MSI acquired Humeril, a fast-growing Toulouse-based company with a proprietary humidity sensing technology that was winning business in the automotive and industrial sectors. The company also reached an agreement to acquire MWS Sensorik GmbH, a German distributor who had been repackaging MSI's accelerometers for the automotive crash-test market (the transaction closed in January 2005). The long-term potential for sensor technology was very promising, and because Guidone was not likely to make the mistakes of his predecessors by adding excessive debt and taking on fixed-cost facilities when making acquisitions, it was very likely that MSI's best days were yet to come.

Principal Divisions

Sensor Division; Consumer Products Division.

Principal Competitors

Bonso Electronics International Inc.; Danaher Corporation; Esterline Technologies Corporation.

Further Reading

Goldblatt, Dan, "Measurement Specialties Weighs in with a Broad Range of Products," *Northern New Jersey Business,* February 8, 1995, p. 6.

Nelson, Jennifer, "Success by Any Measurement," *NJBIZ,* August 23, 2004, p. 8.

Ress, David, "Mismeasured," *Star Ledger,* April 3, 2002, p. 19.

Simon, Ellen, "Measuring Up," *Star-Ledger,* November 26, 2003, p. 21.

Vardi, Nathan, "Mismeasurement," *Forbes,* September 2, 2002, p. 202.

—Ed Dinger

Michaels Stores, Inc.

8000 Bent Branch Drive
Irving, Texas 75063
U.S.A.
Telephone: (972) 409-1300
Toll Free: (800) 642-4235
Fax: (972) 409-1556
Web site: http://www.michaels.com

Public Company
Incorporated: 1962 as Dupey Enterprises, Inc.
Employees: 41,100
Sales: $3.39 billion (2004)
Stock Exchanges: New York
Ticker Symbol: MIK
NAIC: 451120 Hobby, Toy and Game Stores

Michaels Stores, Inc. is the largest specialty retailer of arts, crafts, and home decor in North America. The company operates several different retail and wholesale businesses, led by its mainstay Michaels chain, which comprises more than 850 stores in the United States and Canada. Michaels also operates Aaron Brothers, a 165-store chain that offers custom framing services and an assortment of ready-made frames. Michaels' wholesale business is operated through Star Decorators' Wholesale Warehouse, which is a business-to-business supplier of floral and decorating supplies. In addition, Michaels operates ReCollections, a chain of nine stores that carries supplies for scrapbooks. A smaller version of the mainstay Michaels concept is operated as Village Crafts by Michaels, a format designed for communities with populations ranging between 70,000 and 90,000. Michaels also owns Artistree, a manufacturer of frames with three locations in California, Texas, and North Carolina. Artistree exclusively serves the Michaels and Aaron Brothers chains.

The First Ten Years

Two decades before the 450th Michaels arts and crafts store opened in 1996 the first store was established, its creation the work of a young, enterprising businessman whom retail analysts

would later hail as a "merchandising genius." His name was Michael Dupey, and he got his start in 1973 when he converted one of a group of Ben Franklin stores operated by his father into an arts and craft store that operated under the name Michaels. Located in Dallas, the first store became part of the Dupey family business, a company headed by Michael Dupey's father, Jim Dupey, and aptly named Dupey Enterprises, Inc. Founded in 1962 and the predecessor to Michaels Stores, Inc., Dupey Enterprises controlled the first store and transformed the retail concept into a chain, adding additional stores as the 1970s progressed.

Dupey Enterprises controlled the Michaels retail concept for ten years. With Michael Dupey leading the way, the Dupey family business expanded the number of Michaels stores, assembling a small chain of stores comprising 11 units, nearly all of which were located in Texas, by the time its era of ownership was over. Although the Michaels retail concept enjoyed an encouraging start, the period of Dupey ownership would stand as the least prolific decade in the retailer's first 30 years of existence. Michael Dupey created the concept, but the work of transforming Michaels into a national chain and building it into the largest retailer of its kind in the United States fell to the new owners who took control of the company in 1983. The year marked the beginning of the Wyly era in Michaels' history, a period during which Michaels arts and crafts stores proliferated throughout the United States and into Canada and Puerto Rico.

1983 Acquisition by the Wylys

In 1983, Dupey Enterprises sold Michaels to Peoples Restaurants, Inc., a company controlled by renowned Dallas entrepreneurs Sam Wyly and his older brother Charles J. Wyly, Jr. Among his numerous accomplishments in the business world, Sam Wyly had founded University Computing Company, a computer software and services company, in 1963. He had cofounded Earth Resources Company, an oil refiner and miner of gold and silver, and, along with his brother, had acquired a 20-unit restaurant chain named Bonanza Steakhouse in 1967. Under the stewardship of the Wyly brothers, Bonanza Steakhouse ballooned into a sprawling 600-restaurant chain during the ensuing two decades, recording an impressive rate of expansion that the Wylys would match with their new acquisition, Michaels.

226

Company Perspectives:

Since our founding, the family of Michaels Stores, Inc., the nation's largest retailer of arts and crafts materials, has been helping crafters of all ages express their imaginations with skill and originality. With a broad assortment of products, knowledgeable and friendly associates, in-store events, classrooms, and instructional displays, we offer a shopping experience that inspires our customers to pursue their creative goals. At Michaels Stores, Inc. we provide the ideas and education to complete an array of artistic, leisure, and home décor projects for beginners and experts from start to finish.

As part of the deal that brought Michaels into the Peoples Restaurants fold, Michael Dupey successfully negotiated for ownership of two Dallas Michaels stores and was granted the exclusive, royalty-free rights to open licensed Michaels stores in Dallas and area counties. Other than this proviso, Peoples Restaurants assumed full control over the 11-unit Michaels chain, but the company did not hold on to the retailer for long. In 1984, one year after acquiring the retailer, Peoples Restaurants spun off Michaels to Peoples Restaurants shareholders in a rights offering at $2.50 per share, making the arts and crafts retailer a separate, publicly traded corporate entity. On May 6, 1984, the company began trading its stock on the NASDAQ, with the Wylys ranking as the largest shareholders in Michaels Stores, Inc.

Concurrent with the company's initial public offering, Sam Wyly was named chairman of Michaels and a seat on the company's board of directors was taken by his brother Charles, who was named vice-chairman in 1985. Under the leadership of the Wylys, Michaels expanded aggressively, casting aside the prosaic growth that characterized the first decade of its existence to emerge quickly as a strong, regional competitor in the arts and crafts retail industry. During their first five years of directing the company, the Wylys (with Sam in charge) devoted more than $100 million toward the acquisition of small arts and crafts chains and toward opening new stores, embarking on this course shortly after taking the retailer public.

1980s Acquisitions

In July 1984, two months after the company's initial public offering, Michaels acquired Montiel Corporation, operator of a 13-unit chain with stores scattered across Colorado, Arizona, and New Mexico. Having already doubled the size of their company in eight weeks, the Wylys pressed forward, opening additional Michaels stores while they searched for further acquisitions. In 1985, six more retailers were purchased, and in 1987 the company acquired Moskatel's, Inc., a 28-store chain in California, where the greatest concentration of Michaels stores would be located in the future.

By the time these acquisitions were completed, Michaels already represented a promising chain on the verge of breaking into the ranks of national arts and crafts retailers. The company's vast selection of merchandise, which included silk and dried flowers, oil paints, picture frames, model airplanes and ships, greeting cards, and party favors, attracted a specific and loyal clientele. Nearly all (90 percent) of Michaels's customers were female, and 25 percent patronized a Michaels store at least once a week. Largely due to the popularity of the Michaels retail concept and the ambitious expansion orchestrated by the Wylys, Michaels' sales and earnings rose strongly during the mid-1980s, reaching $167 million and $4.9 million, respectively, in 1987.

In 1988, Michaels acquired a division of Wal-Mart Stores, Inc. named Helen's Arts & Crafts. The sale by Wal-Mart represented the massive retailer's exit from the business of selling arts and crafts supplies, but Michaels was fast on the rise and the addition of another arts and crafts retailer represented yet one more step toward national prominence. By this point in the company's history, Michaels had recorded incredible growth. The 11 stores acquired by the Wyly-controlled Peoples Restaurants in 1983 had grown into a chain comprising more than 100 stores. Much had been achieved, but as the company exited the late 1980s and prepared for the 1990s, a regrettable event interrupted Michaels' otherwise steady rise toward becoming the preeminent arts and crafts chain in the United States.

By the late 1980s, Michaels' success had attracted considerable attention from both those involved in the arts and crafts industry and the business community in general. One of those drawn to the company was famed investor Richard Bass, who with his firm, Arcadia Partners, attempted a leveraged buyout of Michaels. The particulars of the deal were negotiated during much of 1989 before the proposed $225 million transaction was terminated in January 1990. At Michaels' headquarters in Irving, Texas, executives were dismayed, particularly Sam Wyly. After the pain resulting from the foundered deal had ebbed somewhat, Wyly told a reporter from the *Dallas Business Journal*, "We wasted almost a year on that deal that failed. It was a major distraction and we will never do that again."

Because of the failed leveraged buyout, Michaels was forced to take a $5 million pretax charge on its balance sheet, which trimmed earnings from $5.2 million to a paltry $13,000, even as annual revenues rose 20 percent to $290 million. The lesson learned from the failed deal was a hard one, but in the wake of Michaels' "major distraction" the company effected sweeping changes that made its operations stronger than ever before. The changes first became apparent in August 1990 when Michaels President B.B. Tulley was replaced by a Michaels director, Donald G. Thomson. Michael Dupey, who at the time was operating his 24-unit MJDesigns chain, was brought in as a special consultant, marking the return of the "merchandising genius," and purchasing was dramatically streamlined. Quickly, the company was moving forward on all fronts with positive momentum. The Michaels chain comprised 140 stores by the end of 1990, with sales reaching $362 million and debt down from $34 million to $9 million after one year.

Animated Growth During the 1990s

By early 1991, the Michaels empire was flourishing once again, prompting one retail analyst to remark, "They [Michaels] are marketing better and buying better. The management restructuring seems to be helping them; they are running a tighter operation." Merchandising and advertising functions had been centralized, profitability was made a primary focus,

Key Dates:

1962: Dupey Enterprises, Inc. is founded.
1973: Dupey Enterprises converts a Ben Franklin store into an arts-and-crafts store named Michaels.
1983: Dupey Enterprises sells the 11-store Michaels chain to Peoples Restaurant, Inc., which spins off the concept as a separate company the following year.
1990: A leveraged buyout by Richard Bass's Arcadia Partners collapses.
1994: Michaels acquires the 101-store Leewards Creative Crafts chain.
1995: The 71-unit Aaron Brothers chain is acquired.
1996: R. Michael Rouleau is appointed chief executive officer.
2000: Michaels starts a wholesale operation.
2002: Village Crafts by Michaels, a smaller-store format, is introduced.
2003: The first ReCollections store opens in Dallas.
2004: Michaels announces the goal of reaching $5 billion within two years.

and regional and district manager positions had been created. At this point, confidence ran high enough to lead Sam Wyly to project that the company would eclipse the $1 billion-in-sales plateau in the next five years, an objective that, remarkably, Michaels achieved.

With a goal of reaching $1 billion in sales in the next five years, Michaels' strategy was clear as it prepared for 1992 and the remainder of the 1990s: aggressive expansion throughout the United States. Midway through its plan to open 35 stores in 1992, the Michaels chain consisted of 157 stores, each selling more than 30,000 different arts and craft items and each averaging more than $3 million in sales annually, roughly twice the arts supply industry average. During the previous five years, store sales had more than doubled and profits had quadrupled, a rate of financial growth that ranked the company as one of the hottest retail stories during the early 1990s. The popularity of Michaels stores was credited to the retailer's vast product selection, with silk and dried flowers representing its largest product category in terms of sales generated. Product selection told only half the tale of the company's success, however, because much was owed to the service provided by Michaels' store employees. Amid the display booths and product departments that filled the selling space in a Michaels store, employees taught in-store art classes, providing instruction for various arts and crafts projects, including how to create T-shirt designs and how to make festive centerpieces. With service, product mix, and rapid expansion propelling the company forward, it was only a matter of time and money before Michaels stores dotted the nation's landscape.

The stores opened in 1993 extended Michaels' presence from its base in the Southeast and Southwest to Ohio, Virginia, Oklahoma, Washington, and Iowa, and carried the company beyond U.S. borders for the first time, as two Michaels stores made their debut in Toronto, Canada. The strategy was to cover as much territory as possible with Michaels stores before competitors had the time to catch up. In 1994, any hope of catching the Irving-based retailer was lost as Michaels completed an unprecedented year of physical growth by increasing its store count more than 70 percent.

In terms of acquisitions, 1994 got off to a start in March when Michaels acquired Oregon Craft & Floral Supply, staking a presence in the Oregon arts and crafts retail market. The company then purchased H&H Craft & Floral, which fleshed out its presence in southern California. Next, in April 1994, Michaels acquired Seattle, Washington-based Treasure House Stores, Inc., moving the company into Washington where it had little market presence. These three acquisitions added 25 stores to the expanding Michaels chain, but the company's next acquisition quickly overshadowed the gains made during the spring months of 1994. In July, Michaels acquired Leewards Creative Crafts Inc., a 101-unit chain of arts and crafts stores that gave Michaels solid footing in the midwestern and northeastern markets, areas where the company had achieved scant market penetration.

In addition to the stores gained through acquisitions during 1994, Michaels opened 32 new stores on its own, helping drive sales up to $995 million. At the beginning of 1995, there were 380 stores composing the Michaels chain, with stores scattered throughout 41 states and in Canada. For 1995, 55 stores were expected to be added to the chain, including units in Alaska and Puerto Rico, as efforts were underway to round out the company's presence throughout North America, particularly in the Northeast. The company's stores by this point averaged 16,000 square feet and were located in highly visible strip shopping centers near shopping malls. Of the merchandise gracing the company's store shelves—general crafts, home decor items, picture frames, art and hobby supplies, party supplies, wearable art, and seasonal and holiday goods—silk and dried flowers and plants still accounted for the bulk of Michaels' sales, generating a fifth of its annual revenue volume.

As store expansion continued in 1995, Michaels added another retail concept to its widely popular Michaels format. In March 1995, the company acquired Aaron Brothers Holdings, Inc., operator of a 71-unit chain of specialty framing and art supply stores. Located primarily in California, where the greatest number of Michaels stores were located, the Aaron Brothers stores offered professional custom framing services, sold photograph frames, and stocked a full line of ready-made frames, as well as a broad selection of art supplies.

Buoyed by the addition of Aaron Brothers and the more than $50 million in sales the retailer generated the year before its acquisition, Michaels entered 1996 as the country's largest arts and crafts retailer. The $1 billion-in-sales mark had been reached in 1995 when the company recorded $1.29 billion in sales. The company anticipated opening between 50 and 55 new Michaels stores in 1996, but was beginning to scale back its expansion plans to achieve greater operational efficiencies. Between 1991 and 1995, the company's expansion of store units had increased at a compounded annual rate of 33 percent; for the future the store growth rate was targeted at 15 percent. As the company charted its course for the late 1990s and the beginning of the 21st century, Michaels officials saw the potential for 900 stores in the United States and in Canada, an estimate that set the stage for another decade of robust growth for the 23-year-old company.

Diversification with the New Century

Michaels' impressive rate of expansion continued as the 1990s progressed, but only after the company dealt with some serious problems related to its rampant growth. Sales in 1996 reached $1.4 billion, a total that hardly could be celebrated because it coincided with a staggering $31 million loss for the year. Worse still, the company was running out of cash. In late 1996, R. Michael Rouleau arrived as the company's new chief executive officer, inheriting a mess that called on his four decades of retail experience to clean up. Rouleau, who had worked for Target and Lowe's, among other retailers, first directed his attention to the company's cash flow problem, raising $125 million in junk bonds to keep the company alive as he implemented sweeping measures designed to return the sprawling company to profitability. Rouleau revamped the chain's units, met with hundreds of vendors, and devoted more resources to the company's custom framing business, Artistree, which began as two small manufacturing shops started by Michaels in 1993. Rouleau's most significant changes were directed at Michael's single greatest problem: inventory management. The equipment and systems used by the company to track inventory were antiquated, dating back to the earliest days of the personal computer. Rouleau invested $22 million in a state-of-the-art point-of-sale system that kept track of inventory movement and he upgraded the systems used in the company's four warehouses. The changes worked wonders, resulting in an average increase in profits of 35 percent compounded annually during the first five years of his tenure. The average revenues generated by a Michaels store increased substantially as well, swelling from $2.9 million in 1997 to nearly $4 million by 2002.

With the revamped, sophisticated infrastructure to support expansion, Michaels grew aggressively around the end of the century. The company added significantly to its two chains, Michaels and Aaron Brothers, and diversified into new business areas. In 2000, the company purchased a one-store florist and decorating supplies operation in Dallas that became the foundation of its Star Decorators' Wholesale Warehouse business. Through its wholesale operation, Michaels began selling floral supplies and accessories, ribbon, containers, party and wedding supplies, and seasonal décor, targeting floral and gift shop owners, interior decorators, banks, and hotels as its customers. The company envisioned its wholesale business eventually occupying 50 locations. In 2002, the company added another dimension to its business by creating an arts-and-crafts store for smaller markets. The first store, roughly half the size of a typical Michaels store, debuted as Village Crafts by Michaels, a concept designed for communities with populations ranging between 70,000 and 90,000. Rouleau and his team identified 150 markets in the United States as ideal locations for the company's Village Crafts concept. Roughly a year after introducing its smaller-store format, the company introduced yet another concept. In mid-2003, the company opened a pilot store in Dallas named ReCollections, a store catering to those who liked to assemble scrapbooks.

By the end of 2004, Michaels stood as a giant in its industry. There were 850 Michaels stores in operation in North America, with company officials setting 1,300 stores as the concept's saturation point. The company's Aaron Brothers chain, which it had acquired as a 50-store chain located exclusively in Califor-

nia, had flowered in a 165-store chain spread across eight states. The company foresaw Aaron Brothers as a 600-store chain. With the company's three other concepts—Star Decorators', Village Crafts by Michaels, and ReCollections—offering further room for expansion, Michaels had no intention of slowing its pace of expansion. By 2006, the company expected to reach $5 billion in sales. By 2009, Michaels planned to open 1,000 additional stores, an ambitious goal that promised aggressive expansion throughout the decade.

Principal Subsidiaries

Aaron Brothers, Inc.; Michaels Finance Company, Inc.; Michaels of Canada, ULC; Michaels Stores Card Services, LLC; Michaels Stores Procurement Company, Inc.

Principal Competitors

A.C. Moore Arts & Crafts, Inc.; Hobby Lobby Stores, Inc.; Jo-Ann Stores, Inc.

Further Reading

Bond, Helen, ''Management Shake-Up at Michaels Earns Kudos from Stock Analysts,'' *Dallas Business Journal,* April 5, 1991, p. 2.

Chen, Christine Y., ''Hobbies 'R' Michaels: Why Wall Street Says a Fast-Growing Arts-and-Crafts Chain Still Has Plenty of String,'' *Fortune,* November 15, 2004, p. 226.

Coleman, Lisa, ''Glue-On Eyeballs, Anyone?,'' *Forbes,* August 17, 1992, p. 58.

''Corporate Snapshot: Michaels Stores, Inc.,'' *Dallas/Fort Worth Business Journal,* September 14, 1987, p. 13.

Fuquay, Jim, ''Former Book Executive Named President of Irving, Texas-Based Michaels Stores,'' *Forth Worth Star-Telegram,* December 6, 2002, p. B4.

——, ''Michaels Stores to Cooperate with Subpoena on Dallas Investors' Stockholdings,'' *Fort Worth Star-Telegram,* February 24, 2005, p. B1.

Gordon, Joanne, ''Crafty Fellow,'' *Forbes,* November 25, 2002, p. 90.

Hall, Jesse, ''Michaels Shops for New Metroplex Digs,'' *Dallas Business Journal,* February 10, 1995, p. 1.

Howell, Debbie, ''Michaels Crafting an Expansion Plan,'' *DSN Retailing Today,* July 5, 2004, p. 8.

——, ''Michaels Opens ReCollections,'' *DSN Retailing Today,* July 7, 2003, p. 4.

——, ''Michaels Touts Growth, Spells Out Expansion Plan,'' *DSN Retailing Today,* October 2000, p. 4.

''Jack Bush Joins Michaels Stores,'' *Discount Store News,* July 22, 1991, p. 2.

Lisanti, Tony, ''The SPARC Awards Are Where Good Guys Finish First,'' *Discount Store News,* September 18, 1995, p. 15.

Longo, Don, ''Michaels: The Quiet Success Story,'' *Retail Merchandiser,* May 2002, p. 22.

Lundegard, Karen M., ''Texas Crafts-Supply Retailers Bringing Feud to Maryland,'' *Baltimore Business Journal,* September 29, 1995, p. 2.

''Michaels Divisions,'' *DSN Retailing Today,* January 27, 2003, p. 10.

''Michaels Stock Deals Studied,'' *Dallas Morning News,* February 24, 2005, p. B3.

Much, Marilyn, ''Michaels Stores Inc.,'' *Investor's Business Daily,* November 5, 2002, p. A10.

Philippidis, Alex, ''Crafts Retailer Expands with 2 County Stores,'' *Westchester County Business Journal,* January 17, 2005, p. 5.

Recio, Maria, ''Opinions Differ on Link Between Michaels Stores, Sniper,'' *Fort Worth Star-Telegram,* October 17, 2002, p. B3.

Smith, Sarah, "Michaels Stores Inc.," *Fortune,* June 6, 1988, p. 152.

"Taking Stock: Michaels Stores Inc.," *Dallas Business Journal,* August 6, 1990, p. 13.

"13D Highlights: Michaels Stores, Inc.," *Insiders' Chronicle,* April 30, 1990, p. 42.

Wilensky, Dawn, "Michaels Crafts Future with Superior Mix, Service," *Discount Store News,* January 16, 1995, p. 19.

Wilson, Marianne, "Michaels Artfully Crafts High Performance," *Chain Store Age Executive with Shopping Center Age,* November 1995, p. 39.

—update: Jeffrey L. Covell

Millennium & Copthorne Hotels plc

Scarsdale Place, Kensington
London
W8 5SR
United Kingdom
Telephone: +44 20 7872 2444
Fax: +44 20 7872 2460
Web site: http://www.millenniumhotels.com

Public Company
Incorporated: 1995
Employees: 12,328
Sales: £547.1 million ($1.16 billion) (2004)
Stock Exchanges: London
Ticker Symbol: MLC
NAIC: 721110 Hotels (Except Casino Hotels) and Motels

In less than a decade, Millennium & Copthorne Hotels plc (MCH) has built one of the Asian region's largest hotel groups and has taken a place among the global top 40. The company, based in London and listed on the London Stock Exchange, serves as the international arm of Singapore's Hong Leong Group, and its chairman is Kwek Leng Beng. MCH operates some 90 hotels worldwide, chiefly under the Millennium and Copthorne brand names. The company has positioned itself as an operator of "luxury four-star" hotels, enabling it to differentiate its offering from the crowded five-star hotel bracket, particularly by offering lower room rates. The company's portfolio contains many prestigious hotels in 18 countries, including Indonesia, Singapore, Malaysia, Hong Kong, Korea, and Taiwan, as well as in Abu Dhabi and Dubai in the Middle East. New Zealand is a major market for the company, with 30 hotels, including 15 Kingsgate Hotels. Together, the Asia/Pacific region accounts for 36 percent of company revenues, which neared £550 million ($1.2 billion) in 2004. In Europe, the company operates primarily in the United Kingdom, with nearly 20 hotels, as well as two hotels each in France and Germany. Europe accounts for 31 percent of group sales. The company's North American portfolio targets major city markets in the United States. In late 2004 and early 2005, the company sold off its holdings in two U.S. landmark hotels, the Plaza in New York, and the Biltmore in Los Angeles. The United States remains the company's single-largest market, at 33 percent of sales. After a difficult period in the first half of the 2000s, MCH has announced plans for further expansion, including the opening of as many as 20 Copthorne hotels in the United Kingdom.

Founding an Asian Hotel Leader in the Mid-1990s

The origins of Millennium & Copthorne Hotels traced back to the formation of Singapore's City Developments Limited (CDL), the property development and real estate vehicle of the Kwek family's Hong Leong Singapore. Founded in 1941 by Kwek Hong Png, that company grew into a leading Singapore conglomerate. In 1972, Kwek extended his business interests into the real estate market by acquiring control of CDL, which had already completed several prominent developments in Singapore. CDL had been founded in 1963, and grew into one of the country's largest land holders before beginning its expansion onto the international market.

CDL's interest in the hotel market began only in the late 1980s, when the company acquired its first hotel, the King's Hotel, in Singapore in 1989. That acquisition was followed soon after by the purchase of the city's Orchid Hotel. The company continued to seek new hotel purchases in the Asian region. From the start, the company targeted the luxury hotel market, and by the early 1990s its holdings included the Regent in Kuala Lumpur, the Heritage Hotel in Manila, and the Grand Hyatt in Taipei. The expansion of the company's hotel operations began especially after Kwek Leng Beng took over as head of the family empire following his father's death. CDL began acquiring additional properties in the early 1990s. The depressed real estate and tourism markets at the start of the decade enabled the company to build a strong portfolio of choice sites at low prices.

CDL's first foray outside of the Asian region came in 1993. The company turned to London, buying the Gloucester Hotel. Soon after, the company entered the New Zealand market (destined to become one of the group's core markets), buying a chain of 13 hotels there.

Kwek Leng Beng now took CDL on a spending spree, paying out more than $1 billion over the next three years to

Company Perspectives:

It is the 40th largest hotel group in the world and is Singapore's largest hotel chain. The group's range of four-star and four-star deluxe properties as well as their six new five-star hotels reflect the individual characteristics of their location whilst delivering the high standards which today's business and leisure travellers require.

boost its hotels portfolio to some 55 hotels, with more than 14,000 rooms, in 11 countries. Among the group's purchases were its first properties in the United States, including the Hilton and the Broadway in New York City, bought in 1994.

CDL boosted its U.K. presence in 1995, paying £219 million for the Copthorne group of hotels, formerly owned by Aer Lingus. That purchase also gave the company hotel properties in Paris and in Germany. Following the acquisition of Copthorne, CDL launched a new hotel brand, Millennium, and began rebranding a number of its assets, including the Gloucester, as well as its French and German hotels.

Also in 1995, CDL became the leading hotel group in New Zealand, boosting its portfolio there to 21 hotels. In the United States, meanwhile, the company became a joint owner of the prestigious Plaza in New York in partnership with Prince Alwaleed bin Talal of Saudi Arabia and Donald Trump.

In addition to acquiring properties, Kwek also plowed money into renovating and upgrading the hotels in CDL's portfolios, and raising rates in order to stake out what the company called the "luxury four-star" bracket. Positioned just below the heavily lauded five-star segment, CDL's hotels offered extensive amenities, including up-to-date technologies, at lower room rates.

The rise in the hotel market into the mid-1990s brought a surge in value in CDL's hotel holdings. CDL also continued to build up recognition of its new flagship brand, in an effort to place the Millennium name among the world's top hotel brands. An important step in that direction came in 1996, when CDL decided to spin off its 23 non-Pacific region Millennium and Copthorne hotels into a new company, Millennium & Copthorne Hotels, which was then listed on the London Stock Exchange. The new company, with operations focused especially in the United Kingdom, and with properties in the United States, France, and Germany as well, took London as its home base. CDL remained its primary shareholder, with 55 percent of MCH's shares.

Creating a Hotel Leader for the New Century

The successful offering enabled MCH to launch an ambitious expansion program. Soon after its initial public offering of stock, the company announced that it planned to spend as much as £150 million on new hotel acquisitions. The company made good on its intentions by October of that year, paying £81 million to acquire the 318-room Britannia in London.

The extension of the Copthorne brand to some of CDL's hotels in New Zealand in 1997, and then to a group of CDL's

Asian hotels in 1998 set the stage for a merger of CDL's and MCH's hotel portfolios. This took place in April 1999, when MCH announced that it was paying £556 million to acquire CDL's 43 hotels in the Asia Pacific. Following the merger, MCH emerged as a major hotel group, with 67 hotels and 17,000 rooms. The company then confirmed its new presence in the Asian Pacific, paying £219 million to acquire the Seoul Hilton, a five-star hotel.

Soon after the acquisition of CDL's hotels, MCH made a new move to join the world's top hotel companies, paying £450 million to acquire 29 Regal hotels in the United States, as well as a number of smaller hotels under different names, from Regal International, a company registered in Hong Kong. The acquisition boosted the company's portfolio to nearly 100 hotels and placed it into the global top 50 hotel groups. By the end of 1999, MCH's portfolio had swelled to almost 120 hotels. Among the hotels acquired in the Regal deal was the famed Biltmore in Los Angeles.

The company set to work trimming its portfolio in 2000, selling off its less profitable assets, including 12 smaller hotels acquired with the Regal chain. By mid-2001, the company had trimmed back its holdings to a portfolio of 89 hotels, with a total of 24,000 rooms. This made the company one of the largest hotel operations in the Asian Pacific, and placed the company at number 34 among all hotel groups.

As it began integrating its acquisitions—including rebranding most of the Regal chain—MCH sought a new, less expensive means of expanding onto the European continent. In May 2000, the company formed an alliance with Germany's Maritim Hotels, establishing a cross-selling and joint-marketing partnership. Maritim controlled a portfolio of 39 predominantly Germany-based hotels.

In 2001, MCH began rolling out a new hotel brand, the so-called "boutique" brand M Hotel. The new concept targeted business travelers especially. The company began refitting its Copthorne Harbour View Hotel in Singapore (where, because of a trademark conflict, the company was not able to use the Millennium brand) and planned to launch the new hotel format at the end of the year.

In further expansion, the company entered the Middle East for the first time, winning long-term management contracts for two hotels in Morocco and two hotels in the United Arab Emirates. The company also secured three hotel management contracts in Turkey, and another in the Galapagos Islands.

Yet MCH, like most of the global tourism industry, was caught short by the September 11 terrorist attacks that year. MCH was directly affected by the attacks—the company's Millennium Hilton stood just across the street from the World Trade Center. The company also was caught up in the aftermath of the attacks, as the global tourism industry went into freefall.

The Millennium Hilton reopened for business again in 2003 in time to profit from the upswing in the travel and tourism industries as hotel visits began to return to pre-9/11 levels. MCH announced its interest in new acquisitions into mid-decade. But the company also began pruning its own portfolio, taking advantage of the surge in hotel prices. In 2004, the

Key Dates:

company together with partner Alwaleed bin Talal announced that they were selling their stakes in the Plaza Hotel for $675 million—the highest per-room price ever paid for a New York hotel. MCH's profit from the sale came to nearly £52 million ($90 million).

The company, under CEO Tony Potter, admitted that it was "not sentimental" when it came to its hotel portfolio, acknowledging its willingness to negotiate individual purchases of its hotels. This openness led the company to put another of its landmark hotels up for sale, the Biltmore, in March 2005. The sale of that hotel was expected to raise as much as $500 million.

Millennium & Copthorne Hotels by then had secured a place for itself among the world's top hotel groups.

Principal Subsidiaries

ATOS Holdings AG (Austria); CDL Hotels Holdings New Zealand Limited; CDL Hotels New Zealand Limited (70%); CDL Hotels USA Inc; CDL Investments New Zealand Limited (43%); KIN Holdings Limited (New Zealand; 43%); Kingsgate International Corporation Limited (New Zealand; 43%); M&C Management Services (USA) Inc.; Millennium Hotels & Resorts Services Limited (U.K.); Millennium Partnercard Services Limited (U.K.); Quantum Limited (New Zealand; 49%); Tara Hotels Deutschland GmbH.

Principal Competitors

Loews Corporation; Radisson Hotels and Resorts; Orascom Group; Rallye S.A.; Mingly Corporation Limited; Carlson Holdings Inc.; Compass Group PLC; Hilton Group PLC; MARITIM Hotelgesellschaft GmbH; SABMiller; Tokyu Corporation.

Further Reading

Armitage, Jim, "Millennium & Copthorne Books into London Revival," *Evening Standard,* February 21, 2005.

Doebele, Justin, and Heidi Brown, "The Man with the Golden Machine Gun," *Forbes,* July 9, 2001.

"A Hotel Chain Looks Ahead," *Card Technology,* July 3, 2002, p. 10.

"M&C Plans More UK Openings," *Caterer & Hotelkeeper,* February 24, 2005, p. 8.

Moore, Malcolm, "Millennium 'Back on Recovery Path,'" *Daily Telegraph,* August 9, 2002.

Nozar, Robert A., "Growth for Millennium," *Hotel & Motel Management,* June 19, 2000, p. 3.

"Pivotal Year for Top Hotels Group," *Western Daily Press,* February 22, 2005.

Tran, Tini, "Hotelier's Profit Triples on Revival in World Travel," *Financial Post,* November 5, 2004.

Walsh, Dominic, "M&C to Sell Hollywood's Favourite Hotel for $500m," *The Times,* March 23, 2005, p. 50.

——, "Millennium & Copthorne Checks Out of The Plaza in £370m Deal," *The Times,* August 14, 2004, p. 51.

—M.L. Cohen

MSC Industrial Direct Co., Inc.

75 Maxess Road
Melville, New York 11747-3151
U.S.A.
Telephone: (516) 812-2000
Fax: (516) 349-1301
Web site: http://www.mscdirect.com

Public Company
Founded: 1941 as Sid Tool Company
Employees: 2,912
Sales: $955.3 million (2004)
Stock Exchanges: New York
Ticker Symbol: MSM
NAIC: 423830 Industrial Machinery and Equipment
   Merchant Wholesalers

MSC Industrial Direct Co., Inc. is one of the United States' largest direct marketers of MRO (maintenance, repair, and operations) tools and supplies, catering mostly to small and midsize companies. It also sells cutting tools to the machine shop industry, the company's original emphasis. All told, the Melville, New York-based company offers more than 500,000 items, sold through a 4,475-page catalog (The Big Book), as well as by telemarketing and the Internet. MSC maintains 90 sales offices in 37 states, predominantly east of the Mississippi River, and four distribution centers strategically located in Atlanta, Georgia; Elkhart, Indiana; Harrisburg, Pennsylvania; and Reno, Nevada. Although a public company, MSC is majority owned by its founder and his family.

Company Founding: 1940s

MSC was founded by Sidney Jacobson, who was raised in Brooklyn, New York. In 1934, at the age of 16, he went to work for a machine tool shop. In 1941 he decided to strike out on his own, and using $1,100 he had saved and another $3,000 borrowed from his mother, he started Sid Tool Company to sell cutting tools and accessories to New York City machine shops. His small storefront was located at 177 Mulberry Street, now the heart of Manhattan's Little Italy but at the time was located

close to the center of the borough's thriving machine tool industry. Before long, however, the United States was drawn into World War II, and Jacobson was drafted into the Air Force, where he served in the ordnance area loading bombs onto airplanes. He was forced to leave the business in the hands of his brother. When he too was drafted, the reins were handed over to a sister, who ran the company until Jacobson was released from the service after the war was over in 1945.

Sid Tool was doing about $3,000 a month in sales when Jacobson regained control. It was during this period that he landed a pair of significant Long Island customers after becoming friendly with their buyers: Grumman Corporation and Republic Aircraft. Around this time he always became involved in the production of promotional materials. With the help of a friend he learned how to put together brochures, which he used to good effect in promoting special sales items. Like many returning servicemen he moved to the new suburbs to raise a family, relocating to Great Neck on Long Island. Tired of commuting into the lower east side of Manhattan, in 1955 he decided to relocate Sid Tool to Plainview, Long Island, where he was able to find a suitable 25,000-square-foot building. Moreover, most of his business now came from Grumman and Republic, while Manhattan was beginning to undergo some major changes, with traditional manufacturing operations leaving the city and present-day Little Italy and Chinatown neighborhoods beginning to take shape. Sid Tool prospered during the postwar years but gradually the company became overly dependent on Grumman and Republic, which by the early 1960s accounted for 90 percent of all sales.

In 1964 Jacobson decided to use the experience he had acquired in assembling brochures to launch a catalog business to diversify his sales mix, and to reach out to more customers than he could ever hope to visit to drum up new business. What set the catalog apart was that Jacobson was able to offer imported cutting tools at discount prices, something no one else had attempted at that time. He had assembled his slate of imported products by attending trade shows and contacting manufacturers, and with the success of the catalog he would soon be contacted by manufacturers interested marketing via the Sid Tool publication. What would become known as the Big Book was anything but in 1964, roughly 150 pages in length and featuring the most elementary of production values. Recalling the first catalog 40 years later in an interview, Jacobson guessed that he had about 2,000 copies printed, mailed to addresses pulled together from Dun & Bradstreet.

Computerized Inventory Control System: 1969

Within a few years catalog sales surpassed regular sales, and the company reached the peak of its capabilities. It became increasingly difficult to keep a handle on the business, especially since so many of the products Sid Tool offered were imported. According to Jacobson, in the late 1960s there was one particular import item he thought he had in adequate supply; however, he discovered it was out of stock. To replenish his supply from the foreign manufacturer took six months, far too long a lag time to keep customers happy. Believing there had to be a better way to keep track of his inventory, he took the unprecedented step in the industry of installing a computerized inventory control and order processing system in 1969, this during the days of punch-card processing. The competition thought him crazy, Jacobson recalled, but the investment in computers proved to be the crucial element in the company's success, leading to the development of an industry powerhouse while many of Jacobson's carping competitors fell by the wayside.

In 1970 Sid Tool acquired another cutting tool marketer, Manhattan Supply Company, to serve as a vehicle to increase the distribution of its imported cutting tool business. It was the initials of Manhattan Supply that would form the basis of the MSC name, although for many years business would be conducted under both the Sid Tool and MSC names in Plainview, where in 1978 the company opened its first distribution center. It was also in 1978 that MSC became one of the first distributors in the country to launch a fully integrated Quality Assurance Department.

By the mid-1970s MSC was posting $7 million in annual sales. At this point, in 1976, Jacobson's son Mitchell Jacobson, a recent graduate of New York University School of Law, joined the company on a fulltime basis, having previously worked summers and holidays while attending Brandeis University and law school. By the end of the decade Jacobson's wife was experiencing some health problems, which placed a great deal of strain on Jacobson, as he tried to simultaneously run the business and take care of his wife. He decided to devote himself to his wife and withdrew, at least temporarily, from the day-to-day running of the company. He turned to his son, telling him he could either choose to run the business or sell it. Electing to keep the company, Mitchell Jacobson then embarked on a research trip that took him to a number of industrial supply houses, from which he identified their best practices and brought them home to apply to MSC, setting up the company for the exponential growth it would realize over the next quarter-century.

In 1982 Mitchell Jacobson replaced his father as president of the company. Under his leadership, MSC began to add branch

offices at a steady clip, many by way of acquisition, growing from three in the mid-1980s to 26 in 1990, when a second distribution center opened in Atlanta. Also of great importance in 1980 was the introduction of a Total Quality Management (TQM) initiative, dedicated to improving the quality of every aspect of the business. According to *Long Island Business News*, this program "enabled Jacobson to flatten the organization's structure, empower its employees with decision-making responsibilities and streamline its operations." Most importantly, TQM resulted in an improved ability to quickly fill customer orders. The back-end operations had improved so much that by 1991 MSC was able to ship 98 percent of orders on the day they were received, but competitors were also improving their fill rates. MSC found a way to stand out from the crowded field. It guaranteed that any order taken before 4:30 p.m. would be shipped that day, if the item was in stock, or the company would send the customer a check for $50. Although a gimmick, the ploy worked. Fulfillment employees took up the challenge to get orders out the door, so that it was a rare occurrence when a check had to be cut (0.01 percent of all orders in the first three years of the program). As a result of this near perfect fill rate, the company earned a sterling reputation with customers, driving up sales, further stimulated by the 1994 move beyond its traditional cutting tool lines to include MRO product categories, expanded geographic reach, and increased catalog distribution and other mailings. In 1993 the company mailed 2.4 million pieces, a number that increased to 6.6 million two years later. The shifting emphasis to the MRO market was a natural progression, given the declining manufacturing base in the United States that adversely impacted the sale of cutting tools and the fact that MSC's competitors were already offering MRO products and services, making it almost imperative that MSC follow suit.

Net sales grew from $118.9 million in 1991 to $248.5 million in 1995. To spur further growth, the company made plans to go public. In October 1995 MSC Industrial Direct Co., Inc. was formed as a holding company, an initial offering of stock was conducted two months later, and shares began trading on the New York Stock Exchange. Also in that month, the company completed a minor acquisition, picking up Kaja Productions, Inc. for $1,000.

More acquisitions followed in 1996 as MSC looked to continue expanding in the MRO field by adding existing marketers. In June 1996 the company acquired D.T.C. Tool Corp. and Cut-Rite Tool Corp. A month later Swiss Precision Instruments, Inc. was added, followed by the November purchase of Brooks Precision Supply, Inc. Four more acquisitions were completed in 1997: Dolin Supply, Inc.; Anderson Industrial Supply, Inc.; Enco Manufacturing Co.; and Discount Tool and Supply Company. Moreover, MSC expanded its warehouse and distribution capabilities. In 1996 the company opened a 275,000-square-foot facility in Elkhart, Indiana, which not only allowed MSC to better serve the Midwest but also acted as a pilot for a new warehouse and distribution center that opened in Harrisburg, Pennsylvania, a year later. The Harrisburg center then replaced the three facilities the company maintained on Long Island: a 100,000-square-foot shipping and receiving facility in Central Islip, an 83,000 square-foot small parts shipping facility in Plainview, and a 60,000-square-foot small parts receiving facility, also located in Plainview. The leases on all three of the buildings were set to expire over the next few years.

Key Dates:

1941: Sid Jacobson starts Sid Tool Company in New York City.
1955: Business is relocated to Plainview, New York.
1964: First "Big Book" is mailed.
1969: Computerized inventory control system is installed.
1970: Manhattan Supply Company is acquired.
1982: Mitchell Jacobson is named president.
1995: Company is taken public.
1997: Plainview distribution center is relocated to Harrisburg, Pennsylvania.
2000: Company begins Internet marketing.

Technology Aiding Mid-1990s Catalog Publishing

In the mid-1990s MSC also began investing in new technology to improve its catalog business. A fully integrated database allowed MSC to quickly assemble the material. The days of employees taking their own catalog pictures and writing their own copy were all but forgotten. Now suppliers provided copy and photographs, which could be electronically downloaded and laid out for printing. As a result production costs were cut in half. In addition, the catalog turned to a lighter weight paper, a change that allowed the catalog to increase its page count to more than 3,500 in 1997. Although MSC cut down production costs, the Big Book was still a costly affair. Unlike catalogers, who do mass mailings in hopes of achieving a reasonable response rate, a Big Book marketer like MSC looked to trim its mailing, relying almost entirely on buyer files. The goal for such operations was to come as close to a 100 percent response rate as possible. In order to prospect for new customers, MSC began producing a monthly 60-page catalog, containing the best items to lure in new customers. By turning to the smaller catalog instead of the earlier practice of mailing the Big Book, MSC was able to cut its prospecting costs by more than half.

As the Plainview leases expired and the warehousing and distribution operations moved entirely to Harrisburg, MSC transferred its corporate headquarters and customer support center to Melville, New York, in 1998. The company also continued to expand through acquisitions, adding RMG Corporation and Drake-Atwood Tool & Supply Company, Inc. in June 1998, followed by the $6.2 million purchase of Specialty Company, Inc. in October. Sales reached $462.1 million in fiscal 1997 and grew to $614.5 million in 1998, which ended on August 29 of that year. But it was during the summer of 1998 that the company stumbled. According to *Industrial Distribution,* "the combination of a weak industrial economy, aggressive investment, and tight cost controls to manage earnings led to a higher-than-normal employee turnover rate and a temporary decline in customer service. These events further contributed to a decline in MSC's sales and earnings growth, as well as its stock price." Some of the problem was simply timing: Just when sales were trailing off because of the impact of economic problems in Asia, MSC was spending money to open a fourth distribution center in Reno, Nevada, in 1999. In addition, management was reportedly distracted for six months by a major acquisition that failed to be consummated. But Mitchell Ja-

cobson refused to accept excuses for the company's performance during this period, telling *Investor's Business Daily* in 2000, "Our whole operation was not as crisp. We didn't answer the phone quite as quickly. Our people were not quite as well trained as they would have been. There were errors in our catalog. You name it." To get MSC back on the right foot, some organizational changes were made and a new compensation plan was introduced to revitalize customer service.

Although a major acquisition may have fallen through, MSC completed a pair of deals in 1999, paying $428,000 for Direct Line, Inc. and $6.2 million for Corbin Corporation. The company also began turning to the Internet to spur sales, in September 2000 launching MSCdirect.com, which gradually introduced the Big Book to the net. To drive customers to the site, MSC invested in direct mail and telemarketing efforts as well as customer training. While this web business fit in well with MSC's operations, other Internet investments proved ill-fated, given the dotcom meltdown at the time. In June 2001 the company announced it would write off $10.3 million invested in four Internet start-ups: MaterialNet.com, MROLink.COM. Tradaq.com, and Commerx Inc.

Due to the poor economy, sales dipped to $794 million in 2002 from $869.2 million the prior year. But business rebounded in 2003 as sales totaled $844.7 million and net income reached a record $52 million. The balance sheet improved even further in 2004, with sales reaching $955.3 million and net income soaring to $82.2 million. It was also during 2004 that Mitchell Jacobson gave up the presidency to COO David Sandler, relinquishing day-to-day responsibilities to concentrate on strategic planning while retaining the chairmanship and the CEO title. Sidney Jacobson, approaching 90, remained active in the company, continuing to serve as vice-chairman.

Principal Subsidiaries

Sid Tool Co., Inc.; Cut-Rite Tool Corp.; MSC Services Corp.; D.T.C. Tool Corp.; Brooks Precision Supply, Inc.; Anderson Industrial Supply, Inc. Dolin Supply, Inc.; Discount Tool and Supply Company; RMG Corporation; Corbin Corporation; MSC Direct Line, Inc.; Swiss Precision Instruments, Inc.

Principal Competitors

Applied Industrial Technologies, Inc.; J&L Industrial Supply; W.W. Grainger, Inc.

Further Reading

Grugal, Robin, "Buck Stops Here—MSC Industrial Takes the Blame for Recent Woes, Starts Recovery," *Investor's Business Daily,* July 21, 2000, p. A9.

Johnson, John R., "Big Book, New Look," *Industrial Distribution,* June 1998, p. 76.

"A Look at This Year's Finalists," *Long Island Business News,* June 27, 1994, p. 28.

Miller, Paul, "Big Books Thrive," *Catalog Age,* July 1997, p. 153.

——, "MSC Bets $50 on Same-Day Shipping,: *Catalog Age,* December 1995, p. 53.

—Ed Dinger

Mulberry Group PLC

Kilver Court
Shepton Mallet BA4 5NF
United Kingdom
Telephone: 44 17 4934 0500
Fax: 44 1749 345 532
Web site: http://www.mulberry.com
Public Company
Incorporated: 1971
Employees: 464
Sales: $56.6 million (2004)
Stock Exchanges: London
Ticker Symbol: MUL
NAIC: 316993 Personal Leather Goods (Except Women's Handbag and Purse) Manufacturing; 448320 Luggage and Leather Goods Stores; 448150 Clothing Accessories Stores; 316992 Women's Handbag and Purse Manufacturing; 316991 Luggage Manufacturing; 315999 Other Apparel Accessories and Other Apparel Manufacturing

Mulberry Group PLC bases the high-end accessories and select men's and women's apparel that it designs, makes, and sells on English country style. Items are sold through about 13 company-owned stores, select department stores, and the Mulberry web site. The company is best known for its leather-bound Filofaxes, or datebooks, and handbags.

1971 to Late 1990s: The Company Grows from Its Roots in Shepton Mallet

In 1971, Roger Saul decided to go into business using the £500 he had received as a 21st birthday present for capital. His father suggested he sell Christmas trees or donkeys. Instead, Saul, and his mother, Joan, founded a company making leather goods in their garage.

Although a quiet-spoken man, Saul was full of enthusiasm and it was this that became the driving force behind Mulberry. The company drew inspiration for its designs from what was quintessentially English as well as eccentric. "Mulberry whiffs

of all sorts of things," as Saul explained in a 1993 *Times* article. "A certain integrity, a certain reserve, definitely a humourous eccentricity. Quality unquestionably, and perhaps even a little bit aristocratic. People expect that from an English branded product, but you must not be afraid to laugh at yourself."

The company set up headquarters in Shepton Mallet, Somerset, and pulled together a factory workforce of local residents. Other factories in nearby Chilcompton and Walton followed and Mulberry added to its collections of accessories and introduced ready-to-wear items. By the early 1990s, Mulberry was a known entity and in 1991, it added its "At Home" range of interior designs, the precursor of its Home Division. By 1992, the company was drawing in revenues of £50 million.

In 1996, Mulberry opened new stores in Heathrow Airport and Tokyo. These duty-free shops joined the company's other successful duty-free operations in Germany and Denmark. Mulberry also entered into an exclusive distribution agreement with Moonbat Company Limited, one of Japan's largest fashion accessory companies, to import Mulberry's full range of accessories and ready-to-wear products. In May, it sold shares on the Alternative Investment Market, a part of the London stock exchange reserved for newer companies. Sales in Mulberry's retail division climbed 26 percent in 1996, while sales in its home division rose 50 percent. The company as a whole enjoyed a profit of £1.7 million.

Based on the preceding year's strength, in 1997, Mulberry opened the Charlton House Hotel in its home town of Shepton Mallet, Somerset, to showcase the Mulberry Home Collection of interior items and introduce Mulberry to a wider audience. The Georgian-fronted Charlton House dated back to 1630 when merchant Roger Ames built it as a home for his bride. "Having created this environment, it is very important that the detail is right, that things are put together in our way, to emphasize that we could live here," Roger announced in the *Times* March 8, 1997 article. Each of the hotel's 16 bedrooms reflected a different aspect of Mulberry's interior collection; the moldings, pelmets, and Baroque plaster work throughout the building were a sign of Roger's passion for architectural salvage.

Also in 1997, Mulberry opened two new stores: one in Manchester, which became the company's flagship store for the north of England, and its first stand-alone Mulberry Home Store in London.

1998–2000: Rocky Times Following Asian Crisis

By 1998, however, Mulberry was feeling the effects of the 1997 Asian crisis. Sales growth had exceeded 25 percent for each of the previous two years. Now there was an increase in operating costs of nearly 15 percent. Company losses for the year totaled £1 million. Moonbat withdrew from its investment program, and Mulberry had to reorganize its Japanese operations, taking over control of its Tokyo stores.

Mulberry responded by strengthening its management team and laying off some of its 472 staff in 1998. Saul and his wife, Monty, and other directors took 12 percent pay cuts. In order to combat the impact of the strong pound, the company closed its handbag factory in Somerton, laying off 28 workers, and moved production of its leather goods overseas to Italy, Turkey, and Spain. Over the course of the year, the company issued four profit warnings, and late in the year, one of its directors left.

However, such was the demand for Mulberry's Bohemian take on classic English country style that the company continued to open new franchise shops worldwide, including new stores in Japan in 1998. Mulberry also targeted the Middle East for expansion, specifically Bahrain, Kuwait, and Lebanon. It opened a new Mulberry Home Store adjacent to its flagship store in Tokyo, which doubled its total sales area there. Elsewhere in the world, Mulberry continued selling well—in the United States, where only the Home Collection was available, in Europe, and in Dubai, which already had two stores.

In fact, to increase its penetration of the European market, in 1999 Mulberry struck a license and partnership agreement with Kravet, an American home furnishings company, to open a new Mulberry Home showroom in London's Chelsea Harbour. Kravet also agreed to distribute Mulberry fabric, wallpaper, and soft furnishings through its network in the United Kingdom, Europe, and North and South America. To aid in the marketing of its Home Collection, the company also published its first lifestyle book, *Mulberry at Home*. The company also entered into a second partnership with Toray Industries, the world's largest textile manufacturer, to develop the Mulberry brand in Japan. However, all this while, Mulberry continued to issue profit warnings, and dropping share prices and losses led to its decision to suspend dividend payments in 1999.

2000–04: A Return to Accessories and Profitability Under New Management

Management at first made the decision to look to product innovation and the introduction of new product lines in 2000 to improve performance, then sold almost 42 percent of the

family-controlled company to Ong Beng Seng and his wife Christina, Singaporean billionaires, who owned an investment vehicle called Challice. "We had to do a lot of soul-searching, but if we want to be truly successful it is increasingly difficult to stay independent," Saul confided in a 2000 *Financial Times* article. The Ongs ran Club 21 Armani in the United Kingdom and owned a string of other designer licenses throughout the U.S. and Asia. Christina Ong also owned a collection of fashionable shops, hotels, and restaurants, including London's Met Bar. The Ongs agreed to set up a joint venture to promote and sell Mulberry products in the United States.

The decision seemed a good one, counteracting the image that Mulberry had become stuck in a classic time warp and heralding a return to profitability in 2001 with revenues of $39.7 million. With British designer Scott Henshall taking over the design direction for Mulberry, the company stepped up its ready-to-wear line and launched a new menswear line in Italy. It also introduced a new high tech line, which included covers for laptops and portable CD players.

Then in 2002, the company returned to losses for the full year. It canceled plans for five outlets in the United States and closed stores in Brussels and Tokyo, although it went ahead with its scheduled expansion in Russia, the Netherlands, and Scandinavia. On the management front, it split the role of chairman from that of its chief executive officer and began a search for a new chief executive.

A row between Christina Ong and Saul followed, revolving around the agreement reached earlier that specified that Challice would open five stores in the United States in return for increasing its stake in Mulberry to 51 percent. With no American stores on the horizon, Saul demanded that Challice fulfill its commitment or sell its stake in the company. Ong wanted the Mulberry brand to be developed further before expanding overseas. The situation turned somewhat nasty when, following a clash with Saul, Christina Ong demanded a shareholders' extraordinary general meeting to vote on his removal.

In the end, Saul stepped down as chairman, while remaining president and non-executive director. Godfrey Davis became chairman and chief executive officer of Mulberry. Later the Ongs appointed Bernard Lam Kong Heng and Steven Grapstein to become non-executive directors. In 2003 Saul sold the last of his stake in the company to Insight Investment and stepped down from his role as president, with plans to open a spa next to Charlton House Hotel and launch a new range of bath and spa products. "It worried me enormously when it was just ourselves (his family) and the Ongs—it was a very locked-out situation," he said in a 2004 *Financial Times* article. "And now we have an investment structure that should help push [the company] forward. If the Ongs invest in Mulberry and put in good people, Mulberry will go far."

However, Mulberry's losses continued as Challice continued to buy up more of the company. Under Davis, the company refocused on the accessories side of its business—selling leather accessories, handbags and belts—rather than clothes and instituted tighter management controls. Mulberry's strategy, according to Davis, would be "to simplify the business and make deals with experienced people who can develop a brand

Key Dates:

1971: Roger Saul and his mother found Mulberry.
1997: Mulberry opens the Charlton House Hotel in its home town of Shepton Mallet.
1999: Mulberry strikes a license and partnership agreement with Kravet and with Toray Industries in Japan.
2000: Mulberry sells 42 percent of its business to Challice, owned by the Ongs.
2002: Godfrey Davis becomes chairman and chief executive officer of Mulberry.
2003: Ong Beng Seng and Christina Ong purchase the company through Challice; Saul leaves.
2004: The company opens its first U.S. store.
2005: Mulberry signs agreements with Mitsui and Co. and Sanki Shoji Co. for wholesale distribution to selected Japanese stores.

like Mulberry in their home markets.'' The Ongs and management also made plans to develop Mulberry's overseas markets via partnerships and to stem its losses by closing stores, including those in Paris and at some locations in the United Kingdom.

The company returned to profitability in 2003. In 2004, it entered into a partnership with Bergdorf Goodman and opened its first U.S. store. It also set plans to expand into Japan, Asia, and the United States in 2005. It began wholesale distribution to selected Japanese shops in 2005 by signing agreements with Mitsui & Co. and Sanki Shoji Co. When in 2005, Mulberry won the British Fashion Council award for accessory designer of the year for the first time in its history, the honor seemed to bode well for its future.

Principal Subsidiaries

Mulberry Oslo AS; Mulberry USA LLC; Mulberry Company (Design) Limited; Mulberry Company (Europe) Limited; Mulberry Company (Sales) Limited; Mulberry Company (France) SARL; Kilver Street Inc.; Mulberry (UK) Limited; Mulberry Company (Holdings) Limited; Mulberry Fashions Limited; Mulberry Leathers Limited; Mulberry (Shoes) Limited; Mulberry Company (Far East) Limited.

Principal Competitors

Burberry; Dooney and Burke; Etienne Aigner; Gucci; Hermes; Prada; kate spade; Kenneth Cole; LVMH; Pinault-Printemps-Redoute; Tandy Brands.

Further Reading

Buckley, Kevin, and Elizabeth Rigby, ''Roger Saul Finds New Direction As He Cuts Ties with Mulberry,'' *Financial Times*, September 9, 2004, p. 23.

Buckley, Sophy, ''Founder Reduces Mulberry Stake in Sale to Fidelity Household Goods,'' *Financial Times*, October 7, 2003, p. 28.

——, ''Mulberry Seeks Expansion After Returning to Black,'' *Financial Times*, June 25, 2004, p. 25.

Cope, Nigel, ''Mulberry Accuses Christina Ong of Veiled Attempt at Takeover,'' *Independent*, November 18, 2002, p. 17.

Dowdy, Clare, ''Mulberry,'' *Financial Times*, October 2, 2001, p. 22.

Hollinger, Peggy, ''UK: Deal with Ongs in the Bag for Mulberry,'' *Financial Times*, August 18, 2000, p. 21.

Morris, Belinda, ''From Head-to-Toe and Floor-to-Ceiling, a Designer Country Hotel Is Born,'' *Financial Times*, March 8, 1997, p. 11.

Webb, Iain R., ''Fruit of an English Country Garden,'' *Times*, September 27, 1993.

—Carrie Rothburd

Nestlé S.A.

Avenue Nestlé 55
CH-800 Vevey
Switzerland
Telephone: +41-21-924-2111
Fax: +41-21-924-28-13
Web site: http://www.nestle.com

Public Company
Incorporated: 1866 as Anglo-Swiss Condensed Milk
  Company
Employees: 253,000
Sales: CHF 86.76 billion ($76.66 billion) (2004)
Stock Exchanges: Basle Geneva Zurich Amsterdam
  Brussels Frankfurt London Paris Tokyo Vienna OTC
Ticker Symbols: NESN; NSRGY (ADRs)
NAIC: 311514 Dry, Condensed, and Evaporated Dairy
  Product Manufacturing; 311520 Ice Cream and Frozen
  Dessert Manufacturing; 311511 Fluid Milk Manufac-
  turing; 311422 Specialty Canning; 311411 Frozen
  Fruit, Juice, and Vegetable Processing; 311412 Frozen
  Specialty Food Manufacturing; 311230 Breakfast
  Cereal Manufacturing; 311111 Dog and Cat Food
  Manufacturing; 311320 Chocolate and Confectionery
  Manufacturing from Cacao Beans; 312111 Soft Drink
  Manufacturing; 311930 Flavoring Syrup and
  Concentrate Manufacturing; 311920 Coffee and Tea
  Manufacturing; 311823 Dry Pasta Manufacturing;
  311999 All Other Miscellaneous Food Manufacturing;
  325412 Pharmaceutical Preparation Manufacturing;
  325620 Toilet Preparation Manufacturing; 551112
  Offices of Other Holding Companies

Nestlé S.A. is the largest food and beverage company in the
world. With a manufacturing facility or office in nearly every
country of the world, Nestlé often is referred to as "the most
multinational of the multinationals." Nestlé markets approximately 7,500 brands organized into the following categories:
baby foods, breakfast cereals, chocolate and confectionery,
beverages, bottled water, dairy products, ice cream, prepared
foods, foodservice, and pet care.

Early History

While serving as the American consul in Zurich, Charles
Page decided that Switzerland, with its abundant milk supply
and easy access to the whole European market, was the perfect
location for a condensed milk factory. The first canned condensed milk had been produced in the United States by Gail
Borden some ten years before, and originally Page planned to
produce and sell "Borden Milk" in the European market as a
licensee. The plan fell through, however, so in 1866 he established the Anglo-Swiss Condensed Milk Company as a limited
company in Cham, Switzerland.

The company's name was meant to flatter the British, to
whom Page hoped to sell a great deal of his condensed milk.
Anglo-Swiss first expanded its operations beyond Switzerland's
borders in 1872, when it opened a factory in Chippenham,
England. Condensed milk rapidly became a staple product in
European cupboards—the business downturn in 1872 and the
depression of 1875 did not affect the firm's sales. Charles Page
died in 1873, leaving the company in the hands of his brother
George and Anglo-Swiss's other investors. The next year,
Anglo-Swiss undertook further expansion in England by purchasing the Condensed Milk Company in London. By 1876
sales were almost four times their 1872 level.

Meanwhile, in Vevey, Switzerland, in 1867 Henri Nestlé
began selling his newly developed cow's-milk food for infants
who could not be breastfed. Demand for his Farine Lactée
Nestlé soared. Between 1871 and 1873, daily production more
than doubled, from fewer than 1,000 tins a day to 2,000.
Nestlé's goal was to bring his baby food within everyone's
reach, and he spared no effort in trying to convince doctors and
mothers of its benefits. But while his energy and good intentions
were nearly endless, his financial resources were not. By 1873,
demand for Nestlé's product exceeded his production capabilities, resulting in missed delivery dates. At 61, Nestlé was running out of energy, and his thoughts turned to retirement. Jules
Monnerat, a former member of parliament who lived in Vevey,
had long eyed the business, and in 1874 Nestlé accepted Mon-

nerat's offer of CHF 1 million. Thus, in 1875, the company became Farine Lactée Henri Nestlé with Monnerat as chairman.

In 1877 Nestlé faced a new competitor when the Anglo-Swiss Condensed Milk Company—already the leading manufacturer of condensed milk in Europe—decided to broaden its product line and manufacture cheese and milk food for babies. Nestlé quickly responded by launching a condensed milk product of its own. George Page tried to buy the competing company outright, but he was firmly told that Nestlé was not for sale. Turning his attention elsewhere, he purchased the Anglo-Swiss Company's first factory in the United States in 1881. The plant, located in Middletown, New York, was built primarily to escape import duties, and it was soon successful enough to challenge Borden's supremacy in the U.S. condensed milk market. It also presented a drawback: George Page spent so much time there that Anglo-Swiss began to lose its hold on Europe, much to the delight of Nestlé. After George Page's death in 1899, the Anglo-Swiss Condensed Milk Company decided to sell its American business to Borden in 1902 so that it could concentrate on regaining market share in Europe.

Until 1898 Nestlé remained determined to manufacture only in Switzerland and export to its markets around the world. But that year the company finally decided to venture outside Switzerland with the purchase of a Norwegian condensed milk company. Two years later, in 1900, Nestlé opened a factory in the United States, and quickly followed this by entering Britain, Germany, and Spain. Early in the 1900s, Nestlé also became involved in chocolate, a logical step for a company based in Vevey, the center of the Swiss chocolate industry. Nestlé became a partner in the Swiss General Chocolate Company, the maker of the Peter and Kohler brands. Under their agreement, the chocolate company produced the first Nestlé brand milk chocolate, while Nestlé concentrated on selling the Peter, Kohler, and Nestlé brands around the world.

Merger of Nestlé and Anglo-Swiss in 1905

In 1905 Nestlé and the Anglo-Swiss Condensed Milk Company finally quelled their fierce competition by merging to create the Nestlé and Anglo-Swiss Milk Company. The new firm would be run by two registered offices, one in Vevey and one in Cham. With Emile-Louis Roussy as chairman, the company now included seven factories in Switzerland, six in Great Britain, three in Norway, and one each in the United States, Germany, and Spain.

In response to an increase in import duties in Australia—Nestlé's second largest export market—the company decided to begin manufacturing there in 1906 by buying a major condensed milk company, the Cressbrook Dairy Company, in Brisbane. In the next few years production and sales continued to increase as the company began to replace sales agents with subsidiary companies, particularly in the rapidly growing Asian markets.

Most of its factories were located in Europe, however, and when World War I broke out in 1914, Nestlé's operations, particularly in such warring countries as Britain and Germany, were seriously affected. Although production continued in full force during the early months of the war, business soon grew more difficult. By 1916 fresh milk shortages, especially in Switzerland, meant that Nestlé's factories often sold almost all of their milk supplies to meet the needs of local towns. Shipping obstacles, increased manufacturing and operating costs, and restrictions on the use of production facilities added to Nestlé's wartime difficulties, as did a further decrease in fresh milk supplies due to shortages of cattle.

To deal with these problems and meet the increased demand for its products from governments supplying their troops, Nestlé decided to expand in countries less affected by the war and began purchasing existing factories, particularly in the United States, where it established links with several existing firms. By 1917 Nestlé had 40 factories, and in 1918, its world production was more than double what it was in 1914. Nestlé pursued the same strategy in Australia; by 1920 it had acquired a controlling interest in three companies there. That same year, Nestlé began production in Latin America when it established a factory in Araras, Brazil, the first in a series of Latin American factories. By 1921, the firm had 80 factories and 12 subsidiaries and affiliates. It also introduced a new product that year—powdered milk called Lactogen.

It did not take long for the effects of such rapid expansion to catch up with the company, however. Nestlé and Anglo-Swiss reported its first loss in 1921, to which the stock market reacted with panic, making matters worse. The company explained that the CHF 100 million loss was due to the rising prices of raw materials such as sugar and coal, and a trade depression that had caused a steady fall in consumer purchasing power, coupled with falling exchange rates after the war, which forced the company to raise prices.

To battle the storm, the company decided to reorganize both management and production. In 1922 it brought production in line with actual sales by closing some of its factories in the United States, Britain, Australia, Norway, and Switzerland. It also hired Louis Dapples, a banking expert, to put the company back in order. Dapples directed Nestlé with an iron fist, introducing stringent financial controls and reorganizing its administration. By 1923, signs of improvement were already evident, as Nestlé's outstanding bank loans had dropped from CHF 293 million in 1921 to CHF 54.5 million in 1923. Meanwhile in France, Belgium, Italy, Germany, and South Africa, production facilities were expanded. By consolidating certain operations and expanding others, Nestlé was also able to widen its traditional range of products.

Overall, the late 1920s were profitable, progressive times. In addition to adding some new products of its own—including malted milk, a powdered beverage called Milo, and Eledon, a powdered buttermilk for babies with digestive disorders—the company bought interests in several manufacturing firms. Among them were butter and cheese companies, as well as Sarotti A.G., a

Key Dates:

1866: The Anglo-Swiss Condensed Milk Company is founded in Cham, Switzerland.
1867: Henri Nestlé begins selling cow's milk-food in Vevey, Switzerland.
1900: Nestlé opens a factory in the United States.
1905: Nestlé and the Anglo-Swiss Condensed Milk Company merge.
1938: Nestlé introduces Nescafe.
1974: Nestlé enters the nonfood business, becoming a major shareholder of the cosmetics company L'Oréal.
1979: After numerous name changes, Nestlé S.A. is adopted as the official corporate title of the company.
1985: Nestlé acquires Carnation and Hills Brothers Inc.
1992: Nestlé acquires Perrier.
1998: Nestlé acquires the Spillers pet food business belonging to Dalgety PLC, making it the second largest pet food maker in Europe.
2002: Nestlé acquires Ralston-Purina to become co-leader in the global pet food business.
2003: Nestlé acquires Dreyer's Grand Ice Cream.
2005: Chief executive officer Peter Brabeck-Letmathe is named chairman of the board.

Berlin-based chocolate business that began manufacturing Nestlé, Peter, Cailler, and Kohler chocolate. In 1928, under the direction of Chairman Louis Dapples, Nestlé finally merged with Peter, Cailler, Kohler, Chocolats Suisses S.A.—the resulting company of a 1911 merger between the Swiss General Chocolate Company and Cailler, another leading firm—adding 13 chocolate plants in Europe, South America, and Australia to the growing firm.

Expansion During the Great Depression

Nestlé was becoming so strong that it seemed even the Great Depression would have little effect on its progress. In fact, its U.S. subsidiary, Nestlé's Food Company Inc. of New York, barely felt the stock market crash of 1929. In 1930 Nestlé created new subsidiaries in Argentina and Cuba. Despite the Depression, Nestlé added more production centers around the world, including a chocolate manufacturer in Copenhagen and a small factory in Moravia, Czechoslovakia, to manufacture milk food, Nescao, and evaporated milk. Factories were also opened in Chile and Mexico in the mid-1930s.

While profits were down 13 percent in 1930 over the year before, Nestlé faced no major financial problems during the Depression, as its factories generally maintained their output and sales were steady. Although Nestlé's New York-based subsidiary, renamed Nestlé's Milk Products Company, was more affected than those in other countries, U.S. sales of milk products were steady until 1931 and 1932, when a growing public frugality began to cause trouble for more expensive but established brands such as Nestlé's. Profit margins narrowed, prices dropped, and cutthroat competition continued until 1933, when new legislation set minimum prices and conditions of sales.

The markets, such as the United States, that were among the first to feel the effects of the Depression were also the first to

recover from it. The Depression continued in Switzerland, however. Nestlé products manufactured there could no longer compete on international markets since Swiss currency exchanges were made especially difficult from the early 1930s, when many major countries devalued their currencies, until 1936, when Switzerland finally did likewise. The company decided to streamline production and close several factories, including its two oldest, in Cham and Vevey.

Decentralization efforts begun during the Depression continued to modify the company's structure gradually. By 1936, the industrial and commercial activity of the Nestlé and Anglo-Swiss Condensed Milk Company itself was quite limited in comparison with the considerable interests it had in companies manufacturing and selling its products. More than 20 such companies existed on five continents. In effect, the firm had become a holding company. Consequently, the Nestlé and Anglo-Swiss Condensed Milk Company Limited was established to handle production and marketing on the Swiss market; the parent company officially became a holding firm, called the Nestlé and Anglo-Swiss Holding Company Ltd.; and a second holding company, Unilac Inc., was created in Panama by a number of Nestlé's overseas affiliates.

Nescafé Instant Coffee Debuting in 1938

In 1937 Louis Dapples died, and a new management team, whose members had grown up with the organization, took over. The team included Chairman Edouard Muller, formerly managing director; Carl J. Abegg, vice-chairman of the board; and Maurice Paternot, managing director. In 1938 Nestlé introduced its first nonmilk product: Nescafé. The revolutionary instant coffee was the result of eight years of research, which had begun when a representative of the Brazilian Coffee Institute asked Louis Dapples if Nestlé could manufacture ''coffee cubes'' to help Brazil use its large coffee surplus. Although coffee crystals and liquid extracts had been tried before, none had satisfactorily preserved a coffee taste.

Nestlé's product took the form of a soluble powder rather than cubes, allowing users to control the amount of coffee they used. Although Nestlé originally intended to manufacture Nescafé in Brazil, administrative barriers were too great, so Nescafé was first manufactured in Switzerland. Limited production capacity meant that it was launched without the elaborate marketing tactics usually used for products with such potential.

Nescafé quickly acquired a worldwide reputation, however, after it was launched in 1939 in the United States, where it did exceptionally well. Nestea, a soluble powdered tea, also made a successful debut in the early 1940s.

World War II had a dire effect on Nestlé. In 1939 profits plummeted to $6 million, compared to $20 million the year before. As in the last war, the company was plagued by food shortages and insufficient supplies of raw materials. To wage its own battle against the war, the company decided to split its headquarters at Vevey and transfer part of the management and executive team to an office in Stamford, Connecticut, where it could better supervise distant markets. Nestlé continued under control of dual managements until 1945.

But the war was not all bad for Nestlé. When the United States became involved in 1941, Nescafé and evaporated and powdered milk were in heavy demand from American armed forces. Nestlé's total sales jumped from $100 million before the war to $225 million in 1945, with the greatest increase occurring in North America, where sales went from $14 million to $60 million. With the end of the war, Nestlé's European and American branches were able to discuss future plans without fear of censorship, and the company could begin to face the challenge of rebuilding its war-torn subsidiaries. Nestlé also relaunched Nescafé and baby foods and began to research new products extensively. Researchers focused on the three areas Nestlé considered most likely to affect the food industry's future: an increase in world population, rising standards of living in industrialized countries, and the changing social and economic conditions of raw-material-producing countries.

Postwar Growth Through Merger and Acquisition

In 1947 Nestlé merged with Alimentana S.A., the manufacturer of Maggi seasonings, bouillon, and dehydrated soups, and the holding company changed its name to Nestlé Alimentana Company. Edouard Muller became the first chairman of Nestlé Alimentana, but he died in 1948, before the policies he helped formulate put the company on the road to a new future. Carl Abegg assumed leadership of the board.

In 1950 Nestlé acquired Crosse and Blackwell, a British manufacturer of preserves and canned foods. Nestlé hoped its $24 million investment would serve as a marketing outlet for Maggi products, but the plan was less than successful, primarily because Crosse and Blackwell could not compete in the United Kingdom with H.J. Heinz Company. Similar setbacks occurred in 1963, when Nestlé acquired Findus frozen foods in Scandinavia for $32 million. Although the company performed well in Sweden, it encountered difficulties in other markets, where the British-Dutch giant Unilever reigned. While parts of the Findus operation eventually became profitable, Nestlé merged its German, Italian, and Australian Findus branches with Unilever. The development of freeze-drying in 1966 led to Taster's Choice, the first freeze-dried coffee, as well as other instant drinks.

In 1971 Nestlé acquired Libby, a maker of fruit juices, in the United States, and in 1973 it bought Stouffer's, which took Nestlé into the hotel and restaurant field and led to the development of Lean Cuisine, a successful line of low-calorie frozen entrees. Nestlé entered the nonfood business for the first time in 1974 by becoming a major shareholder in the French company L'Oréal, a leading cosmetics company. Nestlé diversified further in 1977 with the acquisition of Alcon Laboratories, a Fort Worth, Texas, pharmaceutical company that specialized in ophthalmic products. Then, two years later, Nestlé purchased Burton, Parsons and Company Inc., an American manufacturer of contact lens products. The company adopted its present name—Nestlé S.A.—in 1979.

Facing Boycott in Late 1970s and Early 1980s

The 1970s saw Nestlé's operations in developing countries increase considerably. Of Nestlé's 303 manufacturing facilities, the 81 factories in developing nations contributed 21 percent of Nestlé's total production. In the mid-1970s, however, the firm faced a new problem as a result of its marketing efforts in these countries, when a boycott against all Nestlé products was started in the United States in 1977. Activists claimed that Nestlé's aggressive baby food promotions made mothers in developing countries so eager to use Nestlé's formula that they used it any way they could. The poverty-stricken areas had high rates of illiteracy, and mothers, unable to read and follow the directions, often mixed the product with local polluted water or used an insufficient amount of the expensive formula, unwittingly starving their infants. Estimates of Nestlé's losses as a result of the boycott, which lasted until the early 1980s, ranged as high as $40 million.

In 1981 Helmut Maucher became managing director of Nestlé and made this controversy one of his top priorities. He met with boycott supporters and complied with the World Health Organization's demands that Nestlé stop promoting the product through advertising and free samples. His direct confrontation of the issue contrasted with Nestlé's earlier low-profile approach and was quite successful in allaying its critics' fears.

Series of Major Acquisitions in the Later 1980s

Maucher also reduced overhead by turning over more authority to operating units and reducing headquarters staff. In addition, he spearheaded a series of major acquisitions. In 1985 Nestlé acquired Carnation, a U.S. manufacturer of milk, pet, and culinary products, for $3 billion, at the time one of the largest acquisitions in the history of the food industry. This was followed in 1985 by the acquisition of Hills Brothers Inc., the third largest U.S. coffee firm, which added ground roast coffee to Nestlé's product line. In the late 1980s, as food companies around the world prepared for the integration of the European Community in 1992, Nestlé continued to make major acquisitions. In 1988 the company paid £2.55 billion ($4.4 billion) for Rowntree Mackintosh PLC—a leading British chocolate manufacturer—marking the largest takeover of a British company by a foreign one to date. That same year Nestlé also purchased the Italian pasta maker Buitoni SpA.

Capital expenditures reached CHF 2.8 billion in 1991. Half was devoted to installation improvements, including data processing and automation, particularly in North America and Europe. The other half was spent expanding plants, primarily in Latin America and the Far East, areas where products were often based on local raw materials, tastes, and habits. That year Nestlé made 31 acquisitions, also adding a new factory in the People's Republic of China. Among the companies purchased were Alco Drumstick, a U.S. ice cream manufacturer with many European activities; Indra, a Swedish frozen-food maker; La Campiña, a Mexican evaporated milk producer; and 97 percent of Intercsokoládé, a Hungarian chocolate maker. The latter was Nestlé's first venture into the newly opened markets of Eastern Europe.

In September 1991 Nestlé and The Coca-Cola Company formed a 50–50 joint-venture, Coca-Cola Nestlé Refreshment Company, to produce and distribute concentrates and bases for the production of ready-to-drink coffee and tea beverages. With an initial capitalization of $100 million the products, to be sold under the Nescafé and Nestea brand names, would be marketed worldwide save for Japan, primarily through Coca-Cola's international network of businesses.

Nescafé, sold in more than 100 countries by 1991, was launched in the Republic of Korea—Coca-Cola and Nestlé's first joint endeavor—as was Nescafé Cappuccino in Europe. Hills Bros. "Perfect Balance," a 50 percent-decaffeinated coffee, began selling in the United States, as did Nestea in cans at the beginning of 1992. By early 1992, a joint venture allowed the company to obtain a majority interest in Cokoladovny, a Czechoslovakian chocolate and biscuit producer. In addition, Nestlé in 1992 battled for and won, with a bid of $2.3 billion in cash, the French mineral water producer Source Perrier, though European regulators forced Nestlé to sell off some Perrier brands. That same year Nestlé took nearly full control of another mineral water concern, Vittel. Nestlé had acquired a 30 percent stake in Vittel in 1969, a move marking the company's first foray into mineral water.

Reemphasis on Core Food Area in Later 1990s

As the 1990s continued, Nestlé recommitted itself to its core food products area, never having been able to grow its healthcare and cosmetics sectors into significant parts of the overall business. The company sold off some of its health and beauty interests, retaining Alcon and the minority holding in L'Oréal—it still hoped to gain full control of the latter, which was privately controlled. Nestlé made other divestments as well, including Wine World Estates, a group of northern California wineries (sold in 1995); canned beans and pasta operations in Canada, a fresh meat business in Germany, and cold meat operations in Sweden (1996); Contadina canned tomato products in the United States, Sarotti chocolate and Dany sandwiches in Germany, and Locatelli brand cheeses in Italy (1997); and Libby's canned meat products, which were sold to International Home Foods for $126 million in 1998.

Acquisitions in the mid-to-late 1990s centered around mineral water, ice cream, and pet foods. In 1993 Nestlé purchased mineral water brands in the United States (Deer Park and Utopia) and Italy (Vera and San Bernardo), as well as ice cream brands in Italy, the Philippines, and South Africa. Added in 1994 were the Alpo pet food company in the United States and Warnke ice creams in Germany; the company also gained a majority stake in chocolate maker Goplana S.A. in Poland. Still further expansion of the ice cream sector came in 1995 with the purchase of Conelsa, the leader in the Spanish market; the chilled dairy products division of Pacific Dunlop in Australia; and Dolce S.A.E., the leading maker of ice cream in Egypt. That year Nestlé also acquired Ortega, a leading brand of Mexican food products in the United States. In 1997 Nestlé entered the Canadian ice cream market through the purchase of Ault and Dairy World, giving the company a 40 percent market share. In early 1998 Nestlé took full control of the San Pellegrino mineral water group and acquired Klim milk powders and Cremora coffee creamers from Borden Brands International. Also in 1998 the company secured the number two position in the European pet food market, trailing only Mars, through the £715 million ($1.2 billion) purchase of the Spillers pet food business of Dalgety PLC.

Despite all of this activity, Nestlé's acquisition pace slowed during the late 1990s as the company shifted toward organic growth starting in 1996. The numerous acquisitions had enabled Nestlé to gain a presence in various product areas in various countries. The company now had fewer countries and products that it wished to add to its portfolio. Other reasons for the shift

to organic growth included the increasing price of acquisitions and antitrust concerns. Meanwhile, in June 1997 Peter Brabeck-Letmathe was named chief executive, taking over the day-to-day management of Nestlé from Maucher. In September 1998 Nestlé announced that Maucher would retire as chairman by the spring of 2000, being replaced by Rainer Gut, then chairman of the Credit Suisse Group.

Nestlé's aggressive marketing of infant formula once again became an issue in 1997 when a report called *Cracking the Code* was issued by the Interagency Group on Breastfeeding Monitoring (IGBM), which had conducted research in Bangladesh, Poland, South Africa, and Thailand. The IGBM concluded that several companies, including Nestlé, were in violation of the World Health Organization's International Code of Marketing of Breastmilk Substitutes, which had been adopted in 1981. According to the report Nestlé's code violations included supplying pregnant women and health workers with materials that promoted formula feeding but did not emphasize the superiority of breastfeeding over formula, and distributing free samples. Nestlé countered by calling the report biased and flawed, and by eliciting a response critical of *Cracking the Code* from an independent marketing research consultant.

At the dawn of the 21st century, Nestlé had about 500 factories in more than 78 countries, boasted sales exceeding CHF 70 billion, and was the undisputed leader in the food industry worldwide. Its portfolio included more than 8,500 brands. The company had set a goal of achieving 4 percent underlying sales growth each year, but failed to meet this target for 1998, largely because of economic downturns in southeast Asia, Latin America, and Eastern Europe.

Consolidation and Expansion in the Early 21st Century

It took several years before the character of the Brabeck-Letmathe era of leadership revealed itself. Initially, Brabeck-Letmathe managed the company in a fashion similar to his predecessor, Maucher. The pair, in fact, had agreed on a list of characteristics to remain unaltered during the two reigns of command, but after several years at the helm, Brabeck-Letmathe realized he needed to break the covenant, making one sweeping change in particular. Maucher had insisted that Nestlé retain its decentralized structure as a way to cater to local markets and tastes (Nestlé, for example, produced 200 different formulations of Nescafé), but Brabeck-Letmathe saw the company becoming uncompetitive so he began to consolidate its operations. The management of factories, which historically had been divided country by country, was broken into regional divisions. Further, products that were similar were organized into strategic business units, adding more cohesion to the operation of Nestlé's global business.

Maucher was remembered as a wheeler and dealer, executing an ambitious acquisition campaign during his decade-and-a-half in charge. Brabeck-Letmathe, in contrast, waited several years before making a major acquisition, preaching growth through internal means during his first years in office. When he did strike out on the acquisition trail, he gravitated toward companies involved in pet care, health, and nutritional products, steering Nestlé toward the higher, value-added market in which the company added basic ingredients to products. Nestlé acquired PowerBar in 2000, but Brabeck-Letmathe's master stroke occurred two years later when he spent $10.3 billion to acquire Ralston-Purina. The acquisition made Nestlé the joint world leader in the pet food business, putting the company alongside Mars, Incorporated, which owned the Pedigree, Sheba, and Whiskas brands. Next, Brabeck-Letmathe turned his attention to Nestlé's ice cream business, completing the acquisition of a German ice cream manufacturer named Schoeller in 2002. The following year, the company spent $2.8 billion to acquire majority control of Dreyer's Grand Ice Cream.

As Nestlé pressed forward under the leadership of Brabeck-Letmathe, the company plotted a future course that distinguished it from its rivals. Rival food conglomerates such as Unilever and Danone focused on narrowing their strategic focus, shedding businesses in an effort to increase their profit margins. Unilever, for example, shuttered more than 100 of its factories and reduced the number of its brands from 1,600 to 400 during the first three years of the decade. Nestlé chose a different path for its future, promising to get bigger as the years passed, emphasizing growth in areas designed to transform it from a food company into a food, health, and wellness company with a deeper involvement in nutritional products. Growth in this direction promised to be the legacy of Brabeck-Letmathe's tenure. The influence of his leadership was expected to increase as he completed his first decade of stewardship. In early 2005, Brabeck-Letmathe was named chairman of Nestlé, giving him the two most powerful positions at one of the largest companies in the world.

Principal Subsidiaries

EUROPE: Nestlé Deutschland AG (Germany; 97.2%); Blaue Quellen Mineral- und Heilbrunnen AG (Germany; 90.6%); Trinks GmbH (Germany; 90.6%); Alcon Pharma GmbH (Germany); Alois Dallmayr Kaffee OHG (Germany; 48.6%); Heimbs & Sohn GmbH & Co. KG (Germany; 48.6%); Azul Kaffee GmbH & Co. KG (Germany; 48.6%); Nüahr-Engel GmbH (Germany; 97.22%); Vittel Mineralwasser GmbH (Germany); Österreichische Nestlé GmbH (Austria); Nestlé Belgilux S.A. (Belgium); Perrier Vittel Belgilux S.A. (Belgium); Alcon-Couvreur S.A. (Belgium); Nestlé Sofia A.D. (Bulgaria; 99%); Nestlé Danmark A/S (Denmark); Premier Is A/S (Denmark); Nestlé España S.A. (Spain); Productos del Café S.A. (Spain); Davigel España S.A. (Spain); EYCAM Perrier S.A. (Spain); Alcon-Cusi S.A. (Spain); Helados y Congelados S.A. (Spain); Compañia del Frio Alimentario S.A. (Spain); Compañia Avidesa S.A. (Spain; 99.43%); Alimentos Congelados S.A. (Spain); Soumen Nestlé Oy (Finland); Nestlé France S.A.; France Glaces-Findus S.A.; Chambourcy S.A. (France; 99.9%); Herta S.A. (France); Davigel S.A. (France; 99.9%); Perrier Vittel France S.A.; S.A. des Eaux Minérales de Ribeauvillé (France; 98.3%); Société Conditionnement et Industrie S.A. (France; 77.9%); Eau Minérale Naturelle de Plancoët "Source Sassay" S.A. (France); Nestlé Coffee Specialties France S.A.; Nestlé Clinical Nutrition S.A. (France); Laboratoires Alcon S.A. (France); Nestlé Dairy Industry S.A.I. (Greece; 85.4%); Alcon Laboratories Hellas E.P.E. (Greece); Nestlé Italiana S.p.A. (Italy; 99.9%); SO.GE.AM S.p.A. (Italy); SO.GE.PLAST S.p.A. (Italy); Alcon Italia S.p.A. (Italy); Nestlé

Hungaria Kft (Hungary); A/S Nestlé Norge (Norway); Nestlé Nederland B.V. (Netherlands); Alcon Nederland B.V. (Netherlands); Goplana S.A. (Poland; 76.97%); Nestlé Polska Sp. zo.o. (Poland); Naleczowianka Spolka zo.o. (Poland; 33.3%); Winiary S.A. (Poland; 83.28%); Nestlé Portugal S.A.; Longa Vida S.A. (Portugal); Sociedade das Aguas de Pisoes Moura S.A. (Portugal); Nestlé (Ireland) Ltd.; Nestlé Food S.r.o. (Czech Republic); Nestlé UK Ltd.; Perrier Vittel UK Ltd.; Buxton Mineral Water Company Ltd. (U.K.); Alcon Laboratories (U.K.) Ltd.; C.U. Rossiya (Russia; 93.21%); Nestlé Zhukovsky Ice Cream LLC (Russia; 80.48%); Nestlé Food LLC (Russia); Nestlé Food S.r.o. (Slovakia; 99.9%); Svenska Nestlé AB (Sweden); Jede AB (Sweden); Zoégas Kaffe AB (Sweden); Société des Produits Nestlé S.A.; Nestlé Suisse S.A.; Frisco-Findus AG (99.8%); Perrier Vittel Suisse S.A.; Alcon Pharmaceuticals Ltd.; Nestlé World Trade Corporation; Food Ingredients Specialities S.A.; Nestlé Coffee Specialties S.A.; Nestlé Türkiye Gida Sanayi A.S. (Turkey). AFRICA: Nestlé (South Africa) (Pty) Ltd.; Alcon Laboratories Pty Ltd. (South Africa); Nestlé Cameroun (Cameroon; 99.6%); Nestlé Côte d'Ivoire (Ivory Coast; 80.9%); Dolce S.A.E. (Egypt); Industrie du Froid S.A.E. (Egypt); Société des eaux minérales Vittor S.A.E. (Egypt; 88.5%); Nestlé Gabon (90%); Nestlé Ghana Ltd. (51%); Nestlé Guinée (Guinea; 99%); Nestlé Foods Kenya Ltd.; Nestlé's Products (Mauritius) Ltd.; Nestlé Maroc S.A. (Morocco; 93.4%); Nestlé Foods Nigeria PLC (57%); Nestlé Sénégal; Nestlé Tunisie (Tunisia; 59.2%); Nestlé Zimbabwe (Pvt) Ltd. AMERICAS: Nestlé Argentina S.A.; Alcon Laboratorios Argentina S.A.; Nestlé Bolivia S.r.l.; Nestlé Industrial e Comercial Ltda. (Brazil); Companhia Produtora de Alimentos (Brazil); Tostines Industrial e Comercial Ltda. (Brazil); Perrier Vittel de Brasil Ltda. (Brazil); Alcon Laboratorios do Brasil S.A. (Brazil); Nestlé Canada, Inc.; Midwest Food Products, Inc. (Canada; 50%); Laura Secord, Inc. (Canada); The Perrier Group of Canada Ltd.; Alcon Canada, Inc.; Nestlé Chile S.A. (99.5%); Alcon Laboratorios Chile Limitada; Nestlé de Colombia S.A.; Laboratorios Alcon de Colombia S.A.; Nestlé Costa Rica S.A.; Nestlé El Salvador S.A.; Nestlé Ecuador S.A. (74.7%); Neslandia S.A. (Ecuador); Nestlé USA, Inc.; Nestlé USA - Food Division, Inc.; Nestlé USA - Beverage Division, Inc.; Food Ingredient Specialities, Inc. (U.S.A.); Great Spring Waters of America, Inc. (U.S.A.); Nestlé Puerto Rico, Inc. (U.S.A.); Alcon Laboratories, Inc. (U.S.A.); Alcon (Puerto Rico), Inc. (U.S.A.); Nestlé Guatemala S.A.; Nestlé Hondureña S.A. (Honduras); Nestlé-JMP Jamaica Ltd.; Cremo Ltd. (Jamaica); Compañá Nestlé S.A. de C.V. (Mexico); Alimentos Findus S.A. de C.V. (Mexico); Industrias Alimenticias Club S.A. de C.V. (Mexico); Manantiales La Asuncion, S.A. de C.V. (Mexico); Alcon Laboratorios S.A. de C.V. (Mexico); Productos Nestlé (Nicaragua) S.A.; Nestlé Panamí S.A.; Nestlé Caribbean, Inc. (Panama); Nestlé Perú S.A. (93.1%); D'Onofrio S.A. (Peru; 80.6%); Sociedad Dominicana de Conservas y Alimentos S.A. (Dominican Republic; 75.7%); Compañia Dominicana de Alimentos Lacteos S.A. (Dominican Republic); Helados Nestlé S.A. (Dominican Republic); Nestlé Trinidad and Tobago Ltd.; Nestlé del Uruguay S.A.; Nestlé Venezuela S.A.; Chocolates Nestlé S.A. (Venezuela); Caramelos Royal C.A. (Venezuela). ASIA: Saudi Food Industries Co. Ltd. (Saudi Arabia; 51%); Nestlé Bangladesh Ltd. (60%); Nestlé Ice Cream L.L.C. (United Arab Emirates; 49%); Nestlé Hong Kong Ltd.; Nestlé Dairy Farm Hong Kong Ltd.; Nestlé India Ltd. (51%); P.T. Nestlé Indonesia

(57.6%); P.T. Nestlé Confectionery Indonesia; P.T. Nestlé Asean (Indonesia) (60%); P.T. Supmi Sakti (Indonesia; 97%); OSEM Investments Ltd. (Israel; 39.7%); Nestlé Japan Ltd.; Nestlé-Mackintosh K.K. (Japan; 66%); Perrier Japon K.K. (Japan); Alcon Japan Ltd.; Nestlé Jordan Trading Co. Ltd. (49%); Nestlé Kuwait General Trading Co. W.L.L. (49%); Société pour l'Exportation des Produits Nestlé S.A. (Lebanon); Nestlé (Malaysia) Bhd. (52.7%); Nestlé Foods (Malaysia) Sdn. Bhd. (51%); Nestlé Products Sdn. Bhd. (Malaysia; 51%); Malaysia Cocoa Manufacturing Sdn. Bhd. (51%); Nestlé Asean (Malaysia) Sdn. Bhd. (60%); Nestlé Cold Storage (Malaysia) Sdn. Bhd. (51%); Milkpak Ltd. (Pakistan; 56.2%); Nestlé Philippines, Inc.; Nestlé Foods Korea Ltd.; Nestlé Shuangcheng Ltd. (China; 90%); Nestlé Dongguan Ltd. (China; 60%); Maggi Dongguan Ltd. (China); Nestlé Tianjin Ltd. (China); Nestlé Qingdao Ltd. (China); Nestlé Dairy Farm Tianjin Ltd. (China; 75%); Nestlé Dairy Farm Qingdao Ltd. (China); Nestlé Dairy Farm Guangzhou Ltd. (China; 60%); Nestlé Singapore (Pte) Ltd.; Nestlé Asean Singapore (Pte) Ltd. (60%); Nestlé Lanka Ltd. (Sri Lanka; 90.8%); Nestlé Taiwan Ltd.; Nestlé Distributors Ltd. (Taiwan); Foremost Foods (Taiwan) Ltd.; Alcon Pharmaceuticals Ltd. (Taiwan); Nestlé Products Thailand, Inc.; Nestlé Asean (Thailand) Ltd. (60%); Quality Coffee Products Ltd. (Thailand; 49%); Nestlé Foods (Thailand) Ltd.; Nestlé Trading (Thailand) Ltd. (49%); Nestlé Manufacturing (Thailand) Ltd.; Nestlé Ice Cream (Thailand) Ltd. (46.3%); Nestlé Vietnam Ltd.; Long An Mineral Water Joint Venture Company (Vietnam; 42.7%). OCEANIA: Nestlé Australia Ltd.; Petersville Australia Ltd.; Nestlé Echuca Pty Ltd. (Australia); Alcon Laboratories (Australia) Pty Ltd.; Nestlé (Fiji) Ltd. (67%); Nestlé Nouvelle-Calédonie S.A. (New Caledonia); Nestlé New Zealand Ltd.; Nestlé (PNG) Ltd. (Papua New Guinea); Nestlé Polynesia S.A. (French Polynesia); Nestlé Purina PetCare Co.

Principal Competitors

ConAgra Foods, Inc.; Groupe Danone; Kraft Foods Inc.

Further Reading

Choi, Candice, "Nestle to Shut Down Three St. Louis Plants," *Daily News*, April 2, 2005, p. 31.

"Daring, Defying, to Grow—Nestlé," *Economist (US)*, August 7, 2004, p. 56US.

Hall, William, "Leading Swiss Banker to Be Nestlé Chairman," *Financial Times*, September 21, 1998, p. 26.

——, "Maucher Keeps His Claws in Nestlé," *Financial Times*, May 7, 1997, p. 26.

——, "Strength of Brands Is Key to Success," *Financial Times*, November 30, 1998, p. SII.

Harrisson, Pierre, *L'Empire Nestlé*, Lausanne, Switzerland: Editions P.-M. Favre, 1983, 493 p.

Heer, Jean, *Nestlé: 125 Years, 1866–1991*, Vevey, Switzerland: Nestlé, 1991.

——, *World Events, 1866–1966: The First Hundred Years of Nestlé*, Vevey, Switzerland: Nestlé, 1966.

Interagency Group on Breastfeeding Monitoring, *Cracking the Code*, UK Committee for UNICEF, 1997.

Maucher, Helmut, *Leadership in Action: Tough-Minded Strategies from the Global Giant*, New York: McGraw-Hill, 1994, 160 p.

Mudd, Tom, "Nestlé Plays to Global Audience," *Industry Week*, August 13, 2001, p. 34.

"Nestlé Closes $2.8 Billion Dreyer's Deal After Clearing Final Hurdle with FTC," *Quick Frozen Foods International*, July 2003, p. 10.

"Nestlé Consolidating Its Chocolate Production," *New York Times*, February 5, 1993.

Oram, Roderick, "Nestlé's Portfolio of Possibilities," *Financial Times*, August 8, 1996, p. 24.

——, "Sweet Success for a Strong Leader," *Financial Times*, September 19, 1995, p. 53.

Pink, Robert "Richenberger Keeps Nestle on Straight and Narrow," *Corporate Finance*, May 2004, p. 18.

Rapoport, Carla, "Nestlé's Brand Building Machine," *Fortune*, September 19, 1994, pp. 147–48, 150, 154, 156.

Richards, Louise, "Repackaging of Nestle Cannot Hide Realities," *Financial Times*, February 25, 2005, p. 12.

Rohwedder, Cacilie, "Nestlé Goes on Investment Diet, Limiting Its Expansion: Emphasis Shifts to Strengthening Core Food Products in European Market," *Wall Street Journal*, September 27, 1994, p. B6.

Steinmetz, Greg, and Tara Parker-Pope, "All Over the Map: At a Time When Companies Are Scrambling to Go Abroad, Nestlé Has Long Been There," *Wall Street Journal*, September 26, 1996, p. R4.

Szabo, Andras, "Nestlé Posts Increased Revenue, Plans Investments," *Europe Intelligence Wire*, March 28, 2005, p. 32.

Templeman, John, Stewart Toy, and Dave Lindorff, "Nestlé: A Giant in a Hurry," *Business Week*, March 22, 1993, pp. 50–51, 54.

Thompson, Stephanie, "Nestlé Warns Stores: Prove It or Lose It," *Advertising Age*, September 13, 2004, p. 1.

Urry, Maggie, and William Hall, "Nestlé Buys Spillers for £715m," *Financial Times*, February 5, 1998, p. 21.

—Anne C. Hughes
—updates: David E. Salamie; Jeffrey L. Covell

Newport Corporation

1791 Deere Avenue
Irvine, California 92606
U.S.A.
Telephone: (949) 863-3144
Toll Free: (800) 222-6440
Fax: (949) 253-1680
Web site: http://www.newport.com

Public Company
Founded: 1969 as Newport Research Corporation
Employees: 942
Sales: $285.8 million (2004)
Stock Exchanges: NASDAQ
Ticker Symbol: NEWP
NAIC: 339111 Laboratory Apparatus and Furniture
   Manufacturing

Newport Corporation serves the semiconductor and micro-electronics, communications, aerospace and defense, healthcare, and research markets, offering a variety of precision components and systems, including lasers, light sources, crystals, spectrographs and monochromators, vibration control worktables and platforms, wafer handling robotics, photonics instruments, motion control equipment, optical filters, and a wide range of optics (such as lenses, mirrors and prisms, and beamsplitters). Each year for more than three decades the company has published the *Newport Catalog,* a major sourcebook for advanced technical products and services. It is now available on the Web as well. Newport maintains 24 sales offices located around the world, and owns nine international subsidiaries in the United Kingdom, Italy, France, The Netherlands, Germany, Switzerland, Singapore, China, and Sweden. Newport is a public company based in Irvine, California, with its shares trading on the NASDAQ.

Company's Founding in the Late 1960s

Newport was founded as Newport Research Corporation in a garage in 1969 by graduates of the California Institute of Technology, John Matthew and Dennis Terry, who were looking for industrial applications for lasers. Just a few years earlier, in 1960, physicist Theodore Harold Maiman had invented the first operable laser, spurring worldwide interest in the technology. Another Cal Tech graduate, Milton Chang, soon joined the company. At school he had worked with Matthews and Terry, and they had become all too aware of a glaring need for equipment specifically designed for laser work. The optical tables at the school were so unstable that the graduate students had to conduct experiments late at night because during the day the building shook too much. Although not noticeable to most people, the building's elevators caused vibrations while traveling up and down in the shafts. The third-shift experiments proved fruitful, however, as the young researchers developed some important techniques that would be put to use at Newport. In the meantime, Chang graduated and worked in the research laboratory at Northrop Corp. for two years before Matthews recruited him to head up Newport's marketing. Given their encounters with troublesome elevators, it was little wonder that Newport's first commercial product was a steel-clad, honeycomb core table for laser experiments, essentially a stabilized platform that counteracted the vibrations emanating from the floor. In the first year of operation, Newport generated sales of $46,000, a modest number, yet the company was now able to move out of the garage and lease industrial space in Fountain Valley, California.

Newport also took advantage of its stabilized table business to launch a catalog in 1971. *Newport Catalog* became a wish book for high-tech clientele, a source for precision optic, electro-optic, and opto-mechanical products. During its first decade Newport pursued opportunities in whatever direction laser research took, such as holography and interferometry. In 1978 the company went public.

In addition to following the leads of others, Newport pursued its own interests. Matthews, for instance, was an avid shooter, and during the 1970s he began developing a laser sight for firearms. He received a patent on a laser sight in 1979, but the initial version was far too cumbersome to have commercial value. Because refining the sight would require far more funds than Newport could invest, Matthews asked the board to sell the laser sight business to him and some staff members who wanted to branch off. After the board agreed, Matthews resigned as Newport's president, replaced by Chang, and founded a new company, Laser Products, which later adopted the name Sure-Fire LLC, makers of the SureFire WeaponLight, a weapon-mounted flashlight for the law enforcement and military markets. In addition, Matthews' company would produce laser sights, shield lights, and baton lights so powerful they could blind and temporarily disable an opponent.

Advances in Holography in the 1980s

One area on which Newport elected to focus was holography, which focused two laser beams on photographic film to produce a three-dimensional image. Holograms were invented in 1948, creating a great deal of enthusiasm about their potential uses, such as 3-D television and movies. Despite massive amounts of money spent on research, holograms were still little more than a curiosity 30 years later, essentially a fascinating technology chasing an application. In the early 1980s, however, they found their way on the front of credit cards, acting as an anti-counterfeiting measure. Newport made one of the few successful applications of hologram technology in the 1980s by developing a holographic camera for mechanical engineers. Coupled with a computerized system the Holocamera, a 70-pound unit suitable for the field, lab, or factory, produced moving holograms that revealed areas of stress and vibration in a product design.

By the mid-1980s Newport was generating sales in excess of $40 million. Chang stepped down as president and CEO in early 1988, indicating that he had been interested in leaving for some time, but only now was he comfortable, having assembled the management team and operational systems needed to sustain the company's long-term growth. He stayed on as chairman of the executive committee for a time, while becoming involved in a number of start-ups and serving on the boards of several optics companies. Chang was replaced as president by Thomas Galantowicz, a former senior president of the company, but the CEO title was eliminated. Overall, Newport fared well during the 1980s, enjoying margins of 11 percent to 24 percent. By the end of the decade, sales reached $57 million.

The early 1990s brought a number of changes and some struggles, however. In 1991 Newport moved its headquarters to Irvine, California, and reinstated the CEO position, naming 59-year-old Richard E. Schmidt to assume the post. He also succeeded 70-year-old Erwin Tomash as chairman of the board. Schmidt was the former CEO and chairman of Milton Roy, manufacturer of environmental and analytical instruments. From 1986 to 1991 he doubled the company's revenues to $150 million, at which point the company was sold. A Milton Roy board member who also served on Newport's board recommended Schmidt for the job at Newport. When Schmidt took over, he inherited the effects of a major acquisition initiated earlier in 1991, the $43 million purchase of the Micro-Positioning Products division of Micro-Controle, a French company. The acquisition placed Newport in the forefront of the positioning and motion control systems field, but the operation was not easily assimilated. Newport was forced to embark on a

costly restructuring of the company, and that coupled with the effects of a recession led to a $14.2 million loss in 1992 and a further loss of $3.7 million in 1993. "The impact of the Micro-Controle acquisition was more than we had thought," Schmidt told the *Orange County Business Journal* in a 1995 profile. "It had too many locations and too many people, and the product lines needed to be rationalized. It was not as profitable as we had thought." At the time the deal had been completed, Newport expected Micro-Controle to double its revenues to $120 million.

To turn around Newport Schmidt consolidated the European operations, reducing the number of segments from seven to three. Employment was trimmed to less than 600 from a headcount of 950 in 1991. As a result of these and other cost-cutting measures, as well as a rebounding economy, Newport returned to profitability in 1994, earning $3.3 million on sales of $85.6 million. At this stage Newport was still very much dedicated to the manufacture of equipment used in research laboratories, with institutional customers including Massachusetts Institute of Technology, Lawrence Livermore Laboratories, and Cal Tech, and corporate clients including Hewlett-Packard, 3M, IBM, and Texas Instruments. More than half of revenues came from the sale of electro-optical products, much of it custom designed, an area in which Newport held a 50 percent market share in the United States and 25 percent worldwide. The main challenge Schmidt now faced was flat sales from Newport's traditional market, U.S. university and government research laboratories. For further growth in this area, the company looked overseas, in particular to Latin America and Asia, where governments were actively investing in research labs to improve their countries' scientific standing. In early 1995, for instance, Newport opened a sales office in Taiwan to take advantage of the emerging market in Asia.

To drum up additional business, Schmidt looked to commercial customers and to achieve growth through acquisitions. In February 1995 Newport acquired RAM Optical Instrumentation, Inc. in a stock exchange. RAM Optical manufactured video-based measurement and inspection systems, essentially projecting microscopic images on a television for inspection and assembly. This deal provided Newport with entry into a new area, one that produced more standardized products with greater appeal for industrial customers. A month later, Newport traded more stock to add Light Control Instruments Incorporated, a San Luis Obispo, California-based company that made laser diode test and control instrumentation. Newport was thus able to expand its ability to serve the growing telecommunications field. To tap into this market, Newport placed high hopes on a product called AutoAlign, which aligned fiber-optic cable to photonic devices such as laser diodes, receivers, and waveguides.

Robert Deuster Becomes CEO in 1996

In 1996 Schmidt stepped down as CEO, turning over the job to 46-year-old Robert Deuster while staying on as chairman. Deuster earned an electrical engineering degree from Marquette University, then went to work for General Electric Company's Medical Systems Group, holding both engineering and marketing positions. In 1985 he was named vice-president of sales and marketing of the Enerpac Division of Applied Power, Inc., then over the next decade held a variety of senior management positions for Applied Power, including president of the

Key Dates:

1969: The company is founded.
1971: The first *Newport Catalog* is issued.
1978: The company is taken public.
1991: Division of Micro-Controle is acquired.
1995: Light Control Instruments and RAM Optical Instruments Incorporated are acquired.
1996: Robert Deuster is named CEO.
2001: Kensington Laboratories is acquired.
2004: Spectra-Physics is acquired.

APITECH Division, president of the Barry Controls Division, and senior vice-president of the Distributed Products Group.

Deuster took over a company that topped the $100 million level in sales in 1995 and recorded a net profit of nearly $3.9 million. A few months before his appointment in 1996, Newport completed another acquisition, adding Minneapolis-based MikroPrecision Instruments, Inc. to increase its presence in the semiconductor equipment and computer peripherals arena. Shortly after taking over, Deuster made his mark by investing $5 million to establish a unit devoted to fiber optics. Although it was a risky move that took about two years before showing any signs of paying off, Deuster was proven correct about the potential of fiber optics, as telephone companies began adding fiber optics to the final connections between customers and the switching offices, rather than relegating the technology to the long-distance sections of the network. The need for a more robust network also would grow as the demand for highspeed Internet service began to gain momentum. Sales in the fiber-optic and semiconductor sectors became increasingly important as lab product sales lessened in importance. The fiber-optics communications sector was strengthened further with the October 1998 acquisition of Environmental Optical Sensors, Inc., maker of high-precision assembly and test equipment for the market. A year later, Newport paid $6.3 million to acquire the Commercial Optics divisions of Corning OCA, which formed the basis of Newport Precision Options, devoted to the production of specialized precision optical products and systems and value-added opto-mechanical subassemblies. As a result of these investments and changes in the marketplace, Newport showed steady improvement on its balance sheet. Sales totaled $143 million in 1997 and net income improved to $10 million. A year later sales were flat, dipping to $142.8 million, but Newport increased earnings to $11.2 million. In 1999 the company recorded sales of $144.1 million and net income of $7.9 million, before enjoying a breakout year in 2000, when sales jumped to $252.9 million and net income more than tripled to $27.8 million.

In 2000 Newport's performance gained the attention of Wall Street, which drove up the price of its stock at a breathtaking rate. Over the first six months of the year, shares rose 581 percent to more than $107, making it the sixth best performing stock on the NASDAQ in the first half of 2000. Newport's ascent was remarkable because so many other tech stocks stumbled during the spring. By late September the price hit a high watermark of $189 (after a three-for-one split, no less), a 1,000 percent increase for the year. Before 2000 closed, however, Newport arranged to use its stock to acquire Kensington Laboratories, maker of robotic

automation systems, serving the semiconductor industry that Newport would adapt to fiber-optic component assembly and automation. The deal closed in February 2001.

The fiber-optics market tailed off dramatically in 2001 as the telecommunications sector entered a severe downturn. With customers postponing investments, Newport was adversely impacted, forcing a number of cost-cutting measures, including a major reduction in the workforce. Fortunately for Newport it could still fall back on its semiconductor and metrology businesses, each enjoying strong success in 2001 while the fiber-optic business stumbled. Nevertheless, the loss of fiber-optic sales was a hard blow, leading to two years of further job cuts and more belt-tightening efforts, such as consolidating six of its 12 plants. Newport lost $6.3 million in 2001 and more than $100 million a year later. Not surprisingly the price of Newport stock plummeted, as far as $10 before rebounding. Sales bottomed out at $134.8 million in 2003, but the company's loss was reduced to $13.2 million for the year.

Newport looked to revive its fortunes in 2004 with the acquisition of laser manufacturer Spectra-Physics for $300 million, a deal that created a single-source supplier by adding more than 5,000 products to the 10,000 Newport already offered. Although Newport faced a major task in integrating Spectra-Physics into its operations, necessitating more reductions in headcount and plant closings, the merger had the potential to create a powerhouse in its field. When the telecommunications sector rebounded, there was every reason to believe that Newport would be well positioned to take advantage of the upturn.

Principal Subsidiaries

Kensington Laboratories, Inc.; Spectra-Physics, Inc.; Micro Robotics Systems, Inc.

Principal Competitors

Agilent Technologies Inc.; Brooks Automation, Inc.; Carl-Zeiss-Stiftung.

Further Reading

Bratt, Dick, "Newport Corp. Leads in Laser Technology," *Orange County Business Journal,* May 26, 1986, p. 23.
Brown, Ken Spencer, "Seeing the Light," *Orange County Business Journal,* June 19–25, 2000, p. 1.
Chuang, Tamara, "Telecommunications Woes Force Irvine, Calif., Fiber-Optics Firm to Cut Jobs," *Orange County Register,* August 21, 2002.
Deckert, Andrea, "Spectra-Physics Boosts Income for California Parent," *Rochester Business Journal,* January 28, 2005, p. 5.
Hector, Gary, "Sighting Profits in Holography," *Fortune,* May 16, 1983, p. 164.
Kelleher, James B., "Irvine, Calif.-Based Fiber Optics Company Performs with Nasdaq's Best," *Orange County Register,* July 1, 2000.
Lyster, Michael, "Changing the Customer Mix," *Orange County Business Journal,* May 8, 1995, p. 1.
Meinel, Carolyn, "Holography: A Technology in Search of an Application." *Technology Review,* April 1983, p. 76.
Simons, Andrew, "After the Boom," *Orange County Business Journal,* March 4–March 10, 2002, p. 1.

—Ed Dinger

NutriSystem, Inc.

200 Welsh Road
Horsham, Pennsylvania 19044
U.S.A.
Telephone: (215) 706-5300
Toll Free: (800) 321-8446
Fax: (215) 706-5388
Web site: http://www.nutrisystem.com

Public Company
Incorporated: 1971 as Shape-Up, Inc.
Employees: 107
Sales: $22.57 million (2003)
Stock Exchanges: American
Ticker Symbol: NSI
NAIC: 541990 All Other Professional, Scientific and
Technical Services

NutriSystem, Inc., formerly an operator of weight-loss centers, offers its services on the Internet, providing diet programs on its web site, www.nutrisystem.com. The company offers counseling online and via telephone, provides weight-loss programs, and distributes prepackaged foods. Through a contract with QVC, Inc., a television shopping network, NutriSystem sells its food on television, deriving more than 20 percent of its total revenues from QVC-related sales. NutriSystem also owns Slim and Tone, a franchiser of fitness clubs.

Origins

For roughly a decade, Harold Katz enjoyed a level of success that most entrepreneurs could only dream of reaching. Quickly, however, his job of running one of the fastest growing companies in the United States became a litigious affair, rife with hostility, and generally a nightmarish ordeal. For Katz, the son of a grocer who received no formal education beyond high school, the path to possessing a personal fortune valued at more than $300 million began in 1971. He was 34 years old at the time, having spent the years after high school floating from one job to another. He started working at his father's grocery store, spent a short time running a specialty sales business, and got involved in the insurance business. By the beginning of the 1970s, Katz was looking for another job, and he got the inspiration for his try at an entrepreneurial career from his mother. Katz had watched his mother gain and lose weight repeatedly, fueling his desire to find a better solution to controlling weight. He decided to integrate behavioral counseling, medical supervision, and low-calorie meals into one business concept, developing weight loss "centers" that looked like medical offices. "I realized then that if you could put all of that under one roof, you'd have a fantastic business," Katz reflected in a May 1985 interview with *Inc.* magazine.

Katz bet everything he had that his business would succeed. He emptied his savings account, totaling $20,000, and took out a second mortgage on his house, giving him another $20,000. With the start-up capital, Katz opened his first weight-loss center in Willow Grove, a suburb of his native Philadelphia, in December 1971. The first center was named Shape Up, Inc. Several months later, he opened a second center, and in September 1972 he discovered the concept's primary growth engine, selling the third center to a franchisee. (Katz's weight-loss centers underwent several name changes during their first decade, becoming Shape-Up Weight Control Centers of America, Inc. in 1976, Weight Loss Medical Centers of America, Inc. in 1977, Nutri-System Weight Loss Medical Centers of America, Inc. in 1979, and Nutri/System, Inc. in 1980.) As the Nutri/System concept quickly blossomed into a nationwide chain of weight-loss centers, it did so largely though franchise agreements, becoming what Katz referred to as a "money-making machine" in his interview with *Inc.*

Each Nutri/System center earned its money through a set-up fee to clients and by charging each client according to the amount of weight lost. The centers earned most of their money from another source, however, recording hefty profits from the sale of private-label food, which Nutri/System clients were obliged to purchase at least five times a week. As one critic of the Katz-led organization put it, as quoted in *Inc.* article on the company, "It was the unconscionable price of the damn food that made Nutri/System."

During the 1970s, there was little controversy about the price of the company's food, at least in comparison to the uproar

Company Perspectives:

NutriSystem now stands as a constant pillar of support and information for those looking to lose weight in a busy world. As an Internet force, its wide-ranging web content, combined with its knowledgeable and professional counselors, equals a powerful resource for all dieting consumers. And it's available 24 hours a day, 7 days a week, with no waiting for weekly meetings or worry about expensive membership fees. NutriSystem believes in its clients and is there to help them, every step of the way. Together with its growing online member community, NutriSystem makes weight loss—and the goal of becoming healthy and fit—a reality for millions.

surrounding the issue a decade later. During the 1970s, everything was fine because everyone was making money, Katz and his franchisees included, several of whom became millionaires during the decade. By the end of the 1970s, Katz's enterprise ranked as one of the 100 fastest growing companies in the country, quickly blanketing the nation with Nutri/System centers. Beginning in 1979, Nutri/System began a four-year period that would see the company record revenue growth at a compound annual rate of 82 percent. Katz took the company public during this period, debuting on the over-the-counter exchange in January 1981, before moving to the more prestigious New York Stock Exchange. By late 1982, Katz, who owned 67 percent of Nutri/System's stock, had parlayed his $40,000 initial investment into a fortune valued at more than $300 million. Katz was immensely wealthy, a stature he relished. He moved the company into a new $2 million headquarters facility in Huntingdon, Pennsylvania, equipped with a lavish office with stained glass, a wet bar, and a model of his corporate jet. Katz bought a massive estate, a $56,000 customized Cadillac Seville, and, lastly, he purchased his hometown basketball team, the Philadelphia 76ers.

Katz's chain operated in 50 states during the early 1980s, comprising 500 weight-loss centers, 400 of which were franchised units. Together, the centers generated nearly $50 million in sales a year, a total that was practically doubling every year. The pressing problem at this point was trying to sustain a phenomenal record of growth, which threatened to become increasingly difficult as the company reached its projected saturation point of between 700 and 800 Nutri/System weight-loss centers. Katz had an enormous flow of cash at his disposal and put it to use to find new areas of growth. He began acquiring other businesses, convinced that his success with Nutri/System reflected a talent that could be grafted onto other businesses. ''I'd been in business for nearly 31 years,'' he said in his *Inc.* interview. ''And I'd hate to think that all I, and the people that I'd surrounded myself with, knew was weight loss. We knew franchising, we knew the service business; we were salesmen, marketers.''

The Turbulent Early 1980s

When Nutri/System was at its peak, Katz began spending some of the money earned from his rousing success. In August 1981, he acquired a Philadelphia-based executive placement firm named Fox-Morris Associates, paying $4.2 million for the com-

pany. In March 1982, he purchased Gloria Marshall Figure Salons for $15.1 million and Nutrient Cosmetic Ltd. for $8.1 million. Katz also started a new business, Tele-Cut, a hair-styling salon he designed as a franchise concept. His foray into other business areas swiftly proved that he was not blessed with a Midas touch. The acquired companies, each generating less profit than they should have before they were acquired, worsened under Katz's control, turning into money-losers. The acquisition of Gloria Marshall, in particular, was a disaster, presenting what many Nutri/System franchisees perceived as a competitor operating within their organization. Despite the anemic state of the chain and Katz's assurances that Gloria Marshall presented no threat to Nutri/System centers, franchisees looked at Gloria Marshall and saw a business offering a computerized diet, a weight-maintenance program, and a diet supplement, which was supplied by Nutri/System. The acquisition, according to Katz's comments in his interview with *Inc.*, ''led to the end of the honeymoon'' between Nutri/System and its franchisees. Within a short time, corporate divorce appeared to be the only solution to resolve the enmity between Katz and his franchisees.

The missteps on the acquisition front were followed by actions that caused further anxiety for Nutri/System franchisees. Senior Nutri/System officials began selling large amounts of stock they held in the company, beginning in January 1983 when Katz sold 670,000 shares. During the ensuing two months, Katz's brother, Nutri/System's vice-president Robert Katz, sold 42,250 shares, the company's marketing vice-president sold 58,250 shares, and its national medical director sold 7,000 shares. In mid-March 1983, nine days after the sale of stock by senior executives ended, the company announced its earnings for the third quarter would drop by as much as $1.8 million, a revelation that led shareholders to file a class-action lawsuit against the company. Meanwhile, another contentious battle was taking place, pitting Katz against a large number of franchisees, who, like their customers, felt gouged by the price of the food they were obliged to buy from Katz. The franchisees formed a federation that sought compromise from Katz, eventually resulting in a lawsuit filed against Nutri/System that counted 280 of the 550 franchised centers as litigants in the antitrust lawsuit.

The good times were through for Katz, as they were for the company he presided over. Nutri/System posted a $17.4 million loss in 1984, one year after reaping a $13 million profit. Katz, exasperated by his experience dealing with an increasingly hostile group of franchisees, looked to sell the company and nearly did so, but the buyer backed out at the last moment, unwilling to pay for a company whose market value was plummeting. Everyone within the organization, including Katz, believed Nutri/System was headed toward an imminent ownership change, but the aborted sale of the company kept the same personalities in place, creating an uncomfortable chemistry within the organization that Katz realized he needed to do something about. ''For the benefit of everyone,'' he said in his interview with *Inc.*, ''it's important that we have a new chief executive officer, some new life, some new thinking, somebody coming in clean.''

The untarnished executive selected by Katz was A. Donald McCulloch, who became chief executive officer of the troubled Nutri/System organization in 1985. McCulloch, 39 years old at the time, possessed a wealth of marketing experience gained while working for General Foods, Wilson Sporting Goods, Pizza Hut, and Hathaway shirt. McCulloch used his experience to develop a turnaround plan, a plan that, if successful, would give him an opportunity to acquire the company, according to his stipulation to Katz in accepting the chief executive officer position. "On an Amtrak napkin on my way back from Nutri/System," McCulloch said in a November 13, 1989 interview with *Forbes*, "I made a list of five things we needed to do: control our finances, bring in new management, innovate marketing, upgrade operations, and restructure the branch network system." McCulloch's influence on the organization produced encouraging results, paving the way for his acquisition of the company and the exit of Katz.

In 1986, the Katz era came to an end. McCulloch and four other executives completed a leveraged buyout of the company, a $69.5 million deal that netted Katz $37.9 million. Although far from impoverished, Katz ended his relationship with his entrepreneurial creation with substantially less than the $300 million he could have taken away only a few years earlier. For Nutri/System, the change in ownership marked a fresh start and a return to a privately-held status. The company expanded aggressively for the remainder of the 1980s, developing into a chain of 1,800 weight-loss centers that generated $764 million in revenues by the decade's conclusion.

Collapse in the Early 1990s

Despite the change in ownership, Nutri/System continued to find itself involved in damaging legal battles. During the early 1990s, the company faced hundreds of lawsuits alleging the Nutri/System weight-loss program created medical problems resulting in the loss of a client's gallbladder. By 1991, the company conceded it faced about 300 lawsuits nationally, while other sources put the number closer to 800, each claiming that the rapid loss of weight increased the saturation of bile with

cholesterol, directly contributing to the formation of symptomatic gallstones and gallbladder disease. In mid-1993, the company succumbed to the forces against it, operating as a debtor in possession under Chapter 11 of the U.S. Bankruptcy Code until it was discharged the following year.

Nutri/System was a shadow of its former self throughout the 1990s. The company operated only a fraction of the weight-loss centers it had operated during the 1980s and it was a perennial money loser. Annual sales, which had neared $800 million in 1989, hovered around the $50 million range throughout the 1990s. As the company entered the late 1990s, the decision was made to abandon its traditional approach to offering weight-loss programs in favor of becoming an Internet-based provider of weight loss solutions. Nutri/System sold its company-owned centers to Complete Wellness Weight Management, Inc. in 1997 and re-emerged as an e-commerce company with a new name, nutrisystem.com inc.

NutriSystem in the 21st Century

The company's web site launched in 1999, beginning a new era for the Nutri/System diet plan. In 2000, the first full year of Internet-based sales, the company generated $20 million in revenue, a total that was nearly matched by the $14 million it lost during the year. The beginning of the new decade was a time of rebuilding, to be sure, requiring new methods and a new approach to running the 30-year-old brand. In an effort to improve its financial health, the company purchased the Sweet Success product line from Nestlé USA. Inc. in August 2000, just before it changed its corporate title to Nutri/System, Inc. Sweet Success was a diet meal replacement line distributed in traditional retail locations such as supermarkets, drugstores, and discount chains, but Nutri/System executives decided to drop the product line four months after acquiring it, officially discontinuing it in June 2001.

The brief and unproductive association with Sweet Success was countered with a more lasting and lucrative relationship forged in 2001. Nutri/System reached an agreement with the shopping network QVC, Inc. to sell the company's food on television, which developed into a sizeable business. By 2004, food sales through QVC accounted for more than one-fifth of Nutri/System's total revenue.

As Nutri/System completed its first 30 years of business, new owners took control of the company. In December 2002, HJM Holdings LLC and NewSpring Ventures L.P. acquired 58.4 percent of Nutri/System, giving the two investment concerns majority control over Nutri/System. HJM Holdings' Michael J. Hagan, the cofounder of VerticalNet, a business-to-business Internet and software company, was named chairman and chief executive officer of Nutri/System. Under his leadership, the company, which changed its name to NutriSystem, Inc. in 2003, introduced its first new food line in a dozen years, a line of more than 100 food selections with a low glycemic index called NutriSystem Nourish. The new program debuted in December 2003. The introduction of NutriSystem Nourish was followed by the acquisition of Slim and Tone, a franchiser of fitness centers, in late 2004. These two new avenues of potential growth represented Hagan's attempt to move the company beyond its past and reinvent a successful business model for the future, something NutriSystem needed as it entered the mid-2000s.

Principal Subsidiaries

Slim and Tone LLC.; NutriSystem Direct, LLC.

Principal Competitors

eDiets.com, Inc.; Jenny Craig, Inc.; Weight Watchers International, Inc.

Further Reading

Davey, Tom, ''Woes Weigh Heavier on Nutri-System Inc.,'' *Business Journal Serving Greater Sacramento,* June 17, 1991, p. 36.

Demery, Paul, ''Weight Watchers: Rival's Ad Is False,'' *Long Island Business News,* July 8, 1991, p. 3.

Diamond, Jonathan, ''Weight-Loss Center Chain Moving into Market,'' *Philadelphia Business Journal,* February 26, 1990, p. 5.

Dooms, Tracey M., ''Indianapolis Woman Joins Ranks of Former Clients Suing Nutri/System,'' *Indianapolis Business Journal,* June 3, 1991, p. 1.

Freifeld, Karen, ''A Minute on the Lips. . . . ,'' *Forbes,* June 16, 1986, p. 150.

Harrison, David J., ''Battle Over Nutri/System Hits Region,'' *Baltimore Business Journal,* January 24, 1992, p. 3.

Parker, Akwell, ''Weight-Loss Company Nutri/System Names New Chairman, CEO,'' *Philadelphia Inquirer,* December 24, 2002, p. 13.

Rogan, Ed, ''Nutri-System's Leveraged Buyout Nets Katz $37.9 M,'' *Philadelphia Business Journal,* February 10, 1986, p. 5.

Schifrin, Matthew, ''Living Off the Fat of the Land,'' *Forbes,* November 13, 1989, p. 186.

Waters, Craig R., ''Slim Pickings,'' *Inc.,* May 1985, p. 94.

''Weight of One Lawsuit Off, Nutri/System Gains Another,'' *Philadelphia Business Journal,* September 16, 1991, p. 12.

—Jeffrey L. Covell

Oaktree Capital Management, LLC

333 South Grand Avenue, 28th Floor
Los Angeles, California 90071
U.S.A.
Telephone: (213) 830-6300
Fax: (213) 830-6393
Web site: http://www.oaktreecapital.com

Private Company
Incorporated: 1995
Employees: 290
Total Assets: $26.86 billion (2004)
NAIC: 523920 Portfolio Management; 523930 Investment
    Advice; 523999 Miscellaneous Financial Investment
    Activities

Oaktree Capital Management, LLC is an investment firm specializing in acquiring the bad debt of financially ailing companies. Oaktree Capital, with nearly $27 billion in assets, has offices in Los Angeles, New York, Tokyo, London, Singapore, and Frankfurt.

Origins

Oaktree Capital was started by a financial analyst whom *American Banker*, in its April 26, 2002 issue, described as "a force in the graveyard of capitalism." Howard S. Marks, who helped pioneer a new angle of attack in the investment community, earned his reputation by pursuing what others retreated from, becoming one of the kings of high-risk, high-yield investments. Marks grew up in the New York borough of Queens in the middle-class neighborhood of Forest Hills. The son of an accountant, Marks followed in his father's footsteps, earning his degree in accounting from The Wharton School at the University of Pennsylvania. After earning an M.B.A. in accounting and marketing from the University of Chicago, Marks accepted a position as an equity analyst at Citibank, beginning his professional career in 1969.

Marks distinguished himself at Citibank, helping to steer the massive financial institution in a new direction. Within a decade, he rose from his entry position as an equity analyst to become the director of equity research. Marks had earned the promotion to director by 1978, a year that marked a turning point in his career. In an interview with *American Banker* on April 26, 2002, Marks explained what happened, describing the pivotal event that opened a new area of business for Citibank and determined the direction his career would take for decades to follow. "Around September," Marks said, "the bank was approached about running a high-yield bond mutual fund. Remember, this was twenty-four years ago and nobody had heard of the junk bond world—then only $2.5 billion of the total." Marks continued: "They said to me, 'There's something called high-yield bonds and the leading figure is some guy named Milken at a small brokerage firm in Los Angeles—would you take it on?' Of course I did," Marks responded. "And that was a lucky moment for me."

Michael Milken, through his exploitation of the junk bond market, became one of the dominant symbols of 1980s-style capitalism. Although Marks garnered less attention than Milken, he was involved in the earliest days of the junk bond market, registering considerable success alongside his Wharton alum, Milken. Marks headed Citibank's involvement in the junk bond market, leading the New York City-based operation even after Citibank allowed him to relocate to Los Angeles in 1980. He found the move to be beneficial from a professional standpoint, explaining in his interview with *American Banker*, "Many times we view New York as being preoccupied with what's going on in the financial markets at the moment, making it easy to not see the whole picture. In California, we're stepped back a bit, and I believe that gives us more perspective."

Marks found a lasting home in Southern California, but not as a Citibank executive. He left the company in 1985, frustrated that the amount of money he brought into Citibank from the junk bond market, which had developed into a $100 billion market the year he left, was not proportionate to his salary. He joined a Los Angeles institutional money manager named Trust Company of the West (TCW) Group, becoming the chief investment officer for the company's distressed debt and president of its subsidiary, TCW Asset Management Co. Marks continued to excel at TCW during the late 1980s and early 1990s—a period that saw his colleague Milken indicted and imprisoned—but he experienced

Company Perspectives:

The mission of Oaktree Capital Management, LLC is to provide highly professional, risk-averse management in a small number of sophisticated investment specialties. Oaktree is a firm involved exclusively in inefficient markets and alternative investments, and among such firms it has a solid track record, a broad product range and substantial assets under management. We are dedicated to the achievement of consistent and superior performance without accepting high risk. Our ultimate objective is investment success, the fruits of which are shared by all of Oaktree's clients and personnel.

the same sort of frustration at TCW as he had experienced at Citibank. In an April 26, 2002 interview with *American Banker*, one of Marks's colleagues explained what happened. "He (Marks) told me that for every dollar his group brought in, they were only allowed to keep 20 cents because they (TCW's senior management) were subsidizing the nonprofitable business at TCW. Howard was in line to be president of TCW, but he left and took everyone in his group with him because he wanted more control over his destiny."

Former TCW Executives Gathering in 1995

Marks left TCW in 1995 determined to end the problems associated with an employer-employee relationship. He founded Oaktree Capital in April, starting the company with six other executives, all of whom worked for TCW. Marks took the title of chairman at the newly formed Oaktree Capital, heading a distinguished investment team that produced a level of success that surprised Marks and the six other principal partners. Joining Marks from TCW was Bruce A. Karsh, who was appointed Oaktree Capital's president. Karsh, a graduate of the University of Virginia School of Law, was a managing director at TCW and the portfolio manager of the TCW Special Credits Funds. Karsh was credited with developing the investment approach and strategies used in TCW's distressed debt investments, possessing skills that made him the natural leader of Oaktree Capital's distressed debt effort. Oaktree Capital's investments in real estate were headed by Russell S. Bernard, a Cornell University graduate who attracted the attention of TCW executives in 1993. Bernard, who started his real estate career in 1983, managed a diversified portfolio of properties located in 40 states by the early 1990s, when he began working with members of TCW's distressed debt team to explore possible joint investments. The collaboration led to Bernard's move from Win Properties, where he served as a partner and vice-president, to TCW in 1994. In his brief stay at TCW, Bernard assembled a staff of real estate professionals, all of whom left with Bernard in 1995 to join Oaktree Capital.

The other members of the founding team added new areas of expertise and strengthened Oaktree Capital's capabilities in its main line of business, distressed debt investments. Richard Masson, a managing director at TCW and co-leader of the company's distressed debt effort, became the head of Oaktree Capital's analytical team, a team responsible for evaluating prospective investments and determining company valuation.

Stephen A. Kaplan, who had helped establish TCW's principal investment strategy, took on similar responsibilities at Oaktree Capital, spearheading the firm's investments that required it to assume managerial control over a particular company. Rounding out the group of seven cofounders were Larry W. Keele and Sheldon M. Stone. Keele, who was in charge of TCW's convertible value portfolios, became the head of Oaktree Capital's convertible securities management. Stone, who directed Oaktree Capital's high-yield bond management group, worked with Marks at Citibank, where he performed credit analysis and managed high-yield bond portfolios. When Marks left Citibank for TCW, Stone followed, and the pair established TCW's high-yield bond department, which Stone led for the ensuing decade.

The brain drain suffered by TCW because of Oaktree Capital's formation was substantial, but the loss suffered by the institutional money manager ran deeper. Within three months of Oaktree Capital's formation, more than 30 TCW clients transferred $1.5 billion in assets to Oaktree Capital. The chief investment officer for one of the clients in the initial group that switched from TCW to Oaktree Capital offered his reason for transferring to the Marks-led firm in the April 26, 2002 *American Banker* article on Oaktree Capital. "It was the team with whom we were investing," the Pennsylvania State Employees Retirement System's Peter Gilbert said. "Howard has the ability to make money from specialized market niches and he knows how to attract and retain very good people." Publicly, TCW officials expressed their displeasure at their loss of business and personnel, but behind the scenes they struck a deal with Oaktree Capital to avoid a complete loss. TCW contracted with Oaktree to manage and to liquidate roughly $2.6 billion in assets that Karsh and Masson had managed.

Oaktree Capital set out with a considerable jump-start over other start-up investment companies. With the talent and assets drawn from TCW, Marks's company became a discernible force in the national investment community shortly after its formation. Within five years, Oaktree Capital came to dominate its market niche, excelling in executing the strategy formulated by Marks and his six other cofounders. From 1995 forward, Marks eschewed investing in companies that required more than a modicum of hands-on management. Oaktree Capital, through the guidance of Marks, favored companies that possessed tangible assets, setting its sights on manufacturers, retailers, and companies involved in industries such as trucking. Investing in companies whose assets consisted largely of real estate became a favorite target of Oaktree Capital. Marks focused on companies with a solid business plan, and then swooped in when the otherwise sound companies ran aground because they had incurred too much debt by overpaying for an acquisition or had faltered financially because of overly ambitious expansion. Both of these scenarios involved the outlay of capital that companies generally did not have in their coffers. They took on debt when completing an acquisition or financing an expansion plan and sometimes suffered serious consequences. A lack of cash flow or, ultimately, bankruptcy resulted from the mistakes made in pursuing growth. When the originators of the debt incurred by the troubled company started looking for an exit strategy, their anxiety piqued to the point where they were willing to accept pennies on the dollar for their debt, Oaktree Capital started looking for an entry strategy. Most fled from financial disaster, cutting their ties from corporate rot, but

Key Dates:

1995: Oaktree Capital Management is formed in April by a group of executives from Trust Company of the West.

2000: Oaktree Capital begins acquiring bankrupt movie theater chains.

2004: Oaktree Capital sells its stake in Loews Cineplex Entertainment Corp.

the misfortune of others was the fortune of Marks, "one of the biggest vulture investors," as described in the April 26, 2002 issue of *American Banker.*

Oaktree Capital invested in a number of different companies during its first decade of business. One of the first investments was the acquisition of the Mountain High Ski Resort in Wrightwood, California, a 90-minute drive from Los Angeles. Marks acquired the ski resort from an Orange County businessman named Terry Tognazzini, and began wooing snowboarders. For years, Mountain High derived roughly 90 percent of its business from skiers, but under Oaktree Capital's management snowboarders accounted for 80 percent of the resort's business, which quadrupled the number of visitors during the first half of the 2000s. Oaktree Capital sold the resort in 2005, executing its strategy of improving an asset's balance sheet and then selling the business for a substantial profit.

Oaktree Capital and the Movie Theater Business in the 2000s

Oaktree Capital's most notable investments in the new millennium involved its pursuit of cinema operators. The largest of the national chains were in poor financial health during the early years of the decade, racking up debilitating debt from overly rapid expansion. Oaktree Capital, in separate partnerships with Denver billionaire Phillip Anschutz and a Canadian investment firm named Onex Corp., bailed out several large movie-theater chains, gaining equity positions at an attractive price. At the beginning of 2001, Oaktree Capital began delving into the movie-theater business, acquiring, along with Anschutz, 35 percent of the bank loans belonging to beleaguered Regal Cinemas Inc., operator of the largest chain in the United States. Before the end of the year, Marks and his team furthered their position in the movie-theater business, pairing with Onex to take control of Loews Cineplex Entertainment Corp., which filed for bankruptcy in February 2001, and bankrupt GC Companies Inc., the owner of General Cinema Theatres Inc., a 73-theater chain operating in 20 states. Oaktree Capital also took control of smaller movie-theater assets, acquiring Silver Cinemas Inc., a discount movie-theater chain that also owned Landmark Theatre Corp., the largest art-house chain in the United States. After acquiring bankrupt Silver Cinemas in mid-2001, the company teamed with Onex again in August 2002 to acquire Cinemex, a Mexico-based movie-theater chain.

As Oaktree Capital completed its first decade in business, the company's investment strategy was reaping substantial re-

wards. The company sold Landmark Theatre Corp. in 2003, profiting on its initial $40 million investment, but registered its greatest profit with the sale of the Loews chain. Oaktree Capital and Onex restructured the chain, spending $35 million on three acquisitions, and brought the chain out of bankruptcy. In mid-2004, the two investment firms sold the chain for $1.46 billion, roughly doubling their money. In the years ahead, the execution of Oaktree Capital's investment strategy promised to see the companies under its control come and go as Marks and the other principals worked to squeeze profits from their nearly $30 billion portfolio of assets. The sale of the Mountain High ski resort in the beginning of 2005, for example, coincided with the arrival of Oaktree Capital's newest asset, a Texas-based industrial cleaning services company named HydroChem Holding Inc. Oaktree Capital's second decade of business promised to include more of the same, as struggling companies were repaired, sold for a profit, and replaced with more struggling companies, each handpicked by Oaktree Capital's squad of vulture investors.

Principal Subsidiaries

OCM Investments, LLC; Oaktree Capital Management Limited.

Principal Competitors

The Anschutz Company; Appola Advisors, L.P.; St. James's Place Capital PLC.

Further Reading

Barry, Kate, "Fore! Sale," *Los Angeles Business Journal,* April 7, 2003, p. 26.

Carey, David, "Anschutz to Gain Control Regal Cinemas," *Daily Deal,* September 5, 2001, p. 4.

Cecil, Mark, "Onex/Oaktree Scope More Movie Targets," *Mergers & Acquisitions Report,* December 10, 2001.

Fixmer, Andy, "Mountain High Ski Resort Goes on Block," *Los Angeles Business Journal,* January 3, 2005, p. 5.

Godinez, Victor, "Dallas Firm to Purchase Art-House Theater Chain," *Dallas Morning News,* September 24, 2003, p. B2.

Holman, Kelly, "Oaktree Buys HydroChem," *Daily Deal,* January 5, 2005, p. 31.

King, Laura, "Ones, Oaktree Buy General Cinema Theatres," *Daily Deal,* June 13, 2001, p. 34.

Kuehner-Herbert, Katie, "A Vulture's Full Plate: Buyer of Bad Debt May Face a Market Glut," *American Banker,* April 26, 2002, p. 1.

Leizens, Leticia, "Investment Firm Is Betting on Big Payoff with Pillowtex," *HFN The Weekly Newspaper for the Home Furnishing Network,* January 14, 2002, p. 28.

Lindemann, Melissa, "Mexican Cinema Operator Cinemax Was Purchased by the United States' Oaktree Capital Management and Canada's Onex Corporation," *Business Mexico,* August 2002, p. 14.

Morris, John E., "Loews' Happy Ending," *Daily Deal,* June 28, 2004, p. 32.

"Onex Agrees to Sell Loews Cineplex for C$2.0 Billion," *Canadian Corporate News,* June 22, 2004, p. 12.

"Onex Completes Sale of Loews Cineplex," *Canadian Corporate News,* August 17, 2004, p. 14.

Stremfel, Michael, "A Bear's Eye View," *Los Angeles Business Journal,* September 24, 2001, p. 30.

—Jeffrey L. Covell

Occidental Petroleum Corporation

10889 Wilshire Boulevard
Los Angeles, California 90024
U.S.A.
Telephone: (310) 208-8800
Toll Free: (800) 622-9231
Fax: (310) 443-6694
Web site: http://www.oxy.com

Public Company
Incorporated: 1920
Employees: 7,209
Sales: $11.36 billion (2004)
Stock Exchanges: New York
Ticker Symbol: OXY
NAIC: 211111 Crude Petroleum and Natural Gas
    Extraction; 324110 Petroleum Refineries; 325181
    Alkalies and Chlorine Manufacturing; 325998 All
    Other Miscellaneous Chemical Product Manufactur-
    ing; 551112 Offices of Other Holding Companies

Occidental Petroleum Corporation, an oil and gas and chemicals company, conducts its business through two major subsidiaries, Occidental Oil and Gas Corporation and Occidental Chemical Corporation. Occidental Oil and Gas, representing the larger of the two business segments, operates in the United States, the Middle East, and Latin America. Domestically, the company ranks as the largest natural gas producer in California and the largest oil producer in Texas. Overseas assets in oil and gas are located in Oman, Qatar, Yemen, Columbia, Ecuador, Russia, and Pakistan. Occidental Chemical manufactures vinyls, chlorine, and caustic soda, relying on 24 manufacturing sites in the United States, two facilities in Canada, and one plant in Chile. Occidental, the governing entity for the oil and gas and chemical operations, derives roughly $7.5 billion in annual sales from its oil and gas interests and $3.6 billion from its chemicals business.

Early History

Occidental Petroleum was founded in 1920 in California. Its early years as an oil-finding entity were largely undistinguished,

with the company almost bankrupt by the mid-1950s. It was Occidental Petroleum's early difficulties, however, that laid the groundwork for its later success. In 1956 Occidental Petroleum came to the attention of Armand Hammer, a millionaire well-known for his savvy and success in business dealings with the Soviet Union in the 1920s. In 1921 Hammer had met Vladimir Lenin, the leader of the Russian Revolution, and had become the first U.S. businessman to establish ties with the Soviet Union. Among other enterprises, Hammer had operated an asbestos mine, imported grain, and manufactured pencils. While in Moscow, he had purchased Russian art treasures at bargain prices, later reselling many art objects in the United States at considerable profit. (Later it was revealed that many of Hammer's treasures were fakes, and he was well aware of it.)

In 1956 Hammer and his wife Frances each invested $50,000 in two oil wells that Occidental planned to drill in California. When both wells struck oil, Hammer, nearly 60, took an active interest in further Occidental oil exploration.

At Hammer's first association with Occidental, the company was run by Dave Harris, Roy Roberts, and John Sullivan. Hammer's increased involvement, his strong personality, and his ability to raise money for oil drilling propelled him more and more into the limelight. By July 1957 Hammer had become company president.

Growth Under Hammer in the 1960s

Hammer's influence played a key role in the development of Occidental. As Steve Weinberg wrote in *Armand Hammer: The Untold Story*, "Few *Fortune* 500 corporations have come so totally under the sway of one person, especially one who owned such a tiny percentage of stock."

From his earliest days as president of Occidental, one of Hammer's overriding drives was for Oxy to diversify. In his autobiography, Hammer reported that a prime rationale for diversifying was to make Oxy too big for the other major oil companies to take over. Acquisitions included energy and chemical companies, as well as meat-producing operations.

At the time Hammer became involved with Occidental, the company was listed on very small stock exchanges on the West

Coast; within several years, however, Oxy was on the American Stock Exchange, boosted by the 1959 Hammer-led acquisition of Gene Reid Drilling Company of Bakersfield, California. This acquisition was to prove fortuitous for the growth of Occidental. Hammer attracted Reid, an engineer, and his son Bud, a geologist, to the cash-poor Occidental by offering them shares of the company. Hammer was to use the stock strategy to attract talent in other acquisitions as well.

In 1961 while working with Occidental employees Richard Vaughn, Robert Teitsworth, and the Reids, Hammer took a chance on drilling the Lathrop field, near San Francisco. It had been drilled previously for natural gas by Texaco and other companies, but only to a depth of about 5,600 feet. Reid and the others suggested that there was gas farther down, and at 6,900 feet they were proven correct. Occidental made one of the largest gas finds in California. Over the course of one night, the company found gas worth hundreds of millions of dollars.

By the end of 1961, Occidental was reporting a $1 million profit on revenues of over $4 million. The company's reputation and fortune were bolstered by continued success in natural gas, as well as through more oil finds. By March 1964 Oxy's shares were trading on the New York Stock Exchange.

Through the mid-1960s, Hammer pushed Oxy more and more to occupy an international position. The company built, for example, a superphosphoric-acid plant in England and helped build a $33 million ammonia and urea plant in Saudi Arabia. Oxy also had dealings with other countries, among them Nicaragua, Venezuela, Morocco, and Turkey.

Throughout the 1960s, Hammer kept up negotiations with Libya's King Idris for the use of Libya's natural resources. This persistence was to pay off handsomely. In 1966 Oxy's potential skyrocketed, with a billion-barrel oilfield find in Libya. The find was vintage Hammer, as he wined and dined important Libyan officials and then took a risk on land previously drilled by others. The Libyan oil finds established Oxy as one of the largest petroleum companies in the world. From early 1967

until November of that same year, Oxy's stock doubled in value to more than $100 a share.

Hammer's skills as a negotiator were put to the test when the Libyan king was overthrown in a bloodless coup in 1969 and replaced by the Revolutionary Command Council, soon to be headed by Muammar Qaddafi. Many analysts feared the new government would nationalize the oilfields. However, Hammer negotiated in late 1970 an agreement by which Libya received an immediate increase of 30 cents per barrel of oil, with another ten-cent increase spread over five years. Some industry observers viewed this agreement as the beginning of the end of cheap energy, as other multinational oil companies quickly signed similar agreements with their host countries. Most petroleum-producing countries called for matching increases, and oil prices headed upward.

Wheeling and Dealing in the 1970s–80s

In the early 1970s, Hammer caused a sensation with a $20 billion long-term deal with the Soviets that featured a barter agreement by which Oxy would supply phosphate fertilizer to the U.S.S.R. in exchange for Soviet ammonia and urea. Many in the U.S. government criticized the deal, saying the agreement helped a communist country, despite the fact that the deal was consummated during a period of détente between the United States and the Soviet Union. Hammer, in fact, considered his dealings as détente through trade, and he continued this notion through trade with the Chinese, with whom he began negotiating in 1979. Oxy ended up with two offshore oil exploration and development contracts and a joint agreement to develop a Chinese coal mine.

In 1981 Oxy moved beyond the energy and chemical fields to acquire Iowa Beef Packers (IBP), the largest meatpacker in the United States. IBP cost Oxy $750 million in stock and proved a sound investment; in 1987 Oxy sold 49.5 percent of IBP to the public for $960 million. The astute business deal would be somewhat overshadowed, however, by numerous union strikes over pay and working conditions, as the United Food and Commercial Workers Union maintained Oxy management was unconcerned with workers at the packing plants.

In 1982 Hammer engineered Oxy's $4 billion acquisition of Cities Service Company, a huge domestic oil company headquartered in Oklahoma. The deal was viewed with skepticism by many investment bankers who, as reported in Hammer's autobiography, *Hammer,* regarded it as "Jonah trying to swallow the whale." Nevertheless, the deal made Occidental the eighth largest oil company in the United States and the country's 12th largest industrial concern. One of Hammer's first steps after the acquisition was to sell off those Cities Service units he felt Occidental did not need, resulting in about $1 billion in revenue for Oxy. Some 16,000 jobs were lost as the Cities Service workforce dropped 80 percent.

In late 1985 Hammer made another multibillion-dollar transaction, acquiring Midcon, the huge domestic natural gas pipeline company, for $3 billion. Shortly after the acquisition, the natural gas industry was deregulated. The industry, as a whole, suffered from strong competition because of deregulation, and Occidental was no exception.

Key Dates:

In a reorganization move in May 1986, Occidental Petroleum Corporation of California became a wholly owned subsidiary of the parent company. Corporate headquarters remained in Los Angeles.

The most successful of Oxy's operations during the mid- to late 1980s was its chemical branch, Occidental Chemical (Oxychem). The chemical operations were built largely through the acquisitions of other companies. Occidental purchased holdings from Diamond Shamrock Chemicals in 1986 and from Du Pont and Shell Chemical in 1987, among others. In the five-year period from 1983 through 1987, Oxychem almost doubled its sales to nearly $3 billion. According to J. Roger Hirl, president and chief operating officer of Oxychem, as reported in *Chemical & Engineering News,* Oxy moved into the chemical industry as a balance to its petroleum business. While noting the cyclical nature of both the petroleum and chemical industries, Hirl said they normally were not in parallel cycles.

In 1988 Occidental, spending $2.2 billion to purchase Cain Chemical, moved up to become the nation's sixth largest chemical producer, with sales accounting for almost 25 percent of Oxy's total. Cain Chemical then became known as Oxy Petrochemicals Inc.

The late 1980s brought challenges in the form of environmental litigations. In February 1988 Oxy was found liable for cleaning up the toxic wastes at the country's most infamous landfill, Love Canal in Niagara Falls, New York. After eight years of deliberations, a federal judge ruled that Occidental was responsible for the improper disposal by Hooker Chemical of more than 21,000 tons of chemicals on the site, during the 1940s and 1950s. Occidental had purchased Hooker Chemical in 1968, unaware of the problems that began to surface in 1978. Before the ruling, Oxy had paid $20 million in damages to 1,300 former Love Canal residents, but nothing toward the cleanup of the site. Total cleanup costs were expected to exceed $100 million.

Also during this time, Oxy was hit by a disaster unequaled in oil production history. In July 1988, the company's Piper Alpha offshore oil platform exploded in Britain's North Sea, killing 167 people. The accident panicked the oil market, already made nervous by the continuing Iran-Iraq War. Oil prices were driven up immediately after the accident by as much as $1 a barrel. The accident was thought to be caused by a leak in a pressurized natural gas line that triggered the massive explosion. Occidental immediately shut down the pipeline that served the platform and five others. In August 1989 Oxy resumed North Sea production. The accident was estimated to have cost over $1 billion, including an approximately $183 million settlement with families of the victims and surviving workers.

During 1989 Oxy restructured its domestic oil and gas operations, which resulted in the loss of 900 jobs, the majority from the Oxy Oil and Gas subsidiary's headquarters in Tulsa, Oklahoma. For the year 1989, however, Oxy reported an overall increase of about 1,000 workers, due primarily to expansion at IBP and Oxychem.

Hammer's Last Years

Hammer's decisions did not always please stockholders. One such circumstance centered around Occidental's funding of a $95 million museum to house Hammer's valuable painting collection. The collection was worth an estimated $250 million. Many shareholders did not see the expense of building and operating a museum as serving the best financial interest of the company. The disagreement ended in the courts, in 1990, and although the Armand Hammer Museum of Art and Cultural Center would be built as planned alongside Occidental's corporate headquarters in Los Angeles, the proposed settlement called for limits on the amount of future contributions by Occidental to the museum and to other charities associated with Hammer.

Throughout his career Hammer had been able to attract talented people to Occidental. Nowhere was this more evident than with Ray Irani, the president and chief operating officer during Hammer's last years at Occidental. In 1983 Hammer had convinced Irani, the president of Olin Corporation, to run Oxychem. When Irani took over, Oxychem had an operating loss of $23 million and supplied about 9 percent of Occidental's total sales. In 1989 Oxychem had an operating profit of $1.2 billion and supplied about one-quarter of Oxy's total sales. In February 1990, the board of directors of Occidental proposed Irani as the successor to Armand Hammer as chairman and chief executive officer whenever Hammer should vacate those offices.

In 1989, Occidental reported that 94 percent of its revenues came from domestic operations compared to 55 percent from the same source in 1980. Still, Oxy continued to be involved in large foreign operations. In June 1990, for example, Oxy was the only U.S. company in a four-country agreement to build a $7 billion petrochemical plant in the Soviet Union, the largest-ever joint Soviet-Western project.

Restructuring in the 1990s

When Armand Hammer died at the age of 92 on December 10, 1990, the changeover in command at the top was expected: Ray Irani, president and chief executive officer under Hammer for six years, took over as chairman of the board. Irani worked quickly to get Oxy out from under Hammer's slew of pet projects, many of which had no place in an oil company's portfolio. He sold the meatpacking business, shed Oxy's investments in Arabian horses, got rid of its 5.4 percent stake in the makers of Arm & Hammer baking soda, and canceled a $485,000 contract for a fourth authorized Hammer biography. The University of California agreed to take over the Armand Hammer Museum, which became known as the UCLA Arts Center. Occidental even sold off the ''Codex Hammer,'' a Leonardo Da Vinci manuscript Hammer had bought with $5.6 million of the company's money and renamed for himself. Irani also announced he was canceling the company's billion-dollar petrochemical deal with the Soviet Union. Perhaps most importantly, Irani outlined a strategy to reduce the company's debt load by 40 percent by 1992. Upon Hammer's death, the company's debt stood at a staggering $8.5 billion, and dealing with this was paramount. Irani's strategy called for selling unneeded assets, and also included slashing stockholder dividends to $1 a share from $2.50.

Occidental's restructuring went on in several stages throughout the early 1990s. By the end of 1992, the company had met its first set of goals, reducing its debt by $3 billion. However, Occidental announced that it still intended to cut its costs by $300 million by cutting capital spending, eliminating jobs, and instituting a salary freeze. At the same time, the company dedicated more money to international oil and gas exploration, increasing its production of oil from abroad, with operations in Yemen, Oman, and Ecuador. At that time, about half of the company's revenues came from its chemical business. In 1995, Oxy announced it was simplifying the management of its oil and gas operations in an attempt to grow that business and get away from its dependence on chemicals. Occidental formed a single operating company to take on all its oil and gas business, and then split this into four divisions: exploration, production, enhanced oil recovery, and finance and administration. The company hoped that by focusing its resources, it could both cut costs and improve future earnings.

Occidental's next big move came in 1997. The company spent $3.65 billion to buy a huge oil field, the Naval Petroleum Reserve, from the U.S. government. The naval reserve, called Elk Hills, produced both oil and natural gas. The field, near Bakersfield, California, had been owned by the government since 1900, as a secure source of domestic oil. Deciding it no longer needed the source, the government auctioned the reserve in a deal that was the largest privatization in U.S. history. Occidental bought 78 percent of Elk Hills; the remainder was already owned by Chevron Corporation. To finance this purchase, Oxy decided to sell its MidCon unit, a huge natural gas

pipeline the company operated between the Gulf and western states and Chicago. Oxy soon sold MidCon to KN Energy Inc. for almost $4 billion. The company also sold off various oil production units it judged unnecessary, including properties in Louisiana, Mississippi, and Wyoming. By mid-1998, Occidental had transformed itself into a much more focused company than it had been during Hammer's reign. It had five major oil and gas operations in the United States, including Elk Hills, which was thought to have huge growth potential. For international growth, the company counted on a blossoming oilfield it ran in Qatar. Only about one-third of Occidental was still invested in chemicals, freeing the company somewhat from the volatility of the chemical business cycle.

Occidental in the 21st Century

Occidental's efforts to realign its operations continued as it entered the 21st century. The process of becoming a more focused oil and gas company with large, long-lived oil and gas assets in three primary regions, the United States, the Middle East, and Latin America, meant Occidental needed both to add to its holdings and to strip away those interests deemed outside its new, refined business scope. At the close of the century, the company ended its involvement in Venezuela and the Dutch North Sea and traded its oil and gas interests in the Philippines and Malaysia for Royal Dutch/Shell interests in Yemen and Columbia. The divestitures made room for additions to the company's portfolio, such as the sale of its 29.2 percent interest in Canadian Occidental, which gave Occidental $700 million to complete an important acquisition in 2000. In April, the company purchased Altura Energy Ltd., the largest oil producer in Texas, with proved reserves of 850 million barrels of oil equivalent. The Altura acquisition was a massive deal, a $3.6 billion purchase that made Occidental the largest oil producer in Texas. The acquisition also added substantially to Occidental's debt, which exceeded $6 billion by the end of 2000.

As Occidental entered a new decade, Irani returned to one of Hammer's favorite haunts. When U.S. sanctions against Libya were lifted in the spring of 2004, Irani sent a negotiating team back to the country that had delivered one of Hammer's greatest successes. Occidental was producing 45,000 barrels of oil per day from three fields in 1986, when it was ordered to leave the country. After declaring he had given up his nuclear ambitions, Qaddafi auctioned off exploration rights in the oil-rich Libyan desert, and Irani's lieutenants were there to secure sizeable holdings for Occidental. Of the 15 blocks up for sale, Occidental acquired nine of them, paying dearly for the right to explore for oil. In early 2005, Occidental agreed to pay signing bonuses of $90 million, far more than any other bidder, and the company agreed to give as much as 89 percent of the hydrocarbons it found back to Libya. There were some industry analysts who wondered if Occidental had given up too much to renew its efforts in Libya, but the company was attracted by the easily accessible crude available in the North African desert. In the coming years, it was up to Irani to see if he could replicate Hammer's success and make Libya a major source of Occidental's oil.

Principal Subsidiaries

Centurion Pipeline GP, Inc; Centurion Pipeline LP, Inc.; Centurion Pipeline L.P.; D.S. Ventures, Inc.; Glenn Springs Holdings, Inc.; INDSPEC Chemical Corporation; INDSPEC Holding Corporation; INDSPEC Technologies, Ltd.; Laguna Petroleum Corporation; La Porte Chemicals Corp.; Occidental Andina, LLC; Occidental C.O.B. Partners; Occidental Chemical Chile Limitada; Occidental Chemical Corporation; Occidental Chemical Holding Corporation; Occidental Chemical Nevis, Inc.; Occidental Chile Investments, LLC; Occidental Crude Sales, Inc. (International); Occidental de Colombia, Inc.; Occidental del Ecuador, Inc.; Occidental Dolphin Holdings Ltd. (Bermuda); Occidental Energy Marketing, Inc.; Occidental Exploration and Production Company; Occidental International Holdings Ltd.; Occidental International Oil and Gas Ltd.; Occidental Mexico Holdings, Inc.; Occidental of Elk Hills, Inc.; Occidental of Oman, Inc.; Occidental Oil and Gas Holding Corporation; Occidental Oil and Gas Pakistan LLC; Occidental OOOI Holder, Inc.; Occidental Overseas Operations, Inc.; Occidental Peninsula, Inc.; Occidental Permian Ltd.; Occidental Petroleum (Pakistan), Inc.; Occidental Petroleum Investment Co.; Occidental Petroleum of Qatar Ltd.; Occidental Pipeline Holding Corporation; Occidental PVC LP, Inc.; Occidental Quimica do Brasil Ltda. (Brazil).

Principal Competitors

E.I. du Pont de Nemours and Company; Exxon Mobil Corporation; Royal Dutch/Shell Group of Companies.

Further Reading

Brown, Christie, "The Master Cynic," *Forbes*, October 17, 1994, pp. 364–68.

Bryant, Adam, "At Occidental, So-So Results But Big Pay for the Boss," *New York Times*, March 19, 1998, pp. D1, D8.

Fan, Aliza, "Occidental Plans Broad Restructuring to Save Firm $100 Million per Year," *Oil Daily*, October 26, 1995, p. 1.

Fritsch, Peter, "Occidental Plans $3.65 Billion Purchase," *Wall Street Journal*, October 7, 1997, pp. A3, A6.

Glover, Kara, "Ray Irani Brings New Ways to Occidental," *Los Angeles Business Journal*, March 23, 1992, p. 12.

Hammer, Armand, and Neil Lyndon, *Hammer*, New York: G.P. Putnam's Sons, 1987.

Helman, Christopher, "Oxy Moron?," *Forbes*, February 28, 2005, p. 46.

Marcial, Gene G., "To the Shores of Tripoli?," *Business Week*, February 16, 2004, p. 97.

"Occidental Awarded Nine Exploration Blocks in Libya," *PrimeZone Media Network*, January 31, 2005, p. 32.

"Oxy Chief Sees Return to Libya This Year," *Oil Daily*, January 25, 2005.

"Oxy Makeover Continues," *International Petroleum Finance*, August 2001, p. 14.

Rundle, Rhonda, "Occidental Acts to Pare Further Its 1993 Costs," *Wall Street Journal*, November 20, 1992, p. A3.

Shook, Barbara, "Chevron Settles with Oxy for $775 Million," *Oil Daily*, November 19, 1999, p. 31.

——, "Oxy Nears Emergence from Restructuring As Simpler Company with New Profile," *Oil Daily*, April 1, 1998, p. 62.

"'Treason' Ups Political Heat," *LatAm Energy*, October 6, 2004, p. 1.

Waldner, Erin, "Occidental Petroleum's Earnings Balloon in Fourth Quarter," *Bakersfield Californian*, January 25, 2005, p. B2.

Weinberg, Steve, *Armand Hammer: The Untold Story*, Boston: Little, Brown and Company, 1989.

—Mark Uri Toch
—updates: A. Woodward; Jeffrey L. Covell

OPPENHEIMER
OPPENHEIMER WOLFF & DONNELLY LLP

Oppenheimer Wolff & Donnelly LLP

Plaza VII, Suite 3300
45 S. 7th Street
Minneapolis, Minnesota 55402
U.S.A.
Telephone: (612) 607-7000
Fax: (612) 607-7100
Web site: http://www.oppenheimer.com

Private Partnership
Founded: 1886 as Lawler and Durment
Employees: 120
Operating Revenues: $102.0 million (2004 est.)
NAIC: 541110 Law Offices

Oppenheimer Wolff & Donnelly LLP offers its legal expertise to businesses operating everything from manufacturing to food to nanotechnology and ranging in size from start-up to global giant. While its scope of services is broad, Oppenheimer has special expertise in the area of technology, a practice that has brought the firm both good times and bad.

River City Roots: 1880s–1950s

The roots of Oppenheimer Wolff & Donnelly LLP were sown in St. Paul, Minnesota, in the late 19th century. Daniel W. Lawler and Edmund S. Durment established a law practice in the river town in 1886. The railroad industry provided business opportunities in those early days. William H. Oppenheimer joined the firm in 1913. Virginia L. Martin wrote in *Oppenheimer Wolff & Donnelly and Its 111-Year History,* "Will Oppenheimer put his imprimatur on the little firm so indelibly that not even its incredible growth, major changes in the law, in the firm itself, and in technology have entirely erased it more than eighty years later." Moreover, Oppenheimer and various firm partners would play important roles in the development of the upper Mississippi River town during the early years of the 20th century.

By 1925, with its early partners gone, the firm became Oppenheimer Dickson Hodgson Brown and Donnelly, the second largest law practice in St. Paul. While individual practice

brought in much of the firm's revenues well into the mid-20th century, Will Oppenheimer built a cache of corporate clients from the 1920s through the 1950s, including The St. Paul Companies, Economics Laboratories (Ecolab), and Brown and Bigelow. But work for a start-up computer company proved to be pivotal.

According to Martin, "Control Data Company (CDC) played two important roles in Oppenheimer Wolff & Donnelly's growth: First it retained the firm as general counsel, initiating a major hiring frenzy; twenty years later, it began hiring its own in-house legal staff, drastically reducing the amount of work the company gave the firm and forcing it to undergo a major reassessment of its path."

The Oppenheimer firm first defended CDC (now Ceridian Corporation) when it faced litigation during the late 1950s into the early 1960s, directed at it from Sperry Rand Corporation (Unisys), the former employer of many CDC executives. But a much larger CDC case followed.

CDC brought an antitrust lawsuit against IBM in 1976. A total of 30 full- and part-time attorneys plus 125 paralegals were engaged in the research and discovery phase of the case. Settled in CDC's favor in 1972, the case drew considerable press coverage and gave the firm national attention.

Oppenheimer's work with CDC on the IBM suit led to the establishment of an office in Brussels in 1969. The city was the home of CDC's European headquarters and became the site of the firm's first expansion outside St. Paul. In 1973, Oppenheimer crossed the river into Minneapolis, opening an office in the new IDS Tower downtown.

Time of Transformation: 1980s

By 1979, Oppenheimer's work with CDC had tapered off. The early 1980s marked a period of change for the company and the legal profession. Oppenheimer began its "transformation from a small law firm to a large international firm," observed Martin. In terms of the legal profession, the number of women practicing law began to grow rapidly, and new types of practices, such as environmental law, were being initiated.

Company Perspectives:

Our Values: All across our firm, Oppenheimer attorneys and staff subscribe to the same set of core values: Relationship-based Client Service; Talent-based Quality; Innovation; Respect: Entrepreneurial Spirit; Team Mindset; Diversity.

Oppenheimer opened its third office in 1983, in Washington, D.C. Offices in New York and Chicago followed three years later, expanding practice areas and diversifying the firm's clientele. Also in 1986, Oppenheimer grew its Minneapolis operation, merging with another of that city's firms. A second international office opened in 1988, in Paris.

In 1977, the U.S. Supreme Court had ruled that attorneys could advertise, subject to state bar association rules. Many law firms were slow to jump on the bandwagon, concerned about the reaction of potential and current clients. But as the number of lawyers grew—725,000 in the U.S. by 1990—so did the need to compete for business. Oppenheimer hired its first marketing director in 1987.

In 1989, as part of an effort to raise the firm's profile and client numbers, Oppenheimer sponsored a dinner with Boris Yeltsin, then deputy to the Supreme Soviet. The following year Polish Solidarity labor union leader Lech Walesa met exclusively with Oppenheimer clients interested in doing business with Poland. ''Both are part of the firm's Eastern European strategy that includes seminars, newsletters and client briefing,'' wrote Carol Kleiman of the *Chicago Tribune*. Oppenheimer Marketing Director James C. Bilwas was quick to point out that high-visibility visits were part of an overall marketing plan. Other activities ranged from producing videos to educating the company's lawyers in marketing techniques. During 1991 the firm ran ads in the *Wall Street Journal,* a move to mitigate the confusion on the part of the public over the two Oppenheimer entities: the law firm and the financial company.

From 1985 to 1991, led by Thomas Kane as managing partner, the number of Oppenheimer attorneys nearly doubled. After six years of aggressive expansion, Kane was voted out of the position. Kane, a 25-year veteran of the firm, planned to stay on as a practicing attorney. But the marketing director who had helped raise the firm's local profile during the period departed.

The shift in leadership had been preceded by the exodus of more than two dozen attorneys. The attrition rate of 12 percent in the course of the year exceeded that of the city's other large law firms. According to *Minneapolis-St. Paul CityBusiness,* the culture of the firm had changed during the period of rapid growth. The influx of new attorneys drove up the level of competition for a coveted role as firm partner.

In the industry at large, growth had been flat. Business declines on the coasts had resulted in layoffs and the culling of attorneys failing to generate business. As for Oppenheimer, its real estate and merger and acquisition work had fallen off, but the firm was elevating its intellectual property and employment law efforts.

Donald Engle, the new managing partner, who had served for 35 years as corporate lawyer for Burlington Northern Inc., looked for a 20 percent increase in revenues by 1993. He envisioned Oppenheimer—the Twin Cities' number three law firm—among the top 75 law firms in the nation.

Technology Driven: The 1990s

An expansion drive begun in 1996 was driven in large part by the technology boom. Oppenheimer entered California in early 1997 via merger with intellectual property firm Poms, Smith, Lande & Rose. Another group of intellectual property attorneys came over from Bronson, Bronson & McKinnon, joining the Oppenheimer Silicon Valley office. Oppenheimer further grew its corporate practice in California during 1998, to keep pace with the rapidly expanding tech industry. The firm merged with Newport Beach-based Bruck & Perry but retained the Oppenheimer Wolff & Donnelly name. The Asian market also became more viable with a significant West Coast location.

On the opposite coast, Oppenheimer merged its Washington, D.C. office with Bayh, Connaughton & Steward, P.C. in 1998, creating Oppenheimer Wolff Donnelly & Bayh LLP. Former U.S. Senator Birch Bayh continued his practice within the combined entity. ''The merger strengthens Oppenheimer's established practice areas and greatly expands the government relations capability of the firm's international network,'' a *PR Newswire* article of April 1998 reported. The D.C. and California mergers were part of an expansion drive begun in 1996.

The 1998 version of the 100-year-old-plus firm consisted of 300 attorneys with offices in Amsterdam, Brussels, Chicago, Geneva, Los Angeles, Minneapolis, New York, Orange County, Paris, St. Paul, Silicon Valley, and Washington, D.C. Strategic alliances were set up in Milan and Rome.

Oppenheimer's expansion of its intellectual law practice garnered the company some of its own legal problems in 1999. Graham & James claimed that Oppenheimer had lured attorneys away from its firm. Oppenheimer closed its two-year-old San Jose office and moved to Palo Alto. Twenty Oppenheimer attorneys were practicing intellectual property law in the Silicon Valley. In 1998, more than one-quarter of the firm's $88 million in revenue had come from intellectual property practice, according to the *Star Tribune* (Minneapolis).

Technology Making a U-Turn: 2000s

During 2000, Oppenheimer earned the distinction as the first Minnesota firm to enter the realm of fee-based online services. Targeting the Internet industry—those clients who were already at home on the Web—the firm offered an ''opinion of patentability'' for a flat fee of $500. An Internet patent infringement assessment for $1,000 was also ready to fly. Oppenheimer employed more than 35 intellectual property attorneys nationally. Requests for computer-related patents had climbed in the United States, rising from 1,300 to 2,600 from 1998 to 1999, according to the *Star Tribune.*

Concurrently, tech-related business failures were on the upswing. On the one hand, the situation increased business opportunities for Oppenheimer Wolff & Donnelly. During the 1990s

Key Dates:

1886: Daniel W. Lawler and Edmund S. Durment found a law firm in St. Paul, Minnesota.
1913: William H. Oppenheimer joins the firm.
1925: The firm is renamed Oppenheimer Dickson Hodgson Brown and Donnelly.
1957: The firm takes on start-up company Control Data Corporation (CDC) as a client.
1968: The CDC antitrust lawsuit against IBM is initiated.
1972: Oppenheimer is nationally known for work with technology companies.
1973: The firm relocates to Minneapolis.
1983: Oppenheimer opens a Washington, D.C. office, beginning a geographical expansion drive.
1996: Another expansion drive begins, with growth on both the East and West Coasts.
2001: The technology industry meltdown devastates the firm's intellectual property practice.
2003: The firm's offices outside of Minneapolis are closed.

the firm had developed business in the area of restructuring public companies, preparing them for the escalation of bankruptcies on both coasts. But dot-com failures had a withering effect on NASDAQ and the flow of private capital into the high-tech industry.

Michael Bleck, who had led Oppenheimer's drive to the technology track, retired from his position as CEO in 2001. One hundred attorneys practiced in California. Technology clients were bringing in more than half of the firm's revenue. Under Bleck's six years of leadership, Oppenheimer's revenue had grown from $60 million to $120 million, according to the *Star Tribune.*

The technology meltdown devastated Oppenheimer's intellectual property practice. The firm closed its Palo Alto office at the end of May 2003 and concurrently shut the doors in New York. Amid rumors about the firm's demise, Oppenheimer determined that it would downsize, leaving only its Minneapolis office open. "Its offices in Paris, Brussels and Geneva are for sale, office furniture included," reported David Phelps for the *Star Tribune* in June 2003. The Orange County office was scheduled to close in mid-July.

While Oppenheimer ranked fifth among Twin Cities law firms in 2002, the reorganization dropped the firm to about tenth in size, with about 120 attorneys in Minneapolis. The firm had left the city of its birth, St. Paul, entirely during 2000. Since Oppenheimer's Minneapolis office had continued to pull in profits even as the satellite offices struggled, the partners believed the firm could continue on successfully as a local firm.

The new and much smaller Oppenheimer Wolff & Donnelly achieved its revenue goals during the year following the reorganization, according to a September 2004 *ABA* article. Continued stability, not a return to growth, was in its immediate future.

Principal Competitors

Cooley Godward; Howrey Simon Arnold & White.

Further Reading

Beal, Dave, "Dave Beal Column," *Saint Paul Pioneer Press,* August 31, 2003.

Chanen, Jill Schachner, "Back from the Brink," *ABA Journal,* September 2004, pp. 34+.

Hoogesteger, John, "Bankruptcy Wave May Follow Tech Cash Trouble," *CityBusiness* (Minneapolis), June 30, 2000, p. 1.

Jean, Sheryl, "Need E-Commerce Advice? Oppenheimer Goes Online," *CityBusiness* (Minneapolis), February 18, 2000, p. 1.

Kleiman, Carol, "Marketing Becomes More in Evidence at Law Firms," *Chicago Tribune,* April 1, 1990, p. 1.

Martin, Virginia L., "Oppenheimer Wolff & Donnelly and Its 111-Year History," *Ramsey County History,* Spring 1997, pp. 4–21.

Nissen, Todd, "Oppenheimer Wolff Feels Growing Pains," *Minneapols-St. Paul CityBusiness,* November 25, 1991, pp. 1+.

"Oppenheimer Expands in California; Grows Silicon Valley Office & Merges with Newport Beach Firm," *PR Newswire,* June 29, 1998.

"Oppenheimer Expands in Washington, D.C.," *PR Newswire,* April 1, 1998, p. 1.

Phelps, David, "Oppenheimer Downsizes, Will Stay in Minneapolis," *Star Tribune* (Minneapolis), June 10, 2003, p. 1D.

——, "Oppenheimer Firm in Legal Dispute Over Expansion," *Star Tribune* (Minneapolis), August 21, 1999, p. 2D.

St. Anthony, Neal, "Tech Slump to Last a While, Execs Say," *Star Tribune* (Minneapolis), March 3, 2001, p. 1D.

Smith, Martin J., "Law Firms' New Tack PR Campaigns Become Necessary in a Competitive Market," *Orange County Register,* August 21, 1991, p. C01.

—Kathleen Peippo

Palm Management Corporation

1730 Rhode Island Avenues, NW, Suite 900
Washington, D.C. 20036
U.S.A.
Telephone: (2020) 775-7256
Toll Free: (800) 795-7256
Fax: (202) 775-9153
Web site: http://www.thepalm.com

Private Company
Founded: 1926
Employees: 1,600
Sales: $125 million (2003 est.)
NAIC: 722110 Full-Service Restaurants

Palm Management Corporation operates 30 upscale steakhouses in major U.S. cities, Mexico, and Puerto Rico, as well as a pair of inns located in the Hamptons area of Long Island. Now based in Washington, D.C., The Palm originated in New York City, where it grew into an institution, known for its huge steaks and lobsters, sawdust strewn floors, walls covered with caricatures of celebrities and prized customers, and theatrical waiters. After expanding to only Washington, D.C., and Los Angeles during the Palm's first 50 years, The Palm has since opened satellite eateries in most major U.S. cities, transferring as much of the charm of the original restaurant, including caricatures of local notables and the gregarious waiters, but forgoing the sawdust on the floors due to local health regulations. Palm Management also operates a mail-order meat business, Palm Pak. The company is owned and operated by the third and fourth generations of The Palm's founding families.

The Palm Dating to the Prohibition Era

The Palm's founders were Pio Bozzi and John Ganzi, immigrants from the Parma region of Italy who met in New York in 1920. They decided to open a restaurant in 1926 at 837 Second Avenue between 44th and 45th streets in the Kips Bay section of Manhattan, what was then an Italian neighborhood and the heart of New York's newspaper district. According to lore, the partners planned to name the restaurant after their native Parma, but when they applied for a business license, a bureaucrat unable, or unwilling, to decipher their thick Italian accents typed in "Palm" as the name of the establishment. Given that The Palm was to become known for its steaks and not its Italian food, the misunderstanding proved to be a stroke of good fortune. Bozzi and Ganzi intended to specialize in northern Italian cuisine, but they were willing to adapt to the times and the taste of their clientele. The Palm started out as a speakeasy during the Prohibition era, serving drinks as well as Italian food, a perfect combination to appeal to the newspaper employees in the neighborhood. When some of the newspapermen wanted an occasional steak, Ganzi was more than willing to please, known to scurry up Second Avenue to a local butcher to buy a steak and then rush back to the kitchen to cook it to order.

The Palm also became a hangout for syndicated newspaper cartoonists, who sold their works to nearby King Features Syndicate, or to Hearst, UPI, and the *Mirror*. For many cartoonists it was a hand-to-mouth existence. Each Wednesday, "look day," the cartoonists peddled their work to magazine editors, and whether they were able to sell their work determined if they could afford to eat. Often The Palm traded a plate of spaghetti for a copy of a freshly drawn cartoon character it could put up on the wall. Since Bozzi and Ganzi could not afford to decorate their place, it was considered a fair trade. The practice evolved into the artists creating a caricature of a famous person or favorite Palm customer. Unlike another New York institution, Sardi's, which mounted framed celebrity caricatures, The Palm simply glued their pictures to the wall in a haphazard manner, lending a comfortable, fraternal air to the restaurant. What started out as a simple bartering arrangement evolved into a tradition, complete with an unveiling ceremony. The Palm values the original artwork so much that it is insured for $500,000.

With the repeal of Prohibition in the early 1930s, The Palm shed its speakeasy existence. It also established itself as an excellent steakhouse, although Italian food remained on the menu. In the early 1940s, the founders stepped down, replaced by their sons, Walter Ganzi and Bruno Bozzi. They brought "surf and turf" to The Palm with the introduction of the three-pound lobster to the menu. Somehow they were able to maintain a supply of steak during the war years of the 1940s, little hindered by meat shortages caused by World War II. Thus The Palm continued to grow its steakhouse reputation, and was so prosperous that during the postwar skyscraper building boom that came to Kips Bay it was able to resist attractive buyout offers and remain in its original location.

Third Generation Becoming Involved in the 1960s

A third generation of the founding families, Bruce Bozzi, Jr., and Wally Ganzi, Jr., came to work at The Palm in 1963 and were instrumental in helping the restaurant to adapt to a changing culture. At the time, New York steakhouses maintained a strict jacket-and-tie dress code. To appeal to a younger market, The Palm eliminated these dress restrictions. In addition, the younger family members made The Palm more open to women, who until that time were almost never seen in the restaurant during lunch. Bruce Bozzi also was credited during this period with introducing the four-pound lobster to The Palm menu, dispelling the notion that larger meant tougher when it came to lobster. As a result, the sale of lobster at The Palm increased dramatically, transforming the image of The Palm into a steak and seafood restaurant. In 1967 the crowded restaurant expanded, opening a second floor dining room. A group of syndicated newspaper cartoonists, at the cost of drinks and lunch, decorated the room with sketches, which one of them arranged to paint. A newly hired busboy, however, mistook the art for graffiti and washed down the walls, necessitating a second round of free drinks and lunch to decorate the new Palm dining room.

The second generation owners of The Palm retired in the late 1960s, leaving the business in the hands of younger, more aggressively minded family members, who would seek to spread The Palm concept. The first move was to Washington, D.C., an idea suggested by George H. Bush, future president of the United States who at the time was the U.S. ambassador to the United Nations, the headquarters of which was located several blocks from The Palm. Bush decried the lack of hearty American fare in capital-area restaurants and urged Ganzi and Bozzi to open a Palm restaurant in Washington. He and several friends each invested $10,000 to launch the new eatery in 1972. It quickly established itself as a place where the city's power brokers convened. In the meantime, the original Kips Bay restaurant continued to thrive, prompting the owners in 1973 to open another Palm Restaurant, Palm Too, across Second Avenue to handle the overflow from the flagship unit.

The fourth Palm Restaurant, located in Los Angeles, was launched once again at the behest of a customer, author William Peter Blatty of *The Exorcist* fame. Because the story was set in

the Georgetown section of Washington, D.C., when the novel was transferred to the screen much of the filming was done on location. Blatty adopted the D.C. Palm as his personal haunt and soon began urging management to open a Palm Restaurant in Los Angeles to cater to its own brand of power brokers. To prove his seriousness he put up $600,000 of his own money. Ganzi and Bozzi agreed and launched a search for a suitable site in Beverly Hills. After a deal fell through, however, they turned their attention to a less exclusive part of town, West Hollywood, where they found a ramshackle, erstwhile auto parts store on Santa Monica Boulevard. The Los Angeles Palm opened in 1975 to little fanfare. A Hollywood publicist was paid to bring his clients to dine—including Farrah Fawcett Majors, who was starring in the hit television series *Charlie's Angels,* and her husband, Lee Majors, star of another series, *The Six Million Dollar Man*—and soon other celebrities began to trickle in. The buzz about The Palm reached critical mass and was soon on its way to making the restaurant a bi-coastal institution. Blatty's faith in the concept was rewarded, as he eventually sold out to Ganzi and Bozzi for $2 million in the 1980s. It was also at the Washington Palm that Ganzi began to relocate himself and his family to the city of a new operation, a practice that would prove taxing over the next 15 years. Bozzi, in the meantime, continued to run the New York operations from offices located above the original restaurant.

With four successful restaurants in the fold, The Palm no longer required the prompting of its patrons to continue its expansion efforts, despite the declining popularity of red meat in the United States (per-capita consumption dropped from 94.4 pounds in 1976 to 77.6 pounds six years later). In 1977 a Palm Restaurant opened in Houston, the Ganzi family residence for two years. Two years later the Palm concept was transplanted to the Hamptons when the company opened a restaurant at the Huntting Inn, also owned by Ganzi and Bozzi, located in a 300-year-old building in trendy East Hampton, a town known for its share of celebrities, including the likes of Billy Joel, Calvin Klein, and Robert De Niro. To serve its growing chain of restaurants, Palm Management acquired its own meat purveyor during the 1970s.

The next Palm Restaurant was opened in 1980 in Chicago, housed in the posh Regent Hotel. A year later a Palm Restaurant opened in Miami, quickly becoming a favorite for transplanted New Yorkers and snowbirds as well as locals. After a Dallas location opened in 1983, The Palm began to slow the pace. The next Palm Restaurant, the chain's tenth, opened in San Francisco on the ground floor of the Hotel Juliana in February 1986. Unlike other locations, however, the Palm concept did not find as fertile ground in the Bay Area. Management tried a number of measures to adapt to the culture, offering smaller steaks and adding more seafood and poultry dishes, but The Palm was never fully embraced by San Franciscan diners. After four years, when the hotel changed owners, The Palm was unable to come to terms on a new lease and management opted to shut down the operation in the summer of 1990.

Third Generation Easing Involvement in the Late 1980s

Ganzi and Bozzi started one more restaurant during the 1980s, opening a Palm in Philadelphia, Pennsylvania, in 1989,

Key Dates:

1926: Pio Bozzi and John Ganzi open New York's Palm Restaurant.
1967: The restaurant opens a second floor dining room.
1972: The Washington, D.C., Palm opens.
1975: The Los Angeles Palm opens.
1983: The Palm Restaurant opens in Dallas.
1990: Alfred Thimm is named chief operating officer.
1996: Restaurants are opened in Boston, Denver, and Chicago.
1999: The third New York City Palm opens in Times Square.
2002: The second Los Angeles Palm Restaurant opens.
2004: The Atlantic City Palm opens.

but the partners, after nearly 40 years of running the business, were growing tired. Bozzi wanted to spend more time with his family and Ganzi, with politics, and to gain some much needed relief from the nomadic life he had been leading since the early 1970s. (It was also during the late 1980s that Palm Management moved its headquarters to Washington, D.C., to be closer to its accountant.) In need of someone to assume day-to-day control of The Palm chain, they decided to recruit a chief operating officer and asked Bozzi's son-in-law, Alfred L. Thimm, Jr., if he was interested in taking on the job.

Thimm's association with The Palm dated to his college years, when as a senior studying modern languages at Union College in Schenectady, New York, he became a part-time server at the East Hampton Palm to earn some extra money while visiting a girlfriend. Having worked at other upstate restaurants, he became enamored of the Palm mystique, so much so that he traveled hundreds of miles to work occasional shifts during his final months as an undergraduate. The son of teachers, Thimm continued his education in Germany but, unsure of what to do with his life, he returned to East Hampton and worked at The Palm during the summers. In the winter, he shifted to Florida, waiting tables at The Palm in Miami. Finally he heeded his family's call and enrolled in the University of Denver's M.B.A. program, concentrating on hotel and restaurant management. It was during this time that he began dating Bozzi's daughter, Andrea, whom he had met originally during his days at East Hampton. After graduation, they were married and he worked for four years with Boston-based Laventhol & Howath's Management Advisory Service, involved in lodging and restaurant consulting work. Then in 1989 he went to work for David Berins and Co., which then became part of Arthur Anderson & Co.'s Real Estate Advisory Group, for which he led several hospitality consulting projects.

Despite his affection for The Palm, when Ganzi called to inquire about his interest in the COO position, he was hesitant to go to work for his wife's family. He finally agreed and began the task of bringing a modern corporate infrastructure to The Palm, which at the time still relied on handwritten checks and lacked a point-of-sales system. According to a 2002 profile in *Nation's Restaurant News*, ''Over time, Thimm would introduce a modern management system, including a uniform sys-

tem of accounts, an innovative, direct-mail marketing plan, a system to update the aging restaurants and a revamped bonus plan for management.'' He encountered some resistance from old-timers Ganzi and Bozzi, but eventually won them over, and after a couple of years The Palm was ready once again to resume its expansion.

In 1993 The Palm opened a restaurant in Las Vegas at the Forum Shops in Caesars Palace, quickly establishing itself as one of the most successful units in the entire chain. Two years later a Palm Restaurant opened in Atlanta's trendy Buckhead district, in the Westin Buckhead hotel, where it became the only Palm location to offer breakfast and a separate bar, The Palm Bar Two. In 1996, The Palm opened two restaurants: in Boston, in the Westin Hotel, Copley Place, located in Boston's Back Bay district; and in Denver, in the Westin Hotel at Tabor Center. The Chicago-area Palm also changed hotels in 1996 to the Swissotel. A year later The Palm opened a restaurant in Charlotte, North Carolina, in the Phillips Place shopping center. In 1998 the concept moved beyond the border when a new Palm Restaurant was opened in Puerto Rico in the El San Juan Hotel and Casino. The chain closed out the 1990s by establishing a unit in Mexico City's Presidente Inter-Continental Hotel and revisiting established markets, opening a restaurant in Tysons Corner, Virginia, to serve the corridor of high-tech companies located in the Washington, D.C., area and adding a third New York City location, this one in the revitalized Times Square district.

As a new century dawned, The Palm continued to expand. In 2000 it opened three restaurants: a third Texas Palm, in San Antonio, as well as a second restaurant/inn located in East Hampton (the James Lane Café at the Hedges Inn) and the first restaurant in Nashville. In 2001 The Palm celebrated its 75th anniversary by opening three more restaurants: in Orlando, Florida, in the Hard Rock Hotel at Universal Studios; in Tampa Bay at the Westshore Plaza; and in Troy, Michigan, to take advantage of recent office development in Troy and Auburn Hills. A second international Palm was opened in Cancun, Mexico, in 2002, as was a second Los Angeles restaurant located close to the new Staples Center. In addition, The Palm opened a restaurant in Coral Gables, Florida, in 2002.

While The Palm saw its business adversely impacted by a downturn in the economy, the deleterious effects that the terrorist attacks of September 11, 2001, had on travel and tourism, and record beef prices, the chain persevered, although it put a temporary hold on its expansion program. Then, in the fall of 2004, The Palm Restaurant opened its 28th location, this one in The Quarter at Tropicana, a mall attached to the Tropicana hotel and casino. In 2005 restaurants opened in Atlantic City and the Gas Lamp district of San Diego, close to the new baseball park.

Principal Subsidiaries

JORM Supply Corporation; Palm Pak.

Principal Competitors

Morton's Restaurant Group, Inc.; Ruth's Chris Steak House, Inc.; The Smith and Wollensky Restaurant Group, Inc.

Further Reading

Frumkin, Paul, ''Palm Prexy Thimm,'' *Nation's Restaurant News,* May 13, 2002, p. 8.

——, ''2002 Golden Chain: Alfred L. Thimm Jr.,'' *Nation's Restaurant News,* September 30, 2002, p. 65.

——, ''West Side Is Best for Latest Times Square-Based Palm,'' *Nation's Restaurant News,* August 2, 1999, p. 80.

Jensen, Elizabeth, ''Sizzling Rivalry: Upscale Steakhouses Get into a Beef War As Chains Grow Fast,'' *Wall Street Journal,* December 24, 1997, p. A1.

Kapner, Suzann, ''The Palm Celebrates 70th Year,'' *Nation's Restaurant News,* June 10, 1996, p. 21.

—Ed Dinger

Paloma Industries Ltd.

6-23 Momozono-cho, Mizuho-ku
Nagoya
467-8585
Japan
Telephone: +81 52 824 5031
Fax: +81 52 824 4366
Web site: http://www.paloma.co.jp

Private Company
Incorporated: 1911
Employees: 10,400
Sales: ¥240 billion ($2.01 billion) (2004)
NAIC: 333414 Heating Equipment (Except Electric and
    Warm Air Furnaces) Manufacturing

Paloma Industries Ltd. is one of the world's leading producers of gas-powered water heaters, boilers, and other appliances. Based in Nagoya, Japan, Paloma has pioneered energy-efficient water heater designs, including the "tankless" water heater, which, because it provides instantaneous hot water, does not require large water tanks. Paloma produces a variety of appliances, primarily for the domestic market, including gas cooking stoves, gas rice cookers, gas space heaters, and bath heating systems, as well as swimming pool heating systems. The company also manufactures air conditioners for the residential market and appliances for industrial and commercial use, as well as road heating systems for public works and other projects. Since the late 1980s, Paloma also has been a force on the international heating market, through its acquisition of the United States' Rheem Manufacturing Company, based in New York, and one of the global central heating and cooling leaders. Paloma also has been acquiring other members of the Rheem licensing group, including Rheem operations in Canada, Mexico, and Singapore, and, since 2002, in Australia and New Zealand. In addition to Rheem, Paloma's international operations include Raypak in the United States and Canada. Paloma Industries is a private company, controlled by the founding Kobayashi family and led by President Toshihiro Kobayashi. In 2004 the company's sales topped ¥240 billion ($2 billion).

Founding a Gas Appliance Leader in the Early 20th Century

Paloma Industries had its start in Nagoya shortly after the dawn of the 20th century. Gas-powered lighting systems had been in use in Japan since being introduced in Osaka in the early 1870s. By the close of the century, most of Japan's major cities had been outfitted with gas-lighting and gas distribution networks, and in 1906 Nagoya, too, opened its gas grid. The new utility provided an opportunity for a new range of business and appliances beyond lighting fixtures.

In 1911, Saburo Kobayashi founded a company for the production of gas-powered appliances, launching a line of water heaters and room heaters. In 1931, the company changed its name to Kobayashi Factory, and in 1933, the next generation of the Kobayashi family, in the form of Shin Kobayashi, took over as head of the company. By 1938, the company had outgrown its original site and added a new production plant in Nagoya, in Mizuho Ku. Soon after, however, Japan's entry into World War II forced the company to suspend production.

Kobayashi resumed production in 1945 almost directly following the end of the war. The company began an effort to expand its production in the postwar period, widening its range and adopting a new brand name, Paloma, in 1952. The company now extended its sales beyond the Nagoya region, quickly developing the Paloma name into a nationally known gas appliance brand. During this period Kobayashi expanded its line of appliances, adding stoves in the early 1950s and, in 1958, a new generation of gas rice cookers.

By the early 1960s, the Paloma brand had become quite well known in Japan, and the company decided to establish a dedicated, independent company, Paloma Industrial Corporation, in 1964. That company later developed into the flagship of what became known as the Paloma Group. In 1968, Paloma added a second factory, in Fukuoka. The company had by then earned recognition for the innovation and quality of its products, win-

Company Perspectives:

Ever since our founding in 1911, Paloma has consistently continued to maintain an unflinching stance about one thing: providing our clientele with products that put priority on safety above all else. No matter how sophisticated or easy to use it may be, we believe that only true technology is also furnished with safety.

People make mistakes. That's precisely why it's Paloma's unchanging corporate mission to adopt this stance in our quest for responsible technology. As a manufacturer, we must engage in product development that is grounded in good conscience as we actively strive to ensure safety.

For this reason, we have always placed safety before cost and productivity. We have established our own stringent standards for safety and tackled safety measures before all else. We have brought into the world such innovations as flame-failure safety devices for portable gas cooking stoves and oxygen depletion safety shut-off devices for gas water heaters. In this way and others, we're seizing the initiative to enlighten the entire industry about safety.

In bringing reliance and comfort into people's daily lives, Paloma's reliable and safe technology makes no compromise. The form and specs of our products are an eloquent testimonial to this.

Key Dates:

1911: Saburo Kobayashi founds the company to produce gas-powered appliances in Nagoya.
1931: The company name becomes Kobayashi Factory.
1933: Son Shin Kobayashi takes over as head of the company.
1938: A second factory is constructed in Nagoya.
1952: The Paloma brand name is launched.
1964: The company name is changed to Paloma Industries.
1973: Paloma Industries Inc. is established in Chicago.
1988: Paloma acquires Rheem Manufacturing Co. in the United States.
1993: Paloma opens a new factory in Hokkaido.
1994: Rheem adds a new production facility in Arkansas.
1998: Paloma opens a new complex in Tokyo.
2002: Paloma and Rheem acquire the Australia, New Zealand, and China water heater operations from Southcorp Holdings.
2004: Paloma reports sales of ¥240 billion ($2 billion).

ning, for example, a design award from the Ministry of Trade and Industry, for a newly launched gas rice cooker in 1972.

International Growth in the 1980s

Paloma entered the international market in the early 1970s, launching a subsidiary in the United States, in Chicago, in 1973 in order to introduce its gas water heaters to the U.S. market. The company remained an innovator in the field, particularly in the development of safety devices and energy efficiency technologies for its gas-powered appliances. In 1977 the company launched a new system for preventing incomplete combustion in its water heaters. The company marked another industry first in 1985 with the début of a pulsating combustion unit that provided greater fuel efficiency. The company then adapted its pulse technology to a line of boilers in 1986.

Despite its presence in the United States for more than a decade, the majority of Paloma's sales remained in Japan into the late 1980s. The company began to make headway into the United States toward the middle of the decade, with its line of instantaneous water heaters. Also known as tankless water heaters, this water heating system eliminated the need for large boilers, which, because they continuously heated water in a reservoir, were not very fuel-efficient. Paloma's instantaneous system provided hot water only at the rate it was being used.

In the late 1980s, Paloma found a new means for expanding its international presence. In 1988, the company agreed to pay more than $770 million to acquire Rheem Manufacturing Co., based in New York. The purchase gave Paloma control of one of the U.S. market's top producers of central heating and

cooling systems. Rheem also produced water heaters, boilers, and steam boilers, with total company sales of more than $800 million.

Rheem was founded in California in the mid-1920s by brothers Donald and Richard Rheem. The Rheems originally operated a galvanizing plant in San Francisco, producing oil drums and other containers. In the early 1930s, Rheem opened a new plant in Los Angeles, producing water heaters. Rheem quickly became a national brand name, with sales across the United States. The company also turned to the international market early on. In 1939 Rheem formed a 50–50 joint venture with Australia's BHP, setting up a factory in Waterloo.

Rheem expanded its product range in the 1940s and 1950s, adding oil furnaces, air conditioners, and space heaters. The company continued to seek new markets, establishing subsidiaries in Chile and Singapore in the 1970s. By then, however, Rheem had sold off parts of its global network, including its share of its Australia operations, to BHP in 1973. Rheem Australia later was acquired by South Australian Brewing Holdings (later known as Southcorp Limited) in 1988.

Global Network in the New Century

Back at home, Paloma continued to build up its domestic operations. In 1988, the company opened its research and development laboratory in Sapporo. The company began building a new factory, in Hokkaido Noboribetsu, which was completed in 1993. The company also began building a new headquarters, which was finished in 1995. Then, in 1998, the company expanded into the Tokyo area with the construction of the Paloma Plaza building in Minato-ku. Leading the company now was a new generation of the founding family, represented by Toshihiro Kobayashi.

Rheem also expanded as part of the Paloma group, opening a new production facility in Arkansas in 1994. The company added Raypac, based in California, a maker of heating systems for swimming pools and spas. In 2002, Rheem returned to Australia, buying back Rheem Australia Ltd., as well as Rheem New Zealand, from Southcorp Holdings. The total purchase price was reported at AUD 540 million. The purchase also gave Paloma control of Hotstream, a manufacturer of water heaters in China, marking Paloma's entry into that market. With sales of more than ¥240 billion ($2 billion), Paloma had established a solid position as one of the world's leading manufacturers of water heaters and related appliances. As it turned to the future, the company remained controlled by the founding Kobayashi family.

Principal Subsidiaries

Paloma Industries, Inc. (U.S.A.); Rheem (Australia); Rheem (New Zealand); Rheem Mamufacturing Company (Singapore) Pte Ltd.; Rheem Manufacturing Company (U.S.A.).

Principal Competitors

John Thompson Boilers; Cochrane Engineering Private Ltd.; Wolseley PLC; TUTCO Inc.; Hitachi Chemical Company Ltd.; ThyssenKrupp Services AG; Alstom Power Sweden AB; Behr GmbH und Company KG; Blue Circle Industries PLC; Lennox International Inc.

Further Reading

"Efficient Technology to Private Label Tankless Water Heater," *Plumbing & Mechanical,* October 2004, p. 26.

Furukawa, Tsukasa, and Michael C. Gabriele, "Paloma Plans to Purchase Rheem Mfg.," *Metalworking News,* April 4, 1988, p. 5.

"Japanese Giant Warms to Heater Deal," *Australian Financial Review,* December 4, 2001.

"Paloma Industries Tankless Gas Water Heater," *PM Engineer,* September 2003, p. 62.

"Rheem Buys Back WH Business Down Under," *Reeves Journal,* February 2002, p. 55.

"Water Heaters Sold," *Australasian Business Intelligence,* February 5, 2002.

—M.L. Cohen

Better Ingredients.
Better Pizza.

Papa John's International, Inc.

2002 Papa John's Boulevard
P.O. Box 99900
Louisville, Kentucky 40299-2334
U.S.A.
Telephone: (502) 261-7272
Toll Free: (888) 777-7272
Fax: (502) 266-2925
Web site: http://www.papajohns.com

Public Company
Incorporated: 1993
Employees: 14,610
Sales: $917.4 million (2003)
Stock Exchanges: NASDAQ
Ticker Symbol: PZZA
NAIC: 722211 Limited-Service Restaurants; 533110
    Lessors of Nonfinancial Intangible Assets (Except
    Copyrighted Works)

Papa John's International, Inc. ranks as the third largest pizza chain in the United States, trailing only Pizza Hut (a division of YUM! Brands, Inc.) and Domino's, Inc. The company has built a chain of more than 2,800 pizza delivery and carry-out restaurants operating under the trademark ''Papa John's'' in 49 states, the District of Columbia, and 20 international markets. Approximately 570 of the outlets are company owned, with the remainder being franchised. The firm also franchises about 115 Perfect Pizza restaurants in the United Kingdom. After the opening of its first store in 1985, Papa John's grew rapidly through the late 1990s before settling in as a more mature company in the following decade. In a highly competitive segment of the restaurant industry, Papa John's has managed to carve out a highly profitable niche by offering a very limited menu consisting of pizza, breadsticks, cheese sticks, chicken strips, chicken wings, and canned or bottled soft drinks; and by using high-quality ingredients and touting them in its trademark slogan ''Better Ingredients. Better Pizza.'' Company founder John Schnatter continues to hold about a 29 percent stake in the company.

From Broom Closet to First Papa John's

Papa John's was born in what was once a broom closet in the back of a southern Indiana tavern. The idea for the company originated in the mind of a 23-year-old entrepreneur who felt that he knew how to make a better pizza. In September 1983, shortly after attaining a business degree from Ball State University in just three years, John Schnatter returned to his hometown of Jeffersonville, Indiana, to take over the management of Mick's Lounge, a bar co-owned by his father. The tavern, noted for its fistfights and biker clientele, was physically and financially decrepit; beer dealers and other vendors even refused to give the establishment credit. In his first week, Schnatter, $64,000 in debt with a long list of angry creditors, cleaned and repainted the bar, determined to make the most of his opportunity. He lowered and simplified beer prices, while adding more pool tables and video games. In addition, he began to market the bar through promotions that resulted in word-of-mouth advertising. In just three months, he had paid off half of his debt.

Although Schnatter quickly succeeded in resurrecting the bar to profitability a month later, his ambitions extended far beyond the walls of a smoke-filled beer joint. In March 1984 he sold his business partner, Bob Ehringer, who had purchased the elder Schnatter's stake in the business, on the idea of supplementing revenues by serving pizza out of the bar's broom closet. With $1,600 worth of equipment and ingredients, Papa John's was born. Schnatter tore down a wall with a sledgehammer to make room for an eight-by-ten-foot kitchen. During those early days Schnatter and his partner worked from 9 a.m. to 1:30 a.m., sleeping in the bar so they would not miss any calls. For the first six months, the pizza business generated only $1,000 to $1,500 a week and was financially dependent on the bar. But as the fledgling establishment became better known, sales increased. By March 1985, the two partners, along with a few helpers, were making 3,000 to 4,000 pizzas a week.

With Mick's Lounge financially sound and not enough room in the ''broom closet'' kitchen to keep up with the growing demand for pizzas, Schnatter and Ehringer set their eyes on an empty retail space next door where they could open their first restaurant. Having gained valuable experience working in several restaurants in high school and in college preparing himself

Company Perspectives:

Papa John's is the most quality-focused pizza company in the world with a simple formula for success: focus on one thing and do it better than anyone else. By keeping the menu simple and by using only superior-quality ingredients, Papa John's is able to focus on the quality of our products. This commitment to quality can be seen in all of Papa John's ingredients, from our fresh traditional pizza dough, to our vine-ripened fresh-packed tomato sauce, 100% real cheese and many other premium ingredients.

for such an opportunity, Schnatter was eager to put his ideas into practice. "One day he sat at his desk in the dorm and had a menu laid out, along with a company logo," recalled Schnatter's college roommate in *Business First-Louisville*. "Papa John's was on his mind even on campus."

But before the 23-year-old entrepreneur could launch his new venture, his father and top supporter died. "You're supposed to feel sorry for yourself, and I could have sat at the bar and moped," he said in *Business First-Louisville*. "But I'm pretty tough on myself, and I got on with it." Having inherited his father's unwavering determination, Schnatter acquired the site for his restaurant through sweat equity. With the help of his uncle, Bill Schnatter, who became a partner in charge of store layout and construction, and Ehringer, who took over operations and maintenance, Schnatter, the firm's president and chief markctcr, opened his first restaurant.

In January 1986 the company was incorporated and able to stand on its own. A year later Schnatter and Ehringer sold Mick's Lounge so they could devote more time to Papa John's. The strategy that brought them such rapid success was simple: make the best pizza and sell it at a competitive price. What Schnatter had learned while working in pizza joints as a teenager and a college student was to keep his product line focused. Although other restaurants offered salad bars and chicken wings, he devoted his energy to producing the "Perfect Pizza" (a slogan that would later become a registered company trademark) and delivering it to customers in a timely fashion. Schnatter also introduced early on a signature bonus that served to signal the quality of the product: each pizza was accompanied by a container of the company's special garlic sauce and two pepperoncinis. Behind the focused strength of this strategy, Papa John's generated revenues of $500,000 in its first year and opened two more restaurants in the "Kentuckiana" region, including the first franchised outlet. (The company headquarters were shifted to Louisville, Kentucky, in 1989.)

To prepare the company for more serious expansion, the visionary Schnatter built a commissary near corporate headquarters in Louisville's Bluegrass Industrial Park to supply his stores with fresh pizza dough and spices. In the commissary, giant mixers turned bags of flour mix and warm water into dough balls of several sizes. The dough was then chilled until it was firm enough to be shipped to individual stores twice a week and shaped into pizza crusts or breadsticks. The commissary system was frequently cited by industry analysts and company

officials as a key factor in the success of Papa John's. The system not only reduced labor costs and reduced waste because the dough was pre-measured; it, perhaps more importantly, maintained control over the consistency of the product. In many other restaurants, for instance, the least experienced employees were responsible for making the dough because it was such a messy job.

Not only did this centralized production facility furnish all of the Papa John's stores with the same high-quality ingredients for their pizzas, but it lowered start-up costs for new restaurants by saving them the cost of expensive equipment. From this early stage in the company's history, Schnatter made sure that he expanded the production capacity of his commissary system before he added new restaurants. Accordingly, four additions were made to the company's first commissary by the end of the decade and the opening of the 23rd Papa John's.

In 1989 Schnatter enlisted the services of pizza industry veteran Dan Holland to help the company strengthen its financial base and fashion a strategy for further growth. A former executive with Mr. Gatti's and Pizza Hut, Holland, who took over as company president in 1990, brought more than a decade of experience in the pizza business to Papa John's. That same year, which brought in $15 million in revenue, Ehringer, who did not share his partner's expansionary vision, sold his 40 percent share in the company to Schnatter.

Phenomenal Growth in the Early 1990s

During the early 1990s the company embarked on a phenomenal pattern of growth, expanding to 200 restaurants and $82 million in sales. At least part of the success was due to a surge in the overall pizza market, which grew at the fastest rate of any major segment of the restaurant industry during the mid-1980s and early 1990s. Pizza sales also benefited from the larger trend toward more off-premise food consumption; pizza was, to some extent, viewed as one of the leading replacements for the home-cooked meal and realized a greater increase in sales than other large quick-service segments, such as hamburgers and chicken. Having established itself from the beginning as primarily a delivery and carry-out restaurant, Papa John's was poised to take full advantage of this growing demand.

Another contributing factor to the company's success during this period was its ability to keep start-up costs low for new franchises during the recession of the early 1990s. Whereas some restaurant franchises cost upwards of $1 million, a Papa John's could be purchased during this period for less than $100,000. This bargain price, combined with the company's profitable history, attracted a number of high-profile franchisees into the Papa John's stable. Such restauranteurs as Rick Sherman, former president of Rally's and Church's Fried Chicken chains; Frank Carney, one of the founders of Pizza Hut; Ed Johnson, founder of Grandy's; and Jack Laughery, former chairman and CEO of Hardee's, all opened several stores.

After recording total revenues of close to $50 million in 1992, having roughly doubled its size every year since 1986, the company looked to raise money to pay off debts and finance continued expansion. In June 1993, Papa John's went public with an initial offering of 1.55 million shares at $13 a share. As

Key Dates:

1984: John Schnatter and partner Bob Ehringer begin selling pizza out of a converted broom closet of Mick's Lounge in Jeffersonville, Indiana.
1985: Schnatter opens the first Papa John's restaurant in a retail space next to the bar.
1986: Franchising of Papa John's begins.
1989: Company headquarters are shifted to Louisville, Kentucky.
1993: Papa John's goes public, raising about $12 million through an initial public offering (IPO).
1996: The thousandth Papa John's is opened.
1998: International expansion begins with opening of units in Mexico and Puerto Rico.
1999: Company opens the 2,000th Papa John's restaurant; the U.K. pizza chain Perfect Pizza Holdings, Ltd. is acquired; Papa John's moves into third place among U.S. pizza chains.
2005: Nigel Travis is hired as president and CEO, with Schnatter remaining chairman.

evidence of the strong faith of the financial community in the company, the stock closed at $20, generating proceeds of about $12 million after costs. The stock sale helped to strengthen the company's financial base while providing capital for entrance into three new markets: Atlanta, Georgia; Orlando, Florida; and Charlotte, North Carolina.

Geographic expansion required the building of two more commissaries to supply the new stores during the early 1990s; one in Orlando and one in Raleigh, North Carolina. The commissaries, which were designed to serve a 400-mile radius, enabled the company to open its 400th store in 1993, nearly doubling the size of the company from the previous year. Total revenue, likewise, increased more than 80 percent, surpassing the $89 million mark.

Just as Papa John's was nearing the 500-store milestone in mid-1994, it was named by *Business Week* as the nation's best-run small business, based on three-year results in sales growth, earnings growth, and return on invested capital. The attention the company received from this report, as well as from other reports by business and industry publications ranging from *Forbes* to *Nation's Restaurant News,* helped the company to attract management talent and gain momentum in the investment community. Taking advantage of this energy, Papa John's completed two common stock offerings during the year, raising an additional $35 million and preparing the way for further expansion.

In keeping with the company's strategy of ensuring that the commissary system was developed to support the growth and geographical expansion of restaurants, Papa John's constructed its fourth commissary in Jackson, Mississippi, during 1994. The company also finalized plans to build a full-service commissary in Orlando to replace the existing dough-producing facility. The additional production capacity provided the infrastructure to serve up to 1,200 restaurants in 20 states. The timely expansion of this system, according to many industry experts, enabled the

company to continue its ability to monitor and control product quality and consistency, while lowering food costs.

Papa John's, having set quality standards for all products used in its restaurants, required all of its franchises to purchase dough and spices from the commissary. What is more, virtually all of the franchises, although they were not required to do so, purchased their other supplies from the commissary as well, taking advantage of the lower prices offered. While the commissaries helped to improve quality control and efficiency by providing each individual franchise with the same products, they also facilitated the growth of the company by lowering start-up costs. With the commissary system, there was no need for franchises to purchase expensive dough-making equipment and train their employees how to use it.

Throughout Papa John's tremendous growth during its first ten years of operation, its marketing programs targeted the delivery area of each restaurant, primarily through print materials in direct mail and store-to-door couponing. In 1994, for instance, approximately 80 percent of all purchases were made using a coupon, at a savings of about 17 percent. As the company became more affluent and attempted to serve a larger geographic area, it increasingly supplemented local marketing efforts with radio and television advertising. To maximize the resources of its individual restaurants, the company also created the Papa John's Marketing Fund, Inc., a nonprofit corporation that handled market-wide marketing programs, such as radio, television, and billboards. The Marketing Fund, which was supported by required contributions from each store, also provided company-owned and franchised restaurants with catalogs and toll free numbers for uniforms and promotional items.

Late 1990s: Maintaining Focus amid Intensifying Pizza Wars

As Papa John's entered the late 1990s, it had no plans to change the simple formula that had placed it in position to become the nation's fourth largest pizza chain. Schnatter promised to keep what Bill McDowell of *Restaurants and Institutions* magazine called "an almost obsessive focus on the core product." No additions to the four core menu items—pizza, breadsticks, cheese sticks, and canned soft drinks—had been planned. As Schnatter stated in a 1995 letter to stockholders, Papa John's did not intend to follow the lead of its competitors who "clutter their menus with chicken wings, salads, pasta and subs." Rather, the company planned to direct its energy and resources toward "delivering the Perfect Pizza" to more people and in a larger geographical region.

More than 250 restaurants opened during 1995, and the company opened a new distribution center in Dallas in early 1996 and a full-service commissary in Denver during the latter part of 1996 to facilitate western expansion. This latest expansion push was aided by two more secondary stock offerings: 800,000 shares at $40 per share in August 1995 and 1.14 million shares at $47.25 per share in May 1996. Another milestone was reached in August 1996 when the 1,000th Papa John's opened for business. In October 1996 the menu was tweaked with the addition of thin crust pizza to go alongside the traditional crust the company had been selling since its founding. Papa John's felt compelled to make this move because one-quarter or more of U.S. pizza eaters preferred thin crust.

By early 1998 the Papa John's system included nine commissaries/distribution centers supporting more than 1,500 units. A tenth commissary opened in Portland, Oregon, during the year, and the facility in Louisville was expanded from 35,000 to 82,500 square feet. The company also expanded internationally for the first time, opening outlets in Mexico and Puerto Rico.

The year also saw the "pizza wars" heat up, particularly a head-to-head battle between Papa John's and Pizza Hut. The battle began in earnest the previous year when Pizza Hut attempted to regain momentum through quality with the introduction of "totally new pizzas" featuring fresh toppings and a reformulated sauce in a direct strike at Papa John's "Better Ingredients. Better Pizza" positioning in the market. Papa John's responded with an advertisement featuring Frank Carney, the Pizza Hut cofounder who was now a Papa John's franchisee. Carney claimed in the ad to have found a "better pizza." Pizza Hut soon filed a complaint with the Better Business Bureau's National Advertising Division (NAD), a mediation board, stipulating that Papa John's slogan was false and damaging to Pizza Hut. After an investigation, the NAD concluded that Papa John's had a "reasonable basis" for its claims. Undeterred, Pizza Hut took its case to federal court, which prompted Papa John's to countersue, charging its rival with misleading advertising. In late 1999 a jury found both companies guilty, and in January of the following year a federal district judge ruled that Papa John's had to stop using the "Better Ingredients. Better Pizza" slogan, though this ruling was stayed while Papa John's filed an appeal. The U.S. Court of Appeals for the Fifth Circuit later overturned the rulings against Papa John's, and in March 2001 the U.S. Supreme Court declined to review the case, thereby enabling the company to continue using the slogan. Papa John's did not come out of these skirmishes completely unscathed, however. Schnatter was forced to admit that his chain used canned tomato sauce and canned mushrooms; Papa John's soon thereafter switched to fresh mushrooms.

Seeking to maintain a mix of 25 percent corporate-owned stores and 75 percent franchised, Papa John's embarked in 1999 on a strategy of acquiring franchises in lieu of developing new corporate markets. That year another 400 Papa John's were opened, including the 2,000th store, located in Denver. Papa John's also made its largest move overseas yet, purchasing Perfect Pizza Holdings, Ltd. for $32.5 million. The U.K. firm operated 205 Perfect Pizza delivery and carry-out pizza restaurants. Conversion to the Papa John's format proceeded slowly over the next several years. For the year, Papa John's reported systemwide sales of $1.42 billion, which for the first time bested the total for Little Caesar Enterprises, Inc., moving Papa John's into third place in the U.S. market, behind only Pizza Hut ($5 billion in U.S. systemwide sales) and Domino's ($2.56 billion). Papa John's corporate revenues reached $805.3 million, while net income climbed to $47.3 million.

Transitioning into More Mature Company in the Early 2000s

In the early 2000s Papa John's considerably slowed down its expansion as it focused more on improving profitability in an environment highlighted by ongoing price competition, a slowing economy, and high cheese costs. The company began closing underperforming units in 2001, countering the more limited store openings. In 2003, for instance, 103 Papa John's restaurants were opened but 105 were shuttered. Growth was targeted to the West and Northeast. Looking for an edge in an increasingly competitive sector of the restaurant industry, Papa John's made another rare addition to the menu in September 2002 with the rollout of Papa's Chickenstrips, made from all-white-meat, boneless, breaded chicken. The company also began introducing specialty pizzas. On the overseas front, Papa John's entered China in 2003, its 14th international market, and it also converted 60 Perfect Pizza restaurants in the United Kingdom to the Papa John's format, reducing the Perfect Pizza chain to 135 locations.

Corporate revenues fell in both 2002 and 2003, dropping from $971.2 million to $917.4 million over that period. Net income fell from $47.2 million to $33.6 million during the same time span. This stagnation continued in 2004 when Papa John's announced plans to shutter about 120 more stores. Late in the year the company cut 70 positions across its corporate staff in order to reduce annual expenses by about $2.3 million. Around this same time, Papa's Wings chicken wings were added to the menu. For the year, systemwide sales increased just 0.1 percent. Five more international markets were entered during 2004: Russia, Trinidad, Peru, Bahrain, and Oman.

In a potential signal of a new era at the company, Papa John's hired Nigel Travis as president and CEO, replacing Schnatter, who remained chairman. Travis had served as president and COO of the Blockbuster Inc. video store chain from 2001 to 2004. A British national, Travis had an earlier five-year stint at Burger King Corporation, serving in various leadership positions for the fast-food company, which at the time was owned by the U.K. firm Grand Metropolitan plc. With sales for 2005 expected to remain stagnant or increase no more than 2 percent, Papa John's kept its expansion plans in check, anticipating opening 80 to 100 domestic units while closing a similar number. International operations were expected to grow by as many as 50 net units. It was clear that Papa John's had entered a much slower growth phase in its evolution, and that it had become nearly impossible for the company to reach a goal that Schnatter had set in the heady days of the late 1990s: overtaking Pizza Hut—thereby becoming the number one pizza chain—within ten years.

Principal Subsidiaries

Papa John's USA, Inc.; PJ Food Service, Inc.; PJFS of Mississippi, Inc.; Papa John's Support Services, Inc.; Risk Services Corp.; Capital Delivery, Ltd.; RSC Insurance Services Ltd. (Bermuda); Colonel's Limited, LLC; Papa John's (U.K.) Ltd.; Perfect Pizza Ltd. (U.K.); Perfect Pizza Holdings, Ltd. (U.K.).

Principal Competitors

Pizza Hut; Domino's, Inc.; Little Caesar Enterprises, Inc.

Further Reading

Cebrzynski, Gregg, "Pizza Power Grab: Papa John's Seizes Third Place from Little Caesars," *Nation's Restaurant News,* June 26, 2000, pp. 104+.

Coeyman, Marjorie, "Papa Grows Up," *Restaurant Business,* February 15, 1997, pp. 29–30, 34.

Cooper, Ron, "Focus Was Key Ingredient in Schnatter's Success," *Business First-Louisville,* June 12, 1995.

——, "Papa John's Rolls Out the Dough," *Business First-Louisville,* December 16, 1991, p. 1.

Eagles, Cynthia, "Papa John's Nears 3,000-Store Milestone," *Business First of Louisville,* November 26, 2001.

Egerton, Judith, "Papa John's at 10: The Growth Is Spectacular," *Louisville Courier-Journal,* April 17, 1995.

George, Eric, "Putting Pop in Papa John's," *Louisville,* January 1994, p. 26.

Goetz, David, "Papa John's Wants Slice of Breakfast Market," *Louisville Courier-Journal,* February 17, 2005, p. 1A.

Greenwald, John, "Slice, Dice, and Devour," *Time,* October 26, 1998, pp. 64–66.

Henderson, Angelo B., "Out of the Broom Closet and into the Oven," *Louisville Courier-Journal,* September 5, 1988, p. E1.

McDowell, Bill, "Papa John's Slice of Success," *Restaurants and Institutions,* February 15, 1995.

"Nobody's Growing Like Papa John's," *Pizza Today,* July 1994, p. 50.

Papiernik, Richard L., "Papa John's 'Simple' Policy Pays Off: Profits up 77%," *Nation's Restaurant News,* March 6, 1995.

Redding, Rick, "Building an Empire Schnatter Style," *Business First of Louisville,* April 2, 1999.

Reichert, Walt, "Pizza on the Move," *Louisville,* September 1991, p. 31.

Roth, Daniel, "This Ain't No Pizza Party," *Fortune,* November 9, 1998, pp. 158–60, 162, 164.

Ruggless, Ron, "John Schnatter: Mom Never Thought There'd Be Days Like This, but Papa John's CEO Is Rolling in Dough," *Nation's Restaurant News,* January 2000, pp. 158, 160.

Schiller, Zachary, "From a Broom Closet in a Bar to 485 Pizza Restaurants," *Business Week,* May 23, 1994, p. 94.

Walkup, Carolyn, "Goal-Setting and Focus Are the Secrets Behind Papa John's Meteoric Rise," *Nation's Restaurant News,* January 1997, pp. 182, 184.

——, "John Schnatter: Focus and Discipline Arm Papa John's Founder in Quest to Keep Chain Rolling in the Dough," *Nation's Restaurant News,* October 14, 1996, pp. 168, 170.

Zuber, Amy, "The Brawl's in Their Court: Pizza Hut, Papa John's Gear Up for Battle," *Nation's Restaurant News,* October 25, 1999, p. 8.

——, "Papa John's Aims for Bigger Slice of Pizza Segment with Product Focus," *Nation's Restaurant News,* November 11, 2002, pp. 4, 93, 98.

——, "Papa John's European Expansion to Mushroom via Perfect Pizza Buy," *Nation's Restaurant News,* December 13, 1999, p. 8.

——, "Papa John's Saucy No Longer As Sales Decline," *Nation's Restaurant News,* November 26, 2001, pp. 4, 60.

——, "Papa John's Still Saucy After Stock Meltdown," *Nation's Restaurant News,* May 8, 2000, pp. 8+.

——, "Papa John's Takes on Pizza Hut, Plans for Growth," *Nation's Restaurant News,* March 30, 1998, pp. 65–66.

——, "Pizza Hut-vs.-Papa John's Battle Signals Intensifying War Among Segment Leaders," *Nation's Restaurant News,* June 22, 1998, pp. 114, 116, 120.

—Jason Gallman
—update: David E. Salamie

PATTON BOGGS LLP
ATTORNEYS AT LAW

www.pattonboggs.com

Patton Boggs LLP

2550 M St. NW
Washington, D.C. 20037
U.S.A.
Telephone: (202) 457-6000
Fax: (202) 457-6315
Web site: http://www.pattonboggs.com

Partnership
Founded: 1962 as Barco, Cook and Patton
Employees: 400
Sales: $202.1 million (2004)
NAIC: 541110 Offices of Lawyers

Patton Boggs LLP is a Washington, D.C.-based full-service law firm best known for its lobbying prowess. The firm employs about 400 attorneys and maintains offices in Anchorage, Dallas, Denver, northern Virginia, and Doha, Qatar. Patton Boggs takes a generalist approach, bringing together teams with diverse expertise to serve client needs. Rather than organizing the firm by departments, Patton Boggs relies on what it calls "relatively porous practice groups." These include Antitrust; Appropriations; Bankruptcy and Restructuring; Business; Defense and National Security; Energy; Environmental, Health and Safety; Food and Drug; Health Care; Intellectual Property; International Trade and Transactions; Litigation and Dispute Resolution; Mergers and Acquisitions; Municipal Representation; Political Law; Public Policy and Lobbying; Tax; Telecommunications and Technology; and Transportation and Infrastructure. Patton Boggs is headed by Chairman Thomas Hale Boggs, Jr., regarded as one of Washington's foremost lobbyists and one of the nation's top lawyers. Well into his 70s, founder James Richard Patton, Jr., remains active in the firm.

Firm Foundation: Early 1960s

James Patton was born in Durham, North Carolina, in 1928. After receiving an undergraduate degree from the University of North Carolina, he earned a law degree from Harvard University in 1951. He then became an embassy attaché and special assistant assigned to Indochina, although it is now widely known that he

was actually working for the Central Intelligence Agency. Patton relocated to Washington in 1954, and was employed by the Office of National Estimates for two years before joining the prestigious Washington, D.C., law firm of Covington & Burling where he became well versed in the practice of international law. In 1962 he decided to strike out on his own, creating a partnership with a pair of attorneys, Charles D. Cook & J.W. "Jim" Barco, to form a general practice focusing on international law called Barco, Cook and Patton. Patton and Barco had known each other from their days at Harvard Law School and had later worked together on a treaty between India and Pakistan. Barco had also served as the deputy to Henry Cabot Lodge, the U.S. ambassador to the United Nations, and had worked with Cook, who was counselor to the U.N. mission. While Patton set up shop in Washington at 1717 Pennsylvania Avenue N.W., Barco and Cook elected to remain in New York City to practice.

Within a few years the New York and Washington division of the partnership proved unwieldy, leading to the departure of Barco and Cook, but in the meantime Patton recruited other attorneys who became key partners of the firm. In October 1963 he hired George Blow, a friend from his days at Covington & Burling. Blow had made a name for himself by successfully arguing in 1957 the Double Jeopardy case (*Green v the United States*) before the United States Supreme Court, in which a man accused of murder was tried for the same crime twice in violation of the Fifth Amendment. The addition of Blow necessitated a further name change to the firm, which now became Barco, Cook, Patton and Blow.

"Tommy" Boggs Joins Firm in 1966

Attorney Chuck Verrill joined the firm as an associate, then in April 1966 Patton added two more young attorneys to the small firm: Joseph L. Brand and "Tommy" Boggs. Along with his sister, radio and television political correspondent Corinne "Cokie" Roberts, and Barbara Sigmund who became mayor of Princeton, New Jersey, Boggs grew up immersed in politics. His father, Thomas Hale Boggs, Sr., had become a Democratic congressman from Louisiana at the age of 26 in 1940 and rose through the ranks of House leadership and the Democratic party, becoming chairman of the Democratic National Commit-

Company Perspectives:

At Patton Boggs, we see opportunities where others see problems. Our ability to see things differently, viewing issues in light of a broader range of possibilities, allows us to translate client ideas and problems into creative results and solutions.

tee in 1958. As a result, the Boggs' home was often frequented by Washington's elite and the Boggs' children were not surprised to have such dinner guests as Lyndon Johnson, John Kennedy, and longtime Speaker of the House Sam Rayburn. The younger Boggs earned his undergraduate and law degrees at Georgetown University. In 1961 he took a position as an economist for the Joint Economic Committee for the U.S. Congress, then in 1965 became special assistant to the director of the Office of Emergency Planning. In 1966 Boggs decided to begin practicing law and interviewed with a large number of Washington-area firms. One of the largest, Hogan and Hartson, offered him a job, but Boggs turned it down in favor of going to work for the much smaller firm of Barco, Cook, Patton and Blow. Less than two years later Barco and Cook departed and the young guns became partners, leading to yet another name change for the firm: Patton, Blow, Verrill, Brand and Boggs.

In these early years, the firm's international clients included Pakistan, Turkey, Uganda, Ireland, and Norway. It was because many of these international clients required advocates in Washington in order to achieve their ends that the firm became involved in lobbying. Boggs was well suited to the task. Not only did he know many leading politicians through his father, his mentor during his tenure on Capital Hill had been Clark Clifford, one of the most famous capital insiders, adept at backroom machinations and cutting deals over drinks and cigars. The old boy network would give way to the era of the super lobbyist, as epitomized by Tommy Boggs. But first he would try his hand at running for office. In 1970 he ran as a Democrat in Maryland for the U.S. House of Representatives but lost. His father, in the meantime, continued to win reelection in Louisiana. He was so well entrenched that he ran unopposed in 1972 and was on the verge of becoming the House speaker. Campaigning for a fellow Democratic congressman in Alaska, the senior Boggs was flying from Anchorage to Juneau when his plane disappeared. It was never found, he was presumed dead, and his wife, Lindy, was elected to replace him—a seat she held until her resignation in 1991.

The firm steadily picked up clients in the late 1960s and early 1970s and added to its roster of attorneys. Timothy May, who would become managing partner, joined in March 1969 and two years later made partner, necessitating yet another name change. But the firm name of Patton, Boggs, Blow, Verrill, Brand & May was clearly too cumbersome, and in 1973 the partners agreed to shorten the name, retaining only the most senior partners. The result was Patton, Boggs and Blow, a name the firm kept for the next quarter-century. The small firm also attempted to expand beyond Washington, D.C., during this period, launching one-man operations in Mexico City and Tehran, but both closed down within a year.

A major project during the early 1970s that solidified Patton Boggs's public policy lobbying practice was the Trans-Alaska Pipeline System, for which it represented both oil companies and construction companies. The election of Democrat Jimmy Carter to the White House in 1976 was also a boon to Patton Boggs's lobbying efforts, as Tommy Boggs forged his reputation as a Democratic rainmaker. A major success in the second half of the 1970s was the firm's work on behalf of a struggling Chrysler, for which Patton Boggs played a key role in arranging a government bailout. During the late 1970s the firm also participated in high-profile, and highly partisan, tax bills.

By 1980 Patton Boggs employed 38 attorneys. In that year Carter was defeated for the presidency by Ronald Reagan, and for a brief time it appeared that lobbyists would have a difficult time finding corporate clients. The prevailing assumption was that a Reagan administration would be so friendly toward business interests that lobbyists would be unnecessary. But control of the Congress remained contentious and those who believed that lobbyists no longer had a role to play were quickly disabused of that notion. Patton Boggs steadily added to its lobbying business and as it became involved in different public policy areas it identified talented government attorneys working in specific fields and began hiring them to assemble a roster of experts, an approach that proved key to the firm's long-term growth. In little more than a year Patton Boggs employed 72 attorneys. Also during the early 1980s, Patton Boggs again attempted to expand geographically. It opened an office in London, but it closed within four years. The firm also established an office in Saudi Arabia to serve a client building a hospital in the country, but once the project was successfully launched, the office was closed in the mid-1980s. Later in the 1980s Patton Boggs opened an office in Baltimore, Maryland, to accommodate a partner who needed to work close to home for personal reasons, but because Baltimore was so close to Washington the new office added nothing to the firm's prospects. A more legitimate attempt at regional expansion was the 1988 acquisition of a Greensboro, North Carolina-based law firm: Foster, Conner, Robson & Gumbiner. Some of the partners were prominent in Republican politics, helping to mitigate the sense that Patton Boggs was a Democratic shop. Once again, however, the attempt to establish a foothold outside of the Beltway failed and the Greensboro and Raleigh, North Carolina offices were eventually closed in the 1990s.

Helping Defeat 1990s Healthcare Reforms

The 1990s saw another Democrat, Bill Clinton, take the presidency but, while the White House may have been in the hands of the Democrats, control of the Congress was swinging to the Republicans. Thus, Patton Boggs made a concerted effort to bring in more Republican-connected attorneys to bolster its lobbying business. Democratic ties not withstanding, Patton Boggs played a major role in thwarting Clinton's effort to implement healthcare reforms, a defeat that crippled his presidency and led to the Democrats losing the House to Republicans in 1994. Patton Boggs's clients in this fight included the Association of Trial Lawyers of America, opposed to the concept of limiting the amount a victim could collect in a malpractice lawsuit, and The National Association of Life Underwriters and the National Association of Health Underwriters, threatened by

Key Dates:

1962: Barco, Cook and Patton is formed.
1963: George Blow joins firm.
1966: Thomas Hale Boggs, Jr., joins firm.
1973: Firm adopts Patton, Boggs and Blow name.
1993: Blow retires.
1997: Stuart Pape is named managing partner.

the idea of mandatory alliances, which would eliminate their lucrative middleman role because consumers would now be able to negotiate directly with purchasing alliances. Despite overwhelming public support for the proposals, all of the reforms were successfully bottled up in committee and no bills were ever passed. According to a 1995 *Washington Monthly* article, ''Not only did [Patton Boggs's] victory confirm their reputation, but the total defeat of all health reform also means that the issue will come around again, and with it, another rush of clients paying top prices to have Patton Boggs on their side. Healthcare reform took good care of Patton Boggs. The firm's total revenue shot up 25 percent in two years, from $49 million to $61 million.''

Other major work for Patton Boggs during the 1990s was a private sector effort to eliminate the 20-year-ban on the export of Alaska North Slope crude oil; retailers' efforts to block quotas on textile imports; the advertising industry's fight to ward off tax increases; and efforts related to the passage of major international trade agreements, GATT (General Agreement on Tariffs and Trade) and NAFTA (North American Free Trade Agreement). The 1990s also saw organizational changes at Patton Boggs. In 1992 the firm hired Dallas-area attorneys with financial service expertise and opened a Dallas office. Blow retired in 1993; later in the decade the firm assumed the name of Patton Boggs LLP. In 1997 the firm's current managing partner, Stuart Pape, took charge; he had joined Patton Boggs in 1980 after working for the Food and Drug Administration, an example of the firm luring away attorneys who possessed inside knowledge about specific subjects. In addition to Dallas, Patton Boggs opened offices in Anchorage and Denver.

In 2000 Patton Boggs opened an office in northern Virginia to become involved in the high-tech boom the area was enjoying. The timing proved unfortunate, however, as the bottom fell out of the industry. Nevertheless, the firm retained the office and added the intellectual property lawyers required by the practice. By now Patton Boggs had effectively shed its reputation as a Democratic-leaning firm, with at least as many Republican public policy lawyers as Democrats. During the contentious 2000 presidential election, in fact, Patton Boggs was on the Supreme Court brief for George W. Bush. Even Tommy Boggs, a lifelong Democrat, admitted to the *Denver Business Journal* in 2001 that ''When the Republicans take over the White House, the business community basically thinks they can get a lot done. . . . So we've always done better as a law firm . . . when the Republicans control the White House.''

Patton Boggs continued to hire high-profile, politically connected attorneys in the new century, including Clinton confidant Lanny Davis, national counsel to the Bush-Cheney presidential campaign Ben Ginsberg, and former Democratic Senator John Breaux. Entering 2005 Patton Boggs employed 400 attorneys and generated revenues in excess of $200 million a year. Of that amount $65.8 million came from lobbying-related fees, making Patton Boggs the highest grossing lobbying firm according to an annual survey conducted by ALM's *Influence* newsletter.

Principal Competitors

Akin, Gump, Strauss, Hauer & Feld, LLP; Cassidy & Associates; Hogan & Hartson; Arnold & Porter LLP.

Further Reading

Abramson, Jill, ''Acquisition by Prominent Washington Law Firm Shows Building Political Links Is a Subtle Craft,'' *Wall Street Journal,* June 22, 1988, p. 1.

Fletcher, Amy, ''Q&A with Patton Boggs' Partner,'' *Denver Business Journal,* May 18, 2001, p. A3.

Franklin, Daniel, ''Tommy Boggs and the Death of Health Care Reform,'' *Washington Monthly,* April 1995, p. 31.

Reilly, Ann M., ''Washington's Super Lobbyists,'' *Dun's Business Month,* August 1983, p. 30.

—Ed Dinger

plante
moran

Plante & Moran, LLP

27400 Northwestern Highway
Southfield, Michigan 48034
U.S.A.
Telephone: (248) 352-2500
Fax: (248) 352-0018
Web site: http://www.plantemoran.com

Private Company
Incorporated: 1924
Employees: 1,450
Sales: $210 million (2005 est.)
NAIC: 541211 Offices of Certified Public Accountants;
541611 Administrative Management and General
Management Consulting Services

Plante & Moran, LLP is the tenth largest accounting firm in the United States. In addition to performing the tasks of accounting, auditing, and tax preparation for its clients, the firm offers management consulting services in a variety of areas including wealth management, human resources, and technology. Plante & Moran serves mid-size businesses in the fields of manufacturing, financial services, health care, construction, real estate, and auto sales, as well as nonprofit organizations and municipal governments. The company has offices in Michigan, Ohio, Illinois, Tennessee, and Shanghai, China. Ownership is vested in the firm's partners, who number nearly 200.

Beginnings

The origins of Plante & Moran date to 1924, when Elorion Plante founded a small accounting firm in Detroit, Michigan. In 1941 he hired Frank Moran to assist him, after having become acquainted with the young man when he tutored his daughter. Moran, who had earned a degree in philosophy but had not studied accounting, worked briefly for Plante, and then for General Motors, before spending three years as a U.S. Navy supply officer during World War II.

After his return from the service, Moran came back to Detroit and began working for Plante once again, also taking

night classes in accounting. After completing his studies he became a Certified Public Accountant (CPA), and in 1950 Plante elevated him to the level of partner, renaming the firm Plante & Moran. At this time their clients were typically small and medium-sized private firms, for which they performed accounting, auditing, and tax preparation.

Moran's background in philosophy led him to approach the job of accounting differently from many in the business, and he began to advise his clients on more than just financial matters. Bill Hermann, a later managing partner of the firm, told *Crain's Detroit Business* that Moran would look at his client's business ''like a hand. Its strengths were the fingers, and the spaces between were gaps. He'd figure out how to help fill in the gaps to help the client.''

To help clients improve their hiring practices, for example, in the early 1950s Moran began working with a psychologist to develop pre-employment tests to give to prospective hires. The tests were used to screen out people who were not likely to mesh with a firm's corporate culture or who were not suited for the work they would be asked to perform.

Moran also believed that his firm should adhere to the highest ethical standards, and he was confident that such a policy would yield long-lasting success. He had a circular view of the value of ethics, believing that hiring good people would result in them doing their work well, which would attract better clients, who in turn would pay good fees, which would enable the firm to pay its staff well, which would enable Plante & Moran to hire the best workers.

Frank Moran, Managing Partner: 1955

In 1955 Frank Moran became managing partner of the firm. He continued to broaden its offerings, such that by the early 1960s one-third of the company's revenues came from services other than auditing and accounting. As Plante & Moran grew it began hiring more staff, and Moran decided to create a hierarchy that was different from most firms of its type. Rather than having a structure with numerous levels of authority, he decided on just three: staff, associate, and partner. He felt that this would encourage employees to work more as a team, with fewer official distinctions between them.

As the company grew it began to open additional offices in other Michigan cities, in some cases by merging with existing firms. To help new employees, by the early 1970s the company began pairing freshly minted CPAs with a senior-level "buddy," who helped them get acclimated to the job. Moran's focus on treating his staff well also extended to allowing them flexible work schedules, and such policies led to a low turnover rate for the firm compared to the rest of the industry.

In 1977 Plante & Moran formed the Financial Planning Group to offer investment advice to its clients. The year 1981 saw Edward M. Parks elected managing partner of the firm, while Frank Moran moved into the role of board chairman. The following year the firm opened a new office in Ann Arbor, and in 1985 the company merged with a Lansing, Michigan-based accounting firm that had several offices, including one in the suburbs of Cleveland, Ohio.

Program to Retain Women Begun in Mid-1980s

In the early 1980s the firm's partners began to take note of the fact that more women than men were leaving the company each year, either for different jobs or to stay home with their children. Looking to boost the number of female partners, which was then less than 5 percent, and to retain women in general, in 1986 Plante & Moran formed the Parenting Tightrope Action Committee. Its job was to look for ways to help parents juggle the demands of their careers and their families, using Moran's chosen term for such a balancing act in its name.

The busiest time of year for an accountant was the so-called "tax season" from January through April 15, during which the company's staff worked up to 70 hours per week, including nights and weekends. Plante & Moran had for some time bought dinners, hired a full-time "gopher" to run personal errands, and treated the entire staff to a semi-annual retreat at a resort after tax season. To help working mothers, the firm also began offering free day care for children on Saturdays. Another new perk added for working parents was a six-month paid leave for either women or men after the birth or adoption of a child.

In 1988 Plante & Moran became a full associate member of Moores Rowland International, a worldwide association of independent accounting firms. The same year saw a merger with Dieterman, Linden, Maske, Strassburger & Co., which became the company's Grand Rapids, Michigan office.

In July 1993 William L. (Bill) Matthews took over for Edward Parks as managing partner. He had joined Plante & Moran in 1961 as a proofreader, and had held a number of other positions, most recently serving as regional managing partner for the firm's four southeast Michigan offices. The year also saw the company incorporate Plante & Moran Financial Advisors, Inc. as a subsidiary.

At this time Plante & Moran was headquartered in the Detroit suburb of Southfield, and had offices in Ann Arbor, Battle Creek, Benton Harbor, Coldwater, Grand Haven, Grand Rapids, Kalamazoo, Lansing, Mount Clemens, Traverse City, and Troy, Michigan, as well as in Cleveland, Ohio. With close to 600 employees, it was the largest independent accounting firm in the state, and the 14th largest in the United States. In addition to serving small businesses, law offices, banks, and manufacturing companies, Plante & Moran also performed work for non-profit organizations, local government agencies, and school systems.

In 1994 Plante & Moran absorbed another Michigan accounting firm, McEndarffer, Hoke & Berhnard, and also formed Plante & Moran CRESA LLC. The latter was a real estate consulting agency aligned with the newly formed CRESA, a national alliance of firms that specialized in tenant representation and related services for commercial real estate.

Partners Surpassing 100 in 1994

In the summer of 1994 Plante & Moran added five more partners, for a total of 104. Four of the new partners were women, a confirmation of the success of the company's programs to retain female employees. Eight percent of the firm's partners were now women, well above the industry average of 5 percent, while close to 40 percent of its total staff was female. Two years later the company was named to *Working Mothers* magazine's list of the 100 Best Companies for Working Mothers in the United States.

In 1996 the firm merged with Gavigan Burkhart Freeman & Co., which employed 30 at offices in Traverse City and Gaylord, Michigan. Plante & Moran now had a staff of more than 750, and annual revenues of almost $70 million.

The year 1996 also saw creation of Plante & Moran Corporate Finance LLC, a new subsidiary which would offer investment banking services, as well as strategic advice for auto industry suppliers. The firm's consultants were now helping companies earn QS-9000 certification (which would soon be made mandatory by several automakers) by assisting with personnel management and the development of procedures to win certification. At this time half of the firm's revenues were derived from auditing and accounting, one-fourth from tax work, and one-fourth from management consulting services.

In April 1997 Frank Moran died of cancer at the age of 78. He had continued to work for the firm as chairman up to the time of his death. In August, Plante & Moran merged with NCOT Accounting and Consulting, Inc. of Toledo, Ohio, which would become known as NCOT Plante & Moran LLP. The 100 employees added in the merger boosted the firm's staff to more than 1,000, and gave it new offices in the Ohio cities of Toledo, Dublin, and Lancaster. All nine of NCOT's shareholders would

Key Dates:

1924: Elorion Plante founds accounting firm in Detroit, Michigan.
1950: Frank Moran is named partner; firm becomes known as Plante & Moran.
1955: Moran becomes managing partner.
1960s: Consulting work grows to account for one-third of revenues.
1977: Financial Planning Group is founded.
1981: Edward Parks is chosen as managing partner; Moran is named chairman.
1984: Merger with Lansing, Michigan firm adds offices there and in Cleveland, Ohio.
1993: William Matthews becomes managing partner.
1994: Plante & Moran CRESA LLC is founded.
1996: Plante & Moran Corporate Finance LLC is founded.
1997: Frank Moran dies; merger occurs with NCOT Accounting and Consulting of Ohio.
1998: Plante & Moran Benefits Administration LLC is founded.
2001: William Herman takes role of managing partner.
2002: Firm is chosen to help investigate Enron collapse; Plante Moran Trust is created.
2004: Merger with GSS&C gives firm three Illinois offices; firms merges with AFME, Inc.

become partners of the merged firm. NCOT specialized in services to long-term care companies and physician-practice management.

Another new development of 1997 was the launch of the Masters Forum, an executive education program for business owners, directors, and senior managers. The program consisted of multiple sessions held over the course of a year, featuring prominent speakers and experts offering strategic advice.

Addition of Benefits Administration Subsidiary: 1998

In early 1998 the firm created a new unit, Plante & Moran Benefits Administration, LLC, which would offer administration and consulting services for retirement and cafeteria plans. The company also formed a joint venture with four other regional accounting firms called Infinet Resources, which was intended to develop products and services for community banks.

During the year the National Survey of Women in Public Accounting named Plante & Moran number one in the country for the percentage of female partners it had, which now stood at 14 percent. The year 1998 also saw the firm ranked 29th on *Fortune* magazine's list of the 100 Best Places to Work in America. Along with flexible scheduling and other employee benefits, *Fortune* praised the Plante & Moran policy which stated that "staff members will not be required to perform work that offends their personal principles." By the end of 1999 the company had nearly 1,200 staff members at 16 offices in Michigan and Ohio. Annual revenues stood at $117 million.

In the spring of 2000 the firm partnered with HMG Healthcare Services of Hudson, Ohio, to offer consulting and data

systems services to health care providers. The spring also saw Plante & Moran in merger discussions with Olive LLP, a large Indianapolis-based accounting firm, but after several months the idea was abandoned. In June the company acquired the Cleveland office of Clifton Gunderson, which gave it a larger presence in that market. Plante & Moran was now the ninth largest CPA firm in the United States.

In the fall the company added space to its headquarters in Southfield and opened a new office in the Detroit suburb of Auburn Hills, where it consolidated the operations of now-closed offices in Troy and Bloomfield Hills. For 2000, revenues hit $142.7 million, an increase of more than 20 percent over the year before.

In July 2001 a new managing partner took the reins. William M. Herman had worked for Plante & Moran for 30 years, and had been a partner for 20. That same year the company formed an alliance with technology consulting firm Brintech, Inc. to expand its community bank service.

In February 2002 the firm formed a new unit, Plante Moran Trust, to help clients set up and manage trusts. In March the company partnered with Swartz & Associates to form Plante & Moran Swartz Group, which would offer technological consulting to the continuing care industry. The firm had been moving up in *Fortune*'s annual list of 100 Best Companies to Work for, and was now in the top ten. It was the highest-ranked accounting company.

Enron Collapse Bringing Work: 2002

In the summer of 2002 Plante & Moran was chosen to help unravel the labyrinthine accounting practices that had allegedly helped cause the dramatic collapse of energy giant Enron, which official auditor Arthur Andersen was accused of turning a blind eye toward. The company sent 25 staff members to Houston, Texas, where they would work for many months with Alston & Bird, an Atlanta-based law firm also assigned to the case.

In 2003 the company formed Plante Moran Insurance Agency, which would operate as a unit of its Family Wealth Advisors group, and in January 2004 the firm merged with Gleeson, Sklar, Sawyers and Cumpata (GSS&C), a Chicago-based accounting firm with three offices in Illinois. The move boosted Plante & Moran's employment ranks to over 1,300 and its annual revenues to $191 million. Also in 2004, the company opened a new office in Columbus, Ohio, and combined its Kalamazoo and Battle Creek offices into a single site in Portage, Michigan.

In June 2004 the company merged with AFME, Inc. of Nashville, Tennessee, a manufacturing consulting firm. Plante & Moran also expanded its Global Services unit during the year by opening an office in Shanghai, China, and formed a joint venture with O/E Systems called PMV Technologies LLC. The latter would offer office technology management services.

In the spring of 2005 Plante & Moran merged with BKR Dupuis & Ryden of Flint, Michigan, which operated offices in that city and in Ann Arbor. The staff of the latter would be transferred to Plante & Moran's existing office there. In May 2005 the company expanded its presence in Chicago by acquiring Wetmore & Associates, a four-person firm with revenues of $700,000 that specialized in employee benefit plan audits.

More than 80 years after its founding, Plante & Moran had become the largest accounting firm in Michigan, and one of the ten largest in the United States. Frank Moran's guiding principles of fairness and high ethical standards toward both clients and employees had set the firm on a course that gave it a firm grounding for continued success.

Principal Subsidiaries

Plante & Moran Financial Advisors, Inc.; Plante & Moran Benefits Administration, LLC; Plante & Moran Corporate Finance LLC; Plante & Moran CRESA, LLC; Plante & Moran Global Services; NCOT Plante & Moran LLC; Plante Moran Trust; Plante Moran Insurance Agency; Financial Institutions Group; Family Wealth Advisors.

Principal Competitors

Crowe Chizek & Company LLC; Clifton Gunderson LLP; UHY Advisors, Inc.; Deloitte & Touche LLP; Ernst & Young LLP; PricewaterhouseCoopers LLP; KPMG LLP.

Further Reading

Alix, Jay, *Life on the Tightrope: A Tribute to Frank S. Moran,* London: Brown Partworks, 1999.

Ashe, John C., "Plante Moran Trust to Debut in February," *Michigan Banker*, January 1, 2002, p. 15.

Beltran, Luisa, "Plante & Moran Named Leader for Working Women," *Accounting Today*, November 11, 1996, p. 26.

Carlino, Bill, "Plante & Moran Seeks Great Lakes Growth," *Accounting Today*, July 26, 2004, p. 1.

Caswell, Christine, "Plante & Moran Makes Staff a Top Priority," *Greater Lansing Business Monthly*, July 1, 1993, p. 14.

Dayasena, Melanie, "Plante & Moran and GSS&C Merger Completes US Coverage for MRI," *International Accounting*, February 6, 2004, p. 4.

Demery, Paul, "Plante's Program Fosters Advancement of CPA Moms," *Accounting Today*, September 26, 1994, p. 14.

Dietderich, Andrew, "O/E Systems Leaves Leasing; Joins Forces with Spinoff from Plante & Moran," *Crain's Detroit Business*, September 6, 2004, p. 3.

Kramer, Mary, "CPA Firm's Founder Set Tone for Excellence," *Crain's Detroit Business*, November 4, 2002, p. 9.

Matthews, William L., "Legacy of Innovative Staff Development Programs Requires Commitment from New Generation of Leaders," *Michigan Banker*, April 1, 1999, p. 50.

McGregor, Jena, "Milk and Cookie Mindset," *Australian CPA*, October 1, 2004, p. 28.

Merx, Katie, "Fast Growth Impels Plante & Moran to Add Space, Offices," *Crain's Detroit Business*, October 23, 2000, p. 31.

——, "Plante & Moran May Hit Top 10 with Merger," *Crain's Detroit Business*, January 12, 2004, p. 1.

——, "Plante & Moran Named to Work on Enron Case," *Crain's Detroit Business*, September 23, 2002, p. 1.

Parks, Ed, "Plante & Moran Chairman Was Mentor to Many," *Crain's Detroit Business*, April 7, 1997, p. 7.

"Plante & Moran Again Ranks High on *Fortune* Magazine's Annual List of 100 Best Employers in America," *Michigan Banker*, February 1, 2000, p. 21.

"Plante & Moran Expands Presence in Midwest," *International Accounting*, March 16, 2005, p. 2.

Rent, Katy, "Plante & Moran Swims Against Accounting Tide," *Grand Rapids Business Journal*, March 18, 2002, p. B3.

Roush, Matt, "Ohio Firm to Merge into Plante & Moran," *Crain's Detroit Business*, August 25, 1997, p. 3.

——, "Plante & Moran to Head South of State Border," *Crain's Detroit Business*, March 3, 1997, p. 17.

Serres, Christopher, "Plante & Moran Hunts for Merger," *Crain's Cleveland Business*, July 24, 2000, p. 3.

Zaslow, Jeff, "Moving On—A Different Kind of Public Accounting: One Firm's Tradition of Goodbye Memos," *Wall Street Journal*, August 1, 2002, p. D1.

—Frank Uhle

Portillo's Restaurant Group, Inc.

2000 Spring Road, Suite 500
Oak Brook, Illinois 60523-3930
U.S.A.
Telephone: (630) 954-3373
Toll Free: (866) 986-2333
Fax: (630) 954-5851
Web site: http://www.portillos.com

Private Company
Founded: 1963
Employees: 3,500
Sales: $175 million (2005 est.)
NAIC: 722110 Full-Service Restaurants; 722210 Limited-Service Eating Places

Mentioning "Portillo's" in the Midwest garners instant recognition and makes mouths water. Portillo's Restaurant Group, Inc. (also known as The Portillo Restaurant Group) consists of its namesake hot dog and sandwich chain, Barnelli's Pasta House, Barney's BBQ, Key Wester Fish & Pasta House, and Luigi's House. Many of Portillo's outlets have a Barnelli's or Barney's sharing space, providing customers with a wide array of delicious, made-to-order fare. Key Wester and Luigi's House are upscale full-service restaurants serving pasta and seafood dishes, the former in a Hemingwayesque atmosphere and the latter in the tradition of northern Italy. After conquering the Midwest, Dick Portillo moved west, opening a Portillo's in Buena Park, California, in 2005.

In the Beginning: 1963–71

Richard "Dick" Portillo was born and raised in the Midwest, specifically Chicago, Illinois. The Portillo family was poor and lived in the city's infamous projects until Dick's father earned enough for the family to move to the southern suburbs. Dick Portillo graduated from high school in 1957 and enlisted with the Marines. Upon his return, he took his savings, little more than $1,000, pooled it with an investment from his older brother Frank, and took on a great American pastime, the hot dog. Using an old trailer with no restroom or running water (a major health

code violation by today's standards), Portillo opened "The Dog House" on North Avenue in Villa Park, Illinois.

In its earliest days the Dog House gained little attention and had only sporadic sales for its limited menu of hot dogs (wrapped with fries), tamales, and soda pop. Portillo slowly learned the ABCs of running a small fast-food establishment, including not buying his supplies from local grocers, since that made it nearly impossible to turn a profit. Portillo visited a competitor and reportedly sneaked into his back room to find out where the rival bought his hot dogs, buns, and condiments. Armed with this information, Portillo began getting what he needed wholesale and set out to make the Dog House the best hot dog vendor in the area. Five months into the business, Dick Portillo repaid his brother's investment and became the hot dog stand's sole owner (Frank bought into another fast-food enterprise, Brown's Chicken).

What the Dog House lacked in atmosphere it made up in the hard work of Dick Portillo and his wife Sharon. They toiled long hours at the stand and did dishes at night in their apartment. Although the next few years were touch-and-go, by 1967 the Dog House was a success. With his profits and help from a local businessman, Harold Reskin, who owned the shopping center where the Dog House was located, Portillo secured a larger trailer and changed the name of his enterprise to "Portillo's."

In 1969 Portillo's had attracted a steady clientele and Reskin helped Dick Portillo finance a freestanding outlet with a counter and kitchen, but no tables or chairs for customers. A second such location was built the following year, 1970. These two hot dog shops soon gained local acclaim and business was good. Portillo was able to finance his own expansion through profits and bank loans, requiring no partners, no investors, and no strings. This self-reliance would turn out to be one of Dick Portillo's most powerful business tools.

Dogs Taking Flight: 1972–89

The success of Portillo's allowed the Portillo family to live well. In the early 1970s, the family took the first of many trips to Key West, Florida, a favorite haunt of writer Ernest Hemingway. Dick Portillo was enchanted by the community's quaint

Company Perspectives:

The Portillo Restaurant Group is the largest privately-owned restaurant company in the Midwest with more than 3,000 employees operating 41 units with 5 separate concepts, plus a catering division. This was all accomplished without franchising or investors. Over the years, Portillo's has remained a family owned business. Dick Portillo attributes much of his success to his hard-working employees and to you, the satisfied customer. He thanks you for your support.

shops and the ambience of its restaurants. Upon his return to Illinois, Portillo began envisioning a new restaurant reflecting the charm of Key West's best seafood eateries. Although it would take Portillo two decades to realize his dream, the inspiration for the Key Wester Fish & Pasta House was born.

While the Key Wester idea was at the back of Dick Portillo's mind, he did, however, try his hand at barbecue. In 1987 Portillo built and opened an eatery called Barney's, serving slow-cooked barbecue ribs, chicken, and sandwiches. He also continued to scout locations for more Portillo's hot dog shops, which he always bought outright, in or near small shopping centers. By this time the "Chicago-style" hot dog had gained fame not only with area residents, but visitors as well. Portillo's served its own version of the Chicago dog—often called the "garden on a bun"—with a variety of vegetables and condiments. Moreover, Portillo's hot dogs were steamed, never grilled, boiled, deep fried, or rolled around a countertop rotisserie.

According to Jeff Smith, of *Frugal Gourmet* fame, there were more than 4,000 hot dog stands in Chicago in the late 1980s. Smith had researched the nation's obsession with hot dogs for his book, *The Frugal Gourmet Cooks American* (William Morrow, 1987), and found that Chicagoans considered their city the "Hot Dog Capital" of the world (New Yorkers, of course, begged to differ). Dick Portillo's success certainly supported the notion, as did other Windy City vendors such as Byron's, Gold Coast Dogs, Murphy's Red Hots, and hundreds of pushcart owners. By 1988, however, Portillo's was the largest hot dog chain in the Chicago area, with 11 outlets, and the company's segue into barbecue, Barney's, was gathering momentum as well.

Portillo's had not established itself by taste alone, but by the unusual old-time décor of its dining rooms and the speed of order fulfillment. While the dining rooms were attractive and scrupulously clean, the drive-in windows were high-tech. Once lines had started curving around buildings and into streets, Portillo pioneered the use of placing order-takers outside with headsets. This allowed orders to go into the kitchen more quickly and kept the lines moving at a faster clip. As Portillo had commented to *Restaurants & Institutions* (May 29, 1989) magazine, "There are 256 ways to dress a hot dog, so operationally, it can be a nightmare."

Portillo's offered hot dogs any way a customer wanted them. For years the Naperville outlet led the thriving group's sales, bringing in an estimated $2 million-plus annually by the end of the decade. Dick Portillo, however, had no plans to slow down

and savor his success. He intended to add a number of new Portillo's in the suburban Chicago area and was in negotiations to franchise a similar chain in Asia with a Japanese firm called, oddly enough, Chicago Foods. Although the venture was later discontinued, due to quality concerns and translating Portillo's appeal, it would be the restaurant group's only failure.

Variety Is the Spice of Life: 1990s

In the new decade, Portillo experimented by putting two of his restaurant concepts together in one unit. Pairing a Barney's barbecue with a Portillo's Hot Dogs proved ideal, providing customers with a wide range of menu items. Another concept was introduced in 1993 with Barnelli's Pasta Bowl, which offered a selection of pasta dishes, homemade breads, salads, and desserts. Soon a dual unit featuring Barnelli's and Portillo's opened, and this combination, too, was a hit with suburban fans. As his eateries thrived in Illinois, Portillo finally realized his dream of opening a full-service seafood restaurant in Florida. The Key Wester Fish & Pasta House opened in Naples, Florida (where Portillo vacationed), in 1995 and offered a nautical décor and seafood selection Papa Hemingway would have admired.

Back home in Illinois, the Portillo's empire had brought in more than $50 million by mid-decade. There were 25 locations sprinkled in and around the Chicago area, almost all Portillo's Hot Dogs, with the exception of the three locations that combined Portillo's and Barnelli's pasta specialties or the barbecue and chicken items of Barney's. The chain's 25th location, a two-story Portillo's/Barnelli's in downtown Chicago, wowed locals with a wide variety of edibles and more than a million dollars' worth of Dick Portillo's sports-themed memorabilia. By this time in its evolution, Portillo's had become equally renowned for its food and the atmosphere of its restaurants. Each location was characterized by a particular Americana theme (sports, music, Prohibition), housing a wide array of early 20th-century objets d'art.

Foodwise, though, Portillo's fame came from its hot dogs (which represented 35 percent of the chain's sales) and an ever-expanding menu of chicken and Italian beef sandwiches, hamburgers, soups, and the chain's famously delicious french fries. In the summer of 1996 Portillo brought his Key Wester concept to Illinois, opening an upscale full-service restaurant a mere block from one of the company's top-performing Portillo's locations in Naperville. Key Wester proved an immediate smash, always filled to capacity, and helped ring up overall group sales of more than $75 million for 1996.

By the late 1990s Portillo's had captured the hearts of Illinoisans and countless visitors to the area. As sales continued to rise, industry analysts wondered if Portillo would eventually franchise or go public. While Portillo had steadfastly rejected the idea of franchising due to quality issues, it seemed taking the firm public was within the realm of possibility.

Multiple Concepts, Same Quality: The 2000s

The dawn of the 21st century ushered in a new era for Portillo's, with sales topping the $100 million mark by 2001. The Illinois fiefdom included two dozen Portillo's Hot Dogs locations, nine Barnelli's Pasta Bowls (all sharing space with a

Key Dates:

1963: The Dog House opens in Villa Park, Illinois.
1967: The Dog House is expanded and renamed Portillo's Hot Dogs.
1987: The first Barney's restaurant, serving ribs and sandwiches, is opened.
1993: The first Barnelli's Pasta Bowl is opened in Schaumburg.
1994: Dick Portillo is crowned *Inc.* magazine's Entrepreneur of the Year.
1995: The Key Wester Fish & Pasta House opens in Naples, Florida.
1996: A second Key Wester opens in Naperville, Illinois.
2000: Luigi's House, an authentic Italian eatery, opens in Illinois.
2004: Portillo's first major advertising campaign is launched.
2005: A Portillo's Hot Dogs opens in Buena Park, California.

Portillo's Hot Dogs unit), two Luigi's House full-service restaurants, the Key Wester Fish & Pasta House, and burgeoning catering services as well.

According to *Restaurant Business* magazine (October 15, 2003), more than 20 billion hot dogs were sold in the United States in 2002, which certainly helped Portillo's leap to sales of a reported $150 million. Dick Portillo continued to expand his chain, moving from the well-represented western and northern suburbs into the neighborhoods south of Chicago. This led to a monumental discovery: not only had many residents of the southern suburbs never been to a Portillo's, but most had never even heard of the brand. To remedy the situation, Portillo did something he had never done in the restaurant group's four-decade history—he initiated a major advertising campaign.

The campaign, produced by the Chicago-based Reilly Group, hit the airwaves in 2004. A series of humorous ads for both radio and television featured Portillo himself describing the history of the local chain and its high-quality food. The ploy apparently worked, as the company's sales continued to climb and Portillo scouted new locations not only in the Chicago area, but outside Illinois as well. In 2004 Portillo announced his intention to take his show on the road, to open a Portillo's in Southern California. The new Portillo's was slated to open in Buena Park, south of Los Angeles, in late 2005. Amazingly, Los Angeles was a major hot dog market despite most people's perception of it as a haven for vegetarians, vegans, and the Hollywood "raw" craze. If the Buena Park restaurant fared well, Portillo planned on opening several more California locations, and perhaps expanding into such southern states as Georgia and Florida. Whereas Portillo's, Barney's, and Barnelli's all seemed to thrive, Portillo did concede

to Wade Daniels of *Nation's Restaurant News* (January 31, 2005) that although his Key Wester concept was still doing exceptionally well, he saw no "future in the fish business" due to escalating prices in fresh seafood.

Dick Portillo, by all accounts, was living the American Dream. The former Marine, who never attended college, had built an empire from one 6- by 12-foot trailer selling hot dogs. The entrepreneur had even prompted a new phrase in restaurant lexicon: "fast-casual dining." Whereas Portillo's may have begun its existence as a tiny fast-food joint, it evolved into a food industry phenomenon. As Dick Portillo had commented to Carolyn Walkup of *Nation's Restaurant News* (January 28, 2002), "I love this business. When you love something, it's not just money; it's a passion." Portillo's passion had become a staple in the diets of many Midwesterners and was on its way to capturing the appetites of Californians and, potentially, many other Americans as well.

Principal Operating Units

Portillo's Hot Dogs; Barnelli's Pasta; Barney's BBQ; Key Wester Fish & Pasta House; Luigi's House.

Principal Competitors

Al's Italian Beef; Byron's Hot Dogs; Gold Coast Dogs; Murphy's Red Hots; JR's Hot Dogs; Pot Belly Sandwich Works.

Further Reading

Andy, Fixmer, "Forget Sprouts, Hot Dog Is L.A.'s Culinary Staple," *Los Angeles Business Journal,* March 14, 2005, pp. 3+.
Baar, Aaron, "Reilly Tells Portillo's Success Story," *ADWEEK Midwest Edition,* June 10, 2004.
Bultman, Janis, "Hot Dogs with Mustard and Glitz," *Forbes,* December 12, 1988, pp. 118+.
Daniels, Wade, "Portillo's Hot Dogs: Barking Up the Right Tree," *Nation's Restaurant News,* January 31, 2005, pp. 170+.
Fixtman, Janis, "Hot Dogs with Mustard and Glitz," *Forbes,* December 12, 1988, pp. 118+.
Murphy, H. Lee, "A Real Hot Dog Hopes to Make Fish Stick," *Crain's Chicago Business,* December 9, 1996, pp. 3+.
Ramseyer, Rick, "Missing Links: Hot Dog Chains Are Building Business," *Restaurant Business,* October 15, 2003, pp. 40+.
Ryan, Nancy Ross, "The Hot Dog," *Restaurants & Institutions,* May 29, 1989, pp. 104+.
Walkup, Caroline, "American Hot Dog Chains Make Global Headway," *Nation's Restaurant News,* July 24, 1995, p. 19.
——, "Hot Dog! It's Twins: Portillo's Launches 25th Restaurant with 2-in-1 Concept," *Nation's Restaurant News,* January 9, 1995, pp. 3+.
——, "Portillo's Hot Dogs," *Nation's Restaurant News,* January 28, 2002, pp. 164+.
——, "Regional Chain Stacks Fast Food Deck with Winning Ways," *Nation's Restaurant News,* April 3, 1995, p. 11.

—Nelson Rhodes

PriceSmart, Inc.

9740 Scranton Road
San Diego, California 92121
U.S.A.
Telephone: (858) 404-8800
Fax: (858) 404-4500
Web site: http://www.pricesmart.com

Public Company
Incorporated: 1997
Employees: 3,314
Sales: $609.7 million (2004)
Stock Exchanges: NASDAQ
Ticker Symbol: PSMT
NAIC: 452910 Warehouse Clubs and Superstores

PriceSmart, Inc. operates membership club stores in Latin America, the Caribbean, and Asia, selling food and consumer goods in approximately 30 warehouse-style stores. Members pay between $20 and $35 to shop at PriceSmart stores, which offer merchandise at reduced prices. The company also licenses 11 stores in China. Father and son Sol and Robert Price own 47 percent of PriceSmart's stock.

Origins

PriceSmart was founded by an individual whom *Forbes*, in a December 22, 2003 article, described as a retailing "demigod," a businessman whose influence on U.S. retailing in the 20th century created a $70 billion industry. PriceSmart was Sol Price's third retail venture, a company started more than 40 years after he first entered the retail sector. Price began his storied career in the mid-1950s, when he was working as an attorney in San Diego. His first venture sprang from the coincidence of two fateful events: the inheritance of a vacant warehouse in his home town and a knock on the door of his law office. Price needed to find a tenant for his warehouse, and the solution to his problem was answered by the knock on his office door. A couple of Price's clients had stopped by to ask him to take a short trip to Los Angeles to give his opinion on an unusual business they had come across. The clients were in-

volved in the wholesale jewelry business, and they had been selling watches to a non-profit, member-owned, retail operation in Los Angeles called Fedco. Price made the trip north and noticed that Fedco's facility was similar to the warehouse he had inherited. He asked his clients to look at his warehouse, suggesting that his building could be used for the same purpose. His clients agreed, marking the beginning of Fedmart and the first traces of the membership club industry.

The business was begun in 1954, started with a $50,000 capital investment. Price solicited the help of eight individuals, who each invested $5,000, and he convinced his law firm to invest the remaining $10,000. Price obtained his inventory from his clients, beginning with the two jewelry wholesalers. Another client, who was involved in the furniture business, provided Price with a small selection of furniture. A third client sold liquor, giving Price's Fedmart the odd merchandise mix of jewelry, furniture, and liquor. He opened membership to government employees of all levels—federal, state, and local. Despite the less than comprehensive selection of goods, Price's business thrived from the start, collecting $4.5 million during its first year in business, four times the total projected by Price and his investors.

Success spawned the establishment of other warehouse stores and a more coherent merchandising strategy. Fedmart developed into a chain of stores, and along the way, Price pioneered several innovations in the retail industry. Fedmart became the first retailer to sell gasoline at wholesale prices. The chain was the first to open an in-store pharmacy. Fedmart also opened in-store optical departments, establishing a format that was aped widely decades later. Aside from developing several industry firsts, Price guided the company into food retailing, a product line that would underpin the chain's development. Price was joined in his business by his son, Robert, who served as Fedmart's executive vice-president until the father-and-son team sold the chain in 1975. After 21 years, Price's start-up had flowered into a 45-store chain with sales exceeding $300 million.

Price Club Debuting in the 1970s

After selling Fedmart, the Prices searched for an idea for their next business venture. "We spent a lot of time walking up and

---

Company Perspectives:

At PriceSmart, the scope of membership shopping has expanded to include merchandise and services. Members realize true value as a result of PriceSmart's efficient and aggressive low cost sourcing, distribution and operations. PriceSmart today is a global, volume-driven, merchandising and services leader delivering value to the member-customer and small businesses.

---

down streets of San Diego talking about it,'' Sol Price remembered in a November 1990 interview with *Supermarket Business.* ''Then,'' Price continued, revealing the inspiration for his second venture, ''we spent a lot of time talking with small business owners—grocery store owners, restaurateurs, the people who ran newspaper and candy stands. We'd ask them where they bought their merchandise, and we discovered a gap in the distribution system just waiting to be filled.'' The gap was filled by The Price Co., started by Sol and Robert Price in 1976. The pair opened their first store, called Price Club, on the outskirts of San Diego. Although Fedmart bore many of the markings of a club warehouse, industry pundits generally ascribed the birth of the industry to the opening of the first Price Club.

Seeking to be a wholesaler to businesses that lacked the financial clout to demand the wholesale prices commanded by larger businesses, the Prices tried to tailor their merchandise mix to meet their customers' needs. Office supplies was first on the list, followed by tires, food, paper products, and a range of other goods, all stacked on metal shelves in a spartan, cavernous, 100,000-square-foot store. To qualify for membership in Price Club, customers were required to show proof of business activity, either presenting a business license or a resale permit.

In contrast to Fedmart's first year of business, Price Club performed terribly. ''We almost went off the cliff for about the first seven months,'' Sol Price admitted in his interview with *Supermarket Business.* By the end of the first year, the San Diego store had collected $16 million in sales, but posted a loss of $750,000. The Prices had no idea what the problem was until a customer suggested opening membership to government employees as Fedmart had done. Soon, membership was opened to employees of the government, hospitals, financial institutions, and utilities, the type of customers who were unlikely to bounce checks (one of Sol Price's enduring business credos was never to accept credit cards: ''it's against my religion for people to go into debt to shop,'' he remarked in a *Supermarket Business* interview). The less discriminatory membership policy turned Price Club into an unmitigated success story, fueling the expansion of the concept into a chain and convincing many onlookers to start membership clubs of their own.

The Prices took Price Co. public in 1980, enabling eager investors to share in the rapid growth of the chain. By the time of the company's initial public offering, the chain was generating nearly $150 million in sales and earning $6 million before taxes. The stores, which looked ''like something the Red Cross might set up for disaster relief,'' according to the April 1985 issue of *Dun's Business Month,* represented the fastest growing

format in U.S. retailing, and Price Co. by far ranked as the segment's dominant player. The stores by this point carried everything from appliances to auto supplies and from liquor to luggage, but the merchandise diversity belied the soundness of the Prices' business strategy. ''Price is the most disciplined retail organization I have ever seen,'' an industry analyst stated in the April 1985 issue of *Dun's Business Month.* Midway through the 1980s, Price Co. had 20 warehouses in operation, 14 of which were located in California. The success of the chain had created many imitators, including Costco Wholesale Club, BJ's Wholesale Club, and Sam's Wholesale Club, but Sol Price and his son enjoyed a large lead over all rivals. The sales of the eight largest companies combined did not equal the revenue volume maintained by Price Co. Put another way, the warehouse club industry had become a $2 billion industry by 1985, the year Price Co. collected $1.8 billion in sales.

By the end of the 1990s, Price Co. operated more than 50 warehouse stores. Its revenue at the beginning of the decade exceeded $5 billion. The company continued to hold sway as an industry leader, but competition inspired by its own success had set the stage for a fierce battle in the 1990s, a battle the Prices opted to wage with the help of a rival. In 1993, when Price Co.'s leadership position had been usurped by Wal-Mart's Sam's Wholesale Club, the Prices decided to merge with Costco. At the time, Price Co.'s revenues totaled $7.5 billion, about a billion dollars more than third place Costco, creating a $16 billion wholesale club that counted Robert Price as its chairman. For less than a year, the merged company operated with two headquarters, one in Kirkland, Washington, where Costco was based, and the other in San Diego, Price Co.'s hometown. The arrangement failed to work, leading to a spinoff that put the company back under the control of the original Costco management team. Robert Price left the organization in 1994, leaving with control over Price/Costco's commercial real estate operations and controlling interests in merchandising opportunities in certain international markets, including Australia, New Zealand, and Central America. These assets became part of a new company, aptly named Newco, but they eventually formed the foundation for another company, PriceSmart.

PriceSmart Is Born in the Late 1990s

Before starting PriceSmart, Robert Price presided over the operations spun off from Costco. Initially organized within Newco, the real estate properties, which consisted primarily of shopping centers in California and Arizona, became known as Price Enterprises, which operated as a real estate investment trust (later renamed Price Legacy Corporation). The other interests gained from the spinoff consisted of the rights to operate membership club stores in certain international markets, giving the Prices the opportunity to express their skills in building another retail chain. They decided to open stores in emerging markets in Latin America and the Caribbean, focusing on regions with a rising middle class free from the competitive likes of Wal-Mart and Carrefour. The Prices opened their first PriceSmart in Los Pueblos, Panama, the first of an expected 30 to 35 warehouse stores. The Prices informed investors that each unit was expected to generate between $20 million and $30 million in sales annually, enabling their retail chain to reach $1 billion in sales within five years. They took PriceSmart public in

Key Dates:

1954: Sol Price starts Fedmart, an early version of Price-Smart.
1976: Sol Price's second venture, Price Club, is started.
1993: The Price Co. and Costco Wholesale Club merge.
1994: Robert Price gains control of the international rights to operate membership club stores in certain international markets.
1996: The first PriceSmart opens in Panama.
1997: PriceSmart completes its initial public offering of stock.
2003: PriceSmart announces it will restate financial results for 2002 and 2003.
2005: PriceSmart settles investors' lawsuit and exits the Mexican market.

September 1997, when the company began trading on the NAS-DAQ. Following the initial public offering, Sol Price owned 33 percent of the company and Robert Price owned 25 percent, giving the pair substantial control over the direction of their new retailing venture.

To lead their company, the Prices selected Gilbert Partida, who joined PriceSmart in December 1997. Partida, like Sol Price, was an attorney by training who also served as the head of the San Diego Chamber of Commerce. Under Partida's leadership, the execution of Price's retailing strategy went according to plan—at first. A second store was opened in Panama the same month Partida arrived, a unit located in Via Brazil. Together, the two stores generated $60 million in sales in 1998, meeting the high end of the Price's revenue projection. No additional stores were opened in 1998, but the company compensated for the lack of activity by assuming an aggressive expansion posture in 1999, when PriceSmart opened seven new warehouse outlets. The stores opened in Panama, Costa Rica, the Dominican Republic, El Salvador, Honduras, and Guatemala, with each grand opening a testament to Partida's skill. He made sure that each grand opening was a celebrated affair, orchestrating spectacular events that often included a visit by the home country's prime minister. Unfortunately for Price-Smart, Partida's talents ended there, and the chain began to suffer from poor management as it entered the 21st century.

PriceSmart in the 21st Century

Partida had never led a company before joining PriceSmart. The 35-year-old attorney had no retailing experience either. When the company began to falter, critics pointed their fingers directly at Partida or at the Prices for having selected someone ill-equipped to manage the development of what promised to be a $1 billion retail business. "He," an analyst said, referring to Partida in a December 22, 2003 interview with *Forbes*, "made a lot of ego-driven decisions that were terrible." PriceSmart opened seven new stores in 2000 and seven more stores in 2001, giving the company a total of 23 stores in 11 countries by the end 2001. Sales for the year reached $489 million, representing substantial growth for the company, but the cracks in the organization already were beginning to show. The profits re-

corded by the chain were meager, and some of Partida's actions were questionable. In August 2001, he flew to New York to solicit interest in a private-equity offering, extolling Price-Smart's strengths to investors. One week later, however, he sold 28 percent of his stake in the company, netting $700,000 from the sale and causing a furor among investors.

In 2002, PriceSmart began straying from its original strategic course, causing further anxiety among shareholders. In January, the company announced it was opening three stores in Mexico, a country dominated by Wal-Mart—the type of competitor the Prices had said they wanted to avoid. Suspicious of the move, and tired of lackluster profitability, the largest Price-Smart shareholders organized a meeting to discuss their grievances. Next, Partida began offering telephone cards at Price-Smart units, turning to a business that yielded exceptionally low profit margins. At the end of the year, the company recorded $648 million in sales, but net income amounted to only $6.3 million, less than 1 percent of sales and well below half the company's projected total.

Partida resigned abruptly in April 2003 before the full extent of PriceSmart's problems were revealed. Robert Price took over as the company's interim chief executive officer and tried to correct some of the mistakes made by Partida, getting PriceSmart out of the telephone card business and closing four stores during the year. The worst was yet to come, however. In November 2003, when losses for the fourth quarter threatened to be as much as $20 million, the company announced it was restating its financial figures for 2002 and 2003 because of improperly booked revenue. Shareholders, who watched PriceSmart's stock value plummet from $49 per share in March 2000 to $6.75 per share at the end of 2003, filed a class-action lawsuit against the company, charging that it had violated federal securities laws by issuing a series of materially false and misleading statements.

As PriceSmart prepared for the future, the company was working to set its operations on a proper course. In February 2005, the company announced it was closing its warehouses in Mexico. "We were late (in entering Mexico) in terms of the number of operators," conceded Robert Price in a February 13, 2005 interview with the *San Diego Union-Tribune*. "We were the last ones in and found it to be a challenging situation," he said. In March 2005, the company settled the lawsuit filed by investors, agreeing to pay $2.35 million. As the company pressed ahead in 2005, Robert Price held onto his title as interim chief executive officer. The search continued for a permanent replacement, one whose task would be ensuring that the Price's third retail chain enjoyed as much success as their first two ventures.

Principal Subsidiaries

PriceSmart (Guatemala) S.A. (66%); PriceSmart Aruba (90%); PriceSmart Barbados; PSMT Caribe, Inc.; PriceSmart Guam; PriceSmart Jamaica (67%); PriceSmart Mexico (50%); Price-Smart Nicaragua (51%); PriceSmart Panama; PriceSmart Philippines (52%); PriceSmart Trinidad (90%); PriceSmart U.S. Virgin Islands; Ventures Services, Inc.

Principal Competitors

Carrefour SA; Royal Ahold N.V.; Wal-Mart Stores, Inc.

Further Reading

Allen, Mike, "PriceSmart Expands," *San Diego Business Journal,* July 24, 2000, p. 4.

——, "PriceSmart Struggles to Regain Once-Profitable Venture," *San Diego Business Journal,* May 31, 2004, p. 6.

Bragaw, Richard S., "At Price Club the Golden Rule Keeps the Customer Satisfied," *Supermarket Business,* November 1990, p. 37.

Crabtree, Penni, "PriceSmart Mulls Going Private to Avert Rules," *San Diego Union-Tribune,* February 26, 2005, p. B3.

Gallagher, Leigh, "Price to Pay," *Forbes,* December 22, 2003, p. 68.

Green, Frank, "San Diego-Based Retailer PriceSmart Experiences Decline in Sales," *San Diego Union-Tribune,* August 7, 2003, p. B4.

"Law Offices of Charles J. Piven, P.A. Announces Class Action Lawsuit Against PriceSmart, Inc. in Behalf of Investors," *PrimeZone Media Network,* December 23, 2003, p. 12.

Levy, Robert, "Make Way for Warehouse Clubs," *Dun's Business Month,* April 1985, p. 76.

McMahon, Shannon, "PriceSmart Settles Investor's Lawsuit," *San Diego Union-Tribune,* March 4, 2004, p. B2.

——, "PriceSmart Pulling Out of Mexico," *San Diego Union-Tribune,* February 13, 2005, p. B3.

Orol, Ron, "Activist Shareholders Eye PriceSmart," *Daily Deal,* September 10, 2002, p. 12.

——, "PriceSmart Founder: We're Not for Sale," *Daily Deal,* September 14, 2002, p. 13.

"San Diego-Based Warehouse Retailer PriceSmart Reports Slump in Sales," *San Diego Union-Tribune,* June 7, 2003, p. B6.

—Jeffrey L. Covell

QLT Inc.

QLT Inc.

887 Great Northern Way
Vancouver, British Columbia V5T 4T5
Canada
Telephone: (604) 707-7000
Toll Free: (800) 663-5486
Fax: (604) 707-7001
Web site: http://www.qltinc.com

Public Company
Incorporated: 1981 as Quadra Logic Technologies
Employees: 329
Sales: $186.1 million (2004)
Stock Exchanges: NASDAQ Toronto
Ticker Symbols: QLTI; QLT
NAIC: 325412 Pharmaceutical Preparation Manufacturing

QLT Inc. is a biotechnology company that develops and markets photodynamic therapeutic products—drugs that are activated by exposure to light. The company has a history of developing treatments for cancer, but its greatest commercial success is Visudyne, a light-activated treatment for age-related macular degeneration, the leading cause of blindness in people over age 50. Other pharmaceutical products in the company's development pipeline include treatments for prostate cancer, skin cancer, and male pattern baldness. The acquisition of Atrix Laboratories in 2004 gave QLT a second marketable pharmaceutical product named Eligard, which is a treatment for advanced prostate cancer.

Origins

Without question, the single most influential figure in QLT's history was Dr. Julia Levy, whose pioneering scientific work achieved commercial success when she was forced to trade her lab coat for the attire of a chief executive officer. Levy was born Julia Coppens in 1934, beginning her life in Singapore, where her father worked as an executive for a Dutch bank. Levy's father, Guillaume Coppens, sent his wife and two daughters to stay with relatives in British Columbia, Canada, on the eve of World War II, fearing for his family's safety. Guillaume

Coppens's anxiety was justified; he was captured by the Japanese and interned in Indonesia, surviving the ordeal but devastated by the experience. He joined his family in British Columbia after the war, unable to work for the remainder of his life. "My recollection of my life was: 'Don't upset your father,'" Levy reflected in a July 23, 2003 interview with *Contemporary Canadian Biographies.*

Levy's mother, who served as the motivation for QLT's greatest commercial success, supported the family by working as a physiotherapist. After high school, Levy spent a year serving as a file clerk at BC Hydro to supplement the scholarships she had earned to attend the University of British Columbia, where she studied microbiology and immunology. After earning her undergraduate degree in 1955, Levy went overseas to obtain her doctorate, attending the University of London's National Institute for Medical Research. She earned her Ph.D. in experimental pathology in 1959 and returned to the University of British Columbia, where she began conducting research on cancer.

After her first marriage ended in divorce, Levy married a physicist at the University of British Columbia named Edwin Levy. The couple married in 1969 and several years later purchased a holiday property on Sonora Island in British Columbia, where they planned to build a cottage. It was the turning point in Levy's career. After a decade of conducting research, Levy had little to show for her efforts, at least in comparison to what she produced after she handed a machete to her son Ben and asked him to clear the weeds on the property. Ben, who was born during Levy's first marriage, was seven years old at the time, and he took to the task with zeal, slashing away at the underbrush with what amounted to a sword. Ben came across some cow parsley and hacked away at it with sufficient enthusiasm to cover his skin in fluid from the plant. "It was a hot day," Ben remembered in a July 6, 1996 interview with the *Vancouver Sun,* describing the fateful day on Sonora Island. "The sun came out, and all of a sudden, I just started blistering everywhere, especially on my arms."

When Levy returned to work, she asked her colleagues at the University of British Columbia about what might have caused her son's skin to blister. She learned that a substance in cow parsley's leaves can attack and destroy certain kinds of tissue, skin cells included, but only when activated by exposure to light. Levy was intrigued and began thinking about the potential of photo-activated drugs, embarking on research that would lead to her co-invention of photodynamic therapy (PDT). Levy's work focused on a two-step process that began with the intravenous injection of a drug. After the drug entered the patient's bloodstream, it collected where abnormal blood vessels were being formed. Once the drug was concentrated around the flawed blood vessels, it was activated by a dose of non-thermal laser light, triggering a process that destroyed abnormal cells.

While Levy's scientific research found a pioneering and focused direction, her work with a team of researchers at the University of British Columbia centered on studying antibodies for treating various forms of cancer. Guiding a drug through development, the various stages of regulatory approval, and through numerous clinical trials represented one of the most arduous and time-consuming achievements in the business world, a monumental task that was even more challenging for the research team in Vancouver. In the beginning of the 1980s, the Canadian biotechnology industry did not exist. At the time, the only way to produce a drug was to sell the rights to a foreign pharmaceutical company. Levy and her colleagues turned to the University of British Columbia for support, but the university refused. With nowhere else to turn, and wishing to remain in control of their discoveries, the research team decided to start their own business. In 1981, Levy mortgaged her house to come up with $50,000, a sum matched by her cofounders, John Brown, Jim Miller, Anthony Phillips, and Ron MacKenzie. They named their company Quadra Logic Technologies, renting one room above a bakery to house their office and laboratory. Each of the founders continued to work at the university, unable to draw a salary from their fledgling venture, and conducted their research above the bakery during off hours.

In many respects, Quadra Logic, or QLT as the company eventually became known, served as Levy's vehicle to deliver her scientific findings to the commercial market. Starting out in 1981, however, Levy and her colleagues were many years away from enjoying any commercial success. The path describing a drug's progression from discovery through development, regulatory approval, and commercialization promised to be an unnerving journey—particularly for a group not versed in the intricacies of clearing regulatory and clinical hurdles. Because the market in the United States was integral to the company's success, approval needed to be obtained from the U.S. Food and Drug Administration (FDA), requiring a process that Levy later described as akin to playing "Russian Roulette," as quoted in the October 22, 2002

issue of *Canadian Chemical News.* "And that's really ugly because you're not the master of your fate," she added.

Photofrin in the Mid-1980s

The young QLT scored its first success with a drug that already had begun progressing along the path toward commercialization. Levy convinced her partners to acquire the rights to Photofrin, a light-activated drug in the midst of clinical trials as a cancer treatment. In 1986, QLT formed an alliance with a larger pharmaceutical company—something nearly every small biotechnology company like QLT needed to do to survive. The company reached an agreement with American Cyanamid to co-develop Photofrin, brokering a deal that gave it equity, which enabled it to fund the drug's development. The alliance was important for another reason because American Cyanamid, practiced in the vagaries of drug development and clinical trials, provided the QLT team with an invaluable tutorial in shepherding a drug through to commercialization. "That was a very fortunate experience for us," Levy reflected in an October 2002 interview with *Canadian Chemical News.* "Because with biotechnology companies they'll take the science forward to a certain level and then they'll license it out to a large pharma company, and the pharma company (will) say, 'Thank you very much, we'll see you later,' and does the development."

The partnership ended before Photofrin gained approval, but it ended on beneficial terms for QLT. American Cyanamid was acquired by another company in the early 1990s, which gave the rights to Photofrin back to QLT, which by that point had another drug in its development pipeline. The idea for the drug came from Levy, who drew her inspiration for developing photodynamic therapy from her son and her motivation for creating what would be her career's crowning achievement from her mother.

The Development of Visudyne in the 1990s

During the mid-1980s, Levy's mother began to lose her sight. She was diagnosed with age-related macular degeneration, an incurable deterioration of the central portion of the retina and the leading cause of blindness in people over the age of 50. Levy had spent her entire career studying cancer and she noticed a similarity between macular degeneration and her chosen field of study: both diseases manifested themselves by forming new, abnormal tissue.

Levy's mother suffered from "wet" macular degeneration, in which flawed blood vessels bleed under the retina, damaging the light-sensitive membrane at the back of the eye. Levy focused her work on developing a drug that targeted the abnormal blood vessels and destroyed them when activated by light, eventually creating QLT's defining pharmaceutical product, Visudyne.

The development of Visudyne became a crusade of sorts for Levy, one whose success was jeopardized when QLT's partnership with American Cyanamid was terminated. Between 1992 and 1995, the company's survival was at stake as it sought to navigate on its own. Levy recalled the period in her October 2002 interview with *Canadian Chemical News,* remembering "really putting on blinkers and just concentrating on trying to get approval for Photofrin, and taking our preclinical work with [Visudyne] forward." She added: "We could have gone under

---

Key Dates:

1981: A group of scientists at the University of British Columbia founds Quadra Logic Technologies, the company that becomes QLT.

1986: QLT forms an alliance with American Cyanamid to develop and market Photofrin.

1995: QLT wins approval to market Photofrin.

2000: The rights to Photofrin are sold and QLT gains clearance to market Visudyne.

2004: QLT merges with Atrix Laboratories, Inc.

---

then if we hadn't taken very major measures to pull ourselves together and focus, focus, focus.''

After a decade of work, QLT received the nod of approval it had labored to obtain in 1995, when Photofrin was accepted by the FDA as a marketable drug. QLT became the only company with approval to market a light-activated pharmaceutical product in the field of photodynamic therapy. Winning approval for her first drug was a celebratory moment for Levy, but she barely had time to mark the occasion before her responsibilities broadened. All of QLT's other founders departed in 1995, leaving Levy, who had served variously as the company's chief scientific officer and vice-president, as the only one to lead the company. Before the year was through, Levy accepted the titles of president and chief executive officer, becoming the company's corporate and scientific leader as it endeavored to win approval for its second drug, Visudyne.

Commercial Success in the 2000s

Under Levy's leadership, QLT recorded the greatest financial growth in its history. Photofrin gave the company the steady stream of revenue it had worked for years to secure, but the lifeblood of its operations, Visudyne, would deliver QLT's most strident financial growth. Visudyne won approval from the FDA in 2000, the same year Levy sold Photofrin to Quebec-based Axcan Pharma Inc. QLT won approval for Visudyne, which it marketed in partnership with Novartis Ophthalmics, in April, recording its first sales from the drug in the second fiscal quarter of 2000, when the company collected $25 million. During the second quarter of 2001, the company generated $56 million from the sale of Visudyne, as its use spread throughout more than 50 countries. The U.S. market represented the company's single biggest market, accounting for two-thirds of Visudyne sales and enabling it to join an elite group of biotechnology companies. "Of the 490 publicly traded biotechnology companies around the world," Levy declared in the Winter 2001 issue of *Buyside,* "only 14 are profitable, and QLT is one of them. Visudyne is an important reason for our growth," she added. "It was the largest ophthalmic product launch on record, with sales of $150 million in the first 12 months."

After years of working to bring Visudyne to market and watching its sales mushroom with each passing fiscal quarter, Levy decided to give up her management responsibilities at QLT. She departed in 2002, after 21 years at the company, passing the titles of president and chief executive officer to Paul Hastings.

Hastings started his career in the pharmaceutical industry in 1984 with Hoffman La Roche, the first of several companies he worked for in the industry. Before joining QLT, Hastings served as president and CEO of Axys Pharmaceuticals.

Hastings's task at QLT was one Levy presumably would not have relished. Sales of Visudyne continued to rise as the reins of leadership passed from Levy to Hastings, but analysts demanded more. QLT was dependent almost entirely on the sale of Visudyne, a dependence that some industry observers described as a weakness. One analyst, in the January 24, 2003 issue of *The America's Intelligence Wire,* typified the assessment of QLT by the financial community, saying, "The big issue for them is what are you going to do next." Although Visudyne was the only treatment for macular degeneration on the market, QLT was expected to contend with its first competition as early as 2005, when Eyetech, a biotechnology company working in collaboration with Pfizer, Inc., was expected to win approval for its macular degeneration drug Macugen.

Hastings's challenge was to build QLT's business beyond Visudyne. The company had two other products under development, Tariquidar, a cancer treatment, and QLT0074, a male baldness treatment, but Hastings realized he needed to take a more aggressive approach to augmenting the company's business. In early 2004, he earmarked $500 million in cash to develop the company's product pipeline and quell analysts' cries for a more diversified product offering. "We are looking to continue to build the pipeline by bringing in-house new technologies, licensing things in, and making acquisitions of products or companies," Hastings announced in the February 2, 2004 issue of *Investor's Business Daily.* Toward this end, Hastings completed a deal that promised a more a balanced QLT in the years ahead. In November 2004, QLT completed a merger with Atrix Laboratories, Inc., a specialty pharmaceutical company with a pipeline of products and drug delivery platforms. Among the immediate gains of the merger was QLT's ability to market one of Atrix's products, Eligard, a treatment for prostate cancer. As Hastings prepared for the future, further deals were expected, as he sought to build on Levy's legacy and create a leading, diversified biotechnology company.

Principal Subsidiaries

QLT USA, Inc.

Principal Competitors

Bausch & Lomb Inc.; DUSA Pharmaceuticals, Inc.; Miravent Medical Technologies.

Further Reading

Alva, Marilyn, "Competition Is Due to Heat Up in Market to Treat Eye Disease," *Investor's Business Daily,* July 12, 2004, p. A13.

"B.C.-Based QLT Completes Merger with Atrix of Colorado," *America's Intelligence Wire,* January 19, 2005, p. 14.

"Blocking Blindness," *Maclean's* May 26, 1997, p. 62.

"Combination Creates Value," *R & D Directions,* January 2005, p. 10.

Gorman, Christine, "Vision Saver," *Time,* November 29, 1999, p. 117.

Greenwood, John, "QLT Eyes a Blockbuster," *National Post,* January 9, 1999, p. D4.

"Julia Levy," *Contemporary Canadian Biographies,* July 2003, p. 32.

Niles, Steve, "Strong Potential in QLT's Hands," *R & D Directions,* May 2004, p. 18.

"On the Way to Full Integration," *R & D Directions,* July-August 2004, p. 14.

"QLT Announces Positive Skin Cancer Results," *Canadian Corporate News,* November 1, 2000.

"QLT: Building Success Through Profitable Biotechnology," *Buyside,* Winter 2001, p. 61.

"QLT CEO Named Entrepreneur of the Year," *Canadian Corporate News,* October 2, 2000.

"QLT Inc.," *Investor's Business Daily,* February 2, 2004, p. A10.

"QLT Inc.," *Market News Publishing,* June 8, 2001.

"QLT to Acquire Kinetek Pharmaceuticals Inc.," *Asia Africa Intelligence Wire,* March 29, 2004, p. 34.

Reichmann, Deb, "QLT Allays Fears About Rival Drug," *America's Intelligence Wire,* September 1, 2004, p. 32.

Sanchez, Mary, "The Levy Legacy," *Canadian Chemical News,* October 2002, p. 30.

Schmucker, Jane, "Watchers Take QLT's Positive Drug News with Grain of Salt," *America's Intelligence Wire,* January 24, 2003, p. 31.

"Shareholder Sues QLT Inc. for Securities Fraud Announces Bernstein Liebhard & Lifshitz, LLP," *Internet Wire,* June 8, 2001.

Svaldi, Aldo, "Canadian Drug Maker QLT Buys Fort Collins, Colo., Biotech Atrix Laboratories," *Denver Post,* June 15, 2004, p. B2.

" 'We've Only Begun to Realize the Potential of Visudyne,' " *Medical Laser Insight,* February 2001, p. 8.

Woolley, Scott, "Here's to Good Health," *Forbes,* May 3, 1999, p. 146.

—Jeffrey L. Covell

The Reader's Digest Association, Inc.

Reader's Digest Road
Pleasantville, New York 10570
U.S.A.
Telephone: (914) 238-1000
Fax: (914) 238-4559
Web site: http://www.rd.com

Public Company
Incorporated: 1922
Employees: 5,000
Sales: $2.38 billion (2004)
Stock Exchanges: New York
Ticker Symbol: RDA
NAIC: 511130 Book Publishers; 454113 Mail-Order
   Houses; 511120 Periodical Publishers; 511140
   Database and Directory Publishers

The Reader's Digest Association, Inc. is a worldwide publisher and distributor of magazines, books, recorded music, and home video packages, which are sold through a variety of distribution channels, including direct mail, display marketing, direct response television, catalogs, retail, and the Internet. Its major publication is the monthly general-interest magazine *Reader's Digest,* which is the world's most widely read magazine with a global readership of more than 100 million, and is available in 48 editions and 19 languages. The company also publishes numerous special-interest magazines and books that include do-it-yourself, cooking, health, gardening, and children's titles. To market its many products, the Reader's Digest Association uses an extensive consumer database that is considered to be one of the largest in the world.

The Early Years

Reader's Digest was founded in 1922 through the joint efforts of DeWitt Wallace and Lila Bell Acheson Wallace. DeWitt Wallace was born on November 12, 1889, in St. Paul, Minnesota, to a father who was a college professor and who later became president of Macalester College. Throughout his

years of early adulthood, DeWitt Wallace read widely, and got in the habit of making notes from his reading to retain ideas. In a job handling inquiries about an agricultural textbook, he began wondering if his reading notes might be useful to others if published. Thus, he conceived the idea of condensing magazine articles and reprinting them in a digest magazine.

In the early 1900s, Wallace produced a 128-page book on farming, providing information about agricultural bulletins available to farmers. He sold 100,000 copies of the book by traveling through five states in an old car, selling the book to banks and feed stores that would give the book to customers as a gift. Due to his success with the book, he saw a market for that type of publication among the public as a whole, and sought to publish condensed versions of articles in a magazine form.

World War I temporarily interrupted Wallace's plans. In October 1918, he was severely wounded in battle in France. During his months of recuperation, he focused on reading from a variety of magazines, distilling the articles down to their essentials. On his return home to St. Paul, he continued to work on digesting other magazine articles, putting together 31 summarized articles in a sample of the type of digest magazine he thought would sell. The cost of printing the sample was paid for with money borrowed from his brother and father. He showed his sample to several publishing houses with the hope that they would use his idea and hire him as editor, but all of them turned him down.

In January 1922, Wallace finally published the magazine on his own, aided by his wife, Lila Bell Acheson Wallace. Acheson had been born in Canada in 1889, but spent most of her early life in the United States while her father preached in a number of midwestern towns. In 1921, she married DeWitt Wallace, and together they began selling his magazine idea to readers by direct mail. The couple rented an apartment in Greenwich Village in New York City, with Lila retaining her job as a social worker to pay the rent. DeWitt Wallace sent out letters to potential subscribers, offering his magazine idea for sale and promising a money-back guarantee if readers were not satisfied. These solicitations brought in 1,500 subscriptions at $3 each, generating enough money to finance the first edition and possibly the second.

The first edition of *Reader's Digest* was dated February 1922, and contained 64 pages. Its small measurements, about 5.5 inches by 7.5 inches, allowed readers to carry it in a pocket or purse and was a unique innovation among magazines at the time. The lead article was by Alexander Graham Bell and was on the importance of self-education as a lifelong habit.

DeWitt Wallace spent much of the magazine's first year in the New York Public Library reading articles to summarize in future issues, while Lila Wallace kept her job. The first edition was judged to be a success when there were no cancellations of subscriptions after its release. By September 1922, the couple was able to rent a garage and apartment for their editorial offices, choosing to live in Pleasantville, New York, where they had been married in 1921. Additional promotional letters brought in new subscribers, and within a year of its first edition, circulation had risen to 7,000. After four years, circulation was up to 20,000, and by 1929 it had risen to an astounding 216,000 subscribers.

The Mid-1900s: A Growing Enterprise

Initially, *Reader's Digest* kept a low profile, partly for fear that envious magazines might stop allowing it to reprint their articles. DeWitt Wallace seemed to have a very good notion of what his readers wanted, and circulation continued to grow, reaching over one million in 1936 and three million in 1939. An edition began appearing in England in 1938. Due to the rapid increase in the size of operations, in 1939 the Wallaces moved their facilities to Chappaqua, New York, located close by, but retained their mailing address in Pleasantville, because of the euphonious nature of its name. The address has remained at Pleasantville ever since.

In 1950, condensed books under the *Reader's Digest* name first appeared. These books, which presented abbreviated versions of popular novels, were an immediate success. Therefore, nine years later the company diversified even further when a series of phonograph record albums of music that was culturally sophisticated yet broadly popular appeared under the *Reader's Digest* banner.

Foreign-language editions of *Reader's Digest* carried advertising from their inception, but in the United States advertising was not introduced until 1955. Furthermore, the magazine did not accept advertising for alcoholic beverages until the late 1970s, and it never ran advertisements for cigarettes. Instead, it began warning readers of the dangers of smoking, well before the surgeon general made his report in 1964.

Reader's Digest owed its initial appeal and continued success to DeWitt's ability to choose articles that reflected the values of its many readers. Many of those readers later told of the hope and inspiration they drew from the optimistic spirit that

pervaded *Reader's Digest*. That spirit reflected the outlook of DeWitt Wallace, who based the magazine's content on what he wanted to read. Even as the publication grew in size and popularity, he retained strict editorial control.

When the magazine became successful, DeWitt Wallace kept up the task of editing it and managing finances. His wife designed the corporate headquarters and purchased many artworks that are still part of the company's collection. She also had a hand in selecting the graphics that adorned the back cover of the *Digest*. In 1956, she formed the Lila Wallace Reader's Digest Fund to support the arts and make them accessible to persons of all income levels. A DeWitt Wallace Reader's Digest Fund was also formed for the purpose of providing education programs for young people.

The 1970s and 1980s: The Changing Face of the Association

In 1973, after over half a century of work, the Wallaces retired, although DeWitt Wallace kept in close contact with the editorial and corporate offices. He died on March 30, 1981, at the age of 91. Lila Wallace survived him by three years. The Wallaces never had children, and therefore most of their stock in the company was willed to charities, including Macalester College. This stock was non-voting, however, and almost all of the Wallace's voting power was placed with the two Wallace trust funds, of which the association management owned 3 percent.

About the time of Lila Wallace's death in 1984, George Grune became head of The Reader's Digest Association. The company was not performing very well, and in a successful effort to improve profitability, he took the company public and began a cost-cutting program that included the termination of foreign editions of *Reader's Digest* that were losing money, the divestiture of weak divisions, and the reduction of the workforce from 10,000 to 7,500. He also decreased the rate at which advertising was being lost.

Members of the staff who had worked during the Wallace years became concerned that Grune's methods departed from Wallace's idea that the company was an association of readers and not just a for-profit venture. There was no doubt that Grune had improved profits; in five years profits increased sevenfold. After years of higher profits, several of the charities that owned non-voting shares of the association's stock sold some of their shares to the public in order to take advantage of the high price the stock would bring. After the sale, in February 1990, 21 percent of the total stock was publicly held, these all being class A non-voting shares. Nearly all of the class B voting shares (98 percent) were still held by the trust funds, with the remainder held by employees of the association.

As the 1980s drew to a close, The Reader's Digest Association remained a global company, with operations located in 50 cities throughout the world. *Reader's Digest* continued as its premiere publication, accounting for nearly a third of the company's revenues. The *Digest* also served to introduce subscribers to other products sold by the company, such as the condensed books and audio or video tapes.

To maintain its subscribers' loyalties, editors of *Reader's Digest* kept coverage diverse and of high quality. The publica-

Key Dates:

1922: DeWitt Wallace and Lila Bell Acheson Wallace publish volume 1, number 1 of *Reader's Digest*.
1938: The first international edition is published in the United Kingdom.
1950: Reader's Digest Condensed Books is established.
1973: The Wallaces retire.
1984: George Grune is appointed chief executive officer.
1996: Reader's Digest World, later renamed www.rd.com, is launched, giving the company its first presence on the Internet.
1998: Thomas O. Ryder is appointed chairman and chief executive officer.
1999: Books Are Fun, Ltd. is acquired amid sweeping restructuring efforts.
2001: Restrictions are imposed against sweepstakes promotions, prompting Reader's Digest to abandon the use of sweepstakes for marketing purposes.
2002: Reiman Publications is acquired, the largest acquisition in the association's history.

tion was earning nearly 70 percent of its revenues from circulation, which was a very high figure given that most magazines rely more heavily on advertising for revenue. But because the *Digest* did not rely so much on its advertisers, its content did not have to be targeted to a market desired by the advertisers, leaving editors free to select articles having the broadest appeal.

In the late 1980s, the association acquired several special-interest magazines, such as *Travel Holiday, The Family Handyman, New Choices for the Best Years,* and *American Health.* In 1990, it expanded this line by purchasing the British magazine *Money,* which was renamed *Moneywise,* and by starting up a French magazine, *Budgets Famille.* The special-interest-magazine line, along with other Reader's Digest books and home entertainment, accounted for the revenues not brought in by the *Reader's Digest* magazine. The company's books were either released individually or in series. Series books included such new product lines in the United States as the AMA Home Medical Library, while general individual books included reference books, how-to books, cookbooks, travel guides, and others.

The 1990s and Beyond

As the global economy was restructured in the 1990s, The Reader's Digest Association made attempts to keep pace. Its products were already well known in 11 of the 12 countries that made up the European single market, although *Budgets Famille* was suspended in May 1990 after six issues because it did not meet circulation or advertising objectives. The company began formulating plans to expand into the new markets of Eastern Europe that were beginning to be important in world trade. For example, when the Berlin Wall was opened in 1989, employees of the *Digest* started distributing complimentary copies of the German-language version of *Reader's Digest* and collecting names for a mailing list of potential subscribers. Then in late 1991, *Reader's Digest* became available in Russian- and Hungarian-language editions to serve readers in those countries.

In this way, the association continued to keep pace with an ever-changing world.

In 1991 the company boasted record sales figures, despite the fact that it was operating in a weak economic climate due to worldwide uncertainty caused by the Persian Gulf War. Aiding the Association in its success were two acquisitions made that year. Both David & Charles, a British book publisher and one of the United Kingdom's leading book clubs, and Joshua Morris Publishing, Inc., an international book publisher with a focus on children's materials, contributed to the Reader's Digest Association's strong financial standing in the early 1990s.

In 1992, as Reader's Digest celebrated its 70th anniversary, the company updated the strategic plan that had been set in place when Grune first took over in 1984. Even greater emphasis was placed on expanding into new markets around the globe, with use of the *Reader's Digest* magazine as an entry tool. The company committed to the idea of releasing at least one new edition of the magazine in each of the following years. Also emphasized in the newly updated plan were cost control measures which led to a 10 percent workforce reduction at the company's headquarters in Pleasantville in 1993. The structure of the company itself was also reorganized into three main operating divisions: Reader's Digest Europe, Reader's Digest U.S.A., and Reader's Digest Pacific, each of which became responsible for the business in its own market area.

The corporation's rejuvenation efforts soon began to show evidence of success. In 1993, after 55 years in the United Kingdom, that edition of *Reader's Digest* became the area's bestselling and most widely read magazine. That same year, *Fortune* magazine called the Reader's Digest Association the United States' most admired publishing company. In the United States, the ABC television network aired a special program entitled "Reader's Digest: On Television," which helped the company's books and home entertainment segment begin to flourish once again, after a slump during the previous few years. Furthermore, in a move designed to coincide with the world's progression into the information age, Reader's Digest began to pursue the development of interactive CD-ROM products.

By 1995, James P. Schadt had succeeded Grune as chairman and CEO of the Reader's Digest Association. Schadt, who moved up from the rank of president upon Grune's retirement to fill the new leadership role, had been with the company throughout its restructuring phase. His position as president was filled by Ken Gordon, a longtime Reader's Digest employee and the head of the U.S.A. operating division. Together, the two continued to focus both on strengthening Reader's Digest's business in the United States, and expanding throughout the world.

The year 1995 also offered unique opportunities for Reader's Digest to participate in cooperative endeavors with other companies. Reader's Digest teamed up with the Meredith Corporation, known widely for its *Better Homes and Gardens* and *Ladies' Home Journal* products, as a means of expanding its consumer database. The company also entered into partnerships with Microsoft, to produce CD-ROMs based on Reader's Digest reference books, and with Dove Audio to produce audio books.

Other operations of the association contributed to the company's total revenue. These operations included a subsidiary,

QSP, Inc., which provided fundraising services for schools and youth groups through the sale of subscriptions to magazines, music products, and candy. Nearing the end of the century, *Reader's Digest* remained the world's best-selling and most widely read magazine. Despite the magazine's popularity, however, it was the books and home-entertainment division that generated the bulk of the association's profits by the late 1990s. Furthermore, with the increasing popularity of the Internet, an entirely new avenue of product development and distribution was opening up for Reader's Digest.

Downsizing and Restructuring at Century's End

New leadership arrived at Reader's Digest as it entered the late 1990s, and the assessment of the association's condition was bleak. In April 1998, Thomas O. Ryder, who was recruited from American Express, was appointed chairman and chief executive officer, ushering in an era of sweeping change at the nearly 70-year-old company. Ryder discovered an organization suffering from bloated overhead, dwindling profits, weak product offerings, poor pricing decisions, and a litany of other ills that prompted him almost immediately to launch a program for recovery that would stretch into the 21st century. Ryder's cost-cutting measures began in July 1998, aimed at trimming between $300 million and $350 million in expenses by 2001. His measures substantially increased operating profits, but in January 2001, as Ryder wrote in the association's 2004 annual report, "suddenly everything went wrong." When the dot.com industry collapsed, Reader's Digest incurred heavy loses because it had invested sizeable sums in Internet-related businesses. Ryder also blamed the effects of 9/11 and the anthrax scare for inflicting damage on the association, but the most devastating development of the year came after regulatory agreements forced Reader's Digest to abandon its sweepstakes promotion business. In 2001, 32 states fined the association for misleading consumers with sweepstakes promotions. Subsequently, the use of sweepstakes marketing was eliminated from all U.S. editions of *Reader's Digest.*

On a more positive note, the years of restructuring also saw Reader's Digest complete several important acquisitions. In 1999, the company acquired Books Are Fun, Ltd. for $380 million. A profitable and fast-growing company, Books Are Fun operated traveling book fairs in office buildings and schools. In 2002, the company completed the largest acquisition in its history, paying $760 million for Greendale, Wisconsin-based Reiman Publications. A publisher of cooking, gardening, country lifestyle, and nostalgia magazines and books, Reiman was expected to add $300 million in annual revenue to Reader's Digest's total volume. Reiman published 12 bimonthly magazines with an aggregate circulation of 16 million subscribers. The company also maintained a 32-million-customer database, 19 million of whom were not in Reader's Digest's database.

As Reader's Digest entered the mid-2000s, Ryder continued his restructuring efforts, endeavoring to create a company that could look forward to a profitable future. Much work needed to be done, but there were signs of improvement, including a $10 million increase in operating profits by the company's North American operations in 2004. Another encouraging sign was the expansion of the company's non-core business, a goal of Ryder's when he took over and the motivation for the acquisi-

tion of Books Are Fun and Reiman. In 1998, Reader's Digest derived 8 percent of its revenue from its non-core operations. In 2004, the company derived 35 percent of its revenue from its non-core businesses. In the years ahead, the success of the company depended heavily on the effectiveness of Ryder's measures, making his tenure of management arguably as important as the legacy of the Wallaces.

Principal Subsidiaries

Reader's Digest Argentina, SRL; The Reader's Digest Association Pty. Limited (Australia); Verlag Das Beste Ges.m.b.H. (Austria); Reader's Digest N.V.-S.A. (Belgium); Reader's Digest Brasil Ltda. (Brazil); The Reader's Digest Association (Canada) Ltd.; Guangdong Pegasus Marketing Information & Service Co. Ltd. (China); Reader's Digest Vyber s.r.o. (Czech Republic); Oy Valitut Palat-Reader's Digest Ab (Finland); Selection du Reader's Digest S.A. (France); Verlag Das Beste GmbH (Germany); Reader's Digest Asia, Ltd. (Hong Kong); Reader's Digest Kiado KFT (Hungary); Libri e Piu, Srl (Italy); The Reader's Digest Ltd. (Japan); Reader's Digest (Malaysia) Sdn. Bhd; Caribe Condor S.A. de C.V. (Mexico); Reader's Digest European Shared Services B.V. (Netherlands); Det Beste A/S (Norway); Reader's Digest (Philippines) Inc.; Reader's Digest Przeglad Sp.z o.o. (Poland); Seleccoes do Reader's Digest (Portugal) S.A.; Editura Reader's Digest SRL (Romania); Publishing House Reader's Digest, JSC (Russia); Reader's Digest Vyber Slovensko, s.r.o. (Slovak Republic); Reader's Digest Selecciones S.A. (Spain); Reader's Digest Aktiebolag (Sweden); Das Beste aus Reader's Digest AG/Selection du Reader's Digest SA (Switzerland); Reader's Digest (Thailand) Limited; LLC Direct Digest (Ukraine); Reader's Digest Europe Limited (U.K.); Ardee Music Publishing, Inc.; Books Are Fun, Ltd.; Christmas Angel Productions, Inc.; Pegasus Asia Investments Inc.; Pegasus Finance Corp; Pegasus Investment, Inc; Pegasus Sales, Inc.; Pleasantville Music Publishing, Inc.; QSP, Inc.; R.D. Manufacturing Corporation; RD Publications, Inc.; Reader's Digest Children's Publishing, Inc.; Reader's Digest Consumer Services, Inc.; Reader's Digest Entertainment, Inc.; Reader's Digest Financial Services, Inc.; Reader's Digest Latinoamerica, S.A.; Reader's Digest Sales and Services, Inc.; Reader's Digest Sub Nine, Inc.; Reader's Digest Young Families, Inc.; SMDDMS, Inc.

Principal Competitors

Bertelsmann AG; Rodale, Inc.; Time Inc.

Further Reading

Ferguson, Charles W., "Unforgettable DeWitt Wallace," *Reader's Digest,* February 1987.

Granatstein, Lisa, "Digesting Change," *MEDIAWEEK,* June 17, 2002, p. 42.

——, "Digesting RDA's Changes," *MEDIAWEEK,* April 29, 2002, p. 5.

Harrington, John, "StockWatch: World of Woe at Reader's Digest," *Crain's New York Business,* August 27, 2001, p. 30.

Lynn, Matthew, "Revolution in Pleasantville," *Management Today,* April 1996, p. 62.

Milliot, Jim, "International Unit Leads Reader's Digest," *Publishers Weekly,* February 7, 2005, p. 10.

——, "More Jobs Go As Reader's Digest Restructures Again," *Publishers Weekly,* August 4, 2003, p. 11.

——, "More Restructuring at RD," *Publishers Weekly,* March 10, 2003, p. 17.

——, "Publishers Discuss Finances, The Future at Conference," *Publishers Weekly,* December 20, 1993, p. 10.

——, "RD Focuses on Expansion," *Publishers Weekly,* November 8, 2004, p. 10.

——, "Reader's Digest 'On Track,'" *Publishers Weekly,* February 2, 2004, p. 16.

——, "Reader's Digest to Acquire Reiman Publications," *Publishers Weekly,* April 1, 2002, p. 9.

——, "Trade Unit Sales Jump at Reader's Digest," *Publishers Weekly,* May 10, 2004, p. 7.

Morais, Richard C., "Hate Selling," *Forbes,* June 5, 1995, p. 142.

——, "Takeover Bait," *Forbes Global,* July 7, 2003, p. 26.

"New Castle," *Westchester County Business Journal,* February 28, 2005, p. 36.

Pogrebin, Robin, "A Magazine Only a Mother Could Love? Seeking Younger Audience, Reader's Digest Tries to Lose Its Stodgy Image," *New York Times,* July 22, 1996, p. C1.

Rothman, Andrea, "The Man Who Rewrote Reader's Digest," *Business Week,* June 4, 1990.

"Ryder Probes RDA's Past Problems," *Direct Marketing,* August 2000, p. 9.

"With the Sale of Its 65-Year-Old Headquarters, 'Reader's Digest' Is Becoming a 'Pleasantville' Tenant," *America's Intelligence Wire,* December 6, 2004, p. 31.

—Donald R. Stabile
—updates: Laura E. Whiteley; Jeffrey L. Covell

Recreational Equipment, Inc.

6750 South 228th Street
Kent, Washington 98032
U.S.A.
Telephone: (253) 395-3780
Fax: (253) 395-4352
Web site: http://www.rei.com

Member-Owned Cooperative
Incorporated: 1938
Employees: 6,500
Sales: $887.8 million (2004)
NAIC: 451110 Sporting Goods Stores; 448140 Family
    Clothing Stores; 454113 Mail-Order Houses

Recreational Equipment, Inc. (REI) is one of the nation's largest consumer cooperatives, selling sports apparel, outdoor sporting equipment, and mountain climbing gear. REI sells its apparel and gear through a chain of 77 stores, a web site, and through a mail-order catalog business. The cooperative is owned by its more than 1.7 million member-customers who receive annual patronage dividends in proportion to their spending. In addition to its involvement with outdoor clothing and equipment, REI operates a full-service adventure travel company named REI Adventures.

Early History

When a group of Pacific Northwest mountain climbers searched for a way to get their hands on highly coveted Swiss ice axes, their solution was the formation of REI, an enterprise destined to become one of the largest consumer cooperatives in the United States. At the time of REI's formation in 1938, serious mountain climbers in the region were in need of quality, European-manufactured mountaineering equipment, but there was little they could do individually to bridge the 5,000-mile gap separating Seattle and the epicenter of European mountaineering manufacturing. Swiss ice axes and other European-manufactured mountain climbing equipment were unavailable in Seattle during the 1930s, forcing area climbers to use inferior mountaineering equipment while their European counterparts enjoyed the advantages of quality equipment designed for seri-

ous use. To open up a distribution conduit from Europe to the Pacific Northwest a group of 23 Seattle, Washington climbers led by Lloyd Anderson took collective action and turned to the roots of the modern cooperative movement for the philosophical backbone to support their group effort.

Anderson, an engineer who served as REI's president during the cooperative's first three decades of existence, looked to England for a way to import Swiss ice axes to the United States. His research uncovered the Rochdale Equitable Partners Society, an organization established in Rochdale, England, during the 19th century that was widely regarded as the progenitor of the modern cooperative movement. From the Rochdale Cooperative, Anderson adopted the principles that would guide REI, creating a cooperative whose membership was open to all, with each active member receiving one vote and annual dividends in proportion to patronage. After paying a modest, one-time membership fee, customers became owners of the cooperative and received a percentage of the amount they spent on merchandise each year, a percentage that was determined by the cooperative's annual profit total. Organized as such, REI represented a bold experiment in the retail industry, an enterprise with an egalitarian perspective pursuing socialist, utopian objectives that were conspicuously out of place in the fast-paced, profit-crazed retail world. The concept worked, however, succeeding in an industry littered with failed businesses whose strategies were more in line with capitalist ideals.

Not surprisingly, REI's development into one of the country's largest consumer cooperatives and into one of the nation's largest retailers was a slow, gradual process. The object was not to create a flourishing chain of retail outlets, but to create a way for Seattle climbers to obtain state-of-the-art European climbing equipment at the best prices possible. The cooperative, in fact, did not operate a retail location until six years after its formation. Initially, REI operated out of Lloyd Anderson's house in West Seattle, but public demand for mountaineering hardware led to the establishment of the cooperative's first store in 1944, a modest operation comprising three shelves situated in the back of a gas station in downtown Seattle.

From this milestone in the company's history, the arrival of the next turning point was nine years away, occurring in 1953 when REI hired its first full-time employee to manage the cooperative's sole store. The store by this point was collecting $72,000 a year in sales, and its stewardship fell to a young local climbing enthusiast named Jim Whittaker, who, along with his twin brother, Lou, had spent his life scaling the myriad mountains dotting the Pacific Northwest. Whittaker joined REI a decade before he became the first American to reach the summit of Mt. Everest, an achievement that earned the inveterate mountain man worldwide fame and local acclaim and drew attention to REI, Whittaker's place of employment (off the mountains) for a quarter of a century. Whittaker's involvement with REI led to the beginning of a new era in the cooperative's history, bringing to a close the decades of Anderson's presidency and marking the beginning of REI's development into a retail giant.

Expansion Beginning in the 1970s

Anderson served as REI's president from its founding year to 1971, overseeing the establishment of the company's first store in 1944 and its relocation to Seattle's Capitol Hill neighborhood in 1962. His departure in 1971 paved the way for Whittaker's ascendancy to the cooperative's presidency and years of unprecedented growth for the sleepy, one-store enterprise. Under Whittaker's leadership, the cooperative diversified and expanded. A product-testing subsidiary named THAW, which was formed in 1967, was built into a clothing manufacturing subsidiary during Whittaker's tenure in the 1970s. A second store was established in Berkeley, California, in 1975, making its debut 31 years after the first store opened its doors. After this lengthy gap separating store openings, Whittaker waited a mere year before opening REI's third store, establishing it in Jantzen Beach, Oregon. Quickly, REI was transforming into a regional retail powerhouse under Whittaker's directorship, executing a common evolutionary leap expected of many retail corporations but not necessarily of a consumer-owned cooperative. For years, certain members of REI's board of directors (elected by active customer-owners) had been growing alarmed at the changes taking place, changes that, according to some, were altering the philosophical foundation upon which REI had been created. As the 1970s progressed, the rancor intensified, pitting a faction of rebellious board members against their president, Jim Whittaker. The resolution of this dispute set the stage for the most prolific growth in REI's history, marking a definitive juncture in the story of the cooperative's life.

Essentially, the philosophical battle waged during the 1970s hinged on the central issue of growth, on whether REI would follow Whittaker's ambitious expansion plans or the desires of those board members who wanted to preserve the cooperative's more simplistic roots. It was a struggle in which Whittaker did not want to participate. Whittaker quit in 1979, later telling a *Forbes* reporter, "A lot of board members were against growth; they wanted it to be the same little store." Whittaker went on to found a new manufacturer of mountain gear, a company whose merchandise was marketed under the "Because It's There" label, but his departure did not signal a return to the more supine years of REI's past. Instead, the cooperative entered the 1980s fully committed to the scale of expansion proposed by Whittaker.

In the election to decide Whittaker's successor, the proponents of no growth lost out to those who clamored for expansion, paving the way for a new president whose professional background determined REI's future. Elected to replace Whittaker was Jerry Horn, a former merchandise executive for Sears who joined REI and immediately began preaching strategic planning. The focus on strategic planning worked wonders for REI's profitability, boosting annual patronage dividends considerably. Horn added a line of children's apparel, replaced the cooperative's full-time clerks with more inexpensive seasonal workers, and in 1981 acquired Mountain Safety Research (MSR), a manufacturer of backpacking stoves, helmets, carabiners, and other mountaineering equipment. In a few short years Horn could point to tangible evidence in support of his work. Patronage dividends increased from a depressed 5 percent when he joined the company to 12 percent by the early 1980s, an increase that validated the shouts for growth during Whittaker's tenure.

Horn resigned from REI in June 1983, opting to leave the cooperative to run a stockholder-owned campsite company. Horn left a rapidly growing company supported by seven stores and a mail-order catalog business that generated roughly 25 percent of the cooperative's annual revenue volume. Sales by this point had marched upward at a 26 percent annual pace for the past three decades, rising to $72 million by 1982, while annual profits neared $9 million, the bulk of which was divided among the cooperative's 465,000 customer-owners. To take charge of this flourishing retail enterprise, the cooperative's board elected 36-year-old Wally Smith to replace Horn, a selection that augured more growth for REI. Smith, whose childhood dream was to become a stockbroker, joined REI as a summer worker in 1965, becoming the first manager of the cooperative's Berkeley store when it opened a decade later. Before being elected as the cooperative's fourth president, Smith earned a business degree from the University of Washington. He then proceeded to use his educational training to orchestrate REI's expansion.

By the time Smith was settling into his new position at REI, the cooperative was selling not only a variety of climbing equipment, apparel items, and sleeping bags, but also items that had little to do with the objectives first articulated by Lloyd Anderson during the 1930s. REI, through its seven retail outlets and the more than five million catalogs it distributed each year, was a purveyor of signed and numbered art reproductions and gourmet popcorn by the time Smith took the helm. To charges that REI was developing into an organization that bore little resemblance to the cooperative formed nearly a half century earlier, Smith expressed no remorse. "The demand for backpacking goods peaked in the 1970s," he explained to a reporter from *Forbes* just after assuming REI's presidential duties. "What responsible company doesn't change with the times?"

Four years after being elected president, Smith had quickly established a legacy of expansion at REI. In 1987, the cooperative operated 17 stores, up substantially from the seven stores Smith inherited in 1983. Expansion on the East Coast was started during the year with the establishment of a store in Reading, Massachusetts, and ambitious expansion scheduled for the immediate future promised to strengthen the cooperative's national presence significantly. Sites selected for REI stores in 1988 (the cooperative's 50th anniversary year) included San Francisco, San Diego, Atlanta, Philadelphia, and California's San Fernando Valley, part of a five-year plan that called for the opening of between 15 and 20 25,000-square-foot stores.

1990s: Growth and a New Flagship Store

Fueled by this prodigious expansion, annual sales swelled to more than $200 million by the end of the decade, reaching $231 million by the beginning of the 1990s. The cooperative's subsidiary operations, THAW and MSR, had also recorded encouraging growth during the 1980s, adding to the luster of the REI organization as it prepared for the decade ahead. THAW's sales volume increased 166 percent during the 1980s, while MSR, one-quarter the size of THAW, registered more prolific growth, increasing its sales volume an astounding 453 percent. By 1990, there were 22 stores spread across 13 states; a year later there were 27 stores scattered throughout 16 states extending from Alaska to New York. Eight years after Smith's election, REI's membership rolls included more than two million registered members, more than 900,000 of whom were designated as active members—twice the number during Smith's inaugural year.

Growth on all fronts necessitated the construction of a state-of-the-art 400,000-square-foot distribution center in Sumner, Washington, in 1991, evidence that the onset of a national economic recession was having little effect on REI. The cooperative, in fact, performed admirably during an economic downturn that devastated many retailers throughout the country. In 1992, when REI operated 32 stores in 18 states and announced plans to double in size by the end of the decade, the cooperative posted record sales, a feat duplicated in 1993, when REI acquired tent manufacturer Walrus, Inc., and again in 1994. The most remarkable news of the early 1990s, however, was the cooperative's announcement in 1993 that it would relocate its

flagship Capitol Hill store and construct a modern store more suited to the needs of the company during the 1990s and the decades ahead.

Since its establishment in 1962, the Capitol Hill store had grown along with the cooperative, but in helter-skelter fashion. As the cooperative grew, the flagship store expanded, swallowing up adjoining buildings along Pike Street and eventually snaking its way through five levels of retail space measuring 37,000 square feet. By the early 1990s, Smith and REI's board had decided the time had come for a new store, a store that would put an end to the nightmares of parking near Pike Street and make a bold statement about the future of REI.

As designs were being developed for the new store, REI continued to experience heartening growth. In 1994, REI operated 40 stores in 18 states, generated $432 million in sales, and ranked as the sixth largest sports apparel retailer in the United States. After two years of registering record sales and averaging 16 percent annual growth during the worst of economic times for retailers, projections for 1995 were justifiably optimistic. In 1995, however, expectations collided with reality. Anticipating growth during the year in excess of 15 percent, Smith was chagrined to record a modest gain in sales of 2.8 percent. Any disappointment stemming from 1995's lackluster sales performance was swept away the following fall when REI celebrated the grand opening of its new flagship store among throngs of disbelieving customers.

REI's new Seattle store opened in September 1996 after more than three years of planning. Measuring nearly 100,000 square feet, the new store contained 80,000 square feet of retail space, or more than twice the space of the cooperative's old and shuttered Capitol Hill store. Aside from increased retail space and an onsite, multilevel parking garage, there were numerous features that put the store in a class of its own and quickly made it a destination point for tourists visiting the Pacific Northwest. On the 1.2-acre site occupied by the flagship store, 21,000 square feet was set aside for native Northwest flora and a pond and waterfall charged with recirculated rainwater. Winding its way through the REI park was a 470-foot outdoor mountain-bike trail for customers to test bikes before purchase. Inside, the store featured a Rain Room that showered water on customers trying on waterproof clothing, a camp-stove-testing and water-filter-testing area next to the store's campsite and stream, and the most eye-catching of all the new features and interactive displays gracing the store, the 110-ton, 65-foot REI Pinnacle, the tallest free-standing indoor climbing structure in the world. Housed in a glass enclosure that offered summit views of the Puget Sound, the Olympic Mountains, and downtown Seattle, the indoor climbing rock accommodated as many as 15 climbers at a time and represented one of the most effective marketing tools for the store.

REI Entering the 2000s

As REI prepared for the late 1990s, there was much to be celebrated. The opening of the new flagship store proved to be a rousing success, fueling confidence in the future. Although some charged that the cooperative had strayed from its roots by opening a store of such scale and grandiosity, others maintained that REI had merely built upon the foundation created by Lloyd

Anderson to produce an enterprise capable of competing and growing during the 1990s and the century ahead. Whatever the feelings of the nearly 1.4 million customer-owners composing the cooperative's membership during the mid-1990s, the spectacle of the new flagship store pointed to the continued evolution of the principles first established by Anderson in 1938.

If the advocates of a less expansion-minded REI were troubled by the cooperative's actions in the mid-1990s, the growth of the retailer during the ensuing decade offered little solace. REI grew robustly at the close of the century, scoring success and registering notable failures as it flirted with $1 billion in sales. REI established a presence on the Internet the same month the Seattle flagship opened, adding a discount site, REI-Outlet.com, in 1998. The following year, the company began building toward one of the boldest moves in its history when it launched a Japanese-language web site. The launch of the site set the stage for the greatest geographic leap in the cooperative's history, leading to the opening of a store in suburban Tokyo in April 2000. The establishment of a retail store in Japan, where the cooperative had built a base of more than 80,000 members during the 1990s, could have ushered in an era of international expansion but the experiment failed quickly. In June 2001, after discovering that outdoor enthusiasts represented a niche market in Japan, REI announced it was liquidating merchandise at the Tokyo store and shutting down its Japanese-language web site.

The entry into Japan proved to be a mistake—not the only misstep taken by the cooperative—but on the whole the story was one of growth. REI operated 59 stores in 14 states by the end of the 1990s, a total that grew in subsequent years by establishing stores in clusters. In 2000, for example, the company opened its fifth store in the Bay Area, establishing a 22,000-square-foot store in Fremont, California. In late 2003, REI opened a store in Durham, the third store in North Carolina. By the end of 2004, there were 77 stores operating under the REI banner. Sales for the year nearly reached $890 million, a 10 percent increase from the total collected in 2003. Profits in 2004 made a more impressive leap, increasing 32 percent to reach $25 million. The financial totals were noteworthy not only because they reflected a vibrant retailer but also because they marked a turning point. In 2004, Dennis Madsen, an REI employee of 39 years, announced his intention to retire as president and chief executive officer the following year, paving the way for new leadership as the cooperative plotted its future course.

Sally Jewell was tapped to replace Madsen as the day-to-day leader of REI. A University of Washington graduate, Jewell spent nearly two decades in the banking industry before becoming REI's chief operations officer in 2000. Jewell officially occupied the presidential post in April 2005, announcing in an April 19, 2005 interview with Tacoma's *News Tribune*, "It's great to have an avocation become a vocation." Looking ahead, Jewell planned to continue to expand by clustering stores in new markets, employing the same expansion strategy used by Madsen. She also embraced a merchandising strategy that emphasized clothes and gear developed for short excursions in the outdoors. Looking ahead, Jewell, through a gradual process, intended to brand the stores according to their local market, seeking to make an REI store reflect the distinguishing characteristics of its particular market. "We want a regional feel with a national presence," she remarked in her interview with the *News Tribune*.

Principal Subsidiaries

THAW; REI Adventures; REI Foundation.

Principal Competitors

L.L. Bean, Inc.; Patagonia; The Sports Authority, Inc.; Bass Pro Outdoor World.

Further Reading

Baldwin, William, "The Money-Minded Mountaineers," *Forbes,* October 24, 1983, p. 73.
Bonner, Paul, "Seattle-Based Outdoor Outfitter REI to Open Store in Durham, N.C.," *Herald-Sun,* November 14, 2003, p. B3.
Button, Graham, "Still Climbing," *Forbes,* May 25, 1992, p. 12.
Carpenter, Kristin, "REI Venturing Out with Off-Price Web Site," *Sporting Goods Business,* August 10, 1998, p. 22.
Clark, Ken, "REI Scales New Heights," *Chain Store Age,* July 2004, p. 26A.
Clements, Barbara, "The Jewell of REI," *News Tribune,* April 19, 2005, p. B1.
——, "REI to Close Tacoma, Wash., Store Due to Declining Sales," *News Tribune,* November 21, 2003, p. B2.
"Dennis Madsen: President and CEO Recreational Equipment, Inc.," *Chain Store Age,* February 2004, p. 24.
Green, Frank, "Concept of Cooperatives Gains Popularity in the Grocery Fields," *Knight-Ridder/Tribune Business News,* August 30, 1994, p. 8.
Flash, Cynthia, "REI Co-Op Opens Flagship Store in Seattle," *Knight-Ridder/Tribune Business News,* September 11, 1996, p. 9.
Kim, Nancy J., "REI Closing Two Lackluster Locations," *Puget Sound Business Journal,* June 19, 1998, p. 3.
——, "Signs, Material Convey a Message at New REI," *Puget Sound Business Journal,* September 11, 1996, p. 4.
Nogaki, Sylvia Wieland, "Seattle's Outdoor Gear Cooperative REI to Move," *Knight-Ridder/Tribune Business News,* December 6, 1993, p. 12.
Prinzing, Debra, "REI Subsidiary: Grown Up and Standing Alone," *Puget Sound Business Journal,* September 2, 1991, p. 2.
Schooley, Tim, "Outdoors Cooperative REI Opens Fifth Bay Area Store," *Business Journal,* September 15, 2000, p. 11.
Seckler, Valerie, "REI Expanding Web Presence in Japan," *Daily News Record,* October 27, 2000, p. 6.
Spector, Robert, "A Steady Climb," *Sporting Goods Business,* July 1991, p. 98.
Tice, Carol, "Poor Results Prompt REI to Bail Out of Japan," *Puget Sound Business Journal,* June 29, 2001, p. 8.
——, "REI Gives Online Biz Its Own Room to Grow," *Puget Sound Business Journal,* August 4, 2000, p. 7.
Volk, David, "Muscle-Powered But Not Muscle-Bound," *Puget Sound Business Journal,* June 24, 1991, p. 39.

—Jeffrey L. Covell

Regency Centers Corporation

121 W. Forsyth Street, Suite 200
Jacksonville, Florida 32202
U.S.A.
Telephone: (904) 598-7000
Toll Free: (800) 950-6333
Fax: (904) 634-3428
Web site: http://www.regencycenters.com

Public Company
Incorporated: 1993 as Regency Corporation
Employees: 385
Sales: $391.9 million (2004)
Stock Exchanges: New York
Ticker Symbol: REG
NAIC: 525930 Real Estate Investment Trusts

Regency Centers Corporation is a Jacksonville, Florida-based real estate investment trust (REIT), one of the largest operators of grocery-anchored shopping centers. Its portfolio consists of more than 390 properties—either wholly owned, jointly owned, or managed—comprising 50 million square feet of space, located in metropolitan markets in 26 states. The REIT maintains strong ties with the major supermarket chains. About 90 percent of its shopping centers are anchored by grocers ranking in the top three of their market. Regency's chairman and chief executive officer, Martin E. Stein, Jr., is the son of the couple that founded the REIT's predecessor, Regency Realty.

Origins Dating to the 1960s

Martin E. Stein, Sr., and Joan Wellhouse were married in 1950. Her father ran a Tampa, Florida company that made paper wrappings used to ship citrus, and involved her in the business early on, something of a tradition with the women in her family. As she explained to the *Business Journal-Jacksonville* in a 1994 profile, "In my family women were always involved, interested and knew about investments. If the men retired or died early, the women just did it." Her husband also came from a well-to-do family, located in Jacksonville, where the Steins ran a

Seagram's distributorship, among other business interests. In 1963 Martin and Joan Stein started the Regency Group, primarily a land and apartment development company. Four years later the company developed the first regional mall in Florida, Jacksonville's Regency Square shopping center, now known as Regency Square Mall. It was anchored originally by May Department Stores and J.C. Penney. Over the next 15 years Regency concentrated on developing office buildings and apartments. In 1981 the company doubled the size of the mall and also began to expand its operations throughout Florida. Regency reached a major turning point in 1988 with the death of Martin Stein. His wife succeeded him as chairman, while their son, Martin E. "Hap" Stein, Jr., took over as chief executive. The younger Stein earned an undergraduate degree at Washington and Lee University in Virginia, followed by a master's degree in business at Dartmouth College in New Hampshire. He returned to Jacksonville in 1976 to join the family business, but at first was put to work in an energy plant that Regency owned at the time. In 1981 he was put in charge of Regency's real estate division. Under his leadership, Regency began to concentrate on what became its niche, grocery-anchored shopping centers located in established neighborhood locations, in the belief that grocery stores were recession-proof and established locations helped to ward off competition. In addition to a 30,000-square-foot grocery store, the shopping centers Regency developed during this period were co-anchored by a 10,000-square-foot drugstore. As larger supermarket formats with pharmacies emerged, the drugstores became out-parcels, no longer serving as anchors.

By 1993 Regency's real estate holdings totaled 24 properties, including 21 shopping centers and three office complexes, half of them owned with investment partners. It was at this point that the Steins, like an increasing number of real estate developers, decided to take their portfolio public with the creation of a REIT, incorporated in July 1993 as Regency Corp. Regency Group then transferred the shopping centers and office properties to Regency Realty Corp., which was then sold to the REIT after it completed its public offering. Regency Group remained an active concern, serving as a private trust for other family interests in Florida land, utility companies, and a printing company.

Company Perspectives:

Founded in 1963, Regency has the experience, resources and flexibility to create value for our grocer partners, our retail partners and our development partners.

Major Changes in Law Regarding REITs in the 1980s

REITs had been established by the U.S. Congress in 1960 as a way for small investors to become involved in real estate in a manner similar to mutual funds. Just like stock companies, REITs could be taken public and their shares traded; they were also subject to regulation by the Securities and Exchange Commission. Unlike other stock companies, however, REITs were required by law to pay out at least 95 percent of their taxable income to shareholders each year, a provision that severely limited the ability of REITs to retain internally generated funds. During the first 25 years of existence, REITs were allowed only to own real estate, a situation that hindered their growth because third parties had to be contracted to manage the properties. Although REITs flourished for brief periods, from 1968 to 1972 and 1985 to 1986, it was not until changes made to the structure by the Tax Reform Act of 1986 altered the nature of real estate investment that REITs began to become truly viable investment vehicles. Limited partnership tax shelter schemes that had competed for potential investments were shut down by the act: interest and depreciation deductions were greatly reduced so that taxpayers could not generate paper losses in order to lower their tax liabilities. Separately, the act also permitted REITs to provide customary services, in effect allowing the trusts to operate and manage the properties they owned. But despite these major changes in law, the REIT form was still not embraced for a few years. In the second half of the 1980s the banks, insurance companies, pension funds, and foreign investors (especially the Japanese) provided the lion's share of real estate investment funds. The resulting glutted marketplace led to a shakeout that hampered many real estate firms. With properties available at distressed prices in the early 1990s, REITs finally became an attractive mainstream investment option and many real estate firms, starting in 1993, now went public to become roll-up vehicles in different segments of the industry. Regency Group was one of several companies to focus on neighborhood shopping centers.

With Salomon Brothers Inc. acting as lead underwriter and St. Petersburg, Florida-based James and Associates and Atlanta-based Robinson-Humphrey Co. as co-managers, Regency sold 5.41 million shares at $20 apiece, raising $108 million. Shares were then listed on the New York Stock Exchange and began trading. The offering allowed Regency Group to retire more than $80 million in debt. It also provided the new REIT with cash and shares that could be used to develop new shopping centers and roll up existing properties. Of the 24 properties in Regency's initial portfolio, 16 were located in Florida, five in Alabama, two in Mississippi, and one in Atlanta. With Martin E. Stein, Jr., serving as CEO, management's goal was to make Regency into a major regional developer of neighborhood shopping centers in Florida and the Southeast.

The REIT padded its war chest in the fall of 1995 with the private placement of $50 million in stock, of which $44 million was used to acquire four shopping centers in St. Petersburg, Tampa, West Palm Beach, and Atlanta. Regency received another infusion of cash in June 1996, when Security Capital Group bought a 43 percent stake at a cost of $132 million. The deal was a turning point for Regency on a number of levels. Aside from the additional capital to fuel ever greater growth, the alliance with Security Capital was significant because the REIT in effect received the imprimatur of the man behind Security Capital, William Sanders, a man with a sterling reputation in real estate. After launching Chicago-based LaSalle Partners in 1968, he reestablished himself in New Mexico in 1990 and within a matter of five years had assembled a $5 billion real estate portfolio among REITs he ran under the Security Capital banner. In the words of the *Florida Times Union,* Regency's association with Sanders ''put the real estate industry on notice that Regency [was] a company to watch.'' Although Regency had delivered high dividends to its shareholders, the price of its stock had languished during its early years. The REIT received a much needed boost from the Sanders connection, providing more buying power with its stock and increased access to capital markets to raise additional funds.

At the end of 1996 Regency owned 50 properties, but in early 1997 the REIT made a significant jump in size when it acquired Branch Properties L.P. in a deal worth more than $200 million that brought with it 26 shopping centers, either existing or in development. Many of them were located in Atlanta, giving Regency a dominant position in the market. Other properties were located in the Nashville area and the Carolinas. Regency was now beginning to raise its sights beyond the Southeast, targeting such Midwest cities as Indianapolis and Cincinnati and Mid-Atlantic markets including Washington, D.C., and Baltimore. Through the rest of 1997, Regency added properties in many of these markets. In April it paid $48.4 million to acquire two supermarket-anchored shopping centers in Charlotte, North Carolina, one in Asheville, North Carolina, and another two in Orlando, Florida. Later in the summer, Regency spent another $63.5 million to add a Cincinnati shopping center and two more Atlanta-area properties. Finally, in the autumn of 1997, Regency acquired two additional Miami shopping centers and a third in Columbus, Ohio, at a cost of nearly $40.6 million. The year 1997 was also noteworthy because Joan Stein stepped down as Regency's chair, and was succeeded by her son.

Creation of Industry Powerhouse; Merger with Pacific Retail Trust in 1998

Regency opened 1998 with another major acquisition, this time spending more than $250 million to add privately held, St. Louis-based developer Midland Group's 21 existing shopping centers and development pipeline of an additional 11 centers, totaling about 3.2 million square feet of retail space. Midland was the largest developer of Kroger grocery-anchored shopping centers, and in addition to St. Louis sites, Regency also picked up shopping centers in Cincinnati and Columbus, Ohio, and Raleigh, North Carolina. Furthermore, Regency entered into a joint venture with The State of Ohio Teacher's Retirement System to acquire Midland's interest in another seven shopping centers located in Texas and Colorado. The Midland deal was also important because it established an important relationship with Kroger, one of the major supermarket chains in the country. Regency's appetite for shopping centers was not sated, however. In September 1998, the REIT acquired Pacific Retail Trust, a William Sanders closely held company with 69 shopping centers, existing or in development, located in western states.

In effect, Sanders was assembling a powerhouse roll-up vehicle with national scope to consolidate a fragmented segment of the real estate industry that all too often involved owners who were underfunded developers, unschooled institutions, or just mom-and-pop operators. Not only would the combined operations save on overhead costs, but also the beefed up Regency would be able to attract more investors to fuel even greater growth. When the merger was completed in early 1999, Security Capital, which had owned 40 percent of Regency and 70 percent of Pacific Retail, owned a controlling 54 percent stake in the combined company. At this stage, Regency owned 192 shopping centers in 22 states, 22.2 million square feet of retail space, and total assets valued at $2.2 million. Nevertheless, the price of Regency shares continued to be undervalued by Wall Street, prompting a buyback effort by the REIT during 1999. At the close of the year, Regency posted revenues of $258 million and net income of nearly $90 million.

Despite an economy that began to slump in 2000, Regency continued to prosper in 2000, supporting the contention that grocery-anchored shopping centers were indeed recession-proof. Much of the REIT's growth was the result of keeping pace with grocer's expansion plans. Regency was keen on high-growth, densely populated markets with above-average incomes, such as Arizona, Texas, and California, especially in the Los Angeles area. All told, Regency spent about $500 million in 2000 on development deals.

In January 2001, Regency Realty Corporation changed its name to Regency Centers Corporation, a brand-building effort to help solidify the REIT's position as a major national grocery-anchored shopping center operator and developer. New markets Regency focused on were Oregon and Washington, where it had

19 shopping centers opened or in development. In the Puget Sound region alone there were ten Regency shopping centers. On the East Coast, Regency was constructing two major shopping centers in northern Virginia, as well as developing projects in Wilmington, Delaware, and Vorhees, New Jersey, part of a plan to build a presence in the Interstate 95 corridor that runs from the Washington, D.C., area through Philadelphia to New York City and Boston. Regency launched a major push in the Philadelphia market in 2003 in the hope of opening a dozen shopping centers within the next two or three years.

In 2002 General Electric Capital Corporation acquired Security Capital Group Inc., in the process gaining majority ownership of Regency. Despite speculation that GE Capital was primed to acquire the remaining Regency shares, the firm opted instead in June 2003 to sell the stock, which had finally begun to rise, reaching a record high around $35 when GE announced its intentions. The decision to sell by GE Capital appeared to be little more than simply an effort to take advantage of a seller's market.

Regency's revenues grew to $353.7 million in 2002 and $377.6 million in 2003, while net income during this period improved to $110.5 million in 2002 and $130.8 million in 2003. The REIT remained aggressive in 2004, completing a major deal in the autumn, paying $406 million to acquire 17 shopping centers from Atlanta-based Branch Capital Partners, thereby doubling Regency's Atlanta portfolio and strengthening its dominant position in the market. In early 2005, Regency was involved in an even larger transaction, teaming up with Australia's Macquarie CountryWide Trust to buy the 101 strip mall portfolio of the California Public Employees' Retirement System at a cost of $2.74 billion. The partners had been involved in some deals a couple of years earlier, but nothing approached this deal in magnitude. Regency took a 35 percent interest and would manage the properties, half of which were located in the Washington, D.C., area and California markets. In addition, the portfolio included shopping centers in Regency target markets such as Philadelphia and Chicago, plus toeholds in new markets in suburbs of New York City and Minneapolis. It was quite likely that Regency would pursue further joint ventures. In this way, the REIT was able to expand its platform while conserving its capital and receiving fees for managing the shopping centers. Given that there were few real estate opportunities in Australia and New Zealand, the prospect of continued cooperation with Macquarie or other Australian firms was highly likely.

Principal Subsidiaries

Regency Centers Texas L.L.C.; Regency Centers, L.P.; K&G/RRG II, L.L.C.; Macquarie CountryWide-Regency, L.L.C.; Columbia Regency Retail Partners, L.L.C.

Principal Competitors

Developers Diversified Realty Corporation; Kimco Realty Corporation; Weingarten Realty Investors.

Further Reading

Basch, Mark, "Acquisition Takes Regency into Midwest," *Florida Times Union,* January 14, 1998, p. B4.

——, "Regency Rolls, Stock Languishes," *Florida Times Union,* May 27, 1998, p. B7.

——, "Regency Set to Move into Midwest and Mid-Atlantic," *Florida Times Union,* June 13, 1997, p. C8.

Chittum, Ryan, and Morag MacKinnon, "Regency Centers Goes Strip-Mall Shopping," *Wall Street Journal,* February 16, 2005, p. C5.

Horak, Kathy, " 'Being a Lady, She Adds a Touch of Class,' " *Business Journal-Jacksonville,* July 15, 1994, p. 11.

——, "Regency Group Takes Trust Public," *Business Journal-Jacksonville,* August 13, 1993, p. 1.

Laird, Susan, "A REIT in a Hurry," *Florida Trend,* August 1997, p. 28.

Lerner, Michele, "Martin 'HAP' Stein, Jr.—Happy Days at Regency Centers," *Real Estate Portfolio,* November/December 2003.

Novelli, Lynn, "Shopping Smart," *Real Estate Portfolio,* January/February 2001.

—Ed Dinger

Rinascente S.p.A.

Strada 8, Palazzo N
Milanofiori
Rozzano
I-20089 MI
Italy
Telephone: +39 02 5758139; 02 57582373
Fax: +39 02 57512468
Web site: http://www.grupporinascente.it

Private Company
Incorporated: 1917
Employees: 29,000
Sales: EUR 925 million ($1.25 billion) (2004)
NAIC: 452111 Department Stores (Except Discount
  Department Stores)

Rinascente S.p.A. is Italy's leading department store group. The Milan-based company operates under two core brands: the upscale La Rinascente and the mid-market Upim. La Rinascente is the company's—and Italy's—oldest department store format, with its flagship store on Milan's Piazza Duomi, opened in 1917. The company operates 17 additional La Rinascente stores throughout Italy, with a focus on high-end clothing fashions and accessories, perfumes and beauty products, as well as some housewares and related items. The La Rinascente brand also represents an important real estate portfolio, with many other prominent city-center locations in addition to the Milan site, including the group's store on Rome's Via del Corso. The La Rinascente chain generates approximately 35 percent of the company's total revenues, which reached EUR 925 million ($1.25 billion) in 2004. The largest part of the group's operation is its chain of 147 Upim department stores, which operate on a national level and represent Italy's largest store chain. The Upim chain targets the mid-market shopping sector. Rinascente S.p.A. itself was put up for sale at the beginning of the 21st century. Formerly a public company, Rinascente came under the control of Eurofind, owned jointly by the Agnelli family (who also control the Fiat automotive group) and Auchan S.A., one of France's leading department store, supermarket, and other retail groups. After Auchan took control of Rinascente's foods business in 2003, Eurofind put the remainder of the business up for sale. In March 2005, a consortium led by Pirelli Real Estate received approval to buy Rinascente for EUR 870 million ($1.2 billion). That consortium included members of the Boretti family, founders of the Rinascente group in 1917.

Founding in 19th Century, Growth During Early 20th Century

La Rinascente represented a pioneering force in Italy's retail sector in the 20th century. Even into the 21st century, the company's department stores retained a distinct presence in a retail market heavily dominated by small, often family-owned shops.

La Rinascente itself started out as a small shop in Milan. In 1865, Ferdinando Bocconi set up shop on the Via Santa Radegonda in Milan's center, calling his store "Alle Città d'Italia." Bocconi's shop differed from the other general goods stores in the area at the time, becoming the first in Italy to focus exclusively on ready-to-wear dresses.

Bocconi's shop remained a fixture in Milan's retail market into the 20th century, later moving to a more prominent location, on the city's Piazza Duomo, across from the city's famous cathedral. The Bocconi family expanded the store into a department store format, before opening other shops. By the outbreak of World War I, the family had become one of the city's leading families, and went on to found Milan's first private business school, Bocconi University.

In 1917, the Bocconis sold their shop to another rising Milan industrialist family, the Borlettis, led by brothers Senatore and Romualdo. The Borlettis had gained status as Italian industrialists through their alarm clock factory, among other interests. During World War I, the family had boosted its fortunes by converting production at their factory from alarm clocks to fuses for hand grenades. The family also developed interests in the Italian media market, adding newspaper and magazine interests, including ownership of the country's leading daily, *Il Secolo*.

The Borletti family continued to expand the Bocconi department stores, introducing a modern department store format. The

308

Borlettis also adopted a new name for the store, turning to famed Italian writer Gabriele D'Annunzio, who dubbed the store "La Rinascente."

The new La Rinascente opened at the end of 1918 to great fanfare. Yet just weeks later the company was struck by disaster, when a fire destroyed the store. The Borlettis set out to rebuild the Duomi site, reopening its doors in 1921. In celebration of that event, the company commissioned artist Marcello Dudovich to create a new series of advertising posters. The first Dudovich poster debuted that year, and through the 1930s, Dudovich's stylized designs became synonymous with La Rinascente.

In the meantime, the Borletti family continued to expand its retail interests. In 1928, the company expanded into a new department store format, Upim. That store chain was based on the fixed-price format launched by Frank Woolworth in the late 19th century. The five-and-dime price format was introduced into Europe at the beginning of the 20th century, most famously by Britain's Marks and Spencer. In Italy, the Upim store adopted price formats ranging from 1 to 4 liras. Upim's family-oriented format became hugely popular among Italian consumers, particularly during the difficult economic years of the 1930s. In 1934, Upim was formally merged into the La Rinascente group.

La Rinascente faced a new setback during World War II when its flagship Piazza Duomi store was bombed by Allied forces in 1943. The rebuilding of the store was completed only in 1950, marking a new era for the company as Italy entered into an extended economic boom period.

Diversification in the 1960s

The growing strength of the Italian economy led La Rinascente to begin exploring other retail areas during the 1960s and 1970s. The company's first diversification came at the beginning of the 1960s, when the company became one of the first in Italy to branch out into the newly developing supermarket sector. First introduced in the United States in the 1930s and 1940s, the self-service supermarket format's appearance in Europe challenged the traditional small grocers. In Italy, the retail sector remained heavily oriented toward its small grocers and retail stores. Nonetheless, the supermarket captured a growing share of consumer spending through the end of the century.

La Rinascente's own entry into the supermarket sector came in 1961, with the launch of Supermercati Sma. The Sma chain grew strongly through the decade. At the beginning of the 1970s, the company extended its supermarket operations into a new direction, borrowing the "hypermarket" format pioneered in France and elsewhere. The hypermarket format enabled La Rinascente to combine its expertise in department store operation with its fast-growing supermarket foods business. In 1972, the company pioneered the hypermarket format in Italy, launching its Citta Mercati, or City Market.

La Rinascente's growth was backed by new majority owners, in the form of the Agnelli family, which also controlled the country's Fiat motor vehicle giant. After suffering through the economic crisis of the late 1970s, the Agnellis temporarily sold off their control of the company, to construction group De Angeli Frua, in 1981. Three years later, however, the Agnellis bought back into La Rinascente, once again acquiring a majority in the company. By this time, La Rinascente was a public company, listed on the Borsa Italiana.

In the meantime, the company had emerged as Italy's leading retail group. This position was boosted by the launch of a new expansion of the Upim chain, notably through the introduction of the first franchise offers in 1975.

In 1983, La Rinascente entered a new sector, launching the Bricocenter chain of do-it-yourself hardware stores. That expansion was followed in 1988 by the acquisition of supermarket rival Sigros e Sagea, which added 77 new supermarkets to La Rinascente's portfolio. The purchase of Sigros e Sagea also enabled the company to extend its interests to the wholesale sector, with eight cash-and-carry stores.

New Owners in the Mid-2000s

La Rinascente continued to expand rapidly into the early 1990s. With its sales topping $3 billion, the company's retail network neared 800 stores. The company also had added to its range of retail offerings, with the electronics and home appliance chain Trony, and the kitchen and home furnishings format Croff. Into the middle of the decade, the company continued to expand its range of operation, notably through the development of a hard discount branch.

The mid-1990s saw a dramatic transformation of the group, however. In 1995, the company acquired regional supermarket group Cedis-Migliarini. This purchase helped tip the balance between food and nonfood sales. By 1996, the company's food sales represented more than 70 percent of total sales. The La Rinascente and Upim chains combined to produce less than 23 percent of sales. By then, the company's total network had topped 900 stores, nearly half of which consisted of franchises.

The Agnelli family, which had transferred its control of La Rinascente to its IFIL holding, had been rumored to be seeking to cash out of its majority holding in La Rinsascente since the difficult years at the beginning of the 1990s. As the Agnellis' core Fiat business continued to experience difficulties through the end of the decade, the Agnelli family stepped up its search for a partner.

In 1997, IFIL announced that it was transferring its stake in La Rinascente to a new joint venture, Eurofind, with France's

Key Dates:

1865: Federico Bocconi opens Italy's first ready-to-wear dress shop in Milan, later transferring the store to the city's Piazza Duomi and expanding it into a department store format.

1917: Senatore and Romualdo Borletti acquire control of Bocconi's store, which is renamed La Rinascente.

1928: Upim, a fixed-price variety goods store, is launched.

1950: The La Rinascente store, destroyed during Allied bombing attacks, reopens in Milan.

1961: The company extends into the supermarket sector with the launch of the Sma supermarket chain.

1972: The company opens the first hypermarket in Italy, Citta Mercati (City Market).

1983: The Bricocenter DIY chain is launched.

1988: Sigros e Sagea, a supermarket and cash-and-carry store group, is acquired.

1995: The company acquires Cedis-Migliarini, a regional supermarket group.

1997: Auchan and IFIL found Eurofind, which becomes the majority shareholder of La Rinascente.

1998: SIB, which takes over Bricocenters and Auchan's Italian Leroy Merlin stores, is created.

2002: Auchan and IFIL launch a buyout of La Rinascente, delisting it from the Borsa Italiana.

2004: Auchan acquires control of La Rinascente's food store operations, leaving only the La Rinascente and Upim store chains.

2005: La Rinascente is acquired by a consortium led by the Borletti family and including Pirelli Real Estate.

Auchan. Under the deal, Auchan agreed to transfer its five Auchan shopping centers, which included both hypermarket and hard discount stores, in Turin, Mestre, Piacenza, Bari, and Milan. In 1998, the two companies agreed to merge their DIY stores, including La Rinascente's Bricocenter stores and Auchan's Leroy Merlin stores, into a new holding company, SIB, or Societa Italiana di Bricolage.

By then, Auchan had gained the controlling stake in Eurofind, which itself built up a shareholding of more than 60 percent in La Rinascente. Under Auchan's leadership, La Rinascente began redeveloping its operations, including launching a refurbishing effort throughout the La Rinascente chain. As part of this effort, La Rinascente began expanding its range of designer labels. The chain also expanded, notably by converting a former Auchan shopping center to the La Rinascente format. By the beginning of the 2000s, the company operated 18 La Rinascente stores throughout Italy. The company also boosted its supermarket holdings with the purchase of supermarket rival Colmark S.p.A.

IFIL and Auchan made a bid to take full control of La Rinascente in 2002, buying up nearly all of the stock Eurofind did not already own and delisting the company. This move preceded a breaking up of La Rinascente, in large part to permit IFIL to exit its shareholding of the company. In 2004, Auchan bought up La Rinascente's food operations, including its supermarket chains.

By the end of that year, IFIL and Auchan announced their intention to sell off the remainder of La Rinascente, which then consisted of the Upim variety goods store chain and the La Rinascente department stores. After receiving a number of bids, the company finally announced that it had reached an agreement to sell La Rinascente to an investment consortium led by the Borletti family, under Maurizio Borletti, a grandson of Romualdo Borletti. Major investors in the consortium included Pirelli Real Estate, while the Borletti family's stake remained at barely more than 1 percent. The purchase, priced at EUR 888 million ($1.2 billion), received approval in March 2005. With a return of the Borletti family to the helm, La Rinascente turned toward further growth in the new century.

Principal Subsidiaries

La Rinascente; Upim.

Principal Competitors

Coin S.p.A.; SME S.p.A.; Standa S.p.A.

Further Reading

"Auchan Buys Share of Rinascente Food Unit for EUR 1 Billion," *just-food.com,* November 5, 2004.

"Aucan et les Agnelli vendent Rinascente," *Le Figaro,* March 14, 2005.

"Bargain of the Century," *Economist,* February 19, 2005, p. 60.

"Consortium Wins Rinascente Auction," *Financial Times,* March 14, 2005, p. 22.

Epiro, Stephanie, "Rinascente's Natural Progression," *WWD,* June 10, 2004, p. 15.

Grassia, Luigi, "IFIL Ratifies Sale of Rinascente," *La Stampa,* March 14, 2005.

"La Pirelli Re conquista I magazzinni Rinascente," *La Stampa,* March 13, 2005.

O'Brian, Heather, "Bidder Would Take Rinascente Private," *Daily Deal,* October 8, 2002.

"Rinascente Continues Growth," *European Cosmetic Markets,* April 1999, p. 129.

"Simon in Joint Venture to Develop Malls in Italy," *HFN The Weekly Newspaper for the Home Furnishing Network,* January 5, 2004, p. 44.

Zargani, Luisa, "Borletti Clan Back at La Rinascente Italian Store Chain," *WWD,* March 15, 2005, p. 3.

——, "Italian Stores' Modern Movement," *WWD,* August 15, 2000, p. 17.

——, "La Rinascente Attracts Many Potential Bidders," *WWD,* December 2, 2004, p. 8.

—M.L. Cohen

The Ritz-Carlton Hotel Company, L.L.C.

4445 Willard Avenue, Suite 800
Chevy Chase, Maryland 20815-3699
U.S.A.
Telephone: (301) 547-4700
Fax: (301) 547-4723
Web site: http://www.ritzcarlton.com

Wholly Owned Subsidiary of Marriott International, Inc.
Incorporated: 1983
Employees: 28,000
Sales: $1.5 billion (2004 est.)
NAIC: 721110 Hotels (Except Casino Hotels) and Motels

The Ritz-Carlton Hotel Company, L.L.C. operates a chain of 57 hotels worldwide—35 located in cities and 23 in resorts. The chain banks on the lustrous image of its name and strives to make each of its locations uniquely luxurious. Its hotels, which Ritz-Carlton only manages for other property owners, are top-rated, including several that earn five stars and five diamonds in domestic rankings. Aside from its 35 hotels across the United States, Ritz-Carlton has locations in Montreal; Santiago, Chile; Montego Bay, Jamaica; Cancún, Mexico; San Juan, Puerto Rico; St. Thomas, U.S. Virgin Islands; Berlin and Wolfsburg, Germany; Sintra, Portugal; Barcelona, Spain; Istanbul, Turkey; Bahrain; Sharm al-Sheikh, Egypt; Doha, Qatar; Dubai, United Arab Emirates; Shanghai and Hong Kong, China; Bali, Indonesia; Osaka, Japan; Seoul, South Korea; Kuala Lumpur, Malaysia; and Singapore. Ritz-Carlton has also expanded beyond its flagship hotels in several additional ventures. It is jointly creating a new luxury chain with the Italian luxury goods maker Bulgari S.p.A., with the first Bulgari Hotel & Resort opening in Milan, Italy, in May 2004. More than 20 Ritz-Carlton hotels now feature spas, and the company has added to several of its hotel properties luxury residential condominiums known as the Residences at The Ritz-Carlton. In addition, the firm has entered the timeshare sector through the Ritz-Carlton Club, which is offering memberships in Aspen and Bachelor Gulch, Colorado; Jupiter, Florida; and St. Thomas, U.S. Virgin Islands. Founded in 1983 when William B. Johnson bought the rights to the famous Ritz-Carlton name, the chain is owned by hotel giant Marriott International, Inc.

Early History

The history of the current Ritz-Carlton Hotel Company properly begins in the 19th century, with the exploits of legendary hotelier César Ritz. The ambitious child of a poor herdsman, Ritz was born in 1850 in the small mountain village of Niederwald, Switzerland. One of 13 children, Ritz left home at the age of 16 to work in the dining room of a hotel in the adjacent town of Brieg. After a few months on the job he was fired, according to his employer, for not possessing even an ''aptitude,'' much less a ''flair,'' for the hotel business. Hired as a waiter in the restaurant of another hotel, Ritz soon was fired once again.

Undismayed, Ritz traveled to Paris, where he worked emptying slops for small hotels. Fired from two more jobs, he finally landed a position at a chic restaurant near the Madeleine and worked his way up from busboy to manager. At the age of 19 he was asked to become a partner by the owner of the restaurant, yet Ritz politely refused the offer. His ambition was still unsatisfied, but now that he knew what he wanted, he rolled up his aprons and sauntered down the street to the most elegant and famous restaurant of the day, Voisin, an international meeting place for royalty and gourmets. Starting at the bottom as an assistant waiter, Ritz learned how to carve a roast and press duck, how to decant wine, and how to serve food in ways that pleased both the eye and the palate.

It was at Voisin that Ritz developed his instincts for high-quality food and service, and his personal touch began to attract influential customers such as Sarah Bernhardt, Alexandre Dumas the younger, and the Rothschilds. When Germany invaded France and laid siege to Paris in 1871, a food scarcity led the city zoo to butcher its two elephants; Voisin purchased the trunks of the animals. When Ritz served them in high style, *trompe sauce chasseur* became a gourmet's rage and Ritz himself an overnight sensation in Parisian culinary circles.

A short time later, Ritz left Paris and worked for three years in resort restaurants and fashionable hotels in Nice, San Remo, Rome, Baden-Baden, and Vienna. Good luck now came his

---

Company Perspectives:

THE CREDO: The Ritz-Carlton Hotel is a place where the genuine care and comfort of our guests is our highest mission.

We pledge to provide the finest personal service and facilities for our guests who will always enjoy a warm, relaxed, yet refined ambience.

The Ritz-Carlton experience enlivens the senses, instills well-being, and fulfills even the unexpressed wishes and needs of our guests.

---

way. Ritz was the restaurant manager at Rigi-Kulm, an Alpine hotel renowned for its location and cuisine, when he was informed one cold winter day that the heating plant had broken down and, at almost the same moment, that a group of 40 wealthy Americans were to arrive soon for lunch. Ritz ordered lunch to be served in the drawing room instead of the dining room—it looked warmer because of the large red curtains that framed the room. He directed the waiters to pour alcohol into large copper pots and then set them afire, and bricks were placed in the ovens. The room was warm when the Americans arrived, and each of them was given a brick wrapped in flannel to warm their feet. By the end of the meal, which started with a peppery hot consommé and ended with flaming crêpes suzette, the guests were gushing with praise for the young manager.

Reports of Ritz's modest miracle of quick thinking and resourcefulness spread among hotelmen throughout Europe and the United States. When the owner of a large hotel in Lucerne heard the story, he immediately hired Ritz to act as his general manager. The hotel had been losing money steadily for some time, but the 27-year-old former peasant revived the hotel in two years. Here he developed and refined the hotel service and methods that made his name famous. ''People like to be served, but invisibly,'' Ritz once said. It was Ritz who originated the phrase, ''The customer is always right.'' Ritz remembered who preferred Turkish cigarettes, who loved gardenias in their room, and who ate chutney during breakfast. If a diner did not like the way his meat was prepared, it was immediately whisked away without any questions asked. For Ritz, no detail was too small and no request too big if it meant satisfying a customer.

In 1892 Ritz journeyed to London to manage the Hotel Savoy, an elegant hotel in the midst of a financial crisis. Ritz brought along his lifelong associate, Auguste Escoffier, a chef whom he had met during one of his jobs in Europe. With Ritz devoting his attention to a myriad of details, sometimes roving from room to room remaking beds to assure his guests the most comfortable night's sleep in London, at other times arranging lavish entertainment for important customers, and with Escoffier whipping up gourmet dishes in the kitchen, the Savoy soon became the toast of London's high society. When Alfred Beit, a diamond mogul from South Africa, asked Ritz to arrange a party for him, Ritz flooded the Savoy's main dining room and transformed it into a miniature Venice, with dinner served to guests as they lounged in gondolas serenaded by native gondoliers. At another party, with Cecil Rhodes, James Gordon Bennett, Lord Randolph Churchill, and Gilbert and Sullivan attending, Ritz arranged for Caruso to sing for their evening

pleasure. After three years, the Savoy's stock rebounded from a few shillings to £20 a share.

When a quarrel broke out one day between Ritz and the directors of the Savoy, Ritz left the hotel never to return again. Ritz's friends reacted immediately with more than 200 telegrams sent to show him their support. The Prince of Wales, a close friend who was later to become King Edward VII, wired the statement, ''Where Ritz goes, we follow.'' With such support from wealthy and influential friends, Ritz decided to pursue a dream he had had for years—to open a hotel of his own that would be the epitome of elegance.

The Ritz Hotel, built in Paris on the Place Vendôme, opened for business in 1898. The lobby was small to discourage idlers, and only 225 rooms were constructed for its guests, but furnishings were exquisite and service meticulous to the last detail. Ritz designed a garden to encourage conversation over coffee and tea; he painted the hotel's walls instead of papering them because it was easier to keep clean; he borrowed the overall color scheme for the hotel from a painting by Van Dyck; and, highly innovative for the time, Ritz equipped many of the rooms with private baths. Ritz also established the traditional apparel for hotel personnel: a black tie for the maître d'hôtel, a white tie for the waiter, and brass buttons for the bellhop's uniform. On opening day people came from miles around Paris to walk through the hotel's corridors.

Ritz prepared an elaborate reception and elegant dinner in 1902 in honor of the coronation of his good friend Edward VII. All the arrangements had been finalized when a telegram informed Ritz that Edward was grievously ill and required an operation. With a heavy heart the great hotelier attended to the details of cancellation and then, exhausted from his exertions, collapsed. He revived and redoubled his efforts to please patrons of the hotel, but suffered a physical and mental breakdown in 1911. Never fully regaining his renowned verve and energy for work, for seven years Ritz was a figurehead at his own hotel. In October 1918, as he lay dying, Ritz thought he saw his wife at the bedside and asked her to take care of their daughter. Ritz and his wife had no daughter—the ''daughter'' was the way both of them referred to Ritz's dream hotel in Paris.

Ritz-Carlton Chain in the Early 20th Century

With the opening of the new century, Ritz had arranged to build and operate the Carlton Hotel in London and, shortly thereafter, opened the Ritz Hotel in Piccadilly. At this time, he also organized a group of hoteliers and financiers and created the tricontinental Ritz-Carlton Management Corporation. The purpose of the group was to lease the Ritz-Carlton name, crest, and stationery to interested parties willing to establish a hotel of their own and abide by the service and culinary standards set by Ritz himself. Under the terms of this agreement, one of the most famous of all the Ritz-Carlton Hotels opened in New York in 1910.

The New York Ritz-Carlton was built for $5 million, and its equipment and furnishings cost $750,000 more. Robert Goelet, a businessman, paid $5,000 for use of the Ritz-Carlton name and nurtured the hotel like one of his children. Soft rugs, gilded mirrors, glittering chandeliers, oversized bathtubs, and vials of

Key Dates:

1898: César Ritz opens the Ritz Hotel in Paris.
c. 1900: Ritz arranges to build and operate the Carlton Hotel in London; the Ritz-Carlton Management Corporation is formed, through which Ritz-Carlton hotels are built in the United States.
1927: The Ritz-Carlton, Boston, opens.
1983: William B. Johnson purchases the rights to the Ritz-Carlton name and the Ritz-Carlton hotel in Boston; Johnson founds The Ritz-Carlton Hotel Company, L.L.C., based in Atlanta, and begins expanding.
1990: Johnson's company is now operating and managing 28 Ritz-Carlton hotels.
1992: Company is awarded the Malcolm Baldridge National Quality Award.
1995: Marriott International, Inc. buys a 49 percent stake in Ritz-Carlton.
1998: Marriott boosts its interest in Ritz-Carlton to 99 percent.
1999: Ritz-Carlton earns its second Baldrige award; company moves into timeshare market with creation of the Ritz-Carlton Club.
2000: First Residences at The Ritz-Carlton luxury residential condominiums debut at the new Washington, D.C., Ritz-Carlton hotel.
2003: Company relocates its headquarters to Chevy Chase, Maryland.
2004: First Bulgari Hotel & Resort debuts in Milan, Italy, from a joint venture with Bulgari S.p.A.

perfume under the seats of the elevators welcomed and rewarded its rich guests. The hotel immediately became renowned for its superb cuisine—Chef M. Diat created vichyssoise in its kitchen in 1912. On every floor two waiters were stationed day and night to attend the needs of customers who preferred to eat in their rooms. The hotel was a mecca for the world's richest and most famous people and, for New York society, was host to a seemingly endless stream of balls, cotillions, and receptions. For one coming-out party, its ballroom was decorated with $10,000 worth of eucalyptus trees; at another, live monkeys helped transform the ballroom into a tropical jungle. Joffre, Foch, Clemenceau, Leopold I of Belgium, the Duke of Windsor, Mrs. George W. Vanderbilt, and Charlie Chaplin were all served at the Ritz-Carlton. The New York Ritz-Carlton remained faithful to César Ritz's imperatives—pamper your guests with lavish surroundings and meticulous service.

During the 1920s, the Ritz-Carlton Management Company leased the use of its name to a number of financiers that wanted to build hotels and also were willing to abide by the standards set down by César Ritz. During this decade the Philadelphia Ritz-Carlton, Montreal Ritz-Carlton, Atlantic City Ritz-Carlton, and Boston Ritz-Carlton opened for business. All of these hotels, in their individual manner, carried on the tradition of fashionable sophistication so important to the Ritz name. Yet those who had known César Ritz would say that none of the hotels ever captured the rococo elegance of the Paris Ritz on the Place Vendôme.

After César Ritz and one of his sons died in 1918, it was assumed that the remaining son, Charles, would take the place of his father and continue managing the Paris and London hotels under the Ritz-Carlton name. But Charles was more inclined to travel, and even before the death of his father he journeyed to the United States and worked in a New London, Connecticut hotel. His jobs over the next several years ranged from working as a night manager at the New York Ritz-Carlton to selling Swiss music boxes to department stores. The rather leisurely pace of Charles Ritz's business activities provided him the time to pursue what interested him most—fly fishing. In 1928 his mother made a pilgrimage across the Atlantic to persuade him to return to Paris and work at his father's hotel. He yielded to his mother's urging, but once in Paris he found that all the top management spots at the hotel were filled, so he worked in the local office of a New York stockbroker. Rather than being disappointed with not working for the hotel, Charles was able to continue developing his expertise in fly fishing. In fact, he had already launched a secondary career as a designer of fishing rods.

After the crash of the New York stock market in 1929, the hotels that bore the Ritz-Carlton name in Europe and the United States suffered from the onset of a worldwide depression. Although the hotels were able to weather the financial hardship, many of them began to lose the elegant luster they so earnestly and carefully cultivated before the Depression. Many millionaires who frequented Ritz-Carlton dining rooms in search of new gustatory delights were no longer millionaires. Indeed, the New York Ritz-Carlton even changed its luncheon and dinner menus from French into English hoping that it would result in more customers. The owner and manager of the Boston Ritz-Carlton, realizing he was almost at the point of insolvency, went from room to room turning on the lights in its empty rooms to impress his wealthy father before the old man arrived to discuss terms of a loan for the hotel.

The difficulties luxury hotels experienced during the depression were compounded by World War II. When leisure travel between Europe and the United States was common in the 1920s and 1930s, many wealthy individuals stayed and dined at Ritz-Carlton hotels. This traffic ceased altogether when the war started in Europe in 1939 and, not surprisingly, Ritz-Carlton hotels suffered as a result. When World War II was at its height, many Ritz-Carlton dining areas and ballrooms on both sides of the Atlantic were used as meeting rooms for military personnel.

Hotels for Businessmen After World War II

Many of the Ritz-Carlton hotels did not survive the combined effects of the depression and World War II. Even though the Paris Ritz celebrated it 50th birthday in 1948 amid diplomats and millionaires drinking champagne, the Philadelphia Ritz-Carlton and Montreal Ritz-Carlton had closed their doors. In 1950, when the New York Ritz-Carlton announced that it would close to make way for a 25-story office building, its former guests protested. The only Ritz-Carlton hotel left in North America was the Boston Ritz-Carlton, and its survival was questionable.

The London Ritz-Carlton and the Paris Ritz prospered during the 1950s and 1960s by gradually adapting to a new breed of guest—the international businessman. When Charles Ritz became chairman of the board of the Ritz-Carlton Management Company in 1953, most of the old wealth and aristocracy were gone. By 1968, 70 percent of the guests staying at the Paris Ritz were American businessmen on expense accounts. With his success in Paris, Ritz was asked to serve as a consultant to the firm of Cabot, Cabot, and Forbes, purchasers of the Boston Ritz-Carlton in 1964. He also served as consultant to the Ritz-Carlton in London.

The Ritz-Carlton Management Company leased its name to financiers in both Lisbon and Madrid, stipulating that the hotels meet acceptable standards. Although Charles Ritz owned only 1 percent of the stock in the company, with the remainder held by British and Continental investors, he was the guardian of the hotel's standards; during the late 1960s, the company sued the Ritz in Rome over use of the name because the hotel did not measure up to those standards.

The hotels operating under the Ritz name in Europe prospered throughout the 1970s, primarily because of the ever increasing presence of international business travelers with corporate expense accounts and a surge in travel by the nouveau riche. Indeed, the company's continued commitment to and cultivation of attentive service to a new generation of guests had the effect of raising revenues for almost all the European operations. The week before Charles Ritz died in July 1976, he was still issuing orders to improve the luxury and elegance that symbolized the Paris hotel.

Revitalized Under Johnson in the 1980s

In 1983 William B. Johnson, a real estate mogul and developer from Atlanta, purchased the rights to the name and the aging Ritz-Carlton in Boston for approximately $70 million. Having already constructed more than 100 Waffle House restaurants and numerous Holiday Inns, Johnson turned his attention to the Boston Ritz-Carlton and spent $22 million to restore the hotel to its original condition. He then established a headquarters for his company, The Ritz-Carlton Hotel Company, L.L.C., in Atlanta and began to arrange financing for new hotels around the country, mostly through partnerships between Johnson and other parties. In a key early move, Johnson brought onboard Horst Schulze as vice-president of operations. Schulze, who came to Ritz-Carlton after spending nine years in various positions at Hyatt Hotels Corporation (and who fittingly had at one time in his career worked at the Savoy in London), was soon named president and would eventually be credited with building Ritz-Carlton into a global luxury chain.

Bumps in the 1990s

By 1990, Johnson's Ritz-Carlton Hotel Company operated and managed 28 Ritz-Carlton hotels. Johnson directly owned the hotels in Boston, Buckhead, Georgia, and Naples, Florida; financing for the remainder of the hotels was through partnerships, including those in Australia, Hawaii, and Cancún. The only Ritz-Carlton Hotel that Johnson did not operate was in Chicago. Built by Four Seasons before Johnson purchased rights to the name, the Chicago Ritz-Carlton also was managed by the rival hotel.

The company won the Malcolm Baldridge National Quality Award in 1992. The Ritz-Carlton Hotel Company was the first

hotel company awarded the highly prestigious prize, given annually by the U.S. Department of Commerce. With 24-hour room service, twice-a-day maid service, complete gymnasium facilities, and menus that continued the tradition of culinary excellence first established by César Ritz, Johnson's company was well prepared for competing with Four Seasons and other hotel groups in the luxury hotel market.

But although the chain was doing extremely well on quality and service, finances were a different matter. The company had expanded aggressively, opening or acquiring eight hotels in 1990 alone, with six the next year and many more planned. By 1992 the company had full or part ownership in 13 of the chain's hotels, and the others were owned by private investors. These investors included financier Willard G. Rouse III, Ford Motor Company's real estate division, Prudential Realty Group, and John F. McDonnell, of McDonnell Douglas. Presumably those who had put money into new Ritz-Carltons were not as happy as some of the pampered guests. The hotel industry as a whole was still suffering from the effects of the late 1980s recession, and many hotels were stuck with empty rooms. The Ritz-Carlton was no exception. The Buckhead Ritz-Carlton in Atlanta, which Johnson himself owned, was said to require an occupancy rate of virtually 100 percent every night of the year to make enough money to cover its debt. The splashy Mauna-Lani Ritz-Carlton in Hawaii was also in debt, having run approximately $13 million over its estimated construction costs, and its occupancy rate for 1991 was only 44 percent. Teachers Insurancy and Annuity Association, a backer of several Ritz-Carltons, sued in 1992 to recover payment on $80 million it had lent the owners of the Tyson Corners (Virginia) Ritz-Carlton and had trouble collecting on its loan to a Kansas City Ritz-Carlton as well. Sources quoted in a July 6, 1992, *Business Week* article claimed the Ritz-Carlton Hotel Company was more than $1 billion in debt. Schulze admitted only that the company was in default on a loan for $70 million and that it was seeking to restructure other debts. The company insisted that the hotels would get over any stumbling blocks caused by the economic downturn and that its money problems were only short-term.

Yet bad news continued to dog the luxury chain. When its Aspen, Colorado, hotel opened in October 1992, it was shadowed by lawsuits from investors and dire reports that the 257-room hotel would have to achieve at least 60 percent occupancy just to break even, in a town where 50 percent occupancy was the average. The Hong Kong Ritz-Carlton was completed in August 1992 but stood empty for months, in receivership, with no prospective buyer. By 1994, a *Wall Street Journal* report (April 22, 1994) quoted sources who claimed that out of the 30 Ritz-Carltons open at the time, all but six or seven were losing money. This was contested by Ritz-Carlton's President Schulze. He allowed that 30 percent of the chain's hotels were unprofitable. Many Ritz-Carltons were in cities that could not really support such a luxury hotel. For example, in Kansas City, the average room rate was $67. The Kansas City Ritz-Carlton charged on average $115, and according to a local hotel consultant, this was still $70 less than the hotel needed to make a profit. The company's distinctive quest for service often led to exorbitant costs, spending lavishly on harpists, flowers, even champagne-stocked limousines for guests turned away on an overbooked night. The Ritz-Carlton Hotel Company continued to take on average 5 percent of its hotel's gross revenues, whether the hotel made money or not, and some investors seemed to think the management company did not really care whether the hotels were profitable, as long as the brand image was maintained.

New Ownership and New Initiatives in the Late 1990s

In 1995 the sprawling hotel chain Marriott International, Inc. bought a 49 percent stake in Ritz-Carlton. The larger company believed it could increase sales and profit margins at the Ritz and that things would eventually look up for the troubled chain. The cost of Marriott's initial investment was estimated to be about $200 million in cash and assumed debt. The next year, Marriott spent $331 million to take over the Ritz-Carlton Atlanta and buy a majority interest in two of the other Ritz-Carltons owned outright by William Johnson.

Following the ownership change, with Schulze still in charge, Ritz-Carlton continued to focus on maintaining its brand image. In August 1997 Schulze terminated, over quality issues, management agreements with a Saudi Arabian businessman who owned four Ritz-Carlton hotels, leaving the brand without a presence in four key markets: Washington, D.C., New York City, Los Angeles, and Aspen, Colorado. To make sure the company stayed on track, Schulze also put the company through the rigors of applying for a second Baldridge award, which Ritz-Carlton received in November 1999. Ritz-Carlton became only the second company to win the award twice, and it did so in the least amount of time possible (because companies cannot be given the award more often than once every seven years). Ritz-Carlton's rigorous training program was given a great deal of the credit for maintaining the high quality of service: New employees had to go through a month-long "certification" program along with 310 hours of training classes. Existing workers needed to be "recertified" every year, a process involving a further 125 hours of class work.

Despite some lingering conflicts with its hotel owners, Ritz-Carlton nevertheless moved ahead with expansion, opening new Ritz-Carltons in Singapore (January 1996); Bali, Indonesia (November 1996); St. Thomas, U.S. Virgin Islands (December 1996); Osaka, Japan (May 1997); Kuala Lumpur, Malaysia (November 1997); San Juan, Puerto Rico (December 1997); Shanghai, China (January 1998); Dubai, United Arab Emirates (September 1998); and Sharm al-Sheikh, Egypt (December 1999). The company also began seeking out new revenue sources in fast-growing sectors of the luxury market. For several new hotels slated for opening in the early 2000s, the company incorporated into the plans adjacent or attached luxury residential condominiums, called the Residences at The Ritz-Carlton. The first such addition was located at the new Washington, D.C., Ritz-Carlton, which opened in October 2000. A second initiative was the creation of the Ritz-Carlton Club in 1999, the brand's first move into the timeshare market. The first two of these were a standalone property in Aspen and one located adjacent to the St. Thomas hotel. Finally, Ritz-Carlton also began adding spas to its existing hotels or incorporating them into planned locations, and it began opening up golf courses near some of its resort hotels, with the first such one debuting in Jamaica in the summer of 2000.

Helping to make these moves financially possible were the deep pockets of Marriott, which also lent its own in-house

expertise in certain areas. For example, Marriott was already well established in timeshares, and was able to shift Robert Phillips from its timeshare operations to overseeing Ritz-Carlton's timeshare startup. There were other benefits for Ritz-Carlton flowing from its relationship with Marriott, such as being able to take advantage of the parent company's reservation system and buying power. The partnership was solidified in 1998 when Marriott boosted its interest in Ritz-Carlton to 99 percent. By 1999 revenues from the 35 hotels it operated around the world totaled about $1.4 billion.

Surviving the Early 2000s Travel Downturn

During 2000 five more Ritz-Carlton hotels opened. In addition to the aforementioned properties on Jamaica and in Washington, D.C., the new hotels were located in New Orleans, Philadelphia, and Wolfsburg, Germany. Late in the year Schulze announced his intention to retire from his operational role at the company in early 2001 at age 60. Schulze's service at Ritz-Carlton was encapsulated in the company slogan he contributed to the company lore: "We are ladies and gentlemen serving ladies and gentlemen." While Schulze temporarily remained onboard in the capacity of vice-chairman, Simon F. Cooper took over as president and chief operating officer. Cooper, a 30-year hotel veteran, had spent ten years as head of the award-winning Canadian chain Delta Hotels & Resorts before joining Marriott International in 1998 as president of Marriott Lodging Canada.

Cooper took leadership of Ritz-Carlton at an inauspicious time. The luxury lodging market, already feeling the effects of the economic slowdown, was further depressed by the travel downturn that followed the tragic events of September 11. The chain's occupancy rate fell from 77.5 percent in 2000 to 66.9 percent in 2001 and would not improve much over the next two years. This dropoff and stagnation was also reflected in the figures for revenue per available room (REVPAR), a key industry statistic. For Ritz-Carlton's North American properties, REVPAR fell each year from 2001 to 2003, bottoming out at $151.85.

Despite the economic travails, the company ploughed ahead with its aggressive expansion plans. More than a dozen additional hotels were opened from 2001 to 2003, including two in New York City that marked the brand's return to that metropolis. A second location in Boston was established, and a smaller, boutique-style Ritz-Carlton with only 75 rooms opened in the Georgetown section of Washington, D.C. Several more Ritz-Carltons debuted in Florida, while new overseas locations included Bahrain; Doha, Qatar; Istanbul, Turkey; Sintra, Portugal; and Santiago, Chile. Another important development in 2003 was the shifting of the company headquarters from Atlanta to Chevy Chase, Maryland. The move was made mainly to achieve operational efficiencies from the proximity to Marriott's base in Bethesda, Maryland. Ritz-Carlton nevertheless maintained a large measure of independence, as evidenced by its not moving into the Marriott headquarters itself.

The luxury hotel market recovered somewhat in 2004, and Ritz-Carlton's results improved in tandem. The occupancy rate for the year of 69.2 percent was 4.3 percentage points better than 2003, while the REVPAR figure of $177.96 represented a 12.9 percent improvement. Expansion slowed considerably in

2004, with the only new Ritz-Carlton opening in Berlin. In May 2004, however, the first Bulgari Hotel & Resort debuted in Milan, Italy. This new property was the first outcome from a 50–50 joint venture formed in early 2001 between Ritz-Carlton and the Italian luxury goods maker Bulgari S.p.A. Whereas the Ritz chain mainly catered to business executives, Bulgari hotels were envisioned more for entertainment celebrities and fashion types. The partners eventually planned to open up to a dozen Bulgari hotels around the world, with the second expected to open in Bali, Indonesia, in 2005.

In the meantime, Ritz-Carlton's less ambitious, but more international, plans for growth called for seven more Ritz-Carltons to open from 2005 to 2007. The only U.S. property on the drawing board was to be located in Dallas. No fewer than three new hotels were scheduled for booming China. The other locations were Grand Cayman, Tokyo, and Jakarta, Indonesia. Late in 2004 the company announced plans to open a 300-room hotel in Hong Kong within the upper 13 floors of a 100-story tower, which at 1,574 feet would make the hotel the highest in the world. This Ritz-Carlton was expected to open in 2009.

Principal Competitors

Four Seasons Hotels Inc.; Starwood Hotels & Resorts Worldwide, Inc.; Wyndham International, Inc.; Hilton Hotels Corporation; Fairmont Hotels & Resorts Inc.; Loews Hotels Holding Corporation.

Further Reading

Alisau, Patricia, "Ritz-Carlton Plans to Move Headquarters Closer to Marriott," *Hotel and Motel Management,* August 2002, p. 15.

Beirne, Mike, "Collins Checks into New Ritz Digs," *Brandweek,* January 4, 1999, p. 33.

Binkley, Christina, "Ritz-Carlton's Schultze to Retire from Overseeing Daily Operations," *Wall Street Journal,* January 23, 2001, p. B10.

Binkley, Christina, and Alessandra Galloni, "A Bitter Suite Mix: Ritz-Carlton's Bulgari Venture Aimed to Elevate Hotel Brand; Now, Divas Duel for Spotlight," *Wall Street Journal,* October 8, 2004, p. B1.

Carey, Susan, "This No-Frills (at Present) Hotel Won't Leave a Light on for You," *Wall Street Journal,* February 24, 1993, p. B1.

Durbin, Fran, "Ritz-Carlton Commissions Study to Examine Meetings Market," *Travel Weekly,* April 18, 1994, p. 56.

Evans, Judith, "Executive with a First-Class Vision: Ritz-Carlton Chief Horst Schulze Still Believes in Old-Fashioned Service," *Washington Post,* August 23, 1999, p. F13.

Fickes, Michael, "Puttin' on a New Ritz," *National Real Estate Investor,* January 2000, p. 82.

Gutner, Toddi, "Puttin' on the Ritz," *Forbes 400,* October 19, 1992, p. 22.

Hirsch, James S., "Of Luxury and Losses: Many Ritz Hotels Are in the Red," *Wall Street Journal,* April 22, 1994, p. B1, B4.

Kent, George, "The Word for Elegance," *Readers Digest,* 1948, pp. 147–50.

Lamb, Robyn, "Ritz-Carlton Hotel Moving Headquarters to Chevy Chase," *Baltimore (Md.) Daily Record,* March 6, 2003.

McDowell, Edwin, "Ritz-Carlton's Keys to Good Service," *New York Times,* March 31, 1993, p. D1, D5.

Poole, Sheila M., "Happy Workers Equal Happy Guests," *Atlanta Journal-Constitution,* June 25, 2000, p. G1.

——, "Marriott Exec Named President of Ritz Unit," *Atlanta Journal-Constitution,* January 23, 2001, p. D1.

Schenke, Jarred, "Ritz-Carlton HQ Checking Out of Atlanta," *Atlanta Business Chronicle,* June 14, 2002.

Shaw, Russell, "Ritz Buyer Touts Deal's Benefits," *Hotel and Motel Management,* April 3, 1995, p. 1.

Spiegel, Peter, "Putting on the Ritz," *Forbes,* April 17, 2000, pp. 165–66.

Touby, Laurel, "Too Many Rooms at the Inn for Ritz-Carlton," *Business Week,* July 6, 1992, pp. 74–76.

Tucker, Katheryn Hayes, "Learning How to Put on the Ritz," *Georgia Trend,* October 2004, pp. 70+.

Walsh, John P., "Ritz-Carlton Enlarges Brand," *Hotel and Motel Management,* February 5, 2001, pp. 3, 29.

"Why the Ritz Caters to a Business Elite," *Business Week,* August 17, 1968, pp. 56–62.

—Thomas Derdak
—updates: A. Woodward; David E. Salamie

Ruby Tuesday, Inc.

150 West Church Avenue
Maryville, Tennessee 37801-4936
U.S.A.
Telephone: (865) 379-5700
Fax: (865) 379-6817
Web site: http://www.rubytuesday.com

Public Company
Incorporated: 1972
Employees: 37,000
Sales: $1.04 billion (2004)
Stock Exchanges: New York
Ticker Symbol: RI
NAIC: 722110 Full-Service Restaurants; 533110 Lessors of Nonfinancial Intangible Assets (Except Copyrighted Works)

Ruby Tuesday, Inc. is a leading company in the bar-and-grill category of the U.S. casual dining restaurant industry. From its original location in Knoxville, Tennessee, the Ruby Tuesday chain has grown to more than 700 units in about 40 states primarily in the Southeast, Northeast, Mid-Atlantic, and Midwest. Nearly 500 of the outlets are company owned with the remainder being franchised. Entrees, ranging in price from $6.49 to $16.99, include ribs, chicken, steak, seafood, pasta, burgers, and sandwiches, and the menu also features soups, a salad bar, and desserts. The restaurants also offer food for carryout via the company's "curb-side to-go" initiative. Ruby Tuesday's relatively small but expanding international operations include about three dozen franchised restaurants in about a dozen countries. Ruby Tuesday was founded in 1972 with the opening of the Knoxville outlet, enjoyed ten years of expansion as an independent company, then spent 14 years as part of Morrison Inc. (later known as Morrison Restaurants Inc.) from 1982 to 1996, and finally became independent again in 1996 when Morrison split up into three separate publicly traded companies, one of which was Ruby Tuesday, Inc.

Origins in Knoxville

That original Knoxville location had its beginnings in a Hollywood-like deathbed scene. In 1972 Samuel E. (Sandy) Beall was a 22-year-old University of Tennessee, Knoxville, student majoring in finance, who on the side helped William Kholmia manage a group of Pizza Hut restaurants. Kholmia suffered a massive heart attack that year. On his deathbed, Kholmia, wanting his protegé to be his own boss, offered Beall $10,000 to open a restaurant.

Beall accepted the offer, and together with four of his college buddies scraped together another $10,000 to open the first Ruby Tuesday, which was located near the university campus in Knoxville. Beall named the restaurant after the then ubiquitous Rolling Stones' song "Ruby Tuesday," which he kept hearing on the jukebox. The restaurant itself, which was a converted old house, featured barn wood walls, fake Tiffany lamps over the tables, and a $1.45 hamburger served on an English muffin. Beall also secured the first liquor-by-drink license in Knoxville, which enhanced the restaurant's popularity with students. Ruby Tuesday's subsequent success made Beall too busy for school, so he dropped out to devote himself full-time to his venture.

Over the next several years, Ruby Tuesday grew slowly, adding a new outlet about every nine months. As the chain expanded, the rustic decor and inexpensive fare proved popular with not only college students but also young couples. By 1982, ten years after its founding, Ruby Tuesday was a 15 restaurant chain. Nearly all the restaurants were located in regional shopping malls. Beall had also begun to develop a second concept called L&N Seafood Grill.

Sold to Morrison in 1982

As Ruby Tuesday's rate of growth began to increase in the early 1980s, Beall realized he needed more capital to expand the flagship chain and develop other concepts. He considered taking the company public, entering the franchising game, or selling the company. It was the last option that he eventually took, following a real estate agent/acquaintance's suggestion that Morrison Inc. might be a likely buyer.

Company Perspectives:

The foundation of our company is built around our mission: To Be The Best Where It Counts. Ruby Tuesday has proven its broad appeal, with a customer base that is a cross-section of the American people and with successful sites that range from the smallest towns to major metropolitan areas.

Morrison was a cafeteria and contract foodservice chain founded in 1920 and headquartered in Mobile, Alabama. An ill-conceived diversification in the 1960s into motels, china and small wares, insurance, and other disparate areas led to confusion and reduced profit margins by the late 1970s. Morrison's fortunes were turned around following the appointment of Ernest Eugene Bishop as CEO in 1980. Bishop quickly divested the company of all its non-restaurant and food-service businesses, and then, in April 1982, enhanced Morrison's restaurant sector by buying Ruby Tuesday for $15 million in cash and stock. At the time, Ruby Tuesday revenue averaged about $1 million a year per restaurant.

Bishop left Beall in control of the day-to-day operations of Ruby Tuesday, making Beall president of the newly created Specialty Restaurant Division of Morrison. Beall soon opened the first L&N Seafood Grill, located in Knoxville, then developed the Silver Spoon Cafe concept, a New York City delicatessen-style restaurant. The first Silver Spoon opened in 1984, also in Knoxville.

Rapid Growth in the Mid- and Late 1980s

By 1985 it was clear that the sale of Ruby Tuesday to Morrison had indeed enabled the restaurant chain to markedly increase its growth rate. At fiscal year-end 1985, there were 35 Ruby Tuesdays in business, more than double the number at the time of the sale, along with seven L&N restaurants. The Specialty Restaurant Division as a whole brought in $70 million in revenue, 11 percent of Morrison's total. More importantly, the Ruby Tuesday restaurants were improving Morrison's overall profitability since the Specialty Restaurant Division's $7.5 million in profits represented 18 percent of the parent company's total.

The increasing importance of the specialty restaurants to Morrison's future was quite evident when Bishop decided in 1985 that Beall should be his successor. That year Bishop made Beall executive vice-president of Morrison's specialty restaurants and cafeteria operations. Since before Ruby Tuesday was sold to Morrison, Beall lived in the resort town of Hilton Head, South Carolina, and commuted to Knoxville, where Ruby Tuesday was still based. In 1986 Bishop asked Beall to relocate to Mobile to become president and COO of Morrison, and Beall agreed, proving his dedication and his desire to succeed Bishop by leaving his beloved Hilton Head.

Meanwhile, the specialty restaurants continued to grow at a rapid pace in the late 1980s, nearing the 200-unit mark, with more than 125 Ruby Tuesdays among them. All of this growth was achieved through company-owned units, keeping Morrison in total control of operations, control that would have been impossible if the company had decided to franchise. As Morrison's

cafeteria operations suffered from a general category-wide decline, the specialty restaurants became even more important, accounting for half of Morrison's profits by the end of the decade.

Revamped Restaurant Lineup in the Early 1990s

In the early 1990s, in order to provide more growth opportunities and to guard against the fluctuations of the retail market, the Ruby Tuesday chain was shifted from an emphasis on shopping mall locations to a longer-term 50–50 mix of mall and freestanding locations. In conjunction with this shift came Ruby Tuesday's inclusion in so-called restaurant parks, clusters of dinner houses that share some development and ongoing operational costs and that provide customers a range of restaurant choices in a small area—even the easy ability to switch their restaurant choice if the wait at one restaurant is too long. One of the first restaurant parks featuring a Ruby Tuesday was located in the Denver suburb of Englewood—with the other dinner houses being Chevys, Grisanti's, and Stanford's.

In 1992 Morrison restructured itself, emphasizing restaurants over cafeterias by changing its name to Morrison Restaurants Inc. The dinner house restaurants—Ruby Tuesday, L&N, and Silver Spoon—were positioned within Morrison Restaurants as the Casual Dining Group, later known as the Ruby Tuesday Group. The year 1992 also saw Beall become CEO of Morrison, and Morrison posted its first $1 billion revenue year.

In the early 1990s, Beall was beginning to become disenchanted with the L&N Seafood concept. Ruby Tuesday's success was largely attributed to its per-person check average of $8.75, and Beall was finding it nearly impossible to get L&N's average even under $10. At the same time, the Silver Spoon concept was not overly successful either, and was considered too similar to Ruby Tuesday itself. Meanwhile, Beall was strongly interested in entering the burgeoning Italian restaurant sector, and signed a letter of intent late in 1992 to acquire Uno Restaurants Corporation and its chain of 110 Italian restaurants. Early the following year, however, Uno pulled out of the deal after a disagreement over the purchase price.

Left without this prize acquisition, Beall decided it was time to abandon Silver Spoon and create a new casual Italian restaurant, to be called Mozzarella's Cafe. In 1993 Silver Spoon units began to be converted to Mozzarella's, which featured a variety of pasta dishes and pizzas, as well as fresh seafood, steak, and grilled chicken selections. The check average—$9.50—was higher than Ruby Tuesday's, but still under the $10 mark. The under $10 category was where Beall wished to position all of the Ruby Tuesday Group concepts.

Beall continued to revamp the Ruby Tuesday Group later in 1993 and in the following two years. The group entered into a joint venture in mid-1993 with the Dallas-based 12-unit Tia's Tex-Mex, founded by Larry Lavine (founder of the highly successful Chili's chain), who needed financing to fund further expansion. As part of the joint venture agreement, the Ruby Tuesday Group was given a five-year option to acquire Tia's, which it did in January 1995 for $9 million in common stock. Tia's restaurants were conceived to be "reminiscent of a grand old Mexican restaurant," featured display kitchens and outdoor patios, and offered various Tex-Mex dishes with a $9 check average.

Key Dates:

1972: Samuel E. (Sandy) Beall and four college buddies open the first Ruby Tuesday restaurant in Knoxville, Tennessee.

1982: Now a 15-unit chain, Ruby Tuesday is acquired by Morrison Inc. for $15 million.

1989: The number of Ruby Tuesdays reaches 125.

1993: Company launches an Italian casual restaurant chain called Mozzarella's Cafe (later American Cafe).

1995: Tia's Tex-Mex chain is acquired; first international Ruby Tuesday opens in Hong Kong.

1996: Morrison splits into three separate public companies, one of which is Ruby Tuesday, Inc., based in Mobile, Alabama.

1997: Franchising of the Ruby Tuesday concept begins.

1998: Company headquarters are reestablished in Maryville, Tennessee.

2000: The Tia's Tex-Mex and American Cafe chains are sold off.

The year 1993 also saw the debut of Sweetpea's, a Southern-style dinner house, in suburban Atlanta. Featuring such home-style and comfort-type meals as country-fried steak and chicken pot pie and a check average in the $7 range, Sweetpea's was positioned to compete with such stalwarts as Cracker Barrel and Shoney's. In 1994, having already grown to four units, the Sweetpea's name was changed to Snapp's because the Ruby Tuesday Group could not secure legal rights to the name and because the Dallas-based Black-eyed Pea (another Southern-style restaurant) raised objections to the name, fearing customer confusion.

In mid-1994, the Ruby Tuesday Group announced that it would phase out the L&N Seafood Grill concept, given that L&N could not conform to the Ruby Tuesday under $10 check average. Most of the L&Ns were subsequently converted to either Ruby Tuesdays or Mozzarella's Cafes, although several were simply closed. Approximately $20 million was set aside to implement the phaseout.

Independent Again in the Late 1990s

In May 1995 Ruby Tuesday entered into a license agreement with Jardine Pacific to develop Ruby Tuesday restaurants in the Asia-Pacific region. The first Ruby Tuesday located outside the United States opened in Hong Kong in July 1995, with additional units planned for mainland China, Singapore, Malaysia, and Australia.

Ruby Tuesday came full circle in 1996 when Morrison was split into three separate public companies: Ruby Tuesday, Inc., the former Ruby Tuesday Group; Morrison Fresh Cooking Inc., comprised of Morrison's cafeterias and quick-service restaurants; and Morrison Health Care Inc., the healthcare foodservice business of Morrison. Of the spinoffs, Beall said, ''Now that our businesses have matured, we no longer need a layer of administrative management between these self-supporting independent operations and the shareholders.'' Legally, Ruby Tues-

day, Inc. was the successor company to Morrison Restaurants Inc.; Beall retained his position as president and CEO of Ruby Tuesday, which remained based in Mobile.

Ruby Tuesday's first year of its second period as an independent company was a rough one. Although revenues increased 20.3 percent to $620.1 million in fiscal 1996, the company posted a net loss of $2.9 million due in part to increased competition in its restaurant sector and in part to $25.9 million in asset impairment and restructuring charges that were posted during the third quarter. The firm bounced back the next year, however, reporting profits of $25 million on sales of $655.4 million. During 1997 the company established an international division to facilitate overseas growth, and it also began franchising. In terms of the latter, the strategy taken was to keep operating company-owned restaurants in core geographic areas while selling off or otherwise establishing units in noncore regions. For example, during the fiscal year ending in June 1998, 48 restaurants in Arizona, Colorado, Florida, and a few other markets were sold to franchisees. At the same time, Ruby Tuesday was opening about 40 new restaurants a year.

In the summer of 1998 the company returned to its roots, moving its corporate headquarters to Maryville, Tennessee, about 15 miles south of Knoxville. The new corporate campus also included an onsite training facility. Revenue growth slowed in the final years of the decade because of the continuing sale of units to franchisees, but profits kept growing. For fiscal year 1999, revenues grew just 1.5 percent, reaching $722.3 million, but profits jumped 25.6 percent, to $36.5 million. That year the poorly performing Mozzarella's Cafe units were converted into a concept called American Cafe. Among the overseas markets being targeted for growth at this time were Chile, Honduras, Iceland, India, and Kuwait. Back home, the number of franchised Ruby Tuesdays neared the 100 mark.

Early 21st-Century Growth Initiatives

Ruby Tuesday began the 21st century with a retrenchment. In April 2000 the company announced plans to sell off the Tia's Tex-Mex (26-unit) and American Cafe (42-unit) chains in order to focus full attention on the flagship operation. In November 2000 Ruby Tuesday completed the sale of the restaurants to Specialty Restaurant Group, LLC in a management-led buyout valued at about $59 million. In anticipation of the sale, the company took a $10.1 million charge, cutting into profits for the fiscal year ending in June 2000. Whereas profits grew only slightly, revenue increased 10 percent, reaching $797.5 million, despite the sale of another 42 Ruby Tuesday restaurants to franchisees.

The early 2000s saw Americans increasingly seeking takeout food higher in quality than typical fast-food fare. A few casual dining chains, including Outback Steakhouse, Inc., pioneered in curbside pickup programs through which a customer could call in an order and then drive to the restaurant and park in one of several designated spaces. These spaces were monitored by restaurant staff, usually via video camera, who would then run the order out to the car. Ruby Tuesday joined this successful trend by launching what was eventually called ''curb-side to-go'' at selected locations in 2001. After finding that takeout revenues had doubled at these units, the company began expanding the program. By late 2003 all the chain's non-mall locations were offering curb-side to-go.

Although Ruby Tuesday saw some softening of sales, particularly at its mall locations, in the immediate aftermath of September 11, 2001, when consumers pulled back on their spending, the overall trend was positive. The company continued to open 45 to 50 company-owned units per year in the eastern United States, while opening about two dozen franchise units each year west of the Mississippi. By early 2004 there were at least 700 Ruby Tuesdays across the country, more than 200 of which were franchise outlets. For the fiscal year ending in May 2004, the company's revenues surpassed the $1 billion mark for the first time. Profits were a record $110 million.

At this time, Ruby Tuesday was in the midst of launching several initiatives aimed at nutrition- and diet-conscious Americans. In late 2003 its restaurants began frying foods in canola oil, which is free of the trans fats that had been linked to heart disease. At the same time, a new menu was introduced featuring several low-carb items aimed at dieters watching their intake of carbohydrates. Then in April 2004, in an unprecedented move, the restaurants began using menus that included nutritional information for every item, listing calories, total fat, net carbs, and fiber. The company backtracked just four months later, however, and removed the listings from the menus, citing the prohibitive cost of printing new menus every time there were changes. Anytime a menu item was altered in any way, such as a portion size change or the amount of a particular ingredient, a menu reprint was necessitated. As a replacement, Ruby Tuesday began printing the data on separate tabletop cards, the updating of which was expected to be quicker and less costly.

The timing of these initiatives was perhaps unfortunate. Simultaneously, Ruby Tuesday also cut its portion sizes on a number of its dishes, which alienated many customers, and it also began a marketing transition from a coupon-based campaign to the chain's first television advertising effort. The elimination of the coupons and the negative customer response to the portion cuts were factors in a 5 percent decline in sales during the second half of the 2004 calendar year. With a consumer backlash against leaner menus apparently building, Ruby Tuesday early in 2005 at least partially reversed course and rolled out heavier fare, including thick-cut onion rings and half-pound burgers. The menu nevertheless still offered more than 30 low-carb, low-fat, and low-calorie choices, and Ruby Tuesday remained the only U.S. casual dining chain with a salad bar. Chairman and CEO Beall was hoping that aggressive television advertising could turn the tide and make this downturn short-lived.

Principal Competitors

Darden Restaurants, Inc.; Brinker International, Inc.; Applebee's International, Inc.; Carlson Restaurants Worldwide, Inc.; Outback Steakhouse, Inc.

Further Reading

Bernstein, Charles, "Beall Puts the 'More' in Morrison: Samuel E. 'Sandy' Beall III Is Determined to Make Morrison Inc. a Casual-Restaurant Chain Empire Every Bit As Strong As Brinker and General Mills Restaurants," *Restaurants and Institutions,* July 1, 1994, pp. 20–22, 26, 30, 34.

——, "Morrison: Hello, Ruby Tuesday," *Restaurants and Institutions,* August 26, 1992, pp. 27–28.

Carlino, Bill, "Forging a New Identity," *Nation's Restaurant News,* March 28, 1994, p. 66.

——, "Morrison Splits into Three Companies," *Nation's Restaurant News,* October 9, 1995, p. 1.

——, "Ruby Tuesday Tunes Trio, Adds Sweetpea's to Stable," *Nation's Restaurant News,* May 24, 1993, p. 5.

Geisel, Amy, "There's No Place Like Home: Ruby's Back to Its Roots," *Knoxville (Tenn.) News-Sentinel,* May 17, 1998, p. D1.

Gordon, Mitchell, "Morrison's Moves: Cafeteria Operator Profiting from Full-Serve Eateries," *Barron's,* September 30, 1985, pp. 50–51.

Gray, Steven, "Dishing Out the Truth: Ruby Tuesday Yanks Listings of Calories, Fat on Its Menus," *Wall Street Journal,* August 31, 2004, p. B1.

Greenwald, Judy, "Profitable Recipe: Morrison Finds Few Things Beat the Cafeteria Trade," *Barron's,* September 13, 1982, pp. 52–53.

Hayes, Jack, "Drive-by Dining: Ruby Tuesday Steers Toward Curbside Takeout," *Nation's Restaurant News,* November 26, 2001, pp. 4, 61.

Kadlec, Daniel, "Chain Reaction," *Time,* June 7, 2004, pp. 99–100.

King, Paul, "Divided They Fall: Former Morrison Cos. Face Drop in Profits," *Nation's Restaurant News,* May 6, 1996, p. 11.

LaVecchia, Gina, "Ruby Tuesday Still Rocks," *Restaurant Hospitality,* May 2002, pp. 53–54, 56, 58.

Palmeri, Christopher, "Hello, Ruby Tuesday," *Forbes,* December 20, 1993, p. 194.

Peters, James, "Ruby Tuesday Deploys Sales, Service Initiatives," *Nation's Restaurant News,* October 21, 2002, pp. 4, 11–12.

——, "Ruby Tuesday Rolls Out Changes to Drive Sales," *Nation's Restaurant News,* July 21, 2003, pp. 4, 11, 95.

Walkup, Carolyn, "Ruby Tuesday Accounts for Content, Serves Up Nutritional Info on Menus," *Nation's Restaurant News,* March 22, 2004, p. 1.

Waters, C. Dickinson, "Ruby Tuesday to Divest Sister Chains in Favor of Core Product," *Nation's Restaurant News,* April 24, 2000, pp. 1, 138.

Yeldell, Cynthia, "Ruby Tuesday to Start Advertising," *Knoxville (Tenn.) News-Sentinel,* July 16, 2004, p. C1.

—David E. Salamie

Safe Flight Instrument Corporation

20 New King Street
White Plains, New York 10604-1206
U.S.A.
Telephone: (914) 946-9500
Fax: (914) 946-7882
Web site: http://www.safeflight.com

Private Company
Incorporated: 1946
Employees: 130
Sales: $25 million (2004 est.)
NAIC: 334511 Search, Detection, Navigation, Guidance,
    Aeronautical, and Nautical System and Instrument
    Manufacturing; 336412 Aircraft Engine and Engine
    Parts Manufacturing

Safe Flight Instrument Corporation produces a wide array of devices to make flying safer and more manageable. From their earliest flying lessons, all pilots are made familiar with the urgent whine of the stall warning indicator, the lifesaving alarm that sounds when airflow over the wings has slowed to a critical level. Safe Flight founder Leonard M. Greene invented that instrument in the late 1940s, and went on to earn more than 100 other patents.

The company has produced more than 600,000 stall warning indicators. Other products include angle-of-attack systems, airborne wind shear warning systems, automatic throttles, and engine monitoring devices. Customers include most aircraft manufacturers, as well as the U.S. military and business jet operators.

Origins

Safe Flight Instrument Corporation founder Leonard M. Greene came from an entrepreneurial family. According to his book, *Inventorship: The Art of Innovation,* his father had started a rubber cement company in a hayloft. Greene, who had four siblings, started inventing toys for himself as a child, according to a profile in *Technology Review.*

Greene presented research to the Institute of Aeronautical Sciences on the problem of breaking the sound barrier while still in his 20s. He was in charge of theoretical aerodynamics for Grumman Aircraft at the time, notes *Aviation Week & Space Technology.* Another critical aviation problem caught his interest after he witnessed an aircraft accident.

Planes need air to flow over their wings in order to fly controllably. If this airflow is disturbed or slowed past a certain point, the wings will lose their lift and the plane will fall—a condition known as a stall. In this case, there is a danger of the aircraft spinning sideways uncontrollably. Stall-spin accidents accounted for more than half of all aviation fatalities in the 1940s. Greene witnessed one of these accidents firsthand at the age of 19.

There are maneuvers to recover from a stall, given sufficient altitude and situational awareness. Greene developed a device—the Stall Warning Indicator—that alerted the pilot whenever a stall was impending. According to *Technology Review,* the design was very simple. A small sensor was installed near the critical point where airflow would separate from the wing in a stall. When wind passed the sensor at a dangerous angle, it would trip a circuit connected to a horn and light in the cockpit.

The first Stall Warning Indicators, introduced in 1946, sold for $17 each, according to Greene. Greene reports that he started his company in a rented carriage house with an initial investment of $14,000. The company had three employees.

The *Saturday Evening Post* (October 25, 1947) dubbed the stall warning indicator perhaps the "greatest lifesaver since the invention of the parachute." The device was made standard equipment in most aircraft by 1950, and the company would sell 500,000 units in the next 50 years.

In the 1950s, Safe Flight led the way in developing automatic throttle systems. These were used in a variety of business aircraft and airliners. The autothrottles led to the development of the SCAT (Speed, Command, Attitude, Thrust) system, which TWA put on its entire fleet in the mid-1960s.

Activism in the 1970s and 1980s

By 1971, Safe Flight was reporting sales of $2.4 million. New products in the early 1970s included an autopilot for sailboats.

321

Company Perspectives:

Over the past five and a half decades, Safe Flight Instrument Corporation has invented some of the most significant safety and performance innovations in aviation. With equipment on two-thirds of the world's aircraft, the company designs, develops and produces a variety of products to enhance performance and safety. Safe Flight equipment can be found on all types of fixed and rotary wing aircraft in the general, corporate, commercial, and military sectors.

The year was 1946.... Safe Flight, a newly formed aviation instrumentation manufacturer, brought to market the industry's first Stall Warning System—all but putting an end to a major cause of aircraft accidents and aviation fatalities. From the invention of wing lift detection to the development of airborne wind shear detection alert and recovery guidance, to the recent innovation of powerline detection and warning for helicopters, Safe Flight has remained devoted to improving aviation performance and safety—worldwide.

With facilities in White Plains, New York, the company employs a full spectrum of engineering, manufacturing, and software disciplines to develop a variety of safety and performance equipment for the world's aviation needs.

In 1972, Greene responded to IBM's new policy of mandatory retirement at age 60 by placing an ad in a local business journal seeking to hire talent from among its displaced executives. This stance against age discrimination was but one aspect of Greene's social activism. Leonard Greene also was known for his efforts to hire the disabled and for writing on ways to end poverty.

In the 1970s, Greene established the Institute for Socioeconomic Studies in White Plains, New York. He advocated replacing most social programs with a direct income supplement, which he believed would be more efficient than the existing cumbersome bureaucracy. Greene helped form Corporate Angel Network in 1981 to provide cancer patients transportation to distant treatment sites using space available on corporate jets.

Warning Against Wind Shear in the 1980s

In the late 1970s, Safe Flight developed an onboard wind shear warning system designed to alert pilots to microbursts—the sudden, forceful downdrafts that were particularly dangerous during landings. The device also could calculate the best maneuver for flying out of wind shear. Unlike airport-based devices of the day (before Doppler radar), the Safe Flight unit was virtually immune to false alarms.

The units cost $10,000 to $13,000 each. By the mid-1980s, Boeing was incorporating Safe Flight's wind shear technology into its new airliners. It had been used by makers of corporate aircraft for several years, and was available as a retrofit for numerous aircraft types.

Ground Proximity in the 1990s

Leonard Greene was named to the National Inventors Hall of Fame in 1991. He continued to work on aviation-related problems.

Key Dates:

1946: Safe Flight Instrument Corporation is organized.
1949: Leonard M. Greene patents the Stall Warning Indicator.
1971: Sales exceed $2 million.
1976: Greene patents the first airborne Wind Shear Warning System.
1991: Leonard Greene is named to the National Inventors Hall of Fame.
2002: Leadership is restructured after the death of Leonard Greene's son Don on September 11, 2001.

Safe Flight teamed with SCI Systems, Inc. of Huntsville, Alabama, to develop an updated ground-proximity warning system (GPWS) in the early 1990s. GPWS had been mandatory equipment on commercial airliners since 1974; new regulations were requiring their installation on 10 to 30 passenger aircraft by 1994. The partnership with SCI was placed on the "back burner," however, when Safe Flight gave priority to its wind shear detection business, reported *Business & Commercial Aviation*.

In 1994, Greene patented an idea for a supersonic aircraft with a reduced sonic boom. He patented a propulsion system for such a plane in 1995, noted *Aviation Week & Space Technology*, assigning these patents to Boeing.

Other projects during the 1990s included "stick shakers" for alerting pilots to engine conditions through vibrations. In 1998 the company began developing a guidance system to help pilots avoid spatial disorientation during the last 30 feet of a landing, Randy Greene later told *Business & Commercial Aviation*.

In 2001, Safe Flight patented a technology to help aircraft avoid collisions with power lines. Safe Flight's device detected the 50- to 60-hertz signal emitted by alternating current. The "Powerline Detection System" was aimed primarily at helicopters. Units sold for $10,000 each, much less than competing products.

Regrouping After 9/11

Safe Flight Executive Vice-President Don Greene, the adopted son of the company's founder, perished in the September 11, 2001 terrorist attacks on the United States. An experienced aviator, he was a passenger on United Airlines Flight 93.

The company leadership was soon restructured. Another one of Leonard Greene's sons, Randall (Randy) Greene, replaced his father as president and chief executive officer. Randall Greene was a very experienced pilot who had led projects at Bendix Avionics and AlliedSignal Aerospace and had developed a new version of the Rockwell Commander aircraft.

Leonard Greene remained chairman. By this time, he had accumulated more than 8,000 flying hours. He was honored by the U.S. Patent and Trademark Office as part of its bicentennial celebrations in 2002.

Safe Flight had about 150 employees at the time. Many stayed with the company for their entire career. Randy Greene told *Business & Commercial Aviation,* "Safe Flight doesn't have layoffs. Ever."

The company was developing new helicopter products, including an Exceedance Warning System to alert pilots when engines were being operated outside accepted parameters. Another device displayed the status of a helicopter's landing light.

Safe Flight was promoting its new AutoPower automatic throttle, a computerized cruise control. Another important system was the N1 Computer, which adjusted jet thrust settings for optimum power based on real time air conditions. This freed pilots from having to look up settings on charts. By May 2004, Safe Flight had sold 600 N1 Computers to Cessna for use in Citation business jets.

Principal Competitors

Honeywell Inc.; Rockwell Collins, Inc.; Teledyne Technologies Incorporated.

Further Reading

"Alerts, Affordably," *Business & Commercial Aviation,* March 1, 2004, p. 54.

Fox, Barry, "Hums and Helicopters," *New Scientist,* August 26, 2000, p. 7.

Garvey, William, "B/CA Fast Five," *Business & Commercial Aviation,* October 2002, p. 16.

Gilbert, Gordon A., "Joint Venture to Produce Ground Prox Box Is On Hold," *Business & Commercial Aviation,* January 1, 1994, p. 20.

Goyer, Robert, "Time Between Failure: 50 Years and Counting," *Flying,* February 1997, p. 34.

Greene, Leonard M., *Free Enterprise Without Poverty,* New York: W.W. Norton, 1981.

——, *Inventorship: The Art of Innovation,* New York: John Wiley & Sons, 2001.

——, *The National Tax Rebate: A New America with Less Government,* Washington, D.C.: Regnery Publishing, 1998.

"Gulfstream Offering Autothrottle As G200 Option, Retrofit," *The Weekly of Business Aviation,* July 19, 2004, p. 27.

Hlotyak, Elizabeth, "A 'Rising Star' and a High Flier: Heineken, Safe Flight Instrument Lauded for Corporate Ethics," *Westchester County Business Journal,* May 20, 2002, pp. 1, 8.

"IBM, Which Reported '71 Sales Figure of $8.3-Billion, Announces Policy Under. . .," *New York Times Abstracts,* October 5, 1972, p. 67.

"Lifetime Achievement: Leonard M. Greene," *Aviation Week & Space Technology,* April 29, 2002, p. 43.

"Manufacturers Urge Interim Implementation of Warning Function," *Aviation Week & Space Technology,* September 22, 1986, p. 78.

Moorman, Robert W., "Ground-Prox Field Filling Up," *Air Transport World,* March 1, 1993, p. 75.

"The Passengers: Donald F. Greene," *Pittsburgh Post-Gazette,* October 28, 2001, p. C9.

"Patent Granted for Supersonic Aircraft with Minimal Sonic Boom," *Aviation Daily,* March 22, 1994, p. 460.

"Republic Testing Shear System," *Aviation Week & Space Technology,* July 4, 1983, p. 78.

"Safe Flight Instrument Announces Executive Restructuring," *The Weekly of Business Aviation,* January 7, 2002, p. 16.

"Sounding an Alarm in the Sky," *Technology Review,* March/April 1999, p. 104.

Stein, Kenneth J., "Wind Shear Development Provides Timely Warning," *Aviation Week & Space Technology,* March 2, 1981, p. 62.

Whitehouse, Franklin, "Corporate Planes to Help Fly Cancer Patients," *New York Times,* Sec. 1, Part 2, December 27, 1981, p. 51.

Witkin, Richard, "Republic Airlines Proposes to Buy Wind Shear Detectors. . .," *New York Times Abstracts,* June 6, 1983, p. 12.

—Frederick C. Ingram

St. James's Place Capital, plc

St. James's Place House, Dollar Street
Cirencester
Gloucestershire GL7 2AQ
United Kingdom
Telephone: +44-1285-640-302
Fax: +44-1285-640-436
Web site: http://www.sjpc.co.uk

Public Company
Founded: 1991 as J. Rothschild Assurance Group
Employees: 1,131
Total Assets: $11.82 billion (2003)
Stock Exchanges: London
Ticker Symbol: SJPC
NAIC: 524113 Direct Life Insurance Carriers; 525990
   Other Financial Vehicles

St. James's Place Capital, plc is a financial services holding company. The self-employed sales force of St. James's Partnership attends to the financial and wealth management services needs of an affluent clientele in the United Kingdom. Companies of the St. James's Place Group subsidiary provide life assurance, trust, and third-party financial services products. HBOS (formerly Halifax) owns approximately 60 percent of St. James's Place Capital.

Rothschild Name on New Financial Entity: 1992–95

A rift between members of the famed Rothschild financial house sent family members off in different directions in 1980. Lord Jacob Rothschild would divide his time among financial ventures, philanthropy, and cultural activities. In 1992, *Institutional Investor* listed his principal financial holdings as J. Rothschild Assurance Group, founded in 1991; a stake in Global Asset Management money management firm; and joint venture J. Rothschild, Wolfensohn & Co., advisor to wealthy European customers of the U.S. investment banking concern James D. Wolfensohn Inc. St. James's Place Capital (SJPC) owned 100 percent of J. Rothschild Group. Since 1977, the SJPC group had

controlled Lord Rothschild's interest in financial services and investment companies.

Control was a factor in the estrangement within the Rothschild financial dynasty. Lord Jacob Rothschild sought to cultivate outside business partners, while others felt that family members should manage the Rothschild financial legacy.

Sir Mark Weinberg, who had already succeeded in growing financial houses Abbey Life and Hambro Life (Allied Dunbar), was St. James's Place and J. Rothschild Group co-chair. Mike Wilson, former CEO of Hambro, was chief executive of J. Rothschild Assurance.

As well as bringing in new blood to manage the financial operations, Rothschild shared control of the assets. *Institutional Investor* reported, ''Though Jacob remains the biggest shareholder in public companies Rothschild Investment Trust (RIT) and St. James's Place Capital, which owns 40% of RIT, he says his colleagues have significant equity stakes in the various businesses. For example, Weinberg has 'a very significant equity stake' in J. Rothschild Assurance.''

Rothschild's SJPC entered into another new partnership in 1994, joining with New York Life Worldwide Holding to form Life Assurance Holding Corporation, a vehicle to acquire U.K. life businesses. SJPC's new partner was a subsidiary of New York Life Insurance Company.

Rothschild's Role Reduced: 1996–99

Holding company St. James's Place Capital entered into reconstruction during 1996. SJPC spun off its £123 million investment portfolio, creating Value Realisation Trust. Ownership remained with existing SJPC shareholders. According to the *Financial Times,* SJPC would concentrate its attention on the life assurance business. The core businesses were J. Rothschild Assurance Holdings, the principal life assurance business; Life Assurance Holding Corporation, the ''vulture fund''; and Global Asset Management, holding £5.8 billion under management.

Lord Rothschild stepped down as joint chairman following the reconstruction. Sir Mark Weinberg continued as sole chair.

Then in October 1996, Rothschild sold more than half of the family's 10.9 percent stake in SJPC. The move allowed Rothschild to turn more of his attention to the National Heritage Memorial Fund and Heritage Lottery Fund, which he chaired. Regarding the sale of the shares Weinberg told the *Financial Times,* "Lord Rothschild felt he had too large a family holding in a company in which he no longer played a managerial role."

J. Rothschild Assurance, seller of life assurance to the wealthy, engaged in a reverse takeover of holding company SJPC in 1997. The *Financial Times* reported, "The enlarged business will be better able to reward the self-employed sales staff of J. Rothschild, called partners, who together with the founders own 34 per cent of the company because of their remuneration in share options."

SJPC, which held 44 percent of J. Rothschild's ordinary share capital, was slated to buy the remaining shares. Prudential, the United Kingdom's largest life assurer, which held a 22 percent stake in J. Rothschild via its ownership of Scottish Amicable, planned to up its holdings to 29.9 percent and gain a greater presence in the affluent end of the life market. Sir Mark Weinberg continued as executive chair and retained his ownership stake, and Lord Rothschild stayed on as president but retired from the board.

During 1999, Life Assurance Holding Corporation announced that it was examining its ownership structure. In addition to SJPC and New York Life's equal split of 46 percent, Chase Investment Bank held 19 percent and Prudential held 15 percent. The move was prompted by a desire to improve the entity's purchase positioning. All four companies needed to approve deals for new companies. Also during the year, SJPC sold its stake in Global Asset Management to UBS.

Halifax Taking Control: 2000–05

Mortgage banker Halifax bought 17 percent of SJPC from Prudential in 2000, paving the way for gaining a controlling interest in the company. Halifax had entered into diversification away from mortgages. The Internet played a part in its new game plan. Halifax was in the process of establishing an online banking program.

SJPC, in turn, had been seeking an Internet partnership, but talks with Prudential did not pan out. Halifax envisioned a private bank operating under the St. James's Place brand linked with its new online program.

The United Kingdom's largest mortgage bank paid £750 million, or $1.2 billion, for 60 percent interest in St. James's Place Capital, the holding company for J. Rothschild Assurance, according to a May 2000 *Private Banker International* article. Intelligent Finance, Halifax's new Internet platform, and the resources of St. James's Place Capital would be the backbone for new wealth management venture St. James's Place Private Bank. Weinberg and Wilson would stay on as SJPC's chair and CEO, respectively.

The St. James's Place Capital purchase gave Halifax "a significant foothold in the UK affluent and high net worth market," according to *Private Banker International.* St. James's Place Capital had been Lord Rothschild's main corporate vehicle but was now primarily a life assurance holding company, with its main asset J. Rothschild Assurance. The 972 direct sales employees of J. Rothschild Partnership served 300,000 clients, for whom they claimed "a 95% 'share of wallet' in terms of clients' life and long-term savings products."

The Halifax connection would give the sales force a banking license, more products, capital backing, and the potential to cross-sell to Halifax retail customers. Potential risks to Halifax lay in its high level of dependency on J. Rothschild's partners to sell the new endeavor.

Intelligent Finance online bank began operation in September 2000. The private bank was scheduled to open in 2001. SJPC management expressed a desire to begin offering services to small businesses as well as wealthy individuals.

Despite a soft market new business sales grew by 42 percent during 2000. SJPC's profits also rose in 2000, to £80 million before exceptionals. In addition, the company's shares outperformed the market during the year by 142 percent. Even as SJPC continued to find success through a direct sales force, others had not. Prudential and Sun Life Financial of Canada exited the channel.

"We are now particularly well placed to be a major force in providing an integrated range of financial services for the 4m or so higher-net-worth and higher-income individuals in the UK," Wilson told the *Financial Times.* SJPC planned to use joint ventures to add general and medical insurance products during 2001.

A merger of Halifax and the Bank of Scotland in 2001 created HBOS, elevating both financial institutions in the process. Increased diversification and a strengthened strategic position yielded the fastest-growing bank revenues in the United Kingdom. The new entity succeeded in "raising profits and dividends when others could not," reported the *Financial Times* in 2003. But concurrently, the value of HBOS's 60 percent interest in SJPC had "fallen substantially."

A lengthy stock market downturn had depressed SJPC's numbers. At the end of March 2003, the market hit eight-year lows, according to the *Yorkshire Post.* But in the later half of 2003 the outlook improved and Weinberg expected to see a return to 15 to 20 percent increases in new business.

Despite the setback, SJPC ranked among the United Kingdom's top wealth management companies, with £8 billion in funds under management. The company was listed in the FTSE 250 Index and served 400,000 clients.

In 2004 the group moved into commercial property for the first time, tapping HBOS's Insight Investment to make £500 million in investments over three years. The action was in response to increased interest in commercial property by private investors. SJPC planned to advise clients to have 10 percent of their portfolio in property. The company's first investments were expected to be in two or three U.K. investment trusts, according to *Property Week*.

In September 2004 Mark Lund was appointed chief executive, succeeding Mike Wilson. Wilson in turn moved into the position of chair with Weinberg moving to the presidency. Plans for expansion of St. James's Place products and services into new areas such as mortgages and protection were in the works.

Total group profit before taxes for the year 2004 increased 37 percent to £142.3 million. The sale of Life Assurance Holding Corporation to Swiss Re accounted for £28 million of that amount. Funds under management rose 20 percent to £9.5 billion.

As for the future, SJPC faced an environment in which there were both challenges and opportunities. The United Kingdom was embarking on wide sweeping regulatory changes in the insurance industry; pension responsibilities were shifting from state and company onto the individual; and life expectancies continued to rise, requiring increased retirement savings.

Principal Subsidiaries

St. James's Place Group.

Principal Competitors

Legal & General Group; Prudential PLC; Standard Life.

Further Reading

Adams, Christopher, "Companies & Markets: J. Rothschild in Market Listing: Reverse Takeover of St. James's Place Makes Weinberg Fresh Fortune," *Financial Times London Edition,* April 10, 1997.

Barkas, Eric, "James's Farewell to Bad Times," *Yorkshire Post,* February 25, 2004, p. 1.

Bolger, Andrew, "Companies & Finance UK: Strong Growth at St. James's Life Assurance New Business Sales Rise 42% in Flat Market," *Financial Times London Edition,* February 20, 2001.

——, "Companies & Finance: UK and Ireland: St. James's Private Bank Starts in January," *Financial Times London Edition,* October 28, 2000.

Brown-Humes, Christopher, "Companies & Finance: UK and Ireland: Rothschild Cuts Stake in St. James's Place," *Financial Times London Edition,* October 16, 1996.

"Companies Reporting Positive Results," *Financial Advisors,* March 3, 2005.

Danaher, Tim, "Wealth Manager in £500m Debut: St. James's Place Capital Appoints HBOS Arm Insight to Acquire Commercial Property Portfolio," *Property Week,* February 20, 2004, pp. 1+.

Denton, Nicholas, "Companies & Finance: UK: St. James's Place to Concentrate on Financial Services," *Financial Times London Edition,* June 5, 1996.

Flanagan, Martin, "St. James's Proves There's Still Room for Personal Touch," *Scotsman,* October 28, 2004, p. 55.

"Halifax Latest to Enter Private Banking Market," *Private Banker International,* May 2000, p. 2.

Halverson, Patrick, "UK Company News: 'Resilient' Core Businesses Help St. James's to £18.7m," *Financial Times London Edition,* June 10, 1995.

"A House Still Divided," *Institutional Investor,* May 1992, p. 82+.

"James's Farewell to Bad Times," *Yorkshire Post,* February 25, 2004, p. 1.

"LAHC Could Cut Backers to Gain Buying Freedom," *Money Marketing,* September 2, 1999.

Love, Bruce, "Mark Lund: The New Chief Executive of St. James's Place Says He Believes That Advice Is the Key to Servicing Clients and That Without a Fresh Stock of Products on Its Shelves, Customers Will Not Buy and Advisors Will Not Want to Stay with the Company," *Money Marketing,* September 2, 2004, p. 25.

Mackintosh, James, and Andrea Felsted, "Companies & Finance: UK: Halifax Bolsters Internet Strategy, Banks Control of St. James's Place Capital Changes Hands in GBP760M Deal," *Financial Times London Edition,* March 23, 2000.

"New York and St. James's Capital Link," *Life Insurance International,* January 8, 1995.

Noonan, Brendan, "U.K.'s Prudential Sells Two Noncore Holdings," *Bestwire,* March 23, 2000.

"Pension Funds Smaller Group Winners," *Money Management,* April 1, 2003.

"St. James's Place Plugs Gaps with Multi-Tie Deals," *Financial Advisor,* February 3, 2005.

Urry, Maggie, "Cricket Fan Keeps His Eye on the Ball: HBOS Has Achieved the Fastest-Growing Revenues Among UK Banks," *Financial Times,* May 17, 2003, p. 22.

—Kathleen Peippo

Shanghai Baosteel Group Corporation

**Fujin Lu-Baoshan District, Guoyuan, Changqian
  Zhonglu**
Shanghai
201900
China
Telephone: +86 21 5664 8648
Fax: +86 21 5664 8046
Web site: http://www.baosteel.com

Government-Owned Company
Incorporated: 1978 as Baoshan Iron & Steel (Group)
  Corporation
Employees: 32,000
Sales: CNY 120.4 billion ($14.5 billion) (2004)
NAIC: 331111 Iron and Steel Mills; 331210 Iron and
  Steel Pipes and Tubes Manufacturing from Purchased
  Steel; 331221 Cold-Rolled Steel Shape Manufacturing

Shanghai Baosteel Group Corporation is the Chinese government-owned holding company for a group of steel, steel products, and steel trading companies, which themselves operate under the publicly listed flagship Shanghai Iron & Steel Co. Ltd. Shanghai Baosteel is China's leading steel producer: In 2005, the company's annual output topped 20 million tons, and the company expects to double that by 2010. As such, the company dominates the Chinese steel industry, controlling some 10 percent of the total market, and ranks among the world's top steel producers. Shanghai Baosteel focuses on the production of steel plate and steel tubing. The company produces high-grade steel for the automobile, shipbuilding, pipeline, household appliance, and other sectors, primarily for the domestic market. The company's steel is also used for tool & die equipment, springs and bearings, and for the aerospace and commercial aviation industries. Shanghai Baosteel has begun investing in developing new steel production technologies, in part in an effort to win a greater share of the international automobile market. The company is a major supplier to international automakers such as Fiat. Shanghai Iron & Steel Co. operates the largest and most modern facility in China, accounting for more than half of the group's

total production. Other companies in the group include Baosteel Shanghai No. 1 Iron & Steel Co., which produces premium stainless steel, among other products; Pudong Steel Corporation, a plate producer; and No. 5 Steel Corporation, a specialty steel products producer. Shanghai Baosteel also has interests in mining, particularly coal mining, both in China and abroad. The company's sales and distribution are handled through subsidiary Shanghai Baosteel International Economic & Trading Corporation Ltd., which operates a marketing network throughout China and in ten countries internationally. Shanghai Baosteel is led by President and Chairwoman Xie Qihua.

Founding a Modern Steel Giant in the 1970s

Prior to the early 1950s, China's iron and steel industry remained undeveloped in large part, with very few plants in operation. The first (and only) modern steel plant had been built by the Japanese in Anshan soon after World War I, and this complex eventually featured nine blast furnaces. Yet total production never topped one million tons. The Anshan complex was mostly destroyed during World War II, and again during the Chinese civil war, and its equipment and machinery were appropriated by the departing Soviets.

With the creation of the People's Republic of China, the country made a new effort to develop an industrial infrastructure. The central government began investing in the construction of new steel plants, for the most part based on Soviet designs and technology. The Anshan complex was rebuilt, and eventually reached a total output of seven million tons. Another large facility was built at Wuhan in the early 1950s. Many small, but modern, steel plants were constructed during this period. At the same time, many local and regional governments began installing a large number of so-called "backyard" furnaces for the production of pig iron. The period launched by the Great Leap Forward saw a dramatic increase in the country's steel output.

The Chinese steel industry collapsed again into the 1960s, in part because the overworking of the country's larger furnaces forced them to be shut down. By 1961, production had dropped to half of its total from the year before. The government began an effort to centralize control of the steel industry, shutting down many of the smaller plants and importing new technology from Austria, Japan, and elsewhere.

The steel industry remained linked to the political situation in the country, with output rising in periods of relative stability, such as the early 1960s, and dropping back during crisis times such as the Cultural Revolution in the late 1960s and the political battles of the post-Mao era. Nonetheless, steel remained an essential component of China's effort to modernize its industrial and economic infrastructure. By 1979, the country's total output topped 34 million tons. Into the 1980s, the country boasted 13 plants capable of producing more than one million tons annually. In addition, some 800 small-scale plants remained in operation.

The Chinese government began instituting economic reforms at the end of the 1970s in an effort to move beyond the disastrous policies of the Great Leap Forward era. Steel continued to play a central role in the government's plans. At the end of the 1970s, the government set a total domestic production target of 80 million tons per year to be reached by the end of the 1980s. For the most part, the government sought to refurbish and modernize its existing plants, including an effort to improve fuel efficiency at the predominantly coal-burning sites.

Yet the new reform era, which, under Deng Xiaoping, began opening the Chinese economy to the foreign market in the late 1970s, also called for the creation of a new, large-scale integrated steel works at Baoshan, near the Shanghai port. The project was developed in close collaboration with the Japanese; indeed, the site was meant to be an exact copy of an existing plant in Kimitsu, operated by Nippon Steel. That plant was considered at the time to be the world's most modern steel facility.

Construction on the new site, which later boasted a total output of 20 million tons, began in 1978. The initial completion date was scheduled for 1982. A series of delays, however, set the commissioning of the facility back to 1985, and then to 1988. From the start, the facility, called Baoshan Iron & Steel Corporation, benefited from its special status as the Chinese government's steel industry flagship. As such, the facility took on the country's best engineers and managers, including Xie Qihua, who joined the company in 1978 and later emerged as its chairwoman. Whereas the country's existing steel plants were burdened by outmoded and inefficient equipment, and forced to produce unprofitable and low-grade steel products, Baoshan was designed from the start to incorporate cutting-edge technology and to produce highly profitable specialty steels.

The company's privileged position also put it first in line for a number of important contracts. In 1989, for example, Baoshan Iron & Steel became the primary supplier to another Chinese government flagship, Shanghai Automotive Industry Group Cor-

poration. The company continued to win important contracts through the 1990s and into the 2000s, such as for the 4,200-kilometer West-East Natural Gas Pipeline, which launched construction in 2003. Baoshan became responsible for producing more than 60 percent of the steel for that massive project.

Becoming a World Leader in the 2000s

China's extraordinary growth during the late 1980s and through the 1990s quickly outpaced its steel production. The country was forced to turn to foreign markets for a significant percentage of its steel and iron needs. Baoshan Iron & Steel, meanwhile, emerged as an important supplier to China's infrastructure projects. As such, the company's production remained entirely focused on the domestic market.

Into the late 1990s, however, Baoshan began to feel the heat from a new generation of competitors. Continued economic reforms had opened up the steel industry to a variety of new players, which established their own modern steel production plants throughout the country. By the mid-2000s, there were more than 4,000 steel producers in China, and the country's total output now topped the world at 200 million tons. Yet even these levels could not keep up with the surge in China's economy during this period, and steel imports remained an important force in the domestic steel market.

In order to retain its leadership in this new marketplace, Baoshan began reorganizing at the end of the 1990s. Leading this effort was Xie Qihua, who was named the company's general manager in 1994. Xie began seeking alliances with other Chinese steel industry companies, as well as strengthening Baoshan's marketing and distribution operations. As such, in 1996 the company added a new trading component, Baosteel Group International Trade Corporation (BGITC), originally founded in 1985. That operation extended its marketing network throughout China, before adding offices in more than ten countries worldwide. The addition of BGITC helped extend Baoshan's production to the export market, with Korea becoming a major customer for the company.

Baoshan changed its name to Baosteel Iron & Steel Corporation at the beginning of 1998, in preparation for its proposed merger with Shanghai Metallurgical Group Corporation. That government-owned company boasted a payroll of some 120,000, compared with Baosteel's 10,000. Yet Shanghai Metallurgical was losing money, a situation the Chinese government hoped to turn around by merging it into profitable Baosteel.

The collapse of the Asian region economies during the crisis of the late 1990s threatened to derail the merger plans. Baosteel's profits faded quickly, as its revenues dived and its export markets disappeared. Yet by the end of 1998, the merger went through, becoming a three-way merger with the addition of another Shanghai-based steel producer, Shanghai Meishan Group Co. Ltd. The enlarged business then changed its name to Shanghai Baosteel Group Corporation, with the former Baoshan taking the lead of the new company. Baosteel now claimed the position as China's largest integrated steel works, with total annual production of nearly 20 million tons and assets of CNY 100 billion.

Baosteel began testing the public market in the late 1990s, listing four subsidiaries on the Shanghai Stock Exchange, in

Key Dates:

1978: Integrated steel works is founded in Shanghai as a flagship for the new era of Chinese economic reform; the original completion date is slated for 1982.
1988: Baoshan plant begins production.
1989: The company becomes the major steel supplier to Shanghai Automotive Industry Group.
1996: A domestic and international marketing arm, Baosteel Group International Trade Corporation, is incorporated.
1998: The company changes its name to Shanghai Baosteel Iron & Steel Corporation, and then merges with Shanghai Metallurgical and Shanghai Meishan, becoming China's leading integrated steelworks.
2000: Shanghai Baosteel Iron & Steel lists stock on the Shanghai Stock Exchange.
2001: The company forms an alliance with Shougang Group and Wuhan Iron and Steel Group Corporation, becoming the world's third largest integrated steel group; a stainless steel production partnership is formed in Shanghai with ThyssenKrupp.
2005: The company receives permission to begin construction of a new steelworks in Guangdong province as part of a goal of doubling capacity to more than 40 million tons by 2010.

limited offerings that remained off-limits for foreign investors. Yet China's decision to join the World Trade Organization—opening up the country and its steel industry to full-fledged foreign competition for the first time—placed new pressure on Baosteel. To remain competitive, Baosteel recognized that it needed to develop its international operations.

As part of that effort, the company reorganized into a listing vehicle, Shanghai Baosteel Iron & Steel, under parent company Shanghai Baosteel Group. In December 2000, Shanghai Baosteel listed its shares on the Shanghai Stock Exchange. Although the listing remained restricted to domestic investors, it became China's largest ever public offering, raising some CNY 7.7 billion. The listing set the stage for a later international listing, most likely on the Hong Kong Stock Exchange, which would open the company's capital to foreign investors.

The listing of Shanghai Baosteel was seen as proof of the Chinese government's commitment to economic reform, especially as it placed a significant share of its flagship steel company, known by some as the Chinese steel industry's "aircraft carrier," on the public market. The listing provided capital for Baosteel's investment program, enabling it to step up its technology and boost its production. The listing also signaled a significant change in corporate culture. As Xie expressed it to the *South China Morning Post:* "It will make us more of a market-driven company." Xie herself was named president and chairwoman of both the publicly listed company and its government-owned parent.

Baosteel now began strengthening its position through a number of strategic alliances. In 2001, for example, the com-

pany entered a union with Shougang Group and Wuhan Iron and Steel Group Corporation. That alliance allowed Baosteel to claim the spot as the world's third largest integrated steel company. In that year, also, the company found a new technological partner in ThyssenKrupp of Germany, when the two companies launched the first phase of a new Shanghai-based stainless steel production partnership. Also in 2001, Baosteel was chosen as a primary supplier of steel to Italy's Fiat, marking a major step forward in Baosteel's efforts to become a supplier to the global automotive industry.

In 2003, Baosteel launched an acquisition drive worth some $270 million, which included the acquisitions of Lubao Steel Pipe Corporation and Baogang Yichang Steel Sheets Corporation. Baosteel previously had held significant stakes in both companies, which had nonetheless continued to compete with Baosteel. In that year, also, Baosteel set up a strategic partnership with Shanghai Automotive Industry Group, seen as an important move in the integration of the country's steel and automotive industries.

Into the mid-decade, Baosteel announced an ambitious new growth target—the doubling of its production capacity in order to claim the position as the world's top steel producer by 2010. In early 2005, the company took a step toward achieving that goal when it received approval to begin construction on a new 20-million-ton facility in Zhanjiang City, in Guangdong province. The integrated steelworks, expected to cost some $10 billion, was expected to launch production by the end of the decade. As part of its growth strategy, Baosteel reaffirmed its intention to launch a global public offering, most likely before the end of 2005. That offering would mean a coming of age for Baosteel, which already had claimed its place among the world's top steel groups.

Principal Subsidiaries

Baoshan Iron & Steel Co., Ltd.; Baosteel Group Shanghai Meishan Co., Ltd.; Baosteel Group Shanghai No.1 Iron & Steel Co., Ltd.; Baosteel Group Shanghai No.5 Steel Co., Ltd.; Baosteel Group Shanghai Pudong Iron & Steel Co., Ltd.; Ningbo Baoxin Stainless Steel Co., Ltd.; Shanghai Baosteel International Economic & Trading Corporation Ltd.

Principal Competitors

Libyan Iron and Steel Co; Capital Iron-Steel Company General; Panzhihua Iron and Steel Group Co.; C Grossmann Eisen- u Stahlwerk AG; Chongqing Special Steel Group Company Ltd.; Forjas de Santa Clara C.A.; Cargill Inc.; Xinyu Steel and Iron Plant General of Jiangxi; Krivorozhstal; Aceros Chile S.A.; ThyssenKrupp AG; Arcelor S.A.; China Steel Corporation; Nippon Steel Corporation; POSCO.

Further Reading

"Baosteel and Jinchuan to Invest in Exploitation of Nickel Mine," *Alestron,* March 29, 2005.
"Baosteel Hasn't Given Up Plan to Be Listed Overseas," *Xinhua News Agency,* April 15, 2005.
"Baosteel—One to Top the World," *China Metallurgy News,* September 18, 2001, p. 1.

"Baosteel Sets Up Mining JV with Brazilian Firm," *AsiaPulse News,* October 24, 2001.

"Baosteel to Buy Affiliated Firms for $422.8m," *Business Daily Update,* August 12, 2004.

"Baosteel to Win Approval for $10b Steel Project," *Business Daily Update,* December 15, 2004.

"China: Baosteel Poised for Domination," *China Daily,* May 16, 2001.

"China's Baosteel Hopes for Smoother IPO at Home," *Business Day,* August 25, 2000.

"China's Baosteel Sets Ambitious Growth Plan," *American Metal Market,* November 13, 2003, p. 5.

Dyer, Geoff, "Baosteel Delays Offering Due to Weak Conditions," *Financial Times,* February 24, 2005, p. 32.

Harding, James, "Baoshan Steels Itself for Asian Turmoil Aftershocks," *Financial Times,* April 22, 1998, p. 38.

Roberts, Dexter, "A Rising Star in Steel," *Business Week,* January 26, 2004, p. 18.

Wang, Annie, "Holding Up Half the Sky," *Fortune,* October 4, 2004, p. 170.

Wong, Lisa, "Baosteel Sets a Target of $1b from Dual Move," *South China Morning Post,* September 10, 1999.

—M.L. Cohen

Shangri-La Asia Ltd.

21/F CITIC Tower
1 Tim Mei Avenue Central
Hong Kong
Telephone: +852 2525 9146
Fax: +852 2523 8842
Web site: http://www.shangri-la.com

Public Company
Incorporated: 1971
Employees: 16,300
Sales: $726.0 million (2004)
Stock Exchanges: Hong Kong Singapore
NAIC: 721110 Hotels (Except Casino Hotels) and Motels

Shangri-La Asia Ltd. is the Asian region's leading and fastest-growing luxury hotel group. The company, part of Malaysia's Kuok Group, operates 45 hotels throughout Asia. In 2005, the company also began a drive into the European and North American markets, including the launch of construction on its first European hotel, in London, expected to be completed in 2009. The company also has opened its first hotel in the Middle East, in Dubai, and in the Maldives. Mainland China, however, forms the heart of the company's empire, with more than 20 hotels in operation, and at least 15 more expected to open before 2010. Shangri-La is unusual among international hotel companies in that it owns a significant proportion of its hotels; of the hotels under the group's management not wholly owned by the company, most are owned by other companies in the Kuok Group, and especially by Shangri-La's own major shareholder, Kerry Properties Ltd. Shangri-La hotels primarily operate under the luxury, five-star Shangri-La brand. The company also operates a smaller number of mid-range, business-oriented Traders hotels. Listed on the Hong Kong and Singapore Stock Exchanges, Shangri-La remains a tiny part of the Kuok business empire. Nonetheless, founder Robert Kuok holds an active interest in the group, and has stated his desire to see Shangri-La reach 100 hotels in his lifetime. In 2004, the company posted revenues of $726 million.

Kuok Family Origins in the 1970s

The Kuok family immigrated to Malaysia, then under British control, from the Fujian province in China in the first decade of the 20th century. Under patriarch Kuok Keng Kang the family entered the trading business, dealing in rice, flour, and sugar. Kuok, like many successful Chinese emigrés, sent his children overseas to study. Son Robert, born in 1927, went to the Raffles school in Singapore, where he became good friends with Tun Abdul Razak and Tun Hussein Onn, both of whom later became Malaysian prime ministers, and Lee Kuan Yew, who became the first prime minister of Singapore after its independence.

Although his education was cut short by World War II, Robert Kuok's friendships were to play an important role in his later career. Kuok's use of ''guanxi'' (which in Chinese refers to having a network of prominent allies) enabled him to build his empire rapidly both during and after the war. Kuok also was gifted with the ability to spot opportunity, and especially to see into the long term. During the Japanese occupation of Malaysia and Singapore during the war, Kuok went to work for Mitsubishi, where he learned Japanese. This enabled him to emerge as an important supplier of basic foodstuffs.

Following the war, Kuok recognized that heavy competition and low margins had made the rice trade unattractive. Instead, Kuok switched his efforts to the sugar trade, and moved to England, where he learned his way around the commodities markets before returning to Malaysia. Following Malaysia's independence in 1957, Kuok's guanxi enabled him to build a true sugar empire, developing significant plantations. In 1959, Kuok entered sugar refining as well. Before long, Kuok had established a reputation as the ''Sugar King,'' controlling as much as 10 percent of the world's sugar supply.

Despite remaining a minority in Malaysia, the ethnic Chinese community had long dominated the country's economy. Growing demands for a more equitable distribution of wealth in the country led Kuok to transfer his business empire to Singapore in the late 1960s and early 1970s. Nonetheless, Kuok supported the need to establish a more equitable distribution of wealth, if only to ensure the country's political and economic stability.

> ## Company Perspectives:
>
> *The name Shangri-La was inspired by James Hilton's legendary novel* Lost Horizon. *A tranquil haven in the mountains of Tibet, Shangri-La casts a spell on all who resided there. Today, Shangri-La stands as a synonym for paradise. And even though mythical in origin, the name perfectly encapsulates the genuine serenity and service for which Shangri-La Hotels and Resorts have come to be recognized.*

At the same time, Kuok had begun to expand his business interests into other areas. In the mid-1960s, for example, Kuok entered flour milling and trading. The Kuok Group, as Kuok's business empire came to be known, also added interests in palm oil (PPB Oil Palms Bhd.), tanker operations (Malaysian Bulk Carries Bhd.), and even media interests, particularly the *South China Morning Post*. Yet among Kuok's most significant and most successful ventures was his entry into the real estate and property development sector in the early 1970s. Kuok's Kerry Properties became his real estate flagship, emerging as one of the leading property groups in Hong Kong, with significant real estate holdings and developments throughout the Asian region, including the Chinese mainland, as well as Australia and elsewhere.

Among Kuok's early real estate purchases was a hotel property in Singapore. Built in 1971, this property became the starting point for the later Shangri-La luxury hotel chain. Initially, the Kuok group turned over the management of its hotel property to Westin Hotels. In 1981, however, the company added its second hotel, in Kowloon. The new hotel marked Kuok's entry into direct hotel management, as well as ownership. Launching the Shangri-La brand, Kuok founded a new company for its hotel interests, Shangri-La Hotels & Resorts, in 1982. An important factor behind Shangri-La's later success was Kuok's willingness to turn over its direction to hotel industry professionals David Hayden and Robert Hutchinson, both of whom had worked for Westin.

Claiming the Chinese Mainland in the 1990s

The combination of Kuok's guanxi and the market experience of Hayden and Hutchinson enabled the company to make a significant move in the mid-1980s. In 1984, the company opened its first hotel on the Chinese mainland, in Hangzhou, on the eastern coast, becoming a pioneer in the country's virtually non-existent luxury hotel market. The company's choice of that market also revealed its ability to plan for the long term. Rather than simply target China's major and most well-known markets, such as Beijing and Shanghai, Shangri-La saw potential in developing its position in lesser-known and smaller cities. In this way, the company's properties became the first—and often only—luxury hotel in a given area. Many of these cities nonetheless had populations of five million or more, and represented important industrial growth areas.

Shangri-La launched a second hotel brand in 1989, with a first site in Beijing. Called Traders, the new hotel chain gave the company a mid-range brand, with sparser accommodations. Nonetheless, the company installed the same level of luxury services at the new Traders hotel, as a part of its creation of a bridge level between the four-star and five-star hotel grades. Traders represented part of the group's long-term strategy as well, targeting locations with no luxury hotels. By introducing the Traders brand, the company hoped to develop a market for luxury hotel services, paving the way for the entry of its Shangri-La brand as well.

Shangri-La grew only slowly during the 1980s, however. By the beginning of the 1990s, the group counted just six hotels. Yet the company had developed a strong foundation for growth into the new decade. In the early 1990s, the company doubled the number of hotels, owned by Kerry Properties and other Kuok companies, adding sites in Hong Kong, the Philippines, and Fiji. In the meantime, the Kuok Group began expanding its property interests in mainland China, launching 12 new developments, including hotels, in the early 1990s.

In the mid-1990s, Kuok set up a second property ownership vehicle, Shangri-La Asia Ltd., which paid the Kuok group HKD $4.2 billion to acquire the existing Shangri-La properties in 1995. Shangri-La Asia was then listed on the Hong Kong and Singapore Stock Exchanges, reducing Kuok's stake to less than 63 percent. The following year, Shangri-La Asia paid another HKD 2.5 billion ($321 million) to buy up the 12 Kuok hotel properties under development in China. Then, in 1997, property-owning Shangri-La Asia took over hotel management company Shangri-La Hotels & Resorts, becoming an integrated hotel management and ownership group.

By the end of the decade, Shangri-La's portfolio had grown to 39 properties, including 17 hotels in operation or under development in China alone. Indeed, the company's early focus on the mainland Chinese market helped shield it from the worst of the Asian economic crisis in the later half of the 1990s, from which China emerged relatively unscathed. The company's strategy of investing in relatively unknown areas of the mainland also had placed it in a strong position to profit from the surge in China's industrial sector and from the country's fast-growing economy in general at the dawn of the 21st century.

Shangri-La also had begun developing its interests beyond the Asian region. At the beginning of the century, the company added its first hotel in the Middle East, in Dubai. The company also acquired its first North American property, the Pacific Palisades in Vancouver, Canada.

Global Luxury Hotel Empire in the New Century

The early 2000s proved a difficult period for the company, however. The global dropoff in tourist and business travel following the terrorist attacks against the United States in 2001 was further exacerbated by the SARS epidemic in much of Asia in 2002 and 2003. Backed by the Kuok Group's deep pockets, Shangri-La nonetheless continued its ambitious development program, led by the desire of Robert Kuok, then in his 70s, to see Shangri-La build its portfolio to more than 100 hotels in his lifetime.

China remained central to Shangri-La's growth plans. In 2005, for example, the company announced that it planned to build 15 new hotels in that country before 2010. At the same time, Shangri-La, by then the largest luxury hotel operator

Key Dates:

1971: Robert Kuok extends interests into property and hotel development, building his first hotel in Singapore.

1981: Kuok establishes a second hotel in Kowloon, launching the Shangri-La brand, and entering direct hotel management.

1982: The company incorporates as Shangri-La Hotels & Resorts.

1984: The company opens its first Shangri-La hotel in Hangzhou, China.

1989: The mid-range Traders Hotel brand is launched, with the first site in Beijing.

1995: The company establishes publicly listed Shangri-La Asia, which acquires the Kuok-owned hotel properties, and then goes public on the Singapore and Hong Kong Stock Exchanges.

1996: Shangri-La Asia buys 15 hotel sites under development in China from the Kuok-owned companies.

1997: Shangri-La Asia acquires Shangri-La Hotels & Resorts, creating an integrated hotel ownership and management group.

2005: Shangri-La Asia announces plans to add 15 new hotels in China, five hotels in Europe, and hotels in North America, in order to reach a total of 100 hotels by 2010.

based in the Asian region, had set its sights on building a global brand, announcing plans to enter Europe and North America during the decade as well. In February 2005, the company announced its first European property, a 30-year lease contract for a hotel in the London Bridge Tower development, scheduled for completion in 2009. The company also announced its interest in establishing hotels in Paris, Frankfurt, and other European cities. Meanwhile, the company was scouting out properties in the United States, targeting at least one property in that country by the end of 2005.

Principal Subsidiaries

Edsa Shangri-La Hotel & Resort, Inc. (Philippines); Fiji Mocambo Limited; Kerry Industrial Company Limited; Mactan Shangri-La Hotel & Resort, Inc. (Philippines); Makati Shangri-La Hotel & Resort, Inc. (Philippines); Shangri-La Asia Treasury Limited; Shangri-La Finance Limited; Shangri-La Hotel (Baotou) Co., Ltd.; Shangri-La Hotel (Chengdu) Co., Ltd.; Shangri-La Hotel (Guangzhou Pazhou) Co., Ltd.; Shangri-La Hotel (Guilin) Co., Ltd.; Shangri-La Hotel (Huhhot) Co., Ltd.; Shangri-La Hotel (Ningbo) Co., Ltd.; Shangri-La Hotel (Shenzhen Futian) Co., Ltd.; Shangri-La Hotel (Wenzhou) Co., Ltd.; Shangri-La Hotel (Xian) Co., Ltd.; Shangri-La Hotel Limited (Singapore); Shangri-La Hotel Management Consultancy (Shanghai) Co., Ltd.; Shangri-La Hotel Public Company Limited (Thailand); Shangri-La Hotels (Malaysia) Berhad; Shangri-La International Hotel Management B.V. (The Netherlands); Shangri-La International Hotel Management Limited (Hong Kong); SLIM International Limited (Cook Islands); Traders Yangon Company (Myanmar) Limited; Yanuca Island Limited (Fiji).

Principal Competitors

Three Cities Group; Nicon Hotels Ltd.; Mingly Corporation Limited; Tokyu Corporation; Mitsui Fudosan Company Ltd.; Beijing Jingxi Tourism Development; Sapporo Holdings Ltd.; The Hongkong and Shanghai Hotels, Limited; Mandarin Oriental International Limited; New World Development Company Limited.

Further Reading

"Business Travelers Are Back in Shangri-La," *Business Asia,* September 2003, p. 12.

Davidson, Tyler, "Shangri-La Hotels Plans Major Asia Expansion," *Travel Weekly,* May 20, 1996, p. 10.

"The Kuok Businesses," *Malaysian Business,* March 16, 2004.

"Profit Returns to Shangri-La As Asia Booms," *Business Asia,* May 5, 2000, p. 9.

"Room Service: Robert Kuok," *Economist,* June 1, 1996, p. 62.

Ruggia, James, "Counting on China," *Travel Agent,* August 9, 1999, p. 80.

——, "Finding the Road to Success," *Travel Agent,* November 4, 1996, p. 54.

"Shangri-La Plans New Hotel," *China Trade News,* April 5, 2001.

"Shangri-La to Build in Mongolian Capital," *Hotels,* March 2005, p. 38.

"Shangri-La to Open Hotel in London in 2009," *FWN,* February 8, 2005.

Teves, Oliver, "Shangri-La Asia Plans Expansion in China, Europe and North America," *AP Worldstream,* February 16, 2005.

—M.L. Cohen

SIG plc

Hillsborough Works, Langsett Road
Sheffield
S6 2LW
United Kingdom
Telephone: + 44 114 285 6300
Fax: + 44 114 285 6385
Web site: http://www.sigplc.co.uk

Public Company
Incorporated: 1956 as Sheffield Insulations Limited
Employees: 7,000
Sales: £1.39 billion ($2.4 billion) (2004)
Stock Exchanges: London
Ticker Symbol: SIG
NAIC: 423330 Roofing, Siding, and Insulation Material
   Merchant Wholesalers; 423310 Lumber, Plywood,
   Millwork, and Wood Panel Merchant Wholesalers;
   423390 Other Construction Material Merchant Whole-
   salers; 423710 Hardware Merchant Wholesalers;
   423720 Plumbing and Heating Equipment and
   Supplies (Hydronics) Merchant Wholesalers; 423730
   Warm Air Heating and Air-Conditioning Equipment
   and Supplies Merchant Wholesalers

SIG plc is one of the world's leading wholesale suppliers of insulation, roofing, and commercial interior products, active in the United Kingdom, Ireland, France, Germany, Benelux, the United States, and Poland. The company operates more than 400 distribution centers. The company's Insulation operations cover the three primary areas of thermal barriers, sound insulation, and smoke and fire barriers; under Roofing, the company carries a full range of roofing materials and accessory products; the company's Commercial Interiors division includes ceilings and wall systems, partitions and other office furnishings, and lighting and storage systems, as well as fully integrated interior packages. SIG has grown strongly during the early 2000s, in part due to an aggressive acquisition program, and in part because of tightening emissions and building code rules and legislation. The company holds leading positions in many of its

markets, including the United Kingdom and Germany, as well as several states in the United States. Founded in 1956 as Sheffield Insulations Limited, SIG is listed on the London Stock Exchange. The company posted revenues of nearly £1.4 billion in 2004. The founding Adsetts family remain significant shareholders in the company.

Insulation Origins in the 1950s

The Adsetts family's background had little to do with building products. Instead, the family, led by Ernest Adsetts, operated a small ice cream family business in Sheffield in the 1950s. That business, however, had already led the family into the distribution sector, notably through the development of a string of sweet shops in the Sheffield area.

Ernest Adsetts's son William Norman Adsetts, born in 1931, did not immediately join his father in business after finishing school. Instead, in 1955, the younger Adsetts went to work for Fibreglass Ltd., a subsidiary of Pilkingtons, then pioneering the use of fiberglass as an insulation material. Norman Adsetts recognized the potential for the new material, especially for the creation of a business serving as a middleman between manufacturers and building contractors. Adsetts convinced his father to launch a new business, the wholesale distribution company Sheffield Insulations Limited, in 1956.

Norman Adsetts joined his father in business only in 1966. The company remained quite small, and focused on the local market. This began to change after Norman Adsetts became the company's managing director in 1970. Adsetts now placed the company on the growth track. By 1985, the year in which Norman Adsetts became company chairman, Sheffield's sales had topped £59 million.

Sheffield continued to grow strongly through the end of that decade, with sales topping £100 million and a network of 30 store branches by 1988. The oil crisis of the 1970s had provided a major boost to the group's growth, as the construction market sought out new insulation materials in order to increase buildings' fuel efficiency. The company's growth also was stimulated by tightening anti-pollution and safety regulations. One such piece of legislation, passed by Parliament in 1989, increased the required insulation levels by some 40 percent.

Sheffield sought to take further advantage of the expanding market for insulation and fireproofing materials by expanding into other regions in the United Kingdom, and also by diversifying its product offerings. In order to fuel this expansion, the company went public in 1989, listing on the London Stock Exchange. At that time, the company changed its name, to Sheffield Insulations Group (SIG). The Adsetts family nonetheless maintained control of the company, with more than 55 percent of its stock.

The listing enabled SIG to begin targeting acquisitions. In 1990, for example, the company acquired Ceilings Distributions (Leeds), a company specialized in the wholesale distribution of ceiling and wall systems, as well as partitions and related office furnishings. The acquisition enabled SIG to expand beyond its core insulation business for the first time.

Nonetheless, the start of the 1990s marked a low point for the company, as the collapse of the U.K. building sector, coupled with the slide into a global recession, sent the company into the red. In response, SIG brought in a new managing director, Bill Forrester, who guided the company back to profitability by 1993. In that year, also, Forrester led the company into a new and larger acquisition, of WMS, an architectural ironmonger company. The WMS acquisition led the company into manufacturing, with WMS's production of fittings and parts for doors. The purchase more than doubled SIG's size in a deal worth nearly £53 million in cash and stock. As a result of the acquisition, the Adsetts family's shareholding in SIG was reduced to just 20 percent. WMS formed the basis for the creation of the group's SIG Architectural Products division.

International Growth in the 1990s

SIG continued to rebuild its sales into the middle of the decade, nearing turnover of £120 million by 1995. The company also made a major new expansion effort, this time through the acquisition of chief U.K. rival Freeman, then the United Kingdom's second largest insulation distributor, for £18 million, in 1994. The Freeman acquisition also proved significant in that it brought the company its first international operations, a shareholding in Isokauf, in Germany.

SIG's foothold in Germany led it to expand its sales to nearby Poland in 1995. In that year, also, the company's U.K. position was boosted with the purchase of Komfort Systems, which produced ceilings and partitions. The company added roofing materials and systems as well, buying up Asphaltic in 1996. That purchase, completed in July 1997, added more than 50 store branches, for a purchase price of £25 million. Norman Adsetts retired in that year, taking on the honorary position of life president. The company also formally adopted the name of SIG plc, in 1995.

In Germany, meanwhile, the company bought the second largest insulation distributor, WKT, as well as full control of Isokauf. SIG also reinforced its entry into Poland with the opening of its first branch in that country. By the end of 1996, the company's market share in the United Kingdom had risen to 30 percent, while its position in Germany had already topped 10 percent of the total market.

SIG exited production, selling off its architectural products division in a management buyout in 1997. The company also faced a takeover attempt from its own management team, which sought to take the company private in a leveraged buyout; the company's shareholders rejected the effort, however. The following year, the company faced a fresh takeover attempt, this time from outside of the company. Those talks, too, came to nothing and were abandoned in 2000.

In the meantime, SIG continued its expansion effort, buying up U.K. building products distribution group Roskel for nearly £25 million in 1997. The signing of the Kyoto Agreement that year, which sought to reduce global greenhouse gas emissions, signaled a new era of growth in SIG's core markets. In order to take advantage of the expected rise in demand for insulation, roofing, and related building materials, SIG entered the United States, buying Distribution International and Branton Industries, both located on the Gulf Coast and specialized in providing materials to the oil and gas industry. In 1998, the group added to its dominance of the U.K. market with the purchase of Colemans Roofing.

Leading Insulation Group in the New Century

SIG entered the Benelux market in 2000, buying The Netherlands' Nouwens Group. The following year, the company added a presence in the Republic of Ireland, buying Capco Holdings for £27 million. The company also added to its U.K. operations, buying up Woods Insulation.

By then, SIG's transformation into a major internationally operating building products distribution group was well underway, as the company's sales neared £1 billion—nearly double its sales from just two years earlier.

David Williams took over as group CEO at the beginning of 2002. The company was once again facing a downturn in the construction industry as the economy softened at the beginning of the new century. Nonetheless, SIG remained on the lookout for new expansion opportunities. In 2002, for example, the company acquired AM Proos and Clydesdale Roofing, based in the United Kingdom.

New legislation, in the European Union and elsewhere, gave SIG reason for continued optimism, with the toughening of

Key Dates:

1956: Ernest Adsetts follows son Norman Adsetts's advice and forms a business distributing insulation products to the building sector in Sheffield, founding Sheffield Insulations Limited.
1966: Norman Adsetts joins his father's business.
1970: Norman Adsetts becomes the company managing director.
1985: Norman Adsetts becomes company chairman.
1988: The company goes public on the London Stock Exchange as Sheffield Insulations Group (SIG).
1990: The company acquires CDL, a supplier of ceiling products in the United Kingdom.
1993: The company acquires the WMS Group, forming the Architectural Products division.
1994: The company acquires the Freeman Group, which also provides entry into Germany through a stake in Isokauf.
1995: The company changes its name to SIG plc; Komfort Systems in the United Kingdom is acquired.
1996: The company acquires WKT, in Germany, and full control of Isokauf.
1997: The company enters the United States through the purchases of Distribution International and Branton Industries along the Gulf Coast.
1998: The company acquires Coleman Roofing in the United Kingdom.
2000: The company enters Benelux with the purchase of the Nouwens Group.
2001: The company acquires Capco Holdings in Ireland.
2004: The company expands into Belgium and Austria; Orion Trent in the United Kingdom is acquired.
2005: The branch network expands to 412 as turnover nears £1.4 billion.

energy efficiency and safety requirements. By 2004, also, the construction sector had begun to expand again. SIG announced its interest in carrying out new acquisitions, earmarking as much as £100 million for new purchases. In the meantime, the company continued its organic growth, extending its operations in Belgium and Austria from its bases in The Netherlands and Germany.

SIG completed a new major acquisition in the United Kingdom in 2004, buying up Orion Trent Insulation. At the same time, the company continued seeking out smaller, bolt-on acquisitions in order to build up its network of distribution branches in the United Kingdom and elsewhere. By early 2005, SIG had added another 42 branches, expanding its total network to 412 worldwide. SIG appeared to be insulated for further growth into the new century.

Principal Subsidiaries

SIG Trading Limited; Miller Pattison Limited; SIG Building Products Limited (ROI); Insulation Distributors Limited; WeGo Dämmstoffe GmbH & Co. Holding OHG (Germany); Société de l'Ouest des Produits Isolants S.A. (Ouest Isol) (France); SIG Nederland B.V.; WKT Polska Sp. z.o.o. (Poland); SIG–Southwest, Inc. (U.S.A.); BWI Group, Inc. (U.S.A.).

Principal Competitors

Hunter Douglas N.V.; Lapeyre Group; Grafton Group PLC; American Builders and Contractors Supply Company Inc.; ZEDACH AG; Pacific Supply; Baustoffimportkontor GmbH; Ditas A/S; Solar Holding A/S; bauMax AG; Esha Nederland B.V.

Further Reading

Brough, Andy, and Tim Steer, ''Roof Insulation Firm Has Lofty Ambitions,'' *Sunday Times,* August 1, 2004, p. 10.
Cole, Robert, ''SIG,'' *The Times,* January 14, 2005, p. 61.
Goff, Sharlene, ''SIG Insulated Against Downturn,'' *Financial Times,* March 10, 2004, p. 24.
Jameson, Angela, ''Investors Balk at SIG's Poor Outlook,'' *The Times,* September 3, 2002, p. 26.
''Sales Keep SIG Group Dancing on the Ceiling,'' *Birmingham Post,* September 9, 2004, p. 23.
''SIG Back on Acquisitions Trail,'' *Birmingham Post,* September 4, 2003, p. 25.
''SIG Swoops to Clean Up,'' *Daily Telegraph,* March 10, 2005.
Smy, Lucy, ''Insulation Demand Fuels SIG,'' *Financial Times,* March 9, 2005, p. 22.

—M.L. Cohen

Sol Meliá

Sol Meliá S.A.

Gremio de Toneleros 24, Poligono
Palma de Mallorca
E-07009
Spain
Telephone: + 34 971 22 45 43
Fax: + 34 971 22 44 98
Web site: http://www.solmelia.com

Public Company
Incorporated: 1956 as Hoteles Mallorquines
Employees: 36,000
Sales: EUR 1.04 billion ($1.3 billion) (2004)
Stock Exchanges: Madrid
Ticker Symbol: SOL
NAIC: 721110 Hotels (Except Casino Hotels) and
    Motels; 551112 Offices of Other Holding Companies

Sol Meliá S.A. owns and manages more than 350 hotels and resorts worldwide, placing it among the top ten international hotel companies. The company, based in Mallorca, Spain, has long been that country's leading hotel group, and Sol Meliá's extensive portfolio of hotels—featuring more than 90,000 rooms across 350 hotels in more than 30 countries—places it among Europe's top three hotel companies. Sol Meliá also claims the spot of the world's leading resort chain operator. Sol Meliá's hotels operate under four core brands. Meliá Hotels & Resorts target the higher-end, four- and five-star hotel bracket. Sol Hoteles offers family-oriented hotel and vacation packages. Tryp hotels are geared toward business travelers in Spain, targeting especially the city market. Paradisus is the group's luxury all-inclusive resort operator. After growing quickly into the early 2000s, notably through acquisitions, Sol Meliá has begun launching a series of partnerships and joint ventures in the difficult post-9/11 hotel and vacation market. In 2003, the company launched its first Hard Rock-themed hotel, in Chicago, in partnership with Hard Rock owner the Rank Group. That opening also marked Sol Meliá's entry into the United States. Two more U.S. hotels are slated to open in the mid-2000s, in San Diego and New York. Sol Meliá also has

teamed up with Warner Bros. to launch a chain of Flintstones-themed hotels, primarily for the European and Asian markets. Sol Meliá is listed on the Madrid Stock Exchange. The founding Escarrer family remains actively involved in the company: founder Gabriel Escarrer Juliá serves as chairman of the board, while son Gabriel Escarrer Jaume, Jr., chief architect of the company's international expansion, is group CEO. In 2004, Sol Meliá posted sales of EUR 1.04 billion ($1.3 billion).

Majorca Origins in the 1950s

Born in 1935 on the island of Majorca, Gabriel Escarrer Juliá embarked on an early career which took him to London in the 1950s, where he worked as an agent for the Thomas Cook Travel agency. In 1956, however, Escarrer, then just 21, returned to Majorca to go into business for himself as a hotelkeeper. Escarrer leased the Altair Hotel, a 60-room building located in the residential area of Palma de Majorca.

Escarrer's timing was right. By the 1960s, Majorca had begun to take off as a popular tourist destination, particularly among British and other northern vacationers. Escarrer's early experience with travel agents led him to develop cooperative efforts with tour operators and travel agencies, increasing the flow of tourists to his hotel. At the same time, Escarrer launched a strategy of plowing profits back into his business, notably in order to finance the purchase of additional hotels and properties.

In this way, Escarrer's company, Hoteles Mallorquines, grew into a full-fledged chain, focused on the Spanish islands, including Majorca, the Canary Islands, and the Balearic Islands. In the mid-1970s, with the continued rise of tourism in Spain—especially after the end of the Franco dictatorship—Escarrer became determined to expand his company onto a national level.

Escarrer now began buying properties in other popular Spanish tourism destinations. By the early 1980s, the company had covered much of Spain, and had developed a new brand and name, becoming Hoteles Sol in 1984.

That year marked the company's emergence as Spain's leading hotel group, as the company completed the acquisition of the Hotasa Hotel chain, backed by Aresbank, the Spanish unit of the KIO Group. The Hotasa added 32 hotels to the Sol group, primarily along the Spanish coast. Yet Hotasa also owned several hotels in the Spanish urban market, marking Sol's introduction to the operation of city-based hotels. The purchase of the Hotasa group also placed Sol among the world's top 50 hotel groups, with a 37th place ranking.

With its growth at home secured, Sol became interested in the international market in the mid-1980s. The company's interest turned to Bali, which at the time had not yet attained its later popularity as a tourist destination. Sol acquired a property at Nosa Dua in Bali and began constructing its first international resort in 1987.

Growing into an International Leader in the 1990s

The year 1987 became still more significant to the company's history. In June of that year, the Escarrer beat out a number of other, larger hotel groups in his bid to acquire the luxury-oriented Meliá hotel group. The Meliá group consisted of 22 four- and five-star hotels, with a strong presence in the European market, but also in the Americas, Caribbean, and Mediterranean. Meliá had been owned by Interport, based in Luxembourg, and run by Giancarlo Parretti. The addition of Meliá encouraged the company to change its name again, becoming Sol Meliá.

Escarrer was joined by son Sebastian Escarrer Jaume. The younger Escarrer, who had completed an MBA at the Wharton School, now led the group into the restructuring of its organization, transforming Sol Meliá into a modern corporation ahead of a renewed growth effort in the 1990s. Among other features introduced to the company and to its growing international hotel chain during the early 1990s were information technology, stricter accounting and financial management controls, and quality control systems. Escarrer also redeveloped Sol Meliá as a holding company for two separate components: Inmotel Inversiones, which owned the company's hotel properties, and Sol Meliá S.A., which became exclusively a hotel management company. The completion of this restructuring led the Escarrers to bring Sol Meliá to the stock market in June 1996, marking the first time a hotel management company in Europe had gone public. Another of Escarrer's sons, Gabriel Escarrer Jaume, Jr., became CEO of Inmotel.

Throughout this period, Sol Meliá had continued to develop its international network of hotels. The company targeted especially markets such as South and Central America, as well as properties in Mexico, while continuing to build up its European holdings. As part of its push into the Latin American market, the company created a second property investment vehicle, Meliá Inversiones Americanas (MIA), which was launched on the Madrid Stock Exchange in 1998. Following the creation of MIA, Inmotel was repositioned to focus on building up the company's European hotel property portfolio.

By the end of the 1990s, the company had extended its hotel empire to more than 260 hotels. In 1999 alone, the company spent more than EUR 605 million building 27 hotels and buying 34 more. This investment campaign enabled the company to secure a presence in most of the major European capitals, including London, Paris, and Rome.

In the meantime, the growing consolidation of the hotel and resorts industries, with a flurry of takeovers and cross-mergers in the late 1990s and early 2000s, encouraged Sol Meliá to adapt its own organizational structure. In 1998, the company launched a new restructuring, integrating its two hotel-owning companies into its core Sol Meliá management arm. That process was completed in 1999, and Sol Meliá S.A. became an integrated hotel group. The move placed Sol Meliá at the number 12 spot among the world's top hotel groups, with operations in 27 countries and a market capitalization of EUR 2.3 billion.

Hotel and Resort Leader in the New Century

Sol Meliá was rumored to have entered takeover talks with Hilton International at the approach of the new century. The takeover of Sol Meliá by Hilton was viewed as a logical strategic move for both companies, giving Hilton access to Sol Meliá's leading position in the fast-growing Spanish tourist market, while adding Sol Meliá's industry-leading resorts holdings.

Yet by September 2000, those talks appeared to have been abandoned. Instead, Sol Meliá struck out on its own, announcing its acquisition of Spanish rival Tryp Hotels. The deal, worth as much as $240 million, gave Sol Meliá control of Tryp's 60 business-class hotels and reinforced Sol Meliá's presence in the Spanish urban market, including 17 hotels in the Madrid area. Tryp also added a number of resorts to Sol Meliá's portfolio, including an entry into the ski resort market for the first time. With the purchase of Tryp, Sol Meliá emerged as Europe's third largest hotel group, while entering the global top ten for the first time.

Following the Tryp acquisition, Sol Meliá streamlined its brand portfolio, cutting in half the number of hotel chains under its control. The company's four brands were now Sol, Tryp, Meliá, and the luxury resorts chain Paradisus. The rebranding effort was completed in 2001.

Yet the collapse of the global tourism industry following the attacks of September 11 that year put a chill on Sol Meliá's growth. The company now focused its efforts on investments meant to improve its portfolio. As part of that process, the company streamlined its holdings, dropping the number of hotels under its controls back from 350 to just 331 by 2002.

Sol Meliá now began seeking partnerships as a means of generating new expansion opportunities. The company joined with the Hard Rock Café company, part of the Rank Group, to launch a new Hard Rock Café hotel concept. The first of these, which opened in Chicago in 2003, also marked Sol Meliá's first

Key Dates:

1956: Gabriel Escarrer Juliá leases the Altair Hotel in Majorca.

1984: The company's name changes to Hoteles Sol and with the acquisition of the Hotasa hotel chain, it becomes the leading Spanish hotel group.

1987: The company opens its first international hotel in Bali; the Meliá hotel group is acquired, and the name is changed to Sol Meliá.

1996: The company is split into Inmotel Inversiones (hotel ownership) and Sol Meliá S.A. (hotel management); Sol Meliá begins trading on the Madrid Stock Exchange.

1998: The company creates Meliá Inversiones Americana (MIA), which is then launched in a public offering as part of an expansion in Latin America.

1999: Inmotel and MIA are integrated into Sol Meliá.

2000: The acquisition of Tryp Hotels places Sol Meliá as the number three European hotel group and number ten in the world.

2001: The company rebrands the hotels under four brands: Sol, Meliá, Paradisus, and Tryp.

2003: The first Hard Rock Hotel is opened in Chicago as part of a partnership with Rank Group; two Spanish hotels are converted to the new Sol Flintstones hotel brand as part of a partnership with Warner Bros.

2005: The company launches a renovation for a Hard Rock Hotel in New York City; a third hotel is opened in the Dominican Republic.

hotel in the North American market. The two companies then began preparations to open two new Hard Rock hotels, in San Diego, expected to be opened in 2006, and in New York, where renovation began in 2005.

In Europe, meanwhile, Sol Meliá teamed up with Warner Bros. to launch another hotel concept, the more family-oriented Sol Flintstones-themed hotels. The first of these hotels involved the renovation of two former Sol hotels in Menorca and Majorca and opened in 2003.

As the tourism industry began to revitalize toward the middle of the 2000s, Sol Meliá continued to seek out partnerships and alliances, such as cooperation agreements with tour oper-

ator Cedant and with online travel agency lastminute.com. The company also returned to organic growth, boosting its number of hotels back to 350, including the opening of its third hotel in the Dominican Republic in February 2005. From a single hotel, Sol Meliá had built one of the world's top hotel groups for the 21st century.

Principal Subsidiaries

Grupo Sol Asia, Ltd. (Hong Kong); Grupo Sol Services (Singapore); Hoteles Meliá, S.L.; Hoteles Paradisus, S.L.; Hoteles Sol Meliá, S.L.; Marktur Turizm, A.S. (Turkey); Meliá Brasil Administraçao; Meliá Inversiones Americanas, N.V. (Netherlands); Meliá Tour, S.L.; Parking Internacional, S.A.; Sol Caribe Tours, S.A. (Panama); Sol Group Corporation (U.S.A.); Sol Group, B.V. (Netherlands); Sol Hoteles U.K., Ltd.; Sol Maninvest, B.V. (Netherlands); Sol Meliá Benelux, B.V. (Belgium); Sol Meliá China, Ltd. (Hong Kong); Sol Meliá Croacia; Sol Meliá Deutschland, GmbH; Sol Meliá Europe, B.V. (Netherlands); Sol Meliá Finance, Ltd. (Cayman Islands); Sol Meliá France, S.A.S.; Sol Meliá Guatemala, S.A.; Sol Meliá Marruecos, S.A. (Morocco); Sol Meliá Perú, S.A.; Sol Meliá Services, S.A. (Switzerland); Sol Meliá Suisse, S.A.; Sol Meliá Travel S.A.; Tenerife Sol, S.A.; Torresol Des. Turísticos, S.A.

Principal Competitors

Loews Corporation; Radisson Hotels and Resorts; Orascom Group; Rallye S.A.; Carlson Holdings Inc; Compass Group PLC; Hilton Group PLC; MARITIM; SABMiller PLC; Protea Hotels and Inns Proprietary Ltd.; Itsui Fudosan Company Ltd.; Southern Sun Group; Marriott International Inc.; ACCOR S.A.

Further Reading

Arellano, Luisa Esquiroz, "The Reign from Spain," *Travel Agent,* October 22, 2001, p. 28.

Dela Cruz, Tony, "Hard Rock, Sol Meliá Plan to Develop 10,000 Hotel Rooms," *Hotel & Motel Management,* August 2004, p. 7.

Fox, Linda, "From Bedrock to Hard Rock," *Travel Trade Gazette,* October 6, 2003, p. 40.

"Ready to Rock," *Travel Weekly,* December 8, 2003, p. 6.

Serlen, Bruce, "Sol Meliá Plants US Flag with Windy City Hard Rock," *Business Travel News,* September 22, 2003, p. 24.

"Sol Meliá's D.R. Hat Trick," *Travel Weekly,* February 14, 2005, p. 6.

Tarpey, David, "Sol Searching," *Caterer & Housekeeper,* January 31, 2002, p. 26.

—M.L. Cohen

Sola International Inc.

10590 West Ocean Air Drive, Suite 300
San Diego, California 92130
U.S.A.
Telephone: (858) 509-9899
Fax: (858) 509-9898
Web site: http://www.sola.com

Division of Carl Zeiss AGG
Incorporated: 1960 as Scientific Optical Laboratories of
  Australia
Employees: 6,634
Sales: $650.1 million (2004)
NAIC: 339115 Ophthalmic Goods Manufacturing;
  423460 Ophthalmic Goods Merchant Wholesalers

Sola International Inc. designs and manufactures eyeglass lenses, primarily focusing on the plastic lens segment of the market, which the company helped develop in the 1960s. The company concentrates on four product segments: progressive lenses, photochromic lenses, coated lenses, and plastic lenses. Sola operates on a global basis, maintaining manufacturing and distribution sites in North and South America, Europe, Australia, and Asia. The company has sales operations in 27 countries. Instead of selling directly to consumers, Sola markets its lenses to retail chains, independent optometrists and opticians, and independent wholesalers.

Origins

Sola, once it reached maturity, perennially ranked as one of the world's largest lens makers, a stature it enjoyed while being affiliated with two companies of entirely different corporate backgrounds. The corporate parentage of Sola included one of the oldest companies in Britain and a unique investment company run by some of the luminaries of capitalism in the 20th century. Sola began operating in Australia, founded after nine optical technicians, working in a garage in Adelaide, helped pioneer the use of plastic lenses. The research team began their work in 1956, hoping to find a replacement for glass lenses, and the incorporation of their company, Scientific Optical Laborato-

ries of Australia, in 1960, heralded a revolutionary development in the eyeglass lens industry. Sola grew for nearly two decades before it became the target of its first corporate parent, a glass manufacturer based in England, Pilkington PLC.

The largest glassmaker in the world, Pilkington was founded in the wake of the Industrial Revolution The company began as part of the St. Helens Crown Glass Company, a concern founded by the Pilkington and Greenall families in 1826. More than a century of quiet existence followed the founding of the company, as successive generations of patrician leadership built Pilkington into an industry leader. The company continued to operate in relative obscurity even after it joined the ranks of publicly held enterprises in 1970, but it began to attract more attention after Sir Antony Pilkington expanded the company's glass business internationally. The company's first diversifying move was the acquisition of an Australian lens maker named Sola International, a purchase made in 1979, four years after Sola had established manufacturing operations in the United States, when it opened a facility in Sunnyvale, California. The acquisition made strategic sense, representing a logical addition to one of the company's ancillary businesses that sold bits of flat glass used to make eyeglass lenses. The only problem with the acquisition of Sola was that it was a success, which encouraged management to make further acquisitions, acquisitions that were far less successful.

Ownership Change in the 1990s

By the end of the 1980s, Pilkington was awash in debt and still reeling from a hostile takeover attempt made on the company in 1987. In late 1990, Sir Antony Pilkington announced the company would begin selling peripheral assets, which eventually led to the sale of Sola. Sola's next parent company was an intensely private investment company that bore resemblance to few other companies around the world. The company was unusual not for the way it conducted its business, but because of its shareholders, who represented the true assets of the company.

The company that acquired Sola was AEA Investors, Inc., an investment firm that began to take shape after a conversation during lunch in November 1963. Seated at the table were J. Richardson Dilworth, the financial adviser to the Rockefeller family, George Love, the chairman of Chrysler Corp. and

Consolidation Coal, and Sir Siegmund Warburg, the heir of an enormously wealthy German banking family. The lunchtime talk centered on gathering together wealthy families, pooling their money, and acquiring companies for investment purposes. It took five years before their conversation materialized into a company, a company originally known as American European Associates. Not long after starting the company, the founders discovered the ideal investors were retired chief executive officers (CEOs), not wealthy families. CEOs of the largest corporations in the world possessed more than ample capital to support AEA and their management skills could be used by placing them on the board of directors of companies acquired by AEA—the attribute that set the investment company apart from others of its ilk. AEA's investors, referred to as ''participants'' by the company, included only the most powerful of the world's CEOs, the leaders of IBM, Exxon, General Motors, and a short list of other industry behemoths. AEA selected its participants a year or two before they retired, signing them on before they agreed to join too many other corporate boards. The strategy created an investment company *Fortune* described in a June 5, 1989 article as ''like a small greenhouse where companies are repotted and refertilized in carefully controlled light and temperature—a place where all the gardeners have green thumbs.''

In 1993, the high minds at AEA turned their attention to Pilkington's Sola, creating a Menlo Park, California, investment partnership, Sola Group Ltd., in September to complete the acquisition of the eyeglass lens manufacturing operations. AEA paid $315 million for Sola, gaining the company's manufacturing and distribution sites in North and South America, Europe, Australia, and Asia.

When AEA acquired Sola, the company was enjoying a sustained period of robust financial growth. In its business, product innovation was central to achieving financial growth because to a large extent the number of people needing glasses did not change much over time. Presenting innovative changes to consumers and convincing them to purchase the often more expensive innovation represented the chief driver of sales and profits. Such was the case with Sola's strident progress when AEA acquired the company, a growth spurt related to the introduction of progressive lenses. Developed in the late 1970s, progressive lenses were bifocal lenses without the seam that many wearers found unappealing. Sola introduced its first progressive lens, called VIP, in 1984, a lens that was ten times more profitable than a standard lens, ushering in an era of strong financial growth that stretched until the late 1990s.

While Sola was still enjoying the financial rewards engendered by VIP, the company completed an initial public offering (IPO) of stock. Sola debuted on the New York Stock Exchange in February 1995, raising $81 million from the offering. In the wake of the IPO, Sola announced two acquisitions, although company officials stressed that the acquisitions did not reflect a strategic decision to accelerate expansion by acquiring other companies. The larger of the two acquisitions was announced first, when Sola revealed in May 1996 that it had agreed to pay $107 million for the worldwide lens division of American Optical Corp. The purchase of American Optical strengthened Sola's position in progressive lens manufacture, but its greatest contribution was to Sola's presence in France and Africa. The second acquisition, announced less than a month after the American Optical deal was revealed, was the $16 million purchase of Neolens, Inc. Although much smaller than the American Optical deal, the Neolens purchase was no less important. Neolens was one of four or five companies with the technology to produce polycarbonate lenses, a type of plastic that could be fitted directly into eyeglass frames. Prior to the Neolens acquisition, Sola's products had to be finished in a lab before they could be fitted into eyeglass frames.

Shortly before the acquisitions were announced, Sola released its first financial figures as a publicly traded company. Sales were up 12 percent to $387.7 million and profits were up 46 percent to $33.7 million, gains that were attributed to the company's progress in expanding internationally. As the company plotted its course for the late 1990s, it was focusing expansion on markets in developing markets, targeting countries in Eastern Europe, Asia, and Africa. ''We have been most active lately in China,'' Sola's chief executive officer, John Heine, said in a June 7, 1996 interview with the *San Francisco Business Times*. ''And we are breaking ground next month for a factory in Guangzhou.''

The years of strident financial growth came to an end in the late 1990s, forcing Sola to search for a way to invigorate its financial growth. In 1998, earnings per share totaled $2, falling to $1.30 per share in 1999, and dropping 30 percent in 2000 to 91 cents per share. The company ranked as the largest maker of eyeglass lenses in both North and South America, but its size was not enough to guarantee financial growth. ''The (lens) market slowed down from the lack of innovation,'' a Sola executive remarked in a June 8, 2001 interview with *Investor's Business Daily*. ''The industry was built on innovation and needs innovation to continue to grow.''

Sola in the 21st Century

The sale of progressive lenses no longer provided the punch to Sola's bottom line, propelling the company's drive to find a new financial stimulant. In mid-2001, Sola unveiled new technology it had developed, designing a pair of glasses with curved lenses instead of flat lenses. Sola formed an alliance with a Parsippany, New Jersey-based frame maker, Safilo USA, to create what was dubbed ''Enigma,'' a pair of eyeglasses whose curvature widened the wearer's field of vision by as much as 40 percent. Together, the lenses and Safilo's frames retailed for between $500 and $600, with the lenses alone selling for 50 times more than standard lenses. The lenses also were 30 times more profitable than standard lenses. Enigma lenses, like progressive lenses, improved optical performance and they were regarded as stylish, fueling optimism that the curved eyeglasses would trigger financial growth.

Sola took other steps beyond Enigma to improve its financial performance during the early 2000s. To reduce costs, the

---

Key Dates:

1956: A group of optical technicians in Adelaide, Australia, begin developing plastic lenses.
1960: Sola is incorporated as Scientific Optical Laboratories of Australia.
1979: Sola is acquired by Pilkington PLC.
1993: AEA Investors acquires Sola from Pilkington.
1995: Sola completes an initial public offering of stock.
2001: In a partnership with Safilo USA, Sola introduces eyeglasses with curved lenses.
2004: Carl Zeiss AGG and EQT Partners AB announce an agreement to acquire Sola.

---

company trimmed its payroll at U.S. production plants and relocated operations to Mexico, Brazil, and China, where labor costs were much lower. The company also consolidated its manufacturing operations, reducing the number of plants it operated from 17 down to 3 by 2002.

The biggest event of the new decade—and a monumental event in the history of Sola—occurred at the end of 2004. In the beginning of December, a competitor, the German optical group Carl Zeiss, and a Swedish private equity firm, EQT Partners AB, announced they had reached an agreement to acquire Sola. Zeiss, comprising a group of companies operating in the optical and opto-electronic industries, conducted business in 30 countries, generating nearly $3 billion in annual revenue. EQT was an equity firm founded in 1994. The transaction was valued at $1.1 billion, 30 percent more than Sola's stock value when the deal was announced. The acquisition, perceived as part of a global trend toward consolidation in the eyeglass industry, promised profound changes for Sola, including moving its headquarters to Aalen, Germany, where Zeiss was based. The new company was expected to have 9,000 employees and slightly more than $1 billion in annual sales.

As Sola entered its 45th year of business, its pending acquisition by Zeiss promised the beginning of a new chapter in its history. In March 2005, the European Union gave its approval to the consolidation, leaving only Switzerland and Australia to approve the proposed takeover.

Principal Subsidiaries

SOLA Agentina S.A.; SOLA Optical Partners (Australia); American Optical Benelux N.V. (Belgium); SOLA Brasil Industria Optica Ltda. (Brazil); American Optical Lens Company Limited (Canada); SOLA Optical CZ S.R.O. (Czech Republic); Sola Nordic A/S (Denmark); SOLA Optical (U.K.) Limited; SOLA Optical Holdings S.A.R.L. (France); SOLA Optical Holdings GmbH (Germany); SOLA Hong Kong Ltd.; SOLA Optical Lens Marketing Pvt. Ltd. (India); SOLA Holdings Ireland Limited; SOLA Optical Italia S.p.A. (Italy); American Optical Japan Limited; Sola Optical Lens Malaysia SDN BHD; Lentes SOLA S.A. de C.V. (Mexico); Optical Sola de Mexico, S. de R.L. de C.V.; Imgo Industries B.V. (Netherlands); Sola Technologies Limited (New Zealand); SOLA Optical (Poland) S.P.Z.O.O.; IOLA Industria Optical S.A. (Portugal; 89%); SOLA Optical Singapore Pte. Ltd.; American Optical Company International A.G. (Switzerland); SOLA Optical Taiwan Ltd. (China); American Optical Lens Company; Copeland Optical Inc.; SOLA Optical Espana Lentese Oftalmicas SL (Spain).

Principal Competitors

Essilor International SA; Bausch & Lomb Incorporated; Hoya Corporation.

Further Reading

Allen, Mike, "Vision Clear As Sola International Acquires New Firm," *San Diego Business Journal,* December 6, 2004, p. 15.
"Britain First to Market with Sola's Teflon Lens," *Optician,* April 5, 2002, p. 2.
Carlsen, Clifford, "Lens Maker Improves Vision with Two Buys," *San Francisco Business Times,* June 7, 1996, p. 3.
"Facing Up to a Cruel World: Pilkington," *Economist (US),* October 12, 1991, p. 78.
Fikes, Bradley J., "Sola Acquisition Approved in Europe," *North County Times,* March 4, 2005, p. 12.
Knowlton, Christopher, "The Richest Little Club in the World," *Fortune,* June 5, 1989, p. 73.
Lau, Gloria, "Sola International Inc.," *Investor's Business Daily,* June 8, 2001, p. A8.
Lauzon, Michael, "Oracle Lens Manufacturing Corp.," *Plastics News,* November 27, 2000, p. 3.
Weston, Paula, "Sola Optical Works to Better Plastic Lenses," *Plastics News,* December 13, 1999, p. 9.

—Jeffrey L. Covell

Southwest Airlines Co.

2702 Love Field Dr.
Dallas, Texas 75235
U.S.A.
Telephone: (214) 792-4000
Toll Free: (800) I-FLY-SWA
Fax: (214) 792-5015
Web site: http://www.southwest.com

Public Company
Incorporated: 1967 as Air Southwest Co.
Employees: 31,011
Sales: $6.53 billion (2004)
Stock Exchanges: New York
Ticker Symbol: LUV
NAIC: 481111 Scheduled Passenger Air Transportation;
    481112 Scheduled Freight Air Transportation

Southwest Airlines Co. (SWA), the model for budget upstarts everywhere, has become the largest domestic airline in the United States, by number of passengers carried. More than 70 million passengers fly SWA each year to about 60 destinations around the country. Passengers have found that Southwest's rock bottom pricing creates almost a new form of transportation, more in competition with the automobile than other airlines. They are willing to forsake in-flight meals, baggage transfers, and other traditional frills for economically amenable wings.

The company flies only Boeing 737s, to simplify maintenance and training, and employee productivity is high. Planes are turned around for their next flight in just 15 minutes, one-third the industry average. Though the airline has boosted its wages and taken on other aspects of a traditional airline, such as its first codeshare arrangement, Southwest remains a maverick in the industry.

Beginning a Labor of Love

Southwest Air was founded in 1966 when a group of Texas investors, including Rollin King, M. Lamar Muse, and Herbert D. Kelleher, pooled $560,000 to form the Air Southwest Company.

Incorporated in 1967, the company was envisioned as a commuter airline serving three cities within Texas: Dallas, Houston, and San Antonio. Although the Texas Aeronautics Commission (TAC), the regulatory body responsible for overseeing aviation within the state, granted the company permission to fly the routes it had requested in February 1968, three competing airlines filed suit to prevent the airline from getting off the ground. Kelleher, an attorney whose stake in the airline was a mere $20,000, took the case all the way to the U.S. Supreme Court, and in December 1970 this court ruled in favor of Air Southwest.

Six months later, after fighting numerous legal battles, changing its name to Southwest Air, and selling stock in the company, the fledgling airline began operations on June 18, 1971. Under the stewardship of President M. Lamar Muse, the airline offered six daily roundtrip flights between Dallas and San Antonio, and 12 daily roundtrip flights between Dallas and Houston. One-way tickets cost $20.

Courting the commuter, the company stressed ''no-frills'' convenience and, in reference to Love Field in Dallas, its home base, made ''love'' its promotional theme. Flight attendants were dressed in hot pants and go-go boots to serve ''love potions'' and ''love bites'' (also known as drinks and peanuts) to the company's clientele of mostly male business fliers. Southwest made much of its scantily clad women, whose pin-up-like images would eventually appear widely, including on the cover of *Esquire* magazine.

By the end of 1971, Southwest owned four aircraft, offered hourly flights between Dallas and Houston, and had inaugurated service between San Antonio and Houston, completing the last leg of a triangular route. In the following year, the company transferred its Houston service from Houston Intercontinental Airport to William P. Hobby Airport, located much closer to the city's downtown, in an effort to become more convenient to commuters. In 1973, Braniff Airlines began a fare war with Southwest over service from this airport to Dallas. Southwest resorted to giveaways of liquor, leather ice buckets, and 50 percent discounts on fares. The company also introduced cargo service between the airports it served and by the end of 1973 had notched its first profitable year, carrying over half a million passengers.

Still More Controversy in the 1970s

Southwest again found itself involved in legal controversy in 1972, when the cities of Dallas and Fort Worth and their Regional Airport Board filed suit to force the airline to move from Love Field to the newly constructed Dallas-Fort Worth regional airport, hoping that by charging higher landing fees and rent there, they could help offset the cost of the expensive project. While all the other airlines had signed a contract to move to the new airport in 1968, Southwest had not done so because it was not in existence at that time. In a big break for Southwest, a federal judge ruled in 1973 that the airline could continue to operate at Love Field in Dallas as long as the airport remained open. Thwarted, the Dallas City Council subsequently passed a law closing the airport to all scheduled airlines, but this law was thrown out in court.

In 1974, Southwest's competitors began moving out to the Dallas-Fort Worth Airport, leaving the airline with a monopoly on service from the cheaper, more convenient airport. After defeating yet another legal challenge, this one from the other carriers, Southwest was able to solidify its presence at Love Field and its newly renovated facilities at Houston's Hobby Airport, making its strong commuter service the basis for broader operations.

This expansion began in 1975, when the airline inaugurated service to the Rio Grande Valley, with four roundtrip flights each day to Harlingen. By the end of that year, the company had acquired a fifth plane, and its stock was listed on the American Stock Exchange under the ticker symbol "LUV." In the following year, Southwest laid plans to extend service to five other Texas cities and again found itself the object of hostile litigation by competitors.

In 1977, the airline put into effect its plan to offer service from Corpus Christi, Lubbock, Midland/Odessa, El Paso, and Austin. Its stock was transferred to the New York Stock Exchange, and the company issued its second and third quarterly dividends, the latter totaling seven cents per share. In May of that year, the airline exceeded the five million passenger mark.

Deregulated at Last

In 1978, Congress passed the Airline Deregulation Act, fundamentally altering the nature of the airline industry. Although Southwest was now legally free to greatly expand its operations, the company planned conservative growth to avoid the perils of taking on large debts.

In early 1978, the airline applied for permission to purchase a wholly owned subsidiary, Midway (Southwest) Airway Company, in order to inaugurate service from Chicago's Midway Airport to six midwestern destinations. Although it received

tentative approval to do so, Southwest abandoned this ambitious attempt at expansion in August. Instead, the company added service to the mid-sized Texas city of Amarillo and the Jefferson County Airport. In July 1978, the company implemented its first fare increase since 1972, adding three dollars to the cost of a one-way ticket, and five dollars for a roundtrip fare. By the end of the year, the airline's fleet had grown to 13 Boeing 737 planes.

In March 1978, significant changes were made in Southwest's upper-level management. After a dispute with the airline's governing board, President M. Lamar Muse, who had largely shaped the company during its early years, was deposed by the board and replaced by lawyer Kelleher, who became chairman. In August, Howard D. Putnam, a United Airlines executive, became president and chief executive officer.

In 1979, Southwest introduced self-ticketing machines in many of its airports to speed up and simplify passenger ticketing, and the airline introduced service to New Orleans, its first destination outside Texas. In late December 1979, earlier opponents of Southwest's continuing use of Love Field won a partial victory in Congress. Speaker of the House Jim Wright, a Congressman from Texas, attached a rider to a federal trade law which forbade traffic between Love Field and any states other than Louisiana, Arkansas, Oklahoma, and New Mexico, the four states surrounding Texas. This severe limitation of Southwest's interstate flights from its hub forced the airline to conform to its established role as a commuter service for the energy belt, now in a severe depression. The airline inaugurated service to Oklahoma City, Tulsa, and Albuquerque in April 1980.

Earlier that year, Southwest was hit by a machinists' strike, which curtailed operations for several weeks. The company brought in temporary workers to keep 12 of its 18 planes flying, and the union eventually settled for what the airline had initially offered.

In 1981, celebrating its tenth year of operation, the airline introduced a multimedia advertising campaign featuring the theme, "Loving you is what we do," and produced an ad picturing six Southwest flight attendants, all purportedly "physical 10s," grouped around a birthday cake, promising, "You ain't seen nothin' yet." In June 1981, the airline was found guilty of sex discrimination in a class action suit filed by a man seeking a job as a ticket agent and ordered to cease its discriminatory hiring practices. Also in 1981, after a series of petition drives, stewardesses won the right in their new contract not to wear hot pants on the job.

In September 1981, President Howard Putnam resigned to become the head of Braniff International Airlines, and was succeeded as president and chief executive officer by Chairman Kelleher, who brought his flamboyant personal style to the job of running the airline. With Kelleher at the helm, the airline's pace of expansion picked up markedly, despite the nationwide recession and difficulties arising from an air traffic controllers' strike. In early 1982, Southwest introduced service from Kansas City, Missouri, to seven destinations. Just a few weeks later, the airline made its entry into the western air travel market when it began flights from San Diego, Las Vegas, and Phoenix. Additional California service was inaugurated that fall, when Los Angeles and San Francisco came on line.

The airline's steady growth continued in 1983, as it added customers, flights, and airplanes. The company ratified a two-tier wage system, secured a one-year pay freeze from its pilots' association, and signed contracts with several of its unions, including its mechanics and flight attendants. Service from Denver began in May 1983.

Stretching Out in the 1980s

In a departure from its previous policy of sticking to short-haul flights, Southwest inaugurated two routes between Texas and California—El Paso to Los Angeles and San Antonio to Los Angeles—as well as a major north-south California route from San Diego to San Francisco. Entry into these long-haul markets, coupled with bad weather throughout the Southwest region, curtailed profits somewhat during this period.

In 1984, helped by ongoing peace with its labor unions, Southwest continued to increase capacity and rack up steady profits, despite growing competition from Continental, Braniff, and Muse Air, founded by the former president of Southwest. In July 1984, the company implemented limited cost-cutting measures, paring back unprofitable flights and reducing new hires. The company took delivery on the first of a new generation of planes, the Boeing 737-300, and introduced service from another midwestern city, Little Rock, Arkansas.

The following year, Southwest further expanded its midwestern network of routes, adding flights to St. Louis and Chicago's Midway airport. The company unveiled its "Just Say When" promotion, touting itself as the most convenient way to travel. The airline also made its first big acquisition when it paid $60 million for Muse Air Corporation, a Houston-based competitor, to prevent another competitor, Continental Airlines, from snatching it up. Unlike Southwest, Muse Air offered longer flights and full service to its customers. Kelleher kept the full-service frills and renamed the airline Transtar. In

its first year, the money-losing company was able to turn a small profit.

By 1986, Southwest had scheduled flights from 25 cities. The airline introduced a number of fare-cutting measures in efforts to maintain its market share in the heavily competitive post-deregulation airline industry. "Incredible Pair Fares," "Fly Now, Pay Less," programs, $25 tickets for senior citizens, and finally "Fun Fares" became part of the strategy to lure more fliers to the skies. In addition, the airline was waging a fare war at its Phoenix hub against America West Airlines, offering flights between California and Arizona for $25.

During the summer of 1986, the airline stepped up the hoopla surrounding its low fares, making "fun" its new corporate byword and implementing a "fun" uniform of golf shirts, surfer shorts, and tennis shoes, along with in-flight games and giveaways. In July, the golf shirts were replaced by red Southwest T-shirts asserting that "Southwest Fliers Have More Fun." In an effort to simplify ticketing, a drive-through ticket window was installed near the airline's Dallas hub in August 1986, and in October tickets became available through automatic teller machines at 7-Eleven stores in Corpus Christi, Texas.

By 1987, Southwest's full-service subsidiary Transtar was locked in head-to-head combat with Continental for service out of Houston's Hobby Airport. The competing airline hit Transtar with cheaper flights scheduled 15 minutes before and after every Transtar departure, and the Southwest subsidiary was soon draining off $2 million in losses every month. In August 1987, after suffering a net loss for the first quarter of the year, Southwest shut down Transtar. The Transtar debacle cut the company's year-end earnings by 60 percent.

Despite aggressive pricing, Southwest found its rapid expansion thwarted in some markets, as full-service rivals drove the airline out of Denver, hampered its ambitious plans for operations in Nashville, and continued to put up stiff resistance in Phoenix. In addition, the airline was fined $402,000 by the Federal Aviation Authority in 1987. Faced with the demands of business fliers, the company introduced its first frequent flier program. Unlike the programs of other airlines, which award prizes based on mileage accrued, Southwest's program was designed to reward the short-haul flier, allotting prizes on the basis of number of trips taken.

In 1988, Southwest President Kelleher announced plans to double the airline's size by 1994. His strategy for accomplishing this was to increase the frequency of flights between cities already on the Southwest route map and to open up new routes in California and the Midwest. In keeping with the airline's policy of flying out of airports that are close to urban centers, Southwest also switched its Detroit flights to Detroit City Airport from the more remote Metro Airport.

Also in 1988, as a sign of the ever growing airline's commitment to lightheartedness, Southwest painted one of its 737s to resemble a killer whale to celebrate the company's agreement to become the official airline of Sea World of Texas. Shamu One, named after Sea World's mascot orca, was eventually joined by Shamu Two and Shamu Three. When Federal anti-smoking regulations went into effect on all domestic flights, Southwest offered its passengers lollipops as a substitute for the now-banned cigarettes. Passengers on flights during the winter holiday season of 1988 reported that flight attendants were dressed as elves and reindeer, and that the pilot sang Christmas carols over the public address system while gently rocking the plane from side to side.

In the spring of 1989, Southwest began its planned assault on the California market and touched off a fare war with much larger carriers, such as American Airlines and United Airlines, when it introduced $19 fares from Oakland International Airport, in the San Francisco Area, to Ontario, a suburb of Los Angeles. Aiming to reach $1 billion in revenues for the year, Southwest planned continued expansion of its fleet of planes and added Indianapolis to its route map. In a novel pairing of businesses, the company offered, for a limited time, a free companion ticket to anyone buying a holiday meal at Kentucky Fried Chicken.

Prudence Prevails in the 1990s

As a result of its steady growth, Southwest entered the 1990s as a major airline, with a fleet of 94 planes serving 27 cities. Relying on conservative financial management, the company was able to avoid the pitfalls of debt that crippled many other carriers in the early 1990s, and despite suffering a loss in its fourth quarter, turned an overall profit in 1990.

Southwest took advantage of the misfortunes of its competitors in 1991, scooping up market share abandoned by ailing US Air in California and by bankrupt America West in Phoenix, and buying gates at Midway Airport from its defunct Chicago competitor, Midway Airlines. By year's end, Southwest had 124 jets flying to 32 cities.

By 1992, the company's concerted push into the California market had proven profitable, and Southwest became the second largest carrier in the state. The company looked to the Midwest as its next largest site of expansion. When the Department of Transportation began ranking airlines based upon baggage handling, customer satisfaction, and on-time performance, Southwest outpaced its larger, more expensive colleagues to win the first "Triple Crown" in 1992. Moreover, it kept winning them year after year. In 1993, when Southwest was expanding to the East Coast via Baltimore/Washington International Airport, Southwest was the only major carrier to take home a profit.

Southwest aggressively pursued non-traditional means of ticketing passengers. It sidestepped Apollo and other established reservation networks in lieu of more direct contact with travel agents. It dubbed its own network SWAT, for Southwest Air Travel.

Takeovers of Morris Air and Arizona One in 1994 expanded the company's network still further. The company continued to add routes to the Midwest and California. Southwest followed suit with its low-budget peers by eliminating paper tickets.

In 1995, the company reached $2.8 billion in operating revenues. Within five years, Southwest had added more than 10,000 employees to its roster. Southwest commemorated its 1996 silver anniversary with a special plane called *Silver One*. Internet ticket sales debuted along with new Florida service, which added the carrier's 50th city in 1997.

For the 25th consecutive year, the carrier posted a profit in 1997, $317.7 million. Due to its low fares, the carrier by entering a market could increase the volume of passenger traffic fourfold, and some businesses used the availability of Southwest service as a prime criterion in choosing new locations. The airline's 2,300 flights per day, impressive safety record, and status as a much admired corporate citizen suggested it would long remain one of the industry's legendary survivors.

Southwest continued its eastern push in the late 1990s, entering New York (Islip) and exploiting a void in the Raleigh-Durham market left by retreating American Airlines and US Airways. It was also adding long-haul flights to its network.

Taking Care of Business After 2000

In 2000, SWA introduced an online booking tool geared toward corporate travel offices called SWABIZ. This offered convenient access to Southwest's low fares rather than corporate discounts per se, an official told *Business Travel News*. Earnings were about $600 million on revenues of $5.6 billion in 2000.

In 2001, Southwest took legal action to prevent the Orbitz online booking site from displaying its fares. This move surprised some observers. Southwest complained of other airlines getting preferential treatment on the site, particularly the ones that owned Orbitz LLC. Southwest did allow the Sabre computer reservations system to list its flights, though reservations had to be made through Southwest.com.

The question of who would follow Southwest's inimitable leader and spokesman, Herb Kelleher, was resolved in June 2001. While retaining the office of chairman, he was replaced as president by the company's general counsel, James F. Parker, and as CEO by former executive vice-president for customers Colleen C. Barrett. (The two had previously worked together for Kelleher's law firm.)

Southwest was not immune to the effects of the September 11, 2001 terrorist attacks on the United States. Increased security following 9/11 made traveling by auto a more attractive choice for many. While its larger rivals laid off tens of thousands of workers, lost billions of dollars, and appealed for bankruptcy protection in the two years following the attack, Southwest remained profitable, avoided layoffs, and kept its employees working.

Southwest allowed the A&E Television Network to film a reality show on its planes beginning in 2003. The show was a clone of a British show centered on easyJet PLC, which itself was closely modeled after Southwest.

Success of the "major" airlines in wresting concessions from labor eroded one area of Southwest's relative competitive advantage as its own unions negotiated more lucrative compensation. Jim Parker retired as CEO in 2004 following contentious contract negotiations with the flight attendants' and mechanics' unions. He was succeeded by former CFO Gary C. Kelly.

After more than 30 years of consistently profitable growth, Southwest was flying more passengers than any other U.S. airline. Its 417 planes were making 2,900 hops a day to 59 destinations. Revenues continued to increase at a 10 percent clip, reaching $6.5 billion in 2004. The company's cargo business, from freight carried in its planes' belly holds, was small but growing, with $117 million in 2004. Earnings of $313 million were no record but were handsome compared to other airlines in the post-9/11 environment.

The airline continued to look for ways to cut costs. It trimmed its reservations staff as Internet booking became more popular. It installed winglets on its planes to cut fuel consumption and benefited greatly from hedging on oil prices.

Southwest entered the Philadelphia market in May 2004, mounting a robust challenge to a US Airways stronghold. The airline was also reviving a challenge to the decades-old law that kept Southwest from operating beyond adjacent states from Love Field. "Growth opportunities have become more precious," CEO Gary Kelly told *Air Transport World*. SWA entered its first codeshare agreement with the much smaller ATA Airlines in December 2004. This type of deal, common in the industry but surprising for the famously independent Southwest, allowed the two carriers to list and sell seats on each other's flights. Southwest also negotiated to buy six gates at Chicago's Midway Airport from ATA, bringing its total there to 25, and a 27.5 percent stake in ATA, which was in bankruptcy. The deal cost $117 million.

Moving into 2005, Southwest was facing many familiar challenges: rising oil prices, intense competition, cumbersome regulations. In the uncertain times that had legacy (traditional) carriers reeling, Southwest was still winging ahead with its ever-popular low-fare formula.

Principal Subsidiaries

API Terminal, Inc.; Southwest ABQ RES Center, Inc.; Southwest Jet Fuel Co.; TranStar Airlines Corporation; Triple Crown Insurance Ltd. (Bermuda).

Principal Competitors

AirTran Holdings, Inc.; AMR Corp.; Continental Airlines, Inc.; Delta Air Lines, Inc.; JetBlue Airways Corporation; United Airlines Inc.

Further Reading

Allen, Margaret, "SW Airlines' President Has a Customer-First Flight Plan," *San Antonio Business Journal*, August 31, 2001, p. 13.

Brooker, Katrina, "Can Anyone Replace Herb?," *Fortune*, April 17, 2000, pp. 186+.

Brown, David A., "Southwest Airlines Gains Major Carrier Status by Using Go-It-Alone Strategy," *Aviation Week & Space Technology*, March 5, 1990.

Chakravarty, Subrata N., "Hit "Em Hardest with the Mostest," *Forbes*, September 16, 1991.

"Corporate Case Study: Southwest Airlines Keeps PR Course with Flying Colors," *PR Week* (US), January 26, 2004.

Donnelly, Sally B., "One Airline's Magic: How Does Southwest Soar Above Its Money-Losing Rivals? Its Employees Work Harder and Smarter, in Return for Job Security and a Share of the Profits," *Time*, October 28, 2002, pp. 45+.

Flint, Perry, "Southwest Keeps It Simple," *Air Transport World*, April 2005, pp. 26+.

Freiberg, Kevin, and Jackie Freiberg, *Nuts! Southwest Airlines' Crazy Recipe for Business and Personal Success*, Austin: Bard, 1996.

Gibney, Frank, Jr., "Southwest's Friendly Skies," *Newsweek*, May 30, 1988.

Gibson, Jane Whitney, and Charles W. Blackwell, "Flying High with Herb Kelleher: A Profile in Charismatic Leadership," *Journal of Leadership Studies*, Summer/Fall 1999, p. 120.

Gruner, Stephanie, "Have Fun, Make Money: How Herb Kelleher Parties Profitably at Southwest Airlines," *Inc.*, May 1998, p. 123.

Jonas, David, and David Meyer, "SW Shines in Light of Biz Changes," *Business Travel News*, December 9, 2002, pp. 1+.

Keating, Peter, "Rating the Airlines: The Best Airlines to Fly Today," *Money*, November 1, 1997.

Kelly, Kevin, "Southwest Airlines: Flying High with 'Uncle Herb'," *Business Week*, July 3, 1989.

Labich, Kenneth, and Ani Hadjian, "Is Herb Kelleher America's Best CEO?," *Fortune*, May 2, 1994.

Levering, Robert, and Milton Moskowitz, *The 100 Best Companies to Work for in America*, New York: Doubleday, 1993.

——, "The 100 Best Companies to Work for in America," *Fortune*, January 12, 1998.

Loeffelholz, Suzanne, "The Love Line," *Financial World*, March 21, 1989.

McKenna, Ed, "Southwest's Cargo Turn: The 'Southwest Effect' Is Being Felt in Bellies, with Revenue Surging, Forwarders Praising," *Traffic World*, February 14, 2005, p. 30.

Maglitta, Joseph, "Lean, Mean Flying Machines," *Computerworld*, July 11, 1994.

Putnam, Howard D., *The Winds of Turbulence*, New York: Harper Business, 1991.

"Southwest: After Kelleher, More Blue Skies," *Business Week*, April 2, 2001, p. 45.

Southwest Airlines Co., *Southwest Airlines History*, Dallas: Southwest Airlines Co., 1991.

"SW CEO: Crisis Opens Door," *Business Travel News*, November 8, 2004, pp. 1+.

Taylor, John H., "Risk Taker," *Forbes*, November 14, 1988.

Troxell, Thomas N., Jr., "Deregulation in Stride," *Barton's*, January 23, 1984.

Walker, Karen, "The King of Low-Cost," *Airline Business*, June 1999, p. 38.

Weber, Joseph, "These Two Airlines Are Doing It Their Way," *Business Week*, September 21, 1987.

"Why Herb Kelleher Gets So Much Respect from Labor," *Business Week*, September 24, 1984.

Zellner, Wendy, "Dressed to Kill . . . Competitors," *Business Week*, February 21, 2005, p. 60.

——, "Striking Gold in the California Skies," *Business Week*, March 30, 1992.

Zellner, Wendy, and Michael Arndt, "Holding Steady; As Rivals Sputter, Can Southwest Stay on Top?," *Business Week*, February 3, 2003, p. 66.

—Elizabeth Rourke
—update: Frederick C. Ingram

Spacelabs Medical, Inc.

5150 20th Avenue, S.E.
Issaquah, Washington 98027
U.S.A.
Telephone: (425) 657-7200
Toll Free: (800) 522-7025
Fax: (425) 657-7212
Web site: http://www.spacelabs.com

Business Segment
Incorporated: 1958
Employees: 750
Sales: $242.1 million (2001)
NAIC: 334510 Electrical and Electrotherapeutic
   Apparatus Manufacturing; 339111 Laboratory
   Apparatus and Furniture Manufacturing; 339112
   Surgical and Medical Instrument Manufacturing;
   339113 Surgical Appliance and Supplies
   Manufacturing; 511210 Software Publishers

Spacelabs Medical, Inc., wholly owned by OSI Systems, Inc., is a leading global provider of patient monitoring systems for critical care, emergency, and perioperative areas. Its integrated solutions include wired and wireless networks, clinical information connectivity, ambulatory blood pressure monitors, and medical data servers.

1958–80s: NASA's Maker of Health Monitoring Systems Enters Acute Care World

Ben Ettelson and James A. Reeves founded Spacelabs in 1958 to collaborate with the U.S. Air Force to develop systems to monitor the vital signs of U.S. astronauts in space. On the historic four-day Gemini IV mission in 1965, astronauts James McDivitt and Edward White wore Spacelabs' gear so that NASA's mission control could monitor their temperature, respiration, and cardiac output.

In the mid-1960s, Spacelabs began to develop monitoring systems for hospitals, and by 1968, the company introduced its first ICU and CCU monitoring systems. From that time onward, the company broadened its scope beyond single, stand-alone patient monitors. During the late 1960s and early 1970s, it made significant advances, culminating in its first monitoring system to incorporate microprocessor technology. Spacelab's "Alpha" was the first modular monitor and the first to allow systems communication via a data bus. Another first occurred in 1979 that changed the direction of critical care monitoring when Spacelabs introduced a bedside arrhythmia detection monitoring module.

In 1980, Squibb acquired Spacelabs as part of a trend on the part of pharmaceutical companies to invest in medical electronic companies. These companies subscribed to the theory that pharmaceutical therapies were synergistic with diagnostic and monitoring businesses. Dennis C. Fill oversaw the creation of the Squibb Medical Systems Group and managed Advanced Technology Laboratories, Squibb Medical Systems, and Spacelabs Inc. In 1981, Spacelabs' sales exceeded $50 million, and the following year it moved its corporate offices from Chatsworth, California, to Redmond, Washington. In the early 1980s, it added significantly to its acute care product line with improvements to its patient data management systems, including noninvasive blood pressure and cardiac output measurement.

In the mid-1980s, the company introduced the Patient Care Management System (PCMS). Based on a completely new system architecture, PCMS allowed for the foundation of a hospital-wide integrated clinical information system and changed the course of patient monitoring with touchscreen controls, Ethernet communication, and "smart" modules that optimized system flexibility and upgradeability. The PCMS was still the industry's only system to integrate with other manufacturers' bedside devices through its bedside monitor.

However, Squibb soon discovered that diagnostic and monitoring equipment were not really synergistic with its pharmaceutical core business and spun off its medical electronics businesses in 1986 into a new company, Westmark International Inc., which was based in Washington state. Fill, who believed in the businesses that Squibb had acquired, left Squibb to head Westmark, which made and distributed diagnostic imaging systems and patient-monitoring systems. Spacelabs, which had grown steadily throughout the last ten years, topped $200 million in revenues by

Company Perspectives:

More time to care is the essence of every Spacelabs solution. Ask caregivers all over the world what is most important in providing the highest standard of care and their answer is the same: time with the patient. As hospitals around the globe are asked to achieve increasingly difficult objectives with tighter budgets, time for patient care grows even more precious. After many years of partnering with caregivers, Spacelabs understands caregivers' needs and consistently delivers these vital efficiencies: fast, accurate, comprehensible patient data; intuitive, easy-to-use monitors; anytime, anywhere access to monitoring information; flexible, open-system technology platforms.

Key Dates:

1958: Ettelson and Reeves found Spacelabs.
1968: Spacelabs introduces the first ICU and CCU monitoring systems.
1974: Spacelabs launches the first monitoring system to incorporate microprocessor technology.
1980: Squibb acquires Spacelabs.
1986: Spacelabs becomes part of Squibb Corp.'s Westmark International Inc.
1992: Westmark spins off Spacelabs, which begins trading under the symbol SLMD.
1995: Spacelabs purchases Consolidated Peritronics Medical, Inc.
1997: The company acquires Burdick and Advanced Medical Systems.
1998: Spacelabs acquires exclusive rights to market and distribute Medical Insight R & D's anesthesia delivery system.
2001: Spacelabs sells its headquarters building in Redmond, Washington.
2002: Spacelabs becomes a division of Instrumentarium, Finland's largest medical equipment maker; GE Medical Systems purchases Instrumentarium and acquires Spacelabs; Quinton Cardiology Systems buys Burdick from Spacelabs.
2004: OSI buys GE Medical Systems.

1991. In 1992, Westmark spun off Spacelabs under Carl A. Lombardi and began trading under the symbol SLMD.

1990s: Broadening Product Lines and International Reach

Throughout the late 1980s, Spacelabs expanded internationally, opening offices in England, Australia, France, and Germany, and, in the early 1990s, offices in Singapore, Hong Kong, and Austria. In 1990, it purchased First Medical Devices Corp., maker of semi-automatic heart defibrillators. The late 1990s saw further expansion with subsidiaries in Beijing and Mexico City and offices in Sweden, Belgium, Italy, Spain, India, and Taiwan. In 1995, Spacelabs also acquired a second company, Consolidated Peritronics Medical, Inc. This last acquisition added labor and delivery clinical information systems, including basic fetal surveillance software, to Spacelabs' offerings.

Spacelabs also continued to expand upon its own systems throughout the 1990s. In 1990, it introduced a compact version of its bedside monitor that allowed monitoring while transporting patients between care areas. In 1994, it brought out its Patient Care Information System (PCIS), which changed the monitoring network into an information network by integrating patient monitors at the patient bedside or at a central station with hospital information systems and resources. In 1995, the first bedside module for continuous cardiac output monitoring debuted as well as a portable monitor for wireless network monitoring. In 1996, the PCIS Physician Workstation Windows compatible software was developed to allow remote, continuous access to a networked patient's waveforms and clinical information via a computer and modem.

Spacelabs once again broadened its product line with strategic acquisitions in 1997. The company purchased Advanced Medical Systems, which expanded its perinatal product line, and Burdick, through which it staked a claim in the self-care and primary care markets. "Getting together with Burdick was a very good fit for us, filling in some of the markets we wanted to address," announced the company's chief executive officer, Carl A. Lombardi, in a 2000 *Repertoire* article. Burdick came with a distribution network, which complemented Spacelabs' own.

Spacelabs also signed an agreement in 1998 with Medical Insight R & D, B.V. for the exclusive rights to market and distribute Medical Insight's anesthesia delivery system. With this agreement in place, Spacelabs became able to offer a complete system for patient management, making it possible for data from anesthesia delivery and patient monitoring to be integrated into the consolidated patient record. Its next generation patient-monitoring platform, the Ultraview Care Network, which appeared in 1998, provided local and remote access to the patient's longitudinal records and allowed doctors to monitor readings from several stand-alone medical instruments at same time.

2000–04: Looking for a Buyer

Yet despite this growth, "[t]he adoption of electronic medical record technology has been slower than expected," Lombardi confessed in a 2000 *MDSI Repertoire* article. According to Lombardi, hospital staffers were preoccupied with Y2K and reimbursement issues. As a result, Spacelab's revenues of $300 million in 1999 amounted to only about $10 million in profits that year. In 2000, revenues decreased to $249 million with $4.7 million in losses. The downward trend continued in 2001 with revenues of $242 million and losses of $2.1 million. In addition, the company's stock price grew only two percentage points from 1992 to 2001, leading Spacelabs' largest shareholder, New York investment firm Tweedy, Browne Co. LLC, to press for a takeover. The company had, in November 2000, rebuffed a hostile takeover attempt when Cardiac Sciences of California offered to buy it for $143 million.

However, by 2002, after Lombardi announced his decision to retire, Spacelabs, faced with ongoing losses and with dramatic consolidation in its industry, began looking to sell itself. It had sold its headquarters building in Redmond, Washington, in 2001 for $80 and then leased back the space. In 2002, it shut down its printed circuit board manufacturing unit and switched to an outside manufacturer.

Finland's largest medical equipment maker, Instrumentarium, which had sales of $920 million in 2001, purchased Spacelabs for $140 million in 2002. As a division of Instrumentarium, Spacelabs continued to serve its U.S. customers directly through existing sales channels. In international sales of critical care systems, the Spacelabs Medical division began to cooperate closely with another division of Instrumentarium that specialized in anesthesia machines and nitric oxide devices, Datex-Ohmeda. With the purchase of both Datex-Ohmeda and Spacelabs, Instrumentarium became the world's largest manufacturer of anesthesia systems.

Later in 2002, two-year-old GE Medical Systems purchased Instrumentarium, acquiring both Datex-Ohmeda and Spacelabs as part of the $2.06 billion purchase. General Electric Co. had formed GE Medical Systems in 2000 as a stand-alone division to offer electronic record-keeping to hospitals. U.S. Justice Department officials, like their counterparts at the European Commission, approved the deal with the stipulation that General Electric divest itself of Spacelabs and a mobile x-ray product line and provide other makers of patient monitors with the information needed to interface with Spacelabs' equipment. General Electric also had to license its gas monitoring modules and other anesthesia supply machines for a period of several years to Spacelab's buyer in order to ensure the emergence of an effective competitor.

Spacelabs itself sold its Burdick acquisition, a division that mainly produced electrocardiographs and heart monitors, to Quinton Cardiology Systems for $24 million in 2002. The two companies set up a sales and marketing partnership to offer hospitals packaged deals on equipment purchases.

In January 2004, General Electric Co. found a buyer for Spacelabs in OSI Systems Inc. OSI agreed to pay $57 million for Spacelabs, which by that date had an installed base of about 100,000 patient monitoring units worldwide. Spacelabs' management was still confident that electronic medical records would find their way into healthcare and that these would improve the timing and accuracy of patient information.

Principal Competitors

Alaris Medical; Cerner; Datascope; GE [Medical Systems] Healthcare; McKesson; Philips Electronics; Siemens Medical Solutions.

Further Reading

Barrett, Rick, "General Electric's Planned Purchase of Finnish Medical Business Is Big Deal," *Knight Ridder Tribune Business News*, December 19, 2002, p. 1.

Dietrich, Heidi, "Spacelabs on the Block Once More," *Puget Sound Business Journal*, September 12, 2003.

Murray, Matt, and James Kanter, "GE's Deal for Instrumentarium Finally Is Cleared by EU Panel," *Wall Street Journal*, September 3, 2003, p. A8.

"Spacelabs Takes the Global View," *MDSI Repertoire*, February 2000, http://www.medicaldistribution.com/rep/Rep.

—Carrie Rothburd

Tecumseh Products Company

100 East Patterson Street
Tecumseh, Michigan 49286
U.S.A.
Telephone: (517) 423-8411
Fax: (517) 423-8760
Web site: http://www.tecumseh.com

Public Company
Incorporated: 1930 as Hillsdale Machine & Tool
  Company
Employees: 22,000
Sales: $1.91 billion (2004)
Stock Exchanges: NASDAQ
Ticker Symbols: TECUA; TECUB
NAIC: 326199 All Other Plastics Product Manufacturing;
  333415 Air-Conditioning and Warm Air Heating
  Equipment and Commercial and Industrial
  Refrigeration Equipment Manufacturing; 333618
  Other Engine Equipment Manufacturing; 333612
  Speed Changer, Industrial High-Speed Drive, and
  Gear Manufacturing; 333911 Pump and Pumping
  Equipment Manufacturing; 335312 Motor and
  Generator Manufacturing; 336312 Gasoline Engine
  and Engine Parts Manufacturing

Tecumseh Products Company manufactures compressors for refrigeration and air conditioning equipment, gasoline engines and automobile transmissions, and pumps and pumping equipment for industrial, commercial, and agricultural use. The second largest domestic manufacturer of engines for small tractors, snow blowers, and lawn mowers, the company is best known for its compressors, machines that compress refrigerants in air conditioners and refrigerators. The town of Tecumseh, Michigan, in which the company is headquartered, has since become known as the ''Refrigeration Capital of the World.''

An early 1990s public offering brought in new capital while allowing the founding Herrick family to retain control. The company has since moved to establish manufacturing hubs in Brazil and India while cutting back on U.S. production. Tecum-seh has acquired some suppliers and is attempting to make its brand more visible to consumers and contractors.

Company Founding in 1930

Tecumseh Products was founded by Ray W. Herrick, a master toolmaker who came to prominence in the 1920s in Michigan's growing auto industry. Herrick's reputation as a knowledgeable and highly skilled toolmaker led to his rapid advancement in the industry. He was given supervisory positions and became a friend and adviser to influential inventors and industrialists such as Henry Ford, Harvey Firestone, and Thomas Edison. In 1928 Herrick was asked to help turn around the struggling Alamo Engine Company in the southeastern Michigan town of Hillsdale, where he served until 1933 as factory manager and eventually as director of sales and production. The company continued to decline, however, and during this time Herrick and a local toolmaker named C.F. (Bill) Sage decided to launch a business of their own, incorporating as Hillsdale Machine & Tool Company in 1930.

The Hillsdale company manufactured high-quality automobile and electric refrigerator parts, as well as small tools and mechanical novelties. Also handling orders that Alamo could not fill, the Hillsdale company went from grossing $26,000 in sales during its first year of operation to $284,000 by 1933. Initially, two-thirds of the company's stock was owned by Sage and his wife, while Herrick owned the remaining third. By 1933, however, Herrick bought out most of their interest and gained control of the company.

Competition in the manufactured parts industry was fierce in 1933, and Hillsdale soon sought larger production facilities. When Alamo went into receivership that year, Herrick leased its plant for one year, hoping to purchase it at the end of the term. The rent paid to Alamo's receivers, however, cut into the Hillsdale company's profits. Furthermore, the Hillsdale company had been founded during the height of the Great Depression, and these early years were characterized by escalating debt and inadequate cash flow. By 1934, Herrick's company was close to bankruptcy.

That year, however, as a result of a concerted effort by Herrick, the Ford Motor Company, private investors, and the city of Tecumseh—located about 60 miles southwest of Detroit—Hillsdale Tool & Machine Company managed to raise a little more than $12,000, with which it acquired a 30,000-square-foot abandoned facility in Tecumseh. Changing the company's name to Tecumseh Products, Herrick had the building renovated, borrowed the necessary machinery, and soon began the mass production of automotive and refrigerator parts. The following year the company gained much needed cash flow leverage when Henry Ford helped Herrick secure a line of credit with a Detroit bank.

In 1936 Tecumseh Products began to focus on manufacturing the product on which its reputation would be built: the hermetically sealed refrigeration compressor. Five years earlier, Herrick had been approached by Frank Smith, an engineer interested in selling Herrick his compressor designs. At that time, Herrick had employed Smith as a machinist, agreeing to consider the prototypes that Smith was developing. Over the next few years, engineers Curtis Brown and Jens Touborg joined Smith, and the three eventually formed an engineering business known as Tresco. Tresco worked closely with Tecumseh Products, providing Herrick with designs for inexpensive and reliable refrigeration compressors that rivaled those of the major manufacturers. By the end of the 1930s, Tecumseh Products was producing more than 100,000 of these compressors a year.

At the onset of World War II, Herrick shifted the focus of Tecumseh Products to the manufacture of defense materials. The company continued to produce compressors, which had applications in military equipment, while also turning out anti-aircraft projectile casings and precision parts for aircraft engines. By 1942, Tecumseh was mainly producing 40-millimeter shell casings, which it supplied to the U.S. Navy. In April of that year the company received the Navy E award for excellence for

its contributions to the war effort; it received several similar awards before the war ended.

Postwar Air Conditioners

In 1945 Herrick's son, Kenneth G. Herrick, returned from the war and went to work for Tecumseh Products as the company resumed its focus on the production of compressors. During this time, competition in the industry intensified, with postwar demand for electric appliances, especially refrigerators, rising dramatically. Becoming known for the high quality of its compressors, as well as for their timely delivery, Tecumseh Products soon emerged as an industry leader. In 1947 a Tecumseh Products compressor was featured in the first window unit air conditioner for the home. By 1950, Tecumseh's sales reached $72 million, and the company was producing more than two million compressors a year.

Throughout the 1950s and 1960s Tecumseh Products sought to expand. First it increased its production capacity with the 1950 and 1952 purchases of Universal Cooler Corp. in Marion, Ohio, and the Acklin Stamping Company of Toledo, respectively. Also involved in finding new uses for its products, the company marketed an air conditioning compressor for automobiles in 1953. The following year, Tecumseh's sales reached $124 million, and in 1955 Herrick is reported to have paid nearly $5 million to purchase Tresco, the engineering business founded by Smith, Brown, and Touborg. At this time, Herrick brought Joseph E. Layton in from International Harvester to serve Tecumseh Products as president and chief executive officer. Herrick remained the company's chairperson.

Purchasing two Wisconsin companies in 1956 and 1957—the Lauson Engine Company of New Holstein and Power Products of Grafton—Tecumseh Products claimed two new divisions designated for the production of gasoline engines. These two acquisitions were provided with new, modern equipment and tools in order to begin production of compact, lightweight engines suitable for use in lawn and garden machinery. Also during this time the company began to establish licensees abroad, planning to one day market its products worldwide.

Establishment of a Canadian Subsidiary in 1960

In 1960 Tecumseh Products of Canada, Ltd. was formed as a sales distribution center for compressors manufactured in the United States. This facility was later expanded into a production facility to handle demand for compressors in Canada. Over the next decade the company acquired the Diecast Division of Sheboygan Falls, Wisconsin, and the Peerless Gear & Machine Company, which it designated as a separate division and provided with a new plant to manufacture transaxles, transmissions, and differentials for lawn and garden equipment. Furthermore, the company set up research and development laboratories at Purdue University and in Ann Arbor, Michigan, to support its divisions, employing scientists in the fields of chemistry and metallurgy, as well as mechanical and electrical engineers.

In 1964 Layton died unexpectedly, and William Hazelwood, a divisional vice-president, was named president of Tecumseh Products. Hazelwood remained in this position until 1966 when the 76-year-old Herrick gave up the chairmanship and, retaining a position for himself as vice-chairman, named his son Kenneth as president. Four years later Kenneth Herrick's son Todd came to work for Tecumseh Products. Kenneth ascended to chairman and CEO, and William MacBeth was named president. By this time the company had manufactured more than 100 million compressors and 25 million small engines.

In 1973 Ray Herrick died. Under Kenneth Herrick, Tecumseh Products built compressor and engine plants in Kentucky, Tennessee, and Mississippi, while continuing to add to its product line. For example, the company acquired M.P. Pumps, Inc., of Detroit, which produced pumps used in agricultural, industrial, and marine environments. Submersible pumps, used as sump pumps and in large cooling systems, were introduced in 1980, with the company's purchase of the Little Giant Pump Company in Oklahoma.

International in the 1980s and 1990s

Tecumseh Products sought to become an international company in the 1980s, and, over the next ten years, foreign sales, both from exports and through European acquisitions, rose to 15 percent of the company's total sales revenues. In 1981 Tecumseh Products entered into a joint venture with the Italian Fiat Settori Componenti, which resulted in the formation of Tecnamotor S.p.A., a manufacturer and marketer of engines for outdoor power equipment. The following year Tecumseh Products increased its holdings in the Sociade Intercontinental de Compressores Hermeticos SICOM, S.A. SICOM was based in Sao Paulo, Brazil, and served world markets through its manufacture of compressors. Tecumseh Products was further able to form a strong European interest through a 1985 joint venture with L'Unite Hermetique S.A. in Paris, a compressor manufacturer and exporter that Tecumseh Products eventually acquired as a subsidiary. The company's expansion into the international market had mixed results. It gained market share and enjoyed financial success, particularly in the engine sales of Tecnamotor, of which it acquired 100 percent ownership in 1989. This new subsidiary went on to become the largest engine manufacturer of its kind in Europe. Nevertheless, the company experienced a sharp decline in earnings during the late 1980s, which it attributed to the undervalued American dollar and delays in new product development.

In the United States, foreign competition in the production of refrigeration components intensified during the late 1980s and early 1990s. Tecumseh Products, though, continued to experience growth. In 1987 the company introduced a new line of air conditioning compressors for residential use, designed to be both quieter and more energy efficient in compliance with the federal government's National Appliance Energy Conservation Act. In 1989 air conditioning compressors were bolstered by a nationwide heat wave, and the company's net income rose to $82 million, up from $70 million the year before.

The company's interest in some foreign markets, however, suffered due to political instabilities during this time, particularly in China, where compressor sales fell almost to zero during the Tiananmen Square riots, as well as in the Middle East, where export sales were threatened by the Persian Gulf War. In 1992 Tecumseh was given an E Star award by the U.S. Department of Commerce for its commitment to international markets during these difficult times.

As Tecumseh Products entered the 1990s, it featured a broad range of products in several divisions. Refrigeration products, which accounted for more than half of its total sales, included compressors sold to the manufacturers of home cooling systems and appliances, water coolers, vending machines, and refrigerated display cases. Engine products mainly featured aluminum diecast engines of 2 to 12 horsepower used in machinery for both home lawn maintenance and farming. Power train products included transmissions, transaxles, and differentials produced for lawn and garden equipment as well as for recreational vehicles. The pump products division featured a variety of pumps made from cast iron, aluminum, stainless steel, or brass, capable of pumping up to 300 gallons per minute, while the company's submersible pumps division produced pumps for use in clothes washers and carpet cleaners as well as kidney dialysis machines.

In 1992 the company faced a new series of federal regulations designed to protect the environment by imposing restrictions on compressor and engine emissions and banning altogether chlorofluorocarbons (CFCs), which were widely used in refrigeration. As the ban on CFCs neared implementation in the mid-1990s, Tecumseh Products began converting its compressors to operate on alternative refrigerants, which, the company asserted, were available but costly. Furthermore, in joint efforts with the Environmental Protection Agency (EPA), Tecumseh Products researched possible improvements to the engine manufacturing process that would lead to less harmful emissions, and also developed new techniques for treating and disposing of contaminated sediments resulting from dangerous industrial wastes being dumped into rivers.

New Capital in 1992

Financially, in March 1992 the stockholders of Tecumseh Products approved a proposal to reclassify its existing shares as voting Class B stock, while creating a new class of nonvoting Class A common stock. The stockholders were issued one share of the Class A stock for each share they already owned. At the time, Edward Wyatt observed in *Barron's* that ''because 45%

of the equity currently outstanding is owned by members of the founding Herrick family, the stock plan will allow them to retain their voting rights while effectively splitting the stock 2-for-1.'' He also observed that the new plan would probably induce analysts to follow the fortunes of Tecumseh Products more closely.

By this time the founding Herrick family had had four generations involved in Tecumseh's management. In 1994, CEO Todd Herrick told *Financial World* the credo of his grandfather that still guided the company: ''We believe in God, we mind our business and we work like hell.''

In the mid-1990s, Tecumseh had revenues of about $2 billion and 15,000 employees. The company was developing its versions of the new, energy-efficient scroll compressors that were beginning to replace traditional reciprocating compressors in the air conditioning industry.

Tecumseh opened a new plant in Georgia in 1995 and a 200,000-square-foot factory in Corinth, Mississippi, in 1997. The latter's initial product was an electric motor for air conditioner compressors that had previously been sourced in Singapore.

The company also was expanding abroad, entering a joint venture with the Shriram Group to set up a plant in Hyderabad, India. It later bought out its partner there and acquired a refrigerator compressor factory near New Delhi from Whirlpool of India.

The company began promoting its brand directly to consumers. It aired ads urging them to look for its motors when they bought snow throwers, a market in which Tecumseh held a lead over rival Briggs & Stratton Corp., which led the lawn mower market.

Restructuring for the New Millennium

Sales were $1.65 billion in 2000. The company's three business segments were each profitable. Strong Brazilian operations saved the Compressor Business, while operations in India were affected by start-up costs and work stoppages. The Engine & Power Train Business had slowed after a Y2K-inspired run on generators the previous year. The smallest unit, the Pump Business, was growing on the popularity of water gardening and industrial sales. During the year, the company entered the residential wastewater collection, transfer, and disposal market through the purchase of the assets of Interon Corporation.

Tecumseh cut 900 jobs in a 2000 restructuring that closed a plant in Somerset, Kentucky. Another 600 were being cut at an Indian factory. The company was expanding its operations in Mississippi, however.

According to one report, Tecumseh controlled 20 percent of the world market for small engines. It was growing its business in Europe, where it was dominant, with a 25 percent market share. Europe made up nearly 40 percent of the world market and was expected to grow due to the opening of Eastern Europe. Tecumseh acquired its Czech carburetor supplier, Motoco, from Motor Jikov in May 2001. Tecumseh had other European operations, including joint ventures and a subsidiary in France.

Tecumseh's subsidiary in India, Tecumseh Products India Ltd. (TPIL), was starting to export to South Africa and West Asia. The Indian market itself was ripe for development, with relatively few owning refrigerators or air conditioners. Tecumseh's plants in India produced compressor components as well as completed units.

Tecumseh acquired a supplier of manufacturing software, Manufacturing Data Systems, Inc. (MDSI), in 2002. The next year, it bought FASCO Motors, Invensys PLC's electric motor operations, for $415 million. FASCO formed the basis of a new business segment, Electrical Components.

Company officials told *Contracting Business* that although Tecumseh had enjoyed a relatively low profile in the past, it was becoming more retail-oriented. It leveraged its expertise in compressors to products such as drinking water systems and cooling towers through its ''Cool Products'' line. Tecumseh's products were distributed through 130 distribution centers and 1,700 outlets in the United States. Tecumseh was phasing out its U.S. manufacturing due to price pressure from customers. The company managed net income of $10 million on sales of $1.9 billion in 2004.

Principal Subsidiaries

Evergy, Inc.; FASCO Australia Pty. Ltd.; FASCO Industries, Inc.; FASCO Motors, Ltd. (Thailand); Little Giant Pump Company; Masterflux; Manufacturing Data Systems, Inc.; Motoco a.s. (Czech Republic); M.P. Pumps, Inc.; Tecumotor/Evergy; Tecumseh do Brasil, Ltda.; Tecumseh Compressor Company; Tecumseh Europa, S.p.A. (Italy); Tecumseh France S.A.; Tecumseh Power Company; Tecumseh Products Company of Canada, Ltd.; Tecumseh Products India Ltd.; TMT Motoco, Ltd. (Brazil).

Principal Divisions

Compressors; Engines & Power Trains; Pumps; Electrical Components.

Principal Competitors

Briggs & Stratton Corporation; Bristol Compressors, Inc.; Copeland Corporation; Matsushita Electric Industrial Corporation.

Further Reading

Content, Thomas, ''Tecumseh Agrees to Superfund Cleanup,'' *Milwaukee Journal Sentinel,* May 8, 2003, p. 3B.

Dawson, John Harper, *A Biography of Ray W. Herrick,* Adrian, Mich.: Lenawee County Historical Society, Inc., 1984.

Dundas, Bill, ''Prototyping Productivity,'' *Modern Machine Shop,* May 2003, p. 80.

Hajewski, Doris, ''Snow Thrower Commercials: Tecumseh Turns to TV,'' *Milwaukee Journal Sentinel,* Bus. Sec., November 27, 1997, p. 1.

Harris, William B., ''Little, Big-Rich Tecumseh,'' *Fortune,* July 1955, p. 98.

Kaushik, Neha, ''Tecumseh to Make India Export Hub,'' *Businessline* (Chennai, India), January 9, 2003, p. 1.

Kumar, V. Rishi, ''Tecumseh India on Broadbase Street,'' *Businessline* (Chennai, India), December 8, 2001, p. 1.

"Old Secret—New Approach," *Contracting Business* (Cleveland), January 2003, pp. 54+.

Paulk, Michael, "Expansion Nets 700 New Jobs," *Memphis Business Journal*, May 12, 2000, p. 1.

Reingold, Jennifer, "Unchanged Melody," *Financial World*, April 26, 1994, pp. 40+.

Richards, J., "EPA and Tecumseh Products Conduct Joint PCB Study," *Northeastern Wisconsin Business Review*, September 1992, p. 6.

Schuyler, David, "Briggs, Tecumseh Vie to Wear European Crown," *Business Journal* (Milwaukee), May 26, 2000, p. 24.

Serwer, Andy, "Ever Heard of Tecumseh?," *Fortune*, April 5, 2004, p. 156.

Sheffield, Christopher, "Tecumseh Announces $40 Million Expansion," *Mississippi Business Journal*, October 21, 1996, p. 1.

"Tecumseh Acquires Motoco," *Access Czech Republic Business Bulletin,* May 15, 2001, p. S10.

"Tecumseh Plans Exports to S. Africa, West Asia," *Businessline* (Chennai, India), April 18, 2001, p. 1.

"Tecumseh Products Co.," *Journal of Commerce,* August 14, 1992.

"Tecumseh Products Says It Will Lay Off 1,500 Workers," *New York Times,* April 26, 2000, p. C4.

"Tecumseh: Relocating to India," *Appliance,* November 2002, p. 22.

"Tecumseh to Move Production Out of US," *New York Times,* April 9, 2003, p. C4.

Wyatt, Edward A., "Here Comes Tecumseh: Renewed Earnings Surge Appears in the Works," *Barron's,* March 2, 1992, pp. 17, 22–24.

—Tina Grant
—update: Frederick C. Ingram

TransPro, Inc.

100 Gando Drive
New Haven, Connecticut 06513
U.S.A.
Telephone: (203) 401-6450
Fax: (203) 401-6470
Web site: http://www.transpro.com

Public Company
Incorporated: 1995
Employees: 1,545
Sales: $268.1 million (2004)
Stock Exchanges: American
Ticker Symbol: TPR
NAIC: 336399 All Other Motor Vehicle Parts
    Manufacturing

TransPro, Inc. manufactures and distributes heat transfer and temperature control products for automobiles, light- and heavy-duty trucks, as well as industrial applications, with the business divided between two business groups. The Automotive and Light Truck Strategic Business Group manufactures aftermarket automotive heating, cooling, and air-conditioning products sold to auto parts retailers (such as AutoZone and Pep Boys), wholesalers, and radiator shops. Brands include Ready-Aire Heater Cores, Ready-Rad Radiators, and a complete line of Ready-Aire Temperature Control Products. The Heavy Duty Strategic Business Group sells aftermarket products—complete truck radiators, radiator cores, engine cooling systems, and charge air coolers—for on-highway, off-highway, and industrial applications. Until 2005 the group also manufactured original equipment, but TransPro sold this aspect of the group to concentrate on the aftermarket. In a related deal, TransPro padded its aftermarket business, adding locomotive and military equipment as new markets, and gained international scope by adding plants in Mexico and Europe. Domestically, the company operates production facilities in Connecticut, New York, and Texas, and regional facilities in California, Colorado, Connecticut, Florida, Georgia, Illinois, Ohio, Texas, and Washing-

ton. TransPro maintains its headquarters in New Haven, Connecticut, and its stock trades on the American Stock Exchange.

Roots Reaching Back to the 1920s

Although TransPro was launched in 1995 as a spinoff from The Allen Group Inc., its heritage dates to the 1928 incorporation of Allen Electric & Equipment Company. Over the next four decades Allen picked up dozens of unrelated assets, transforming itself into an unwieldy conglomerate. Subsidiaries manufactured portable steel buildings, car-wash equipment, hydraulic activators for submarines, chain conveyor belts for factories, military electronics, and aftermarket automobile test equipment. In 1968, Walter B. Kissinger joined the board of the Chicago-based company and proceeded to bring some order to Allen's chaotic affairs. Now overshadowed by his world-famous older brother, diplomat Henry Kissinger, at the time Walter, an accomplished corporate turnaround artist, was actually better known.

In 1938, when he was just 14 years old, Walter and his family fled Nazi Germany to England and then the United States, settling in New York City, where he and his brother attended high school. Both brothers joined the U.S. military during World War II, with Henry assigned to the European theater and Walter to the Pacific. Henry, who had been studying accounting before the war, became involved with Army intelligence, the first step in his diplomatic career. Ironically, Walter aspired to become a diplomat and ended up a businessman. After his stint in the military he enrolled at Princeton's Woodrow Wilson School of Public and International Affairs. In another stroke of irony, his 1951 senior thesis broached the possibility of Detente between the United States and China, an idea his brother would introduce to the Nixon White House two decades later. But the mood of Washington during the early 1950s, characterized by the Communist witch hunts and rise of Senator Eugene McCarthy, disillusioned Walter Kissinger about government service. Instead, he opted to enter Harvard Business School. After becoming quickly disenchanted with a job at a large corporation, Kissinger in 1957 took over a failed small electronics company, Advanced Vacuum Products. He built up the business, sold it to a larger company, and at the age of 38 was wealthy enough to retire. Instead he took on a new challenge in the 1960s, turning around an auto parts maker, Jervis Corp. He successfully narrowed its focus to car mirrors and again walked away with a sizable sum of money. His next stop was the Allen Group board.

Because of Kissinger's intervention, Allen dismissed the investment bankers who were responsible for many of the company's misguided acquisitions, and pulled the plug on an R&D project, a diagnostic computer for auto engines intended to be sold to repair shops. Kissinger recognized it as a concept far ahead of the market, one that was draining cash with no hope of a return. Kissinger's efforts in sorting out Allen's tangled business affairs were appreciated by his fellow board members, who convinced him to take over as chief executive officer. He agreed, but only if certain directors were axed and Allen's headquarters were relocated to Long Island, where he resided along with his stable of prized Arabian horses.

Once in charge of Allen, Kissinger cleaned house, casting off 40 operations that accounted for $190 million in annual sales, opting instead to concentrate on some of the assets relating to the automotive industry. His primary goal was to be the number one or number two company in whatever business Allen elected to stay in. He kept Crown Steel Products Co., which performed pickup truck conversions and installed specialized interiors in utility trucks and vans for fleets, as well as making metal parts for light trucks. He also kept the money-losing automobile test-equipment division, dumped its management team, and turned it around. Kissinger added to the automotive assets in 1970, acquiring G&O Manufacturing Company, a New Haven, Connecticut-based radiator maker. G&O was founded in 1915 by Charles Oppe and Frederick Gargiulio. It started out making custom-built automobile radiators, but as car manufacturing moved increasingly to Detroit the company turned its attention to truck radiators and, later, airplane radiators.

Another venture Kissinger kept was the car wash equipment company, but in the wake of the energy crisis in the early 1970s, he exited this business as well. Many service stations had been offering free car washes as a way to boost gas sales, but with drivers now lining up for blocks for a chance to fill their tanks, there was little need for such incentives. Another unit sold auto accessories, ranging from mag wheels to Snoopy key rings, a successful area for Allen until the early 1980s when cheap competition from the Far East destroyed the market. Allen also operated a Mobile Communications division, producing antennas for two-way radio communication, used by truckers and the police. With the citizens band (CB) craze of the mid-1970s, this unit experienced a splash of success before the market dried up. After a few years of losses, the unit began to rebound in the 1980s with the rise of cellular mobile telecommunications, which unlike CB radios proved to be a long-term growth area.

Allen achieved record profits in 1985, and then suffered through two money-losing years. Despite the losses, Allen continued to invest a great deal of money on research and development, a strategy that paid off in the long run but in the short term cost Kissinger his job in 1988. Two of the successful sectors were replacement automobile radiators and the mobile communications division. In the early 1990s, Allen moved its headquarters to Cleveland and began focusing on these two areas. Taking advantage of its car telephone antenna business, Allen expanded further into the quickly growing cellular communications field, offering products such as antennas, filters, repeaters, and power amplifiers that allowed cellular providers to cut back on the number of stations needed to service a territory. On the automotive side, in 1990 Allen established GO/DAN Industries (GDI), a joint venture that manufactured aftermarket automotive heat transfer products.

In March 1995 the Federal Communications Commission sold 99 licenses for the development of wireless communications networks, an event that was a boon to Allen and its two mobile communications subsidiaries. One of them, Comsearch, offered software that the license holders needed to develop a frequency and determine the location of transmission stations when designing a system. The other subsidiary, Allen Telecom Group, also expected higher demand for its antennas, filters, and amplifiers. Already, the wireless communications business was contributing about 64 percent of Allen's $330 million in annual revenues. It was not surprising, therefore, that management decided it was in the best interest of both businesses to split and go their separate ways.

Allen Group's Spinoff of TransPro in 1995

In June 1995 Allen announced that it would spin off its automotive and truck product units in order to concentrate on the growing wireless communication business. The new company, taking the name of TransPro, Inc., was incorporated in Delaware in July 1995. It was composed of three Allen businesses: the Crown metal fabrication unit (which in addition to its automotive work would continue to fabricate cabinets for the telecommunications industry); G&O Manufacturing Company, maker of heat transfer products for trucks; and GDI, whose joint venture partner Allen bought out before spinning off TransPro. Pro forma sales for these businesses in 1995 totaled $247.3 million.

TransPro established its headquarters in New Haven, Connecticut, where GDI was based, and GDI's CEO, Henry P. McHale, took charge of the newly independent company. The first major step in growing TransPro was the 1996 $5.2 million purchase of Los Angeles-based Rahn Industries Inc., a deal that added aftermarket automotive air-conditioning components, such as condensers and evaporators, to TransPro's product offerings. Rahn also produced tube and fin heat exchangers for industrial applications. Next, in December 1997 TransPro paid $1 million for Vehicle Management Systems Inc. (VMS), a Canadian company that specialized in utility van conversions. TransPro added to its automotive air-conditioning parts business with the 1998 acquisition of Evap Inc., an Arlington, Texas-based manufacturer of the Ready Aire line of aftermarket automotive temperature control products. Several months later, in February 1999, TransPro paid $2.25 million to pick up another Arlington company, A/C Plus, Inc., a remanufacturer of air-conditioning compressors.

Key Dates:

1928: Allen Electric & Equipment Co. is formed.
1969: CEO Walter Kissinger begins to concentrate on automotive products.
1972: Allen Electric changes its name to Allen Group.
1995: Allen spins off automotive assets, forming TransPro.
1999: A/C Plus is acquired.
2000: The Crown division is sold.
2004: The aftermarket business of Modine Manufacturing Company is acquired, and the heavy-duty OEM business is sold to Modine.

In 1997 TransPro recorded revenues of $288.9 million and net income of $7.9 million. While Rahn, VMS, and Evap made a significant contribution to the balance sheet in 1998, it was not enough to offset the loss of a major contract with Ford to perform cab conversions. As a result, sales in 1998 declined 17 percent to $240.1 million, and net income dropped to $1.6 million. TransPro took steps in 1999 to devote more resources to the automotive aftermarket, in particular air-conditioning parts. It began the development of a 223,000-square-foot state-of-the-art plant in the Dallas area to remanufacture car air-conditioning compressors, and also hired an investment bank, Minneapolis-based Goldsmith Agio Helms, to help it sell off the Crown and G&O units. The proceeds were earmarked to pay down debt, thus allowing TransPro to borrow additional funds for further strategic acquisitions. In 1999 TransPro also closed a pair of plants located in Philadelphia, Pennsylvania, and Atlanta, Georgia, moving their condenser manufacturing operations to a new manufacturing line in Mexico. For the year, TransPro regained much of the losses suffered in 1998, increasing sales 9 percent to $261.6 million, resulting in a profit of $6.8 million.

Divesting the Crown Division in 2000

TransPro found a buyer for Crown in April 2000 when Legett & Platt Inc. agreed to pay $28.6 million in cash and assume $8.9 million of debt to acquire the unit. On other fronts, however, TransPro was not faring as well in 2000. During the first half of the year sales of aftermarket heating and cooling products dropped off, the result according to the company of moderate weather in the Northeast and upper Midwest and customers' high inventory levels. A few weeks after reporting disappointing second quarter numbers, TransPro announced that it would not meet estimates for the rest of the year and was suspending its quarterly cash dividend. Subsequently, McHale resigned as president and CEO, leaving the board as well, to "pursue other opportunities," his departure slated for the end of the year. The company immediately began a search for his replacement. In February 2001, concurrent with the announcement of the company's 2000 results, McHale's successor was named, 54-year-old Charles E. Johnson, a former Allen Group executive with extensive experience in the automotive aftermarket. Johnson had served as president of the Equion Corporation, maker of aftermarket and OEM heating and cooling systems, and prior to taking over at TransPro had been CEO of Canadian General Tower, which made polymer films and composite materials to the automotive and other markets.

Johnson took over at a time when a softening economy and mild weather combined to hinder TransPro's efforts to improve its balance sheet. Nevertheless, he took a number of steps to help turn around the company. He divided the business into three strategic business units: the automotive and light truck aftermarket; heavy-duty products; and air-conditioning replacement parts. This organization would be later refined, resulting in the current pair of business units. The company also implemented more stringent controls on inventory levels, aided by the installation of uniform inventory information systems; began manufacturing some parts it had outsourced; closed a California condenser plant and transferred most of the production to the less expensive Mexico operation; and established a new hub-and-spoke distribution system that allowed the company to close down two branches while lowering costs and improving service.

Following the divestiture of Crown, Transpro reported sales of $203.3 million in 2000 and 2001, and net losses of $9.2 million and $20.8 million, respectively. The changes Johnson initiated began to bear fruit in 2002, as TransPro increased revenues by 13.4 percent to $230.6 million and returned to profitability, netting nearly $2 million. The company was strong enough that at the end of the year it was able to acquire the assets of Fedco Automotive Components Company, a Buffalo, New York-based company that manufactured OEM and aftermarket automotive and truck heaters. To finance the deal, TransPro relied on its newly restructured and increased line of credit that afforded greater latitude in the way management grew the company.

On the balance sheet, TransPro took a step back in 2003, with revenues dropping slightly to $228.7 million, the result of the company phasing out some OEM customer programs, mild weather, and a soft industrial market that adversely impacted the heavy-duty aftermarket unit. As a result the company lost $4.5 million. The heavy-duty unit bounced back in 2004, adding more than $20 million in sales over the previous year and leading the way to an overall 17.2 percent gain in revenues to $268.1 million, coupled with net income of nearly $5.2 million.

Still facing challenging conditions—rising interest rates, increasing fuel and raw material costs, and stiff competition resulting in lower prices and tight margins—TransPro elected to focus its efforts on the aftermarket. In the fall of 2004 it agreed to acquire the aftermarket business of Wisconsin-based Modine Manufacturing Company, to be spun off from Modine and then merged with TransPro. The deal brought with it manufacturing and distribution operations in Europe and Mexico. At the same time, TransPro sold to Modine its heavy-duty OEM business for $17 million. The transaction closed in 2005, a year in which TransPro continued to tweak its operations, opening a new distribution facility in Southaven, Mississippi, while closing an acquired Fedco plant in Buffalo and moving heater production to Mexico. Whether these changes would have the desired effect remained an unanswered question.

Principal Subsidiaries

G&O Manufacturing Company, Inc.; GO/DAN Industries, Inc.; TransPro, Inc. de Mexico, S.A. de C.V.; Radiadores GDI, S.A. de C.V.; Ready Aires, Inc.

Principal Competitors

Delphi Corporation; Lennox International Inc.; Standard Motor Products, Inc.

Further Reading

Berkowitz, Harry, ''How a Chairman Made Allen Regroup,'' *Newsday,* October 27, 1986, p. 3.

Gordon, Mitchell, ''Shifting into High Gear,'' *Barron's National Business and Financial Weekly,* October 19, 1981, p. 50.

Higgins, Steve, ''New Haven, Conn.-Based Heating, Cooling Firm's Profits Rise 24 Percent,'' *New Haven Register,* August 17, 2004.

———, ''New Haven, Conn.-Based Manufacturer Gains Auto Part Firm's Aftermarket Business,'' *New Haven Register,* October 30, 2004.

Jaffe, Thomas, ''Tow Truck on the Way?,'' *Forbes,* April 4, 1988, p. 154.

Kraar, Louis, 'The Younger, Richer Kissinger,'' *Fortune,* February 8, 1982, p. 90.

Talley, Karen, ''Allen Group in a Growth Period,'' *Long Island Business News,* August 20, 1990, p. 1.

—Ed Dinger

Trex Company, Inc.

160 Exeter Drive
Winchester, Virginia 22603
U.S.A.
Telephone: (540) 542-6300
Toll Free: (800) 289-8739
Fax: (540) 542-6885
Web site: http://www.trex.com

Public Company
Incorporated: 1998
Employees: 615
Sales: $253.6 million (2004)
Stock Exchanges: New York
Ticker Symbol: TWP
NAIC: 326122 Plastics Pipe and Pipe Fitting Manufacturing

Trex Company, Inc. manufactures decking and railing using a combination of reclaimed wood and recycled plastic. The company's decking is sold under the Trex brand in three varieties, Trex Origins, Trex Accents, and Trex Brasilia. Its railing systems are sold in three varieties as well, a Traditional Series, an Artisan Series, and a Trex Designer Series. The company's products are manufactured at plants in Winchester, Virginia; Fernley, Nevada; and Olive Branch, Mississippi. Trex materials are sold at more than 3,300 contractor-oriented lumberyards in the United States and Canada. The company's products are also available at Home Depot stores, either directly or via special order, throughout the United States.

Origins

Roger Wittenberg never claimed to be motivated by a need to protect the environment, but his entrepreneurial career reflected a concern for just that. "Recycling is the best way I know to make money," he said in a June 1, 2003 interview with *FSB,* shrugging off the label of an environmentalist. Wittenberg, an organic chemist by training, made his living by using the waste of others to produce marketable products, something he did with his first company, which converted scrap metal into parts for knitting machinery. His next venture found a use for old baked goods, which were used to make poultry feed and

sold to companies such as Perdue and Polly Farms. Wittenberg's poultry-feed business provided the inspiration for another business, a bread-crumb business that, in turn, helped spawn Trex. To make bread crumbs, which were sold to food companies such as Progresso and 4-C, Wittenberg pulverized 20-tractor loads of unwanted bread loaves on a daily basis, a production process that produced a prodigious amount of its own waste: the plastic bags holding the bread loaves. Wittenberg quickly became awash in plastic bags, prompting him to search for a remedy to his problem. The solution became Trex.

Wittenberg, ever ready to find a use for what others no longer wanted, began experimenting with his mounds of plastic bags. He discovered that if he shredded the plastic and mixed it with sawdust, the result, after heating the mixture and pressing it through a die, produced something similar in appearance to wood but superior to wood in numerous ways. "It's like making a great big strand of spaghetti," he remarked in his interview with *FSB.* Wittenberg perfected his production process in 1988, calling his recycled material Rivenite, a product he believed would perform well as a substitute for fire logs. Rivenite, however, did not burn easily, so Wittenberg thought of other uses for his material, briefly entertaining the idea of making park benches out of Rivenite before abandoning the plan because the market for park benches was too small. Wittenberg's company, Rivenite Corp., eked out a living while its founder searched for a suitable application for the material, selling Rivenite to customers who used it for industrial flooring.

Acquired by Mobil: 1992

Wittenberg's business was small, but his reclaimed polyethylene and wood composite caught the attention of one of the largest companies in the world. Mobil Corporation, through its Mobil Chemical Co. subsidiary, owned the largest plastics operation in the United States, a business that accumulated vast amounts of recycled plastic. As the owner of Hefty, the company also ranked as the largest producer of disposable plastic products in the country. During the early 1990s, the company was searching for a way to commercialize its recycled plastic and it came across Wittenberg's Rivenite Corp. Mobil paid $10 million to acquire Rivenite in 1992, hiring Wittenberg in the process. The company used the acquisition to form its Compos-

Key Dates:

1988: Roger Wittenberg combines sawdust and shredded plastic bags, creating a material he calls Rivenite.
1992: Mobil Chemical Co. acquires Wittenberg's technology and re-brands the material Timbrex.
1994: Mobil focuses on the residential decking market, changing the name of the composite to Trex as part of the new market orientation.
1996: Four Mobil executives complete a leveraged buyout of the decking assets.
1999: Trex completes its initial public offering (IPO) of stock and opens a second manufacturing facility in Fernley, Nevada.
2004: Construction begins on a third manufacturing facility in Olive Branch, Mississippi.

ite Products Division, attempting to find a synergy connection between waste and a commercial product that mirrored Wittenberg's business philosophy. Initially, Mobil's management experienced the same dilemma that had confronted Wittenberg: company executives struggled to find a suitable application for the technology they had acquired. Mobil officials experimented with different uses for Rivenite, making noise barriers, constructing stop-sign posts, and manufacturing picnic tables. Eventually, the company settled on using Rivenite as a material for residential and commercial decking, a decision that positioned Wittenberg's creation in a $2 billion market.

Rivenite was re-branded as Timbrex under Mobil's control, making its debut as material used in municipal, government, and commercial projects. A production plant was constructed in Winchester, Virginia, to produce the material, yielding the first batch of planks branded under the name Timbrex. After being used by municipalities and, notably, to build walking trails in the Florida Everglades, Timbrex gained exposure, prompting Mobil executives to focus on the market for residential construction in 1994. The name of the material was shortened to Trex in anticipation of the concentration on residential decking, a move that also was supported by a program touting the benefits of using Trex, a message directed at home-builders and contractors. Trex decking was roughly twice the cost of traditional southern yellow pine, but Trex required almost no maintenance. Wittenberg's material did not need to be sealed. It was immune to rot, did not split or splinter, and termites found nothing appetizing about a mash of plastic and sawdust. Mobil backed an effort to preach the advantages of Trex to its targeted audience, placing educational advertisements in trade publications read by contractors and dispatching a sales force to building-supply distributors and professional lumberyards. By the end of 1994, Trex had won nearly $8 million worth of orders, exponentially higher than the $600,000 the Timbrex brand attracted two years earlier.

Independence in 1996

Trex showed promise under Mobil's control, but the business did not have the chance to fully express its potential as a tiny component of a multibillion-dollar company. The brand's greatest success was achieved when it gained independence.

Independence arrived after Mobil divested its plastics business, which lessened the company's interest in Trex. In 1996, four Mobil executives, including Wittenberg and Robert Matheny, who would serve as Trex's chief executive officer, completed a leveraged buyout of the decking assets, paying $29.5 million to gain control of a company they named Trex Company, LLC. Matheny, a 26-year Mobil veteran and the general manager of the Composite Products Division, immediately launched a promotional program to increase awareness of Trex. Advertisements were placed in magazines such as *Southern Living* and *Better Homes and Gardens*, as the company sought to develop brand identification in a market largely devoid of brand names.

Once on its own, Trex began to record remarkable growth. Trex's most pressing perennial problem was keeping up with the demand for its decking material, a problem that would hound the company during its first decade as a separate entity. To help finance expansion, the company began preparing for an initial public offering (IPO) of stock, taking its first step in September 1998, when Trex Company Inc. was formed to acquire Trex Company, LLC. In December 1998, with its IPO slated for the following spring, the company announced it had acquired a 37-acre parcel of land in Fernley, Nevada, where it planned to build a new, 150,000-square-foot manufacturing facility. The new plant, expected to open in the fall of 1999, promised to increase manufacturing capacity by more than 25 percent and relieve some of the strain at the company's Winchester plant, which was being inundated with orders for Trex decking. The number of lumberyards carrying Trex had increased dramatically in the space of a few years, growing from 500 in 1995 to more than 2,000 in 1998, pushing the Winchester facility to its limits.

On April 7, 1999, Trex Company, Inc. acquired the limited liability company Trex Company, LLC, and organized the acquisition as its wholly owned subsidiary. One week later, Trex Company, Inc. completed its IPO, giving it the financial resources to fund a high-profile print advertising campaign and to help pay for the Fernley plant. The new plant opened before the end of the year, a year in which Trex sales reached $78 million, or more than twice the total collected two years earlier. The company by this point ranked as the largest manufacturer of non-wood decking in the United States, dominating a highly fragmented industry. The company competed against roughly 20 other non-wood decking companies, but less than half of its rivals generated more than $5 million in annual sales.

Trex management began discussing the establishment of a third manufacturing plant almost immediately after opening the Fernley plant. In May 2000, the company announced it would not build a third plant, but in February 2001 the company renewed its commitment to constructing another facility, announcing it had signed a purchase agreement for 100 acres in Knoxville, Tennessee. Plans for the Knoxville plant were dropped, however, after the costs projected for the construction ran too high. Finally, in early 2004, the company made good on its promise to build a third manufacturing facility, selecting a site in Olive Branch, Mississippi, to help meet escalating demand for Trex products, which had increased 30 percent each year for the previous five years. In a February 2, 2004 interview with the *Mississippi Business Journal*, Matheny commented on the addition of a third facility. "The Olive Branch site," he said, "offers many of the attributes we have been seeking—an ideal transportation center, an excellent local workforce, and favorable access to raw materials. It will also help us control the various components of our costs, including raw materials. We plan to build the new facility out gradually, in step with our marketing plan, and expect to grow it substantially over time.''

Robust Growth in the 21st Century

As Trex went back and forth with the establishment of a third manufacturing plant, the company recorded remarkable growth. Sales eclipsed $100 million in 2000, reaching $117.5 million, and more than doubled by 2004, when the company collected $253.6 million. The company's products by this point were sold in more than 3,300 lumberyards in North America. The company's production plants were consuming prodigious amounts of waste material and converting it into long planks and, a new dimension of the company's business, railing systems. Trex collected 1.3 billion plastic bags each year, about half of all available recycled grocery bags in the country. For its sawdust, the company collected between 200 million and 300 million pounds of wood scraps from furniture and cabinet-makers every year.

As Trex eagerly awaited the completion of its Olive Branch facility, demand for Trex decking continued to grow. Entering the mid-2000s, the company was working to develop a network of retailers to sell decking and railing systems in the United Kingdom, Norway, and Ireland. Domestically, the company forged an important agreement in 2004. After several years of negotiations, the company signed an agreement with Home Depot to sell Trex products in select Home Depot stores. Consumers also were given the opportunity to order Trex products at any Home Depot store in the country by placing a special order. Matheny hailed the agreement, remarking in an April 19, 2004 interview with *Home Channel News NewsFax*, ''Home Depot represents an exciting new opportunity for Trex to expand our distribution channels and reach a whole new set of consumers and contractors.'' Matheny also said the partnership with Home Depot would ''dramatically accelerate'' demand for Trex, creating even greater need for the addition of the company's third manufacturing facility. The Olive Branch plant, which was expected to serve markets in the South and Midwest, was slated for its grand opening in mid-2005.

Principal Subsidiaries

Winchester Capital, Inc.; Trex Wood Polymer Espana, S.L. (Spain); Winchester SP, Inc.

Further Reading

Adler, Carlye, ''Roger Wittenberg, Co-Founder, Trex Company,'' *FSB*, June 1, 2003, p. 88.

DeRosa, Angie, ''Trex Zeros in on New Plant Site,'' *Plastics News*, October 27, 2003, p. 3.

Doba, Jinida, ''Trex Plans to Build 3rd Lumber Facility,'' *Plastics News*, February 26, 2001, p. 4.

Gillette, Becky, ''Wood Planking Company Expands to Northwest Mississippi,'' *Mississippi Business Journal*, February 2, 2004, p. 12.

Schonfeld, Erick, ''Building on Innovation,'' *Business 2.0*, November 2004, p. 82.

''Trex Building Plant in DeSoto County,'' *Mississippi Business Journal*, January 12, 2004, p. A8.

''Trex Partners with Home Depot,'' *Home Channel News NewsFax*, April 19, 2004, p. 1.

Truini, Joe, ''Trex Ventures into Miss.,'' *Waste News*, January 5, 2004, p. 5.

—Jeffrey L. Covell

24 Hour Fitness Worldwide, Inc.

12647 Alcosta Boulevard, 5th Floor
San Ramon, California 94583
U.S.A.
Telephone: (925) 543-3100
Fax: (925) 543-3200
Web site: http://www.24hourfitness.com

Private Company
Founded: 1983
Employees: 16,000
Sales: $1 billion (2003 est.)
NAIC: 713990 All Other Amusement and Recreation
   Industries

Based in San Ramon, California, 24 Hour Fitness Worldwide, Inc. is the largest privately owned and operated chain of fitness centers, with more than 300 clubs located in 16 states and Asia and a membership in excess of 2.7 million. As the company name implies, the centers are open 24 hours a day, seven days a week. They come in five types. "Active" clubs are basic fitness centers up to 25,000 square feet in size, offering cardio equipment, free weights and other weight training machines, and group exercise classes. Somewhat larger, from 35,000 to 50,000 square feet, are the "Sport" clubs, which also include a basketball court and swimming pool. Somewhat larger than these facilities, the "Super-sport" category is able to offer massage, sauna, and steam room amenities. 24 Hour Fitness's "Ultra-sport" clubs are in the 100,000-square-foot range, large enough to feature day spas, racquetball courts, rock climbing, and a running track in addition to the "Super-sport" offerings. At the other end of the spectrum is a new club type geared toward women, the Express Club, just 6,000 to 10,000 square feet in size, offering limited weight equipment, while emphasizing cardio equipment, group exercise, and personal training. 24 Hour Fitness is majority owned by private equity firm McCown De Leeuw & Co., which in February 2005 put the company up for sale.

Company's Founding Dating to the Early 1980s

The man behind the founding of 24 Hour Fitness is its chief executive officer and chairman, Mark S. Mastrov. He was born in Oakland, California, and raised in nearby Castro Valley. While attending junior college, Mastrov played on the basketball team and blew out his knee; to rehabilitate his injury he relied on Nautilus machines. While earning a business administration degree from California State University at Hayward, Mastrov began working out at a small health club, 5,000 square feet in size, in San Leandro, California. Because he was familiar with the club's Nautilus equipment through his rehab, the owner offered Mastrov a job training the staff on how to properly use the machines. Instead, Mastrov agreed to work four hours a week at the club in exchange for a free membership. He completed his degree and found work as a natural foods salesman, but switched to the fitness industry when the club owner decided to sell out in 1983 and asked if Mastrov was interested in becoming an investor. Mastrov raised $25,000 ($15,000 of which he borrowed from his grandmother), bought a stake in the business, and became the new manager of the club. His partner was a software programmer, and together they developed a front-end system for managing a fitness club, which they then sold to other clubs in the area. The project provided a valuable education, helping Mastrov to gain the fundamental business skills needed to run a fitness club. But perhaps of more importance was his feel for the business. After seeing that members were always lined up at the door when the club opened in the morning, while others were reluctant to leave at closing time, he figured that keeping the club open 24 hours was a selling point and could provide a competitive edge. The club made the change and took the name 24 Hour Nautilus.

A year after Mastrov and his partner took over the club, they recruited a third partner, Leonard Schlemm, who held a Harvard MBA in finance. Schlemm served as Mastrov's mentor, in many ways rounding out his partner's business education, so that in addition to knowing how to run a single club, Mastrov learned how to manage a large organization. The three partners soon fell out, however, with the programmer taking the software business and leaving Mastrov and Schlemm to run the club. While seeming modest in retrospect, Mastrov and Schlemm's goal at the time was to build a chain of ten Northern California health clubs. Mastrov began to raise his sights, however, after attending a Club Industry convention in the mid-1980s. Meeting with other club owners and gaining a better understanding of the industry fueled his creative instincts and competitive drive. Because

Company Perspectives:

Convenient locations, the latest equipment, affordable pricing, knowledgeable staff, and outstanding service—all available up to 24 hours a day, seven days a week—contributed to the company's tremendous growth and success.

banks refused to provide the funding he needed to grow a large chain of fitness clubs, the partners developed a business model that could fund expansion through cash flow, while keeping the company free of debt. A major component of the plan was the pioneering use of electronic fund transfers. This was coupled with the adoption of month-to-month payment plans that opened up club membership to a large number of people who could not afford a large outlay of cash.

Mastrov and Schlemm steadily added 24 Hour Nautilus clubs in California through the rest of the 1980s. In 1991 the chain spurred further growth by hiring Mark Golob as vice-president of marketing. Golob, who started out in the music industry promoting the likes of Bruce Springsteen and Fleetwood Mac, turned to the fitness industry in the 1970s and became involved in promoting Jane Fonda's live workouts when her exercise videotapes were bestsellers. During his brief tenure at 24 Hour Nautilus, Golob drew on his experience with celebrities to develop promotional campaigns using Pamela Anderson, Arnold Schwarzenegger, and Mike Tyson, resulting in a sharp increase in club memberships.

By 1994 Mastrov and Schlemm were operating 32 Northern California clubs. Along the way, the chain focused on membership retention, eschewing the traditional "churn and burn" mentality of the health club industry that devoted more energy signing up new members than keeping existing members happy. The chain also attracted new business by offering membership fees well below the industry average. Given these beliefs, it was not surprising that Mastrov turned to the fast-food industry for inspiration on how to deliver a consistent product that kept customers coming back. In fact, he once told a reporter that the person he was most interested in meeting was McDonald's founder Ray Kroc, noting, "It would be interesting to see how he could keep quality in so many places around the world." Mastrov also took a page from fast food by only targeting markets that he could dominate by building a cluster of clubs. In this way members could find a club close to home as well as where they worked, permitting them to conveniently schedule their exercise sessions during the week and weekends. The company also began to develop a hub-and-spoke approach, offering different types of clubs and price points in the same market, so that some locations offered basketball courts and swimming pools while others provided the basic, cardio machines and weight training equipment.

Major Expansion in the Mid-1990s

The 24 Hour Nautilus chain was stable enough that Mastrov could now approach McCown De Leeuw & Co., a Menlo Park, California private equity investment firm, for funds to accelerate the company's expansion. McCown invested $30 million, money

that was then put to use in 1995 when 24 Hour Nautilus acquired the Ray Wilson Family Fitness Center chain and its 68 Southern California units. A year later the company changed its name to 24 Hour Fitness, although many of the clubs continued to operate under the 24 Hour Nautilus name. During this period the company also began to expand beyond the California market, acquiring smaller chains in the Pacific Northwest and Southwest, as well as Hawaii. Schlemm also departed the company to pursue other opportunities, leaving Mastrov to run the enterprise.

In 1997 24 Hour Fitness filed to make an initial public offering (IPO) of stock. The decline of the stock market in October of that year, however, scuttled the offering. Instead, the company conducted another equity round, raising $75 million. 24 Hour Fitness then used some of that money to take its first international steps. In 1997 Fitness Holdings Europe Ltd. was formed, followed a year later by Fitness Holdings Asia. In 2000 these entities were merged with the domestic operation to create the present-day 24 Hour Fitness Worldwide, Inc. In 1998 and 1999 the company acquired health clubs in Sweden, Norway, and Denmark, then in 2000 opened centers in Germany and Spain. But management soon grew wary of the European market and elected to pull out. In the meantime, Ray Wilson, who had sold his fitness chain to 24 Hour Fitness in 1995 and briefly worked for the company, had built a new chain of fitness centers in Asia, which he then sold to 24 Hour Fitness in 2000. Some of these units were shed, but the company continued to operate centers in Hong Kong, Singapore, Korea, and Taiwan.

Although the company was still thwarted in its efforts to stage an IPO, 24 Hour Fitness had little difficulty finding backers. In 1999, new investors were brought in during a recapitalization of it, concurrent with another equity round. In 2001 24 Hour Fitness completed its seventh round of private investment, raising another $85 million. All told, since McCown De Leeuw's first investment in the mid-1990s, 24 Hour Fitness had amassed more than $500 million in equity from the likes of New York firms Triumph Capital, Lexington Capital, Blackstone Group, and Teachers Pension Fund, and Houston-based Rice Capital.

At this point, the company was opening 20 to 25 clubs a year, as revenues approached the $1 billion mark. In addition to attracting investors, 24 Hour Fitness was forging alliances with celebrity athletes. Basketball star Magic Johnson joined forces with 24 Hour Fitness to open athletic facilities in underserved urban neighborhoods. The first Magic Johnson Sports Club opened in Richmond, California, in 2001, and over the next two years five others followed, the facilities located in Los Angeles, Dallas, and the San Francisco Bay area. Tennis player Andre Agassi also became involved with 24 Hour Fitness, developing his own signature fitness club. The first of four 24 Hour Fitness Agassi Super Sports Club facilities opened in Las Vegas in February 2004. A key reason Agassi chose to partner with 24 Hour Fitness was the chain's 2003 agreement with the U.S. Olympic Committee in which the company became a sponsor for the next three Olympics. In addition, 24 Hour Fitness established a Commitment to Athletes Support Program, which granted club memberships to eligible athletes training for both the summer and winter Olympic Games. The company also donated equipment to upgrade U.S. Olympic training centers in Colorado Springs, Colorado; Lake Placid, New York; and

Key Dates:

1983: The company is founded.
1994: McCown De Leeuw makes an initial investment.
1995: Ray Wilson Family Fitness Center chain is acquired.
2000: 24 Hour Fitness Worldwide, Inc. is formed.
2005: The chain is put up for sale and Forstmann Little & Co. emerges as the buyer.

Chula Vista, California, as well as provided training equipment at High Performance Centers.

Introducing Xpress Zone in 2004

Moreover, 24 Hour Fitness agreed to work with the Olympic Committee's Sports Science and Sports Medicine Divisions to create specialized training programs for U.S. athletes. This research also helped the chain to develop exercise programs for its regular members. In 2004, for example, 24 Hour Fitness introduced its Xpress Zone circuit training regimen: 30 minutes of exercises designed to be completed in a specific order to provide a full-body workout for club members pressed for time. Such an idea was typical for the innovative chain. Mastrov, a frequent traveler because of the international scope of 24 Hour Fitness, thought there might be a market for fitness centers located inside airports. As a result, 24 Hour Fitness opened a 14,000-square-foot center called Fitness on the Fly, at Las Vegas's McCarran International Airport. The chain also was willing to pick up on the ideas of others, such as Curves, a company that developed smaller clubs that catered to people intimidated by standard health clubs, offering timed workout programs. This studio approach to the fitness center led to the creation of 24 Hour Fitness's Express Club concept.

24 Hour Fitness added another sports star to its signature line of sports club in 2004, signing an agreement with basketball player Shaquille O'Neal to open a 24 Hour Fitness Shaq Sports Clubs facility in Miami, the first 24 Hour Fitness center in the Miami market. In January 2005, 24 Hour Fitness added to the fold cyclist Lance Armstrong, five-time winner of the Tour de France. The first 24 Hour Fitness Lance Armstrong Sport Clubs facility was scheduled to open in Austin, Texas, in the summer of 2005. These centers were to include large indoor cycling rooms. In addition, 24 Hours Fitness became a sponsor of Armstrong's Discovery Channel Pro Cycling Team.

According to press accounts in 2005, McCown De Leeuw retained Merrill Lynch & Co. to seek out buyers for 24 Hour Fitness. The *New York Post* reported, ''Firms such as Apollo Advisors, Bain Capital, Cerberus Capital Management and Texas Pacific Group are said to be interested in taking a look at the fitness outfit. Other potential buyers could include some hotel, leisure and recreation companies. . . . Buyout firms are drawn to health clubs because they have proven to be stable cash flow generators, and also generally reflect high returns on investment.'' By May the company had found a buyer in Forstmann Little & Co., which had pledged $1.6 billion to take control, planning to continue to operate and grow the 24 Hour Fitness chain.

Principal Operating Units

Express; Active; Sport; Super-Sport; Ultra-Sport.

Principal Competitors

Bally Total Fitness Holding Corporation; The Sports Club Company, Inc.; World Gym International, Inc.

Further Reading

Bole, Kristen, ''24 Hour Nautilus Is Now a Heavyweight on Club Circuit,'' *San Francisco Business Times,* July 11, 1997, p. 8A.

Calandra, Bob, ''Winning 24/7,'' *Fitness Business Pro,* August 1, 2004.

Hindman, Jon, ''Being Privately Held Is Working Out,'' *California CEO,* Fall 2004.

——, ''Financial Deals 2001: Deal of the Year: Private Equity, 24 Hour Fitness Pumps Up Its Balance Sheet,'' *San Francisco Business Times,* March 1, 2002, p. S5.

''Investment Firm Buying 24 Hour Fitness,'' *Ventura County Star,* May 5, 2005.

Kafka, Peter, ''Time to Shape Up,'' *Forbes,* March 9, 1998, p. 74.

Leuty, Ron, ''Executive Profile: Mark Mastrov,'' *San Francisco Business Times,* January 25, 2002, p. 7.

—Ed Dinger

Ulster Television PLC

Havelock House, Ormeau Road
Belfast
BT7 1EB
United Kingdom
Telephone: +44 28 9032 8122
Fax: 44 28 9024 6695
Web sites: http://www.utvplc.com
http://www.utv.co.uk

Public Company
Incorporated: 1958
Employees: 376
Sales: £63 million ($110 million) (2004)
Stock Exchanges: London Irish
Ticker Symbol: UTV
NAIC: 515120 Television Broadcasting

Ulster Television PLC (known as the less politically sensitive UTV) is Northern Ireland's leading television broadcasting group, and one of the top television broadcasters in the entire Irish television market. UTV is also the Northern Ireland ITV (Independent Television) license holder. As such the company is one of the smallest of the ITV licensees and, together with Channel, one of the last of the true independents. UTV more or less limited its operations to its ITV franchise from its founding in 1958 to the end of the 1990s. The company's broadcasts also are available to much of the Republic of Ireland, and the company has long been one of the most-watched stations in that market. Since the beginning of the 2000s, however, UTV has begun to redevelop itself as a full-fledged media group. The company's primary expansion has been into radio, particularly in Ireland's radio market. UTV now controls radio stations in Cork (96FM and 103FM), Limerick (Live 95FM), Dublin (Q102), and in Liverpool, England (Juice FM). In 2005, the company acquired Coderidge Limited, which operates the LMFM radio station in Drogheda, Dundalk. In March 2005, the company was awarded a license to operate a radio station in Belfast as well. In addition to its television and radio operations, UTV has extended into the New Media market. In 2000, the company acquired Internet provider Direct Net Access, which was renamed as UTV Internet. That company provides broadband Internet services to both Northern Ireland and the Republic of Ireland. UTV also operates the BOCOM International joint venture, which provides satellite broadcasting services to plasma screens, such as at the Dublin Airport. Television remains the group's largest activity, generating some 74 percent of the group's 2004 sales of £63 million ($110 million). Radio revenues added 17 percent to sales, while New Media contributed nearly 9 percent to group sales. UTV is listed on the Irish and London Stock Exchanges.

Independent Television Broadcaster in the 1950s

In the late 1950s, the British broadcasting authority created a rival network to the state-owned British Broadcasting Corporation. The new network, known as the Independent Television network, or ITV, was established in 1958, under the auspices of the Independent Television Authority (ITA). That body then assigned licenses to the various regions in the United Kingdom, including a license for the Northern Ireland broadcast area. The Northern Ireland license was awarded to Ulster Television in 1958.

Ulster Television formally incorporated in February 1959. The company launched its first broadcast on October 31, 1959. The first transmission was hosted by Sir Laurence Olivier. Ulster Television went public in 1961, listing its shares at first on the Belfast Stock Exchange, before extending its listing to the London Stock Exchange as well. The company remained quite modest; in 1966, the company's advertising revenues barely topped £1.25 million.

Over the next decade, television came to play an increasingly important role in Northern Ireland, as penetration of households increased, and as television came into its own—particularly as a source of immediate images reflecting world events. This became especially true for Ulster Television, with the eruption of the Troubles, and the beginnings of a near-war that tore apart Northern Ireland. Ulster Television at times found itself embroiled in the conflict between loyalists and nationalists, often accused of partiality by one side or the other. Indeed, near the end of the 1970s, the company's headquarters were bombed in a terrorist attack. The company's journalists, as well as its management, often found their lives under threat.

<table>
<tr><td colspan="2">

Company Perspectives:

UTV is one of the most successful media groups in Ireland incorporating Television, Radio and New Media.

</td></tr>
</table>

The situation led the group to de-politicize its name, as it began to refer to itself, both on-air and off, as UTV. In 1993, this appellation, at least on-air, was made more or less official. By the end of that decade, the company had begun to call itself UTV Group.

The new name reflected in part the company's expanding focus. In the 1990s, UTV had remained the smallest member of the Independent Television Group. By 1995, the company's sales remained at slightly more than £34 million. The company, which was subsidized by the larger ITV players, including Granada and Carlton, also was accused of being "unambitious," in that it invested comparatively little in new production and focused its existing broadcast production on regional programming.

The liberalization of ownership rules among the ITV members in the mid-1990s appeared to place UTV's future as an independent company in doubt. The company was considered one of the most obvious candidates for takeover, especially by one of the larger ITV groups. Indeed, in 1997, Scottish Media Group (SMG), holder of the ITV franchise in Scotland, appeared to be in the process of a takeover attempt, building up its stake in UTV to more than 18 percent.

By 1998, however, SMG, denying it had ever been interested in an outright takeover of UTV, sold its stake in the Northern Ireland broadcaster to CanWest Global Communication, a broadcasting group based in Canada, which was involved in establishing TV3 in the Republic of Ireland. CanWest's acquisition of SMG's stake boosted its own shareholding position in UTV to slightly less than 30 percent. Nonetheless, CanWest announced its shareholding to be no more than a strategic investment, and not the prelude to an outright takeover. In the meantime, UTV's association with TV3 through its major shareholder allowed the company to begin planning a strategy of cooperation to reinforce the company's position in Ireland. UTV had long been one of the most popular broadcasters in Ireland, and by the 2000s, UTV's broadcasts were estimated to reach nearly 80 percent of the Republic of Ireland.

Full-Fledged Media Group in the New Century

Through the 1990s, UTV had become interested in expanding its range of operations, targeting areas such as interactive television services and future digital terrestrial television services. As part of that effort, the company acquired a stake in the European satellite broadcasting network, SES, operator of the Astra satellite service. UTV sold off its stake in SES, however, in early 2000, for £10 million.

That sale enabled the company to make its first real expansion effort soon after, when the company turned to a new market—Internet services. In March 2000, the company acquired Direct Net Access, paying £4.25 million for the Northern Ireland market's largest Internet services provider. UTV quickly moved to roll out its Internet services across greater Ireland, renaming its service as UTV Internet and launching the market's first free web service in June 2000. UTV Internet also became an early entrant into the race to offer broadband Internet access services.

UTV now began to target another area as it rolled out a strategy to re-develop itself as a full-fledged media group. At the beginning of 2001, the company launched a takeover offer for County Media, which operated three radio stations in Cork, in the Irish Republic. The company's offer was initially blocked by the Irish government, because of existing media ownership rules restricting cross-media ownership. Those rules were slated for review in March 2001, and the lowering of restrictions during that review enabled UTV to complete its purchase of County Media in April 2001. By July of that year, UTV had boosted its stake in County Media to more than 60 percent, before taking full control of the company in early 2002. The purchase gave UTV control of Cork's 96FM and 103FM, as well as the radio sales service, Broadcast Media Sales.

UTV next turned to Limerick, where it paid £10.5 million to acquire that city's Treaty Radio, and its Live95FM station. That acquisition gave UTV control of Limerick county's leading radio station, with a market share of more than 38 percent. UTV's next media extension came later in 2002, when the company acquired the newly launched LiteFM radio station in Dublin. The company then renamed the station as Q102.

The growth of UTV Internet, which emerged as a leading broadband provider in both Northern Ireland and the Republic of Ireland, encouraged UTV to expand its New Media interests. In March 2002, the company acquired a 50 percent stake in

<table>
<tr><td colspan="2">

Key Dates:

</td></tr>
<tr><td>**1958:**</td><td>Ulster Television is created as the license holder for the Northern Ireland part of the Independent Television network.</td></tr>
<tr><td>**1959:**</td><td>Ulster Television begins broadcasting.</td></tr>
<tr><td>**1961:**</td><td>Ulster Television goes public on the Belfast Stock Exchange.</td></tr>
<tr><td>**2000:**</td><td>Direct Net Access is acquired as part of an expansion into other media markets; UTV Internet is launched.</td></tr>
<tr><td>**2001:**</td><td>Ulster Television acquires County Media Ltd. in Cork, entering the radio broadcasting market in the Republic of Ireland.</td></tr>
<tr><td>**2002:**</td><td>Treaty Radio, based in Limerick, and LiteFM (renamed as Q102) in Dublin are acquired; 50 percent of BOCOM International is acquired.</td></tr>
<tr><td>**2003:**</td><td>Ulster Television joins the Absolute Radio UK partnership, which acquires Juice fm in Liverpool, England.</td></tr>
<tr><td>**2005:**</td><td>Ulster Television acquires Coderidge Limited in Drogheda, Dundalk; UTV wins a radio broadcasting license in Belfast.</td></tr>
</table>

BOCOM International. That company specialized in providing satellite broadcasting services to public-area plasma screens, such as those found in airports, train stations, and the like.

In 2003, UTV teamed up with Absolute Radio International and Eurocast to launch Absolute Radio UK. That partnership then acquired the license to Juice FM in Liverpool, England, marking UTV's first extension outside of the greater Irish market.

UTV's continued independence once appeared under threat as the two largest members of the ITV consortium, Granada and Carlton, agreed to merge, creating ITV PLC. The new company then announced its interest in acquiring its smaller, regionally oriented ITV partners in order to refocus the ITV network as a unified, national broadcaster. Yet UTV, joined by SMG and Channel, resisted ITV PLC's takeover plans.

Instead, UTV continued to seek out new expansion opportunities of its own. In early 2005, the company grew again, with the acquisition of Coderidge Limited, an operator of an independent local radio station in Drogheda, Dundalk. Soon after, UTV announced that it had been awarded a license to operate a radio station in the Belfast market as well. While television broadcasting advertising revenues continued to represent nearly 75 percent of the group's turnover, which topped £63 million ($110 million) in 2004, UTV had successfully reinvented itself as one of the greater Ireland market's major media groups.

Principal Subsidiaries

96FM; 103FM; Live 95FM; Q102; Absolute Radio UK; Juice FM; UTV Internet; BOCOM International (50%).

Principal Competitors

British Broadcasting Corporation; News Corporation Ltd.; British Sky Broadcasting Group PLC; ITV PLC; SMG PLC.

Further Reading

Aldrick, Philip, "Ulster TV Gets in the Picture," *Daily Telegraph,* September 20, 2003.

Foley, Stephen, "Picture's on Hold at Ulster TV," *Independent,* September 16, 2003, p. 21.

"Granada Moves to Mop Up TV Minnows," *Independent,* October 15, 2002, p. 21.

Jay, Adam, "Ulster Still Tops ITV League," *Daily Telegraph,* September 16, 2003.

Kennedy, Billy, "Window Watching a Conflict Unfold," *Newsletter,* October 4, 2003.

"Ulster Television Shows That Small Can Be Beautiful," *Independent,* March 18, 2003, p. 25.

"Ulster TV Buys Treaty Radio for Pounds 10.5m," *Independent,* April 9, 2002, p. 22.

"UTV Wins License for New Radio Station in Belfast," *Campaign,* March 11, 2005, p. 8.

White, Dominic, "Don't Press Ulster TV Button," *Daily Telegraph,* September 17, 2002, p. 34.

—M.L. Cohen

Ultra Petroleum Corporation

363 N. Sam Houston Parkway East, Suite 1200
Houston, Texas 77060
U.S.A.
Telephone: (281) 876-0120
Fax: (281) 876-2831
Web site: http://www.ultrapetroleum.com

Public Company
Incorporated: 1979
Employees: 31
Sales: $258.03 million (2004)
Stock Exchanges: American
Ticker Symbol: UPL
NAIC: 211111 Crude Petroleum and Natural Gas
   Extraction

With its headquarters in Houston, Texas, Ultra Petroleum Corporation is an independent oil and gas company focusing on two core properties: southwestern Wyoming and Bohai Bay, China. Ultra holds interests in more than 100,000 acres in Wyoming, intersecting the Jonah natural gas field and the Pinedale Anticline region, where since 2000 the company has enjoyed tremendous success drilling for gas, leading to a dramatic rise in the valuation of the company's stock. Ultra also is developing properties in the shallow waters of Bohai Bay, an area with excellent prospects and one that the company's management team likens to the Gulf of Mexico in the early 1960s. The production of oil from nine already discovered fields in Bohai Bay are expected to represent an increasing percentage of the company's reserves and production in the years to come. Given the potential for even more discoveries in Bohai Bay, and China's growing demand for oil, it is little wonder that investors have taken notice of a company that for most of its history has been little more than a bit player in the energy industry. Ultra is a publicly traded company, listed on the American Stock Exchange.

Company Origins Dating to 1970s' Canada

Ultra was incorporated in Canada in 1979 and was listed later on the Vancouver Stock Exchange, but by 1990 was noth-ing more than a corporate shell. At this point some real estate developers made use of Ultra for three years, then turned it over to another management team, which reorganized it as an oil and gas investment vehicle, bent on achieving growth in reserves through the drill bit rather than acquisition. The company was based in both Vancouver and Granbury, Texas, although its production focus was in the United States—in Texas, New Mexico, and Louisiana. In the first couple of years under its new regime, Ultra enjoyed modest oil and gas production. The only property that offered much hope was the Cedar Creek Field in east Texas, in which Ultra held a 50 percent working interest.

Ultra reached a major turning point in 1996 when it became involved in the Rocky Mountains for the first time. The president of Consolidated Natural Gas Co. (CNG), Jerry Albertus, chose to take early retirement and informed Ultra, which was looking to expand its efforts beyond east Texas, about assets in Wyoming that CNG was interested in divesting. Ultra bought 130,000 acres in the Rockies and named Albertus the company's new president. According to a *Denver Post* company profile in 1998, "The land position involved sections in Jonah Field, a prolific natural gas play, and plenty more acreage reaching into the Pinedale Anticline area in Sublette County. Ultra took the deal, then leased the acreage it could in the play, spudded some wells and hooked up with service giant Halliburton Co. Halliburton funds the majority of the costs of drilling, taking its payment out of cash flow generated from the well drilled."

Wyoming's Pinedale Anticline was an unconventional gas deposit because of the area's geography. It possessed great potential but for decades had frustrated all attempts to tap into its vast reserves. Pinedale was part of the Green River Basin, composed of different layers of gas-charged sand and shale, deposited eons ago by a major river system that flowed from the highlands of Idaho. The thickest section of these gas-rich sands lay beneath the Pinedale Anticline. Although the area possessed an abundance of gas deposits, it was virtually impossible to establish wells that could produce enough gas to make the process economically viable. Normally, gas and oil flow from an underground reservoir to a well because of the difference in pressure, but natural gas located in dense formations like the Pinedale had difficultly flowing to the wells. As early as the 1960s wells had been drilled

Company Perspectives:

Ultra Petroleum is a publicly traded (AMEX - UPL), rapidly growing independent exploration and production company focused on its core properties in the Green River Basin of southwestern Wyoming and the shallow waters of Bohai Bay, China.

here, but they produced a trickle of natural gas rather than a stream and did not justify the cost of constructing a pipeline needed to move the product to market. According to a 2005 article on the Pinedale in *Oil & Gas Investor,* "For decades dating from the 1960s to the mid-1990s, operators in western Wyoming's Pinedale Anticline wrestled with the problem of which technology to apply to uncork the anticline's huge natural gas production and reserve potential. One operator in the 1970s actually considered nuclear stimulation as a way to shake loose the anticline's treasure-trove of tightsands gas." In the neighboring Jonah Field, in the meantime, producers began to enjoy success by employing multi-frac technology to unlock gas deposits trapped in that play's Lance formation of sand deposits, coupled with new horizontal drilling techniques. In essence, multi-frac technology fractured dense structures all along a horizontal wellbore, creating much shorter distances for the gas to travel before being pumped to the surface.

Successfully Tapping Pinedale in 1997

In 1997, operating under a farm-out agreement with giant energy company Questar Corp., Ultra became the first independent oil and gas company to apply multi-frac technology to the entire length of the Lance formation at Pinedale, an area that had seen only six wells dug in the previous 30 years. Ultra was so pleased with its success, that it exercised the right to buy back additional interests in the play, and completed other deals that allowed it to dominate the area. By the end of 1998 Ultra had dug nine wells in an identified sweet spot, 12 miles long and 2 miles wide. The company also was waiting on an environmental impact statement for as many as 700 surface wells on its Wyoming acreage, representing a great deal of future potential.

But before Ultra could take advantage of its Wyoming holdings, it had to get its house in order. The company was burdened with debt and spending excessively, much to the distress of investors. In January 1999 a new chief executive officer was installed, Michael D. Watford, the former CEO of Houston's Nuevo Energy Company from 1994 to 1997, and a 20-year veteran of the oil and gas business. Upon taking over at Ultra, he decided that for the company to succeed in the long run, it would have to shrink before it could grow. "In his first 90 days with Ultra," according to *Oil & Gas Journal,* "Watford cut the payroll from 36 people in three offices to 13 people in one office, he sold some properties to raise cash and worked to regain the confidence of investors and creditors." He did not, however, sell off all of the company's position in the Pinedale Anticline, which he determined should be Ultra's long-term focus.

By mid-2000 Ultra's finances were stable enough to allow the resumption of growth. The first significant act was to reduce the spacing of wells in the Jonah Field, from 80 acres per well to 40, effectively doubling the size of the company's reserves. Next, Ultra was able to take advantage of the long-awaited environmental impact statement for drilling in the Pinedale area. After two years of waiting, Ultra finally was able to start drilling development wells, using a 75-square-mile 3-D seismic survey of the anticline. Ultra also was able to take the experience gained in drilling additional wells in the Jonah Field and apply it to the company's program in Pinedale. As a result Ultra enjoyed a 100 percent success rate in its Wyoming drilling for the next year and longer. The company's drilling program was further strengthened in 2001 with the acquisition of a new 100-square-mile 3-D seismic survey covering the west flank on the Pinedale Anticline, information that would be received over the course of the next year. Armed with data that covered most of the company's Pinedale Anticline acreage, Ultra was well positioned to maintain its sterling success rate in drilling.

Wholly dependent on the U.S. natural gas market, Ultra in 2001 took advantage of an opportunity to become involved in an oil play on the other side of the world to achieve some diversity. In January 2001, Ultra acquired Houston-based Pendaries Petroleum Ltd. in a $40 million stock swap. Pendaries was a small independent but it held interests in three concessions in China's Bohai Bay, covering 766,000 offshore acres. Such concessions were granted by the China National Offshore Oil Company, with a maximum term of 30 years divided into three periods: exploration for seven years, development with no time limit, and a production period of no more than 15 years, although extensions might be negotiated. Through Pendaries, Ultra inherited interests in three blocks, ranging from 10 percent to 18.2 percent. At the time Ultra became involved, three oil discoveries had been made on the blocks, all of which were undergoing evaluation, aided by a recently acquired 3-D seismic survey that covered the area.

Soaring Stock Price in 2001

Investors took notice of Ultra's potential and began bidding up the price of the company's stock. At one time trading under $2 a share in 1999, by mid-2001 the stock topped the $11 mark. Although prospects in China were intriguing, the company's continued success in the Pinedale Anticline remained Ultra's greatest selling point to investors. In January 2001, Ultra's stock gained a listing on the American Stock Exchange, making it more readily available to institutional investors and equity analysts, who in turn brought it to the attention of individual investors. What they saw in 2001 was a great deal of success, especially in Ultra's Wyoming interests. Over the course of the year, the company participated in the drilling of 32 new wells, all but one of which were successful. That one failure was due to a mechanical error. Of these wells, 24 were located on the Pinedale Anticline. The company hoped to deliver 300 billion cubic feet equivalent (Bcfe) of natural gas and crude oil and liquid gas of proved reserves from its combined operations in Wyoming and China, but by year-end it had reached reserves of 445 Bcfe, a significant increase over the 168 Bcfe achieved at the end of the previous year. Moreover, this was accomplished with the results of Wyoming alone, as the company elected to defer the booking of the reserves of its China drilling program. For the year Ultra recorded $38.2 million in revenues and net income of $17.9 million.

Key Dates:

1979: The company is incorporated in Canada.
1996: Wyoming interests are acquired.
1999: Michael Watford is named CEO.
2001: Bohai Bay interests are acquired.
2003: Ultra exceeds the Tcfe (trillion cubic feet equivalent) mark in reserves.

Ultra continued to enjoy success with the drill bit in 2002. In Wyoming it participated in 26 new and successful wells. Since acquiring its initial 3-D seismic data in 2000, Ultra had been involved in the drilling of 82 out of 83 successful wells. In addition, in 2002 the company participated in the drilling of five wells and the discovery of two new fields, for a total now of seven discovered fields. The China National Offshore Oil Company also granted permission to begin the development of the first two fields, allowing Ultra and its partners to drill development wells in 2003. The company again delivered more than it promised in 2002, exceeding its year-end target of proved reserves, which now totaled 700 Bcfe, a 58 percent increase over the prior year. Ultra's successful year was not fully reflected on the balance sheet in 2002, due to a drop in natural gas prices. As a result, revenues were flat, increasing to just $38.5 million, while net income fell to $8 million.

Ultra enjoyed another record-breaking year in 2003, with reserves increasing some 50 percent to more than 1.03 trillion cubic feet equivalent (Tcfe) of natural gas and crude oil and liquid gas, a goal that management had hoped to achieve in 2004. Again, Wyoming production led the way, but the Bohai Bay efforts were gaining increasing importance. Ultra and its partners began building production platforms on two approved sites, and pipelines were laid in anticipation of productions. Additional exploratory drilling took place, and two new fields were discovered. Two earlier finds also were getting set to enter the development phase. With a rebound in Wyoming natural gas prices, Ultra was able to post revenues of $121.6 million in 2003, as well as net income of $45.3 million.

The two Bohai Bay fields drilled their first wells in July 2004, initially producing some 30,000 barrels of oil a day with expectations that the level would increase to 65,000 barrels in 2005. All told in 2004, Ultra increased its production through the drill bit by more than 70 percent. Coupled with higher oil and gas prices, the company also experienced an exceptional year financially, posting revenues of $258 million and net income of $109.1 million. With hundreds of drilling sites identified in Wyoming and the Bohai Bay properties just beginning to produce oil—and a rising demand for oil from the rapidly growing Chinese economy—Ultra Petroleum was well positioned to enjoy continued success for years to come.

Principal Subsidiaries

UP Energy Corporation; Ultra Resources, Inc.; Sino-American Energy Corporation.

Principal Competitors

Apache Corporation; BP p.l.c.; Cabot Oil & Gas Corporation.

Further Reading

Dittrick, Paula, "Ultra Petroleum's Growth Relies on Long-Life US Gas, Chinese Oil," *Oil & Gas Journal*, October 25, 2004, p. 29.

Isaac, David, "From Wyoming to China, It Knows the Drill," *Investor's Business Daily*, August 30, 2004, p. A08.

Klann, Susan, "Ultra Petroleum Seeks New CEO," *Denver Post*, December 20, 1998, p. L6.

Toal, Brian A., "Pumped Up on the Pinedale," *Oil & Gas Investor*, January 2005, p. 75.

"Ultra Petroleum Corp.," *Oil & Gas Investor*, October 2001, p. 22.

"Ultra Petroleum Takes Long-Term Approach to Future Growth," *Oil & Gas Journal*, October 27, 2003, p. 39.

—Ed Dinger

United Online, Inc.

21301 Burbank Boulevard
Woodland Hills, California 91367
U.S.A.
Telephone: (818) 287-3000
Fax: (818) 287-3001
Web site: http://www.unitedonline.net

Public Company
Incorporated: 2001
Employees: 742
Sales: $448.61 million (2004)
Stock Exchanges: NASDAQ
Ticker Symbol: UNTD
NAIC: 514191 Online Information Services

United Online, Inc. offers consumer Internet subscription services through several brands, including NetZero, Juno, and Classmates Online. The company operates as an Internet service provider (ISP) through NetZero, Juno, and BlueLight, offering several packages ranging from free, ad-supported Internet access to moderately priced Internet access. United Online's Internet access services are available in more than 8,200 cities in the United States and Canada. Through its MegaWeb Services subsidiary, the company offers web hosting and domain services, marketing its services under the brands FreeServers.com, BizHosting.com, GlobalServers, and MySite.com. Classmates Online is a community-based network connecting friends and acquaintances from school, work, and the military. United Online operates offices in New York City; Renton, Washington; San Francisco; Orem, Utah; Munich, Germany; Jarfalla, Sweden; and Hyderabad, India. The company is the product of a merger of Juno Online and NetZero, Inc. in 2001, a union that joined the histories of two of the most prominent competitors in the free ISP industry.

Building Subscriber Base with Free E-mail: The Launch of Juno Online in 1995

Juno Online Services L.P. was established in June 1995 as a subsidiary of investment firm D.E. Shaw & Co. with a $20 million investment. Charles Ardai, then 25 years old, was president, and David E. Shaw was the company's chairman. Shaw was also CEO of D.E. Shaw & Co., where Ardai was employed as senior vice-president. It was reportedly Ardai who convinced Shaw that free e-mail would be a "killer app" around which to build an entire business. Within a month Juno announced that it would provide free e-mail service that would be supported by advertising revenue. Another company, FreeMark Communications of Cambridge, Massachusetts, announced that it would offer a similar service by the end of 1995.

On April 22, 1996, Juno launched its free e-mail service. Customers would receive free e-mail in exchange for permitting advertising on their computer screens and providing demographic information about themselves. This information would be provided to advertisers, who could then target their advertising messages appropriately. Initial reaction was skeptical since the software was not downloadable over the Internet; Juno would send it on a disk via regular mail. Through an arrangement with AT&T Corp., Juno's service began with 200 points of presence, or local access telephone numbers, as well as a toll-free telephone number.

Juno began with 15 sponsoring advertisers, including Snapple and Land's End. Advertisers would pay Juno only for ads that were delivered to Juno subscribers. The company was seeking to have its software bundled with computers and had signed deals with two of the top ten PC makers by the April launch. FreeMark's competing e-mail service launched on May 6, 1996.

By June 1996 it was announced that WorldCom Inc., the fourth largest long-distance provider in the United States, would provide the fiber-optic network for Juno's e-mail service. In its first months Juno's service proved very popular and was expected to have a six-figure membership by the end of June. Juno spread the word about its service through traditional advertising methods, including ads in magazines, newspapers, and billboards.

Juno was attracting numerous advertisers as well. Advertisers could target their messages and be assured that they were at least seen, if not read. Since Juno's service was free, it was felt that customers would not abandon the service, as they were doing with paid services such as America Online (AOL) and CompuServe (which would ultimately be acquired by AOL).

In September modem manufacturer U.S. Robotics agreed to include Juno software on CD-ROMs that were shipped with the company's modems. Juno also signed software distribution agreements with Blockbuster Video, the Sam Goody chain of music stores, mail-order music service BMG Direct, and the Billboard Music Guide.

Other companies also were offering free e-mail service. In September *PC Magazine* reviewed three services: Juno, Freemark Mail, and HotMail. Juno and Freemark were dial-up services, whereas HotMail was accessible from any computer with a web browser. In a sense, HotMail was not actually free, because it required Internet access. The magazine found that Juno offered more features, allowing users to save messages as text files, save addresses to an address book, and import entire message folders. Its interface resembled Windows, and users could change fonts, text, and background colors. Mercury Mail was another company offering free e-mail.

By December 1996 Juno had 800,000 subscribers and about 30 advertisers. They included some large firms such as Ford Motor Co. and Miramax Films. For the year Juno reported revenue of about $100,000 and a net loss of $23 million, mainly due to operating expenses.

By mid-1997 Juno claimed to have 2.2 million users. Juno's 1997 advertising revenue was estimated at $4 million by research firm Jupiter Communications, and the company was spending more than that on membership growth, software, and market research. Freemark Mail had failed, and two other available services—HotMail and NetAddress—required Internet access. Juno's subscriber base climbed to 3.5 million by early 1998, then a reported 4.5 million by the end of March. The number of advertisers rose to more than 100. Juno signed a five-year, multimillion-dollar marketing deal with long-distance carrier LCI International Inc. for exclusive rights to advertise its phone services. One survey indicated that Juno's service was used by 14.7 percent of all Web and online users, compared with 6.1 percent for HotMail, which recently had been acquired by The Microsoft Network. For 1997 Juno reported revenue of $9.1 million and a net loss of $33.7 million.

Juno continued to actively defend its users from unwanted e-mail and vigorously prosecuted spammers (junk mail marketers). The company had adopted a "zero-tolerance" approach to unsolicited commercial e-mail in late 1997. In February 1998 it filed a lawsuit against five companies for allegedly forging Juno's domain name and making it appear that their unsolicited e-mail messages were coming from Juno. A similar suit was filed in May 1998 against a New York-based pornography spammer.

In April 1998 Juno introduced the Juno Advocacy Network, which was aimed at political lobbying and advocacy groups. Through the Juno Advocacy Network, such groups could reach Juno's subscribers with their messages based on congressional district, age, gender, hobbies, income, and other demographic data.

Offering More Services and Forming New Alliances: 1998–2000

Juno introduced premium service levels, for which customers paid subscription fees, in 1998. The first billable services were introduced on July 22, 1998. At the time Juno had 5.4 million users. In addition to basic free e-mail service, Juno began offering Juno Gold, an enhanced e-mail service that would allow users to attach files to e-mails, for $2.95 per month. Juno Web, the highest level of service, offered Internet access and full e-mail capabilities for $19.95 a month, a price comparable with other ISPs. Since the beginning of 1998 Juno had more than doubled its points of presence from 500 to 1,200 by purchasing dial-up access from a variety of providers, including Concentric Network, AT&T, Sprint, and WorldCom.

In December 1998 the Hartford Financial Services Group began advertising insurance services to Juno's 6.1 million members under a five-year agreement. Online queries could be answered with a quote within ten minutes. For 1998 Juno's revenue more than doubled to $21.7 million, but the company reported a net loss of $31.6 million.

In 1999 Juno formed marketing alliances with America Online and with WingspanBank.com, the Internet banking subsidiary of Bank One Corp. The agreement with WingspanBank.com gave it the exclusive right to market credit cards and certain banking services to Juno's e-mail subscribers, which had reached seven million by mid-1999. In a deal with America Online announced in August 1999, Juno would start offering a co-branded version of AOL's proprietary instant messaging service. Juno hoped that instant messaging would help attract people to its recently introduced online community, JunoLand.

Juno went public in May 1999 with an initial public offering (IPO) on NASDAQ at $13 a share. For the rest of the year the stock traded in a range between less than $10 and more than $27 before spiking to $87 a share in December 1999. After the first quarter of 2000, though, it was trading back in the $7 to $16 range and heading progressively lower to barely more than $2 a share in late 2000.

In mid-1999 Juno selected Rapp Collins Worldwide of New York to handle its $10 million direct response campaign. The campaign utilized direct response TV and direct mail. Juno's brand advertising was handled by DDB Worldwide. Both agencies were owned by Omnicom Group. By September Juno had about 7.2 million subscribers.

News Corp., which owned about 9 percent of Juno, announced in October 1999 that its News Digital Media subsidiary would supply Juno users with entertainment, news, sports, and business content through Juno's portal site, www.juno.com.

In December 1999 Juno launched version 4.0 of its software and expanded the functionality of all three service levels. Internet access was added to those levels that previously offered only e-mail. As with its free e-mail service, free Internet service was supported by advertisers. Juno Express was introduced as the company's highest service level. With Juno Express, customers in select markets could get high-speed broadband access to the Internet through a deal Juno made earlier in the year with Covad Communications, which operated one of the largest DSL networks. In May 2000 Juno announced that Juno Express was available in 22 U.S. markets. The company planned to roll out Juno Express over Covad's DSL network in new markets throughout the year. Juno Express was priced at $49.95 a month.

In offering free, ad-supported Internet access, Juno faced competition from several other free ISPs. The leader in the field was NetZero Inc., which was backed by a $144 million investment from Qualcomm Inc. Juno hoped to distinguish itself from other free providers by offering a range of billable services to which users could migrate after becoming more sophisticated. When one free ISP, WorldSpy.com, ceased operations, Juno offered to pay it a fee for every WorldSpy subscriber that transferred to a Juno account. WorldSpy had about 260,000 subscribers when it went out of business in mid-2000. For 1999 Juno's revenue again more than doubled to $52 million, with a net loss of $55.8 million.

Until 2000, Juno's advertising had been handled by DDB Worldwide. Following a review in early 2000, Juno awarded its $20 million advertising account to Hampel/Stefanides in New York. The agency produced four 15-second spots to air on CNBC and Fox Network in the fourth quarter of 2000.

In February 2000 Juno teamed with Mail.com Inc. to launch Juno WebMail, a web-based e-mail service that would utilize Mail.com's web-based e-mail technology. Juno WebMail would enable Juno subscribers to send and receive e-mail from any computer connected to the Web, using their juno.com e-mail address.

Later in the year Juno announced that it would host a co-branded version of Mall.com, with the eponymous Austin, Texas-based company, on its shopping channel. Mall.com would be featured on Juno's home page, shopping pages, and product category pages, and Juno also would launch a marketing campaign to promote Mall.com to its members through pop-up and banner ads. More than 120 vendors were affiliated with Mall.com.

In June 2000 Juno filed a lawsuit against free ISP NetZero and wireless telecommunications giant Qualcomm for allegedly violating its advertising technology patents. The lawsuit raised important issues regarding Internet-related patents, their enforceability, and whether they would stifle competition among companies seeking to offer free Internet access. Other major Internet-patent suits filed in 2000 included Amazon.com's suit against BarnesandNoble.com regarding its online ordering system and Priceline.com's suit against Microsoft regarding online purchasing.

With Juno's technology, subscribers logged on and downloaded their e-mail messages and received ads. The connection was then terminated while users read their e-mail and viewed the ads offline. Juno's suit charged that Qualcomm's latest Eudora e-mail software violated Juno's patents in this area.

In October 2000 Juno formed an alliance with Activeworlds.com to provide real-time 3-D chat capabilities to Juno's 3.4 million subscribers. Meanwhile, Juno's stock was floundering, though the company had managed to secure a $125 million financing commitment from an unnamed private source. It also formed alliances with IBM, Time Warner, and Barnes & Noble in the second half of 2000.

The alliance with Time Warner was expected to give Juno access to Time Warner's broadband pipeline. Juno was the second company behind Road Runner to gain access to Time Warner's broadband cable network. The two companies, along with America Online, were to participate in a trial being conducted in Columbus, Ohio, to see if Time Warner's cable system could handle multiple ISPs. In order for Juno to gain full deployment over Time Warner's cable system—and thus offer cable Internet access to its members—Time Warner would have to restructure its exclusive arrangement with Road Runner. At the time Time Warner was under pressure from the Federal Communications Commission to provide open access to ISPs to gain approval for its pending merger with America Online.

Juno's partnership with IBM was announced in August 2000. Under the agreement free Internet access from Juno would be offered on IBM personal computers. The deal was part of Juno's strategy to reduce its subscriber acquisition costs, which were $45 million in the most recent quarter, to less than $20 million in the current quarter. At the time Juno had about 3.4 million subscribers. About 730,000 Juno members were paying for billable services. For the second quarter of 2000, 62 percent of Juno's revenue came from billable services, and 38 percent came from ads and electronic commerce. The company continued to post losses, however.

The Rise of NetZero in the Late 1990s

Juno's rival and legal combatant, NetZero, could relate to years of financial losses, a trait shared by all of the free ISP companies that sprouted up in the late 1990s. NetZero posted an annual loss of $91.3 million on $55.5 million in revenue in June 2000, the latest of a string of deficits recorded by the company in its three-year history. Despite its woeful financial record, the company was still in business, something few other free ISPs could claim. The list of failed companies that offered free Internet access was growing with each passing month. BOSnet, USFreeway, and Cyber Freeway had folded. Freewwweb and WorldSpy.com had collapsed. The industry had imploded, leaving Juno and NetZero as the only concerns with a chance of proving that the free Internet business model could survive. The two companies ultimately put their differences aside (each was suing the other for patent infringement at the dawn of the 21st century) and decided their best chance at survival was to join forces rather than battle against one another. The union added NetZero's history to the heritage of the merged company, a history that began one year after Juno first offered its free e-mail service.

NetZero was formed in July 1997, beginning with roughly two dozen employees in Westlake Village, California. A little more than one year later, on October 19, 1998, the company joined the free ISP fray, launching its ad-supported service on a national basis. NetZero used its own targeting system for delivering ads to its subscribers, a proprietary technology called zCast. zCast software streamed ads to subscribers' desktops, displaying them in a window separated from the main browser. The ads were rotated every 30 seconds and targeted toward an individual subscriber based on details that helped advertisers reach particular consumers. To sign up for NetZero service, a subscriber was required to provide his or her age and income. The geographic location of a subscriber was identified by the telephone number used to access the Internet. Further, NetZero's technology tracked every web site visited by a subscriber, enabling the company to offer advertisers detailed information about a subscriber's interests. "What we're really about," NetZero CEO Ronald Burr explained in a November 9, 1998 interview with *ISP Business News,* "is delivering a quality advertising vehicle to American business."

NetZero quickly became a popular choice for those seeking access to the Internet. Within six months, more than 700,000 customers signed up for its ad-supported service, well toward reaching its goal of signing up one million subscribers during its first year. The company, unlike many of its peers, outsourced its network to Level 3, AGIS, and GTE, saving millions of dollars on infrastructure costs. A September 1999 IPO, coupled with a $144 million investment by wireless technology developer Qualcomm, gave the company much needed cash, but cash infusions only represented a temporary fix to what was proving to be a perennial problem. Every time a NetZero subscriber accessed the Internet, the company lost money. NetZero paid 45 cents an hour for access. Ad revenue only covered roughly half of the expense, resulting in losses that mounted anytime the company provided the service it was created to provide.

A new chief executive officer was hired in 1999 to lead the company toward a profitable future. Mark R. Goldston arrived in March, bringing his marketing and leadership talents to bear on the struggling company. Goldston was a high-profile executive, renowned for leading the team that developed the hugely popular Reebok Pump while serving as chief marketing officer of Reebok International Ltd. in 1988. After his brief but successful stint at Reebok, Goldston served as a principal partner at a private equity firm, Odyssey Partners, L.P., leaving in 1991 to become president and chief operating officer of L.A. Gear Inc. Goldston scored another marketing success at L.A. Gear, intro-

ducing L.A. Lights, a line of children's shoes that lit up when they touched the ground, but after Minnesota's Attorney General derided the company for putting mercury in the sneakers, Goldston was let go. Next, he spent several years working as a consultant before taking the helm at Einstein/Noah Bagel Corp., a spinoff of Boston Chicken. He departed Einstein/Noah Bagel after 21 months, leaving a company that was suffering from profound financial problems.

Under Goldston's direction, NetZero inched closer to profitability. By negotiating deals to buy bandwidth in bulk, the company was able to reduce its access costs to 27 cents per hour by May 2000, tantalizingly close to Goldston's break-even point of 24 cents per hour. In the fall of 2000, the company added substantially to its membership rolls by completing two deals within the space of several days. NetZero forged an agreement with an Arizona-based ISP, iFreedom.com, to refer its subscribers to NetZero. Next, the company agreed to buy the subscriber list of FreeInternet.com, a failed Seattle-based ISP. Together, the two deals added 3.5 million subscribers to NetZero's base of five million subscribers.

Merger of NetZero and Juno in 2001

Despite the progress toward profitability, NetZero, like Juno, was battling for survival as the new century began. In March 2001, NetZero followed Juno's move toward offering a pay subscription service, introducing its Platinum package for $9.95 per month. Several months later, in June 2001, NetZero and Juno put aside their differences and announced their agreement to merge, a move regarded by most industry pundits as necessary for the survival of both companies. "You have to look at this as a final step in the free ISP market," one analyst remarked in an August 1, 2001 interview with *Upstart.* "Through it all, these two came out, and it didn't look like these companies were going to come out of the trenches alone."

Under the terms of the merger, Juno and NetZero were organized as wholly owned subsidiaries of United Online, Inc. The new company, which would develop a portfolio of Internet subscription services, was the combination of two equals, but the new entity drew much from NetZero. United Online's main office occupied NetZero's headquarters in Westlake Village. Goldston, who had become director, chairman, and chief executive officer of NetZero, became United Online's principal executive, serving as the company's president, chief executive officer, and chairman. When the merger was completed in September 2001, United Online boasted more than 6.7 million active users in the United States and Canada, ranking as one of the largest ISPs in North America.

In the wake of the merger, the free ISP business model was given perhaps its best chance at success, but as United Online developed, Goldston increasingly moved the company away from free services. The market for Internet advertising—the sole source of revenue for a free ISP—was slumping, offering Goldston little choice but to guide United Online into other revenue-generating areas. In February 2002, Goldston brokered a deal with Comcast Corp. to buy service from the cable and Internet-access company and sell the service under its two brands, Juno and NetZero. A third brand was added in November 2002, when Goldston acquired the Internet access and e-mail assets of BlueLight.com from Kmart Corporation. The following year, United Online responded to the increasing popularity of broadband Internet access by introducing dial-up accelerator services. NetZero HiSpeed and Juno SpeedBand debuted in April, each costing $14.95 per month, or $5 more than the company's standard $9.95 per month package. United Online continued to offer free Internet access, but the free service was offered primarily as a way to promote the company.

As United Online prepared for the future, the company reached a turning point in its brief history and in the legacies of Juno and NetZero. United Online recorded a profit in 2003 and 2004, offering the first tangible evidence that Goldston's efforts were producing desirable results. The company also completed several important deals as it entered the mid-2000s, offering further encouragement that the revamped business model was built to succeed. In April 2004, the company acquired the consumer web hosting business belonging to About.com. The acquisition added a handful of brands to the company's portfolio of Internet properties, giving it a new subsidiary, MegaWeb Services, that offered web hosting and domain services. In mid-2004, United Online signed a multi-year distribution agreement with RadioShack Corporation that allowed it to offer its subscription Internet access at 5,000 Radio Shack stores nationwide. In November 2004, the company acquired Classmates .com, a community-based network connecting friends and acquaintances from school, work, and the military. In March 2005, United Online acquired PhotoSite, an online photograph-sharing business that offered free and subscription packages enabling photographers to display their photographs on their own web sites. In the future, Goldston was expected to add to the company's collection of subscription Internet services, ensuring that United Online could collect revenue from a variety of sources in the years ahead.

Principal Subsidiaries

NetZero, Inc.; Juno Online Services, Inc.; NetBrands, Inc.; Classmates Online, Inc.; Classmates Advertising, Inc.; MegaWeb Services, Inc.; Juno Online Services Private Development Limited.

Principal Competitors

America Online, Inc.; EarthLink, Inc.; Microsoft Corporation.

Further Reading

Abercrombie, Paul, "Suit Claims Bay Area Firm Sent 'Spam,'" *Tampa Bay Business Journal,* February 6, 1998, p. 3.

"AOL Extends High-Speed Access Via GTE," *Content Factory,* July 28, 1999.

"Bank One Unit, E-mail Firm in Marketing Alliance," *American Banker,* July 21, 1999, p. 12.

Barlas, Pete, "Free Net Access King Migrates to For-Free Broadband Using Comcast's Cable," *Investor's Business Daily,* March 14, 2002, p. A6.

"The Battle of His Life," *Business Week,* March 18, 2002, p. EB18.

Berry, Kate, "United Online Dials for Dollars, But Future May Be Broadband," *Los Angeles Business Journal,* February 23, 2004, p. 45.

"Briefly: Juno Spreads Out," *Telephony,* May 8, 2000.

Busch, Melanie, "WorldCom Inc. Provides Hardware for First Free E-mail Service to Be Offered," *Knight-Ridder/Tribune Business News,* June 4, 1996.

Charski, Mindy, "Free E-mail: A Viable Option for Careful Consumers," *PC World,* July 1997, p. 76.

Coulton, Antoinette, "B of A Advertising Its Cards on E-mail Service," *American Banker,* June 9, 1998, p. 18.

Crum, Rex, "Juno Marches On," *Upside Today,* August 14, 2000, http://www.upside.com/Ebiz/398fl81a0.html.

Deagon, Brian, "With Lean Business Model, United Online Takes on AOL," *Investor's Business Daily,* March 28, 2003, p. A4.

"Free-mail," *Economist (US),* April 27, 1996, p. 71.

Fusaro, Roberta, "AOL, Juno Fend Off Spammers," *Computerworld,* January 11, 1999, p. 24.

Gabriel, Frederick, "Millionaires of Silicon Alley: David E. Shaw," *Crain's New York Business,* November 29, 1999, p. 49.

Gimein, Mark, "Seeking Redemption on the Internet," *Fortune,* May 1, 2000, p. 315.

"Hample/Stefanides Wins Juno Account," *Adweek Eastern Edition,* May 1, 2000, p. 86.

Harris, Roger, "Westlake Village, Calif.-Based Internet Access Firm Buys Seattle-Area Rival," *Ventura County Star,* October 11, 2000, p. 3.

——, "Westlake Village, Calif.-Based Internet Service Firm Gets Restraining Order," *Ventura County Star,* January 9, 2001, p. 2.

Hogan, Mike, "Forget E-mail, Try Free Mail," *PC/Computing,* November 1996, p. 76.

Hopkins, Brent, "Westlake Village, Calif.-Based United Online Sees Revenue Rise, Stock Drop," *Daily News,* August 5, 2004, p. 21.

"IBM Deal Helps Juno Get Subs," *ISP Business News,* August 21, 2000.

"ISP Profile: Here's Something for Nothing from NetZero," *ISP Business News,* November 9, 1998, p. 32.

"Juno in Deal with U.S. Robotics," *Mediaweek,* September 2, 1996, p. 30.

"Juno Online Services, AT&T Team Up for Free E-mail Service Via the Net," *PC Week,* March 25, 1996, p. 59.

"Juno Online Taps Rapp for Direct Response," *Advertising Age,* July 5, 1999, p. 13.

"Juno Opens Review for $20 Mil Account," *Advertising Age,* February 14, 2000, p. 1.

"Juno Strategy Called into Question," *ISP Business News,* August 7, 2000.

"Juno Will Deliver for Fox Media," *Content Factory,* October 27, 1999.

Krause, Jason, "In Flat Market, ISP Says 'We're Not Dead Yet,'" *Standard,* September 11, 2000, http://www.thestandard.com/article/display/0,1151,18345,00.html.

Ladley, Eric, "Free ISP Broaches DSL Offerings," *ISP Business News,* May 8, 2000.

——, "Juno Charges Qualcomm, NetZero Violated Patent," *ISP Business News,* June 19, 2000.

"Mail.Com and Juno Launch Web-Based E-mail Service for Juno Subscribers," *Direct Marketing,* February 2000, p. 15.

McAdams, Deborah, "Juno Gains Access to TW Broadband Pipe," *Broadcasting & Cable,* August 7, 2000, p. 41.

Messina, Judith, "Delivering On-Line," *Crain's New York Business,* March 30, 1998, p. 3.

Moch, Chrissy, "Download: Time Warner Throws FCC a Bone," *Telephony,* August 7, 2000.

——, "Staking a Claim: Free ISPs Fight for Market Share in Wake of Consolidation Trend," *Telephony,* September 11, 2000.

Neelakantan, Shailaja, "Freemail," *Forbes,* August 12, 1996, p. 140.

"NetZero and Juno Complete Merger Creating Online United," *PrimeZone Media Network,* September 25, 2001.

"Newswire Roundup," *Adweek Eastern Edition,* August 28, 2000, p. 35.

Plotnikoff, David, "New Company Offers Free E-mail Service," *Knight-Ridder/Tribune Business News,* April 30, 1996.

Pondel, Evan, "Westlake Village, Calif.-Based United Online Signs Deal with Best Buy," *Daily News,* August 7, 2003, p. 12.

Randall, Neil, "Free-mail: E-mail Services Meet Madison Avenue," *PC Magazine,* September 24, 1996, p. 44.

Riedman, Patricia, "Juno Advocacy Network Eyes Political Ad Dollars," *Advertising Age,* April 6, 1998, p. 35.

——, "Juno Bolsters Free E-mail Service with Internet Access," *Advertising Age,* July 20, 1998, p. 21.

Savage, Sean, "Free E-mail Available If You Don't Mind the Ads," *Knight-Ridder/Tribune Business News,* September 6, 1995.

"Short Takes: Hartford in Sales Deal with Web Dial-up Firm," *American Banker,* December 15, 1998.

Siegmann, Ken, "The Case of Ardai's Juno," *PC Week,* December 9, 1996, p. A3.

"Something for Nothing," *Business Week,* April 26, 1999, p. 94.

Spangler, Todd, "Juno Bids to Be a Top Consumer ISP Brand," *Internet World,* July 27, 1998, p. 38.

"Synchronized Swimming," *Upstart,* August 1, 2004, p. 4.

Taylor, Cathy, "You've Got Mail, But First a Word from Our Sponsor," *Mediaweek,* April 22, 1996, p. 14.

"3-D Chat Pact Formed," *Mediaweek,* October 9, 2000, p. 39.

"Trans World Entertainment Corp.," *Billboard,* September 4, 1999, p. 86.

Tsao, Amy, "United Online: Value ISP, Pricey Stock," *Business Week Online,* May 5, 2003, p. 32.

"TW Signs Juno for Multiple ISP Trial," *Television Digest,* August 7, 2000.

"Under FCC Pressure, Cable Giants Test Open Networks," *ISP Business News,* August 7, 2000.

"United Online Acquires Online Digital Photo Sharing Business from Homestead Technologies," *PrimeZone Media Network,* March 28, 2005, p. 43.

Vargas, Alexia, "Digital New York," *Crain's New York Business,* July 17, 2000, p. 14.

"VC Visions—On the Upswing," *Computer Reseller News,* October 23, 2000, p. 51.

Walsh, Mark, "Local Firms Join Instant Message Duel," *Crain's New York Business,* August 23, 1999, p. 3.

Weiss, Jeff, "Winners and Losers," *San Fernando Valley Business Journal,* December 20, 2004, p. 12.

Wilcox, Gregory J., "Revenues Soar for Westlake Village, Calif.-Based Discount Internet Provider," *Daily News,* October 31, 2003, p. 15.

——, "Woodland Hills, Calif.-Based ISP United Online to Buy Seattle-Based Classmates," *Daily News,* October 26, 2004, p. 13.

Wingfield, Nick, "Juno Offers Free E-mail Service to End-Users," *InfoWorld,* July 10, 1995, p. 10.

Young, Vicki M., "Juno Online, Mall.com in Joint Web Enterprise," *WWD,* June 20, 2000, p. 5.

—David P. Bianco
—update: Jeffrey L. Covell

UNOCAL 76

Unocal Corporation

2141 Rosecrans Avenue, Suite 4000
El Segundo, California 90245-4746
U.S.A.
Telephone: (310) 726-7600
Fax: (310) 726-7817
Web site: http://www.unocal.com

Public Company
Incorporated: 1890 as Union Oil Company of California
Employees: 6,590
Sales: $8.2 billion (2004)
Stock Exchanges: New York Pacific Zurich
Ticker Symbol: UCL
NAIC: 211111 Crude Petroleum and Natural Gas
   Extraction

Unocal Corporation ranks as one of the world's largest independent energy exploration and production companies. Its principal oil and gas exploration and production sites are in Asia (Thailand, Myanmar, Indonesia, Azerbaijan, Bangladesh, and Vietnam) and North America (the United States, the Gulf of Mexico, and Canada) as well as the Netherlands and the Democratic Republic of the Congo. Reserves in 2005 stood at 1.754 billion barrels of oil equivalent, while production was 410,670 barrels of oil equivalent per day. Among other activities, Unocal is involved in the production of geothermal energy and has various petroleum pipeline interests. A fully integrated oil company until the mid- to late 1990s, Unocal has shed most of its downstream operations. Having survived three major hostile takeover battles in its history, Unocal reached an agreement in April 2005 to be acquired by ChevronTexaco Corporation in a deal initially valued at $16.8 billion.

Formed Through Three-Way 1890 Merger

Unocal was founded on October 17, 1890, as Union Oil Company of California from the merger of three California oil companies: Sespe Oil and Torrey Canyon Oil, both of which were owned by oil and land baron Thomas Bard of Ventura County, and Hardison & Stewart Oil. Hardison & Stewart began as a "gentlemen's agreement" partnership between Lyman Stewart and Wallace Hardison in 1883 and incorporated later that year. In constant need of cash to finance exploration, Hardison and Stewart were referred to Bard by their bankers in 1885. Bard became their partner and operated his companies in an informal alliance with theirs. Hardison & Stewart frequently ran short of cash, however, and Bard finally proposed that they merge their companies. Hardison and Stewart consented, and Union incorporated in Santa Paula, California, as a mining company, with Bard as president, Stewart as vice-president, and Hardison as treasurer. The Santa Paula plant was, in 1891, the site of the first petroleum research facility in the western United States.

The merger proved to be anything but stable. Hardison, who had been gradually losing enthusiasm for the oil business, sold his interest in 1892 and left Union to engage in fruit growing. His shares found their way into the possession of Stewart's family. This, in turn, bred in Stewart a conviction that the company was his by rights and led to a conflict with Bard. Although both were Pennsylvania-born wildcatters who had been drawn to California by geologist Benjamin Silliman's predictions of vast oil deposits there, Stewart and Bard differed in temperament. Stewart had lost his savings in a youthful oil venture in his native state; despite this early failure, he flung himself into the oil business with the zeal of one who believed that worldly success was a sign of God's salvation. Bard was a calm and shrewd negotiator who would later become a U.S. senator. Stewart wanted Union to put more effort into marketing petroleum products; Bard wanted it to remain a producer and wholesaler of crude.

In 1894 Bard resigned as president to protest an expansion of Union's refining capacity that Stewart initiated and that was approved by other directors. Bard was succeeded by D.T. Perkins, his hand-picked successor. Stewart, however, faced Perkins down at an annual meeting several months later, and Stewart assumed the presidency himself. Bard, still a director, continued to object to Stewart's free-spending expansion schemes but was outvoted time after time. Finally, he sold out his interest in Union in 1900 and began his political career. In 1901 Union moved to Los Angeles.

Company Perspectives:

Our vision is to be the world's leading energy resource and project development company—the best people, the best partner, and the best performance. We combine the global reach and technical and financial resources of a major with the agility and aggressiveness of a small independent.

Unocal produces and sells a broad array of essential energy resources and develops major energy projects that help improve the quality of life for our customers around the world. Our primary mission is to maximize—ethically and responsibly—the total returns to the owners of the company, our stockholders.

With Stewart as president, his son Will Stewart, a former University of California football star, became general manager. Under the Stewarts, Union continued to expand both its production and retailing operations. Union spent much money on technological advances, organizing the first petroleum-geology department in the American West in 1900, launching a prototypical tanker in 1903, and completing the first successful cemented oil well in 1905. In 1913 the company opened its first service station, at the corner of Sixth and Mateo Streets in Los Angeles. In time, Union came to miss Thomas Bard's fiscal sobriety. As Lyman Stewart continued to buy up real estate with alarming aggressiveness, the company remained poor in cash. To keep up bond payments Union had to borrow ever larger sums from local banks and financiers. As the situation worsened, creditors forced the elder Stewart to resign in 1914, and the board of directors elected his more conservative son to succeed him.

Surviving First Takeover Attempt: Early 1920s

Under Will Stewart, Union continued to expand. In 1917 it acquired Pinal-Dome Oil, a local company that added 20 service stations in Los Angeles and Orange County to its retail network. Union also opened a refinery in Wilmington, California, near Long Beach Harbor, in 1917, just as U.S. involvement in World War I increased the demand for fuels. The company emerged from the war still in vulnerable financial condition. A speculative scramble for Union shares in 1920 generated takeover rumors, and the next year a foreign syndicate headed by what later became Royal Dutch/Shell Group formally launched an acquisition attempt. In response, Lyman Stewart and two other directors, banker Henry Robinson and retired Borden executive Isaac Milbank, organized Union Oil Associates, the sole purpose of which was to accumulate Union shares and prevent them from falling into Shell's grasp. The contest took on jingoistic overtones and came down to a proxy vote at a stockholders meeting in March 1922. When the votes were counted, Union Oil Associates won. Union Oil Associates began to merge with Union itself, and two years later, Shell dumped its Union shares on the open market.

The last great battle of his life over, Lyman Stewart died in 1923. Winning that same fight had left Union in stronger financial condition than ever, and the company continued to prosper. In 1928 it joined with Atlantic Refining to form Atlantic-Union Oil, a marketing venture in Australia and New Zealand. By the end of the decade, Union's annual sales had reached $90 million, and it was pumping more than 18 million barrels of oil per year. The Great Depression abruptly ended the good times for Union. Will Stewart died suddenly in 1930. He was succeeded as president by Vice-President Press St. Clair, who pursued a cautious strategy in response to the worsened business climate. In 1931 Union sold its interest in Pantepec Oil, which held leases for exploration in Venezuela. Two years later, the company sold its share of Atlantic-Union.

Union emerged from the Great Depression with an advertising motif that stood the test of time. In 1932 the company was looking for a distinctive brand name for its gasoline. Robert Matthews, a director and British national who was studying U.S. history to qualify for citizenship, suggested "Union '76," as in "The Spirit of '76" for its patriotic connotations. The octane rating of Union's most potent gasoline also happened to be 76, and the marketing department adopted Matthews's idea.

Provincialism Prevailing: 1938–64

Press St. Clair retired in 1938 and was succeeded by Reese Taylor, president of Consolidated Steel and a Union director. Taylor, who was something of a regional chauvinist, would run Union with an iron hand for 24 years. Under his direction, the company would take St. Clair's caution to an extreme and remain tucked into its geographical niche, rejecting expansion. It would eventually pay for this provincialism, falling behind in the game when other major oil companies embarked on worldwide expansion. First, however, World War II broke out, and Union boosted its crude production in response to increased demand for petroleum products. The production of aviation fuels was increased to seven times prewar levels. The company was well located to keep U.S. Navy ships operating in the Pacific Ocean supplied with fuel.

It was after the war that most of the U.S. oil giants began to develop overseas sources of crude, while Union concentrated its operations in North America. In 1949 Union acquired Los Nietos Company, an oil and gas concern with holdings concentrated in California. It also discovered and began exploiting substantial fields in Louisiana. Nevertheless, Union could not find enough crude to keep up with increasing demand for petroleum products, and it had to dip into its reserves to keep customers happy.

Union made some sporadic attempts to find oil in Latin America, North Africa, and Australia. It got nothing but dry holes for its trouble. Injecting steam into abandoned California wells added 70 million barrels to its reserves, but by 1956 the company was strapped for both oil and cash. That year, Taylor turned to a friend, Gulf Oil President William Whiteford, and swung a deal to acquire Gulf's surplus crude in exchange for convertible debt securities. Those debentures, however, could be exchanged for enough Union stock for Gulf to control Union. Gulf, cash and oil rich, sought entry into the western market and Union once more became a takeover target, all the more so because it accounted for at least 10 percent of gasoline sales in the Pacific Coast market. As Gulf mulled over the possibilities, in 1959 Oklahoma-based Phillips Petroleum Company began acquiring Union stock and became Union's largest shareholder the next year with 15 percent. Union bought back the Gulf

```
┌─────────────────────────────────────────────────────────┐
│                      Key Dates:                           │
│                                                           │
│  1890:  Union Oil Company of California is formed from    │
│         the merger of three California oil companies.     │
│  1901:  Originally based in Santa Paula, California, head-│
│         quarters are moved to Los Angeles.                │
│  1905:  Company completes the first successful cemented   │
│         oil well.                                         │
│  1913:  Union opens its first service station, in Los     │
│         Angeles.                                          │
│  1922:  Takeover attempt by what would later be the Royal │
│         Dutch/Shell Group is thwarted.                    │
│  1932:  The 76 retail brand is introduced.                │
│  1960:  Company moves to block a takeover threat from     │
│         Phillips Petroleum Company.                       │
│  1965:  Union acquires Pure Oil Company, gaining an ex-   │
│         tensive distribution network in the Midwest and   │
│         Southeast.                                        │
│  1969:  A Union Oil drilling platform off the coast of Cali-│
│         fornia near Santa Barbara leaks hundreds of thousands of│
│         gallons of oil into the water and onto the beaches.│
│  1983:  Company reorganizes under a holding company       │
│         called Unocal Corporation.                        │
│  1985:  Unocal fends off another takeover attempt, this one│
│         initiated by T. Boone Pickens, Jr., but only by   │
│         running its debt up to $5.3 billion.              │
│  1989:  Unocal and Petróleos de Venezuela form Uno-Ven,   │
│         a marketing and refining partnership in the midwest-│
│         ern United States.                                │
│  1996:  Company sells off the last of its California oilfields.│
│  1997:  Unocal divests its downstream operations: its West│
│         Coast refining, marketing, and transportation assets│
│         are sold to Tosco Corporation, and it sells off its│
│         interest in Uno-Ven.                              │
│  2004:  Company reaches a settlement to end a lawsuit      │
│         stemming from abuses by Myanmarese military       │
│         during the construction of a pipeline the company │
│         was helping to build.                             │
│  2005:  Unocal agrees to be acquired by ChevronTexaco     │
│         Corporation in a $16.8 billion deal.              │
└─────────────────────────────────────────────────────────┘
```

debentures for $120 million—$50 per share—and got a federal court to bar Phillips from acquiring any more of its stock, ending the second major threat to Union's independence.

None of this, however, addressed the problem of expanding the company's oil reserves and marketing presence. At the end of the 1950s, two-thirds of Union's production was still coming from California, including the Torrey Canyon field discovered by Lyman Stewart in 1889, but a prolonged management shuffle prompted by Reese Taylor's sudden death in 1962 distracted the company from finding a solution. Union's board brought back Albert C. Rubel, who had retired as president in 1960 (Taylor had become chairman in 1956), to take over until a permanent successor could be found. Under Rubel, Union entered into merger talks with Atlantic Refining in 1963, but Atlantic called off the deal because it did not want Union to be the surviving company, losing as it would then its own identity in its East Coast markets. Finally, in 1964, Rubel appointed Senior Vice-President Fred Hartley to take over as CEO.

Stepped-Up Exploration Efforts in the Late 1960s and 1970s

Blunt and outspoken, Hartley was a chemical engineer by training but had shown good business instincts as head of the marketing division. His first actions as CEO were to improve Union's bottom line through layoffs and closing unprofitable service stations. The company also broke out of its provincialism in 1965 by acquiring Pure Oil Company, a struggling oil concern that nonetheless had an extensive distribution network in the Midwest and Southeast. Hartley concluded the deal over the objections of shipping magnate Daniel Ludwig, who had become a Union director when he bought Phillips' 15 percent stake in 1963. The company quickly raised $146 million and bought up all of Ludwig's shares at $36.50 per share.

Hartley saw the need for increased exploration. "If we don't explore we'll go backward and if we don't explore with success we'll go backward and broke," he was fond of saying at the time, as quoted in *Fortune* in April 1967. Union cast a wide exploration net, but it mostly dredged up dry holes. In 1969 the company suffered a public relations disaster when one of its drilling platforms off the coast of California leaked hundreds of thousands of gallons of oil into the water and onto the beaches of Santa Barbara. It took months for Union to get the seepage down to a manageable level. The company maintained that it responded to the leak promptly and had minimized environmental damage, but the incident helped turn public and political opinion against offshore drilling. Various governmental authorities sued Union, Mobil, Gulf, Texaco, and Peter Bawden Drilling, and in an out-of-court settlement reached in 1974, the defendants agreed to pay a total of $9.7 million in damages to the state of California, Santa Barbara County, and the cities of Santa Barbara and Carpinteria.

The Santa Barbara spill and Union's peppery response to criticisms stemming from it gained the company a bad reputation among environmentalists. Throughout the 1970s, even before oil prices began to skyrocket, Union had charted an aggressive course in research and development of alternative energy sources. Union spent substantial sums on developing geothermal power and liquefied natural gas as an automotive fuel. Hartley stopped using a Cadillac as his company car in favor of an Audi, complaining about U.S. automakers' unwillingness to build cars with better gas mileage. In 1974 Union began building an experimental oil shale processing plant in Colorado. Many oil companies turned to shale in the 1970s as a potential source of crude. It was an old enthusiasm of Hartley's; he had written a thesis on it while a student at the University of British Columbia. In 1980, while others were still marking time, Union announced that it would begin constructing a commercial-scale oil shale plant in Parachute Creek, Colorado.

In the 1970s Union joined with Standard Oil of New Jersey, Atlantic Richfield, Standard Oil of Ohio, Mobil, Phillips, and Amerada Hess to form Alyeska Pipeline Service, which would build the TransAlaska pipeline. Union, which was already drilling in Alaska's Cook Inlet, would thus participate in the exploitation of the immense deposits lying under Prudhoe Bay. Union entered a niche of the metals industry in 1977 when it acquired Molycorp, Inc., a producer of rare-earth metals used in high-tech applications.

1980s Brought Third Takeover Attempt

After 15 years under the guidance of Fred Hartley, Union approached the 1980s in a state of financial strength, giving its shareholders a higher-than-average return on assets. Its exploration efforts had begun to pay off, making it rich in oil and gas reserves. At the same time, Hartley's age—he turned 65 in 1980—and the lack of an heir apparent made Union the subject of takeover speculation on Wall Street. To thwart any such attempts, it reorganized in 1983, creating Unocal Corporation as a holding company and reincorporating in Delaware, where incorporation laws made it harder for outsiders to gain control of a company without approval by its directors.

None of this, however, deterred Mesa Petroleum Chairman and corporate raider T. Boone Pickens, Jr., who launched the third major threat to Unocal's independence. Pickens began acquiring Unocal shares in late 1984, even as he was beginning a separate takeover bid for Phillips Petroleum, and eventually accumulated a 13.6 percent stake of Unocal. The Phillips bid failed, but when Pickens walked away from it in January 1985 he did so with a hefty greenmail payment and more than $1 billion in unused credit lines and potential margin loans on his Unocal stock. In the meantime, Hartley refused to sacrifice the money Unocal was pumping into exploration to initiate a stock buyback and inflate its price, although institutional shareholders were clamoring for such a move. Observers speculated that it was only a matter of time before Pickens and Mesa pounced.

Hartley knew that something was up. In early April, the two met by chance as they waited to testify in congressional hearings on the recent spate of hostile takeover bids for major oil companies. *Business Week,* April 15, 1985, reported that Pickens extended his hand in greeting but Hartley refused it, growling, "Go away." "Fred, you're talkin' to your largest stockholder," Pickens said. "Isn't that a shame," Hartley shot back.

Later that month, Mesa announced that it was offering $54 per share in cash for the 37 percent of Unocal stock that it would need for a controlling interest and the same amount in debt securities for the remaining shares. Unocal responded with an offer to buy back 49 percent of its stock for $72 worth of debt per share, but only if Mesa reached its target of 37 million shares. Any shares in Mesa's possession were excluded from this deal, meaning that Pickens could not sell them back to Unocal at a hefty profit. Pickens challenged this last provision in court and initiated a proxy battle to delay the company's annual meeting until he could field his own slate of candidates for the board of directors. Loyal shareholders, however, voted Pickens down in May and reelected Hartley as chairman.

Several days later, the Delaware Supreme Court ruled that Unocal had no legal obligation to include Mesa's holdings in its partial buyback offer. Unocal had stalemated Pickens. To get rid of him, the company agreed to buy back one-third of Mesa's shares at $72 per share; other stockholders would be allowed to sell back some of their holdings as well. Pickens admitted that he would do well to break even on the deal. The most ambitious attempt in his campaign to restructure the oil business—and his first genuine failure—had ended. For its part, Unocal was anything but triumphant in victory. To finance the stock buyback, it had increased its debt load from $1.2 billion to $5.3 billion. Cuts in capital outlays would be necessary.

Fred Hartley was forced to retire in 1988 (he died in October 1990). He had built Unocal into the 14th largest oil company in the United States, but it was left to his successor, CEO Richard Stegemeier, to cope with the bulk of the debt load incurred in the battle against Pickens. Under Stegemeier, Unocal closed unprofitable production and refining facilities and sold off real estate that did not hold oil or gas, including its headquarters building in downtown Los Angeles. Unocal also exited from the no longer promising oil shale business, having spent nearly $1 billion since the mid-1990s and seeing little in return. By the end of the decade, the company was ready for further expansion. In 1989 Unocal joined with Petróleos de Venezuela to form Uno-Ven, a marketing and refining partnership in the midwestern United States. In May 1990 Unocal added to its gas reserves by acquiring Prairie Holding Company from gold-mining concern Placer Dome.

Transformative 1990s

Overall, however, Unocal continued to be haunted by the Pickens takeover attempt well into the 1990s. At the end of 1991 long-term debt stood at a still-high $4.54 billion, resulting in annual interest expenses of about $300 million, which led to a lack of cash for capital projects. For example, the company's California gas stations were long neglected, leading to a market share drop from 13 percent in 1985 to 11 percent in 1993. Stegemeier thus was forced to sell additional assets, $527 million worth in 1993 alone. But these moves were not nearly the dramatic steps needed to turn the company's fortunes around, and at the end of 1993 debt had been reduced only to $3.45 billion.

It was under Roger C. Beach, who took over as CEO in May 1994, that Unocal finally found the strong leadership needed to extricate itself—in dramatic fashion—from its troubled past. Although longtime employee Beach had headed the company's domestic gasoline refining and marketing unit from 1986 to 1992, overseas was where he saw Unocal's future. He began to aggressively expand the company's oil and gas exploration and production outside of the United States, particularly in Asia and Latin America, while concentrating domestic efforts offshore, in the Gulf of Mexico. The quintessential California oil company cut its California production roots in late 1996 when it sold the last of its Golden State fields. Even more dramatic was Beach's rapid divestment of the company's domestic downstream operations. In March 1997 Unocal sold virtually all of its West Coast refining, marketing, and transportation assets to Tosco Corporation for $1.4 billion in cash. Later that year, Unocal sold off its interest in Uno-Ven, the Midwest refiner and marketer. Then, in another move aiming to refocus the company's exploration and production activities, Unocal sold the bulk of its Canadian oil and gas production assets to Tarragon Oil and Gas Ltd. in exchange for a 28.7 percent stake in Tarragon. These divestments enabled Unocal to trim its debt load to $2.2 billion.

While he was leading the company through this amazing transformation, Beach also was stepping up Unocal's presence in such high-growth, high-yield areas as geothermal energy, electrical power plants, and pipelines, often through international joint ventures. In October 1997, for example, a Unocal-led consortium, called Central Asia Gas Pipeline Ltd., was formed to build a $1.9 billion, 790-mile gas pipeline from a field in Turkmenistan to Multan, Pakistan, crossing Afghanistan in the process. With these projects, Unocal faced the challenge of gaining approval from politically unstable governments, such as that of Afghanistan. Even more troubling in the case of the Central Asia Gas Pipeline was that Unocal immediately was slapped with a $15 billion lawsuit from the Argentina-based Bridas S.A., which had plans for a natural gas pipeline of its own and alleged that Unocal had interfered with its Turkmen operations.

Unocal also had to contend with challenges from human rights advocates when it proposed projects for nations with repressive governments, most notably that of Myanmar (Burma). That nation's military regime had led the U.S. government to impose sanctions on it in April 1997. Unocal had a 28 percent interest in an international consortium, led by TOTAL S.A. of France, which was developing a natural gas field in the Andaman Sea off the coast of Myanmar and was constructing a pipeline from this field to Rathaburi, Thailand. In response to political pressure and in a possible first step toward "de-Americanization," Unocal in April 1997 opened a "twin corporate headquarters" in Kuala Lumpur, Malaysia, where the company president, John F. Imle, Jr., and several other senior executives would be based, with Beach remaining at the El Segundo, California, headquarters.

By this time having left the provincialism of its past far behind, the company looked to Asia for its future, where it was doing two-thirds of its capital spending. With the unexpected outbreak of the Asian economic crisis in 1997, Unocal faced some setbacks and delays in certain projects, particularly in two of the hardest hit nations, Thailand and Indonesia, where it had major operations. At the same time, the company was contending with shrinking revenue thanks to a drop in oil prices, which had fallen below $15 a barrel by early 1998. In response Unocal announced in April 1998 that it would cut its 1998 capital-spending budget by about $175 million, or 11.5 percent. Because of the oil price drop, Unocal saw its revenues for the year fall about 10 percent, while net income plunged from $581 million to $130 million.

Early 2000s: The Apparent End of the Road

Buoyed by surging oil and gas prices, Unocal posted its best results ever in 2000: $760 million in earnings on revenue of $8.91 billion. That year the company won a victory in a U.S. federal appeals court on a case involving a series of controversial patents that Unocal had received in the mid-1990s for methods of blending newly mandated cleaner-burning gasoline. The company hoped to eventually pull in between $75 million and $150 million in patent royalties each year from the major U.S. gasoline refiners and marketers. The U.S. Supreme Court in 2001 declined to review the lower court ruling. In the meantime, Beach retired at the end of 2000. Taking over the CEO spot on the first day of 2001 was Charles R. Williamson, who had been executive vice-president for international operations. Since joining Unocal in 1977, Williamson had spent his entire career on the exploration and production side, holding various management positions in the United Kingdom, the Netherlands, and Thailand.

Under Williamson's leadership, Unocal failed to make any major new discoveries in the early 2000s, despite billions in

capital spent drilling mainly deep-water wells. Production steadily declined through 2004 as did reserves. Several deals were completed during this period. Back in 2000 Unocal and Titan Exploration Inc. had merged their respective oil and gas operations in the Permian and San Juan Basins of west Texas and New Mexico, forming Pure Resources, Inc. In 2002 Unocal paid about $410 million in stock to take full control of Pure. The following year the company sold 70 of its properties in the Gulf of Mexico and onshore Louisiana to Forest Oil Corporation for $295 million. This sale was part of a larger divestiture program aimed at improving the profitability and sustainability of the firm's continental U.S. exploration and production operations.

At the same time, Unocal continued to be saddled with a bad reputation stemming from its activities in countries in turmoil from repressive governments. The company received much negative press from revelations that it had been dealing with the Taliban regime before September 11, 2001, in connection with the proposed pipeline across Afghanistan. Unocal had gone so far as to host Taliban officials at the company's offices in Sugar Land, Texas, in 1997—at a time when the Taliban were harboring Osama bin Laden. (Evidently, Unocal dropped the pipeline plan following the bombings of U.S. embassies in Kenya and Tanzania carried out by al-Qaeda in 1998.)

Unocal was also a defendant in a lawsuit alleging that it had turned a blind eye to the actions of the Myanmarese military during the construction of the $1.2 billion pipeline that the TOTAL-Unocal consortium was building. By most accounts, the military had forced villagers to clear the jungle for the pipeline, brutally resorting to torture, rape, and murder to enslave them. Unocal's exact role was in dispute, but a suit was filed in California in 1996 under the Alien Tort Claims Act of 1789, which allowed foreign litigants to seek damages in U.S. courts for crimes against "the law of nations"—acts of genocide, torture, kidnapping, and slavery. Lawyers for the 15 villager-plaintiffs asserted that Unocal was aware of the abuses by the Myanmarese military and therefore should be held legally liable. In June 2004 the U.S. Supreme Court upheld the use of the Alien Tort Claims Act in these sorts of lawsuits. Then in December of that year, on the eve of the California case heading for a jury trial, Unocal suddenly reached a settlement in the case, agreeing to pay the plaintiffs an undisclosed amount of money and to fund programs to improve the living conditions of persons residing near the pipeline "who may have suffered hardships."

Perhaps not coincidentally, soon after this settlement was announced, rumors began flying about Unocal being a takeover target. Despite further drops in both net reserves and daily production, record-high oil prices were more than compensating, helping the firm earn a record $1.21 billion in 2004, nearly double the $643 million mark of the previous year. It also appeared that Unocal was poised to finally begin increasing its production in 2005 as several major long-term projects were on the verge of paying off. Most of these were in Asia, where half of the company's proven reserves resided, and included Attaka, the largest oil and gas field in Indonesia; Unocal's natural gas production in Thailand, which powered 30 percent of Thai electricity production; the Pattani oilfield in Thailand, where production was expected to double to 15,000 barrels per day in 2005; and the firm's 10 percent interest in a consortium controlling four billion barrels of oil in the Caspian Sea. These assets looked increasingly attractive to a number of oil majors struggling to keep their reserve figures from slipping in a period in which it was becoming increasingly difficult and expensive to uncover new petroleum fields.

Although Unocal never disclosed that it was officially "for sale," an auction of sorts had developed by March 2005 with three main suitors involved: China National Offshore Oil Corporation (CNOOC), ChevronTexaco Corporation, and the Italian firm Eni S.p.A. Although it was reported that CNOOC made a bid that included much more cash—but that abruptly fell through at the last minute for undisclosed reasons—Unocal reached an agreement in early April 2005 to be acquired by ChevronTexaco for $16.8 billion in stock and cash. Following shareholder and regulatory approval, ChevronTexaco was expected to sell off some of Unocal's less desirable assets, such as its onshore fields in North America, its Asian power plants, and perhaps the controversial assets in Myanmar. ChevronTexaco appeared mainly interested in Unocal's offshore fields in the Gulf of Mexico, Indonesia, and Thailand. In any event, the deal if consummated would represent the final event for a company that tenaciously if sometimes controversially had managed to stay independent for more than 100, frequently precarious, years.

Principal Subsidiaries

Union Oil Company of California; Molycorp, Inc.; Pure Resources, Inc.; Unocal Energy Trading Inc.; Unocal Foreign Investments Inc.; Unocal Geothermal of Indonesia, Ltd. (Bermuda); Unocal International Corporation; Unocal BTC Pipeline, Ltd. (Bermuda); Unocal Canada Limited; Northrock Resources Ltd. (Canada); Unocal Canada Alberta Hub Limited; Unocal Congo (DRC), Ltd. (Bermuda); Unocal Donggala, Ltd. (Bermuda); Unocal Ganal, Ltd. (Bermuda); Unocal Global Ventures, Ltd. (Bermuda); Unocal Bangladesh, Ltd. (Bermuda); Unocal Khazar, Ltd. (Bermuda); Unocal Makassar, Ltd. (Bermuda); Unocal Myanmar Offshore Co., Ltd. (Bermuda); Unocal Indonesia, Ltd. (Bermuda); Unocal Indonesia Company (Bermuda); Unocal Netherlands B.V.; Unocal Rapak, Ltd. (Bermuda); Unocal Thailand, Ltd. (Bermuda); Unocal International Supply & Trading Co.; Unocal Philippines, Inc.; Unocal Pipeline Company.

Principal Operating Units

North American Energy Operations; International Energy Operations; Geothermal Operations; Unocal Midstream & Trade.

Principal Competitors

BP p.l.c.; Exxon Mobil Corporation; Royal Dutch/Shell Group of Companies; ChevronTexaco Corporation; TOTAL S.A.; ConocoPhillips; Marathon Oil Corporation.

Further Reading

Abramson, David, "Unocal Nears U.S. Downstream Exit with Deal to Sell Uno-Ven to PDVSA," *Oil Daily,* December 30, 1996, pp. 1+.

Bancroft, Thomas, "Playing It Safe," *Forbes,* January 20, 1992, p. 101.

Barrionuevo, Alexei, "Exhausting Feud: A Patent Fracas Pits Unocal Corp. Against Big U.S. Oil Producers," *Wall Street Journal,* August 17, 2000, p. A1.

Byrnes, Nanette, "Scorched Earth," *Financial World,* August 2, 1994, pp. 32+.

Collin, Jane, "Unocal Sets Preparation for Dividing Headquarters Between Malaysia, L.A.," *Oil Daily,* April 10, 1997, pp. 3+.

Culbertson, Katherine, "Unocal Heads Overseas, But Plans to Keep Home Fires Burning," *Oil Daily,* January 13, 1997, pp. 1+.

Cummins, Chip, "Unocal Hopes Deep Water Will Deliver It from Doldrums," *Wall Street Journal,* April 13, 2001, p. B4.

Darlin, Damon, "Getting the Lead Out," *Forbes,* July 17, 1995, pp. 106+.

Eisen, Peter, "Unocal, Bridas Set for Battle in Houston Court over Turkmen Project," *Oil Daily,* November 5, 1997, p. 4.

Ewing, Terzah, "Unocal to Slice Capital Spending As Oil Prices Sag," *Wall Street Journal,* March 20, 1998, p. A4.

Fairclough, Gordon, "Troubled Waters: International Oil Firms in Middle of Burma Battle," *Far Eastern Economic Review,* August 15, 1996, p. 66.

Fan, Aliza, "Unocal Realigns Operations to Focus on Growth in Its Overseas Business," *Oil Daily,* August 19, 1996, pp. 1+.

——, "Unocal's Shift Toward High-Growth Projects to Include Sale of Dutch North Sea Assets," *Oil Daily,* March 7, 1996, pp. 1+.

Fine, Howard, "Unocal's Boss Takes Off the Gloves: Stegemeier Sheds Units, Refocuses, Spars with Critics," *Orange County Business Journal,* March 2, 1992, pp. 1+.

George, Dev, "Unocal Becoming Largest Gas Producer in the Growing Asian Market," *Offshore,* November 1994, pp. 34+.

Girion, Lisa, "Unocal to Settle Rights Claims," *Los Angeles Times,* December 14, 2004, p. A1.

Gold, Russell, "ChevronTexaco Bets on Lofty Crude-Oil Prices," *Wall Street Journal,* April 8, 2005, pp. C1, C2.

——, "ChevronTexaco to Acquire Unocal," *Wall Street Journal,* April 5, 2005, p. A3.

Gordon, Mitchell, "Strength in Union Oil," *Barron's,* November 9, 1970, pp. 9+.

Grover, Ronald, "Can Unocal Move Its Mountain of Debt in Time?," *Business Week,* October 10, 1988, p. 80.

Hartley, Fred L., *"The Spirit of 76": The Story of the Union Oil Company of California,* New York: Newcomen Society in North America, 1977, 20 p.

Holloway, Nigel, "Long Arm of the Law: Unocal Faces Novel Suit over Its Burma Activities," *Far Eastern Economic Review,* September 19, 1996, p. 61.

Hutchinson, W.H., *Oil, Land and Politics: The California Career of Thomas Robert Bard,* Norman: University of Oklahoma Press, 1965.

Kovski, Alan, "Tosco to Acquire West Coast Refining, Marketing, Shipping Assets from Unocal," *Oil Daily,* November 19, 1996, pp. 1+.

Kravetz, Stacy, "Unocal Receives $70 Million Award in Gasoline Suit," *Wall Street Journal,* November 4, 1997, p. B5.

"The Luck of the Drill Bit," *Forbes,* January 15, 1970.

Mack, Toni, "Wildcat Drilling," *Forbes,* June 16, 1997, p. 52.

MacSearraigh, Stephen, "Unocal, Total Actions Prepare Them for World of Sanctions," *Oil Daily,* March 4, 1997, pp. 2+.

O'Hanlon, Thomas, "Fred Hartley and His Well-Oiled Multiplying Machine," *Fortune,* April 1967.

Palmeri, Christopher, "On a Fast Boat to China?: Why Unocal—and Its Rich Reserves—May Be Snapped Up," *Business Week,* January 24, 2005, pp. 62–63.

——, "Through Thick and Thin," *Forbes,* June 15, 1998, pp. 46–47.

Pasztor, Andy, and Stacy Kravetz, "Unocal Is Shifting Strategy to International Operations," *Wall Street Journal,* November 20, 1996, p. B4.

Pederson, Barbara L., *A Century of Spirit: Unocal, 1890–1990,* Los Angeles: Unocal Corporation, 1990, 326 p.

Peltz, James F., "Unocal Eyed for Takeover," *Los Angeles Times,* January 17, 2005, p. C1.

Pope, Hugh, "Unocal Group Plans Central Asia Pipeline," *Wall Street Journal,* October 27, 1997, p. A17.

Prasso, Sheri, and Larry Armstrong, "A Company Without a Country?: Unocal Says It Won't Leave Burma, But It May De-Americanize," *Business Week,* May 5, 1997, p. 40.

Rose, Frederick, and Pauline Yoshihashi, "Unocal Plans Another Round of Asset Sales, Job Cuts," *Wall Street Journal,* April 28, 1992, p. B4.

Sanger, David E., "Unocal Signs Burmese Gas Deal; U.S. May Ban Such Accords," *New York Times,* February 1, 1997, p. 4.

Saunders, Jay, "Unocal Chooses Difficult Road, Tough Times to Transform Itself," *Oil Daily,* September 8, 1998, p. 8.

Toal, Brian A., "Reinventing Unocal," *Oil and Gas Investor,* September 1998, pp. 45–48.

"Trouble in the Pipeline," *Economist,* January 18, 1997, p. 39.

"Unocal Pursues Plans to Shed Refining Unit," *Wall Street Journal,* October 30, 1996, p. A6.

"Unocal Still Struggling with Independent Life," *International Petroleum Finance,* April 2001, pp. 3–5.

Welty, Earl M., and Frank J. Taylor, *The 76 Bonanza: The Fabulous Life and Times of the Union Oil Company of California,* Menlo Park, Calif.: Lane Magazine and Book Company, 1966, 351 p.

Wolcott, Barbara, *David, Goliath, and the Beach-Cleaning Machine: How a Small California Town Fought an Oil Giant and Won!,* Sterling, Va.: Capital Books, 2003, 245 p.

—Douglas Sun
—update: David E. Salamie

VALERO ENERGY CORPORATION

Valero Energy Corporation

One Valero Way
San Antonio, Texas 78249-1112
U.S.A.
Telephone: (210) 246-2000
Toll Free: (800) 531-7911
Fax: (210) 246-2646
Web site: http://www.valero.com

Public Company
Incorporated: 1980
Employees: 19,797
Sales: $54.62 billion (2004)
Stock Exchanges: New York
Ticker Symbol: VLO
NAIC: 324110 Petroleum Refineries; 422710 Petroleum
   Bulk Stations and Terminals; 424720 Petroleum and
   Petroleum Products Merchant Wholesalers (Except
   Bulk Stations and Terminals); 447110 Gasoline
   Stations with Convenience Stores; 447190 Other
   Gasoline Stations; 454311 Heating Oil Dealers

Valero Energy Corporation is the leading independent oil refiner in the United States. The company owns and operates 15 refineries with a combined capacity of 2.5 million barrels per day. About 60 percent of this capacity is in the Gulf Coast region through refineries in Texas, Louisiana, and Aruba. The remaining refineries are on the West Coast, the Mid-Continent region, and in the Northeast. Valero also markets refined products on a wholesale basis through a bulk and rack marketing network and via more than 4,700 retail sites branded as Valero, Diamond Shamrock, Ultramar, Beacon, and Total. About 1,500 of the retail sites are company-operated outlets combining a fuel station with a convenience store. Valero's marketing reach extends to 40 U.S. states, Canada, Latin America, and the Caribbean region. The company also owns a 46 percent interest in Valero L.P., a publicly traded limited partnership that owns and operates crude oil and refined product pipelines, refined product terminals, and crude oil storage facilities mainly located in Texas, Oklahoma, New Mexico, Colorado, and California.

Valero Energy was founded as a natural gas pipeline on the first day of 1980. In an effort to diversify itself into a broad-based energy firm, the company purchased a petroleum refinery shortly after its inception. Renovation and start-up of this facility in a difficult world petroleum market nearly put Valero out of business. The company subsequently sold off its natural gas properties to a limited partnership to retain financial stability and concentrate on its refining activities. Conditions in the petroleum industry repaid this gamble, and Valero Energy thrived in the late 1980s and early 1990s. From there, the Valero of the early 21st century was largely engineered through acquisitions. From 1997 to 2004 the company acquired 14 of the 15 refineries it now operates. The biggest of these deals came in December 2001 when Valero bought Ultramar Diamond Shamrock Corporation for about $6 billion in cash, stock, and assumed debt, thereby gaining six refineries and vastly enlarging its retail operations.

Gas Gathering Pipeline Beginnings As Coastal States Spinoff

The company was created by the Texas Railroad Commission, the state's energy-regulating authority, to rectify the misdeeds of the Lo-Vaca Gathering Company, one subsidiary of the Coastal States Gas Corporation, Valero's corporate precursor. In the 1960s Coastal's chairman, Oscar S. Wyatt, Jr., had signed contracts to deliver gas to many customers, including several large Texas cities, at low prices, with the expectation that costs for gas would not rise. By 1972 and 1973, however, gas prices had risen dramatically, and the company was not able to fulfill its contracts. The Texas regulatory board allowed Coastal to pass on its higher prices to customers and to make a small profit, rather than see the company go out of business. The question of the penalty for Coastal's broken contracts became a matter of litigation that stretched through the mid-1970s.

Finally, in December 1977, the commission ruled that Coastal would have to refund $1.6 billion—more than the company was worth—to its customers. To satisfy this ruling, Coastal's intrastate Texas gas-gathering pipeline was spun off into a new company, Valero. Former Coastal customers were awarded 55 percent of the new company's equity, while the other half went to Coastal's shareholders, with the exception of Wyatt. In addition,

---

Company Perspectives:

Valero is a premier refining and marketing company that leads in shareholder value growth through innovative, efficient upgrading of low-cost feedstocks into high-value, high-quality products.

Coastal was ordered to spend $230 million exploring for new gas over the next decade and a half. Any new gas found would be sold to Valero at a rate 15 percent below the current market price. Valero also got a $110 million chunk of Coastal stock.

Thus, at its birth, Valero became the largest intrastate pipeline in Texas, with 8,000 miles of transmission lines, assets worth $700 million, and start-up revenues exceeding $1 billion. In addition, Valero had the right to charge customers ten cents per million cubic feet (mcf) over its cost of gas in its first year, and 15 cents over mcf in its second, guaranteeing the company a profit of at least $23 million. Valero's stock was slated to be listed on the New York Stock Exchange shortly after its formal inaugural.

To separate itself from its corporate parent, Valero chose to locate its headquarters in San Antonio. The city was both the company's largest customer and an outpost 200 miles from Coastal's Houston home. The company's name was taken from the Mission of San Antonio de Valero, the original name of the Alamo. As its president, the company chose Bill Greehey, formerly the court-appointed head of Lo-Vaca. Greehey had been instrumental in negotiating the out-of-court settlement that resulted in Valero's formation.

Beyond Valero's basic gas business, Greehey planned to expand into gas storage and oil and gas exploration, as well as coal and oil refining. He planned to make Valero a "fully integrated energy company," as he told a *Fortune* correspondent in January 1980.

In its first year of existence, Valero moved quickly to solidify its position and expand into the nonregulated areas of its industry. The company tapped into new supplies of gas, signing contracts in Mexico and Texas, and also added new storage facilities. Announcing that it would spend $14 million expanding its production of natural gas liquids—which at the time were selling at high prices—the company planned to build a $10.2 million processing facility and construct a 25-mile pipeline. Valero also spent $4 million on tentative moves into the gas exploration and drilling business.

First Move into Refining, Early 1980s

Valero made its most significant investment late in 1980 when it bought a one-half interest in Saber Energy, Inc., a small marketer of gasoline, for $51 million. With its new partner, Valero planned to turn Saber's tiny gasoline-producing operation in Corpus Christi, Texas, into a state-of-the-art specialized refinery. The facility was designed to use the product at the bottom of a barrel of crude oil—a high-sulfur, tar-like substance known as atmospheric residual oil (abbreviated "resid")—as its raw material, or "feedstock." Resid was obtained as a byproduct of the processing of raw crude oil and generally cost significantly less

than a barrel of crude, which was the feedstock of a conventional refinery. By cracking resid in a complicated and expensive process, Saber's refinery would create high-quality gasoline. In the Saber partnership, the company made its bid to become a broad-based energy concern.

In 1981 Valero embarked on the construction of the new refining facility, which was slated to cost $100 million. In addition, the company revamped its somewhat ineffective exploration and production operation, moving aggressively to get underway and opening regional offices in Midland and Houston, Texas; Denver, Colorado; and New Orleans, Louisiana. By the end of the fiscal year, Valero's net income had risen to $97.3 million, an increase of more than 50 percent from the previous year.

By 1983 Texas was in the grip of a severe recession, and Valero's outlook was growing less rosy. The company's earnings from its core businesses—gas sales and transportation of other people's gas through Valero's pipelines—went into decline. In an effort to counteract losses, Valero joined in industry efforts to encourage the shipment of gas directly to large commercial customers, which helped somewhat to prop up its earnings.

In its new endeavors, Valero had mixed success. Although the company had spent $100 million on exploration, it had yet to benefit from these efforts. Valero's natural gas liquids business, however, proved prosperous. The company had increased its gas liquids capabilities by 50 percent, building eight plants at a cost of $150 million to stockpile ethane, butane, and propane, and these facilities contributed significantly to Valero's profits. "If not for gas liquids," Greehey told *Business Week* in 1983, "we would have been in trouble."

Mid-1980s Travails

The biggest problem proved to be Valero's large investment in the Saber gasoline refinery. Two years into the project, estimated costs had reached $617 million, the most ever spent per barrel of oil on a refinery. Valero had taken on $550 million in debt to finance construction, and by 1983 the project was behind schedule. Experiencing difficulties meeting federal air pollution standards, the company was forced repeatedly to postpone full start-up of the facility. In addition, the economics of the refinery had shifted significantly since the project's inception. When Valero had started out, resid had been very cheap, while gasoline, the refined product, had been selling at a relatively high price. This justified large expenditures to convert one into the other. By 1983, however, the cost of Valero's raw materials had risen, and an oversupply of gasoline had driven prices for its end product down, dramatically reducing the potential profitability of the refinery.

The cost of raw materials for Valero's refinery was driven up further in 1984 when Great Britain suffered a coal strike. Unable to use coal as a fuel, British industry turned to resid instead, driving the demand and the cost of Valero's feedstock to unexpected heights, which at times exceeded the cost of straight crude oil. As a result of this stroke of bad luck, Valero's Saber refinery had still not become profitable by the middle of 1984.

Valero had certified to its lenders that the refinery was up and running two months after it had originally planned, but even after this step was taken, low gasoline prices meant that the

Key Dates:

1980:   Valero Energy Corporation is formed as a spinoff of Coastal States Gas Corporation, specifically Coastal's intrastate Texas gas-gathering pipeline; based in San Antonio, Valero moves into refining by acquiring an interest in Saber Energy, Inc., which operates a small refinery in Corpus Christi, Texas.
1981:   Valero begins a massive expansion of the Corpus Christi facility into a state-of-the-art refinery.
1984:   The expanded Corpus Christi refinery is up and running.
1987:   Valero spins off its natural gas pipeline and natural gas liquids business into Valero Natural Gas Partners, L.P., in which it holds a 49 percent share; company shuts down its exploration activities.
1994:   Company buys the 51 percent of Valero Natural Gas Partners it does not already own.
1997:   Valero divests its natural gas business in a deal with PG&E valued at $1.5 billion; company acquires Basis Petroleum, Inc. and its three Gulf Coast refineries.
1998:   Refinery in Paulsboro, New Jersey, is purchased from Mobil Corporation.
2000:   Valero buys a refinery in Benicia, California, from Exxon Mobil Corporation, along with 350 gasoline stations—marking the firm's entry into retailing.
2001:   Ultramar Diamond Shamrock Corporation is acquired in a $6.1 billion deal.
2003:   A refinery in St. Charles Parish, Louisiana, is purchased from Orion Refining Corporation.
2004:   Valero acquires El Paso Corporation's Aruba refinery.
2005:   Valero announces a definitive agreement to acquire Premcor Inc. for $6.9 billion in cash and stock.

plant was operating at a loss. In August 1984 heavy trading of Valero's stock prompted speculation that the company would be the target of a takeover.

Saber posted losses of $53 million in the first half of 1984, and by that fall, its rapidly weakening financial condition had obligated Valero to buy out its partner. In doing so, Valero added Saber's substantial debts to its own large tally of borrowed funds, doubling its overall level of long-term indebtedness. As a result, the company was forced to omit a dividend to its shareholders in the quarter in which the consolidation was made. To placate its worried bankers, Valero agreed to limit its spending on other areas of its business while it postponed payments to the bank on its loans. With this news, the price of the company's stock sank to its lowest point, as investors anticipated the company's possible bankruptcy.

In an effort to shore up its financial condition, in February 1985, Valero entered into an agreement with Techniques d'Avant Garde Group SA, known as TAG, a holding company controlled by Saudi Arabian Akkram Ojjeh. TAG invested $15 million in Valero as part of an agreement that the Saudi investor would raise its interest in the company to one-third if Valero could locate a cheap source of raw materials for its refinery. In a second bid to raise funds, Valero sold off a 50 percent interest in

its West Texas pipeline system to InterNorth, an energy company based in Omaha, Nebraska. The sale brought the financially beleaguered company $68 million.

By late spring of 1985, more favorable conditions in the energy industry as a whole had begun to lift Valero's prospects. As costs for crude oil byproducts fell and the price of gasoline rose, the Saber refinery was able to increase its earnings, posting a small operating profit for March. Despite this good news, the company temporarily suspended its production of gasoline at the Saber facility, resuming operations in June. The following month, Valero's agreement with TAG, the Saudi investor, was called off. At the end of 1985 Valero reported losses of $16.1 million.

By early 1986 Valero was also suffering from a glut in its original field, natural gas. Unable to sell the gas it had contracted at its founding in 1979 to buy from its corporate parent, Coastal, Valero refused to fulfill its contracts and in January, was sued by Coastal for $243 million in the first of a number of "take-or-pay" suits over gas purchase agreements that would not be resolved until the end of the decade.

In an effort to strengthen its financial position, Valero restructured $700 million of its debt in April 1986 and got out of the coal business by selling off the mine it owned in Indiana. Unable to make its expensive Saber refinery profitable given conditions in the world oil market, Valero began to informally hunt for a buyer for the facility. Despite the drain on funds by the unprofitable refinery, however, improved performance in Valero's pipeline operations enabled the company to finish the year in the black, posting profits of $34.7 million.

Restructuring and Turnaround in the Late 1980s

Faced with the problem of a profitable gas business that was carrying a money-losing refinery, Valero significantly restructured itself in early 1987. The company spun off its natural gas pipeline and natural gas liquids businesses into a limited partnership, Valero Natural Gas Partners, L.P., in which it would hold a 49 percent share. For this portion, Valero turned over $184 million of its own money, as well as $191 million contributed by public equity investors. The remainder of the gas partnership's funding was raised through the issuance of $550 million in notes. In addition to these moves, Valero abandoned its attempts to find oil and gas reserves, shutting down its exploration activities.

With the money from the divestiture of its gas assets, Valero was able to reduce its dangerously crippling debt load by more than $700 million, restoring its balance sheet to relative health. This meant, however, that the core of the company was its money-losing refinery. Valero lost $13.3 million in the first six months of 1987 on its refining and gasoline marketing activities.

By 1988, however, the climate for petroleum refining had improved, and Valero began to see a turnaround in its fortunes. Lower prices for its raw materials, coupled with reduced gasoline inventories and growing customer demand, enabled the company to turn a profit of $13.2 million in the first half of the year. Noting that the recent turmoil in the oil and gas industry had put many refineries out of business, Valero's leaders were confident that domestic demand for gasoline would continue to exceed refining capacity, keeping prices high. In addition, the company counted on the fact that the product it refined was high-quality, high-octane, clean-burning unleaded gas, for which it anticipated a growing demand.

On the supply side, Valero noted that prices for resid had fallen as stockpiles had grown, and the company moved to upgrade its refinery, increasing capacity. To assure future steady supplies of raw materials, the company sought to take on a foreign petroleum producer as a joint owner in the refinery. Valero ended 1988 with $30.6 million in posted profits.

The company's fortunes continued to improve in the following year. Valero's half-owned natural gas operations had profited from the deregulation of the gas industry; it increased its sales by adding customers outside Texas. The company was able to transport, through interstate gas pipeline linkups, and sell gas to clients in other states and in Mexico. Its number of gas processing plants had grown to 11.

Valero also continued to upgrade its oil-refining facilities. The company added a device that enhanced the octane level of the gas it produced and also constructed a natural gas processing plant that split the gas into products to be used in petrochemicals or oil refining activities. In 1989 Valero announced that it would own a 20 percent stake in a planned $104 million plant for processing gases given off in the refining process in Corpus Christi, Texas. These measures, along with the reduction in Valero's debt load, allowed the company to reduce its break-even point for a barrel of refined oil from $6.00, when the plant had started up, to $3.60 in 1989. As a result of refinery upgrades and the strengthened market, Valero was able to restore its dividend payment in a sign of fiscal health in the second quarter of that year. The company finished 1989 with profits of $41.5 million.

Continuing Recovery in the Early 1990s

Valero's recovery from the severe difficulties it had experienced in the mid-1980s continued as the company moved into the 1990s. The world oil industry was thrown into turmoil in August 1990 when Iraq invaded major oil producer Kuwait, driving up the prices of both crude oil and refined petroleum products. With this increased activity, Valero contracted for an additional $200 million investment in its refinery facilities. The company ended the year with earnings of $94.7 million, nearly double those of the year before. In a reversal of earlier conditions, petroleum refining accounted for a vast portion of the profits, while the company's interest in its natural gas partnership contributed only 20 percent of the company's returns.

The launching of the Allied offensive in the Persian Gulf in early 1991 immediately drove petroleum prices down. In anticipation of this effect, however, Valero had sold much of its first quarter production in advance at inflated prices and added $30 million to its balance sheet. Although Valero lost money when it was forced to shut down part of its production to make improvements to its plant, the company completed 1991 with record profits of $98.7 million.

Looking to profit from the general move toward more environmentally conscious, cleaner-burning fuels, such as natural gas and the high-octane products refined at its Corpus Christi facility, Valero continued to upgrade its plants in 1992. In addition, the company expected that by 1994 their entire gaso-

line output would be made up of reformulated gasoline. With an eye to further expansion, the company solidified its balance sheet by repurchasing the outstanding shares of an old stock offering and sought permission to raise money for expansion by issuing new stocks. Valero also opened an office in Mexico City, in an effort to enhance its relationship with the Mexican government and assist it in its search for clean energy.

In May 1994 the company bought the 51 percent of Valero Natural Gas Partners it did not already own for about $117 million. Valero said that it wanted to expanded the natural gas business, but that the limited partnership structure inhibited growth. Valero soon began seeking a buyer for the business, however, an effort that continued into 1996.

Late 1990s: Separation of Natural Gas Operations, Launch of Refining Acquisition Spree

Late in 1996 Valero officially announced plans to split the company up in order to concentrate solely on oil refining and marketing. In mid-1998 Valero completed a transaction whereby it sold its natural gas business to PG&E Corporation for $720 million in stock and the assumption of $780 million in debt. The deal was structured such that Valero's oil refining and marketing unit was first spun off to existing shareholders prior to consummation of the PG&E transaction. This spun-off unit retained the Valero Energy Corporation name, and the old Valero Energy was then merged into PG&E. The $1.5 billion Valero gained thereby was immediately leveraged to begin a massive, multiyear acquisition spree that would catapult the company into position as one of the largest refiners in the United States.

The first acquisition of this buying binge also occurred in 1997. Valero bought the Basis Petroleum, Inc. oil refining unit of Salomon Inc. for about $485 million in cash and stock. Basis operated three refineries on the U.S. Gulf Coast, two in Texas, in Texas City and Houston, and one in Louisiana, in Krotz Springs. The three refineries had a combined capacity of 260,000 barrels per day, more than doubling Valero's existing output from its original refinery. Although the Basis refineries had been operating at a loss for Salomon, this was in a way a positive for Valero: The facilities were in need of improvements, giving Valero an opportunity to overhaul the refineries just as it had done with the Corpus Christi plant. Already in late 1997, the company announced plans to increase capacity at all three Basis facilities.

After losing out to fellow San Antonio refining company Tesoro Petroleum Corporation in the bidding for a Shell Oil Company refinery in Anacortes, Washington, Valero succeeded in a September 1998 deal that saw it acquire a Mobil Corporation refinery in Paulsboro, New Jersey. Purchased for about $328 million, the refinery was located about 15 miles south of Philadelphia on the Delaware River and produced 155,000 barrels per day, increasing Valero's refining base by 25 percent. The deal geographically diversified Valero's production facilities and provided it with entrée into the markets of the Northeast.

A Blockbuster Deal and Blockbuster Earnings in the Early 2000s

After seeing its bottom line suffer in the late 1990s because of low crude oil prices, Valero, along with the rest of the U.S.

refining industry, entered a new era of fat profits in the new century. Soaring crude oil prices, surging demand for refined products, and refineries operating at or near their capacities produced a volatile mix leading to higher prices at the pump and soaring net income for the refiners. As this new era began, Valero accelerated its strategic spending spree, which centered on buying plants for a slim fraction of their replacement value.

In 2000 the company gained further geographic diversity by buying Exxon Mobil Corporation's refinery in Benicia, California, for $895 million. The 165,000-barrel-a-day refinery, located near San Francisco, was a very good fit for Valero because it could process heavy crude oil and nearly 70 percent of its output was cleaner-burning gasoline, specifically the reformulated gasoline required by the California Air Resources Board. The deal also marked Valero's entry into the retailing market as it included about 350 gasoline stations, mainly in northern California. Valero envisioned the gasoline retailing business providing it with a buffer against the more volatile refining sector. It soon debuted the Valero retail brand at some of the acquired stations.

Valero truly catapulted itself into retailing—and into the ranks of the major players in the U.S. oil industry—through its unexpected acquisition of Ultramar Diamond Shamrock Corporation (UDS) in a deal completed on the last day of 2001. The price was shocking for a company that just a few years earlier had only one refinery: about $4 billion in cash and stock and the assumption of $2.1 billion in debt. Valero gained from UDS six refineries with a combined capacity of 682,000 barrels per day; they were located in Wilmington, California; Three Rivers and McKee, Texas; Ardmore, Oklahoma; Denver, Colorado; and Quebec, Canada. The deal also included UDS's nearly 5,000 retail gasoline stations operating under such names as Diamond Shamrock, Ultramar, and Beacon. Valero also gained control of Shamrock Logistics L.P. (soon renamed Valero L.P.), which owned and operated a 3,600-mile network of crude oil and refined products pipelines. Valero was now the top independent refiner in the United States and one of the leading gasoline retailers as well. With the completion of the UDS deal, Valero saw its revenues soar, jumping from $14.99 billion in 2001 to $26.98 billion the following year.

To gain regulatory approval for the UDS acquisition, Valero had to sell UDS's Golden Eagle refinery located in the San Francisco area along with 70 northern California service stations. These assets were sold to Tesoro Petroleum in 2002 for $945 million. The integration of UDS into Valero was completed without layoffs—a hallmark of the way Greehey did business. Even when Greehey sold the natural gas business to PG&E, he insisted on extracting a promise from the acquirer that none of his former employees would be laid off. Although in each of the several huge mergers that rocked the oil industry in the late 1990s and early 2000s, thousands of employees had lost their jobs as a result, Greehey, according to the *San Antonio Express-News,* simply said, "That's not the Valero way." The company under Greehey's leadership was also well known for its generous corporate giving program.

Two more refinery acquisitions followed in the wake of the UDS deal. In July 2003 Valero spent about $549 million for a refinery in St. Charles Parish, Louisiana, that had daily capacity

of 215,000 barrels. Purchased from the financially troubled Orion Refining Corporation for 20 percent of its replacement cost, this refinery, located adjacent to the Mississippi River, was again a perfect fit for Valero in that it could process cheaper heavy, sour crude oil while meeting environmental regulations. In March 2004 Valero bought a 315,000-barrel-per-day refinery located on Aruba from El Paso Corporation for $465 million plus about $168 million for working capital—a price that represented only about 15 percent of the replacement cost. This refinery too was capable of processing heavy, sour crude.

Valero's strategy of basing its feedstock largely on sour crude oil, which was selling at a large discount to sweet crude oil—the discount having averaged more than $11 per barrel in 2004—paid off big in 2003 and 2004. After posting profits of $622 million on $37.97 billion in revenues in the former year, Valero then nearly tripled its profits one year later, making $1.8 billion on revenues of $54.62 billion. By 2004 the company, every day, was turning two million barrels of crude oil into 40 million gallons of gasoline, which amounted to 10 percent of the U.S. supply. While there were many skeptics who believed the next oil industry bust was right around the corner, Greehey for one remained quite optimistic, contending that the conditions that had created the boom—high crude oil prices, increasing demand for refined products, and refinery utilization at or near capacity—were likely to continue. He told the *San Antonio Express-News* in July 2004, "I think at least for the next four or five years, the refining business is going to be absolutely the best business to be in." Underscoring this conviction, and catapulting it into the lead in domestic crude oil refining, the company inked a deal in May 2005 to acquire Premcor Inc. by the end of the year for $3.4 billion in cash and $3.5 billion in stock. Valero was likely to pursue additional acquisitions of refinery assets as well as increase the capacity of a number of its existing refineries in the years to come.

Principal Subsidiaries

Colorado Refining Company; Valero Canada L.P.; Valero Refining and Marketing Company; Valero Refining Company—Aruba N.V.; Valero Refining Company—California; Valero Refining Company—Louisiana; Valero Refining Company—New Jersey; Valero Refining—New Orleans, L.L.C.; Valero Refining–Texas L.P.

Principal Competitors

BP p.l.c.; Exxon Mobil Corporation; Royal Dutch/Shell Group of Companies; ChevronTexaco Corporation; TOTAL S.A.; ConocoPhillips; Marathon Oil Corporation; CITGO Petroleum Corporation; Motiva Enterprises LLC; Amerada Hess Corporation; Sunoco, Inc.; Tesoro Corporation.

Further Reading

Andrew, John, "Valero Energy Remains a Risky Investment Despite Recent Improvements, Analysts Say," *Wall Street Journal,* April 15, 1985.
Barrionuevo, Alexei, "Tesoro Expands to California in Agreeing to Buy Valero Refinery for $945 Million," *Wall Street Journal,* February 5, 2002, p. B11.
Barrionuevo, Alexei, and Nikhil Deogun, "Valero Agrees to Acquire Rival Ultramar," *Wall Street Journal,* May 7, 2001, p. A3.

"Birth of a Natural-Gas Giant," *Fortune,* January 14, 1980, pp. 15+.

Culbertson, Katherine, "Valero Plans Balanced Growth As Greehey Hands Reins of Firm to New CEO Becraft," *Oil Daily,* April 1, 1996, pp. SW1, SW6.

Day, Bill, "Valero-UDS Set to Form World's Largest Refiner," *San Antonio Express-News,* May 7, 2001, p. 1A.

——, "The Valero Way: Under the Leadership of Bill Greehey, the Energy Giant Is Going to the Top," *San Antonio Express-News,* May 13, 2001, p. 1K.

Ewing, Terzah, "Valero Energy Plans to Separate Refining Business," *Wall Street Journal,* November 22, 1996, p. B2.

Fohn, Joe, "Valero Strikes $1.5 Billion Gas Deal," *San Antonio Express-News,* February 1, 1997, p. 1A.

Gordon, Mitchell, "Free, Fat, and Sassy: Valero Energy Is Enjoying Its Independence," *Barron's,* January 4, 1982, pp. 42+.

Helman, Christopher, "$2 Gas? We Love It," *Forbes,* June 21, 2004, pp. 72, 77.

Kiernan, Peter, and Paul Merolli, "Valero Makes Surprise $6 Billion Bid for UDS," *Oil Daily,* May 8, 2001.

Margolis, Dan, "Valero Chief Forced Out: Founder and Former CEO Returns to Lead Restructured Oil Company," *San Antonio Express-News,* November 22, 1996, p. 1A.

Nazareno, Analisa, "The Valero Way: When Valero Started Buying Oil Refineries Two Decades Ago, Critics Hooted. No One's Laughing Now," *San Antonio Express-News,* July 24, 2004, p. 10H.

Poling, Travis E., "Valero to Buy Mobil Unit," *San Antonio Express-News,* May 22, 1998, p. 1E.

Poole, Claire, "Stubbornness Rewarded," *Forbes,* April 13, 1992, p. 54.

Reid, Keith, "Valero: The UDS Merger Was Only the Beginning for This Ambitious Refiner/Marketer," *National Petroleum News,* January 2004, pp. 18–19.

Rosenberg, Hilary, "A Rough Time for Valero Energy," *Financial World,* August 8, 1984, pp. 35+.

Saunders, Barbara, "PG&E to Buy Valero's Natural Gas Unit," *Oil and Gas Journal,* February 10, 1997, pp. 24, 26.

Schwartz, Nelson, "Pumping Out Profits," *Fortune,* October 1, 2001, pp. 122–24+.

Shook, Barbara, "Valero Energy to Buy Three Basis Refineries in Deal Worth $600 Million," *Oil Daily,* March 18, 1997, pp. 1+.

"Take That, Oscar Wyatt!," *Forbes,* August 21, 1978.

"Valero Acquires California Refinery, Outlets," *Oil and Gas Journal,* March 13, 2000, pp. 28–29.

"Valero Energy: A Newly Independent Pipeliner's Plan to Diversify," *Business Week,* April 7, 1980, pp. 103+.

"Valero Energy Corporation," *Wall Street Transcript,* October 16, 1989.

"Valero Energy: Gambling on a State-of-the-Art Refinery," *Business Week,* October 24, 1983, p. 96.

—Elizabeth Rourke
—update: David E. Salamie

Watts of Lydney Group Ltd.

High Street
Lydney
GL15 5DB
United Kingdom
Telephone: +44 1594 847100
Fax: 44 1594 847401
Web site: http://www.wattsonline.co.uk

Private Company
Incorporated: 1880
Employees: 655
Sales: £60 million ($104 million) (2002 est.)
NAIC: 326211 Tire Manufacturing (Except Retreading);
325212 Synthetic Rubber Manufacturing; 423130 Tire
and Tube Merchant Wholesalers; 423830 Industrial
Machinery and Equipment Merchant Wholesalers;
441110 New Car Dealers; 441310 Automotive Parts
and Accessories Stores; 447110 Gasoline Stations with
Convenience Stores; 531190 Lessors of Other Real
Estate Property; 551112 Offices of Other Holding
Companies; 811111 General Automotive Repair

Watts of Lydney Group Ltd. is the holding company for a group of businesses predominantly focused on the production of industrial and specialist tires for the aviation, materials handling, and related markets. The company's main tire production subsidiary is Watts Industrial Tyres, which produces a wide range of industrial tires, including both solid and pneumatic tires, as well as puncture proofing systems, wheels, tire fitting presses, and the like. This company operates a small production site in Lydney, England, where the company was founded, but has shifted the bulk of its production to joint ventures in Sri Lanka, China, and Brazil. Watts Industrial accounts for approximately one-third of the group's sales, which topped £60 million ($104 million) in 2002. Watts Aviation is responsible for the group's production of aviation and aircraft tires and tubes, including for commercial and corporate aircraft. Watts Polymers is a leading producer of rubber compounds for use in the OEM and retread sectors. Watts Truck & Van Centres special-

izes in sales of DAF Trucks and LDV vans. The company also owns Watts Urethane, a manufacturer of castable polyurethane-based products, including squeegees. Another subsidiary is Watts Plysolene, which produces polycarbonate sheeting, insulation materials, and other specialist waterproofing materials for the construction industry. Privately held Watts remains controlled by the founding Watts family, under the leadership of John Thurston, chairman, Cecil Watts, director, and Melville Watts, president.

Founding a Local Dynasty in the 1850s

The Watts family arrived in Lydney, in Gloucestershire, England, in the mid-1850s and quickly became one of the driving forces behind the region's local industrial development. The first of the family to come to Lydney was David Lazarus Watts, a native of Devon, who traveled to Lydney in 1850 at the age of 39. Watts married local resident Elizabeth Stephens, and the couple opened a general store together in 1851. Watts died in 1862, and Elizabeth Watts took over management of the store, aided by her five children. The family then opened a bakery, and later added a supply store as well.

One of the Watts sons, 14-year-old Josiah, left home to become an apprentice in an ironmonger's shop in Bristol in 1870. After completing his apprenticeship, Josiah Watts returned to Lydney to set up in business on his own. Borrowing £300 from an uncle, Watts launched his own ironmonger's shop near the Lydney port. Watts's business flourished, with orders coming not only from the town's port operations, but also from the nearby railroad. The company also began providing parts and equipment for the town's main industry, a tin plate factory.

Josiah Watts's sons Arthur and John, born in 1887 and 1890, respectively, inherited the Watts family talent for entrepreneurship. The brothers joined their father's business at the dawn of the 20th century, and the company became known as JS Watts & Sons. Arthur Watts went on to become an apprentice to a motor dealership in Bristol, before returning to Lydney to add that business to JS Watts & Sons. Meanwhile, the Watts family continued to operate its original grocery and supply shops and bakery. The family's presence in the town's commercial life led to the adoption of the slogan: ''You can get it from Watts.''

Company Perspectives:

Watts Group of Companies—History and Ethos
Over a century has elapsed since a single-minded young man, with £300 borrowed from his uncle, purchased a small ironmongery shop in Lydney, Gloucestershire. Josiah Watts and his wife Clara, the driving force behind the Company's early success, both have a lot to answer for. The ambition, inspiration, dedication and pride they took in owning their own business have been the cornerstones for the success of one of the few great family businesses remaining in Britain today.
A commitment to customer service, the quality of innovation and the pursuit of excellence now manifest themselves in a high performance group of companies serving industry across the world.

The family continued to display its entrepreneurial drive in the years leading up to World War I. In 1910, for example, JS Watts & Sons began operating a motor vehicle service garage in Lydney. At the same time, the Watts family began a mail collection and delivery service for the local areas. By 1912, the family had branched out again, now launching a Ford automobile dealership.

Both brothers served in the British armed forces during the war; Arthur joined the air force, while John Watts joined the Army's Motor Transport Division. That experience was to serve the brothers in good stead after the war, as the family's involvement in motor vehicles deepened. In 1920, Arthur Watts arranged to buy a fleet of more than 200 surplus vehicles, including support workshops and spare parts, left behind by the departing U.S. troops. The fleet provided the basis for John Watts's launch of a bus service in 1921. That company initially served a route between Ebbw Vale and Tredegar, but by 1922 had been expanded to include the Forest of Dean area. The family's involvement in busing led it to spearhead the merger of a number of area bus companies, creating the Red & White Bus Company, in 1937.

In the meantime, Arthur Watts had emerged as a prominent player in the local motor vehicle sales and service market. Watts had also entered manufacturing by this time, producing, among other things, Watney motorcycles. In 1938, Watts formed a new business, which served as the basis of the later Watts of Lydney group: a tire remolding and retreading business that became known as the Watts Tyre and Rubber Co. The Watts family interest in tire retreading led to the formation of Tyresoles Limited in 1941.

Continued expansion of its tires operation led to the opening of new warehouses in Cardiff and Neath in 1948. By 1948, Watts Tyre & Rubber Co. had opened a new, larger retreading facility in Lydney at the site of the town's old tin plate factory. The family's retread business was boosted again when it acquired a franchise for the Vaculug retread process, introduced in England just one year earlier. That method, pioneered in the United States, was initially developed to retread agricultural tires. The process was later expanded for use with other vehicles, particularly heavy construction and other industrial vehicles.

Tire Manufacturing in the 1950s

Watts's interests in tires expanded beyond retreads and into manufacturing in the early 1950s. In 1953 the company began producing its first industrial tires, under the Duratrack brand. This led the company to establish a new dedicated Tyre division the same year. By the mid-1960s, the company's production of tires for the industrial market had grown strongly. In 1966, the Watts family founded a new dedicated tire company, Watts Industrial Tyres Limited. In the meantime, the Watts family continued to expand their business interests, notably establishing its first service stations in 1958, and then adding the Watts Truck Centre in 1960. In 1968, Watts Tyre & Rubber formed a partnership with Avon Rubber to create a nationally operating tire and battery service.

The company's interest in tire making led it to diversify into new materials. In 1974, Watts established a new subsidiary, Watts Urethane, which began processing castable polyurethane. Watts Urethane later added a range of products, including squeegees. The diversification led Watts to adopt a new structure, placing its operations under a new holding company, Watts of Lydney Group. The company also had come under the leadership of a new generation of the Watts family, including Melville and Cecil Watts and John Thurston.

Watts's expansion continued through the 1990s. In 1983, for example, the company built a new rubber compounding plant. In the mid-1990s, Watts extended its tire operations into the retail sector, launching Watts Tyre and Autocentres. That year, also, the company opened a new tire manufacturing plant. The company's tire and other production operations were then regrouped under a new subsidiary, Watts Industrial Group, in 1998. In that year, the company spent some £4.5 million to expand its production capacity to some 18,000 tires per week.

Watts's industrial operations were expanded again in 1999 with the acquisition of the rubber compounding division of Wellington Holding. The acquisition gave Watts control of two Ondura Ltd. tire compound plants in Yorkshire and a rubber compounder in Hertford. These operations were placed into a new subsidiary, Watts Industrial Polymers, together with Watts's own rubber compounding operations. Also joining the company as part of the Wellington sale was Plysolene Ltd., a company specialized in the production of waterproofing materials and products for the construction industry.

Outsourcing Manufacturing in the New Century

Into the mid-2000s, Watts remained one of Europe's top producers of industrial tires. More than 60 percent of the company's revenues now came from outside of the United Kingdom, with strong sales not only throughout Europe, but in the United States as well.

Yet Watts began a transition during the early 2000s as it, too, entered the United Kingdom's post-industrial age. In the early 2000s, the company announced its intention to reduce its manufacturing presence to a minimum in England. As Doug Pearson, the division's managing director, told *European Rubber Journal:* "Our intention is to retain a limited manufacturing capability in the UK, but substantially we will source our manufactured products from the Far East. The UK is just not a competitive base in which to manufacture."

Key Dates:

1851: David Lazarus Watts opens a general store in Lydney.

1880: Son Josiah Watts founds an ironmonger's shop in Lydney.

1905: The company becomes J.S. Watts & Sons as sons Arthur and John Watts join.

1910: The company opens a garage in Lydney.

1912: The company begins Ford motor car sales.

1921: The company acquires a fleet of 200 surplus vehicles, including mobile workshops and spare parts.

1938: The Watts Tyre and Rubber Co. retreading factory is founded in Lydney.

1951: The company receives a franchise for the Vaculug retreading process.

1953: The company begins manufacturing Duracraft industrial tires, forming the new Tyre Division.

1966: Watts Industrial Tyres Ltd. is formed.

1974: The company diversifies with Watts Urethane Product Ltd.

1979: The business reorganizes under holding company Watts of Lydney Group.

1983: A new rubber compounding plant is opened.

1996: A new tire production site is established.

1998: The company spends £4.5 million expanding tire production.

1999: The rubber compounding division is acquired from Wellington Holdings.

2001: The company announces production joint ventures in China and Brazil and its intention to reduce tire production operations in the United Kingdom.

2004: The company acquires 50 percent of tire producer and retreader Eu-retec in Sri Lanka and shuts down the remaining tire production in the United Kingdom.

As part of the group's new strategy, the company reached its first outsourcing agreement in 2001, setting up a joint venture with China's Guizhou Tyres Inc., establishing the largest industrial tire manufacturing operation in China. Under terms of the deal, Guizhou provided the manufacturing deal while Watts controlled the technology and designs, as well as sales and distribution.

Watts continued looking for new joint venture partners in China, and in Sri Lanka, which had emerged as a major tire manufacturing center. The company also formed a joint venture in Brazil, with that country's Souza Pinto Industria e Comercio de Artefatos de Borracha Ltda. The new subsidiary began production of Watts's solid industrial tires for the South American market.

In 2004, Watts acquired a 50 percent stake in Sri Lanka's Eu-retec, a tire manufacturer and retreader. The purchase marked the end of Watts's tire production in the United Kingdom, as it shut down its rubber tire production at the beginning of May in that year. The companies' manufacturing presence in Sri Lanka enabled it to compete in the OEM market as well, leading to an agreement to produce solid tires for Germany's Continental AG in December 2004. As John Thurston, chairman of the company and a member of the founding Watts family, told *European Rubber Journal:* "We have transformed our tyre company business model over the past few years and this has allowed us to cooperate with Continental in this way. Supply chain agreements between competitors are not unusual in other industries and it is a trend we are keen to develop." Given the Watts' family's long history of entrepreneurship, Watts of Lydney appeared in a strong position as it entered the new century.

Principal Subsidiaries

Watts Aviation; Watts Industrial; Watts Plysolene; Watts Polymers; Watts Truck & Van; Watts Urethane.

Principal Competitors

Bridgestone Corporation; Compagnie Financiere Michelin; Goodyear Tire and Rubber Co.; Sibtyazhmash Joint Stock Co.; Continental AG; Guizhou Rubber Industry Co.; Pirelli C S.p.A.; Yokohama Tire Corporation; Hangzhou Zhongce Rubber Company Ltd.; Liaoning Tyre Factory; Carlisle Tire and Wheel Co.; Trelleborg AB.

Further Reading

Raleigh, Patrick, "Watts Embarks on Overseas Ventures," *European Rubber Journal,* December 2001, p. 14.

——, "Watts to Buy Compounding Unit," *Rubber & Plastics News,* November 1, 1999, p. 4.

"Watts Closes Mixing Plant," *Rubber & Plastics News,* July 9, 2001, p. 18.

"Watts Shifting Output," *Rubber & Plastics News,* November 19, 2001, p. 6.

White, Liz, "UK Firm in Solid-Tyre Deal with Conti," *European Rubber Journal,* December 1, 2004, p. 10.

—M.L. Cohen

Zippo Manufacturing Company

33 Barbour Street
Bradford, Pennsylvania 16701-1973
U.S.A.
Telephone: (814) 368-2700
Fax: (800) 362-3598
Web site: http://www.zippo.com

Private Company
Incorporated: 1932
Employees: 777
Sales: $200 million (2004 est.)
NAIC: 339999 All Other Miscellaneous Manufacturing;
339911 Jewelry (Except Costume) Manufacturing;
332211 Cutlery and Flatware (Except Precious)
Manufacturing; 339941 Pen and Mechanical Pencil
Manufacturing

Zippo Manufacturing Company is world famous for its Zippo windproof lighter, its lifetime guarantee, and the distinctive "click" it makes when opened. The company has sold more than 400 million lighters since its founding in 1932 and each year produces thousands of different designs, including ones aimed specifically at collectors. In addition to its trademark rectangular pocket lighter, the design of which has been little changed since its early 1930s launch, Zippo in 2002 introduced the MPL (or Multi-Purpose Lighter), a long, slender model designed to light candles, grills, fireplaces, and the like—a break from the traditional idea of the "cigarette lighter." The dominant maker of refillable lighters in the United States, with an estimated market share of 40 percent, Zippo also sells its lighters in more than 120 other countries, with Japan being its largest export market. Following the launch of a big overseas push in the mid-1980s, Zippo began to derive 60 percent of its sales from exports. Since diversifying for the first time in 1962 (when a tape measure was introduced), Zippo manufacturers and sells such items as pocket knives, money clips, and writing instruments. The company owns W.R. Case & Sons Cutlery Company, a venerable maker of high-quality pocket, hunting, fishing, camping, and utility knives that, like Zippo, is based in the small Allegheny Mountain town of Bradford, Pennsylvania. Another subsidiary, Zippo Fashion Italia S.r.l., based in Vicenza, Italy, produces a variety of Zippo-branded leather goods, including handbags, belts, wallets, and briefcases, for sale through more than 1,500 boutiques and shops in Europe.

Entrepreneurial Beginnings

George Grant Blaisdell, Zippo's founder, had a checkered career in business prior to focusing on lighters. His father ran a machine shop in Blaisdell's hometown of Bradford, Pennsylvania, where Blaisdell started work as a machinist at age 16 (working a 56-hour week at 10 cents an hour), then became a salesman, and at age 20 took over the business. He managed to keep the business afloat during World War I through government contracts, then sold out in 1920. Blaisdell headed for New York; having failed to strike it rich playing the stock market, he returned to Bradford and invested what money remained in local oil wells (through his co-ownership, with his brother Walter, of Blaisdell Oil Company), making a modest living over the next ten years from the proceeds. Thereupon, in the early 1930s he was waiting for the right business opportunity.

On a muggy summer night in Bradford in 1932, Blaisdell and a friend stepped out on the terrace of the Pennhill Country Club. Blaisdell's friend used a cumbersome-looking Austrian lighter with a removable brass top to light a cigarette. Blaisdell proceeded to chide his friend: "You're all dressed up. Why don't you get a lighter that looks decent?" In an enthusiastic reply, his friend said: "Well, George, it works!"

Blaisdell was suitably impressed and decided to try to sell the lighters himself. He obtained rights to distribute the product in the United States, imported them for 12 cents each, and attempted to sell them for $1 each. But this venture failed, mainly because of the clumsy nature of the lighter's design. Blaisdell then decided to design his own lighter, one that was attractive, easy to use, and dependable.

The resulting original model was rectangular in shape—made from brass tubing with soldered tops and bottoms and square corners—with a chrome-plated hinge soldered on the outside for easy opening and closing. Sized to fit comfortably in a hand, the lighter featured a windhood to protect the wick. Blaisdell liked the name of another recent invention, the zipper, so he christened his lighter the "Zippo" (and his new firm, Zippo Manufacturing Company).

Production of Zippos began in 1933 in a $10 per month rented room over the Rickerson & Pryde garage in Bradford. The shop had $260 in equipment and two employees, from which came lighters retailing for $1.95 with the backing of a lifetime guarantee.

Struggling Early Years

Sales of the lighters got off to a slow start, with only 1,100 sold during the inaugural production year. Blaisdell tried all kinds of methods to move his brainchild. He gave away samples and gifts to long-distance bus drivers, jewelers, and tobacconists. In December 1937 he paid $3,000 of mostly borrowed money for a full-page ad in *Esquire* magazine after he found that retailers shied away from products that were not advertised. Unfortunately, Blaisdell did not yet have sufficient distribution to take advantage of the effect of such advertising so this gambit failed to pay off.

While handling sales himself and struggling to develop a market for his windproof lighter, Blaisdell also tinkered with the design. The lighter was shortened by a quarter inch in 1933, decorative diagonal lines were added in 1934, the hinge was placed on the inside of the case in 1936, and rounded tops and bottoms replaced the square corners of the original design in 1937. This last alteration was important from a production standpoint as the lid and bottom could now be formed as a whole, eliminating the soldering process.

Blaisdell achieved his first big sales break in 1934 when he started selling Zippos on punchboards, two-cents-per-play gambling games popular in U.S. tobacco and confectionery shops, poolrooms, and cigar stands. Before punchboards were outlawed in 1940, more than 300,000 Zippos were sold through this game of chance, enough for Zippo Manufacturing to achieve its first profits, modest though they were.

While punchboards were a short-lived chapter in Zippo history, another of Blaisdell's marketing methods had a much longer-lasting impact. In 1936 an Iowa life insurance company ordered 200 engraved lighters that it gave to its agents as contest prizes. Bradford's own Kendall Oil Company ordered 500 engraved lighters for its customers and employees. Thus began Zippo's specialty advertising business, which would become an increasingly important venture in the coming decades.

With sales increasing thanks to the punchboards and the special markets deals, Blaisdell expanded his operations. First, the production facility expanded into the entire second floor of the Rickerson & Pryde building; Blaisdell also added a new office elsewhere in Bradford. Then in 1938 the factory and offices were both moved into a former garage on Barbour Street in Bradford. That same year, Zippo's first table lighter debuted, a four-and-a-half inch tall model that held four times the fuel of a pocket lighter. The following year Zippo introduced a sophisticated new lighter model, the 14-karat solid gold Zippo, available in both plain and engine-turned models.

World War II Brought Zippo Fame

With the onset of U.S. involvement in World War II, the U.S. government forced the halt in production of many consumer products. Blaisdell continued Zippo production, but as he had during World War I, he again moved into government contracting—all Zippos became destined for the U.S. military. With brass reserved for military uses only, the wartime lighters were made of a low-grade steel. Since this provided a poor finish, they were spray-painted black then baked, which produced a crackle finish.

Blaisdell sold some of these Zippos to the military post exchanges at such a low price that they were then resold for $1.00, making them the most affordable lighter available. He also sent hundreds of lighters to celebrities, including the famous war correspondent Ernie Pyle who then gave them away to servicemen overseas. (Pyle gave Blaisdell the nickname "Mr. Zippo.") Through these actions, the Zippo became the favorite lighter of GIs, whose loyalty to the product would help fuel postwar sales. Numerous war stories also helped cement the Zippo as an American icon—the Zippo that stopped a bullet, that cooked soup in helmets, that illuminated the darkened instrument panel of an Army pilot's disabled plane, enabling him to land safely. Zippos also began making frequent appearances in Hollywood movies—notably war movies, such as *Casablanca* (1942), at first but later films noir—enhancing their iconic status. Meanwhile, wartime production peaked in 1945 when three million Zippos were made.

Postwar Design Improvements, Expansions, and Diversification

The Zippo repair clinic became famous in its own right by backing up the Zippo guarantee. Repaired lighters were returned at no cost to the customer, not even return postage. The clinic provided more than just customer goodwill. It also provided invaluable information about design flaws. Over the long run, the repair clinic found that a faulty or broken hinge was the most common reason for a Zippo to be returned. But soon after World War II, in 1946, Blaisdell discovered that the most frequent repairs were for worn striking wheels—wheels that had been coming from an outside supplier. Blaisdell immediately stopped production to address the problem. He decided to bring production of the wheels in-house and spent $300,000 on a new flint wheel capable of firing a lighter as many as 78,000 times. This top-quality wheel was produced by a knurling operation that remained a company secret.

Zippo continued to develop new lighter models following the war. In 1947 Town and Country designs were introduced

Key Dates:
1932: George Grant Blaisdell founds Zippo Manufacturing Company.
1933: After an attempt to sell lighters imported from Austria fails, Blaisdell designs his own lighter, which he christens the ''Zippo,'' and begins manufacturing in Bradford, Pennsylvania.
1941: Following U.S. entry into World War II, Zippo continues to produce lighters but all are now destined for the U.S. military, through which the brand will achieve fame.
1950: Blaisdell establishes his own sales force; first foreign subsidiary is established in Canada.
1962: Zippo diversifies for the first time, producing a pocket tape measure.
1978: Upon Blaisdell's death, ownership of Zippo passes to his two daughters.
1993: W.R. Case & Sons Cutlery Company is acquired; through a license agreement, a line of Zippo clothing is offered in Japan.
2000: George B. Duke, grandson of the founder, gains control of the company.
2002: Zippo launches its Multi-Purpose Lighter (MPL).
2003: First Zippo retail store opens in Hangzhou, China.
2004: DDM Italia S.r.l., maker of Zippo brand leather goods, is acquired and renamed Zippo Fashion Italia S.r.l.

that featured images of pheasants, mallards, geese, sailboats, trout, setters, and horses. Three years later, full cover leather lighters and sterling silver lighters made their debuts.

Meanwhile, Blaisdell sought to improve his sales force. From 1939 to 1950 Zippo's entire sales operation consisted of two cigar salesmen, who sold Zippos as a sideline mainly to tobacco wholesalers. The two men each were charged with a vast selling territory. In 1950 Blaisdell established his own sales force, with district managers assigned specific regions. This sales force was not restricted to tobacco wholesalers, but also called on jewelry, drugstore, and grocery wholesalers.

Also in 1950, Zippo set up its first foreign subsidiary, Zippo Manufacturing Company of Canada Limited. Located in Niagara Falls, Ontario, the company consisted of a small production facility that helped increase overall Zippo capacity, which reached 20,000 lighters a day by 1952. Annual revenues had reached $9.5 million and the company enjoyed healthy after-tax profits of almost 10 percent.

Zippo continued to expand its facilities in the 1950s and 1960s to meet the growing demand, both domestic and foreign. In 1954 a new building for chrome plating and fabricating, located on Congress Street in Bradford, was completed. New corporate offices were built in 1955 next to the Barbour Street factory in Bradford. During the 1960s the Congress Street plant underwent a series of additions and eventually became the main location for fabricating and assembling Zippo products.

After 30 years as a lighter-only company, Zippo in 1962 diversified for the first time when it introduced a six-foot

flexible-steel pocket tape measure. This was followed by a compact pocketknife and nail file, a money-clip knife, a golf ball, a key holder, a magnifier, and a letter opener. Unlike Zippo lighters, however, none of these products were made available for retail purchase; they were available only through Zippo's specialty advertising operation, which by the mid-1960s accounted for 40 percent of overall company volume. Zippo boasted of more than 27,000 commercial accounts at the time. All of Zippo's metal products were backed by the same Zippo pledge: ''If for any reason your Zippo will not work, regardless of age or condition—we'll fix it free.'' (For unfixable items, the company sent the customer a replacement.) Zippo even guaranteed its golf ball as playable for 180 holes.

End of Blaisdell Era in the 1970s

After introducing the first of a series of lighters with space designs in 1969—the first honoring the landing on the moon—Zippo ushered in the 1970s appropriately enough with a Zodiac lighter series. In 1976 a commemorative bicentennial lighter hit the market, as did an in-fashion denim-like lighter.

The year 1978 marked the end of an era when Blaisdell died. Ownership of Zippo Manufacturing passed to Blaisdell's daughters, Harriet Wick and Sarah Dorn, who had worked for the company for years and would continue to do so for years to come but did not wish to run it. They entrusted the presidency to a longtime employee, Robert Galey.

Unfortunately, throughout the 1970s and into the early 1980s, Zippo's sales stagnated at about $30 million a year. The firm was manufacturing-oriented and needed to become more marketing-focused in order to get past this plateau. As it turned out, Galey's stint as president was short-lived since he retired in 1986. Zippo's third president was Michael Schuler, who had joined the company as controller shortly after Blaisdell's death and then was promoted to vice-president and controller in 1982. Under Schuler's leadership, Zippo's revenues increased fivefold within ten years.

Schuler Era: 1986 to 2000

The spectacular growth of this period was generated by a combination of increased exports, the aggressive targeting of the collector's and gift/souvenir markets, and creative line extensions. On the export front, Japan remained the top market—one of every four Zippos made in the late 1980s went to Japan—and Western European sales were strong also, but Schuler targeted such emerging areas as China and South Asia and Eastern Europe following the fall of communism. Many of these emerging nations had high percentages of smokers, making them prime Zippo territory. This contrasted sharply with Zippo's domestic market, where antismoking crusades continued to gain momentum throughout the 1990s. Overall, whereas exports constituted only 40 percent of total company sales in the mid-1980s, by 1995 65 percent of sales originated outside the United States.

Credit for Zippo's ''discovery'' of the collector's and gift markets for Zippo lighters goes to the person Schuler hired in 1991 as head of sales and marketing, James Baldo. Soon after taking the job, Baldo commissioned customer surveys that showed that 30 percent of Zippo's customers defined themselves as "collectors." The surveys also showed that many buyers gave the lighters away as gifts. In response, Zippo began offering premium-priced—$19 to $40—gift/souvenir lighter sets, including ones with licensed brands (Harley-Davidson, Corvette) or images of tourist destinations (Niagara Falls, Empire State Building).

Then Zippo began offering limited edition "collector" Zippos, directly targeting the collector's market. In 1992, a 60th anniversary lighter appeared, followed by 1993's Varga Girl lighter, 1994's D-Day commemorative lighter, 1995's Mysteries of the Forest, and 1996's Zippo Salutes Pinup Girls. Zippo also began producing a collector's guide and, starting in 1993, sponsored an annual July swap meet at the Bradford headquarters. In 1994 the company took the further step of opening in Bradford the Zippo Family Store and Museum, highly popular with collectors, which was expanded to five times its original size in 1996.

Zippo had been criticized at times throughout its history for being too conservative, in particular in regard to line extensions. But under Schuler, Zippo began a more aggressive diversification approach, beginning in 1993 with the acquisition of the crosstown W.R. Case & Sons Cutlery Company, a firm with annual sales of $15 million. Case was founded in 1889 in Little Valley, New York, but relocated to Bradford in 1905, where it developed a line of pocket knives, hunting knives, household cutlery, and commemoratives. The company had filed for bankruptcy after a difficult period and then was bought out of bankruptcy by a limited partnership, River Associates, in 1990. Case's products meshed well with Zippo's and provided Zippo with another avenue into the retail market. Soon after the acquisition, in fact, dual gift sets that included a Case knife and a Zippo lighter were soon being retailed at prices ranging from $50 to $200.

A much more dramatic extension came via the 1993 license agreement with Japanese clothing manufacturer Itochu Fashion System Co. Itochu gained the right to the Zippo name and soon offered Zippo jeans, gloves, and leather jackets in Japan.

With antismoking forces gaining steam in the United States, Zippo came up in 1995 with a creative way to keep its brand strong. It introduced the ZipLight pocket flashlight, which was simply a traditional lighter casing with a replaceable battery pack inside. Zippo spent $500,000 on a television advertising campaign to launch this new product, one of its largest campaigns ever.

The Zippo brand, prematurely declared dead by *USA Today* in 1989, was clearly alive and well and seemed as ubiquitous as ever. Revenues for 1996 were estimated to have reached a record $150 million. The company was now producing 80,000 lighters a day, and the 300 millionth Zippo lighter rolled off the assembly line that year. One year later, the company opened the Zippo/Case Visitors Center to replace the previous Family Store and Museum. The new visitors center encompassed the Zippo/Case Museum and the Zippo/Case Store and also offered visitors a chance to view repair technicians practicing their craft in the Zippo Repair Clinic.

Unfortunately for the company, 1996 turned out to be a peak year, as sales dropped off in the late 1990s and into the new century. Zippo's diversification drive, including the heavily promoted ZipLight, never produced any big winners, and even the push into the collectibles market, while meeting with the approval of many customers, failed to nudge sales higher. Certainly in the U.S. market, part of the problem was the steady decline in smoking: 42 percent of American adults were smokers in 1965, a figure that was down to 24 percent by 1998 and then to 20 percent by 2001. Finally, the muddled ownership situation was another key hindrance. The two daughters of the founder, plus their four children, all had equal control of the company, and all worked there as well. Having six persons equally in charge made it difficult for Zippo to adopt new strategies and led to a certain malaise, particularly following some of the failed attempts to ramp up sales.

New Ownership, New Management, New Strategies for the New Century

One of the grandchildren of the founder, George B. Duke, began negotiating to buy out his relatives in 1998. By 2000 he, along with his mother, Sarah Dorn, had gained control of the company. Feeling that the firm needed to become more marketing oriented, Duke in 2001 replaced Schuler, the CEO, with Greg Booth, who had years of marketing experience with Kendall Motor Oil, Sunoco, Inc., and the Zippo subsidiary W.R. Case & Sons. The new owner and new manager soon commissioned studies by two outside consulting firms, both of which reached the same conclusion, that the Zippo brand was extremely strong and that there were tremendous possibilities for creating a broader line of Zippo products through licensing deals. Based on this research, and to counter the antismoking trends that were hurting sales of lighters, Duke and Booth set an ambitious goal of deriving half of the company's revenues from products unrelated to tobacco by 2010. They also aimed to double the company's overall revenues by that same year.

Ironically, the first new product to come out of this new strategy was in fact a lighter—just not a traditional cigarette lighter. Zippo launched its Multi-Purpose Lighter (MPL) in 2002 via a major television advertising campaign led off on the Home & Garden Television cable channel. The MPL was part of the rapidly growing multipurpose lighter category, but it was the first premium refillable model on the market. Offered in two models carrying suggested retail prices of $14.95 and $19.95, the MPL featured a long, slender, ergonomic design with a window showing the level of the butane fuel. With its adjustable flame, the MPL was designed to light candles, lanterns, grills, fireplaces, stoves, campfires, and more. In another break with tradition, Zippo contracted with a Chinese company to make the MPL, but it nonetheless backed it with the usual lifetime guarantee. The company continued to make its traditional pocket lighters in Bradford, despite increasing cut-price competition from low-wage countries.

Sales of the MPL got off to a good start, with about two million units sold the first year—far exceeding company expectations. Even more encouraging than the numbers, however, was that the people buying the new lighter skewed mostly female and younger than the average Zippo customer. The MPL's child-resistant safety button was seen to be a key feature in attracting female buyers. Another plus was that the MPL expanded Zippo's base of retailers as such chains as Bed Bath & Beyond Inc. became Zippo sellers for the first time. Unfortunately, in October

2004 Zippo was forced to recall about 100,000 MPLs because in some cases fuel was spilling out of the nozzle when the lighter was first used. The company set up a system to send out replacement lighters to consumers who had purchased the affected models. At the same time, Zippo was developing for release in 2005 a second version of the MPL, one geared to outdoor use when hiking or camping, for example, and featuring a more durable, windproof design and a built-in flashlight.

While launching the MPL, Zippo also continued to pursue opportunities in the collectors market. In 2002 the company founded an international club for Zippo collectors, Zippo Click, naming it after the distinctive sound of a Zippo lighter opening. For a $20 membership fee, collectors received a number of benefits, including a subscription to a quarterly magazine; access to a members-only web site providing opportunities for communicating with other collectors and for buying, selling, and trading merchandise; and the chance to purchase products available only to members. Just a couple years after its formation, Zippo Click had gained more than 7,000 members. There were also by this time dozens of independent lighter collectors' clubs with thousands of members around the world.

In September 2003 Zippo Manufacturing reached another milestone with the production of its 400 millionth lighter. That same year, the company elected to consolidate its North American production in Bradford by shutting down the plant in Niagara Falls, Canada, which had been producing about 500,000 lighters per year for the Canadian market. Also, Zippo was the subject of criticism that year stemming from its sponsorship of a web site, zippotricks.com, featuring hundreds of tricks that can be performed with a Zippo lighter. The National Fire Protection Association and others in the fire safety industry contended that the company, through the web site, was encouraging people to play with fire. Although Zippo officials disagreed with this criticism, they pulled the plug on the site under withering pressure. The web site's original creator subsequently transformed it into the more generic lightertricks.com, which was unaffiliated with Zippo.

In the early 2000s Zippo's leaders were becoming increasingly concerned about the production of cheap knockoff lighters, many of which were being made in China. The company estimated that it was losing as much as a third of its potential worldwide sales to counterfeiters, particularly factories in southern China that were capable of churning out 45,000 fake Zippos a day. Zippo therefore accelerated an effort to trademark the distinctive shape of its lighter—a rectangular metal shell with beveled edges and a gently curving flip-top—around the world. Trademark protection in the United States was granted in 2002. The company pulled back from a related effort to trademark the distinctive Zippo click.

Coincidentally or not, China was at the center of another development in 2003, the opening of the first Zippo retail store. Located in Hangzhou, a city of several million people located about 110 miles southeast of Shanghai, the store sold only Zippo products but more than just lighters and lighter accessories. It offered Zippo clothing, watches, sunglasses, and leather goods such as wallets and belts. Zippo products were already available in 450 outlets throughout China, a rapidly growing market in which it was estimated that one-third of all

the world's tobacco was consumed and where 40 percent of the adult population were smokers. The company planned to open several more Zippo stores in China.

In stepping up its efforts to protect its precious brand, Zippo discovered that a family-owned company in Italy called DDM Italia S.r.l. had been selling a line of leather goods—handbags, belts, wallets, and the like—under the Zippo name since the late 1980s. Zippo Manufacturing had not registered the name under clothing and leather categories, which led to a lengthy trademark dispute and contentious court battles. In early 2004 Zippo settled the matter by acquiring DDM Italia for an undisclosed sum. The Italian firm was renamed Zippo Fashion Italia S.r.l., and it continued to operate separately and sell Zippo brand fashion accessories throughout Europe. The Italian subsidiary also began exploring the idea of producing men's leather accessories for sale both in Europe and elsewhere.

Zippo at this time was also working hard to develop its first line of Zippo licensed products for release in 2005. These brand-extending items were to be produced under license by other manufacturers, and Booth told the *Bradford Era* in June 2003 that they would be ''stainless steel, rugged, durable, and premium grade products that come with extended or lifetime warranties.'' Zippo was particularly investigating flame-related outdoor products, such as grills, patio heaters, and Tiki torches, for the initial launch, to be followed most likely by camping equipment and other outdoor gear, perhaps even mountain bikes. Eventually, the hope was to be able to set up in-store boutiques within retailers offering the entire range of Zippo products. Concurrently under development was a refillable butane pocket lighter aimed at customers not enamored of the smell or messiness of the traditional Zippo lighter fluid.

As Zippo Manufacturing pursued its aggressive growth and diversification goals, it faced a new challenge. In April 2005 the U.S. Transportation Security Administration began implementing a ban on all lighters within the cabin of aircraft and in checked luggage. Zippo agreed that lighters posed a potential threat within passenger cabins, but objected to the ban on packing them in checked luggage. The firm released a statement in which Booth said, ''We have not uncovered one instance in which lighters in checked luggage exploded, caught fire, or otherwise posed a danger to the aircraft.'' He said that the ban could potentially cut total Zippo sales by 20 to 30 percent. The ban threatened the company's gift business, as well as its sales in airports and duty-free shops, and also prevented collectors from taking their wares to and from swap meets and shows when traveling by air. This latest threat seemed to provide added impetus to the drive to extend the Zippo brand beyond lighters.

Principal Subsidiaries

W.R. Case & Sons Cutlery Company; Zippo Canada Sales, Ltd.; Zippo France S.A.; Zippo GmbH (Germany); Zippo Fashion Italia S.r.l. (Italy); Zippo Italia S.r.l. (Italy); Zippo Japan; Zippo South Africa; Zippo U.K. Limited.

Principal Competitors

Société BIC; Swedish Match AB; Tokai Corporation; Swiss Army Brands, Inc.; Ronson Corporation; Buck Knives Inc.

Further Reading

Amster, Robin, "Zippo Lighter: American Classics," *Popular Mechanics,* August 1994, pp. 44–46.

Baker, Stephen, "How Zippo Keeps the Flame Lit," *Business Week,* November 20, 1995.

Beardi, Cara, "Zippo's Eternal Flame: New Campaign Uses Emotion to Take on Disposables," *Advertising Age,* August 13, 2001, p. 4.

Brown, Christie, "Flaming Success," *Forbes,* November 18, 1996, pp. 214–16.

Carlino, Maria, "Zippo Manufacturing Co.," *Journal of Commerce and Commercial,* February 3, 1995, p. 4A.

Collins, Lisa, "Keeping Zippo's Flame: Name Is Hot, Marketing Lacks Spark," *USA Today,* August 11, 1989, pp. 1B-2B.

Dininny, Paulette, "Keepers of the Flame," *Smithsonian,* December 1998, p. 44.

Dipazquale, Cara B., "Rebel Has New Cause," *Advertising Age,* July 8, 2002, p. 3.

Fogarty, Thomas A., "Keeping Zippo's Flame Eternal," *USA Today,* June 24, 2003, p. B3.

Fuller, Nicole, and Jim McKay, "Travelers Lightened of Their Lighters," *Pittsburgh Post-Gazette,* April 15, 2005.

Galloni, Alessandra, "Lighter Lovers Flip Their Tops at a Zippo Collectors' Convention," *Wall Street Journal,* August 4, 1995, p. B1.

Kaplan, Andrew, "Scorching Demand for Lighters," *U.S. Distribution Journal,* April 15, 1996, p. 14.

Levy, Robert, "The Mark of Zippo," *Dun's Review,* October 1966, pp. 53–54, 59.

Lindeman, Teresa F., "Ketchum's New Zippo Campaign Lights Everything but Cigarettes," *Pittsburgh Post-Gazette,* September 11, 1998, p. D1.

McGrath, Molly Wade, *Top Sellers, U.S.A.: Success Stories Behind America's Best-Selling Products from Alka-Seltzer to Zippo,* New York: Morrow, 1983, pp. 156–57.

McKenzie, Bob, "Zippo Lighters a Low-Tech Legend," *Financial Post,* January 1, 1994, p. 8.

Meabon, Linda L., *Zippo Manufacturing Company,* Charleston, S.C.: Arcadia Publishing, 2003, 128 p.

Pasinski, Jim, "Booth Talks About Zippo," *Bradford (Pa.) Era,* June 5, 2003.

——, "Despite Rumors, Booth Says Zippo Business Is on the Upswing," *Bradford (Pa.) Era,* June 6, 2003.

"Mr. Zippo," *Fortune,* October 1952, p. 220.

Neuborne, Ellen, "Hands-on Case Study—The Problem: Zippo Has a Strong Brand Name, but Stagnant Sales. Can the Fabled Firm Market Its Way Out of the Doldrums?," *Inc.,* September 2004, pp. 42, 44.

Poore, David, *Zippo: The Great American Lighter,* Atglen, Pa.: Shiffer, 1997, 216 p.

Schellhammer, Marcie, "Counterfeiting of Zippo Lighters in China Affecting Bradford," *Bradford (Pa.) Era,* August 3, 2004.

Sheehan, Charles, "Zippo Fired Up over Cheap Chinese Lighter Knockoffs," *Pittsburgh Post-Gazette,* August 3, 2004, p. C9.

Sorkin, Andrew Ross, "Ketchum's Challenge Is How to Remake the Zippo As Something Other Than a Cigarette Lighter," *New York Times,* March 18, 1999, p. C7.

Spangler, Todd, "Zippo Gets Tough on Lighter Pirates," *Harrisburg (Pa.) Patriot,* February 25, 2003, p. D6.

Stranahan, Susan Q., "Zippo Makes a Comeback," *Fortune,* September 8, 1997, pp. 40+.

Teather, David, "Old Flame Still Burning," *Guardian* (London), January 29, 2005, p. 30.

"Zippo: A History of Progress," Bradford, Pa.: Zippo Manufacturing Company, 1995.

"The Zippo Lighter Collector's Guide," Bradford, Pa.: Zippo Manufacturing Company, 1996.

—David E. Salamie

Zondervan Corporation

5300 Patterson Avenue, S.E.
Grand Rapids, Michigan 49530
U.S.A.
Telephone: (616) 698-6900
Fax: (616) 698-3223
Web site: http://www.zondervan.com

Wholly Owned Subsidiary of HarperCollins Publishers
Inc.
Incorporated: 1931
Employees: 400
Sales: $160 million (2005 est.)
NAIC: 511130 Book Publishers; 511210 Software
Publishing; 511199 All Other Publishers; 512120
Motion Picture and Video Distribution

Zondervan Corporation, a wholly owned subsidiary of HarperCollins Publishers, is one of the largest Christian publishing companies in the world. Its products range from the top selling *New International Version of the Bible*, to inspirational fiction, self-help, reference, biography, history, and textbooks, to gift products and a wide range of multimedia products. Since becoming a subsidiary of HarperCollins in 1988, Zondervan has concentrated its energies on traditional religious publishing, while extending its reach beyond the evangelical market with such bestsellers as Rick Warren's *The Purpose-Driven Life* and the Veggie Tales books for children. Having divested itself of a bookstore chain and a music company, Zondervan has found its niche as the nation's leading Bible publisher and continues to develop products for its evolving Christian market.

A Family Business: 1930s–60s

Zondervan was created in 1931 by brothers Pat and Bernard Zondervan, in their mother's Grandville, Michigan farmhouse as a religious bookselling company. In 1932 the brothers opened their first bookstore in neighboring Grand Rapids. The following year saw the first two books published under the Zondervan imprint. The company's home base of western Michigan was particularly religious and conservative, a perfect locale for such a

business. Grand Rapids, known as the city with the most churches per capita in the United States, was home to a number of seminaries and church-affiliated colleges, and was the headquarters of the Reformed Church in America, the Dutch Protestant sect founded on the principles of John Calvin.

From the 1930s through the 1950s the company expanded. In 1959 Zondervan bought a religious music company, Singspiration. The following year the company took over publication of *Halley's Bible Handbook* from a private firm, eventually selling over four million copies of the title. Over the years Zondervan's bookstore operation had expanded to a number of locations and in the early 1960s the first outlet was opened in a shopping mall. The success of this store led the company to open in other malls, eventually placing all new outlets in such locations.

In 1966 Zondervan purchased the Bible department from the larger Harper & Row publishing company, which brought the company a number of specialized Bibles and related textbooks, including the popular *Harper Study Bible*. During the same year cofounder Bernie Zondervan died, but brother Pat continued to lead the company. Zondervan's publishing efforts included a somewhat broad range of material, not always books with a strictly conservative, religious bent. Titles such as *The Act of Marriage* by Tim and Beverly LaHaye from 1959 and *Sexual Happiness in Marriage* by Herbert Miles from 1967 were published alongside more typical fare such as biographies of missionaries, discussions of theological issues, Bible encyclopedias and concordances, and tracts on the evils of tobacco or communism.

Further Expansion: 1970–87

Zondervan occasionally published religious titles with mass appeal, such as Hal Lindsey's *The Late Great Planet Earth* from 1970, which eventually sold some ten million copies. The following year, 1971, Zondervan made an investment in the financially troubled International Bible Society's translation of the *New International Version of the Bible*, a move that would later repay itself many times over. The New Testament of the *New International Version* was published in 1973, with Zondervan given exclusive rights in the United States. The entire Bible was ready in 1978, and was a sensation, quickly

Company Perspectives:

To be the leading Christian communications company meeting the needs of people with resources that glorify Jesus Christ and promote biblical principles. Zondervan is a leading international Christian communications company, producing bestselling and awardwinning Bibles, books, children's products, software, audio, video, multimedia, and a broad line of gift products.

rising on the bestseller lists to second place behind the King James version. Zondervan was suddenly vaulted to the forefront of religious publishing houses. The *NIV*, as it was known, was a scrupulous translation from the original languages into contemporary English, and it appealed to many Christians of different branches of the faith. Within a few years it was adopted as the Bible of choice by a wide range of churches, from Baptists to Episcopalians. With the *NIV* also came the opportunity to create many derivative works such as concordances and study materials, all of which found a ready market.

Zondervan went public in 1976, issuing stock on the NAS-DAQ. Following the success of the *NIV* Bible, the company began to acquire other businesses. In 1980 religious music publisher John T. Benson Company was purchased, making Zondervan the second largest producer of religious recordings in the United States. In the early 1980s other acquisitions included religious publishers Chosen Books, Francis Asbury Press, and Fleming H. Revell Company, and a specialty bindery, Tapley-Rutter Company.

Zondervan's business, while based on the apparently steady and predictable religious book market, was actually more tenuous than it appeared. In 1979 there were difficulties related to the bookstore chain, resulting in unexpected losses. Though sales and profits more than doubled within the next five years, with annual revenues in 1983 of $93 million, in 1984 accounting irregularities hid losses of several million dollars. These were ultimately attributed to poor inventory control and unanticipated expenses such as unrecoverable publishing advances, but the company's chief financial officer was dismissed and Zondervan was sanctioned by the Securities and Exchange Commission. A lawsuit from a disgruntled New Jersey investor followed, eventually settled out of court for $3.6 million in 1989.

Just before the discovery of its financial problems, Zondervan had chosen James Buick as its chief executive, replacing Pat Zondervan's successor, Peter Kladder, who had been with the company since 1956. Buick, a former executive of Brunswick Corporation, immediately had his hands full. Zondervan posted losses for the next several years following the bookkeeping debacle, and in 1986 a hostile takeover attempt was organized by British financier Christopher Moran. After months of wheeling and dealing, including a visit from Moran to Pat Zondervan and an emergency prayer session held by employees, the company's board reached an agreement with its stockholders to seek a third-party buyer. Not long afterwards, Moran began quietly selling off his shares. The stock price, which had been driven up by the takeover attempt, plummeted when Moran's selloff was discov-

ered. Many investors were angry and when the company was finally sold over a year later for $56.7 million to Harper & Row, other lawsuits were initiated on behalf of investors who felt the board had accepted an unfairly low price. During the course of the takeover attempt, Zondervan had also sold off its Revell and Chosen Books subsidiaries, and had closed a Grand Rapids-based printing operation.

Acquisition and Prosperity: 1988 to the Early 1990s

Harper & Row (which soon merged with British religious book company Collins Publishing to become HarperCollins) was owned by News Corporation Ltd., headed by Rupert Murdoch. Murdoch's other interests included the Fox film and television studios and several tabloid news publications. Zondervan employees and the company's chairman emeritus expressed concerns that the publisher's traditional religious, evangelic focus would be changed as part of a more aggressive pursuit of profits, much as they had also worried about Moran's intentions several years earlier.

Fortunately for Zondervan, there was no apparent downside to the change of ownership as the company's editorial policy was not altered. Instead, there was an enhancement of Zondervan's ability to cross-market titles into the mainstream. Successful books such as the memoirs of Dave Dravecky (a baseball pitcher who had lost his pitching arm), Oliver North, Colin Powell, and Dan Quayle were marketed with HarperCollins, enabling them to reach a larger audience. In some cases Zondervan secured authors it might not have been able to attract on its own, because of its association with HarperCollins. By 1991 the company's estimated annual sales were $175 million, up from $106 million just four years earlier. The publishing division issued an average of 130 new titles a year, including Bible editions tailored to specific audiences such as women and teens, and maintained a healthy backlist of some 1,000 titles.

Though business had been on a more even keel since its acquisition by HarperCollins, Zondervan's management still had doubts about the relationship. In early 1992 amid slumping sales and layoffs, Zondervan sought investors to help buy the company back from HarperCollins. Then rival Word Publishing came up for sale and Zondervan placed its buyout plans on hold to court Word. Word, however, was bought by the country's top religious publisher, Thomas Nelson, and Zondervan abandoned its buyout aspirations. Apparently satisfied it could remain editorially independent, Zondervan concentrated on streamlining operations and developing new products. At the end of 1992, the company sold its Benson Music subsidiary and left the music business completely.

In September 1993 major change came to Zondervan when the company split in two, with the publishing operations retaining the name of Zondervan Publishing House, and the bookstore chain becoming a separate entity (though still owned by Harper-Collins and with offices in the same building as Zondervan). Chief executive James Buick, who had directed the company for almost ten years and had been instrumental in the breakup, retired, and management of Zondervan went to Bruce Ryskamp.

With sales of personal computers beginning to surge in the late 1980s, the company had created a software division to

Key Dates:

1931: Zondervan is founded by Pat and Bernard Zondervan in Grandville, Michigan.
1932: The first Zondervan bookstore is opened in Grand Rapids, Michigan.
1933: Two books are published under the Zondervan name.
1959: Zondervan buys an inspirational music company.
1966: Zondervan acquires the Bible division of Harper & Row.
1971: The company invests in the International Bible Society.
1973: Zondervan publishes the New Testament portion of the International Bible Society's *New International Version* (*NIV*) of the Bible.
1976: Zondervan goes public on the NASDAQ.
1978: Zondervan publishes the entire *NIV*.
1980: John T. Benson, a religious music company, is purchased.
1986: Zondervan fights off a hostile takeover attempt.
1987: Harper & Row buys Zondervan in the aftermath of the takeover attempt; Zondervan ultimately becomes a subsidiary of HarperCollins.
2000: Zondervan publishes its first e-books.
2002: Rick Warren's *The Purpose-Driven Life* is published by Zondervan.
2004: A gender-neutral edition of the *NIV* causes controversy.
2005: *Rolling Stone* magazine causes a media firestorm after refusing a Zondervan ad.

market computer-formatted Bibles and study aids. Other divisions had been founded to create video and audio products, and these operations were merged in early 1995 to form ZPH New Media. Products included BibleSource for Windows, macBible, several series of religious studies and children's videos, and audio versions of some of the company's books. The products were primarily distributed to Christian bookstores.

Fluctuating Bible Sales: Mid- to Late 1990s

The *NIV* Bible, which had been Zondervan's crown jewel since 1978, had remained a consistent bestseller and in 1986 had eclipsed the King James version as the top-selling Bible. The company continued to capitalize on its success, issuing many derivative works and variant versions. Increasingly, Bible sales were being targeted to specific niche groups. One method of repackaging the *NIV* was to create a "Devotional Bible," which added numerous prayers and commentaries directed toward a specific audience, such as mothers with young children or retirees. In late 1994 the Christian Booksellers Association's sales chart of bestselling Bibles, which had been topped by the *NIV* for several years, saw Zondervan products holding all of the top ten slots. It was estimated that 45 percent of all Bibles sold were *NIV*s, especially those directed to niche markets such as women, teens, and children.

Zondervan continued to seek new markets, purchasing Editorial Vida (known in the United States as Vida Publishers) in

August 1995, a distributor of Bibles in French, Spanish, and Portuguese. In addition, Zondervan announced a new *NIV* version called the *New International Reader's Bible* (or *NIrV*), which was written at a third grade reading level. The audience for this version was people with poor reading skills and new immigrants with a limited command of English—it was an instant success.

With so many different niche Bibles on the market (from Zondervan as well as its rivals), it was hardly surprising sales had begun to slump by 1996. Several newly published translations did poorly and Zondervan's former chain of bookstores (now owned by its management following the 1995 buyout) reported shipping more than $200,000 worth of King James Bibles back to publishers. Despite the industrywide slowdown, Zondervan was only slightly affected, and unveiled plans for Devotional Bibles targeted at college students and African Americans. Another Bible project, however, embroiled the company in controversy.

In the years since it had been introduced, the *NIV* had been subject to occasional revisions, as new discoveries of ancient sources were made or new Bible scholarship was published. In the spring of 1997 a committee of scholars wanted to make changes to a number of gender-specific terms in the translation, removing references to "man" and substituting gender-neutral language when a particular passage actually referred to all of humankind. This was not an especially radical move, as the committee was composed of respected, conservative scholars, and changes of this type had already been incorporated into several Bible translations including the recently published *NIrV* and the U.K. version of the *NIV*. When a report in a Christian publication implied the changes were being made to satisfy feminists, anger was stirred up among fundamentalists and Zondervan put the project on the backburner. The International Bible Society, which was responsible for the *NIV* and *NIrV*, also announced it would revise the *NIrV* back to the older *NIV* language standards to appease fundamentalists.

Despite this setback Zondervan continued to do well, with the successful publication of the *African-American Devotional Bible* in the fall of 1997 and the *Collegiate Devotional Bible* in mid-1998. The company also renamed its children's division Zonderkidz and increased its range of products, which included the acquisition of the Gold 'n' Honey unit of Multnomah Publishers. By the end of the decade Zondervan was releasing a total of some 2,000 publications and had renewed its contract with the International Bible Society to continue publishing the *NIV* through the year 2023.

A New Century: Early 2000s

At the dawn of the 21st century, Zonderkidz gained recognition and market share for its age-appropriate Bibles (including the *NIrV* new kids' edition), software and video products, and picture books. Zondervan also expanded its presence in electronic media, not only establishing its own website capable of taking and processing orders, but teaming up with Amazon.com to create an online "Bible store" (www.amazon.com/zondervan) as well. Zondervan also issued two e-books in November 2000, one of which was available only in electronic form. Next came the launch of Inspirio, Zondervan's renamed gifts division, offering a variety of inspirationally themed products including bookmarks, Bible covers, figurines, gift books, candles, cards, and more.

In early 2001 Zondervan absorbed the publishing and marketing duties for Marshall Pickering, an evangelical imprint of HarperCollins based in the United Kingdom. In hopes of broadening Zondervan's international appeal, Marshall Pickering's titles, as well as those of its Anglican imprint, Fount, were folded into Zondervan's catalogue. In the early part of the year, the company rehauled its image and introduced a new logo. Instead of separate logos for each division, the new logo was simply "Zondervan," and was launched at the Christian Booksellers Association convention in July. Though Christian publishing as a whole experienced an industry slowdown for the first three quarters of the year, the aftermath of the terrorist attacks in September 2001 caused a surge in sales for Bibles and inspirational titles. Zondervan finished the year with revenues of $165 million, with its *NIV* editions accounting for a major chunk of its sales.

Zondervan scored several coups in 2002 including a Zonderkidz joint venture with Big Idea Productions, the licensor of the wildly popular Veggie Tales; issuing its first electronic version of the *NIV*; and publishing Rick Warren's book *The Purpose-Driven Life.* The latter proved an astounding success, topping Christian bestseller lists and crossing over to mainstream publishing lists as well. *The Purpose-Driven Life* was to adults what the Veggie Tales phenomenon was to kids— with Zondervan cashing in on both. Zonderkidz planned to publish 30 new Veggie Tales books over the next two years, including several tie-in titles for the first big screen Veggie Tales movie, released in late 2002.

By 2003 Zondervan continued to ride high with *The Purpose-Driven Life,* which had sold 100,000 copies in a matter of months and was slated for translation into several languages. Not only had the title remained at the top of both Christian and general bestseller lists, but it was named Christian Book of the Year by the Christian Booksellers Association. Zondervan's gift division, Inspirio, signed a deal with Running Press in mid-2003 to issue miniature versions of the bestseller. Though the new imprint contained both names, Inspirio marketed its editions to Christian bookstores while Running Press sold to conventional bookstores and retailers. Zondervan did, however, run into controversy with *Today's New International Version* (*TNIV*), its gender-neutral *NIV* which had been resurrected despite running afoul of fundamentalists.

Zondervan believed the translation mirrored societal changes and would appeal to the 18- to 34-year-old demographic, though offended conservatives asked religious bookstores to boycott the title. Thus Zondervan turned to mass merchandisers including Wal-mart, Kmart, and Target for distribution to market the progressive *TNIV.* In keeping with its more traditional products, Zondervan signed Anne Graham Lotz, daughter of Billy Graham, to a four-book deal and partnered with Mel Gibson to handle DVD and VHS sales of his hit movie *The Passion of the Christ* to Christian markets (Twentieth-Century Fox handled nonreligious sales). With *The Passion of the Christ* earning hundreds of millions of dollars at the box office, Zondervan executives expected orders and sales for the

DVDs and videos to skyrocket upon release in August 2004. By the end of the year *The Purpose-Driven Life* had sold more than 15 million copies worldwide and had been named Christian Book of the Year for a second time, propelling Zondervan's sales and in turn accounting for 15 percent of parent company HarperCollins' revenues.

Keeping the Faith, 2005 and Beyond

In January 2005 Zondervan was once again in the news with its *TNIV* after initiating a $1 million advertising campaign and approaching *Rolling Stone* magazine with an ad for the "hip" bible. *Rolling Stone,* long the bastion for free speech and often outrageous content, refused the ad, believing its audience would not appreciate a Bible advertisement. News of the refusal sent shockwaves throughout the magazine's readership and beyond. As *Rolling Stone* faced angry readers and advertisers, Zondervan benefited from numerous publications clamoring to show their political correctness and carry ads for the *TNIV.* In the end, *Rolling Stone* caved and Zondervan had a plethora of media outlets for the controversial *TNIV.* Other Zondervan hits during the year included a glossy, new edition of the *NIV* for women that looked more like an issue of *Glamour* or *Vogue,* and Rick Warren's still popular *The Purpose-Driven Life,* which remained on both the Christian and mainstream bestseller lists.

Into the 21st century Zondervan continued to rule the Bible segment of Christian publishing, putting out Bibles tailored to the evolving needs of its readers. Bibles came in all shapes and sizes—from traditional leather bindings to neon or flower-printed softcovers, from e-books for handheld devices to audio, video, or DVD formats. The *NIV,* its most popular line of Bibles, had sold more than 150 million copies worldwide by 2005. In addition to its mainstay Bibles, Zondervan provided a myriad of religious-themed materials from its Inspirio line's bookmarks, candles, and home décor products to Zonderkidz's chapter books, picture books, and ABC primers.

Principal Operating Units

Bibles; Books; New Media; Zonderkidz; Inspirio; Vida Publishers.

Principal Competitors

Canon Press; Multnomah Publishers; Thomas Nelson Inc.; Tyndale House Publishers, Inc.; W Publishing Group.

Further Reading

"Baptists Irate Over Zondervan Plan for New Bible," *Grand Rapids Press,* May 14, 1997, p. A1.

"Bible Bust: Publishers Are Making Too Many Bibles for Too Few Christians," *Grand Rapids Press,* November 9, 1996, p. B1.

Buss, Dale, "A New Bible for Sale," *Sales & Marketing Management,* April 2003, p. 16.

——, "Fight to Take Over a Religious Publisher Becomes a Holy War," *Wall Street Journal,* August 14, 1986.

Couretas, John, "Zondervan Cuts 49 from Work Force," *Grand Rapids Press,* February 11, 1992, p. B6.

Crosby, Cindy, "Harper Moves UK Religion to Zondervan," *Publishers Weekly,* April 23, 2001, p. 11.

Crossen, Cynthia, "Harper & Row Says It Will Acquire Zondervan, Expand Religious Line," *Wall Street Journal,* July 14, 1988.

Dart, John, "New Bible Woos Young Adults, Skirts Critics," *Christian Century,* March 8, 2005, pp. 14+.

Fine, Jon, "Bible Publisher Turns *Rolling Stone* Ad Ban into PR Gold," *Advertising Age,* January 24, 2005, p. 3.

Garrett, Lynn, et al., "Smooth Sailing for CBA in Atlanta," *Publishers Weekly,* July 23, 2001, p. 16.

——, "Surfing for Bibles," *Publishers Weekly,* March 13, 2001, p.40.

——, "Zondervan Forms New Children's Publishing Group," *Publishers Weekly,* November 16, 1998, p. 18.

Grenier Guiles, Melinda, "Zondervan Says Financial Chief Relieved of Job," *Wall Street Journal,* December 17, 1984.

Harger, Jim, "Turning the Page: Zondervan's Breakup into Publishing, Bookstore Firms Is Success Story," *Grand Rapids Press,* May 10, 1994, p. E1.

——, "Zondervan Gets 28 Year Contract to Publish Bible," *Grand Rapids Press,* June 13, 1995, p. B8.

——, "Zondervan Splitting into Two Companies," *Grand Rapids Press,* September 3, 1993.

Knorr, David, "Litigation Fails to Block Zondervan Merger," *Grand Rapids Business Journal,* August 15, 1988, p. 1.

LeBlanc, Doug, "Hands Off My *NIV*," *Christianity Today,* June 16, 1997, p. 52.

Maryles, Daisy, "The Purpose-Driven Campaign," *Publishers Weekly,* February 10, 2003, p. 60.

Meehan, Chris, "Selling the Word," *Grand Rapids Press,* December 28, 1997, p. G1.

——, "Zondervan's Mission and Marketing Goals Translate into Retail Expansion," *Publishers Weekly,* March 9, 1984, pp. 90–93.

Milliot, Jim, "HarperCollins Has Record Fiscal 2004; Zondervan Drives Gains in Sales and Earnings," *Publishers Weekly,* August 16, 2004, p. 15(2).

Perlman, Lisa, "Christian Publisher Says Chapter on Its Woes Is Closed," *Los Angeles Times,* September 11, 1988, p. 7.

Raugust, Karen, "Veggie Tales from Zonderkidz," *Publishers Weekly,* August 26, 2002, p. 10.

Reed, Eric, "Southern Baptists Blast *TNIV*," *Christianity Today,* August 5, 2002, p. 17.

Ruark, James E., and Theodore W. Engstrom, *The House of Zondervan,* Grand Rapids, Mich.: Zondervan Publishing House, 1981.

"Running Press Inks Mini Deal with Zondervan," *Publishers Weekly,* June 2, 2003, p. 13.

Shepherd, Forrest, "What It Means for Now: A Popular Bible Translation Offends Readers and Scholars by Going Gender-Neutral," *Alberta Report,* March 18, 2002, p. 50.

Rublin, Lauren R., "Do Zondervan Shareholders Have a Prayer? The Unorthodox Behavior of a Bible Publisher's Stock," *Barron's,* October 19, 1987, p. 18.

Schifrin, Matthew, "Bible Bungle," *Forbes,* March 11, 1985, p. 123.

Simmons, Rebecca, "Diversity—New Bible Aimed at Blacks," *Dayton Daily News,* October 4, 1997, p. 6C.

Steel, Johannes, "Zondervan May Prove an Investment Made in Heaven," *Oklahoma City Times,* November 11, 1983.

Terbel, John, "A History of Book Publishing in the United States," New York: R.R. Bowker, 1981.

Veverka, Amber, "James G. Buick: Inside Track," *Grand Rapids Business Journal,* May 28, 1991, p. 5.

——, "Zondervan Nixes Plan for Management Buyout," *Grand Rapids Business Journal,* October 5, 1992, p. 3.

"Zondervan Adds to Kids Line," *Publishers Weekly,* May 17, 1999, p. 15.

"Zondervan Corp. Finally Finds Suitable Suitor," *Grand Rapids Business Journal,* July 18, 1988, p. 1.

"Zondervan Corp. Says It Expects to Post Loss of $3.5 Million for 1984," *Wall Street Journal,* April 17, 1985.

"Zondervan Ready to Sell Its Benson Music Business," *Grand Rapids Press,* November 17, 1992, p. A7.

"Zondervan's $3.5 Million Settlement Approved by Judge," *Associated Press,* February 27, 1989.

—Frank Uhle
—update: Nelson Rhodes

INDEX TO COMPANIES

Index to Companies

Listings in this index are arranged in alphabetical order under the company name. Company names beginning with a letter or proper name such as Eli Lilly & Co. will be found under the first letter of the company name. Definite articles (The, Le, La) are ignored for alphabetical purposes as are forms of incorporation that precede the company name (AB, NV). Company names printed in bold type have full, historical essays on the page numbers appearing in bold. Updates to entries that appeared in earlier volumes are signified by the notation (upd.). Company names in light type are references within an essay to that company, not full historical essays. This index is cumulative with volume numbers printed in bold type.

INDEX TO INDUSTRIES ———————————————

Index to Industries

ADVERTISING & OTHER BUSINESS SERVICES (continued)

AEROSPACE

FOOD PRODUCTS

FOOD SERVICES & RETAILERS

FOOD SERVICES & RETAILERS
(*continued*)

Fresh Enterprises, Inc., 66
Fresh Foods, Inc., 29
Friendly Ice Cream Corp., 30
Frisch's Restaurants, Inc., 35
Fuller Smith & Turner P.L.C., 38
Furr's Restaurant Group, Inc., 53
Furr's Supermarkets, Inc., 28
Garden Fresh Restaurant Corporation, 31
Gate Gourmet International AG, 70
The Gateway Corporation Ltd., II
Genuardi's Family Markets, Inc., 35
George Weston Limited, II; 36 (upd.)
Ghirardelli Chocolate Company, 30
Giant Food Inc., II; 22 (upd.)
Godfather's Pizza Incorporated, 25
Golden Corral Corporation, 10; 66 (upd.)
Golden Krust Caribbean Bakery, Inc., 68
Golden State Foods Corporation, 32
The Golub Corporation, 26
Gordon Food Service Inc., 8; 39 (upd.)
The Grand Union Company, 7; 28 (upd.)
The Great Atlantic & Pacific Tea
    Company, Inc., II; 16 (upd.); 55 (upd.)
Greggs PLC, 65
Gristede's Foods Inc., 31; 68 (upd.)
Ground Round, Inc., 21
Groupe Promodès S.A., 19
Guyenne et Gascogne, 23
H.E. Butt Grocery Co., 13; 32 (upd.)
Haggen Inc., 38
Hannaford Bros. Co., 12
Hard Rock Cafe International, Inc., 12
Harris Teeter Inc., 23
Harry's Farmers Market Inc., 23
Hickory Farms, Inc., 17
Holberg Industries, Inc., 36
Holland Burgerville USA, 44
Hooters of America, Inc., 18; 69 (upd.)
Hops Restaurant Bar and Brewery, 46
Hoss's Steak and Sea House Inc., 68
Hotel Properties Ltd., 71
Houchens Industries Inc., 51
Hughes Markets, Inc., 22
Hungry Howie's Pizza and Subs, Inc., 25
Hy-Vee, Inc., 36
ICA AB, II
Iceland Group plc, 33
IHOP Corporation, 17; 58 (upd.)
Il Fornaio (America) Corporation, 27
In-N-Out Burger, 19
Ingles Markets, Inc., 20
Inserra Supermarkets, 25
Inter Link Foods PLC, 61
International Dairy Queen, Inc., 10; 39
    (upd.)
ITM Entreprises SA, 36
Ito-Yokado Co., Ltd., 42 (upd.)
J Sainsbury plc, II; 13 (upd.); 38 (upd.)
J. Alexander's Corporation, 65
Jamba Juice Company, 47
JD Wetherspoon plc, 30
Jerry's Famous Deli Inc., 24
Jitney-Jungle Stores of America, Inc., 27
John Lewis Partnership plc, 42 (upd.)
Johnny Rockets Group, Inc., 31
KFC Corporation, 7; 21 (upd.)
King Kullen Grocery Co., Inc., 15
Koninklijke Ahold N.V. (Royal Ahold), II;
    16 (upd.)
Koo Koo Roo, Inc., 25
The Kroger Co., II; 15 (upd.); 65 (upd.)
The Krystal Company, 33
Kwik Save Group plc, 11
La Madeleine French Bakery & Café, 33
Landry's Restaurants, Inc., 15; 65 (upd.)

The Laurel Pub Company Limited, 59
Laurus N.V., 65
LDB Corporation, 53
Leeann Chin, Inc., 30
Levy Restaurants L.P., 26
Little Caesar Enterprises, Inc., 7; 24 (upd.)
Loblaw Companies Limited, 43
Logan's Roadhouse, Inc., 29
Lone Star Steakhouse & Saloon, Inc., 51
Long John Silver's, 13; 57 (upd.)
Luby's, Inc., 17; 42 (upd.)
Lucky Stores, Inc., 27
Lund Food Holdings, Inc., 22
Madden's on Gull Lake, 52
Maid-Rite Corporation, 62
Maines Paper & Food Service Inc., 71
Marie Callender's Restaurant & Bakery,
    Inc., 28
Marsh Supermarkets, Inc., 17
Matt Prentice Restaurant Group, 70
Max & Erma's Restaurants Inc., 19
McAlister's Corporation, 66
McCormick & Schmick's Seafood
    Restaurants, Inc., 71
McDonald's Corporation, II; 7 (upd.); 26
    (upd.); 63 (upd.)
Megafoods Stores Inc., 13
Meijer Incorporated, 7
Metcash Trading Ltd., 58
Metromedia Companies, 14
Mexican Restaurants, Inc., 41
The Middleby Corporation, 22
Minyard Food Stores, Inc., 33
MITROPA AG, 37
Monterey Pasta Company, 58
Morrison Restaurants Inc., 11
Morton's Restaurant Group, Inc., 30
Mrs. Fields' Original Cookies, Inc., 27
Musgrave Group Plc, 57
Nash Finch Company, 8; 23 (upd.); 65
    (upd.)
Nathan's Famous, Inc., 29
National Convenience Stores Incorporated,
    7
New World Restaurant Group, Inc., 44
New York Restaurant Group, Inc., 32
Noble Roman's Inc., 14
Noodles & Company, Inc., 55
NPC International, Inc., 40
O'Charley's Inc., 19; 60 (upd.)
Old Spaghetti Factory International Inc., 24
The Oshawa Group Limited, II
Outback Steakhouse, Inc., 12; 34 (upd.)
P&C Foods Inc., 8
P.F. Chang's China Bistro, Inc., 37
Palm Management Corporation, 71
Pancho's Mexican Buffet, Inc., 46
Panda Management Company, Inc., 35
Panera Bread Company, 44
Papa John's International, Inc., 15; 71
    (upd.)
Papa Murphy's International, Inc., 54
Pathmark Stores, Inc., 23
Peapod, Inc., 30
Penn Traffic Company, 13
Performance Food Group Company, 31
Perkins Family Restaurants, L.P., 22
Peter Piper, Inc., 70
Petrossian Inc., 54
Phillips Foods, Inc., 63
Piccadilly Cafeterias, Inc., 19
Piggly Wiggly Southern, Inc., 13
Pizza Hut Inc., 7; 21 (upd.)
Planet Hollywood International, Inc., 18;
    41 (upd.)
Players International, Inc., 22
Ponderosa Steakhouse, 15

Portillo's Restaurant Group, Inc., 71
Provigo Inc., II; 51 (upd.)
Publix Super Markets Inc., 7; 31 (upd.)
Pueblo Xtra International, Inc., 47
Quality Dining, Inc., 18
Quality Food Centers, Inc., 17
The Quizno's Corporation, 42
Rally's, 25; 68 (upd.)
Ralphs Grocery Company, 35
Randall's Food Markets, Inc., 40
Rare Hospitality International Inc., 19
Raving Brands, Inc., 64
Red Robin Gourmet Burgers, Inc., 56
Restaurant Associates Corporation, 66
Restaurants Unlimited, Inc., 13
RFC Franchising LLC, 68
Richfood Holdings, Inc., 7
Richtree Inc., 63
The Riese Organization, 38
Riser Foods, Inc., 9
Roadhouse Grill, Inc., 22
Rock Bottom Restaurants, Inc., 25; 68
    (upd.)
Romacorp, Inc., 58
Roundy's Inc., 58 (upd.)
RTM Restaurant Group, 58
Rubio's Restaurants, Inc., 35
Ruby Tuesday, Inc., 18; 71 (upd.)
Ruth's Chris Steak House, 28
Ryan's Restaurant Group, Inc., 15; 68
    (upd.)
Safeway PLC, II; 24 (upd.); 50 (upd.)
Santa Barbara Restaurant Group, Inc., 37
Sbarro, Inc., 16; 64 (upd.)
Schlotzsky's, Inc., 36
Schultz Sav-O Stores, Inc., 21
Schwan's Sales Enterprises, Inc., 26 (upd.)
Seaway Food Town, Inc., 15
Second Harvest, 29
See's Candies, Inc., 30
Seneca Foods Corporation, 17
Service America Corp., 7
SFI Group plc, 51
Shaw's Supermarkets, Inc., 56
Shells Seafood Restaurants, Inc., 43
Shoney's, Inc., 7; 23 (upd.)
ShowBiz Pizza Time, Inc., 13
Skyline Chili, Inc., 62
Smart & Final, Inc., 16
Smith's Food & Drug Centers, Inc., 8; 57
    (upd.)
Sodexho Alliance SA, 29
Somerfield plc, 47 (upd.)
Sonic Corporation, 14; 37 (upd.)
The Southland Corporation, II; 7 (upd.)
Spaghetti Warehouse, Inc., 25
SPAR Handels AG, 35
Spartan Stores Inc., 8
Stater Bros. Holdings Inc., 64
The Steak n Shake Company, 41
Steinberg Incorporated, II
Stew Leonard's, 56
The Stop & Shop Supermarket Company,
    II; 68 (upd.)
Subway, 32
Super Food Services, Inc., 15
Supermarkets General Holdings
    Corporation, II
Supervalu Inc., II; 18 (upd.); 50 (upd.)
SWH Corporation, 70
SYSCO Corporation, II; 24 (upd.)
Taco Bell Corp., 7; 21 (upd.)
Taco Cabana, Inc., 23
Taco John's International, Inc., 15; 63
    (upd.)
TelePizza S.A., 33
Tesco PLC, II

HEALTH & PERSONAL CARE PRODUCTS

INFORMATION TECHNOLOGY

INFORMATION TECHNOLOGY
(*continued*)

INSURANCE

LEGAL SERVICES

GEOGRAPHIC INDEX

Geographic Index

NOTES ON CONTRIBUTORS ─────────────────────────

Notes on Contributors

COHEN, M.L. Novelist and researcher living in Paris.

COVELL, Jeffrey L. Seattle-based writer.

CULLIGAN, Susan B. Minnesota-based writer.

DINGER, Ed. Writer and editor based in Bronx, New York.

HALASZ, Robert. Former editor in chief of *World Progress* and *Funk & Wagnalls New Encyclopedia Yearbook*; author, *The U.S. Marines* (Millbrook Press, 1993).

INGRAM, Frederick C. Utah-based business writer who has contributed to *GSA Business, Appalachian Trailway News,* the *Encyclopedia of Business,* the *Encyclopedia of Global Industries,* the *Encyclopedia of Consumer Brands,* and other regional and trade publications.

PEIPPO, Kathleen. Minneapolis-based writer.

RHODES, Nelson. Editor, writer, and consultant in the Chicago area.

ROTHBURD, Carrie. Writer and editor specializing in corporate profiles, academic texts, and academic journal articles.

SALAMIE, David E. Part-owner of InfoWorks Development Group, a reference publication development and editorial services company.

UHLE, Frank. Ann Arbor-based writer; movie projectionist, disc jockey, and staff member of *Psychotronic Video* magazine.

WOODWARD, A. Wisconsin-based writer.